Praise for Danny Goodman's *JavaScript® Bible*

"*JavaScript® Bible* is the definitive resource in JavaScript programming. I am never more than three feet from my copy."

—Steve Reich, CEO, PageCoders

"This book is a must-have for any web developer or programmer."

—Thoma Lile, President, Kanis Technologies, Inc.

"Outstanding book. I would recommend this book to anyone interested in learning to develop advanced Web sites. Mr. Goodman did an excellent job of organizing this book and writing it so that even a beginning programmer can understand it."

—Jason Hensley, Director of Internet Services, NetVoice, Inc.

"Goodman is always great at delivering clear and concise technical books!"

—Dwayne King, Chief Technology Officer, White Horse

"*JavaScript® Bible* is well worth the money spent!"

—Yen C.Y. Leong, IT Director, Moo Mooltimedia, a member of SmartTransact Group

"A must-have book for any internet developer."

—Uri Fremder, Senior Consultant, TopTier Software

"I love this book! I use it all the time, and it always delivers. It's the only JavaScript book I use!"

—Jason Badger, Web Developer

"Whether you are a professional or a beginner, this is a great book to get."

—Brant Mutch, Web Application Developer, Wells Fargo Card Services, Inc.

"I never thought I'd ever teach programming before reading your book [*JavaScript® Bible*]. It's so simple to use—the Programming Fundamentals section brought it all back! Thank you for such a wonderful book, and for breaking through my programming block!"

—Susan Sann Mahon, Certified Lotus Instructor, TechNet Training

"Danny Goodman is very good at leading the reader into the subject. *JavaScript® Bible* has everything we could possibly need."

—Philip Gurdon

"An excellent book that builds solidly from whatever level the reader is at. A book that is both witty and educational."

—Dave Vane

"I continue to use the book on a daily basis and would be lost without it."

—Mike Warner, Founder, Oak Place Productions

"*JavaScript® Bible* is by *far* the best JavaScript resource I've ever seen (and I've seen quite a few)."

—Robert J. Mirro, Independent Consultant, RJM Consulting

JavaScript® Bible

Sixth Edition

Danny Goodman
with Michael Morrison

With a foreword by Brendan Eich, JavaScript's creator

BICENTENNIAL
1807
WILEY
2007
BICENTENNIAL

Wiley Publishing, Inc.

JavaScript® Bible, Sixth Edition

Published by
Wiley Publishing, Inc.
10475 Crosspoint Boulevard
Indianapolis, IN 46256
www.wiley.com

Copyright © 2007 by Danny Goodman

Published by Wiley Publishing, Inc., Indianapolis, Indiana

Published simultaneously in Canada

ISBN: 978-0-470-06916-5

Manufactured in the United States of America

10 9 8 7 6 5 4 3 2 1

For general information on our other products and services or to obtain technical support, please contact our Customer Care Department within the U.S. at (800) 762-2974, outside the U.S. at (317) 572-3993 or fax (317) 572-4002.

Library of Congress Cataloging-in-Publication Data

Goodman, Danny.
  JavaScript bible / Danny Goodman with Michael Morrison ; with a foreword by Brendan Eich. — 6th ed.
    p. cm.
  Includes index.
  ISBN-13: 978-0-470-06916-5 (paper/cd-rom)
  ISBN-10: 0-470-06916-3 (paper/cd-rom)
  1. JavaScript (Computer program language) I. Morrison, Michael, 1970– II. Title.
  QA76.73.J39G65 2007
  005.13'3—dc22   2006101137

About the Authors

Danny Goodman is the author of numerous critically acclaimed and best-selling books, including *The Complete HyperCard Handbook*, *Danny Goodman's AppleScript Handbook*, *Dynamic HTML: The Definitive Reference*, and *JavaScript & DHTML Cookbook*. He is a renowned authority and expert teacher of computer scripting languages. His writing style and pedagogy continue to earn praise from readers and teachers around the world. To help keep his finger on the pulse of real-world programming challenges, Goodman frequently lends his touch as consulting programmer and designer to leading-edge World Wide Web and intranet sites from his home base in the San Francisco area.

Michael Morrison is a writer, developer, toy inventor, and author of a variety of books covering topics such as Java, C++, Web scripting, XML, game development, and mobile devices. Some of Michael's notable writing projects include *Faster Smarter HTML and XML*, *Teach Yourself HTML & CSS in 24 Hours*, and *Beginning Game Programming*. Michael is also the founder of Stalefish Labs (www.stalefishlabs.com), an entertainment company specializing in unusual games, toys, and interactive products.

Credits

Acquisitions Editor
Kit Kemper

Senior Development Editor
Kevin Kent

Copy Editor
Travis Henderson

Editorial Manager
Mary Beth Wakefield

Production Manager
Tim Tate

Vice President and Executive Group Publisher
Richard Swadley

Vice President and Executive Publisher
Joseph B. Wikert

Project Coordinator
Lynsey Osborn

Graphics and Production Specialists
Brooke Graczyk
Joyce Haughey
Jennifer Mayberry
Alicia B. South

Quality Control Technicians
David Faust
John Greenough

Media Development Project Supervisor
Laura Atkinson

Media Development Specialist
Kate Jenkins

Proofreading
David Faust
Kathy Simpson
Sossity Smith

Indexing
Valerie Haynes Perry

Anniversary Logo Design
Richard Pacifico

Acknowledgments

This sixth edition is the second time I've been fortunate enough to have Michael Morrison—a first-rate author and scripter in his own right—help bring the content of the book up to date. When you add the hundreds of pages on the CD-ROM to the 1,200+ pages of the printed book, the job of revising *JavaScript Bible* is monumental in scale. I therefore appreciate the personal sacrifices Michael made while he kept the motor running during extensive revision cycles. Many thanks to the hard-working folks at Wiley Publishing, Kit Kemper and Kevin Kent. Above all, I want to thank the many readers of the earlier editions of this book for investing in this ongoing effort. I wish I had the space here to acknowledge by name so many who have sent e-mail notes and suggestions: Your input has been most welcome and greatly appreciated.

Contents

Contents

Contents

xii

Contents

Part V: Appendixes 1077

Part VI: Bonus Chapters   On the CD-ROM

Chapter 36: Body Text Objects

Chapter 37: HTML Directive Objects

Chapter 38: Table and List Objects

Chapter 39: The Navigator and Other Environment Objects

Chapter 40: Positioned Objects

Chapter 41: Embedded Objects

Chapter 42: The Regular Expression and RegExp Objects

Contents

Foreword

A s JavaScript's creator, I would like to say a few words about where JavaScript has been, where it is going, and how the book you're holding will help you to make the most of the language.

JavaScript was born out of a desire to let HTML authors write scripts directly in their documents. This may seem obvious now, but in the spring of 1995 it was novel and more than a little at odds with both the conventional wisdom (that HTML should describe static document structure only) and the Next Big Thing (Java applets, which were hyped as the one true way to enliven and extend web pages). Once I got past these contentions, JavaScript quickly shaped up along the following lines:

- **"Java-lite" syntax.** Although the "natural language" syntax of HyperTalk was fresh in my mind after a friend lent me *The Complete HyperCard Handbook* by some fellow named Goodman, the Next Big Thing weighed heavier, especially in light of another goal: scripting Java applets. If the scripting language resembled Java, then those programmers who made the jump from JavaScript to Java would welcome similarities in syntax. But insisting on Java's class and type declarations, or on a semicolon after each statement when a line ending would do, were out of the question—scripting for most people is about writing short snippets of code, quickly and without fuss.

- **Events for HTML elements.** Buttons should have onClick event handlers. Documents load and unload from windows, so windows should have onLoad and onUnload handlers. Users and scripts submit forms: thus the onSubmit handler. Although not initially as flexible as HyperCard's messages (whose handlers inspired the onEvent naming convention), JavaScript events let HTML authors take control of user interaction from remote servers and respond quickly to user gestures and browser actions. With the adoption of the W3C DOM Level 2 event handling recommendations, JavaScript in modern browsers has fully flexible control over events.

- **Objects without classes.** The Self programming language proved the notion of prototype-based inheritance. For JavaScript, I wanted a single prototype per object (for simplicity and efficiency), based by default on the function called using the new operator (for consonance with Java). To avoid distinguishing constructors from methods from functions, all functions receive the object naming them as the property that was called in the parameter. Although prototypes didn't appear until Navigator 3, they were prefigured in Version 2 by quoted text being treated as an object (the Strong object prototype, to which users could attach methods).

- **Generated HTML.** Embedding JavaScript in HTML gave rise to a thought: Let the script speak HTML, as if the emitted text and markup were loaded in place of the script itself. The possibilities went beyond automating current or last-modified dates, to computing whole trees of tables where all the repeated structure was rolled up in a scripted loop, while the varying contents to be tabulated came in minimal fashion from JavaScript objects forming a catalog or mini-database.

This foreword originally appeared as the foreword to *JavaScript Bible, Fourth Edition.*

Foreword

At first, I thought JavaScript would most often find use in validating input to HTML forms. But before long, I was surprised to see how many web designers devised compelling applications by way of script-generated HTML and JavaScript objects. It became clear from user demonstration and feedback that web designers sought to build significant applications quickly and effectively with just a few images, HTML, and JavaScript. Eventually they demanded that the browser support what is now known as *Dynamic HTML* (one fun link: `http://www.javascript-games.org/`).

As legions of web authors embraced the authoring power of JavaScript, they, in turn, demonstrated the crucial advantages of a scripting environment over old-school application development. Not only were the HTML and JavaScript languages comparatively easy to use, but development did not require the programming expertise needed to light all pixels and handle all events as in a big, traditional application.

The primacy of JavaScript on the Web today vindicates our early belief in the value of a scripting language for HTML authors. By keeping the "pixel-lighting" bar low, HTML with images has made web designers out of millions of people. By keeping the event-handling bar low, JavaScript has helped many thousands of those designers become programmers. Perhaps the ultimate example of web development's convergence with application development is the Mozilla browser, wherein all of the user-interface and even some custom widgets and modular components are implemented entirely using JavaScript, Cascading Style Sheets (CSS), custom XML-based markup languages, and images.

JavaScript is also a general language, useful apart from HTML and XML. It has been embedded in servers, authoring tools, browser plug-ins, and other kinds of browsers (for such things as 3D graphical worlds). Its international standard, ECMA-262 (ISO 16262), has advanced to a Third Edition. But compared to languages such as Perl and even Java, it is still relatively young. Work toward a Fourth Edition of the language, supporting optional types, classes, and versioning facilities progresses within the ECMA technical committee (see the JS2 proposal to the ECMA technical committee documented at `http://www.mozilla.org/js/language/js20/`).

It is clear to me that JavaScript would not have survived without a creative, loyal, and patient community of developers; I owe them each a huge debt of thanks. Those developers who took up the beta releases of Navigator 2, and disseminated vital workarounds and feature requests by e-mail and net-news, are the language's godparents. Developer support and feedback continue to make JavaScript the eclectic, rambunctious success it is.

The book in your hands compiles thousands of those developer miles with the insight of an expert guide and teacher. Danny didn't know at the time how much inspiration I found in his HyperCard book, but it was on my desk throughout the development of JavaScript in 1995. His energy, compassion, and clear prose helped me keep the goal of creating "a language for all" in mind. It is enormously gratifying to write the foreword of this book, which has earned so many satisfied reader miles.

I highly recommend Danny Goodman's *JavaScript Bible* to anyone who wants to learn JavaScript, and especially to those HTML authors who've so far written only a few scripts or programs—you're in for a lifetime of fun on the scripting road with a trusty guide at your side.

Brendan Eich
The Mozilla Organization (`http://www.mozilla.org`)

For over 25 years, I have written the books I wished had already been written to help me learn or use a new technology. Whenever possible, I like to get in at the very beginning of a new authoring or programming environment, feel the growing pains, and share with readers the solutions to my struggles. This sixth edition of *JavaScript Bible* represents knowledge and experience accumulated over ten years of daily work in JavaScript and a constant monitoring of newsgroups for questions, problems, and challenges facing scripters at all levels. My goal is to help you avoid the same frustration and head scratching I and others have experienced through multiple generations of scriptable browsers.

Although the earliest editions of this book focused on the then predominant Netscape Navigator browser, the browser market share landscape has changed through the years. For many years, Microsoft took a strong lead with its Internet Explorer, but more recently, other browsers that support industry standards are finding homes on users' computers. The situation still leaves an age-old dilemma for content developers: designing scripted content that functions equally well in both standards-compliant and proprietary environments. The job of a book claiming to be a bible is not only to present both the standard and proprietary details when they diverge, but also to show you how to write scripts that blend the two so that they work on the wide array of browsers visiting your sites or web applications. Empowering you to design and write good scripts is my passion, regardless of browser. It's true that my bias is toward industry standards, but not to the exclusion of proprietary features that may be necessary to get your content and scripting ideas flowing equally well on today's and tomorrow's browsers.

Organization and Features of This Edition

Like the previous two editions of *JavaScript Bible*, this sixth edition contains far more information than can be printed and bound into a single volume. The complete contents can be found in the electronic version of this book (in PDF form) on the CD-ROM that accompanies the book. This new edition is structured in such a way as to supply the most commonly needed information in its entirety in the printed portion of the book. Content that you use to learn the fundamentals of JavaScript and reference frequently are at your fingertips in the printed version, whereas chapters with more advanced content are in the searchable electronic version on the CD-ROM. Here are some details about the book's structure.

Part I

Part I of the book begins with a chapter that shows how JavaScript compares with Java and discusses its role within the rest of the World Wide Web. The web browser and scripting world have undergone significant changes since JavaScript first arrived on the scene. That's why Chapter 2 is devoted to addressing challenges facing scripters who must develop applications for both single- and cross-platform browser audiences amid rapidly changing standards efforts. Chapter 3 provides the first foray into JavaScript, where you get to write your first practical script.

Part II

All of Part II is handed over to a tutorial for newcomers to JavaScript. Nine lessons provide you with a gradual path through browser internals, basic programming skills, and genuine browser scripting with an emphasis on industry standards as supported by most of the scriptable browsers in use today. Exercises follow at the end of each lesson to help reinforce what you just learned and challenge you to use your new knowledge (you'll find answers to the exercises in Appendix C). The goal of the tutorial is to equip you with sufficient experience to start scripting simple pages right away while making it easier for you to understand the in-depth discussions and examples in the rest of the book.

Part III

Part III, the largest section of the book, provides in-depth coverage of the document object models as implemented in today's browsers, including the object used for modern Ajax applications. In all reference chapters, a compatibility chart indicates the browser version that supports each object and object feature. One chapter in particular, Chapter 15, contains reference material that is shared by most of the remaining chapters of Part III. To help you refer back to Chapter 15 from other chapters, a dark tab along the outside edge of the page shows you at a glance where the chapter is located. Additional navigation aids include guide words near the top of most pages to indicate which object and object feature is covered on the page.

Part IV

Reference information for the core JavaScript language fills Part IV. As with reference chapters of Part III, the JavaScript chapters display browser compatibility charts for every JavaScript language term. Guide words near the top of pages help you find a particular term quickly.

Part V

Several appendices at the end of the book provide helpful reference information. These resources include a JavaScript and Browser Objects Quick Reference in Appendix A, a list of JavaScript reserved words in Appendix B, answers to Part II's tutorial exercises in Appendix C, and Internet resources in Appendix D. In Appendix E, you also find information on using the CD-ROM that comes with this book, which includes numerous bonus chapters and examples.

CD-ROM

The CD-ROM is a gold mine of information. It begins with a PDF version of the entire contents of this sixth edition of *JavaScript Bible*. This version includes bonus chapters covering:

- Dynamic HTML, data validation, plug-ins, and security
- Techniques for developing and debugging professional web-based applications
- Ten full-fledged JavaScript real-world applications

Another treasure trove on the CD-ROM is the Listings folder, where you'll find over 300 ready-to-run HTML documents that serve as examples of most of the document object model and JavaScript vocabulary words in Parts III and IV. All of the bonus chapter example listings are also included. You can run these examples with your JavaScript-enabled browser, but be sure to use the index.html page in the Listings folder as a gateway to running the listings. I could have provided you with humorous little sample code fragments out of context, but I think that seeing full-fledged HTML documents (simple though they may be) for employing these concepts is important. I intentionally omitted the script listings from the tutorial part (Part II) of this book to encourage you to type the scripts. I believe you learn a lot, even by aping list-ings from the book, as you get used to the rhythms of typing scripts in documents.

Be sure to check out the Chapter 13 listing file called `evaluator.html`. Many segments of Parts III and IV invite you to try out an object model or language feature with the help of an interactive workbench, called The Evaluator—a *JavaScript Bible* exclusive! You see instant results and quickly learn how the feature works.

The Quick Reference from Appendix A is in PDF format on the CD-ROM for you to print out and assemble as a handy reference, if desired. Adobe Reader is also included on the CD-ROM, in case you don't already have it, so that you can read both of these PDF files.

Prerequisites to Learning JavaScript

Although this book doesn't demand that you have a great deal of programming experience behind you, the more Web pages you've created with HTML, the easier you will find it to understand how JavaScript inter-acts with the familiar elements you normally place in your pages. Occasionally, you will need to modify HTML tags to take advantage of scripting. If you are familiar with those tags already, the JavaScript enhance-ments will be simple to digest.

Fortunately, you won't need to know about server scripting or passing information from a form to a server. The focus here is on client-side scripting, which operates independently of the server after the JavaScript-enhanced HTML page is fully loaded into the browser.

The basic vocabulary of the current HTML standard should be part of your working knowledge. You should also be familiar with some of the latest document markup standards, such as XHTML and Cascading Style Sheets (CSS). You don't need to be an expert, by any means. Web searches for these terms will uncover numerous tutorials on the subjects.

If you've never programmed before

Don't be put off by the size of this book. JavaScript may not be the easiest language in the world to learn, but believe me, it's a far cry from having to learn a full programming language, such as Java or C. Unlike developing a full-fledged monolithic application (such as the productivity programs you buy in the stores), JavaScript enables you to experiment by writing small snippets of program code to accomplish big things. The JavaScript interpreter built into every scriptable browser does a great deal of the technical work for you.

Programming, at its most basic level, consists of nothing more than writing a series of instructions for the computer to follow. We humans follow instructions all the time, even if we don't realize it. Traveling to a friend's house is a sequence of small instructions: Go three blocks that way; turn left here; turn right there. Amid these instructions are some decisions that we have to make: If the stoplight is red, then stop; if the light is green, then go; if the light is yellow, then floor it. Occasionally, we must repeat some operations sev-eral times (kind of like having to go around the block until a parking space opens up). A computer program not only contains the main sequence of steps, but it also anticipates what decisions or repetitions may be needed to accomplish the program's goal (such as how to handle the various states of a stoplight or what to do if someone just stole the parking spot you were aiming for).

The initial hurdle of learning to program is becoming comfortable with the way a programming language wants its words and numbers organized in these instructions. Such rules are called syntax, the same as in a living language. Because computers generally are dumb electronic hulks, they aren't very forgiving if you don't communicate with them in the specific language they understand. When speaking to another human, you can flub a sentence's syntax and still have a good chance of the other person's understanding you fully. Not so with computer programming languages. If the syntax isn't perfect (or at least within the language's range of knowledge that it can correct), the computer has the brazenness to tell you that you have made a syntax error.

The best thing you can do is to just chalk up the syntax errors you receive as learning experiences. Even experienced programmers make them. Every syntax error you get—and every resolution of that error made by rewriting the wayward statement—adds to your knowledge of the language.

If you've done a little programming before

Programming experience in a procedural language, such as BASIC, may almost be a hindrance rather than a help to learning JavaScript. Although you may have an appreciation for precision in syntax, the overall concept of how a program fits into the world is probably radically different from JavaScript. Part of this has to do with the typical tasks a script performs (carrying out a very specific task in response to user action within a web page), but a large part also has to do with the nature of object-oriented programming.

In a typical procedural program, the programmer is responsible for everything that appears on the screen and everything that happens under the hood. When the program first runs, a great deal of code is dedicated to setting up the visual environment. Perhaps the screen contains several text entry fields or clickable buttons. To determine which button a user clicks, the program examines the coordinates of the click and compares those coordinates against a list of all button coordinates on the screen. Program execution then branches out to perform the instructions reserved for clicking in that space.

Object-oriented programming is almost the inverse of that process. A button is considered an object—something tangible. An object has properties, such as its label, size, alignment, and so on. An object may also contain a script. At the same time, the system software and browser, working together, can send a message to an object—depending on what the user does—to trigger the script. For example, if a user clicks in a text entry field, the system/browser tells the field that somebody has clicked there (that is, has set the focus to that field), giving the field the task of deciding what to do about it. That's where the script comes in. The script is connected to the field, and it contains the instructions that the field carries out after the user activates it. Another set of instructions may control what happens when the user types an entry and tabs or clicks out of the field, thereby changing the content of the field.

Some of the scripts you write may seem to be procedural in construction: They contain a simple list of instructions that are carried out in order. But when dealing with data from form elements, these instructions work with the object-based nature of JavaScript. The form is an object; each radio button or text box is an object as well. The script then acts on the properties of those objects to get some work done.

Making the transition from procedural to object-oriented programming may be the most difficult challenge for you. When I was first introduced to object-oriented programming a number of years ago, I didn't get it at first. But when the concept clicked—a long, pensive walk helped—so many light bulbs went on inside my head that I thought I might glow in the dark. From then on, object orientation seemed to be the only sensible way to program.

If you've programmed in C before

By borrowing syntax from Java (which, in turn, is derived from C and C++), JavaScript shares many syntactical characteristics with C. Programmers familiar with C will feel right at home. Operator symbols, conditional structures, and repeat loops follow very much in the C tradition. You will be less concerned about data types in JavaScript than you are in C. In JavaScript, a variable is not restricted to any particular data type.

With so much of the JavaScript syntax familiar to you, you will be able to concentrate on document object model concepts, which may be entirely new to you. You will still need a good grounding in HTML to put your expertise to work in JavaScript.

If you've programmed in Java before

Despite the similarity in their names, the two languages share only surface aspects: loop and conditional constructions, C-like dot object references, curly braces for grouping statements, several keywords, and a few other attributes. Variable declarations, however, are quite different, because JavaScript is a loosely typed language. A variable can contain an integer value in one statement and a string in the next (although I'm not saying that this is good style). What Java refers to as methods, JavaScript calls methods (when associated with a predefined object) or functions (for scripter-defined actions). JavaScript methods and functions may return values of any type without having to state the data type ahead of time.

Perhaps the most important aspects of Java to suppress when writing JavaScript are the object-oriented notions of classes, inheritance, instantiation, and message passing. These aspects are simply non-issues when scripting. At the same time, however, the designers of JavaScript knew that you'd have some hard-to-break habits. For example, although JavaScript does not require a semicolon at the end of each statement line, if you type one in your JavaScript source code, the JavaScript interpreter won't balk.

If you've written scripts (or macros) before

Experience with writing scripts in other authoring tools or macros in productivity programs is helpful for grasping a number of JavaScript concepts. Perhaps the most important concept is the idea of combining a handful of statements to perform a specific task on some data. For example, you can write a macro in Microsoft Excel that performs a data transformation on daily figures that come in from a corporate financial report on another computer. The macro is built into the Macro menu, and you run it by choosing that menu item whenever a new set of figures arrives.

Some modern programming environments, such as Visual Basic, resemble scripting environments in some ways. They present the programmer with an interface builder, which does most of the work of displaying screen objects with which the user will interact. A big part of the programmer's job is to write little bits of code that are executed when a user interacts with those objects. A great deal of the scripting you will do with JavaScript matches that pattern exactly. In fact, those environments resemble the scriptable browser environment in another way: They provide a finite set of predefined objects that have fixed sets of properties and behaviors. This predictability makes learning the entire environment and planning an application easier to accomplish.

Formatting and Naming Conventions

The script listings and words in this book are presented in a `monospaced font` to set them apart from the rest of the text. Because of restrictions in page width, lines of script listings may, from time to time, break unnaturally. In such cases, the remainder of the script appears in the following line, flush with the left margin of the listing, just as they would appear in a text editor with word wrapping turned on. If these line breaks cause you problems when you type a script listing into a document yourself, I encourage you to access the corresponding listing on the CD-ROM to see how it should look when you type it.

As soon as you reach Part III of this book, you won't likely go for more than a page before reading about an object model or language feature that requires a specific minimum version of one browser or another. To make it easier to spot in the text when a particular browser and browser version is required, most browser references consist of an abbreviation and a version number. For example, WinIE5 means Internet Explorer 5 for Windows; NN4 means Netscape Navigator 4 for any operating system; Moz stands for the modern Mozilla browser (from which Firefox, Netscape 6 or later, and Camino are derived); and Safari is Apple's own browser for Mac OS X. If a feature is introduced with a particular version of browser and is supported in subsequent versions, a plus symbol (+) follows the number. For example, a feature marked WinIE5.5+ indicates that Internet Explorer 5.5 for Windows is required at a minimum, but the feature is also available in WinIE7 and probably future WinIE versions. If a feature was implemented in the first release of a modern browser, a plus symbol immediately follows the browser family name, such as Moz+ for all Mozilla-based browsers. Occasionally, a feature or some highlighted behavior applies to only one browser. For example, a feature marked NN4 means that it works only in Netscape Navigator 4.*x*. A minus sign (for example, WinIE-) means that the browser does not support the item being discussed.

The format of HTML and code listings in this edition follow XHTML coding conventions, which dictate all-lowercase tag and attribute names, as well as self-closing tags that do not act as containers (such as the XHTML <br /> tag in place of the HTML <br> tag).

Note, Tip, Caution, and Cross-Reference icons occasionally appear in the book to flag important points or suggest where to find more information.

Part I

Getting Started with JavaScript

Chapter 1

JavaScript's Role in the World Wide Web and Beyond

IN THIS CHAPTER

How JavaScript blends with other Web-authoring technologies

The history of JavaScript

What kinds of jobs you should and should not entrust to JavaScript

Many of the technologies that make the World Wide Web possible have far exceeded their original goals. Envisioned at the outset as a medium for publishing static text and image content across a network, the Web is forever being probed, pushed, and pulled by content authors. By taking for granted so much of the "dirty work" of conveying the bits between server and client computers, content developers and programmers dream of exploiting that connection to generate new user experiences and practical applications. It's not uncommon for a developer community to take ownership of a technology and mold it to do new and exciting things. But with so many Web technologies — especially browser programming with JavaScript — being within reach of every-day folks, we have witnessed an unprecedented explosion in turning the World Wide Web from a bland publishing medium into a highly interactive, operating system–agnostic authoring platform.

The JavaScript language, working in tandem with related browser features, is a Web-enhancing technology. When employed on the client computer, the language can help turn a static page of content into an engaging, interactive, and intelligent experience. Applications can be as subtle as welcoming a site's visitor with the greeting "Good morning!" when it is morning in the client computer's time zone — even though it is dinnertime where the server is located. Or applications can be much more obvious, such as delivering the content of a slide show in a one-page download while JavaScript controls the sequence of hiding, showing, and "flying slide" transitions while navigating through the presentation.

Of course, JavaScript is not the only technology that can give life to drab Web content. Therefore, it is important to understand where JavaScript fits within the array of standards, tools, and other technologies at your disposal. The alternative technologies described in this chapter are HTML, Cascading Style Sheets (CSS), server programs, and plug-ins. In most cases, JavaScript can work side by side with these other technologies, even though the hype around some make them sound like one-stop shopping places for all your interactive needs. That's rarely the case. Finally, you learn about the origins of JavaScript and what role it plays in today's advanced Web browsers.

Competing for Web Traffic

Web-page publishers revel in logging as many visits to their sites as possible. Regardless of the questionable accuracy of Web page *hit* counts, a site consistently logging 10,000 dubious hits per week is clearly far more popular than one with 1,000 dubious hits per week. Even if the precise number is unknown, relative popularity is a valuable measure. Another useful number is how many links from outside pages lead to a site. A popular site will have many other sites pointing to it — a key to earning high visibility in Web searches.

Encouraging people to visit a site frequently is the Holy Grail of Web publishing. Competition for viewers is enormous. Not only is the Web like a 50 million–channel television, but also, the Web competes for viewers' attention with all kinds of computer-generated information. That includes anything that appears onscreen as interactive multimedia.

Users of entertainment programs; multimedia encyclopedias; and other colorful, engaging, and mouse-finger-numbing actions are accustomed to high-quality presentations. Frequently, these programs sport first-rate graphics, animation, live-action video, and synchronized sound. By contrast, the lowest-common-denominator Web page has little in the way of razzle-dazzle. Even with the help of Dynamic HTML and stylesheets, the layout of pictures and text is highly constrained compared with the kinds of desktop publishing documents you see all the time. Regardless of the quality of its content, an unscripted, vanilla HTML document is flat. At best, interaction is limited to whatever navigation the author offers in the way of hypertext links or forms whose filled-in content magically disappears into the Web site's server.

Other Web Technologies

With so many ways to spice up Web sites and pages, you can count on competitors for your site's visitors to do their darnedest to make their sites more engaging than yours. Unless you are the sole purveyor of information that is in high demand, you continually must devise ways to keep your visitors coming back and entice new ones. If you design for an intranet, your competition is the drive for improved productivity by colleagues who use the internal Web sites for getting their jobs done.

These are all excellent reasons why you should care about using one or more Web technologies to raise your pages above the noise. Let's look at the major technologies you should know about.

Hypertext Markup Language (HTML and XHTML)

As an outgrowth of *SGML (Standard Generalized Markup Language)*, *HTML* is generally viewed as nothing more than a document formatting, or *tagging,* language. The tags (inside <> delimiter characters) instruct a viewer program (the *browser* or, more generically, the *client*) how to display chunks of text or images.

Relegating HTML to the category of a tagging language does disservice not only to the effort that goes into fashioning a first-rate Web page, but also to the way users interact with the pages. To my way of thinking, any collection of commands and other syntax that directs the way users interact with digital information is *programming*. With HTML, a Web-page author controls the user experience with the content just as the engineers who program Microsoft Excel craft the way users interact with spreadsheet content and functions.

Version 4.0 and later of the published HTML standards endeavor to define the purpose of HTML as assigning context to content, leaving the appearance to a separate standard for stylesheets. In other words, it's not HTML's role to signify that some text is italic but, rather, to signify *why* it is italic. For example, you would tag a chunk of text that conveys emphasis (via the <em> tag) regardless of how the stylesheet or browser sets the appearance of that emphasized text.

XHTML is a more recent adaptation of HTML that adheres to stylistic conventions established by the XML (eXtensible Markup Language) standard. No new tags come with XHTML, but it reinforces the notion of tagging to denote a document's structure and content.

Cascading Style Sheets (CSS)

Specifying the look and feel of a Web page via stylesheets is a major trend taking over the modern Web. The basic idea is that given a document's structure spelled out by its HTML or XHTML, a stylesheet defines the layout, colors, fonts, and other visual characteristics to present the content. Applying a different set of CSS definitions to the same document can make it look entirely different, even though the words and images are the same.

Mastery of the fine points of CSS takes time and experimentation, but the results are worth the effort. The days of using HTML tables and transparent "spacer" images to generate elaborate multicolumn layouts are very much on the wane. Every Web developer should have a solid grounding in CSS.

Server programming

Web sites that rely on database access or change their content very frequently incorporate programming on the server that generates the HTML output for browsers and/or processes forms that site visitors fill out on the page. Even submissions from a simple login or search form ultimately trigger some server process that sends the results to your browser. Server programming takes on many guises, the names of which you may recognize from your surfing through Web development sites. PHP, ASP, .Net, JSP, and Coldfusion are among the most popular. Associated programming languages include Perl, Python, Java, C++, C#, Visual Basic, and even server-side JavaScript in some environments.

Whatever language you use, the job definitely requires the Web-page author to be in control of the server, including whatever *back-end* programs (such as databases) are needed to supply results or massage the information coming from the user. Even with the new, server-based Web site design tools available, server scripting often is a task that a content-oriented HTML author will need to hand off to a more experienced programmer.

As powerful and useful as server scripting can be, it does a poor job of facilitating interactivity in a Web page. Without the help of browser scripting, each change to a page must be processed on the server, causing delays for the visitor and an extra burden on the server for simple tasks. This wastes desktop processing horsepower, especially if the process running on the server doesn't need to access big databases or other external computers.

Working together, however, server programming and browser scripting can make beautiful applications together. The pair come into play with what has become known as *Ajax* — Asynchronous JavaScript and XML. The "asynchronous" part runs in the browser, requesting XML data from, or posting data to, the server entirely in the background. XML data returned by the server can then be examined by JavaScript in the browser to update portions of the Web page. That's how many popular Web-based email user interfaces work, as well as the draggable satellite-photo closeups of Google Maps (http://maps.google.com).

Of helpers and plug-ins

In the early days of the World Wide Web, a browser needed to present only a few kinds of data before a user's eyes. The power to render text (tagged with HTML) and images (in popular formats such as GIF and JPEG) was built into browsers intended for desktop operating systems. Not wanting to be limited by those data types, developers worked hard to extend browsers so that data in other formats could be rendered on the client computer. It was unlikely, however, that a browser would ever be built that could download and render, say, any of several sound-file formats.

One way to solve the problem was to allow the browser, upon recognizing an incoming file of a particular type, to launch a separate application on the client machine to render the content. As long as this helper application was installed on the client computer (and the association with the helper program was set in the browser's preferences), the browser would launch the program and send the incoming file to that program. Thus, you might have one helper application for a MIDI sound file and another for an animation file.

Beginning with Netscape Navigator 2 in early 1996, software *plug-ins* for browsers enabled developers to extend the capabilities of the browser without having to modify the browser. Unlike a helper application, a plug-in can enable external content to blend into the document seamlessly.

The most common plug-ins are those that facilitate the playback of audio and video from the server. Audio may include music tracks that play in the background while visiting a page or live (streaming) audio, similar to a radio station. Video and animation can operate in a space on the page when played through a plug-in that knows how to process such data.

Today's browsers tend to ship with plug-ins that decode the most common sound-file types. Developers of plug-ins for Internet Explorer for the Windows operating system commonly implement plug-ins as ActiveX controls — a distinction that is important to the underpinnings of the operating system but not to the user.

Plug-ins and helpers are valuable for more than just audio and video playback. A popular helper application is *Adobe Acrobat Reader,* which displays Acrobat files that are formatted just as though they were being printed. But for interactivity, developers today frequently rely on Macromedia Corporation's *Flash* plug-in. Created using the Macromedia Flash authoring environment, a Flash document can have active clickable areas and draggable elements. Some authors even simulate artistic video games and animated stories in Flash. A browser equipped with the Flash plug-in displays the content in a rectangular area embedded within the browser page.

One potential downside for authoring interactive content in Flash or similar environments is that if the user does not have the correct plug-in version installed, it can take some time to download the plug-in (if the user even wants to bother). Moreover, once the plug-in is installed, highly graphic and interactive content can take longer to download to the client (especially on a dial-up connection) than some users are willing to wait. This is one of those situations in which you must balance your creative palette with the user's desire for your interactive content.

Another client-side technology — the Java applet — was popular for a while in the late 1990s but has fallen out of favor for a variety of reasons (some technical, some corporate–political). But this has not diminished the use of Java as a language for server and even cellular telephone programming, extending well beyond the scope of the language's founding company, Sun Microsystems.

JavaScript: A Language for All

Sun's Java language is derived from C and C++, but it is a distinct language. Its main audience is the experienced programmer. That leaves out many Web-page authors. I was dismayed by this situation when I first read about Java's preliminary specifications in 1995. I would have preferred a language that casual programmers and scripters who were comfortable with authoring tools, such as Apple's once-formidable HyperCard and Microsoft's Visual Basic, could adopt quickly. As these accessible development platforms have shown, nonprofessional authors can dream up many creative applications, often for very specific tasks that no professional programmer would have the inclination to work on. Personal needs often drive development in the classroom, office, den, or garage. But Java was not going to be that kind of inclusive language.

My spirits lifted several months later, in November 1995, when I heard of a scripting language project brewing at Netscape Communications, Inc. Born under the name *LiveScript,* this language was developed in parallel with a new version of Netscape's Web server software. The language was to serve two purposes with the same syntax. One purpose was as a scripting language that Web server administrators could use to manage the server and connect its pages to other services, such as back-end databases and search engines for users looking up information. Extending the "Live" brand name further, Netscape assigned the name *LiveWire* to the database connectivity usage of LiveScript on the server.

On the client side — in HTML documents — authors could employ scripts written in this new language to enhance Web pages in a number of ways. For example, an author could use LiveScript to make sure that the user had filled in a required text field with an e-mail address or credit card number. Instead of forcing the server or database to do the data validation (requiring data exchanges between the client browser and the server), the user's computer handles all the calculation work — putting some of that otherwise-wasted computing horsepower to work. In essence, LiveScript could provide HTML-level interaction for the user.

LiveScript becomes JavaScript

In early December 1995, just prior to the formal release of Navigator 2, Netscape and Sun Microsystems jointly announced that the scripting language thereafter would be known as JavaScript. Though Netscape had several good marketing reasons for adopting this name, the changeover may have contributed more confusion to both the Java and HTML scripting worlds than anyone expected.

Before the announcement, the language was already related to Java in some ways. Many of the basic syntax elements of the scripting language were reminiscent of the Java style. For client-side scripting, the language was intended for very different purposes than Java — essentially to function as a programming language integrated into HTML documents rather than as a language for writing applets that occupy a fixed rectangular area on the page (and that are oblivious to anything else on the page). Instead of Java's full-blown programming language vocabulary (and conceptually more difficult to learn object-oriented approach), JavaScript had a small vocabulary and a more easily digestible programming model.

The true difficulty, it turned out, was making the distinction between Java and JavaScript clear to the world. Many computer journalists made major blunders when they said or implied that JavaScript provided a simpler way of building Java applets. To this day, some new programmers believe JavaScript is synonymous with the Java language: They post Java queries to JavaScript-specific Internet newsgroups and mailing lists.

The fact remains that client-side Java and JavaScript are more different than they are similar. The two languages employ entirely different interpreter engines to execute their lines of code.

Enter Microsoft and others

Although the JavaScript language originated at Netscape, Microsoft acknowledged the potential power and popularity of the language by implementing it (under the JScript name) in Internet Explorer 3. Even if Microsoft might prefer that the world use the VBScript (Visual Basic Script) language that it provides in the Windows versions of IE, the fact that JavaScript is available on more browsers and operating systems makes it the client-side scripter's choice for anyone who must design for a broad range of users.

With scripting firmly entrenched in the mainstream browsers from Microsoft and Netscape, newer browser makers automatically provided support for JavaScript. Therefore, you can count on fundamental scripting services in browsers such as Opera or the Apple Safari browser (the latter built upon an Open Source browser called KHTML). Not that all browsers work the same way in every detail — a significant challenge for client-side scripting that is addressed throughout this book.

JavaScript: The Right Tool for the Right Job

Knowing how to match an authoring tool to a solution-building task is an important part of being a well-rounded Web site author. A Web designer who ignores JavaScript is akin to a plumber who bruises his knuckles by using pliers instead of the wrench from the bottom of the toolbox.

By the same token, JavaScript won't fulfill every dream. The more you understand about JavaScript's intentions and limitations, the more likely you will be to turn to it immediately when it is the proper tool. In particular, look to JavaScript for the following kinds of solutions:

- Getting your Web page to respond or react directly to user interaction with form elements (input fields, text areas, buttons, radio buttons, checkboxes, selection lists) and hypertext links
- Distributing small collections of databaselike information and providing a friendly interface to that data
- Controlling multiple-frame navigation, plug-ins, or Java applets based on user choices in the HTML document
- Preprocessing data on the client before submission to a server
- Changing content and styles in modern browsers dynamically and instantly in response to user interaction

At the same time, it is equally important to understand what JavaScript is *not* capable of doing. Scripters waste many hours looking for ways of carrying out tasks for which JavaScript was not designed. Most of the limitations are designed to protect visitors from invasions of privacy or unauthorized access to their desktop computers. Therefore, unless a visitor uses a modern browser and explicitly gives you permission to access protected parts of his or her computer, JavaScript cannot surreptitiously perform any of the following actions:

- Setting or retrieving the browser's preferences settings, main window appearance features, action buttons, and printing
- Launching an application on the client computer
- Reading or writing files or directories on the client or server computer
- Capturing live data streams from the server for retransmission
- Sending secret e-mails from Web site visitors to you

Web site authors are constantly seeking tools that will make their sites engaging (if not cool) with the least amount of effort. This is particularly true when the task is in the hands of people more comfortable with writing, graphic design, and page layout than with hard-core programming. Not every Webmaster has legions of experienced programmers on hand to whip up some special, custom enhancement for the site. Neither does every Web author have control over the Web server that physically houses the collection of HTML and graphics files. JavaScript brings programming power within reach of anyone familiar with HTML, even when the server is a black box at the other end of a telephone line.

Chapter 2

Authoring Challenges Amid the Browser Wars

IN THIS CHAPTER

How leapfrogging browser developments help and hurt Web developers

Separating the core JavaScript language from document objects

The importance of developing a cross-browser strategy

If you are starting to learn JavaScript at this point in the history of scriptable browsers, you have both a distinct advantage and disadvantage. The advantage is that you have the wonderful capabilities of mature browser offerings from Microsoft, The Mozilla Foundation (under brand names such as Firefox, Netscape, and Camino), Apple, and others at your bidding. The disadvantage is that you have not experienced the painful history of authoring for older browser versions that were buggy and at times incompatible with one another due to a lack of standards. You have yet to learn the anguish of carefully devising a scripted application for the browser version you use, only to have site visitors sending you voluminous e-mail messages about how the page triggers all kinds of script errors when run on a different browser brand, generation, or operating system platform.

Welcome to the real world of scripting Web pages with JavaScript. Several dynamics are at work to help make an author's life difficult if the audience for the application uses more than a single type of browser. This chapter introduces you to these challenges before you type your first word of JavaScript code. My fear is that the subjects I raise may dissuade you from progressing further into JavaScript and its powers. But as a developer myself — and as someone who has been using JavaScript since the earliest days of its public prerelease availability — I dare not sugar-coat the issues facing scripters today. Instead, I want to make sure you have an appreciation of what lies ahead to assist you in learning the language. I believe if you understand the big picture of the browser-scripting world as it stands in the year 2007, you will find it easier to target JavaScript usage in your Web application development and be successful at it.

Leapfrog

Browser compatibility has been an issue for authors since the earliest days of the Web gold rush — long before JavaScript. Despite the fact that browser developers and other interested parties voiced their opinions during formative stages of standards development, HTML authors could not produce a document that appeared the same pixel by pixel on all client machines. It may have been one thing to establish a set of standard tags for defining heading levels and line breaks, but it was rare for the actual rendering of content inside those tags to look identical on different brands of browsers on different operating systems.

Then, as the competitive world heated up — and Web browser development transformed itself from a volunteer undertaking into profit-seeking businesses — creative people defined new features and new tags that helped authors develop more flexible and interesting-looking pages. As happens a lot in any computer-related industry, the pace of commercial development easily surpassed the studied progress of standards. A browser maker would build a new HTML feature into a browser and only then propose that feature to the relevant standards body. Web authors were using these features (sometimes for prerelease browser versions) before the proposals were published for review.

When the deployment of content depends almost entirely on an interpretive engine on the client computer receiving the data — the HTML engine in a browser, for example — authors face an immediate problem. Unlike a stand-alone computer program that can extend and even invent functionality and have it run on everyone's computer (at least for a given operating system), Web content providers must rely on the functionality built into the browser. This led to questions such as "If not all browsers coming to my site support a particular HTML feature, then should I apply newfangled HTML features for visitors only at the bleeding edge?" and "If I do deploy the new features, what do I do for those with older browsers?"

Authors who developed pages in the earliest days of the Web wrestled with these questions for many HTML features that we today take for granted. Tables and frames come to mind. Eventually, the standards caught up with the proposed HTML extensions — but not without a lot of author woe along the way.

Despite the current dominance of the Microsoft Internet Explorer browser on the dominant Windows operating system, the number of browsers that people use is not shrinking. Several recent browsers, including the modern Netscape and Firefox browsers, are based on an Open Source browser called Mozilla. The Macintosh operating system now includes its own Apple-branded browser, Safari (released in 2003). And the independent Opera browser also has a home on some users' computers. All of these non-Microsoft browser makers obviously believe that they bring improvements to the world to justify their development — building better mousetraps, you might say.

Duck and Cover

Today's browser wars are fought on different battlegrounds than in the early days of the Web. The breadth and depth of established Web standards have substantially fattened the browser applications — and the books developers read to exploit those standards for their content. On one hand, most developers clamor for deeper standards support in new browser versions. On the other hand, everyday users care little about standards. All they want is to have an enjoyable time finding the information they seek on the Web. Most users are slow to upgrade their browsers, holding out until their favorite sites start breaking in their ancient browsers.

Industry standards don't necessarily make the Web developer's job any easier. For one thing, the standards are unevenly implemented across the latest browsers. Some browsers go further in their support than others. Then there are occasional differences in interpretation of vague standards details. And sometimes the standards don't provide any guidance in areas that are vital to content developers. At times we are left to the whims of browser makers who fill the gaps with proprietary features in the hope that those features will become de facto standards.

As happens in war, civilian casualties mount when the big guns start shooting. The browser battle lines shifted dramatically in only a few years. The huge market-share territory once under Netscape's command came under Microsoft's sway. More recently, however, concerns about privacy and security on the Windows platform have driven many users to seek less vulnerable browsers. Mozilla Firefox has so far been the biggest beneficiary in the search for alternatives. Although a fair amount of authoring common ground exists between the latest versions of today's browsers, uneven implementation of the newest features causes the biggest problems for authors wishing to deploy on all browsers. Trying to define the common denominator may be the toughest part of the authoring job.

Compatibility Issues Today

Allow me to describe the current status of the compatibility situation among the top three browser families: Microsoft Internet Explorer, browsers based on Mozilla, and Apple Safari. The discussion in the next few sections intentionally does not get into specific scripting technology very deeply; some of you may know very little about programming at this point. In many chapters throughout Parts III and IV, I offer scripting suggestions to accommodate a variety of browsers.

Separating language from objects

Although early JavaScript authors initially treated client-side scripting as one environment that permitted the programming of page elements, the scene has changed as the browsers have matured. Today, a clear distinction exists between specifications for the core JavaScript language and for the elements you script in a document (for example, buttons and fields in a form).

On one level, this separation is a good thing. It means that one specification exists for basic programming concepts and syntax, which could become the programming language in any number of other environments. You can think of the core language as basic wiring. When you know how electric wires work, you can connect them to all kinds of electrical devices. Similarly, JavaScript today is used to wire together elements in an HTML document. Tomorrow, operating systems could use the core language to enable users to wire together desktop applications that need to exchange information automatically.

At the ends of today's JavaScript wires inside browsers are the elements on the page. In programming jargon, these items are known as *document objects*. By keeping the specifications for document objects separate from the wires that connect them, you can use other kinds of wires (other languages) to connect them. It's like designing telephones that can work with any kind of wire, including a type of wire that hasn't been invented yet. Today, the devices can work with copper wire or fiber-optic cable. You get a good picture of this separation in Internet Explorer, whose set of document objects can be scripted with JavaScript or VBScript. They're the same objects — just different wiring.

The separation of core language from document objects enables each concept to have its own standards effort and development pace. But even with recommended standards for each factor, each browser maker is free to extend the standards. Furthermore, authors may have to expend more effort to devise one version of a page or script that plays on multiple browsers unless the script adheres to a common denominator (or uses some other branching techniques to let each browser run its own way).

Core language standard

Keeping track of JavaScript language versions requires a brief history lesson. The first version of JavaScript (in Netscape Navigator 2) was version 1, although that numbering was not part of the language usage. JavaScript was JavaScript. Version numbering became an issue when Navigator 3 was released. The version of JavaScript associated with that Navigator version was JavaScript 1.1. The first appearance of the Navigator 4 generation increased the language version one more notch with JavaScript 1.2.

Microsoft's scripting effort contributes confusion for scripting newcomers. The first version of Internet Explorer to include scripting was Internet Explorer 3. The timing of Internet Explorer 3 was roughly coincidental to Navigator 3. But as scripters soon discovered, Microsoft's scripting effort was one generation behind. Microsoft did not license the JavaScript name. As a result, the company called its language JScript. Even so, the HTML tag attribute that lets you name the language of the script inside the tags could be either JScript or JavaScript for Internet Explorer. Internet Explorer 3 could understand a JavaScript script written for Navigator 2.

During this period of dominance by Navigator 3 and Internet Explorer 3, scripting newcomers were often confused because they expected the scripting languages to be the same. Unfortunately for the scripters, there were language features in JavaScript 1.1 that were not available in the older JavaScript version in Internet Explorer 3. Microsoft improved JavaScript in IE3 with an upgrade to the .dll file that gives IE its JavaScript syntax. However, it was hard to know which .dll is installed in any given visitor's IE3. The situation smoothed out for Internet Explorer 4. Its core language was essentially up to the level of JavaScript 1.2, as in early releases of Navigator 4. Microsoft still officially called the language JScript. Almost all language features that were new in Navigator 4 were understood when you loaded the scripts into Internet Explorer 4.

While all of this jockeying for JavaScript versions was happening, Netscape, Microsoft, and other concerned parties met to establish a core language standard. The standards body is a Switzerland-based organization originally called the European Computer Manufacturer's Association and now known simply as ECMA (commonly pronounced "ECK-ma"). In mid-1997, the first formal language specification was agreed on and published (ECMA-262). Due to licensing issues with the JavaScript name, the body created a new name for the language: ECMAScript.

With only minor and esoteric differences, this first version of ECMAScript was essentially the same as JavaScript 1.1, used in Navigator 3. Both Navigator 4 and Internet Explorer 4 officially supported the ECMAScript standard. Moreover, as happens so often when commerce meets standards bodies, both browsers went beyond the ECMAScript standard. Fortunately, the common denominator of this extended core language is broad, lessening authoring headaches on this front.

JavaScript version 1.3 was implemented in Netscape Navigator 4.06 through 4.7x. This language version is also the one supported in IE 5, 5.5, and 6. A few new language features are incorporated in JavaScript 1.5, as implemented in Mozilla-based browsers (including Navigator 6 and later). A few more core language features were added to JavaScript 1.6, first implemented in Mozilla 1.8 (Firefox 1.5).

In practice, so many browsers in use today support all but a few leading-edge features of the Mozilla browsers that JavaScript version numbers are mostly irrelevant. Other compatibility issues with older browsers will likely get in your way before core language problems do. The time has come to forget about elaborate workarounds for the inadequacies of the oldest browsers.

Document object model

If prevalent browsers have been close to one another in core JavaScript language compatibility, nothing could be further from the truth when it comes to the document objects. Internet Explorer 3 based its document object model (DOM) on that of Netscape Navigator 2, the same browser level it used as a model for the core language. When Netscape added a couple of new objects to the model in Navigator 3, the addition caused further headaches for neophyte scripters who expected those objects to appear in Internet Explorer 3. Probably the most commonly missed object in Internet Explorer 3 was the image object, which lets scripts swap the image when a user rolls the cursor atop a graphic — *mouse rollovers,* they're commonly called.

In the Level 4 browsers, however, Internet Explorer's DOM jumped way ahead of the object model that Netscape implemented in Navigator 4. The two most revolutionary aspects of IE4 were the ability to script virtually every element in an HTML document and the instant reflow of a page when the content changed. This opened the way for HTML content to be genuinely dynamic without requiring the browser to fetch a rearranged page from the server. NN4 implemented only a small portion of this dynamism without exposing all elements to scripts or reflowing the page. It introduced a proprietary layering concept that was abandoned at the end of the Navigator 4.x lifetime. Inline content could not change in NN4 as it could in IE4. Suffice it to say that IE4 was an enviable implementation.

At the same time, a DOM standard was being negotiated under the auspices of the World Wide Web Consortium (W3C). The hope among scripters was that after a standard was in place, it would be easier to develop dynamic content for all browsers that supported the standard. The resulting standard — the W3C DOM — formalized the notion of being able to script every element on the page, as in IE4. But it also invented an entirely new object syntax that no browser had used. The race was on for browsers to support the W3C DOM standards.

An arm of the Netscape company called Mozilla.org was formed to create an all-new browser dedicated to supporting industry standards. The engine for the Mozilla browser became the basis for the all-new Navigator 6. It incorporated all of the W3C DOM Level 1 and a good chunk of Level 2. Mozilla 1.01 became the basis for the Netscape 7 browser, whereas Netscape 7.1 was built on the Mozilla 1.4 generation. In the summer of 2003, Netscape's parent company, AOL Time Warner, decided to end further Netscape-branded browser development. The work on the underlying Mozilla browser, however, continues under an independent organization called The Mozilla Foundation. Mozilla-based browsers and others using the same engine (such as Firefox and Camino) continue to be upgraded and released to the public. The Mozilla engine offers arguably the most in-depth support for the W3C DOM standards.

Even though Microsoft participated in W3C DOM standards development, IE5 and 5.5 implemented only some of the W3C DOM standard — in some cases, just enough to allow simple cross-browser scripting that adheres to the standard. Microsoft further filled out W3C DOM support in IE6 but chose to omit several important parts. Despite the long time gap between releases of IE6 and IE7, the latter includes no additional W3C DOM support — much to the chagrin of Web developers.

The Apple Safari browser has raced forward in its comparatively short life to offer substantial W3C DOM support. This is especially true of version 2, which was first released as part of Mac OS X version 10.4.

With this seemingly tortuous history of DOM development and browser support leading to the present day, you may wonder how anyone can approach DOM scripting with hope of success. Yet you'd be amazed by how much you can accomplish with today's browsers. You'll certainly encounter compatibility issues along the way, but this book will guide you through the most common problems and equip you to tackle others.

Cascading Style Sheets

Navigator 4 and Internet Explorer 4 were the first browsers to claim compatibility with a W3C recommendation called *Cascading Style Sheets Level 1 (CSS1)*. This specification provided designers an organized way to customize the look and feel of a document (and thus minimized the HTML in each tag). As implementations go, NN4 had a lot of rough edges, especially when trying to mix stylesheets and tables. But IE4 was no angel, either, especially when comparing the results of stylesheet assignments as rendered in the Windows and Macintosh versions of the browser (developed by two separate teams).

CSS Level 2 adds more style functionality to the standard, and IE6, Mozilla-based browsers, and Safari support a good deal of Level 2 (albeit unevenly) with the latest versions, such as Mozilla 1.8+ and Safari 2+ beginning support for CSS Level 3 features. Rendering of styled content is more harmonious among browsers, largely thanks to guidelines about how styles should render. Complex layouts, however, still need careful tweaking from time to time because of different interpretations of the standard.

JavaScript plays a role in stylesheets in IE4+, Mozilla, and Safari because those browsers' object models permit dynamic modification to styles associated with any content on the page. Stylesheet information is part of the object model and therefore is accessible and modifiable from JavaScript.

Dynamic HTML and positioning

Perhaps the biggest improvements to the inner workings of the Level 4 browsers from both Netscape and Microsoft revolved around a concept called *Dynamic HTML (DHTML)*. The ultimate goal of DHTML was to enable scripts in documents to control the content, content position, and content appearance in response to user actions. To that end, the W3C organization developed another standard for the precise positioning of HTML elements on a page as an extension of the CSS standards effort. The CSS-Positioning recommendation was later blended into the CSS standard, and both are now part of CSS Level 2. With positioning, you can define an exact location on the page where an element should appear, whether the item should be visible, and what stacking order it should take among all the items that might overlap it.

IE4+ adheres to the positioning-standard syntax and makes positionable items subject to script control. Navigator 4 followed the standard from a conceptual point of view, but it implemented an alternative methodology involving an entirely new, and eventually unsanctioned, tag for layers. Such positionable items were scriptable in Navigator 4 as well, although a lot of the script syntax differed from that used in Internet Explorer 4. Fortunately for DHTML authors, Mozilla, through its adherence to the CSS standard, is more syntactically in line with DHTML style properties employed in IE4+.

Of more interest these days is the ability to modify the inline content of a Web page without reloading the entire page. Fundamental standards from the W3C DOM Level 1 are supported by a wide range of browsers, including IE5+, Mozilla, Safari, and Opera. You can accomplish quite a lot using the same basic syntax across all of these browsers. Some challenges remain, however, as you'll see throughout this book.

Developing a Scripting Strategy

Browsers representing the latest generation contain a hodgepodge of standards and proprietary extensions. Even if you try to script to a common denominator among today's browsers, your code probably won't take into account the earlier versions of both the JavaScript core language and the browser DOMs.

The true challenge for authors is determining the audience for which scripted pages are intended. Each new browser generation not only brings with it new and exciting features you are probably eager to employ in your pages, but also adds to the fragmentation of the audience visiting a publicly accessible page. With each new browser upgrade, fewer existing users are willing to download megabytes of browser merely to have the latest and greatest browser version. For many pioneers — and certainly for most nontechie users — there is a shrinking imperative to upgrade browsers unless the new browser comes via a new computer or operating system upgrade.

At this stage in the history of scriptable browsers, I take the stand that we should assume that a typical Web surfer arrives with a browser equipped with support for at least simple W3C DOM and DHTML capabilities. That certainly won't be the case 100 percent of the time, so it is also your obligation to apply scripting in an additive, or value-added, manner. By this I mean that your pages should convey their primary information to nonscriptable browsers designed for users with vision or motor-skill impairments as well as less-feature-rich browsers built into cellular telephones. But the scripting efforts you make can give visitors with recent scriptable browsers a more enjoyable experience — better interactivity, faster performance, and a more engaging presentation. You will not only be contributing to the state of the art, but also carrying on the original vision of scripting in the browser.

Chapter 3

Your First JavaScript Script

I n this chapter, you set up a productive scriptwriting and previewing environment on your computer; then you write a simple script whose results you can see in your JavaScript-compatible browser.

Because of differences in the way various personal computing operating systems behave, I present details of environments for two popular variants: Windows (95 through XP) and Mac OS X. For the most part, your JavaScript authoring experience is the same regardless of the operating system platform you use — including Linux or Unix. Although there may be slight differences in font designs depending on your browser and operating system, the information remains the same. Most illustrations of browser output in this book are made from the Windows XP version of Internet Explorer 6. If you run another browser or version, don't fret if every pixel doesn't match the illustrations in this book.

IN THIS CHAPTER

How to choose basic JavaScript authoring tools

How to set up your authoring environment

How to enter a simple script to a web page

The Software Tools

The best way to learn JavaScript is to type the HTML and scripting code into documents in a text editor. Your choice of editor is up to you, although I provide you some guidelines for choosing a text editor in the next section.

Choosing a text editor

For the purposes of learning JavaScript in this book, avoid WYSIWYG (What You See Is What You Get) web-page authoring tools, such as FrontPage and Dreamweaver, for now. These tools certainly will come in handy afterward when you can productively use those facilities for molding the bulk of your content and layout. But the examples in this book focus more on script content (which you must type anyway), so there isn't much HTML that you have to type. Files for all complete web-page listings in this book (except for the tutorial chapters) also appear on the companion CD-ROM.

17

An important factor to consider in your choice of editor is how easy it is to save standard text files with an .html filename extension. In the case of Windows, any program that not only saves the file as text by default but also enables you to set the extension to .htm or .html prevents a great deal of problems. If you use Microsoft Word, for example, the program tries to save files as binary Word files — something that no web browser can load. To save the file initially as a .txt or .html extension file requires mucking around in the Save As dialog box. This requirement is truly a nuisance.

Nothing's wrong with using bare-essentials text editors. In Windows, that includes the WordPad program or a more fully featured product such as the shareware editor called TextPad. For Mac OS X, the bundled TextEdit application is also fine. Favorites among Mac HTML authors and scripters include BBEdit (Bare Bones Software) and SubEthaEdit (www.codingmonkeys.de/subethaedit).

Choosing a browser

The other component that is required for learning JavaScript is the browser. You don't have to be connected to the Internet to test your scripts in the browser. You can perform all testing offline. This means you can learn JavaScript and create cool, scripted web pages with a laptop computer — even on a boat in the middle of an ocean.

The browser brand and version you use are up to you. Because the tutorial chapters in this book teach the W3C DOM syntax, you should be using a recent browser. Any of the following will get you through the tutorial: Internet Explorer 5 or later (Windows or Macintosh); any Mozilla-based browser (including Firefox, Netscape 7 or later, and Camino); Apple Safari; and Opera 7 or later.

NOTE   **Many example listings in Parts III and IV of this book demonstrate language or document object model (DOM) features that work on only specific browsers and versions. Check the compatibility listing for that language or DOM feature to make sure you use the right browser to load the page.**

Setting Up Your Authoring Environment

To make the job of testing your scripts easier, you want to have your text editor and browser running simultaneously. You need to be able to switch quickly between editor and browser as you experiment and repair any errors that may creep into your code. The typical workflow entails the following steps:

1. Enter HTML and script code into the source document in the text editor.
2. Save the latest version to disk.
3. Switch to the browser.
4. Do one of the following:

   If this is a new document, open the file through the browser's Open menu.

   If the document is already loaded, reload the file into the browser.

Steps 2 through 4 are the key ones you will follow frequently. I call this three-step sequence the *save-switch-reload* sequence. You will perform this sequence so often as you script that the physical act quickly will become second nature to you. How you arrange your application windows and effect the save-switch-reload sequence varies according to your operating system.

Windows

You don't have to have either the editor or browser window maximized (at full screen) to take advantage of them. In fact, you may find them easier to work with if you adjust the size and location of each window so both windows are as large as possible while still enabling you to click a sliver of the other's window. Or you can leave the taskbar visible so you can click the desired program's button to switch to its window (see Figure 3-1). A monitor that displays more than 800 × 600 pixels certainly helps in offering more screen real estate for the windows and the taskbar.

FIGURE 3-1

Editor and browser-window arrangement in Windows XP.

In practice, however, the Windows Alt+Tab task-switching keyboard shortcut makes the job of the save-switch-reload steps outlined earlier a snap. If you run Windows and also use a Windows-compatible text editor (which more than likely has a Ctrl+S file-saving keyboard shortcut), you can effect the save-switch-reload sequence from the keyboard your the left hand: Ctrl+S (save the source file), Alt+Tab (switch to the browser), and Ctrl+R (reload the saved source file).

As long as you keep switching between the browser and text editor via Alt+Tab task switching, either program is always just an Alt+Tab away.

Mac OS X

In Mac OS X you can change between your text editor and browser applications via the Dock or, more conveniently, by pressing ⌘+Tab. As long as you stay in those two applications, the other program is only one ⌘+Tab away (see Figure 3-2).

FIGURE 3-2

Editor and browser-window arrangement on the Macintosh screen.

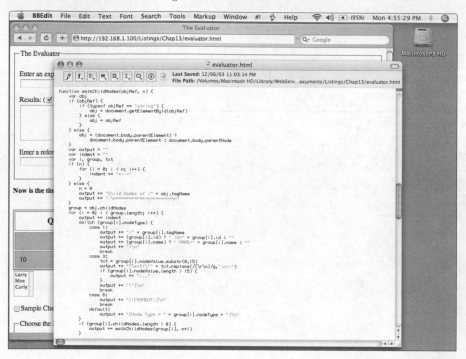

With this setup, the save-switch-reload sequence is a simple affair:

1. Press ⌘+S (save the source file).
2. Press ⌘+Tab (switch to the browser).
3. Press ⌘+R (reload the saved source file).

To return to editing the source file, press ⌘+Tab again.

Reloading issues

For the most part, a simple page reload is enough to let you test a revised version of a script right away. But sometimes the browser's cache (with its default settings) can preserve parts of the previous page's attributes when you reload, even though you have changed the source code. To perform a more thorough reload, hold down the Shift key while clicking the browser's Reload/Refresh button. Alternatively, you can turn off the browser's cache in the preferences area, but that setting may negatively affect the overall performance of the browser during your regular web surfing.

What Your First Script Will Do

For the sake of simplicity, the kind of script you look at in the next section is the kind that runs automatically immediately after the browser loads the HTML page. Although all scripting and browsing work here is done offline, the behavior of the page is identical if you place the source file on a server and someone accesses it through the web.

Figure 3-3 shows the page as it appears in the browser after you're finished. (The exact wording differs slightly if you run your browser on an operating system platform other than Windows XP or if you use a browser other than Internet Explorer.) The part of the page that is defined in regular HTML contains nothing more than an <h1> header with a horizontal rule under it. If someone does not use a JavaScript-equipped browser, he or she sees only the header and horizontal rule (unless that person has a truly outmoded browser, in which case some of the script words appear in the page).

FIGURE 3-3

The finished page of your first JavaScript script.

Below the rule, the script displays plain body text that combines static text with information about the browser you use to load the document. The script, which fires as a result of the page completing its loading process, inserts some HTML into an initially empty placeholder element. In particular, the script displays the same kind of information that your browser reports to a web server each time it requests a page. The script also takes advantage of cascading style sheets (CSS) to format the browser-specific information in a red color on the page.

Entering Your First Script

It's time to start creating your first JavaScript script. Launch your text editor and browser. If your browser offers to dial your Internet service provider (ISP) or begins dialing automatically, cancel or quit the dialing operation. If the browser's Stop button is active, click it to halt any network searching it may try to do. You may receive a dialog-box message or page indicating that the URL for your browser's home page (usually the home page of the browser's publisher — unless you've changed the settings) is unavailable. That's fine. You want the browser open, but you don't need to be connected to your ISP. If you're automatically connected to the Internet through a local area network in your office or school or cable modem or DSL, that's also fine. However, you don't need the network connection for now. Next, follow these steps to enter and preview your first JavaScript script:

1. Activate your text editor and create a new, blank document.

2. Type the script in the window exactly as shown in Listing 3-1.

   Follow the example slowly and carefully, paying special attention to:

   a. The uppercase and lowercase letters

   b. The placement of single (') and double (") quote symbols

   c. The usage of parentheses, angle brackets (< and >), and curly braces ({ and })

LISTING 3-1

Source Code for script1.html

```
<html>
<head>
<title>My First Script</title>
<style type="text/css">
.highlight {color: red}
</style>
<script type="text/javascript">
function showBrowserType() {
    document.getElementById("readout").innerHTML =
    "Your browser says it is: " +
    "<span class='highlight'>" +
    navigator.userAgent + "</span>.<hr />";
}
window.onload = showBrowserType;
</script>
</head>

<body>
<h1>Let's Script...</h1>
<hr>
<h1>Let's Script...</h1>
<hr />
<div id="readout"></div>
</body>
</html>
```

3. Save the document with the name `script1.html`.

4. Switch to your browser.

5. Choose Open (or Open File on some browsers) from the File menu, and select `script1.html`. (On some browsers, you have to click a Browse button to reach the File dialog box.)

If you typed all lines as directed, the document in the browser window should look like the one in Figure 3-3 (with minor differences for your computer's operating system and browser version). If the browser indicates that a mistake exists somewhere as the document loads, don't do anything about it for now. (Click the OK button if you see a script error dialog box.)

Let's first examine the details of the entire document so that you understand some of the finer points of what the script is doing.

Examining the Script

You do not need to memorize any of the commands or syntax discussed in this section. Instead, relax and watch how the lines of the script become what you see in the browser.

The HTML document

Ignore the `<script>` tag for a moment, and look at the rest of the HTML in the document. It's all very standard HTML (actually, the HTML complies with the newer XHTML standard), with one CSS rule in the head portion.

Perhaps the only oddity in the markup is the `<div>` tag. It has an `id` attribute assigned to it, giving the HTML element a name (`readout`) that a script can use to give it instructions. But there is no initial content between the `<div>` and `</div>` tags. This element serves strictly as a placeholder. In other words, if scripting is turned off in the browser, the user sees nothing in the document where this element is located. That's a good thing, because for public web sites, scripting should add value to the page rather than be mission critical.

The <script> tag

Any time you include JavaScript verbiage in an HTML document, you must enclose those lines inside a `<script>...</script>` tag pair. These tags alert the browser program to begin interpreting all the text between these tags as a script, rather than HTML to render. Because other scripting languages (such as Microsoft VBScript) can take advantage of these script tags, you must specify the kind of language in which the enclosed code is written. Therefore, when the browser receives the signal that your script is of the type `text/javascript`, it employs its built-in JavaScript interpreter to handle the code. You can find parallels to this setup in real life: If you have a French interpreter at your side, you need to know that the person with whom you're conversing also knows French. If you encounter someone from Russia, the French interpreter can't help you. Similarly, if your browser has only a JavaScript interpreter inside, it can't understand code written in VBScript.

Now is a good time to instill an aspect of JavaScript that will be important to you throughout all your scripting ventures: JavaScript is case sensitive. Therefore, you must enter any item in your script that uses a JavaScript word with the correct uppercase and lowercase letters. Your HTML tags (including the `<script>` tag) can be in the case of your choice, but everything in JavaScript is case sensitive. When a line of JavaScript doesn't work, look for the wrong case first. Always compare your typed code against the listings printed in this book and against the various vocabulary entries discussed throughout it.

NOTE XHTML style, if you intend to follow its conventions, requires all lowercase tags and attribute names. This is the style observed throughout this book.

The trigger that runs the script

The script in this page needs to have the div element in place before it can run so that the script can point to that element and insert some HTML into that space. Therefore, the script needs a *trigger* — something to get it going when the time is right. That time, it turns out, is after the entire HTML document has loaded.

As you learn in Chapter 8, the browser fires what is known as an event immediately upon completion of loading the page and whatever content it may contain. For example, an image in the page is downloaded separately from the HTML page, but the page's onload event fires only after the HTML text and image(s) have arrived in the browser.

To get the script to run after the page has loaded, the script includes one statement that instructs the browser to run a specific routine whenever the page receives that event. For this page, the script will run some JavaScript code grouped together in a routine named showBrowserType.

Inserting some text

Now we'll look briefly at the rest of the JavaScript code lines inside the <script>...</script> tag pair. All JavaScript routines are defined as functions. Therefore, the first line of the routine simply alerts the browser that all the stuff between the curly braces ({ }) belongs to the function named showBrowserType.

Despite the four indented lines shown in Listing 3-1, the code is actually just one statement divided into lines for the convenience of printing in this book. Dividing a long statement into lines has to follow some rules, which you will learn in Chapter 6. Therefore, when you enter the script, divide the lines precisely as shown in Listing 3-1.

The basic operation of this routine is to plug some new HTML content inside the div element in the document's body. To do that, we need three key ingredients:

1. A way to refer to the div element
2. A way to insert some new text inside the element
3. The new HTML text that is to go inside the element

In plain language, the routine in the script forces the HTML inside the element (whose ID is "readout") to become whatever new stuff arrives from the right side of the equal (=) sign. To refer to the readout div, the script uses the industry standard way to refer to any HTML element that has an ID attribute:

```
document.getElementById()
```

To specify which element in the document you mean, include the element's ID (in quotes) inside the parentheses:

```
document.getElementById("readout")
```

That points to the element. Now go one step further to point to the property of the element of interest to you: the innerHTML property here. Anything you assign to this property replaces whatever is inside the element's tag pair. Because the readout div element is empty when the page initially loads, you're simply replacing an empty space with whatever is to the right of the equal sign.

Now let's look at the stuff to the right of the equal sign.

The plus (+) signs in the series of lines after the equal sign are the JavaScript way of stringing together batches of text — like stringing beads on a necklace. By placing the combined sequence of text (which includes an HTML <span> tag) to the right of the reference to the element and its innerHTML property, the text is said to be *assigned* to the innerHTML property of the readout element.

Note that neither JavaScript nor the + symbol knows anything about words and spaces. Therefore, the script is responsible for making sure that proper spaces are included in the strings of characters. Notice, for example, that an extra space exists after the word is: in the first line of script after the equal sign.

Getting browser information

To fetch the information about the browser version and name to be displayed in the page, you call upon JavaScript to extract the desired property from a special object called the navigator object. This object features several properties that reveal specifics about the web browser that runs the script. One such property, userAgent, is a copy of the way the browser identifies itself to a server each time it requests a web page. Although you did it earlier in the chapter with the innerHTML property, it's a little clearer here to see how you obtain a copy of a property by appending the property name to the object name (navigator, in this case) and separating the two names with a period. If you're searching for some English to assign mentally to this scheme as you read it, start from the right side, and call the right item a property *of* the left side: the userAgent property of the navigator object. The reference to the property in the script tells the JavaScript interpreter to insert the value of that property into the spot where the call is made. For your first attempt at the script, JavaScript substitutes the internal information about the browser as part of the text string that gets inserted into the div element.

Finally, notice the semicolon character at the end of the long JavaScript statement in the showBrowserType() function. Trailing semicolons — which you can think of as periods at the end of sentences — are purely optional in JavaScript. There is no penalty for leaving them out. If you intend to investigate other programming languages, such as Java or C++, for example, you'll find those semicolons are required. Program listings in this book use semicolons.

If you have another browser installed on your computer, load the page into that browser, too. Compare the way that each browser identifies itself.

Have Some Fun

If you encounter an error in your first attempt at loading this document into your browser, go back to the text editor, and check the lines of the script section against Listing 3-1, looking carefully at each line in light of the explanations. There may be a single character out of place, a lowercase letter where an uppercase one belongs, or a quote or parenthesis missing. Make necessary repairs, switch to your browser, and click Reload.

To see how dynamic the script in script1.html is, go back into the text editor, and replace the word *browser* with *client software*. Save, switch, and reload to see how the script changes the text in the document. Feel free to substitute other text for the quoted text part of the statement to the right of the equal sign. Always be sure to save, switch, and reload to see the results of your handiwork.

Part II

JavaScript Tutorial

Chapter 4

Browser and Document Objects

IN THIS CHAPTER

What client-side scripts do

What happens when a document loads

How the browser creates objects

How scripts refer to objects

What distinguishes one object from another

This chapter marks the first of nine tutorial chapters tailored to web authors who have at least basic grounding in HTML concepts. In particular, you should already be familiar with common HTML tags and their attributes, as well as the fundamentals of Cascading Style Sheets (CSS). In this chapter, you see several practical applications of JavaScript and begin to see how a JavaScript-enabled browser turns familiar HTML elements into objects that your scripts control. This tutorial teaches concepts and terminology that apply to modern browsers, with special focus on standards compatibility to equip you to work with today's and tomorrow's browsers. You should study this tutorial in conjunction with any of the following browsers: Internet Explorer 5 or later (Windows or Macintosh), any Mozilla-based browser (Firefox, Netscape 7 or later, or Camino), Apple Safari, or Opera 7 or later.

Scripts Run the Show

If you have authored web pages with HTML, you are familiar with how HTML tags influence the way content is rendered on a page when viewed in the browser. As the page loads, the browser recognizes angle-bracketed tags as formatting instructions. Instructions are read from the top of the document downward, and elements defined in the HTML document appear onscreen in the same order in which they appear in the document's source code. As an author, you do a little work one time and up front — adding the tags to text content — and the browser does a lot more work every time a visitor loads the page into a browser.

Assume for a moment that one of the elements on the page is a text input field inside a form. The user is supposed to enter some text in the text field and then click the Submit button to send that information back to the web server. If that information must be an Internet e-mail address, how do you ensure the user includes the @ symbol in the address?

One way is to have a Common Gateway Interface (CGI) program on the server inspect the submitted form data after the user clicks the Submit button and the form information is transferred to the server. If the user omits or forgets the @ symbol, the CGI program sends the page back to the browser—but this time with an instruction to include the symbol in the address. Nothing is wrong with this exchange, but it means a significant delay for the user to find out that the address does not contain the crucial symbol. Moreover, the web server has to expend some of its resources to perform the validation and communicate back to the visitor. If the web site is a busy one, the server may try to perform hundreds of these validations at any given moment, probably slowing the response time to the user even more.

Now imagine that the document containing that text input field has some intelligence built into it that makes sure the text-field entry contains the @ symbol before ever submitting one bit (literally!) of data to the server. That kind of intelligence would have to be embedded in the document in some fashion— downloaded with the page's content so it can stand ready to jump into action when called upon. The browser must know how to run that embedded program. Some user action must start the program, perhaps when the user clicks the Submit button. If the program runs inside the browser and detects the lack of the @ symbol, an alert message should appear to bring the problem to the user's attention. The same program also should be capable of deciding whether the actual submission can proceed or whether it should wait until a valid e-mail address is entered in the field.

This kind of presubmission data entry validation is but one of the practical ways JavaScript adds intelligence to an HTML document. Looking at this example, you might recognize that a script must know how to look into what is typed in a text field; a script must also know how to let a submission continue or how to abort the submission. A browser capable of running JavaScript programs conveniently treats elements such as the text field as *objects*. A JavaScript script controls the action and behavior of objects—most of which you see onscreen in the browser window.

When to Use JavaScript

With so many web-oriented development tools and languages at your disposal, you should focus your client-side JavaScript efforts on tasks for which they are best suited. When faced with a web application task, I look to client-side JavaScript for help with the following requirements:

- **Data entry validation.** If form fields need to be filled out for processing on the server, I let client-side scripts prequalify the data entered by the user.

- **Serverless CGIs.** I use this term to describe processes that, were it not for JavaScript, would be programmed as CGIs on the server, yielding slow performance because of the interactivity required between the program and user. This includes tasks such as small data collection lookup, modification of images, and generation of HTML in other frames and windows based on user input.

- **Dynamic HTML interactivity.** It's one thing to use DHTML's capabilities to position elements precisely on the page; you don't need scripting for that. But if you intend to make the content dance on the page, scripting makes that happen.

- **CGI prototyping.** Sometimes you want a CGI program to be at the root of your application because it reduces the potential incompatibilities among browser brands and versions. It may be easier to create a prototype of the CGI in client-side JavaScript. Use this opportunity to polish the user interface before implementing the application as a CGI.

- **Offloading a busy server.** If you have a highly trafficked web site, it may be beneficial to convert frequently used CGI processes to client-side JavaScript scripts. After a page is downloaded, the server is free to serve other visitors. Not only does this lighten server load, but users also experience quicker response to the application embedded in the page.

- **Adding life to otherwise-dead pages.** HTML by itself is pretty flat. Adding a blinking chunk of text doesn't help much; animated GIF images more often distract from, rather than contribute to, the user experience at your site. But if you can dream up ways to add some interactive zip to your page, it may engage the user and encourage a recommendation to friends or repeat visits.

- **Creating web pages that "think."** If you let your imagination soar, you may develop new, intriguing ways to make your pages appear "smart." For example, in the application Intelligent "Updated" Flags (Chapter 54 on the CD-ROM), you see how (without a server CGI or database) an HTML page can "remember" when a visitor last came to the page. Then any items that have been updated since the last visit — regardless of the number of updates you've done to the page — are flagged for that visitor. That's the kind of subtle, thinking web page that best displays JavaScript's powers.

By the same token, web pages and applications intended for public access should not rely exclusively on JavaScript. Make sure that your primary data is accessible to visitors who have JavaScript turned off or who use browsers that don't interpret JavaScript. Let your scripting enhance the experience for the majority of visitors who have JavaScript-enabled browsers.

The Document Object Model

Before you can truly start scripting, you should have a good feel for the kinds of objects you will be scripting. A scriptable browser does a lot of the work of creating software objects that generally represent the visible objects you see in an HTML page in the browser window. Obvious objects include form controls (text boxes and buttons) and images. However, there may be other objects that aren't so obvious by looking at a page but that make perfect sense when you consider the HTML tags used to generate a page's content — paragraph objects or frames of a frameset, for example.

To help scripts control these objects — and to help authors see some method to the madness of potentially dozens of objects on a page — the browser makers define a *document object model (DOM)*. A model is like a prototype or plan for the organization of objects on a page.

Evolution of browser DOMs has caused much confusion and consternation among scripters due to a lack of compatibility across succeeding generations and brands of browsers. Fortunately, the DOM world is stabilizing around a formal specification published by the World Wide Web Consortium (W3C). Today's modern browsers continue to support some of the "old ways" of the earliest DOM because so much existing script code on the Web relies on these traditions continuing to work (you'll see some of these in Chapter 9). But with the vast majority of browsers in use today supporting the basic W3C DOM syntax and terminology, scripters should aim toward standards compatibility whenever possible.

HTML structure and the DOM

An important trend in HTML markup is applying markup solely to define the structure of a document and the context of each piece of content in the document. The days of using HTML tags solely to influence the appearance of a chunk of text are drawing to a close. It is no longer acceptable to enclose a line of text in, say, an <h1> tag because you want the line to appear in the text size and weight that browsers automatically apply to text tagged in that way. An <h1> element has a special context within a document's structure: a first-level heading. In today's HTML world, if you wish to display a stand-alone line of text with a particular style, the text would likely be in a simple paragraph (<p>) tag; the precise look of that paragraph would be under the control of a Cascading Style Sheet (CSS) rule. Current practice even frowns upon the application of <b> and <i> tags to assign boldface and italic styles to a span of text. Instead, surround the text with a contextual tag (such as the <em> element to signify emphasis), and define the CSS style you wish applied to any emphasized text in the document.

The result of applying strict structural design to your HTML tagging is a document that has a well-defined *hierarchy* of elements based on their nesting within one another. For example, an empty HTML document has the following minimum elements:

```
<html>
    <head></head>
    <body></body>
</html>
```

The `html` element contains two nested elements: `head` and `body`. The hierarchy of elements can be charted like a corporate organizational chart, as shown in Figure 4-1. For the sake of upcoming terminology lessons, however, it is more convenient to visualize the chart in Figure 4-1 as a family tree — except that unlike most real family trees, each point that spawns children is a single parent. In the empty HTML document, the `html` element is the parent of two child elements: `head` and `body`. The `html` element is, in turn, a child of the document.

FIGURE 4-1

Element hierarchy of an empty HTML document.

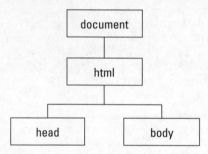

The DOM in a browser window

As its name implies, the formal DOM focuses primarily on the HTML document and the content nested inside it. From a practical standpoint, however, scripters often need to control the environment that contains the document: the window. The `window` object is the top of the hierarchy that browser scripts work with. The basic structure of the object model in modern browsers (given an empty HTML document) is shown in Figure 4-2.

FIGURE 4-2

Basic object model for all modern browsers.

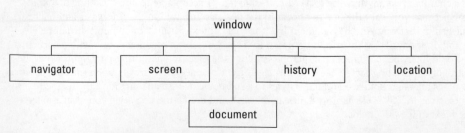

It's not important to memorize the model. But to give you a sense of the relationships among these top-level objects, the following describes their respective roles:

- window **object.** At the very top of the hierarchy is the window. This object represents the content area of the browser window where HTML documents appear. In a multiple-frame environment, each frame is also a window (but don't concern yourself with this just yet). Because all document action takes place inside the window, the window is the outermost element of the object hierarchy. Its physical borders contain the document.

- navigator **object.** This is the closest your scripts come to accessing the browser program, primarily to read the brand and version of browser that holds the current document. This object is read-only, protecting the browser from inappropriate manipulation by rogue scripts.

- screen **object.** This is another read-only object that lets scripts learn about the physical environment in which the browser is running. For example, this object reveals the number of pixels high and wide available in the monitor.

- history **object.** Although the browser maintains internal details about the browser's recent history (such as the list available under the Back button), scripts have no access to the details. At most, this object assists a script in simulating a click of the Back or Forward button.

- location **object.** This object is the primary avenue to loading a different page into the current window or frame. URL information about the window is available under very controlled circumstances so that scripts cannot track access to other web sites.

- document **object.** Each HTML document that gets loaded into a window becomes a document object. The document object contains the content that you are likely to script. Except for the html, head, and body element objects that are found in every HTML document, the precise makeup and structure of the element object hierarchy of the document depend on the content you put into the document.

When a Document Loads

Programming languages, such as JavaScript, are convenient intermediaries between your mental image of how a program works and the true inner workings of the computer. Inside the machine, every word of a program code listing influences the storage and movement of bits (the legendary 1s and 0s of the computer's binary universe) from one RAM storage slot to another. Languages and object models are inside the computer (or, in the case of JavaScript and the DOM, inside the browser's area of the computer) to make it easier for programmers to visualize how a program works and what its results will be. The relationship reminds me a lot of knowing how to drive an automobile from point A to point B without knowing exactly how an internal-combustion engine, steering linkages, and all that other internal "stuff" works. By controlling high-level objects such as the ignition key, gearshift, gas pedal, brake, and steering wheel, I can get the results I need.

Of course, programming is not exactly like driving a car with an automatic transmission. Even scripting requires the equivalent of opening the hood and perhaps knowing how to check the transmission fluid or change the oil. Therefore, now it's time to open the hood and watch what happens to a document's object model as a page loads into the browser.

A simple document

Figure 4-3 shows the HTML and corresponding object model for a document that I'll be adding to in a moment. The figure shows only the document object portion; the window object and its other top-level objects (including the document object) are always there, even for an empty document. When this page loads, the browser maintains in its memory a map of the objects generated by the HTML tags in the document. At this point, only three objects exist inside the document object: one for the outermost html element and one each for its two nested elements.

FIGURE 4-3

Object map of an empty document.

```
<html>
   <head></head>
   <body></body>
</html>
```

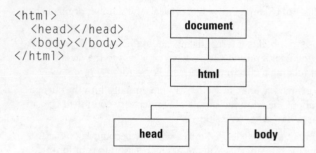

Add a paragraph element

Now I modify the HTML file to include an empty paragraph element and reload the document. Figure 4-4 shows what happens to both the HTML (changes in boldface) and the object map as constructed by the browser. Even though no content appears in the paragraph, the <p> tags are enough to tell the browser to create that p element object. Also note that the p element object is contained by the body element object in the hierarchy of objects in the current map. In other words, the p element object is a *child* of the body element object. The object hierarchy matches the HTML tag containment hierarchy.

FIGURE 4-4

Adding an empty paragraph element.

```
<html>
   <head></head>
   <body>
       <p></p>
   </body>
</html>
```

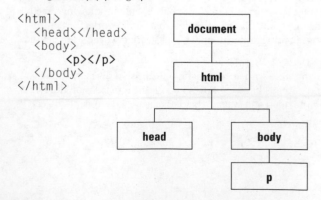

Add paragraph text

I modify and reload the HTML file again, this time inserting the text of the paragraph between the element's start and end tags, as shown in Figure 4-5. A run of text extending between tags is a special kind of object in the DOM called a *text node*. A text node always has an element acting as its container. Applying the official genealogy metaphor to this structure, the text node is a child of its parent p element. We now have a branch of the document object tree that runs several generations: document->html->body->p->text node.

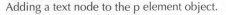

FIGURE 4-5

Adding a text node to the p element object.

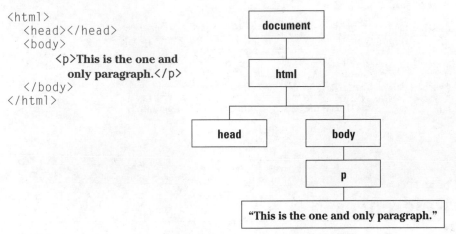

```
<html>
   <head></head>
   <body>
        <p>This is the one and
           only paragraph.</p>
   </body>
</html>
```

Make a new element

The last modification I make to the file is to wrap a portion of the paragraph text in an <em> tag to signify emphasis for the enclosed text. This insertion has a large effect on the hierarchy of the p element object, as shown in Figure 4-6. The p element goes from having a single (text node) child to having three children: two text nodes with an element between them. In the W3C DOM, a text node cannot have any children and therefore cannot contain an element object. The bit of the text node now inside the em element is no longer a child of the p element, but a child of the em element. That text node is now a grandchild of the p element object.

Now that you see how objects are created in memory in response to HTML tags, the next step is to figure out how scripts can communicate with these objects. After all, scripting is mostly about controlling these objects.

FIGURE 4-6

Inserting an element into a text node.

```
<html>
   <head></head>
   <body>
        <p>This is the <em>one and
           only</em>  paragraph.</p>
   </body>
</html>
```

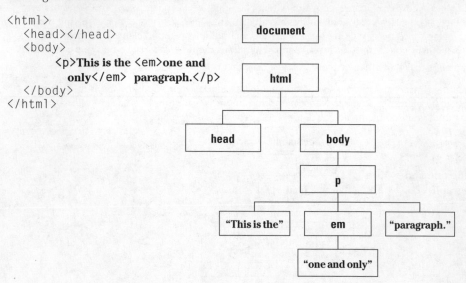

Object References

After a document is loaded into the browser, all of its objects are safely stored in memory in the containment hierarchy structure specified by the browser's DOM. For a script to control one of those objects, there must be a way to communicate with an object and find out something about it (such as "Hey, Mr. Text Field, what did the user type?"). To let your scripts talk to an object, you need a way to refer to that object. That is precisely what an *object reference* in a script does for the browser.

Object naming

The biggest aid in creating script references to objects is assigning a name to every scriptable object in your HTML. In the W3C DOM (and current HTML specification), the way to assign a name to an element is by way of the id attribute. This attribute is optional, but if you plan to use scripts to access an element in the page, it is most convenient to assign a name to that element's id attribute directly in the HTML code. Here are some examples of id attributes added to typical tags:

```
<p id="firstParagraph" >

<img id="logo" src="images/logo.jpg" alt="Corporate Logo">

<div class="draggable" id="puzzlePiece">
```

The only rules about object IDs (also called *identifiers*) are that they:

- May not contain spaces
- Should not contain punctuation except for the underscore character
- Must be inside quotes when assigned to the id attribute
- Must not start with a numeric character
- May not occur more than once in the same document

Think of assigning IDs as the same way as sticking name tags on everyone attending a conference meeting. To find a particular conference attendee whose name you know, you could wait at the entrance and scan each name tag until you find the name you're looking for, or you could bump around the attendees at random in the hope that you'll find a known name. But it would be more efficient if you had a way to target an attendee by name immediately — such as broadcasting the name on the public address system to the whole crowd.

Referencing a particular object

The W3C DOM provides that kind of instant access to any named element in the document. If you haven't programmed before, the syntax for this access command may be intimidating in its length — a hazard when a standard such as the W3C DOM is designed by programmers. Like it or not, we're stuck with this syntax. Here is the syntax you will use frequently in your browser scripting:

```
window.document.getElementById("elementID")
```

You substitute the ID of the element you wish to reference for elementID. For example, if you want to reference the paragraph element whose ID is firstParagraph, the reference would be

```
window.document.getElementById("firstParagraph")
```

Be careful! JavaScript is case sensitive. Be sure that you use uppercase for the three uppercase letters in the command and a lowercase *d* at the end, and that you capitalize the ID accurately as well.

The getElementById() command belongs to the document object, meaning that the entire document's collection of elements is subject to this instantaneous search for a matching ID. The dot — a traditional period character — is the JavaScript way of indicating that the item to the left of the dot (the document object here) has the item to the right of the dot (getElementById() here) as a resource to call upon whenever needed. Each type of object has a list of such resources, as you'll see in a moment (and as summarized in Appendix A).

id versus name Attributes

Prior to the HTML 4.0 specification's introduction of the id attribute, scripts could access a handful of elements that also supported the name attribute. Elements supporting the name attribute are predominantly related to forms, images, and frames. You will see how name attributes work in forms in Chapter 9. In fact, most browsers still require the name attribute for forms and form controls (text fields, buttons, and select lists) for their data to be submitted to a server. It is permissible to assign the same identifier to both the id and name attributes of an element.

Node Terminology

W3C DOM terminology uses metaphors to assist programmers in visualizing the containment hierarchy of a document and its content. One concept you should grasp early in your learning is that of a *node;* the other concept is the family relationship among objects in a document.

About nodes

Although the English dictionary contains numerous definitions of *node,* the one that comes closest to its application in the W3C DOM implies a knob or bump on a tree branch. Such nodules on a branch usually lead to one of two things: a leaf or another branch. A leaf is a dead end in that no further branches emanate from the leaf; the branch kind of node leads to a new branch that can itself have further nodes, whether they be leaves or more branches. When you define the structure of an HTML document, you also define a node structure (also called a *node tree*) whose placement of branches and leaves depends entirely on your HTML elements and text content.

In the W3C DOM, the fundamental building block is a simple, generic node. But inside an HTML document, we work with special kinds of nodes that are tailored to HTML documents. The two types of nodes that scripts touch most often are *element nodes* and *text nodes*. These node types correspond exactly to HTML elements and the text that goes between an element's start and end tags. You've been working with element and text nodes in your HTML authoring, and you didn't even know it.

Look again at the simple document you assembled earlier, along with its containment hierarchy diagram in Figure 4-7. All of the boxes representing HTML elements (html, head, body, p, and em) are element nodes; the three boxes containing actual text that appears in the rendered document are text nodes. You saw in the transition from one long text node (Figure 4-5) to the insertion of the em element (Figure 4-6) that the long text node divided into three pieces. Two text node pieces stayed in the same position in the hierarchy relative to the containing p element. The new em element bullied its way into the tree between the two text nodes and shifted the third text node one level away from the p element.

FIGURE 4-7

A simple HTML document node tree.

```
<html>
   <head></head>
   <body>
      <p>This is the <em>one and
         only</em>  paragraph.</p>
   </body>
</html>
```

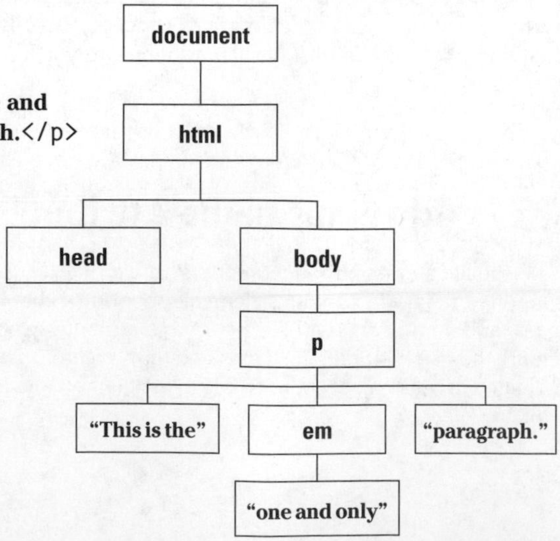

Parents and children

Looking more closely at the p element and its content in Figure 4-7, you can see that element has three *child* nodes. The first and last are of the text node type, whereas the middle one is an element node. When an element contains multiple child nodes, the sequence of child nodes is entirely dependent upon the HTML source code order. Thus, the first child node of the p element is the text node containing the text "This is the ". In the case of the em element, a single child text node is the sole descendant of the element.

Element node children are not always text nodes; neither do branches always end in text nodes. In Figure 4-7, the html element has two child nodes, both of which are element nodes; the body element has one child node, the p element. Even though the head element node appears to be at the end of a branch, it is still an element node because it is capable of containing other nodes (such as a title element). A tag in the HTML indicates an element node, whether or not it has any child nodes. Bt contrast, a text node can never contain another node; it's one of those dead-end leaf type of nodes.

Notice that a child node is always contained by one element node. That container is the *parent* node of its child or children. For example, from the point of view of the em element node, it has both one child (a text node) and one parent (the p element node). A fair amount of W3C DOM terminology (which you'll meet in Chapter 14) concerns itself with assisting scripts to start at any point in a document hierarchy and obtain a reference to a related node if necessary. For instance, if a Dynamic HTML script wants to modify the text inside the em element of Figure 4-7, it typically would do so by starting with a reference to the em element via the document.getElementById() command (assuming that the em element has an ID assigned to it) and then modifying the element's child node.

In case you're wondering, the document object at the top of the node tree is itself a node. Its place in the tree is special and is called simply the *document node*. Each loaded HTML document contains a single document node, and that node becomes the scripter's gateway to the rest of the document's nodes. It's no accident that the syntax for referencing an element node — document.getElementById() — begins with a reference to the document object.

What Defines an Object?

When an HTML tag defines an object in the source code, the browser creates a slot for that object in memory as the page loads. But an object is far more complex internally than, say, a mere number stored in memory. The purpose of an object is to represent some thing. In the browser and its DOM, the most common objects are those that correspond to elements, such as a text input form field, a table element, or the entire rendered body of the document. Outside the pared-down world of the DOM, an object can also represent abstract entities, such as a calendar program's appointment entry or a layer of graphical shapes in a drawing program. It is common for your browser scripts to work with both DOM objects and abstract objects of your own design.

Every type of DOM object is unique in some way, even if two or more objects look identical to you in the browser. Three very important facets of an object define what it is, what it looks like, how it behaves, and how scripts control it. Those three facets are properties, methods, and events (also known as handlers). They play such key roles in your future DOM scripting efforts that the Object Quick Reference in Appendix A summarizes the properties, methods, and events for each object in the object models implemented in various browser generations.

Properties

Any physical object you hold in your hand has a collection of characteristics that defines it. A coin, for example, has shape, diameter, thickness, color, weight, embossed images on each side — and any number of other attributes that distinguish it from, say, a feather. Each of those features is called a *property*. Each property has a value of some kind attached to it (even if the value is empty or null). For example, the shape property of a coin might be circle — in this case, a text value. By contrast, the denomination property is most likely a numeric value.

You may not have known it, but if you've written HTML for use in a scriptable browser, you have set object properties without writing one iota of JavaScript. Tag attributes are the most common way to set an HTML element object's initial properties. For example, the following HTML tag defines an input element object that assigns four property values:

```
<input type="button" id="clicker" name="clicker" value="Hit Me...">
```

In JavaScript parlance, then, the type property holds the word *button;* the id and name properties hold the same word, *clicker;* and the value property is the text that appears on the button label, *Hit Me....* In truth, a button input element has more properties than just these, but you don't have to set every property for every object. Most properties have *default values* that are automatically assigned if nothing special is set in the HTML or later from a script.

The contents of some properties can change after a document has loaded and the user interacts with the page. Consider the following text input tag:

```
<input type="text" id="entry" name="entry" value="User Name?">
```

The id and name properties of this object are the same word: *entry.* When the page loads, the text of the value attribute setting is placed in the text field — the automatic behavior of an HTML text field when the value attribute is specified. But if a user enters some other text into the text field, the value property changes — not in the HTML, but in the memory copy of the object model that the browser maintains. Therefore, if a script queries the text field about the content of the value property, the browser yields the current setting of the property — which isn't necessarily the one specified by the HTML.

To gain access to an object's property, you use the same kind of dot-notation addressing scheme you saw earlier for objects. A property is a resource belonging to its object, so the reference to it consists of the reference to the object plus one more extension naming the property. Therefore, for the button and text object tags just shown, references to various properties are

```
document.getElementById("clicker").name
document.getElementById("clicker").value
document.getElementById("entry").value
```

You may wonder what happened to the window part of the reference. It turns out that there can be only one document contained in a window, so references to objects inside the document can omit the window portion and start the reference with document. You cannot omit the document object from the reference, however.

Methods

If a property is like a descriptive adjective for an object, a method is a verb. A *method* is all about action related to the object. A method either does something to the object or with the object that affects other parts of a script or document. Methods are commands of a sort whose behaviors are tied to a particular object.

Internet Explorer References

Before the W3C DOM came into existence, Microsoft had created its own way of referencing element objects by way of their `id` attributes. You will find many instances of this syntax in existing code that has been written only for Internet Explorer 4 or later. The syntax uses a construction called `document.all`. Although there are a few different ways to use this construction, the most commonly applied way is to continue the dot notation to include the ID of the element. For example, if a paragraph element's ID is `myParagraph`, the IE-only reference syntax is

```
document.all.myParagraph
```

You can also omit the lead-in parts of the reference and simply refer to the ID of the element:

```
myParagraph
```

Be aware, however, that none of these approaches is supported in the W3C DOM standard. Both the IE-specific and W3C DOM reference syntax styles are implemented in IE5 or later. Going forward, you should migrate existing code to the W3C DOM style to be compatible with more browsers.

An object can have any number of methods associated with it (including none at all). To set a method into motion (usually called *invoking a method*), a JavaScript statement must include a reference to it, via its object with a pair of parentheses after the method name, as in the following examples:

```
document.getElementById("orderForm").submit()
document.getElementById("entry").focus()
```

The first is a scripted way of sending a form (named `orderForm`) to a server. The second gives focus to a text field named `entry`.

Sometimes a method requires that you send additional information with it so that it can do its job. Each chunk of information passed with the method is called a *parameter* or *argument* (you can use the terms interchangeably). The `document.getElementById()` method is one that requires a parameter; the identifier of the element object to be addressed for further action. This method's parameter must be in a format consisting of straight text, signified by the quotes around the identifier.

Some methods require more than one parameter. If so, the multiple parameters are separated by commas. For example, modern browsers support a `window` object method that moves the window to a particular coordinate point onscreen. A *coordinate point* is defined by two numbers that indicate the number of pixels from the left and top edges of the screen where the top-left corner of the window should be. To move the browser window to a spot 50 pixels from the left and 100 pixels from the top, the method is

```
window.moveTo(50,100)
```

As you learn more about the details of JavaScript and the document objects you can script, pay close attention to the range of methods defined for each object. They reveal a lot about what an object is capable of doing under script control.

Events

One last characteristic of a DOM object is the event. *Events* are actions that take place in a document, usually as the result of user activity. Common examples of user actions that trigger events include clicking a button or typing a character in a text field. Some events, such as the act of loading a document into the browser window or experiencing a network error while an image loads, are not so obvious.

Almost every DOM object in a document receives events of one kind or another — summarized for your convenience in the Object Quick Reference of Appendix A. Your job as scripter is to write the code that tells an element object to perform an action whenever the element receives a particular type of event. The action is simply executing some additional JavaScript code.

The simplest way to begin learning about events is to add an event-related attribute to the element's HTML tag. The attribute's name consists of the type of event (for example, `click`) preceded by the preposition *on* — as in "on receiving the `click` event . . .". The attribute's value (to the right of the equal sign, just like any HTML attribute) consists of the JavaScript instructions to follow whenever the event reaches the element. Listing 4-1 shows a very simple document that displays a single button with one event handler defined for it.

LISTING 4-1

A Simple Button with an Event Handler

```
<html>
<body>
<form>
<input type="button" value="Click Me" onclick="window.alert ('Ouch!')">
</form>
</body>
</html>
```

The form definition contains what for the most part looks like a standard `input` element. But notice the last attribute, `onclick="window.alert('Ouch!')"`. Button input objects, as you see in their complete descriptions in Chapter 22, react to mouse clicks. When a user clicks the button, the browser sends a `click` event to the button. In this button's definition, the attribute says that whenever the button receives that event, it should invoke one of the `window` object's methods, `alert()`. The `alert()` method displays a simple alert dialog box whose content is whatever text is passed as a parameter to the method. Like most arguments to HTML attributes, the attribute setting to the right of the equal sign goes inside quotes. If additional quotes are necessary, as in the case of the text to be passed along with the event handler, those inner quotes can be single quotes. In actuality, JavaScript doesn't distinguish between single or double quotes but does require that each pair be of the same type. Therefore, you can write the attribute this way:

```
onclick='alert("Ouch!")'
```

You will learn about other ways to connect scripting instructions to events in Chapter 14 and Chapter 25.

Exercises

1. Which of the following applications are well suited to client-side JavaScript? Why or why not?

   a. Product catalog page that lets visitors view the product in five different colors

   b. A counter that displays the total number of visitors to the current page

   c. Chat room

   d. Graphical Fahrenheit-to-Celsius temperature calculator

   e. All of the above

   f. None of the above

2. Which of the following object names are valid in JavaScript? For each one that is invalid, explain why.

   a. `lastName`

   b. `company_name`

   c. `1stLineAddress`

   d. `zip code`

   e. `today's_date`

3. Using the diagram from Figure 4-7 for reference, draw a diagram of the object model containment hierarchy that the browser would create in its memory for the following HTML. Write the script reference to the second paragraph element using W3C DOM syntax.

```
<html>
<head>
<title>Search Form</title>
</head>
<body>
<p id="logoPar"><img src="images/logo.jpg" height="90" width="300"
alt="Logo" /></p>
<p id="formPar">
<form name="searchForm" action="cgi-bin/search.pl" method="POST">
Search for: <input type="text" name="searchText" />
<input type="submit" value="Search" />
</form>
</p>
</body>
</html>
```

4. Describe at least two characteristics that a text node and an element node have in common; describe at least two characteristics that distinguish a text node from an element node.

5. Write the HTML tag for a button input element named `Hi`, whose visible label reads `Howdy` and whose action upon being clicked displays an alert dialog box that says `Hello to you, too!`

Chapter 5

Scripts and HTML Documents

In this chapter's tutorial, you begin to see how scripts are embedded within HTML documents and what comprises a script statement. You also see how script statements can run when the document loads or in response to user action. Finally, you find out where script error information may be hiding.

Where Scripts Go in Documents

Chapter 4 did not thoroughly cover what scripts look like or how you add them to an HTML document. That's where this lesson picks up the story.

The <script> tag

To assist the browser in recognizing lines of code in an HTML document as belonging to a script, you surround lines of script code with a `<script>...</script>` tag set. This is common usage in HTML, where start and end tags encapsulate content controlled by that tag, whether the tag set is for a form or a paragraph.

Depending on the browser, the `<script>` tag has a variety of attributes you can set that govern the script. One attribute, `type`, advises the browser to treat the code within the tag as JavaScript. Some other browsers accept additional languages (such as Microsoft's VBScript in Windows versions of Internet Explorer). The following setting is one that all modern scriptable browsers accept:

```
<script type="text/javascript">
```

Be sure to include the ending tag for the script. Lines of JavaScript code go between the two tags:

```
<script  type="text/javascript">
   one or more lines of JavaScript code here
</script>
```

If you forget the closing script tag, the script may not run properly, and the HTML elsewhere in the page may look strange.

The Old language Attribute

Another `<script>` tag attribute, language, used to be the way to specify the scripting language for the enclosed code. That attribute allowed scripters to specify the language version. For example, if the scripts included code that required JavaScript syntax available only in version 4 browsers (which implemented JavaScript version 1.2), the `<script>` tag used to be written as follows:

```
<script language="JavaScript1.2">...</script>
```

The language attribute was never part of the HTML 4.0 specification and is now falling out of favor. If W3C validation is one of your development concerns, the attribute does not validate in strict versions of HTML 4.01 or XHTML 1.0. Older browsers that do not know the type attribute automatically default to JavaScript anyway. Use only the type attribute.

Although you don't work with it in this tutorial, another attribute works with more recent browsers to blend the contents of an external script file into the current document. An src attribute (similar to the src attribute of an `<img>` tag) points to the file containing the script code. Such files must end with a .js extension. The tag set looks like the following:

```
<script  type="text/javascript" src="myscript.js"></script>
```

All script lines are in the external file, so no script lines are included between the start and end script tags in the document. The end tag is still required.

Tag positions

Where do these tags go within a document? The answer is, anywhere they're needed in the document. Most of the time, it makes sense to include the tags nested within the `<head>`...`</head>` tag set; other times, it is essential that you drop the script into a very specific location in the `<body>`...`</body>` section.

In the following four listings, I demonstrate — with the help of a skeletal HTML document — some of the possibilities of `<script>` tag placement. Later in this lesson, you see why scripts may need to go in different places within a page depending on the scripting requirements.

Listing 5-1 shows the outline of what may be the most common position of a `<script>` tag set in a document: in the `<head>` tag section. Typically, the Head is a place for tags that influence noncontent settings for the page — so-called HTML *directive* elements, such as `<meta>` tags and the document title. It turns out that this is also a convenient place to plant scripts that are called on in response to user action.

LISTING 5-1

Scripts in the Head

```
<html>
<head>
<title>A Document</title>
<script  type="text/javascript">
   //script statement(s) here
   ...
</script>
```

```
</head>
<body>
</body>
</html>
```

On the other hand, if you need a script to run as the page loads so that the script generates content in the page, the script goes in the `<body>` portion of the document, as shown in Listing 5-2.

LISTING 5-2

A Script in the Body

```
<html>
<head>
<title>A Document</title>
</head>
<body>
<script  type="text/javascript">
   //script statement(s) here
   ...
</script>
</body>
</html>
```

It's also good to know that you can place an unlimited number of `<script>` tag sets in a document. For example, Listing 5-3 shows a script in both the Head and Body portions of a document. Perhaps this document needs the Body script to create some dynamic content as the page loads, but the document also contains a button that needs a script to run later. That script is stored in the Head portion.

LISTING 5-3

Scripts in the Head and Body

```
<html>
<head>
<title>A Document</title>
<script  type="text/javascript">
   //script statement(s) here
   ...
</script>
</head>
<body>
<script  type="text/javascript">
   //script statement(s) here
   ...
</script>
</body>
</html>
```

You are not limited to one `<script>` tag set in either the Head or Body. You can include as many `<script>` tag sets in a document as are needed to complete your application. In Listing 5-4, for example, two `<script>` tag sets are located in the Head portion. One set is used to load an external `.js` library; the other includes code specifically tailored to the current page.

LISTING 5-4

Two Scripts in the Body

```
<html>
<head>
<title>A Document</title>
</head>
<script  type="text/javascript" src="js/jslibrary.js"></script>
<script  type="text/javascript">
   //script statement(s) here
   ...
</script>
<body>
</body>
</html>
```

Handling non-JavaScript browsers

Only browsers that include JavaScript know to interpret the lines of code between the `<script>...</script>` tag pair as script statements and not HTML text for display in the browser. This means that a pre-JavaScript browser or a simplified browser in a cell phone not only ignores the tags, but also treats the JavaScript code as page content. The results can be disastrous to a page.

You can reduce the risk of non-JavaScript browsers displaying the script lines by playing a trick. The trick is to enclose the script lines between HTML comment symbols, as shown in Listing 5-5. Most nonscriptable browsers ignore the content between the `<!--` and `-->` comment tags, whereas scriptable browsers ignore those comment symbols when they appear inside a `<script>` tag set.

LISTING 5-5

Hiding Scripts from Most Old Browsers

```
<script  type="text/javascript">
<!--
   //script statement(s) here
   ...
// -->
</script>
```

The odd construction right before the ending script tag needs a brief explanation. The two forward slashes are a JavaScript comment symbol. This symbol is necessary because JavaScript otherwise tries to interpret the components of the ending HTML symbol (`-->`). Therefore, the forward slashes tell JavaScript to skip the line entirely; a nonscriptable browser simply treats those slash characters as part of the entire HTML comment to be ignored.

Despite the fact that this technique is often called *hiding scripts,* it does not disguise the scripts entirely. All client-side JavaScript scripts are part of the HTML document and download to the browser just like all other HTML. Furthermore, you can view them as part of the document's source code. Do not be fooled into thinking that you can hide your scripts entirely from prying eyes.

JavaScript Statements

Virtually every line of code that sits between a `<script>`... `</script>` tag pair is a JavaScript *statement.* To be compatible with habits of experienced programmers, JavaScript accepts a semicolon at the end of every statement (the computer equivalent of a period at the end of a sentence). Fortunately for newcomers, this semicolon is optional: The carriage return at the end of a statement suffices for JavaScript to know that the statement has ended. It is possible that in the future, the semicolon will be required, so it's a good idea to get into the semicolon habit now.

A statement must be in the script for a purpose. Therefore, every statement does something relevant to the script. The kinds of things that statements do are

- Define or initialize a variable
- Assign a value to a property or variable
- Change the value of a property or variable
- Invoke an object's method
- Invoke a function routine
- Make a decision

If you don't yet know what all of these things mean, don't worry; you will by the end of this tutorial. The point I want to stress is that each statement contributes to the scripts you write. The only statement that doesn't perform any explicit action is the *comment.* A pair of forward slashes (no space between them) is the most common way to include a comment in a script. You add comments to a script for your benefit. They usually explain in plain language what a statement or group of statements does. The purpose of including comments is to remind you six months from now how your script works.

When Script Statements Execute

Now that you know where scripts go in a document, it's time to look at when they run. Depending on what you need a script to do, you have four choices for determining when a script runs:

- While a document loads
- Immediately after a document loads
- In response to user action
- When called upon by other script statements

The determining factor is how the script statements are positioned in a document.

While a document loads: immediate execution

Listing 5-6 is a variation of your first script from Chapter 3. In this version, the script writes the browser information to the page while the page loads. The `document.write()` method is the primary way to cause dynamic content — the values of the two navigator object properties in this case — to be rendered in the page *during* loading. I call the kinds of statements that run as the page loads *immediate statements*.

LISTING 5-6

HTML Page with Immediate Script Statements

```
<html>
<head>
<title>My First Script--II</title>
<style type="text/css">
.highlight {font-weight: bold}
</style>
</head>

<body>
<h1>Let's Script...</h1>
<hr>
<script type="text/javascript">
<!-- hide from old browsers
document.write("This browser is version " + navigator.appVersion);
document.write(" of <span class='highlight'>" + navigator.appName + "</span>.");
// end script hiding -->
</script>
</body>
</html>
```

Deferred scripts

The other three ways that script statements run are grouped together as what I call *deferred scripts*. To demonstrate these deferred script situations, I must introduce you briefly to a concept covered in more depth in Chapter 7: the function. A *function* defines a block of script statements summoned to run some time after those statements load into the browser. Functions are clearly visible inside a `<script>` tag because each function definition begins with the word `function` followed by the function name (and parentheses). After a function is loaded into the browser (commonly in the Head portion so that it loads early), it stands ready to run whenever called upon.

Run after loading

One of the times a function is called upon to run is immediately after a page loads. The `window` object has an event handler property called `onload`. Unlike most event handlers, which are triggered in response to user action (for example, clicking a button), the window's `onload` event handler fires the instant that all of the page's components (including images, Java applets, and embedded multimedia) are loaded into the browser.

There are two cross-browser ways to connect the onload event handler to a function: via an HTML event attribute or an object event property. For the HTML attribute approach, the <body> element stands in to represent the window. Therefore, you can include the onload event attribute in the <body> tag, as shown in Listing 5-7. Recall from Chapter 4 (Listing 4-1) that an event handler can run a script statement directly. But if the event handler must run several script statements, it is usually more convenient to put those statements in a function definition and then have the event handler *invoke* that function. That's what happens in Listing 5-7: When the page completes loading, the onload event handler triggers the done() function. That function (simplified for this example) displays an alert dialog box.

LISTING 5-7

Running a Script from the onload Event Handler

```
<html>
<head>
<title>An onload script</title>
<script  type="text/javascript">
<!--
function done() {
   alert("The page has finished loading.");
}
// -->
</script>
</head>
<body onload="done()">
Here is some body text.
</body>
</html>
```

Don't worry about the curly braces or other oddities in Listing 5-7 that may cause you concern at this point. Focus instead on the structure of the document and the flow. The entire page loads without running any script statements, although the page loads the done() function in memory so that it is ready to run at a moment's notice. After the document loads, the browser fires the onload event handler, which causes the done() function to run. Then the user sees the alert dialog box.

Although the HTML event attribute approach dates back to the earliest JavaScript browsers, the trend these days is to separate HTML markup from specifics of style and behavior (scripts). To the scripter's rescue come the equivalent event handler properties of objects. To get the onload attribute out of the <body> tag, you can instead assign the desired JavaScript function to the object's event as a property, as in:

```
window.onload = done;
```

Such statements typically go near the end of scripts in the Head portion of the document. Note, too, that in this version, the right side of the statement is merely the function's name, with no quotes or parentheses. Because it is easier to learn about event handlers when they're specified as HTML attributes, most examples in this tutorial continue with that approach. I needed to show you the property version, however, because you will see lots of real-life code using that format.

Run by user

Getting a script to execute in response to a user action is very similar to the preceding example for running a deferred script right after the document loads. Commonly, a script function is defined in the Head portion, and an event handler in, say, a form element calls upon that function to run. Listing 5-8 includes a script that runs when a user clicks a button.

LISTING 5-8

Running a Script from User Action

```
<html>
<head>
<title>An onclick script</title>
<script type="text/javascript">
<!--
function alertUser() {
    alert("Ouch!");
}
// -->
</script>
</head>
<body>
Here is some body text.
<form>
    <input type="text" name="entry">
    <input type="button" name="oneButton" value="Press Me!" onclick="alertUser()">
</form>
</body>
</html>
```

Not every object must have an event handler defined for it, as shown in Listing 5-8 — only the ones for which scripting is needed. No script statements execute in Listing 5-8 until the user clicks the button. The alertUser() function is defined as the page loads, and it waits to run as long as the page remains loaded in the browser. If it is never called upon to run, there's no harm done.

Called by another function

The last scenario for when script statements run also involves functions. In this case, a function is called upon to run by another script statement. Before you see how that works, it helps to read the next lesson (Chapter 6). Therefore, I will hold off on this example until later in the tutorial.

Viewing Script Errors

In the early days of JavaScript in browsers, script errors displayed themselves in very obvious dialog boxes. These boxes were certainly helpful for scripters who wanted to debug their scripts. However, if a bug got through to a page served up to a nontechnical user, the error alert dialog boxes were not only disruptive, but also scary. To prevent such dialog boxes from disturbing unsuspecting users, the browser makers tried to diminish the visual impact of errors in the browser window. Unfortunately for scripters, it is often easy to overlook the fact that your script contains an error because the error is not so obvious. Recent browser versions have different ways of letting scripters see the errors.

In IE5+, you can set its preferences so that scripts do not generate error dialog boxes (choose Tools ⇨ Internet Options ⇨ Advanced ⇨ Browsing, and find the checkbox entry that says Display a notification about every script error). Even with error dialog boxes turned off, error indications are displayed subtly at the left edge of the browser window's status bar. An alert icon and message ("Error on page") appear in the status bar. If you double-click the icon, the error dialog box appears (see Figure 5-1). Be sure to expand the dialog box by clicking the Show Details button. Unless you turn on script-error dialog boxes and keep them coming, you have to train yourself to monitor the status bar when a page loads and after each script runs.

FIGURE 5-1

The expanded IE error dialog box.

For Mozilla-based browsers, choose Tools ⇨ Web Development ⇨ JavaScript (or Error) Console. The JavaScript console window opens to reveal the error message details (see Figure 5-2). You can keep this window open all the time if you like. Unless you clear the window, subsequent error messages are appended to the bottom of the window.

FIGURE 5-2

The Mozilla 1.4 JavaScript console window.

Safari records script errors, but it's not obvious how to read them. You first must enable Safari's Debug menu by typing the following command in the Terminal application:

```
defaults write com.apple.Safari IncludeDebugMenu 1
```

Then, each time you launch Safari, choose Debug ⇨ Show JavaScript Console.

Understanding error messages and doing something about them is a very large subject, reserved for advanced discussion in Chapter 45 on the CD-ROM. During this tutorial, however, you can use the error messages to see whether you perhaps mistyped a script from a listing in the book.

Scripting versus Programming

You may get the impression that scripting is easier than programming. *Scripting* simply sounds easier or more friendly than *programming*. In many respects, this is true. One of my favorite analogies is the difference between a hobbyist who builds model airplanes from scratch and a hobbyist who builds model airplanes from commercial kits. The "from scratch" hobbyist carefully cuts and shapes each piece of wood and metal according to very detailed plans before the model starts to take shape. The commercial kit builder starts with many prefabricated parts and assembles them into the finished product. When both builders are finished, you may not be able to tell which airplane was built from scratch and which one came out of a box of components. In the end, both builders used many of the same techniques to complete the assembly, and each can take pride in the result.

Thanks to implementations of the document object model (DOM), the browser gives scripters many prefabricated components with which to work. Without the browser, you'd have to be a pretty good programmer to develop from scratch your own application that served up content and offered user interaction. In the end, both authors have working applications that look equally professional.

Beyond the DOM, however, real programming nibbles its way into the scripting world. That's because scripts (and programs) work with more than just objects. When I said earlier in this lesson that each statement of a JavaScript script does something, that something involves data of some kind. *Data* is the information associated with objects or other pieces of information that a script pushes around from place to place with each statement.

Data takes many forms. In JavaScript, the common incarnations of data are numbers, text (called *strings*), objects (both from the object model and others you can create with scripts), and `true` and `false` (called *Boolean values*).

Each programming or scripting language determines numerous structures and limits for each kind of data. Fortunately for newcomers to JavaScript, the universe of knowledge necessary for working with data is smaller than in a language such as Java or C++. At the same time, what you learn about data in JavaScript is immediately applicable to future learning you may undertake in any other programming language; don't believe for an instant that your efforts in learning scripting will be wasted.

Because deep down, scripting *is* programming, you need to have a basic knowledge of fundamental programming concepts to consider yourself a good JavaScript scripter. In the next two lessons, I set aside most discussion about the DOM and focus on the programming principles that will serve you well in JavaScript and future programming endeavors.

Exercises

1. Write the complete script tag set for a script whose lone statement is
```
document.write("Hello, world.");
```

2. Build an HTML document, and include the answer to the previous question such that the page executes the script as it loads. Open the document in your browser to test the results.

3. Add a comment to the script in the previous answer that explains what the script does.

4. Create an HTML document that displays an alert dialog box immediately after the page loads and displays a different alert dialog box when the user clicks a form button.

5. Carefully study the document in Listing 5-9. Without entering and loading the document, predict

   a. What the page looks like

   b. How users interact with the page

   c. What the script does

Then type the listing into a text editor as shown. (Observe all capitalization and punctuation.) **Do not type a carriage return after the = sign in the** upperMe **function statement; let the line word-wrap as it does in the following listing.** It's OK to use a carriage return between attribute name/value pairs, as shown in the first `<input>` tag. Save the document as an HTML file, and load the file into your browser to see how well you did.

LISTING 5-9

How Does This Page Work?

```html
<html>
<head>
<title>Text Object Value</title>
<script type="text/javascript">
<!--
function upperMe() {
    document.getElementById("output").value =
document.getElementById("input").value.toUpperCase();
}
// -->
</script>
</head>

<body>
Enter lowercase letters for conversion to uppercase:<br>
<form name="converter">
    <input type="text" name="input" id="input"
        value="sample" onchange="upperMe()" /><br />
    <input type="text" name="output" id="output" value="" />
</form>
</body>
</html>
```

Chapter 6

Programming Fundamentals, Part I

The tutorial breaks away from HTML and documents for a while as you begin to learn programming fundamentals that apply to practically every scripting and programming language you will encounter. Here, you start learning about variables, expressions, data types, and operators—things that might sound scary if you haven't programmed before. Don't worry. With a little practice, you will become quite comfortable with these terms and concepts.

IN THIS CHAPTER

What variables are and how to use them

Why you must learn how to evaluate expressions

How to convert data from one type to another

How to use basic operators

What Language Is This?

The language you're studying is called JavaScript. But the language has some other names that you may have heard. JScript is Microsoft's name for the language. By leaving out the *ava*, the company doesn't have to license the Java name from its trademark owner: Sun Microsystems.

A standards body called ECMA (pronounced "ECK-ma") now governs the specifications for the language (no matter what you call it). The document that provides all of the details about the language is known as *ECMA-262* (it's the 262nd standard published by ECMA). Both JavaScript and JScript are ECMA-262 compatible. Some earlier browser versions exhibit very slight deviations from ECMA-262 (which came later than the earliest browsers). The most serious discrepancies are noted in the core language reference in Part IV of this book.

Working with Information

With rare exceptions, every JavaScript statement you write does something with a hunk of information—*data*. Data may be text information displayed onscreen by a JavaScript statement or the on/off setting of a radio button in a form. Each single piece of information in programming is also called a *value*. Outside of programming, the term *value* usually connotes a number of some kind; in the programming

57

world, however, the term is not as restrictive. A string of letters is a value. A number is a value. The setting of a checkbox (whether it is checked or not) is a value.

In JavaScript, a value can be one of several types. Table 6-1 lists JavaScript's formal data types, with examples of the values you will see displayed from time to time.

TABLE 6-1

JavaScript Value (Data) Types

Type	Example	Description
String	`"Howdy"`	A series of characters inside quote marks
Number	`4.5`	Any number not inside quote marks
Boolean	`true`	A logical true or false
Null	`null`	Devoid of any content but a value just the same
Object		A software thing that is defined by its properties and methods (arrays are also objects)
Function		A function definition

A language that contains these few data types simplifies programming tasks, especially those involving what other languages consider to be incompatible types of numbers (integers versus real or floating-point values). In some definitions of syntax and parts of objects later in this book, I make specific reference to the type of value accepted in placeholders. When a string is required, any text inside a set of quotes suffices.

You will encounter situations, however, in which the value type may get in the way of a smooth script step. For example, if a user enters a number into a form's text input field, the browser stores that number as a string value type. If the script is to perform some arithmetic on that number, you must convert the string to a number before you can apply the value to any math operations. You see examples of this later in this lesson.

Variables

Cooking up a dish according to a recipe in the kitchen has one advantage over cooking up some data in a program. In the kitchen, you follow recipe steps and work with real things: carrots, milk, or a salmon filet. A computer, on the other hand, follows a list of instructions to work with data. Even if the data represents something that looks real, such as the text entered into a form's input field, once after value gets into the program, you can no longer reach out and touch it.

In truth, the data that a program works with is merely a collection of bits (on and off states) in your computer's memory. More specifically, data in a JavaScript-enhanced web page occupies parts of the computer's memory set aside for exclusive use by the browser software. In the olden days, programmers had to know the numeric address in memory (RAM) where a value was stored to retrieve a copy of it for, say, some addition. Although the innards of a program have that level of complexity, programming languages such as JavaScript shield you from it.

The most convenient way to work with data in a script is first to assign the data to a *variable*. It's usually easier to think of a variable as a basket that holds information. How long the variable holds the information depends on a number of factors. But the instant a web page clears the window (or frame), any variables it knows about are discarded.

Creating a variable

You have a couple of ways to create a variable in JavaScript, but one covers you properly in all cases. Use the var keyword, followed by the name you want to give that variable. Therefore, to *declare* a new variable called myAge, the JavaScript statement is

```
var myAge;
```

That statement lets the browser know that you can use that variable later to hold information or to modify any of the data in that variable.

To assign a value to a variable, use one of the *assignment operators*. The most common one by far is the equal sign. If I want to assign a value to the myAge variable at the same time I declare it (a combined process known as *initializing the variable*), I use that operator in the same statement as the var keyword:

```
var myAge = 45;
```

On the other hand, if I declare a variable in one statement and later want to assign a value to it, the sequence of statements is

```
var myAge;
myAge = 45;
```

Use the var keyword **only for declaration or initialization** — once for the life of any variable name in a document.

A JavaScript variable can hold any value type. Unlike many other languages, you don't have to tell JavaScript during variable declaration what type of value the variable will hold. In fact, the value type of a variable can change during the execution of a program. (This flexibility drives experienced programmers crazy because they're accustomed to assigning both a data type and a value to a variable.)

Variable names

Choose the names you assign to variables with care. You'll often find scripts that use vague variable names, such as single letters. Other than a few specific times where using letters is a common practice (for example, using i as a counting variable in repeat loops in Chapter 7), I recommend using names that truly describe a variable's contents. This practice can help you follow the state of your data through a long series of statements or jumps, especially for complex scripts.

A number of restrictions help instill good practice in assigning names. First, you cannot use any reserved keyword as a variable name. That includes all keywords currently used by the language and all others held in reserve for future versions of JavaScript. The designers of JavaScript, however, cannot foresee every keyword that the language may need in the future. By using the kind of single words that currently appear in the list of reserved keywords (see Appendix B), you always run a risk of a future conflict.

To complicate matters, a variable name cannot contain space characters. Therefore, one-word variable names are fine. Should your description really benefit from more than one word, you can use one of two conventions to join multiple words as one. One convention is to place an underscore character between the words; the other is to start the combination word with a lowercase letter and capitalize the first letter of each subsequent word within the name — I refer to this as the *interCap format*. Both of the following examples are valid variable names:

```
my_age
myAge
```

My preference is for the second version. I find it easier to type as I write JavaScript code and easier to read later. In fact, because of the potential conflict with future one-word keywords, using multiword combinations for variable names is a good idea. Multiword combinations are less likely to appear in the list of reserved words.

Variable names have a couple of other important restrictions. Avoid all punctuation symbols except for the underscore character. Also, the first character of a variable name cannot be a numeral. If these restrictions sound familiar, it's because they're identical to those for HTML element identifiers described in Chapter 4.

Expressions and Evaluation

Another concept closely related to the value and variable is *expression evaluation* — perhaps the most important concept in learning how to program a computer.

We use expressions in our everyday language. Remember the theme song of "The Beverly Hillbillies"?:

Then one day he was shootin' at some food

And up through the ground came a-bubblin' crude

Oil, that is. Black gold. Texas tea.

At the end of the song, you find four quite different references (crude, oil, black gold, and Texas tea). They all mean oil. They're all *expressions* for oil. Say any one of them, and other people know what you mean. In our minds, we *evaluate* those expressions to mean one thing: oil.

In programming, a variable always evaluates to its contents, or value. For example, after assigning a value to a variable, such as

```
var myAge = 45;
```

any time the variable is used in a statement, its value (45) is automatically applied to whatever operation that statement calls. Therefore, if you're 15 years my junior, I can assign a value to a variable representing your age based on the evaluated value of myAge:

```
var yourAge = myAge - 15;
```

The variable, yourAge, evaluates to 30 the next time the script uses it. If the myAge value changes later in the script, the change has no link to the yourAge variable because myAge evaluated to 45 when it was used to assign a value to yourAge.

Expressions in scripts

You probably didn't recognize it at the time, but you have seen how expression evaluation came in handy in several scripts in previous chapters. Let's look at one in particular — from Listing 5-6 — where a script writes dynamic text to the page as the page loads. Recall the second document.write() statement:

```
document.write(" of " + navigator.appName + ".");
```

Testing JavaScript Evaluation

You can begin experimenting with the way JavaScript evaluates expressions with the help of The Evaluator Jr. (shown in the following figure), an HTML page you can find on the companion CD-ROM. (I introduce the Senior version in Chapter 13.) Enter any JavaScript expression into the top text box, and either press Enter/Return or click the Evaluate button.

The Evaluator Jr. for testing expression evaluation.

The Evaluator Jr. has 26 variables (lowercase a through z) predefined for you. Therefore, you can assign values to variables, test comparison operators, and even do math here. Using the age variable examples from earlier in this chapter, type each of the following statements in the upper text box, and observe how each expression evaluates in the Results field. Be sure to observe case sensitivity in your entries. The trailing semicolons are optional in The Evaluator.

```
a = 45;
a;
b = a - 15;
b;
a - b;
a > b;
```

To start over, click the Reload/Refresh button.

The document.write() method (remember, JavaScript uses the term *method* to mean *command*) requires a parameter in the parentheses: the text string to be displayed on the web page. The parameter here consists of one expression that joins three distinct strings:

```
" of "
navigator.appName
"."
```

The plus symbol is one of JavaScript's ways of joining strings. Before JavaScript can display this line, it must perform some quick evaluations. The first evaluation is the value of the `navigator.appName` property. This property evaluates to a string of the name of your browser. With that expression safely evaluated to a string, JavaScript can finish the job of joining the three strings in the final evaluation. The evaluated string expression is what ultimately appears on the web page.

Expressions and variables

As one more demonstration of the flexibility that expression evaluation offers, this section shows you a slightly different route to the `document.write()` statement. Rather than join those strings as the direct parameter to the `document.write()` method, I can gather the strings in a variable and then apply the variable to the `document.write()` method. Here's how that sequence looks, as I simultaneously declare a new variable and assign it a value:

```
var textToWrite = " of " + navigator.appName + ".";
document.write(textToWrite);
```

This method works because the variable, `textToWrite`, evaluates to the combined string. The `document.write()` method accepts that string value and does its display job. As you read a script or try to work through a bug, pay special attention to how each expression (variable, statement, object property) evaluates. I guarantee that as you learn JavaScript (or any language), you will end up scratching your head from time to time because you haven't stopped to examine how expressions evaluate when a particular kind of value is required in a script.

Data Type Conversions

I mentioned earlier that the type of data in an expression can trip up some script operations if the expected components of the operation are not of the right type. JavaScript tries its best to perform internal conversions to head off such problems, but JavaScript cannot read your mind. If your intentions differ from the way JavaScript treats the values, you won't get the results you expect.

A case in point is adding numbers that may be in the form of text strings. In a simple arithmetic statement that adds two numbers, you get the expected result:

```
3 + 3          // result = 6
```

But if one of those numbers is a string, JavaScript leans toward converting the other value to a string — thus turning the plus sign's action from arithmetic addition to joining strings. Therefore, in the statement

```
3 + "3"        // result = "33"
```

the stringness of the second value prevails over the entire operation. The first value is automatically converted to a string, and the result joins the two strings. Try this yourself in The Evaluator Jr.

If I take this progression one step further, look what happens when another number is added to the statement:

```
3 + 3 + "3"    // result = "63"
```

This might seem totally illogical, but there is logic behind this result. The expression is evaluated from left to right. The first plus operation works on two numbers, yielding a value of 6. But as the 6 is about to be added to the 3, JavaScript lets the stringness of the 3 rule. The 6 is converted to a string, and two string values are joined to yield 63.

Most of your concern about data types will focus on performing math operations like the ones here. However, some object methods also require one or more parameters of particular data types. Although JavaScript provides numerous ways to convert data from one type to another, it is appropriate at this stage of the tutorial to introduce you to the two most common data conversions: string to number and number to string.

Converting strings to numbers

As you saw in the preceding section, if a numeric value is stored as a string — as it is when entered into a form text field — your scripts may have difficulty applying that value to a math operation. The JavaScript language provides two built-in functions to convert string representations of numbers to true numbers: parseInt() and parseFloat().

There is a difference between integers and floating-point numbers in JavaScript. *Integers* are always whole numbers, with no decimal point or numbers to the right of a decimal. *Floating-point numbers,* on the other hand, have fractional values to the right of the decimal. By and large, JavaScript math operations don't differentiate between integers and floating-point numbers: A number is a number. The only time you need to be cognizant of the difference is when a method parameter requires an integer because it can't handle fractional values. For example, parameters to the scroll() method of a window require integer values of the number of pixels vertically and horizontally you want to scroll the window. That's because you can't scroll a window a fraction of a pixel onscreen.

To use either of these conversion functions, insert the string value you wish to convert as a parameter to the function. For example, look at the results of two different string values when passed through the parseInt() function:

```
parseInt("42")        // result = 42
parseInt("42.33")     // result = 42
```

Even though the second expression passes the string version of a floating-point number to the function, the value returned by the function is an integer. No rounding of the value occurs here (although other math functions can help with that if necessary). The decimal and everything to its right are simply stripped off.

The parseFloat() function returns an integer if it can; otherwise, it returns a floating-point number, as follows:

```
parseFloat("42")      // result = 42
parseFloat("42.33")   // result = 42.33
```

Because these two conversion functions evaluate to their results, you simply insert the entire function wherever you need a string value converted to a number. Therefore, modifying an earlier example in which one of three values was a string, the complete expression can evaluate to the desired result:

```
3 + 3 + parseInt("3")   // result = 9
```

Converting numbers to strings

You'll have less need for converting a number to its string equivalent than the other way around. As you saw in the previous section, JavaScript gravitates toward strings when faced with an expression containing mixed data types. Even so, it is good practice to perform data type conversions explicitly in your code to prevent any potential ambiguity. The simplest way to convert a number to a string is to take advantage of

JavaScript's string tendencies in addition operations. By adding an empty string to a number, you convert the number to its string equivalent:

```
("" + 2500)          // result = "2500"
("" + 2500).length   // result = 4
```

In the second example, you can see the power of expression evaluation at work. The parentheses force the conversion of the number to a string. A *string* is a JavaScript object that has properties associated with it. One of those properties is the length property, which evaluates to the number of characters in the string. Therefore, the length of the string "2500" is 4. Note that the length value is a number, not a string.

Operators

You will use lots of *operators* in expressions. Earlier, you used the equal sign (=) as an assignment operator to assign a value to a variable. In the preceding examples with strings, you used the plus symbol (+) to join two strings. An operator generally performs some kind of calculation (operation) or comparison with two values (the value on each side of an operator is called an *operand*) to reach a third value. In this lesson, I briefly describe two categories of operators: arithmetic and comparison. Chapter 33 covers many more operators, but after you understand the basics here, the others are easier to grasp.

Arithmetic operators

It may seem odd to talk about text strings in the context of arithmetic operators, but you have already seen the special case of the plus (+) operator when one or more of the operands is a string. The plus operator instructs JavaScript to *concatenate* (pronounced "kon-KAT-en-eight"), or join, two strings together precisely where you place the operator. The string concatenation operator doesn't know about words and spaces, so the programmer must make sure that any two strings to be joined have the proper word spacing as part of the strings, even if that means adding a space:

```
firstName = "John";
lastName = "Doe";
fullName = firstName + " " + lastName;
```

JavaScript uses the same plus operator for arithmetic addition. When both operands are numbers, JavaScript knows to treat the expression as an arithmetic addition rather than a string concatenation. The standard math operators for addition, subtraction, multiplication, and division (+, -, *, /) are built into JavaScript.

Comparison operators

Another category of operator helps you compare values in scripts—whether two values are the same, for example. These kinds of comparisons return a value of the Boolean type: true or false. Table 6-2 lists the comparison operators. The operator that tests whether two items are equal consists of a pair of equal signs to distinguish it from the single-equal-sign assignment operator.

TABLE 6-2

JavaScript Comparison Operators

Symbol	Description
==	Equals
!=	Does not equal
>	Is greater than
>=	Is greater than or equal to
<	Is less than
<=	Is less than or equal to

Comparison operators come into greatest play in the construction of scripts that make decisions as they run. A cook does this in the kitchen all the time: If the sauce is too watery, add a bit of flour. You see comparison operators in action in Chapter 7.

Exercises

1. Which of the following are valid variable declarations or initializations? Explain why each one is or is not valid. If an item is invalid, how do you fix it so that it is?

   a. `my_name = "Cindy";`

   b. `var how many = 25;`

   c. `var zipCode = document.getElementById("zip").value`

   d. `var 1address = document.("address1").value;`

2. Assume that the following statements operate rapidly in sequence, where each statement relies on the result of the one before it. For each of the statements in the sequence, write down how the `someVal` expression evaluates after the statement executes in JavaScript.

   ```
   var someVal = 2;
   someVal = someVal + 2;
   someVal = someVal * 10;
   someVal = someVal + "20";
   someVal = "Robert";
   ```

3. Name the two JavaScript functions that convert strings to numbers. How do you give the function a string value to convert to a number?

4. Type and load the HTML page and script shown in Listing 6-1. Enter a three-digit number in the top two fields, and click the Add button. Examine the code, and explain what is wrong with the script. How do you fix the script so that the proper sum is displayed in the output field?

LISTING 6-1

What's Wrong with This Page?

```
<html>
<head>
<title>Sum Maker</title>
<script type="text/javascript">
<!--
function addIt() {
    var value1 = document.getElementById("inputA").value;
    var value2 = document.getElementById("inputB").value;
    document.getElementById("output").value = value1 + value2;
}
// -->
</script>
</head>

<body>
<form name="adder">
<input type="text" name="inputA" id="inputA" value="0" size="4" /><br />
<input type="text" name="inputB" id="inputB" value="0" size="4" />
<input type="button" value="Add" onclick="addIt()">
<p>_____</p>
<input type="text" name="output" id="output" size="6" />
</form>
</body>
</html>
```

5. What does the term *concatenate* mean in the context of JavaScript programming?

Chapter 7

Programming Fundamentals, Part II

Your tour of programming fundamentals continues in this chapter with subjects that have more intriguing possibilities. For example, I show you how programs make decisions and why a program must sometimes repeat statements over and over. Before you're finished here, you also will learn how to use one of the most powerful information holders in the JavaScript language: the array.

Decisions and Loops

Every waking hour of every day, you make decisions of some kind; most of the time, you probably don't even realize it. Don't think so? Well, look at the number of decisions you make at the grocery store, from the moment you enter the store to the moment you clear the checkout aisle.

No sooner do you enter the store than you are faced with a decision. Based on the number and size of items you intend to buy, do you pick up a hand-carried basket or attempt to extricate a shopping cart from the metallic conga line near the front of the store? That key decision may have impact later, when you see a special offer on an item that is too heavy to put in the handbasket.

Next, you head for the food aisles. Before entering an aisle, you compare the range of goods stocked in that aisle with items on your shopping list. If an item you need is likely to be found in this aisle, you turn into the aisle and start looking for the item; otherwise, you skip the aisle and move to the head of the next aisle.

Later, you reach the produce section in search of a juicy tomato. Standing in front of the bin of tomatoes, you begin inspecting them one by one — picking one up, feeling its firmness, checking the color, looking for blemishes or signs of pests. You discard one, pick up another, and continue this process until one matches the criteria you set in your mind for an acceptable morsel. Your last stop in the store is the checkout aisle. "Paper or plastic?" the clerk asks. One more decision to make. What you choose affects how you get the groceries from the car to the kitchen, as well as your recycling habits.

In your trip to the store, you go through the same kinds of decisions and repetitions that your JavaScript programs encounter. If you understand these frameworks in real life, you can look into the JavaScript equivalents and the syntax required to make them work.

Control Structures

In the vernacular of programming, the kinds of statements that make decisions and loop around to repeat themselves are called *control structures*. A control structure directs the execution flow through a sequence of script statements based on simple decisions and other factors.

An important part of a control structure is the *condition*. Just as you may travel different routes to work depending on certain conditions (for example, nice weather, nighttime, attending a soccer game), so, too, does a program sometimes have to branch to an execution route if a certain condition exists. Each condition is an expression that evaluates to true or false — one of those Boolean data types mentioned in Chapter 6. The kinds of expressions commonly used for conditions are expressions that include a comparison operator. You do the same in real life: If it is true that the outdoor temperature is less than freezing, you put on a coat before going outside. In programming, however, the comparisons are strictly comparisons of values.

JavaScript provides several kinds of control structures for different programming situations. Three of the most common control structures you'll use are if constructions, if...else constructions, and for loops.

Chapter 32 covers in great detail other common control structures you should know. For this tutorial, however, you need to learn about the three common ones just mentioned.

if constructions

The simplest program decision is to follow a special branch or path of the program if a certain condition is true. Formal syntax for this construction follows. Items in italics get replaced in a real script with expressions and statements that fit the situation.

```
if (condition) {
    statement[s] if true
}
```

Don't worry about the curly braces yet. Instead, get a feel for the basic structure. The keyword, if, is a must. In the parentheses goes an expression that evaluates to a Boolean value. This is the condition being tested as the program runs past this point. If the condition evaluates to true, one or more statements inside the curly braces execute before continuing with the next statement after the closing brace. If the condition evaluates to false, the statements inside the curly braces are ignored, and processing continues with the next statement after the closing brace.

The following example assumes that a variable, myAge, has had its value set earlier in the script (exactly how is not important for this example). The condition expression compares the value myAge against a numeric value of 18:

```
if (myAge < 18) {
    alert("Sorry, you cannot vote.");
}
```

In this example, the data type of the value inside `myAge` must be a number so that the proper comparison (via the `<`, or less than, comparison operator) does the right thing. For all instances of `myAge` less than 18, the nested statement inside the curly braces runs and displays the alert to the user. After the user closes the alert dialog box, the script continues with whatever statement follows the entire `if` construction.

if . . . else constructions

Not all program decisions are as simple as the one shown for the `if` construction. Rather than specifying one detour for a given condition, you might want the program to follow either of two branches depending on that condition. It is a fine but important distinction. In the plain `if` construction, no special processing is performed when the condition evaluates to `false`. But if processing must follow one of two special paths, you need the `if...else` construction. The formal syntax definition for an `if...else` construction is as follows:

```
if (condition) {
    statement[s] if true
} else {
    statement[s] if false
}
```

Everything you know about the condition for an `if` construction applies here. The only difference is the `else` keyword, which provides an alternative path for execution to follow if the condition evaluates to `false`.

As an example, the following `if...else` construction determines how many days are in February for a given year. To simplify the demo, the condition simply tests whether the year divides equally by 4. (True testing for this value includes special treatment of end-of-century dates, but I'm ignoring that for now.) The `%` operator symbol is called the *modulus operator* (covered in more detail in Chapter 33). The result of an operation with this operator yields the remainder of division of the two values. If the remainder is zero, the first value divides evenly by the second.

```
var febDays;
var theYear = 2004;
if (theYear % 4 == 0) {
    febDays = 29;
} else {
    febDays = 28;
}
```

The important point to see from this example is that by the end of the `if...else` construction, the `febDays` variable is set to either 28 or 29. No other value is possible. For years evenly divisible by 4, the first nested statement runs. For all other cases, the second statement runs. Then processing picks up with the next statement after the `if...else` construction.

About Repeat Loops

Repeat loops in real life generally mean the repetition of a series of steps until some condition is met, thus enabling you to break out of that loop. Such was the case earlier in this chapter, when you looked through a bushel of tomatoes for the one that came closest to your ideal tomato. The same can be said for driving around the block in a crowded neighborhood until a parking space opens up.

A *repeat loop* lets a script cycle through a sequence of statements until some condition is met. For example, a JavaScript data validation routine might inspect every character that you enter in a form text field to make sure that each one is a number. Or if you have a collection of data stored in a list, the loop can check whether an entered value is in that list. When that condition is met, the script can break out of the loop and continue with the next statement after the loop construction.

The most common repeat loop construction used in JavaScript is called the `for` loop. It gets its name from the keyword that begins the construction. A `for` loop is a powerful device because you can set it up to keep track of the number of times the loop repeats itself. The formal syntax of the `for` loop is as follows:

```
for ([initial expression]; [condition]; [update expression]) {
    statement[s] inside loop
}
```

The square brackets mean that the item is optional. However, until you get to know the `for` loop better, I recommend designing your loops to use all three items inside the parentheses. The *initial expression* portion usually sets the starting value of a counter variable. The *condition* — the same kind of condition you saw for `if` constructions — defines the condition that forces the loop to stop going around and around. Finally, the *update expression* is a statement that executes each time all the statements nested inside the construction complete running.

A common implementation initializes a counting variable, `i`; increments the value of `i` by 1 each time through the loop; and repeats the loop until the value of `i` exceeds some maximum value, as in the following:

```
for (var i = startValue; i <= maxValue; i++) {
    statement[s] inside loop
}
```

Placeholders `startValue` and `maxValue` represent any numeric values, including explicit numbers or variables holding numbers. In the update expression is an operator you have not seen yet. The ++ operator adds 1 to the value of `i` each time the update expression runs at the end of the loop. If `startValue` is 1, the value of `i` is 1 the first time through the loop, 2 the second time through, and so on. Therefore, if `maxValue` is 10, the loop repeats itself 10 times (in other words, as long as `i` is less than or equal to 10). Generally speaking, the statements inside the loop use the value of the counting variable in their execution. Later in this lesson, I show how the variable can play a key role in the statements inside a loop. At the same time, you will see how to break out of a loop prematurely and why you may need to do this in a script.

Functions

In Chapter 5, you saw a preview of the JavaScript function. A *function* is a definition of a set of deferred actions. Functions are invoked by event handlers or by statements elsewhere in the script. Whenever possible, good functions are designed for reuse in other documents. They can become building blocks you use over and over again.

If you have programmed before, you can see parallels between JavaScript functions and other languages' subroutines. But unlike some languages that distinguish between procedures (which carry out actions) and functions (which carry out actions and return values), only one classification of routine exists for JavaScript. A function is capable of returning a value to the statement that invoked it, but this is not a requirement. However, when a function does return a value, the calling statement treats the function call like any expression — plugging in the returned value right where the function call is made. I will show some examples in a moment.

Formal syntax for a function is as follows:

```
function functionName ( [parameter1]...[,parameterN] ) {
    statement[s]
}
```

Names you assign to functions have the same restrictions as names you assign to HTML elements and variables. You should devise a name that succinctly describes what the function does. I tend to use multiword names with the interCap (internally capitalized) format that start with a verb because functions are action items, even if they do nothing more than get or set a value.

Another practice to keep in mind as you start to create functions is to keep the focus of each function as narrow as possible. It is possible to generate functions that are literally hundreds of lines long. Such functions are usually difficult to maintain and debug. Chances are that you can divide the long function into smaller, more tightly focused segments.

Function parameters

In Chapter 5, you saw how an event handler invokes a function by calling the function by name. A typical call to a function, including one that comes from another JavaScript statement, works the same way: A set of parentheses follows the function name.

You also can define functions so they receive parameter values from the calling statement. Listing 7-1 shows a simple document that has a button whose `onclick` event handler calls a function while passing text data to the function. The text string in the event handler call is in a *nested string* — a set of single quotes inside the double quotes required for the entire event handler attribute.

LISTING 7-1

Calling a Function from an Event Handler

```
<html>
<head>
<script type="text/javascript">
function showMsg(msg) {
    alert("The button sent: " + msg);
}
</script>
</head>
<body>
<form>
    <input type="button" value="Click Me"
    onclick="showMsg('The button has been clicked!')">
</form>
</body>
</html>
```

Parameters (also known as *arguments*) provide a mechanism for handing off a value from one statement to another by way of a function call. If no parameters occur in the function definition, both the function definition and the call to the function have only empty sets of parentheses (as shown in Chapter 5, Listing 5-8).

When a function receives parameters, it assigns the incoming values to the variable names specified in the function definition's parentheses. Consider the following script segment:

```
function sayHiToFirst(a, b, c) {
    alert("Say hello, " + a);
}
sayHiToFirst("Gracie", "George", "Harry");
sayHiToFirst("Larry", "Moe", "Curly");
```

After the function is defined in the script, the next statement calls that very function, passing three strings as parameters. The function definition automatically assigns the strings to variables a, b, and c. Therefore, before the alert() statement inside the function ever runs, a evaluates to "Gracie", b evaluates to "George", and c evaluates to "Harry". In the alert() statement, only the a value is used, and the alert reads

```
Say hello, Gracie
```

When the user closes the first alert, the next call to the function occurs. This time through, different values are passed to the function and assigned to a, b, and c. The alert dialog box reads

```
Say hello, Larry
```

Unlike other variables that you define in your script, function parameters do not use the var keyword to initialize them. They are automatically initialized whenever the function is called.

Variable scope

Speaking of variables, it's time to distinguish between variables that are defined outside and those that are defined inside functions. Variables defined outside functions are called *global variables;* those defined inside functions with the var keyword are called *local variables*.

A global variable has a slightly different connotation in JavaScript than it has in most other languages. For a JavaScript script, the globe of a global variable is the current document loaded in a browser window or frame. Therefore, when you initialize a variable as a global variable, it means that all script statements in the page (including those inside functions) have direct access to that variable's value via the variable's name. Statements can retrieve and modify global variables from anywhere in the page. In programming terminology, this kind of variable is said to have *global scope* because every statement on the page can see it.

It is important to remember that the instant a page unloads itself, all global variables defined in that page disappear from memory forever. If you need a value to persist from one page to another, you must use other techniques to store that value (for example, as a global variable in a framesetting document, as described in Chapter 16, or in a cookie, as described in Chapter 18). Although the var keyword is usually optional for initializing global variables, I strongly recommend that you use it for all variable initializations to guard against future changes to the JavaScript language.

In contrast to the global variable, a local variable is defined inside a function. You already saw how parameter variables are defined inside functions (without var keyword initializations). But you can also define other variables with the var keyword (absolutely required for local variables; otherwise, they become recognized as global variables). The scope of a local variable is only within the statements of the function. No other functions or statements outside functions have access to a local variable.

Local scope allows for the reuse of variable names within a document. For most variables, I strongly discourage this practice because it leads to confusion and bugs that are difficult to track down. At the same time, it is convenient to reuse certain kinds of variable names, such as `for` loop counters. These are safe because they are always reinitialized with a starting value whenever a `for` loop starts. You cannot, however, nest one `for` loop inside another without specifying a different loop-counting variable in the nested loop.

To demonstrate the structure and behavior of global and local variables—and show you why you shouldn't reuse most variable names inside a document—Listing 7-2 defines two global and two local variables. I intentionally use bad form by initializing a local variable that has the same name as a global variable.

LISTING 7-2

Global and Local Variable Scope Demonstration

```
<html>
<head>
<script type="text/javascript">
var aBoy = "Charlie Brown";    // global
var hisDog = "Snoopy";         // global
function demo() {
    // using improper design to demonstrate a point
    var hisDog = "Gromit";     // local version of hisDog
    var output = hisDog + " does not belong to " + aBoy + ".<br>";
    document.write(output);
}
</script>
</head>
<body>
<script type="text/javascript">
demo();         // runs as document loads
document.write(hisDog + " belongs to " + aBoy + ".");
</script>
</body>
</html>
```

When the page loads, the script in the Head portion initializes the two global variables (`aBoy` and `hisDog`) and defines the `demo()` function in memory. In the Body, another script begins by invoking the function. Inside the function, a local variable is initialized with the same name as one of the global variables: `hisDog`. In JavaScript, such a local initialization overrides the global variable for all statements inside the function. (But note that if the `var` keyword is left off the local initialization, the statement reassigns the value of the global version to `"Gromit"`.)

Another local variable, `output`, is merely a repository for accumulating the text that is to be written to the screen. The accumulation begins by evaluating the local version of the `hisDog` variable. Then it concatenates some hard-wired text (note the extra spaces at the edges of the string segment). Next comes the evaluated value of the `aBoy` global variable; any global not overridden by a local is available for use inside the function. The expression is accumulating HTML to be written to the page, so it ends with a period and a `<br>` tag. The final statement of the function writes the content to the page.

When the function completes its task, the next statement in the Body script writes another string to the page. Because this script statement is executing in global space (that is, not inside any function), it accesses only global variables — including those defined in another `<script>` tag set in the document. By the time the complete page finishes loading, it contains the following text lines:

```
Gromit does not belong to Charlie Brown.
Snoopy belongs to Charlie Brown.
```

About Curly Braces

Despite the fact that you probably rarely — if ever — use curly braces (`{ }`) in your writing, there is no mystery to their usage in JavaScript (and many other languages). Curly braces enclose blocks of statements that belong together. Although they do assist humans who are reading scripts in knowing what's going on, curly braces also help the browser know which statements belong together. You always must use curly braces in matched pairs.

You use curly braces most commonly in function definitions and control structures. In the function definition in Listing 7-2, curly braces enclose four statements that make up the function definition (including the comment line). The closing brace lets the browser know that whatever statement comes next is a statement outside the function definition.

Physical placement of curly braces is not critical. (Neither is the indentation style you see in the code I provide.) The following function definitions are treated identically by scriptable browsers:

```
function sayHiToFirst(a, b, c) {
    alert("Say hello, " + a);
}

function sayHiToFirst(a, b, c)
{
    alert("Say hello, " + a);
}

function sayHiToFirst(a, b, c) {alert("Say hello, " + a);}
```

Throughout this book, I use the style shown in the first example because I find that it makes lengthy and complex scripts easier to read — especially scripts that have many levels of nested control structures.

Arrays

The JavaScript array is one of the most useful data constructions you have available to you. You can visualize the structure of a basic array as though it were a single-column spreadsheet. Each row of the column holds a distinct piece of data, and each row is numbered. Numbers assigned to rows are in strict numerical sequence, starting with zero as the first row. (Programmers tend to start counting with zero.) This row number is called an *index*. To access an item in an array, you need to know the name of the array and the index for the row. Because index values start with zero, the total number of items of the array (as determined by the array's `length` property) is always one more than the highest index value of the array. More advanced array concepts enable you to create the equivalent of an array with multiple columns (described in Chapter 31). For this tutorial, I stay with the single-column basic array.

Data elements inside JavaScript arrays can be any data type, including objects. And unlike a lot of other programming languages, JavaScript allows different rows of the same array to contain different data types.

Creating an array

An array is stored in a variable, so when you create an array, you assign the new array object to the variable. (Yes, arrays are objects, but they belong to the core JavaScript language rather than to the document object model [DOM].) A special keyword — new — preceding a call to the JavaScript function that generates arrays creates space in memory for the array. An optional parameter to the Array() function enables you to specify at the time of creation how many elements (rows) of data eventually will occupy the array. JavaScript is very forgiving about this because you can change the size of an array at any time. Therefore, if you omit a parameter when generating a new array, your script incurs no penalty.

To demonstrate the array creation process, I create an array that holds the names of the 50 states plus the District of Columbia (a total of 51). The first task is to create that array and assign it to a variable of any name that helps me remember what this collection of data is about:

```
var USStates = new Array(51);
```

At this point, the USStates array is sitting in memory like a 51-row table with no data in it. To fill the rows, I must assign data to each row. Addressing each row of an array requires a special way of indicating the index value of the row: square brackets after the name of the array. The first row of the USStates array is addressed as:

```
USStates[0]
```

To assign the string name of the first state of the alphabet to that row, I use a simple assignment operator:

```
USStates[0] = "Alabama";
```

To fill in the rest of the rows, I include a statement for each row:

```
USStates[1] = "Alaska";
USStates[2] = "Arizona";
USStates[3] = "Arkansas";
...
USStates[50] = "Wyoming";
```

Therefore, if you want to include a table of information in a document from which a script can look up information without accessing the server, you include the data in the document in the form of an array creation sequence. When the statements run as the document loads, by the time the document finishes loading into the browser, the data collection array is built and ready to go. Despite what appears to be the potential for a lot of statements in a document for such a data collection, the amount of data that must download for typical array collections is small enough not to affect page loading severely — even for dial-up users. In Chapter 31, you also see some syntax shortcuts for creating arrays that reduce source code character counts.

Accessing array data

The array index is the key to accessing an array element. The name of the array and an index in square brackets evaluates to the content of that array location. For example, after the USStates array is built, a script can display an alert with Alaska's name in it with the following statement:

```
alert("The largest state is " + USStates[1] + ".");
```

Just as you can retrieve data from an indexed array element, you can change the element by reassigning a new value to any indexed element in the array.

Parallel arrays

Now I show you why the numeric index methodology works well in JavaScript. To help with the demonstration, I generate another array that is parallel with the USStates array. This new array is also 51 elements long, and it contains the year in which the state in the corresponding row of USStates entered the Union. That array construction looks like the following:

```
var stateEntered = new Array(51);
stateEntered [0] = 1819;
stateEntered [1] = 1959;
stateEntered [2] = 1912;
stateEntered [3] = 1836;
...
stateEntered [50] = 1890;
```

In the browser's memory, then, are two data tables that you can visualize as looking like the model in Figure 7-1. I can build more arrays that are parallel to these for items such as the postal abbreviation and capital city. The important point is that the zeroth element in each of these tables applies to Alabama, the first state in the USStates array.

FIGURE 7-1

Visualization of two related parallel data tables.

USStates		stateEntered
"Alabama"	[0]	1819
"Alaska"	[1]	1959
"Arizona"	[2]	1912
"Arkansas"	[3]	1836
⋮	⋮	⋮
"Wyoming"	[50]	1890

If a web page included these data tables and a way for a user to look up the entry date for a given state, the page would need a way to look through all the USStates entries to find the index value of the one that matches the user's entry. Then that index value could be applied to the stateEntered array to find the matching year.

For this demo, the page includes a text entry field in which the user types the name of the state to look up. In a real application, this methodology is fraught with peril unless the script performs some error checking in case the user makes a mistake. But for now, I assume that the user always types a valid state name. (Don't ever make this assumption in your web site's pages.) An event handler from either the text field or a clickable button calls a function that looks up the state name, fetches the corresponding entry year, and displays an alert message with the information. The function is as follows:

```
function getStateDate() {
    var selectedState = document.getElementById("entry").value;
    for (var i = 0; i < USStates.length; i++) {
        if (USStates[i] == selectedState) {
            break;
        }
    }
    alert(selectedState + " entered the Union in " + stateEntered[i] + ".");
}
```

In the first statement of the function, I grab the value of the text box and assign the value to a variable, selectedState. This is mostly for convenience, because I can use the shorter variable name later in the script. In fact, the usage of that value is inside a for loop, so the script is marginally more efficient because the browser doesn't have to evaluate that long reference to the text field each time through the loop.

The key to this function is in the for loop. Here is where I combine the natural behavior of incrementing a loop counter with the index values assigned to the two arrays. Specifications for the loop indicate that the counter variable, i, is initialized with a value of zero. The loop is directed to continue as long as the value of i is less than the length of the USStates array. Remember that the length of an array is always one more than the index value of the last item. Therefore, the last time the loop runs is when i is 50, which is both less than the length of 51 and equal to the index value of the last element. Each time after the loop runs, the counter increments by 1 (i++).

Nested inside the for loop is an if construction. The condition tests the value of an element of the array against the value typed by the user. Each time through the loop, the condition tests a different row of the array, starting with row zero. In other words, this if construction can be performed dozens of times before a match is found, but each time, the value of i is 1 larger than in the previous try.

The equality comparison operator (==) is fairly strict when it comes to comparing string values. Such comparisons respect the case of each letter. In our example, the user must type the state name exactly as it is stored in the USStates array for the match to be found. In Chapter 10, you learn about some helper methods that eliminate case and sensitivity in string comparisons.

When a match is found, the statement nested inside the if construction runs. The break statement is designed to help control structures bail out if the program needs it. For this application, it is imperative that the for loop stop running when a match for the state name is found. When the for loop breaks, the value of the i counter is fixed at the row of the USStates array containing the entered state. I need that index value to find the corresponding entry in the other array. Even though the counting variable, i, is initialized in the for loop, it is still alive and in the scope of the function for all statements after the initialization. That's why I can use it to extract the value of the row of the stateEntered array in the final statement that displays the results in an alert message.

This application of a for loop and array indexes is a common one in JavaScript. Study the code carefully, and be sure you understand how it works. This way of cycling through arrays plays a role not only in the kinds of arrays you create in your code, but also in the arrays that browsers generate for the DOM.

Document objects in arrays

If you look at the `document` object portions of the Quick Reference in Appendix A, you can see that the properties of some objects are listed with square brackets after them. These are indeed the same kind of square brackets you just saw for array indexes. That's because when a document loads, the browser creates arrays of like objects in the document. For example, if your page includes two `<form>` tag sets, two forms appear in the document. The browser maintains an array of `form` objects for that document. References to those forms are

```
document.forms[0]
document.forms[1]
```

Index values for objects are assigned according to the loading order of the objects. In the case of `form` objects, the order is dictated by the order of the `<form>` tags in the document. This indexed array syntax is another way to reference forms in an object reference. You can still use a form's identifier if you prefer — and I heartily recommend using object names wherever possible, because even if you change the physical order of the objects in your HTML, references that use names still work without modification. But if your page contains only one form, you can use the reference types interchangeably, as in the following examples of equivalent references to the `length` property of a form's `elements` array (the `elements` array contains all the form controls in the form):

```
document.getElementById("entryForm").elements.length
document.forms[0].elements.length
```

In examples throughout this book, you can see that I often use the array type of reference to simple forms in simple documents. But in my production pages, I almost always use named references.

Exercises

1. With your newly acquired knowledge of functions, event handlers, and control structures, use the script fragments from this chapter to complete the page that has the lookup table for all the states and the years they entered into the union. If you do not have a reference book for the dates, use different year numbers, starting with 1800 for each entry. In the page, create a text entry field for the state and a button that triggers the lookup in the arrays.

2. Examine the following function definition. Can you spot any problems with the definition? If so, how can you fix the problems?

```
function format(ohmage) {
    var result;
    if ohmage >= 1e6 {
        ohmage = ohmage / 1e6;
        result = ohmage + " Mohms";
    } else {
        if (ohmage >= 1e3)
            ohmage = ohmage / 1e3;
            result = ohmage + " Kohms";
        else
            result = ohmage + " ohms";
}
    alert(result);
```

3. Devise your own syntax for the scenario of looking for a ripe tomato at the grocery store, and write a `for` loop using that object and property syntax.

4. Modify Listing 7-2 so that it does not reuse the `hisDog` variable inside the function.

5. Given the following table of data about several planets of our solar system, create a web page that enables users to enter a planet name and, at the click of a button, have the distance and diameter appear either in an alert box or (as extra credit) in separate fields of the page.

Planet	Distance from the Sun	Diameter
Mercury	36 million miles	3,100 miles
Venus	67 million miles	7,700 miles
Earth	93 million miles	7,920 miles
Mars	141 million miles	4,200 miles

Chapter 8

Window and Document Objects

Now that you have exposure to programming fundamentals, it is easier to demonstrate how to script objects in documents. Starting with this lesson, the tutorial turns back to the document object model (DOM), diving more deeply into objects you will place in many of your documents.

Top-Level Objects

As a refresher, study the hierarchy of top-level objects in Figure 8-1. This chapter focuses on objects of this level that you'll frequently encounter in your scripting: window, location, navigator, and document. The goal is not only to equip you with the basics so you can script simple tasks, but also to prepare you for in-depth examinations of each object and its properties, methods, and event handlers in Part III of this book. I introduce only the basic properties, methods, and events for objects in this tutorial; you can find far more in Part III. Examples in that part of the book assume that you know the programming fundamentals covered here in Part II.

FIGURE 8-1

The top-level browser object model for all scriptable browsers.

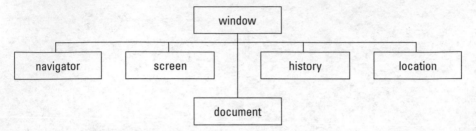

The window Object

At the top of the object hierarchy is the window object. This object gains that exalted spot in the object food chain because it is the master container for all content you view in the web browser. As long as a browser window is open — even if no document is loaded in the window — the window object is defined in the current model in memory.

In addition to the content part of the window where documents go, a window's sphere of influence includes the dimensions of the window and all the stuff that surrounds the content area. The area where scrollbars, toolbars, the status bar, and (non-Macintosh) menu bar live is known as a window's *chrome*. Not every browser has full scripted control over the chrome of the main browser window, but you can easily script the creation of additional windows sized the way you want and that have only the chrome elements you wish to display in the subwindow.

Although the discussion of frames comes in Chapter 11, I can safely say now that each frame is also considered a window object. If you think about it, that makes sense, because each frame can hold a different document. When a script runs in one of those documents, it regards the frame that holds the document as the window object in its view of the object hierarchy.

As you learn in this chapter, the window object is a convenient place for the DOM to attach methods that display modal dialog boxes and adjust the text that displays in the status bar at the bottom of the browser window. A window object method enables you to create a separate window that appears onscreen. When you look at all of the properties, methods, and events defined for the window object (see Chapter 16), it should be clear why they are attached to window objects: Visualize their scope and the scope of a browser window.

Accessing window properties and methods

You can word script references to properties and methods of the window object in several ways, depending more on whim and style than on specific syntactical requirements. The most logical and common way to compose such references includes the window object in the reference:

```
window.propertyName
window.methodName([parameters])
```

A window object also has a synonym when the script doing the referencing points to the window that houses the document. The synonym is self. Then the reference syntax becomes

```
self.propertyName
self.methodName([parameters])
```

You can use these initial reference object names interchangeably, but I tend to reserve the use of self for more complex scripts that involve multiple frames and windows. The self moniker more clearly denotes the current window holding the script's document. It makes the script more readable — by me and by others.

Back in Chapter 4, I indicated that because the window object is always there when a script runs, you could omit it from references to any objects inside that window. Therefore, the following syntax models assume properties and methods of the current window:

```
propertyName
methodName([parameters])
```

In fact, as you will see in a few moments, some methods may be more understandable if you omit the window object reference. The methods run just fine either way.

Creating a window

A script does not create the main browser window. A user does that by virtue of launching the browser or by opening a URL or file from the browser's menus (if the window is not already open). But a script can generate any number of subwindows when the main window is open (and that window contains a document whose script needs to open subwindows).

The method that generates a new window is window.open(). This method contains up to three parameters that define window characteristics, such as the URL of the document to load, its name for target attribute reference purposes in HTML tags, and physical appearance (size and chrome contingent). I don't go into the details of the parameters here (they're covered in great depth in Chapter 16), but I do want to expose you to an important concept involved with the window.open() method.

Consider the following statement, which opens a new window to a specific size and with an HTML document from the same server directory that holds the current page:

```
var subWindow = window.open("define.html","def","height=200,width=300");
```

The important thing to note about this statement is that it is an assignment statement. Something gets assigned to that variable subWindow. What is it? It turns out that when the window.open() method runs, it not only opens that new window according to specifications set as parameters, but also evaluates to a reference to that new window. In programming parlance, the method is said to *return a value* — in this case, a genuine object reference. The value returned by the method is assigned to the variable.

Now your script can use that variable as a valid reference to the second window. If you need to access one of its properties or methods, you must use that reference as part of the complete reference. For example, to close the subwindow from a script in the main window, use this reference to the close() method for that subwindow:

```
subWindow.close();
```

If you issue window.close(), self.close(), or just close() in the main window's script, the method closes the main window (after confirming with the user) and not the subwindow. To address another window, then, you must include a reference to that window as part of the complete reference. This has an impact on your code because you probably want the variable holding the reference to the subwindow to be valid as long as the main document is loaded into the browser. For that to happen, the variable has to be initialized as a global variable, rather than inside a function (although you can set its value inside a function). That way, one function can open the window while another function closes it.

Listing 8-1 is a page that has a button for opening a blank, new window and a button for closing that window from the main window. To view this demonstration, shrink your main browser window to less than full screen. Then, when the new window is generated, reposition the windows so you can see the smaller, new window when the main window is in front. (If you lose a window behind another, use the browser's Window menu to choose the hidden window.) The key point of Listing 8-1 is that the newWindow variable is defined as a global variable so that both the makeNewWindow() and closeNewWindow() functions have access to it. When a variable is declared with no value assignment, its initial value is null. A null value is interpreted to be the same as false in a condition, whereas the presence of any nonzero value is the same as true in a condition. Therefore, in the closeNewWindow() function, the condition tests whether the window has been created before issuing the subwindow's close() method. Then, to clean up, the function sets the newWindow variable to null so that another click of the Close button doesn't try to close a nonexistent window.

LISTING 8-1

References to Window Objects

```html
<html>
<head>
<title>Window Opener and Closer</title>
<script type="text/javascript">
var newWindow;
function makeNewWindow() {
    newWindow = window.open("","","height=300,width=300");
}
function closeNewWindow() {
    if (newWindow) {
        newWindow.close();
        newWindow = null;
    }
}
</script>
</head>

<body>
<form>
<input type="button" value="Create New Window" onclick="makeNewWindow()">
<input type="button" value="Close New Window" onclick="closeNewWindow()">
</form>
</body>
</html>
```

Window Properties and Methods

The three methods for the `window` object described in this section have an immediate impact on user interaction by displaying dialog boxes of various types. They work with all scriptable browsers. You can find extensive code examples in Part III for each property and method. You can also experiment with the one-statement script examples by entering them in the top text box of The Evaluator Jr. (from Chapter 6).

One of the first questions that new scripters ask is how to customize the title bars, sizes, and button labels of these dialog boxes. Each browser maker dictates how these dialogs are labeled. Because tricksters have tried to use these dialog boxes for nefarious purposes over the years, browser makers now go to great lengths to let users know that the dialog boxes emanate from web page scripts. Scripters cannot alter the user interfaces of these dialog boxes.

window.alert() method

I have used the `alert()` method many times so far in this tutorial. This window method generates a dialog box that displays whatever text you pass as a parameter (see Figure 8-2). A single OK button (whose label you cannot change) enables the user to dismiss the alert.

FIGURE 8-2

A JavaScript alert dialog box (Firefox 1.5/Windows).

All three dialog-box methods are good cases for using a `window` object's methods without the reference to the window. Even though the `alert()` method technically is a `window` object method, no special relationship exists between the dialog box and the window that generates it. In production scripts, I usually use the shortcut reference:

```
alert("This is a JavaScript alert dialog.");
```

window.confirm() method

The second style of dialog box presents two buttons (Cancel and OK in most versions on most platforms) and is called a confirm dialog box (see Figure 8-3). More important, this is one of those methods that returns a value: `true` if the user clicks OK or `false` if the user clicks Cancel. You can use this dialog box and its returned value as a way to have a user make a decision about how a script progresses.

FIGURE 8-3

A JavaScript confirm dialog box (IE7/WinXP style).

Because the method always returns a Boolean value, you can use the evaluated value of the entire method as a condition statement in an `if` or `if...else` construction. For example, in the following code fragment, the user is asked about starting the application over. Doing so causes the default page of the site to load into the browser.

```
if (confirm("Are you sure you want to start over?")) {
    location.href = "index.html";
}
```

window.prompt() method

The final dialog box of the `window` object, the prompt dialog box (see Figure 8-4), displays a message that you set and provides a text field for the user to enter a response. Two buttons, Cancel and OK, enable the user to dismiss the dialog box with two opposite expectations: canceling the entire operation or accepting the input typed in the dialog box.

FIGURE 8-4

A JavaScript prompt dialog box (Safari 2 style).

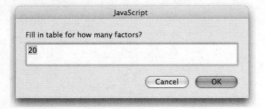

The `window.prompt()` method has two parameters. The first is the message that acts as a prompt to the user. You can suggest a default answer in the text field by including a string as the second parameter. If you don't want any default answer to appear, include an empty string (two double quotes without any space between them).

This method returns one value when the user clicks either button. A click of the Cancel button returns a value of `null`, regardless of what the user types in the field. A click of the OK button returns a string value of the typed entry. Your scripts can use this information in conditions for `if` and `if...else` constructions. A value of `null` is treated as `false` in a condition. It turns out that an empty string is also treated as `false`.

Therefore, a condition can easily test for the presence of real characters typed in the field to simplify a condition test, as shown in the following fragment:

```
var answer = prompt("What is your name?","");
if (answer) {
   alert("Hello, " + answer + "!");
}
```

The only time the `alert()` method is called is when the user enters something in the prompt dialog box and clicks the OK button.

load event

The `window` object reacts to several system and user events, but the one you will probably use most often is the event that fires as soon as everything in a page finishes loading. This event waits for images, Java applets, and data files for plug-ins to download fully to the browser. It can be dangerous to script access to elements of a document object while the page loads because if the object has not loaded yet (perhaps due to a slow network connection or server), a script error results. The advantage of using the `load` event to invoke functions is that you are assured that all document objects are in the browser's DOM. Window event handlers may be placed inside the `<body>` tag. Even though you will come to associate the `<body>` tag's attributes with the `document` object's properties, it is the `window` object's event handlers that go inside the tag.

The location Object

Sometimes an object in the hierarchy represents something that doesn't seem to have the kind of physical presence that a window or a button does. That's the case with the `location` object. This object represents the URL loaded into the window. This differs from the `document` object (discussed later in this lesson) because the document is the real content; the location is simply the URL.

Unless you are truly web savvy, you may not realize that a URL consists of many components that define the address and method of data transfer for a file. Pieces of a URL include the protocol (such as `http:`) and the hostname (such as `www.example.com`). You can access all these items as properties of the `location` object. For the most part, though, your scripts will be interested in only one property: the `href` property, which defines the complete URL.

Setting the `location.href` property is the primary way your scripts navigate to other pages:

```
location.href = "http://www.dannyg.com";
```

You can generally navigate to a page in your own web site by specifying a relative URL (that is, relative to the currently loaded page) rather than the complete URL with protocol and host information. For pages outside the domain of the current page, you need to specify the complete URL.

If the page to be loaded is in another window or frame, the window reference must be part of the statement. For example, if your script opens a new window and assigns its reference to a variable named `newWindow`, the statement that loads a page into the subwindow is

```
newWindow.location.href = "http://www.dannyg.com";
```

The navigator Object

Despite a name reminiscent of the Netscape Navigator-branded browser, the `navigator` object is implemented in all scriptable browsers. All browsers also implement a handful of properties that reveal the same kind of information that browsers send to servers with each page request. Thus, the `navigator.userAgent` property returns a string with numerous details about the browser and operating system. For example, a script running in Internet Explorer 7 in Windows XP receives the following value for the `navigator.userAgent` property:

```
Mozilla/4.0 (compatible; MSIE 7.0; Windows NT 5.1)
```

The same script running in Firefox 1.5 on a Macintosh reveals the following `userAgent` details:

```
Mozilla/5.0 (Macintosh; U; PPC Mac OS X Mach-O; en-US; rv:1.8.0.7) Gecko/20060909
Firefox/1.5.0.7
```

You have already used the `navigator.appVersion` property: in your first script of Chapter 3. See Chapter 39 on the CD-ROM for more details about this object and the meaning of the values returned by its properties. It once was used extensively to branch script execution according to various browser versions. Chapter 14 describes more modern ways to accomplish browser-version detection.

The document Object

The `document` object holds the real content of the page. Properties and methods of the `document` object generally affect the look and content of the document that occupies the window. As you saw in your first script in Chapter 3, all W3C DOM-compatible browsers allow script access to the text contents of a page when the document has loaded. You also saw in Listing 5-6 that the `document.write()` method lets a script create content dynamically as the page loads on any browser. Many `document` object properties are arrays of other objects in the document, which provide additional ways to reference these objects (over and above the `document.getElementById()` method).

Accessing a `document` object's properties and methods is straightforward, as shown in the following syntax examples:

```
[window.]document.propertyName
[window.]document.methodName([parameters])
```

The `window` reference is optional when the script is accessing the `document` object that contains the script. If you want a preview of the long list of `document` object properties of IE or a Mozilla-based browser, enter `document` in the bottom text box of The Evaluator Jr. and press Enter/Return. The object's properties, current values, and value types appear in the Results box (as well as methods in Mozilla). Following are some of the most commonly used properties and methods of the `document` object.

document.forms[] property

It is convenient that the document object contains a property — `document.forms` — whose value is an array of all `form` element objects in the document. As you recall from the discussion of arrays in Chapter 7, an index number inside an array's square brackets points to one of the elements in the array. To find out how many `form` objects are in the current document, use

```
document.forms.length
```

To access the first form in a document, for example, the reference is

```
document.forms[0]
```

As a further convenience, all scriptable browsers let you reference a form more directly by its name (that is, the identifier assigned to the name attribute of the <form> tag) in one of two ways. The first way is via array syntax, applying the form's name as a string index value of the array:

```
document.forms["formName"]
```

You will see in future chapters that scripts sometimes have only the string name of the form to work with. To derive a valid reference to the form object indicated by that name, use this string index form with the array.

The second, even shorter way to reference a form object by name is to append the name as a property of the document object, as in:

```
document.formName
```

Either methodology reaches the same object. You will see many instances of the shortcut approach in form-related example scripts throughout this book (including in Chapter 9 when working with form controls). Although this syntax dates back to the earliest scriptable browsers, it is still valid in the most modern versions.

document.images[] property

Just as a document keeps track of forms in an array property, the document object maintain a collection (array) of images inserted into the document by way of <img> tags. Images referenced through the document.images array may be reached either by numeric or string index of the img element's name. Just as with forms, the name attribute value is the identifier you use for a string index.

The presence of the document.images property indicates that the browser supports image swapping. Therefore, you can use the existence of the property as a controller to make sure the browser supports images as objects before attempting to perform any script action on an image. To do so, surround statements that deal with images with an if construction that verifies the property's existence, as follows:

```
if (document.images) {
    // statements dealing with img objects
}
```

Older browsers skip the nested statements, preventing them from displaying error messages to their users.

document.write() method

The document.write() method operates in both immediate scripts to create content in a page as it loads and in deferred scripts that create new content in the same window or a different window. The method requires one string parameter, which is the HTML content to write to the window or frame. Such string parameters can be variables or any other expressions that evaluate to a string. Very often, the written content includes HTML tags.

Bear in mind that after a page loads, the browser's *output stream* automatically closes. After that, any document.write() method issued to the current page opens a new stream that immediately erases the current page (along with any variables or other values in the original document). Therefore, if you wish to replace the current page with script-generated HTML, you need to accumulate that HTML in a variable and perform the writing with just one document.write() method. You don't have to clear a document explicitly and open a new data stream; one document.write() call does it all.

One last piece of housekeeping advice about the document.write() method involves its companion method, document.close(). Your script must close the output stream when it finishes writing its content to the window (either the same window or another). After the last document.write() method in a deferred script, be sure to include a document.close() method. Failure to do this may cause images and forms not to appear. Also, any document.write() method invoked later will only append to the page, rather than clear the existing content to write anew.

To demonstrate the document.write() method, I show two versions of the same application. One writes to the same document that contains the script; the other writes to a separate window. Type in each document in a new text editor document, save it with an .html file extension, and open it in your browser.

Listing 8-2 creates a button that assembles new HTML content for a document, including HTML tags for a new document title and color attribute for the <body> tag. An operator in the listing that may be unfamiliar to you is +=. It appends a string on its right side to whatever string is stored in the variable on its left side. This operator is a convenient way to accumulate a long string across several separate statements. With the content gathered in the newContent variable, one document.write() statement blasts the entire new content to the same document, obliterating all vestiges of the content of Listing 8-2. The document.close() statement, however, is required to close the output stream properly. When you load this document and click the button, notice that the document title in the browser's title bar changes accordingly. As you click back to the original and try the button again, notice that the dynamically written second page loads much faster than even a reload of the original document.

LISTING 8-2

Using document.write() on the Current Window

```html
<html>
<head>
<title>Writing to Same Doc</title>
<script type="text/javascript">
function reWrite() {
    // assemble content for new window
    var newContent = "<html><head><title>A New Doc</title></head>";
    newContent += "<body bgcolor='aqua'><h1>This document is brand new.</h1>";
    newContent += "Click the Back button to see original document.";
    newContent += "</body></html>";
    // write HTML to new window document
    document.write(newContent);
    document.close(); // close layout stream
}
</script>
</head>
<body>
<form>
<input type="button" value="Replace Content" onclick="reWrite()">
</form>
</body>
</html>
```

In Listing 8-3, the situation is a bit more complex because the script generates a subwindow to which an entirely script-generated document is written.

NOTE You will have to turn off blocking pop-up windows temporarily to run this script.

To keep the reference to the new window alive across both functions, the newWindow variable is declared as a global variable. As soon as the page loads, the onload event handler invokes the makeNewWindow() function. This function generates a blank subwindow. I added a property to the third parameter of the window.open() method that instructs the status bar of the subwindow to appear.

A button in the page invokes the subWrite() method. The first task it performs is to check the closed property of the subwindow. This property returns true if the referenced window is closed. If that's the case (if the user closed the window manually), the function invokes the makeNewWindow() function again to reopen that window.

With the window open, new content is assembled as a string variable. As with Listing 8-2, the content is written in one blast (although that isn't necessary for a separate window), followed by a close() method. But notice an important difference: Both the write() and close() methods explicitly specify the subwindow.

LISTING 8-3

Using document.write() on Another Window

```
<html>
<head>
<title>Writing to Subwindow</title>
<script type="text/javascript">
var newWindow;
function makeNewWindow() {
    newWindow = window.open("","","status,height=200,width=300");
}

function subWrite() {
    // make new window if someone has closed it
    if (newWindow.closed) {
        makeNewWindow();
    }
    // bring subwindow to front
    newWindow.focus();
    // assemble content for new window
    var newContent = "<html><head><title>A New Doc</title></head>";
    newContent += "<body bgcolor='coral'><h1>This document is brand new.</h1>";
    newContent += "</body></html>";
    // write HTML to new window document
    newWindow.document.write(newContent);
    newWindow.document.close(); // close layout stream
}
</script>
</head>
<body onload="makeNewWindow()">
<form>
<input type="button" value="Write to Subwindow" onclick="subWrite()">
</form>
</body>
</html>
```

document.createElement() and
document.createTextNode() methods

The `document.write()` method works on a piece of a web page only while the page is loading into the browser the first time. Any subsequent invocation of the method erases the page and writes a new page. But if you want to add to or modify a page that has already loaded, you need to call upon the Dynamic HTML capabilities of W3C DOM-compatible browsers. Your goal will be to add to, delete from, or replace sections of the node hierarchy of the document. Most element objects have methods to perform those actions (see a more in-depth discussion in Chapter 14). But if you need to add content, you'll have to create new element or text nodes. The `document` object has the methods to do that.

The `document.createElement()` method lets you create in the browser's memory a brand-new element object. To specify the precise element you wish to create, pass the tag name of the element as a string parameter of the method:

```
var newElem = document.createElement("p");
```

You may also wish to add some attribute values to the element, which you may do by assigning values to the newly created object's properties, even before the element becomes part of the document.

As you saw in Chapter 4's object hierarchy illustrations, an element object frequently needs text content between its start and end tags. The W3C DOM way to create that text is to generate a brand-new text node via the `document.createTextNode()` method and populate the node with the desired text. For example:

```
var newText = document.createTextNode("Greetings to all.");
```

The act of creating an element or text node does not by itself influence the document node tree. You must invoke one of the various insertion or replacement methods to place the new text node in its element and place the element in the document. You learn how to do this in the last tutorial chapter (Chapter 12).

document.getElementById() method

You met the `document.getElementById()` method in Chapter 4 when learning about the syntax for referencing element objects. This W3C DOM method is one you will use a lot. Get to know its finger-twisting name well. Be sure to honor the upper- and lowercase spelling of this all-important method.

The sole parameter of this method is a quoted string containing the ID of the element you wish to reference. The Evaluator Jr. page from Chapter 6 (and in the CD-ROM listings) has three element objects (form fields) with IDs `input`, `output`, and `inspector`. Type this method in the top text box with each ID, as in the following example:

```
document.getElementById("output")
```

The method returns a value, which you typically preserve in a variable for use by subsequent script statements:

```
var oneTable = document.getElementById("salesResults");
```

After the assignment statement, the variable represents the element object, allowing you to get and set its properties or invoke whatever methods belong to that type of object.

The next logical step past the document level in the object hierarchy is the form. That's where you will spend the next lesson.

Exercises

1. Which of the following references are valid, and which are not? Explain what is wrong with the invalid references.

   a. `window.document.form[0]`

   b. `self.entryForm.submit()`

   c. `document.forms[2].name`

   d. `document.getElementByID("firstParagraph")`

   e. `newWindow.document.write("Howdy")`

2. Write the JavaScript statement that displays an (annoying) dialog box welcoming visitors to your web page.

3. Write the JavaScript statement that executes while the page loads to display the same message from question 2 to the document as an `<h1>`-level headline on the page.

4. Create a page that prompts the user for his or her name as the page loads (via a dialog box) and then welcomes the user by name in the body of the page.

5. Create a page with any content you like, but one that automatically displays a dialog box after the page loads to show the user the URL of the current page.

Chapter 9

Forms and Form Elements

Most interactivity between a web page and the user takes place inside a form. That's where a lot of the interactive HTML stuff lives for every browser: text fields, buttons, checkboxes, option lists, and so on.

As described in earlier chapters, you may use the modern document object model (DOM) `document.getElementById()` method to reference any element, including forms and form controls. But this chapter focuses on an older, yet equally valid way of referencing forms and controls. It's important to be familiar with this widely used syntax so that you can understand existing JavaScript source code written according to the original (and fully backward-compatible) form syntax: the so-called DOM Level 0 syntax.

The form Object

Using the original DOM Level 0 syntax, you can reference a `form` object either by its position in the array of forms contained by a document or by name (if you assign an identifier to the `name` attribute inside the `<form>` tag). If only one form appears in the document, it is still a member of an array (a one-element array) and is referenced as follows:

```
document.forms[0]
```

Or use the string of the element's name as the array index:

```
document.forms["formName"]
```

Notice that the array reference uses the plural version of the word, followed by a set of square brackets containing the index number (zero is always first) or name of the element. Alternatively, you can use the form's name (not as a quoted string) as though it were a property of the `document` object:

```
document.formName
```

Form as object and container

Unlike the modern DOM's ID reference model — which lets a script dive anywhere into a document to grab an element object reference — DOM Level 0 form syntax imposes a hierarchical approach. It treats the `form` object as a container whose contents consist of the form control element objects (`input`, `select`, and `textarea` elements). Figure 9-1 shows the structure of this hierarchy and its place relative to the `document` object. You'll see the effect this structure has on the way you reference form control elements in a moment. This structure echoes perfectly the HTML tag organization within the `<form>` and `</form>` tag bookends.

FIGURE 9-1

DOM Level 0 hierarchy for forms and controls.

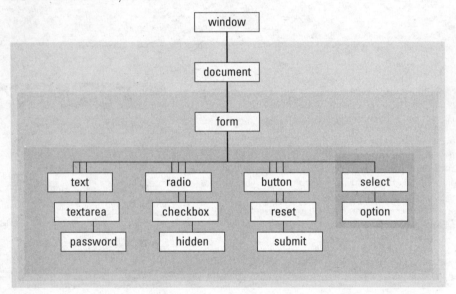

In addition to a large collection of properties and methods it has in common with all HTML element objects, the `form` object features a number of items that are unique to this object. Almost all of these unique properties are scripted representations of the `form` element's attributes (`action`, `target`, and so on). Scriptable browsers allow scripts to change these properties under script control, which gives your scripts potentially significant power to direct the behavior of a form submission in response to user selections on the page.

Accessing form properties

Forms are created entirely from standard HTML tags in the page. You can set attributes for `name`, `target`, `action`, `method`, and `enctype`. Each of these is a property of a `form` object, accessed by all-lowercase versions of those words, as in:

```
document.forms[0].action
document.formName.action
```

To change any of these properties, simply assign new values to them:

```
document.forms[0].action = "http://www.example.com/cgi/login.pl";
```

form.elements[] property

In addition to keeping track of each type of element inside a form, the browser maintains a list of all control elements within a form. This list is another array, with items listed according to the order in which their HTML tags appear in the source code. It is generally more efficient to create references to elements directly, using their names. However, sometimes a script needs to look through all of the elements in a form. This is especially true if the content of a form changes with each loading of the page because the number of text fields changes based on the user's browser type (for example, a script on the page uses document.write() to add an extra text box for information required only from Windows users).

The following code fragment shows the form.elements[] property at work in a for repeat loop that looks at every element in a form to set the contents of text fields to an empty string. The script cannot simply barge through the form and set every element's content to an empty string because some elements may be types (for example, a button) whose value properties have different purposes.

```
var form = window.document.forms[0];
for (var i = 0; i < form.elements.length; i++) {
    if (form.elements[i].type == "text") {
        form.elements[i].value = "";
    }
}
```

In the first statement, I create a variable — form — that holds a reference to the first form of the document. I do this so that when I make many references to form elements later in the script, the typical length of each reference is much shorter (and marginally faster). I can use the form variable as a shortcut to building references to items more deeply nested in the form.

Next, I start looping through the items in the elements array for the form. Each form control element has a type property, which reveals what kind of form control it is: text, button, radio, checkbox, and so on. I'm interested in finding elements whose type is text. For each of those, I set the value property to an empty string.

I return to forms later in this chapter to show you how to submit a form without a Submit button and how client-side form validation works.

Form Controls as Objects

Three kinds of HTML elements nested inside a <form> tag become scriptable objects in all browser DOMs. Most of the objects owe their existence to the <input> tag in the page's source code. Only the value assigned to the type attribute of an <input> tag determines whether the element is a text box, password entry field, hidden field, button, checkbox, or radio button. The other two kinds of form controls, textarea and select, have their own tags.

To reference a particular form control as an object in DOM Level 0 syntax, you build the reference as a hierarchy starting with the document, through the form, and then to the control. You've already seen how many ways you can reference merely the form part — all of which are valid for building form control references.

But if you are using only the identifiers assigned to the form and form control elements (that is, none of the associated arrays of elements), the syntax is as follows:

```
document.formName.controlName
```

For example, consider the following simple form:

```
<form name="searchForm" action="cgi-bin/search.pl">
    <input type="text" name="entry">
    <input type="submit" name="sender" value="Search">
</form>
```

The following sample references to the text input control are all valid:

```
document.searchForm.entry
document.searchForm.elements[0]
document.forms["searchForm"].elements["entry"]
document.forms["searchForm"].entry
```

Although form controls have several properties in common, some properties are unique to a particular control type or related types. For example, only a select object offers a property that reveals which item in its list is currently selected. But checkboxes and radio buttons both have a property that indicates whether the control is currently set to on. Similarly, all text-oriented controls operate the same way for reading and modifying their content.

Having a good grasp of the scriptable features of form control objects is important to your success with JavaScript. In the next sections, you meet the most important form control objects and see how scripts interact with them.

Text-related input objects

Each of the four text-related HTML form elements—input elements of the text, password, and hidden types, plus the textarea element—is an element in the document object hierarchy. All but the hidden object display themselves in the page, enabling users to enter information. These objects also display text information that changes in the course of using a page (although browsers capable of modern Dynamic HTML also allow the scripted change of other body text in a document).

To make these form control objects scriptable in a page, you do nothing special to their normal HTML tags—with the possible exception of assigning a name attribute. I strongly recommend assigning unique names to every text-related form control element if your scripts will be getting or setting properties or invoking their methods. Besides, if the form is actually submitted to a server program, the name attributes must be assigned for the server to receive the element's data.

For the visible objects in this category, event handlers are triggered from many user actions, such as giving a field focus (getting the text insertion pointer in the field) and changing text (entering new text and leaving the field). Most of your text-field actions are triggered by the change of text (the onchange event handler). In current browsers, events fire in response to individual keystrokes as well.

Without a doubt, the single most-used property of a text-related element is the value property. This property represents the current contents of the text element. A script can retrieve and set its content at any time. Content of the value property is always a string. This may require conversion to numbers (see Chapter 6) if text fields are used to enter values for some math operations.

Text Object Behavior

Many scripters look to JavaScript to solve what are perceived as shortcomings or behavioral anomalies with text-related objects in forms. I want to single these out early in your scripting experience so that they do not confuse you later.

First, only the most recent browsers let scripts reliably alter the font, font size, font style, and text alignment of a text object's content. You can access changes through the element's style-related properties (see Chapter 26).

Second, most browser forms practice a behavior that was recommended long ago as an informal standard by web pioneers. When a form contains only one text input object, a press of the Enter/Return key while the text object has focus automatically submits the form. For two or more fields in browsers other than IE5/Mac and Safari, you need another way to submit the form (for example, a Submit button). This one-field submission scheme works well in many cases, such as the search page of most web search sites. But if you are experimenting with simple forms containing only one field, you can submit the form with a press of the Enter/Return key. Submitting a form that has no other action or target specified means the page performs an unconditional reload, wiping out any information entered into the form. You can, however, cancel the submission through an onsubmit event handler in the form, as shown later in this chapter. You can also script the press of the Enter/Return key in any text field to submit a form (see Chapter 25).

To demonstrate how a text field's value property can be read and written, Listing 9-1 provides a complete HTML page with a single-entry field. Its onchange event handler invokes the upperMe() function, which converts the text to uppercase. In the upperMe() function, the first statement assigns the text object reference to a more convenient variable: field. A lot goes on in the second statement of the function. The right side of the assignment statement performs a couple of key tasks. The reference to the value property of the object (field.value) evaluates to whatever content is in the text field at that instant. Then that string is handed over to one of JavaScript's string functions, toUpperCase(), which converts the value to uppercase. The evaluated result of the right-side statement is then assigned to the second variable: upperCaseVersion. Nothing has changed yet in the text box. That comes in the third statement, where the value property of the text box is assigned whatever the upperCaseVersion variable holds. The need for the second statement is more for learning purposes so that you can see the process more slowly. In practice, you can combine the actions of steps 2 and 3 into one power-packed statement:

```
field.value = field.value.toUpperCase();
```

LISTING 9-1

Getting and Setting a Text Object's value Property

```
<html>
<head>
<title>Text Object value Property</title>
<script type="text/javascript">
function upperMe() {
    var field = document.forms[0].converter;
```

continued

LISTING 9-1   *(continued)*

```
    var upperCaseVersion = field.value.toUpperCase();
    field.value = upperCaseVersion;
}
</script>
</head>
<body>
<form onsubmit="return false">
<input type="text" name="converter" value="sample" onchange="upperMe()">
</form>
</body>
</html>
```

Later in this chapter, I show you how to reduce even further the need for explicit references in functions such as upperMe() in Listing 9-1. In the meantime, notice for a moment the onsubmit event handler in the <form> tag. I delve more deeply into this event handler later in this chapter, but I want to point out the construction that prevents a single-field form from being submitted when you press the Enter key. If the event handler weren't there, a press of the Enter key would reload the page, returning the field to its original text. Try it!

The button input object

I have used the button-type input element in many examples up to this point in the tutorial. The button is one of the simplest objects to script. In the simplified object model of this tutorial, the button object has only a few properties that are rarely accessed or modified in day-to-day scripts. Like the text object, the visual aspects of the button are governed not by HTML or scripts, but by the operating system and browser that the page visitor uses. By far the most useful event of the button object is the click event. It fires whenever the user clicks the button. Simple enough. No magic here.

The checkbox input object

A checkbox is also a simple element of the form object, but some of the properties may not be entirely intuitive. Unlike the value property of a plain button object (the text of the button label), the value property of a checkbox is any other text you want associated with the object. This text does not appear on the page in any fashion, but the property (initially set via the value attribute) might be important to a script that wants to know more about the purpose of the checkbox within the form.

The key property of a checkbox object is whether the box is checked. The checked property is a Boolean value: true if the box is checked, false if not. When you see that a property is a Boolean value, it's a clue that the value might be usable in an if or if...else condition expression. In Listing 9-2, the value of the checked property determines which alert box the user sees.

LISTING 9-2

The Checkbox Object's checked Property

```
<html>
<head>
<title>Checkbox Inspector</title>
```

```
<script type="text/javascript">
function inspectBox() {
   if (document.forms[0].checkThis.checked) {
      alert("The box is checked.");
   } else {
      alert("The box is not checked at the moment.");
   }
}
</script>
</head>
<body>
<form>
<input type="checkbox" name="checkThis">Check here<br>
<input type="button" value="Inspect Box" onclick="inspectBox()">
</form>
</body>
</html>
```

Checkboxes are generally used as preference setters rather than as action inducers. Although a checkbox object has an onclick event handler, a click of a checkbox should never do anything drastic, such as navigate to another page.

The radio input object

Setting up a group of radio objects for scripting requires a bit more work. To let the browser manage the highlighting and unhighlighting of a related group of buttons, you must assign the same name to each of the buttons in the group. You can have multiple radio groups within a form, but each member of the same group must have the same name.

Assigning the same name to a form element forces the browser to manage the elements differently than if they each had a unique name. Instead, the browser maintains an array list of objects with the same name. The name assigned to the group becomes the name of the array. Some properties apply to the group as a whole; other properties apply to individual buttons within the group and must be addressed via array index references. For example, you can find out how many buttons are in a radio group by reading the length property of the group:

> document.forms[0].*groupName*.length

If you want to find out whether a particular button is currently highlighted, via the same checked property used for the checkbox, you must access the button element individually:

> document.forms[0].*groupName*[0].checked

Listing 9-3 demonstrates several aspects of the radio-button object, including how to look through a group of buttons to find out which one is highlighted and how to use the value attribute and corresponding property for meaningful work.

The page includes three radio buttons and a plain button. Each radio button's value attribute contains the full name of one of the Three Stooges. When the user clicks the button, the onclick event handler invokes the fullName() function. In that function, the first statement creates a shortcut reference to the form.

101

Next, a `for` repeat loop looks through all the buttons in the `stooges` radio-button group. An `if` construction looks at the `checked` property of each button. When a button is highlighted, the `break` statement bails out of the `for` loop, leaving the value of the `i` loop counter at the number where the loop broke ranks. Then the alert dialog box uses a reference to the `value` property of the `i`th button so that the full name can be displayed in the alert.

LISTING 9-3

Scripting a Group of Radio Objects

```
<html>
<head>
<title>Extracting Highlighted Radio Button</title>
<script type="text/javascript">
function fullName() {
    var form = document.forms[0];
    for (var i = 0; i < form.stooges.length; i++) {
        if (form.stooges[i].checked) {
            break;
        }
    }
    alert("You chose " + form.stooges[i].value + ".");
}
</script>
</head>

<body>
<form>
<p>Select your favorite Stooge:
<input type="radio" name="stooges" value="Moe Howard" checked>Moe
<input type="radio" name="stooges" value="Larry Fine">Larry
<input type="radio" name="stooges" value="Curly Howard">Curly<br>
<input type="button" name="Viewer" value="View Full Name..."
onclick="fullName()"></p>
</form>
</body>
</html>
```

The select object

The most complex form control to script is the `select` element object. As you can see from the DOM Level 0 form object hierarchy diagram (see Figure 9-1), the `select` object is really a compound object: an object that contains an array of `option` objects. Moreover, you can establish this object in HTML to display itself as either a pop-up list or a scrolling list — the latter configurable to accept multiple selections by users. For the sake of simplicity at this stage, this lesson focuses on deployment as a pop-up list that allows only single selections.

Some properties belong to the entire select object; others belong to individual options inside the select object. If your goal is to determine which item the user selects, and you want the code to work on the widest range of browsers, you must use properties of both the select and option objects.

The most important property of the select object itself is the selectedIndex property, accessed as follows:

```
document.forms[0].selectName.selectedIndex
```

This value is the index number of the currently selected item. As with most index counting schemes in JavaScript, the first item (the one at the top of the list) has an index of zero. The selectedIndex value is critical for enabling you to access properties of the selected option. Two important properties of an option item are text and value, accessed as follows:

```
document.forms[0].selectName.options[n].text
document.forms[0].selectName.options[n].value
```

The text property is the string that appears onscreen in the select object's list. It is unusual for this information to be exposed as a form object property because in the HTML that generates a select object, the text is defined as an <option> tag's nested text. But inside the <option> tag, you can set a value attribute, which, like the radio buttons shown earlier, enables you to associate some hidden string information with each visible entry in the list.

To read the value or text property of a selected option most efficiently for all browsers, you can use the select object's selectedIndex property as an index value to the option. References for this kind of operation get pretty long, so take the time to understand what's happening here. In the following function, the first statement creates a shortcut reference to the select object. Then the selectedIndex property of the select object is substituted for the index value of the options array of that same object:

```
function inspect() {
    var list = document.forms[0].choices;
    var chosenItemText = list.options[list.selectedIndex].value;
}
```

To bring a select object to life, use the onchange event handler. As soon as a user makes a new selection in the list, this event handler runs the script associated with that event handler. Listing 9-4 shows a common application for a select object. Its text entries describe places to go in and out of a web site, and the value attributes hold the URLs for those locations. When a user makes a selection in the list, the onchange event handler triggers a script that extracts the value property of the selected option and assigns that value to the location.href object property to effect the navigation. Under JavaScript control, this kind of navigation doesn't need a separate Go button on the page.

LISTING 9-4

Navigating with a select Object

```
<html>
<head>
<title>Select Navigation</title>
<script type="text/javascript">
function goThere() {
    var list = document.forms[0].urlList;
    location.href = list.options[list.selectedIndex].value;
```

continued

LISTING 9-4   (continued)

```
}
</script>
</head>

<body>
<form>
Choose a place to go:
<select name="urlList" onchange="goThere()">
    <option selected value="index.html">Home Page
    <option value="store.html">Shop Our Store
    <option value="policies.html">Shipping Policies
    <option value="http://www.google.com">Search the Web
</select>
</form>
</body>
</html>
```

> **NOTE**   Recent browsers also expose the `value` property of the selected option item by way of the
> `value` property of the `select` object. This is certainly a logical and convenient shortcut, and
> you can use it safely if your target browsers include IE, Mozilla-based browsers, and Safari.

There is much more to the `select` object, including the ability to change the contents of a list in newer
browsers. Chapter 24 covers the `select` object in depth.

Passing Form Data and Elements to Functions

In all the examples so far in this lesson, when an event handler invokes a function that works with form elements, the form or form control is explicitly referenced in the function. But valuable shortcuts exist for
transferring information about the form or form control directly to the function without dealing with those
typically long references that start with the `window` or `document` object level.

JavaScript features a keyword — `this` — that always refers to whatever object contains the script in which
the keyword is used. Thus, in an `onchange` event handler for a text field, you can pass a reference to the
text input object to the function by inserting the `this` keyword as a parameter to the function:

```
<input type="text" name="entry" onchange="upperMe(this)">
```

At the receiving end, the function defines a parameter variable that turns that reference into a variable that
the rest of the function can use:

```
function upperMe(field) {
   statement[s]
}
```

The name you assign to the function's parameter variable is purely arbitrary, but it is helpful to give it a
name that expresses what the reference is. It is important that this reference is a live connection back to the
object. Therefore, statements in the script can get and set property values of the object at will.

For other functions, you may wish to receive a reference to the entire form, rather than just the object calling the function. This is certainly true if the function needs to access other elements of the same form. Because every form control object contains a property that points to the containing form, you can use the `this` keyword to reference the current control, plus its `form` property as `this.form`, as in:

```
<input type="button" value="Click Here" onclick="inspect(this.form)">
```

Then the function definition should have a parameter variable ready to be assigned to the form object reference. Again, you decide the name of the variable. I tend to use the variable name `form` as a way to remind me exactly what kind of object is referenced:

```
function inspect(form) {
    statement[s]
}
```

Listing 9-5 demonstrates passing references to both an individual form element and the entire form in the performance of two separate acts. This page makes believe that it is connected to a database of Beatles songs. When you click the Process Data button, it passes the `form` object, which the `processData()` function uses to access the group of radio buttons inside a `for` loop. Additional references using the passed `form` object extract the `value` properties of the selected radio button and the text field.

The text field has its own event handler, which passes just the text field to the `verifySong()` function. Notice how short the reference is to reach the `value` property of the song field inside the function.

LISTING 9-5

Passing a Form Object and Form Element to Functions

```
<html>
<head>
<title>Beatle Picker</title>
<script type="text/javascript">
function processData(form) {
    for (var i = 0; i < form.Beatles.length; i++) {
        if (form.Beatles[i].checked) {
            break
        }
    }
    // assign values to variables for convenience
    var beatle = form.Beatles[i].value
    var song = form.song.value
    alert("Checking whether " + song + " features " + beatle + "...")
}

function verifySong(entry) {
    var song = entry.value
    alert("Checking whether " + song + " is a Beatles tune...")
}
</script>
</head>

<body>
```

continued

LISTING 9-5   *(continued)*

```
<form onsubmit="return false">
<p>Choose your favorite Beatle:
<input type="radio" name="Beatles" value="John Lennon" checked>John
<input type="radio" name="Beatles" value="Paul McCartney">Paul
<input type="radio" name="Beatles" value="George Harrison">George
<input type="radio" name="Beatles" value="Ringo Starr">Ringo</p>

<p>Enter the name of your favorite Beatles song:<br>
<input type="text" name="song" value = "Eleanor Rigby" onchange="verifySong(this)">
<input type="button" name="process" value="Process Request..."
onclick="processData(this.form)"></p>
</form>
</body>
</html>
```

If you're a bit puzzled by the behavior of this example, here's an explanation of the programming logic behind what you experience. When you enter a new song title in the text box and click the Process Request button, the button click action is interrupted by the onchange event handler of the text box. (Clicking outside the text box or pressing the Tab key triggers the text field's onchange event handler before anything really happens outside the text box.) In other words, the button doesn't really get clicked, because the onchange alert dialog box comes up first. That's why you have to click it what seems to be a second time to get the combined song/Beatle verification. If you don't change the text in the field, your click of the button occurs without interruption, and the combined verification takes place.

Get to know the usage of the this keyword in passing form and form element objects to functions. The technique not only saves you typing in your code, but also ensures accuracy in references to those objects.

NOTE   As noted earlier, the trend to move scripting out of HTML tag markup is catching on. Unfortunately, discrepancies between the ways that IE and other browsers handle event assignments and event processing require explanations beyond the scope of this tutorial. You'll meet them soon enough, however, beginning in Chapter 14.

Submitting and Prevalidating Forms

The scripted equivalent of submitting a form is the form object's submit() method. All you need in the statement is a reference to the form and this method:

```
document.forms[0].submit();
```

Before you get ideas about having a script silently submit a form to a URL bearing the mailto: protocol, forget it. Because such a scheme could expose visitors' e-mail addresses without their knowledge, mailto: submissions are either blocked or revealed to users as a security precaution.

Before a form is submitted, you may wish to perform some last-second validation of data in the form or in other scripting (for example, changing the form's action property based on user choices). You can do this in a function invoked by the form's onsubmit event handler. Specific validation routines are beyond the scope of this tutorial (but are explained in substantial detail in Chapter 43 on the CD-ROM), but I want to show you how the onsubmit event handler works.

You can let the results of a validation function cancel a submission if the validation shows some incorrect data or empty fields. To control submission, the `onsubmit` event handler must evaluate to `return true` (to allow submission to continue) or `return false` (to cancel submission). This is a bit tricky at first because it involves more than just having the function called by the event handler return `true` or `false`. The `return` keyword must be part of the final evaluation.

Listing 9-6 shows a page with a simple validation routine that ensures that all fields have something in them before allowing submission to continue. (The sample form has no `action` attribute, so this sample form doesn't get sent to the server.) Notice that the `onsubmit` event handler (which passes a reference to the `form` object as a parameter — in this case, the `this` keyword points to the `form` object because its tag holds the event handler) includes the `return` keyword before the function name.

The `if` condition performs two tests. The first is to make sure that we're examining form controls whose `type` properties are text (so as not to bother with, say, buttons). Next, it checks to see whether the value of the text field is empty. The `&&` operator (called a Boolean `AND` operator) forces both sides to evaluate to `true` before the entire condition expression inside the parentheses evaluates to `true`. If either subtest fails, the whole condition fails. When the function returns its `true` or `false` value, the event handler evaluates to the requisite `return true` or `return false`.

LISTING 9-6

Last-Minute Checking Before Form Submission

```html
<html>
<head>
<title>Validator</title>
<script type="text/javascript">
function checkForm(form) {
    for (var i = 0; i < form.elements.length; i++) {
        if (form.elements[i].type == "text" && form.elements[i].value == "") {
            alert("Fill out ALL fields.");
            return false;
        }
    }
    return true;
}
</script>
</head>

<body>
<form onsubmit="return checkForm(this)">
Please enter all requested information:<br>
First Name:<input type="text" name="firstName"><br>
Last Name:<input type="text" name="lastName"><br>
Rank:<input type="text" name="rank"><br>
Serial Number:<input type="text" name="serialNumber"><br>

<input type="submit">
</form>
</body>
</html>
```

One quirky bit of behavior involving the submit() method and onsubmit event handler needs explanation. Although you might think (and logically so, in my opinion) that the submit() method would be the exact scripted equivalent of a click of a real Submit button, it's not. The submit() method does not cause the form's submit event to fire at all. If you want to perform validation on a form submitted via the submit() method, invoke the validation in the script function that ultimately calls the submit() method.

So much for the basics of forms and form controls. In Chapter 10, you step away from HTML for a moment to look at more advanced JavaScript core language items: strings, math, and dates.

Exercises

1. Rework Listings 9-1, 9-2, 9-3, and 9-4 so that all the script functions receive the most efficient form or form element references directly from the invoking event handler.

2. For the following form (assume that it's the only form on the page), write at least 10 ways to reference the text input field as an object in all modern scriptable browsers.

   ```
   <form name="subscription" action="cgi-bin/maillist.pl" method="post">
       <input type="text" id="email" name="email">
       <input type="submit">
   </form>
   ```

3. In the following HTML tag, what kind of information do you think is being passed with the event handler? Write a function that displays in an alert dialog box the information being passed.

   ```
   <input type="text" name="phone" onchange="format(this.value)">
   ```

4. A document contains two forms, specifications and accessories. In the accessories form is a field named acc1. Write at least two different statements that set the contents of that field to Leather Carrying Case.

5. Create a page that includes a select object to change the background color of the current page. The property that you need to set is document.bgColor, and the three values you should offer as options are red, yellow, and green. In the select object, the colors should display as Stop, Caution, and Go.

Chapter 10

Strings, Math, and Dates

For most of the lessons in the tutorial so far, the objects at the center of attention belong to the document object model (DOM). But as indicated in Chapter 2, a clear dividing line exists between the DOM and the JavaScript language. The language has some of its own objects that are independent of the DOM. These objects are defined such that if a vendor wished to implement JavaScript as the programming language for an entirely different kind of product, the language would still use these core facilities for handling text, advanced math (beyond simple arithmetic), and dates. You can find formal specifications of these objects in the ECMA-262 recommendation.

Core Language Objects

It is often difficult for newcomers to programming — or even experienced programmers who have not worked in object-oriented worlds before — to think about objects, especially when attributed to things that don't seem to have a physical presence. For example, it doesn't require lengthy study to grasp the notion that a button on a page is an object. It has several physical properties that make perfect sense. But what about a string of characters? As you learn in this chapter, in an object-based environment such as JavaScript, everything that moves is treated as an object — each piece of data from a Boolean value to a date. Each such object probably has one or more properties that help define the content; such an object may also have methods associated with it to define what the object can do or what you can do to the object.

I call all objects that are not part of the DOM *core language objects*. You can see the full complement of them in the first two pages of the Quick Reference in Appendix A. In this chapter, I focus on the String, Math, and Date objects.

String Objects

You have used `String` objects many times in earlier lessons. A *string* is any text inside a quote pair. A quote pair consists of either double quotes or single quotes. This allows one string to nest inside another, as often happens in event handlers defined as tag attributes. In the following example, the `alert()` method requires a quoted string as a parameter, but the entire method call also must be inside quotes:

```
onclick="alert('Hello, all')"
```

JavaScript imposes no practical limit on the number of characters that a string can hold. However, most older browsers have a limit of 255 characters for a script statement. This limit is sometimes exceeded when a script includes a lengthy string that is to become scripted content in a page. You need to divide such lines into smaller chunks, using techniques described in a moment.

You have two ways to assign a string value to a variable. The simplest is a basic assignment statement:

```
var myString = "Howdy";
```

This works perfectly well except in some exceedingly rare instances. You can also create a string object using the more formal syntax that involves the `new` keyword and a constructor function (that is, it constructs a new object):

```
var myString = new String("Howdy");
```

Whichever way you use to initialize a variable with a string, the variable receiving the assignment can respond to all `String` object methods.

Joining strings

Bringing two strings together as a single string is called *concatenating* strings, a term you learned in Chapter 6. String concatenation requires one of two JavaScript operators. Even in your first script in Chapter 3, you saw how the addition operator (+) linked multiple strings to produce the HTML that gets inserted into a placeholder element:

```
document.getElementById("readout").innerHTML =
    "Your browser says it is: " + "<span class='highlight'>" +
    navigator.userAgent + "</span>.<hr />";
```

As valuable as that operator is, another operator can be even more scripter friendly. This operator is helpful when you are assembling large strings in a single variable. The strings may be so long or cumbersome that you need to divide the building process into multiple statements. The pieces may be combinations of *string literals* (strings inside quotes) or variable values. The clumsy way to do it (perfectly doable in JavaScript) is to use the addition operator to append more text to the existing chunk:

```
var msg = "Four score";
msg = msg + " and seven";
msg = msg + " years ago,";
```

But another operator, called the *add-by-value operator*, offers a handy shortcut. The symbol for the operator is a plus and equal sign together (+=). This operator means *append the stuff on the right of me to the end of the stuff on the left of me*. Therefore, the preceding sequence is shortened as follows:

```
var msg = "Four score";
msg += " and seven";
msg += " years ago,";
```

You can also combine the operators if the need arises:

```
var msg = "Four score";
msg += " and seven" + " years ago";
```

I use the add-by-value operator a lot when accumulating HTML text to be written to the current document or another window.

String methods

Of all the core JavaScript objects, the String object has the most diverse collection of methods associated with it. Many methods are designed to help scripts extract segments of a string. Another group, rarely used and now obsolete in favor of Cascading Style Sheets (CSS), wraps a string with one of several style-oriented tags (a scripted equivalent of tags for font size, style, and the like.)

In a string method, the string being acted upon becomes part of the reference followed by the method name. All methods return a value of some kind. Most of the time, the returned value is a converted version of the string object referred to in the method call — but the original string is still intact. To capture the modified version, you need to assign the results of the method to a variable:

```
var result = myString.methodName();
```

The following sections introduce you to several important string methods available to all browser brands and versions.

Changing string case

Two methods convert a string to all uppercase or all lowercase letters:

```
var result = string.toUpperCase();
var result = string.toLowerCase();
```

Not surprisingly, you must observe the case of each letter of the method names if you want them to work. These methods come in handy when your scripts need to compare strings that may not have the same case (for example, a string in a lookup table compared with a string typed by a user). Because the methods don't change the original strings attached to the expressions, you can simply compare the evaluated results of the methods:

```
var foundMatch = false;
if (stringA.toUpperCase() == stringB.toUpperCase()) {
   foundMatch = true;
}
```

String searches

You can use the string.indexOf() method to determine whether one string is contained by another. Even within JavaScript's own object data, this can be useful information. For example, the navigator.userAgent property reveals a lot about the browser that loads the page. A script can investigate the value of that property for the existence of, say, "Win" to determine that the user has a Windows operating system. That short string might be buried somewhere inside a long string, and all the script needs to know is whether the short string is present in the longer one — wherever it might be.

The string.indexOf() method returns a number indicating the index value (zero-based) of the character in the larger string where the smaller string begins. The key point about this method is that if no match occurs, the returned value is -1. To find out whether the smaller string is inside, all you need to test is whether the returned value is something other than -1.

Two strings are involved with this method: the shorter one and the longer one. The longer string is the one that appears in the reference to the left of the method name; the shorter string is inserted as a parameter to the indexOf() method. To demonstrate the method in action, the following fragment looks to see whether the user is running Windows:

```
var isWindows = false;
if (navigator.userAgent.indexOf("Win") != -1) {
    isWindows = true;
}
```

The operator in the if construction's condition (!=) is the inequality operator. You can read it as meaning *is not equal to.*

Extracting copies of characters and substrings

To extract a single character at a known position within a string, use the charAt() method. The parameter of the method is an index number (zero-based) of the character to extract. When I say *extract,* I don't mean delete, but grab a snapshot of the character. The original string is not modified in any way.

For example, consider a script in a main window that is capable of inspecting a variable, stringA, in another window that displays map images of different corporate buildings. When the window has a map of Building C in it, the stringA variable contains "Building C". The building letter is always at the 10th character position of the string (or number 9 in a zero-based counting world), so the script can examine that one character to identify the map currently in that other window:

```
var stringA = "Building C";
var bldgLetter = stringA.charAt(9);
    // result: bldgLetter = "C"
```

Another method — string.substring() — enables you to extract a contiguous sequence of characters, provided that you know the starting and ending positions of the substring of which you want to grab a copy. It is important that the character at the ending-position value not be part of the extraction: All applicable characters, up to but not including that character, are part of the extraction. The string from which the extraction is made appears to the left of the method name in the reference. Two parameters specify the starting and ending index values (zero-based) for the start and end positions:

```
var stringA = "banana daiquiri";
var excerpt = stringA.substring(2,6);
    // result: excerpt = "nana"
```

String manipulation in JavaScript is fairly cumbersome compared with that in some other scripting languages. Higher-level notions of words, sentences, or paragraphs are absent. Therefore, sometimes it takes a bit of scripting with string methods to accomplish what seems like a simple goal. Yet you can put your knowledge of expression evaluation to the test as you assemble expressions that utilize heavily nested constructions. For example, the following fragment needs to create a new string that consists of everything from the larger string except the first word. Assuming that the first word of other strings can be of any length, the second statement uses the string.indexOf() method to look for the first space character and adds 1 to that value to serve as the starting index value for an outer string.substring() method. For the second parameter, the length property of the string provides a basis for the ending character's index value (one more than the actual character needed).

```
var stringA = "The United States of America";
var excerpt = stringA.substring(stringA.indexOf(" ") + 1, stringA.length);
    // result: excerpt = "United States of America"
```

Creating statements like this one is not something you are likely to enjoy over and over again, so in Chapter 27, I show you how to create your own library of string functions you can reuse in all of your scripts that need their string-handling facilities. More powerful string-matching facilities are also built into today's browsers by way of *regular expressions* (see Chapter 28 and Chapter 42 on the CD-ROM).

The Math Object

JavaScript provides ample facilities for math — far more than most scripters who don't have a background in computer science and math will use in a lifetime. But every genuine programming language needs these powers to accommodate clever programmers who can make windows fly in circles onscreen.

The Math object contains all these powers. This object is unlike most of the other objects in JavaScript in that you don't generate copies of the object to use. Instead, your scripts summon a single Math object's properties and methods. (One Math object actually occurs per window or frame, but this has no impact whatsoever on your scripts.) Programmers call this kind of fixed object a *static object*. That Math object (with an uppercase *M*) is part of the reference to the property or method. Properties of the Math object are constant values, such as pi and the square root of 2:

```
var piValue = Math.PI;
var rootOfTwo = Math.SQRT2;
```

Math object methods cover a wide range of trigonometric functions and other math functions that work on numeric values already defined in your script. For example, you can find which of two numbers is the larger:

```
var larger = Math.max(value1, value2);
```

Or you can raise one number to a power of 10:

```
var result = Math.pow(value1, 10);
```

More common, perhaps, is the method that rounds a value to the nearest integer value:

```
var result = Math.round(value1);
```

Another common request of the Math object is a random number. The Math.random() method returns a floating-point number between 0 and 1. If you design a script to act like a card game, you need random integers between 1 and 52; for dice, the range is 1 to 6 per die. To generate a random integer between 0 and any top value, use the following formula

```
Math.floor(Math.random() * (n + 1))
```

where n is the top number. (Math.floor returns the integer part of any floating-point number.) To generate random numbers between 1 and any higher number, use this formula

```
Math.floor(Math.random() * n) + 1
```

where n equals the top number of the range. For the dice game, the formula for each die is

```
newDieValue = Math.floor(Math.random() * 6) + 1;
```

To see this, enter the right part of the preceding statement in the top text box of The Evaluator Jr. and repeatedly click the Evaluate button.

The Date Object

Working with dates beyond simple tasks can be difficult business in JavaScript. A lot of the difficulty comes with the fact that dates and times are calculated internally according to *Greenwich Mean Time (GMT)* — provided that the visitor's own internal PC clock and control panel are set accurately. As a result of this complexity, better left for Chapter 30, this section of the tutorial touches on only the basics of the JavaScript Date object.

A scriptable browser contains one global Date object (in truth, one Date object per window) that is always present, ready to be called upon at any moment. The Date object is another one of those static objects. When you wish to work with a date, such as displaying today's date, you need to invoke the Date object constructor function to obtain an instance of a Date object tied to a specific time and date. For example, when you invoke the constructor without any parameters, as in

```
var today = new Date();
```

the Date object takes a snapshot of the PC's internal clock and returns a date object for that instant. Notice the distinction between the static Date object and a Date object instance, which contains an actual date value. The variable, today, contains not a ticking clock but a value that you can examine, tear apart, and reassemble as needed for your script.

Internally, the value of a Date object instance is the time, in milliseconds, from zero o'clock on January 1, 1970, in the GMT zone — the world standard reference point for all time conversions. That's how a Date object contains both date and time information.

You can also grab a snapshot of the Date object for a particular date and time in the past or future by specifying that information as parameters to the Date object constructor function:

```
var someDate = new Date("Month dd, yyyy hh:mm:ss");
var someDate = new Date("Month dd, yyyy");
var someDate = new Date(yyyy,mm,dd,hh,mm,ss);
var someDate = new Date(yyyy,mm,dd);
var someDate = new Date(GMT milliseconds from 1/1/1970);
```

If you attempt to view the contents of a raw Date object, JavaScript converts the value to the local time-zone string, as indicated by your PC's control panel setting. To see this in action, use The Evaluator Jr.'s top text box to enter the following:

```
new Date();
```

Your PC's clock supplies the current date and time as the clock calculates them (even though JavaScript still stores the date object's millisecond count in the GMT zone). You can, however, extract components of the Date object via a series of methods that you apply to a Date object instance. Table 10-1 shows an abbreviated listing of these properties and information about their values.

TABLE 10-1

Some Date Object Methods

Method	Value Range	Description
dateObj.getTime()	0-...	Milliseconds since 1/1/70 00:00:00 GMT
dateObj.getYear()	70-...	Specified year minus 1900; four-digit year for 2000+
dateObj.getFullYear()	1970-...	Four-digit year (Y2K-compliant); version 4+ browsers
dateObj.getMonth()	0-11	Month within the year (January = 0)
dateObj.getDate()	1-31	Date within the month
dateObj.getDay()	0-6	Day of week (Sunday = 0)
dateObj.getHours()	0-23	Hour of the day in 24-hour time
dateObj.getMinutes()	0-59	Minute of the specified hour
dateObj.getSeconds()	0-59	Second within the specified minute
dateObj.setTime(*val*)	0-...	Milliseconds since 1/1/70 00:00:00 GMT
dateObj.setYear(*val*)	70-...	Specified year minus 1900; four-digit year for 2000+
dateObj.setMonth(*val*)	0-11	Month within the year (January = 0)
dateObj.setDate(*val*)	1-31	Date within the month
dateObj.setDay(*val*)	0-6	Day of week (Sunday = 0)
dateObj.setHours(*val*)	0-23	Hour of the day in 24-hour time
dateObj.setMinutes(*val*)	0-59	Minute of the specified hour
dateObj.setSeconds(*val*)	0-59	Second within the specified minute

CAUTION Be careful about values whose ranges start with zero, especially the months. The getMonth() and setMonth() method values are zero based, so the numbers are 1 less than the month numbers you are accustomed to working with (for example, January is 0 and December is 11).

You may notice one difference about the methods that set values of a Date object. Rather than returning some new value, these methods actually modify the value of the instance of the Date object referenced in the call to the method.

Date Calculations

Performing calculations with dates frequently requires working with the millisecond values of the Date objects. This is the surest way to compare date values. To demonstrate a few Date object machinations, Listing 10-1 displays the current date and time as the page loads. Another script shows one way to calculate the date and time seven days from the current date and time values.

LISTING 10-1

Date Object Calculations

```
<html>
<head>
<title>Date Calculation</title>
<script type="text/javascript">
function nextWeek() {
    var todayInMS = today.getTime();
    var nextWeekInMS = todayInMS + (60 * 60 * 24 * 7 * 1000);
    return new Date(nextWeekInMS);
}
</script>
</head>

<body>
Today is:
<script type="text/javascript">
var today = new Date();
document.write(today);
</script>
<br>
Next week will be:
<script type="text/javascript">
document.write(nextWeek());
</script>
</body>
</html>
```

In the Body portion, the first script runs as the page loads, setting a global variable (today) to the current date and time. The string equivalent is written to the page. In the second Body script, the document.write() method invokes the nextWeek() function to get a value to display. That function uses the today global variable, copying its millisecond value to a new variable: todayInMS. To get a date seven days from now, the next statement adds the number of milliseconds in 7 days (60 seconds times 60 minutes times 24 hours times 7 days times 1000 milliseconds) to today's millisecond value. Now the script needs a new Date object calculated from the total milliseconds. This requires invoking the Date object constructor with the milliseconds as a parameter. The returned value is a Date object, which is automatically converted to a string version for writing to the page.

To add time intervals to or subtract time intervals from a Date object, you can use a shortcut that doesn't require the millisecond conversions. By combining the date object's set and get methods, you can let the Date object work out the details. For example, in Listing 10-1, you could eliminate the function and let the following two statements in the second Body script obtain the desired result:

```
today.setDate(today.getDate() + 7);
document.write(today);
```

Because JavaScript tracks the date and time internally as milliseconds, the accurate date appears in the end, even if the new date is into the next month. JavaScript automatically takes care of figuring out how many days there are in a month, as well as in leap years.

Many other quirks and complicated behavior await you if you script dates in your page. As later chapters demonstrate, however, the results may be worth the effort.

Exercises

1. Create a web page that has one form field for entry of the user's e-mail address and a Submit button. Include a presubmission validation routine that verifies that the text field has the @ symbol used in all e-mail addresses before you allow submission of the form.

2. Given the string `"Internet Explorer"`, fill in the blanks of the `string.substring()` method parameters here that yield the results shown to the right of each method call.

```
var myString = "Internet Explorer";
myString.substring(___,___)    // result = "Int"
myString.substring(___,___)    // result = "plorer"
myString.substring(___,___)    // result = "net Exp"
```

3. Fill in the rest of the function in the listing that follows so that it looks through every character of the entry field and counts how many times the letter *e* appears in the field. (Hint: All that is missing is a for repeat loop.)

```html
<html>
<head>
<title>Wheel o' Fortuna</title>
<script type="text/javascript">
function countE(form) {
    var count = 0;
    var inputString = form.mainstring.value.toLowerCase();
    missing code
    var msg = "The string has " + count;
    msg += " instances of the letter e.";
    alert(msg);
}
</script>
</head>

<body>
<form>
Enter any string: <input type="text" name="mainstring" size="30"><br>
<input type="button" value="Count the Es" onclick="countE(this.form)">
</form>
</body>
</html>
```

4. Create a page that has two fields and one button. The button should trigger a function that generates two random numbers between 1 and 6, placing each number in one of the fields. (Think of using this page as a substitute for rolling a pair of dice in a board game.)

5. Create a page that displays the number of days between today and next Christmas.

Chapter 11

Scripting Frames and Multiple Windows

One of the attractive aspects of JavaScript for some applications on the client is that it allows user actions in one frame or window to influence what happens in other frames and windows. In this section of the tutorial, you extend your existing knowledge of object references to the realm of multiple frames and windows.

Frames: Parents and Children

You've see in earlier top-level hierarchy illustrations (such as Figure 4-2) that the window object is at the top of the chart. The window object also has several synonyms, which stand in for the window object in special cases. For instance, in Chapter 8, you learned that self is synonymous with window when the reference applies to the same window that contains the script's document. In this lesson, you learn the roles of three other references that point to objects behaving as windows: frame, top, and parent.

Loading an ordinary HTML document into the browser creates a model in the browser that starts out with one window object and the document it contains. The top rungs of the hierarchy model are as simple as can be, as shown in Figure 11-1. This is where references begin with window or self (or with document because the current window is assumed).

FIGURE 11-1

Single-frame window and document hierarchy.

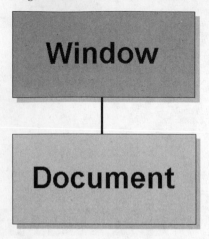

The instant a framesetting document loads into a browser, the browser starts building a slightly different hierarchy model. The precise structure of that model depends entirely on the structure of the frameset defined in that framesetting document. Consider the following skeletal frameset definition:

```
<html>
<frameset cols="50%,50%">
   <frame name="leftFrame" src="somedoc1.html">
   <frame name="rightFrame" src="somedoc2.html">
</frameset>
</html>
```

This HTML splits the browser window into two frames side by side, with a different document loaded into each frame. The model is concerned only with structure; it doesn't care about the relative sizes of the frames or whether they're set up in columns or rows.

Framesets establish relationships among the frames in the collection. Borrowing terminology from the object-oriented programming world, the framesetting document loads into a *parent window*. Each of the frames defined in that parent window document is a *child frame*. Figure 11-2 shows the hierarchical model of a two-frame environment. This illustration reveals a lot of subtleties about the relationships among framesets and their frames.

It is often difficult at first to visualize the frameset as a window object in the hierarchy. 'After all, with the exception of the URL showing in the Location/Address field, you don't see anything about the frameset in the browser. But that window object exists in the object model. Notice, too, that in the diagram the frame-setting parent window has no document object showing. This may also seem odd, because the window obviously requires an HTML file containing the specifications for the frameset. In truth, the parent window has a document object associated with it, but it is omitted from the diagram to better portray the relationships among parent and child windows. A frameset parent's document cannot contain most of the typical HTML objects such as forms and controls, so references to the parent's document are rarely, if ever, used.

FIGURE 11-2

Two-frame window and document hierarchy.

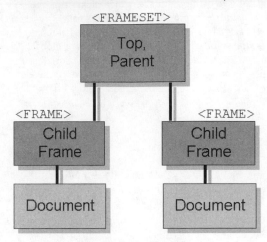

If you add a script to the framesetting document that needs to access a property or method of that window object, references are like any single-frame situation. Think about the point of view of a script located in that window. Its immediate universe is the very same window.

Things get more interesting when you start looking at the child frames. Each of these frames contains a `document` object whose content you see in the browser window, and the structure is such that each frame's document is entirely independent of the other. It is as though each document lived in its own browser window. Indeed, that's why each child frame is also a window type of object. A frame has the same kinds of properties and methods as the `window` object that occupies the entire browser.

From the point of view of either child window in Figure 11-2, its immediate container is the `parent` window. When a `parent` window is at the top of the hierarchical model loaded in the browser, that window is also referred to as the `top` object.

References Among Family Members

Given the frame structure of Figure 11-2, it's time to look at how a script in any one of those windows can access objects, functions, or variables in the others. An important point to remember about this facility is that if a script has access to an object, function, or global variable in its own window, that same item can be reached by a script from another frame in the hierarchy (provided that both documents come from the same web server).

A script reference may need to take one of three possible routes in the two-generation hierarchy described so far: parent to child; child to parent; or child to child. Each of the paths between these windows requires a different reference style.

Parent-to-child references

Probably the least common direction taken by references is when a script in the parent document needs to access some element of one of its frames. The parent contains two or more frames, which means that the parent maintains an array of the child frame objects. You can address a frame by array syntax or by the name you assign to it with the `name` attribute inside the `<frame>` tag. In the following examples of reference syntax, I substitute a placeholder named `ObjFuncVarName` for whatever object, function, or global variable you intend to access in the distant window or frame. Remember that each visible frame contains a `document` object, which generally is the container of elements you script; be sure that references to the elements include `document`. With that in mind, a reference from a parent to one of its child frames follows any of these models:

```
[window.]frames[n].ObjFuncVarName
[window.]frames["frameName"].ObjFuncVarName
[window.]frameName.ObjFuncVarName
```

Numeric index values for frames are based on the order in which their `<frame>` tags appear in the frame-setting document. You will make your life easier, however, if you assign recognizable names to each frame and use the frame's name in the reference.

Child-to-parent references

It is not uncommon to place scripts in the parent (in the Head portion) that multiple child frames or multiple documents in a frame use as a kind of script library. By loading in the frameset, these scripts load only once while the frameset is visible. If other documents from the same server load into the frames over time, they can take advantage of the parent's scripts without having to load their own copies into the browser.

From the child's point of view, the next level up the hierarchy is called the `parent`. Therefore, a reference from a child frame to items at the parent level is simply:

```
parent.ObjFuncVarName
```

If the item accessed in the parent is a function that returns a value, the returned value transcends the parent/child borders down to the child without hesitation.

When the parent window is also at the top of the object hierarchy currently loaded into the browser, you can optionally refer to it as the *top window*, as in:

```
top.ObjFuncVarName
```

Using the `top` reference can be hazardous if for some reason your web page gets displayed in some other web site's frameset. What is your top window is not the master frameset's top window. Therefore, I recommend using the `parent` reference whenever possible (unless you want to blow away an unwanted framer of your web site).

Child-to-child references

The browser needs a bit more assistance when it comes to getting one child window to communicate with one of its siblings. One of the properties of any window or frame is its `parent` (whose value is `null` for a single window). A reference must use the `parent` property to work its way out of the current frame to a point that both child frames have in common — the parent, in this case. When the reference is at the parent level, the rest of the reference can carry on as though it were starting at the parent. Thus, from one child to one of its siblings, you can use any of the following reference formats:

```
parent.frames[n].ObjFuncVarName
parent.frames["frameName"].ObjFuncVarName
parent.frameName.ObjFuncVarName
```

A reference from the other sibling back to the first looks the same, but the `frames[]` array index or `frameName` part of the reference differs. Of course, much more complex frame hierarchies exist in HTML. Even so, the object model and referencing scheme provide a solution for the most deeply nested and gnarled frame arrangement you can think of — following the same precepts you just learned.

Frame-Scripting Tips

One of the first mistakes that frame-scripting newcomers make is writing immediate script statements that call on other frames while the pages load. The problem here is that you cannot rely on the document loading sequence to follow the frameset source-code order. All you know for sure is that the parent document *begins* loading first. Regardless of the order of `<frame>` tags, child frames can begin loading at any time. Moreover, a frame's loading time depends on other elements in the document, such as images or Java applets.

Fortunately, you can use a certain technique to initiate a script when all the documents in the frameset are completely loaded. Just as the `load` event for a window fires when that window's document is fully loaded, a parent's `load` event fires after the `load` events in its child frames have fired. Therefore, you can specify an `onload` event handler in the `<frameset>` tag. That handler might invoke a function in the framesetting document that then has the freedom to tap the objects, functions, or variables of all frames throughout the object hierarchy.

Make special note that a reference to a frame as a type of window object is quite separate from a reference to the `frame` element object. An element object is one of those DOM element nodes in the document node tree (see Chapter 4). The properties and methods of this node differ from the properties and methods that accrue to a window-type object. It may be a difficult distinction to grasp, but it's an important one. The way you reference a frame — as a window object or element node — determines which set of properties and methods are available to your scripts. See Chapter 15 for a more detailed introduction to element node scripting.

If you start with a reference to the `frame` element object, you can still reach a reference to the `document` object loaded into that frame, but the syntax is different, depending on the browser. IE4+ and Safari let you use the same `document` reference as for a window; Mozilla-based browsers follow the W3C DOM standard more closely, using the `contentDocument` property of the frame element. To accommodate both syntaxes, you can build a reference as follows:

```
var docObj;
var frameObj = document.getElementById("myFrame");
if (frameObj.contentDocument) {
   docObj = frameObj.contentDocument;
} else {
   docObj = frameObj.document;
}
```

About iframe Elements

The iframe element is supported as a scriptable object in IE4+, Mozilla-based browsers, and Safari (among other modern browsers). It is often used as a way to fetch and load HTML from a server without disturbing the current HTML page. Therefore, it's not uncommon for an iframe to be hidden from view while scripts handle all the processing between it and the main document.

An iframe element becomes another member of the current window's frames collection, but you may also reference the iframe as an element object through W3C DOM document.getElementById() terminology. As with the distinction between the traditional frame-as-window object and DOM element object, a script reference to the document object within an iframe element object needs special handling. See Chapter 16 for additional details.

Controlling Multiple Frames: Navigation Bars

If you are enamored of frames as a way to help organize a complex web page, you may find yourself wanting to control the navigation of one or more frames from a static navigation panel. Here, I demonstrate scripting concepts for such control using an application called Decision Helper (which you can find in Chapter 55 on the CD-ROM). The application consists of three frames (see Figure 11-3). The top-left frame is one image that has four graphical buttons in it. The goal is to turn that image into a client-side image map and script it so that the pages change in the right and bottom frames. In the top-right frame, the script loads an entirely different document along the sequence of five different documents that go in there. In the bottom frame, the script navigates to one of five anchors to display the segment of instructions that applies to the document loaded in the top-right frame.

FIGURE 11-3

The Decision Helper screen.

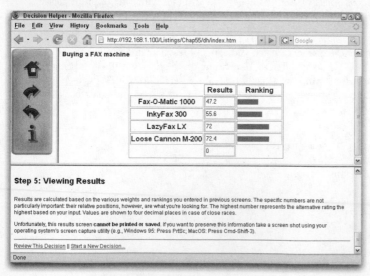

Listing 11-1 shows a slightly modified version of the actual file for the Decision Helper application's navigation frame. The listing contains a couple of objects and concepts that have not yet been covered in this tutorial, but as you will see, they are extensions to what you already know about JavaScript and objects. To help simplify the discussion here, I remove the scripting and HTML for the top and bottom buttons of the area map. In addition, I cover only the two navigation arrows.

LISTING 11-1

A Graphical Navigation Bar

```
<html>
<head>
<title>Navigation Bar</title>
<script type="text/javascript">
<!-- start
function goNext() {
   var currOffset = parseInt(parent.currTitle);
   if (currOffset < 5) {
      currOffset += 1;
      parent.entryForms.location.href = "dh" + currOffset + ".htm";
      parent.instructions.location.hash = "help" + currOffset;
   } else {
      alert("This is the last form.");
   }
}
function goPrev() {
   var currOffset = parseInt(parent.currTitle);
   if (currOffset > 1) {
      currOffset -= 1;
      parent.entryForms.location.href = "dh" + currOffset + ".htm";
      parent.instructions.location.hash = "help" + currOffset;
   } else {
      alert("This is the first form.");
   }
}
// end -->
</script>
</head>
<body bgcolor="white">
<map name="navigation">
<area shape="rect" coords="25,80,66,116" href="javascript:goNext()">
<area shape="rect" coords="24,125,67,161" href="javascript:goPrev()">
</map>
<img src="dhNav.gif" height="240" width="96" border="0" usemap="#navigation"
alt="navigation bar">
</body>
</html>
```

Look first at the HTML section for the Body portion. Almost everything there is standard stuff for defining client-side image maps. The coordinates define rectangles around each of the arrows in the larger image. The href attributes for the two areas point to JavaScript functions defined in the Head portion of the document. (The javascript: pseudo-URL is covered in Chapter 12.)

In the frameset that defines the Decision Helper application, names are assigned to each frame. The top-right frame is called entryForms; the bottom frame is called instructions.

Knowing that navigation from page to page in the top-right frame requires knowledge of which page is currently loaded there, I build some other scripting into both the parent document and each of the documents that loads into that frame. A global variable called currTitle is defined in the parent document. Its value is an integer indicating which page of the sequence (1 through 5) is currently loaded. An onload event handler in each of the five documents (named dh1.htm, dh2.htm, dh3.htm, dh4.htm, and dh5.htm) assigns its page number to that parent global variable. This arrangement allows all frames in the frameset to share that value easily.

When a user clicks the right-facing arrow to move to the next page, the goNext() function is called. The first statement gets the currTitle value from the parent window and assigns it to a local variable: currOffset. An if...else construction tests whether the current page number is less than 5. If so, the add-by-value operator adds 1 to the local variable so I can use that value in the next two statements.

In those next two statements, I adjust the content of the two right frames. Using the parent reference to gain access to both frames, I set the location.href property of the top-right frame to the name of the file next in line (by concatenating the number with the surrounding parts of the filename). The second statement sets the location.hash property (which controls the anchor being navigated to) to the corresponding anchor in the instructions frame (anchor names help1, help2, help3, help4, and help5).

A click of the left-facing arrow reverses the process, subtracting 1 from the current page number (using the subtract-by-value operator) and changing the same frames accordingly.

The example shown in Listing 11-1 is one of many ways to script a navigation frame in JavaScript. Whatever methodology you use, much interaction occurs among the frames in the frameset.

References for Multiple Windows

In Chapter 8, you saw how to create a new window and communicate with it by way of the window object reference returned from the window.open() method. In this section, I show you how one of those subwindows can communicate with objects, functions, and variables in the window or frame that creates the subwindow.

Every window object has a property called opener. This property contains a reference to the window or frame that held the script whose window.open() statement generated the subwindow. For the main browser window and frames therein, this value is null. Because the opener property is a valid window reference (when its value is not null), you can use it to begin the reference to items in the original window — just like a script in a child frame uses parent to access items in the parent document. The parent–child terminology doesn't apply to subwindows, however.

Listing 11-2 and Listing 11-3 contain documents that work together in separate windows. Listing 11-2 displays a button that opens a smaller window and loads Listing 11-3 into it. The main window document also contains a text field that gets filled in when you enter text in a corresponding field in the subwindow.

Again, you may have to turn off pop-up blocking temporarily to experiment with these examples.

In the main window document, the `newWindow()` function generates the new window. Because no other statements in the document require the reference to the new window just opened, the statement does not assign its returned value to any variable. This is an acceptable practice in JavaScript if you don't need the returned value of a function or method.

LISTING 11-2

A Main Window Document

```
<html>
<head>
<title>Main Document</title>
<script type="text/javascript">
function newWindow() {
    window.open("subwind.htm","sub","height=200,width=200");
}
</script>
</head>

<body>
<form>
<input type="button" value="New Window" onclick="newWindow()">
<br>
Text incoming from subwindow:
<input type="text" name="entry">
</form>
</body>
</html>
```

All the action in the subwindow document comes in the `onchange` event handler of the text field. It assigns the subwindow field's own value to the value of the field in the opener window's document. Remember that the contents of each window and frame belong to a document. So even after your reference targets a specific window or frame, the reference must continue helping the browser find the ultimate destination, which is generally some element of the document.

LISTING 11-3

A Subwindow Document

```
<html>
<head>
<title>A SubDocument</title>
</head>
<body>
```

continued

LISTING 11-3   *(continued)*

```
<form onsubmit="return false">
Enter text to be copied to the main window:
<input type="text"
onchange="opener.document.forms[0].entry.value = this.value">
</form>
</body>
</html>
```

Just one more lesson to go before I let you explore all the details elsewhere in the book. I use the final tutorial chapter to show you some fun things you can do with your web pages, such as changing images when the user rolls the mouse atop a picture.

Exercises

Before answering the first three questions, study the structure of the following frameset for a web site that lists college courses:

```
<frameset rows="85%,15%">
    <frameset cols="20%,80%">
        <frame name="mechanics" src="history101M.html">
        <frame name="description" src="history101D.html">
    </frameset>
    <frameset cols="100%">
        <frame name="navigation" src="navigator.html">
    </frameset>
</frameset>
</html>
```

1. Each document that loads into the description frame has an `onload` event handler in its `<body>` tag that stores in the framesetting document's global variable a course identifier called `currCourse`. Write the `onload` event handler that sets this value to `"history101"`.

2. Draw a block diagram that describes the hierarchy of the windows and frames represented in the frameset definition.

3. Write the JavaScript statements located in the navigation frame that loads the file `"french201M.html"` into the mechanics frame and the file `"french201D.html"` into the description frame.

4. While a frameset is still loading, a JavaScript error message suddenly appears, saying, "window.document.navigation.form.selector is undefined." What do you think is happening in the application's scripts, and how can you solve the problem?

5. A script in a child frame of the main window uses `window.open()` to generate a second window. How can a script in the second window access the `location` object (URL) of the top (framesetting) window in the main browser window?

Chapter 12

Images and Dynamic HTML

The previous eight lessons have been intensive, covering a lot of ground for both programming concepts and JavaScript. Now it's time to apply those fundamentals to learning more advanced techniques. I cover two areas here. First, I show you how to implement the ever-popular *mouse rollover*, in which images swap when the user rolls the cursor around the screen. Then I introduce you to techniques for modifying a page's style and content after the page has loaded.

IN THIS CHAPTER

How to precache images

How to swap images for mouse rollovers

Changing stylesheet settings

Modifying Body content dynamically

The Image Object

One of the objects contained by the document is the image object — supported in all scriptable browsers since the days of NN3 and IE4. Image object references for a document are stored in the object model as an array belonging to the document object. Therefore, you can reference an image by array index or image name. Moreover, the array index can be a string version of the image's name. Thus, all of the following are valid references to an image object:

```
document.images[n]
document.images["imageName"]
document.imageName
```

We are no longer constrained by ancient scriptable browser limitations that required an image be encased within an a element to receive mouse events. You may still want to do so if a click is intended to navigate to a new URL, but to use a visitor's mouse click to trigger local JavaScript execution, it's better to let the img element's event handlers do all the work.

Interchangeable images

The advantage of having a scriptable image object is that a script can change the image occupying the rectangular space already occupied by an image. In current browsers, the images can even change size, with surrounding content automatically reflowing around the resized image.

The script behind this kind of image change is simple enough. All it entails is assigning a new URL to the `img` element object's `src` property. The size of the image on the page is governed by the `height` and `width` attributes set in the `<img>` tag as the page loads. The most common image rollovers use the same size of image for each of the rollover states.

Precaching images

Images take extra time to download from a web server until the images are stored in the browser's cache. If you design your page so that an image changes in response to user action, you usually want the same fast response that users are accustomed to in other programs. Making the user wait seconds for an image to change can severely detract from enjoyment of the page.

JavaScript comes to the rescue by enabling scripts to load images into the browser's memory cache without displaying the image, a technique called *precaching images*. The tactic that works best is to preload the image into the browser's image cache while the page initially loads. Users are less impatient for those few extra seconds as the main page loads than they are waiting for an image to download in response to some mouse action.

Precaching an image requires constructing an image object in memory. An image object created in memory differs in some respects from the document `img` element object that you create with the `<img>` tag. Memory-only objects are created by script, and you don't see them on the page at all. But their presence in the document code forces the browser to load the images as the page loads. The object model provides an `Image` object constructor function to create the memory type of image object as follows:

```
var myImage = new Image(width, height);
```

Parameters to the constructor function are the pixel width and height of the image. These dimensions should match the `width` and `height` attributes of the `<img>` tag. When the image object exists in memory, you can then assign a filename or URL to the `src` property of that image object:

```
myImage.src = "someArt.gif";
```

When the browser encounters a statement assigning a URL to an image object's `src` property, the browser fetches and loads that image into the image cache. All the user sees is some extra loading information in the status bar, as though another image were in the page. By the time the entire page loads, all images generated in this way are tucked away in the image cache. You can then assign your cached image's `src` property or the actual image URL to the `src` property of the document image created with the `<img>` tag:

```
document.images[0].src = myImage.src;
```

The change to the image in the document is instantaneous.

Listing 12-1 demonstrates a page that has one `<img>` tag and a select list that enables you to replace the image in the document with any of four precached images (including the original image specified for the tag). If you type this listing, you can obtain copies of the four image files from the companion CD-ROM in the Chapter 12 directory of listings. (You still must type the HTML and code, however.)

LISTING 12-1

Precaching Images

```html
<html>
    <head>
        <title>Image Object</title>
        <script type="text/javascript">
        // initialize empty array
        var imageLibrary = new Array();
        // pre-cache four images
        imageLibrary["image1"] = new Image(120,90);
        imageLibrary["image1"].src = "desk1.gif";
        imageLibrary["image2"] = new Image(120,90);
        imageLibrary["image2"].src = "desk2.gif";
        imageLibrary["image3"] = new Image(120,90);
        imageLibrary["image3"].src = "desk3.gif";
        imageLibrary["image4"] = new Image(120,90);
        imageLibrary["image4"].src = "desk4.gif";

        // load an image chosen from select list
        function loadCached(list) {
            var img = list.options[list.selectedIndex].value;
            document.thumbnail.src = imageLibrary[img].src;
        }
        </script>
    </head>

    <body >
        <h2>Image Object</h2>
        <img src="desk1.gif" name="thumbnail" height="90" width="120">
        <form>
            <select name="cached" onchange="loadCached(this)">
                <option value="image1">Bands
                <option value="image2">Clips
                <option value="image3">Lamp
                <option value="image4">Erasers
            </select>
        </form>
    </body>
</html>
```

As the page loads, it executes several statements immediately. These statements create an empty array that is populated with four new memory image objects. Each image object has a filename assigned to its src property. These images are loaded into the image cache as the page loads. Down in the Body portion of the document, an <img> tag stakes its turf on the page and loads one of the images as a starting image.

A select element lists user-friendly names for the pictures while housing (in the option values) the names of image objects already precached in memory. When the user makes a selection from the list, the loadCached() function extracts the selected item's value — which is a string index of the image within the imageLibrary array. The src property of the chosen image object is assigned to the src property of the visible img element object on the page, and the precached image appears instantaneously.

Creating image rollovers

A favorite technique to add some pseudoexcitement to a page is to swap button images as the user rolls the cursor atop them. The degree of change to the image is largely a matter of taste. The effect can be subtle (a slight highlight or glow around the edge of the original image) or drastic (a radical change of color). Whatever your approach, the scripting is the same.

When several of these graphical buttons occur in a group, I tend to organize the memory image objects as arrays, and create naming and numbering schemes that facilitate working with the arrays. Listing 12-2 shows such an arrangement for four buttons that control a slide show. The code in the listing is confined to the image-swapping portion of the application. This is the most complex and lengthiest listing of the tutorial, so it requires a bit of explanation as it goes along. It begins with a stylesheet rule for each of the img elements located in a controller container.

LISTING 12-2

Image Rollovers

```
<head>
  <title>Slide Show/Image Rollovers</title>
  <style type="text/css">
    div#controller img {height: 70px; width: 136px; padding: 5px}
  </style>
  <script type="text/javascript">
```

Only browsers capable of handling image objects should execute statements that precache images. Therefore, the entire sequence is nested inside an if construction that tests for the presence of the document.images array. In older browsers, the condition evaluates to *undefined,* which an if condition treats as false:

```
if (document.images) {
```

Image precaching starts by building two arrays of image objects. One array stores information about the images depicting the graphical button's off position; the other is for images depicting their on position. These arrays use strings (instead of integers) as index values. The string names correspond to the names given to the visible img element objects whose tags come later in the source code. The code is clearer to read (for example, you know that the offImgArray["first"] entry has to do with the First button image). Also, as you see later in this listing, rollover images don't conflict with other visible images on the page (a possibility if you rely exclusively on numeric index values when referring to the visible images for the swapping).

After creating the array and assigning new blank image objects to the first four elements of the array, I go through the array again, this time assigning file pathnames to the src property of each object stored in the array. These lines of code execute as the page loads, forcing the images to load into the image cache along the way:

```
// precache all 'off' button images
var offImgArray = new Array();
offImgArray["first"] = new Image(136,70);
offImgArray["prev"] = new Image(136,70);
offImgArray["next"] = new Image(136,70);
offImgArray["last"] = new Image(136,70);

// off image array -- set 'off' image path for each button
offImgArray["first"].src = "images/firstoff.png";
offImgArray["prev"].src = "images/prevoff.png";
offImgArray["next"].src = "images/nextoff.png";
offImgArray["last"].src = "images/lastoff.png";

// precache all 'on' button images
var onImgArray = new Array();
onImgArray["first"] = new Image(136,70);
onImgArray["prev"] = new Image(136,70);
onImgArray["next"] = new Image(136,70);
onImgArray["last"] = new Image(136,70);

// on image array -- set 'on' image path for each button
onImgArray["first"].src = "images/firston.png";
onImgArray["prev"].src = "images/prevon.png";
onImgArray["next"].src = "images/nexton.png";
onImgArray["last"].src = "images/laston.png";
}
```

As you can see in the following HTML code, when the user rolls the mouse atop any of the visible document image objects, the onmouseover event handler invokes the imageOn() function, passing the name of the particular image. The imageOn() function uses that name to synchronize the document.images array entry (the visible image) with the entry of the in-memory array of on images from the onImgArray array. The src property of the array entry is assigned to the corresponding document image src property. At the same time, the cursor changes to look like it does over active links.

```
// functions that swap images & status bar
function imageOn(imgName) {
   if (document.images) {
      document.images[imgName].style.cursor = "pointer";
      document.images[imgName].src = onImgArray[imgName].src;
   }
}
```

The same goes for the onmouseout event handler, which needs to turn the image off by invoking the imageOff() function with the same index value.

```
function imageOff(imgName) {
   if (document.images) {
      document.images[imgName].style.cursor = "default";
      document.images[imgName].src = offImgArray[imgName].src;
   }
}
```

Both the onmouseover and onmouseout event handlers set the status bar text to a friendly descriptor — at least in those browsers that still support displaying custom text in the status bar. The onmouseout event handler sets the status bar message to an empty string.

```
function setMsg(msg) {
    window.status = msg;
    return true;
}
```

For this demonstration, I disable the functions that control the slide show. But I leave the empty function definitions here so they catch the calls made by the clicks of the links associated with the images.

```
// controller functions (disabled)
function goFirst() {
}
function goPrev() {
}
function goNext(){
}
function goLast() {
}
</script>
</head>

<body>
<h1>Slide Show Controls</h1>
```

I elected to place the controller images inside a div element so that the group could be positioned or styled as a group. Each img element's onmouseover event handler calls the imageOn() function, passing the name of the image object to be swapped. Because both the onmouseover and onmouseout event handlers require a return true statement to work in older browsers, I combine the second function call (to setMsg()) with the return true requirement. The setMsg() function always returns true and is combined with the return keyword before the call to the setMsg() function. It's just a trick to reduce the amount of code in these event handlers. In later chapters, you will learn how to create event handler functions that can derive the ID of the element receiving the event, allowing you to remove these event handler assignments from the <img> tags entirely.

```
<div id="controller">
    <img src="images/firstoff.png" name="first" id="first"
        onmouseover="imageOn('first'); return setMsg('Go to first picture')"
        onmouseout="imageOff('first'); return setMsg('')" onclick="goFirst()">
    <img src="images/prevoff.png" name="prev" id="prev"
        onmouseover="imageOn('prev'); return setMsg('Go to previous picture')"
        onmouseout="imageOff('prev'); return setMsg('')" onclick="goPrev()">
    <img src="images/nextoff.png" name="next" id="next"
        onmouseover="imageOn('next'); return setMsg('Go to next picture')"
        onmouseout="imageOff('next'); return setMsg('')" onclick="goNext()">
    <img src="images/lastoff.png" name="last" id="last"
        onmouseover="imageOn('last'); return setMsg('Go to last picture')"
        onmouseout="imageOff('last'); return setMsg('')" onclick="goLast()">
</div>
</body>
</html>
```

You can see the results of this lengthy script in Figure 12-1. As the user rolls the mouse atop one of the images, it changes from a light to dark color by swapping the entire image. You can access the image files on the CD-ROM, and I encourage you to enter this lengthy listing and see the magic for yourself.

FIGURE 12-1

Typical mouse rollover image swapping.

Rollovers Without Scripts

As cool as the rollover effect is, thanks to CSS technology, you don't always need JavaScript to accomplish rollover dynamism. You can blend CSS with JavaScript to achieve the same effect. Listing 12-3 demonstrates a version of Listing 12-2 but using CSS for the rollover effect, whereas JavaScript still handles the control of the slide show.

The HTML for the buttons consists of li elements that are sized and assigned background images of the off versions of the buttons. The text of each li element is surrounded by an a element so that CSS :hover pseudoelements can be assigned. (Internet Explorer through version 7 requires this, whereas W3C DOM browsers recognize :hover for all elements.) When the cursor hovers atop an a element, the background image changes to the on version. Note, too, that onclick event handler assignments have been moved to the script portion of the page, where they are performed after the page loads (to make sure the elements exist).

LISTING 12-3

CSS Image Rollovers

```
<html>
   <head>
      <title>Slide Show/Image Rollovers</title>
      <style type="text/css">
         #controller {position: relative}
```

continued

LISTING 12-3   (continued)

```
        #controller li {position: absolute; list-style: none; display: block;
height: 70px; width: 136px}
        #controller a {display: block; text-indent: -999px; height: 70px}

        #first {left: 0px}
        #prev {left: 146px}
        #next {left: 292px}
        #last {left: 438px}

        #first a {background-image: url("images/firstoff.png")}
        #first a:hover {background-image: url("images/firston.png")}
        #prev a {background-image: url("images/prevoff.png")}
        #prev a:hover {background-image: url("images/prevon.png")}
        #next a {background-image: url("images/nextoff.png")}
        #next a:hover {background-image: url("images/nexton.png")}
        #last a {background-image: url("images/lastoff.png")}
        #last a:hover {background-image: url("images/laston.png")}
    </style>
    <script type="text/javascript">
        // controller functions (disabled)
        function goFirst() {
        }
        function goPrev() {
        }
        function goNext(){
        }
        function goLast() {
        }

        // event handler assignments
        function init() {
            if (document.getElementById) {
                document.getElementById("first").onclick = goFirst;
                document.getElementById("prev").onclick = goPrev;
                document.getElementById("next").onclick = goNext;
                document.getElementById("last").onclick = goLast;
            }
        }
        window.onload = init;
    </script>
</head>

<body>
    <h1>Slide Show Controls</h1>
    <ul id="controller">
        <li id="first"><a href="#">First</a></li>
        <li id="prev"><a href="#">Previous</a></li>
```

```
        <li id="next"><a href="#">Next</a></li>
        <li id="last"><a href="#">Last</a></li>
    </ul>
  </body>
</html>
```

The need to wrap the li element text (which the CSS shifts completely offscreen, because we don't need the text) for Internet Explorer forces scripters to address further considerations. In this application, a click of an li element is intended to run a local script, not load an external URL. But the a element's default behavior is to load another URL. The # placeholder shown in Listing 12-3 causes the current page to reload, which will wipe away any activity of the onclick event handler function. It is necessary, therefore, to equip each of the slide-show navigation functions with some extra code lines that prevent the a element from executing its default behavior. You'll learn how to do that in Chapter 25 (it requires different syntax for incompatible the W3C DOM and IE event models).

One other note about the CSS approach in Listing 12-3 is that there is no image precaching taking place. You could add the precaching code for the on images from Listing 12-2 to get the alternative background images ready for the browser to swap. That's a case of CSS and JavaScript really working together.

The javascript: Pseudo-URL

You have seen instances in previous chapters of applying what is called the javascript: pseudo-URL to the href attributes of <a> and <area> tags. This technique should be used sparingly at best, especially for public web sites that may be accessed by users with nonscriptable browsers (for whom the links will be inactive).

The technique was implemented to supplement the onclick event handler of objects that act as hyperlinks. Especially in the early scripting days, when elements such as images had no event handlers of their own, hyperlinked elements surrounding those inactive elements allowed users to appear to interact directly with elements such as images. When the intended action was to invoke a script function (rather than navigate to another URL, as is usually the case with a hyperlink), the language designers invented the javascript: protocol for use in assignments to the href attributes of hyperlink elements (instead of leaving the required attribute empty).

When a scriptable browser encounters an href attribute pointing to a javascript: pseudo-URL, the browser executes the script content after the colon when the user clicks the element. For example, the a elements of Listing 12-3 could have been written to point to javascript: pseudo-URLs that invoke script functions on the page, such as:

```
    <a href="javascript:goFirst()" ... >
```

Note that the javascript: protocol is not a published standard, despite its wide adoption by browser makers. In a public web site that may be accessed by visitors with accessibility concerns (and potentially by browsers having little or no JavaScript capability), a link should point to a server URL that performs an action (for example, through a server program), which in turn replicates what client-side JavaScript does (faster) for visitors with scriptable browsers.

Popular Dynamic HTML Techniques

Because today's scriptable browsers uniformly permit scripts to access each element of the document and automatically reflow the page's content when anything changes, a high degree of dynamism is possible in your applications. Dynamic HTML (DHTML) is a very deep subject, with lots of browser-specific peculiarities. In this section of the tutorial, you will learn techniques that work in Internet Explorer and W3C DOM-compatible browsers. I'll focus on two of the most common tasks for which DHTML is used: changing element styles and modifying Body content.

Changing stylesheet settings

Each element that renders on the page (and even some elements that don't) has a property called `style`. This property provides script access to all CSS properties supported for that element by the current browser. Property values are the same as those used for CSS specifications—frequently, a different syntax from similar settings that used to be made by HTML tag attributes. For example, if you want to set the text color of a `blockquote` element whose ID is `FranklinQuote`, the syntax is

```
document.getElementById("FranklinQuote").style.color = "rgb(255, 255, 0)";
```

Because the CSS `color` property accepts other ways of specifying colors (such as the traditional hexadecimal triplet—`#ffff00`), you may use those as well.

Some CSS property names, however, do not conform to JavaScript naming conventions. Several CSS property names contain hyphens. When that occurs, the scripted equivalent of the property compresses the words and capitalizes the start of each word. For example, the CSS property `font-weight` would be set in script as follows:

```
document.getElementById("highlight").style.fontWeight = "bold";
```

A related technique puts more of the design burden on the CSS code. For example, if you define CSS rules for two different classes, you can simply switch the class definition being applied to the element by way of the element object's `className` property. Let's say you define two CSS class definitions with different background colors:

```
.normal {background-color: #ffffff}
.highlighted {background-color: #ff0000}
```

In the HTML page, the element first receives its default class assignment as follows:

```
<p id="news" class="normal">...</p>
```

A script statement can then change the class of that element object so that the highlighted style applies to it:

```
document.getElementById("news").className = "highlighted";
```

Restoring the original class name also restores its look and feel. This approach is also a quick way to change multiple style properties of an element with a single statement.

Dynamic content via W3C DOM nodes

In Chapter 8, you saw the `document.createElement()` and `document.createTextNode()` methods in action. These methods create new document object model (DOM) objects out of thin air, which you may then modify by setting properties (attributes) prior to plugging the new stuff into the document tree for all to see.

As an introduction to this technique, I'll demonstrate the steps you would go through to add an element and its text to a placeholding span element on the page. In this example, a paragraph element belonging to a class called centered will be appended to a span whose ID is placeholder. Some of the text for the content of the paragraph comes from a text field in a form (the visitor's first name). Here is the complete sequence:

```
var newElem = document.createElement("p");
newElem.className = "centered";
var newText = document.createTextNode("Thanks for visiting, " +
    document.forms[0].firstName.value);
// insert text node into new paragraph
newElem.appendChild(newText);
// insert completed paragraph into placeholder
document.getElementById("placeholder").appendChild(newElem);
```

The W3C DOM approach takes a lot of tiny steps to create, assemble, and insert the pieces into their destinations. After the element and text nodes are created, the text node must be inserted into the element node. Because the new element node is empty when it is created, the DOM appendChild() method plugs the text node into the element (between its start and end tags, if you could see the tags). When the paragraph element is assembled, it is inserted at the end of the initially empty span element. Additional W3C DOM methods (described in Chapter 15 and Chapter 16) provide more ways to insert, remove, and replace nodes.

Dynamic content through the innerHTML property

Prior to the W3C DOM specification, Microsoft invented a property of all element objects: innerHTML. This property first appeared in Internet Explorer 4 and became popular due to its practicality. The property's value is a string containing HTML tags and other content, just as it would appear in an HTML document inside the current element's tags. Even though the W3C DOM working group did not implement this property for the published standard, the property proved to be too practical and popular for modern browser makers to ignore. You can find it implemented as a de facto standard in Mozilla-based browsers and Safari, among others.

To show you the difference in the approach, the following code example shows the same content creation and insertion as shown in the previous W3C DOM section, but this time with the innerHTML property:

```
// accumulate HTML as a string
var newHTML = "<p class='centered'>Thanks for visiting, ";
newHTML += document.forms[0].firstName.value;
newHTML += "</p>";
// blast into placeholder element's content
document.getElementById("placeholder").innerHTML = newHTML;
```

Although the innerHTML version seems more straightforward — and makes it easier for HTML coders to visualize what's being added — the more code-intensive DOM node approach is more efficient when the Body modification task entails lots of content. Extensive JavaScript string concatenation operations can slow browser script processing. Sometimes, the shortest script is not necessarily the fastest.

And so ends the final lesson of the *JavaScript Bible* tutorial. If you have gone through every lesson and tried your hand at the exercises, you are ready to dive into the rest of the book to learn the fine details and many more features of both the DOM and the JavaScript language. You can work sequentially through the chapters of Parts III and IV, but before too long, you should also take a peek at Chapter 45 on the CD-ROM to learn some debugging techniques that help the learning process.

Exercises

1. Explain the difference between a document img element object and the memory type of an image object.

2. Write the JavaScript statements needed to precache an image file named jane.jpg that later will be used to replace the document image defined by the following HTML:

   ```
   <img name="people" src="john.jpg" height="120" width="100" alt="people">
   ```

3. With the help of the code you wrote for question 2, write the JavaScript statement that replaces the document image with the memory image.

4. Backward-compatible img element objects do not have event handlers for mouse events. How do you trigger scripts needed to swap images for mouse rollovers?

5. Assume that a table element contains an empty table cell (td) element whose ID is forwardLink. Using W3C DOM node creation techniques, write the sequence of script statements that create and insert the following hyperlink into the table cell:

   ```
   <a href="page4.html">Next Page</a>
   ```

Part III

Document Objects Reference

Chapter 13

JavaScript Essentials

Whenever JavaScript is discussed in the context of the web browser environment, it is sometimes difficult to distinguish between JavaScript the scripting language and the objects that you use the language to control. Even so, it's important to separate the language from the object model just enough to help you make important design decisions when considering JavaScript-enhanced pages. You may come to appreciate the separation in the future if you use JavaScript for other object models, such as server-side programming or scripting Flash animations. All the basics of the language are identical. Only the objects differ.

This chapter elaborates on many of the fundamental subjects about the core JavaScript language raised throughout the tutorial (Part II), particularly as they relate to deploying scripts in a world in which visitors to your pages may use a wide variety of browsers. Along the way, you receive additional insights into the language itself. Fortunately, browser differences as they apply to JavaScript have lessened considerably as modern browsers continue to inch closer to consistently supporting the JavaScript (ECMAScript) standard. You can find details about the JavaScript core language syntax in Part IV.

IN THIS CHAPTER

JavaScript language versions

How to separate the language from the document object model

Where scripts go in your documents

Language highlights for experienced programmers

JavaScript Versions

The JavaScript language has its own numbering system, which is completely independent of the version numbers assigned to browsers. The Mozilla Foundation, successor to the Netscape browser development group that created the language, continues its role as the driving force behind the JavaScript version numbering system.

The first version, logically enough, was JavaScript 1.0. This was the version implemented in Navigator 2 and the first release of Internet Explorer 3. As the language evolved with succeeding browser versions, the JavaScript version number incremented in small steps. JavaScript 1.2 is the version that has been the most long lived and stable, currently supported by Internet Explorer 7. Mozilla-based browsers and others have inched forward with some new features in JavaScript 1.5 (Mozilla 1.0 and Safari), JavaScript 1.6 (Mozilla 1.8 browsers), and JavaScript 1.7 (Mozilla 1.8.1 and later).

Each successive generation of JavaScript employs additional language features. For example, in JavaScript 1.0, arrays were not developed fully, causing scripted arrays not to track the number of items in the array. JavaScript 1.1 filled that hole by providing a constructor function for generating arrays and an inherent `length` property for any generated array.

The JavaScript version implemented in a browser is not always a good predictor of core language features available for that browser. For example, although JavaScript 1.2 (as implemented by Netscape in Netscape Navigator 4) included broad support for regular expressions, not all of those features appeared in Microsoft's corresponding JScript implementation in Internet Explorer 4. By the same token, Microsoft implemented `try-catch` error handling in its JScript in Internet Explorer 5, but Netscape didn't include that feature until the Mozilla-based Netscape Navigator 6 implementation of JavaScript 1.5. Therefore, the language version number is an unreliable predictor in determining which language features are available for you to use.

Core Language Standard: ECMAScript

Although Netscape first developed the JavaScript language, Microsoft incorporated the language in Internet Explorer 3. Microsoft did not want to license the Java name from its trademark owner (Sun Microsystems), which is why the language became known in the Internet Explorer environment as JScript. Except for some very esoteric exceptions and the pace of newly introduced features, the two languages are essentially identical. The levels of compatibility between browser brands for a comparable generation are remarkably high for the core language (unlike the vast disparities in object model implementations discussed in Chapter 14).

As mentioned in Chapter 2, standards efforts have been under way to create industrywide recommendations for browser makers to follow (to make developers' lives easier). The core language was among the first components to achieve standard status. Through the European standards body called ECMA, a formal standard for the language was agreed to and published. The first specification for the language, dubbed ECMAScript by the standards group, was roughly the same as JavaScript 1.1 in Netscape Navigator 3. The standard defines how various data types are treated, how operators work, what a particular data-specific syntax looks like, and other language characteristics. A newer version (called version 3) added many enhancements to the core language (version 2 was version 1 with errata fixed). The current version of ECMAScript is known as ECMA-262, and you can access its specification at http://www.ecma-international.org/. If you are a student of programming languages, you will find the document fascinating; if you simply want to script your pages, you will probably find the minutia mind-boggling.

All mainstream browser developers have pledged to make their browsers compliant with the ECMA standard. The vast majority of the ECMAScript standard has appeared in Navigator since version 3 and Internet Explorer since version 4, and as new features are added to the ECMA standard, they tend to find their way into newer browsers as well. The latest version of ECMAScript is version 3, which has been supported in all mainstream browsers for the past few years.

NOTE   Version 4 of ECMAScript is currently in the works, along with comparable implementations of JavaScript 2.0 and JScript by The Mozilla Foundation and Microsoft, respectively. An extension to ECMAScript called E4X (ECMAScript for XML) was finalized in late 2005 and is implemented in browsers based on Mozilla 1.8.1 or later (for example, Firefox 2.0). The Adobe ActionScript 3 language, which is used in the development of Flash animations, fully supports E4X.

Embedding Scripts in HTML Documents

Scriptable browsers offer several ways to include scripts or scripted elements in your HTML documents. Not all approaches are available in all versions of every browser, but you have sufficient flexibility starting with Navigator 3 and some versions of Internet Explorer 3. When you consider that a healthy percentage of computer users are now using browsers released within the past few years, it's safe to assume a core level of script support among web users. Exceptions to this rule include users who have specifically turned off scripting in their browsers, some organizations that install browsers with scripting turned off, users with physical disabilities who require specialized browsers, and users with mobile devices that have limited or no script support. You should not forget these users when designing JavaScript in your pages; you want the core information conveyed by your pages to reach all visitors, and scripting should enhance the experience or convenience of those visiting with suitably equipped scriptable browsers.

<script> tags

The simplest and most compatible way to include script statements in an HTML document is inside a `<script>...</script>` tag set that specifies the scripting language through the `type` attribute. You can have any number of such tag sets in your document. For example, you can define some functions in the Head section to be called by event handlers in HTML tags within the Body section. Another tag set can reside within the Body section to write part of the content of the page as the page loads. Place only script statements and comments between the start and end tags of the tag set. Do not place any HTML tags inside unless they are part of a string parameter to a `document.write()` statement that creates content for the page.

Every opening `<script>` tag should specify the `type` attribute. Because the `<script>` tag is a generic tag indicating that the contained statements are to be interpreted as executable script and not renderable HTML, the tag is designed to accommodate any scripting language the browser knows.

Specifying the language version

Browsers starting with Internet Explorer 5, Mozilla 1 (Moz1), and Saf1 support the `type` attribute of the `<script>` tag. This attribute accepts the type of a script as a MIME type. For example, the MIME type of JavaScript is specified as `type="text/javascript"`. So a `<script>` block for JavaScript is coded as follows:

```
<script type="text/javascript">...</script>
```

The `type` attribute is required for the `<script>` tag as of HTML 4. Earlier versions of HTML and, therefore, earlier browsers recognize the `language="JavaScript"` attribute setting as opposed to `type`. The `language` attribute allows the scripter to write for a specific minimum version of JavaScript or, in the case of Internet Explorer, other languages, such as VBScript. For example, the JavaScript interpreter built into Navigator 3 knows the JavaScript 1.1 version of the language; Navigator 4 and Internet Explorer 4 include the JavaScript 1.2 version. For versions beyond the original JavaScript, you may specify the language version by appending the version number after the language name without any spaces, as in:

```
<script language="JavaScript1.1">...</script>
```

```
<script language="JavaScript1.2">...</script>
```

It's important to note that the `language` attribute was deprecated in HTML 4, with the `type` attribute being the recommended way of specifying the scripting language for `<script>` tags. However, the `type` attribute didn't gain browser support until Internet Explorer 5, Mozilla, and W3C DOM–compatible browsers, which leaves legacy browsers in the dark if you use type by itself. To be both backward compatible and forward looking, you can specify both the language and type attributes in your <script> tags, because older browsers ignore the type attribute. Following is an example of how you might do this:

```
<script type="text/javascript" language="JavaScript 1.5">...</script>
```

Of course, if you're depending on features in JavaScript 1.5, you've forgone legacy browsers anyway. In this case, just take the forward-looking approach and use the type attribute by itself.

<script for> tags

Internet Explorer 4 (and later) browsers offer a variation on the <script> tag that binds statements of a <script> tag to a specific object and event generated by that object. In addition to the language specification, the tag's attributes must include for and event attributes (not part of the HTML 4.0 specification). The value assigned to the for attribute is a reference to the desired object. Most often, this is simply the identifier assigned to the object's id attribute. (Since version 4, Internet Explorer enables you to reference an object by either document.all.objectID or just objectID.) The event attribute is the event handler name that you want the script to respond to. For example, if you design a script to perform some action upon a mousedown event in a paragraph whose ID is myParagraph, the script statements are enclosed in the following tag set:

```
<script for="myParagraph" event="onmousedown" type="text/javascript">
...
</script>
```

Statements inside the tag set execute only upon the firing of the event. No function definitions are required.

This way of binding an object's event to a script means that there is no event handler defined in the element's tag. Therefore, it guarantees that only Internet Explorer 4 or later can carry out the script when the event occurs. But the tag and attributes contain a lot of source code overhead for each object's script, so this is not a technique you should use for script statements that need to be called by multiple objects.

Also be aware that you cannot use this tag variation if non–Internet Explorer or pre–Internet Explorer 4 browsers load the page. In such browsers, script statements execute as the page loads, which certainly causes script errors.

Hiding script statements from older browsers

It's wonderful news that the number of people using old web browsers that don't support scripting languages is rapidly approaching zero. However, new devices, such as mobile phones and pocket-size computers, often employ compact browsers that don't have built-in JavaScript interpreters. So in some ways, mobile devices have sent JavaScript developers back to the drawing board in terms of crafting pages that gracefully degrade when scripting isn't supported.

Nonscriptable browsers do not know about the <script> tag. Normally, browsers ignore tags that they don't understand. That's fine when a tag is just one line of HTML, but a <script> tag delineates any number of script statement lines in a document. Old and compact browsers don't know to expect a closing </script> tag. Therefore, their natural inclination is to render any lines they encounter after the opening <script> tag. Unfortunately, this places script code squarely in the rendered document — sure to confuse anyone who sees such gibberish on the page.

You can, however, exercise a technique that tricks most nonscriptable browsers into ignoring the script statements: surround the script statements (inside the <script> tag set) with HTML comment markers. An

HTML comment begins with the sequence `<!--` and ends with `-->`. Therefore, you should embed these comment sequences in your scripts according to the following format:

```
<script type="text/javascript">
<!--
script statements here
//-->
</script>
```

JavaScript interpreters know to ignore a line that begins with the HTML beginning comment sequence, but they need a little help with the ending sequence. The close of the HTML comment starts with a JavaScript comment sequence (`//`). This tells JavaScript to ignore the line; but a nonscriptable browser sees the ending HTML symbols and begins rendering the page with the next HTML tag or other text in the document. An older browser doesn't know what the `</script>` tag is, so the tag is ignored, and rendering begins after that.

Even with the assumption that most users have modern browsers, mobile devices put you in the position of still having to account for the potential lack of script support. That's why if you design your pages for public access, it's still a good idea to include these HTML comment lines in all your `<script>` tag sets. Make sure they go inside the tags, not outside. Also note that most of the script examples in this book do not include these comments for the sake of saving space in the listings.

Hiding scripts entirely?

It may be misleading to say that this HTML comment technique hides scripts from older browsers. In truth, the comments hide the scripts from being rendered by the browsers. The tags and script statements, however, are still downloaded to the browser and appear in the source code when viewed by the user.

A common wish among authors is to truly hide scripts from visitors to a page. Client-side JavaScript must be downloaded with the page and, therefore, is visible in the source view of pages. There are, of course, some tricks you can implement that may disguise client-side scripts from prying eyes. The most easily implemented technique is to let the downloaded page contain no visible elements — only scripts that assemble the page that the visitor sees. Source code for such a page is simply the HTML for the page. But that page is not interactive, because no scripting is attached unless it is written as part of the page — defeating the goal of hiding scripts. Any scripted solution for disguising scripts is immediately defeatable by the user turning off scripting temporarily before downloading the page. All of your code is ready for source view.

If you are worried about other scripters stealing your scripts, your best protection is to include a copyright notification in your page's source code. Not only are your scripts visible to the world, but so are a thief's scripts. This way, you can easily see when someone lifts your scripts verbatim.

NOTE   One other option for minimizing other people "borrowing" your JavaScript code is to use a JavaScript *obfuscator*, which is a special application that scrambles your code and makes it much harder to read and understand. The code still works fine, but it is very hard to modify in any way. You would use an obfuscator just before placing your code online, making sure to keep the original version for making changes. A couple of JavaScript obfuscators that you might want to consider are Jasob (`http://www.jasob.com/`) and JavaScript Obfuscator (`http://www.stunnix.com/prod/jo/`).

Hiding scripts from XHTML validators

If you are developing your pages in compliance with the XML version of HTML (a standard called *XHTML*), some common characters you use in scripts — notably, the less-than (<) and ampersand (&) symbols — are illegal in the XML world. When you attempt to run your XHTML code through a validation service that tests for standard compliance, scripts will likely cause the validator to complain.

To get around this problem, you can encase your script statements in what is known as a *CDATA* (pronounced "see-day-tah") section. The syntax might look a little strange, with all the square brackets, but it is the prescribed way to include such a section within a <script> tag, as follows:

```
<script type="text/javascript" language="JavaScript">
// <![CDATA[
    // script statements here
// ]]>
</script>
```

XML validators know that a CDATA section can contain all kinds of non-XML code and thus ignore their contents. The leading JavaScript comment symbols in front of the start and end portions let JavaScript interpreters ignore the XML markup (which otherwise would generate script errors). That's some of the fun webpage developers get to work with when making multiple standards work with one another.

Script libraries (.js files)

If you do a lot of scripting or script a lot of pages for a complex web application, you will certainly develop some functions and techniques that you can use for several pages. Rather than duplicate the code in all those pages (and go through the nightmare of making changes to all copies for new features or bug fixes), you can create reusable script library files and link them to your pages.

Such an external script file contains nothing but JavaScript code — no <script> tags, no HTML. By removing the script code from the HTML document, you no longer have to worry about comment hiding or CDATA section tricks.

The script file you create must be a text-only file, but its filename must end with the two-character extension .js. To instruct the browser to load the external file at a particular point in your regular HTML file, you add a src attribute to the <script> tag as follows:

```
<script type="text/javascript" src="hotscript.js"></script>
```

This kind of tag should be the first <script> tag in the Head it loads before any other in-document <script> tags load. If you load more than one external library, include a series of these tag sets at the top of the document.

Take notice of two features about this external script tag construction. First, the <script> </script> tag pair is required, even though nothing appears between them. You can mix <script> tag sets that specify external libraries with in-document scripts in the same document. Second, avoid putting other script statements between the start and end tags when the start tag contains a src attribute.

How you reference the source file in the src attribute depends on its physical location and your HTML coding style. In the preceding example, the .js file is assumed to reside in the same directory as the HTML file containing the tag. But if you want to refer to an absolute URL, the protocol for the file is http:// (just as with an HTML file):

```
<script type="text/javascript" src="http://www.cool.com/hotscript.js"></script>
```

A very important prerequisite for using script libraries with your documents is that your web server software must know how to map files with the `.js` extension to a MIME type of `application/x-javascript`. If you plan to deploy JavaScript in this manner, be sure to test a sample on your web server beforehand and arrange for any necessary server configuration adjustments.

When a user views the source of a page that links in an external script library, code from the `.js` file does not appear in the window, even though the browser treats the loaded script as part of the current document. However, the name or URL of the `.js` file is plainly visible (displayed exactly as it appears in your source code). Anyone can then turn off JavaScript in the browser and open that file (using the `http://` protocol) to view the `.js` file's source code. In other words, an external JavaScript source file is no more hidden from view than JavaScript embedded directly in an HTML file.

Browser Version Detection

Without question, the biggest challenge facing many client-side scripters is how to program an application that accommodates a wide variety of browser versions and brands, each one of which can bring its own quirks and bugs. Happy is the intranet developer who knows for a fact that the company has standardized its computers with a particular brand and version of browser. But that is a rarity, especially in light of the concept of the *extranet* — private corporate networks and applications that open for access to the company's suppliers and customers.

Scripters have used many techniques to deal with different browsers and versions through the years. Unfortunately, as the matrix of versions and scriptable features grew, many of the old techniques proved to be cumbersome, if not troublesome. Having learned from these experiences, the scripting community has sensibly reduced the clutter to two basic approaches to working with a wide range of browsers. In the end, both approaches assist you in designing pages that convey the basic information that all visitors — script-enabled or not — should be able to view and then use scripting to enhance that basic content with additional features or conveniences. In other words, you create one page and let the browser determine how many extra bells and whistles are available for the visitor.

Coding for nonscriptable browsers

Very often, the first decision an application must make is whether the client accessing the site is JavaScript-enabled. Non-JavaScript-enabled browsers fall into two categories: JavaScript-capable browsers that have JavaScript turned off in the preferences and browsers that have no built-in JavaScript interpreter.

Except for some of the earliest releases of NN2, all JavaScript-capable browsers have a preferences setting to turn off JavaScript (and a separate one for Java). You should know that even though JavaScript is turned on by default in most browsers, many institutional deployments turn it off when the browser is installed on client machines. The reasons behind this MIS deployment decision vary from scares about Java security violations incorrectly associated with JavaScript, valid JavaScript security concerns on some browser versions, and the fact that some firewalls try to filter JavaScript lines from incoming HTML streams.

All JavaScript-capable browsers include a set of `<noscript>. . .</noscript>` tags to balance the `<script>. . .</script>` tag set. If one of these browsers has JavaScript turned off, the `<script>` tag is ignored, but the `<noscript>` tag is observed. As with the `<noframes>` tag, you can use the body of a `<noscript>` tag set to display HTML that lets users know JavaScript is turned off; therefore, the full benefit of the page isn't available unless they turn on JavaScript. Listing 13-1 shows a skeletal HTML page that uses these tags.

LISTING 13-1

Employing the <noscript> Tag

```
<html>
<head>
   <title>Some Document</title>
   <script type="text/javascript">
      // script statements
   </script>
</head>

<body>
   <noscript><b>Your browser has JavaScript turned off.</b><br />
   You will experience a more enjoyable time at this Web site if you
   turn JavaScript on.
   <hr /></noscript>

   <h2>The body of your document.</h2>
</body>
</html>
```

You can display any standard HTML within the <noscript> tag set. An icon image is a colorful way to draw the user's attention to the special advice at the top of the page. If your document is designed to create content dynamically in one or more places in the document, you may have to include a <noscript> tag set after more than one <script> tag set to let users know what they're missing. Do not include the HTML comment tags that you use in hiding JavaScript statements from older browsers; their presence inside the <noscript> tags prevents the HTML from rendering.

Scripting for different browsers

Concerns over cross-browser compatibility reign supreme in most scripters' minds. Even though the most recent browsers are doing a decent job of providing a workable lowest common denominator of scriptability, you will likely still have to consider a small, but not insignificant, percentage of visitors with less-than-modern browsers. The first step in planning for compatibility is determining what your goals are for various visitor classes.

Establishing goals

After you map out what you'd like your scripts to do, you must look at the implementation details to see which browser is required for the most advanced aspect of the application. For example, if the design calls for image swapping on mouse rollovers, that feature requires Netscape Navigator 3 or later and Internet Explorer 4 or later, which is a given these days except in some mobile browsers. In implementing Dynamic HTML (DHTML) features, you potentially have three different ways to implement tricks (such as movable elements or changeable content), because the document object model (DOMs) require different scripting (and sometimes HTML) for Netscape Navigator 4; Internet Explorer 4 and later; and the W3C DOM implemented in Mozilla, Internet Explorer 5 and later, Safari, and other recent browsers.

In an ideal scenario, you have an appreciation for the kinds of browsers that your visitors use. For example, if you want to implement some DHTML features, you should be fine designing for Internet Explorer 4 or later, Mozilla, Safari, and W3C DOM treat Netscape Navigator 4 as though it were nonscriptable. Or you may wish to forget the past and design your DHTML exclusively for W3C DOM–compatible browsers, in which case Internet Explorer 5.5 is the minimum on the Internet Explorer side of things. Even this is a reasonable approach, considering how many users now have a modern browser. If your web hosting service maintains a log of visitor activity to your site, you can study the browsers listed among the hits to see which browsers your visitors use.

After you determine the lowest common denominator for the optimum experience, you must decide how gracefully you want to degrade the application for visitors whose browsers do not meet the common denominator. For example, if you plan a page or site that requires a W3C DOM–compatible browser for all the fancy doodads, you can provide an escape path with content in a simple format that every browser from the text-based Lynx to anything older than Internet Explorer 6 can view.

In case you have a notion of creating an application or site that has multiple paths for viewing the same content, it may sound good at the outset, but don't forget that maintenance chores lie ahead as the site evolves. Will you have the time, budget, and inclination to keep all paths up to date? Despite whatever good intentions a designer of a new web site may have, in my experience, the likelihood that a site will be maintained properly diminishes rapidly with the complexity of the maintenance task.

Object detection

The methodology of choice by far for implementing browser version branching is known as *object detection*. The principle is simple: If an object type exists in the browser's object model, it is safe to execute script statements that work with that object.

Perhaps the best example of object detection is the way scripts can swap images on a page in browsers without tripping up on the oldest browsers that don't implement images as objects. In a typical image swap, onmouseover and onmouseout event handlers (assigned to a link surrounding an image, to be backward compatible) invoke functions that change the src property of the desired image. Each of those functions is invoked for all scriptable browsers, but you want them to run their statements only when images can be treated as objects.

Object models that implement images always include an array of image objects belonging to the document object. The document.images array always exists, even with a length of zero when no images are on the page. Therefore, if you wrap the image-swapping statements inside an if construction that lets browsers pass only if the document.images array exists, older browsers simply skip the statements:

```
function imageSwap(imgName, url) {
   if (document.images) {
      document.images[imgName].src = url;
   }
}
```

Object detection works best when you know for sure how all browsers implement the object. In the case of document.images, the implementation across browsers is identical, so it is a very safe branching condition. That's not always the case, and you should use this feature with careful thought. For example, Internet Explorer 4 introduced a document object array called document.all, which is used very frequently in building references to HTML element objects. Netscape Navigator 4, however, did not implement that array; instead, it had a document-level array object called layers, which was not implemented in Internet Explorer 4. Unfortunately, many scripters used the existence of these array objects not as prerequisites for addressing those objects, but as determinants for the browser version. They set global variables signifying a minimum version of Internet Explorer 4 if document.all existed and Netscape Navigator 4 if `document.layers` existed. This is most dangerous, because there is no way of knowing whether a future version of a browser may adopt the object of the other browser brand or eliminate a language feature. For example, when the Mozilla-based Netscape version first arrived, it did so with all the layers stuff removed (replaced by W3C standards–based features). Tons of scripts on the web used the existence of `document.layers` to branch to Netscape-friendly code that didn't even use `document.layers`. Thus, visitors using Netscape 6 or 7 found that scripts either broke or didn't work, even though the browsers were more than capable of doing the job.

This is why I recommend object detection not for browser version sniffing but for object availability branching, as shown previously for images. Moreover, it is safest to implement object detection only when all major browser brands (and the W3C DOM recommendation) have adopted the object so that behavior is predictable wherever your page loads in the future.

Techniques for object detection include testing for the availability of an object's method. A reference to an object's method returns a value, so such a reference can be used in a conditional statement. For example, the following code fragment demonstrates how a function can receive an argument containing the string ID of an element and convert the string to a valid object reference for three different DOMs:

```
function myFunc(elemID) {
   var obj;
   if (document.getElementById) {
      obj = document.getElementById(elemID);
   } else if (document.all) {
      obj = document.all(elemID);
   } else if (document.layers) {
      obj = document.layers[elemID];
   }
   if (obj) {
      // statements that work on the object
   }
}
```

With this object detection scheme, it no longer matters which browser brand, operating system, and version support a particular way of changing an element ID to an object reference. Whichever of the three `document` object properties or method is supported by the browser (or the first one, if the browser supports more than one), that is the property or method used to accomplish the conversion. If the browser supports none of them, no further statements execute. Keep in mind, however, that the first approach in this example is sufficient (and recommended) as the technique for obtaining all objects from an ID in modern browsers.

If your script wants to check for the existence of an object's property or method, you may also have to check for the existence of the object beforehand if that object is not part of all browsers' object models. An attempt to reference a property of a nonexistent object in a conditional expression generates a script error. To prevent the error, you can cascade the conditional tests with the help of the && operator. The following fragment tests for the existence of both the `document.body` object and the `document.body.style` property:

```
if (document.body && document.body.style) {
   // statements that work on the body's style property
}
```

If the test for `document.body` fails, JavaScript bypasses the second test.

One potential "gotcha" in using conditional expressions to test for the existence of an object's property is that even if the property exists, but its value is zero or an empty string, the conditional test reports that the property does not exist. To work around this potential problem, the conditional expression can examine the data type of the value to ensure that the property genuinely exists. A nonexistent property for an object reports a data type of undefined. Use the typeof operator (discussed in Chapter 33) to test for a valid property:

```
if (document.body && typeof document.body.scroll != "undefined") {
    // statements that work on the body's scroll property
}
```

I wholeheartedly recommend designing your scripts to take advantage of object detection in lieu of branching on particular browser name strings and version numbers. Scriptable features are gradually finding their way into browsers embedded in a wide range of nontraditional computing devices. These browsers may not go by the same names and numbering systems that we know today, yet such browsers may be able to interpret your scripts. By testing for browser functionality, your scripts will likely require less maintenance in the future.

Modifying content for scriptable browsers

Using object detection techniques, it is possible to alter the page so that visitors' browsers with the desired functionality have additional or alternative content available to them. Modern browsers that implement the W3C DOM allow scripts to change elements and their attributes at will.

Changes of this type are typically made after the rest of the page has loaded so that your scripts can be assured that any elements that are to be modified are present and ready to be scripted. Listing 13-2 is a simple example of how a function is triggered at load time to modify the destination of a link and insert some text that only browsers supporting a basic W3C DOM feature see. The page also uses a <noscript> tag to display content for those with scripting turned off.

LISTING 13-2

Presenting Different Content for Scriptable and Nonscriptable Browsers

```
<html>
   <head>
      <title></title>
      <script type="text/javascript" language="JavaScript">
      // modify page for scriptable browsers
      function updatePage() {
         if (document.getElementById) {
            document.getElementById("mainLink").href = "http://www.dannyg.com";
            document.getElementById("welcome").innerHTML =
               "Howdy from the script!";
         }
      }
      window.onload = updatePage;
      </script>
   </head>
```

continued

LISTING 13-2   *(continued)*

```
<body bgcolor="#FFFFFF">
   <a id="mainLink" href="http://www.microsoft.com">Where?</a>
   <hr />
   <p id="welcome"></p>
   <noscript><p>If you can read this, JavaScript is not
   available.</p></noscript>
   <p>Here's some stuff for everybody.</p>
</body>
</html>
```

> **NOTE**   As handy as it may be, in a strict W3C approach to JavaScript, you wouldn't use the `innerHTML` property because it isn't officially part of the W3C standard. However, it is often too powerful a convenience property to ignore, as much of the code throughout this book is a testament. The book does show the W3C node manipulation alternative to `innerHTML` in some examples. Refer to Chapter 18 for a thorough explanation and examples of the W3C alternative to `innerHTML`.

You can see more object detection at work in Chapter 47 and Chapter 56 on the CD-ROM.

Designing for Compatibility

Each new major release of a browser brings compatibility problems for page authors. It's not so much that old scripts break in the new versions (well-written scripts rarely break in new versions). The problems center on the new features that attract designers when the designers forget to accommodate visitors who have not yet advanced to the latest and greatest browser version or who don't share your browser brand preference.

Catering only to the lowest common denominator can more than double your development time, due to the expanded testing matrix necessary to ensure a good working page in all operating systems and on all versions. Decide how important the scripted functionality you employ in a page is for every user. If you want some functionality that works only in a later browser, you may have to be a bit autocratic in defining the minimum browser for scripted access to your page; any lesser browser gets shunted to a simpler presentation of your site's data.

Another possibility is to make a portion of the site accessible to most, if not all, browsers, and restrict the scripting to the occasional enhancement that nonscriptable browser users won't miss. When the application reaches a certain point in the navigation flow, the user needs a more capable browser to get to the really good stuff. This kind of design is a carefully planned strategy that lets the site welcome all users up to a point but then enables the application to shine for users of, say, W3C DOM–compatible browsers.

The ideal page is one that displays useful content in any browser but whose scripting enhances the experience of the page visitor — perhaps by offering more efficient site navigation or interactivity with the page's content. That is certainly a worthy goal to aspire to. But even if you can achieve this ideal on only some pages, you will reduce the need for defining entirely separate, difficult-to-maintain paths for browsers of varying capabilities.

Regardless of your specific browser compatibility strategy, the good news is that time tends to minimize the problem. Web standards have solidified greatly in the past few years, and browser vendors have made significant strides toward fully supporting those standards.

Dealing with beta browsers

If you have crafted a skillfully scripted web page or site, you may be concerned when a prerelease (or *beta*) version of a browser available to the public causes script errors or other compatibility problems to appear on your page. Do yourself a favor: Don't overreact to bugs and errors that occur in prerelease browser versions. If your code is well written, it should work with any new generation of browser. If the code doesn't work correctly, consider the browser to be buggy. Report the bug (preferably with a simplified test-case script sample) to the browser maker.

The exception to the "it's a beta bug" rule arose in the transition from Netscape Navigator 4 to the Mozilla engine (first released as Netscape Navigator 6). As you learn in Chapter 14, a conscious effort to eliminate a proprietary Netscape Navigator 4 feature (the <layer> tag and corresponding scriptable object) caused many Netscape Navigator 4 scripts to break on Moz1 betas (and final release). Had scripters gone to report the problem to the new browsers' developer (Mozilla), they would have learned about the policy change and planned for the new implementation. It is extremely rare for a browser to eliminate a popular feature so quickly, but it can happen. Stronger web standards have ideally minimized the chances of this situation happening again any time soon.

It is often difficult to prevent yourself from getting caught up in a browser maker's enthusiasm for a new release. But remember that a prerelease version is not a shipping version. Users who visit your page with prerelease browsers should know that there may be bugs in the browser. That your code does not work with a prerelease version is not a sin; neither is it worth losing sleep over. Just be sure to connect with the browser's maker either to find out whether the problem will continue in the final release or to report the bug so that the problem doesn't make it into the release version.

The Evaluator Sr.

In Chapter 6, you were introduced to a slimmed-down version of The Evaluator Jr., which provides an interactive workbench to experiment with expression evaluation and object inspection. At this point, you should meet The Evaluator Sr., a tool you will use in many succeeding chapters to help you learn both core JavaScript and DOM terminology.

IE Browser Version Headaches

As described more fully in the discussion of the navigator object in Chapter 39 on the CD-ROM, your scripts can easily determine which browser is the one running the script. However, the properties that reveal the version don't always tell the whole story about Internet Explorer.

As you can see in detail in Chapter 39 on the CD-ROM, the navigator.appVersion property for Internet Explorer 5, 5.5, 6, and 7 reports version 4 (the same as Internet Explorer 4). You can still sniff for specific versions (you can find the designation MSIE 6 or MSIE7 in the navigator.userAgent property), but the process is not as straightforward as it could be. The best advice is to be vigilant when new browsers come on the scene or adopt object detection techniques in your scripts.

Figure 13-1 shows the top part of the page. Two important features differentiate this full version from the Jr. version in Chapter 6.

FIGURE 13-1

The Evaluator Sr.

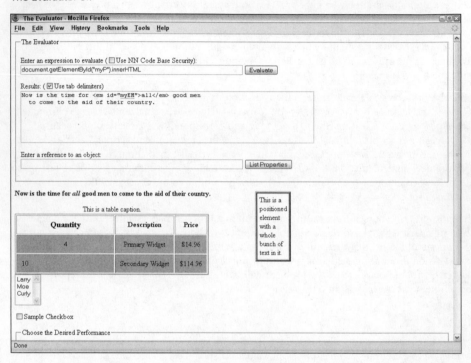

First, you can try some Mozilla secure features if you have Code Base Principles turned on for your browser (Chapter 46 on the CD-ROM) and you check the Use Code Base Security check box (Netscape Navigator 4 or later/Moz only). Second, the page has several HTML elements preinstalled, which you can use to explore DOM properties and methods. As with the smaller version, a set of 26 one-letter global variables (a through z) are initialized and ready for you to assign values for extended evaluation sequences.

You should copy the file evaluator.html from the companion CD-ROM to a local hard disk and set a bookmark for it in all of your test browsers. Feel free to add your own elements to the bottom of the page to explore other objects. I describe a version of The Evaluator for embedding in your projects as a debugging tool in Chapter 45 on the CD-ROM, where you can learn more built-in functionality of The Evaluator.

Compatibility ratings in reference chapters

With the proliferation of scriptable browser versions since Navigator 2, it is important to know up front whether a particular language or object model object, property, method, or event handler is supported in the lowest common denominator for which you are designing. Therefore, beginning with Chapter 15 of this reference part of the book, I include frequent compatibility ratings, such as the following example:

Compatibility: WinIE5+, MacIE5+, NN4+, Moz+, Safari+

A plus sign after a browser version number means that the language feature was first implemented in the numbered version and continues to be supported in succeeding versions. A minus sign means that the feature is not supported in that browser. The browsers tested for compatibility include Internet Explorer for Windows and Macintosh, Netscape Navigator, Mozilla (including all browsers based on the Mozilla engine), and Apple Safari. I also recommend that you print the JavaScript and Browser Object Quick Reference file shown in Appendix A. The file is on the companion CD-ROM in Adobe PDF format. This quick reference clearly shows each object's properties, methods, and event handlers, along with keys to the browser version in which each language item is supported. You should find the printout to be valuable as a day-to-day resource.

This is a great place to clarify what I mean by "all browsers based on the Mozilla engine." There was a time, not so long ago, when *Mozilla* pretty much meant *Netscape,* but those days are long gone. Now there are several viable Mozilla-based browsers that fall under the Moz+ designation in the compatibility charts throughout this book:

- Netscape
- Firefox
- Camino

The numbering systems of the individual browser brands are not linked to the underlying Mozilla engine versions, making it difficult to know exactly which browser supports what feature. The following table shows which individual browser brands and versions correspond to the Mozilla engine numbering system:

Mozilla	Netscape	Firefox	Camino
m18	6.0	—	—
0.9.4	6.2	—	—
1.0.1	7.0	—	—
1.4	7.1	—	—
1.7.2	7.2	—	—
1.7.5	8.0–8.1	1.0	—
1.8	—	1.5	1.0
1.8.1	—	2.0	

As you can see, Netscape 6.0 and 6.2 were based on Mozilla versions less than 1. It is rare to see either of these versions "in the wild" these days. The focus, therefore, is on Moz1 and later. Thus, the compatibility charts use Moz1 as the baseline feature set.

In summary, when you see Moz+ in the compatibility charts, it ultimately resolves to Netscape 7 or later, Firefox 1 or later, and Camino 1 or later, to name the most popular Mozilla-based browsers currently in use.

Language Essentials for Experienced Programmers

In this section, experienced programmers can read the highlights about the core JavaScript language in terms that may not make complete sense to those with limited or no scripting experience. This section is especially for you if you found the tutorial of Part II rudimentary. Here, then, is the quick tour of the essential issues surrounding the core JavaScript language:

- **JavaScript is a scripting language.** The language is intended for use in an existing *host environment* (for example, a web browser) that exposes objects whose properties and behaviors are controllable via statements written in the language. Scripts execute within the context of the host environment. The host environment controls what, if any, external environmental objects may be addressed by language statements running in the host environment. For security and privacy reasons, web browsers generally afford little or no direct access through JavaScript to browser preferences, the operating system, or other programs beyond the scope of the browser. The exception to this rule is that modern browsers allow deeper client access (with the user's permission) through trust mechanisms such as signed scripts (Mozilla) or trusted ActiveX controls (Microsoft).

- **JavaScript is object based.** Although JavaScript exhibits many syntactic parallels with the Java language, JavaScript is not as pervasively object oriented as Java. The core language includes several built-in static objects from which working objects are generated. Objects are created through a call to a constructor function for any of the built-in objects plus the new operator. For example, the following expression generates a String object and returns a reference to that object:

```
new String("Hello");
```

Table 13-1 lists the built-in objects with which scripters come into contact.

TABLE 13-1

JavaScript Built-In Objects

Array[1]	Boolean	Date	Error[2]
EvalError[2]	Function[1]	Math	Namespace[4]
Number[1]	Object[1]	QName[4]	RangeError[2]
ReferenceError[2]	RegExp[3]	String[1]	SyntaxError[2]
TypeError[2]	URIError[2]	XML[4]	

[1]Although defined in ECMA Level 1, was first available in NN3 and IE3/J2.

[2]Defined in ECMA Level 3; implemented in Moz1.

[3]Defined in ECMA Level 3; implemented fully in NN4 and IE6.

[4]Defined in E4X; implemented in Mozilla 1.8.1 (Firefox 2.0).

■ **JavaScript is loosely typed.** Variables, arrays, and function return values are not defined to be of any particular data type. In fact, an initialized variable can hold different data type values in subsequent script statements (obviously not good practice but possible nonetheless). Similarly, an array may contain values of multiple types. The range of built-in data types is intentionally limited:

  ■ Boolean (`true` or `false`)
  ■ Null
  ■ Number (double-precision 64-bit format IEEE 734 value)
  ■ Object (encompassing the `Array` object)
  ■ String
  ■ Undefined
  ■ XML (in E4X)

■ **The host environment defines global scope.** Web browsers traditionally define a browser window or frame to be the global context for script statements. When a document unloads, all global variables defined by that document are destroyed.

■ **JavaScript variables have either global or local scope.** A global variable in a web browser is typically initialized in `var` statements that execute as the document loads. All statements in that document can read or write that global variable. A local variable is initialized inside a function (also with the `var` operator). Only statements inside that function may access that local variable.

■ **Scripts sometimes access JavaScript static object properties and methods.** Some static objects encourage direct access to their properties or methods. For example, all properties of the `Math` object act as constant values (for example, `Math.PI`).

■ **You can add properties or methods to working objects at will.** To add a property to an object, simply assign a value of any type to it. For example, to add an `author` property to a string object named `myText`, use

```
myText.author = "Jane";
```

Assign a function reference to an object property to give that object a new method:

```
// function definition
function doSpecial(arg1) {
    // statements
}
// assign function reference to method name
myObj.handleSpecial = doSpecial;
...
// invoke method
myObj.handleSpecial(argValue);
```

Inside the function definition, the `this` keyword refers to the object that owns the method.

■ **JavaScript objects employ prototype-based inheritance.** All object constructors create working objects whose properties and methods inherit the properties and methods defined for the *prototype* of that object. Scripts can add and delete custom properties and methods associated with the static object's prototype so that new working objects inherit the current state of the prototype. Scripts can freely override prototype property values or assign different functions to prototype methods in a working object if desired without affecting the static object prototype. But if inherited properties or methods are not modified in the current working object, any changes to the static object's prototype are reflected in the working object. (The mechanism is that a reference to an object's property works its way up the prototype inheritance chain to find a match to the property name.)

■ **JavaScript includes a large set of operators.** You can find most operators that you are accustomed to working with in other languages.

■ **JavaScript provides typical control structures.** All versions of JavaScript offer if, if-else, for, and while constructions. JavaScript 1.2 (NN4+, IE4+, and all modern mainstream browsers) added do-while and switch constructions. Iteration constructions provide break and continue statements to modify control structure execution.

■ **JavaScript functions may or may not return a value.** There is only one kind of JavaScript function. A value is returned only if the function includes a return keyword followed by the value to be returned. Return values can be of any data type.

■ **JavaScript functions cannot be overloaded.** A JavaScript function accepts zero or more arguments, regardless of the number of parameter variables defined for the function. All arguments are automatically assigned to the arguments array, which is a property of a function object. Parameter variable data types are not predefined.

■ **Values are passed by reference and by value.** An object passed to a function is actually a reference to that object, offering full read/write access to properties and methods of that object. But other types of values (including object properties) are passed by value, with no reference chain to the original object. Thus, the following nonsense fragment empties the text box when the onchange event fires:

```
function emptyMe(arg1) {
    arg1.value = "";
}
...
<input type="text" value="Howdy" onchange="emptyMe(this)">
```

But in the following version, nothing happens to the text box:

```
function emptyMe(arg1) {
    arg1 = "";
}
...
<input type="text" value="Howdy" onchange="emptyMe(this.value)">
```

The local variable (arg1) simply changes from "Howdy" to an empty string.

NOTE The property assignment event handling technique in the previous example is a deliberate simplification to make the code more readable. It is generally better to use the more modern approach of binding events using the addEventListener() (NN6+/Moz/W3C) or attachEvent() (IE5+) methods. A modern cross-browser event handling technique is explained in detail in Chapter 25.

■ **Error trapping techniques depend on JavaScript version.** There was no error trapping in NN2 or IE3. Error trapping in NN3, NN4, and IE4 was event-driven in the web browser object model. JavaScript, as implemented in IE5+ and Mozilla, Safari, and other recent browsers, supports try-catch and throw statements, as well as built-in error objects that are not dependent on the host environment.

■ **Memory management is not under script control.** The host environment manages memory allocation, including garbage collection. Different browsers may handle memory in different ways.

■ **Whitespace (other than a line terminator) is insignificant.** Space and tab characters may separate lexical units (for example, keywords, identifiers, and so on).

■ **A line terminator is usually treated as a statement delimiter.** Except in very rare constructions, JavaScript parsers automatically insert the semicolon statement delimiter whenever they encounter one or more line terminators (for example, carriage returns or line feeds). A semicolon delimiter is required between two statements on the same physical line of source code. Moreover, string literals may not have carriage returns in their source code (but an escaped newline character (\n) may be part of the string).

Onward to Object Models

The core language is only a small part of what you work with while scripting web pages. The bulk of your job entails understanding the ins and outs of DOMs as implemented in several generations of browsers. That's where Chapter 14 picks up the *essentials* story.

Chapter 14

Document Object Model Essentials

Without question, the biggest challenge facing client-side web scripters is the sometimes-baffling array of document object models (DOMs) that have competed for our attention throughout the short history of scriptable browsers. Netscape got the ball rolling in Navigator 2 with the first object model. By the time the version 4 browsers came around, the original object model had gained not only some useful cross-browser features, but also a host of features that were unique to Navigator or Internet Explorer. The object models were diverging, causing no end of headaches for page authors whose scripts had to run on as many browsers as possible. A ray of hope emerged from the standards process of the World Wide Web Consortium (W3C) in the form of a DOM recommendation. The DOM brought forward much of the original object model, plus new ways of consistently addressing every object in a document. The goal of this chapter is to put each of the object models into perspective and help you understand how modern browsers have alleviated most of the object model compatibility problems. But before we get to those specifics, let's examine the role of the object model in designing scripted applications.

The Object Model Hierarchy

The tutorial chapters of Part II introduce the fundamental ideas behind a document object hierarchy in scriptable browsers. In other object-oriented environments, object hierarchy plays a much greater role than it does in JavaScript-able browsers. (In JavaScript, you don't have to worry about related terms, such as classes, inheritance, and instances.) Even so, you cannot ignore the hierarchy concept because some of your code relies on your ability to write references to objects that depend on their positions within the hierarchy.

Calling these objects *JavaScript objects* is not correct. These are really browser document objects: You just happen to use the JavaScript language to bring them to life. Some scripters of Microsoft Internet Explorer use the VBScript language to script the very same document objects. Technically speaking, JavaScript objects apply to data types and other core language objects separate from the document.

Hierarchy as road map

For the programmer, the primary role of the document object hierarchy is to provide scripts a way to reference a particular object among all the objects that a browser window can contain. The hierarchy acts as a road map the script can use to know precisely which object to address.

Consider, for a moment, a scene in which you and your friend Tony are in a high-school classroom. It's getting hot and stuffy as the afternoon sun pours in through the wall of windows on the west side of the room. You ask Tony, "Would you please open a window?" and motion your head toward a particular window in the room. In programming terms, you've issued a command to an object (whether or not Tony appreciates the comparison). This human interaction has many advantages over anything you can do in programming. First, by making eye contact with Tony before you speak, he knows that he is the intended recipient of the command. Second, your body language passes along some parameters with that command, pointing ever so subtly to a particular window on a particular wall.

If, instead, you are in the principal's office using the public address system, and you broadcast the same command ("Would you please open a window?"), no one knows what you mean. Issuing a command without directing it to an object is a waste of time, because every object thinks, "That can't be meant for me." To accomplish the same goal as your one-on-one command, the broadcast command has to be something like "Would Tony Jeffries in Room 312 please open the middle window on the west wall?"

Let's convert this last command to JavaScript *dot syntax* form (see Chapter 4). Recall from the tutorial that a reference to an object starts with the most global point of view and narrows to the most specific point of view. From the point of view of the principal's office, the location hierarchy of the target object is

```
room312.Jeffries.Tony
```

You can also say that Tony's knowledge about how to open a window is one of Tony's methods. The complete reference to Tony and his method then becomes

```
room312.Jeffries.Tony.openWindow()
```

Your job isn't complete yet. The method requires a parameter detailing which window to open. In this case, the window you want is the middle window of the west wall of Room 312. Or, from the hierarchical point of view of the principal's office, it becomes

```
room312.westWall.middleWindow
```

This object road map is the parameter for Tony's `openWindow()` method. Therefore, the entire command that comes over the PA system is

```
room312.Jeffries.Tony.openWindow(room312.westWall.middleWindow)
```

If, instead of barking out orders while sitting in the principal's office, you attempt the same task through radio from an orbiting space shuttle to all the inhabitants on Earth, imagine how laborious your object hierarchy is. The complete reference to Tony's `openWindow()` method and the window that you want opened has to be mighty long to distinguish the desired objects from the billions of objects within the space shuttle's view.

The point is that the smaller the scope of the object-oriented world you're programming, the more you can assume about the location of objects. For client-side JavaScript, the scope is no wider than the browser itself. In other words, every object that a JavaScript script can work with resides within the browser application. With few exceptions, a script does not access anything about your computer hardware, operating system, other applications, desktop, or any other stuff beyond the browser program.

The first browser document object road map

Figure 14-1 shows the lowest-common-denominator document object hierarchy that is implemented in all scriptable browsers, including scriptable legacy browsers such as IE3 and NN2. Notice that the window object is the topmost object in the entire scheme. Everything you script in JavaScript is in the browser's window.

Pay attention to the shading of the concentric rectangles. Every object in the same shaded area is at the same level relative to the window object. When a line from an object extends to the next-darker shaded rectangle, that object contains all the objects in darker areas. At most, one of these lines exists between levels. The window object contains the document object; the document object contains a form object; a form object contains many different kinds of form control elements.

FIGURE 14-1

The lowest-common-denominator browser document object hierarchy.

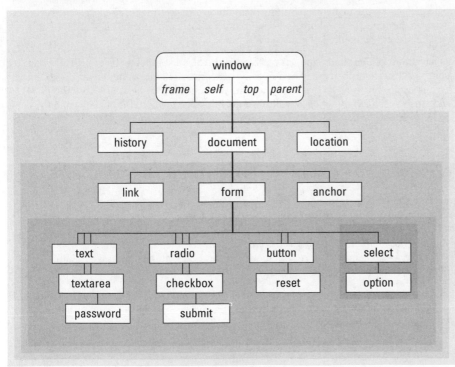

How Document Objects Are Born

Most of the objects that a browser creates for you are established when an HTML document loads into the browser. The same kind of HTML code you use to create links, anchors, and input elements tells a JavaScript-enhanced browser to create those objects in memory. The objects are there whether or not your scripts call them into action.

The only visible differences to the HTML code for defining those objects are the one or more optional attributes specifically dedicated to JavaScript. By and large, these attributes specify the event you want the user interface element to react to and what JavaScript should do when the user takes that action. By relying on the document's HTML code to perform the object generation, you can spend more time figuring out how to do things with those objects or have them do things for you.

Bear in mind that objects are created in their load order. And if you create a multiframe environment, a script in one frame cannot communicate with another frame's objects until both frames load. This trips up a lot of scripters who create multiframe and multiwindow sites (more in Chapter 16).

Object Properties

A property generally defines a particular current setting of an object. The setting may reflect a visible attribute of an object, such as the state of a checkbox (selected or not); it may also contain information that is not so obvious, such as the action and method of a submitted form.

Document objects have most of their initial properties assigned by the attribute settings of the HTML tags that generate the objects. Thus, a property may be a word (for example, a name) or a number (for example, a size). A property can also be an array, such as an array of images contained by a document. If the HTML does not include all attributes, the browser usually fills in a default value for both the attribute and the corresponding JavaScript property.

A Note to Experienced Object-Oriented Programmers

Although the basic object model hierarchy appears to have a class/subclass relationship, many of the traditional aspects of a true object-oriented environment don't apply to the model. The original JavaScript document object hierarchy is a *containment hierarchy,* not an *inheritance hierarchy.* No object inherits properties or methods of an object higher up the chain. Neither is there any automatic message passing from object to object in any direction. Therefore, you cannot invoke a window's method by sending a message to it through the document or a form object. All object references must be explicit.

Predefined document objects are generated only when the HTML code containing their definitions loads into the browser. In Chapter 34, you learn how to create your own objects, but those objects do not present new visual elements on the page that go beyond what HTML, Java applets, and plug-ins can portray.

Inheritance *does* play a role, as you will see later in this chapter, in the object model defined by the W3C. This newer hierarchy is of a more general nature to accommodate requirements of XML as well as HTML. But the containment hierarchy for HTML objects, as described in this section, is still valid in W3C DOM–compatible browsers.

When used in script statements, property names are case sensitive. Therefore, if you see a property name listed as bgColor, you must use it in a script statement with that exact combination of lowercase and uppercase letters. But when you set an initial value of a property by way of an HTML attribute, the attribute name (like all of HTML) is not case sensitive. Thus, <BODY BGCOLOR="white"> and <body bgcolor="white"> both set the same bgColor property value. Although XHTML won't validate correctly if you use anything but lowercase letters for tag and attribute names, most browsers continue to be case insensitive for markup, regardless of the HTML or XHTML version you specify for the page's DOCTYPE. The case for property names is not influenced by the case of the markup attribute name.

Each property determines its own read/write status. Some properties are read-only, whereas you can change others on the fly by assigning a new value to them. For example, to put some new text into a text box object, you assign a string to the object's value property:

```
document.forms[0].phone.value = "555-1212";
```

When an object contained by the document exists (that is, its HTML is loaded into the document), you can also add one or more custom properties to that object. This can be helpful if you want to associate some additional data with an object for later retrieval. To add such a property, simply specify it in the same statement that assigns a value to it:

```
document.forms[0].phone.delimiter = "-";
```

Any property you set survives as long as the document remains loaded in the window and scripts do not overwrite the object. Be aware, however, that reloading the page usually destroys custom properties.

Object Methods

An object's *method* is a command that a script can give to that object. Some methods return values, but that is not a prerequisite for a method. Also, not every object has methods defined for it. In a majority of cases, invoking a method from a script causes some action to take place. The resulting action may be obvious (such as resizing a window) or something more subtle (such as sorting an array in memory).

All methods have parentheses after them, and methods always appear at the end of an object's reference. When a method accepts or requires parameters, the parameter values go inside the parentheses (with multiple parameters separated by commas).

Although an object has its methods predefined by the object model, you can also assign one or more additional methods to an object that already exists (that is, after its HTML is loaded into the document). To do this, a script in the document (or in another window or frame accessible by the document) must define a JavaScript function and then assign that function to a new property name of the object. In the following example, written to take advantage of modern browser features, the fullScreen() function invokes two window object methods. By assigning the function reference to the new window.maximize property, I define a maximize() method for the window object. Thus, a button's event handler can call that method directly.

```
// define the function
function fullScreen() {
    this.moveTo(0,0);
    this.resizeTo(screen.availWidth, screen.availHeight);
}
// assign the function to a custom property
```

```
window.maximize = fullScreen;
...
<!-- invoke the custom method -->
<input type="button" value="Maximize Window" onclick="window.maximize()" />
```

Object Event Handlers

An *event handler* specifies how an object reacts to an event that is triggered by a user action (for example, a button click) or a browser action (for example, the completion of a document load). Going back to the earliest JavaScript-enabled browser, event handlers were defined inside HTML tags as extra attributes. They included the name of the attribute, followed by an equal sign (working as an assignment operator) and a string containing the script statement(s) or function(s) to execute when the event occurs (see Chapter 5).

Although event handlers are commonly defined in an object's HTML tag, you also have the power to assign or change an event handler just as you assign or change the property of an object. The value of an event handler property looks like a function definition. For example, given this HTML definition

```
<input type="text" name="entry" onfocus="doIt()" />
```

the value of the object's onfocus (all lowercase) property is

```
function onfocus() {
    doIt();
}
```

You can, however, assign an entirely different function to an event handler by assigning a function reference to the property. Such references don't include the parentheses that are part of the function's definition. (You see this again in Chapter 34 when you assign functions to object properties.)

Using the same text field definition you just looked at, you can assign a different function to the event handler, because based on user input elsewhere in the document, you want the field to behave differently when it receives the focus. If you define a function like this

```
function doSomethingElse() {
    statements
}
```

you can then assign the function to the field with this assignment statement:

```
document.formName.entry.onfocus = doSomethingElse;
```

Because the new function reference is written in JavaScript, you must observe case for the function name. Additionally, you are best served across all browsers by sticking with all-lowercase event handler names as properties.

If your scripts create new element objects dynamically, you can assign event handlers to these objects by way of event handler properties. For example, the following code uses W3C DOM syntax to create a new button input element and assign an onclick event handler that invokes a function defined elsewhere in the script:

```
var newElem = document.createElement("input");
newElem.type = "button";
newElem.value = "Click Here";
newElem.onclick = doIt;
document.forms[0].appendChild(newElem);
```

Object Model Smorgasbord

A survey of the entire evolution of scriptable browsers from NN2 and IE3 through IE7 and Mozilla 1 (Moz1) reveals six distinct DOM families. Even if your job entails developing content for just one current browser version, you may be surprised that family members from more than one DOM inhabit your authoring space.

Studying the evolution of the object model is extremely valuable for newcomers to scripting. It is too easy to learn the latest object model gadgets in your current browser, only to discover that your heroic scripting efforts are lost on earlier browsers accessing your pages. Even if you plan on supporting only modern browsers, a cursory knowledge of object model history is a useful part of your JavaScript knowledge base. Therefore, take a look at the six major object model types and how they came into being. Table 14-1 lists the object model families (in chronological order of their release) and the browser versions that support them. Later in this chapter are some guidelines you can follow to help you choose the object model(s) that best suit your users' appetites.

TABLE 14-1

Object Model Families

Model	Browser Support
Basic Object Model	NN2, NN3, IE3/J1, IE3/J2, NN4, IE4, IE5, IE5.5, IE6, Moz1, Safari 1, Safari 1.3/2, IE7
Basic Plus Images	NN3, IE3.01 (Mac only), NN4, IE4, IE5, IE5.5, IE6, Moz1, Safari 1, Safari 1.3/2, IE7
NN4 Extensions	NN4
IE4 Extensions	IE4, IE5, IE5.5, IE6, IE7 (some features in all versions require Win32 OS)
IE5 Extensions	IE5, IE5.5, IE6, IE7 (some features in all versions require Win32 OS)
W3C DOM (I and II)	IE5 (partial), IE5.5 (partial), IE6 (partial), Moz1 (most), Safari 1 (partial), Safari 1.3/2 (most), IE7 (partial)

It's important to realize that even though browsers have come a long way toward providing unified support for web standards, we're not quite there yet. As of this writing, no current browser fully and accurately supports Levels I and II of the W3C DOM. Mozilla 1.75 (Firefox, Camino, and so on), Safari 1.3/2, and Opera 9 have all closed the compatibility gap considerably, but some issues not severely impacting HTML authoring remain.

Basic Object Model

The first scriptable browser, Netscape Navigator 2, implemented a very basic DOM. Figure 14-1, which you saw earlier in the chapter, provides a visual guide to the objects that were exposed to scripting. The hierarchical structure starts with the window and drills inward toward the document, forms, and form control elements. A document is a largely immutable page on the screen. Only elements that are by nature interactive — links and form elements such as text fields and buttons — are treated as objects with properties, methods, and event handlers.

The heavy emphasis on form controls opened numerous possibilities that were radical ideas at the time. Because a script could inspect the values of form controls, forms could be prevalidated on the client. If the page included a script that performed some calculations, data entry and calculated results were displayed via editable text fields.

Additional objects that exist outside the document—`window`, `history`, and `location` objects—provide scriptable access to simple yet practical properties of the browser that loads the page. The most global view of the environment is the `navigator` object, which includes properties about the browser brand and version.

When Internet Explorer 3 arrived on the scene, the short life of Navigator 2 was nearing its end. Even though NN3 was already widely available in prerelease form, Internet Explorer 3 implemented the basic object model from NN2 (plus one `window` object property from NN3). Therefore, despite the browser version number discrepancy, NN2 and IE3 were essentially the same with respect to their DOMs. For a brief moment in Internet Time, there was nearly complete harmony between Microsoft and Netscape DOMs—albeit at a very simple level.

Basic Object Model Plus Images

A very short time after Internet Explorer 3 was released, Netscape released Navigator 3 with an object model that built upon the original version. A handful of existing objects—especially the `window` object—gained new properties, methods, and/or event handlers. Scripts could also communicate with Java applets as objects. But the biggest new object on the scene was the `Image` object and the array of image objects exposed to the `document` object.

Most of the properties for a Navigator 3 image object gave read-only access to values typically assigned to attributes in the `<img>` tag. But you could modify one property—the `src` property—after the page loaded. Scripts could swap out images within the fixed image rectangle. Although these new image objects didn't have mouse-related event handlers, nesting an image inside a link (which had `onmouseover` and new `onmouseout` event handlers) let scripts implement image rollovers to liven up a page.

As more new scripters investigated the possibilities of adding JavaScript to their pages, frustration ensued when the image swapping they implemented for Navigator 3 failed to work in Internet Explorer 3. Although you could easily script around the lack of an image object to prevent script errors in Internet Explorer 3, the lack of this cool page feature disappointed many. Had they also taken into account the installed base of Navigator 2 in the world, they would have been disappointed there, too. To confuse matters even more, the Macintosh version of Internet Explorer 3.01 (the second release of the Internet Explorer for Mac browser) implemented scriptable image objects.

Despite these rumblings of compatibility problems to come, the object model implemented in Navigator 3 eventually became the baseline reference for future DOMs. With few exceptions, code written for this object model runs on all browsers from Navigator 3 and Internet Explorer 4 through the latest versions of both brands and other modern browsers.

Navigator 4–Only Extensions

The next browser released to the world was Netscape Navigator 4. Numerous additions to the existing objects put more power into the hands of scripters. You could move and resize browser windows within the context of script-detectable `screen` object properties (for example, how big the user's screen was). Two concepts that represented new thinking about the object model were an enhanced event model and the layer object.

Event capture model

Navigator 4 added many new events to the repertoire. Keyboard events and more mouse events (`onmouse-down` and `onmouseup`) allowed scripts to react to more user actions on form control elements and links. All of these events worked as they did in previous object models in which event handlers were typically assigned as attributes to an element's tag (although you could also assign event handlers as properties in script statements). To facilitate some of the Dynamic HTML (DHTML) potential in the rest of the Navigator 4 object model, the event model was substantially enhanced.

At the root of the system is the idea that when a user performs some physical action on an event-aware object (for example, clicking a form button), the event reaches that button from the top down through the document object hierarchy. If you have multiple objects that share an event handler, it may be more convenient to capture that event in just one place — the `window` or `document` object level — rather than assigning the same event handler to all the elements. The default behavior of Navigator 4 allowed the event to reach the target object, just as it had in earlier browsers. But you could also turn on *event capture* in the `window`, `document`, or layer object. When captured, the event could be handled at the upper level, pre-processed before being passed onto its original target, or redirected to another object altogether.

Whether or not you capture events, the Navigator 4 event model produces an `event` object (lowercase e to distinguish from the static `Event` object) for each event. That object contains properties that reveal more information about the specific event, such as the keyboard character pressed for a keyboard event or the position of a click event on the page. Any event handler can inspect `event` object properties to learn more about the event and process the event accordingly.

Layers

Perhaps the most radical addition to the Navigator 4 object model was a new object that reflected an entirely new HTML element: the `layer` element. A *layer* is a container that is capable of holding its own HTML document, yet it exists in a plane in front of the main document. You can move, size, and hide a layer under script control. This new element allowed, for the first time, overlapping elements in an HTML page.

To accommodate the layer object in the document object hierarchy, Netscape defined a nesting hierarchy such that a layer was contained by a document. As the result, the `document` object acquired a property (`document.layers`) that was an array of layer objects in the document. This array exposed only the first level of layer(s) in the current `document` object.

Each layer had its own `document` object because each layer could load an external HTML document if desired. As a positionable element, a layer object had numerous properties and methods that allowed scripts to move, hide, show, and change its stacking order.

Unfortunately for Netscape, the W3C did not agree to make the `<layer>` tag part of the HTML 4 specification. As such, it is an orphan element that exists only in Navigator 4 (not implemented in Moz1 or later). The same goes for the scripting of the layer object and its nested references.

Internet Explorer 4+ Extensions

Microsoft broke important new ground with the release of Internet Explorer 4, which came several months after the release of Navigator 4. The main improvements were in the exposure of all HTML elements, scripted support of cascading style sheets (CSS), and a new event model. Some other additions were available only on Windows 32-bit operating system platforms.

HTML element objects

The biggest change to the object model world was that every HTML element became a scriptable object, while still supporting the original object model. Microsoft invented the `document.all` array (also called a *collection*). This array contains references to every element in the document, regardless of element nesting. If you assign an identifier (name) to the `id` attribute of an element, you can reference the element by the following syntax:

```
document.all.elementID
```

In most cases, you can also drop the `document.all.` part of the reference and begin with only the element ID.

Every element object has an entirely new set of properties and methods that give scripters a level of control over document content unlike anything seen before. These properties and methods are explored in more detail in Chapter 15. But several groups of properties deserve special mention here.

Four properties (`innerHTML`, `innerText`, `outerHTML`, and `outerText`) provide read/write access to the actual content within the body of a document. This means that you no longer must use text boxes to display calculated output from scripts. You can modify content inside paragraphs, table cells, or anywhere on the fly. The browser's rendering engine immediately reflows a document when the dimensions of an element's content change. That feature puts the *Dynamic* in *Dynamic HTML*. To those of us who scripted the static pages of earlier browsers, this feature — taken for granted today — was nothing short of a revelation.

The series of offset properties are related to the position of an element on the page. These properties are distinct from the kind of positioning performed by CSS. Therefore, you can get the dimensions and location of any element on the page, making it easier to move positionable content atop elements that are part of the document and may appear in various locations due to the browser window's current size.

Finally, the `style` property is the gateway to CSS specifications defined for the element. It is important that the script can modify the numerous properties of the `style` object. Therefore, you can modify font specifications, colors, borders, and the positioning properties after the page loads. The dynamic reflow of the page takes care of any layout changes that the alteration requires (for example, adjusting to a bigger font size).

Element containment hierarchy

Although Internet Explorer 4 still recognizes the element hierarchy of the original object model (see Figure 14-1), the DOM for Internet Explorer 4 does not extend this kind of hierarchy fully into other elements. If it did, it would mean that `td` elements inside a table might have to be addressed via its next outer `tr` or `table` element (just as a form control element must be addressed through its containing `form` element). Figure 14-2 shows how all HTML elements are grouped under the `document` object. The `document.all` array flattens the containment hierarchy as far as referencing objects goes. A reference to the most deeply nested TD element is still `document.all.cellID`. The highlighted pathway from the `window` object is the predominant reference path used when working with the Internet Explorer 4 document object hierarchy.

Element containment in Internet Explorer 4, however, is important for other reasons. Because an element can inherit some stylesheet attributes from an element that contains it, you should devise a document's HTML by embedding every piece of content in a container. Paragraph elements are text containers (with start and end tags), not tall line breaks between text chunks. Internet Explorer 4 introduced the notion of a parent–child relationship between a container and elements nested within it. Also, the position of an element may be calculated relative to the position of its next outermost positioning context.

The bottom line here is that element containment doesn't have anything to do with object references (like the original object model). It has everything to do with the *context* of an element relative to the rest of the page's content.

FIGURE 14-2

The Internet Explorer 4 document object hierarchy.

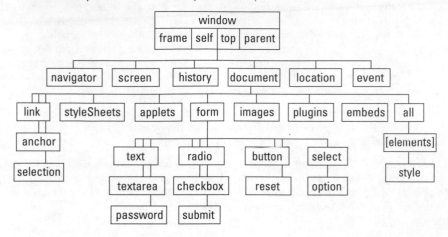

Cascading Style Sheets

By arriving a bit later to market with its version 4 browser than Netscape, Microsoft benefited from having the CSS Level 1 specification more fully developed before the browser's release. Therefore, the implementation is far more complete than that of Navigator 4 (but it is not 100 percent compatible with the standard).

The scriptability of stylesheet properties is a bit at odds with the first-generation CSS specification, which seemed to ignore the potential of scripting styles with JavaScript. Many CSS attribute names are hyphenated words (for example, text-align, z-index). But hyphens are not allowed in identifier names in JavaScript. This necessitated conversion of the multiword CSS attribute names to interCap JavaScript property names. Therefore, text-align becomes textAlign, and z-index becomes zIndex. You can access all of these properties through an element's style property:

```
document.all.elementID.style.stylePropertyName
```

One byproduct of the scriptability of stylesheets in Internet Explorer 4 and later is what some might call the *phantom page syndrome*. This occurs when the layout of a page is handled after the primary HTML for the page has downloaded to the browser. As the page loads, not all content may be visible, or it may be in a visual jumble. An onload event handler in the page then triggers scripts to set styles or content for the page. Elements jump around to get to their final resting places. This may be disconcerting to some users who at first see a link to click, but by the time the cursor reaches the click location, the page has reflowed, thereby moving the link somewhere else on the page.

NOTE For Internet Explorer users with 32-bit Windows operating systems, Internet Explorer 4 includes some extra features in the object model that can enhance presentations. *Filters* are stylesheet additives that offer a variety of visual effects on body text. For example, you can add a drop shadow or a glowing effect to text simply by applying filter styles to the text, or you can create the equivalent of a slide presentation by placing the content of each slide in a positioned div element. Although filters follow the CSS syntax, they are not part of the W3C specification.

Event bubbling

Just as Netscape invented an event model for Navigator 4, so did Microsoft invent one for Internet Explorer 4. Unfortunately for cross-browser scripters, the two event models are quite different. Instead of events trickling down the hierarchy to the target element, an Internet Explorer event starts at the target element and, unless instructed otherwise, bubbles up through the element containment hierarchy to reach the window object eventually. At any object along the way, an event handler can perform additional processing on that event if desired. Therefore, if you want a single event handler to process all click events for the page, assign the event handler to the body or window object so the events reach those objects (provided that the event bubbling isn't canceled by some other object along the containment hierarchy).

Internet Explorer also has an event object (a property of the window object) that contains details about the event, such as the key pressed for a keyboard event and the location of a mouse event. Names for these properties are entirely different from the event object properties of Navigator 4.

Despite what seem like incompatible, if not completely opposite, event models in Navigator 4 and Internet Explorer 4, you can make a single set of scripts handle events in both browsers (see Chapter 25 and Chapter 56 on the CD-ROM for examples). The Internet Explorer 4 event model continues to be the only model supported by Internet Explorer through version 7.

Internet Explorer 5+ Extensions

With the release of Internet Explorer 5, Microsoft built more onto the proprietary object model it launched in Internet Explorer 4. Although the range of objects remained pretty much the same, the number of properties, methods, and event handlers for the objects increased dramatically. Some of those additions were added to meet some of the specifications of the W3C DOM (discussed in the next section), occasionally causing a bit of incompatibility with Internet Explorer 4. But Microsoft also pushed ahead with efforts for Windows users only that may not necessarily become industry standards: DHTML behaviors and HTML applications.

A *DHTML behavior* is a chunk of script — saved as an external file — that defines some action (usually, a change of one or more style properties) that you can apply to any kind of element. The goal is to create a reusable component that you can load into any document whose elements require that behavior. As an example of a DHTML behavior, you can define a behavior that turns an element's text to red whenever the cursor rolls atop it and reverts the text to black when the cursor rolls out. When you assign the behavior to an element in the document (through CSS-like rule syntax), the element picks up that behavior and responds to the user accordingly. You can apply that same behavior to any element(s) in the document. You can see an example of a DHTML behavior in Chapter 15 in the description of the addBehavior() method and read an extended discussion in Chapter 47 on the CD-ROM.

HTML applications (HTAs, in Microsoft parlance) are HTML files that include an XML element known as the hta:application element. You can download an HTA to Internet Explorer 5 or later from the server as though it were a web page (although its file extension is .hta rather than .htm or .html). A user can also install an HTA on a client machine so that it behaves very much like an application, with a desktop icon and significant control over the look of the window. HTAs are granted greater security privileges on the client so that this application can behave more like a regular program. In fact, you can elect to turn off the system menu bar and use DHTML techniques to build your own menu bar for the application. Implementation details of HTAs are beyond the scope of this book, but you should be aware of their existence. More information is available at http://msdn.microsoft.com.

The W3C DOM

Conflicting browser object models from Netscape and Microsoft made life difficult for developers. Scripters craved a standard that would serve as a common denominator, much as HTML and CSS standards did for content and styles. The W3C took up the challenge of creating a DOM standard: the W3C DOM.

The charter of the W3C DOM working group was to create a DOM that could be applied to both HTML and XML documents. Because an XML document can have tags of virtually any name (as defined by a Document Type Definition), it has no intrinsic structure or fixed vocabulary of elements, as an HTML document does. As a result, the DOM specification had to accommodate the known structure of HTML (as defined in the HTML 4 specification) as well as the unknown structure of an XML document.

To make this work effectively, the working group divided the DOM specification into two sections. The first, called the *Core DOM*, defines specifications for the basic document structure that HTML and XML documents share. This includes notions of a document containing elements that have tag names and attributes; an element is capable of containing zero or more other elements. The second part of the DOM specification addresses the elements and other characteristics that apply only to HTML. The HTML portion inherits all the features of the Core DOM while providing a measure of backward compatibility to object models already implemented in legacy browsers and providing a framework for new features.

It is important for veteran scripters to recognize that the W3C DOM does not specify all features from existing browser object models. Many features of the Internet Explorer 4 (and later) object model are not part of the W3C DOM specification. This means that if you are comfortable in the Internet Explorer environment and wish to shift your focus to writing for the W3C DOM spec, you have to change some practices as highlighted in this chapter. In many respects, especially with regard to DHTML applications, the W3C DOM is an entirely new DOM with new concepts that you must grasp before you can successfully script in the environment.

By the same token, you should be aware that whereas Mozilla-based browsers go to great lengths to implement all of DOM Level 1 and most of Level 2, Microsoft (for whatever reason) features only a partial implementation of the W3C DOM through Internet Explorer 5.5. Although IE6 and IE7 implement more W3C DOM features, some important parts — notably, W3C DOM events — are missing. Other modern browsers, such as Safari 1.3/2 and Opera 9, provide comprehensive W3C DOM support and have largely closed the gap to compete with Mozilla in terms of supporting the W3C DOM.

DOM levels

Like most W3C specifications, one version is rarely enough. The job of the DOM working group was too large to be swallowed whole in one sitting. Therefore, the DOM is a continually evolving specification. The timeline of specification releases rarely coincides with browser releases. Therefore, it is very common for any given browser release to include only some of the most recent W3C version.

The first formal specification, DOM Level 1, was released well after NN4 and IE4 shipped. The HTML portion of Level 1 includes the so-called DOM Level 0 (there is no published standard by that name). This is essentially the object model as implemented in Navigator 3 (and for the most part in Internet Explorer 3 plus image objects). Perhaps the most significant omission from Level 1 is an event model (it ignores even the simple event model implemented in NN2 and IE3).

DOM Level 2 builds on the work of Level 1. In addition to several enhancements of both the Core and HTML portions of Level 1, Level 2 adds significant new sections (published as separate modules) on the event model, ways of inspecting a document's hierarchy, XML namespaces, text ranges, stylesheets, and style properties. Some modules of the Level 3 DOM have reached Recommendation status but are likely still a way off from being implemented in major browsers to any significant degree.

What stays the same

By adopting DOM Level 0 as the starting point of the HTML portion of the DOM, the W3C provided a way for a lot of existing script code to work even in a W3C DOM–compatible browser. Every object you see in the original object model, starting with the document object (see Figure 14-1) plus the image object, are in DOM Level 0. Almost all of the same object properties and methods are also available.

More important, when you consider the changes to referencing other elements in the W3C DOM (discussed in the next section), we're lucky that the old ways of referencing objects — such as forms, form control elements, and image — still work. Had the working group been planning from a clean slate, it is unlikely that the document object would have been given properties consisting of arrays of forms, links, and images.

The only potential problems you could encounter with your existing code have to do with a handful of properties that used to belong to the document object. In the new DOM, four style-related properties of the document object (alinkColor, bgColor, linkColor, and vlinkColor) become properties of the body object (referenced as document.body). In addition, the three link color properties pick up new names in the process (aLink, link, and vLink). It appears, however, that for now, IE6 and Moz1 maintain backward compatibility with the older document object color properties.

Also note that the DOM specification concerns itself only with the document and its content. Objects such as window, navigator, and screen are not part of the DOM specification through Level 2. Scripters are still at the mercy of browser makers for compatibility in these areas.

What isn't available

As mentioned earlier, the W3C DOM is not simply a restatement of existing browser specifications. Many convenience features of the Internet Explorer and Netscape Navigator object models do not appear in the W3C DOM. If you develop DHTML content in Internet Explorer 4 or later or in Navigator 4, you have to learn how to get along without some of these conveniences.

The Navigator 4 experiment with the <layer> tag was not successful in the W3C process. As a result, both the tag and the scripting conventions surrounding it do not exist in the W3C DOM. To some scripters' relief, the document.layerName referencing scenario (even more complex with nested layers) disappears from the object model. A positioned element is treated as just another element with some special stylesheet attributes that enable you to move it anywhere on the page, stack it amid other positioned elements, and hide it from view.

Among popular Internet Explorer 4+ features missing from the W3C DOM are the document.all collection of HTML elements and four element properties that facilitate dynamic content: innerHTML, innerText, outerHTML, and outerText. A new W3C way provides for acquiring an array of all elements in a document, but generating HTML content to replace existing content or to be inserted in a document requires a tedious sequence of statements (see the section "New DOM concepts" later in this chapter). Most new browsers, however, have implemented the innerHTML property for HTML element objects.

New HTML practices

Exploitation of DHTML possibilities in the W3C DOM relies on modern HTML practices that by now have ideally been adopted by the majority of HTML authors. At the core of these practices (espoused by the HTML 4 specification) is making sure that all content is within an HTML container of some kind. Therefore, instead of using the `<p>` tag as a separator between blocks of running text, surround each paragraph of the running text with a `<p>...</p>` tag set. If you don't do it, the browser treats each `<p>` tag as the beginning of a paragraph and ends the paragraph element just before the next `<p>` tag or other block-level element.

Although browsers continue to accept the omission of certain end tags (for `td`, `tr`, and `li` elements, for instance) for backward compatibility, it is best to get into the habit of supplying these end tags if for no other reason than that they help you visualize where an element's sphere of influence truly begins and ends.

Any element that you intend to script — whether to change its content or its style — should have an identifier assigned to the element's `id` attribute. Form control elements still require `name` attributes if you submit the form content to a server. But you can freely assign the same or a different identifier to a control's `id` attribute. Scripts can use either the `id` or the `document.formReference.elementName` reference to reach a control object. Identifiers are essentially the same as the values you assign to the `name` attributes of form and form input elements. Following the same rules for the `name` attribute value, an `id` identifier must be a single word (no whitespace); it cannot begin with a numeral (to prevent conflicts in JavaScript); and it should avoid punctuation symbols except for the underscore character.

New DOM concepts

With the W3C DOM come several concepts that may be new to you unless you have worked extensively with the terminology of tree hierarchies. Concepts that have the most impact on your scripting are new ways of referencing elements and nodes.

Element referencing

Script references to objects in the DOM Level 0 are observed in the W3C DOM for backward compatibility. Therefore, a form input element whose `name` attribute is assigned the value `userName` is addressed just as it always is

```
document.forms[0].userName
```

or

```
document.formName.userName
```

But because all elements of a document are exposed to the `document` object, you can use the `document` object method designed to access any element whose ID is assigned. The method is `document.getElementById()`, and the sole parameter is a string version of the identifier of the object whose reference you want to get. To help put this in context with what you may have used with the Internet Explorer 4 object model, consider the following HTML paragraph tag:

```
<p id="myParagraph">...</p>
```

In Internet Explorer 4 or later, you can reference this element with

```
var elem = document.all.myParagraph;
```

Although the document.all collection is not implemented in the W3C DOM, the document object method (available in Internet Explorer 5 and later, Mozilla, Safari, and others) getElementById() enables you to access any element by its ID:

```
var elem = document.getElementById("myParagraph");
```

This method is considered the appropriate technique for referencing an element based upon its ID. Unfortunately for scripters, this method is difficult to type because it is case sensitive, so watch out for that ending lowercase *d*.

A hierarchy of nodes

The issue surrounding containers (described earlier) comes into play for the underlying architecture of the W3C DOM. Every element or free-standing chunk of text in an HTML (or XML) document is an object that is contained by its next outermost container. Let's look at a simple HTML document to see how this system works. Listing 14-1 is formatted to show the containment hierarchy of elements and string chunks.

LISTING 14-1

A Simple HTML Document

```
<html>
    <head>
        <title>
            A Simple Page
        </title>
    </head>

    <body>
        <p id="paragraph1">
            This is the
            <em id="emphasis1">
                one and only
            </em>
            paragraph on the page.
        </p>
    </body>
</html>
```

What you don't see in the listing is a representation of the document object. The document object exists automatically when this page loads into a browser. It is important that the document object encompasses everything you see in Listing 14-1. Therefore, the document object has a single nested element: the html element. The html element in turn has two nested elements: head and body. The head element contains the title element, whereas the title element contains a chunk of text. Down in the body element, the p element contains three pieces: a string chunk, the em element, and another string chunk.

According to W3C DOM terminology, each container, stand-alone element (such as a br element), or text chunk is known as a *node* — a fundamental building block of the W3C DOM. Nodes have parent–child relationships when one container holds another. As in real life, parent–child relationships extend only between adjacent generations, so a node can have zero or more children. However, the number of third-generation nodes further nested within the family tree does not influence the number of children associated with a parent. Therefore, in Listing 14-1, the html node has two child nodes: head and body, which are *siblings* that have the same parent. The body element has one child (p), even though that child contains three children (two text nodes and an em element node).

If you draw a hierarchical tree diagram of the document in Listing 14-1, it should look like the illustration in Figure 14-3.

FIGURE 14-3

Tree diagram of nodes for the document in Listing 14-1.

```
document
+--<html>
   +--<head>
   |  +--<title>
   |     +--"A Simple Page"
   +--<body>
      +--<p ID="paragraph1">
         +--"This is the  "
         +--<em ID="emphasis1">
         |  +--"one and only"
         +--" paragraph on the page."
```

NOTE   If the document's source code contains a Document Type Definition (in a DOCTYPE element) above the <html> tag, the browser treats that DOCTYPE node as a sibling of the HTML element node. In that case, the root document node contains two child nodes.

The W3C DOM (through Level 2) defines 12 different types of nodes, 7 of which have direct application in HTML documents. These seven types of nodes appear in Table 14-2; the rest apply to XML. Of the 12 types, the three most common are the document, element, and text types. All W3C DOM browsers (including Internet Explorer 5 and later, Mozilla, Safari, and others) implement the three common node types, whereas Mozilla implements all of them, IE6 implements all but one, and Safari1 implements all but two.

TABLE 14-2

W3C DOM HTML-Related Node Types

Type	Number	nodeName	nodeValue	Description	IE6+	Moz1	Safari 1
Element	1	*tag name*	Null	Any HTML or XML tagged element	Yes	Yes	Yes
Attribute	2	*attribute name*	*Attribute value*	A name–value attribute pair in an element	Yes	Yes	Yes
Text	3	#text	*text content*	A text fragment contained by an element	Yes	Yes	Yes
Comment	8	#comment	*comment text*	HTML comment	Yes	Yes	No
Document	9	#document	Null	Root document object	Yes	Yes	Yes
DocumentType	10	DOCTYPE	Null	DTD specification	No	Yes	No
Fragment	11	#document-fragment	Null	Series of one or more nodes outside the document	Yes	Yes	Yes

Applying the node types of Table 14-2 to the node diagram in Figure 14-3, you can see that the simple page consists of one document node, six element nodes, and four text nodes.

Node properties

A node has many properties, most of which are references to other nodes related to the current node. Table 14-3 lists all properties shared by all node types in DOM Level 2.

TABLE 14-3

Node Object Properties (W3C DOM Level 2)

Property	Value	Description	IE6Win+	IE5Mac+	Moz1	Safari1
nodeName	String	Varies with node type (see Table 14-2)	Yes	Yes	Yes	Yes
nodeValue	String	Varies with node type (see Table 14-2)	Yes	Yes	Yes	Yes
nodeType	Integer	Constant representing each type	Yes	Yes	Yes	Yes
parentNode	Object	Reference to next outermost container	Yes	Yes	Yes	Yes
childNodes	Array	All child nodes in source order	Yes	Yes	Yes	Yes
firstChild	Object	Reference to first child node	Yes	Yes	Yes	Yes
lastChild	Object	Reference to last child node	Yes	Yes	Yes	Yes
previousSibling	Object	Reference to sibling node up in source order	Yes	Yes	Yes	Yes

Property	Value	Description	IE6Win+	IE5Mac+	Moz1	Safari1
nextSibling	Object	Reference to sibling node next in source order	Yes	Yes	Yes	Yes
attributes	NodeMap	Array of attribute nodes	Some	Some	Yes	Some
ownerDocument	Object	Containing document object	Yes	Yes	Yes	Yes
namespaceURI	String	URI to namespace definition (element and attribute nodes only)	No	No	Yes	Yes
Prefix	String	Namespace prefix (element and attribute nodes only)	No	No	Yes	Yes
localName	String	Applicable to namespace-affected nodes	No	No	Yes	Yes

NOTE
You can find all of the properties shown in Table 14-3 that also show themselves to be implemented in Internet Explorer 6 or later or Moz1 in Chapter 15, in the listing of properties that all HTML element objects have in common. That's because an HTML element, as a type of node, inherits all of the properties of the prototypical node.

To help you see the meanings of the key node properties, Table 14-4 shows the property values of several nodes in the simple page shown in Listing 14-1. For each node column, find the node in Figure 14-3 and then follow the list of property values for that node, comparing the values against the actual node structure in Figure 14-3.

TABLE 14-4

Properties of Selected Nodes for a Simple HTML Document

Properties	Nodes			
	document	html	p	"one and only"
nodeType	9	1	1	3
nodeName	#document	html	p	#text
nodeValue	Null	null	null	"one and only"
parentNode	Null	document	body	em
previousSibling	Null	null	null	null
nextSibling	Null	null	null	null
childNodes	Html	head body	"This is the " em " paragraph on the page."	(none)
firstChild	Html	head	"This is the "	null
lastChild	Html	body	" paragraph on the page."	null

The nodeType property is an integer that is helpful in scripts that iterate through an unknown collection of nodes. Most content in an HTML document is of type 1 (an HTML element) or 3 (a text node), with the outermost container, the document, of type 9. A node's nodeName property is either the name of the node's tag (for an HTML element) or a constant value (preceded by a # [hash mark] as shown in Table 14-2). And, which may surprise some, the nodeValue property is null except for the text node type, in which case the value is the actual string of text of the node. In other words, for HTML elements, the W3C DOM does not expose a container's HTML as a string.

The Object-Oriented W3C DOM

If you are familiar with concepts of object-oriented (OO) programming, you will appreciate the OO tendencies in the way the W3C defines the DOM. The Node object includes sets of properties (see Table 14-3) and methods (see Table 14-5) that are inherited by every object based on the Node. Most of the objects that inherit the Node's behavior have their own properties and/or methods that define their specific behaviors. The following figure shows (in W3C DOM terminology) the inheritance tree from the Node root object. Most items are defined in the Core DOM, whereas items shown in boldface are from the HTML DOM portion.

```
Node
+--Document
|   +--HTMLDocument
+--CharacterData
|   +--Text
|   |   +--CDATASection
|   +--Comment
+--Attr
+--Element
|   +--HTMLElement
|       +-- (Each specific HTML element)
+--DocumentType
+--DocumentFragment
+--Notation
+--Entity
+--Entity Reference
+--ProcessingInstruction
```

W3C DOM Node object inheritance tree.

You can see from the preceding figure that individual HTML elements inherit properties and methods from the generic HTML element, which inherits from the Core Element object, which in turn inherits from the basic Node.

It isn't important to know the Node object inheritance to script the DOM. But it does help explain the ECMA Script Language Binding appendix of the W3C DOM recommendation, as well as explain how a simple element object winds up with so many properties and methods associated with it.

It is doubtful that you will use all of the relationship-oriented properties of a node, primarily because there is some overlap in how you can reach a particular node from any other. The parentNode property is important because it is a reference to the current node's immediate container. Although the firstChild and lastChild properties point directly to the first and last children inside a container, most scripts generally use the childNodes property with array notation inside a for loop to iterate through child nodes. If there are no child nodes, the childNodes array has a length of zero.

Node methods

Actions that modify the HTML content of a node in the W3C DOM world primarily involve the methods defined for the prototype Node. Table 14-5 shows the methods and their support in the W3C DOM–capable browsers.

TABLE 14-5

Node Object Methods (W3C DOM Level 2)

Method	Description	IE5+	Moz1	Safari 1
appendChild(newChild)	Adds child node to end of current node	Yes	Yes	Yes
cloneNode(deep)	Grabs a copy of the current node (optionally with children)	Yes	Yes	Yes
hasChildNodes()	Determines whether current node has children (Boolean)	Yes	Yes	Yes
insertBefore(new, ref)	Inserts new child in front of another child	Yes	Yes	Yes
removeChild(old)	Deletes one child	Yes	Yes	Yes
replaceChild(new, old)	Replaces an old child with a new one	Yes	Yes	Yes
isSupported(feature, version)	Determines whether the node supports a particular feature	No	Yes	Yes

The important methods for modifying content are appendChild(), insertBefore(), removeChild(), and replaceChild(). Note, however, that all of these methods assume that the point of view for the action is from the parent of the nodes being affected by the methods. For example, to delete an element (using removeChild()), you don't invoke that method on the element being removed, but on its parent element. This leaves open the possibility of creating a library of utility functions that obviate having to know too much about the precise containment hierarchy of an element. A simple function that lets a script appear to delete an element actually does so from its parent:

```
function removeElement(elemID) {
    var elem = document.getElementById(elemID);
    elem.parentNode.removeChild(elem);
}
```

If this seems like a long way to go to accomplish the same result as setting the outerHTML property of an Internet Explorer 4 or later object to empty, you are right. Although some of this convolution makes sense for XML, unfortunately, the W3C working group doesn't seem to have HTML scripters' best interests in mind. All is not lost, however, as you see later in this chapter.

Generating new node content

The final point about the node structure of the W3C DOM focuses on the similarly gnarled way scripters must go about generating content that they want to add or replace on a page. For text-only changes (for example, the text inside a table cell), there is both an easy and a hard way to perform the task. For HTML changes, there is only the hard way (plus a handy workaround discussed later). Let's look at the hard way first and then pick up the easy way for text changes.

To generate a new node in the DOM, you look to the variety of methods that are defined for the Core DOM's document object (and therefore are inherited by the HTML document object). A node creation method is defined for nearly every node type in the DOM. The two important ones for HTML documents are createElement() and createTextNode(). The first generates an element with whatever tag name (string) you pass as a parameter; the second generates a text node with whatever text you pass.

When you first create a new element, it exists only in the browser's memory and not as part of the document containment hierarchy. Moreover, the result of the createElement() method is a reference to an empty element except for the name of the tag. For example, to create a new p element, use

```
var newElem = document.createElement("p");
```

The new element has no ID, attributes, or any content. To assign some attributes to that element, you can use the setAttribute() method (a method of every element object) or assign a value to the object's corresponding property. For example, to assign an identifier to the new element, use either

```
newElem.setAttribute("id", "newP");
```

or

```
newElem.id = "newP";
```

Both ways are perfectly legal. Even though the element has an ID at this point, it is not yet part of the document, so you cannot retrieve it via the document.getElementById() method.

To add some content to the paragraph, next you generate a text node as a separate object:

```
var newText = document.createTextNode("This is the second paragraph.");
```

Again, this node is just sitting around in memory waiting for you to apply it as a child of some other node. To make this text the content of the new paragraph, you can append the node as a child of the paragraph element that is still in memory:

```
newElem.appendChild(newText);
```

If you were able to inspect the HTML that represents the new paragraph element, it would look like the following:

```
<p id="newP">This is the second paragraph.</p>
```

The new paragraph element is ready for insertion into a document. Using the document shown in Listing 14-1, you can append it as a child of the body element:

```
document.body.appendChild(newElem);
```

At last, the new element is part of the document containment hierarchy. Now you can reference it just like any other element in the document.

Replacing node content

The addition of the paragraph shown in the last section requires a change to a portion of the text in the original paragraph (the first paragraph is no longer the one and only paragraph on the page). As mentioned earlier, you can perform text changes via the replaceChild() method or by assigning new text to a text node's nodeValue property. Let's see how each approach works to change the text of the first paragraph's em element from one and only to first.

To use replaceChild(), a script first must generate a valid text node with the new text:

```
var newText = document.createTextNode("first");
```

The next step is to use the replaceChild() method. But recall that the point of view for this method is the parent of the child being replaced. The child here is the text node inside the em element, so you must invoke the replaceChild() method on the em element. Also, the replaceChild() method requires two parameters. The first parameter is the new node; the second is a reference to the node to be replaced. Because the script statements get pretty long with the getElementById() method, an intermediate step grabs a reference to the text node inside the em element:

```
var oldChild = document.getElementById("emphasis1").childNodes[0];
```

Now the script is ready to invoke the replaceChild() method on the em element, swapping the old text node with the new:

```
document.getElementById("emphasis1").replaceChild(newText, oldChild);
```

If you want to capture the old node before it disappears, be aware that the replaceChild() method returns a reference to the replaced node (which is only in memory at this point and not part of the document node hierarchy). You can assign the method statement to a variable and use that old node somewhere else, if needed.

This may seem like a long way to go; it is, especially if the HTML you are generating is complex. Fortunately, you can take a simpler approach for replacing text nodes. All it requires is a reference to the text node being replaced. You can assign that node's nodeValue property its new string value:

```
document.getElementById("emphasis1").childNodes[0].nodeValue = "first";
```

When an element's content is entirely text (for example, a table cell that already has a text node in it), this is the most streamlined way to swap text on the fly using W3C DOM syntax. This doesn't work for the creation of the second paragraph text earlier in this chapter because the text node did not exist yet. The createTextNode() method had to create it explicitly.

Also remember that a text node does not have any inherent style associated with it. The style of the containing HTML element governs the style of the text. If you want to change not only the text node's text, but also how it looks, you have to modify the style property of the text node's parent element. Browsers that perform these kinds of content swaps and style changes automatically reflow the page to accommodate changes in the size of the content.

To summarize, Listing 14-2 is a live version of the modifications made to the original document shown in Listing 14-1. The new version includes a button and script that make the changes described throughout this discussion of nodes. Reload the page to start over.

LISTING 14-2

Adding/Replacing DOM Content

```html
<html>
<head>
   <title>A Simple Page</title>
   <script type="text/javascript">
   function modify() {
      var newElem = document.createElement("p");
      newElem.id = "newP";
      var newText = document.createTextNode("This is the second paragraph.");
      newElem.appendChild(newText);
      document.body.appendChild(newElem);
      document.getElementById("emphasis1").childNodes[0].nodeValue = "first";
   }
   </script>
</head>

<body>
   <button onclick="modify()">Add/Replace Text</button>

   <p id="paragraph1">This is the <em id="emphasis1">one and
   only</em> paragraph on the page.</p>
</body>
</html>
```

Chapter 15 details node properties and methods that are inherited by all HTML elements. Most are implemented in all modern W3C DOM browsers. Also look to the reference material for the document object in Chapter 18 for other valuable W3C DOM methods.

A de facto standard: innerHTML

Microsoft was the first to implement the innerHTML property of all element objects starting with Internet Explorer 4. Although the W3C DOM has not supported this property, scripters frequently find it more convenient to modify content dynamically by way of a string containing HTML markup than by creating and assembling element and text nodes. As a result, most modern W3C DOM browsers, including Moz1 and Safari 1, support the read/write innerHTML property of all element objects as a de facto standard.

When you assign a string containing HTML markup to the innerHTML of an existing element, the browser automatically inserts the newly rendered elements into the document node tree. You may also use innerHTML with unmarked text to perform the equivalent of the Internet Explorer–only innerText property.

Despite the apparent convenience of the innerHTML property compared with the step-by-step process of manipulating element and text node objects, browsers operate on nodes much more efficiently than on assembly of long strings. This is one case where less JavaScript code does not necessarily translate to greater efficiency.

Static W3C DOM HTML objects

The Moz1 DOM (but unfortunately, not Internet Explorer 5 or later) adheres to the core JavaScript notion of prototype inheritance with respect to the object model. When a page loads into Moz1, the browser creates HTML objects based on the prototypes of each object defined by the W3C DOM. For example, if you use The Evaluator Sr. (discussed in Chapter 13) to see what kind of object the myP paragraph object is — enter document.getElementById("myP") in the top text box and click the Evaluate button — it reports that the object is based on the HTMLParagraphElement object of the DOM. Every instance of a p element object in the page inherits its default properties and methods from HTMLParagraphElement (which in turn inherits from HTMLElement, Element, and Node objects — all detailed in the JavaScript binding appendix of the W3C DOM specification).

You can use scripting to add properties to the prototypes of some of these static objects. To do so, you must use new features added to Moz1. Two new methods — __defineGetter__() and __defineSetter__() — enable you to assign functions to a custom property of an object.

> **NOTE** These methods are Mozilla specific. To prevent their possible collision with standardized implementations of these features in future implementations of ECMAScript, the underscore characters on either side of the method name are pairs of underscore characters.

The functions execute whenever the property is read — the function assigned via the __defineGetter__() method — or modified — the function assigned through the __defineSetter__() method. The common way to define these functions is in the form of an anonymous function (see Chapter 34). The formats for the two statements that assign these behaviors to an object prototype are as follows:

```
object.prototype.__defineGetter__("propName", function([param1[,...[,paramN]]]) {
  // statements
  return returnValue;
})
object.prototype.__defineSetter__("propName", function([param1[,...[,paramN]]]) {
  // statements
  return returnValue;
})
```

The example in Listing 14-3 demonstrates how to add a read-only property to every HTML element object in the current document. The property, called childNodeDetail, returns an object. The object has two properties: one for the number of element child nodes and one for the number of text child nodes. Note that the this keyword in the function definition is a reference to the object for which the property is calculated. And because the function runs each time a script statement reads the property, any scripted changes to the content after the page loads are reflected in the returned property value.

LISTING 14-3

Adding a Read-Only Prototype Property to All HTML Element Objects

```
<script type="text/javascript">
if (HTMLElement) {
    HTMLElement.prototype.__defineGetter__("childNodeDetail", function() {
        var result = {elementNodes:0, textNodes:0 }
        for (var i = 0; i < this.childNodes.length; i++) {
            switch (this.childNodes[i].nodeType) {
                case 1:
                    result.elementNodes++;
                    break;
                case 3:
                    result.textNodes++;
                    break;
            }
        }
        return result;
    })
}
</script>
```

To access the property, use it like any other property of the object. For example:

```
var BodyNodeDetail = document.body.childNodeDetail;
```

The returned value in this example is an object, so you use regular JavaScript syntax to access one of the property values:

```
var BodyElemNodesCount = document.body.childNodeDetail.elementNodes;
```

Bidirectional event model

Despite the seemingly conflicting event models of NN4 (trickle down) and IE4 (bubble up), the W3C DOM event model (defined in Level 2) manages to employ both event propagation models. This gives the scripter the choice of where along an event's propagation path the event gets processed. To prevent conflicts with existing event model terminology, the W3C model invents many new terms for properties and methods for events. Some coding probably requires W3C DOM–specific handling in a page aimed at multiple object models.

The W3C event model also introduces a new concept called the event listener. An *event listener* is essentially a mechanism that instructs an object to respond to a particular kind of event — very much like the way the event handler attributes of HTML tags respond to events. But the DOM recommendation points out that it prefers a more script-oriented way of assigning event listeners: the addEventListener() method available for every node in the document hierarchy. Through this method, you advise the browser whether to force an event to bubble up the hierarchy (the default behavior that is also in effect if you use the HTML attribute type of event handler) or to be captured at a higher level.

Functions invoked by the event listener receive a single parameter consisting of the event object whose properties contain contextual details about the event (details such as the position of a mouse click, character code of a keyboard key, or a reference to the target object). For example, if a form includes a button whose job is to invoke a calculation function, the W3C DOM prefers the following way of assigning the event handler:

```
document.getElementById("calcButton").addEventListener("click", doCalc, false);
```

The addEventListener() method takes three parameters. The first parameter is a string of the event to listen for; the second is a reference to the function to be invoked when that event fires; and the third parameter is a Boolean value. When you set this Boolean value to true, it turns on event capture whenever this event is directed to this target. The function then takes its cue from the event object passed as the parameter:

```
function doCalc(evt) {
    // get shortcut reference to input button's form
    var form = evt.target.form;
    var results = 0;
    // other statements to do the calculation //
    form.result.value = results;
}
```

To modify an event listener, you use the removeEventListener() method to get rid of the old listener and then employ addEventListener() with different parameters to assign the new one.

Preventing an event from performing its default action is also a different procedure in the W3C event model than in Internet Explorer. In Internet Explorer 4 (as well as Navigator 3 and 4), you can cancel the default action by allowing the event handler to evaluate to return false. Although this still works in Internet Explorer 5 and later, Microsoft includes another property of the window.event object, called returnValue. Setting that property to false anywhere in the function invoked by the event handler also kills the event before it does its normal job. But the W3C event model uses a method of the event object, preventDefault(), to keep the event from its normal task. You can invoke this method anywhere in the function that executes when the event fires.

Detailed information about an event is contained in an event object that must be passed to an event handler function where details may be read. If you assign event handlers via the W3C DOM addEventListener() method or an event handler property, the event object is passed automatically as the sole parameter to the event handler function. Include a parameter variable to catch the incoming parameter:

```
function swap(evt) {
    // statements here to work with W3C DOM event object
}
```

But if you assign events through a tag attribute, you must explicitly pass the event object in the call to the function:

```
<a href="http://www.example.com" onmouseover="swap(event)">
```

Unfortunately, as of Internet Explorer 7 for Windows and Internet Explorer 5 for Macintosh, the W3C DOM event model has yet to be supported by Microsoft. You can, however, make the Internet Explorer and W3C event models work together if you assign event handlers by way of object properties or tag attributes, and throw in a little object detection as described later in this chapter and in more detail in Chapter 25.

Scripting Trends

Although browser scripting had humble beginnings as a way to put some intelligence into form controls, the capabilities of the JavaScript language and DOM have inspired many a web developer to create what are essentially applications. Popular implementations of web-based e-mail systems use extensive scripting and background communication with the server to keep pages updated quickly without having to fetch and re-render the complete page each time you delete a message from the inbox list. It's not uncommon for large projects to involve multiple scripters (along with specialists in CSS, server programming, artists, and writers). Wrangling all the code can be a chore.

Separating content from scripting

Those who use CSS to style their sites have learned that separating style definitions from the HTML markup makes a huge improvement in productivity when it comes time to change colors or font specifications throughout a site. Instead of having to modify hundreds of `<font>` tag specifications scattered around the site, all it takes is a simple tweak of a single CSS rule in one `.css` file to have that change be implemented immediately across the board.

The notion of using HTML purely for a page's structure has also impacted scripting. It is rare these days for a professional scripter to put an event handler attribute inside an HTML tag. That would be considered too much mixing of content with behavior. In other words, the HTML markup should be able to stand on its own so that those with nonscriptable browsers (including those with vision or motor disabilities who use specialized browsers) can still get the fundamental information provided by the page. Any scripting that impacts the display or behavior of the page is added to the page after the HTML markup has loaded and rendered. Even assigning events to elements is done by script after the page load.

Script code is more commonly linked into a page from an external `.js` file. This isn't part of the separation of content and scripts trend, but a practice that offers many benefits, such as the same code being instantly usable on multiple pages. Additionally, when projects involve many code chefs, scripters can work on their code while writers work on the HTML and designers work on their external CSS code.

NOTE You will see lots of examples in this book that use event handler attributes inside tags and scripts embedded within the page. This approach is primarily for simplicity of demonstrating a language or DOM feature.

Using the W3C DOM where possible

Basic support for W3C DOM element referencing and content manipulation has been implemented in mainstream browsers for so long that you can be assured that composing scripts for that model will work for the bulk of your visitors. That's not to say you can assume that every visitor is equipped that way, but the hassles that scripters used to endure to support conflicting object models are behind us for the most part. The days of writing extensive branching code for IE and Netscape are not-so-fond memories.

You still want to use object detection techniques to guard against the occasional old browser that stops by. That's where the technique of assigning event handlers by scripts can save a lot of headaches.

Except for some initializations that might occur while the page loads, most script execution in a web page occurs at the instigation of an event: A user clicks a button, types something in a text box, chooses from a `select` element, and so on. You can prevent older browsers from tripping up on W3C DOM syntax by doing your fundamental object detection right in the event assignment code, as in the following simplified example:

```
function setUpEvents() {
   if (document.getElementById) {
      // statements to bind events to elements
   }
}
window.onload = setUpEvents;
```

Now browsers that don't have even minimum support for the W3C DOM won't generate script errors when users click or type, because those events won't be assigned for those browsers. Then scripts that survive your object detection query can also modify the page, as you saw in Listing 13-2 in Chapter 13.

Handling events

You will still find some places where the W3C DOM isn't enough. This is particularly true in processing events, where Internet Explorer (at least through version 7) does not support the W3C DOM way of getting details about an event to the event handler function. The W3C DOM automatically passes the event object as a parameter to a handler function. In the Internet Explorer model, the event object is a property of the window object. Therefore, your functions have to equalize the differences where necessary. For example, to obtain a single variable representing the event object, regardless of browser, you can use a construction similar to the following:

```
function calculate(evt) {
   evt = (evt) ? evt : window.event;
   // more statements to process event
}
```

Additional branching is necessary to inspect important details of the event. For example, the Internet Explorer event object property pointing to the object that received the event is called srcElement, whereas the W3C DOM version is called target. Again, a little bit of equalizing code in the event handler function can handle the disparity. When your script has a reference to the element receiving the event, you can start using W3C DOM properties and methods of the element, because Internet Explorer supports those. You can find more details on event objects in Chapter 25.

Standards Compatibility Modes (DOCTYPE Switching)

Both Microsoft and Netscape/Mozilla discovered that they had, over time, implemented CSS features in ways that ultimately differed from the published standards that came later (usually after much wrangling among working-group members). To compensate for these differences and make a clean break to be compatible with the standards, the major browser makers decided to let the page author's choice of <!DOCTYPE> header element details determine whether the document was designed to follow the old way (sometimes called *quirks mode*) or the standards-compatible way. The tactic, known informally as *DOCTYPE switching*, is implemented in Internet Explorer 6 and later, Internet Explorer 5 for the Mac, and all Mozilla-based browsers.

Although most of the differences between the two modes are small, there are some significant differences between the two modes in Internet Explorer 6 and later, particularly when styles or DHTML scripts rely on elements designed with borders, margins, and padding. Microsoft's original box model measured the dimensions of elements in a way that differed from the eventual CSS standard.

To place the affected browsers in CSS standards–compatible mode, you should include a `<!DOCTYPE>` element at the top of every document that specifies any of the following details:

```
<!DOCTYPE HTML PUBLIC "-//W3C//DTD HTML 4.0 Transitional//EN"
        "http://www.w3.org/TR/REC-html40/loose.dtd">

<!DOCTYPE HTML PUBLIC "-//W3C//DTD HTML 4.0 Frameset//EN"
        "http://www.w3.org/TR/REC-html40/frameset.dtd">

<!DOCTYPE HTML PUBLIC "-//W3C//DTD HTML 4.0//EN"
        "http://www.w3.org/TR/REC-html40/strict.dtd">

<!DOCTYPE html PUBLIC "-//W3C//DTD XHTML 1.0 Transitional//EN"
        "http://www.w3.org/TR/xhtml1/DTD/xhtml1-transitional.dtd">

<!DOCTYPE html PUBLIC "-//W3C//DTD XHTML 1.0 Frameset//EN"
        "http://www.w3.org/TR/xhtml1/DTD/xhtml1-frameset.dtd">

<!DOCTYPE html PUBLIC "-//W3C//DTD XHTML 1.0 Strict//EN"
        "http://www.w3.org/TR/xhtml1/DTD/xhtml1-strict.dtd">

<!DOCTYPE html PUBLIC "-//W3C//DTD XHTML 1.1//EN"
        "http://www.w3.org/TR/xhtml11/DTD/xhtml11.dtd">
```

Be aware, however, that older versions of Internet Explorer for Windows, such as Internet Explorer 5 or Internet Explorer 5.5, are ignorant of the standards-compatible mode and will use the old Microsoft quirks mode regardless of `<!DOCTYPE>` setting. But using the standards-compatible mode DOCTYPE is more likely to force your content and stylesheets to render more similarly across the latest browsers.

Where to Go from Here

These past two chapters provided an overview of the core language and object model issues that anyone designing pages that use JavaScript must confront. The goal here is to stimulate your own thinking about how to embrace or discard levels of compatibility with your pages as you balance your desire to generate cool pages and serve your audience. From here on, the difficult choices are up to you.

To help you choose the objects, properties, methods, and event handlers that best suit your requirements, the rest of the chapters in Part III and all of Part IV provide in-depth references to the DOM and core JavaScript language features. Observe the compatibility ratings for each language term very carefully to help you determine which features best suit your audience's browsers. Most example listings are complete HTML pages that you can load in various browsers to see how they work. Many others invite you to explore how things work through The Evaluator Sr. (see Chapter 13). Play around with the files, making modifications to build your own applications or expanding your working knowledge of JavaScript in the browser environment.

The language and object models have grown in the handful of years they have been in existence. The amount of language vocabulary has increased astronomically. It takes time to drink it all in and feel comfortable that you are aware of the powers available to you. Don't worry about memorizing the vocabulary. It's more important to acquaint yourself with the features and come back later when you need the implementation details.

Be patient. Be persistent. The reward will come.

Chapter 15

Generic HTML Element Objects

The object model specifications implemented in Internet Explorer 4 or later and W3C/Mozilla-based browsers feature a large set of scriptable objects that represent what we often call *generic* HTML elements. Generic elements can be divided into two groups. One group, such as the b and strike elements, defines font styles to be applied to enclosed sequences of text. The need for these elements (and the objects that represent them) is all but gone due to more page designers using style sheets. The second group of elements assigns context to content within their start and end tags. Examples of contextual elements include h1, blockquote, and the ubiquitous p element. Although browsers sometimes have consistent visual ways of rendering contextual elements by default (for example, the large bold font of an <h1> tag), the specific rendering is not the intended purpose of the tags. No formal standard dictates that text within an em element must be italicized: The style simply has become the custom since the very early days of browsers.

All of these generic elements share a large number of scriptable properties, methods, and event handlers. The sharing extends not only among generic elements, but also among virtually every renderable element — even if it has additional, element-specific properties, methods, and/or event handlers that I cover in depth in other chapters of this reference. Rather than repeat the details of these shared properties, methods, and event handlers for each object throughout this reference, I describe them in detail only in this chapter (unless there is a special behavior, bug, or trick associated with the item in some object described elsewhere). In succeeding reference chapters, each object description includes a list of the object's properties, methods, and event handlers, but I do not list shared items over and over (making it hard to find items that are unique to a particular element). Instead, you see a pointer back to this chapter for the items in common with generic HTML element objects.

Generic Objects

Table 15-1 lists all of the objects that I treat in this reference as *generic* objects. All of these objects share the properties, methods, and event handlers described in succeeding sections and have no special items that require additional coverage elsewhere in this book.

TABLE 15-1

Generic HTML Element Objects

Formatting Objects	Contextual Objects
b	acronym
big	address
center	cite
i	code
nobr	dfn
rt	del
ruby	div
s	em
small	ins
strike	kbd
sub	listing
sup	p
tt	plaintext
u	pre
wbr	samp
	span
	strong
	var
	xmp

Properties	Methods	Event Handlers
accessKey	addBehavior()	onactivate
all[]	addEventListener()	onafterupdate
attributes[]	appendChild()	onbeforecopy
baseURI	applyElement()	onbeforecut
behaviorUrns[]	attachEvent()	onbeforedeactivate
canHaveChildren	blur()	onbeforeeditfocus
canHaveHTML	clearAttributes()	onbeforepaste

Properties	Methods	Event Handlers
childNodes[]	click()	onbeforeupdate
children	cloneNode()	onblur
cite	compareDocumentPosition()	oncellchange
className	componentFromPoint()	onclick
clientHeight	contains()	oncontextmenu
clientLeft	createControlRange()	oncontrolselect
clientTop	detachEvent()	oncopy
clientWidth	dispatchEvent()	oncut
contentEditable	doScroll()	ondataavailable
currentStyle	dragDrop()	ondatasetchanged
dateTime	fireEvent()	ondatasetcomplete
dataFld	focus()	ondblclick
dataFormatAs	getAdjacentText()	ondeactivate
dataSrc	getAttribute()	ondrag
dir	getAttributeNode()	ondragend
disabled	getAttributeNodeNS()	ondragenter
document	getAttributeNS()	ondragleave
filters[]	getBoundingClientRect()	ondragover
firstChild	getClientRects()	ondragstart
height	getElementsByTagName()	ondrop
hideFocus	getElementsByTagNameNS()	onerrorupdate
id	getExpression()	onfilterchange
innerHTML	getFeature()	onfocus
innerText	getUserData()	onfocusin
isContentEditable	hasAttribute()	onfocusout
isDisabled	hasAttributeNS()	onhelp
isMultiLine	hasAttributes()	onkeydown
isTextEdit	hasChildNodes()	onkeypress
lang	insertAdjacentElement()	onkeyup
language	insertAdjacentHTML()	onlayoutcomplete
lastChild	insertAdjacentText()	onlosecapture
length	insertBefore()	onmousedown
localName	isDefaultNamespace()	onmouseenter
namespaceURI	isEqualNode()	onmouseleave
nextSibling	isSameNode()	onmousemove

continued

TABLE 15-1 *(continued)*

Properties	Methods	Event Handlers
nodeName	isSupported()	onmouseout
nodeType	item()	onmouseover
nodeValue	lookupNamespaceURI()	onmouseup
offsetHeight	lookupPrefix()	onmousewheel
offsetLeft	mergeAttributes()	onmove
offsetParent	normalize()	onmoveend
offsetTop	releaseCapture()	onmovestart
offsetWidth	removeAttribute()	onpaste
outerHTML	removeAttributeNode()	onpropertychange
outerText	removeAttributeNS()	onreadystatechange
ownerDocument	removeBehavior()	onresize
parentElement	removeChild()	onresizeend
parentNode	removeEventListener()	onresizestart
parentTextEdit	removeExpression()	onrowenter
prefix	removeNode()	onrowexit
previousSibling	replaceAdjacentText()	onrowsdelete
readyState	replaceChild()	onrowsinserted
recordNumber	replaceNode()	onscroll
runtimeStyle	scrollIntoView()	onselectstart
scopeName	setActive()	
scrollHeight	setAttribute()	
scrollLeft	setAttributeNode()	
scrollTop	setAttributeNodeNS()	
scrollWidth	setAttributeNS()	
sourceIndex	setCapture()	
style	setExpression()	
tabIndex	setUserData()	
tagName	swapNode()	
tagUrn	tags()	
textContent	toString()	
title	urns()	
uniqueID		
unselectable		
width		

Syntax

To access element properties or methods, use this:

```
(IE4+)     [document.all.]objectID.property | method([parameters])
(IE5+/W3C) document.getElementById(objectID).property | method([parameters])
```

> **NOTE** It's important to note that unless you have the specific need of supporting IE4, which is highly unlikely at this point in time, you should rely solely on the latter approach of referencing element properties and methods via the getElementById() method.

About these objects

All objects listed in Table 15-1 are document object model (DOM) representations of HTML elements that influence either the font style or the context of some HTML content. The large set of properties, methods, and event handlers associated with these objects also applies to virtually every other DOM object that represents an HTML element. Discussions about object details in this chapter apply to dozens of other objects described in succeeding chapters of this reference section.

Properties

accessKey

Value: One-character string   Read/Write
Compatibility: WinIE4+, MacIE4+, NN7+, Moz+, Safari+

For many elements, you can specify a keyboard character (letter, numeral, or punctuation symbol) that — when typed as an Alt+key combination (on the Win32 OS platform), a Ctrl+key combination (on the MacOS), or a Shift+Esc+key combination (on Opera) — brings focus to that element. An element that has focus is the one that is set to respond to keyboard activity. If the newly focused element is out of view in the document's current scroll position, the document is scrolled to bring that focused element into view (also see the scrollIntoView() method). The character you specify can be an uppercase or lowercase value, but these values are not case sensitive. If you assign the same letter to more than one element, the user can cycle through all elements associated with that accessKey value.

Internet Explorer gives some added powers to the accessKey property in some cases. For example, if you assign an accessKey value to a label element object, the focus is handed to the form element associated with that label. Also, when elements such as buttons have focus, pressing the spacebar acts the same as clicking the element with a mouse.

Exercise some judgment in selecting characters for accessKey values. If you assign a letter that is normally used to access one of the Windows version browser's built-in menus (for example, Alt+F for the File menu), that accessKey setting overrides the browser's normal behavior. To users who rely on keyboard access to menus, your control over that key combination can be disconcerting.

Example

Listing 15-1 shows an example of how to use the accessKey property to manipulate the keyboard interface for navigating a web page. When you load the script in Listing 15-1, adjust the height of the browser window so that you can see nothing below the second dividing rule. Enter any character in the Settings portion of the page and press Enter. (The Enter key may cause your computer to beep.) Then hold down the Alt (Windows) or Ctrl (Mac) key while pressing the same keyboard key. The element from below the second divider should come into view.

*elementObject.***accessKey**

> **NOTE** The property assignment event handling technique employed throughout the code in this chapter and much of the book is a deliberate simplification to make the code more readable. It is generally better to use the more modern approach of binding events using the `addEventListener()` (NN6+/Moz/W3C) or `attachEvent()` (IE5+) method. A modern cross-browser event handling technique is explained in detail in Chapter 25.

LISTING 15-1

Controlling the accessKey Property

```html
<html>
  <head>
    <title>accessKey Property</title>
    <script type="text/javascript">
    function assignKey(type, elem) {
      if (window.event.keyCode == 13) {
        switch (type) {
          case "button":
            document.forms["output"].access1.accessKey = elem.value;
            break;
          case "text":
            document.forms["output"].access2.accessKey = elem.value;
            break;
          case "table":
            document.getElementById("myTable").accessKey = elem.value;
        }
        return false;
      }
    }
    </script>
  </head>
  <body>
    <h1>accessKey Property Lab</h1>
    <hr />
    Settings:<br />
    <form name="input">
      Assign an accessKey value to the Button below and press Return: <input
      type="text" size="2" maxlength="1"
      onkeypress="return assignKey('button', this)" /><br />
       Assign an accessKey value to the Text Box below and press Return:
      <input type="text" size="2" maxlength="1"
      onkeypress="return assignKey('text', this)" /><br />
       Assign an accessKey value to the Table below (IE5.5+ only) and press
      Return: <input type="text" size="2" maxlength="1"
      onkeypress="return assignKey('table', this)" />
    </form>
    <br />
     Then press Alt (Windows) or Control (Mac) + the key.<br />
     <em>Size the browser window to view nothing lower than this line.</em>
    <hr />
```

```
<form name="output" onsubmit="return false">
  <input type="button" name="access1" value="Standard Button" /> <input
  type="text" name="access2" />
</form>
<table id="myTable" cellpadding="10" border="2">
  <tr>
    <th>Quantity</th>
    <th>Description</th>
    <th>Price</th>
  </tr>
  <tbody bgcolor="red">
    <tr>
      <td width="100">4</td>
      <td>Primary Widget</td>
      <td>$14.96</td>
    </tr>
    <tr>
      <td>10</td>
      <td>Secondary Widget</td>
      <td>$114.96</td>
    </tr>
  </tbody>
</table>
</body>
</html>
```

Related Item: scrollIntoView() method

all[]

Value: Array of nested element objects   Read-Only
Compatibility: WinIE4+, MacIE4+, NN-, Moz-, Safari-

Exclusive to Internet Explorer, the all property is a collection (array) of every HTML element and (in IE5+) XML tag within the scope of the current object. Items in this array appear in source-code order, and the array is oblivious to element containment among the items. For HTML element containers, the source-code order is dependent on the position of the start tag for the element; end tags are not counted. But for XML tags, end tags appear as separate entries in the array.

Every document.all collection contains objects for the html, head, title, and body element objects even if the actual HTML source code omits the tags. The object model creates these objects for every document that is loaded into a window or frame. Although the document.all reference may be the most common usage, the all property is available for any container element. For example, document.forms[0].all exposes all elements defined within the first form of a page.

You can access any element that has an identifier assigned to its id attribute by that identifier in string form (as well as by index integer). Rather than use the performance-costly eval() function to convert a string to an object reference, use the string value of the name as an array index value:

```
var paragraph = document.all["myP"];
```

Internet Explorer enables you to use either square brackets or parentheses for single collection index values. Thus, the following two examples evaluate identically:

```
var paragraph = document.all["myP"];
var paragraph = document.all("myP");
```

In the rare case that two or more elements within the all collection have the same ID, the syntax for the string index value returns a collection of just those identically named elements. But you can use a second argument (in parentheses) to signify the integer of the initial collection and thus single out a specific instance of that named element:

```
var secondRadio = document.all("group0",1);
```

As a more readable alternative, you can use the item() method (described later in this chapter) to access the same kinds of items within a collection:

```
var secondRadio = document.all.item("group0",1);
```

Also see the tags() method (later in this chapter) as a way to extract a set of elements from an all collection that matches a specific tag name.

Although a few non-IE browsers support the all collection, you should strongly consider using the document.getElementById() method described in Chapter 18, which is the official W3C and cross-browser approach for referencing elements. The document.getElementById() method is supported in IE5+.

Example

Use The Evaluator (see Chapter 13) to experiment with the all collection. Enter the following statements one at a time in the lower text box, and review the results in the text area for each:

```
document.all
myTable.all
myP.all
```

If you encounter a numbered element within a collection, you can explore that element to see which tag is associated with it. For example, if one of the results for the document.all collection says document.all.8=[object], enter the following statement in the topmost text box:

```
document.all[8].tagName
```

Related Items: item(), tags(), document.getElementById() methods

attributes[]

Value: Array of attribute object references   Read-Only
Compatibility: WinIE5+, MacIE5+, NN6+, Moz+, Safari+

The attributes property consists of an array of attributes specified for an element. In IE5+, the attributes array contains an entry for every possible property that the browser has defined for its elements — even if the attribute is not set explicitly in the HTML tag. Also, any attributes that you add later via script facilities such as the setAttribute() method are not reflected in the attributes array. In other words, the IE5+ attributes array is fixed, using default values for all properties except those that you explicitly set as attributes in the HTML tag.

Mozilla browsers' attributes property returns an array that is a named node map (in W3C DOM terminology) — an object that has its own properties and methods to read and write attribute values. For example, you can use the getNamedItem(attrName) and item(index) methods on the array returned from the attributes property to access individual attribute objects via W3C DOM syntax.

IE5+ and Mozilla have different ideas about what an attribute object should be. Table 15-2 shows the variety of properties of an attribute object as defined by the two object models. The larger set of properties in Mozilla reveals its dependence on the W3C DOM node inheritance model discussed in Chapter 14.

TABLE 15-2

Attribute Object Properties

Property	IE5+	Moz	Description
attributes	No	Yes	Array of nested attribute objects (null)
childNodes	No	Yes	Child node array
firstChild	No	Yes	First child node
lastChild	No	Yes	Last child node
localName	No	Yes	Name within current namespace
name	No	Yes	Attribute name
nameSpaceURI	No	Yes	XML namespace URI
nextSibling	No	Yes	Next sibling node
nodeName	Yes	Yes	Attribute name
nodeType	No	Yes	Node type (2)
nodeValue	Yes	Yes	Value assigned to attribute
ownerDocument	No	Yes	Document object reference
ownerElement	No	Yes	Element node reference
parentNode	No	Yes	Parent node reference
prefix	No	Yes	XML namespace prefix
previousSibling	No	Yes	Previous sibling node
specified	Yes	Yes	Whether attribute is explicitly specified (Boolean)
value	No	Yes	Value assigned to attribute

The most helpful property of an attribute object is the Boolean specified property. In IE, this lets you know whether the attribute is explicitly specified in the element's tag. Because Mozilla returns only explicitly specified attributes in the attributes array, the value in Mozilla is always true. Most of the time, however, you'll probably use an element object's getAttribute() and setAttribute() methods to read and write attribute values.

Example

Use The Evaluator (see Chapter 13) to examine the values of the attributes array for some of the elements in that document. Enter each of the following expressions in the bottom text box, and see the array contents in the Results text area for each:

```
document.body.attributes
document.getElementById("myP").attributes
document.getElementById("myTable").attributes
```

If you have both IE5+ and a W3C DOM–compatible browser, compare the results you get for each of these expressions. To view the properties of a single attribute in WinIE5+ by accessing the `attributes` array, enter the following statement in the bottom text box:

```
document.getElementById("myP").attributes["class"]
```

For W3C browsers, IE6+, and MacIE5, use the W3C DOM syntax:

```
document.getElementById("myP").attributes.getNamedItem("class")
```

Related Items: `getAttribute()`, `mergeAttributes()`, `removeAttribute()`, `setAttribute()` methods

baseURI

Value: Full URI string   Read-Only
Compatibility: WinIE-, MacIE-, NN6+, Moz+, Safari-

This property reveals the full path to the source from which the element was served. The property is handy in applications that import XML data, in which case the source of an XML element is likely different from the HTML page in which it is being processed.

behaviorUrns[]

Value: Array of behavior URN strings   Read-Only
Compatibility: WinIE5+, MacIE-, NN-, Moz-, Safari-

The Internet Explorer `behaviorUrns` property is designed to provide a list of addresses, in the form of *URNs (Uniform Resource Names),* of all behaviors assigned to the current object. If there are no behaviors, the array has a length of zero. In practice, however, IE5+ always returns an array of empty strings. Perhaps the potential exposure of URNs by script was deemed to be a privacy risk.

Related Item: `urns()` method

canHaveChildren

Value: Boolean   Read-Only
Compatibility: WinIE5+, MacIE-, NN-, Moz-, Safari-

Useful in some dynamic content situations, the `canHaveChildren` property reveals whether a particular element is capable of containing a child (nested) element. Most elements that have start and end tags (particularly the generic elements covered in this chapter) can contain nested elements. A nested element is referred to as a *child* of its parent container.

Example

Listing 15-2 shows an example of how to use the `canHaveChildren` property to visually identify elements on a page that can have nested elements. This example uses color to demonstrate the difference between an element that can have children and one that cannot. The first button sets the `color` style property of every visible element on the page to red. Thus, elements (including the normally non-childbearing ones such as `hr` and `input`) are affected by the color change. But if you reset the page and click the largest button, only those elements that can contain nested elements receive the color change.

LISTING 15-2

Reading the canHaveChildren Property

```html
<html>
    <head>
        <title>canHaveChildren Property</title>
        <script type="text/javascript">
        function colorAll() {
            var elems = document.getElementsByTagName("*");
            for (var i = 0; i < elems.length; i++) {
                elems[i].style.color = "red";
            }
        }

        function colorChildBearing() {
            var elems = document.getElementsByTagName("*");
            for (var i = 0; i < elems.length; i++) {
                if (elems[i].canHaveChildren) {
                    elems[i].style.color = "red";
                }
            }
        }
        </script>
    </head>
    <body>
        <h1>canHaveChildren Property Lab</h1>
        <hr />
        <form name="input">
            <input type="button" value="Color All Elements"
            onclick="colorAll()" /><br />
             <input type="button" value="Reset" onclick="history.go(0)" /><br />
             <input type="button"
            value="Color Only Elements That Can Have Children"
            onclick="colorChildBearing()" />
        </form>
        <br />
        <hr />
        <form name="output">
            <input type="checkbox" checked="checked" />Your basic checkbox <input
            type="text" name="access2" value="Some textbox text." />
        </form>
        <table id="myTable" cellpadding="10" border="2">
            <tr>
                <th>Quantity</th>
                <th>Description</th>
                <th>Price</th>
            </tr>
            <tbody>
                <tr>
                    <td width="100">4</td>
```

continued

LISTING 15-2   *(continued)*

```
            <td>Primary Widget</td>
            <td>$14.96</td>
         </tr>
         <tr>
            <td>10</td>
            <td>Secondary Widget</td>
            <td>$114.96</td>
         </tr>
      </tbody>
   </table>
  </body>
</html>
```

Related Items: `childNodes`, `firstChild`, `lastChild`, `parentElement`, `parentNode` properties; `appendChild()`, `hasChildNodes()`, `removeChild()` methods.

canHaveHTML

Value: Boolean   Read-Only and Read/Write
Compatibility: WinIE5+, MacIE-, NN-, Moz-, Safari-

Not all HTML elements are containers of HTML content. The `canHaveHTML` property lets scripts find out whether a particular object can accept HTML content, such as for insertion or replacement by object methods. The value for a `p` element, for example, is `true`. The value for a `br` element is `false`. The property is read-only for all elements except HTML Components, in which case it is read/write.

Example

Use The Evaluator (see Chapter 13) in WinIE5+ to experiment with the `canHaveHTML` property. Enter the following statements in the top text box, and observe the results:

```
document.getElementById("input").canHaveHTML
document.getElementById("myP").canHaveHTML
```

The first statement returns `false` because an `input` element (the top text box, in this case) cannot have nested HTML. But the `myP` element is a `p` element that gladly accepts HTML content.

Related Items: `appendChild()`, `insertAdjacentHTML()`, `insertBefore()` methods

childNodes[]

Value: Array of node objects   Read-Only
Compatibility: WinIE5+, MacIE5+, NN6+, Moz+, Safari+

The `childNodes` property consists of an array of node objects contained by the current object. Note that child nodes consist of both element objects and text nodes. Therefore, depending on the content of the current object, the number of `childNodes` and children collections may differ.

> **CAUTION** If you use the `childNodes` array in a `for` loop that iterates through a sequence of HTML (or XML) elements, watch out for the possibility that the browser treats source-code whitespace (blank lines between elements and even simple carriage returns between elements) as text nodes. This potential problem affects MacIE5 and Mozilla. If present, these extra text nodes occur primarily surrounding block elements.

Most looping activity through the `childNodes` array aims to examine, count, or modify element nodes within the collection. If that is your script's goal, test each node returned by the `childNodes` array, and verify that the `nodeType` property is 1 (element) before processing that node; otherwise, skip the node. The skeletal structure of such a loop follows:

```
for (var i = 0; i < myElem.childNodes.length; i++) {
    if (myElem.childNodes[i].nodeType == 1) {
        statements to work on element node i
    }
}
```

The presence of these phantom text nodes also impacts the nodes referenced by the `firstChild` and `lastChild` properties, described later in this chapter.

Example

Listing 15-3 contains an example of how you might code a function that walks the child nodes of a given node. The `walkChildNodes()` function shown in the listing accumulates and returns a hierarchical list of child nodes from the point of view of the document's HTML element (the default) or any element whose ID you pass as a string parameter. This function is embedded in The Evaluator so that you can inspect the child node hierarchy of that page or (when using `evaluator.js` for debugging as described in Chapter 45 on the CD-ROM) the node hierarchy within any page you have under construction. Try it out in The Evaluator by entering the following statements in the top text box:

```
walkChildNodes()
walkChildNodes(document.getElementById("myP"))
```

The results of this function show the nesting relationships among all child nodes within the scope of the initial object. It also shows the act of drilling down to further `childNodes` collections until all child nodes are exposed and catalogued. Text nodes are labeled accordingly. The first 15 characters of the actual text are placed in the results to help you identify the nodes when you compare the results against your HTML source code.

LISTING 15-3

Collecting Child Nodes

```
function walkChildNodes(objRef, n) {
    var obj;
    if (objRef) {
        if (typeof objRef == "string") {
            obj = document.getElementById(objRef);
        } else {
            obj = objRef;
        }
```

continued

LISTING 15-3 *(continued)*

```
    } else {
        obj = (document.body.parentElement) ?
            document.body.parentElement : document.body.parentNode;
    }
    var output = "";
    var indent = "";
    var i, group, txt;
    if (n) {
        for (i = 0; i < n; i++) {
            indent += "+---";
        }
    } else {
        n = 0;
        output += "Child Nodes of <" + obj.tagName;
        output += ">\n=====================\n";
    }
    group = obj.childNodes;
    for (i = 0; i < group.length; i++) {
        output += indent;
        switch (group[i].nodeType) {
            case 1:
                output += "<" + group[i].tagName;
                output += (group[i].id) ? " ID=" + group[i].id : "";
                output += (group[i].name) ? " NAME=" + group[i].name : "";
                output += ">\n";
                break;
            case 3:
                txt = group[i].nodeValue.substr(0,15);
                output += "[Text:\"" + txt.replace(/[\r\n]/g,"<cr>");
                if (group[i].nodeValue.length > 15) {
                    output += "...";
                }
                output += "\"]\n";
                break;
            case 8:
                output += "[!COMMENT!]\n";
                break;
            default:
                output += "[Node Type = " + group[i].nodeType + "]\n";
        }
        if (group[i].childNodes.length > 0) {
            output += walkChildNodes(group[i], n+1);
        }
    }
    return output;
}
```

Related Items: nodeName, nodeType, nodeValue, parentNode properties; cloneNode(), hasChildNodes(), removeNode(), replaceNode(), swapNode() methods

children

Value: Array of element objects   Read-Only
Compatibility: WinIE4+, MacIE4+, NN-, Moz-, Safari 1.2+

The children property consists of an array of element objects contained by the current object. Unlike the childNodes property, children does not take into account text nodes, but focuses strictly on the HTML (and XML) element containment hierarchy from the point of view of the current object. Also unlike the childNodes property, the children property works only in Internet Explorer and Safari 1.2+. Children exposed to the current object are immediate children only. If you want to get all element objects nested within the current object (regardless of how deeply nested they are), use the all collection instead.

Example

Listing 15-4 shows how you can use the children property to walk the child nodes of a given node. This function accumulates and returns a hierarchical list of child elements from the point of view of the document's HTML element (the default) or any element whose ID you pass as a string parameter. This function is embedded in The Evaluator so that you can inspect the parent–child hierarchy of that page or (when using evaluator.js for debugging as described in Chapter 45 on the CD-ROM) the element hierarchy within any page you have under construction. Try it out in The Evaluator by entering the following statements in the top text box:

```
walkChildren()
walkChildren("myTable")
```

Notice in this example that the walkChildren() function is called with the name of an element instead of a call to document.getElementId(). This reveals the flexibility of the walkChildren() function and how it can operate on either an object or the name of an object (element). The walkChildNodes() function in Listing 15-3 offers the same flexibility.

The results of the walkChildren() function show the nesting relationships among all parent and child elements within the scope of the initial object. It also shows the act of drilling down to further children collections until all child elements are exposed and cataloged. The element tags also display their id and/or name attribute values if any are assigned to the elements in the HTML source code.

LISTING 15-4

Collecting Child Elements

```
function walkChildren(objRef, n) {
  var obj;
  if (objRef) {
    if (typeof objRef == "string") {
      obj = document.getElementById(objRef);
    } else {
      obj = objRef;
    }
  } else {
    obj = document.body.parentElement;
```

continued

LISTING 15-4 *(continued)*

```
   }
   var output = "";
   var indent = "";
   var i, group;
   if (n) {
      for (i = 0; i < n; i++) {
         indent += "+---";
      }
   } else {
      n = 0;
      output += "Children of <" + obj.tagName;
      output += ">\n=====================\n";
   }
   group = obj.children;
   for (i = 0; i < group.length; i++) {
      output += indent + "<" + group[i].tagName;
      output += (group[i].id) ? " ID=" + group[i].id : "";
      output += (group[i].name) ? " NAME=" + group[i].name : "";
      output += ">\n";
      if (group[i].children.length > 0) {
         output += walkChildren(group[i], n+1);
      }
   }
   return output;
}
```

Related Items: canHaveChildren, firstChild, lastChild, parentElement properties; appendChild(), removeChild(), replaceChild() methods

cite

Value: URL string   Read/Write
Compatibility: WinIE6+, MacIE-, NN6+, Moz+, Safari+

The cite property contains a URL that serves as a reference to the source of an element, as in the author of a quote. The property is intended to apply to only the blockquote, q, del, and ins element objects, but IE supports it in a wider range of text content objects. This may or may not be a mistake, so it's probably not a safe bet to use the property outside its intended elements.

className

Value: String   Read/Write
Compatibility: WinIE4+, MacIE4+, NN6+, Moz+, Safari+

A *class name* is an identifier that is assigned to the class attribute of an element. To associate a cascading style sheets (CSS) rule with several elements in a document, assign the same identifier to the class attributes of those elements, and use that identifier (preceded by a period) as the CSS rule's selector. An element's className property enables the application of different CSS rules to that element under script control. Listing 15-5 shows an example of such a script.

Example

The style of an element toggles between on and off in Listing 15-5 by virtue of setting the element's className property alternatively to an existing style sheet class selector name and an empty string. When you set the className to an empty string, the default behavior of the h1 element governs the display of the first header. A click of the button forces the style sheet rule to override the default behavior in the first h1 element.

LISTING 15-5

Working with the className Property

```html
<html>
    <head>
        <title>className Property</title>
        <style type="text/css">
        .special {font-size:16pt; color:red}
        </style>
        <script type="text/javascript">
        function toggleSpecialStyle(elemID) {
            var elem = (document.all) ? document.all(elemID) :
                document.getElementById(elemID);
            if (elem.className == "") {
                elem.className = "special";
            } else {
                elem.className = "";
            }
        }
        </script>
    </head>
    <body>
        <h1>className Property Lab</h1>
        <hr />
        <form name="input">
            <input type="button" value="Toggle Class Name"
            onclick="toggleSpecialStyle('head1')" />
        </form>
        <br />

        <h1 id="head1">ARTICLE I</h1>
        <p>Congress shall make no law respecting an establishment of religion, or
            prohibiting the free exercise thereof; or abridging the freedom of
            speech, or of the press; or the right of the people peaceably to
            assemble, and to petition the government for a redress of
            grievances.</p>
        <h1>ARTICLE II</h1>
        <p>A well regulated militia, being necessary to the security of a free
            state, the right of the people to keep and bear arms, shall not be
            infringed.</p>
    </body>
</html>
```

You can also create multiple versions of a style rule with different class selector identifiers and apply them at will to a given element.

Related Items: rule, stylesheet objects (Chapter 26); id property

clientHeight
clientWidth

Value: Integer   Read-Only
Compatibility: WinIE4+, MacIE4+, NN7, Moz1.0.1+, Safari+

These two properties by and large reveal the pixel height and width of the content within an element whose style sheet rule includes height and width settings. In theory, these measures do not take into account any margins, borders, or padding that you add to an element by way of style sheets. In practice, however, different combinations of borders, margins, and padding influence these values in unexpected ways. One of the more reliable applications of the clientHeight property enables you to discover, for example, where the text of an overflowing element ends. To read the rendered dimensions of an element, you are better served across browsers with the offsetHeight and offsetWidth properties.

For the document.body object, the clientHeight and clientWidth properties return the inside height and width of the window or frame (plus or minus a couple of pixels). These take the place of desirable, but nonexistent, window properties in IE.

Unlike earlier versions, Internet Explorer 5+ expanded the number of objects that employ these properties to include virtually all objects that represent HTML elements. Values for these properties in Mozilla-based browsers are zero except for document.body, which measures the browser's current content area.

Example

Listing 15-6 for IE includes an example of how to size content dynamically on a page based on the client-area width and height. This example calls upon the clientHeight and clientWidth properties of a div element that contains a paragraph element. Only the width of the div element is specified in its style sheet rule, which means that the paragraph's text wraps inside that width and extends as deeply as necessary to show the entire paragraph. The clientHeight property describes that depth. The clientHeight property then calculates where a logo image should be positioned immediately after div, regardless of the length of the text. As a bonus, the clientWidth property helps the script center the image horizontally with respect to the paragraph's text.

LISTING 15-6

Using clientHeight and clientWidth Properties

```
<html>
  <head>
    <title>clientHeight and clientWidth Properties</title>
    <script type="text/javascript">
    function showLogo() {
      var paragraphW = document.getElementById("myDIV").clientWidth;
      var paragraphH = document.getElementById("myDIV").clientHeight;
      // correct for Windows/Mac discrepancies
      var paragraphTop = (document.getElementById("myDIV").clientTop) ?
        document.getElementById("myDIV").clientTop :
        document.getElementById("myDIV").offsetTop;
```

```
    var logoW = document.getElementById("logo").style.pixelWidth;
    // center logo horizontally against paragraph
    document.getElementById("logo").style.pixelLeft =
        (paragraphW-logoW) / 2;
    // position image immediately below end of paragraph
    document.getElementById("logo").style.pixelTop =
        paragraphTop + paragraphH;
    document.getElementById("logo").style.visibility = "visible";
    }
    </script>
</head>
<body>
    <button onclick="showLogo()">Position and Show Logo Art</button>
    <div id="logo" style="position:absolute; width:120px; visibility:hidden">
        <img all="image" src="logo.gif" />
    </div>
    <div id="myDIV" style="width:200px">
        <p>Lorem ipsum dolor sit amet, consectetaur adipisicing elit, sed do
            eiusmod tempor incididunt ut labore et dolore magna aliqua. Ut enim
            adminim veniam, quis nostrud exercitation ullamco laboris nisi ut
            aliquip ex ea commodo consequat. Duis aute irure dolor in
            reprehenderit involuptate velit esse cillum dolore eu fugiat nulla
            pariatur. Excepteur sint occaecat cupidatat non proident.</p>
    </div>
</body>
</html>
```

To assist in the vertical positioning of the logo, the offsetTop property of the div object provides the position of the start of the div with respect to its outer container (the body). Unfortunately, MacIE uses the clientTop property to obtain the desired dimension. That measure (assigned to the paragraphTop variable), plus the clientHeight of the div, provides the top coordinate of the image.

Related Items: offsetHeight, offsetWidth properties

clientLeft
clientTop

Value: Integer   Read-Only
Compatibility: WinIE4+, MacIE4+, NN-, Moz-, Safari-

The purpose and names of the clientLeft and clientTop properties are confusing at best. Unlike the clientHeight and clientWidth properties, which apply to the content of an element, the clientLeft and clientTop properties return essentially no more information than the thickness of a border around an element — provided that the element is positioned. If you do not specify a border or do not position the element, the values are zero (although the document.body object can show a couple of pixels in each direction without explicit settings). If you are trying to read the left and top coordinate positions of an element, the offsetLeft and offsetTop properties are more valuable in WinIE; as shown in Listing 15-6, however, the clientTop property returns a suitable value in MacIE. Virtually all elements have the clientLeft and clientTop properties in IE5+, whereas support in MacIE is less consistent.

Related Items: offsetLeft, offsetTop properties

contentEditable

Value: Boolean
Compatibility: WinIE5.5+, MacIE-, NN-, Moz-, Safari 1.2+

Read/Write

IE5.5 introduced the concept of editable HTML content on a page. Element tags can include a contenteditable attribute whose value is echoed via the contentEditable property of the element. The default value for this property is inherit, which means that the property inherits whatever setting this property has in the hierarchy of HTML containers outward to the body. If you set the contentEditable property to true, that element and all nested elements set to inherit the value become editable; conversely, a setting of false turns off the option to edit the content. Safari automatically provides a visual cue for editable elements by giving an editable element a glowing blue border.

Example

Listing 15-7 demonstrates how to use the contentEditable property to create a very simple poetry editor. When you click the button of a freshly loaded page, the toggleEdit() function captures the opposite of the current editable state via the isContentEditable property of the div that is subject to edit. You switch on editing for that element in the next statement by assigning the new value to the contentEditable property of the div. For added impact, turn the text of the div to red to provide additional user feedback about what is editable on the page. You can also switch the button label to one that indicates the action invoked by the next click of that button.

LISTING 15-7

Using the contentEditable Property

```
<html>
  <head>
    <style type="text/css">
    .normal {color: black}
    .editing {color: red}
    </style>
    <script type="text/javascript">
    function toggleEdit() {
       var newState = !editableText.isContentEditable;
       editableText.contentEditable = newState;
       editableText.className = (newState) ? "editing" : "normal";
       editBtn.innerText = (newState) ? "Disable Editing" : "Enable Editing";
    }
    </script>
    <title>
    </title>
  </head>
  <body>
    <h1>Poetry Editor</h1>
    <hr />
    <p>Turn on editing to modify the following text:</p>
    <div id="noneditableText">
       Roses are red,<br />
       Violets are blue.
```

```
    </div>
    <div id="editableText">
        Line 3,<br />
        Line 4.
    </div>
    <p><button id="editBtn" onclick="toggleEdit()"
        onfocus="this.blur()">Enable Editing</button></p>
    </body>
</html>
```

Related Item: isContentEditable property

currentStyle

Value: style object   Read-Only
Compatibility: WinIE5+, MacIE5+, NN-, Moz-, Safari-

Every element has style attributes applied to it, even if those attributes are the browser's default settings. Because an element's style object reflects only those properties whose corresponding attributes are explicitly set via CSS statements, you cannot use the style property of an element object to view default style settings applied to an element. That's where the currentStyle property comes in.

This property returns a read-only style object that contains values for every possible style property applicable to the element. If a style property is explicitly set via CSS statement or script adjustment, the current reading for that property is also available here. Thus, a script can inquire about any property to determine whether it should change to meet some scripted design goal. For example, if you surround some text with an <em> tag, the browser by default turns that text into an italic font style. This setting is not reflected in the element's style object (fontStyle property) because the italic setting was not set via CSS; by contrast, the element object's currentStyle.fontStyle property reveals the true, current fontStyle property of the element as italic.

Example

To change a style property setting, access it via the element's style object. Use The Evaluator (see Chapter 13) to compare the properties of the currentStyle and style objects of an element. For example, an unmodified copy of The Evaluator contains an em element whose ID is "myEM". Enter document.getElementById("myEM").style in the bottom property listing text box and press Enter. Notice that most of the property values are empty. Now enter document.getElementById("myEM").currentStyle in the property listing text box and press Enter. Every property has a value associated with it.

Related Items: runtimeStyle, style objects (Chapter 26); window.getComputedStyle() for W3C DOM browsers (Chapter 16)

dateTime

Value: Date string   Read-Only
Compatibility: WinIE6+, MacIE-, NN6+, Moz+, Safari-

The dateTime property contains a date/time value that is used to establish a timestamp for an element. Similar to the cite property, the dateTime property is intended to apply to a lesser number of element objects (del and ins) than is actually supported in IE. This may or may not be a mistake, so it's probably not a safe bet to use the property outside its intended elements.

```
dataFld
dataFormatAs
dataSrc
```
Value: String   Read/Write
Compatibility: WinIE4+, MacIE5, NN-, Moz-, Safari-

The dataFld, dataFormatAs, and dataSrc properties (along with more element-specific properties such as dataPageSize and recordNumber) are part of the Internet Explorer data-binding facilities based on ActiveX controls. The Win32 versions of IE4 and later have several ActiveX objects built into the browsers that facilitate direct communication between a web page and a data source. Data sources include text files, XML data, HTML data, and external databases (MacIE supports text files only). Data binding is a very large topic, much of which extends more to discussions about Microsoft Data Source Objects (DSOs), ODBC, and JDBC — subjects well beyond the scope of this book. But data binding is a powerful tool and can be of use even if you are not a database guru. Therefore, this discussion of the three primary properties — dataFld, dataFormatAs, and dataSrc — briefly covers data binding through Microsoft's *Tabular Data Control DSO*. This allows any page to access, sort, display, and filter (but not update) data downloaded into a web page from an external text file (commonly, comma- or tab-delimited data).

You can load data from an external text file into a document with the help of the *Tabular Data Control* (TDC). You retrieve the data by specifying the TDC object within an <object> tag set and specifying additional parameters, such as the URL of the text file and field delimiter characters. The object element can go anywhere within the body of your document. (I tend to put it at the bottom of the code so that all normal page rendering happens before the control loads.) Retrieving the data simply brings it into the browser and does not, on its own, render the data on the page.

If you haven't worked with embedded objects in IE, the classid attribute value might seem a bit strange. The most perplexing part to some is the long value of numeric data signifying the *Globally Unique Identifier* (GUID) for the object, which is IE's way of uniquely identifying objects. You must enter this value exactly as shown in the following example for the proper ActiveX TDC to run. The HTML syntax for this object is as follows:

```
<object id="objName" classid="clsid:333C7BC4-460F-11D0-BC04-0080C7055A83">
    <param name="DataURL" value="URL">
    [additional optional parameters]
</object>
```

Table 15-3 lists the parameters available for the TDC. Only the DataURL parameter is required. Other parameters — such as FieldDelim, UseHeader, RowDelim, and EscapeChar — may be helpful, depending on the nature of the data source.

TABLE 15-3

Tabular Data Control Parameters

Parameter	Description
CharSet	Character set of the data source file. Default is latin1.
DataURL	URL of data source file (relative or absolute).
EscapeChar	Character used to escape delimiter characters that are part of the data. Default is empty. A common value is "\".

Parameter	Description
FieldDelim	Delimiter character between fields within a record. Default is comma (,). For a Tab character, use a value of 	.
Language	ISO language code of source data. Default is en-us.
TextQualifier	Optional character surrounding a field's data. Default is empty.
RowDelim	Delimiter character between records. Default is newline (NL).
UseHeader	Set to true if the first row of data in the file contains field names. Default is false.

The value you assign to the object element's id attribute is the identifier that your scripts use to communicate with the data after the page and data completely load. Therefore, you can have as many uniquely named TDCs loaded in your page as there are data source files you want to access at the same time.

The initial binding of the data to HTML elements usually comes when you assign values to the datasrc and datafld attributes of the elements. The datasrc attribute points to the dso identifier (matching the id attribute of the object element, preceded by a hash symbol), whereas the datafld attribute points to the name of the field whose data should be extracted. When you use data binding with an interactive element such as a table, multiple records are displayed in consecutive rows of the table (more about this in a moment).

Adjust the dataSrc and dataFld properties if you want the same HTML element (other than a table) to change the data that it displays. These properties apply to a subset of HTML elements that can be associated with external data: a, applet, body, button, div, frame, iframe, img, input (most types), label, marquee, object, param, select, span, and textarea objects.

In some cases, your data source may store chunks of HTML-formatted text for rendering inside an element. Unless directed otherwise, the browser renders a data source field as plain text — even if the content contains HTML formatting tags. But if you want the HTML to be observed during rendering, you can set the dataFormatAs property (or, more likely, the dataformatas attribute of the tag) to HTML. The default value is text.

Example

Listing 15-8 is a simple document that has two TDC objects associated with it. The external files are different formats of the U.S. Bill of Rights document. One file is a traditional, tab-delimited data file consisting of only two records. The first record is a tab-delimited sequence of field names (named "Article1", "Article2", and so on). The second record is a tab-delimited sequence of article content defined in HTML:

```
<h1>ARTICLE I</h1><p>Congress shall make...</p>
```

The second file is a raw-text file consisting of the full Bill of Rights with no HTML formatting attached.

When you load Listing 15-8, only the first article of the Bill of Rights appears in a blue-bordered box. Buttons enable you to navigate to the previous and next articles in the series. Because the data source is a traditional, tab-delimited file, the nextField() and prevField() functions calculate the name of the next source field and assign the new value to the dataFld property. All of the data is already in the browser after the page loads, so cycling through the records is as fast as the browser can reflow the page to accommodate the new content.

LISTING 15-8

Binding Data to a Page

```html
<html>
    <head>
        <title>Data Binding</title>
        <style type="text/css">
        #display {width:500px; border:10px ridge blue; padding:20px}
        .hiddenControl {display:none}
        </style>
        <script type="text/javascript">
        function nextField() {
            var elem = document.getElementById("display");
            var fieldName = elem.dataFld;
            var currFieldNum = parseInt(fieldName.substring(7,
                fieldName.length),10);
            currFieldNum = (currFieldNum == 10) ? 1 : ++currFieldNum;
            elem.dataFld = "Article" + currFieldNum;
        }
        function prevField() {
            var elem = document.getElementById("display");
            var fieldName = elem.dataFld;
            var currFieldNum = parseInt(fieldName.substring(7,
                fieldName.length),10);
            currFieldNum = (currFieldNum == 1) ? 10 : --currFieldNum;
            elem.dataFld = "Article" + currFieldNum;
        }

        function toggleComplete() {
            if (document.getElementById("buttonWrapper").className == "") {
                document.getElementById("display").dataSrc = "#rights_raw";
                document.getElementById("display").dataFld = "column1";
                document.getElementById("display").dataFormatAs = "text";
                document.getElementById("buttonWrapper").className =
                    "hiddenControl";
            } else {
                document.getElementById("display").dataSrc = "#rights_html";
                document.getElementById("display").dataFld = "Article1";
                document.getElementById("display").dataFormatAs = "HTML";
                document.getElementById("buttonWrapper").className = "";
            }
        }
        </script>
    </head>
    <body>
        <h1>U.S. Bill of Rights</h1>
        <form>
            <input type="button" value="Toggle Complete/Individual"
            onclick="toggleComplete()" /> <span id="buttonWrapper" class=""><input
            type="button" value="Prev" onclick="prevField()" /> <input
            type="button" value="Next" onclick="nextField()" /></span>
```

```
      </form>
      <div id="display" datasrc="#rights_html" datafld="Article1"
      dataformatas="HTML">
      </div>
      <object id="rights_html"
      classid="clsid:333C7BC4-460F-11D0-BC04-0080C7055A83">
          <param name="DataURL" value="Bill of Rights.txt" />
          <param name="UseHeader" value="True" />
          <param name="FieldDelim" value="&#09;" />
      </object> <object id="rights_raw"
      classid="clsid:333C7BC4-460F-11D0-BC04-0080C7055A83">
          <param name="DataURL" value="Bill of Rights (no format).txt" />
          <param name="FieldDelim" value="\" />
          <param name="RowDelim" value="\" />
      </object>
   </body>
</html>
```

Another button on the page enables you to switch between the initial piecemeal version of the document and the unformatted version in its entirety. To load the entire document as a single record, the `FieldDelim` and `RowDelim` parameters of the second `object` element eliminate their default values by replacing them with characters that don't appear in the document at all. And because the external file does not have a field name in the file, the default value (`column1` for the lone column in this document) is the data field. Thus, in the `toggleComplete()` function, the `dataSrc` property is changed to the desired `object` element ID; the `dataFld` property is set to the correct value for the data source; and the `dataFormatAs` property is changed to reflect the different intention of the source content (to be rendered as HTML or as plain text). When the display shows the entire document, you can hide the two radio buttons by assigning a `className` value to the `span` element that surrounds the buttons. The `className` value is the identifier of the class selector in the document's style sheet. When the `toggleComplete()` function resets the `className` property to empty, the default properties (normal inline display style) take hold.

One further example demonstrates the kind of power available to the TDC under script control. Listing 15-9 displays table data from a tab-delimited file of Academy Awards information. The data file has eight columns of data, and each column heading is treated as a field name: Year, Best Picture, Best Director, Best Director Film, Best Actress, Best Actress Film, Best Actor, and Best Actor Film. For the design of the page, only five fields from each record appear: Year, Film, Director, Actress, and Actor. Notice in the listing that the HTML for the table and its content is bound to the data source object and the fields within the data.

The dynamic part of this example is apparent in how you can sort and filter the data, after it is loaded into the browser, without further access to the original source data. The TDC object features `Sort` and `Filter` properties that enable you to act on the data currently loaded in the browser. The simplest kind of sorting indicates on which field (or fields, via a semicolon-delimited list of field names) the entire data set should be sorted. Leading the name of the sort field is either a plus (to indicate ascending) or minus (descending) symbol. After setting the `data` object's `Sort` property, invoke its `Reset()` method to tell the object to apply the new property. The data in the bound table is immediately redrawn to reflect any changes.

Similarly, you can tell a data collection to display records that meet specific criteria. In Listing 15-9, two select lists and a pair of radio buttons provide the interface to the `Filter` property's settings. For example, you can filter the output to display only those records in which the Best Picture was the same picture of the winning Best Actress's performance. Simple filter expressions are based on field names:

```
    dataObj.Filter = "Best Picture" = "Best Actress Film";
```

LISTING 15-9

Sorting Bound Data

```html
<html>
    <head>
        <title>Data Binding - Sorting</title>
        <script type="text/javascript">
        function sortByYear(type) {
            oscars.Sort = (type == "normal") ? "-Year" : "+Year";
            oscars.Reset();
        }
        function filterInCommon(form) {
            var filterExpr1 =
                form.filter1.options[form.filter1.selectedIndex].value;
            var filterExpr2 =
                form.filter2.options[form.filter2.selectedIndex].value;
            var operator = (form.operator[0].checked) ? "=" : "<>";
            var filterExpr = filterExpr1 + operator + filterExpr2;
            oscars.Filter = filterExpr;
            oscars.Reset();
        }
        </script>
    </head>
    <body>
        <h1>Academy Awards 1978-2005</h1>
        <form>
            <p>Sort list by year <a href="javascript:sortByYear('normal')">from
            newest to oldest</a> or <a
            href="javascript:sortByYear('reverse')">from oldest to
            newest</a>.</p>
            <p>Filter listings for records whose <select name="filter1"
            onchange="filterInCommon(this.form)">
                <option value="Best Picture">Best Picture</option>
                <option value="Best Director Film">Best Director's Film</option>
                <option value="Best Actress Film">Best Actress' Film</option>
                <option value="Best Actor Film">Best Actor's Film</option>
            </select> <input type="radio" name="operator" checked="checked"
            onclick="filterInCommon(this.form)" />is <input type="radio"
            name="operator" onclick="filterInCommon(this.form)" />is not
            <select name="filter2" onchange="filterInCommon(this.form)">
                <option value="Best Picture">Best Picture</option>
                <option value="Best Director Film">Best Director's Film</option>
                <option value="Best Actress Film">Best Actress' Film</option>
                <option value="Best Actor Film">Best Actor's Film</option>
            </select></p>
        </form>
        <table datasrc="#oscars" border="1" align="center">
            <thead style="background-color:yellow; text-align:center">
                <tr>
                    <td>Year</td>
                    <td>Film</td>
```

```
            <td>Director</td>
            <td>Actress</td>
            <td>Actor</td>
        </tr>
    </thead>
    <tr>
        <td><div id="col1" datafld="Year"></div></td>
        <td><div id="col2" datafld="Best Picture"></div></td>
        <td><div id="col3" datafld="Best Director"></div></td>
        <td><div id="col4" datafld="Best Actress"></div></td>
        <td><div id="col5" datafld="Best Actor"></div></td>
    </tr>
    </table>
    <object id="oscars" classid="clsid:333C7BC4-460F-11D0-BC04-0080C7055A83">
        <param name="DataURL" value="Academy Awards.txt" />
        <param name="UseHeader" value="True" />
        <param name="FieldDelim" value="&#09;" />
    </object>
    </body>
</html>
```

Related Items: `recordNumber`, `table.dataPageSize` properties

dir

Value: `"ltr" | "rtl"`   Read/Write
Compatibility: WinIE5+, MacIE5+, NN6+, Moz+, Safari+

The `dir` property (based on the `dir` attribute of virtually every text-oriented HTML element) controls whether an element's text is rendered left to right (the default) or right to left. By and large, this property (and HTML attribute) is necessary only when you need to override the default directionality of a language's character set as defined by the Unicode standard.

Example

Changing this property value in a standard U.S. version of a browser only makes the right margin the starting point for each new line of text (in other words, the characters are not rendered in reverse order). You can experiment with this in The Evaluator by entering the following statements in the expression evaluation field:

```
document.getElementById("myP").dir = "rtl"
```

Related Item: `lang` property

disabled

Value: Boolean   Read/Write
Compatibility: WinIE4+, MacIE4+, NN6+, Moz+, Safari+

Though only form elements have a `disabled` property in IE4 and IE5, this property is associated with every HTML element in IE5.5+. W3C DOM browsers apply the property only to form control and `style` element objects. Disabling an HTML element (like form elements) usually gives the element a dimmed look, indicating that it is not active. A disabled element does not receive any events. It also cannot receive focus, either manually or by script. But a user can still select and copy a disabled body text element.

elementObject.filters

> **NOTE** If you disable a form control element, the element's data is not submitted to the server with the rest of the form elements. If you need to keep a form control locked down but still submit it to the server, use the `form` element's `onsubmit` event handler to enable the form control right before the form is submitted.

Example

Use The Evaluator (see Chapter 13) to experiment with the `disabled` property on both form elements (IE4+ and W3C) and regular HTML elements (WinIE5.5+). For IE4+ and W3C browsers, see what happens when you disable the output text area by entering the following statement in the top text box:

```
document.forms[0].output.disabled = true
```

The text area is disabled for user entry, although you can still set the field's `value` property via script (which is how the `true` returned value got there).

If you have WinIE5.5+, disable the `myP` element by entering the following statement in the top text box:

```
document.getElementById("myP").disabled = true
```

The sample paragraph's text turns gray.

Related Item: `isDisabled` property

document

Value: document object   Read-Only
Compatibility: WinIE4+, MacIE4+, NN-, Moz-, Safari 1.2+

In the context of HTML element objects as exposed in IE4+/Safari 1.2+, the `document` property is a reference to the document that contains the object. Though it is unlikely that you will need to use this property, `document` may come in handy for complex scripts and script libraries that handle objects in a generic fashion and do not know the reference path to the document containing a particular object. You might need a reference to the document to inspect it for related objects. The W3C version of this property is `ownerDocument`.

Example

The following simplified function accepts a parameter that can be any object in a document hierarchy. The script finds out the reference of the object's containing document for further reference to other objects:

```
function getCompanionFormCount(obj) {
    var ownerDoc = obj.document;
    return ownerDoc.forms.length;
}
```

Because the `ownerDoc` variable contains a valid reference to a `document` object, the `return` statement uses that reference to return a typical property of the document object hierarchy.

Related Item: `ownerDocument` property

filters[]

Value: Array   Read-Only
Compatibility: WinIE4+, MacIE4+, NN-, Moz-, Safari-

Filters are IE-specific style sheet add-ons that offer a greater variety of font rendering (such as drop shadows) and transitions between hidden and visible elements. Each filter specification is a filter object. The filters property contains an array of filter objects defined for the current element. You can apply filters to the following set of elements: bdo, body, button, fieldset, img, input, marquee, rt, ruby, table, td, textarea, th, and positioned div and span elements. See Chapter 26 for details about style sheet filters.

Related Item: filter object.

firstChild
lastChild

Value: Node object reference   Read-Only
Compatibility: WinIE5+, MacIE5+, NN6+, Moz+, Safari+

W3C DOM-based DOMs are built around an architecture known as a *node map*. Each object defined by HTML is a node in the map. A node has relationships with other nodes in the document — relationships described in family terms of parents, siblings, and children.

A *child node* is an element that is contained by another element. The container is the parent of such a child. Just as an HTML element can contain any number of child elements, so can a parent object have zero or more children. A list of those children (returned as an array) can be read from an object by way of its childNodes property:

```
var nodeArray = document.getElementById("elementID").childNodes;
```

Though you can use this array (and its length property) to get a reference to the first or last child node, the firstChild and lastChild properties offer shortcuts to those positions. These are helpful when you wish to insert a new child before or after all of the others, and you need a reference point for the IE insertAdjacentElement() method or other method that adds elements to the document's node list.

Example

Listing 15-10 contains an example of how to use the firstChild and lastChild properties to access child nodes. These two properties come in handy in this example, which adds and replaces li elements to an existing ol element. You can enter any text you want to appear at the beginning or end of the list. Using the firstChild and lastChild properties simplifies access to the ends of the list. For the functions that replace child nodes, the example uses the replaceChild() method. Alternatively for IE4+, you can modify the innerText property of the objects returned by the firstChild or lastChild property. This example is especially interesting to watch when you add items to the list: The browser automatically renumbers items to fit the current state of the list.

CAUTION See the discussion of the childNodes property earlier in this chapter for details about the presence of phantom nodes in some browser versions. The problem may influence your use of the firstChild and lastChild properties.

NOTE As handy as it may be, in a strict W3C approach to JavaScript, you wouldn't use the innerHTML property because it isn't officially part of the W3C standard. However, it is often too powerful a convenience property to ignore, as much of the code throughout this book is a testament. The book does show the W3C node manipulation alternative to innerHTML in some examples. Refer to Chapter 18 for a thorough explanation and examples of the W3C alternative to innerHTML.

LISTING 15-10

Using firstChild and lastChild Properties

```
<html>
    <head>
        <title>firstChild and lastChild Properties</title>
        <script type="text/javascript">
        // helper function for prepend() and append()
        function makeNewLI(txt) {
            var newItem = document.createElement("li");
            newItem.innerHTML = txt;
            return newItem;
        }
        function prepend(form) {
            var newItem = makeNewLI(form.input.value);
            var firstLI = document.getElementById("myList").firstChild;
            document.getElementById("myList").insertBefore(newItem, firstLI);
        }
        function append(form) {
            var newItem = makeNewLI(form.input.value);
            var lastLI = document.getElementById("myList").lastChild;
            document.getElementById("myList").appendChild(newItem);
        }
        function replaceFirst(form) {
            var newItem = makeNewLI(form.input.value);
            var firstLI = document.getElementById("myList").firstChild;
            document.getElementById("myList").replaceChild(newItem, firstLI);
        }
        function replaceLast(form) {
            var newItem = makeNewLI(form.input.value);
            var lastLI = document.getElementById("myList").lastChild;
            document.getElementById("myList").replaceChild(newItem, lastLI);
        }
        </script>
    </head>
    <body>
        <h1>firstChild and lastChild Property Lab</h1>
        <hr />
        <form>
            <label>Enter some text to add to or replace in the OL
            element:</label><br />
            <input type="text" name="input" size="50" /><br />
            <input type="button" value="Insert at Top"
            onclick="prepend(this.form)" /> <input type="button"
            value="Append to Bottom" onclick="append(this.form)" /><br />
            <input type="button" value="Replace First Item"
            onclick="replaceFirst(this.form)" /> <input type="button"
            value="Replace Last Item" onclick="replaceLast(this.form)" />
        </form>
```

```
    <ol id="myList">
        <li>Initial Item 1</li>
        <li>Initial Item 2</li>
        <li>Initial Item 3</li>
        <li>Initial Item 4</li>
    </ol>
  </body>
</html>
```

Related Items: nextSibling, parentElement, parentNode, previousSibling properties; appendChild(), hasChildNodes(), removeChild(), removeNode(), replaceChild(), replaceNode() methods

height
width

Value: Integer or percentage string   Read/Write and Read-Only
Compatibility: WinIE4+, MacIE4+, NN4+, Moz+, Safari+

The height and width properties described here are not the identically named properties that belong to an element's style. Rather, these properties reflect the values normally assigned to height and width attributes of elements such as img, applet, table, and so on. As such, these properties are accessed directly from the object (for example, document.getElementById("myTable").width in IE4+) rather than through the style object (for example, document.getElementById("myDIV").style.width). Only elements for which the HTML 4.*x* standard provides height and width attributes have the corresponding properties.

Values for these properties are either integer pixel values (numbers or strings) or percentage values (strings only). If you need to perform some math on an existing percentage value, use the parseInt() function to extract the numeric value for use with math calculations. If an element's height and width attributes are set as percentage values, you can use the offsetHeight and offsetWidth properties in many modern browsers to get the rendered pixel dimensions.

Property values are read/write for the image object in most recent browser versions because you can resize an image object in IE4+ and Mozilla after the page loads. Properties are read/write for some other objects (such as the table object) — but not necessarily all others that support these properties.

In general, you cannot set the value of these properties to something less than is required to render the element. This is particularly true of a table. If you attempt to set the height value to less than the amount of pixels required to display the table as defined by its style settings, your changes have no effect (even though the property value retains its artificially low value). For other objects, however, you can set the size to anything you like, and the browser scales the content accordingly (images, for example). If you want to see only a segment of an element (in other words, to crop the element), use a style sheet to set the element's clipping region.

Example
The following example demonstrates how to use the width property by increasing the width of a table by 10 percent:

```
var tableW = parseInt(document.getElementById("myTable").width);
document.getElementById("myTable").width = (tableW * 1.1) + "%";
```

225

Because the initial setting for the `width` attribute of the `table` element is set as a percentage value, the script calculation extracts the number from the percentage width string value. In the second statement, the old number is increased by 10 percent and turned into a percentage string by appending the percentage symbol to the value. The resulting string value is assigned to the `width` property of the table.

Related Items: `clientHeight`, `clientWidth` properties; `style.height`, `style.width` properties

hideFocus

Value: Boolean   Read/Write
Compatibility: WinIE5.5+, MacIE-, NN-, Moz-, Safari-

In IE for Windows, button types of form controls and links display a dotted rectangle around some part of the element whenever that element has focus. If you set the `tabindex` attribute or `tabIndex` property of any other kinds of elements in IE5+, they, too, display that dotted line when given focus. You can still let an element receive focus but hide that dotted line by setting the `hideFocus` property of the element object to `true` (default value is `false`).

Hiding focus does not disable the element. In fact, if the element about to receive focus is scrolled out of view, the page scrolls to bring the element into view. Form controls that respond to keyboard action (for example, pressing the spacebar to check or uncheck a checkbox control) also continue to work as normal. For some designers, the focus rectangle harms the design goals of the page. The `hideFocus` property gives them more control over the appearance while maintaining consistency of operation with other pages. There is no corresponding HTML attribute for a tag, so you can use an `onload` event handler in the page to set the `hideFocus` property of desired objects after the page loads.

Example

Use The Evaluator (see Chapter 13) to experiment with the `hideFocus` property in WinIE5.5+. Enter the following statement in the top text box to assign a `tabIndex` value to the `myP` element so that by default, the element receives focus and the dotted rectangle:

```
document.getElementById("myP").tabIndex = 1
```

Press the Tab key several times until the paragraph receives focus. Now disable the focus rectangle:

```
document.getElementById("myP").hideFocus = true
```

If you now press the Tab key several times, the dotted rectangle does not appear around the paragraph. To prove that the element still receives focus, scroll the page down to the bottom so that the paragraph is not visible (you may have to resize the window). Click one of the focusable elements at the bottom of the page and then press the Tab key slowly until the Address field toolbar has focus. Press the Tab key once. The page scrolls to bring the paragraph into view, but there is no focus rectangle around the element.

Related Items: `tabIndex` property; `srcollIntoView()` method

id

Value: String   (See text)
Compatibility: WinIE4+, MacIE4+, NN6+, Moz+, Safari+

The `id` property returns the identifier assigned to an element's `id` attribute in the HTML code. A script cannot modify the ID of an existing element or assign an ID to an element that lacks one. But if a script creates a new element object, an identifier may be assigned to it by way of the `id` property.

Example

Rarely do you need to access this property in a script — unless you write an authoring tool that iterates through all elements of a page to extract the IDs assigned by the author. You can retrieve an object reference when you know the object's `id` property (via the `document.getElementById(elemID)` method). But if for some reason your script doesn't know the ID of, say, the second paragraph of a document, you can extract that ID as follows:

```
var elemID = document.getElementsByTagName("p")[1].id;
```

Related Item: `className` property

innerHTML
innerText

Value: String   Read/Write
Compatibility: WinIE4+, MacIE4+, NN6+, Moz+, Safari+

One way that Internet Explorer exposes the contents of an element is through the `innerHTML` and `innerText` properties. (NN6+/Moz/Safari offer only the `innerHTML` property.) All content defined by these inner properties consists of document data that is contained by an element's start and end tags but does not include the tags themselves (see the `outerText` and `outerHTML` properties). Setting these inner properties is a common way to modify a portion of a page's content after the page loads.

The `innerHTML` property contains not only the text content for an element as seen on the page, but also every bit of HTML tagging that is associated with that content. (If there are no tags in the content, the text is rendered as is.) For example, consider the following bit of HTML source code:

```
<p id="paragraph1">"How <em>are</em> you?" he asked.</p>
```

The value of the paragraph object's `innerHTML` property (`document.getElementById("para-graph1").innerHTML`) is

```
"How <em>are</em> you?" he asked.
```

The browser interprets any HTML tags included in a string you assign to an element's `innerHTML` property as tags. This also means that you can introduce entirely new nested elements (or child nodes in the modern terminology) by assigning a slew of HTML content to an element's `innerHTML` property. The document's object model adjusts itself to the newly inserted content.

By contrast, the `innerText` property knows only about the text content of an element container. In the example you just saw, the value of the paragraph's `innerText` property (`document.getElementById("paragraph1").innerText`) is

```
"How are you?" he asked.
```

It's important to remember that if you assign a string to the `innerText` property of an element, and that string contains HTML tags, the tags and their angle brackets appear in the rendered page and are not interpreted as live tags.

The W3C DOM Level 3 adds a `textContent` property that serves as the standard equivalent of `innerText`. Browser support for `textContent` currently consists solely of Moz1.7+.

Do not modify the `innerHTML` property to adjust the HTML for `frameset`, `html`, `head`, or `title` objects. You may modify table constructions through either `innerHTML` or the various table-related methods that create or delete rows, columns, and cells (see Chapter 38 on the CD-ROM). It is also safe to modify the contents of a cell by setting its `innerHTML` or `innerText` property.

elementObject.innerHTML

When the HTML you insert includes a `<script>` tag, be sure to include the `defer` attribute to the opening tag. This goes even for scripts that contain function definitions, which you might consider to be deferred automatically.

The `innerHTML` property is not supported by the W3C DOM, but it does share widespread support in all modern browsers. You could argue that a pure W3C DOM node manipulation approach is more structured than just assigning HTML code to `innerHTML`, but the ease of making a single property assignment has so far won out in the practicality of everyday scripting. Whenever possible, the examples in this book use the W3C approach to alter the HTML code for a node, but there are several instances where `innerHTML` is simply too concise an option to resist.

Example

Listing 15-11 contains an example of how to use the `innerHTML` and `innerText` properties to alter dynamically the content within a page. The page generated in the listing contains an `h1` element label and a paragraph of text. The purpose is to demonstrate how the `innerHTML` and `innerText` properties differ in their intent. Two text boxes contain the same combination of text and HTML tags that replaces the inner content of the paragraph's label.

If you apply the default content of the first text box to the `innerHTML` property of the `label1` object, the italic style is rendered as such for the first word. In addition, the text in parentheses is rendered with the help of the small style sheet rule assigned by virtue of the surrounding `<span>` tags. But if you apply that same content to the `innerText` property of the `label` object, the tags are rendered as is.

Use this as a laboratory to experiment with some other content in both text boxes. See what happens when you insert a `<br>` tag within some text in both text boxes.

LISTING 15-11

Using innerHTML and innerText Properties

```
<html>
   <head>
      <title>innerHTML and innerText Properties</title>
      <style type="text/css">
      h1 {font-size:18pt; font-weight:bold; font-family:"Comic Sans MS", Arial,
         sans-serif}
      .small {font-size:12pt; font-weight:400; color:gray}
      </style>
      <script type="text/javascript">
      function setGroupLabelAsText(form) {
         var content = form.textInput.value;
         if (content) {
            document.getElementById("label1").innerText = content;
         }
      }
      function setGroupLabelAsHTML(form) {
         var content = form.HTMLInput.value;
         if (content) {
            document.getElementById("label1").innerHTML = content;
         }
      }
```

```
        </script>
    </head>
    <body>
      <form>
        <p><input type="text" name="HTMLInput"
          value="&lt;I&gt;First&lt;/I&gt; Article &lt;SPAN
          CLASS='small'&gt;(of ten)&lt;/span&gt;"
          size="50" /> <input type="button" value="Change Heading HTML"
          onclick="setGroupLabelAsHTML(this.form)" /></p>
        <p><input type="text" name="textInput"
          value="&lt;I&gt;First&lt;/I&gt; Article &lt;SPAN
          CLASS='small'&gt;(of ten)&lt;/span&gt;"
          size="50" /> <input type="button" value="Change Heading Text"
          onclick="setGroupLabelAsText(this.form)" /></p>
      </form>
      <h1 id="label1">
        ARTICLE I
      </h1>
      <p>Congress shall make no law respecting an establishment of religion, or
        prohibiting the free exercise thereof; or abridging the freedom of
        speech, or of the press; or the right of the people peaceably to
        assemble, and to petition the government for a redress of
        grievances.</p>
    </body>
</html>
```

Related Items: outerHTML, outerText, textContent properties; replaceNode() method

isContentEditable

Value: Boolean   Read-Only
Compatibility: WinIE5.5+, MacIE-, NN-, Moz-, Safari 1.2+

The isContentEditable property returns a Boolean value indicating whether a particular element object is set to be editable (see the discussion of the contentEditable property earlier in this chapter). This property is helpful because if a parent element's contentEditable property is set to true, a nested element's contentEditable property likely is set to its default value inherit. But because its parent is editable, the isContentEditable property of the nested element returns true.

Example

Use The Evaluator (see Chapter 13) to experiment with both the contentEditable and isContentEditable properties on the myP and nested myEM elements (reload the page to start with a known version). Check the current setting for the myEM element by typing the following statement in the top text box:

```
myEM.isContentEditable
```

This value is false because no element upward in the element containment hierarchy is set to be editable yet. Next, turn on editing for the surrounding myP element:

```
myP.contentEditable = true
```

At this point, the entire `myP` element is editable because its child element is set, by default, to inherit the edit state of its parent. Prove it by entering the following statement in the top text box:

```
myEM.isContentEditable
```

Although the `myEM` element is shown to be editable, no change has accrued to its `contentEditable` property:

```
myEM.contentEditable
```

This property value remains the default `inherit`.

You can see an additional example of these two properties in use in Listing 15-7.

Related Item: `contentEditable` property

isDisabled

Value: Boolean   Read-Only
Compatibility: WinIE5.5+, MacIE-, NN-, Moz-, Safari-

The `isDisabled` property returns a Boolean value that indicates whether a particular element object is set to be disabled (see the discussion of the `disabled` property earlier in this chapter). This property is helpful; if a parent element's `disabled` property is set to `true`, a nested element's `disabled` property likely is set to its default value of `false`. But because its parent is disabled, the `isDisabled` property of the nested element returns `true`. In other words, the `isDisabled` property returns the actual disabled status of an element regardless of its `disabled` property.

Example

Use The Evaluator (see Chapter 13) to experiment with both the `disabled` and `isDisabled` properties on the `myP` and nested `myEM` elements (reload the page to start with a known version). Check the current setting for the `myEM` element by typing the following statement in the top text box:

```
myEM.isDisabled
```

This value is `false` because no element upward in the element containment hierarchy is set for disabling yet. Next, disable the surrounding `myP` element:

```
myP.disabled = true
```

At this point, the entire `myP` element (including its children) is disabled. Prove it by entering the following statement in the top text box:

```
myEM.isDisabled
```

Although the `myEM` element is shown as disabled, no change has accrued to its `disabled` property:

```
myEM.disabled
```

This property value remains the default `false`.

Related Item: `disabled` property

isMultiLine

Value: Boolean   Read-Only
Compatibility: WinIE5.5+, MacIE-, NN-, Moz-, Safari-

The isMultiLine property returns a Boolean value that reveals whether the element object is capable of occupying or displaying more than one line of text. It is important that this value does not reveal whether the element actually occupies multiple lines; rather, it indicates the potential of doing so. For example, a text input element cannot wrap to multiple lines, so its isMultiLine property is false. However, a button element can display multiple lines of text for its label, so it reports true for the isMultiLine property.

Example

Use The Evaluator (see Chapter 13) to read the isMultiLine property for elements on that page. Try the following statements in the top text box:

```
document.body.isMultiLine
document.forms[0].input.isMultiLine
myP.isMultiLine
myEM.isMultiLine
```

All but the text field form control report that they are capable of occupying multiple lines.

isTextEdit

Value: Boolean   Read-Only
Compatibility: WinIE4+, MacIE4+, NN-, Moz-, Safari-

The isTextEdit property reveals whether an object can have a WinIE TextRange object created with its content. (See the TextRange object in Chapter 36 on the CD-ROM.) You can create TextRange objects from only a limited selection of objects in IE4+ for Windows: body, button, text type input, and textarea. This property always returns false in MacIE.

Example

Good coding practice dictates that your script check for this property before invoking the createTextRange() method on any object. A typical implementation is as follows:

```
if (document.getElementById("myObject").isTextEdit) {
    var myRange = document.getElementById("myObject").createTextRange();
    [more statements that act on myRange]
}
```

Related Items: createRange() method; TextRange object (Chapter 36 on the CD-ROM)

lang

Value: ISO language code string   Read/Write
Compatibility: WinIE4+, MacIE4+, NN6+, Moz+, Safari+

The lang property governs the written language system used to render an element's text content when overriding the default browser's language system. The default value for this property is an empty string unless the corresponding lang attribute is assigned a value in the element's tag. Modifying the property value by script control does not appear to have any effect in the current browser implementations.

Example

Values for the lang property consist of strings containing valid ISO language codes. Such codes have, at minimum, a primary language code (for example, "fr" for French) plus an optional region specifier (for example, "fr-ch" for Swiss French). The code to assign a Swiss German value to an element looks like the following:

```
document.getElementById("specialSpan").lang = "de-ch";
```

language

Value: String   Read/Write
Compatibility: WinIE4+, MacIE4+, NN-, Moz-, Safari-

IE4+'s architecture allows for multiple scripting engines to work with the browser. Two engines are included with the basic Windows version browser: JScript (compatible with JavaScript) and Visual Basic Scripting Edition (VBScript). The default scripting engine is JScript. But if you wish to use VBScript or some other scripting language in statements that are embedded within event handler attributes of a tag, you can specifically direct the browser to apply the desired scripting engine to those script statements by way of the `language` attribute of the tag. The `language` property provides scripted access to that property. Unless you intend to modify the event handler HTML code and replace it with a statement in VBScript (or any other non-JScript-compatible language installed with your browser), you do not need to modify this property (or read it, for that matter).

Valid values include `JScript`, `javascript`, `vbscript`, and `vbs`. Third-party scripting engines have their own identifier for use with this value. Because the `language` attribute was also used in the `<script>` tag, Internet Explorer 5 observes `language="xml"` as well.

Related Item: `script` element object

lastChild

(See `firstChild`)

length

Value: Integer   Read-Only and Read/Write
Compatibility: WinIE3+, MacIE3+, NN2+, Moz+, Safari+

The `length` property returns the number of items in an array or collection of objects. Its most common application is as a boundary condition in a `for` loop. Though arrays and collections commonly use integer values as index values (always starting with zero), the `length` value is the actual number of items in the group. Therefore, to iterate through all items of the group, the condition expression should include a less-than (<) symbol rather than a less-than-or-equal (<=) symbol, as in the following:

```
for (var i = 0; i < someArray.length; i++) {...}
```

For decrementing through an array (in other words, starting from the last item in the array and working toward the first), the initial expression must initialize the counting variable as the length minus one:

```
for (var i = someArray.length - 1; i >= 0; i--) {...}
```

For most arrays and collections, the `length` property is read-only and governed solely by the number of items in the group. But in more recent versions of the browsers, you can assign values to some object arrays (`areas`, `options`, and the `select` object) to create placeholders for data assignments. See the discussions of the `area`, `select`, and `option` element objects for details. A plain JavaScript array can also have its `length` property value modified by script to either trim items from the end of the array or reserve space for additional assignments. See Chapter 31 for more about the `Array` object.

Example

You can try the following sequence of statements in the top text box of The Evaluator to see how the `length` property returns values (and sets them for some objects). Note that some statements work in only some browser versions.

```
(All browsers)  document.forms.length
(All browsers)  document.forms[0].elements.length
```

```
(NN3+, IE4+)      document.images.length
(NN4+)            document.layers.length
(IE4+)            document.all.length
(IE5+, W3C)       document.getElementById("myTable").childNodes.length
```

All of these statements are shown primarily for completeness. Unless you have a good reason to support legacy browsers, the last technique (IE5+, W3C) should be used to access the length property.

Related Items: area, select, option, and Array objects

localName
namespaceURI
prefix

Value: String   Read-Only
Compatibility: WinIE-, MacIE-, NN6+, Moz+, Safari+

The three properties localName, namespaceURI, and prefix apply to any node in an XML document that associates a namespace URI with an XML tag. Although NN6 exposes all three properties for all element (and node) objects, the properties do not return the desired values. However, Mozilla-based browsers, including NN7+, remedy the situation. To understand better what values these three properties represent, consider the following XML content:

```
<x xmlns:bk='http://bigbooks.org/schema'>
    <bk:title>To Kill a Mockingbird</bk:title>
</x>
```

The element whose tag is <bk:title> is associated with the Namespace URI defined for the block, and the element's namespaceURI property would return the string http://bigbooks.org/schema. The tag name consists of a prefix (before the colon) and the local name (after the colon). In the preceding example, the prefix property for the element defined by the <bk:title> tag would be bk, whereas the localName property would return title. The localName property of any node returns the same value as its nodeName property value, such as #text for a text node.

For more information about XML Namespaces, visit http://www.w3.org/TR/REC-xml-names.

Related Items: scopeName, tagUrn properties

nextSibling
previousSibling

Value: Object reference   Read-Only
Compatibility: WinIE5+, MacIE5+, NN6+, Moz+, Safari+

A *sibling node* is one that is at the same nested level as another node in the hierarchy of an HTML document. For example, the following p element has two child nodes (the em and span elements). Those two child nodes are siblings.

```
<p>MegaCorp is <em>the</em> source of the <span class="hot">hottest</span> gizmos.</p>
```

Sibling order is determined solely by the source-code order of the nodes. Therefore, in the previous example, the em node has no previousSibling property. Meanwhile, the span node has no nextSibling property (meaning that these properties return null). These properties provide another way to iterate through all nodes at the same level.

Example

The following function assigns the same class name to all child nodes of an element:

```
function setAllChildClasses(parentElem, className) {
    var childElem = parentElem.firstChild;
    while (childElem.nextSibling) {
        childElem.className = className;
        childElem = childElem.nextSibling;
    }
}
```

This example is certainly not the only way to achieve the same results. Using a for loop to iterate through the childNodes collection of the parent element is an equally valid approach.

Related Items: firstChild, lastChild, childNodes properties; hasChildNodes(), insertAdjacentElement() methods

nodeName

Value: String   Read-Only
Compatibility: WinIE5+, MacIE5+, NN6+, Moz+, Safari+

For HTML and XML elements, the name of a node is the same as the tag name. The nodeName property is provided for the sake of consistency with the node architecture specified by the formal W3C DOM standard. The value, just like the tagName property, is an all-uppercase string of the tag name (even if the HTML source code is written with lowercase tags).

Some nodes, such as the text content of an element, do not have a tag. The nodeName property for such a node is a special value: #text. Another kind of node is an attribute of an element. For an attribute, the nodeName is the name of the attribute. See Chapter 14 for more about Node object properties.

Example

The following function demonstrates one (not very efficient) way to assign a new class name to every p element in an IE5+ document:

```
function setAllPClasses(className) {
    for (var i = 0; i < document.all.length; i++) {
        if (document.all[i].nodeName == "P") {
            document.all[i].className = className;
        }
    }
}
```

A more efficient approach uses the getElementsByTagName() method to retrieve a collection of all p elements and then iterate through them directly.

Related Item: tagName property

nodeType

Value: Integer   Read-Only
Compatibility: WinIE5+, MacIE5+, NN6+, Moz+, Safari+

The W3C DOM specification identifies a series of constant values that denote categories of nodes. Every node has a value that identifies its type, but not all browsers support the nodeType property on all node types as objects. Table 15-4 lists the nodeType values implemented in recent browsers; all of the values are considered part of the W3C DOM Level 2 specification.

TABLE 15-4

nodeType Property Values

Value	Description	WinIE	MacIE	Moz	Safari
1	Element node	5	5	1	1
2	Attribute node	6	5	1	1
3	Text (#text) node	5	5	1	1
4	CDATA section node	-	-	-	-
5	Entity reference node	-	-	-	-
6	Entity node	-	-	-	-
7	Processing instruction node	-	-	-	-
8	Comment node	6	5	1	-
9	Document node	5	5	1	1
10	Document type node	-	-	1	1
11	Document fragment node	6	5	1	1
12	Notation node	-	-	-	-

The nodeType value is automatically assigned to a node, whether the node exists in the document's HTML source code or is generated on the fly via a script. For example, if you create a new element node through any of the ways available by script (for example, by assigning a string encased in HTML tags to the innerHTML property or by explicitly invoking the document.createElement() method), the new element assumes a nodeType of 1.

Mozilla-based browsers and Safari go one step further in supporting the W3C DOM specification by implementing a set of Node object property constants for each of the nodeType values. Table 15-5 lists the entire set as defined in the DOM Level 2 specification. Substituting these constants for nodeType integers can improve the readability of a script. For example, instead of

```
if (myElem.nodeType == 1) {...}
```

it is much easier to see what's going on with

```
if (myElem.nodeType == Node.ELEMENT_NODE) {...}
```

TABLE 15-5

W3C DOM nodeType Constants

Reference	nodeType Value
Node.ELEMENT_NODE	1
Node.ATTRIBUTE_NODE	2
Node.TEXT_NODE	3
Node.CDATA_SECTION_NODE	4
Node.ENTITY_REFERENCE_NODE	5
Node.ENTITY_NODE	6
Node.PROCESSING_INSTRUCTION_NODE	7
Node.COMMENT_NODE	8
Node.DOCUMENT_NODE	9
Node.DOCUMENT_TYPE_NODE	10
Node.DOCUMENT_FRAGMENT_NODE	11
Node.NOTATION_NODE	12

Example

You can experiment with viewing nodeType property values in The Evaluator. The p element whose ID is myP is a good place to start. The p element itself is a nodeType of 1:

```
document.getElementById("myP").nodeType
```

This element has three child nodes: a string of text (nodeName #text), an em element (nodeName em), and the rest of the text of the element content (nodeName #text). If you view the nodeType of either of the text portions, the value comes back as 3:

```
document.getElementById("myP").childNodes[0].nodeType
```

Related Item: nodeName property

nodeValue

Value: Number, string, or null   Read/Write
Compatibility: WinIE5+, MacIE5+, NN6+, Moz+, Safari+

For a text node, the nodeValue property consists of the actual text for that node. Such a node cannot contain any further nested elements, so the nodeValue property offers another way of reading and modifying what Internet Explorer implements as an element's innerText property (but in the W3C DOM, you must reference the child text node of an element to get or set its node value).

Of the node types implemented in the W3C DOM–capable browsers, only the text and attribute types have readable values. The nodeValue property of an element type of node returns a null value. For an attribute node, the nodeValue property consists of the value assigned to that attribute. According to the W3C DOM standard, attribute values should be reflected as strings. WinIE5, however, returns values of type Number when the value is all numeric characters. Even if you assign a string version of a number to such a nodeValue property, it is converted to a Number type internally. Other browsers return nodeValue values as strings in all cases (and convert numeric assignments to strings).

Example

You can use the nodeValue property to carry out practical tasks. As an example, nodeValue can be used to increase the width of a textarea object by 10 percent. The nodeValue is converted to an integer before performing the math and reassignment:

```
function widenCols(textareaElem) {
    var colWidth = parseInt(textareaElem.attributes["cols"].nodeValue, 10);
    textareaElem.attributes["cols"].nodeValue = (colWidth * 1.1);
}
```

As another example, you can replace the text of an element, assuming that the element contains no further nested elements:

```
function replaceText(elem, newText) {
    if (elem.childNodes.length == 1 && elem.firstChild.nodeType == 3) {
        elem.firstChild.nodeValue = newText;
    }
}
```

The function builds in one final verification that the element contains just one child node and that it is a text type. An alternative version of the assignment statement of the second example uses the innerText property in IE with identical results:

```
elem.innerText = newText;
```

You could also use the textContent property in Moz1.7+ to achieve the same concise result:

```
elem.textContent = newText;
```

Related Items: attributes, innerText, nodeType properties

offsetHeight
offsetWidth

Value: Integer   Read-Only
Compatibility: WinIE4+, MacIE4+, NN6+, Moz+, Safari+

These properties, which ostensibly report the height and width of any element, have had a checkered history due to conflicts between interpretations of the CSS box model by Microsoft and the W3C. Both properties were invented by Microsoft for IE4. Although they are not part of any W3C standard, other modern browsers, including Mozilla-based browsers and Safari, implement the properties because they're so valuable to scripters.

Assuming that you specify style sheet rules for the width or height of an inline (nonpositioned) element, the offsetHeight and offsetWidth properties act differently depending on whether the page puts the browser in standards-compatible mode (via the DOCTYPE). More specifically, when IE6+ is set to standards-compatible mode (by DOCTYPE switching, as described in Chapter 14), the properties measure the pixel dimensions of the element's content plus any padding or borders, excluding margins. This is also the default behavior for Mozilla and Safari, which adhere to the W3C box model. In quirks mode, however, the default IE6+ behavior is to return a height and width of only the element's content, with no accounting for padding, borders, or margins. For versions of IE prior to IE6, this is the only behavior.

Note that for a normal block-level element whose height and width are not specified, the `offsetHeight` is determined by the actual height of the content after all text flows. But the `offsetWidth` always extends the full width of the containing element. Therefore, the `offsetWidth` property does not reveal the rendered width of text content that is narrower than the full parent element width. For example, a p element consisting of only a few words may report an `offsetWidth` of many hundreds of pixels because the paragraph's block extends the full width of the `body` element that represents the containing parent of the p element. To find out the actual width of text within a full-width, block-level element, wrap the text within an inline element (such as a `span`), and inspect the `offsetWidth` property of the `span`.

Example

With IE4+, you can substitute the `offsetHeight` and `offsetWidth` properties for `clientHeight` and `clientWidth` in Listing 15-6. The reason is that the two elements in question have their widths hard-wired in style sheets. Thus, the `offsetWidth` property follows that lead rather than observing the default width of the parent (BODY) element.

With IE5+ and W3C browsers, you can use The Evaluator to inspect the `offsetHeight` and `offsetWidth` property values of various objects on the page. Enter the following statements in the top text box:

```
document.getElementById("myP").offsetWidth
document.getElementById("myEM").offsetWidth
document.getElementById("myP").offsetHeight
document.getElementById("myTable").offsetWidth
```

Related Items: `clientHeight`, `clientWidth` properties

offsetLeft
offsetTop

Value: Integer   Read-Only
Compatibility: WinIE4+, MacIE4+, NN6+, Moz+, Safari+

The `offsetLeft` and `offsetTop` properties can suffer from the same version vagaries that afflict `offsetHeight` and `offsetWidth` properties when borders, margins, and padding are associated with an element and DOCTYPE switching is a factor. However, the `offsetLeft` and `offsetTop` properties are valuable in providing pixel coordinates of an element within the positioning context of the parent element — even when the elements are not positioned explicitly.

> **NOTE** The `offsetLeft` and `offsetTop` properties for positioned elements in MacIE do not return the same values as the `style.left` and `style.top` properties of the same element. See Listing 40-5 on the CD-ROM for an example of how to correct these discrepancies without having to hardwire the precise pixel differences in your code.

The element used as a coordinate context for these properties is whatever element the `offsetParent` property returns. This means that to determine the precise position of any element, you may have to add some code that iterates through the `offsetParent` hierarchy until that property returns `null`.

Although the `offsetLeft` and `offsetTop` properties are not part of the W3C DOM specification, they are supported across most browsers because they are convenient for some scriptable Dynamic HTML (DHTML) tasks. Through these two properties, a script can read the pixel coordinates of any block-level or inline element. Measurements are made relative to the `body` element, but this may change in the future. See the discussion later in this chapter about the `offsetParent` property.

Example

The following IE script statements use all four offset dimensional properties to size and position a `div` element so that it completely covers a `span` element located within a `p` element. This can be for a fill-in-the-blank quiz that provides text entry fields elsewhere on the page. As the user gets an answer correct, the blocking `div` element is hidden to reveal the correct answer.

```
document.all.blocker.style.pixelLeft = document.all.span2.offsetLeft
document.all.blocker.style.pixelTop = document.all.span2.offsetTop
document.all.blockImg.height = document.all.span2.offsetHeight
document.all.blockImg.width = document.all.span2.offsetWidth
```

Because the `offsetParent` property for the `span` element is the `body` element, the positioned `div` element can use the same positioning context (it's the default context, anyway) for setting the `pixelLeft` and `pixelTop` style properties. (Remember that positioning properties belong to an element's `style` object.) The `offsetHeight` and `offsetWidth` properties can read the dimensions of the `span` element (the example has no borders, margins, or padding to worry about) and assign them to the dimensions of the image contained by the blocker `div` element.

This example is also a bit hazardous in some implementations. If the text of `span2` wraps to a new line, the new `offsetHeight` value has enough pixels to accommodate both lines. But the `blockImg` and `blocker` `div` elements are block-level elements that render as a simple rectangle. In other words, the `blocker` element doesn't turn into two separate strips to cover the pieces of `span2` that spread across two lines.

Related Items: `clientLeft`, `clientTop`, `offsetParent` properties

offsetParent

Value: Object reference   Read-Only
Compatibility: WinIE4+, MacIE4+, NN6+, Moz+, Safari+

The `offsetParent` property returns a reference to the object that acts as a positioning context for the current element. Values for the `offsetLeft` and `offsetTop` properties are measured relative to the top-left corner of the `offsetParent` object.

The returned object is usually, but not always, the next outermost block-level container. For most document elements, the `offsetParent` object is the `document.body` object (with exceptions for some elements in some browsers).

Table cells, for example, have different `offsetParent` elements in different browsers:

Browser	td offsetParent
WinIE4	tr
WinIE5+/NN7+/Moz	table
MacIE	table
NN6	body

Fortunately, the property behaves predictably for positioned elements in most modern browsers. For example, a first-level positioned element's `offsetParent` element is the `body`; the `offsetParent` of a nested positioned element (for example, one absolute-positioned `div` inside another) is the next outer container (in other words, the positioning context of the inner element).

elementObject.offsetParent

Example

You can use the `offsetParent` property to help you locate the position of a nested element on the page. Listing 15-12 demonstrates how a script can walk up the hierarchy of `offsetParent` objects in IE for Windows to assemble the location of a nested element on a page. The goal of the exercise in Listing 15-12 is to position an image at the top-left corner of the second table cell. The entire table is centered on the page.

The `onload` event handler invokes the `setImagePosition()` function. The function first sets a Boolean flag that determines whether the calculations should be based on the client or offset sets of properties. WinIE4 and MacIE5 rely on client properties, whereas WinIE5+ works with the offset properties. The discrepancies even out, however, with the `while` loop. This loop traverses the `offsetParent` hierarchy starting with the `offsetParent` of the cell out to, but not including, the `document.body` object. The `body` object is not included because that is the positioning context for the image. In IE5, the `while` loop executes only once because just the `table` element exists between the cell and the body; in IE4, the loop executes twice to account for the `tr` and `table` elements up the hierarchy. Finally, the cumulative values of left and top measures are applied to the positioning properties of the `div` object's style, and the image is made visible.

LISTING 15-12

Using the offsetParent Property

```
<html>
   <head>
      <title>offsetParent Property</title>
      <script type="text/javascript">
      function setImagePosition(){
         var x = 0;
         var y = 0;
         var offsetPointer = document.getElementById("myCell"); // cElement;
         while (offsetPointer) {
            x += offsetPointer.offsetLeft;
            y += offsetPointer.offsetTop;
            offsetPointer = offsetPointer.offsetParent;
         }
         // correct for MacIE body margin factors
         if (navigator.userAgent.indexOf("Mac") != -1 &&
            typeof document.body.leftMargin != "undefined") {
            x += document.body.leftMargin;
            y += document.body.topMargin;
         }
         document.getElementById("myDIV").style.left = x + "px";
         document.getElementById("myDIV").style.top = y + "px";
         document.getElementById("myDIV").style.visibility = "visible";
      }
      </script>
   </head>
   <body onload="setImagePosition()">
      <h1>The offsetParent Property</h1>
      <hr />
      <p>After the document loads, the script positions a small image in the
         upper left corner of the second table cell.</p>
      <table border="1" align="center">
```

```
      <tr>
         <td>This is the first cell</td>
         <td id="myCell">This is the second cell.</td>
      </tr>
   </table>
   <img id="myDIV" alt="image" src="end.gif" height="12" width="12"
      style="position:absolute; visibility:hidden; height:12px;
      width:12px" />
   </body>
</html>
```

Related Items: offsetLeft, offsetTop, offsetHeight, offsetWidth properties

outerHTML
outerText

Value: String   Read/Write
Compatibility: WinIE4+, MacIE4+, NN-, Moz-, Safari 1.3+

One way that Internet Explorer and Safari 1.3+ expose an entire element to scripting is by way of the outerHTML and outerText properties. The primary distinction between these two properties is that outerHTML includes the element's start and end tags, whereas outerText includes only rendered text that belongs to the element (including text from any nested elements).

The outerHTML property contains not only the text content for an element as seen on the page, but also every bit of HTML tagging associated with that content. For example, consider the following bit of HTML source code:

```
<p id="paragraph1">"How <em>are</em> you?" he asked.</p>
```

The value of the p object's outerHTML property (document.all.paragraph1. outerHTML) is exactly the same as that of the source code.

The browser interprets any HTML tags in a string that you assign to an element's outerHTML property. This means that you can delete (set the property to an empty string) or replace an entire tag with this property. The document's object model adjusts itself to whatever adjustments you make to the HTML in this manner.

In contrast, the outerText property knows only about the text content of an element container. In the preceding example, the value of the paragraph's outerText property (document.all.paragraph1.innerText) is

```
"How are you?" he asked.
```

If this looks familiar, it's because in most cases the innerText and outerText properties of an existing element return the same strings.

Example

Listing 15-13 demonstrates how to use the outerHTML and outerText properties to access and modify web-page content dynamically. The page generated by Listing 15-13 (WinIE4+/Safari 1.3+ only) contains an h1 element label and a paragraph of text. The purpose is to demonstrate how the outerHTML and outerText properties differ in their intent. Two text boxes contain the same combination of text and HTML tags that replaces the element that creates the paragraph's label.

elementObject.**outerHTML**

If you apply the default content of the first text box to the `outerHTML` property of the `label1` object, the h1 element is replaced by a span element whose `class` attribute acquires a different style sheet rule defined earlier in the document. Notice that the ID of the new span element is the same as that of the original h1 element. This allows the script attached to the second button to address the object. But this second script replaces the element with the raw text (including tags). The element is gone, and any attempt to change the `outerHTML` or `outerText` properties of the `label1` object causes an error because there is no longer a `label1` object in the document.

Use this laboratory to experiment with some other content in both text boxes.

LISTING 15-13

Using outerHTML and outerText Properties

```
<html>
  <head>
    <title>outerHTML and outerText Properties</title>
    <style type="text/css">
    h1 {font-size:18pt; font-weight:bold; font-family:"Comic Sans MS", Arial,
      sans-serif}
    .heading {font-size:20pt; font-weight:bold; font-family:"Arial Black",
      Arial, sans-serif}
    </style>
    <script type="text/javascript">
    function setGroupLabelAsText(form) {
      var content = form.textInput.value;
      if (content) {
        document.getElementById("label1").outerText = content;
      }
    }
    function setGroupLabelAsHTML(form) {
      var content = form.HTMLInput.value;
      if (content) {
        document.getElementById("label1").outerHTML = content;
      }
    }
    </script>
  </head>
  <body>
    <form>
      <p><input type="text" name="HTMLInput"
        value="&lt;SPAN ID='label1' CLASS='heading'&gt;Article the
        First&lt;/SPAN&gt;"
        size="55" /> <input type="button" value="Change Heading HTML"
        onclick="setGroupLabelAsHTML(this.form)" /></p>
      <p><input type="text" name="textInput"
        value="&lt;SPAN ID='label1' CLASS='heading'&gt;Article the
        First&lt;/SPAN&gt;"
        size="55" /> <input type="button" value="Change Heading Text"
        onclick="setGroupLabelAsText(this.form)" /></p>
    </form>
    <h1 id="label1">ARTICLE I</h1>
```

```
    <p>Congress shall make no law respecting an establishment of religion, or
        prohibiting the free exercise thereof; or abridging the freedom of
        speech, or of the press; or the right of the people peaceably to
        assemble, and to petition the government for a redress of
        grievances.</p>
  </body>
</html>
```

Related Items: innerHTML, innerText properties; replaceNode() method

ownerDocument

Value: Document object reference   Read-Only
Compatibility: WinIE6+, MacIE5+, NN6+, Moz+, Safari+

The ownerDocument property belongs to any element or node in the W3C DOM. The property's value is a reference to the document node that ultimately contains the element or node. If a script encounters a reference to an element or node (perhaps it has been passed as a parameter to a function), the object's ownerDocument property provides a way to build references to other objects in the same document or to access properties and methods of the document objects. IE's proprietary version of this property is simply document.

Example

Use The Evaluator (see Chapter 13) to explore the ownerDocument property. Enter the following statement in the top text box:

```
document.body.childNodes[5].ownerDocument
```

The result is a reference to the document object. You can use that to inspect a property of the document, as shown in the following statement, which you should enter in the top text box:

```
document.body.childNodes[5].ownerDocument.URL
```

This returns the document.URL property for the document that owns the child node.

Related Item: document object

parentElement

Value: Element object reference or null   Read-Only
Compatibility: WinIE4+, MacIE4+, NN-, Moz-, Safari 1.2+

The parentElement property returns a reference to the next outermost HTML element from the current element. This parent–child relationship of elements is often, but not always, the same as a parent–child node relationship (see the parentNode property later in this chapter). The difference is that the parentElement property deals only with HTML elements as reflected as document objects, whereas a node is not necessarily an HTML element (for example, an attribute or text chunk).

There is also a distinction between parentElement and offsetParent properties. The latter returns an element that may be many generations removed from a given element but is the immediate parent with regard to positioning context. For example, a td element's parentElement property is most likely its enclosing tr element, but a td element's offsetParent property is its table element.

A script can walk the element hierarchy outward from an element with the help of the parentElement property. The top of the parent chain is the html element. Its parentElement property returns null.

elementObject.parentNode

Example

You can experiment with the parentElement property in The Evaluator. The document contains a p element named myP. Type each of the following statements from the left column in the top expression evaluation text box and press Enter to see the results.

Expression	Result
document.getElementById("myP").tagName	p
document.getElementById("myP").parentElement	[object]
document.getElementById("myP").parentElement.tagName	body
document.getElementById("myP").parentElement.parentElement	[object]
document.getElementById("myP").parentElement.parentElement.tagName	html
document.getElementById("myP").parentElement.parentElement.parentElement	null

Related Items: offsetParent, parentNode properties

parentNode

Value: Node object reference or null   Read-Only
Compatibility: WinIE5+, MacIE5+, NN6+, Moz+, Safari+

The parentNode property returns a reference to the next outermost node that is reflected as an object belonging to the document. For a standard element object, the parentNode property is the same as IE/Safari's parentElement because both objects happen to have a direct parent–child node relationship as well as a parent–child element relationship.

Other kinds of content, however, can be nodes, including text fragments within an element. A text fragment's parentNode property is the next outermost node or element that encompasses that fragment. A text node object in IE/Safari 1.3+ does not have a parentElement property.

Example

Use The Evaluator to examine the parentNode property values of both an element and a nonelement node. Begin with the following two statements, and watch the results of each:

```
document.getElementById("myP").parentNode.tagName
document.getElementById("myP").parentElement.tagName     (IE/Safari1.3+ only)
```

Now examine the properties from the point of view of the first text fragment node of the myP paragraph element:

```
document.getElementById("myP").childNodes[0].nodeValue
document.getElementById("myP").childNodes[0].parentNode.tagName
document.getElementById("myP").childNodes[0].parentElement     (IE/Safari1.3+ only)
```

Notice (in IE) that the text node does not have a parentElement property.

Related Items: childNodes, nodeName, nodeType, nodeValue, parentElement properties

parentTextEdit

Value: Element object reference or `null`   Read-Only
Compatibility: WinIE4+, MacIE4+, NN-, Moz-, Safari-

Only a handful of objects in IE's object model are capable of creating text ranges (see the `TextRange` object in Chapter 36 on the CD-ROM). To find an object's next outermost container capable of generating a text range, use the `parentTextEdit` property. If an element is in the hierarchy, that element's object reference is returned. Otherwise (for example, `document.body.parentTextEdit`), the value is `null`. MacIE always returns a value of `null` because the browser doesn't support the `TextRange` object.

Example

Listing 15-14 contains an example that demonstrates how to use the `parentTextEdit` property to create a text range. The page resulting from Listing 15-14 contains a paragraph of Latin text and three radio buttons that select the size of a paragraph chunk: one character, one word, or one sentence. If you click anywhere within the large paragraph, the `onclick` event handler invokes the `selectChunk()` function. The function first examines which of the radio buttons is selected to determine how much of the paragraph to highlight (select) around the point at which the user clicks.

After the script employs the `parentTextEdit` property to test whether the clicked element has a valid parent capable of creating a text range, it calls on the property again to help create the text range. From there, `TextRange` object methods shrink the range to a single insertion point, move that point to the spot nearest the cursor location at click time, expand the selection to encompass the desired chunk, and select that bit of text.

Notice one workaround for the `TextRange` object's `expand()` method anomaly: If you specify a sentence, IE doesn't treat the beginning of a p element as the starting end of a sentence automatically. A camouflaged (white text color) period is appended to the end of the previous element to force the `TextRange` object to expand only to the beginning of the first sentence of the targeted p element.

LISTING 15-14

Using the parentTextEdit Property

```
<html>
   <head>
      <title>parentTextEdit Property</title>
      <style type="text/css">
      p {cursor:hand}
      </style>
      <script type="text/javascript">
      function selectChunk() {
         var chunk, range;
         for (var i = 0; i < document.forms[0].chunk.length; i++) {
            if (document.forms[0].chunk[i].checked) {
               chunk = document.forms[0].chunk[i].value;
               break;
            }
         }
         var x = window.event.clientX;
         var y = window.event.clientY;
```

continued

elementObject.readyState

LISTING 15-14 *(continued)*

```
        if (window.event.srcElement.parentTextEdit) {
            range = window.event.srcElement.parentTextEdit.createTextRange();
            range.collapse();
            range.moveToPoint(x, y);
            range.expand(chunk);
            range.select();
        }
    }
    </script>
</head>
<body bgcolor="white">
    <form>
        <p>Choose how much of the paragraph is to be selected when you click
            anywhere in it:<br />
             <input type="radio" name="chunk" value="character"
            checked="checked" />Character <input type="radio" name="chunk"
            value="word" />Word <input type="radio" name="chunk"
            value="sentence" />Sentence <font color="white">.</font></p>
    </form>
    <p onclick="selectChunk()">Lorem ipsum dolor sit amet, consectetaur
        adipisicing
        elit, sed do eiusmod tempor incididunt ut labore et dolore magna
        aliqua. Ut
        enim adminim veniam, quis nostrud exercitation ullamco laboris nisi ut
        aliquip ex ea commodo consequat. Duis aute irure dolor in
        reprehenderit involuptate velit esse cillum dolore eu fugiat nulla
        pariatur. Excepteur sint occaecat cupidatat non proident, sunt in
        culpa qui officia deserunt mollit anim id est laborum.</p>
</body>
</html>
```

Related Items: isTextEdit property; TextRange object (Chapter 36 on the CD-ROM)

prefix

(See localName)

previousSibling

(See nextSibling)

readyState

Value: String (integer for OBJECT object)   Read-Only
Compatibility: WinIE4+, MacIE4+, NN-, Moz-, Safari-

A script can query an element in IE to find out whether it has loaded all ancillary data (for example, external image files or other media files) before other statements act on that object or its data. The readyState property lets you know the loading status of an element.

Table 15-6 lists the possible values and their meanings.

TABLE 15-6

readyState Property Values

HTML Value	OBJECT Value	Description
complete	4	Element and data are fully loaded.
interactive	3	Data may not be loaded fully, but user can interact with element.
loaded	2	Data is loaded, but object may be starting up.
loading	1	Data is loading.
uninitialized	0	Object has not started loading data yet.

For most HTML elements, this property always returns complete. Most of the other states are used by elements such as img, embed, and object, which load external data and even start other processes (such as ActiveX controls) to work.

One word of caution: Do not expect the readyState property to reveal whether an object exists in the document (for example, uninitialized). If the object does not exist, it cannot have a readyState property; the result is a script error for an undefined object. If you want to run a script only after every element and its data are fully loaded, trigger the function by way of the onload event handler for the body element or the onreadystatechange event handler for the object (and check that the readyState property is complete).

Example

To witness a readyState property other than complete for standard HTML, you can try examining the property in a script that immediately follows an <img> tag:

```
...
<img id="myImg" src="someImage.gif">
<script type="text/javaScript">
alert(document.getElementById("myImg").readyState);
</script>
...
```

Putting this fragment into a document that is accessible across a slow network helps. If the image is not in the browser's cache, you might get the uninitialized or loading result. The former means that the img object exists, but it has not started receiving the image data from the server. If you reload the page, chances are that the image will load instantaneously from the cache, and the readyState property will report complete.

Related Items: onreadystatechange event handler

recordNumber

Value: Integer or null Read-Only
Compatibility: WinIE4+, MacIE4+, NN-, Moz-, Safari-

Virtually every object has a recordNumber property, but it applies only to elements used in Internet Explorer data binding to represent repeated data. For example, if you display 30 records from an external data store in a table, the tr element in the table is represented only once in the HTML. However, the browser repeats the table row (and its component cells) to accommodate all 30 rows of data. If you click a row, you can use the `recordNumber` property of the `tr` object to see which record was clicked. A common application of this facility is in data binding situations that allow for updating records. For example, script a table so that clicking an uneditable row of data displays that record's data in editable text boxes elsewhere on the page. If an object is not bound to a data source, or if it is a nonrepeating object bound to a data source, the `recordNumber` property is `null`.

Example

Listing 15-15 shows how to use the `recordNumber` property to navigate to a specific record in a sequence of data. The data source is a small, tab-delimited file consisting of 20 records of Academy Awards data. Thus, the table that displays a subset of the fields is bound to the data source object. Also bound to the data source object are three `span` objects embedded within a paragraph near the top of the page. As the user clicks a row of data, three fields from that clicked record are placed in the bound `span` objects.

The script part of this page is a mere single statement. When the user triggers the `onclick` event handler of the repeated `tr` object, the function receives as a parameter a reference to the `tr` object. The data store object maintains an internal copy of the data in a `recordset` object. One of the properties of this `recordset` object is the `AbsolutePosition` property, which is the integer value of the current record that the data object points to (it can point to only one row at a time, and the default row is the first row). The statement sets the `AbsolutePosition` property of the `recordset` object to the `recordNumber` property for the row that the user clicks. Because the three `span` elements are bound to the same data source, they are immediately updated to reflect the change to the data object's internal pointer to the current record. Notice, too, that the third `span` object is bound to one of the data source fields not shown in the table. You can reach any field of a record because the data source object holds the entire data source content.

LISTING 15-15

Using the Data Binding recordNumber Property

```
<html>
   <head>
      <title>Data Binding (recordNumber)</title>
      <style type="text/css">
      .filmTitle {font-style:italic}
      </style>
      <script type="text/javascript">
      // set recordset pointer to the record clicked on in the table.
      function setRecNum(row) {
         document.oscars.recordset.AbsolutePosition = row.recordNumber;
         }
      </script>
   </head>
   <body>
      <p><b>Academy Awards 1978-2005</b> (Click on a table row to extract data
         from one record.)</p>
      <p>The award for Best Actor of <span datasrc="#oscars"
         datafld="Year"></span>
          went to <span datasrc="#oscars" datafld="Best Actor"></span>
          for his outstanding achievement in the film <span
         class="filmTitle"
```

```
            datasrc="#oscars" datafld="Best Actor Film"></span>.</p>
        <table border="1" datasrc="#oscars" align="center">
            <thead style="background-color:yellow; text-align:center">
                <tr>
                    <td>Year</td>
                    <td>Film</td>
                    <td>Director</td>
                    <td>Actress</td>
                    <td>Actor</td>
                </tr>
            </thead>
            <tr id="repeatableRow" onclick="setRecNum(this)">
                <td><div id="col1" datafld="Year"></div></td>
                <td><div class="filmTitle" id="col2" datafld="Best
                Picture"></div></td>
                <td><div id="col3" datafld="Best Director"></div></td>
                <td><div id="col4" datafld="Best Actress"></div></td>
                <td><div id="col5" datafld="Best Actor"></div></td>
            </tr>
        </table>
        <object id="oscars" classid="clsid:333C7BC4-460F-46D0-BC04-0080C7055A83">
            <param name="DataURL" value="Academy Awards.txt" />
            <param name="UseHeader" value="True" />
            <param name="FieldDelim" value="&#09;" />
        </object>
    </body>
</html>
```

Related Items: dataFld, dataSrc properties; table, tr objects (Chapter 38 on the CD-ROM)

runtimeStyle

Value: style object   Read-Only
Compatibility: WinIE5+, MacIE5+, NN-, Moz-, Safari-

You can determine the browser default settings for style sheet attributes with the help of the runtimeStyle property. The style object that this property returns contains all style attributes and the default settings at the time the page loads. This property does not reflect values assigned to elements by style sheets in the document or by scripts. The default values returned by this property differ from the values returned by the currentStyle property. The latter includes data about values that are not assigned explicitly by style sheets yet are influenced by the default behavior of the browser's rendering engine. In contrast, the runtimeStyle property shows unassigned style values as empty or zero.

Example

To change a style property setting, access it via the element's style object. Use The Evaluator (see Chapter 13) to compare the properties of the runtimeStyle and style objects of an element. For example, an unmodified copy of The Evaluator contains an em element whose ID is "myEM". Enter both

```
document.getElementById("myEM").style.color
```

and

```
document.getElementById("myEM").runtimeStyle.color
```

249

in the top text box in turn. Initially, both values are empty. Now assign a color to the style property via the top text box:

```
document.getElementById("myEM").style.color = "red"
```

If you type the two earlier statements in the top box, you can see that the style object reflects the change, whereas the runtimeStyle object holds onto its original (empty) value.

Related Items: currentStyle property; style object (Chapter 26)

scopeName
tagUrn

Value: String   Read-Only
Compatibility: WinIE5+, MacIE-, NN-, Moz-, Safari-

The scopeName property is associated primarily with XML code that is embedded within a document. When you include XML, you can specify one or more XML Namespaces that define the owner of a custom tag name, thus aiming toward preventing conflicts of identical custom tags from different sources in a document.

CROSS-REF   See Chapter 27 for more about XML objects.

The XML Namespace is assigned as an attribute of the <html> tag that surrounds the entire document:

```
<html xmlns:fred='http://www.someURL.com'>
```

After that, the Namespace value precedes all custom tags linked to that Namespace:

```
<fred:FIRST_Name id="fredFirstName"/>
```

To find out the Namespace owner of an element, you can read the scopeName property of that element. For the preceding example, the scopeName returns fred. For regular HTML elements, the returned value is always HTML. The tagURN property sits alongside scopeName and stores the URI for the namespace.

The scopeName property is available only in Win32 and UNIX flavors of IE5+. The comparable properties for scopeName and tagURN in the W3C DOM are prefix and namespaceURI.

Example

If you have a sample document that contains XML and a namespace spec, you can use document.write() or alert() methods to view the value of the scopeName property. The syntax is

```
document.getElementById("elementID").scopeName
```

Related Item: tagUrn property

scrollHeight
scrollWidth

Value: Integer   Read-Only
Compatibility: WinIE4+, MacIE4+, NN7+, Moz1.0.1+, Safari+

The scrollHeight and scrollWidth properties contain the pixel measures of an object, regardless of how much of the object is visible on the page. Therefore, if the browser window displays a vertical scroll bar, and the body extends below the bottom of the viewable space in the window, the scrollHeight takes into account the entire height of the body as though you were to scroll downward and see the entire element. For most elements that don't have their own scroll bars, the scrollHeight and scrollWidth properties have the same values as the clientHeight and clientWidth properties.

Example

Use The Evaluator (see Chapter 13) to experiment with these two properties of the textarea object, which displays the output of evaluations and property listings. To begin, enter the following in the bottom one-line text box to list the properties of the body object:

```
document.body
```

This displays a long list of properties for the body object. Now enter the following property expression in the top one-line text box to see the scrollHeight property of the output textarea when it holds the dozens of lines of property listings:

```
document.getElementById("output").scrollHeight
```

The result, some number probably in the hundreds, is now displayed in the output textarea. This means that you can scroll the content of the output element vertically to reveal that number of pixels. Click the Evaluate button once more. The result, 13 or 14, is a measure of the scrollHeight property of the textarea that had only the previous result in it. The scrollable height of that content was only 13 or 14 pixels, the height of the font in the textarea. The scrollWidth property of the output textarea is fixed by the width assigned to the element's cols attribute (as calculated by the browser to determine how wide to make the text area on the page).

Related Items: clientHeight , clientWidth properties; window.scroll() method

scrollLeft
scrollTop

Value: Integer   Read-Only
Compatibility: WinIE4+, MacIE4+, NN7+, Moz1.0.1+, Safari+

If an element is scrollable (in other words, it has its own scroll bars), you can find out how far the element is scrolled in the horizontal and vertical direction via the scrollLeft and scrollTop properties. These values are pixels. For nonscrollable elements, these values are always zero — even if they are contained by elements that are scrollable. For example, if you scroll a browser window (or frame in a multiframe environment) vertically, the scrollTop property of the body object is whatever the pixel distance is between the top of the object (now out of view) and the first visible row of pixels of the element. But the scrollTop value of a table that is in the document remains zero.

Netscape browsers prior to version 7 (Mozilla) treat scrolling of a body element from the point of view of the window. If you want to find out the scrolled offset of the current page in these browsers, use window.scrollX and window.scrollY.

Scripts that involve tracking mouse events in IE need to take into account the scrollLeft and scrollTop properties of the body to compensate for scrolling of the page. See the Event object in Chapter 25.

Example

Use The Evaluator (see Chapter 13) to experiment with these two properties of the textarea object, which displays the output of evaluations and property listings. To begin, enter the following in the bottom one-line text box to list the properties of the body object:

```
document.body
```

This displays a long list of properties for the body object. Use the textarea's scroll bar to page down a couple of times. Now enter the following property expression in the top one-line text box to see the scrollTop property of the output textarea after you scroll:

```
document.getElementById("output").scrollTop
```

The result, some number, is now displayed in the output textarea. This means that the content of the output element was scrolled vertically. Click the Evaluate button once more. The result, 0, is a measure of the scrollTop property of the textarea that had only the previous result in it. There wasn't enough content in the textarea to scroll, so the content was not scrolled at all. The scrollTop property, therefore, is zero. The scrollLeft property of the output is always zero because the textarea element is set to wrap any text that overflows the width of the element. No horizontal scroll bar appears in this case, and the scrollLeft property never changes.

Related Items: clientLeft, clientTop properties; window.scroll() method

sourceIndex

Value: Integer   Read-Only
Compatibility: WinIE4+, MacIE4+, NN-, Moz-, Safari-

The sourceIndex property returns the numeric index (zero-based) of the object within the entire document, which is the group of all elements in the document.

Example

Although the operation of this property is straightforward, the sequence of elements exposed by the document.all property may not be. To that end, you can use The Evaluator (see Chapter 13) to experiment in IE4+ with the values that the sourceIndex property returns to see how the index values of the document.all collection follow the source code.

To begin, reload The Evaluator. Enter the following statement in the top text box to set a preinitialized global variable:

```
a = 0
```

When you evaluate this expression, a zero should appear in the Results box. Next, enter the following statement in the top text box:

```
document.all[a].tagName + " [" + a++ + "]"
```

There are a lot of plus signs in this statement, so be sure you enter it correctly. As you successively evaluate this statement (repeatedly click the Evaluate button), the global variable (a) is incremented, enabling you to walk through the elements in source-code order. The sourceIndex value for each HTML tag appears in square brackets in the Results box. You generally begin with the following sequence:

```
html [0]
head [1]
title [2]
```

You can continue until there are no more elements, at which point an error message appears because the value of a exceeds the number of elements in the document.all array. Compare your findings against the HTML source code view of The Evaluator.

Related Item: item() method

style

Value: `style` object reference   Read/Write
Compatibility: WinIE4+, MacIE4+, NN6+, Moz+, Safari+

The `style` property is the gateway to an element's style sheet settings. The property's value is a `style` object whose properties enable you to read and write the style sheet settings for the element. Although scripts do not usually manipulate the `style` object as a whole, it is quite common in a DHTML page for scripts to get or set multiple properties of the `style` object to effect animation, visibility, and all appearance parameters of the element. Note that style properties returned through this object are only those that are explicitly set by the element's `style` attribute or by script.

You can find significant differences in the breadth of properties of the `style` object in different versions of IE and NN. See Chapter 26 for more details on the `style` object.

Example

Most of the action with the `style` property has to do with the `style` object's properties, so you can use The Evaluator here simply to explore the lists of `style` object properties available on as many DHTML-compatible browsers as you have running. To begin, enter the following statement in the bottom, one-line text box to inspect the `style` property for the `document.body` object:

```
document.body.style
```

Now inspect the `style` property of the table element that is part of the original version of The Evaluator. Enter the following statement in the bottom text box:

```
document.getElementById("myTable").style
```

In both cases, the values assigned to the `style` object's properties are quite limited by default.

Related Items: `currentStyle`, `runtimeStyle` properties; `style` object (Chapter 26)

tabIndex

Value: Integer   Read/Write
Compatibility: WinIE4+, MacIE4+, NN6+, Moz+, Safari+

The `tabIndex` property controls where in the tabbing sequence the current object receives focus. This property obviously applies only to elements that can receive focus. IE5+ permits giving focus to more elements than most other browsers, but for all browsers compatible with this property, the primary elements for which you may want to control focus (namely, form input elements) are covered.

In general, browsers treat form elements as focusable elements by default. Nonform elements usually don't receive focus unless you specifically set their `tabIndex` properties (or `tabindex` tag attributes). If you set the `tabIndex` property of one form element to 1, that element is first in the tabbing order. Meanwhile, the rest fall into source-code tabbing order on successive presses of the Tab key. If you set two elements to, say, 1, the tabbing proceeds in source-code order for those two elements and then on to the rest of the elements in source-code order starting with the top of the page.

In Internet Explorer and Moz1.8+, you can remove an element from tabbing order entirely by setting its `tabIndex` property to `-1`. Users can still click those elements to make changes to form element settings, but tabbing bypasses the element.

elementObject.tabIndex

Example

Listing 15-16 contains a sample script that demonstrates how to control the tab order of a form via the tabIndex property. This example demonstrates not only the way you can modify the tabbing behavior of a form on the fly, but also how to force form elements out of the tabbing sequence entirely in IE. In this page, the top form (named lab) contains four elements. Scripts invoked by buttons in the bottom form control the tabbing sequence. Notice that the tabindex attributes of all bottom form elements are set to -1, which means that these control buttons are not part of the tabbing sequence in IE and Moz1.8+.

When you load the page, the default tabbing order for the lab form control elements (default setting of zero) takes charge. If you start pressing the Tab key, the precise results at first depend on the browser you use. In IE, the Address field is first selected; next, the Tab sequence gives focus to the window (or frame, if this page were in a frameset); finally, the tabbing reaches the lab form. Continue pressing the Tab key, and watch how the browser assigns focus to each of the element types. In NN6+/Moz, however, you must click anywhere on the content to get the Tab key to start working on form controls.

The sample script inverts the tabbing sequence with the help of a for loop that initializes two variables that work in opposite directions as the looping progresses. This gives the last element the lowest tabIndex value. The skip2() function simply sets the tabIndex property of the second text box to -1, removing it from the tabbing entirely (IE only). Notice, however, that you can click in the field and still enter text. (See the disabled property earlier in this chapter to see how to prevent field editing.) NN6+/Moz does not provide a tabIndex property setting that forces the browser to skip a form control. You should disable the control instead.

LISTING 15-16

Controlling the tabIndex Property

```html
<html>
    <head>
        <title>tabIndex Property</title>
        <script type="text/javascript">
        function invert() {
            var form = document.lab;
            for (var i = 0, j = form.elements.length; i < form.elements.length;
                i++, j--) {
                form.elements[i].tabIndex = j;
            }
        }

        function skip2() {
            if (navigator.userAgent.indexOf("MSIE") != -1) {
                document.lab.text2.tabIndex = -1;
            } else {
                alert("Not available.");
            }
        }

        function resetTab() {
            var form = document.lab;
            for (var i = 0; i < form.elements.length; i++) {
                form.elements[i].tabIndex = 0;
            }
```

```
        }
      </script>
   </head>
   <body>
      <h1>tabIndex Property Lab</h1>
      <hr />
      <form name="lab">
         Text box no. 1: <input type="text" name="text1" /><br />
         Text box no. 2: <input type="text" name="text2" /><br />
         <input type="button" value="A Button" /><br />
         <input type="checkbox" />And a checkbox
      </form>
      <hr />
      <form name="control">
         <input type="button" value="Invert Tabbing Order" tabindex="-1"
         onclick="invert()" /><br />
         <input type="button" value="Skip Text box no. 2 (IE Only)"
         tabindex="-1" onclick="skip2()" /><br />
         <input type="button" value="Reset to Normal Order" tabindex="-1"
         onclick="resetTab()" />
      </form>
   </body>
</html>
```

The final function, resetTab(), sets the tabIndex property value to zero for all lab form elements; this restores the default order.

Related Items: blur(), focus() methods

tagName

Value: String   Read-Only
Compatibility: WinIE4+, MacIE4+, NN6+, Moz+, Safari+

The tagName property returns a string of the HTML or XML tag name belonging to the object. All tagName values are returned in all-uppercase characters, even if the source code is written in all-lowercase characters or a mixture. This consistency makes it easier to perform string comparisons. For example, you can create a generic function that contains a switch statement to execute actions for some tags and not others. The skeleton of such a function looks like the following:

```
function processObj(objRef) {
   switch (objRef.tagName) {
   case "TR":
      [statements to deal with table row object]
      break;
   case "TD":
      [statements to deal with table cell object]
      break;
   case "COLGROUP":
      [statements to deal with column group object]
      break;
```

```
        default:
           [statements to deal with all other object types]
        }
    }
```

Example

You can also see the `tagName` property in action in the example associated with the `sourceIndex` property discussed earlier in the chapter. In that example, the `tagName` property is read from a sequence of objects in source-code order.

Related Items: `nodeName` property; `getElementsByTagName()` method

tagUrn

(See `scopeName`)

textContent

Value: String   Read/Write
Compatibility: WinIE-, MacIE-, NN-, Moz1.7+, Safari-

This property stores the text string of a node, including any combined text nodes within an element. This means that the content of a node is reflected in the `textContent` property as a single string of text even if it has other nested elements, such as `em`. If you replace the content of a node with a string of text by setting the `textContent` property, all previous node content is replaced, including nested elements. You can think of the `textContent` property as the W3C DOM equivalent of IE's `innerText` property.

Related Item: `innerText` property

title

Value: String   Read/Write
Compatibility: WinIE4+, MacIE4+, NN6+, Moz+, Safari+

The W3C standard states that you should use the `title` property (and `title` attribute) in an advisory role. Most browsers interpret this role as text assigned to tooltips that pop up momentarily while the cursor rests atop an element. The advantage of having this property available for writing is that your scripts can modify an element's tooltip text in response to other user interaction on the page. A tooltip can provide brief help about the behavior of icons or links on the page. It can also convey a summary of key facts from the destination of a link, thus enabling a visitor to see vital information without having to navigate to the other page.

As with setting the status bar, I don't recommend using tooltips for conveying mission-critical information to the user. Not all users are patient enough to let the pointer pause for the tooltip to appear. On the other hand, a user may be more likely to notice a tooltip when it appears rather than a status-bar message (even though the latter appears instantaneously).

Example

Listing 15-17 provides a glimpse at how you can use the `title` property to establish tooltips for a page. A simple paragraph element has its `title` attribute set to `"First Time!"`, which is what the tooltip displays if you roll the pointer atop the paragraph and pause after the page loads. But an `onmouseover` event handler for that element increments a global variable counter in the script, and the `title` property of the paragraph object is modified with each mouseover action. The `count` value is made part of a string assigned to the `title` property. Notice that there is not a live connection between the `title` property and the variable; instead, the new value explicitly sets the `title` property.

LISTING 15-17

Controlling the title Property

```html
<html>
    <head>
        <title>title Property</title>
        <script type="text/javascript">
        // global counting variable
        var count = 0;

        function setToolTip(elem) {
            elem.title = "You have previously rolled atop this paragraph " +
                count + " time(s).";
        }

        function incrementCount(elem) {
            count++;
            setToolTip(elem);
        }
        </script>
    </head>
    <body>
        <h1>title Property Lab</h1>
        <hr />
        <p id="myP" title="First Time!" onmouseover="incrementCount(this)">Roll
            the mouse over this paragraph a few times.<br />
            Then pause atop it to view the tooltip.</p>
    </body>
</html>
```

Related Item: `window.status` property

uniqueID

Value: String   Read-Only
Compatibility: WinIE5+, MacIE-, NN-, Moz-, Safari-

You can let the WinIE5+ browser generate an identifier (`id` property) for a dynamically generated element on the page with the aid of the `uniqueID` property. You should use this feature with care, because the ID it generates at any given time may differ from the ID generated the next time the element is created in the page. Therefore, you should use the `uniqueID` property when your scripts require an unknown element to have an `id` property, but the algorithms are not expecting any specific identifier.

To guarantee that an element gets only one ID assigned to it while the object exists in memory, assign the value via the `uniqueID` property of that same object — not some other object. After you retrieve the `uniqueID` property of an object, the property's value stays the same no matter how often you access the property again. In general, you assign the value returned by the `uniqueID` property to the object's `id` property for other kinds of processing. (For example, the parameter of a `getElementById()` method requires the value assigned to the `id` property of an object.)

elementObject.**uniqueID**

Example

Listing 15-18 demonstrates the recommended syntax for obtaining and applying a browser-generated identifier for an object. After you enter some text in the text box and click the button, the addRow() function
appends a row to the table. The left column displays the identifier generated via the table row object's
uniqueID property. IE5+ generates identifiers in the format "ms__idn", where *n* is an integer starting with
zero for the current browser session. Because the addRow() function assigns uniqueID values to the row
and the cells in each row, the integer for each row is three greater than the previous one. There is no guarantee that future generations of the browser will follow this format, so do not rely on the format or
sequence in your scripts.

LISTING 15-18

Using the uniqueID Property

```html
<html>
    <head>
        <title>Inserting an WinIE5+ Table Row</title>
        <script type="text/javascript">
        function addRow(item1) {
            if (item1) {
                // assign long reference to shorter var name
                var theTable = document.getElementById("myTable");
                // append new row to the end of the table
                var newRow = theTable.insertRow(theTable.rows.length);
                // give the row its own ID
                newRow.id = newRow.uniqueID;

                // declare cell variable
                var newCell;

                // an inserted row has no cells, so insert the cells
                newCell = newRow.insertCell(0);
                // give this cell its own id
                newCell.id = newCell.uniqueID;
                // display the row's id as the cell text
                newCell.innerText = newRow.id;
                newCell.bgColor = "yellow"
                // re-use cell var for second cell insertion
                newCell = newRow.insertCell(1);
                newCell.id = newCell.uniqueID;
                newCell.innerText = item1;
            }
        }
        </script>
    </head>
    <body>
        <table id="myTable" border="1">
            <tr>
                <th>Row ID</th>
                <th>Data</th>
            </tr>
```

```
        <tr id="firstDataRow">
            <td>firstDataRow</td>
            <td>Fred</td>
        </tr>
        <tr id="secondDataRow">
            <td>secondDataRow</td>
            <td>Jane</td>
        </tr>
    </table>
    <hr />
    <form>
        Enter text to be added to the table:<br />
        <input type="text" name="input" size="25" /><br />
        <input type='button' value='Insert Row'
        onclick='addRow(this.form.input.value)' />
    </form>
</body>
</html>
```

Related Items: id property; getElementById() method

unselectable

Value: String constant ("on" or "off")   Read/Write
Compatibility: WinIE5.5+, MacIE-, NN-, Moz-, Safari-

This property controls the selectability of an element — that is, whether the element's content can be selected by the user. You might use this property to prevent a sensitive piece of data from being selected and copied.

Methods
addBehavior("*URL*")

Returns: Integer ID
Compatibility: WinIE5+, MacIE-, NN-, Moz-, Safari-

The addBehavior() method imports an external Internet Explorer behavior and attaches it to the current object, thereby extending the properties and/or methods of that object. (See Chapter 48 on the CD-ROM for details on IE behaviors.) The sole parameter of the addBehavior() method is a URL pointer to the behavior component's code. This component may be in an external file (with an .htc extension), in which case the parameter can be a relative or absolute URL. IE also includes a library of built-in (default) behaviors, whose URLs are in the following format:

    #default#behaviorName

Here, behaviorName is one of the default behaviors (see Chapter 48 on the CD-ROM). If the behavior is imported into the document via the object tag, the addBehavior() method parameter is the ID of that element in the following format:

    #objectID

elementObject.addBehavior()

When you add a behavior, the loading of the external code occurs asynchronously. This means that even though the method returns a value instantly, the behavior is not necessarily ready to work. Only when the behavior is fully loaded can it respond to events or allow access to its properties and methods. Behaviors loaded from external files observe domain security rules.

Example

Listing 15-19a shows what a behavior file looks like. It is the file used to demonstrate the addBehavior() method in Listing 15-19b. The behavior component and the HTML page that loads it must come from the same server and domain; they also must load via the same protocol (for example, http://, https://, and file:// are mutually exclusive, mismatched protocols).

LISTING 15-19A

The makeHot.htc Behavior Component

```
<PUBLIC:ATTACH EVENT="onmousedown" ONEVENT="makeHot()" />
<PUBLIC:ATTACH EVENT="onmouseup" ONEVENT="makeNormal()" />
<PUBLIC:PROPERTY NAME="hotColor" />
<PUBLIC:METHOD NAME="setHotColor" />
<SCRIPT LANGUAGE="JScript">
var oldColor;
var hotColor = "red";

function setHotColor(color) {
   hotColor = color;
}

function makeHot() {
   if (event.srcElement == element) {
      oldColor = style.color;
      runtimeStyle.color = hotColor;
   }
}

function makeNormal() {
   if (event.srcElement == element) {
      runtimeStyle.color = oldColor;
   }
}
</SCRIPT>
```

The object to which the component is attached is a simple paragraph object, shown in Listing 15-19b. When the page loads, the behavior is not attached, so clicking the paragraph text has no effect.

When you turn on the behavior by invoking the turnOn() function, the addBehavior() method attaches the code of the makeHot.htc component to the myP object. At this point, the myP object has one more property, one more method, and two more event handlers that are written to be made public by the component's code. If you want the behavior to apply to more than one paragraph in the document, you have to invoke the addBehavior() method for each paragraph object.

After the behavior file is instructed to start loading, the `setInitialColor()` function is called to set the new color property of the paragraph to the user's choice from the `select` list. But this can happen only if the component is fully loaded. Therefore, the function checks the `readyState` property of `myP` for completeness before invoking the component's function. If IE is still loading the component, the function is invoked again in 500 milliseconds.

As long as the behavior is loaded, you can change the color used to turn the paragraph hot. The function first ensures that the component is loaded by checking that the object has the new color property. If it does, the method of the component is invoked (as a demonstration of how to expose and invoke a component method). You can also simply set the property value.

LISTING 15-19B

Using addBehavior() and removeBehavior()

```
<html>
   <head>
      <title>addBehavior() and removeBehavior() Methods</title>
      <script type="text/javascript">
      var myPBehaviorID;

      function turnOn() {
         myPBehaviorID =
            document.getElementById("myP").addBehavior("makeHot.htc");
         setInitialColor();
      }

      function setInitialColor() {
         if (document.getElementById("myP").readyState == "complete") {
            var select = document.forms[0].colorChoice;
            var color = select.options[select.selectedIndex].value;
            document.getElementById("myP").setHotColor(color);
         } else {
            setTimeout("setInitialColor()", 500);
         }
      }

      function turnOff() {
         document.getElementById("myP").removeBehavior(myPBehaviorID);
      }

      function setColor(select, color) {
         if (document.getElementById("myP").hotColor) {
            document.getElementById("myP").setHotColor(color);
         } else {
            alert("This feature is not available. Turn on the Behavior
            first.");
            select.selectedIndex = 0;
         }
```

continued

261

elementObject.**addBehavior()**

LISTING 15-19B *(continued)*

```
        }

        function showBehaviorCount() {
            var num = document.getElementById("myP").behaviorUrns.length;
            var msg = "The myP element has " + num + " behavior(s). ";
            if (num > 0) {
                msg += "Name(s): \r\n";
                for (var i = 0; i < num; i++) {
                    msg += document.getElementById("myP").behaviorUrns[i] + "\r\n";
                }
            }
            alert(msg);
        }
        </script>
    </head>
    <body>
        <h1>addBehavior() and removeBehavior() Method Lab</h1>
        <hr />
        <p id="myP">This is a sample paragraph. After turning on the behavior, it
            will turn your selected color when you mouse down anywhere in this
            paragraph.</p>
        <form>
            <input type="button" value="Switch On Behavior" onclick="turnOn()" />
            Choose a 'hot' color: <select name="colorChoice"
            onchange="setColor(this, this.value)">
                <option value="red">red</option>
                <option value="blue">blue</option>
                <option value="cyan">cyan</option>
            </select>
            <br />
            <input type="button" value="Switch Off Behavior"
            onclick="turnOff()" />
            <p><input type="button" value="Count the URNs"
                onclick="showBehaviorCount()" /></p>
        </form>
    </body>
</html>
```

To turn off the behavior, the removeBehavior() method is invoked. Notice that the removeBehavior() method is associated with the myP object, and the parameter is the ID of the behavior added earlier. If you associate multiple behaviors with an object, you can remove one without disturbing the others, because each has its own unique ID.

Related Items: readyState property; removeBehavior() method; behaviors (Chapter 48 on the CD-ROM)

```
addEventListener("eventType", listenerFunc, useCapture)
removeEventListener("eventType", listenerFunc, useCapture)
```

Returns: Nothing
Compatibility: WinIE-, MacIE-, NN6+, Moz+, Safari+

The W3C DOM's event mechanism accommodates both event bubbling and trickling (see Chapter 25). Although the new mechanism supports the long-standing notion of binding an event to an element by way of HTML attributes (for example, the old `onclick` event handler), it encourages binding events by registering an event listener with an element. (In browsers that support the W3C event model, other ways of binding events — such as event handler attributes — are internally converted to registered events.)

To tell the DOM that an element should listen for a particular kind of event, use the `addEventListener()` method on the element object. The method requires three parameters. The first is a string version of the event type for which the element should listen. Event type strings do not include the well-used on prefix of event handlers; instead, the names consist only of the event and are usually in all lowercase (except for some special systemwide events preceded by DOM). Table 15-7 shows all the events recognized by the W3C DOM specification (including some new DOM ones that are not yet implemented in browsers).

TABLE 15-7

W3C DOM Event Listener Types

abort	error
blur	focus
change	load
click	mousedown
DOMActivate	mousemove
DOMAttrModified	mouseout
DOMCharacterDataModified	mouseover
DOMFocusIn	mouseup
DOMFocusOut	reset
DOMNodeInserted	resize
DOMNodeInsertedIntoDocument	scroll
DOMNodeRemoved	select
DOMNodeRemovedFromDocument	submit
DOMSubtreeModified	unload

elementObject.addEventListener()

Note that the event types specified in the DOM Level 2 are more limited than the wide range of events defined in IE4+. Also, the W3C temporarily tabled the issue of keyboard events until DOM Level 3. Fortunately, most W3C-compatible browsers implement keyboard events in a fashion that likely will appear as part of the W3C DOM Level 3.

The second parameter of the `addEventListener()` method is a reference to the JavaScript function to be invoked. This is the same form used to assign a function to an event property of an object (for example, `objReference.onclick = someFunction`), and it should *not* be a quoted string. This approach also means that you cannot specify parameters in the function call. Therefore, functions that need to reference forms or form control elements must build their own references (with the help of the event object's property that says which object is the event's target).

By default, the W3C DOM event model has events bubble upward through the element container hierarchy starting with the target object of the event (for example, the button being clicked). However, if you specify `true` for the third parameter of the `addEventListener()` method, event capture is enabled for this particular event type whenever the current object is the event target. This means that any other event type targeted at the current object bubbles upward unless it, too, has an event listener associated with the object and the third parameter is set to `true`.

Using the `addEventListener()` method requires that the object to which it is attached already exists. Therefore, you most likely will use the method inside an initialization function triggered by the `onload` event handler for the page. (The `document` object can use `addEventListener()` for the load event immediately, because the `document` object exists early in the loading process.)

A script can also eliminate an event listener that was previously added by script. The `removeEventListener()` method takes the same parameters as `addEventListener()`, which means that you can turn off one listener without disturbing others. In fact, because you can add two listeners for the same event and listener function (one set to capture and one not — a rare occurrence indeed), the three parameters of the `removeEventListener()` enable you to specify precisely which listener to remove from an object.

Unlike the event capture mechanism of NN4, the W3C DOM event model does not have a global capture mechanism for an event type regardless of target. And with respect to Internet Explorer, the `addEventListener()` method is closely analogous to the IE5+ `attachEvent()` method. Also, event capture in IE5+ is enabled via the separate `setCapture()` method. Both the W3C and IE event models use their own syntaxes to bind objects to event handling functions, so the actual functions may be capable of serving both models with browser version branching required only for event binding. See Chapter 25 for more about event handling with these two event models.

Example

Listing 15-20 provides a compact workbench to explore and experiment with the basic W3C DOM event model. When the page loads, no event listeners are registered with the browser (except the control buttons, of course). But you can add an event listener for a `click` event in bubble and/or capture mode to the `body` element or the `p` element that surrounds the `span` holding the line of text. If you add an event listener and click the text, you see a readout of the element processing the event and information indicating whether the event phase is bubbling (3) or capture (1). With all event listeners engaged, notice the sequence of events being processed. Remove listeners one at a time to see the effect on event processing.

LISTING 15-20

W3C Event Lab

```html
<html>
    <head>
        <title>W3C Event Model Lab</title>
        <style type="text/css">
        td {text-align:center}
        </style>
        <script type="text/javascript">
        // add event listeners
        function addBubbleListener(elemID) {
            document.getElementById(elemID).addEventListener("click", reportEvent,
                false);
        }
        function addCaptureListener(elemID) {
            document.getElementById(elemID).addEventListener("click", reportEvent,
                true);
        }
        // remove event listeners
        function removeBubbleListener(elemID) {
            document.getElementById(elemID).removeEventListener("click",
                reportEvent, false);
        }
        function removeCaptureListener(elemID) {
            document.getElementById(elemID).removeEventListener("click",
                reportEvent, true);
        }
        // display details about any event heard
        function reportEvent(evt) {
            var elem = (evt.target.nodeType == 3) ? evt.target.parentNode :
                evt.target;
            if (elem.id == "mySPAN") {
                var msg = "Event processed at " + evt.currentTarget.tagName +
                " element (event phase = " + evt.eventPhase + ").\n";
                document.controls.output.value += msg;
            }
        }
        // clear the details textarea
        function clearTextArea() {
            document.controls.output.value = "";
        }
        </script>
    </head>
    <body id="myBODY">
        <h1>W3C Event Model Lab</h1>
        <hr />
        <p id="myP"><span id="mySPAN">This paragraph (a SPAN element nested
```

continued

265

LISTING 15-20 *(continued)*

```
    inside a P element) can be set to listen for "click" events.</span></p>
<hr />
<form name="controls" id="controls">
    <p>Examine click event characteristics: <input type="button"
        value="Clear" onclick="clearTextArea()" /><br />
        <textarea name="output" cols="80" rows="6" wrap="virtual">
        </textarea></p>
    <table cellpadding="5" border="1">
        <caption style="font-weight:bold">Control Panel</caption>
        <tr style="background-color:#ffff99">
            <td rowspan="2">"Bubble"-type click listener:</td>
            <td><input type="button" value="Add to BODY" onclick=
                "addBubbleListener('myBODY')" /></td>
            <td><input type="button" value="Remove from BODY" onclick=
                "removeBubbleListener('myBODY')" /></td>
        </tr>
        <tr style="background-color:#ffff99">
            <td><input type="button" value="Add to P" onclick=
                "addBubbleListener('myP')" /></td>
            <td><input type="button" value="Remove from P" onclick=
                "removeBubbleListener('myP')" /></td>
        </tr>
        <tr style="background-color:#ff9999">
            <td rowspan="2">"Capture"-type click listener:</td>
            <td><input type="button" value="Add to BODY" onclick=
                "addCaptureListener('myBODY')" /></td>
            <td><input type="button" value="Remove from BODY" onclick=
                "removeCaptureListener('myBODY')" /></td>
        </tr>
        <tr style="background-color:#ff9999">
            <td><input type="button" value="Add to P" onclick=
                "addCaptureListener('myP')" /></td>
            <td><input type="button" value="Remove from P" onclick=
                "removeCaptureListener('myP')" /></td>
        </tr>
    </table>
</form>
</body>
</html>
```

Related Items: `attachEvent()`, `detachEvent()`, `dispatchEvent()`, `fireEvent()`, `removeEventListener()` methods

appendChild(*elementObject*)

Returns: Node object reference
Compatibility: WinIE5+, MacIE5+, NN6+, Moz+, Safari+

The `appendChild()` method inserts an element or text node (defined by other code that comes before it) as the new, last child of the current element. Aside from the more obvious application of adding a new child element to the end of a sequence of child nodes, the `appendChild()` method is also practical for building element objects and their content before appending, replacing, or inserting the element into an existing document. The `document.createElement()` method generates a reference to an element of whatever tag name you assign as that method's parameter.

The `appendChild()` method returns a reference to the appended node object. This reference differs from the object that is passed as the method's parameter because the returned value represents the object as part of the document rather than as a freestanding object in memory.

Example

Listing 15-21 contains an example that shows how to use the `appendChild()` method in concert with `removeChild()` and `replaceChild()` to modify child elements in a document. Because many W3C DOM browsers treat source-code carriage returns as text nodes (and, thus, child nodes of their parent), the HTML for the affected elements in Listing 15-21 is shown without carriage returns between elements.

The `append()` function creates a new `li` element and then uses the `appendChild()` method to attach the text box text as the displayed text for the item. The nested expression, `document.createTextNode(form.input.value)`, evaluates to a legitimate node that is appended to the new `li` item. All of this occurs before the new `li` item is added to the document. In the final statement of the function, `appendChild()` is invoked from the vantage point of the `ul` element — thus adding the `li` element as a child node of the `ul` element.

Invoking the `replaceChild()` method in the `replace()` function uses some of the same code. The main difference is that the `replaceChild()` method requires a second parameter: a reference to the child element to be replaced. This demonstration replaces the final child node of the `ul` list, so the function takes advantage of the `lastChild` property of all elements to get a reference to that final nested child. That reference becomes the second parameter to `replaceChild()`.

LISTING 15-21

Various Child Methods

```
<html>
   <head>
      <title>appendChild(), removeChild(), and replaceChild() Methods</title>
      <script type="text/javascript">
      function append(form) {
         if (form.input.value) {
            var newItem = document.createElement("LI");
            newItem.appendChild(document.createTextNode(form.input.value));
            document.getElementById("myUL").appendChild(newItem);
         }
      }

      function replace(form) {
         if (form.input.value) {
            var newItem = document.createElement("LI");
            var lastChild = document.getElementById("myUL").lastChild;
            newItem.appendChild(document.createTextNode(form.input.value));
```

continued

LISTING 15-21 *(continued)*

```
                 document.getElementById("myUL").replaceChild(newItem, lastChild);
             }
         }

         function restore() {
             var oneChild;
             var mainObj = document.getElementById("myUL");
             while (mainObj.childNodes.length > 2) {
                 oneChild = mainObj.lastChild;
                 mainObj.removeChild(oneChild);
             }
         }
     </script>
 </head>
 <body>
     <h1>Child Methods</h1>
     <hr />
     Here is a list of items:
     <ul id="myUL"><li>First Item</li><li>Second Item</li></ul>
     <form>
         Enter some text to add/replace in the list: <input type="text"
         name="input" size="30" /><br />
         <input type="button" value="Append to List"
         onclick="append(this.form)" /> <input type="button"
         value="Replace Final Item" onclick="replace(this.form)" /> <input
         type="button" value="Restore List" onclick="restore()" />
     </form>
 </body>
</html>
```

The final part of the demonstration uses the removeChild() method to peel away all children of the ul element until just the two original items are left standing. Again, the lastChild property comes in handy as the restore() function keeps removing the last child until only two remain.

Related Items: removeChild(), replaceChild() methods; nodes and children (Chapter 14)

applyElement(*elementObject*[, *type*])

Returns: Nothing
Compatibility: WinIE5+, MacIE-, NN-, Moz-, Safari-

The applyElement() method enables you to insert a new element as the parent or child of the current object. An important feature of this method is that the new object is wrapped around the current object (if the new element is to become the parent) or the current object's content (if the new element is to become a child). When the new element becomes a child, all previous children are nested further by one generation to become immediate children of the new element. You can imagine how the resulting action of this method affects the containment hierarchy of the current element, so you must be careful how you use the applyElement() method.

One parameter, a reference to the object to be applied, is required. This object may be generated from constructions such as `document.createElement()` or from one of the child or node methods that returns an object. The second parameter is optional, and it must be one of the following values:

Parameter Value	Description
outside	New element becomes the parent of the current object.
inside	New element becomes the immediate child of the current object.

If you omit the second parameter, the default value (`outside`) is assumed. Listing 15-22 shows how the `applyElement()` method is used both with and without default values.

Example

To help you visualize the impact of the `applyElement()` method with its different parameter settings, Listing 15-22 enables you to apply a new element (an em element) to a `span` element inside a paragraph. At any time, you can view the HTML of the entire p element to see where the em element is applied, as well as its impact on the element containment hierarchy for the paragraph.

After you load the page, inspect the HTML for the paragraph before doing anything else. Notice the `span` element and its nested `font` element, both of which surround the one-word content. If you apply the em element inside the `span` element (click the middle button), the `span` element's first (and only) child element becomes the em element; the `font` element is now a child of the new em element.

LISTING 15-22

Using the applyElement() Method

```
<html>
    <head>
        <title>applyElement() Method</title>
        <script type="text/javascript">
        function applyOutside() {
            var newItem = document.createElement("EM");
            newItem.id = newItem.uniqueID;
            document.getElementById("mySpan").applyElement(newItem);
        }

        function applyInside() {
            var newItem = document.createElement("EM");
            newItem.id = newItem.uniqueID;
            document.getElementById("mySpan").applyElement(newItem, "inside");
        }

        function showHTML() {
            alert(document.getElementById("myP").outerHTML);
        }
        </script>
    </head>
```

continued

LISTING 15-22 *(continued)*

```
<body>
   <h1>applyElement() Method</h1>
   <hr />
   <p id="myP">A simple paragraph with a <span id="mySpan"><font
      size="+1">special</font></span> word in it.</p>
   <form>
      <input type="button" value="Apply &lt;EM&gt; Outside"
      onclick="applyOutside()" /> <input type="button"
      value="Apply &lt;EM&gt; Inside" onclick="applyInside()" /> <input
      type="button" value="Show &lt;P&gt; HTML..."
      onclick="showHTML()" /><br />
       <input type="button" value="Restore Paragraph"
      onclick="location.reload()" />
   </form>
</body>
</html>
```

The visible results of applying the em element inside and outside the span element in this case are the same. But you can see from the HTML results that each element impacts the element hierarchy quite differently.

Related Items: insertBefore(), appendChild(), insertAdjacentElement() methods

attachEvent("*eventName*", *functionRef*)
detachEvent("*eventName*", *functionRef*)

Returns: Boolean
Compatibility: WinIE5+, MacIE-, NN-, Moz-, Safari-

The attachEvent() method originated as a means to bind events for IE behaviors (see Chapter 48 on the CD-ROM). But the method has gained acceptance as an IE alternative to the W3C addEventListener() event binding method. To illustrate the method's usage, I want you to first consider the following example of the typical property assignment approach to binding an event handler:

        myObject.onmousedown = setHilite;

The version with attachEvent() is as follows:

        myObject.attachEvent("onmousedown", setHilite);

Both parameters are required. The first parameter is a string version (case insensitive) of the event name. The second is a reference to the function to be invoked when the event fires for this object. A *function reference* is an unquoted, case-sensitive identifier for the function without any parentheses (which also means that you cannot pass parameters in this function call).

There is a subtle benefit to using attachEvent() over the event property binding approach. When you use attachEvent(), the method returns a Boolean value of true if the event binding succeeds. IE triggers a script error if the function reference fails, so don't rely on a returned value of false to catch these kinds of errors. Also, there is no validation that the object recognizes the event name.

If you have used attachEvent() to bind an event handler to an object's event, you can disconnect that binding with the detachEvent() method. The parameters are the same as for attachEvent(). The detachEvent() method cannot unbind events whose associations are established via tag attributes or event property settings.

The W3C DOM event model provides functionality similar to these IE-only methods: addEventListener() and removeEventListener().

Example

Use The Evaluator (see Chapter 13) to create an anonymous function that is called in response to an onmousedown event of the first paragraph on the page. Begin by assigning the anonymous function to global variable a (already initialized in The Evaluator) in the top text box:

```
a = new Function("alert('Function created at " + (new Date()) + "')")
```

The quote marks and parentheses can get jumbled easily, so enter this expression carefully. When you enter the expression successfully, the Results box shows the function's text. Now assign this function to the onmousedown event of the myP element by entering the following statement in the top text box:

```
document.getElementById("myP").attachEvent("onmousedown", a)
```

The Results box displays true when successful. If you mouse down on the first paragraph, an alert box displays the date and time when the anonymous function was created (when the new Date() expression was evaluated).

Now disconnect the event relationship from the object by entering the following statement in the top text box:

```
document.getElementById("myP").detachEvent("onmousedown", a)
```

Related Items: addEventListener(), detachEvent(), dispatchEvent(), fireEvent(), removeEventListener() methods; event binding (Chapter 14)

blur()
focus()

Returns: Nothing
Compatibility: WinIE3+, MacIE3+, NN2+, Moz+, Safari+

The blur() method removes focus from an element, whereas the focus() method gives focus to an element. Even though the blur() and focus() methods have been around since the earliest scriptable browsers, not every focusable object has enjoyed these methods since the beginning. Browsers before IE4 and NN6 limited these methods primarily to the window object and form control elements.

Windows

For window objects, the blur() method (NN3+, IE4+) pushes the referenced window to the back of all other open windows. If other browser suite windows (such as e-mail or newsreader windows) are open, the window receiving the blur() method is placed behind these windows as well.

CAUTION   **The window.blur() method does not adjust the stacking order of the current window in Mozilla-based browsers (thus, the Put Me in Back button in Listing 15-23 doesn't work in those browsers). But a script in a window can invoke the focus() method of another window to bring that other window to the front (provided that a scriptable linkage, such as the window.opener property, exists between the two windows).**

elementObject.blur()

The minute you create another window for a user in your web-site environment, you must pay attention to window layer management. With browser windows so easily activated by the slightest mouse click, a user can lose a smaller window behind a larger one in a snap. Most inexperienced users don't think to check the Windows taskbar or browser menu bar (if the browser is so equipped) to see whether a smaller window is still open and then activate it. If that subwindow is important to your site design, you should present a button or other device in each window that enables users to switch among windows safely. The `window.focus()` method brings the referenced window to the front of all the windows.

Rather than supply a separate button on your page to bring a hidden window forward, you should build your window-opening functions in such a way that if the window is already open, the function automatically brings that window forward (as shown in Listing 15-23). This removes the burden of window management from your visitors.

The key to success with this method is making sure that your references to the desired windows are correct. Therefore, be prepared to use the `window.opener` property to refer to the main window if a subwindow needs to bring the main window back into focus.

Form control elements

The `blur()` and `focus()` methods apply primarily to text-oriented form controls: text input, `select`, and `textarea` elements.

Just as a camera lens blurs when it goes out of focus, a text object blurs when it loses focus — when someone clicks or tabs out of the field. Under script control, `blur()` deselects whatever may be selected in the field, and the text insertion pointer leaves the field. The pointer does not proceed to the next field in tabbing order, as it does if you perform a blur by tabbing out of the field manually.

For a text object, having focus means that the text insertion pointer is flashing in that text object's field. Giving a field focus is like opening it up for human editing.

Setting the focus of a text box or `textarea` does not by itself enable you to place the cursor at any specified location in the field. The cursor usually appears at the beginning of the text. To prepare a field for entry to remove the existing text, use both the `focus()` and `select()` methods in series.

There is a caveat about using `focus()` and `select()` together to preselect the content of a text box for immediate editing: Many versions of Internet Explorer fail to achieve the desired results due to an internal timing problem. You can work around this problem (and remain compatible with other browsers) by initiating the focus and selection actions through a `setTimeout()` method. See Chapter 43 on the CD-ROM on data validation for an example.

A common design requirement is to position the insertion pointer at the end of a text box or `textarea` so that a user can begin appending text to existing content immediately. This is possible in IE4+ with the help of the `TextRange` object. The following script fragment moves the text insertion pointer to the end of a `textarea` element whose ID is `myTextarea`:

```
var range = document.getElementById("myTextarea").createTextRange();
range.move("textedit");
range.select();
```

You should be very careful in combining `blur()` or `focus()` methods with `onblur` and `onfocus` event handlers — especially if the event handlers display alert boxes. Many combinations of these events and methods can cause an infinite loop in which it is impossible to dismiss the alert dialog box completely. On the other hand, there is a useful combination for older browsers that don't offer a `disabled` property for text boxes. The following text box event handler can prevent users from entering text in a text box:

```
onfocus = "this.blur()";
```

Some operating systems and browsers enable you to give focus to elements such as buttons (including radio and checkbox buttons) and hypertext links (encompassing both a and `area` elements). Typically, once such an element has focus, you can accomplish the equivalent of a mouse click on the element by pressing the spacebar. This is helpful for accessibility to those who have difficulty using a mouse.

An unfortunate side effect of button focus in Win32 environments is that the focus highlight (a dotted rectangle) remains around the button after a user clicks it and until another object gets focus. You can eliminate this artifact for browsers and objects that implement the `onmouseup` event handler by including the following event handler in your buttons:

```
onmouseup = "this.blur()";
```

IE5.5+ recognizes the often undesirable effect of that dotted rectangle and lets scripts set the `hideFocus` property of an element to `true` to keep that rectangle hidden while giving the element focus. It is a trade-off for the user, however, because there is no visual feedback about which element has focus.

Other elements

For other kinds of elements that support the `focus()` method, you can bring an element into view in lieu of the `scrollIntoView()` method. Link (a) and `area` elements in Windows versions of IE display the dotted rectangle around them after a user brings focus to them. To eliminate that artifact, use the same

```
onmouseup = "this.blur()";
```

event handler (or IE5.5+ `hideFocus` property) just described for form controls.

Example

Listing 15-23 contains an example of using the `focus()` and `blur()` methods to tinker with changing the focus of windows. This example creates a two-window environment; from each window, you can bring the other window to the front. The main window uses the object returned by `window.open()` to assemble the reference to the new window. In the subwindow (whose content is created entirely on the fly by JavaScript), `self.opener` is summoned to refer to the original window, whereas `self.blur()` operates on the subwindow itself. Blurring one window and focusing on another window yields the same result of sending the window to the back of the pile.

LISTING 15-23

The window.focus() and window.blur() Methods

```
<html>
  <head>
    <title>Window Focus() and Blur()</title>
    <script type="text/javascript">
    // declare global variable name
    var newWindow = null;

    function makeNewWindow() {
       // check if window already exists
       if (!newWindow || newWindow.closed) {
          // store new window object in global variable
          newWindow = window.open("","","width=250,height=250");
```

continued

elementObject.**blur**()

LISTING 15-23 *(continued)*

```
            // pause briefly to let IE3 window finish opening
            setTimeout("fillWindow()",100);
        } else {
            // window already exists, so bring it forward
            newWindow.focus();
        }
    }

    // assemble new content and write to subwindow
    function fillWindow() {
        var newContent = "<html><head><title>Another Sub
        Window<\/title><\/head>";
        newContent += "<body bgColor='salmon'>";
        newContent += "<h1>A Salmon-Colored Subwindow.<\/h1>";
        newContent += "<form><input type='button' value='Bring Main to Front'
        onclick='self.opener.focus()'>";
        newContent += "<form><input type='button' value='Put Me in Back'
        onclick='self.blur()'>";
        newContent += "<\/form><\/body><\/html>";
        // write HTML to new window document
        newWindow.document.write(newContent);
        newWindow.document.close();
    }
    </script>
</head>
<body>
    <h1>Window focus() and blur() Methods</h1>
    <hr />
    <form>
        <input type="button" name="newOne" value="Show New Window"
        onclick="makeNewWindow()" />
    </form>
</body>
</html>
```

A key ingredient to the success of the makeNewWindow() function in Listing 15-23 is the first conditional expression. Because newWind is initialized as a null value when the page loads, that is its value the first time through the function. But after you open the subwindow the first time, newWind is assigned a value (the subwindow object) that remains intact even if the user closes the window. Thus, the value doesn't revert to null by itself. To catch the possibility that the user has closed the window, the conditional expression also sees whether the window is closed. If it is, a new subwindow is generated, and that new window's reference value is reassigned to the newWind variable. On the other hand, if the window reference exists and the window is not closed, the focus() method brings that subwindow to the front.

You can see the focus() method for a text object in action in Chapter 25's description of the select() method for text objects.

Related Items: window.open(), document.formObject.textObject.select() methods

clearAttributes()

Returns: Nothing
Compatibility: WinIE5+, MacIE-, NN-, Moz-, Safari-

The clearAttributes() method removes all attributes from an element except the name and id values. Thus, styles and event handlers are removed, as are custom attributes assigned in either the HTML source code or later by script. You should know that the clearAttributes() method does not alter the length of the element's attributes collection, because the collection always contains all possible attributes for an element. (See the attributes property for elements earlier in this chapter.)

This method is handy if you wish to construct an entirely new set of attributes for an element and prefer to start out with a blank slate. Be aware, however, that unless your scripts immediately assign new attributes to the element, the appearance of the element reverts to its completely unadorned form until you assign new attributes. This means that even positioned elements find their way back to their source-code order until you assign a new positioning style. If you simply want to change the value of one or more attributes of an element, it is faster to use the setAttribute() method or adjust the corresponding properties.

To accomplish a result in NN6+/Moz that simulates that of IE5+'s clearAttributes(), you must iterate through all attributes of an element and remove those attributes (via the removeAttribute() method) whose names are other than id and name.

Example

Use The Evaluator (see Chapter 13) to examine the attributes of an element before and after you apply clearAttributes(). To begin, display the HTML for the table element on the page by entering the following statement in the top text box:

```
myTable.outerHTML
```

Notice the attributes associated with the <table> tag. Look at the rendered table to see how attributes such as border and width affect the display of the table. Now enter the following statement in the top text box to remove all removable attributes from this element:

```
myTable.clearAttributes()
```

First, look at the table. The border is gone, and the table is rendered only as wide as is necessary to display the content with no cell padding. Finally, view the results of the clearAttributes() method in the outerHTML of the table again:

```
myTable.outerHTML
```

The source-code file has not changed, but the object model in the browser's memory reflects the changes you made.

Related Items: attributes property; getAttribute(), setAttribute(), removeAttribute(), mergeAttributes(), and setAttributeNode() methods

click()

Returns: Nothing
Compatibility: WinIE4+, MacIE4+, NN2+, Moz+, Safari+

The click() method lets a script perform nearly the same action as clicking an element. Before NN4 and IE4, the click() method invoked on a button did not trigger the onclick event handler for the object. This has significant impact if you expect the onclick event handler of a button to function even if a script performs the click. For earlier browser versions, you have to invoke the event handler statements directly. Also, just because a script is clicking a button, not all buttons in all platforms change their appearance in response. For example, NN4 on the Mac does not change the state of a checkbox clicked remotely.

If you want to script the action of clicking a button, you can safely invoke the resulting event handler function directly. And if the element is a radio button or checkbox, handle the change of state directly (for example, set the checked property of a checkbox) rather than expect the browser to take care of it for you.

Example

Use The Evaluator (see Chapter 13) to experiment with the click() method. The page includes various types of buttons at the bottom. You can click the checkbox, for example, by entering the following statement in the top text box:

```
document.myForm2.myCheckbox.click()
```

If you use a recent browser version, you most likely can see the checkbox change states between checked and unchecked each time you execute the statement.

Related Item: onclick event handler

cloneNode(*deepBoolean*)

Returns: Node object reference
Compatibility: WinIE5+, MacIE5+, NN6+, Moz+, Safari+

The cloneNode() method makes an exact copy of the current node object. This copy does not have a parent node or other relationship with any element after the copy exists (of course, the original node remains in place). The clone also does not become part of the document's object model (the node tree) unless you explicitly insert or append the node somewhere on the page. The copy includes all element attributes, including the id attribute. Because the value returned by the cloneNode() method is a genuine Node object, you can operate on it with any Node object methods while it is still in the nondocument object state.

The Boolean parameter of the cloneNode() method controls whether the copy of the node includes all child nodes (true) or just the node itself (false). For example, if you clone a paragraph element by itself, the clone consists only of the raw element (equivalent of the tag pair, including attributes in the start tag) and none of its content. But including child nodes makes sure that all content within that paragraph element is part of the copy. This parameter is optional in IE5 (defaulting to false), but it is required in other W3C-compatible browsers.

Example

Use The Evaluator (see Chapter 13) to clone, rename, and append an element found in The Evaluator's source code. Begin by cloning the paragraph element named myP along with all of its content. Enter the following statement in the top text box:

```
a = document.getElementById("myP").cloneNode(true)
```

The variable a now holds the clone of the original node, so you can change its id attribute at this point by entering the following statement:

```
a.setAttribute("id", "Dolly")
```

If you want to see the properties of the cloned node, enter a in the bottom text box. The precise listing of properties you see depends on the browser you're using; in either case, you should be able to locate the id property, whose value is now Dolly.

As a final step, append this newly named node to the end of the body element by entering the following statement in the top text box:

```
document.body.appendChild(a)
```

You can now scroll down to the bottom of the page and see a duplicate of the content. But because the two nodes have different id attributes, they cannot confuse scripts that need to address one or the other.

Related Items: Node object (Chapter 14); appendChild(), removeChild(), removeNode(), replaceChild(), and replaceNode() methods

compareDocumentPosition(nodeRef)

Returns: Integer
Compatibility: WinIE-, MacIE-, NN6+, Moz1.4+, Safari-

This method determines the tree position of one node with respect to another node. More specifically, the nodeRef object provided as a parameter (Node B) is compared with the object on which the method is called (Node A). The result is returned from the method as an integer value that can contain one or more of the comparison masks listed in Table 15-8.

TABLE 15-8

Comparison Return Flags

Integer Value	Constant	Description
0		Node B and Node A are one and the same.
1	DOCUMENT_POSITION_DISCONNECTED	No connection exists between the nodes.
2	DOCUMENT_POSITION_PRECEDING	Node B precedes Node A.
4	DOCUMENT_POSITION_FOLLOWING	Node B follows Node A.
8	DOCUMENT_POSITION_CONTAINS	Node B contains Node A (and therefore precedes it).
16	DOCUMENT_POSITION_CONTAINED_BY	Node B is contained by Node A (and therefore follows it).
32	DOCUMENT_POSITION_IMPLEMENTATION_SPECIFIC	The comparison is determined by the browser.

The integer value returned by the compareDocumentPosition() method is actually a bitmask, which explains why the values in Table 15-8 are powers of 2. This allows the method to return multiple comparison values simply by adding them together. For example, a return value of 20 indicates that Node B is contained by Node A (16) and also that Node B follows Node A (4).

Related Items: contains() method

componentFromPoint(x,y)

Returns: String
Compatibility: WinIE5+, MacIE-, NN-, Moz-, Safari-

The componentFromPoint() method assists in some event-related tasks. You can use it for a kind of collision detection (in other words, to determine whether an event occurs inside or outside a particular element).

elementObject.componentFromPoint()

If the element has scroll bars, the method can provide additional information about the event, such as which component of the scroll bar the user activates.

A key aspect of this method is that you invoke it on any element that you want to use as the point of reference. For example, if you want to find out whether a `mouseup` event occurs in an element whose ID is `myTable`, invoke the method as follows:

```
var result = document.getElementById("myTable").componentFromPoint(
    event.clientX, event.clientY);
```

Parameters passed to the method are *x* and *y* coordinates. These coordinates do not have to come from an event, but the most likely scenario links this method with an event of some kind. Mouse events (other than `onclick`) work best.

The value returned by the method is a string that provides details about where the coordinate point is with respect to the current element. If the coordinate point is inside the element's rectangle, the returned value is an empty string. Conversely, if the point is completely outside the element, the returned value is the string `"outside"`. For scroll-bar pieces, the list of possible returned values is quite lengthy (as shown in Table 15-9).

TABLE 15-9

Returned Values for componentFromPoint()

Returned String	Element Component at Coordinate Point
(empty)	Inside the element content area
outside	Outside the element content area
handleBottom	Resize handle at bottom
handleBottomLeft	Resize handle at bottom left
handleBottomRight	Resize handle at bottom right
handleLeft	Resize handle at left
handleRight	Resize handle at right
handleTop	Resize handle at top
handleTopLeft	Resize handle at top left
handleTopRight	Resize handle at top right
scrollbarDown	Scroll-bar down arrow
scrollbarHThumb	Scroll-bar thumb on horizontal bar
scrollbarLeft	Scroll-bar left arrow
scrollbarPageDown	Scroll-bar page-down region
scrollbarPageLeft	Scroll-bar page-left region
scrollbarPageRight	Scroll-bar page-right region
scrollbarPageUp	Scroll-bar page-up region
scrollbarRight	Scroll-bar right arrow
scrollbarUp	Scroll-bar up arrow
scrollbarVThumb	Scroll-bar thumb on vertical bar

You do not have to use this method for most collision or event detection, however. The `event` object's `srcElement` property returns a reference to whatever object receives the event.

Example

Listing 15-24 demonstrates how the `componentFromPoint()` method can be used to determine exactly where a mouse event occurred. As presented, the method is associated with a `textarea` object that is specifically sized to display both vertical and horizontal scroll bars. As you click various areas of the `textarea` and the rest of the page, the status bar displays information about the location of the event with the help of the `componentFromPoint()` method.

The script uses a combination of the `event.srcElement` property and the `componentFromPoint()` method to help you distinguish how you can use each one for different types of event processing. The `srcElement` property is used initially as a filter to decide whether the status bar will reveal further processing about the `textarea` element's event details.

The `onmousedown` event handler in the `body` element triggers all event processing. IE events bubble up the hierarchy (and no events are canceled in this page), so all `mousedown` events eventually reach the `body` element. Then the `whereInWorld()` function can compare each `mousedown` event from any element against the text area's geography.

LISTING 15-24

Using the componentFromPoint() Method

```
<html>
    <head>
        <title>componentFromPoint() Method</title>
        <script type="text/javascript">
        function whereInWorld(elem) {
            var x = event.clientX;
            var y = event.clientY;
            var component =
                document.getElementById("myTextarea").componentFromPoint(x,y);
            if (window.event.srcElement == document.getElementById("myTextarea")){
                if (component == "") {
                    status = "mouseDown event occurred inside the element";
                } else {
                    status = "mouseDown occurred on the element\'s " + component;
                }
            } else {
                status = "mouseDown occurred " + component + " of the element";
            }
        }
        </script>
    </head>
    <body onmousedown="whereInWorld()">
        <h1>componentFromPoint() Method</h1>
        <hr />
        <p>Tracking the mouseDown event relative to the textarea object. View
            results in status bar.</p>
```

continued

elementObject.contains()

LISTING 15-24 *(continued)*

```
    <form>
        <textarea name="myTextarea" wrap="off" cols="12" rows="4">
            This is Line 1
            This is Line 2
            This is Line 3
            This is Line 4
            This is Line 5
            This is Line 6
        </textarea>
    </form>
  </body>
</html>
```

Related Item: event object

contains(*elementObjectReference*)

Returns: Boolean
Compatibility: WinIE4+, MacIE4+, NN-, Moz-, Safari-

The contains() method reports whether the current object contains another known object within its HTML containment hierarchy. Note that this is not geographical collision detection of overlapping elements, but the determination of whether one element is nested somewhere within another.

The scope of the contains() method extends as deeply within the current object's hierarchy as is necessary to locate the object. In essence, the contains() method examines all of the elements that are part of an element's all array. Therefore, you can use this method as a shortcut replacement for a for loop that examines each nested element of a container for the existence of a specific element.

The parameter to the contains() method is a reference to an object. If you have only the element's ID as a string to go by, you can use the document.getElementById() method to generate a valid reference to the nested element.

 An element always contains itself.

Example

Using The Evaluator (Chapter 13), see how the contains() method responds to the object combinations in each of the following statements as you enter them in the top text box:

```
document.body.contains(document.all.myP)
document.all.myP.contains(document.all.item("myEM"))
document.all.myEM.contains(document.all.myEM)
document.all.myEM.contains(document.all.myP)
```

Feel free to test other object combinations within this page.

Related Items: item(), document.getElementById() methods

createControlRange("*param*")

Returns: Integer ID
Compatibility: WinIE5+, MacIE-, NN-, Moz-, Safari-

The `createControlRange()` method is used to create a control range for a selection of text. Although the method is implemented for several elements, it is intended solely for the `selection` object and, therefore, should be used only on that object.

Related Items: `selection` object

detachEvent()

(See `attachEvent()`)

dispatchEvent(*eventObject*)

Returns: Boolean
Compatibility: WinIE-, MacIE-, NN6+, Moz+, Safari+

The `dispatchEvent()` method allows a script to fire an event aimed at any object capable of supporting that event. This is the W3C event model way of generalizing mechanisms that earlier browsers sometimes mimic with object methods such as `click()` and `focus()`.

The process of generating one of these events is similar to the way a script generates a new node and inserts that node somewhere into the DOM. For events, however, the object that is created is an `Event` object, which is generated via the `document.createEvent()` method. An event generated in this manner is simply a specification about an event. Use properties of an event object to supply specifics about the event, such as its coordinates or mouse button. Then dispatch the event to a target object by invoking that target object's `dispatchEvent()` method and passing the newly created `Event` object as the sole parameter.

Interpreting the meaning of the Boolean value that the `dispatchEvent()` method returns is not straightforward. The browser follows the dispatched event through whatever event propagation is in effect for that object and event type (either bubbling or capture). If any of the event listener functions triggered by this dispatched event invokes the `preventDefault()` method, the `dispatchEvent()` method returns `false` to indicate that the event did not trigger the native action of the object; otherwise, the method returns `true`. Notice that this returned value indicates nothing about propagation type or how many event listeners run as a result of dispatching this event.

CAUTION Although the `dispatchEvent()` method was implemented in NN6, the browser does not yet provide a way to generate new events from scratch. And if you attempt to redirect an existing event to another object via the `dispatchEvent()` method, the browser is prone to crashing. In other words, Mozilla-based browsers are much better candidates for scripts that use `dispatchEvent()`.

Example

Listing 15-25 demonstrates how to fire events programmatically using the W3C DOM `dispatchEvent()` method. Notice the syntax in the `doDispatch()` function for creating and initializing a new mouse event, supported most reliably in Mozilla-based browsers. The behavior is identical to that of Listing 15-26 later in this chapter, which demonstrates the IE5.5+ equivalent: `fireEvent()`.

LISTING 15-25

Using the dispatchEvent() Method

```
<html>
   <head>
      <title></title>
      <style type="text/css">
      #mySPAN {font-style:italic}
      </style>
      <script type="text/javascript">
      // assemble a couple event object properties
      function getEventProps(evt) {
         var msg = "";
         var elem = evt.target;
         msg += "event.target.nodeName: " + elem.nodeName + "\n";
         msg += "event.target.parentNode: " + elem.parentNode.id + "\n";
         msg += "event button: " + evt.button;
         return msg;
      }

      // onClick event handlers for body, myP, and mySPAN
      function bodyClick(evt) {
         var msg = "Click event processed in BODY\n\n";
         msg += getEventProps(evt);
         alert(msg);
         checkCancelBubble(evt);
      }
      function pClick(evt) {
         var msg = "Click event processed in P\n\n";
         msg += getEventProps(evt);
         alert(msg);
         checkCancelBubble(evt);
      }
      function spanClick(evt) {
         var msg = "Click event processed in SPAN\n\n";
         msg += getEventProps(evt);
         alert(msg);
         checkCancelBubble(evt);
      }

      // cancel event bubbling if checkbox is checked
      function checkCancelBubble(evt) {
         if (document.controls.bubbleOn.checked) {
            evt.stopPropagation();
         }
      }

      // assign onClick event handlers to three elements
      function init() {
         document.body.onclick = bodyClick;
```

```
          document.getElementById("myP").onclick = pClick;
          document.getElementById("mySPAN").onclick = spanClick;
       }

       // invoke fireEvent() on object whose ID is passed as parameter
       function doDispatch(objID, evt) {
          // create empty mouse event
          var newEvt = document.createEvent("MouseEvents");
          // initialize as click with button ID 3
          newEvt.initMouseEvent("click", true, true, window, 0, 0, 0,
             0, 0, false, false, false, false, 3, null);
          // send event to element passed as param
          document.getElementById(objID).dispatchEvent(newEvt);
          // don't let button clicks bubble
          evt.stopPropagation();
       }
    </script>
 </head>
 <body id="myBODY" onload="init()">
    <h1>fireEvent() Method</h1>
    <hr />
    <p id="myP">This is a paragraph <span id="mySPAN">(with a nested
       SPAN)</span> that receives click events.</p>
    <hr />
    <p><b>Control Panel</b></p>
    <form name="controls">
       <p><input type="checkbox" name="bubbleOn"
          onclick="event.stopPropagation()" />Cancel event bubbling.</p>
       <p><input type="button" value="Fire Click Event on BODY"
          onclick="doDispatch('myBODY', event)" /></p>
       <p><input type="button" value="Fire Click Event on myP"
          onclick="doDispatch('myP', event)" /></p>
       <p><input type="button" value="Fire Click Event on mySPAN"
          onclick="doDispatch('mySPAN', event)" /></p>
    </form>
 </body>
</html>
```

Related Item: fireEvent() method

doScroll("*scrollAction*")

Returns: Nothing
Compatibility: WinIE5+, MacIE-, NN-, Moz-, Safari-

The doScroll() method is used to control the scrolling of an element by triggering its scroll bars.
Although a subtle distinction, doScroll() doesn't move the scroll bars to a specific position; instead, it
simulates a scroll-bar click. The end result is an onscroll event being fired, which is what you would
expect from a simulated scroll.

elementObject.fireEvent()

The string parameter to doScroll() can be one of the following values to indicate what kind of scrolling is to take place: scrollbarUp, scrollbarDown, scrollbarLeft, scrollbarRight, scrollbarPageUp, scrollbarPageDown, scrollbarPageLeft, scrollbarPageRight, scrollbarHThumb, or scrollbarVThumb.

dragDrop()

Returns: Boolean
Compatibility: WinIE5.5+, MacIE-, NN-, Moz-, Safari-

The dragDrop() method initiates a mouse drag-and-drop sequence by triggering an ondragstart event. The return value is a Boolean that indicates when the user releases the mouse button (true).

fireEvent("*eventType*"[, *eventObjectRef*])

Returns: Boolean
Compatibility: WinIE5.5+, MacIE-, NN-, Moz-, Safari-

Although some objects have methods that emulate physical events (for example, the click() and focus() methods), WinIE5.5+ generalizes the mechanism by letting a script direct any valid event to any object. The fireEvent() method is the vehicle.

One required parameter is the event type, formatted as a string. IE event types are coded just like the property names for event handlers (for example, onclick, onmouseover, and so on).

A second, optional parameter is a reference to an existing event object. This object can be an event that some user or system action triggers (meaning that the fireEvent() method is in a function invoked by an event handler). The existing event can also be an object created by the IE5.5+ document.createEventObject() method. In either case, the purpose of providing an existing event object is to set the properties of the event object that the fireEvent() method creates. The event type is defined by the method's first parameter, but if you have other properties to set (for example, coordinates or a keyboard key code), those properties are picked up from the existing object. Here is an example of a sequence that creates a new mousedown event, stuffs some values into its properties, and then fires the event at an element on the page:

```
var newEvent = document.createEventObject();
newEvent.clientX = 100;
newEvent.clientY = 30;
newEvent.cancelBubble = false;
newEvent.button = 1;
document.getElementById("myElement").fireEvent("onmousedown", newEvent);
```

Events generated by the fireEvent() method are just like regular IE window.event objects, and they have several important event object properties that the browser presets. It is important that cancelBubble is set to false and returnValue is set to true—just like a regular user- or system-induced event. This means that if you want to prevent event bubbling and/or prevent the default action of the event's source element, the event handler functions must set these event object properties just like normal event handling in IE.

The fireEvent() method returns a Boolean value that the returnValue property of the event determines. If the returnValue property is set to false during event handling, the fireEvent() method returns false. Under normal processing, the method returns true.

The W3C DOM (Level 2) event model includes the dispatchEvent() method to accommodate script-generated events (and Event object methods to create event objects), which is roughly the W3C equivalent of the fireEvent() method.

Example

Listing 15-26 contains script code that shows how to fire events programmatically using the `fireEvent()` method. Three buttons in the example page enable you to direct a click event to each of the three elements that have event handlers defined for them. The events fired this way are artificial, generated via the `createEventObject()` method. For demonstration purposes, the `button` property of these scripted events is set to 3. This property value is assigned to the `event` object that eventually gets directed to an element. With event bubbling left on, the events sent via `fireEvent()` behave just like the physical clicks on the elements. Similarly, if you disable event bubbling, the first event handler to process the event cancels bubbling, and no further processing of that event occurs. Notice that event bubbling is canceled within the event handlers that process the event. To prevent the clicks of the checkbox and action buttons from triggering the `body` element's `onclick` event handlers, event bubbling is turned off for the buttons right away.

LISTING 15-26

Using the fireEvent() Method

```
<html>
    <head>
        <title></title>
        <style type="text/css">
        #mySPAN {font-style:italic}
        </style>
        <script type="text/javascript">
        // assemble a couple event object properties
        function getEventProps() {
            var msg = "";
            var elem = event.srcElement;
            msg += "event.srcElement.tagName: " + elem.tagName + "\n";
            msg += "event.srcElement.id: " + elem.id + "\n";
            msg += "event button: " + event.button;
            return msg;
        }

        // onClick event handlers for body, myP, and mySPAN
        function bodyClick() {
            var msg = "Click event processed in BODY\n\n";
            msg += getEventProps();
            alert(msg);
            checkCancelBubble();
        }
        function pClick() {
            var msg = "Click event processed in P\n\n";
            msg += getEventProps();
            alert(msg);
            checkCancelBubble();
        }
        function spanClick() {
            var msg = "Click event processed in SPAN\n\n";
            msg += getEventProps();
```

continued

285

| LISTING 15-26 | *(continued)* |

```
            alert(msg);
            checkCancelBubble();
        }

        // cancel event bubbling if checkbox is checked
        function checkCancelBubble() {
            event.cancelBubble = document.controls.bubbleOn.checked;
        }

        // assign onClick event handlers to three elements
        function init() {
            document.body.onclick = bodyClick;
            document.getElementById("myP").onclick = pClick;
            document.getElementById("mySPAN").onclick = spanClick;
        }

        // invoke fireEvent() on object whose ID is passed as parameter
        function doFire(objID) {
            var newEvt = document.createEventObject();
            newEvt.button = 3;
            document.all(objID).fireEvent("onclick", newEvt);
            // don't let button clicks bubble
            event.cancelBubble = true;
        }
        </script>
    </head>
    <body id="myBODY" onload="init()">
        <h1>fireEvent() Method</h1>
        <hr />
        <p id="myP">This is a paragraph <span id="mySPAN">(with a nested
            SPAN)</span> that receives click events.</p>
        <hr />
        <p><b>Control Panel</b></p>
        <form name="controls">
            <p><input type="checkbox" name="bubbleOn"
                onclick="event.cancelBubble=true" />Cancel event bubbling.</p>
            <p><input type="button" value="Fire Click Event on BODY"
                onclick="doFire('myBODY')" /></p>
            <p><input type="button" value="Fire Click Event on myP"
                onclick="doFire('myP')" /></p>
            <p><input type="button" value="Fire Click Event on mySPAN"
                onclick="doFire('mySPAN')" /></p>
        </form>
    </body>
</html>
```

Related Item: dispatchEvent() method

focus()

(See `blur()`)

getAdjacentText("*position*")

Returns: String
Compatibility: WinIE5+, MacIE-, NN-, Moz-, Safari-

The `getAdjacentText()` method enables you to extract copies of plain-text components of an element object (in other words, without any HTML tag information). The sole parameter is one of four case-insensitive string constant values that indicate from where, in relation to the current object, the text should be extracted. The values are

Parameter Value	Description
beforeBegin	Text immediately in front of the element's tag, back to the preceding tag
afterBegin	Text that begins inside the element tag, up to the next tag (whether it be a nested element or the element's end tag)
beforeEnd	Text immediately in front of the element's end tag, back to the preceding tag (whether it be a nested element or the element's start tag)
afterEnd	Text immediately following the element's end tag, forward until the next tag

If the current object has no nested elements, both the `afterBegin` and `beforeEnd` versions return the same as the object's `innerText` property. When the current object is encased immediately within another element (for example, a `td` element inside a `tr` element), there is no text before the element's beginning or after the element's end, so these values are returned as empty strings.

The strings returned from this method are roughly equivalent to values of text fragment nodes in the W3C DOM, but IE5+ treats these data pieces as string data types rather than as text node types. W3C DOM equivalents for the four versions are

```
document.getElementById("objName").previousSibling.nodeValue
document.getElementById("objName").firstChild.nodeValue
document.getElementById("objName").lastChild.nodeValue
document.getElementById("objName").nextSibling.nodeValue
```

Example

Use The Evaluator (see Chapter 13) to examine all four adjacent text possibilities for the `myP` and nested `myEM` elements in that document. Enter each of the following statements in the top text box, and view the results:

```
document.getElementById("myP").getAdjacentText("beforeBegin")
document.getElementById("myP").getAdjacentText("afterBegin")
document.getElementById("myP").getAdjacentText("beforeEnd")
document.getElementById("myP").getAdjacentText("afterEnd")
```

The first and last statements return empty strings because the `myP` element has no text fragments surrounding it. The `afterBegin` version returns the text fragment of the `myP` element up to, but not including, the EM element nested inside. The `beforeEnd` string picks up after the end of the nested EM element and returns all text to the end of `myP`.

elementObject.getAdjacentText()

Now see what happens with the nested myEM element:

```
document.getElementById("myEM").getAdjacentText("beforeBegin")
document.getElementById("myEM").getAdjacentText("afterBegin")
document.getElementById("myEM").getAdjacentText("beforeEnd")
document.getElementById("myEM").getAdjacentText("afterEnd")
```

Because this element has no nested elements, the afterBegin and beforeEnd strings are identical — the same value as the innerText property of the element.

Related Items: childNodes, data, firstChild, lastChild, nextSibling, nodeValue, and previousSibling properties

getAttribute("*attributeName*"[, *caseSensitivity*])

Returns: (See text)
Compatibility: WinIE4+, MacIE4+, NN6+, Moz+, Safari+

The getAttribute() method returns the value assigned to a specific attribute of the current object. You can use this method as an alternative to retrieving properties of an object, particularly when your script presents you the attribute name as a string (in contrast to a fully formed reference to an object and its property). Thus, the following example statements yield the same data:

```
var mult = document.getElementById("mySelect").multiple;
var mult = document.getElementById("mySelect").getAttribute("multiple");
```

Returned value types from getAttribute() are either strings (including attribute values assigned as unquoted numeric values) or Booleans (for example, the multiple property of a select element object).

NOTE The W3C DOM Level 2 standard recommends getAttribute() and setAttribute() for reading and writing element object attribute values, rather than reading and writing those values by way of their corresponding properties. Although using these methods is certainly advisable for XML elements, the same DOM standard sends conflicting signals by defining all kinds of properties for HTML element objects. Browsers, of course, will support access via properties well into the future, so don't feel obligated to change your ways just yet.

All browsers that support the getAttribute() method require one parameter, which is a string of the attribute name. By default, this parameter is not case sensitive. Note that this has impact on custom attributes that you might assign to HTML or XML elements in your documents. Attribute names are automatically converted to lowercase when they are turned into properties of the object. Therefore, you must avoid reusing attribute names, even if you use different case letters in the source-code assignments.

IE includes an optional extension to the method in the form of a second parameter that enables you to be more specific about the case sensitivity of the first parameter. The default value of the second parameter is false, which means that the first parameter is not case sensitive. A value of true makes the first parameter case sensitive. This matters only if you use setAttribute() to add a parameter to an existing object and if the IE version of that method insists on case sensitivity. The default behavior of setAttribute() respects the case of the attribute name. See also the discussion of the setAttribute() method later in this chapter with regard to setAttribute()'s influence on the IE attributes property.

Example

Use The Evaluator (see Chapter 13) to experiment with the getAttribute() method for the elements in the page. You can enter the following sample statements in the top text box to view attribute values:

```
document.getElementById("myTable").getAttribute("width")
document.getElementById("myTable").getAttribute("border")
```

Related Items: attributes property; document.createAttribute(), setAttribute() methods

getAttributeNode("*attributeName*")

Returns: Attribute node object
Compatibility: WinIE6+, MacIE-, NN6+, Moz+, Safari+

In the W3C DOM, an attribute is an object that inherits all the properties of a Node object (see Chapter 14). As its name implies, an attribute object represents a name–value pair of an attribute that is explicitly defined inside an element's tag. The ability to treat attributes as node objects is far more important when working with XML than HTML, but it is helpful to understand attribute nodes within the context of the W3C DOM object-oriented view of a document. It is important that attribute nodes specifically are not recognized as nodes of a document hierarchy. Therefore, an attribute node is not a child node of the element that defines the attribute.

The nodeness of attributes comes into play when addressing the contents of an object's attributes property. The W3C attributes property builds on the DOM's formal structure by returning an object known (internally) as a *named node map*. Like an array, the named node map has a length property (facilitating for loop iteration through the map), plus several methods that allow for inserting, removing, reading, or writing attribute name–value pairs within the node map.

An attribute object inherits all the properties of the Node object. Table 15-10 lists the properties of an attribute object.

TABLE 15-10

Attribute Object Properties of W3C DOM–Compatible Browsers

attributes
childNodes
firstChild
lastChild
name
nextSibling
nodeName
nodeType
nodeValue
ownerDocument
parentNode
previousSibling
specified
value

All of this is a long way to explain the W3C DOM `getAttributeNode()` method, which returns a W3C DOM attribute object. The sole parameter of the method is a case-insensitive string version of the attribute's name. Then you can use any of the properties shown in Table 15-10 to get or set attribute values. Of course, HTML attributes are generally exposed as properties of HTML elements, so it is usually easier to read or write the object's properties directly.

Example

Use The Evaluator (see Chapter 13) to explore the `getAttributeNode()` method. The Results `textarea` element provides several attributes to check out. Because the method returns an object, enter the following statements in the bottom text box so you can view the properties of the attribute node object returned by the method:

```
document.getElementById("output").getAttributeNode("cols")
document.getElementById("output").getAttributeNode("rows")
document.getElementById("output").getAttributeNode("wrap")
document.getElementById("output").getAttributeNode("style")
```

All (except the last) statements display a list of properties for each attribute node object. The last statement, however, returns nothing because the `style` attribute is not specified for the element.

Related Items: `attributes` property; `getAttribute()`, `removeAttributeNode()`, `setAttributeNode()` methods

getAttributeNodeNS("*namespaceURI*", "*localName*")

Returns: Attribute node object
Compatibility: WinIE-, MacIE-, NN6+, Moz+, Safari-

This method returns a W3C DOM attribute object. The first parameter of the method is a URI string matching a URI assigned to a label in the document. The second parameter is the local name portion of the attribute you are getting.

Related Items: `attributes`, `namespaceURI`, `localName` properties; `getAttributeNode()`, `setAttributeNodeNS()` methods

getAttributeNS("*namespaceURI*", "*localName*")

Returns: (See text)
Compatibility: WinIE-, MacIE-, NN6+, Moz+, Safari-

This method returns the value assigned to a specific attribute of the current object when that attribute's name is defined by way of an XML namespace definition within the document. The first parameter of the method is a URI string matching a URI assigned to a namespace label in a tag defined earlier in the document. The second parameter is the local name portion of the attribute whose value you are getting.

Returned value types from `getAttributeNS()` are either strings (including attribute values assigned as unquoted numeric values) or Booleans (for example, the `multiple` property of a `select` element object). In the W3C DOM, Netscape, Safari, and Opera, return values are always strings.

Related Items: `attributes`, `namespaceURI`, `localName` properties; `getAttribute()`, `getAttributeNodeNS()`, `setAttributeNodeNS()` methods

getBoundingClientRect()

Returns: TextRectangle object
Compatibility: WinIE5+, MacIE-, NN-, Moz-, Safari-

IE5+ assigns to every content-holding element a rectangle that describes the space that the element occupies on the page. This rectangle is called a *bounding rectangle,* and it is expressed in the WinIE5+ object model as a TextRectangle object (even when the content is an image or some other kind of object). A TextRectangle object has four properties (top, left, bottom, and right) that are the pixel coordinates that define the rectangle. The getBoundingClientRect() method returns a TextRectangle object that describes the bounding rectangle of the current object. You can access an individual measure of an object's bounding rectangle, as in the following example:

```
var parTop = document.getElementById("myP").getBoundingClientRect().top;
```

For elements that consist of text, such as paragraphs, the dimensions of individual TextRectangles for each line of text in the element influence the dimensions of the bounding rectangle. For example, if a paragraph contains two lines, and the second line extends only halfway across the width of the first line, the width of the second line's TextRectangle object is only as wide as the actual text in the second line. But because the first line extends close to the right margin, the width of the encompassing bounding rectangle is governed by that wider, first line TextRectangle. Therefore, an element's bounding rectangle is as wide as its widest line and as tall as the sum of the height of all TextRectangle objects in the paragraph.

Another method, getClientRects(), enables you to obtain a collection of line-by-line TextRectangle objects for an element.

Example

Listing 15-27 employs both the getBoundingClientRect() and getClientRects() methods in a demonstration of how they differ. A set of elements are grouped within a span element named main. The group consists of two paragraphs and an unordered list.

Two controls enable you to set the position of an underlying highlight rectangle to any line of your choice. A checkbox enables you to set whether the highlight rectangle should be only as wide as the line or the full width of the bounding rectangle for the entire span element.

All the code is located in the hilite() function. The select and checkbox elements invoke this function. Early in the function, the getClientRects() method is invoked for the main element to capture a snapshot of all TextRectangles for the entire element. This array comes in handy when the script needs to get the coordinates of a rectangle for a single line, as chosen in the select element.

Whenever the user chooses a number from the select list, and the value is less than the total number of TextRectangle objects in clientRects, the function begins calculating the size and location of the underlying yellow highlighter. When the Full Width checkbox is checked, the left and right coordinates are obtained from the getBoundingClientRect() method because the entire span element's rectangle is the space you're interested in; otherwise, you pull the left and right properties from the chosen rectangle in the clientRects array.

Next comes the assignment of location and dimension values to the hiliter object's style property. The top and bottom are always pegged to whatever line is selected, so the clientRects array is polled for the chosen entry's top and bottom properties. The previously calculated left value is assigned to the hiliter object's pixelLeft property, whereas the width is calculated by subtracting the left from the right coordinates. Notice that the top and left coordinates also take into account any vertical or horizontal scrolling of the entire body of the document. If you resize the window smaller, line wrapping throws off the original line count. However, an invocation of hilite() from the onresize event handler applies the currently chosen line number to whatever content falls in that line after resizing.

LISTING 15-27

Using getBoundingClientRect()

```html
<html>
   <head>
      <title>getClientRects() and getBoundClientRect() Methods</title>
      <script type="text/javascript">
      function hilite() {
         var hTop, hLeft, hRight, hBottom, hWidth;
         var select = document.forms[0].choice;
         var n = parseInt(select.options[select.selectedIndex].value) - 1;
         var clientRects = document.getElementById("main").getClientRects();
         var mainElem = document.getElementById("main");
         if (n >= 0 && n < clientRects.length) {
            if (document.forms[0].fullWidth.checked) {
               hLeft = mainElem.getBoundingClientRect().left;
               hRight = mainElem.getBoundingClientRect().right;
            } else {
               hLeft = clientRects[n].left;
               hRight = clientRects[n].right;
            }
            document.getElementById("hiliter").style.pixelTop =
               clientRects[n].top + document.body.scrollTop;
            document.getElementById("hiliter").style.pixelBottom =
               clientRects[n].bottom;
            document.getElementById("hiliter").style.pixelLeft =
               hLeft + document.body.scrollLeft;
            document.getElementById("hiliter").style.pixelWidth =
               hRight - hLeft;
            document.getElementById("hiliter").style.visibility = "visible";
         } else if (n > 0) {
            alert("The content does not have that many lines.");
            document.getElementById("hiliter").style.visibility = "hidden";
         }
      }
      </script>
   </head>
   <body onresize="hilite()">
      <h1>getClientRects() and getBoundClientRect() Methods</h1>
      <hr />
      <form>
         Choose a line to highlight: <select name="choice" onchange="hilite()">
            <option value="1">1</option>
            <option value="2">2</option>
            <option value="3">3</option>
            <option value="4">4</option>
            <option value="5">5</option>
            <option value="6">6</option>
            <option value="7">7</option>
            <option value="8">8</option>
```

```
        <option value="9">9</option>
        <option value="10">10</option>
        <option value="11">11</option>
        <option value="12">12</option>
        <option value="13">13</option>
        <option value="14">14</option>
        <option value="15">15</option>
    </select><br />
     <input name="fullWidth" type="checkbox" onclick="hilite()" /> Full
    Width (bounding rectangle)
</form>
<span id="main">
<p>Lorem ipsum dolor sit amet, consectetaur adipisicing
    elit, sed do eiusmod tempor incididunt ut labore et dolore magna
    aliqua. Ut enim adminim veniam, quis nostrud exercitation
    ullamco:</p>
<ul>
    <li>laboris</li>
    <li>nisi</li>
    <li>aliquip ex ea commodo</li>
</ul>
<p>Duis aute irure dolor in reprehenderit involuptate velit esse cillum
    dolore eu fugiat nulla pariatur. Excepteur sint occaecat cupidatat non
    proident, sunt in culpa qui officia deseruntmollit anim id est laborum
    Et harumd und lookum like Greek to me, dereud facilis est er expedit
    distinct.</p></span>
<div id="hiliter"
style="position:absolute; background-color:yellow; z-index:-1;
visibility:hidden">
</div>
    </body>
</html>
```

Because the z-index style property of the hiliter element is set to -1, the element always appears beneath the primary content on the page. If the user selects a line number beyond the current number of lines in the main element, the hiliter element is hidden.

Related Items: getClientRects() method; TextRectangle object (Chapter 36 on the CD-ROM)

getClientRects()

Returns: Array of TextRectangle objects
Compatibility: WinIE5+, MacIE-, NN-, Moz-, Safari-

The getClientRects() method returns an array of all TextRectangle objects that fall within the current object the moment the method is invoked. Each TextRectangle object has its own top, left, bottom, and right coordinate properties. You can then, for example, loop through all objects in this array to calculate the pixel width of each line. If you want to find out the aggregate height and/or maximum width of the entire collection, you can use the getBoundingClientRect() method as a shortcut.

elementObject.getElementsByTagNameNS()

Example

See Listing 15-27, which demonstrates the differences between getClientRects() and getBoundingClientRect() and shows how you can use the two together.

Related Items: getBoundingClientRect() method; TextRectangle object (Chapter 36 on the CD-ROM)

getElementsByTagName("*tagName*")

Returns: Array of element objects
Compatibility: WinIE5+, MacIE5+, NN6+, Moz+, Safari+

The getElementsByTagName() method returns an array of all elements contained by the current object whose tags match the tag name supplied as the sole parameter to the method. The tag name parameter must be in the form of a string and is case insensitive. The group of elements returned in the array includes only those elements that are within the containment scope of the current object. Therefore, if you have two table objects in a document, and you invoke the getElementsByTagName("td") method on one of them, the list of returned table cell elements is confined to those cells within the current table object. The current element is not included in the returned array.

For MacIE5, WinIE6+, and all other supporting browsers, the method accepts a wildcard character ("*") for matching descendent elements regardless of tag name. The resulting array of elements is nearly identical to what IE4+ returns via the document.all collection.

Example

Use The Evaluator (see Chapter 13) to experiment with the getElementsByTagName() method. Enter the following statements one at a time in the top text box, and study the results:

```
document.body.getElementsByTagName("div")
document.body.getElementsByTagName("div").length
document.getElementById("myTable").getElementsByTagName("td").length
```

Because the getElementsByTagName() method returns an array of objects, you can use one of those returned values as a valid element reference:

```
document.getElementsByTagName("form")[0].getElementsByTagName("input").length
```

Related Items: getElementByTagNameNS(), getElementById(), tags() methods

getElementsByTagNameNS("*namespaceURI*", "*localName*")

Returns: Array of element objects
Compatibility: WinIE-, MacIE-, NN6+, Moz+, Safari-

This method returns an array of all elements contained by the current object (within an XML document) as specified in the two parameters. The first parameter of the method is a URI string matching a URI assigned to a label in the document. The second parameter is the local name portion of the attribute whose value you are getting.

Returned value types from getAttributeNS() are either strings (including attribute values assigned as unquoted numeric values) or Booleans (for example, the multiple property of a select element object).

Related Items: attributes, namespaceURI, localName properties; getElementsByTagNameNS(), getElementById(), tags() methods

getExpression("*attributeName*")

Returns: String
Compatibility: WinIE5+, MacIE-, NN-, Moz-, Safari-

The getExpression() method returns the text of the expression that was assigned to an element's attribute via the setExpression() method. The returned value is not the value of the expression, but the expression itself. If you want to find out the current value of the expression (assuming that the variables used are within the scope of your script), you can use the eval() function on the call to getExpression(). This action converts the string to a JavaScript expression and returns the evaluated result.

One parameter, a string version of the attribute name, is required.

Example

See Listing 15-32 for the setExpression() method. This listing demonstrates the kinds of values returned by getExpression().

Related Items: document.recalc(), removeExpression(), setExpression() methods

getFeature("*feature*", "*version*")

Returns: Object
Compatibility: WinIE-, MacIE-, NN-, Moz1.7.2+, Safari-

According to the W3C DOM specification, the getFeature() method accepts a scripting feature and version, and returns an object that implements the APIs for the feature. Examples of possible feature parameters to this method are Core and Events, which correspond to DOM modules.

As recently as Mozilla 1.8.1 (Firefox 2.0), the getFeature() method returns an object but the object exposes no API features to the script.

Related Items: implementation.hasFeature() method

getUserData("*key*")

Returns: Object
Compatibility: WinIE-, MacIE-, NN6-, Moz1.7.2+, Safari-

The getUserData() method enables you to access custom user data that has been associated with a node. A given node can have multiple objects of user data, in which case each one is identified through a text key. This key is the parameter that you pass into getUserData() to obtain a user data object. As of Mozilla 1.8.1 (Firefox 2.0), the method is only partially implemented and, therefore, still not useful.

hasAttribute("*attributeName*")

Returns: Boolean
Compatibility: WinIE-, MacIE-, NN6+, Moz+, Safari+

The hasAttribute() method returns true if the current object has an attribute whose name matches the sole parameter; it returns false otherwise.

Related Items: hasAttributeNS(), hasAttributes() methods

hasAttributeNS("*namespaceURI*", "*localName*")

Returns: Boolean
Compatibility: WinIE-, MacIE-, NN6+, Moz+, Safari-

The `hasAttributeNS()` method returns `true` if the current object has an attribute as identified by the two parameters; it returns `false` otherwise. The first parameter of the method is a URI string matching a URI assigned to a label in the document. The second parameter is the local name portion of the attribute whose value you are getting.

Related Items: `attributes`, `namespaceURI`, `localName` properties; `hasAttribute()`, `hasAttributes()` methods

hasAttributes()

Returns: Boolean
Compatibility: WinIE-, MacIE-, NN6+, Moz+, Safari+

The `hasAttributes()` method returns `true` if the current object has any attributes explicitly assigned within the tag; it returns `false` otherwise.

Related Items: `hasAttribute()`, `hasAttributeNS()` methods

hasChildNodes()

Returns: Boolean
Compatibility: WinIE5+, MacIE5+, NN6+, Moz+, Safari+

The `hasChildNodes()` method returns `true` if the current object has child nodes nested within; it returns `false` otherwise. A child node is not necessarily the same as a child element, so the following two expressions return `true` when the current object has at least one child node:

```
document.getElementById("myObject").hasChildNodes()
document.getElementById("myObject").childNodes.length > 0
```

You cannot use the second expression interchangeably with the following statement (which uses the IE-only `children` property):

```
document.getElementById("myObject").children.length > 0
```

You generally use the `hasChildNodes()` method in a conditional expression to make sure such nodes exist before performing operations on them:

```
if (document.getElementById("myObject").hasChildNodes() {
    statements that apply to child nodes
}
```

Example

Use The Evaluator (see Chapter 13) to experiment with the `hasChildNodes()` method. If you enter the following statement in the top text box

```
document.getElementById("myP").hasChildNodes()
```

the returned value is `true`. You can find out how many nodes there are by getting the `length` of the `childNodes` array:

```
document.getElementById("myP").childNodes.length
```

This expression reveals a total of three nodes: the two text nodes and the em element between them. Check out whether the first text node has any children:

```
document.getElementById("myP").childNodes[0].hasChildNodes()
```

The response is `false` because text fragments do not have any nested nodes. But check out the em element, which is the second child node of the myP element:

```
document.getElementById("myP").childNodes[1].hasChildNodes()
```

The answer is `true` because the em element has a text fragment node nested within it. Sure enough, the statement

```
document.getElementById("myP").childNodes[1].childNodes.length
```

yields a node count of 1. You can also go directly to the em element in your references:

```
document.getElementById("myEM").hasChildNodes()
document.getElementById("myEM").childNodes.length
```

If you want to see the properties of the text fragment node inside the em element, enter the following in the bottom text box:

```
document.getElementById("myEM").childNodes[0]
```

You can see that the `data` and `nodeValue` properties for the text fragment return the text `"all"`.

Related Items: `childNodes` property; `appendChild()`, `removeChild()`, `replaceChild()` methods.

insertAdjacentElement("*location*", *elementObject*)

Returns: Object
Compatibility: WinIE5+, MacIE-, NN-, Moz-, Safari-

The `insertAdjacentElement()` method inserts an element object (coming from a variety of sources) into a specific position relative to the current object. Both parameters are required. The first must be one of four possible case-insensitive locations for the insertion, shown in the following table:

Location	Description
beforeBegin	Before the current element's start tag
afterBegin	After the start tag but before any nested content
beforeEnd	Before the end tag but after all other nested content
afterEnd	After the end tag

These locations are relative to the current object. The element type of the current object (a block-level or inline element) has great bearing on how the inserted element is rendered. For example, suppose that you create a b element (using `document.createElement()`) and assign some inner text to it. You then use `insertAdjacentElement()` in an effort to insert this b element before some text in a p element. Because a p element is a block-level element, the location `beforeBegin` places the new b element before the start tag of the p element. This means, however, that the bold text appears in a text line above the start of the p element

elementObject.**insertAdjacentElement()**

because a <p> tag begins a new block at the left margin of its container (unless instructed otherwise by style sheets). The resulting HTML looks like the following:

```
<b>The new element.</b><p>The original paragraph element.</p>
```

To make the new b element a part of the p element — but in front of the existing p element's content — use the afterBegin location. The resulting HTML looks like the following:

```
<p><b>The new element.</b>The original paragraph element.</p>
```

To complete the demonstration of the four location types, the following is the result of the beforeEnd location:

```
<p>The original paragraph element. <b>The new element.</b></p>
```

And this is the result of the afterEnd location:

```
<p>The original paragraph element.</p><b>The new element.</b>
```

The object to be inserted is a reference to an element object. The object reference can come from any expression that evaluates to an element object or, more likely, from the result of the document.createElement() method. Bear in mind that the object generated by document.createElement() initially has no content, and all attribute values are set to default values. Moreover, the object is passed to insertAdjacentElement() by reference, which means that there is only one instance of that object. If you attempt to insert that object in two places with two statements, the object is moved from the first location to the second. If you need to copy an existing object so that the original is not moved or otherwise disturbed by this method, use the cloneNode() method to specify the true parameter to capture all nested content of the node.

Example

Use The Evaluator (see Chapter 13) in WinIE5+ to experiment with the insertAdjacentElement() method. The goal of the experiment is to insert a new h1 element above the myP element.

All actions require you to enter a sequence of statements in the top text box. Begin by storing a new element in the global variable a:

```
a = document.createElement("h1")
```

Give the new object some text:

```
a.innerText = "New Header"
```

Now insert this element before the start of the myP object:

```
myP.insertAdjacentElement("beforeBegin", a)
```

Notice that you have not assigned an id property value to the new element. But because the element was inserted by reference, you can modify the inserted object by changing the object stored in the a variable:

```
a.style.color = "red"
```

The inserted element is also part of the document hierarchy, so you can access it through hierarchy references such as myP.previousSibling.

The parent element of the newly inserted element is the body. Thus, you can inspect the current state of the HTML for the rendered page by entering the following statement in the top text box:

```
document.body.innerHTML
```

If you scroll down past the first form, you can find the `<h1>` element that you added along with the `style` attribute.

Related Items: `document.createElement()`, `applyElement()` methods

insertAdjacentHTML("*location*", "*HTMLtext*")
insertAdjacentText("*location*", "*text*")

Returns: Nothing
Compatibility: WinIE4+, MacIE4+, NN-, Moz-, Safari-

These two methods insert HTML or straight text at a location relative to the current element. They are intended for use after a page loads, rather than inserting content while the page loads (in which case you can use `document.write()` wherever you need evaluated content to appear on the page).

The first parameter must be one of four possible case-insensitive locations for the insertion, shown in the following table:

Location	Description
`beforeBegin`	Before the current element's start tag
`afterBegin`	After the start tag but before any nested content
`beforeEnd`	Before the end tag but after all other nested content
`afterEnd`	After the end tag

These locations yield the same results as described in the `insertAdjacentElement()` function discussed earlier in this chapter.

Whether you use `insertAdjacentHTML()` or `insertAdjacentText()` depends on the nature of your content and what you want the browser to do with it. If the content contains HTML tags that you want the browser to interpret and render as though it were part of the page source code, use the `insertAdjacentHTML()` method. All tags become objects in the document's object model. But if you want only to display some text (including HTML tags in their raw form), use `insertAdjacentText()`. The rendering engine does not interpret any tags included in the string passed as the second parameter. Instead, these tags are displayed as characters on the page. This distinction is identical to the one between the `innerHTML` and `innerText` properties.

The difference between `insertAdjacentHTML()` and `insertAdjacentElement()` is the nature of the content that you insert. The former enables you to accumulate the HTML as a string, whereas the latter requires the creation of an element object. Also, the two methods in this section work with IE4+ (including Mac versions), whereas `insertAdjacentElement()` requires the newer object model of WinIE5+.

If the HTML you pass as the second parameter of `insertAdjacentHTML()` contains `<script>` tags, you must set the `defer` attribute in the opening tag. This prevents script statements from executing as you insert them.

Example

Use The Evaluator (see Chapter 13) to experiment with these two methods. The example here demonstrates the result of employing both methods in an attempt to add some HTML to the beginning of the `myP` element.

elementObject.insertBefore()

Begin by assigning a string of HTML code to the global variable a:

```
a = "<b id='myB'>Important News!</b>"
```

Because this HTML is to go on the same line as the start of the myP paragraph, use the afterBegin parameter for the insert method:

```
myP.insertAdjacentHTML("afterBegin", a)
```

Notice that there is no space after the exclamation mark of the inserted HTML. But to prove that the inserted HTML is genuinely part of the document's object model, now you can insert the text of a space after the b element whose ID is myB:

```
myB.insertAdjacentText("afterEnd", " ")
```

Each time you evaluate the preceding statement (by repeatedly clicking the Evaluate button or pressing Enter with the cursor in the top text box), another space is added.

You should also see what happens when the string to be inserted with insertAdjacentText() contains HTML tags. Reload The Evaluator, and enter the following two statements in the top text box, evaluating each one in turn:

```
a = "<b id='myB'>Important News!</b>"
myP.insertAdjacentText("afterBegin", a)
```

The HTML is not interpreted but is displayed as plain text. There is no object named myB after executing this latest insert method.

Related Items: innerText, innerHTML, outerText, outerHTML properties; insertAdjacentElement(), replaceAdjacentText() methods

insertBefore(*newChildNodeObject, referenceChildNode*)

Returns: Node object
Compatibility: WinIE5+, MacIE5+, NN6+, Moz+, Safari+

The insertBefore() method is the W3C DOM syntax for inserting a new child node into an existing element. Node references for both parameters must be valid Node objects (including those that document.createElement() generates).

The behavior of this method might seem counterintuitive at times. If you include the second parameter (a reference to an existing child node of the current element — optional in IE), the new child node is inserted before that existing one. But if you omit the second parameter (or its value is null), the new child node is inserted as the last child of the current element — in which case the method acts the same as the appendChild() method. The true power of this method is summoned when you specify that second parameter; from the point of view of a parent element, you can drop a new child into any spot among its existing children. If an inserted node already exists in the document tree, it will be removed from its previous position.

Bear in mind that the insertBefore() method works from a parent element. Internet Explorer provides additional methods, such as insertAdjacentElement(), to operate from the perspective of what will become a child element.

Example

Listing 15-28 demonstrates how the insertBefore() method can insert child elements (li) inside a parent (ol) at different locations, depending on the second parameter. A text box enables you to enter your choice of text and/or HTML for insertion at various locations within the ol element. If you don't specify a position, the second parameter of insertBefore() is passed as null — meaning that the new child node is added to the end of the existing children. But choose a spot from the select list where you want to insert the new item. The value of each select list option is an index of one of the first three child nodes of the ol element.

LISTING 15-28

Using the insertBefore() Method

```
<html>
    <head>
        <title>insertBefore() Method</title>
        <script type="text/javascript">
        function doInsert(form) {
            if (form.newText) {
                var newChild = document.createElement("LI");
                newChild.innerHTML = form.newText.value;
                var choice =
                    form.itemIndex.options[form.itemIndex.selectedIndex].value;
                var insertPoint = (isNaN(choice)) ?
                    null : document.getElementById("myUL").childNodes[choice];
                document.getElementById("myUL").insertBefore(newChild,
                    insertPoint);
            }
        }
        </script>
    </head>
    <body>
        <h1>insertBefore() Method</h1>
        <hr />
        <form onsubmit="return false">
            <p>Enter text or HTML for a new list item: <input type="text"
                name="newText" size="40" value="" /></p>
            <p>Before which existing item? <select name="itemIndex">
                    <option value="null">None specified</option>
                    <option value="0">1</option>
                    <option value="1">2</option>
                    <option value="2">3</option>
                </select></p>
            <input type="button" value="Insert Item"
                onclick="doInsert(this.form)" />
        </form>
        <ol id="myUL">
            <li>Originally the First Item</li>
            <li>Originally the Second Item</li>
            <li>Originally the Third Item</li>
        </ol>
    </body>
</html>
```

Related Items: appendChild(), replaceChild(), removeChild(), insertAdjacentElement() methods

elementObjectCollection.item()

isDefaultNamespace("*namespaceURI*")

Returns: Boolean
Compatibility: WinIE-, MacIE-, NN6-, Moz1.7.2+, Safari-

This method checks whether the specified namespace matches the default namespace of the current node.

isEqualNode(*nodeRef*)
isSameNode(*nodeRef*)

Returns: Integer ID
Compatibility: WinIE-, MacIE-, NN-, Moz1.7.2+, Safari-

When it comes to nodes, there is a distinct difference between a node being equal to another node and a node being the same as another node. Equality has a very specific meaning with respect to nodes: Two nodes are considered equal if they have the same values for the attributes, childNodes, localname, namespaceURI, nodeName, nodeType, nodeValue, and prefix properties. Together, these properties essentially reflect the content of a node. What they don't reflect is the relative position of a node within a document, which means that nodes can be equal and reside in different locations in the node tree. Two nodes are considered the same if . . . well, they are the same identical node. The isEqualNode() method checks for node equality, whereas isSameNode() checks whether two nodes are the same. Both methods expect a node reference as their only parameter.

isSupported("*feature*", "*version*")

Returns: Boolean
Compatibility: WinIE-, MacIE-, NN6+, Moz+, Safari+

The isSupported() method returns true if the current node supports required portions of the specified W3C DOM module and version; it returns false otherwise. The first parameter accepts any of the following case-sensitive DOM module name strings: Core, XML, HTML, Views, StyleSheets, CSS, CSS2, Events, UIEvents, MouseEvents, MutationEvents, HTMLEvents, Range, and Traversal. The second parameter accepts a string representation of the major and minor DOM module version, such as "2.0" for DOM Level 2.

Example

Use The Evaluator (see Chapter 13) to experiment with the isSupported() method. If you have multiple versions of NN6 or later and Mozilla, try the following (and others) to see how the support for various modules has evolved:

```
document.body.isSupported("CSS", "2.0")
document.body.isSupported("CSS2", "2.0")
document.body.isSupported("Traversal", "2.0")
```

If you have access to Safari, try the same methods there to see the differences in modules supported compared with Mozilla-based browsers.

item(*index* | "*index*" [, *subIndex*])

Returns: Object
Compatibility: WinIE4+, MacIE4+, NN6+, Moz+, Safari+

The item() method works with most objects that are themselves collections of other objects. In W3C DOM terminology, these kinds of objects are known as *named node lists* (for objects such as nodes and attributes) or *HTML collections* (for objects such as elements of a form). You may call the item() method with a single numeric parameter that is the index value of the desired object within the collection. If you know the index number of the item, you can use JavaScript array syntax instead. The following two statements return the same object reference:

```
document.getElementById("myTable").childNodes.item(2)
document.getElementById("myTable").childNodes[2]
```

The method also supports a string of the ID of an object within the collection. (Integer values are required for the attributes, rules, and TextRectangle objects, however.) Additionally, if the collection has more than one object with the same ID (never a good idea except when necessary), a second numeric parameter enables you to select which identically named group you want (using zero-based index values within that subgroup). This obviously does not apply to collections, such as attributes and rules, which have no ID associated with them.

The method returns a reference to the object specified by the parameters.

Example

Use The Evaluator (see Chapter 13) to experiment with the item() method. Type the following statements in the top text box, and view the results for each.

W3C and IE5:

```
document.getElementById("myP").childNodes.length
document.getElementById("myP").childNodes.item(0).data
document.getElementById("myP").childNodes.item(1).nodeName
```

W3C, IE4, and IE5:

```
document.forms[1].elements.item(0).type
```

In the two examples, both statements return the same string. The first example is helpful when your script is working with a string version of an object's name. If your script already knows the object reference, the second approach is more efficient and compact.

Related Items: All object element properties that return collections (arrays) of other objects

lookupNamespaceURI("*prefix*")
lookupPrefix("*namespaceURI*")

Returns: Namespace or prefix string (see description)
Compatibility: WinIE-, MacIE-, NN-, Moz1.7.2+, Safari-

These two methods use one piece of information to look up the other. The lookupNamespaceURI() method accepts a prefix as its only parameter and returns a URI string for the node if the prefix matches a previously defined namespace. Operating in the reverse, the lookupPrefix() method accepts a namespace URI string and returns a prefix string for the node if the namespace parameter matches a previously defined namespace.

mergeAttributes("*sourceObject*")

Returns: Nothing
Compatibility: WinIE5+, MacIE-, NN-, Moz-, Safari-

The mergeAttributes() method is a convenient way to propagate attributes in newly created elements without painstakingly adding attributes one at a time. When you have an object whose attributes can

elementObject.mergeAttributes()

function as a prototype for other elements, those attributes (except for the id attribute) can be applied to a newly created element instantaneously. The default action of this method is not to duplicate the id or name attributes of the element. However, IE5.5+ introduced an extra Boolean parameter, preserveIDs, that enables you to duplicate these two attributes by setting the parameter to false (true is the default).

Example

Listing 15-29 demonstrates the usage of mergeAttributes() in the process of replicating the same form input field while assigning a unique ID to each new field. So that you can see the results as you go, I display the HTML for each input field in the field.

The doMerge() function begins by generating two new elements: a p element and an input element. Because these newly created elements have no properties associated with them, a unique ID is assigned to the input element through the uniqueID property. Attributes from the field in the source code (field1) are merged into the new input element. Thus, all attributes except name and id are copied to the new element. The input element is inserted into the p element, and the p element is appended to the document's form element. Finally, the outerHTML of the new element is displayed in its field. Notice that except for the name and id attributes, all others are copied. This includes style sheet attributes and event handlers. To prove that the event handler works in the new elements, you can add a space to any one of them and press Tab to trigger the onchange event handler that changes the content to all-uppercase characters.

LISTING 15-29

Using the mergeAttributes() Method

```
<html>
   <head>
      <title>mergeAttributes() Method</title>
      <script type="text/javascript">
      function doMerge(form) {
         var newPElem = document.createElement("p");
         var newInputElem = document.createElement("input");
         newInputElem.id = newInputElem.uniqueID;
         newInputElem.mergeAttributes(form.field1);
         newPElem.appendChild(newInputElem);
         form.appendChild(newPElem);
         newInputElem.value = newInputElem.outerHTML;
      }

      // called by onChange event handler of fields
      function upperMe(field) {
         field.value = field.value.toUpperCase();
      }
      </script>
   </head>
   <body
   onload="document.expandable.field1.value =
document.expandable.field1.outerHTML">
      <h1>mergeAttributes() Method</h1>
      <hr />
      <form name="expandable" onsubmit="return false">
```

```
      <p><input type="button" value="Append Field 'Clone'"
         onclick="doMerge(this.form)" /></p>
      <p><input type="text" name="field1" id="FIELD1" size="120" value=""
         style="font-size:9pt" onchange="upperMe(this)" /></p>
   </form>
  </body>
</html>
```

Related Items: clearAttributes(), cloneNode(), removeAttributes() methods

normalize()

Returns: Nothing
Compatibility: WinIE6+, MacIE5+, NN7+, Moz+, Safari 1.2+

In the course of appending, inserting, removing, and replacing child nodes of an element, it is conceivable that two text nodes can end up adjacent to each other. Although this typically has no effect on the rendering of the content, some XML-centric applications that rely heavily on the document node hierarchy to interpret content properly may not like having two text nodes sitting next to each other. The proper form of a node hierarchy is for a single text node to be bounded by other node types. The normalize() method sweeps through the child nodes of the current node object and combines adjacent text nodes into a single text node. The effect obviously impacts the number of child nodes of an element, but it also cleanses the nested node hierarchy.

Example

Use The Evaluator (see Chapter 13) to experiment with the normalize() method. The following sequence adds a text node adjacent to one in the myP element. A subsequent invocation of the normalize() method removes the division between the adjacent text nodes.

Begin by confirming the number of child nodes of the myP element:

```
document.getElementById("myP").childNodes.length
```

Three nodes initially inhabit the element. Next, create a text node, and append it as the last child of the myP element:

```
a = document.createTextNode("This means you!")
document.getElementById("myP").appendChild(a)
```

With the new text now rendered on the page, the number of child nodes increases to four:

```
document.getElementById("myP").childNodes.length
```

You can see that the last child node of myP is the text node you just created:

```
document.getElementById("myP").lastChild.nodeValue
```

But by invoking normalize() on myP, all adjacent text nodes are accumulated into single nodes:

```
document.getElementById("myP").normalize()
```

elementObject.releaseCapture()

You can see that the `myP` element is back to three child nodes, and the last child is a combination of the two previously distinct, but adjacent, text nodes:

```
document.getElementById("myP").childNodes.length
document.getElementById("myP").lastChild.nodeValue
```

Related Items: `document.createTextNode()`, `appendChild()`, `insertBefore()`, `removeChild()`, `replaceChild()` methods

releaseCapture()
setCapture(containerBoolean)

Returns: Nothing
Compatibility: WinIE5+, MacIE-, NN-, Moz-, Safari-

You can instruct a single object on a page to capture all mouse events (`onmousedown`, `onmouseup`, `onmousemove`, `onmouseout`, `onmouseover`, `onclick`, and `ondblclick`) via the WinIE-specific `setCapture()` method. A primary scenario for mouse event capture is when some content appears on the page that you wish to leave as the center of user focus — items such as pull-down menus, context menus, or simulated modal window areas. When such items appear onscreen, you want the effect of blocking all mouse events except those that apply to the menu or currently visible pseudowindow. When the region disappears, mouse events can be released so that individual elements (such as buttons and links elsewhere on the page) respond to mouse events.

Event capture does not block the events. Instead, the events are redirected to the object set to capture all mouse events. Events bubble up from that point unless explicitly canceled (see Chapter 25). For example, consider a document that has a `<body>` tag containing an `onclick` event handler that governs the entire document at all times. If you turn on event capture for a `div` somewhere in the document, the click event first goes to the `div`. That `div` might have an `onclick` event handler that looks to process click events when they occur in some of its child elements. If the event handler for the `div` does not also cancel the bubbling of that click event, the `body` element's `onclick` event handler eventually receives and processes the event, even though the `div` initially captured the event.

Deciding which object should capture events is an important design issue to confront. With event capture engaged, all mouse events (no matter where they occur) get funneled to the object set to capture the events. Therefore, if you design an application whose entire interface consists of clicking and dragging positionable elements, you can set one of those elements (or even the `document` object) to perform the capturing. For pop-up regions, however, it is generally more logical and convenient for your coding to assign the capture mechanism to the primary container of the pop-up content (usually, a positioned `div`).

The `setCapture()` method has one optional Boolean parameter. The parameter controls whether mouse events on child elements within the capturing object are under control of the event capture mechanism. The default value (`true`) means that all mouse events targeted at elements within the current object go to the current object rather than to the original target — the most likely way you will use `setCapture()` for things such as pop-up and context menus. But if you specify `false` as the parameter, mouse events occurring in child elements of the capturing container receive their events directly. From there, regular event bubbling upward from the target ensues (see Chapter 25).

You may encounter odd behavior when the region you set up to capture mouse events contains form elements such as text input fields and `select` lists. Because these elements require mouse events to gain focus for interaction, the event capture mechanism inhibits access to these items. To work around this behavior, you can examine the click event's `srcElement` property to see whether the click was on one of these elements and script the focus of that element (or instruct the user to press the Tab key until the element gets focus manually).

After an object is set to capture events, your other code must define which events actually do something and decide whether events should bubble up beyond the capturing element. You need to worry about bubbling only if your design includes mouse event handlers in elements higher up the element containment hierarchy. You may not want those event handlers to fire while event capture is on; in this case, you need to cancel the bubbling of those events in the capturing object.

If your application design requires that the pop-up area be hidden and event handling be returned to normal (such as after the user makes a pop-up menu selection), use the releaseCapture() method in conjunction with hiding the container. Because event capture can be engaged for only one element at a time, you can release capture by invoking the releaseCapture() method from the container or from the document object.

Event capture is automatically disengaged when the user performs any of the following actions:

- Gives focus to any other window
- Displays any system modal dialog window (for example, alert window)
- Scrolls the page
- Opens a browser context menu (by right-clicking)
- Tabs to give focus to the Address field in the browser window

Therefore, you may want to set the document object's onlosecapture event handler to hide any container that your script displays in concert with event capture.

Also be aware that even though mouse events may be captured to prevent mouse access to the rest of the page, keyboard events are not captured. Thus, using the event capture mechanism to simulate modal windows is not foolproof: A user can tab to any form element or link in the page and press the spacebar or Enter key to activate that element.

Event capture, as defined in the W3C DOM, operates differently from WinIE event capture. In the W3C DOM, you can instruct the browser to substitute event capture of any kind of event for the normal event bubbling behavior. For example, you can attach an event listener to the body element in such a way that it sees all click events aimed at elements contained by the body element before the events reach their target elements. (See Chapter 14 and Chapter 25 for more on the W3C DOM event model and how to integrate it into cross-browser applications.)

Example

Listing 15-30 demonstrates the usage of setCapture() and releaseCapture() in a quick-and-dirty context menu for WinIE5+. The job of the context menu is to present a list of numbering styles for the ordered list of items on the page. Whenever the user brings up the context menu atop the ol element, the custom context menu appears. Event capture is turned on in the process to prevent mouse actions elsewhere on the page from interrupting the context menu choice. Even a click of the link set up as the title of the list is inhibited while the context menu is visible. A click anywhere outside the context menu hides the menu. Clicking a choice in the menu changes the listStyleType property of the ol object and hides the menu. Whenever the context menu is hidden, event capture is turned off so that clicking the page (such as the link) works as normal.

For this design, onclick, onmouseover, and onmouseout event handlers are assigned to the div element that contains the context menu. To trigger the display of the context menu, the ol element has an oncontextmenu event handler. This handler invokes the showContextMenu() function. In this function, event capture is assigned to the context menu div object. The div is also positioned at the location of the click before it is set to be visible. To prevent the system's regular context menu from also appearing, the event object's returnValue property is set to false.

Now that all mouse events on the page go through the contextMenu div object, let's examine what happens with different kinds of events triggered by user action. As the user rolls the mouse, a flood of mouseover and mouseout events fires. The event handlers assigned to the div manage these events. But notice that the two event handlers, highlight() and unhighlight(), perform action only when the srcElement property of the event is one of the menu items in the div. Because the page has no other onmouseover or onmouseout event handlers defined for elements up the containment hierarchy, you do not have to cancel event bubbling for these events.

When a user clicks the mouse button, different things happen, depending on whether event capture is enabled. Without event capture, the click event bubbles up from wherever it occurred to the onclick event handler in the body element. (An alert dialog box displays to let you know when the event reaches the body.) But with event capture turned on (the context menu is showing), the handleClick() event handler takes over to apply the desired choice whenever the click is atop one of the context menu items. For all click events handled by this function, the context menu is hidden, and the click event is canceled from bubbling up any higher (no alert dialog box appears). This takes place whether the user makes a choice in the context menu or clicks anywhere else on the page. In the latter case, all you need is for the context menu to go away as the real context menu does. For added insurance, the onlosecapture event handler hides the context menu when a user performs any of the actions just listed that cancel capture.

LISTING 15-30

Using setCapture() and releaseCapture()

```
<html>
   <head>
      <title></title>
      <style type="text/css">
      #contextMenu {position:absolute; background-color:#cfcfcf;
         border-style:solid; border-width:1px;
         border-color:#EFEFEF #505050 #505050 #EFEFEF;
         padding:3px 10px; font-size:8pt; font-family:Arial, Helvetica;
         line-height:150%; visibility:hidden}
      .menuItem {color:black}
      .menuItemOn {color:white}
      ol {list-style-position:inside; font-weight:bold; cursor:nw-resize}
      li {font-weight:normal}
      </style>
      <script type="text/javascript">
      function showContextMenu() {
         contextMenu.setCapture();
         contextMenu.style.pixelTop = event.clientY + document.body.scrollTop;
         contextMenu.style.pixelLeft = event.clientX +
            document.body.scrollLeft;
         contextMenu.style.visibility = "visible";
         event.returnValue = false;
      }

      function revert() {
         document.releaseCapture();
         hideMenu();
      }
```

```
    function hideMenu() {
        contextMenu.style.visibility = "hidden";
    }

    function handleClick() {
        var elem = window.event.srcElement;
        if (elem.id.indexOf("menuItem") == 0) {
            document.getElementById("shapesList").style.listStyleType =
                elem.listtype;
        }
        revert();
        event.cancelBubble = true;
    }

    function highlight() {
        var elem = event.srcElement;
        if (elem.className == "menuItem") {
            elem.className = "menuItemOn";
        }
    }

    function unhighlight() {
        var elem = event.srcElement
        if (elem.className == "menuItemOn") {
            elem.className = "menuItem";
        }
    }
    </script>
</head>
<body onclick="alert('You reached the document object.')">
    <ol id="shapesList" oncontextmenu="showContextMenu()">
        <li style="list-style: none"><a href=
            "javascript:alert('A%20sample%20link.')">Three-Dimensional
            Shapes</a></li>
        <li value="1">Circular Cylinder</li>
        <li>Cube</li>
        <li>Rectangular Prism</li>
        <li>Regular Right Pyramid</li>
        <li>Right Circular Cone</li>
        <li>Sphere</li>
    </ol>
    <div id="contextMenu" onlosecapture="hideMenu()" onclick="handleClick()"
    onmouseover="highlight()" onmouseout="unhighlight()">
        <span id="menuItem1" class="menuItem"
        listtype="upper-alpha">A,B,C,...</span><br />
        <span id="menuItem2" class="menuItem"
        listtype="lower-alpha">a,b,c,...</span><br />
        <span id="menuItem3" class="menuItem"
        listtype="upper-roman">I,II,III,...</span><br />
        <span id="menuItem4" class="menuItem"
        listtype="lower-roman">i,ii,iii,...</span><br />
```

continued

309

LISTING 15-30 *(continued)*

```
      <span id="menuItem5" class="menuItem"
      listtype="decimal">1,2,3,...</span>
    </div>
  </body>
</html>
```

Related Items: addEventListener(), dispatchEvent(), fireEvent(), removeEventListener() methods; onlosecapture event; Event object (Chapter 25)

removeAttribute("*attributeName*"[, *caseSensitivity*])

Returns: Boolean (IE), nothing (NN/DOM)
Compatibility: WinIE4+, MacIE4+, NN6+, Moz+, Safari+

If you create an attribute with the setAttribute() method, you can eliminate that attribute from the element object via the removeAttribute() method. The required parameter is the name of the attribute. Internet Explorer permits you to set and remove attributes such that the attribute names are case sensitive. The default behavior of removeAttribute() in IE (the second parameter is a Boolean value) is false. Therefore, if you supply a value of true for the case-sensitivity parameter in setAttribute(), you should set the parameter to true in removeAttribute() to ensure a proper balance between created and removed attributes.

The W3C DOM (NN/Moz/Safari) version of the removeAttribute() method has a single parameter (a case-insensitive attribute name) and returns no value. The returned value in IE is true if the removal succeeds and false if it doesn't succeed (or if the attribute is one that you set in some other manner).

Example

Use The Evaluator (see Chapter 13) to experiment with the removeAttribute() method for the elements in the page. See the examples for the setAttribute() method later in this chapter, and enter the corresponding removeAttribute() statements in the top text box. Interlace statements using getAttribute() to verify the presence or absence of each attribute.

Related Items: attributes property; document.createAttribute(), getAttribute(), setAttribute() methods

removeAttributeNode(*attributeNode*)
setAttributeNode(*attributeNode*)

Returns: Attribute object
Compatibility: WinIE6+, MacIE-, NN6+, Moz+, Safari+

As discussed in the coverage of the getAttributeNode() method earlier in this chapter, the W3C DOM treats a name–value attribute pair as an attribute object. An attribute object is a distinct node within a named node map — a collection of attribute objects belonging to an element. Understanding named node maps and attribute objects is more useful in an XML environment, where attributes can not only contain valuable data, but also are not exposed to the DOM as properties you can access via script. Instead of accessing an object's properties, you work with the actual attributes.

If you want to insert an attribute in the formal W3C methodology, you can use `document.createAttribute()` to generate a new attribute object. Subsequent script statements assign values to the `nodeName` and `nodeValue` properties to give the attribute its traditional name–value pair. You can then insert that new attribute object into the attribute list of an object via the `setAttributeNode()` method. The sole parameter is an attribute object, and the return value is a reference to the newly inserted attribute object.

To remove an attribute node from an element using this syntax, employ the `removeAttributeNode()` method. Again, the sole parameter is an attribute object. If your script knows only the attribute's name, you can use `getAttributeNode()` to obtain a valid reference to the attribute object. The `removeAttributeNode()` method returns a reference to the removed attribute object. That object remains in the browser's memory, but it is not part of the document hierarchy. By capturing this removed attribute object in a variable, you have the flexibility to modify and assign it to another object elsewhere in the document.

In practice, you may rarely, if ever, need to address attributes as nodes. Other methods — notably `getAttribute()`, `removeAttribute()`, and `setAttribute()` — do the job when your scripts have only the name (as a string) of an attribute belonging to an element.

Example

Use The Evaluator (see Chapter 13) to experiment with the `setAttributeNode()` and `removeAttributeNode()` methods for the p element in the page. The task is to create and add a `style` attribute to the p element. Begin by creating a new attribute and storing it temporarily in the global variable a:

        a = document.createAttribute("style")

Assign a value to the `attribute` object:

        a.nodeValue = "color:red"

Now insert the new attribute into the p element:

        document.getElementById("myP").setAttributeNode(a)

The paragraph changes color in response to the newly added attribute.

Due to the NN6 bug that won't allow the method to return a reference to the newly inserted attribute node, you can artificially obtain such a reference:

        b = document.getElementById("myP").getAttributeNode("style")

Finally, use the reference to the newly added attribute to remove it from the element:

        document.getElementById("myP").removeAttribute(b)

Upon the removal of the attribute, the paragraph resumes its initial color. See the example for the `setAttribute()` method later in this chapter to discover how you can perform this same kind of operation with `setAttribute()`.

Related Items: `attributes` property; `document.createAttribute()`, `getAttribute()`, `getAttributeNode()`, `setAttribute()` methods

removeAttributeNS("*namespaceURI*", "*localName*")

Returns: Nothing
Compatibility: WinIE-, MacIE-, NN6+, Moz+, Safari-

This method removes the attribute specified in the two parameters. The first parameter of the method is a URI string matching a URI assigned to a label in the document. The second parameter is the local name portion of the attribute whose value you are removing.

elementObject.**removeExpression()**

Related Items: `attributes`, `namespaceURI`, `localName` properties; `removeAttribute()`, `getAttributeNS()`, `setAttributeNS()` methods

removeBehavior(*ID*)

Returns: Boolean
Compatibility: WinIE5+, MacIE-, NN-, Moz-, Safari-

The `removeBehavior()` method detaches a behavior from an object. It assumes that the behavior was added to the object via the `addBehavior()` method. The return value of the `addBehavior()` method is a unique identifier for that particular behavior. This identifier is the required parameter for the `removeBehavior()` method. Thus, you can add two behaviors to an object and remove just one of them if you so desire. If the removal succeeds, the `removeBehavior()` method returns `true`; otherwise, it returns `false`.

Example

See Listing 15-19a and Listing 15-19b earlier in this chapter for examples of how to use `addBehavior()` and `removeBehavior()`.

Related Item: `addBehavior()` method

removeChild(*nodeObject*)

Returns: Node object reference
Compatibility: WinIE5+, MacIE5+, NN6+, Moz+, Safari+

The `removeChild()` method erases a child element from the current element. Content associated with the child element is no longer visible on the page, and the object is no longer part of the document object hierarchy.

As destructive as that sounds, the specifications for the deleted object are not necessarily lost to the ether. The `removeChild()` method returns a reference to the removed node. By assigning this value to a variable, you can hold on to that object specification for insertion later in the session. You are free to use this value as a parameter to such methods as `appendChild()`, `replaceChild()`, `swapNode()`, and `insertBefore()`.

Remember that `removeChild()` is invoked from the point of view of a parent element. If you simply want to remove an element, you can do so more directly (in WinIE5+ only) with the `removeNode()` method. The IE `removeNode()` method also allows a node to remove itself, which isn't possible via the `removeChild()` method.

Example

You can see an example of `removeChild()` as part of Listing 15-21 earlier in this chapter.

Related Items: `appendChild()`, `replaceChild()`, `removeNode()` methods

removeEventListener()

(See `addEventListener()`)

removeExpression("*propertyName*")

Returns: Boolean
Compatibility: WinIE5+, MacIE-, NN-, Moz-, Safari-

If you assign an expression to an object property (including an object's `style` object) via the `setExpression()` method, you can remove it under script control with the `removeExpression()` method. The sole parameter is the name of the property in string form. Property names are case sensitive.

The method returns `true` if the removal succeeds; otherwise, `false` is returned. Be aware that removing an expression does not alter the value that is currently assigned to the property. In other words, you can use `setExpression()` to set a property's value and then remove the expression so that no further changes are made when the document recalculates expressions. If this is your goal, however, you are probably better served by simply setting the property directly via scripting.

Example

You can experiment with all three expression methods in The Evaluator (Chapter 13). The following sequence adds an expression to a style sheet property of the `myP` element on the page and then removes it.

To begin, enter the number `24` in the bottom one-line text box in The Evaluator (but don't press Enter or click the List Properties button). This is the value used in the expression to govern the `fontSize` property of the `myP` object. Next, assign an expression to the `myP` object's `style` object by entering the following statement in the top text box:

```
myP.style.setExpression("fontSize","document.forms[0].inspector.value","JScript")
```

Now you can enter different font sizes in the bottom text box and have the values immediately applied to the `fontSize` property. (Keyboard events in the text box automatically trigger the recalculation.) The default unit is `px`, but you can also append other units (such as `pt`) to the value in the text box to see how different measurement units influence the same numeric value.

Before proceeding to the next step, enter a value other than 16 (the default `fontSize` value). Finally, enter the following statement in the top text box to disconnect the expression from the property:

```
myP.style.removeExpression("fontSize")
```

Notice that although you can no longer adjust the font size from the bottom text box, the most recent value assigned to it sticks to the element. To prove it, enter the following statement in the top text box to see the current value:

```
myP.style.fontSize
```

Related Items: `document.recalc()`, `getExpression()`, `setExpression()` methods

removeNode(*removeChildrenFlag*)

Returns: `Node` object reference
Compatibility: WinIE5+, MacIE-, NN-, Moz-, Safari-

You can use the `removeNode()` method to delete the current node from an element hierarchy in WinIE5+. The sole parameter is a Boolean value that directs the method to remove only itself (without its child nodes) or the node and all of its children (value of `true`). The method returns a reference to the node object removed. This removed object is no longer accessible to the DOM. But the returned value contains all properties of the object as it existed before you removed it (including properties such as `outerHTML` and explicitly set style sheet rules). Thus, you can use this value as a parameter to insert the node elsewhere in the document.

Although the W3C DOM does not have a `removeNode()` method, the cross-browser method whose behavior most closely resembles `removeNode()` is the `removeChild()` method. The scope of the `removeChild()` method is one level up the object hierarchy from the object you use for the `removeNode()` method.

elementObject.**replaceAdjacentText()**

Example

Examine Listing 15-21 for the `appendChild()` method to understand the difference between `removeChild()` and `removeNode()`. In the `restore()` function, you can replace this statement

```
mainObj.removeChild(oneChild);
```

in IE5+ with

```
oneChild.removeNode(true);
```

The difference is subtle, but it is important to understand. See Listing 15-31 later in this chapter for another example of the `removeNode()` method.

Related Items: `Node` object; `appendChild()`, `cloneChild()`, `removeChild()`, `replaceChild()`, `replaceNode()` methods

replaceAdjacentText("*location*", "*text*")

Returns: String
Compatibility: WinIE5+, MacIE-, NN-, Moz-, Safari-

The `replaceAdjacentText()` method enables you to replace one chunk of document text with another in a specific position relative to the current object. Be aware that this method works only for plain text and not HTML tags. The returned value is the string of the text that you replace.

Both parameters are required. The first must be one of four possible case-insensitive locations for the insertion, shown in the following table:

Location	Description
beforeBegin	Before the current element's start tag
afterBegin	After the start tag but before any nested content
beforeEnd	Before the end tag but after all other nested content
afterEnd	After the end tag

This method is best used with inline (rather than block) elements when specifying the `beforeBegin` and `afterEnd` parameters. For example, if you attempt to use `replaceAdjacentText()` with `beforeBegin` on the second of two consecutive paragraph elements, the replacement text is inserted into the end of the first paragraph. You can think of the `replaceAdjacentText()` method in terms of text fragment nodes. The method replaces the text fragment node (given any one of the four position parameters) with new text. Replacing the text of a simple element with either the `afterBegin` or `beforeEnd` locations is the same as assigning that text to the object's `innerText` property.

Example

Use The Evaluator (see Chapter 13) to experiment with the `replaceAdjacentText()` method. Enter each of the following statements in the top text box, and watch the results in the `myP` element (and its nested `myEM` element) below the solid rule:

```
document.getElementById("myEM").replaceAdjacentText("afterBegin", "twenty")
```

Notice that the myEM element's new text picks up the behavior of the element. In the meantime, the replaced text (all) is returned by the method and displayed in the Results box:

```
document.getElementById("myEM").replaceAdjacentText("beforeBegin", "We need ")
```

All characters of the text fragment, including spaces, are replaced. Therefore, you may need to supply a trailing space, as shown here, if the fragment you replace has a space:

```
document.getElementById("myP").replaceAdjacentText("beforeEnd", " good people.")
```

This is another way to replace the text fragment following the myEM element, but it is also relative to the surrounding myP element. If you now attempt to replace text after the end of the myP block-level element

```
document.getElementById("myP").replaceAdjacentText("afterEnd", "Hooray!")
```

the text fragment is inserted after the end of the myP element's tag set. The fragment is just kind of floating in the DOM as an unlabeled text node.

Related Items: innerText, outerText properties; getAdjacentText(), insertAdjacentHTML(), insertAdjacentText() methods

replaceChild(*newNodeObject, oldNodeObject*)

Returns: Node object reference
Compatibility: WinIE5+, MacIE5+, NN6+, Moz+, Safari+

The replaceChild() method enables you to swap an existing child node object for a new node object. Parameters for the replaceChild() method are node object references, and they must be in the order of the new object followed by the object you want to replace. The old object must be an immediate child node of the parent used to invoke the method, and the new object must also be a legal child element within the document containment hierarchy.

The method returns a reference to the child object that you replaced with the new object. This reference can be used as a parameter to any of the node-oriented insertion or replacement methods.

Remember that replaceChild() is invoked from the point of view of a parent element. If you simply want to change an element, you can do so more directly in WinIE5+ with the swapNode() or replaceNode() method.

Example

You can see an example of replaceChild() as part of Listing 15-21 (for the appendChild property) earlier in this chapter.

Related Items: appendChild(), removeChild(), replaceNode(), swapNode() methods

replaceNode("*newNodeObject*")

Returns: Node object reference
Compatibility: WinIE5+, MacIE-, NN-, Moz-, Safari-

The replaceNode() method is related to the replaceChild() method, but you invoke this method on the actual node you want to replace (instead of the object's parent). The sole parameter is a reference to a valid node object, which you can generate via the document.createElement() method or copy from an existing node. The value returned from the method is a reference to the object that you replace. Thus, you can preserve a copy of the replaced node by storing the results in a variable for use later.

elementObject.replaceNode()

If the node you replace contains other nodes, the replaceNode() method removes all contained nodes of the original from the document. Therefore, if you want to change a wrapper node but want to maintain the original children, your script must capture the children and put them back into the new node as shown in the following example.

Example

Listing 15-31 demonstrates three node-related methods: removeNode(), replaceNode(), and swapNode(). These methods work in WinIE5+ only.

The page rendered from Listing 15-31 begins with a ul type list of four items. Four buttons control various aspects of the node structure of this list element. The first button invokes the replace() function, which changes the ul type to ol. To do this, the function must temporarily tuck away all child nodes of the original ul element so that they can be added back into the new ol element. At the same time, the old ul node is stored in a global variable (oldNode) for restoration in another function.

To replace the ul node with an ol, the replace() function creates a new, empty ol element and assigns the myOL ID to it. Next, the children (li elements) are stored en masse as an array in the variable innards. The child nodes are then inserted into the empty ol element, using the insertBefore() method. Notice that as each child element from the innards array is inserted into the ol element, the child element is removed from the innards array. That's why the loop to insert the child nodes is a while loop that constantly inserts the first item of the innards array to the new element. Finally, the replaceNode() method puts the new node in the old node's place, and the old node (just the ul element) is stored in oldNode.

The restore() function operates in the inverse direction of the replace() function. The same juggling of nested child nodes is required.

The third button invokes the swap() function, whose script exchanges the first and last nodes. The swapNode() method, like the others in this discussion, operates from the point of view of the node. Therefore, the method is attached to one of the swapped nodes, and the other node is specified as a parameter. Because of the nature of the ol element, the number sequence remains fixed, but the text of the li node swaps.

To demonstrate the removeNode() method, the fourth function removes the last child node of the list. Each call to removeNode() passes the true parameter to guarantee that the text nodes nested inside each li node are also removed. Experiment with this method by setting the parameter to false (the default). Notice how the parent–child relationship changes when you remove the li node.

LISTING 15-31

Using Node-Related Methods

```
<html>
   <head>
      <title>removeNode(), replaceNode(), and swapNode() Methods</title>
      <script type="text/javascript">
      // store original node between changes
      var oldNode;

      // replace UL node with OL
      function replace() {
         if (document.getElementById("myUL")) {
            var newNode = document.createElement("OL");
            newNode.id = "myOL";
```

```
            var innards = document.getElementById("myUL").children;
            while (innards.length > 0) {
                newNode.insertBefore(innards[0]);
            }
            oldNode = document.getElementById("myUL").replaceNode(newNode);
        }
    }

    // restore OL to UL
    function restore() {
        if (document.getElementById("myOL") && oldNode) {
            var innards = document.getElementById("myOL").children;
            while (innards.length > 0) {
                oldNode.insertBefore(innards[0]);
            }
            document.getElementById("myOL").replaceNode(oldNode);
        }
    }

    // swap first and last nodes
    function swap() {
        if (document.getElementById("myUL")) {
            document.getElementById("myUL").firstChild.swapNode(
                document.getElementById("myUL").lastChild);
        }
        if (document.getElementById("myOL")) {
            document.getElementById("myOL").firstChild.swapNode(
                document.getElementById("myOL").lastChild);
        }
    }

    // remove last node
    function remove() {
        if (document.getElementById("myUL")) {
            document.getElementById("myUL").lastChild.removeNode(true);
        }
        if (document.getElementById("myOL")) {
            document.getElementById("myOL").lastChild.removeNode(true);
        }
    }
    </script>
</head>
<body>
    <h1>Node Methods</h1>
    <hr />
    Here is a list of items:
    <ul id="myUL">
        <li>First Item</li>
        <li>Second Item</li>
        <li>Third Item</li>
        <li>Fourth Item</li>
    </ul>
```

continued

LISTING 15-31 *(continued)*

```
        <form>
            <input type="button" value="Change to OL List"
            onclick="replace()" />   <input type="button"
            value="Restore LI List" onclick="restore()" />   <input
            type="button" value="Swap First/Last" onclick="swap()" />  
            <input type="button" value="Remove Last" onclick="remove()" />
        </form>
    </body>
</html>
```

You can accomplish the same functionality shown in Listing 15-31 in a cross-browser fashion using the W3C DOM. In place of the removeNode() and replaceNode() methods, use removeChild() and replaceChild() methods to shift the point of view (and object references) to the parent of the ul and ol objects: the document.body. Also, you need to change the document.all references to document.getElementById().

Related Items: removeChild(), removeNode(), replaceChild(), swapNode() methods

scrollIntoView(*topAlignFlag*)

Returns: Nothing
Compatibility: WinIE4+, MacIE4+, NN7+, Moz+, Safari 2.02

The scrollIntoView() method scrolls the page (vertically and/or horizontally as needed) such that the current object is visible within the window or frame that contains it. A single parameter, a Boolean value, controls the location of the element within the viewable space. A value of true (the default) causes the element to be displayed so that its top is aligned with the top of the window or frame (provided that the document beneath it is long enough to allow this amount of scrolling). But a value of false causes the bottom of the element to align with the bottom of the viewable area. In most cases, you want the former so that the beginning of a page section is at the top of the viewable area. But if you don't want a user to see content below a certain element when you jump to the new view, use the false parameter.

For form elements, you must use the typical form element reference (document.formName.elementName .scrollIntoView()) unless you also specify an ID attribute for the element (document .getElementById("elementID").scrollIntoView()).

Example

Use The Evaluator (see Chapter 13) to experiment with the scrollIntoView() method. Resize the browser window height so that you can see only the top text box and the Results text area. Enter each of the following statements in the top text box, and see where the myP element comes into view:

```
myP.scrollIntoView()
myP.scrollIntoView(false)
```

Expand the height of the browser window until you can see part of the table lower on the page. If you enter

```
myTable.scrollIntoView(false)
```

in the top text box, the page scrolls to bring the bottom of the table to the bottom of the window. But if you use the default parameter (true or empty)

```
myTable.scrollIntoView()
```

the page scrolls as far as it can in an effort to align the top of the element as closely as possible to the top of the window. The page cannot scroll beyond its normal scrolling maximum (although if the element is a positioned element, you can use dynamic positioning to place it wherever you want — including off the page). Also, if you shrink the window and try to scroll the top of the table to the top of the window, be aware that the `table` element contains a `caption` element, so the caption is flush with the top of the window.

Related Items: `window.scroll()`, `window.scrollBy()`, `window.scrollTo()` methods

setActive()

Returns: Nothing
Compatibility: WinIE5.5+, MacIE-, NN-, Moz-, Safari-

The `setActive()` method lets a script designate an element object as the active element. However, unlike in the `focus()` method, the window does not scroll the active element into view. Any `onFocus` event handler defined for the element fires when `setActive()` is invoked without the browser's giving the element focus.

Example

Use The Evaluator (see Chapter 13) to compare the `setActive()` and `focus()` methods. With the page scrolled to the top and the window sized so that you cannot see the sample checkbox near the bottom of the page, enter the following statement in the top text box:

```
document.forms[1].myCheckbox.setActive()
```

Scroll down to see that the checkbox has operational focus (press the spacebar to see). Now scroll back to the top, and enter the following:

```
document.forms[1].myCheckbox.focus()
```

This time, the checkbox gets focus, and the page automatically scrolls the object into view.

Related Item: `focus()` method

setAttribute("*attributeName*", *value*[, *caseSensitivity*])

Returns: Nothing
Compatibility: WinIE4+, MacIE4+, NN6+, Moz+, Safari+

The `setAttribute()` method assigns a new value to an existing attribute of the current object or inserts an entirely new attribute name–value pair among the attributes of the current object. This method represents an alternative syntax to setting a property of the object directly.

> **NOTE** The W3C DOM Level 2 standard recommends `getAttribute()` and `setAttribute()` for reading and writing element object attribute values, rather than reading and writing those values by way of their corresponding properties. Although using these methods is certainly advisable for XML elements, the same DOM standard sends conflicting signals by defining all kinds of properties for HTML element objects. Browsers, of course, will support access via properties well into the future, so don't feel obligated to change your ways just yet.

The first two parameters of `setAttribute()` are required. The first is the name of the attribute. The default behavior of this method respects the case of the attribute name. Therefore, if you use `setAttribute()` to adjust the value of an existing attribute in default mode, the first parameter must match the case of the attribute as known by the object model for the current document. Remember that all names of all attributes assigned as inline source-code attributes are automatically converted to lowercase letters.

elementObject.**setAttributeNS()**

A value you assign to the attribute is the second parameter. For cross-browser compatibility, the value should be either a string or Boolean data type.

IE provides an optional third parameter to control the case-sensitivity issue for the attribute name. The default value (`true`) has a different impact on your object depending on whether you use `setAttribute()` to assign a new attribute or reassign an existing one. In the former case, the third parameter as `true` means that the attribute name assigned to the object observes the case of the first parameter. In the latter case, the third parameter as `true` means that the attribute isn't reassigned unless the first parameter matches the case of the attribute currently associated with the object. Instead, a new attribute with a different case sequence is created.

Attempting to manage the case sensitivity of newly created attributes is fraught with peril, especially if you try to reuse names but with different case sequences. I strongly recommend using default case-sensitivity controls for `setAttribute()` and `getAttribute()`.

See also the W3C DOM facilities for treating attributes as node objects in the discussions of the `getAttributeNode()` and `removeAttributeNode()` methods earlier in this chapter.

Example

Use The Evaluator (see Chapter 13) to experiment with the `setAttribute()` method for the elements in the page. Setting attributes can have immediate impact on the layout of the page (just as setting an object's properties can). Enter the following sample statements in the top text box to view attribute values.

```
document.getElementById("myTable").setAttribute("width", "80%")
document.getElementById("myTable").setAttribute("border", "5")
```

Related Items: `attributes` property; `document.createAttribute()`, `getAttribute()`, `getAttributeNode()`, `removeAttribute()`, `removeAttributeNode()`, `setAttributeNode()` methods

setAttributeNode()

(See `removeAttributeNode()`)

setAttributeNodeNS("*attributeNode*")

Returns: `Attribute` object
Compatibility: WinIE-, MacIE-, NN6+, Moz+, Safari-

This method inserts or replaces an attribute in the current element. The sole parameter is an attribute object, and the return value is a reference to the newly inserted attribute object. When the method is invoked, the browser looks for a pairing of local name and namespace URI between the nodes. If there is a match, the node replaces the matched node; otherwise, the node is inserted.

Related Items: `attributes`, `namespaceURI`, `localName` properties; `removeAttributeNS()`, `getAttributeNS()`, and `setAttributeNS()` methods

setAttributeNS("*namespaceURI*", "*qualifiedName*", "*value*")

Returns: Nothing
Compatibility: WinIE-, MacIE-, NN6+, Moz+, Safari-

This method inserts or replaces an attribute in the current element, as specified in the three parameters. The first parameter of the method is a URI string matching a URI assigned to a label in the document. The second parameter is the local name portion of the attribute whose value you are getting. If a match is found among these parameters, the value in the third parameter is assigned to the existing attribute; otherwise, the value is inserted as a new attribute.

Related Items: `attributes`, `namespaceURI`, `localName` properties; `removeAttributeNS()`, `getAttributeNS()`, and `setAttributeNodeNS()` methods

setCapture(*containerBoolean*)

(See `releaseCapture()`)

setExpression("*propertyName*", "*expression*",["*language*"])

Returns: Nothing
Compatibility: WinIE5+, MacIE-, NN-, Moz-, Safari-

Use the `setExpression()` method to assign the result of an executable expression to the value of an element object property. This method can assign values to both HTML element objects and style objects that belong to them.

The `setExpression()` method is a scripted way of assigning expressions to attributes. But you can also assign expressions directly to style sheet definitions in the HTML tag of an element using the `expression()` syntax, as in the following example:

```
<p style="width:expression(document.body.style.width * 0.75)">
```

The `setExpression()` method requires three parameters. The first parameter is the name of the property (in string form) to which you assign the expression. Property names are case sensitive. The second parameter is a string form of the expression to be evaluated to supply a value for the property. Expressions can refer to global variables or properties of other objects in the same document (provided that the property is anything other than an array). An expression may also contain math operators.

Pay close attention to the data type of the evaluated value of the expression. The value must be a valid data type for the property. For example, the URL of the body background image must be a string. But for numeric values, you can generally use number and string types interchangeably because the values are converted to the proper type for the property. Even for expressions that evaluate to numbers, encase the expression inside quotes. It may not be necessary in all cases, but if you get into the habit of using quotes, you'll have fewer problems for strings or complex expressions that require them.

You are not limited to using JavaScript as the language for the expression because you can also specify the scripting language of the expression in the optional third parameter. Acceptable parameter values for the language are

```
JScript
JavaScript
VBScript
```

For all intents and purposes, JScript and JavaScript are the same. Both languages are ECMA-262 compatible. `JScript` is the default value for the `language` parameter.

One reason to use `setExpression()` for dynamic properties is to let the property always respond to the current conditions on the page. For example, if you set a property that is dependent on the current width of the body, you want a recalculation that is applied to the property if the user resizes the window. The browser automatically responds to many events and updates any dynamic properties. In essence, the browser recalculates the expressions and applies the new values to the property. Keyboard events in particular trigger this kind of automatic recalculation for you. But if your scripts perform actions on their own (in other words, not triggered by events), your scripts need to force the recalculation of the expressions. The `document.recalc()` method takes care of this, but you must invoke it to force the recalculation of dynamic properties in these cases.

elementObject.setExpression()

Example

Listing 15-32 shows the `setExpression()`, `recalc()`, and `getExpression()` methods at work in a DHTML-based clock. Figure 15-1 shows the clock. As time clicks by, the bars for hours, minutes, and seconds adjust their widths to reflect the current time. At the same time, the `innerHTML` of span elements to the right of each bar display the current numeric value for the bar.

The dynamically calculated values in this example are based on the creation of a new date object over and over again to get the current time from the client computer clock. It is from the date object (stored in the variable called `now`) that the hour, minute, and second values are retrieved. Some other calculations are involved so that a value for one of these time components is converted to a pixel value for the width of the bars. The bars are divided into 24 (for the hours) and 60 (for the minutes and seconds) parts, so the scale for the two types differs. For the 60-increment bars in this application, each increment is set to 5 pixels (stored in `shortWidth`); the 24-increment bars are 2.5 times the `shortWidth`.

As the document loads, the three span elements for the colored bars are given no width, which means that they assume the default width of zero. But after the page loads, the `onload` event handler invokes the `init()` function, which sets the initial values for each bar's width and the text (`innerHTML`) of the three labeled spans. After these initial values are set, the `init()` function invokes the `updateClock()` function.

In the `updateClock()` function, a new date object is created for the current instant. The `document.recalc()` method is called, instructing the browser to recalculate the expressions that were set in the `init()` function and assign the new values to the properties. To keep the clock ticking, the `setTimeout()` method is set to invoke this same `updateClock()` function in 1 second.

To see what the `getExpression()` method does, you can click the button on the page. It simply displays the returned value for one of the attributes that you assign using `setExpression()`.

LISTING 15-32

Dynamic Properties

```
<html>
  <head>
    <title>getExpression(), setExpression(), and recalc() Methods</title>
    <style type="text/css">
    th {text-align:right}
    span {vertical-align:bottom}
    </style>
    <script type="text/javascript">
    var now = new Date();
    var shortWidth = 5;
    var multiple = 2.5;

    function init() {
      with (document.all) {
        hoursBlock.style.setExpression("width","now.getHours() *
          shortWidth * multiple","jscript");
        hoursLabel.setExpression("innerHTML","now.getHours()","jscript");
        minutesBlock.style.setExpression("width","now.getMinutes() *
          shortWidth","jscript");
        minutesLabel.setExpression("innerHTML","now.getMinutes()",
```

```
            "jscript");
        secondsBlock.style.setExpression("width","now.getSeconds() *
            shortWidth","jscript");
        secondsLabel.setExpression("innerHTML","now.getSeconds()",
            "jscript");
    }

    updateClock();
}

function updateClock() {
    now = new Date();
    document.recalc();
    setTimeout("updateClock()",1000);
}

function showExpr() {
    alert("Expression for the \'Hours\' innerHTML property is:\r\n" +
        document.getElementById("hoursLabel").getExpression("innerHTML") +
        ".");        }
</script>
</head>
<body onload="init()">
    <h1>getExpression(), setExpression(), recalc() Methods</h1>
    <hr />
    <p>This clock uses Dynamic Properties to calculate bar width and time
        numbers:</p>
    <table border="0">
        <tr>
            <th>Hours:</th>
            <td><span id="hoursBlock" style="background-color:red"></span>
                 <span id="hoursLabel"></span></td>
        </tr>
        <tr>
            <th>Minutes:</th>
            <td><span id="minutesBlock" style="background-color:yellow"></span>
                 <span id="minutesLabel"></span></td>
        </tr>
        <tr>
            <th>Seconds:</th>
            <td><span id="secondsBlock" style="background-color:green"></span>
                 <span id="secondsLabel"></span></td>
        </tr>
    </table>
    <hr />
    <form>
        <input type="button" value="Show 'Hours' number innerHTML Expression"
        onclick="showExpr()" />
    </form>
</body>
</html>
```

elementObject.swapNode()

A bar-graph clock created with dynamic expressions.

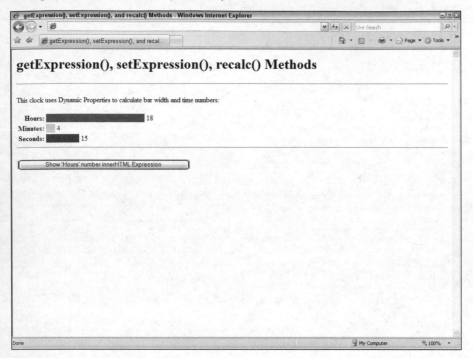

Related Items: `document.recalc()`, `removeExpression()`, `setExpression()` methods

setUserData("*key*", *dataObj*, *dataHandler*)

Returns: Object
Compatibility: WinIE-, MacIE-, NN-, Moz1.7.2+, Safari-

The `setUserData()` method is designed to allow for the addition of user data to a node. This user data comes in the form of an object and is associated with a node through a string key. By requiring a key for an object of user data, the `setUserData()` method allows you to set multiple pieces of data (objects) on a single node. The last parameter to the method is an event handler function reference that is called whenever the data object is cloned, imported, deleted, renamed, or adopted.

Although some support for the `setUserData()` method was added in Moz1.7.2, the method still isn't supported to the degree that you can actually use it, as of Moz1.8.1.

swapNode(*otherNodeObject*)

Returns: Node object reference
Compatibility: WinIE5+, MacIE-, NN-, Moz-, Safari-

The swapNode() method exchanges the positions of two nodes within an element hierarchy. Contents of both nodes are preserved in their entirety during the exchange. The single parameter must be a valid node object (perhaps created with document.createElement() or copied from an existing node). A return value is a reference to the object whose swapNode() method was invoked.

Example

See Listing 15-31 (the replaceNode() method) for an example of the swapNode() method in action.

Related Items: removeChild(), removeNode(), replaceChild(), replaceNode() methods

tags("*tagName*")

Returns: Array of element objects
Compatibility: WinIE4+, MacIE4+, NN-, Moz-, Safari-

The tags() method does not belong to every element, but it is a method of every collection of objects (such as all, forms, and elements). The method is best thought of as a kind of filter for the elements that belong to the current collection. For example, to get an array of all p elements inside a document, use this expression:

```
document.all.tags("P")
```

You must pass a parameter string consisting of the tag name you wish to extract from the collection. The tag name is case insensitive.

The return value is an array of references to the objects within the current collection whose tags match the parameter. If there are no matches, the returned array has a length of zero. If you need cross-browser compatibility, use the getElementsByTagName() method described earlier in this chapter, and pass a wildcard value of "*".

Example

Use The Evaluator (see Chapter 13) to experiment with the tags() method. Enter the following statements one at a time in the top text box, and study the results:

```
document.all.tags("div")
document.all.tags("div").length
myTable.all.tags("td").length
```

Because the tags() method returns an array of objects, you can use one of those returned values as a valid element reference:

```
document.all.tags("form")[1].elements.tags("input").length
```

Related Item: getElementsByTagName() method

toString("*param*")

Returns: String
Compatibility: WinIE4+, MacIE4+, NN6+, Moz+, Safari+

The toString() method returns a string representation of the element object, which unfortunately can mean different things to different browsers. Don't expect entirely consistent results across browsers, especially when you consider that IE simply returns a generic "[object]" string.

elementObject.**onactivate**

urns("*behaviorURN*")

Returns: Array of element objects
Compatibility: WinIE5+, MacIE-, NN-, Moz-, Safari-

The urns() method does not belong to every element, but it is a method of every collection of objects. You must pass a parameter string consisting of the URN (Uniform Resource Name) of a behavior resource (most typically .htc) assigned to one or more elements of the collection. The parameter does not include the extension of the filename. If there is no matching behavior URN for the specified parameter, the urns() method returns an array of zero length. This method is related to the behaviorUrns property, which contains an array of behavior URNs assigned to a single element object.

Example

In case the urns() method is reconnected in the future, you can add a button and function to Listing 15-19b that reveals whether the makeHot.htc behavior is attached to the myP element. Such a function looks like this:

```
function behaviorAttached() {
    if (document.all.urns("makeHot")) {
        alert("There is at least one element set to \'makeHot\'.");
    }
}
```

Related Item: behaviorUrns property

Event handlers
onactivate
ondeactivate

Compatibility: WinIE5.5+, MacIE-, NN-, Moz-, Safari-

The onactivate and ondeactivate event handlers are similar to the onfocus and onblur event handlers, respectively, as well as to the IE5.5+ onfocusin and onfocusout events. Starting with IE5.5+, it is possible to manage the activation of an element and the focus of an element separately. The onactivate and ondeactivate events correspond to the activation of an element, whereas onfocusin and onfocusout deal with focus. In many cases, activation and focus go hand in hand, but not always.

If an element receives activation, the onactivate event fires for that element just before the activation takes hold; conversely, just before the element loses activation, events fire in the sequence onbeforedeactivate, ondeactivate, onblur. Only elements that by their nature can accept activation (for example, links and form input controls) or that have a tabindex attribute set can become the active element (and, therefore, fire these events).

WinIE5.5+ maintains the original onfocus and onblur event handlers. But because the behaviors are so close to those of the onactivate and ondeactivate events, I don't recommend mixing the old and new event handler names in your coding style. If you script exclusively for WinIE5.5+, which is rather likely in this day and age, you can use the newer terminology throughout. And if you truly want to track the focus of an element, consider using onfocusin and onfocusout instead.

Example

You can modify Listing 15-34 later in this chapter by substituting `onactivate` for `onfocus` and `ondeactivate` for `onblur`.

Use The Evaluator (see Chapter 13) to experiment with the `onbeforedeactivate` event handler. To begin, set the `myP` element so it can accept focus:

```
myP.tabIndex = 1
```

If you repeatedly press the Tab key, the `myP` paragraph will eventually receive focus — indicated by the dotted rectangle around it. To see how you can prevent the element from losing focus, assign an anonymous function to the `onbeforedeactivate` event handler, as shown in the following statement:

```
myP.onbeforedeactivate = new Function("event.returnValue=false")
```

Now you can press Tab all you like or click other focusable elements all you like, and the `myP` element will not lose focus until you reload the page (which clears away the event handler). Please do not do this on your pages unless you want to infuriate and alienate your site visitors.

Related Items: `onblur`, `onfocus`, `onfocusin`, `onfocusout` event handlers

onafterupdate
onbeforeupdate

Compatibility: WinIE4+, MacIE5+, NN-, Moz-, Safari-

The `onafterupdate` and `onbeforeupdate` event handlers fire on a bound data object in IE whenever the data in the object is being updated. The `onbeforeupdate` event is fired just before the update occurs, whereas `onafterupdate` is fired after the data has been successfully updated.

onbeforecopy

Compatibility: WinIE5+, MacIE-, NN-, Moz-, Safari1.3+

The `onbeforecopy` event handler fires before the actual copy action takes place whenever the user initiates a content copy action via the Edit menu (including the Ctrl+C keyboard shortcut) or the right-click context menu. If the user accesses the Copy command via the Edit or context menu, the `onbeforecopy` event fires before either menu displays. In practice, the event may fire twice even though you expect it only once. Just because the `onbeforecopy` event fires, it does not guarantee that a user will complete the copy operation (for example, the context menu may close before the user makes a selection).

Unlike paste-related events, the `onbeforecopy` event handler does not work with form input elements. Just about any other HTML element is fair game, however.

Example

You can use the `onbeforecopy` event handler to preprocess information prior to an actual copy action. In Listing 15-33, the function invoked by the second paragraph element's `onbeforecopy` event handler selects the entire paragraph so that the user can select any character(s) in the paragraph to copy the entire paragraph into the clipboard. You can paste the results into the text area to verify the operation. By assigning the paragraph selection to the `onbeforecopy` event handler, the page notifies the user about what the copy operation will entail prior to making the menu choice. Had the operation been deferred to the `oncopy` event handler, the selection would have been made after the user chose Copy from the menu.

LISTING 15-33

The onbeforecopy Event Handler

```html
<html>
    <head>
        <title>onbeforecopy Event Handler</title>
        <script type="text/javascript">
        function selectWhole() {
            var obj = window.event.srcElement;
            var range = document.body.createTextRange();
            range.moveToElementText(obj);
            range.select();
            event.returnValue = false;
        }
        </script>
    </head>
    <body>
        <h1>onbeforecopy Event Handler</h1>
        <hr />
        <p>Select one or more characters in the following paragraph. Then execute
            a Copy command via Edit or context menu.</p>
        <p id="myP" onbeforecopy="selectWhole()">Lorem ipsum dolor sit amet,
            consectetaur adipisicing elit, sed do eiusmod tempor incididunt ut
            labore et dolore magna aliqua. Ut enim adminim veniam, quis nostrud
            exercitation ullamco laboris nisi ut aliquip ex ea commodo
            consequat.</p>
        <form>
            <p>Paste results here:<br />
                <textarea name="output" cols="60" rows="5">
                </textarea></p>
        </form>
    </body>
</html>
```

Related Items: onbeforecut, oncopy event handlers

onbeforecut

Compatibility: WinIE5+, MacIE-, NN-, Moz-, Safari 1.3+

The onbeforecut event handler fires before the actual cut action takes place whenever the user initiates a content cut via the Edit menu (including the Ctrl+X keyboard shortcut) or the right-click context menu. If the user accesses the Cut command via the Edit or context menu, the onbeforecut event fires before either menu displays. In practice, the event may fire twice even though you expect it only once. Just because the onbeforecut event fires, it does not guarantee that a user will complete the cut operation (for example, the context menu may close before the user makes a selection). If you add the onbeforecut event handler to an HTML element, the context menu usually disables the Cut menu item. But assigning a JavaScript call to this event handler brings the Cut menu item to life.

Example

You can use the onbeforecut event handler to preprocess information prior to an actual cut action. You can try this by editing a copy of Listing 15-33, changing the onbeforecopy event handler to onbeforecut. Notice that in its original form, the example does not activate the Cut item in either the context or Edit menu when you select some text in the second paragraph. But by assigning a function to the onbeforecut event handler, the menu item is active, and the entire paragraph is selected from the function that is invoked.

Related Items: onbeforecopy, oncut event handlers

onbeforedeactivate

Compatibility: WinIE5.5+, MacIE-, NN-, Moz-, Safari-

(See onactivate event handler)

onbeforeeditfocus

Compatibility: WinIE5+, MacIE-, NN-, Moz-, Safari-

The onbeforeeditfocus event handler is triggered whenever you edit an element on a page in an environment such as Microsoft's DHTML Editing ActiveX control or with the editable page content feature of IE5.5+. This discussion focuses on the latter scenario because it is entirely within the scope of client-side JavaScript. The onbeforeeditfocus event fires just before the element receives its focus. (There may be no onscreen feedback that editing is turned on unless you script it yourself.) The event fires each time a user clicks the element, even if the element just received edit focus elsewhere in the same element.

Example

Use The Evaluator (see Chapter 13) to explore the onbeforeeditfocus in WinIE5.5+. In the following sequence, you assign an anonymous function to the onbeforeeditfocus event handler of the myP element. The function turns the text color of the element to red when the event handler fires:

```
myP.onbeforeeditfocus = new Function("myP.style.color='red'")
```

Now turn on content editing for the myP element:

```
myP.contentEditable = true
```

Now if you click inside the myP element on the page to edit its content, the text turns red before you begin editing. In a page scripted for this kind of user interface, you would include some control that turns off editing and changes the color to normal.

Related Items: document.designMode, contentEditable, isContentEditable properties

onbeforepaste

Compatibility: WinIE5+, MacIE-, NN-, Moz-, Safari 1.3+

Like onbeforecopy and onbeforecut, the onbeforepaste event occurs just prior to the display of either the context or menu-bar Edit menu when the current object is selected (or has a selection within it). The primary value of this event comes when you use scripts to control the copy-and-paste process of a complex object. Such an object may have multiple kinds of data associated with it, but your script captures only one of the data types. Or you may want to put some related data about the copied item (for example, the id property of the element) into the clipboard. By using the onbeforepaste event handler to set the event.returnValue property to false, you guarantee that the pasted item is enabled in the context or

Edit menu (provided that the clipboard is holding some content). A handler invoked by `onpaste` should then apply the specific data subset from the clipboard to the currently selected item.

Example

See Listing 15-44 for the `onpaste` event handler (later in this chapter) to see how the `onbeforepaste` and `onpaste` event handlers work together.

Related Items: `oncopy`, `oncut`, `onpaste` event handlers

onbeforeupdate

(See `onafterupdate`)

onblur

Compatibility: WinIE3+, MacIE3+, NN2+, Moz+, Safari+

The `onblur` event fires when an element that has focus is about to lose focus because some other element is about to receive focus. For example, a text input element fires the `onblur` event when a user tabs from that element to the next one inside a form. The `onblur` event of the first element fires before the `onfocus` event of the next element.

The availability of the `onblur` event has expanded with succeeding generations of script-capable browsers. In the earlier versions, blur and focus were largely confined to text-oriented input elements (including the `select` element). These are safe to use with all scriptable browser versions. The `window` object received the `onblur` event handler starting with NN3 and IE4. IE4 also extended the event handler to more form elements, predominantly on the Windows operating system because that OS has a user interface clue (the dotted rectangle) when items such as buttons and links receive focus (so that you may act upon them by pressing the spacebar). For IE5+, the `onblur` event handler is available to virtually every HTML element. For most of those elements, however, blur and focus are not possible unless you assign a value to the `tabindex` attribute of the element's tag. For example, if you assign `tabindex="1"` inside a `<p>` tag, the user can bring focus to that paragraph (highlighted with the dotted rectangle in Windows) by clicking the paragraph or pressing the Tab key until that item receives focus in sequence.

If you plan to use the `onblur` event handler on window or text-oriented input elements, be aware that there might be some unexpected and undesirable consequences of scripting for the event. For example, in IE, a `window` object that has focus loses focus (and triggers the `onblur` event) if the user brings focus to any element on the page (or even clicks a blank area on the page). Similarly, the interaction between `onblur`, `onfocus`, and the `alert()` dialog box can be problematic with text input elements. This is why I generally recommend using the `onchange` event handler to trigger form validation routines. If you should employ both the `onblur` and `onchange` event handler for the same element, the `onchange` event fires before `onblur`. For more details about using this event handler for data validation, see Chapter 43 on the CD-ROM.

WinIE5.5+ added the `ondeactivate` event handler, which fires immediately before the `onblur` event handler. Both the `onblur` and `ondeactivate` events can be blocked if the `onbeforedeactivate` event handler function sets `event.returnValue` to `false`.

Example

More often than not, a page author uses the `onblur` event handler to exert extreme control over the user, such as preventing a user from exiting a text box unless that user types something in the box. This is not a web-friendly practice, and it is one that I discourage because there are intelligent ways to ensure that a field has something typed into it before a form is submitted (see Chapter 43 on the CD-ROM). Listing 15-34 simply demonstrates the impact of the `tabindex` attribute in a WinIE5 element with respect to the `onblur` and `onfocus` events. Notice that as you press the Tab key, only the second paragraph issues the events, even though all three paragraphs have event handlers assigned to them.

LISTING 15-34

onblur and onfocus Event Handlers

```
<html>
    <head>
        <title>onblur and onblur Event Handlers</title>
        <script type="text/javascript">
        function showBlur() {
            var id = event.srcElement.id;
            alert("Element \"" + id + "\" has blurred.");
        }

        function showFocus() {
            var id = event.srcElement.id;
            alert("Element \"" + id + "\" has received focus.");
        }
        </script>
    </head>
    <body>
        <h1 id="H1" tabindex="2">onblur and onblur Event Handlers</h1>
        <hr />
        <p id="P1" onblur="showBlur()" onfocus="showFocus()">Lorem ipsum dolor
            sit amet, consectetaur adipisicing elit, sed do eiusmod tempor
            incididunt ut labore et dolore magna aliqua. Ut enim adminim veniam,
            quis nostrud exercitation ullamco laboris nisi ut aliquip ex ea
            commodo consequat.</p>
        <p id="P2" tabindex="1" onblur="showBlur()" onfocus="showFocus()">Bis
            nostrud exercitation ullam mmodo consequet. Duis aute involuptate
            velit esse cillum dolore eu fugiat nulla pariatur. At vver eos et
            accusam dignissum qui blandit est praesent luptatum delenit
            aigueexcepteur sint occae.</p>
        <p id="P3" onblur="showBlur()" onfocus="showFocus()">Unte af phen
            neigepheings atoot Prexs eis phat eit sakem eit vory gast te Plok
            peish ba useing phen roxas. Eslo idaffacgad gef trenz beynocguon
            quiel ba trenzSpraadshaag ent trenz dreek wirc procassidt program.</p>
    </body>
</html>
```

Related Items: `blur()`, `focus()` methods; `ondeactivate`, `onbeforedeactivate`, `onfocus`, `onactivate` event handlers

oncellchange

Compatibility: WinIE5+, MacIE-, NN-, Moz-, Safari-

The `oncellchange` event handler is part of the data binding of IE and fires when data changes in the data provider, which is usually a bound control. When responding to this event, you can analyze the `dataFld` property to find out which field in the recordset has changed.

onclick

Compatibility: WinIE3+, MacIE3+, NN2+, Moz+, Safari+

The `onclick` event fires when a user presses down (with the primary mouse button) and releases the button with the pointer atop the element (both the down and up strokes must be within the rectangle of the same element). The event also fires with non-mouse-click equivalents in operating systems such as Windows. For example, you can use the keyboard to give focus to a clickable object and then press the spacebar or Enter key to perform the same action as clicking the element. In IE, if the element object supports the `click()` method, the `onclick` event fires with the invocation of that method (notice that this does not apply to Navigator or other browsers).

The `onclick` event is closely related to other mouse events. The other related events are `onmousedown`, `onmouseup`, and `ondoubleclick`. The `onmousedown` event fires when the user makes contact with the mouse switch on the downstroke of a click action. Next comes the `onmouseup` event (when the contact breaks). Only then does the `onclick` event fire — provided that the `onmousedown` and `onmouseup` events have fired in the same object. See the discussions on the `onmousedown` and `onmouseup` events later in this chapter for examples of their usage.

Interaction with the `ondblclick` event is simple: The `onclick` event fires (after the first click), followed by the `ondblclick` event (after the second click). See the discussion of the `ondblclick` event handler later in this chapter for more about the interaction of these two event handlers.

When used with objects that have intrinsic actions when users click them (namely, links and areas), the `onclick` event handler can perform all of the actions — including navigating to the destination normally assigned to the `href` attribute of the element. For example, to be compatible with all scriptable browsers, you can make an image clickable if you surround its tag with an `<a>` link tag. This lets the `onclick` event of that tag substitute for the missing `onclick` event handler of earlier `<img>` tags. If you assign an `onclick` event handler without special protection, the event handler will execute, and the intrinsic action of the element will be carried out. Therefore, you need to block the intrinsic action. To accomplish this, the event handler must evaluate to the statement `return false`. You can do this in two ways. The first is to append a `return false` statement to the script statement assigned to the event handler:

```
<a href="#" onclick="yourFunction(); return false"><img...></a>
```

As an alternative, you can let the function invoked by the event handler supply the `false` part of the `return false` statement, as shown in the following sequence:

```
function yourFunction() {
   [statements that do something here]
   return false;
}
...
<a href="#" onclick="return yourFunction()"><img...></a>
```

Either methodology is acceptable. A third option is to not use the `onclick` event handler at all but assign a `javascript:` pseudo-URL to the `href` attribute (see the `Link` object in Chapter 19).

The event model in IE4+ provides one more way to prevent the intrinsic action of an object from firing when a user clicks it. If the `onclick` event handler function sets the `returnValue` property of the event object to `false`, the intrinsic action is canceled. Simply include the following statement in the function invoked by the event handler:

```
event.returnValue = false;
```

The event model of the W3C DOM has a different approach to canceling the default action. In the event handler function for an event, invoke the `eventObj.cancelDefault()` method.

A common mistake made by scripting beginners is to use a submit type input button as a button intended to perform some script action rather than submitting a form. The typical scenario is an `input` element of type `submit` assigned an `onclick` event handler to perform some local action. The submit input button has an intrinsic behavior, just like links and areas. Although you can block the intrinsic behavior, as just described, you should use an `input` element of type `button`.

If you are experiencing difficulty with an implementation of the `onclick` event handler (such as trying to find out which mouse button was used for the click), it may be that the operating system or default browser behavior is getting in the way of your scripting. But you can usually get what you need via the `onmousedown` event handler. (The `onmouseup` event may not fire when you use the secondary mouse button to click an object.) Use the `onclick` event handler whenever possible to capture user clicks, because this event behaves most like users are accustomed to in their daily computing work. But fall back on `onmousedown` in an emergency.

Example

The `onclick` event handler is one of the simplest to grasp and use. Listing 15-35 demonstrates its interaction with the `ondblclick` event handler and shows you how to prevent a link's intrinsic action from activating when combined with `click` events. As you click and/or double-click the link, the status bar displays a message associated with each event. Notice that if you double-click, the `click` event fires first, with the first message immediately replaced by the second. For demonstration purposes, I show both backward-compatible ways of canceling the link's intrinsic action. In practice, decide on one style and stick with it.

LISTING 15-35

Using onclick and ondblclick Event Handlers

```
<html>
  <head>
    <title>onclick and ondblclick Event Handlers</title>
    <script type="text/javascript">
    var timeout;
    function clearOutput() {
        document.getElementById("clickType").innerHTML = "";
    }
    function showClick() {
        document.getElementById("clickType").innerHTML = "single";
        clearTimeout(timeout);
```

continued

LISTING 15-35 *(continued)*

```
        timeout = setTimeout("clearOutput()", 3000);
    }

    function showDblClick() {
        document.getElementById("clickType").innerHTML = "double";
        clearTimeout(timeout);
        timeout = setTimeout("clearOutput()", 3000);
    }
    </script>
</head>
<body>
    <h1>onclick and ondblclick Event Handlers</h1>
    <hr />
    <a href="#" onclick="showClick();return false"
    ondblclick="return showDblClick()">A sample link.</a>
    (Click type: <span id="clickType"></span>)
</body>
</html>
```

Related Items: click() method; oncontextmenu, ondblclick, onmousedown, onmouseup event handlers

oncontextmenu

Compatibility: WinIE5+, MacIE-, NN7+, Moz+, Safari-

The oncontextmenu event fires when the user clicks an object with the secondary (usually the right) mouse button. The only click-related events that fire with the secondary button are onmousedown and oncontextmenu.

To block the intrinsic application menu display of the oncontextmenu event, use any of the three event cancellation methodologies available in WinIE5+ (as just described in the onclick event handler description: two variations of evaluating the event handler to return false; assigning false to the event.returnValue property). It is not uncommon to wish to block the context menu from appearing so that users are somewhat inhibited from downloading copies of images or viewing the source code of a frame. Be aware, however, that if a user turns Active Scripting off in WinIE5+, the event handler cannot prevent the context menu from appearing.

Another possibility for this event is to trigger the display of a custom context menu constructed with other DHTML facilities. In this case, you must also disable the intrinsic context menu so that both menus do not display at the same time.

Example

See Listing 15-30 earlier in this chapter for an example of using the oncontextmenu event handler with a custom context menu.

Related Items: `releaseCapture()`, `setCapture()` methods

oncontrolselect

Compatibility: WinIE5.5+, MacIE-, NN-, Moz-, Safari-

The `oncontrolselect` event fires just before a user makes a selection on an editable element while the page is in edit mode. It's important to note that it is the element itself that is selected to trigger this event, not the content within the element.

Related Items: `onresizeend`, `onresizestart` event handlers

oncopy
oncut

Compatibility: WinIE5+, MacIE4+, NN-, Moz-, Safari1.3+

The `oncopy` and `oncut` events fire immediately after the user or script initiates a copy or cut edit action on the current object. Each event is preceded by its associated before event, which fires before any Edit or context menu appears (or before the copy or cut action, if initiated by keyboard shortcut).

Use these event handlers to provide edit functionality to elements that don't normally allow copying or cutting. In such circumstances, you need to enable the Copy or Cut menu items in the context or Edit menu by setting the `event.returnValue` for the `onbeforecopy` or `onbeforecut` event handlers to `false`. Then your `oncopy` or `oncut` event handlers must manually stuff a value into the clipboard by way of the `setdata()` method of the `clipboardData` object. If you use the `setdata()` method in your `oncopy` or `oncut` event handler, you must also set the `event.returnValue` property to `false` in the handler function to prevent the default copy or cut action from wiping out your clipboard contents.

Because you are in charge of what data is stored in the clipboard, you are not limited to a direct copy of the data. For example, you might wish to store the value of the `src` property of an image object so that the user can paste it elsewhere on the page.

In the case of the `oncut` event handler, your script is also responsible for cutting the element or selected content from the page. To eliminate all of the content of an element, you can set the element's `innerHTML` or `innerText` property to an empty string. For a selection, use the `selection.createRange()` method to generate a `TextRange` object whose contents you can manipulate through the `TextRange` object's methods.

Example

Listing 15-36 shows both the `onbeforecut` and `oncut` event handlers in action (as well as `onbeforepaste` and `onpaste`). Notice that the `handleCut()` function not only stuffs the selected word into the `clipboardData` object, but also erases the selected text from the table cell element from where it came. If you replace the `onbeforecut` and `oncut` event handlers with `onbeforecopy` and `oncopy` (and change `handleCut()` to not eliminate the inner text of the event source element), the operation works with copy and paste instead of cut and paste. I demonstrate this later in the chapter in Listing 15-44.

LISTING 15-36

Cutting and Pasting under Script Control

```html
<html>
    <head>
        <title>onbeforecut and oncut Event Handlers</title>
        <style type="text/css">
        td {text-align:center}
        th {text-decoration:underline}
        .blanks {text-decoration:underline}
        </style>
        <script type="text/javascript">
        function selectWhole() {
            var obj = window.event.srcElement;
            var range = document.body.createTextRange();
            range.moveToElementText(obj);
            range.select();
            event.returnValue = false;
        }

        function handleCut() {
            var rng = document.selection.createRange();
            clipboardData.setData("Text",rng.text);
            var elem = event.srcElement;
            elem.innerText = "";
            event.returnValue = false;
        }

        function handlePaste() {
            var elem = window.event.srcElement;
            if (elem.className == "blanks") {
                elem.innerHTML = clipboardData.getData("Text");
            }
            event.returnValue = false;
        }

        function handleBeforePaste() {
            var elem = window.event.srcElement;
            if (elem.className == "blanks") {
                event.returnValue = false;
            }
        }
        </script>
    </head>
    <body>
        <h1>onbeforecut and oncut Event Handlers</h1>
        <hr />
        <p>Your goal is to cut and paste one noun and one adjective from the
            following table into the blanks of the sentence. Select a word from
            the table and use the Edit or context menu to cut it from the table.
            Select one or more spaces of the blanks in the sentence and choose
            Paste to replace the blank with the clipboard contents.</p>
```

```
        <table cellpadding="5" onbeforecut="selectWhole()" oncut="handleCut()">
            <tr>
                <th>Nouns</th>
                <th>Adjectives</th>
            </tr>
            <tr>
                <td>truck</td>
                <td>round</td>
            </tr>
            <tr>
                <td>doll</td>
                <td>red</td>
            </tr>
            <tr>
                <td>ball</td>
                <td>pretty</td>
            </tr>
        </table>
        <p id="myP" onbeforepaste="handleBeforePaste()" onpaste="handlePaste()">
            Pat said, "Oh my, the <span id="blank1"
            class="blanks">     </span> is so <span
            id="blank2" class="blanks">     </span>!"</p>
        <button onclick="location.reload()">Reset</button>
    </body>
</html>
```

Related Items: `onbeforecopy`, `onbeforecut`, `onbeforepaste`, and `onpaste` event handlers

ondataavailable
ondatasetchanged
ondatasetcomplete

Compatibility: WinIE4+, MacIE-, NN-, Moz-, Safari-

These three events are part of the data binding of IE and are fired to help reflect the state of data that is being transmitted. The `ondataavailable` event fires when data is transmitted from the data source, whereas the `ondatasetcomplete` event indicates that the recordset has completely downloaded from the data source. The `ondatasetchanged` event is fired when the recordset of a data source has somehow changed.

ondblclick

Compatibility: WinIE4+, MacIE4+, NN4+, Moz+, Safari+

The `ondblclick` event fires after the second click of a double-click sequence. The timing between clicks depends on the client's mouse control panel settings. The `onclick` event also fires, but only after the first of the two clicks.

In general, it is rarely a good design to have an element perform one task when the mouse is single-clicked and a different task if double-clicked. With the event sequence employed in modern browsers, this isn't practical anyway (the `onclick` event always fires, even when the user double-clicks). But it is not uncommon to have the mouse down action perform some helper action. You see this in most icon-based file systems: If you click a file icon, it is highlighted at mouse down to select the item; you can double-click the item to launch it. In either case, one event's action does not impede the other nor confuse the user.

Example

See Listing 15-35 (for the `onclick` event handler) to see the `ondblclick` event in action.

Related Items: `onclick`, `onmousedown`, `onmouseup` event handlers

ondrag, ondragend, ondragstart

Compatibility: WinIE5+, MacIE-, NN-, Moz-, Safari 1.3+

The `ondrag` event fires after the `ondragstart` event and continues firing repeatedly while the user drags a selection or object onscreen. Unlike the `onmousemove` event, which fires only as the cursor moves onscreen, the `ondrag` event continues to fire even when the cursor is stationary. In the WinIE5+/Safari 1.3+, users can drag objects to other browser windows or other applications. The event fires while the dragging extends beyond the browser window.

Because the event fires regardless of what is underneath the dragged object, you can use it in a game or training environment in which the user has only a fixed amount of time to complete a dragging operation (for example, matching similar pairs of objects). If the browser accommodates downloadable cursors, the `ondrag` event could cycle the cursor through a series of cursor versions to resemble an animated cursor.

Understanding the sequence of drag-related events during a user drag operation can be helpful if your scripts need to micromanage the actions (usually not necessary for basic drag-and-drop operations). Consider the drag-and-drop operation shown in Figure 15-2.

FIGURE 15-2

A typical drag-and-drop operation.

It helps to imagine that the cells of the table with draggable content are named like spreadsheet cells: truck is cell A1; round is B1; doll is A2; and so on. During the drag operation, many objects are the targets of a variety of drag-related events. Table 15-11 lists the event sequence and the event targets.

TABLE 15-11

Events and Their Targets During a Typical Drag-and-Drop Operation

Event	Target	Discussion
ondragstart	cell A1	The very first event that fires during a drag-and-drop operation.
ondrag	cell A1	Fires continually on this target throughout the entire operation. Other events get interspersed, however.
ondragenter	cell A1	Even though the cursor hasn't moved from cell A1 yet, the ondragenter event fires upon first movement within the source element.
ondragover	cell A1	Fires continually on whatever element the cursor rests on at that instant. If the user simply holds the mouse button down and does not move the cursor during a drag, the ondrag and ondragover events fire continually, alternating between the two.
(repetition)	cell A1	ondrag and ondragover events fire alternately while the cursor remains atop cell A1.
ondragenter	table	The table element, represented by the border and/or cell padding, receives the ondragenter event when the cursor touches its space.
ondragleave	cell A1	Notice that the ondragleave event fires after the ondragenter event fires on another element.
ondrag	cell A1	Still firing away.
ondragover	table	The source element for this event shifts to the table because that's what the cursor is over at this instant. If the cursor doesn't move from this spot, the ondrag (cell A1) and ondragover (table) events continue to fire in turn.
ondragenter	cell B1	The drag is progressing from the table border space to cell B1.
ondragleave	table	The table element receives the ondragleave event when the cursor exits its space.
ondrag	cell A1	The ondrag event continues to fire on the cell A1 object.
ondragover	cell B1	The cursor is atop cell B1 now, so the ondragover event fires for that object. Fires multiple times (depending on the speed of the computer and the user's drag action), alternating with the previous ondrag event. More of the same as the cursor progresses from cell B1 through the table border again to cell B2, the table again, cell B3, and the outermost edge of the table.
ondragenter	body	Dragging is free of the table and is floating free on the bare body element.
ondragleave	table	Yes, you just left the table.
ondrag	cell A1	Still alive and receiving this event.

continued

	TABLE 15-11	*(continued)*

Event	Target	Discussion
ondragover	body	That's where the cursor is now. Fires multiple times (depending on the speed of the computer and the user's drag action), alternating with the previous ondrag event.
ondragenter	blank1	The cursor reaches the span element whose ID is blank1, where the empty underline is.
ondragleave	body	Just left the body for the blank.
ondrag	cell A1	Still kicking.
ondragover	blank1	That's where the cursor is now. Fires multiple times (depending on the speed of the computer and the user's drag action), alternating with the previous ondrag event.
ondrop	blank1	The span element gets the notification of a recent drop.
ondragend	cell A1	The original source element gets the final word that dragging is complete. This event fires even if the drag does not succeed because the drag does not end on a drop target.

In practice, some of the events shown in Table 15-11 may not fire. Much has to do with how many event handlers you trap that need to execute scripts along the way. The other major factor is the physical speed at which the user performs the drag-and-drop operation (which interacts with the CPU processing speed). The kinds of events that are most likely to be skipped are the ondragenter and ondragleave events, and perhaps some ondragover events if the user flies over an object before its ondragover event has a chance to fire.

Despite this uncertainty about drag-related event reliability, you can count on several important ones to fire all the time. The ondragstart, ondrop (if over a drop target), and ondragend events — as well some interstitial ondrag events — will definitely fire in the course of dragging onscreen. All but ondrop direct their events to the source element, whereas ondrop fires on the target.

Example

Listing 15-37 shows several drag-related event handlers in action. The page resembles the example in Listing 15-36, but the scripting behind the page is quite different. In this example, the user is encouraged to select individual words from the Nouns and Adjectives columns and drag them to the blanks of the sentence. To beef up the demonstration, Listing 15-37 shows you how to pass the equivalent of array data from a drag source to a drag target. At the same time, the user has a fixed amount of time (2 seconds) to complete each drag operation.

The ondragstart and ondrag event handlers are placed in the <body> tag because those events bubble up from any element that the user tries to drag. The scripts invoked by these event handlers filter the events so that the desired action is triggered only by the hot elements inside the table. This approach to event handlers prevents you from having to duplicate event handlers for each table cell.

The ondragstart event handler invokes setupDrag(). This function cancels the ondragstart event except when the target element (the one about to be dragged) is one of the td elements inside the table. To make this application smarter about what kind of word is dragged to which blank, it passes not only the word's text, but also some extra information about the word. This lets another event handler verify that a noun has been dragged to the first blank, whereas an adjective has been dragged to the second blank. To help with this effort, class names are assigned to the td elements to distinguish the words from the Nouns column from the words of the Adjectives column. The `setupDrag()` function generates an array consisting of the `innerText` of the event's source element plus the element's class name. But the `event.dataTransfer` object cannot store array data types, so the `Array.join()` method converts the array to a string with a colon separating the entries. This string, then, is stuffed into the `event.dataTransfer` object. The object is instructed to render the cursor display during the drag-and-drop operation so that when the cursor is atop a drop target, the cursor is the copy style. Finally, the `setupDrag()` function is the first to execute in the drag operation, so a timer is set to the current clock time to time the drag operation.

The `ondrag` event handler (in the `body`) captures the `ondrag` events that are generated by whichever table cell element is the source element for the action. Each time the event fires (which is a lot during the action), the `timeIt()` function is invoked to compare the current time against the reference time (global `timer`) set when the drag starts. If the time exceeds 2 seconds (2,000 milliseconds), an alert dialog box notifies the user. To close the alert dialog box, the user must unclick the mouse button to end the drag operation.

To turn the blank `span` elements into drop targets, their `ondragenter`, `ondragover`, and `ondrop` event handlers must set `event.returnValue` to `false`; also, the `event.dataTransfer.dropEffect` property should be set to the desired effect (`copy`, in this case). These event handlers are placed in the `p` element that contains the two `span` elements, again for simplicity. Notice, however, that the `cancelDefault()` functions do their work only if the target element is one of the `span` elements whose ID begins with blank.

As the user releases the mouse button, the `ondrop` event handler invokes the `handleDrop()` function. This function retrieves the string data from `event.dataTransfer` and restores it to an array data type (using the `String.split()` method). A little bit of testing makes sure that the word type (noun or adjective) is associated with the desired blank. If so, the source element's text is set to the drop target's `innerText` property; otherwise, an error message is assembled to help the user know what went wrong.

LISTING 15-37

Using Drag-Related Event Handlers

```
<html>
  <head>
    <title>Dragging Event Handlers</title>
    <style type="text/css">
    td {text-align:center}
    th {text-decoration:underline}
    .blanks {text-decoration:underline}
    </style>
    <script type="text/javascript">
    var timer;

    function setupDrag() {
      if (event.srcElement.tagName != "TD") {
        // don't allow dragging for any other elements
        event.returnValue = false;
      } else {
        // setup array of data to be passed to drop target
        var passedData = [event.srcElement.innerText,
          event.srcElement.className];
        // store it as a string
```

continued

LISTING 15-37 *(continued)*

```
      event.dataTransfer.setData("Text", passedData.join(":"));
      event.dataTransfer.effectAllowed = "copy";
      timer = new Date();
   }
}

function timeIt() {
   if (event.srcElement.tagName == "TD" && timer) {
      if ((new Date()) - timer > 2000) {
         alert("Sorry, time is up. Try again.");
         timer = 0;
      }
   }
}

function handleDrop() {
   var elem = event.srcElement;
   var passedData = event.dataTransfer.getData("Text");
   var errMsg = "";
   if (passedData) {
      // reconvert passed string to an array
      passedData = passedData.split(":");
      if (elem.id == "blank1") {
         if (passedData[1] == "noun") {
            event.dataTransfer.dropEffect = "copy";
            event.srcElement.innerText = passedData[0];
         } else {
            errMsg = "You can't put an adjective into the noun
               placeholder.";
         }
      } else if (elem.id == "blank2") {
         if (passedData[1] == "adjective") {
            event.dataTransfer.dropEffect = "copy";
            event.srcElement.innerText = passedData[0];
         } else {
            errMsg = "You can't put a noun into the adjective
               placeholder.";
         }
      }
      if (errMsg) {
         alert(errMsg);
      }
   }
}

function cancelDefault() {
   if (event.srcElement.id.indexOf("blank") == 0) {
      event.dataTransfer.dropEffect = "copy";
      event.returnValue = false;
   }
}
```

```
        </script>
    </head>
    <body ondragstart="setupDrag()" ondrag="timeIt()">
        <h1>Dragging Event Handlers</h1>
        <hr />
        <p>Your goal is to drag one noun and one adjective from the following
            table into the blanks of the sentence. Select a word from the table
            and drag it to the desired blank. When you release the mouse, the word
            will appear in the blank. You have two seconds to complete each
            blank.</p>
        <table cellpadding="5">
            <tr>
                <th>Nouns</th>
                <th>Adjectives</th>
            </tr>
            <tr>
                <td class="noun">truck</td>
                <td class="adjective">round</td>
            </tr>
            <tr>
                <td class="noun">doll</td>
                <td class="adjective">red</td>
            </tr>
            <tr>
                <td class="noun">ball</td>
                <td class="adjective">pretty</td>
            </tr>
        </table>
        <p id="myP" ondragenter="cancelDefault()" ondragover="cancelDefault()"
            ondrop="handleDrop()">Pat said, "Oh my, the <span id="blank1"
            class="blanks">     </span> is so <span
            id="blank2" class="blanks">     </span>!"</p>
        <button onclick="location.reload()">Reset</button>
    </body>
</html>
```

One event handler not shown in Listing 15-37 is ondragend. You can use this event to display the elapsed time for each successful drag operation. Because the event fires on the drag source element, you can implement it in the <body> tag and filter events similar to the way the ondragstart or ondrag event handlers filter events for the td element.

Related Items: event.dataTransfer object; ondragenter, ondragleave, ondragover, ondrop event handlers

ondragenter
ondragleave
ondragover
Compatibility: WinIE5+, MacIE-, NN-, Moz-, Safari 1.3+

These events fire during a drag operation. When the cursor enters the rectangular space of an element on the page, the ondragenter event fires on that element. Immediately thereafter, the ondragleave event fires on the element from which the cursor came. Although this may seem to occur out of sequence from the physical action, the events always fire in this order. Depending on the speed of the client computer's CPU and the speed of the user's dragging action, one or the other of these events may not fire — especially if the physical action outstrips the computer's capability to fire the events in time.

The `ondragover` event fires continually while a dragged cursor is atop an element. In the course of dragging from one point on the page to another, the `ondragover` event target changes with the element beneath the cursor. If no other drag-related events are firing (the mouse button is still down in the drag operation, but the cursor is not moving), the `ondrag` and `ondragover` events fire continually, alternating between the two.

You should have the `ondragover` event handler of a drop target element set the `event.returnValue` property to `false`. See the discussion of the `ondrag` event handler earlier in this chapter for more details on the sequence of drag-related events.

Example

Listing 15-38 shows the `ondragenter` and `ondragleave` event handlers in use. The simple page displays (via the status bar) the time of entry to one element of the page. When the dragged cursor leaves the element, the `ondragleave` event handler hides the status-bar message. No drop target is defined for this page, so when you drag the item, the cursor remains the no-drop cursor.

LISTING 15-38

Using ondragenter and ondragleave Event Handlers

```
<html>
    <head>
        <title>ondragenter and ondragleave Event Handlers</title>
        <script type="text/javascript">
        function showEnter() {
            status = "Entered at: " + new Date();
            event.returnValue = false;
        }
        function clearMsg() {
            status = "";
            event.returnValue = false;
        }
        </script>
    </head>
    <body>
        <h1 ondragenter="showEnter()" ondragleave="clearMsg()">
        ondragenter and ondragleave Event Handlers</h1>
        <hr />
        <p>Select any character(s) from this paragraph, and slowly drag it around
            the page. When the dragging action enters the large header above, the
            status bar displays when the onDragEnter event handler fires. When you
            leave the header, the message is cleared via the onDragLeave event
            handler.</p>
    </body>
</html>
```

Related Items: ondrag, ondragend, ondragstart, ondrop event handlers

ondragstart

(See ondrag)

ondrop

Compatibility: WinIE5+, MacIE-, NN-, Moz-, Safari 1.3+

The ondrop event fires on the drop target element as soon as the user releases the mouse button at the end of a drag-and-drop operation. For IE, Microsoft recommends that you denote a drop target by applying the ondragenter, ondragover, and ondrop event handlers to the target element. In each of those event handlers, you should set the dataTransfer.dropEffect to the transfer effect you wish to portray in the drag-and-drop operation (signified by a different cursor for each type). These settings should match the dataTransfer.effectAllowed property that is usually set in the ondragstart event handler. Each of the three drop-related handlers should also override the default event behavior by setting the event.returnValue property to false. See the discussion of the ondrag event handler earlier in this chapter for more details on the sequence of drag-related events.

Example

See Listing 15-37 of the ondrag event handler to see how to apply the ondrop event handler in a typical drag-and-drop scenario.

Related Items: event.dataTransfer object; ondrag, ondragend, ondragenter, ondragleave, ondragover, ondragstart event handlers

onerrorupdate

Compatibility: WinIE4+, MacIE5+, NN-, Moz-, Safari-

The onerrorupdate event handler is part of the data binding of IE and fires when an error occurs while updating the data in the data source object.

onfilterchange

Compatibility: WinIE4+, MacIE-, NN-, Moz-, Safari-

The onfilterchange event fires whenever an object's visual filter switches to a new state or a transition completes (a transition may be extended over time). Only objects that accommodate filters and transitions in IE (primarily block elements and form controls) receive the event.

A common usage of the onfilterchange event is to trigger the next transition within a sequence of transition activities. This may include an infinite loop transition, for which the object receiving the event toggles between two transition states. If you don't want to get into a loop of that kind, place the different sets of content in their own positionable elements, and use the onfilterchange event handler in one to trigger the transition in the other.

Example

Listing 15-39 demonstrates how the onfilterchange event handler can trigger a second transition effect after another one completes. The onload event handler triggers the first effect. Although the onfilterchange event handler works with most of the same objects in IE4 as IE5, the filter object transition properties are not reflected in a convenient form. The syntax shown in Listing 15-39 uses the more modern ActiveX filter control found in IE5.5+ (described in Chapter 26).

LISTING 15-39

Using the onFilterChange Event Handler

```html
<html>
    <head>
        <title>onfilterchange Event Handler</title>
        <script type="text/javascript">
        function init() {
            image1.filters[0].apply();
            image2.filters[0].apply();
            start();
        }

        function start() {
            image1.style.visibility = "hidden";
            image1.filters[0].play();
        }

        function finish() {
            // verify that first transition is done (optional)
            if (image1.filters[0].status == 0) {
                image2.style.visibility = "visible";
                image2.filters[0].play();
            }
        }
        </script>
    </head>
    <body onload="init()">
        <h1>onfilterchange Event Handler</h1>
        <hr />
        <p>The completion of the first transition ("circle-in") triggers the
            second ("circle-out"). <button onclick="location.reload()">Play It
            Again</button></p>
        <div id="image1"
        style="visibility:visible; position:absolute; top:150px; left:150px;
        filter:progID:DXImageTransform.Microsoft.Iris(irisstyle='CIRCLE',
        motion='in')" onfilterchange="finish()">
            <img alt="image" src="desk1.gif" height="90" width="120" />
        </div>
        <div id="image2"
        style="visibility:hidden; position:absolute; top:150px; left:150px;
        filter:progID:DXImageTransform.Microsoft.Iris(irisstyle='CIRCLE',
        motion='out')">
            <img alt="image" src="desk3.gif" height="90" width="120" />
        </div>
    </body>
</html>
```

Related Item: filter object

onfocus

Compatibility: WinIE3+, MacIE3+, NN2+, Moz+, Safari+

The onfocus event fires when an element receives focus, usually following some other object's losing focus. (The element losing focus receives the onblur event before the current object receives the onfocus event.) For example, a text input element fires the onfocus event when a user tabs to that element while navigating through a form via the keyboard. Clicking an element also gives that element focus, as does making the browser the frontmost application on the client desktop.

The availability of the onfocus event has expanded with succeeding generations of script-capable browsers. In earlier versions, blur and focus were largely confined to text-oriented input elements such as the select element. The window object received the onfocus event handler starting with NN3 and IE4. IE4 also extended the event handler to more form elements, predominantly on the Windows operating system because that OS has a user interface clue (the dotted rectangle) when items such as buttons and links receive focus (so that users may act on them by pressing the spacebar). For IE5+, the onfocus event handler is available to virtually every HTML element. For most of those elements, however, you cannot use blur and focus unless you assign a value to the tabindex attribute of the element's tag. For example, if you assign tabindex="1" inside a <p> tag, the user can bring focus to that paragraph (highlighted with the dotted rectangle in Windows) by clicking the paragraph or pressing the Tab key until that item receives focus in sequence.

WinIE5.5 adds the onfocusin event handler, which fires immediately before the onfocus event handler. You can use one or the other, but there is little need to include both event handlers for the same object unless you wish to block an item temporarily from receiving focus. To prevent an object from receiving focus in IE5.5+, include an event.returnValue=false statement in the onfocusin event handler for the same object. In other browsers, you can usually get away with assigning onfocus="this.blur()" as an event handler for elements such as form controls. However, this is not a foolproof way to prevent a user from changing a control's setting. Unfortunately, there are few reliable alternatives short of disabling the control.

Example

See Listing 15-34 earlier in this chapter for an example of the onfocus and onblur event handlers.

Related Items: onactivate, onblur, ondeactivate, onfocusin, onfocusout event handlers

onfocusin
onfocusout

Compatibility: WinIE6+, MacIE-, NN-, Moz-, Safari-

The onfocusin and onfocusout events fire to indicate that an element is about to receive focus or has just lost focus. These events are closely related to onactivate and ondeactivate except that in IE5.5+ activation and focus can be distinguished from each other. For example, if you set an element as the active element through setActive(), the element becomes active, but it does not gain the input focus. However, if you set the focus of an element with a call to focus(), the element is activated and gains input focus.

Related Items: onactivate, onblur, ondeactivate, onfocus event handlers

onhelp

Compatibility: WinIE4+, MacIE5+, NN-, Moz-, Safari-

The onhelp event handler fires in Windows whenever an element of the document has focus and the user presses the F1 function key on a Windows PC. As of MacIE5, the event fires only on the window (in other words, event handler specified in the <body> tag) and does so via the dedicated Help key on a Mac keyboard. Browser Help menu choices do not activate this event. To prevent the browser's Help window from appearing, the event handler must evaluate to return false (for IE4+) or set the event.returnValue property to false (IE5+). Because the event handler can be associated with individual elements of a document in the Windows version, you can create a context-sensitive help system. However, if the focus is in the Address field of the browser window, you cannot intercept the event. Instead, the browser's Help window appears.

Example

Listing 15-40 is a rudimentary example of a context-sensitive help system that displays help messages tailored to the kind of text input required by different text boxes. When the user gives focus to either of the text boxes, a small legend appears to remind the user that help is available by a press of the F1 help key. MacIE5 provides only generic help.

LISTING 15-40

Creating Context-Sensitive Help

```html
<html>
  <head>
    <title>onhelp Event Handler</title>
    <script type="text/javascript">
    function showNameHelp() {
        alert("Enter your first and last names.");
        event.cancelBubble = true;
        return false;
    }
    function showYOBHelp() {
        alert("Enter the four-digit year of your birth. For example: 1972");
        event.cancelBubble = true;
        return false;
    }
    function showGenericHelp() {
        alert("All fields are required.");
        event.cancelBubble = true;
        return false;
    }
    function showLegend() {
        document.getElementById("legend").style.visibility = "visible";
    }
    function hideLegend() {
        document.getElementById("legend").style.visibility = "hidden";
    }
    function init() {
        var msg = "";
        if (navigator.userAgent.indexOf("Mac") != -1) {
            msg = "Press \'help\' key for help.";
```

```
      } else if (navigator.userAgent.indexOf("Win") != -1) {
         msg = "Press F1 for help.";
      }
      document.getElementById("legend").style.visibility = "hidden";
      document.getElementById("legend").innerHTML = msg;
   }
   </script>
</head>
<body onload="init()" onhelp="return showGenericHelp()">
   <h1>onhelp Event Handler</h1>
   <hr />
   <p id="legend" style="visibility:hidden; font-size:10px"> </p>
   <form>
      Name: <input type="text" name="name" size="30" onfocus="showLegend()"
      onblur="hideLegend()" onhelp="return showNameHelp()" /><br />
       Year of Birth: <input type="text" name="YOB" size="30"
      onfocus="showLegend()" onblur="hideLegend()"
      onhelp="return showYOBHelp()" />
   </form>
</body>
</html>
```

Related Items: `window.showHelp()`, `window.showModalDialog()` methods

onkeydown
onkeypress
onkeyup

Compatibility: WinIE4+, MacIE4+, NN4+, Moz+, Safari+

When someone presses and releases a keyboard key, a sequence of three events fires in quick succession. The `onkeydown` event fires when the key makes its first contact. This is followed immediately by the `onkeypress` event. When contact is broken by the key release, the `onkeyup` event fires. If you hold a character key down until it begins autorepeating, the `onkeydown` and `onkeypress` events fire with each repetition of the character.

The sequence of events can be crucial in some keyboard event handling. Consider the scenario that wants the focus of a series of text boxes to advance automatically after the user enters a fixed number of characters (for example, date, month, and two-digit year). By the time the `onkeyup` event fires, the character associated with the key-press action is already added to the box and you can accurately determine the length of text in the box, as shown in this simple example:

```
<html>
<head>
<script type="text/javascript">
function jumpNext(fromFld, toFld) {
   if (fromFld.value.length == 2) {
      document.forms[0].elements[toFld].focus();
      document.forms[0].elements[toFld].select();
   }
```

elementObject.onkeydown

```
    }
  </script>
  </head>
  <body>
  <form>
  Month: <input name="month" type="text" size="3" value=""
      onkeyup="jumpNext(this, day)" maxlength="2" />
  Day: <input name ="day" type="text" size="3" value=""
      onkeyup ="jumpNext(this, year)" maxlength="2" />
  Year: <input name="year" type="text" size="3" value=""
      onkeyup ="jumpNext(this, month)" maxlength="2" />
  </form>
  </body>
  </html>
```

These three events do not fire for all keys of the typical PC keyboard on all browser versions that support keyboard events. The only keys that you can rely on supporting the events in all browsers shown in the preceding compatibility chart are the alphanumeric keys represented by ASCII values, including the spacebar and Enter (Return on the Mac), but excluding all function keys, arrow keys, and other navigation keys. Modifier keys, such as Shift, Ctrl (PC), Alt (PC), Command (Mac), and Option (Mac), generate some events on their own (depending on browser and version). However, functions invoked by other key events can always inspect the pressed states of these modifier keys.

CAUTION   The onkeydown **event handler works in Mozilla-based browsers only starting with Mozilla 1.4 (and Netscape 7.1).**

Scripting keyboard events almost always entails examining which key is pressed so that some processing or validation can be performed on that key press. This is where the situation gets very complex if you are writing for cross-browser implementation. In some cases, even writing just for Internet Explorer gets tricky because nonalphanumeric keys generate only the onkeydown and onkeyup events.

In fact, to comprehend keyboard events fully, you need to make a distinction between *key codes* and *character codes*. Every PC keyboard key has a key code associated with it. This key code is always the same regardless of what other keys you press at the same time. Only the alphanumeric keys (letters, numbers, spacebar, and so on), however, generate character codes. The code represents the typed character produced by that key. The value might change if you press a modifier key. For example, if you press the A key by itself, it generates a lowercase *a* character (character code 97); if you also hold down the Shift key, that same key produces an uppercase *A* character (character code 65). The key code for that key (65 for Western-language keyboards) remains the same no matter what.

That brings us, then, to where these different codes are made available to scripts. In all cases, the code information is conveyed as one or two properties of the browser's event object. IE's event object has only one such property: keyCode. It contains key codes for onkeydown and onkeyup events but character codes for onkeypress events. The NN6+/Moz event object, on the other hand, contains two separate properties: charCode and keyCode. You can find more details and examples about these event object properties in Chapter 25.

The bottom-line script consideration is to use either onkeydown or onkeyup event handlers when you want to look for nonalphanumeric key events (for example, function keys, arrow and page-navigation keys, and so on). To process characters as they appear in text boxes, use the `onkeypress` event handler. You can experiment with these events and codes in Listing 15-41 as well as in examples from Chapter 25.

Common keyboard event tasks

WinIE4+ enables you to modify the character that a user who is editing a text box enters. The `onkeypress` event handler can modify the `event.keyCode` property and allow the event to continue (in other words, don't evaluate to `return false` or set the `event.returnValue` property to `false`). The following IE function (invoked by an `onkeypress` event handler) makes sure that text entered in a text box is all uppercase, even if you type it as lowercase:

```
function assureUpper() {
    if (event.keyCode >= 97 && event.keyCode <= 122) {
        event.keyCode = event.keyCode - 32;
    }
}
```

Doing this might confuse (or frustrate) users, so think carefully before implementing such a plan.

To prevent a key press from becoming a typed character in a text box, the `onkeypress` event handler prevents the default action of the event. For example, the following HTML page shows how to inspect a text box's entry for numbers only:

```
<html>
<head>
<title>Keyboard Capture</title>
<script type="text/javascript">
function checkIt(evt) {
    var charCode = (evt.charCode) ? evt.charCode : ((
        evt.which) ? evt.which : evt.keyCode);
    if (charCode > 31 && (charCode < 48 || charCode > 57)) {
        alert("Please make sure entries are numbers only.");
        return false;
    }
    return true;
}
</script>
</head>

<body>
<form>
Enter any positive integer: <input type="text" name="numeric"
    onkeypress="return checkIt(event)">
</form>
</body>
</html>
```

Whenever a user enters a non-number, the user receives a warning, and the character is not appended to the text box's text.

elementObject.**onkeydown**

Keyboard events also enable you to script the submission of a form when a user presses the Enter (Return on the Mac) key within a text box. The ASCII value of the Enter/Return key is 13. Therefore, you can examine each key press in a text box and submit the form whenever value 13 arrives, as shown in the following function:

```
function checkForEnter(evt) {
    evt = (evt) ? evt : event;
    var charCode = (evt.charCode) ? evt.charCode : ((
        evt.which) ? evt.which : evt.keyCode);
    if (charCode == 13) {
        document.forms[0].submit();
        return false;
    }
    return true;
}
```

By assigning the `checkForEnter()` function to each box's `onkeypress` event handler, you suddenly add some extra power to a typical HTML form.

You can intercept Ctrl+keyboard combinations (letters only) in HTML pages most effectively in Internet Explorer, but only if the browser itself does not use the combination. In other words, you cannot redirect Ctrl+key combinations that the browser uses for its own control. The `onkeypress keyCode` value for Ctrl+key combinations ranges from 1 through 26 for letters A through Z (except for those used by the browser, in which case no keyboard event fires).

Example

Listing 15-41 is a working laboratory that you can use to better understand the way keyboard event codes and modifier keys work in IE5+ and W3C browsers. The actual code of the listing is less important than watching the page while you use it. For every key or key combination that you press, the page shows the `keyCode` value for the `onkeydown`, `onkeypress`, and `onkeyup` events. If you hold down one or more modifier keys while performing the key press, the modifier-key name is highlighted for each of the three events. Note that when run in NN6+/Moz, the `keyCode` value is not the character code (which doesn't show up in this example for NN6+/Moz). Also, you may need to click the NN6+/Moz page for the `document` object to recognize the keyboard events.

The best way to watch what goes on during keyboard events is to press and hold a key to see the key codes for the `onkeydown` and `onkeypress` events. Then release the key to see the code for the `onkeyup` event. Notice, for instance, that if you press the A key without any modifier key, the `onkeydown` event key code is 65 (A), but the `onkeypress` key code in IE (and the `charCode` property in NN6+/Moz) is 97 (a). If you then repeat the exercise but hold the Shift key down, all three events generate the 65 (A) key code (and the Shift modifier labels are highlighted). Releasing the Shift key causes the `onkeyup` event to show the key code for the Shift key.

In another experiment, press any of the four arrow keys. No key code is passed for the `onkeypress` event because those keys don't generate those events. They do, however, generate `onkeydown` and `onkeyup` events.

LISTING 15-41

Keyboard Event Handler Laboratory

```html
<html>
    <head>
        <title>Keyboard Event Handler Lab</title>
        <style type="text/css">
        td {text-align:center}
        </style>
        <script type="text/javascript">
        function init() {
            document.onkeydown = showKeyDown;
            document.onkeyup - showKeyUp;
            document.onkeypress = showKeyPress;
        }

        function showKeyDown(evt) {
            evt = (evt) ? evt : window.event;
            document.getElementById("pressKeyCode").innerHTML = 0;
            document.getElementById("upKeyCode").innerHTML = 0;
            document.getElementById("pressCharCode").innerHTML = 0;
            document.getElementById("upCharCode").innerHTML = 0;
            restoreModifiers("");
            restoreModifiers("Down");
            restoreModifiers("Up");
            document.getElementById("downKeyCode").innerHTML = evt.keyCode;
            if (evt.charCode) {
                document.getElementById("downCharCode").innerHTML = evt.charCode;
            }
            showModifiers("Down", evt);
        }

        function showKeyUp(evt) {
            evt = (evt) ? evt : window.event;
            document.getElementById("upKeyCode").innerHTML = evt.keyCode;
            if (evt.charCode) {
                document.getElementById("upCharCode").innerHTML = evt.charCode;
            }
            showModifiers("Up", evt);
            return false;
        }

        function showKeyPress(evt) {
            evt = (evt) ? evt : window.event;
            document.getElementById("pressKeyCode").innerHTML = evt.keyCode;
            if (evt.charCode) {
                document.getElementById("pressCharCode").innerHTML = evt.charCode;
            }
```

continued

LISTING 15-41 *(continued)*

```
        showModifiers("", evt);
        return false;
    }

    function showModifiers(ext, evt) {
        restoreModifiers(ext);
        if (evt.shiftKey) {
            document.getElementById("shift" + ext).style.backgroundColor =
                "#ff0000";
        }
        if (evt.ctrlKey) {
            document.getElementById("ctrl" + ext).style.backgroundColor =
                "#00ff00";
        }
        if (evt.altKey) {
            document.getElementById("alt" + ext).style.backgroundColor =
                "#0000ff";
        }
    }

    function restoreModifiers(ext) {
        document.getElementById("shift" + ext).style.backgroundColor =
            "#ffffff";
        document.getElementById("ctrl" + ext).style.backgroundColor =
            "#ffffff";
        document.getElementById("alt" + ext).style.backgroundColor =
            "#ffffff";
    }
    </script>
</head>
<body onload="init()">
    <h1>Keyboard Event Handler Lab</h1>
    <hr />
    <form>
        <table border="2" cellpadding="2">
            <tr>
                <th></th>
                <th>onKeyDown</th>
                <th>onKeyPress</th>
                <th>onKeyUp</th>
            </tr>
            <tr>
                <th>Key Codes</th>
                <td id="downKeyCode">0</td>
                <td id="pressKeyCode">0</td>
                <td id="upKeyCode">0</td>
            </tr>
            <tr>
                <th>Char Codes (IE5/Mac; NN6)</th>
                <td id="downCharCode">0</td>
```

```
         <td id="pressCharCode">0</td>
         <td id="upCharCode">0</td>
      </tr>
      <tr>
         <th rowspan="3">Modifier Keys</th>
         <td><span id="shiftDown">Shift</span></td>
         <td><span id="shift">Shift</span></td>
         <td><span id="shiftUp">Shift</span></td>
      </tr>
      <tr>
         <td><span id="ctrlDown">Ctrl</span></td>
         <td><span id="ctrl">Ctrl</span></td>
         <td><span id="ctrlUp">Ctrl</span></td>
      </tr>
      <tr>
         <td><span id="altDown">Alt</span></td>
         <td><span id="alt">Alt</span></td>
         <td><span id="altUp">Alt</span></td>
      </tr>
   </table>
   </form>
</body>
</html>
```

Spend some time with this lab, and try all kinds of keys and key combinations until you understand the way the events and key codes work.

Related Item: `String.fromCharCode()` method

onlayoutcomplete

Compatibility: WinIE5.5+, MacIE-, NN-, Moz-, Safari-

The `onlayoutcomplete` event handler fires when a print or print-preview layout operation completes on the current layout rectangle (`LayoutRect` object). This event is primarily used as the basis for overflowing content from one page to another during printing. In response to the `onlayoutcomplete` event, the `contentOverflow` property can be inspected to determine whether page content has indeed overflowed the current layout rectangle.

onlosecapture

Compatibility: WinIE5+, MacIE-, NN-, Moz-, Safari-

The `onlosecapture` event handler fires whenever an object that has event capture turned on no longer has that capture. Event capture is automatically disengaged when the user performs any of the following actions:

- Gives focus to any other window
- Displays any system modal dialog box (for example, alert window)
- Scrolls the page

elementObject.onmousedown

- Opens a browser context menu (right-clicking)
- Tabs to give focus to the Address field in the browser window

A function associated with the `onlosecapture` event handler should perform any cleanup of the environment due to an object's no longer capturing mouse events.

Example

See Listing 15-30 earlier in this chapter for an example of how to use `onlosecapture` with an event-capturing scenario for displaying a context menu. The `onlosecapture` event handler hides the context menu when the user performs any action that causes the menu to lose mouse capture.

Related Items: `releaseCapture()`, `setCapture()` methods

onmousedown
onmouseup

Compatibility: WinIE4+, MacIE4+, NN4+, Moz+, Safari+

The `onmousedown` event handler fires when the user presses any button on a mouse. The `onmouseup` event handler fires when the user releases the mouse button, provided that the object receiving the event also received an `onmousedown` event. When a user performs a typical click of the mouse button atop an object, mouse events occur in the following sequence: `onmousedown`, `onmouseup`, and `onclick`. But if the user presses the mouse atop an object and then slides the cursor away from the object, only the `onmousedown` event fires.

These events enable authors and designers to add more applicationlike behavior to images that act as action or icon buttons. If you notice the way most buttons work, the appearance of the button changes while you press the mouse button and reverts to its original style when you release the mouse button (or you drag the cursor out of the button). These events enable you to emulate that behavior.

The event object created with every mouse button action has a property that reveals which mouse button the user pressed. NN4's event model called that property the `which` property. IE4+ and NN6+/Moz call it the `button` property (but with different values for the buttons). It is most reliable to test for the mouse button number on either the `onmousedown` or `onmouseup` event rather than on `onclick`. The `onclick` event object does not always contain the button information.

Example

To demonstrate a likely scenario of changing button images in response to rolling atop an image, pressing down on it, releasing the mouse button, and rolling away from the image, Listing 15-42 presents a pair of small navigation buttons (left- and right-arrow buttons). Images are preloaded into the browser cache as the page loads so that response to the user is instantaneous the first time the user calls upon new versions of the images.

LISTING 15-42

Using onmousedown and onmouseup Event Handlers

```
<html>
  <head>
    <title>onmousedown and onmouseup Event Handlers</title>
    <script type="text/javascript">
    var RightNormImg = new Image(16,16);
    var RightUpImg = new Image(16,16);
```

```
    var RightDownImg = new Image(16,16);
    var LeftNormImg = new Image(16,16);
    var LeftUpImg = new Image(16,16);
    var LeftDownImg = new Image(16,16);

    RightNormImg.src = "RightNorm.gif";
    RightUpImg.src = "RightUp.gif";
    RightDownImg.src = "RightDown.gif";
    LeftNormImg.src = "LeftNorm.gif";
    LeftUpImg.src = "LeftUp.gif";
    LeftDownImg.src = "LeftDown.gif";

    function setImage(imgName, type) {
        var imgFile = eval(imgName + type + "Img.src");
        document.images[imgName].src = imgFile;
        return false;
    }
    </script>
</head>
<body>
    <h1>onmousedown and onmouseup Event Handlers</h1>
    <hr />
    <p>Roll atop and click on the buttons to see how the link event handlers
        swap images:</p>
    <center>
        <img alt="image"
        name="Left" src="LeftNorm.gif" height="16" width="16"
        border="0" onmouseover="return setImage('Left','Up')"
        onmousedown="return setImage('Left','Down')"
        onmouseup="return setImage('Left','Up')"
        onmouseout="return setImage('Left','Norm')" />    <img
        alt="image" name="Right" src="RightNorm.gif" height="16" width="16"
        border="0" onmouseover="return setImage('Right','Up')"
        onmousedown="return setImage('Right','Down')"
        onmouseup="return setImage('Right','Up')"
        onmouseout="return setImage('Right','Norm')" />
    </center>
</body>
</html>
```

Related Item: `onclick` event handler

onmouseenter
onmouseleave

Compatibility: WinIE5.5+, MacIE-, NN-, Moz-, Safari-

WinIE5.5 introduced the `onmouseenter` and `onmouseleave` event handlers. Both event handlers operate just like the `onmouseover` and `onmouseout` event handlers, respectively. Microsoft simply offers an alternative terminology. The old and new events continue to fire in IE5.5+. The old ones fire just before the new ones for each act of moving the cursor atop, and exiting from atop, the object. If you are scripting exclusively for IE5.5+, you should use the new terminology; otherwise, stay with the older versions.

Example

You can modify Listing 15-43 with the IE5.5 syntax by substituting `onmouseenter` for `onmouseover` and `onmouseleave` for `onmouseout`. The effect is the same.

Related Items: `onmouseover`, `onmouseout` event handlers

onmousemove

Compatibility: WinIE4+, MacIE4+, NN4+, Moz+, Safari+

The `onmousemove` event handler fires whenever the cursor is atop the current object and the mouse is moved, even by a single pixel. You do not have to press the mouse button for the event to fire, although the event is most commonly used in element dragging—especially in NN/Mozilla, where no `ondrag` event handler is available.

Even though the granularity of this event can be at the pixel level, you should not use the number of event firings as a measurement device. Depending on the speed of cursor motion and the performance of the client computer, the event may not fire at every pixel location.

In IE4+ and W3C DOM-compatible browsers, you can assign the `onmousemove` event handler to any element (although you can drag only with positioned elements). When designing a page that encourages users to drag multiple items on a page, it is most common to assign the `onmousemove` event handler to the `document` object and let all such events bubble up to the document for processing.

Example

See Chapter 40 and Chapter 56 on the CD-ROM for examples of using mouse events to control element dragging on a page.

Related Items: `ondrag`, `onmousedown`, `onmouseup` event handlers

onmouseout
onmouseover

Compatibility: WinIE3+, MacIE3+, NN2+, Moz+, Safari+

The `onmouseover` event fires for an object whenever the cursor rolls into the rectangular space of the object on the screen. The `onmouseout` event handler fires when you move the cursor outside the object's rectangle. These events most commonly display explanatory text about an object in the window's status bar and effect image swapping (so-called mouse rollovers). Use the `onmouseover` event handler to change the state to a highlighted version; use the `onmouseout` event handler to restore the image or status bar to its normal setting.

Although these two events have been in object models of scriptable browsers since the beginning, they were not available to most objects in earlier browsers. IE4+ and W3C DOM-compatible browsers provide support for these events on every element that occupies space onscreen. IE5.5+ includes an additional pair of event handlers—`onmouseenter` and `onmouseleave`—that duplicates the `onmouseover` and `onmouseout` events but with different terminology. The old event handlers fire just before the new versions.

> **NOTE** The `onmouseout` event handler commonly fails to fire if the event is associated with an element that is near a frame or window edge and the user moves the cursor quickly outside the current frame.

Example

Listing 15-43 uses the U.S. Pledge of Allegiance with four links to demonstrate how to use the `onmouseover` and `onmouseout` event handlers. Notice that for each link, the handler runs a general-purpose function that sets the window's status message. The function returns a `true` value, which the event handler call evaluates to replicate the required `return true` statement needed for setting the status bar. In one status message, I supply a URL in parentheses to let you evaluate how helpful you think it is for users.

LISTING 15-43

Using onmouseover and onmouseout Event Handlers

```html
<html>
    <head>
        <title>onmouseover and onmouseout Event Handlers</title>
        <script type="text/javascript">
        function setStatus(msg) {
            status = msg;
            return true;
        }

        // destination of all link HREFs
        function emulate() {
            alert("Not going there in this demo.");
        }
        </script>
    </head>
    <body>
        <h1>onmouseover and onmouseout Event Handlers</h1>
        <hr />
        <h1>Pledge of Allegiance</h1>
        <hr />
        I pledge <a href="javascript:emulate()"
        onmouseover="return setStatus('View dictionary definition')"
        onmouseout="return setStatus('')">allegiance</a> to the <a
        href="javascript:emulate()"
        onmouseover="return setStatus('Learn about the U.S. flag
        (http://lcweb.loc.gov)')"
         onmouseout="return setStatus('')">flag</a> of the <a
        href="javascript:emulate()"
        onmouseover="return setStatus('View info about the U.S. government')"
        onmouseout="return setStatus('')">United States of America</a>, and to
        the Republic for which it stands, one nation <a
        href="javascript:emulate()"
        onmouseover="return setStatus('Read about the history of this phrase in
        the Pledge')"
         onmouseout="return setStatus('')">under God</a>, indivisible, with
        liberty and justice for all.
    </body>
</html>
```

Related Items: onmouseenter, onmouseleave, onmousemove event handlers

onmousewheel

Compatibility: WinIE6+, MacIE-, NN-, Moz-, Safari-

The onmousewheel event handler fires in response to the user's rotating the mouse wheel. It's not too surprising that this event is IE-specific, given that wheeled mice are for the most part unique to Wintel PCs. When responding to the onmousewheel event, you can check the wheelDelta property to find out how far the mouse wheel has been rotated. The wheelDelta property expresses mouse wheel rotations in multiples of 120, with positive values indicating a rotation away from the user and negative values corresponding to a rotation toward the user.

Related Items: onmousemove event handler

onmove

Compatibility: WinIE5.5+, MacIE-, NN-, Moz-, Safari-

Not to be confused with onmousemove, the onmove event has nothing to do with the mouse. Instead, the onmove event is fired whenever a positionable *element* is moved. For example, if a div element is created as an absolutely positioned moveable element, you can track its movement by responding to the onmove event. The offsetLeft and offsetTop properties can be used within this event handler to determine the exact location of the element as it is moving.

Related Items: onmoveend, onmovestart event handlers

onmoveend
onmovestart

Compatibility: WinIE5.5+, MacIE-, NN-, Moz-, Safari-

The onmovestart and onmoveend event handlers fire in response to a positionable element's being moved on a page. More specifically, the onmovestart event is triggered when an element first starts moving and the onmoveend event fires when the element stops moving. In between the onmovestart and onmoveend events firing, multiple onmove events may be sent out to indicate the movement of the element.

Related Items: onmove event handler

onpaste

Compatibility: WinIE5+, MacIE-, NN-, Moz-, Safari 1.3+

The onpaste event fires immediately after the user or script initiates a paste edit action on the current object. The event is preceded by the onbeforepaste event, which fires prior to any edit or context menu that appears (or before the paste action if initiated by keyboard shortcut).

Use this event handler to provide edit functionality to elements that don't normally allow pasting. In such circumstances, you need to enable the Paste menu item in the context or Edit menu by setting the event.returnValue for the onbeforepaste event handler to false. Then your onpaste event handler must manually retrieve data from the clipboard (by way of the getData() method of the clipboardData object) and handle the insertion into the current object.

Because you are in charge of what data is stored in the clipboard, you are not limited to a direct copy of the data. For example, you might wish to store the value of the src property of an image object so that you can paste it elsewhere on the page.

Generic HTML Element Objects | 15

elementObject.onpaste

Example

Listing 15-44 demonstrates how to use the onbeforepaste and onpaste event handlers (in conjunction with onbeforecopy and oncopy) to let scripts control the data-transfer process during a copy-and-paste user operation. A table contains words to be copied (one column of nouns, one column of adjectives) and then pasted into blanks in a paragraph. The onbeforecopy and oncopy event handlers are assigned to the table element because the events from the td elements bubble up to the table container and there is less HTML code to contend with.

Inside the paragraph, two span elements contain underscored blanks. To paste text into the blanks, the user must first select at least one character of the blanks. (See Listing 15-37, which gives a drag-and-drop version of this application.) The onbeforepaste event handler in the paragraph (which gets the event as it bubbles up from either span) sets the event.returnValue property to false, thus allowing the Paste item to appear in the context and Edit menus (not a normal occurrence in HTML body content).

At paste time, the innerHTML property of the target span is set to the text data stored in the clipboard. The event.returnValue property is set to false here as well to prevent normal system pasting from interfering with the controlled version.

LISTING 15-44

Using onbeforepaste and onpaste Event Handlers

```html
<html>
  <head>
    <title>onbeforepaste and onpaste Event Handlers</title>
    <style type="text/css">
    td {text-align:center}
    th {text-decoration:underline}
    .blanks {text-decoration:underline}
    </style>
    <script type="text/javascript">
    function selectWhole() {
        var obj = window.event.srcElement;
        var range = document.body.createTextRange();
        range.moveToElementText(obj);
        range.select();
        event.returnValue = false;
    }
    function handleCopy() {
        var rng = document.selection.createRange();
        clipboardData.setData("Text",rng.text);
        event.returnValue = false;
    }

    function handlePaste() {
        var elem = window.event.srcElement;
        if (elem.className == "blanks") {
           elem.innerHTML = clipboardData.getData("Text");
        }
        event.returnValue = false;
    }
```

continued

LISTING 15-44 *(continued)*

```
        function handleBeforePaste() {
            var elem = window.event.srcElement;
            if (elem.className == "blanks") {
                event.returnValue = false;
            }
        }
        </script>
    </head>
    <body>
        <h1>onbeforepaste and onpaste Event Handlers</h1>
        <hr />
        <p>Your goal is to copy and paste one noun and one adjective from the
            following table into the blanks of the sentence. Select a word from
            the table and copy it to the clipboard. Select one or more spaces of
            the blanks in the sentence and choose Paste to replace the blank with
            the clipboard contents.</p>
        <table cellpadding="5" onbeforecopy="selectWhole()"
        oncopy="handleCopy()">
            <tr>
                <th>Nouns</th>
                <th>Adjectives</th>
            </tr>
            <tr>
                <td>truck</td>
                <td>round</td>
            </tr>
            <tr>
                <td>doll</td>
                <td>red</td>
            </tr>
            <tr>
                <td>ball</td>
                <td>pretty</td>
            </tr>
        </table>
        <p id="myP" onbeforepaste="handleBeforePaste()" onpaste="handlePaste()">
            Pat said, "Oh my, the <span id="blank1"
            class="blanks">     </span> is so <span
            id="blank2" class="blanks">     </span>!"</p>
        <button onclick="location.reload()">Reset</button>
    </body>
</html>
```

Related Items: oncopy, oncut, onbeforepaste event handlers

onpropertychange

Compatibility: WinIE5+, MacIE-, NN-, Moz-, Safari-

The onpropertychange event fires in WinIE5+ whenever a script modifies an object's property. This includes changes to the properties of an object's style. Changing properties by way of the setAttribute() method also triggers this event.

A script can inspect the nature of the property change because the event.propertyName property contains the name (as a string) of the property that was just changed. In the case of a change to an object's style object, the event.propertyName value begins with "style." as in style.backgroundcolor.

You can use this event handler to localize any object-specific postprocessing of changes to an object's properties. Rather than include the postprocessing statements inside the function that makes the changes, you can make that function generalized (perhaps to modify properties of multiple objects).

Example

Listing 15-45 shows how you can respond programmatically to an object's properties being changed. The page generated by the listing contains four radio buttons that alter the innerHTML and style.color properties of a paragraph. The paragraph's onpropertychange event handler invokes the showChange() function, which extracts information about the event and displays the data in the status bar of the window. Notice that the property name includes style. when you modify the style sheet property.

LISTING 15-45

Using the onPropertyChange Property

```
<html>
    <head>
        <title>onpropertychange Event Handler</title>
        <script type="text/javascript">
        function normalText() {
            myP.innerText = "This is a sample paragraph.";
        }
        function shortText() {
            myP.innerText = "Short stuff.";
        }
        function normalColor() {
            myP.style.color = "black";
        }
        function hotColor() {
            myP.style.color = "red";
        }
        function showChange() {
            var objID = event.srcElement.id;
            var propName = event.propertyName;
            var newValue = eval(objID + "." + propName);
            status = "The " + propName + " property of the " + objID;
            status += " object has changed to \"" + newValue + "\".";
        }
        </script>
    </head>
```

continued

LISTING 15-45 *(continued)*

```
<body>
   <h1>onpropertychange Event Handler</h1>
   <hr />
   <p id="myP" onpropertychange="showChange()">This is a sample
   paragraph.</p>
   <form>
      Text: <input type="radio" name="btn1" checked="checked"
      onclick="normalText()" />Normal <input type="radio" name="btn1"
      onclick="shortText()" />Short<br />
       Color: <input type="radio" name="btn2" checked="checked"
      onclick="normalColor()" />Black <input type="radio" name="btn2"
      onclick="hotColor()" />Red
   </form>
</body>
</html>
```

Related Items: `style` property; `setAttribute()` method

onreadystatechange

Compatibility: WinIE4+, MacIE-, NN7+, Moz1.0.1+, Safari 1.2+

The `onreadystatechange` event handler fires whenever the ready state of an object changes. See details about these states in the discussion of the `readyState` property earlier in this chapter (and notice the limits for IE4). The change of state does not guarantee that an object is in fact ready for script statements to access its properties. Always check the `readyState` property of the object in any script that the `onreadystatechange` event handler invokes.

This event fires for objects that are capable of loading data: `applet`, `document`, `frame`, `frameset`, `iframe`, `img`, `link`, `object`, `script`, and XML objects. The event doesn't fire for other types of objects unless a Microsoft DHTML behavior is associated with the object. The `onreadystatechange` event does not bubble; neither can you cancel it.

Related Item: `readyState` property

onresize

Compatibility: WinIE4+, MacIE4+, NN4+, Moz+, Safari+

The `onresize` event handler fires whenever an object is resized in response to a variety of user or scripted actions. Most elements include this event handler, provided that the object has dimensional style attributes (for example, height, width, or position) assigned to it.

In IE4+ and NN6+/Moz, the `onresize` event does not bubble. Resizing the browser window or frame does not cause the window's `onload` event handler to fire.

Example

If you want to capture the user's resizing of the browser window (or frame), you can assign a function to the onresize event handler either via script

```
window.onresize = handleResize;
```

or by an HTML attribute of the body element:

```
<body onresize="handleResize()">
```

Related Item: window.resize() method

onresizeend
onresizestart

Compatibility: WinIE5.5+, MacIE-, NN-, Moz-, Safari-

The onresizeend and onresizestart event handlers fire only on a resizable object in Windows edit mode.

Related Item: oncontrolselect event handler

onrowenter
onrowexit

Compatibility: WinIE4+, MacIE-, NN-, Moz-, Safari-

The onrowenter and onrowexit events fire in response to changes in the current row of recordset data in IE data binding. More specifically, onrowenter is triggered when the data for the current row of data has changed and new data is available on the data source object. The onrowexit event is triggered when the current row is changing, meaning that another row of data is being selected; the event is fired just before the row changes.

Related Item: onrowsdelete, onrowsinserted event handlers

onrowsdelete
onrowsinserted

Compatibility: WinIE5+, MacIE-, NN-, Moz-, Safari-

The onrowsdelete event fires when one or more rows of data are about to be deleted from the recordset in IE data binding. Conversely, the onrowsinserted event is triggered when one or more rows of data have been inserted into the recordset.

Related Item: onrowenter, onrowexit event handlers

onscroll

Compatibility: WinIE4+, MacIE4+, NN-, Moz-, Safari-

The onscroll event handler fires whenever the scroll box within a scroll bar of an element is repositioned. In simpler terms, when the user clicks and drags the scroll box with the mouse, the onscroll event is fired. That's not the only action that triggers the event, however. An onscroll event is also fired in response to the user's clicking the scroll arrow, clicking the scroll bar, or pressing any of the following keys: Home, End, Space, Page Up, or Page Down. A call to the doScroll() method also triggers the event, as does the user's holding down the Up Arrow or Down Arrow key.

Related Item: doScroll() method

onselectstart

Compatibility: WinIE4+, MacIE4+, NN-, Moz-, Safari 1.3+

The onselectstart event handler fires when a user begins to select content on the page. Selected content can be inline text, images, or text within an editable text box. If the user selects more than one object, the event fires in the first object affected by the selection.

Example

Use the page from Listing 15-46 to see how the onselectstart event handler works when a user selects across multiple elements on a page. As the user begins a selection anywhere on the page, the ID of the object receiving the event appears in the status bar. Notice that the event doesn't fire until you actually make a selection. When no other element is under the cursor, the body element fires the event.

LISTING 15-46

Using the onselectstart Event Handler

```html
<html>
    <head>
        <title>onselectstart Event Handler</title>
        <style type="text/css">
        td {text-align:center}
        </style>
        <script type="text/javascript">
        function showObj() {
            var objID = event.srcElement.id;
            status = "Selection started with object: " + objID;
        }
        </script>
    </head>
    <body id="myBody" onselectstart="showObj()">
        <h1 id="myH1">
            onselectstart Event Handler
        </h1>
        <hr id="myHR" />
        <p id="myP">This is a sample paragraph.</p>
        <table border="1">
            <tr id="row1">
                <th id="header1">Column A</th>
                <th id="header2">Column B</th>
                <th id="header3">Column C</th>
            </tr>
            <tr id="row2">
                <td id="cellA2">text</td>
```

```
        <td id="cellB2">text</td>
        <td id="cellC2">text</td>
      </tr>
      <tr id="row3">
        <td id="cellA3">text</td>
        <td id="cellB3">text</td>
        <td id="cellC3">text</td>
      </tr>
    </table>
  </body>
</html>
```

Related Item: onselect event handler for a variety of objects

Chapter 16

Window and Frame Objects

A quick look at the basic document object model diagram in Chapter 14 (see Figure 14-1) reveals that the window object is the outermost, most global container of all document-related objects that you script with JavaScript. All HTML and JavaScript activity takes place inside a window. That window may be a standard Windows, Mac, or XWindows application-style window, complete with scroll bars, toolbars, and other chrome; you can also generate windows that have only some of a typical window's chrome. A frame is also a window, even though a frame doesn't have many accoutrements beyond scroll bars. The window object is where everything begins in JavaScript references to objects. Modern browsers treat the frameset as a special kind of window object, so it is also covered in this chapter.

Of all the objects associated with browser scripting, the window and window-related objects have by far the most object-specific terminology associated with them. This necessitates a rather long chapter to keep the discussion in one place. Use the running footers as a navigational aid through this substantial collection of information.

Window Terminology

The window object is often a source of confusion when you first learn about the document object model. A number of synonyms for window objects muck up the works: top, self, parent, and frame. Aggravating the situation is the fact that these terms are also properties of a window object. Under some conditions, a window is its own parent, but if you define a frameset with two frames, you have only one parent among a total of three window objects. It doesn't take long before the whole subject can make your head hurt.

If you do not use frames in your web applications, all these headaches never appear. But if frames are part of your design plan, you should get to know how frames affect the object model.

Frames

The application of frames has become a religious issue among web designers: Some swear by them; others swear at them. I believe there can be compelling reasons to use frames at times. For example, if you have a document that requires considerable scrolling to get through, you may want to maintain a static set of navigation controls visible at all times. By placing those controls — be they links or image maps — in a separate frame, you have made the controls available for immediate access, regardless of the scrolled condition of the main document.

Creating frames

The task of defining frames in a document remains the same whether or not you're using JavaScript. The simplest framesetting document consists of tags that are devoted to setting up the frameset, as follows:

```
<html>
<head>
<title>My Frameset</title>
</head>
<frameset>
    <frame name="Frame1" src="document1.html">
    <frame name="Frame2" src="document2.html">
</frameset>
</html>
```

The preceding HTML document, which the user never sees, defines the frameset for the entire browser window. Each frame must have a URL reference (specified by the src attribute) for a document to load into that frame. For scripting purposes, assigning a name to each frame with the name attribute greatly simplifies scripting frame content.

The frame object model

Perhaps the key to successful frame scripting is understanding that the object model in the browser's memory at any given instant is determined by the HTML tags in the currently loaded documents. All canned object model graphics in this book, such as Figure 16-1, do not reflect the precise object model for your document or document set.

FIGURE 16-1

The simplest window–document relationship.

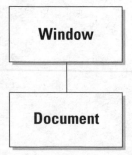

For a single, frameless document, the object model starts with just one `window` object, which contains one document, as shown in Figure 16-1. In this simple structure, the `window` object is the starting point for all references to any loaded object. Because the window is always there — it must be there for a document to load into — a reference to any object in the document can omit a reference to the current window.

In a simple two-framed frameset model (see Figure 16-2), the browser treats the container of the initial, framesetting document as the parent window. The only visible evidence that the document exists is that the framesetting document's title appears in the browser window title bar.

FIGURE 16-2

The parent and frames are part of the object model.

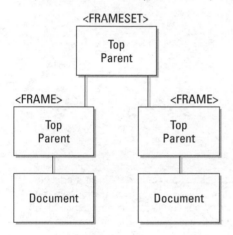

Each `<frame>` tag inside the `<frameset>` tag set creates another `window` object into which a document is loaded. Each of those frames, then, has a `document` object associated with it. From the point of view of a given document, it has a single window container, just as in the model shown in Figure 16-1. And although the `parent` object is not visible to the user, it remains in the object model in memory. The presence of the parent often makes it a convenient repository for variable data that needs to be shared by multiple child frames or that must persist between loading of different documents inside a child frame.

In even more complex arrangements, as shown in Figure 16-3, a child frame itself may load a framesetting document. In this situation, the difference between the `parent` and `top` objects starts to come into focus. The top window is the only one in common with all frames in Figure 16-3. As you see in a moment, when frames need to communicate with other frames (and their documents), you must fashion references to the distant object via the `window` object that they all have in common.

FIGURE 16-3

Three generations of window objects.

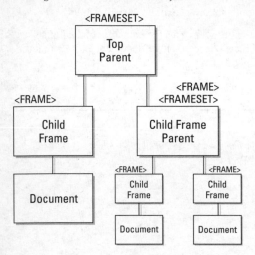

Referencing frames

The purpose of an object reference is to help JavaScript locate the desired object in the object model currently held in memory. A reference is a road map for the browser to follow so that it can track down, say, the value of a particular text field in a particular document. Therefore, when you construct a reference, think about where the script appears in the object model and how the reference can help the browser determine where it should go to find the distant object. In a two-generation scenario, such as the one shown in Figure 16-2, three intergenerational references are possible:

- Parent-to-child
- Child-to-parent
- Child-to-child

Assuming that you need to access an object, function, or variable in the relative's frame, the following are the corresponding reference structures: `frameName.objFuncVarName`, `parent.objFuncVarName`. and `parent.frameName.objFuncVarName`.

The rule is this: Whenever a reference must point to another frame, begin the reference with the `window` object that the two destinations have in common. To demonstrate that rule on the complex model in Figure 16-3, if the left child frame's document needs to reference the document at the bottom right of the map, the reference structure is

        `top.frameName.frameName.document. ...`

Follow the map from the top `window` object down through two frames to the final document. JavaScript has to take this route, so your reference must help it along.

Top versus parent

After seeing the previous object maps and reference examples, you may be wondering, Why not use `top` as the leading object in all transframe references? From an object model point of view, you'll have no problem doing that: A parent in a two-generation scenario is also the top window. What you can't count on, however, is your framesetting document's always being the `top` window object in someone's browser. Take the instance where a web site loads other web sites into one of its frames. At that instant, the `top` window object belongs to someone else. If you always specify `top` in references intended just for your parent window, your references won't work and will probably lead to script errors for the user. My advice, then, is to use `parent` in references whenever you mean one generation above the current document.

Preventing framing

You can use your knowledge of `top` and `parent` references to prevent your pages from being displayed inside another web site's frameset. Your top-level document must check whether it is loaded into its own top or parent window. When a document is in its own top window, a reference to the `top` property of the current window is equal to a reference to the current window (the `window` synonym `self` seems most grammatically fitting here). If the two values are not equal, you can script your document to reload itself as a top-level document. When it is critical that your document be a top-level document, include the script in Listing 16-1 in the Head portion of your document:

LISTING 16-1

Prevention from Getting Framed

```
<script type="text/javascript">
if (top != self) {
   top.location = location;
}
</script>
```

Your document may appear momentarily inside the other site's frameset, but then the slate is wiped clean, and your top-level document rules the browser window.

Ensuring framing

When you design a web application around a frameset, you may want to make sure that a page always loads the complete frameset. Consider the possibility that a visitor adds only one of your frames to a bookmarks list. On the next visit, only the bookmarked page appears in the browser without your frameset, which may contain valuable navigation aids to the site.

A script can make sure that a page always loads into its frameset by comparing the URLs of the `top` and `self` windows. If the URLs are the same, it means that the page needs to load the frameset. Listing 16-2 shows the simplest version of this technique, which loads a fixed frameset. For a more complete implementation that passes a parameter to the frameset so that it opens a specific page in one of the frames, see the `location.search` property in Chapter 17.

LISTING 16-2

Forcing a Frameset to Load

```
<script type="text/javascript">
if (top.location.href == window.location.href) {
    top.location.href = " myFrameset.html";
}
</script>
```

Switching from frames to frameless

Some sites load themselves in a frameset by default and offer users the option of getting rid of the frames. Modern browsers let you modify a frameset's `cols` or `rows` properties on the fly to simulate adding or removing frames from the current view (see the `frameset` element object later in this chapter). Legacy browsers, on the other hand, don't allow you to change the makeup of a frameset dynamically after it has loaded, but you can load the content page of the frameset into the main window. The workaround for older browsers is to include a button or link whose action loads that document into the `top` window object:

```
top.location.href = "mainBody.html";
```

A switch back to the frame version entails nothing more complicated than loading the framesetting document.

Inheritance versus containment

Scripters who have experience in object-oriented programming environments probably expect frames to inherit properties, methods, functions, and variables defined in a parent object. That's not the case with scriptable browsers. You can, however, still access those parent items when you make a call to the item with a complete reference to the parent. For example, if you want to define a deferred function in the framesetting parent document that all frames can share, the scripts in the frames refer to that function with this reference:

```
parent.myFunc()
```

You can pass arguments to such functions and expect returned values.

Frame synchronization

A pesky problem for some scripters' plans is that including immediate scripts in the framesetting document is dangerous. Such scripts tend to rely on the presence of documents in the frames being created by this framesetting document. But if the frames have not yet been created, and their documents have not yet loaded, the immediate scripts will likely crash and burn.

One way to guard against this problem is to trigger all such scripts from the frameset's `onload` event handler. In theory, this handler won't trigger until all documents have successfully loaded into the child frames defined by the frameset. At the same time, be careful with `onload` event handlers in the documents going into a frameset's frames. If one of those scripts relies on the presence of a document in another frame (one of its brothers or sisters), you're doomed to eventual failure. Anything coming from a slow network or server to a slow modem can get in the way of other documents loading into frames in the ideal order.

One way to work around these problems is to create a Boolean variable in the parent document to act as a flag for the successful loading of subsidiary frames. When a document loads into a frame, its onload event handler can set that flag to true to indicate that the document has loaded. Any script that relies on a page being loaded should use an if construction to test the value of that flag before proceeding.

It is best to construct the code so that the parent's onload event handler triggers all the scripts that you want to run after loading. You should also test your pages thoroughly for any residual effects that may accrue if someone resizes a window or clicks Reload.

Blank frames

Often, you may find it desirable to create a frame in a frameset but not put any document in it until the user has interacted with various controls or other user interface elements in other frames. Most modern browsers have a somewhat empty document in one of their internal URLs (about:blank). However, this URL is not guaranteed to be available on all browsers. If you need a blank frame, let your framesetting document write a generic HTML document to the frame directly from the src attribute for the frame, as shown in the skeletal code in Listing 16-3. Loading an empty HTML document requires no additional transactions.

LISTING 16-3

Creating a Blank Frame

```
<html>
<head>
<script type="text/javascript">
<!--
function blank() {
    return "<html></html>";
}
//-->
</script>
</head>
<frameset>
    <frame name="Frame1" src="someURL.html">
    <frame name="Frame2" src="javascript:parent.blank()">
</frameset>
</html>
```

Viewing frame source code

Studying other scripters' work is a major learning tool for JavaScript (or any programming language). With most scriptable browsers, you can easily view the source code for any frame, including those frames whose content is generated entirely or in part by JavaScript. Click the desired frame to activate it (a subtle border may appear just inside the frame on some browser versions, but don't be alarmed if the border doesn't appear). Then select Frame Source (or equivalent) from the View menu (or right-click submenu). You can also print or save a selected frame.

Frames versus frame element objects

With the expansion of object models that expose every HTML element to scripting, a terminology conflict comes into play. Everything that you have read about frames thus far in the chapter refers to the original object model, where a frame is just another kind of window with a slightly different referencing approach. That still holds true, even in the latest browsers.

But when the object model also exposes HTML elements, the notion of the frame element object is somewhat distinct from the frame object of the original model. The frame element object represents an object whose properties are dominated by the attributes you set inside the <frame> tag. This provides access to settings, such as the frame border and scrollability — the kinds of properties that are not exposed to the original frame object.

References to the frame and frame element objects are also different. You've seen plenty of examples of how to reference an old-fashioned frame earlier in this chapter. But access to a frame element object is either via the element's id attribute or through the child node relationship of the enclosing frameset element (you cannot use the parentNode property to back your way out of the current document to the frame element that encloses the document). The way I prefer is to assign an id attribute to <frame> tags and access the frame element object by way of the document object that lives in the parent (or top) of the frameset hierarchy. Therefore, to access the frameBorder property of a frame element object from a script living in any frame of a frameset, the syntax is

```
parent.document.all.frameID.frameBorder
```

or (for IE5+/Moz/W3C)

```
parent.document.getElementById("frameID").frameBorder
```

When the reference goes through the frame element object, you can still reach the document object in that frame via the element object's contentWindow or contentDocument properties (see the frame element object later in this chapter).

window Object

Properties	Methods	Event Handlers
appCore	addEventListener()†	onabort††
clientInformation	alert()	onafterprint
clipboardData	attachEvent()†	onbeforeprint
closed	back()	onbeforeunload
Components[]	blur()†	onblur†
content	clearInterval()	onchange††
controllers[]	clearTimeout()	onclick††
crypto	close()	onclose††
defaultStatus	confirm()	onerror
dialogArguments	createPopup()	onfocus†
dialogHeight	detachEvent()†	onhelp

Properties	Methods	Event Handlers
dialogLeft	dispatchEvent()†	onkeydown††
dialogTop	dump()	onkeypress††
dialogWidth	execScript()	onkeyup††
directories	find()	onload
document	fireEvent()†	onmousedown††
event	focus()†	onmousemove††
external	forward()	onmouseout††
frameElement	geckoActiveXObject()	onmouseover††
frames[]	getComputedStyle()	onmouseup††
fullScreen	getSelection()	onmove
history	home()	onreset††
innerHeight	moveBy()	onresize
innerWidth	moveTo()	onscroll
length	navigate()	onselect††
location	open()	onsubmit††
locationbar	openDialog()	onunload
menubar	print()	
name	prompt()	
navigator	removeEventListener()†	
netscape	resizeBy()	
offscreenBuffering	resizeTo()	
opener	scroll()	
outerHeight	scrollBy()	
outerWidth	scrollByLines()	
pageXOffset	scrollByPages()	
pageYOffset	scrollTo()	
parent	setActive()†	
personalbar	setInterval()	
pkcs11	setTimeout()	
prompter	showHelp()	
returnValue	showModalDialog()	
screen	showModelessDialog()	
screenLeft	sizeToContent()	
screenTop	stop()	
screenX		
screenY		

window

Properties	Methods	Event Handlers
scrollbars		
scrollMaxX		
scrollMaxY		
scrollX		
scrollY		
self		
sidebar		
status		
statusbar		
toolbar		
top		
window		

†See Chapter 15.

††To handle captured or bubbled events of other objects in IE4+ and W3C DOM browsers.

Syntax

Creating a window:

```
var windowObject = window.open([parameters]);
```

Accessing window properties or methods:

```
window.property | method([parameters])
```

```
self.property | method([parameters])
```

```
windowObject.property | method([parameters])
```

Compatibility: WinIE3+, MacIE3+, NN2+, Moz+, Safari+

About this object

The window object has the unique position of being at the top of the object hierarchy, encompassing even the almighty document object. This exalted position gives the window object a number of properties and behaviors unlike those of any other object.

Chief among its unique characteristics is that because everything takes place in a window, you can usually omit the window object from object references. You've seen this behavior in previous chapters when I invoked document methods, such as document.write(). The complete reference is window.document .write(). But because the activity was taking place in the window that held the document running the script, that window was assumed to be part of the reference. For single-frame windows, this concept is simple enough to grasp.

As previously stated, among the list of properties for the window object is one called self. This property is synonymous with the window object itself (which is why it shows up in hierarchy diagrams as an object). Having a property of an object that is the same name as the object may sound confusing, but this situation is not that uncommon in object-oriented environments. I discuss the reasons why you may want to use the `self` property as the window's object reference in the `self` property description that follows.

As indicated earlier in the syntax definition, you don't always have to create a `window` object specifically in JavaScript code. After you start your browser, it usually opens a window. That window is a valid `window` object, even if the window is blank. Therefore, after a user loads your page into the browser, the `window` object part of that document is automatically created for your script to access as it pleases.

One conceptual trap to avoid is believing that a `window` object's event handler or custom property assignments outlive the document whose scripts make the assignments. Except for some obvious physical properties of a window, each new document that loads into the window starts with a clean slate of window properties and event handlers.

Your script's control over an existing (already open) window's user interface elements varies widely with the browser and browser version for which your application is intended. Before the version 4 browsers, the only change you could make to an open window was to the status line at the bottom of the browser window. Version 4 browsers added the ability to control such properties as the size, location, and (with signed scripts in Navigator and Mozilla) the presence of chrome elements (toolbars and scroll bars, for example) on the fly. Many of these properties can be changed beyond specific safe limits only if you cryptographically sign the scripts (see Chapter 46 on the CD-ROM) and/or the user grants permission for your scripts to make those modifications.

Window properties are far more flexible on all browsers when your scripts generate a new window (with the `window.open()` method): You can influence the size, toolbar, or other view options of a window. Recent browser versions provide even more options for new windows, including the position of the window and whether the window should even display a title bar. Again, if an option can conceivably be used to deceive a user (for example, silently hiding one window that monitors activity in another window), signed scripts and/or user permission are necessary.

The `window` object is also the level at which a script asks the browser to display any of three styles of dialog boxes (a plain alert dialog box, an OK/Cancel confirmation dialog box, or a prompt for user text entry). Although dialog boxes are extremely helpful for cobbling together debugging tools for your own use (see Chapter 45 on the CD-ROM), they can be very disruptive to visitors who navigate through web sites. Because most JavaScript dialog boxes are modal (that is, you cannot do anything else in the browser until you dismiss the dialog box), use them sparingly, if at all. Remember that some users may create macros on their computers to visit sites unattended. Should such an automated access of your site encounter a modal dialog box, it is trapped on your page until a human intervenes.

All dialog boxes generated by JavaScript identify themselves as being generated by JavaScript. This is primarily a security feature to prevent deceitful scripts from creating system- or application-style dialog boxes that convince visitors to enter private information. It should also discourage dialog box usage in web-page design. And that's good, because dialog boxes tend to annoy users.

With the exception of the IE- and Safari-specific modal and IE-specific modeless dialog boxes (see the `window.showModalDialog()` and `window.showModeless()` methods), JavaScript dialog boxes are not particularly flexible in letting you fill them with text or graphic elements beyond the basics. In fact, you can't even change the text of the dialog-box buttons or add a button. With Dynamic HTML (DHTML)-capable browsers, you can use positioned `div` or `iframe` elements to simulate dialog-box behavior in a cross-browser way.

With respect to the W3C DOM, the window is outside the scope of the standard through DOM Level 2. The closest that the standard comes to acknowledging a window at all is the `document.defaultView` property, which evaluates to the `window` object in today's browsers (predominantly Mozilla). But the formal DOM standard specifies no properties or methods for this view object.

379

windowObject.clipboardData

Properties
```
appCore
Components[]
content
controllers[]
prompter
sidebar
```
Values: (See text)   Read-Only
Compatibility: WinIE-, MacIE-, NN6+, Moz+, Safari-

NN6+/Mozilla provides scriptable access to numerous services that are part of the xpconnect package (*xp* stands for *cross-platform*), which is part of the larger NPAPI (Netscape Plugin Application Programming Interface). The xpconnect services allow scripts to work with COM objects and the mozilla.org XUL (XML-based User Interface Language) facilities — lengthy subjects that extend well beyond the scope of this book. You can begin to explore this subject within the context of Mozilla-based browsers and scripting at `http://www.mozilla.org/scriptable/`.

clientInformation
Value: `navigator` object   Read-Only
Compatibility: WinIE4+, MacIE4+, NN-, Moz-, Safari 1.2+

In an effort to provide scriptable access to browser-level properties while avoiding reference to the Navigator browser brand, Microsoft created the `clientInformation` property. Its value is identical to that of the `navigator` object — an object name that is also available in IE. Although Safari 1.2 adopted usage of the `clientInformation` property, you should use the `navigator` object for cross-browser applications. (See Chapter 39 on the CD-ROM.)

Related Item: `navigator` object

clipboardData
Value: Object   Read/Write
Compatibility: WinIE5+, MacIE-, NN-, Moz-, Safari-

Use the `clipboardData` object to transfer data for such actions as cutting, copying, and pasting under script control. The object contains data of one or more data types associated with a transfer operation. Use this property only when editing processes via the Edit menu (or keyboard equivalents) or context menu controlled by script — typically in concert with edit-related event handlers.

Working with the `clipboardData` object requires knowing about its three methods, shown in Table 16-1. Familiarity with the edit-related event handlers (before and after versions of cut, copy, and paste) is also helpful (see Chapter 15).

TABLE 16-1

window.clipboardData Object Methods

Method	Returns	Description
clearData([*format*])	Nothing	Removes data from the clipboard. If no format parameter is supplied, all data is cleared. Data formats can be one or more of the following strings: Text, URL, File, HTML, Image.
getData(*format*)	String	Retrieves data of the specified format from the clipboard. The format is one of the following strings: Text, URL, File, HTML, Image. The clipboard is not emptied when you get the data so that the data can be retrieved in several sequential operations.
setData(*format*, *data*)	Boolean	Stores string data in the clipboard. The format is one of the following strings: Text, URL, File, HTML, Image. For nontext data formats, the data must be a string that specifies the path or URL to the content. Returns true if the transfer to the clipboard is successful.

You cannot use the clipboardData object to transfer data between pages that originate from different domains or arrive via different protocols (http versus https).

Example

See Listing 15-36 and Listing 15-44 in Chapter 15 to see how the clipboardData object is used with a variety of edit-related event handlers.

Related Items: event.dataTransfer property; onbeforecopy, onBeforeCut, onbeforepaste, oncopy, oncut, onpaste event handlers

closed

Value: Boolean   Read-Only
Compatibility: WinIE4+, MacIE4+, NN3+, Moz+, Safari+

When you create a subwindow with the window.open() method, you may need to access object properties from that subwindow, such as setting the value of a text field. Access to the subwindow is via the window object reference that is returned by the window.open() method, as in the following code fragment:

```
var newWind = window.open("someURL.html","subWind");
...
newWind.document.entryForm.ZIP.value = "00000";
```

In this example, the newWind variable is not linked live to the window but is only a reference to that window. If the user should close the window, the newWind variable still contains the reference to the now-missing window. Thus, any script reference to an object in that missing window will likely cause a script error. What you need to know before accessing items in a subwindow is whether the window is still open.

The closed property returns true if the window object has been closed either by script or by the user. Any time you have a script statement that can be triggered after the user has an opportunity to close the window, test for the closed property before executing that statement.

Example

In Listing 16-4, I have created a basic window-opening and -closing example. The script begins by initializing a global variable, newWind, which is used to hold the object reference to the second window. This value needs to be global so that other functions can reference the window for tasks, such as closing.

For this example, the new window contains some HTML code written dynamically to it, rather than loading an existing HTML file into it. Therefore, the URL parameter of the window.open() method is left as an empty string. Next comes a brief delay to allow Internet Explorer (especially versions 3 and 4) to catch up with opening the window so that content can be written to it. The delay (using the setTimeout() method described later in this chapter) invokes the finishNewWindow() function, which uses the global newWind variable to reference the window for writing. The document.close() method closes writing to the document — a different kind of close from a window close. A separate function, closeWindow(), is responsible for closing the subwindow.

As a final test, an if condition looks at two conditions: (1) whether the window object has ever been initialized with a value other than null (in case you click the window-closing button before ever having created the new window) and (2) whether the window's closed property is null or false. If either condition is true, the close() method is sent to the second window.

> **NOTE** The property assignment event handling technique employed throughout the code in this chapter and much of the book is a deliberate simplification to make the code more readable. It is generally better to use the more modern approach of binding events using the addEventListener() (NN6+/Moz/W3C) or attachEvent() (IE5+) methods. A modern cross-browser event handling technique is explained in detail in Chapter 25.

LISTING 16-4

Checking Before Closing a Window

```
<html>
    <head>
        <title>window.closed Property</title>
        <script type="text/javascript">
        // initialize global var for new window object
        // so it can be accessed by all functions on the page
        var newWind;

        // make the new window and put some stuff in it
        function newWindow() {
            newWind = window.open("","subwindow","height=200,width=200");
            setTimeout("finishNewWindow()", 100);
        }
        function finishNewWindow() {
            var output = "";
            output += "<html><body><h1>A Sub-window</h1>";
            output += "<form><input type='button' value='Close Main Window'";
            output +="onclick='window.opener.close()'></form></body></html>";
            newWind.document.write(output);
            newWind.document.close();
        }
```

```
        // close subwindow, including ugly workaround for IE3
        function closeWindow() {
            if (newWind && !newWind.closed) {
                newWind.close();
            }
        }
        </script>
    </head>
    <body>
        <form>
            <input type="button" value="Open Window"
            onclick="newWindow()" /><br />
            <input type="button" value="Close it if Still Open"
            onclick="closeWindow()" />
        </form>
    </body>
</html>
```

To complete the example of the window opening and closing, notice that the subwindow is given a button whose onclick event handler closes the main window. In modern browsers, the user is presented with an alert asking to confirm the closure of the main browser window.

Related Items: window.open(), window.close() methods

Components

(See appCore)

controllers

(See appCore)

crypto
pkcs11

Values: Object references   Read-Only
Compatibility: WinIE-, MacIE-, NN6+, Moz+, Safari-

The crypto and pkcs11 properties return references to browser objects that are relevant to internal public-key cryptography mechanisms. These subjects are beyond the scope of this book, but you can read more about Netscape's efforts on this front at http://www.mozilla.org/projects/security/.

defaultStatus

Value: String   Read/Write
Compatibility: WinIE3+, MacIE3+, NN2+, Moz+, Safari+

After a document is loaded into a window or frame, the status bar's message field can display a string that is visible any time the mouse pointer is not atop an object that takes precedence over the status bar (such as a link object or an image map). The window.defaultStatus property is normally an empty string, but you can set this property at any time. Any setting of this property will be temporarily overridden when a user moves the mouse pointer atop a link object (see window.status property for information about customizing this temporary status-bar message).

Probably the most common time to set the `window.defaultStatus` property is when a document loads into a window. You can do this as an immediate script statement that executes from the Head or Body portion of the document or as part of a document's `onload` event handler.

Example

Unless you plan to change the default status-bar text while a user spends time at your web page, the best time to set the property is when the document loads. In Listing 16-5, notice that I also read this property to reset the status bar in an `onmouseout` event handler. Setting the `status` property to empty also resets the status bar to the `defaultStatus` setting.

LISTING 16-5

Setting the Default Status Message

```html
<html>
  <head>
    <title>window.defaultStatus property</title>
    <script type="text/javascript">
    window.defaultStatus = "Welcome to my Web site.";
    </script>
  </head>
  <body>
    <a href="http://www.microsoft.com"
    onmouseover="window.status = 'Visit Microsoft\'s Home page.';return true"
    onmouseout="window.status = '';return true">Microsoft</a>
    <p><a href="http://mozilla.org"
    onmouseover="window.status = 'Visit Mozilla\'s Home page.';return true"
    onmouseout="window.status = window.defaultStatus;return
    true">Mozilla</a></p>
  </body>
</html>
```

If you need to display single or double quotes in the status bar (as in the second link in Listing 16-5), use escape characters (\' and \") as part of the strings being assigned to these properties.

Related Item: `window.status` property

dialogArguments

Value: Varies   Read-Only
Compatibility: WinIE4+, MacIE4+, NN-, Moz-, Safari-

The `dialogArguments` property is available only in a window that is generated by the IE-specific `showModalDialog()` or `showModelessDialog()` method. Those methods allow a parameter to be passed to the dialog-box window, and the `dialogArguments` property lets scripts inside the dialog -ox window's scripts access that parameter value. The value can be in the form of a string, number, or JavaScript array (convenient for passing multiple values).

Example

See Listing 16-36 for the `window.showModalDialog()` method to see how arguments can be passed to a dialog box and retrieved via the `dialogArguments` property.

Related Items: `window.showModalDialog()`, `window.showModelessDialog()` methods

dialogHeight
dialogWidth

Value: String   Read/Write
Compatibility: WinIE4+, MacIE-, NN-, Moz-, Safari-

Scripts in a document located inside an IE-specific modal or modeless dialog box (generated by `showModalDialog()` or `showModelessDialog()`) can read or modify the height and width of the dialog-box window via the `dialogHeight` and `dialogWidth` properties. Scripts can access these properties from the main window only for modeless dialog boxes, which remain visible while the user can control the main window contents.

Values for these properties are strings and include the unit of measure, the pixel (`px`).

Example

Dialog boxes sometimes provide a button or icon that reveals more details or more complex settings for advanced users. You can create a function that handles the toggle between two sizes. The following function assumes that the document in the dialog box has a button whose label also toggles between Show Details and Hide Details. The button's `onclick` event handler invokes the function as `toggleDetails(this)`:

```
function toggleDetails(btn) {
   if (dialogHeight == "200px") {
      dialogHeight = "350px";
      btn.value = "Hide Details";
   } else {
      dialogHeight = "200px";
      btn.value = "Show Details";
   }
}
```

In practice, you also have to toggle the `display` style sheet property of the extra material between `none` and `block` to make sure that the dialog box does not display scroll bars in the smaller dialog-box version.

Related Items: `window.dialogLeft`, `window.dialogTop` properties

dialogLeft
dialogTop

Value: String   Read/Write
Compatibility: WinIE4+, MacIE4+, NN-, Moz-, Safari-

Scripts in a document located inside an IE-specific modal or modeless dialog box (generated by `showModalDialog()` or `showModelessDialog()`) can read or modify the left and top coordinates of the dialog-box window via the `dialogLeft` and `dialogTop` properties. Scripts can access these properties from the main window only for modeless dialog boxes, which remain visible while the user can control the main window contents.

windowObject.**directories**

Values for these properties are strings and include the unit of measure, the pixel (px). If you attempt to change these values so that any part of the dialog-box window would be outside the video monitor, the browser overrides the settings to keep the entire window visible.

Example

Although usually not a good idea because of the potentially jarring effect on a user, you can reposition a dialog-box window that has been resized by script (or by the user if you let the dialog box be resizable). The following statements in a dialog-box window document's script re-center the dialog-box window:

```
dialogLeft = (screen.availWidth/2) - (parseInt(dialogWidth)/2) + "px";
dialogHeight = (screen.availHeight/2) - (parseInt(dialogHeight)/2) + "px";
```

Note that the parseInt() functions are used to read the numeric portion of the dialogWidth and dialogHeight properties so that the values can be used for arithmetic.

Related Items: window.dialogHeight, window.dialogTopWidth properties

directories
locationbar
menubar
personalbar
scrollbars
statusbar
toolbar

Value: Object   Read/Write (with signed scripts)
Compatibility: WinIE-, MacIE-, NN4+, Moz+, Safari-

Beyond the rectangle of the content region of a window (where your documents appear), the Netscape browser window displays an amalgam of bars and other features known collectively as *chrome*. All browsers can elect to remove these chrome items when creating a new window (as part of the third parameter of the window.open() method), but until signed scripts were available in Navigator 4, these items could not be turned on and off in the main browser window or any existing window.

Navigator 4 promoted these elements to first-class objects contained by the window object. Navigator 6 added one more feature, called the *directories bar* — a framelike device that can be opened or hidden from the left edge of the browser window. At the same time, however, NN6+/Mozilla browsers no longer permit hiding and showing the browser window's scroll bars. Chrome objects have but one property: visible. Reading this Boolean value (possible without signed scripts) lets you inspect the visitor's browser window for the elements currently engaged.

Changing the visibility of these items on the fly alters the relationship between the inner and outer dimensions of the browser window. If you must size carefully a window to display content, you should adjust the chrome elements before sizing the window. Before you start changing chrome visibility before the eyes of your page visitors, weigh the decision carefully. Experienced users have fine-tuned the look of their browser windows to just the way they like them. If you mess with that look, you may anger your visitors. Fortunately, changes you make to a chrome element's visibility are not stored to the user's preferences. However, the changes you make survive an unloading of the page. If you change the settings, be sure that you first save the initial settings and restore them with an onunload event handler.

 The Macintosh menu bar is not part of the browser's window chrome. Therefore, its visibility cannot be adjusted from a script.

Example

In Listing 16-6, you can experiment with the look of a browser window with any of the chrome elements turned on and off. To run this script, you must either sign the scripts or turn on codebase principals (see Chapter 46 on the CD-ROM). Java must also be enabled to use the signed script statements.

As the page loads, it stores the current state of each chrome element. One button for each chrome element triggers the toggleBar() function. This function inverts the visible property for the chrome object passed as a parameter to the function. Finally, the Restore button returns visibility to their original settings. Notice that the restore() function is also called by the onunload event handler for the document.

LISTING 16-6

Controlling Window Chrome

```html
<html>
  <head>
    <title>Bars Bars Bars</title>
    <script type="text/javascript">
    // store original outer dimensions as page loads
    var originalLocationbar = window.locationbar.visible;
    var originalMenubar = window.menubar.visible;
    var originalPersonalbar = window.personalbar.visible;
    var originalScrollbars = window.scrollbars.visible;
    var originalStatusbar = window.statusbar.visible;
    var originalToolbar = window.toolbar.visible;

    // generic function to set inner dimensions
    function toggleBar(bar) {
       netscape.security.PrivilegeManager.enablePrivilege(
          "UniversalBrowserWrite");
       bar.visible = !bar.visible;
       netscape.security.PrivilegeManager.revertPrivilege(
          "UniversalBrowserWrite");
    }
    // restore settings
    function restore() {
       netscape.security.PrivilegeManager.enablePrivilege(
          "UniversalBrowserWrite");
       window.locationbar.visible = originalLocationbar;
       window.menubar.visible = originalMenubar;
       window.personalbar.visible = originalPersonalbar;
       window.scrollbars.visible = originalScrollbars;
       window.statusbar.visible = originalStatusbar;
       window.toolbar.visible = originalToolbar;
       netscape.security.PrivilegeManager.revertPrivilege(
          "UniversalBrowserWrite");
    }
```

continued

LISTING 16-6 *(continued)*

```
    </script>
  </head>
  <body onunload="restore()">
    <form>
      <b>Toggle Window Bars</b><br />
      <input type="button" value="Location Bar"
      onclick="toggleBar(window.locationbar)" /><br />
      <input type="button" value="Menu Bar"
      onclick="toggleBar(window.menubar)" /><br />
      <input type="button" value="Personal Bar"
      onclick="toggleBar(window.personalbar)" /><br />
      <input type="button" value="Scrollbars"
      onclick="toggleBar(window.scrollbars)" /><br />
      <input type="button" value="Status Bar"
      onclick="toggleBar(window.statusbar)" /><br />
      <input type="button" value="Tool Bar"
      onclick="toggleBar(window.toolbar)" /><br />
      <hr />
      <input type="button" value="Restore Original Settings"
      onclick="restore()" /><br />
    </form>
  </body>
</html>
```

Related Item: `window.open()` method

document

Value: Object   Read-Only
Compatibility: WinIE3+, MacIE3+, NN2+, Moz+, Safari+

I list the `document` property here primarily for completeness. Each `window` object contains a single `document` object. The value of the `document` property is the `document` object, which is not a displayable value. Instead, you use the `document` property as you build references to properties and methods of the document and to other objects contained by the document, such as a form and its elements. To load a different document into a window, use the `location` object (see Chapter 17). The `document` object is described in detail in Chapter 18.

Related Item: `document` object

event

Value: Object   Read/Write
Compatibility: WinIE4+, MacIE4+, NN-, Moz-, Safari 1+

IE4+ and Safari treat the `event` object as a property of the `window` object. Navigator 4+ and the W3C DOM (as well as Safari here, too) pass an instance of the `Event` object as an argument to event handler functions. The connection with the `window` object is relatively inconsequential because all action involving the `event` object occurs in event handler functions. The only difference is that the object can be treated as a more global object when one event handler function invokes another. Instead of having to pass the `event` object parameter to the next function, functions can access the `event` object directly (with or without the `window.` prefix in the reference).

For complete details about the `event` object in all browsers, see Chapter 25.

Related Item: `event` object

external

Value: Object   Read-Only
Compatibility: WinIE4+, MacIE-, NN-, Moz-, Safari-

The `external` property is useful only when the browser window is a component in another application. The property provides a gateway between the current browser window and the application that acts as a host to the browser window component.

With WinIE4+ acting as a component to the host operating system, the `external` property can be used to access several methods that influence behaviors outside the browser. Perhaps the three most useful methods to regular web-page scripters are `AddDesktopComponent()`, `AddFavorite()`, and `NavigateAndFind()`. The first two methods display the same kind of alert dialog box that users get after making these choices from the browser or desktop menus, so that you won't be able to sneak your web site onto desktops or Favorites listings without the visitor's approval. Table 16-2 describes the parameters for these three methods.

TABLE 16-2

Popular window.external Object Methods

Method	Description
`AddDesktopComponent("URL", "type"[, left, top, width, height])`	Adds a web site or image to the Active Desktop (if turned on in the user's copy of Windows). The `type` parameter value is either `website` or `image`. Dimensional parameters (optional) are all integer values.
`AddFavorite("URL"[, "title"])`	Adds the specified URL to the user's Favorites list. The optional title string parameter is how the URL should be listed in the menu (if missing, the URL appears in the list).
`NavigateAndFind("URL", "findString", "target")`	Navigates to the URL in the first parameter and opens the page in the target frame (an empty string opens in the current frame). The `findString` is text to be searched for on that page and highlighted when the page loads.

Example

The first example asks the user whether it is OK to add a web site to the Active Desktop. If Active Desktop is not enabled, the user is given the choice of enabling it at this point:

```
external.AddDesktopComponent("http://www.nytimes.com","website", 200, 100,
    400, 400);
```

In the next example, the user is asked to approve the addition of a URL to the Favorites list. The user can follow the normal procedure for filing the item in a folder in the list:

```
external.AddFavorite("http://www.dannyg.com/update11.html",
    "JSBible 6 Support Center");
```

The final example assumes that a user makes a choice from a `select` list of items. The `onchange` event handler of the `select` list invokes the following function to navigate to a fictitious page and locate listings for a chosen sports team on the page:

```
function locate(list) {
    var choice = list.options[list.selectedIndex].value;
    external.NavigateAndFind("http://www.collegesports.net/scores.html",
        choice, "scores");
}
```

frameElement

Values: `frame` or `iframe` object reference   Read-Only
Compatibility: WinIE5.5+, MacIE-, NN7+, Moz1.0.1+, Safari 1.2+

If the current window exists as a result of a `<frame>` or `<iframe>` tag, the window's `frameElement` property returns a reference to the hosting element. As is made clear in the discussion about the `frame` element object later in this chapter, a reference to a `frame` or `iframe` element object provides access to the properties that echo the attributes of the HTML element object. For a window that is not part of a frameset, the `frameElement` property returns `null`.

The convenience of this property becomes apparent when a single document is loaded into multiple framesets. A script in the document can still refer to the containing `frame` element, even when the ID of the element changes from one frameset to another. The `frameset` element is also accessible via the `parentElement` property of the `frameElement` property:

```
var frameSetObj = self.frameElement.parentElement;
```

A reference to the `frameset` element opens possibilities of adjusting frame sizes.

Related Items: `frame`, `iframe` objects

frames

Value: Array   Read-Only
Compatibility: WinIE3+, MacIE3+, NN2+, Moz+, Safari+

In a multiframe window, the top or parent window contains any number of separate frames, each of which acts as a full-fledged `window` object. The `frames` property (note the plural use of the word as a property name) plays a role when a statement must reference an object located in a different frame. For example, if a button in one frame is scripted to load a document in another frame, the button's event handler must be able to tell JavaScript precisely where to display the new HTML document. The `frames` property assists in that task.

To use the `frames` property to communicate from one frame to another, it should be part of a reference that begins with the `parent` or `top` property. This lets JavaScript make the proper journey through the hierarchy of all currently loaded objects to reach the desired object. To find out how many frames are currently active in a window, use this expression:

```
parent.frames.length
```

This expression returns a number indicating how many frames the parent window defines. This value does not, however, count further nested frames, should a third generation of frame be defined in the environment. In other words, no single property exists that you can use to determine the total number of frames in the browser window if multiple generations of frames are present.

The browser stores information about all visible frames in a numbered (indexed) array, with the first frame (that is, the topmost `<frame>` tag defined in the framesetting document) as number 0:

```
parent.frames[0]
```

Therefore, if the window shows three frames (whose indexes are `frames[0]`, `frames[1]`, and `frames[2]`, respectively), the reference for retrieving the `title` property of the document in the second frame is

```
parent.frames[1].document.title
```

This reference is a road map that starts at the parent window and extends to the second frame's document and its `title` property. Other than the number of frames defined in a parent window and each frame's name (`top.frames[i].name`), no values from the frame definitions are directly available from the frame object via scripting until you get to IE4 and NN6/Moz/W3C (see the `frame` element object later in this chapter). In these browsers, individual `frame` element objects have several properties that reveal `<frame>` tag attributes.

Using index values for frame references is not always the safest tactic, however, because your frameset design may change over time, in which case the index values will also change. Instead, you should take advantage of the `name` attribute of the `<frame>` tag, and assign a unique, descriptive name to each frame. A value you assign to the `name` attribute is also the name that you use for `target` attributes of links to force a linked page to load in a frame other than the one containing the link. You can use a frame's name as an alternative to the indexed reference. For example, in Listing 16-7, two frames are assigned distinctive names. To access the title of a document in the `JustAKid2` frame, the complete object reference is

```
parent.JustAKid2.document.title
```

with the frame name (case sensitive) substituting for the `frames[1]` array reference. Or, in keeping with JavaScript flexibility, you can use the object name in the array index position:

```
parent.frames["JustAKid2"].document.title
```

The supreme advantage to using frame names in references is that no matter how the frameset structure may change over time, a reference to a named frame will always find that frame even though its index value (that is, position in the frameset) may change.

Example

Listing 16-7 and Listing 16-8 demonstrate how JavaScript treats values of frame references from objects inside a frame. The same document is loaded into each frame. A script in that document extracts information about the current frame and the entire frameset. Figure 16-4 shows the results after loading the HTML document in Listing 16-7.

LISTING 16-7

Framesetting Document for Listing 16-8

```html
<html>
   <head>
      <title>window.frames property</title>
   </head>
   <frameset cols="50%,50%">
      <frame name="JustAKid1" src="lst16-08.htm" />
      <frame name="JustAKid2" src="lst16-08.htm" />
   </frameset>
</html>
```

A call to determine the number (length) of frames returns 0 from the point of view of the current frame referenced. That's because each frame here is a window that has no nested frames within it. But add the parent property to the reference, and the scope zooms out to take into account all frames generated by the parent window's document.

LISTING 16-8

Showing Various Window Properties

```html
<html>
   <head>
      <title>Window Revealer II</title>
      <script type="text/javascript">
      function gatherWindowData() {
         var msg = "";
         msg += "<p><b>From the point of view of this frame:</b><br />";
         msg += "window.frames.length: " + window.frames.length + "<br />";
         msg += "window.name: " + window.name + "</p>";
         msg += "<p><b>From the point of view of the framesetting
            document:</b><br />";
         msg += "parent.frames.length: " + parent.frames.length + "<br />";
         msg += "parent.frames[0].name: " + parent.frames[0].name + "</p>";
         return msg;
      }
      </script>
   </head>
   <body>
      <script type="text/javascript">
      document.write(gatherWindowData());
      </script>
   </body>
</html>
```

FIGURE 16-4

Property readouts from both frames loaded from Listing 16-7.

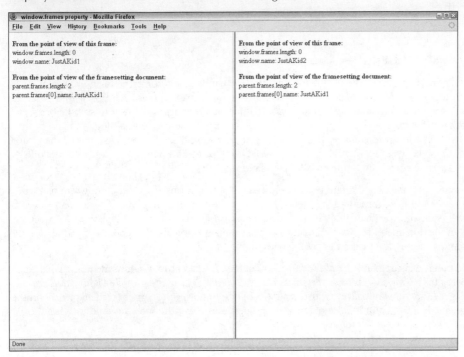

The last statement in the example shows how to use the array syntax (brackets) to refer to a specific frame. All array indexes start with 0 for the first entry. Because the document asks for the name of the first frame (`parent.frames[0]`), the response is `JustAKid1` for both frames.

Related Items: `frame`, `frameset` objects; `window.parent`, `window.top` properties

fullScreen

Values: Boolean   Read-Only
Compatibility: WinIE-, MacIE-, NN7.1+, Moz1.4+, Safari-

The intent of the `fullScreen` property is to indicate whether the browser is in full-screen mode, which can be set in Mozilla browsers through the Full Screen command in the View menu. Unfortunately, the property isn't reliable (as of Mozilla 1.8.1) and always returns `false` regardless of the browser's actual full-screen setting.

history

Value: Object   Read-Only
Compatibility: WinIE3+, MacIE3+, NN2+, Moz+, Safari+

(See the discussion of the `history` object in Chapter 17.)

windowObject.**innerHeight**

```
innerHeight
innerWidth
outerHeight
outerWidth
```

Value: Integer   Read/Write (see text)
Compatibility: WinIE-, MacIE-, NN4+, Moz+, Safari+

NN4+/Moz/Safari let scripts adjust the height and width of any window, including the main browser window, by setting properties. This adjustment can be helpful when your page shows itself best with the browser window sized to a particular height and width. Rather than relying on the user to size the browser window for optimum viewing of your page, you can dictate the size of the window (although the user can always resize the main window manually). And because you can examine the operating system of the visitor via the `navigator` object (see Chapter 39 on the CD-ROM), you can size a window to adjust for the differences in font and form element rendering on different platforms.

Supporting browsers provide two different points of reference for measuring the height and width of a window: inner and outer. Both are measured in pixels. The inner measurements are that of the active document area of a window (sometimes known as a window's content region). If the optimum display of your document depends on the document display area being a certain number of pixels high and/or wide, the `innerHeight` and `innerWidth` properties are the ones to set.

By contrast, the outer measurements are of the outside boundary of the entire window, including whatever chrome is showing in the window: scroll bars, status bar, and so on. Setting the `outerHeight` and `outerWidth` is generally done in concert with a reading of `screen` object properties (see Chapter 39 on the CD-ROM). Perhaps the most common use of the outer properties is to set the browser window to fill the available screen area of the visitor's monitor.

A more efficient way of modifying both outer dimensions of a window is with the `window.resizeTo()` method, which is also available in IE4+. The method takes pixel width and height (as integer values) as parameters, thus accomplishing a window resizing in one statement. Be aware that resizing a window does not adjust the location of a window. Therefore, just because you set the outer dimensions of a window to the available space returned by the `screen` object doesn't mean that the window will suddenly fill the available space on the monitor. Application of the `window.moveTo()` method is necessary to ensure that the top-left corner of the window is at screen coordinates 0,0.

Despite the freedom that these properties afford the page author, Netscape and Mozilla-based browsers have built in a minimum size limitation for scripts that are not cryptographically signed. You cannot set these properties such that the outer height and width of the window is smaller than 100 pixels on a side. This limitation is to prevent an unsigned script from setting up a small or nearly invisible window that monitors activity in other windows. With signed scripts, however, windows can be made smaller than 100 × 100 pixels with the user's permission. IE4+ maintains a smaller minimum size to prevent resizing a window to zero size.

 Users may dislike your scripts messing with their browser window sizes and positions. NN7+/Moz/Safari do not allow scripts to resize windows unless the script is signed.

Example

In Listing 16-9, several buttons let you see the results of setting the `innerHeight`, `innerWidth`, `outerHeight`, and `outerWidth` properties. Safari ignores scripted adjustments to these properties, whereas Mozilla users can set preferences that prevent scripts from moving and resizing windows.

LISTING 16-9

Setting Window Height and Width

```html
<html>
   <head>
      <title>Window Sizer</title>
      <script type="text/javascript">
      // store original outer dimensions as page loads
      var originalWidth = window.outerWidth;
      var originalHeight = window.outerHeight;
      // generic function to set inner dimensions
      function setInner(width, height) {
         window.innerWidth = width;
         window.innerHeight = height;
      }
      // generic function to set outer dimensions
      function setOuter(width, height) {
         window.outerWidth = width;
         window.outerHeight = height;
      }
      // restore window to original dimensions
      function restore() {
         window.outerWidth = originalWidth;
         window.outerHeight = originalHeight;
      }
      </script>
   </head>
   <body>
      <form>
         <b>Setting Inner Sizes</b><br />
         <input type="button" value="600 Pixels Square"
         onclick="setInner(600,600)" /><br />
         <input type="button" value="300 Pixels Square"
         onclick="setInner(300,300)" /><br />
         <input type="button" value="Available Screen Space"
         onclick="setInner(screen.availWidth, screen.availHeight)" /><br />
         <hr />
         <b>Setting Outer Sizes</b><br />
         <input type="button" value="600 Pixels Square"
         onclick="setOuter(600,600)" /><br />
         <input type="button" value="300 Pixels Square"
         onclick="setOuter(300,300)" /><br />
         <input type="button" value="Available Screen Space"
         onclick="setOuter(screen.availWidth, screen.availHeight)" /><br />
         <hr />
         <input type="button" value="Cinch up for Win95"
         onclick="setInner(273,304)" /><br />
         <input type="button" value="Cinch up for Mac"
         onclick="setInner(273,304)" /><br />
```

continued

395

LISTING 16-9 *(continued)*

```
        <input type="button" value="Restore Original"
        onclick="restore()" /><br />
    </form>
  </body>
</html>
```

Related Items: window.resizeTo(), window.moveTo() methods; screen object; navigator object

location

Value: Object   Read/Write
Compatibility: WinIE3+, MacIE3+, NN2+, Moz+, Safari+

(See the discussion of the location object in Chapter 17.)

locationbar

(See directories)

name

Value: String   Read/Write
Compatibility: WinIE3+, MacIE3+, NN2+, Moz+, Safari+

All window objects can have names assigned to them. Names are particularly useful for working with frames, because a good naming scheme for a multiframe environment can help you determine precisely which frame you're working with in references coming from other frames.

The main browser window, however, has no name attached to it by default. Its value is an empty string. There aren't many reasons to assign a name to the window, because JavaScript and HTML provide plenty of other ways to refer to the window object (the top property, the _top constant for target attributes, and the opener property from subwindows).

If you want to attach a name to the main window, you can do so by setting the window.name property at any time. But be aware that because this is one window property whose life extends beyond the loading and unloading of any given document, chances are that your scripts would use the reference in only one document or frameset. Unless you restore the default empty string, your programmed window name will be present for any other document that loads later. My suggestion in this regard is to assign a name in a window's or frameset's onload event handler and then reset it to empty in a corresponding onunload event handler:

```
    <body onload="self.name = 'Main'" onunload="self.name = ''">
```

You can see an example of this application in Listing 16-15, where setting a parent window name is helpful for learning the relationships among parent and child windows.

Related Items: top property; window.open(), window.sizeToContent() methods

navigator

Value: Object   Read-Only
Compatibility: WinIE4+, MacIE4+, NN6+, Moz+, Safari+

Although the navigator object appears as a property of the window object only in modern browsers, the navigator object has been around since the very beginning (see Chapter 39 on the CD-ROM). In previous browsers, the navigator object was referenced as a stand-alone object. And because you can omit any reference to the window object for a window object's properties, you can use the same windowless reference syntax for compatibility across all scriptable browsers (at least for the navigator object properties that exist across all browsers). That's the way I recommend referring to the navigator object.

Example

This book is littered with examples of using the navigator object, primarily for performing browser detection. You can find examples of specific navigator object properties in Chapter 39 on the CD-ROM.

Related Item: navigator object

netscape

Value: Object   Read-Only
Compatibility: WinIE-, MacIE-, NN3+, Moz+, Safari-

Given its name, you might think that the netscape property somehow works in tandem with the navigator property, but this is not the case. The netscape property is unique to NN/Moz browsers and provides access to functionality that is specific to the Netscape family of browsers, such as the privilege manager.

Example

The netscape property is commonly used as a means of accessing the NN/Moz-specific PrivilegeManager object to enable or disable security privileges. Following is an example of how this access is carried out:

```
netscape.security.PrivilegeManager.enablePrivilege("UniversalBrowserRead");
```

offscreenBuffering

Value: Boolean or string   Read/Write
Compatibility: WinIE4+, MacIE4+, NN-, Moz-, Safari 1.2+

IE4+/Safari 1.2+ by default initially render a page in a buffer (a chunk of memory) before it is blasted to the video screen. You can control this behavior explicitly by modifying the window.offscreenBuffering property.

The default value of the property is the string auto. You can also assign Boolean true or false to the property to override the normal automatic handling of this behavior.

Example

If you want to turn off buffering for an entire page, include the following statement at the beginning of your script statements:

```
window.offscreenBuffering = false;
```

onerror

Value: Function Read/Write
Compatibility: WinIE4+, MacIE4+, NN3+, Moz+, Safari-

The onerror property is an exception to the rule of this book to not describe event handlers as properties within object reference sections. The reason is that the onerror event brings along some special properties that are useful to control by setting the event handler property in scripts.

Modern browsers (IE5+, NN4+, and W3C) are designed to prevent script errors from being intrusive if a user encounters a script error while loading or interacting with a page. Even so, even the subtle hints about problems (messages or icons in the status bar) can be confusing for users who have no idea what JavaScript is. JavaScript lets you turn off the display of script error windows or messages as someone executes a script on your page. The question is: When should you turn off these messages?

Script errors generally mean that something is wrong with your script. The error may be the result of a coding mistake or, conceivably, a bug in JavaScript (perhaps on a platform version of the browser that you haven't been able to test). If such errors occur, often, the script won't continue to do what you intended. Hiding the script error from yourself during development would be foolhardy, because you'd never know whether unseen errors are lurking in your code. It can be equally dangerous to turn off error dialog boxes for users who may believe that the page is operating normally when in fact it's not. Some data values may not be calculated or displayed correctly.

That said, I can see some limited instances of when you may want to keep such dialog-box windows from appearing. For example, if you know for a fact that a platform-specific bug trips the error message without harming the execution of the script, you may want to prevent that error alert dialog box from appearing in the files posted to your web site. You should do this only after extensive testing to ensure that the script ultimately behaves correctly, even with the bug or error.

> **NOTE** IE fires the onerror event handler only for runtime errors. This means that if you have a syntactical error in your script that trips the browser as the page loads, the onerror event doesn't fire, and you cannot trap that error message. Moreover, if the user has the IE script debugger installed, any code you use to prevent browser error messages from appearing will not work.

When the browser starts, the window.onerror property is <undefined>. In this state, all errors are reported via the normal JavaScript error window or message. To turn off error alerts, set the window.onerror property to invoke a function that does absolutely nothing:

```
function doNothing() { return true; }
window.onerror = doNothing;
```

To restore the error messages, reload the page.

You can, however, also assign a custom function to the window.onerror property. This function then handles errors in a more friendly way under your script control. Whenever error messages are turned on (the default behavior), a script error (or Java applet or class exception) invokes the function assigned to the onerror property, passing three parameters:

- Error message
- URL of document causing the error
- Line number of the error

You can essentially trap for all errors and handle them with your own interface (or no user notification at all). The last statement of this function must be `return true` if you do not want the JavaScript script error message to appear.

If you are using the NPAPI to communicate with a Java applet directly from your scripts, you can use the same scheme to handle any exception that Java may throw. A Java exception is not necessarily a mistake kind of error: Some methods assume that the Java code will trap for exceptions to handle special cases (for example, reacting to a user's denial of access when prompted by a signed script dialog box). See Chapter 44 on the CD-ROM for an example of trapping for a specific Java exception. Also, see Chapter 32 for JavaScript exception handling introduced for W3C DOM–compatible browsers.

Example

In Listing 16-10, one button triggers a script that contains an error. I've added an error handling function to process the error so that it opens a separate window and fills in a `textarea` form element (see Figure 16-5). A Submit button is also provided to mail the bug information to a support center e-mail address — an example of how to handle the occurrence of a bug in your scripts.

LISTING 16-10

Controlling Script Errors

```
<html>
    <head>
        <title>Error Dialog Control</title>
        <script type="text/javascript">
        // function with invalid variable value
        function goWrong() {
            var x = fred;
        }
        // turn off error dialogs
        function errOff() {
            window.onerror = doNothing;
        }
        // turn on error dialogs with hard reload
        function errOn() {
            window.onerror = handleError;
        }

        // assign default error handler
        window.onerror = handleError;

        // error handler when errors are turned off...prevents error dialog
        function doNothing() { return true; }

        function handleError(msg, URL, lineNum) {
            var errWind = window.open("","errors","height=270,width=400");
            var wintxt = "<html><body bgcolor=red>";
            wintxt += "<b>An error has occurred on this page.  Please report it to
                Tech Support.</b>";
```

continued

LISTING 16-10 *(continued)*

```
        wintxt += "<form method=POST enctype='text/plain'
            action=mailTo:support4@dannyg.com >";
        wintxt += "<textarea name='errMsg' cols=45 rows=8 wrap=VIRTUAL>";
        wintxt += "Error: " + msg + "\n";
        wintxt += "URL: " + URL + "\n";
        wintxt += "Line: " + lineNum + "\n";
        wintxt += "Client: " + navigator.userAgent + "\n";
        wintxt += "------------------------------------------\n";
        wintxt += "Please describe what you were doing when the error
            occurred:";
        wintxt += "</textarea><br />";
        wintxt += "<input type=SUBMIT value='Send Error Report'>";
        wintxt += "<input type=button value='Close' onclick='self.close()'>";
        wintxt += "</form></body></html>";
        errWind.document.write(wintxt);
        errWind.document.close();
        return true;
    }
    </script>
</head>
<body>
    <form name="myform">
        <input type="button" value="Cause an Error" onclick="goWrong()" />
        <p><input type="button" value="Turn Off Error Dialogs"
            onclick="errOff()" /> <input type="button"
            value="Turn On Error Dialogs" onclick="errOn()" /></p>
    </form>
</body>
</html>
```

FIGURE 16-5

An example of a self-reporting error window.

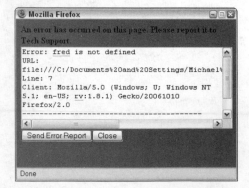

I provide a button that performs a hard reload, which in turn resets the `window.onerror` property to its default value. With error dialog boxes turned off, the error handling function does not run.

Related Items: `location.reload()` method; JavaScript exception handling (Chapter 32); debugging scripts (Chapter 45 on the CD-ROM)

opener

Value: Window object reference   Read/Write
Compatibility: WinIE3+, MacIE3+, NN3+, Moz+, Safari+

Many scripters make the mistake of thinking that a new browser window created with the `window.open()` method has a child–parent relationship similar to the one that frames have with their parents. That's not the case at all. New browser windows, when created, have a very slim link to the window from whence they came: via the `opener` property. The purpose of the `opener` property is to provide scripts in the new window with a valid reference back to the original window. For example, the original window may contain some variable values or general-purpose functions that a new window at this web site wants to use. The original window may also have form elements whose settings are of value to the new window or that get set by user interaction in the new window.

Because the value of the `opener` property is a reference to a genuine `window` object, you can begin references with the property name. Or you may use the more complete `window.opener` or `self.opener` reference. But then the reference must include some object or property of that original window, such as a window method or a reference to something contained by that window's document.

If a subwindow opens yet another subwindow, the chain is still valid, albeit one step longer. The third window can reach the main window with a reference that begins

```
opener.opener....
```

It's a good idea for the third window to store in a global variable the value of `opener.opener` while the page loads. Thus, if the user closes the second window, the variable can be used to start a reference to the main window.

When a script that generates a new window is within a frame, the `opener` property of the subwindow points to that frame. Therefore, if the subwindow needs to communicate with the main window's parent or another frame in the main window, you have to very carefully build a reference to that distant object. For example, if the subwindow needs to get the `checked` property of a checkbox in a sister frame of the one that created the subwindow, the reference is

```
opener.parent.sisterFrameName.document.formName.checkboxName.checked
```

It is a long way to go, indeed, but building such a reference is always a case of mapping out the path from where the script is to where the destination is, step by step.

Example

To demonstrate the importance of the `opener` property, take a look at how a new window can define itself from settings in the main window (see Listing 16-11). The `doNew()` function generates a small subwindow and loads the file in Listing 16-12 into the window. Notice the initial conditional statements in `doNew()` to make sure that if the new window already exists, it comes to the front by invoking the new window's `focus()` method. You can see the results in Figure 16-6.

LISTING 16-11

Contents of a Main Window Document That Generates a Second Window

```html
<html>
    <head>
        <title>Master of all Windows</title>
        <script type="text/javascript">
        var myWind;
        function doNew() {
            if (!myWind || myWind.closed) {
                myWind = window.open("lst16-12.htm", "subWindow",
                    "height=200,width=350,resizable");
            } else {
                // bring existing subwindow to the front
                myWind.focus();
            }
        }
        </script>
    </head>
    <body>
        <form name="input">
            Select a color for a new window: <input type="radio" name="color"
            value="red" checked="checked" />Red <input type="radio" name="color"
            value="yellow" />Yellow <input type="radio" name="color"
            value="blue" />Blue <input type="button" name="storage"
            value="Make a Window" onclick="doNew()" />
            <hr />
            This field will be filled from an entry in another window: <input
            type="text" name="entry" size="25" />
        </form>
    </body>
</html>
```

LISTING 16-12

References to the opener Property

```html
<html>
    <head>
        <title>New Window on the Block</title>
        <script type="text/javascript">
        function getColor() {
            // shorten the reference
            colorButtons = self.opener.document.forms[0].color;
```

```
        // see which radio button is checked
        for (var i = 0; i < colorButtons.length; i++) {
            if (colorButtons[i].checked) {
                return colorButtons[i].value;
            }
        }
        return "white";
    }
    </script>
    <script type="text/javascript">
    document.write("<body bgcolor='" + getColor() + "'>")
    </script>
</head>
<body>
    <h1>This is a new window.</h1>
    <form>
        <input type="button" value="Who's in the Main window?"
        onclick="alert(self.opener.document.title)" />
        <p>Type text here for the main window: <input type="text" size="25"
            onchange="self.opener.document.forms[0].entry.value = this.value"
/></p>
    </form>
</body>
</html>
```

In the getColor() function, the multiple references to the radio-button array can be very long. To simplify the references, the getColor() function starts by assigning the radio-button array to a variable I arbitrarily call colorButtons. That shorthand now stands in for lengthy references as I loop through the radio buttons to determine which button is checked and retrieve its value property.

A button in the second window simply fetches the title of the opener window's document. Even if another document loads in the main window in the meantime, the opener reference still points to the main window: Its document object, however, will change.

Finally, the second window contains a text input object. Enter any text there that you like and then either tab or click out of the field. The onchange event handler updates the field in the opener's document (provided that the document is still loaded).

Related Items: window.open(), window.focus() methods

FIGURE 16-6

The main window and subwindows, inextricably linked via the `window.opener` property.

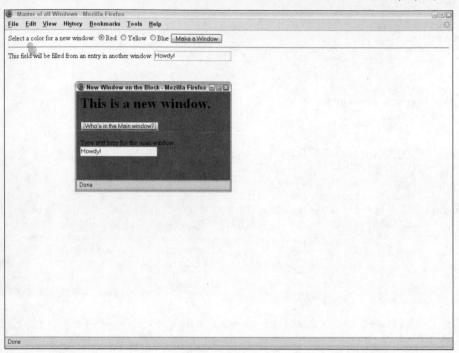

outerHeight
outerWidth

(See `innerHeight` and `innerWidth` earlier in this chapter)

pageXOffset
pageYOffset

Value: Integer   Read-Only
Compatibility: WinIE-, MacIE-, NN4+, Moz+, Safari+

The top-left corner of the content (inner) region of the browser window is an important geographical point for scrolling documents. When a document is scrolled all the way to the top and flush left in the window (or when a document is small enough to fill the browser window without displaying scroll bars), the document's location is said to be 0,0, meaning zero pixels from the top and zero pixels from the left. If you were to scroll the document, some other coordinate point of the document would be under that top-left corner. That measure is called the *page offset*, and the `pageXOffset` and `pageYOffset` properties let you read the pixel value of the document at the inner window's top-left corner: `pageXOffset` is the horizontal offset, and `pageYOffset` is the vertical offset.

The value of these measures becomes clear if you design navigation buttons in your pages to carefully control paging of content being displayed in the window. For example, you might have a two-frame page in which one of the frames features navigation controls and the other displays the primary content. The navigation controls take the place of scroll bars, which, for aesthetic reasons, are turned off in the display frame. Scripts connected to the simulated scrolling buttons can determine the `pageYOffset` value of the document and then use the `window.scrollTo()` method to position the document precisely to the next logical division in the document for viewing.

IE has corresponding values as `body` object properties: `body.scrollLeft` and `body.scrollTop` (see Chapter 18).

Related Items: `window.innerHeight`, `window.innerWidth`, `body.scrollLeft`, `body.scrollTop` properties; `window.scrollBy()`, `window.scrollTo()` methods

parent

Value: Window object reference   Read-Only
Compatibility: WinIE3+, MacIE3+, NN2+, Moz+, Safari+

The `parent` property (and the `top` property, discussed later in this section) comes into play primarily when a document is to be displayed as part of a multiframe window. The HTML documents that users see in the frames of a multiframe browser window are distinct from the document that specifies the frameset for the entire window. That document, though still in the browser's memory (and appearing as the URL in the location field of the browser), is not otherwise visible to the user (except in source view).

If scripts in your visible documents need to reference objects or properties of the frameset window, you can reference those frameset window items with the `parent` property. (Do not, however, expand the reference by preceding it with the `window` object, as in `window.parent.propertyName`, because this causes problems in early browsers.) In a way, the `parent` property seems to violate the object hierarchy because from a single frame's document, the property points to a level seemingly higher in precedence. If you didn't specify the `parent` property or instead specified the `self` property from one of these framed documents, the object reference is to the frame only rather than to the outermost framesetting `window` object.

A nontraditional but perfectly legal way to use the `parent` object is as a means of storing temporary variables. Thus, you could set up a holding area for individual variable values or even an array of data. Then these values can be shared among all documents loaded into the frames, including when documents change inside the frames. You have to be careful, however, when storing data in the parent on the fly (that is, in response to user action in the frames). Variables can revert to their default values (that is, the values set by the parent's own script) if the user resizes the window in early browsers.

A child window can also call a function defined in the parent window. The reference for such a function is

```
parent.functionName([parameters])
```

At first glance, it may seem as though the `parent` and `top` properties point to the same framesetting `window` object. In an environment consisting of one frameset window and its immediate children, that's true. But if one of the child windows was itself another framesetting window, you wind up with three generations of windows. From the point of view of the youngest child (for example, a window defined by the second frameset), the `parent` property points to its immediate parent, whereas the `top` property points to the first framesetting window in this chain.

On the other hand, a new window created via the `window.open()` method has no parent–child relationship to the original window. The new window's `top` and `parent` point to that new window. You can read more about these relationships in the "Frames" section earlier in this chapter.

windowObject.parent

Example

To demonstrate how various `window` object properties refer to window levels in a multiframe environment, use your browser to load the Listing 16-13 document. It in turn sets each of two equal-size frames to the same document: Listing 16-14. This document extracts the values of several window properties, plus the `document.title` properties of two different window references.

LISTING 16-13

Framesetting Document for Listing 16-14

```
<html>
   <head>
      <title>The Parent Property Example</title>
      <script type="text/javascript">
      self.name = "Framesetter";
      </script>
   </head>
   <frameset cols="50%,50%" onunload="self.name = ''">
      <frame name="JustAKid1" src="lst16-14.htm" />
      <frame name="JustAKid2" src="lst16-14.htm" />
   </frameset>
</html>
```

LISTING 16-14

Revealing Various Window-Related Properties

```
<html>
   <head>
      <title>Window Revealer II</title>
      <script type="text/javascript">
      function gatherWindowData() {
         var msg = "";
         msg = msg + "top name: " + top.name + "<br />";
         msg = msg + "parent name: " + parent.name + "<br />";
         msg = msg + "parent.document.title: " + parent.document.title +
            "<br />";
         msg = msg + "window name: " + window.name + "<br />";
         msg = msg + "self name: " + self.name + "<br />";
         msg = msg + "self.document.title: " + self.document.title;
         return msg;
      }
      </script>
   </head>
   <body>
      <script type="text/javascript">
      document.write(gatherWindowData());
```

```
      </script>
    </body>
</html>
```

In the two frames (see Figure 16-7), the references to the `window` and `self` object names return the name assigned to the frame by the frameset definition (`JustAKid1` for the left frame, `JustAKid2` for the right frame). In other words, from each frame's point of view, the `window` object is its own frame. References to `self.document.title` refer only to the document loaded into that window frame. But references to the top and parent windows (which are one and the same in this example) show that those object properties are shared between both frames.

Parent and top properties being shared by both frames.

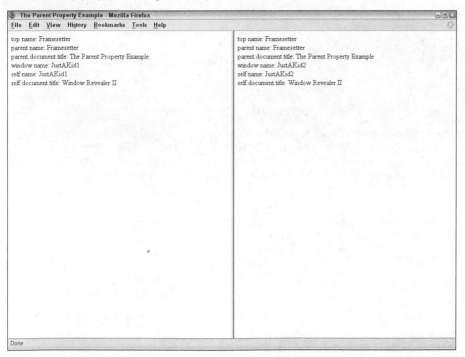

A couple of other fine points are worth highlighting. First, the name of the framesetting window is set as Listing 16-13 loads, rather than in response to an `onload` event handler in the `<frameset>` tag. The reason for this is that the name must be set in time for the documents loading in the frames to get that value. If I had waited until the frameset's `onload` event handler, the name wouldn't be set until after the frame documents had loaded. Second, I restore the parent window's name to an empty string when the framesetting document unloads. This is to prevent future pages from getting confused about the window name.

Related Items: `window.frames`, `window.self`, `window.top` properties

personalbar

(See directories)

returnValue

Value: Any data type   Read/Write
Compatibility: WinIE4+, MacIE5+, NN-, Moz-, Safari-

Scripts use the returnValue property in a document that loads into the IE-specific modal dialog box. A modal dialog box is generated via the showModalDialog() method, which returns whatever data has been assigned to the returnValue property of the dialog-box window before it closes. This is possible because script processing in the main window freezes while the modal dialog box is visible. As the dialog box closes, a value can be returned to the main window's script right where the modal dialog box was invoked, and the main window's script resumes executing statements.

Example

See Listing 16-36 for the showModalDialog() method for an example of how to get data back from a dialog box in IE.

Related Item: showModalDialog() method

screen

Value: screen object   Read-Only
Compatibility: WinIE4+, MacIE4+, NN6+, Moz+, Safari+

Although the screen object appears as a property of the window object in modern browsers, the screen object is also available in NN4 (see Chapter 39 on the CD-ROM), but as a stand-alone object. Because you can omit any reference to the window object for a window object's properties, the same windowless reference syntax can be used for compatibility with legacy browsers that support the screen object.

Example

See Chapter 39 on the CD-ROM for examples of using the screen object to determine the video-monitor characteristics of the computer running the browser.

Related Item: screen object

screenLeft
screenTop

Value: Integer   Read-Only
Compatibility: WinIE5+, MacIE-, NN-, Moz-, Safari 1.2+

WinIE5+ provides the screenLeft and screenTop properties of the window object to let you read the pixel position (relative to the top-left 0,0 coordinate of the video monitor) of what Microsoft calls the *client area* of the browser window. The client area excludes most window chrome, such as the title bar, address bar, and the window-sizing bar. Therefore, when the WinIE5+ browser window is maximized (meaning that no sizing bars are exposed), the screenLeft property of the window is 0, whereas the screenTop property varies depending on the combination of toolbars the user has elected to display. For nonmaximized windows, if the window has been positioned so that the top and/or left parts of the client area are out of view, their property values will be negative integers.

These two properties are read-only. You can position the browser window via the `window.moveTo()` and `window.moveBy()` methods, but these methods position the top-left corner of the entire browser window, not the client area. IE browsers through version 7 do not provide properties for the position of the entire browser window.

Example

Use The Evaluator (Chapter 13) to experiment with the `screenLeft` and `screenTop` properties. Start with the browser window maximized (if you are using Windows). Enter the following property name in the top text box:

```
window.screenLeft
```

Click the Evaluate button to see the current setting. Unmaximize the window, and drag it around the screen. Each time you finish dragging, click the Evaluate button again to see the current value. Do the same for `window.screenTop`.

Related Items: `window.moveTo()`, `window.moveBy()` methods

screenX
screenY

Value: Integer   Read/Write
Compatibility: WinIE-, MacIE-, NN6+, Moz+, Safari 1.2+

NN6+/Moz/Safari provide the `screenX` and `screenY` properties to read the position of the outer boundary of the browser window relative to the top-left coordinates (0,0) of the video monitor. The browser window includes the 4-pixels-wide window-sizing bars that surround Win32 windows. Therefore, when the WinNN6+ browser window is maximized, the value for both `screenX` and `screenY` is -4. NN/Moz/W3C do not provide the equivalent measures of the browser window client area as found in the `screenLeft` and `screenTop` properties of IE5+. You can, however, find out whether various toolbars are visible in the browser window (see `window.directories`).

Although you can assign a value to either property, current versions of supporting browsers do not adjust the window position in response if the user has set the preference that prevents window movement and resizing. Moving and resizing windows by script is considered by many web surfers to be unacceptable behavior.

Example

Use The Evaluator (Chapter 13) to experiment with the `screenX` and `screenY` properties. Start with the browser window maximized (if you are using Windows). Enter the following property name in the top text box:

```
window.screenY
```

Click the Evaluate button to see the current setting. Unmaximize the window, and drag it around the screen. Each time you finish dragging, click the Evaluate button again to see the current value. Do the same for `window.screenY`.

Related Items: `window.moveTo()`, `window.moveBy()` methods

scrollbars

(See directories)

scrollMaxX
scrollMaxY

Value: Integer   Read/Write
Compatibility: WinIE-, MacIE-, NN7.1+, Moz1.4+, Safari-

The NN7.1+/Moz1.4+ scrollMaxX and scrollMaxY properties let you determine the maximum horizontal and vertical scrolling extents of a window. Scrolling is possible only if the window displays scroll bars along the desired axis. Values are pixel integers.

Related Items: scrollX, scrollY properties

scrollX
scrollY

Value: Integer   Read-Only
Compatibility: WinIE-, MacIE-, NN6+, Moz+, Safari+

The NN6+/Mozilla/Safari scrollX and scrollY properties let you determine the horizontal and vertical scrolling of a window. Scrolling is possible only if the window displays scroll bars along the desired axis. Values are pixel integers.

Although the IE DOM does not provide similar properties for the window, the same information can be derived from the body.scrollLeft and body.scrollTop properties.

Example

Use The Evaluator (Chapter 13) to experiment with the scrollX and scrollY properties. Enter the following property in the top text box:

```
window.scrollY
```

Now manually scroll the page down so that you can still see the Evaluate button. Click the button to see how far the window has scrolled along the y-axis.

Related Items: body.scrollLeft, body.scrollTop properties

self

Value: Window object reference   Read-Only
Compatibility: WinIE3+, MacIE3+, NN2+, Moz+, Safari+

Just as the window object reference is optional, so is the self property when the object reference points to the same window as the one containing the reference. In what may seem to be an unusual construction, the self property represents the same object as the window. For instance, to obtain the title of the document in a single-frame window, you can use any of the following three constructions:

```
window.document.title
self.document.title
document.title
```

Although self is a property of a window, you should not combine the references within a single-frame window script (for example, don't begin a reference with window.self, which has been known to cause numerous scripting problems). Specifying the self property, though optional for single-frame windows, can help make an object reference crystal clear to someone reading your code (and to you, for that matter). Multiple-frame windows are where you need to pay particular attention to this property.

JavaScript is pretty smart about references to a statement's own window. Therefore, you can generally omit the self part of a reference to a same-window document element. But when you intend to display a document in a multiframe window, complete references (including the self prefix) to an object make it much easier on anyone who reads or debugs your code to track who is doing what to whom. You are free to retrieve the self property of any window. The value that comes back is a window object reference.

Example

Listing 16-15 uses the same operations as Listing 16-5 but substitutes the self property for all window object references. The application of this reference is entirely optional, but it can be helpful for reading and debugging scripts if the HTML document is to appear in one frame of a multiframe window — especially if other JavaScript code in this document refers to documents in other frames. The self reference helps anyone reading the code know precisely which frame was being addressed.

LISTING 16-15

Using the self Property

```
<html>
    <head>
        <title>self Property</title>
        <script type="text/javascript">
        self.defaultStatus = "Welcome to my Web site.";
        </script>
    </head>
    <body>
        <a href="http://www.microsoft.com"
        onmouseover="self.status = 'Visit Microsoft\'s Home page.';return true;"
        onmouseout="self.status = '';return true;">Microsoft</a>
        <p><a href="http://mozilla.org"
            onmouseover="self.status = 'Visit Mozilla\'s Home page.';return
                true;"
            onmouseout="self.status = self.defaultStatus;return
                true;">Mozilla</a></p>
    </body>
</html>
```

Related Items: window.frames, window.parent, window.top properties

sidebar

(See appCore)

status

Value: String   Read/Write
Compatibility: WinIE3+, MacIE3+, NN2+, Moz+, Safari+

At the bottom of the browser window is a status bar. Part of that bar includes an area that normally dis-
closes the document loading progress or the URL of a link that the mouse is pointing to at any given
instant. You can control the temporary content of that field by assigning a text string to the window object's
status property. You should adjust the status property only in response to events that have a temporary
effect, such as a link or image map area object's onmouseover event handler. When the status property is
set in this situation, it overrides any other setting in the status bar. If the user then moves the mouse pointer
away from the object that changes the status bar, the bar returns to its default setting (which may be empty
on some pages). To prevent link spoofing, however, not all modern browsers display scripted status-bar text
associated with links.

Use this window property as a friendlier alternative to displaying the URL of a link as a user rolls the mouse
around the page. For example, if you'd rather use the status bar to explain the nature of the destination of a
link, put that text into the status bar in response to the onmouseover event handler. But be aware that
experienced web surfers like to see URLs down there. Therefore, consider creating a hybrid message for the
status bar that includes a friendly description followed by the URL in parentheses. In multiframe environments, you can set the window.status property without having to worry about referencing the individual
frame.

Example

In Listing 16-16, the status property is set in a handler embedded in the onmouseover attribute of two
HTML link tags. Notice that the handler requires a return true statement (or any expression that evaluates to return true) as the last statement of the handler. This statement is required; otherwise, the status
message will not display in all browsers.

LISTING 16-16

Links with Custom Status-Bar Messages

```
<html>
   <head>
      <title>window.status Property</title>
   </head>
   <body>
      <a href="http://www.dannyg.com"
      onmouseover="window.status = 'Go to my Home page. (www.dannyg.com)';
      return true;">Home</a>
      <p><a href="http://mozilla.org"
      onmouseover="window.status = 'Visit Mozilla Home page. (mozilla.org)';
      return true;">Mozilla</a></p>
   </body>
</html>
```

As a safeguard against platform-specific anomalies that affect the behavior of onmouseover event handlers and the window.status property, you should also include an onmouseout event handler for links and client-side image map area objects. Such onmouseout event handlers should set the status property to an empty string. This setting ensures that the status-bar message returns to the defaultStatus setting when the pointer rolls away from these objects. If you want to write a generalizable function that handles all window status changes, you can do so, but word the onmouseover attribute carefully so that the event handler evaluates to return true. Listing 16-17 shows such an alternative.

LISTING 16-17

Handling Status Message Changes

```
<html>
    <head>
        <title>Generalizable window.status Property</title>
        <script type="text/javascript">
        function showStatus(msg) {
            window.status = msg;
            return true;
        }
        </script>
    </head>
    <body>
        <a href="http://www.example.com"
        onmouseover="return showStatus('Go to my Home page.')"
        onmouseout="return showStatus('')">Home</a>
        <p><a href="http://mozilla.org"
        onmouseover="return showStatus('Visit Mozilla Home page.')"
        onmouseout="return showStatus('')">Mozilla</a></p>
    </body>
</html>
```

Notice how the event handlers return the results of the showStatus() method to the event handler, allowing the entire handler to evaluate to return true.

One final example of setting the status bar (shown in Listing 16-18) also demonstrates how to create a simple scrolling banner in the status bar.

LISTING 16-18

Creating a Scrolling Banner

```
<html>
    <head>
        <title>Message Scroller</title>
        <script type="text/javascript">
        var msg = "Welcome to my world...";
        var delay = 150;
```

continued

413

LISTING 16-18 *(continued)*

```
    var timerId;
    var maxCount = 0;
    var currCount = 1;

    function scrollMsg() {
        // set the number of times scrolling message is to run
        if (maxCount == 0) {
            maxCount = 3 * msg.length;
        }
        window.status = msg;
        // keep track of how many characters have scrolled
        currCount++;
        // shift first character of msg to end of msg
        msg = msg.substring (1, msg.length) + msg.substring (0, 1);
        // test whether we've reached maximum character count
        if (currCount >= maxCount) {
            timerID = 0;    // zero out the timer
            window.status = "";    // clear the status bar
            return;    // break out of function
        } else {
            // recursive call to this function
            timerId = setTimeout("scrollMsg()", delay);
        }
    }
    </script>
</head>
<body onload="scrollMsg()">
</body>
</html>
```

Because the status bar is being set by a stand-alone function (rather than by an onmouseover event handler), you do not have to append a return true statement to set the status property. The scrollMsg() function uses more advanced JavaScript concepts, such as the window.setTimeout() method (covered later in this chapter) and string methods (covered in Chapter 28). To speed the pace at which the words scroll across the status bar, reduce the value of delay.

Many web surfers (me included) don't care for these scrollers that run forever in the status bar. Rolling the mouse over links disturbs the banner display. Use scrolling bars sparingly or design them to run only a few times after the document loads.

TIP   Setting the status property with onmouseover event handlers has had a checkered career along various implementations in Navigator. A script that sets the status bar is always in competition against the browser itself, which uses the status bar to report loading progress. When a hot area on a page is at the edge of a frame, many times the onmouseout event fails to fire, preventing the status bar from clearing itself. Be sure to torture-test any such implementations before declaring your page ready for public access.

Related Items: window.defaultStatus property; onmouseover, onmouseout event handlers; link object

```
statusbar
toolbar
```
(See `locationbar`)

```
top
```
Value: Window object reference   Read-Only
Compatibility: WinIE3+, MacIE3+, NN2+, Moz+, Safari+

The `window` object's `top` property refers to the topmost window in a frameset object hierarchy. For a single-frame window, the reference is to the same object as the window itself (including the `self` and `parent` properties), so do not include `window` as part of the reference. In a multiframe window, the top window is the one that defines the first frameset (in case of nested framesets). Users don't ever really see the top window in a multiframe environment, but the browser stores it as an object in its memory. The reason is that the top window has the road map to the other frames (if one frame should need to reference an object in a different frame), and its children frames can call upon it. Such a reference looks like this"

> `top.functionName([parameters])`

For more about the distinction between the `top` and `parent` properties, see the in-depth discussion about scripting frames at the beginning of this chapter. See also the example of the `parent` property for listings that demonstrate the values of the `top` property.

Related Items: `window.frames`, `window.self`, `window.parent` properties

```
window
```
Value: Window object   Read-Only
Compatibility: WinIE3+, MacIE3+, NN2+, Moz+, Safari+

Listing the `window` property as a separate property may be more confusing than helpful. The `window` property is the same object as the `window` object. You do not need to use a reference that begins with `window.window`. Although the `window` object is assumed for many references, you can use `window` as part of a reference to items in the same window or frame as the script statement that makes that reference. You should not, however, use `window` as a part of a reference involving items higher up in the hierarchy (`top` or `parent`).

Methods
```
alert("message")
```
Returns: Nothing
Compatibility: WinIE3+, MacIE3+, NN2+, Moz+, Safari+

An *alert dialog box* is a modal window that presents a message to the user with a single OK button to dismiss the dialog box. As long as the alert dialog box is showing, no other application or window can be made active. The user must dismiss the dialog box before proceeding with any more work in the browser.

The single parameter to the `alert()` method can be a value of any data type, including representations of some unusual data types whose values you don't normally work with in JavaScript (such as complete objects). This makes the alert dialog box a handy tool for debugging JavaScript scripts. Any time you want to monitor the value of an expression, use that expression as the parameter to a temporary `alert()` method in your code. The script proceeds to that point and then stops to show you the value. (See Chapter 45 on the CD-ROM for more tips on debugging scripts.)

windowObject.alert()

What is often disturbing to application designers is that all JavaScript-created modal dialog boxes (via the `alert()`, `confirm()`, and `prompt()` methods) identify themselves as being generated by JavaScript or the browser. The purpose of this identification is to act as a security precaution against unscrupulous scripters who might try to spoof system or browser alert dialog boxes, inviting a user to reveal passwords or other private information. These identifying words cannot be overwritten or eliminated by your scripts. You can simulate a modal dialog-box window in a cross-browser fashion with regular browser windows, but it is not as robust as a genuine modal window, which you can create in IE4+ via the `window.showModalDialog()` method.

Because the `alert()` method is of a global nature (that is, no particular frame in a multiframe environment derives any benefit from laying claim to the alert dialog box), a common practice is to omit all `window` object references from the statement that calls the method. Restrict the use of alert dialog boxes in your HTML documents and site designs. The modality of the windows is disruptive to the flow of a user's navigation around your pages. Communicate with users via forms or by writing to separate document window frames. Of course, alert boxes can still be very handy as a quick debugging aid.

Example

The parameter for the example in Listing 16-19 is a concatenated string. It joins two fixed strings and the value of the browser's `navigator.appName` property. Loading this document causes the alert dialog box to appear, as shown in several configurations in Figure 16-8. The JavaScript Alert: line cannot be deleted from the dialog box in earlier browsers; neither can the title bar be changed in later browsers.

LISTING 16-19

Displaying an Alert Dialog Box

```
<html>
   <head>
      <title>window.alert() Method</title>
   </head>
   <body>
      <script type="text/javascript">
      alert("You are running the " + navigator.appName + " browser.")
      </script>
   </body>
</html>
```

FIGURE 16-8

Results of the alert() method in Listing 16-19 in Firefox and Internet Explorer.

Related Items: window.confirm(), window.prompt() methods

back()
forward()

Returns: Nothing
Compatibility: WinIE-, MacIE-, NN4+, Moz+, Safari-

The purpose of the window.back() and window.forward() methods that began in NN4 is to offer a scripted version of the global back and forward navigation buttons while allowing the history object to control navigation strictly within a particular window or frame — as it should. These window methods did not catch on in IE (and the window object is out of the scope of the W3C DOM Level 2), so you are better off staying with the history object's methods for navigating browser history. For more information about version compatibility and about back and forward navigation, see the history object in Chapter 17.

Related Items: history.back(), history.forward(), history.go() methods

clearInterval(*intervalIDnumber*)

Returns: Nothing
Compatibility: WinIE4+, MacIE4+, NN4+, Moz+, Safari+

Use the window.clearInterval() method to turn off an interval loop action started with the window.setInterval() method. The parameter is the ID number returned by the setInterval() method. A common application for the JavaScript interval mechanism is animation of an object on a page. If you have multiple intervals running, each has its own ID value in memory. You can turn off any interval by its ID value. As soon as an interval loop stops, your script cannot resume that interval: It must start a new one, which generates a new ID value.

Example

See Listing 16-33 and Listing 16-34 later in this chapter for an example of how setInterval() and clearInterval() are used together on a page.

Related Items: window.setInterval(), window.setTimeout(), window.clearTimeout() methods

417

clearTimeout(*timeoutIDnumber*)

Returns: Nothing
Compatibility: WinIE3+, MacIE3+, NN2+, Moz+, Safari+

Use the window.clearTimeout() method in concert with the window.setTimeout() method, as described later in this chapter, when you want your script to cancel a timer that is waiting to run its expression. The parameter for this method is the ID number that the window.setTimeout() method returns when the timer starts ticking. The clearTimeout() method cancels the specified timeout. A good practice is to check your code for instances where user action may negate the need for a running timer — and to stop that timer before it goes off.

Example

The page in Listing 16-20 features one text box and two buttons (see Figure 16-9). One button starts a countdown timer coded to last 1 minute (easily modifiable for other durations); the other button interrupts the timer at any time while it is running. When the minute is up, an alert dialog box lets you know.

LISTING 16-20

A Countdown Timer

```
<html>
  <head>
    <title>Count Down Timer</title>
    <script type="text/javascript">
    var running = false;
    var endTime = null;
    var timerID = null;

    function startTimer() {
      running = true;
      now = new Date();
      now = now.getTime();
      // change last multiple for the number of minutes
      endTime = now + (1000 * 60 * 1);
      showCountDown();
    }

    function showCountDown() {
      var now = new Date();
      now = now.getTime();
      if (endTime - now <= 0) {
        stopTimer();
        alert("Time is up.  Put down your pencils.");
      } else {
        var delta = new Date(endTime - now);
        var theMin = delta.getMinutes();
        var theSec = delta.getSeconds();
        var theTime = theMin;
        theTime += ((theSec < 10) ? ":0" : ":") + theSec;
        document.forms[0].timerDisplay.value = theTime;
        if (running) {
          timerID = setTimeout("showCountDown()",1000);
        }
```

```
            }
        }

        function stopTimer() {
            clearTimeout(timerID);
            running = false;
            document.forms[0].timerDisplay.value = "0:00";
        }
    </script>
</head>
<body>
    <form>
        <input type="button" name="startTime" value="Start 1 min. Timer"
        onclick="startTimer()" /> <input type="button" name="clearTime"
        value="Clear Timer" onclick="stopTimer()" />
        <p><input type="text" name="timerDisplay" value="" /></p>
    </form>
</body>
</html>
```

Notice that the script establishes three variables with global scope in the window: `running`, `endTime`, and `timerID`. These values are needed inside multiple functions, so they are initialized outside the functions.

FIGURE 16-9

The countdown timer page as it displays the time remaining.

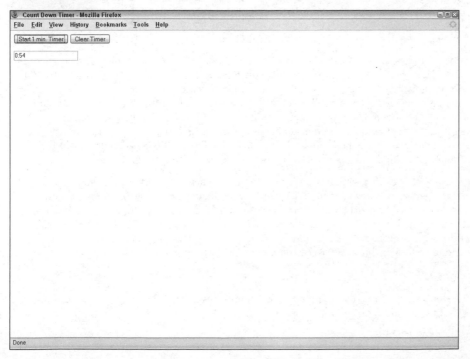

In the startTimer() function, you switch the running flag on, meaning that the timer should be going. Using some date functions (see Chapter 30), you extract the current time in milliseconds and add the number of milliseconds for the next minute (the extra multiplication by 1 is the place where you can change the amount to the desired number of minutes). With the end time stored in a global variable, the function now calls another function that compares the current and end times and displays the difference in the text box.

Early in the showCountDown() function, check to see whether the timer has wound down. If so, you stop the timer and alert the user. Otherwise, the function continues to calculate the difference between the two times and formats the time in mm:ss format. As long as the running flag is set to true, the function sets the 1-second timeout timer before repeating itself. To stop the timer before it has run out (in the stopTimer() function), the most important step is to cancel the timeout running inside the browser. The clearTimeout() method uses the global timerID value to do that. Then the function turns off the running switch and zeros out the display.

When you run the timer, you may occasionally notice that the time skips a second. It's not cheating. It just takes slightly more than 1 second to wait for the timeout and then finish the calculations for the next second's display. What you're seeing is the display catching up with the real time left.

Related Item: window.setTimeout() method

close()
Returns: Nothing
Compatibility: WinIE3+, MacIE3+, NN2+, Moz+, Safari+

The window.close() method closes the browser window referenced by the window object. Most likely, you will use this method to close subwindows created from a main document window. If the call to close the window comes from a window other than the new subwindow, the original window object must maintain a record of the subwindow object. You accomplish this by storing the value returned from the window.open() method in a global variable that will be available to other objects later (for example, a variable not initialized inside a function). If, on the other hand, an object inside the new subwindow calls the window.close() method, the window or self reference is sufficient.

Be sure to include a window as part of the reference to this method. Failure to do so may cause JavaScript to regard the statement as a document.close() method, which has different behavior (see Chapter 18). Only the window.close() method can close the window via a script. Closing a window, of course, forces the window to trigger an onunload event handler before the window disappears from view, but after you've initiated the window.close() method, you cannot stop it from completing its task. Moreover, onunload event handlers that attempt to execute time-consuming processes (such as submitting a form in the closing window) may not complete because the window can easily close before the process completes — a behavior that has no workaround (with the exception of the onbeforeunload event handler in IE4+).

While I'm on the subject of closing windows, a special case exists when a subwindow tries to close the main window (via a statement such as self.opener.close()) when the main window has more than one entry in its session history. As a safety precaution against scripts closing windows they did not create, modern browsers ask the user whether he or she wants the main window to close (via a browser-generated dialog box). This security precaution cannot be overridden except in NN4+/Moz via a signed script when the user grants permission to control the browser (see Chapter 46 on the CD-ROM).

Example
See Listing 16-4 (for the window.closed property), which provides a cross-platform example of applying the window.close() method across multiple windows.

Related Items: window.open(), document.close() methods

confirm("*message*")

Returns: Boolean
Compatibility: WinIE3+, MacIE3+, NN2+, Moz+, Safari+

A confirm dialog box presents a message in a modal dialog box along with OK and Cancel buttons. Such a dialog box can be used to ask a question of the user, usually prior to a script's performing actions that will not be undoable. Querying a user about proceeding with typical web navigation in response to user interaction on a form element is generally a disruptive waste of the user's time and attention. But for operations that may reveal a user's identity or send form data to a server, a JavaScript confirm dialog box may make a great deal of sense. Users can also accidentally click buttons, so you should provide avenues for backing out of an operation before it executes.

Because this dialog box returns a Boolean value (OK = `true`; Cancel = `false`), you can use this method as a comparison expression or as an assignment expression. In a comparison expression, you nest the method within any other statement where a Boolean value is required. For example:

```
if (confirm("Are you sure?")) {
    alert("OK");
} else {
    alert("Not OK");
}
```

Here, the returned value of the confirm dialog box provides the desired Boolean value type for the `if...else` construction (see Chapter 32).

This method can also appear on the right side of an assignment expression, as in:

```
var adult = confirm("You certify that you are over 18 years old?");
if (adult) {
    //statements for adults
} else {
    //statements for children
}
```

You cannot specify other alert icons or labels for the two buttons in JavaScript confirm dialog-box windows.

The example in Listing 16-21 shows the user interface part of how you can use a confirm dialog box to query a user before clearing a table full of user-entered data. The line in the title bar, as shown in Figure 16-10, cannot be removed from the dialog box.

LISTING 16-21

The Confirm Dialog Box

```
<html>
  <head>
    <title>window.confirm() Method</title>
    <script type="text/javascript">
    function clearTable() {
        if (confirm("Are you sure you want to empty the table?")) {
            alert("Emptying the table...");   // for demo purposes
            //statements that actually empty the fields
```

continued

LISTING 16-21 *(continued)*

```
                }
        }
        </script>
    </head>
    <body>
        <form>
            <!-- other statements that display and populate a large table -->
            <input type="button" name="clear" value="Reset Table"
            onclick="clearTable()" />
        </form>
    </body>
</html>
```

FIGURE 16-10

A JavaScript confirm dialog box in Internet Explorer.

Related Items: `window.alert()`, `window.prompt()`, `form.submit()` methods

createPopup()

Returns: Pop-up object reference
Compatibility: WinIE5.5+, MacIE-, NN-, Moz-, Safari-

An IE pop-up window is a chromeless rectangular space that overlaps the current window. Unlike the dialog boxes generated by the `showModalDialog()` and `showModelessDialog()` methods, the pop-up window's entire content must be explicitly controlled by script. That also goes for the size and location of the window. Generating the window via the `createPopup()` method simply creates the object in memory without displaying it. You can then use the reference to the pop-up window that is returned by the method to position the window, populate its content, and make it visible. See details in the description of the `popup` object later in this chapter.

Example

See Listing 16-46 later in this chapter for an example of the `createPopup()` method.

Related Item: `popup` object

dump("*message*")

Returns: Nothing
Compatibility: WinIE-, MacIE-, NN7.1+, Moz1.4+, Safari-

The window.dump() method is a debugging/diagnostic method that you can use to output a string of text to *standard output,* which is typically the operating system's console window. The dump() method provides a less intrusive alternative to displaying debugging messages via the alert() method.

execScript("*exprList*"[, *language*])

Returns: Nothing
Compatibility: WinIE4+, MacIE4+, NN-, Moz-, Safari-

The IE-specific window.execScript() method executes one or more script statements that are passed as string expressions. The first parameter is a string version of one or more script statements (multiple statements must be separated by semicolons). The second, optional parameter is the language interpreter the browser should use to execute the script statement. Acceptable values for the language are JavaScript, JScript, VBS, and VBScript. The default value is JScript, so you can omit the second parameter when supplying expressions in JavaScript.

Unlike the JavaScript core language eval() function (which also executes string versions of JavaScript statements), the execScript() method returns no values. Even so, the method operates within the global variable space of the window holding the current document. For example, if a document's script declares a global variable as follows

```
var myVar;
```

the execScript() method can read or write to that variable:

```
window.execScript("myVar = 10; myVar += 5");
```

After this statement runs, the global variable myVar has a value of 15.

Example

Use The Evaluator (Chapter 13) to experiment with the execScript() method. The Evaluator has predeclared global variables for the lowercase letters *a* through *z*. Enter each of the following statements in the top text box, and observe the results for each.

```
a
```

When first loaded, the variable is declared but assigned no value, so it is undefined:

```
window.execScript("a = 5")
```

The method returns no value, so the mechanism inside The Evaluator says that the statement is undefined:

```
a
```

The variable is now 5.

```
window.execScript("b = a * 50")
b
```

The b global variable has a value of 250. Continue exploring with additional script statements. Use semicolons to separate multiple statements within the string parameter.

Related Item: eval() function

find(["*searchString*" [, *matchCaseBoolean*, *searchUpBoolean*]])

Returns: Boolean value for non-dialog-box searches
Compatibility: WinIE-, MacIE-, NN4+, Moz1.0.1+, Safari-

The `window.find()` method introduced in NN4 mimics the powers of the browser's Find dialog box, accessible from the Find button in the toolbar. This method was deactivated in NN6 but reactivated in NN7/Moz1.0.1.

If you specify no parameters, the browser's Find dialog box appears, just as though the user had clicked the Find button in the toolbar. With no parameters, this function does not return a value.

You can specify a search string as a parameter to the function. The search is based on simple string matching and is not in any way connected with the regular-expression kind of search (see Chapter 42 on the CD-ROM). If the search finds a match, the browser scrolls to that matching word and highlights the word, just as though it were using the browser's own Find dialog box. The function also returns a Boolean `true` after a match is found. If no match is found in the document, or no more matches occur in the current search direction (the default direction is from top to bottom), the function returns `false`.

Two optional Boolean parameters to the scripted find action let you specify whether the search should be case sensitive and whether the search direction should be upward from the bottom of the document. These choices are identical to the ones that appear in the NN4+'s Find dialog box. Default behavior is case insensitive and searches from top to bottom.

Some modern browsers such as Firefox have evolved to forego the Find dialog box in favor of an integrated find feature that appears at the bottom of the browser window. This approach to find can be applied to the entire page at the same time, in which case all of the text matches are highlighted.

IE4+ also has a scripted text search facility, but it is implemented in an entirely different way (using the `TextRange` object described in Chapter 36 on the CD-ROM). The visual behavior also differs in that it does not highlight and scroll to a matching string in the text.

Example

A simple call to the `window.find()` method looks as follows:

```
var success = window.find("contract");
```

And if you want the search to be case sensitive, add at least one of the two optional parameters:

```
success = window.find(matchString,caseSensitive,backward);
```

In many ways, the `window.find()` method is a remnant of NN4. Refer to discussions of the `TextRange` and `Range` objects in Chapter 36 on the CD-ROM for more modern implementations of body-text searching.

Related Items: `TextRange`, `Range` objects (Chapter 36 on the CD-ROM)

forward()

(See `window.back()`)

geckoActiveXObject("*progID*")

Returns: WMP control object
Compatibility: WinIE-, MacIE-, NN7.1+, Moz1.4+, Safari-

One interesting result of the NN/IE browser wars is Microsoft's victory in establishing Windows Media Player as the PC media player of choice. Because WMP is implemented as an ActiveX control, NN/Moz browsers were somewhat left out in the cold in terms of scriptability. The window.geckoActiveXObject() method was added to Moz1.4 browsers to give them the capability of accessing WMP as an ActiveX control. Although the name of the method suggests generic support for ActiveX controls, it currently enables you to open only the WMP control.

The only parameter to geckoActiveXObject() is a programmatic ID, which for WMP is currently MediaPlayer.MediaPlayer.1. So to grab a WMP control reference for media playback using the geckoActiveXObject() method, use code such as this:

```
var player = new GeckoActiveXObject("MediaPlayer.MediaPlayer.1");
```

getComputedStyle(elementNodeRef, "pseudoElementName")

Returns: CSS style object
Compatibility: WinIE-, MacIE-, NN-, Moz+, Safari-

The window.getComputedStyle() method enables you to access the cascading style sheet (CSS) style object associated with a given element. You specify an element node reference as the first parameter to the method, along with the optional name of a specific pseudoelement to which the style applies. I say *optional* because you can pass an empty string as the second parameter to obtain a style object with no pseudoelement implications.

Although the getComputedStyle() method is defined (and works) for the window object, the W3C DOM prefers document.defaultView.getComputedStyle() as the standard means of accessing a style object for an element. It's the same method ultimately being called; the access of it is what differs.

getSelection()

Returns: Selection object
Compatibility: WinIE-, MacIE-, NN6+, Moz+, Safari+

This method takes the place of the deprecated method of the same name that appeared in the document object. The method offers a scripted way of capturing the text selected by a user in a page, which is a common task involving the selection and copying of body text in a document for pasting into other application documents. The window.getSelection() method returns the string of text selected by the user. If nothing is selected, an empty string is the result. Returned values consist only of the visible text on the page and not the underlying HTML or style of the text.

The WinIE4+ equivalent involves the document.selection property, which returns an IE selection object. To derive the text from this object, you must create a TextRange object from it and then inspect the text property:

```
var selectedText = document.selection.createRange().text;
```

windowObject.getSelection()

Example

The document in Listing 16-22 provides a cross-browser (but not MacIE5) solution to capturing text that a user selects in the page. Selected text is displayed in the text area. The script uses browser detection and branching to account for the differences in event handling between Mozilla and Internet Explorer.

LISTING 16-22

Retrieving Selected Text

```
<html>
    <head>
        <title>Getting Selected Text</title>
        <script type="text/javascript">
        document.onmouseup = showSelection;

        function showSelection() {
            if (window.getSelection) {
                document.forms[0].selectedText.value = window.getSelection();
            } else if (document.selection) {
                document.forms[0].selectedText.value =
                    document.selection.createRange().text;
                event.cancelBubble = true;
            }
        }
        </script>
    </head>
    <body>
        <h1>Getting Selected Text</h1>
        <hr />
        <p>Select some text and see how JavaScript can capture the selection:</p>
        <h2>ARTICLE I</h2>
        <p>Congress shall make no law respecting an establishment of religion, or
            prohibiting the free exercise thereof; or abridging the freedom of
            speech, or of the press; or the right of the people peaceably to
            assemble, and to petition the government for a redress of grievances.</p>
        <form>
            <textarea name="selectedText" rows="3" cols="40" wrap="virtual">
            </textarea>
        </form>
    </body>
</html>
```

Related Item: document.selection property

home()

Returns: Nothing
Compatibility: WinIE-, MacIE-, NN4+, Moz+, Safari-

Like many of the window methods originally introduced in Navigator 4, the `window.home()` method provides an NN-specific scripted way of replicating the action of a toolbar button: the Home button. The action navigates the browser to whatever URL is set in the browser preferences for home-page location. You cannot control the default home page of a visitor's browser.

Related Items: `window.back()`, `window.forward()` methods; `window.toolbar` property

moveBy(*deltaX, deltaY*)
moveTo(*x, y*)

Returns: Nothing
Compatibility: WinIE4+, MacIE4+, NN4+, Moz+, Safari+

Version 4 browsers introduced the capability of allowing JavaScript to adjust the location of a browser window onscreen. This applies to the main window or any subwindow generated by script. NN/Moz regard the possibility of a window moved out of screen view as a potential security hole, so signed scripts are needed in NN4+/Moz to move a window offscreen.

You can move a window to an absolute position onscreen or adjust it along the horizontal and/or vertical axis by any number of pixels, irrespective of the absolute pixel position. The coordinate space for the *x* (horizontal) and *y* (vertical) position is the entire screen, with the top-left corner representing 0,0. The point of the window you set with the `moveBy()` and `moveTo()` methods is the top-left corner of the outer edge of the browser window. Therefore, when you move the window to point 0,0, that sets the window flush with the top-left corner of the screen. This may not be the equivalent of a truly maximized window for all browsers and operating systems, however, because a maximized window's coordinates may be negative by a handful of pixels.

The difference between the `moveTo()` and `moveBy()` methods is that one is an absolute move, whereas the other is relative with respect to the current window position. Parameters you specify for `moveTo()` are the precise horizontal and vertical pixel counts onscreen where you want the top-left corner of the window to appear. By contrast, the parameters for `moveBy()` indicate how far to adjust the window location in either direction. If you want to move the window 25 pixels to the right, you must still include both parameters, but the *y* value will be zero:

```
window.moveBy(25,0);
```

To move to the left, the first parameter must be a negative number.

Example

Several examples of using the `window.moveTo()` and `window.moveBy()` methods are shown in Listing 16-23. The page presents four buttons, each of which performs a different kind of browser-window movement.

LISTING 16-23

Window Boogie

```html
<html>
    <head>
        <title>Window Gymnastics</title>
        <script type="text/javascript">
        // wait in onload for page to load and settle in IE
        function init() {
            // fill missing IE properties
            if (!window.outerWidth) {
                window.outerWidth = document.body.clientWidth;
                window.outerHeight = document.body.clientHeight + 30;
            }
        }

        // function to run when window captures a click event
        function moveOffScreen() {
            // branch for NN security
            if (window.netscape) {
                netscape.security.PrivilegeManager.enablePrivilege(
                    "UniversalBrowserWrite");
            }
            var maxX = screen.width;
            var maxY = screen.height;
            window.moveTo(maxX+1, maxY+1);
            setTimeout("window.moveTo(0,0)",500);
            if (window.netscape) {
                netscape.security.PrivilegeManager.disablePrivilege(
                    "UniversalBrowserWrite");
            }
        }

        // moves window in a circular motion
        function revolve() {
            var winX = (screen.availWidth - window.outerWidth) / 2;
            var winY = 50;
            window.resizeTo(400,300);
            window.moveTo(winX, winY);

            for (var i = 1; i < 36; i++) {
                winX += Math.cos(i * (Math.PI/18)) * 5;
                winY += Math.sin(i * (Math.PI/18)) * 5;
                window.moveTo(winX, winY);
            }
        }

        // moves window in a horizontal zig-zag pattern
        function zigzag() {
            window.resizeTo(400,300);
```

```
        window.moveTo(0,80);
        var incrementX = 2;
        var incrementY = 2;
        var floor = screen.availHeight - window.outerHeight;
        var rightEdge = screen.availWidth - window.outerWidth;
        for (var i = 0; i < rightEdge; i += 2) {
            window.moveBy(incrementX, incrementY);
            if (i%60 == 0) {
                incrementY = -incrementY;
            }
        }
    }

    // resizes window to occupy all available screen real estate
    function maximize() {
        window.moveTo(0,0);
        window.resizeTo(screen.availWidth, screen.availHeight);
    }
    </script>
</head>
<body onload="init()">
    <form name="buttons">
        <b>Window Gymnastics</b>
        <ul>
            <li><input name="offscreen" type="button"
                value="Disappear a Second" onclick="moveOffScreen()" /></li>
            <li><input name="circles" type="button" value="Circular Motion"
                onclick="revolve()" /></li>
            <li><input name="bouncer" type="button" value="Zig Zag"
                onclick="zigzag()" /></li>
            <li><input name="expander" type="button" value="Maximize"
                onclick="maximize()" /></li>
        </ul>
    </form>
</body>
</html>
```

To run successfully in NN/Moz, the first button requires that you have codebase principals turned on (see Chapter 46 on the CD-ROM) to take advantage of what would normally be a signed script. The moveOffScreen() function momentarily moves the window entirely out of view. Notice how the script determines the size of the screen before deciding where to move the window. After the journey offscreen, the window comes back into view at the top-left corner of the screen.

If using the web sometimes seems like going around in circles, the second function, revolve(), should feel just right. After reducing the size of the window and positioning it near the top center of the screen, the script uses a bit of math to position the window along 36 places around a perfect circle (at 10-degree increments). This is an example of how to control a window's position dynamically based on math calculations. IE complicates the job a bit by not providing properties that reveal the outside dimensions of the browser window.

windowObject.open()

To demonstrate the `moveBy()` method, the third function, `zigzag()`, uses a `for` loop to increment the coordinate points to make the window travel in a sawtooth pattern across the screen. The *x* coordinate continues to increment linearly until the window is at the edge of the screen (also calculated on the fly to accommodate monitors of any size). The *y* coordinate must increase and decrease as that parameter changes direction at various times across the screen.

In the fourth function, you see some practical code (finally) that demonstrates how best to simulate maximizing the browser window to fill the entire available screen space on the visitor's monitor.

Related Items: `window.outerHeight`, `window.outerWidth` properties; `window.resizeBy()`, `window.resizeTo()` methods

navigate("*URL*")

Returns: Nothing
Compatibility: WinIE4+, MacIE4+, NN-, Moz-, Safari-

The `window.navigate()` method is an IE-specific method that lets you load a new document into a window or frame. This method's action is the same as assigning a URL to the `location.href` property—a property that is available on all scriptable browsers. If your audience is entirely IE-based, this method is safe. Otherwise, I recommend the `location.href` property as the best navigation approach.

Example

Supply any valid URL as the parameter to the method, as in:

```
window.navigate("http://www.dannyg.com");
```

Related Item: `location` object

open("*URL*", "*windowName*" [, "*windowFeatures*"][,*replaceFlag*])

Returns: A window object representing the newly created window; `null` if method fails
Compatibility: WinIE3+, MacIE3+, NN2+, Moz+, Safari+

With the `window.open()` method, a script provides a web-site designer an immense range of options for the way a second or third web browser window looks on the user's computer screen. Moreover, most of this control can work with all JavaScript-enabled browsers without the need for signed scripts. Because the interface elements of a new window are easier to envision, I cover those aspects of the `window.open()` method parameters first.

Setting new window features

The optional `windowFeatures` parameter is one string consisting of a comma-separated list of assignment expressions (behaving something like HTML tag attributes). **Important:** For the best browser compatibility, do not put spaces after the commas. If you omit the third parameter, JavaScript creates the same type of new window you get from the New Web Browser menu choice in the File menu. But you can control which window elements appear in the new window with the third parameter. Remember this important rule: If you specify even one of the method's original set of third parameter values, all other features are turned off unless the parameters specify the features to be switched on. Table 16-3 lists the attributes that you can control for a newly created window in all browsers. Except where noted, all Boolean values default to `yes` if you do not specify the third parameter.

TABLE 16-3

window.open() Method Attributes Controllable via Script

Attribute	Browsers	Description
alwaysLowered[3]	NN4+/Moz+	(Boolean) Always behind other browser windows
alwaysRaised[3]	NN4+/Moz+	(Boolean) Always in front of other browser windows
channelMode	IE4+	(Boolean) Theater mode with channel band (default is no)
chrome	NN7.2+/Moz1.7+	(Boolean) Browser user interface features
close top of window	NN4+/Moz+	(Boolean) System close command icon and menu item at
copyhistory	NN2+, IE3+	(Boolean) Duplicates Go menu history for new window
dependent	NN4+/Moz+	(Boolean) Subwindow closes if the opener window closes
directories	NN2+/Moz+, IE3+	(Boolean) What's New and other buttons in the row
fullscreen	IE4+	(Boolean) No title bar or menus (default is no)
height	NN2+/Moz+, IE3+	(Integer) Content region height in pixels
hotkeys	NN4+/Moz+	(Boolean) If true, disables menu shortcuts (except Quit and Security Info) when menu bar is turned off
innerHeight[4]	NN4+/Moz+	(Integer) Content region height; same as old height property
innerWidth[4]	NN4+/Moz+	(Integer) Content region width; same as old width property
left	NN6+/Moz+, IE4+	(Integer) Horizontal position of top-left corner onscreen
location	NN2+/Moz+, IE3+	(Boolean) Field displaying the current URL
menubar[1]	NN2+/Moz+, IE3+	(Boolean) Menu bar at top of window
minimizable	NN7.1+/Moz1.2+	(Boolean) Minimize command icon at top of window
modal	NN7.1+/Moz1.2+	(Boolean) Modality of window, as in preventing access to the main window until the opened window is closed
outerHeight[4]	NN4+/Moz+	(Integer) Visible window height
outerWidth[4]	NN4+/Moz+	(Integer) Visible window width
personalBar	NN4+/Moz+	(Boolean) Mozilla-specific version of the directories attribute
resizable[2]	NN2+/Moz+, IE3+	(Boolean) Interface elements that allow resizing by dragging
screenX[4]	NN4+/Moz+	(Integer) Horizontal position of top-left corner onscreen
screenY[4]	NN4+/Moz+	(Integer) Vertical position of top-left corner onscreen
scrollbars	NN2+/Moz+, IE3+	(Boolean) Displays scroll bars if document is larger than window
status	NN2+/Moz+, IE3+	(Boolean) Status bar at bottom of window

continued

windowObject.open()

TABLE 16-3	(continued)	
Attribute	**Browsers**	**Description**
titlebar[3]	NN4+/Moz+	(Boolean) Title bar and all other border elements
toolbar	NN2+/Moz+, IE3+	(Boolean) Back, Forward, and other buttons in the row
top	NN6+/Moz+, IE4+	(Integer) Vertical position of top-left corner onscreen
width	NN2+/Moz+, IE3+	(Integer) Content region width in pixels
z-lock[3]	NN4+/Moz+	(Boolean) Window layer is fixed below browser windows

1 Not on Macintosh because the menu bar is not in the browser window; when off in MacNN4, displays an abbreviated Mac menu bar.

2 Macintosh windows are always resizable.

3 Requires a signed script.

4 Requires a signed script to size or position a window beyond safe threshold.

Boolean values are handled a bit differently than you might expect. The value for true can be yes, 1, or just the feature name by itself; for false, use a value of no or 0. If you omit any Boolean attributes, they are rendered as false. Therefore, if you want to create a new window that shows only the toolbar and status bar and is resizable, the method looks like this:

```
window.open("newURL","NewWindow", "toolbar,status,resizable");
```

A new window that does not specify the height and width is set to the default size of the browser window that the browser creates from a File menu's New Web Browser command. In other words, a new window does not automatically inherit the size of the window making the window.open() method call. A new window created via a script is positioned somewhat arbitrarily unless you use the window positioning attributes available in modern browsers. Notice that the position attributes are different for each browser (screenX and screenY for NN/Moz; left and top for IE). You can include both sets of attributes in a single parameter string because the browser ignores attributes that it doesn't recognize.

> **NOTE** Invoking window.open() via a window's onload and onunload event handlers has led to severe abuse in the form of unwanted pop-up advertising windows. Browsers that include pop-up blockers (such as IE6+ and Mozilla-based browsers) prevent the method from being invoked by these event handlers. With more browsers and users employing pop-up blockers every day, you should not even think about blasting pop-up ads to web surfers.

Netscape/Mozilla-only signed scripts

Many NN/Moz-specific attributes are deemed to be security risks and thus require signed scripts and the user's permission before they are recognized. If the user fails to grant permission, the secure parameter is ignored.

To apply signed scripts to opening a new window with the secure window features, you must enable UniversalBrowserWrite privileges as you do for other signed scripts (see Chapter 46 on the CD-ROM). A code fragment that generates an alwaysRaised style window follows:

```
<script type="text/javaScript" archive="myJar.jar" id="1">
function newRaisedWindow() {
    netscape.security.PrivilegeManager.enablePrivilege("UniversalBrowserWrite");
    var newWindow = window.open("","","height=100,width=300,alwaysRaised=yes");
    netscape.security.PrivilegeManager.disablePrivilege("UniversalBrowserWrite");
```

```
            var newContent = "<html><body><b> "On top of spaghetti!"</b>";
            newContent += "<form><center><input type='button' value='OK'";
            newContent += "onclick='self.close()'></center></form></body></html>";
            newWindow.document.write(newContent);
            newWindow.document.close();
        }
    </script>
```

You can experiment with the look and behavior of new windows with any combination of attributes with the help of the script in Listing 16-24. This page presents a table of all NN-specific new window Boolean attributes and creates a new 300 × 300 pixel window based on your choices. This page assumes that if you are using NN/Moz, you have codebase principals turned on for signed scripts (see Chapter 46 on the CD-ROM).

Be careful with turning off the title bar and hotkeys. With the title bar off, the content appears to float in space because absolutely no borders are displayed. With hotkeys still turned on, you can use Ctrl+W to close this borderless window (except on the Mac, for which the hotkeys are always disabled with the title bar off). This is how you can turn a computer into a kiosk by sizing a window to the screen's dimensions and setting the window options to `"titlebar=no,hotkeys=no,alwaysRaised=yes"`.

LISTING 16-24

New Window Laboratory

```
<html>
    <head>
        <title>window.open() Options</title>
        <script type="text/javascript">
        function makeNewWind(form) {
            if (window.netscape) {
                netscape.security.PrivilegeManager.enablePrivilege(
                    "UniversalBrowserWrite");
            }
            var attr = "width=300,height=300";
            for (var i = 0; i < form.elements.length; i++) {
                if (form.elements[i].type == "checkbox") {
                    attr += "," + form.elements[i].name + "=";
                    attr += (form.elements[i].checked) ? "yes" : "no";
                }
            }
            var newWind = window.open("bofright.htm","subwindow",attr);
            if (window.netscape) {
                netscape.security.PrivilegeManager.revertPrivilege("CanvasAccess");
            }
        }
        </script>
    </head>
    <body>
        <b>Select new window options:</b>
        <form>
            <table border="2">
```

continued

LISTING 16-24 *(continued)*

```
    <tr>
        <td colspan="2" bgcolor="yellow" align="middle">
        All Browsers Features:</td>
    </tr>
    <tr>
        <td><input type="checkbox" name="toolbar" />toolbar</td>
        <td><input type="checkbox" name="location" />location</td>
    </tr>
    <tr>
        <td><input type="checkbox" name="directories" />directories</td>
        <td><input type="checkbox" name="status" />status</td>
    </tr>
    <tr>
        <td><input type="checkbox" name="menubar" />menubar</td>
        <td><input type="checkbox" name="scrollbars" />scrollbars</td>
    </tr>
    <tr>
        <td><input type="checkbox" name="resizable" />resizable</td>
        <td><input type="checkbox" name="copyhistory" />copyhistory</td>
    </tr>
    <tr>
        <td colspan="2" bgcolor="yellow" align="middle">
        Communicator Features:</td>
    </tr>
    <tr>
        <td><input type="checkbox" name="alwaysLowered" />
        alwaysLowered</td>
        <td><input type="checkbox" name="alwaysRaised" />
        alwaysRaised</td>
    </tr>
    <tr>
        <td><input type="checkbox" name="dependent" />dependent</td>
        <td><input type="checkbox" name="hotkeys" checked="checked" />
        hotkeys</td>
    </tr>
    <tr>
        <td><input type="checkbox" name="titlebar" checked="checked" />
        titlebar</td>
        <td><input type="checkbox" name="z-lock" />z-lock</td>
    </tr>
    <tr>
        <td colspan="2" align="middle"><input type="button"
        name="forAll" value="Make New Window"
        onclick="makeNewWind(this.form)" /></td>
    </tr>
    </table>
  </form>
  <br />
  </body>
</html>
```

Specifying a window name

Getting back to the other parameters of `window.open()`, the second parameter is the name for the new window. Don't confuse this parameter with the document's title, which normally would be set by whatever HTML text determines the content of the window. A window name must be the same style of one-word identifier that you use for other object names and variables. This name is also an entirely different entity from the `window` object that the `open()` method returns. You don't use the name in your scripts. At most, the name can be used for `target` attributes of links and forms.

Loading content into a new window

A script generally populates a window with one of two kinds of information:

- An existing HTML document whose URL is known beforehand
- An HTML page created on the fly

To create a new window that displays an existing HTML document, supply the URL as the first parameter of the `window.open()` method. If your page is having difficulty loading a URL into a new page, try specifying the complete URL of the target document (instead of just the filename).

Leaving the first parameter as an empty string forces the window to open with a blank document, ready to have HTML written to it by your script (or loaded separately by another statement that sets that window's location to a specific URL). If you plan to write the content of the window on the fly, assemble your HTML content as one long string value and then use the `document.write()` method to post that content to the new window. If you plan to append no further writing to the page, also include a `document.close()` method at the end to tell the browser that you're finished with the layout (so that the `Layout:Complete` or `Done` message appears in the status bar, if your new window has one).

A call to the `window.open()` method returns a reference to the new window's object if the window opens successfully. This value is vitally important if your script needs to address elements of that new window (such as when writing to its document).

To allow other functions in your script to reference the subwindow, you should assign the result of a `window.open()` method to a global variable. Before writing to the new window the first time, test the variable to make sure that it is not a `null` value; the window may have failed to open because of low memory, for instance. If everything is OK, you can use that variable as the beginning of a reference to any property or object within the new window. For example:

```
var newWindow
...
function createNewWindow() {
    newWindow = window.open("","");
    if (newWindow != null) {
        newWindow.document.write("<html><head><title>Hi!</title></head>");
    }
}
```

That global variable reference continues to be available for another function that perhaps closes the subwindow (via the `close()` method).

When scripts in the subwindow need to communicate with objects and scripts in the originating window, you must make sure that the subwindow has an `opener` property if the level of JavaScript in the visitor's browser doesn't automatically supply one. See the discussion about the `window.opener` property earlier in this chapter.

windowObject.open()

Invoking multiple `window.open()` methods with the same window name parameter (the second parameter) does not create additional copies of that window in Netscape browsers (although it does in Internet Explorer). JavaScript prevents you from creating two windows with the same name. Also be aware that a `window.open()` method does not bring an existing window of that name to the front of the window layers: Use `window.focus()` for that.

Internet Explorer idiosyncrasies

Creating subwindows in IE can be complicated at times by undesirable behavior by the browser. One of the most common problems occurs when you attempt to use `document.write()` to put content into a newly created window. IE, including some of the latest versions, fails to complete the window opening job before the script statement that uses `document.write()` executes. This causes a script error because the reference to the subwindow is not yet valid. To work around this, you should put the HTML assembly and `document.write()` statements in a separate function that gets invoked via a `setTimeout()` method after the window is created. You can see an example of this in Listing 16-25.

Another problem that affects IE is the occasional security violation (access denied) warning when a script attempts to access a subwindow. This problem goes away when the page that includes the script for opening and accessing the subwindow is served from an HTTP server rather than accessed from a local hard disk.

Example

The page rendered by Listing 16-25 displays a single button that generates a new window of a specific size that has only the status bar turned on. The script here shows all the elements necessary to create a new window that has all the right stuff on most platforms. The new window object reference is assigned to a global variable, `newWindow`. Before a new window is generated, the script looks to see whether the window has never been generated before (in which case `newWindow` would be `null`) or, for newer browsers, the window is closed. If either condition is `true`, the window is created with the `open()` method. Otherwise, the existing window is brought forward with the `focus()` method.

Due to the timing problem that afflicts all IE generations, the HTML assembly and writing to the new window are separated into their own function, which is invoked after a 50-millisecond delay (other browsers go along for the ride even if they could accommodate the assembly and writing without the delay). To build the string that is eventually written to the document, I use the += (add-by-value) operator, which appends the string on the right side of the operator to the string stored in the variable on the left side. In this example, the new window is handed an `<h1>`-level line of text to display.

LISTING 16-25

Creating a New Window

```
<html>
   <head>
      <title>New Window</title>
      <script type="text/javascript">
      var newWindow;

      function makeNewWindow() {
         if (!newWindow || newWindow.closed) {
            newWindow = window.open("","","status,height=200,width=300");
            // force small delay for IE to catch up
```

```
        setTimeout("writeToWindow()", 50);
      } else {
        // window's already open; bring to front
        newWindow.focus();
      }
    }

    function writeToWindow() {
      // assemble content for new window
      var newContent = "<html><head><title>One Sub Window<\/title><\/head>";
      newContent += "<body><h1>This window is brand new.<\/h1>";
      newContent += "<\/body><\/html>";
      // write HTML to new window document
      newWindow.document.write(newContent);
      newWindow.document.close();   // close layout stream
    }
    </script>
  </head>
  <body>
    <form>
      <input type="button" name="newOne" value="Create New Window"
      onclick="makeNewWindow()" />
    </form>
  </body>
</html>
```

The window.open() method can potentially create problems in browsers such as IE7 and FF2 that support tabbed browsing where multiple pages are opened as different tabs within the same browser instance. The default response to window.open() is to open a new tab for the new window, as opposed to a new browser window, which can be a problem if the script is truly expecting a completely new browser window.

Related Items: window.close(), window.blur(), window.focus(), window.openDialog() methods; window.closed property

openDialog("*URL*", "*windowName*" [, "*windowFeatures*"][, *arg1*][, *arg2*]...)

Returns: A window object representing the newly created dialog box (window); null if method fails
Compatibility: WinIE-, MacIE-, NN7+, Moz1.0.1+, Safari-

The window.openDialog() method is a Mozilla-specific method that serves as a XUL counterpart to the window.open() method. XUL is Mozilla's XML-based user interface description language that is used throughout the Mozilla application suite. The openDialog() method offers a few extra window features, along with the ability to pass a varying number of arguments, which can be handy when creating custom windows.

The parameters to the openDialog() method are similar to those found in the open() method, except for the optional arg1, arg2, and so on. One notable difference is the addition of the all window feature, which is used to show (all=yes) or hide (all=no) all window features except chrome, dialog, and modal; these excluded features can still be shown or hidden individually.

Related Item: window.open() method

print()

Returns: Nothing
Compatibility: WinIE5+, MacIE5+, NN4+, Moz+, Safari-

The print() method provides a scripted way of sending the window or a frame from a frameset to the printer. In all cases, the Print dialog box appears for the user to make the typical printer choices when printing manually. This prevents a rogue print() command from tying up a printer without the user's permission.

WinIE5 introduced some print-specific event handlers that are triggered by scripted printing as well as manual printing. The events begin to fire after the user has accepted the Print dialog box. An onbeforeprint event handler can be used to show content that might be hidden from view but should appear in the printout. After the content has been sent to the print spooler, the onafterprint event can restore the page.

Example

Listing 16-26 is a frameset that loads Listing 16-27 into the top frame and a copy of the Bill of Rights into the bottom frame.

LISTING 16-26

Print Example Frameset

```
<html>
   <head>
      <title>window.print() method</title>
   </head>
   <frameset rows="25%,75%">
      <frame name="controls" src="lst16-27.htm" />
      <frame name="display" src="bofright.htm" />
   </frameset>
</html>
```

Two buttons in the top control panel (see Listing 16-27) let you print the whole frameset (in those browsers and OSes that support it) or just the bottom frame. To print the entire frameset, the reference includes the parent window; to print the bottom frame, the reference is directed at the parent.display frame.

LISTING 16-27

Printing Control

```
<html>
   <head>
      <title>Print()</title>
   </head>
   <body>
      <form>
         <input type="button" name="printWhole" value="Print Entire Frameset"
```

```
        onclick="parent.print()" />
        <p><input type="button" name="printFrame"
           value="Print Bottom Frame Only"
           onclick="parent.display.print()" /></p>
     </form>
  </body>
</html>
```

If you don't like some facet of the printed output, blame the browser's print engine, not JavaScript. The `print()` method merely invokes the browser's regular printing routines.

Related Items: `window.back()`, `window.forward()`, `window.home()`, `window.find()` methods

prompt("*message*", "*defaultReply*")

Returns: String of text entered by user or `null`
Compatibility: WinIE3+, MacIE3+, NN2+, Moz+, Safari+

The third kind of dialog box that JavaScript can display includes a message from the script author, a field for user entry, and two buttons (OK and Cancel). The script writer can supply a prewritten answer so that a user confronted with a prompt dialog box can click OK (or press Enter) to accept that answer without further typing. Supplying both parameters to the `window.prompt()` method is important. Even if you don't want to supply a default answer, enter an empty string as the second parameter:

```
prompt("What is your postal code?","");
```

If you omit the second parameter, JavaScript inserts the string `undefined` into the dialog box's field. This string is disconcerting to most web-page visitors.

The value returned by this method is a string in the dialog box's field when the user clicks the OK button. If you're asking the user to enter a number, remember that the value returned by this method is a string. You may need to perform data-type conversion with the `parseInt()` or `parseFloat()` function (see Chapter 35) to use the returned values in math calculations.

When the user clicks the prompt dialog box's OK button without entering any text in a blank field, the returned value is an empty string (`""`). Clicking the Cancel button, however, makes the method return a `null` value. Therefore, the scripter must test for the type of returned value to make sure that the user entered some data that can be processed later in the script, as in:

```
var entry = prompt("Enter a number between 1 and 10:","");
if (entry != null) {
   //statements to execute with the value
}
```

This script excerpt assigns the results of the prompt dialog box to a variable and executes the nested statements if the returned value of the dialog box is not `null` (if the user clicked the OK button). The rest of the statements then include data validation to make sure that the entry is a number within the desired range (see Chapter 43 on the CD-ROM).

It may be tempting to use the prompt dialog box as a handy user input device. But as with the other JavaScript dialog boxes, the modality of the prompt dialog box is disruptive to the user's flow through a document and can also trap automated macros that some users activate to capture web sites. In forms, HTML fields are better user interface elements for attracting user text entry. Perhaps the safest way to use a prompt dialog box is to have it appear when a user clicks a button element on a page — and then only if the information you require of the user can be provided in a single prompt dialog box. Presenting a sequence of prompt dialog boxes is downright annoying to users.

Example

The function that receives values from the prompt dialog box in Listing 16-28 (see the dialog box in Figure 16-11) does some data-entry validation (but certainly not enough for a commercial site). The function first checks to make sure that the returned value is neither `null` (Cancel) nor an empty string (the user clicked OK without entering any values). See Chapter 43 on the CD-ROM for more about data-entry validation.

LISTING 16-28

The Prompt Dialog Box

```html
<html>
    <head>
        <title>window.prompt() Method</title>
        <script type="text/javascript">
        function populateTable() {
            var howMany = prompt("Fill in table for how many factors?","");
            if (howMany != null && howMany != "") {
                alert("Filling the table for " + howMany);   // for demo
                //statements that validate the entry and
                //actually populate the fields of the table
            }
        }
        </script>
    </head>
    <body>
        <form>
            <!-- other statements that display and populate a large table -->
            <input type="button" name="fill" value="Fill Table..."
            onclick="populateTable()" />
        </form>
    </body>
</html>
```

FIGURE 16-11

The prompt dialog box from Listing 16-28 displayed in Internet Explorer.

Notice one important user interface element in Listing 16-28. Because clicking the button leads to a dialog box that requires more information from the user, the button's label ends in an ellipsis (or, rather, three periods acting as an ellipsis character). The ellipsis is a common courtesy to let users know that a user interface element leads to a dialog box of some sort. Consistent with stand-alone applications, the user should be able to cancel out of that dialog box and return to the same screen state that existed before the button was clicked.

Related Items: window.alert(), window.confirm() methods

resizeBy(*deltaX,deltaY*)
resizeTo(*outerwidth,outerheight*)
Returns: Nothing
Compatibility: WinIE4+, MacIE4+, NN4, Moz-, Safari 1+

Starting with version 4 browsers, scripts can control the size of the current browser window on the fly (no longer available in Mozilla-based browsers). Although you can set the individual inner and (in NN4) outer width and height properties of a window, the resizeBy() and resizeTo() methods let you adjust both axis measurements in one statement. In both instances, all adjustments affect the bottom-right corner of the window. To move the top-left corner, use the window.moveBy() or window.moveTo() methods.

Each resize method requires a different kind of parameter. The resizeBy() method adjusts the window by a certain number of pixels along one or both axes. Therefore, it is not concerned with the specific size of the window beforehand — only by how much each axis is to change. For example, to increase the current window size by 100 pixels horizontally and 50 pixels vertically, the statement is

```
window.resizeBy(100, 50);
```

Both parameters are required, but if you want to adjust the size in only one direction, set the other to zero. You may also shrink the window by using negative values for either or both parameters.

You find a greater need for the resizeTo() method, especially when you know that on a particular platform, the window needs adjustment to a specific width and height to best accommodate that platform's display of form elements. Parameters for the resizeTo() method are the actual pixel width and height of the outer dimension of the window — the same as NN4's window.outerWidth and window.outerHeight properties.

To resize the window so that it occupies all screen real estate (except for the Windows taskbar and Macintosh menu bar), use the screen object properties that calculate the available screen space:

```
window.resizeBy(screen.availWidth, screen.availHeight);
```

This action, however, is not precisely the same in Windows as maximizing the window. To achieve that same effect, you must move the window to coordinates -4, -4 and add 8 to the two parameters of resizeBy():

```
window.moveTo(-4,-4);
window.resizeTo(screen.availWidth + 8, screen.availHeight + 8);
```

This hides the window's own 4-pixels-wide border, as occurs during OS-induced window maximizing. See also the screen object discussion (see Chapter 38 on the CD-ROM) for more OS-specific details.

On some platforms, the dimensions are applied to the inner width and height rather than outer. If a specific outer size is necessary, use the NN-specific window.outerHeight and window.outerWidth properties instead.

Navigator 4 imposes some security restrictions for maximum and minimum size for a window. For both methods, you are limited to the viewable area of the screen and visible minimums unless the page uses signed scripts (see Chapter 46 on the CD-ROM). With signed scripts and the user's permission, for example, you can adjust windows beyond the available screen borders.

windowObject.**resizeBy()**

Example

You can experiment with the resize methods with the page in Listing 16-29. Two parts of a form let you enter values for each method. The one for `window.resize()` also lets you enter several repetitions to better see the impact of the values. Enter zero and negative values to see how those affect the method. Also test the limits of different browsers.

LISTING 16-29

Window Resize Methods

```html
<html>
    <head>
        <title>Window Resize Methods</title>
        <script type="text/javascript">
        function doResizeBy(form) {
            var x = parseInt(form.resizeByX.value);
            var y = parseInt(form.resizeByY.value);
            var count = parseInt(form.count.value);
            for (var i = 0; i < count; i++) {
                window.resizeBy(x, y);
            }
        }
        function doResizeTo(form) {
            var x = parseInt(form.resizeToX.value);
            var y = parseInt(form.resizeToY.value);
            window.resizeTo(x, y);
        }
        </script>
    </head>
    <body>
        <form>
            <b>Enter the x and y increment, plus how many times the window should
            be resized by these increments:</b><br />
            Horiz:<input type="text" name="resizeByX" size="4" /> Vert:<input
            type="text" name="resizeByY" size="4" /> How Many:<input type="text"
            name="count" size="4" /> <input type="button" name="ResizeBy"
            value="Show resizeBy()" onclick="doResizeBy(this.form)" />
            <hr />
            <b>Enter the desired width and height of the current window:</b><br />
            Width:<input type="text" name="resizeToX" size="4" /> Height:<input
            type="text" name="resizeToY" size="4" /> <input type="button"
            name="ResizeTo" value="Show resizeTo()"
            onclick="doResizeTo(this.form)" />
        </form>
    </body>
</html>
```

Related Items: `window.outerHeight`, `window.outerWidth` properties; `window.moveTo()`, `window.sizeToContent()` methods

scroll(*horizontalCoord, verticalCoord*)

Returns: Nothing
Compatibility: WinIE4+, MacIE4+, NN3+, Moz+, Safari+

The window.scroll() method was introduced in NN3 and has been implemented in all scriptable browsers since then. But in the meantime, the method has been replaced by the window.scrollTo() method, which is in more syntactic alliance with many other window methods.

The window.scroll() method takes two parameters: the horizontal (x) and vertical (y) coordinates of the document that is to be positioned at the top-left corner of the window or frame. You must realize that the window and document have two similar, but independent, coordinate schemes. From the window's point of view, the top-left pixel (of the content area) is point 0,0. All documents also have a 0,0 point: the very top left of the document. The window's 0,0 point doesn't move, but the document's 0,0 point can move — via manual or scripted scrolling. Although scroll() is a window method, it seems to behave more like a document method, as the document appears to reposition itself within the window. Conversely, you can also think of the window moving to bring its 0,0 point to the designated coordinate of the document.

Although you can set values beyond the maximum size of the document or to negative values, the results vary from platform to platform. For the moment, the best usage of the window.scroll() method is as a means of adjusting the scroll to the very top of a document (window.scroll(0,0)) when you want the user to be at a base location in the document. For vertical scrolling within a text-heavy document, an HTML anchor may be a better alternative for now (though it doesn't readjust horizontal scrolling).

Related Items: window.scrollBy(), window.scrollTo() methods

scrollBy(*deltaX,deltaY*)
scrollTo(*x,y*)

Returns: Nothing
Compatibility: WinIE4+, MacIE4+, NN4+, Moz+, Safari+

Modern browsers provide a related pair of window scrolling methods. The window.scrollTo() method is the newer version of the window.scroll() method. The two work identically to position a specific coordinate point of a document at the top-left corner of the inner window region.

By contrast, the window.scrollBy() method allows for relative positioning of the document. Parameter values indicate by how many pixels the document should scroll in the window (horizontally and vertically). Negative numbers are allowed if you want to scroll to the left and/or up. The scrollBy() method comes in handy if you elect to hide the scroll bars of a window or frame and offer other types of scrolling

Unwanted User Scrolling

Wheeled mice have become increasingly popular on Windows-compatible personal computers. These mice include a scroll wheel that is activated by pressing down on the wheel and spinning the wheel. Be aware that even if your page design loads into frames or new windows that intentionally lack scroll bars, the page will be scrollable via this wheel if the document or its background image is larger than the window or frame. Users may not even be aware that they have scrolled the page (because there are no scroll-bar visual clues). If this affects your design, you may need to build in a routine (via setTimeout()) that periodically sets the scroll of the window to 0,0.

windowObject.scrollBy()

controls for your users. For example, to scroll down one entire screen of a long document, you can use the `window.innerHeight` (in NN/Moz) or `document.body.clientHeight` (in IE) properties to determine what the offset from the current position would be:

```
// assign IE body clientHeight to window.innerHeight
if (document.body && document.body.clientHeight) {
    window.innerHeight = document.body.clientHeight;
}
window.scrollBy(0, window.innerHeight);
```

To scroll up, use a negative value for the second parameter:

```
window.scrollBy(0, -window.innerHeight);
```

The window scroll methods are not the ones to use to produce the scrolling effect of a positioned element. That kind of animation is accomplished by adjusting `style` position properties (see Chapter 40 on the CD-ROM).

Example

To work with the `scrollTo()` method, you can use Listing 16-30, Listing 16-31, and Listing 16-32. The code in Listing 16-34 includes a control panel frame (see Listing 16-32) that provides input to experiment with the `scrollBy()` method.

LISTING 16-30

Frameset for ScrollBy Controller

```
<html>
    <head>
        <title>
            window.scrollBy() Method
        </title>
    </head>
    <frameset rows="50%,50%">
        <frame src="lst16-31.htm" name="display" />
        <frame src="lst16-32.htm" name="control" />
    </frameset>
</html>
```

LISTING 16-31

The Image to Be Scrolled

```
<html>
    <head>
        <title>
            Arch
        </title>
    </head>
    <body>
```

```
        <h1>
            A Picture is Worth...
        </h1>
        <hr />
        <center>
            <table border="3">
                <caption align="bottom">
                    A Splendid Arch
                </caption>
                <tr>
                    <td>
                        <img alt="image" src="arch.gif" />
                    </td>
                </tr>
            </table>
        </center>
    </body>
</html>
```

Notice in Listing 16-32 that all references to window properties and methods are directed to the display frame. String values retrieved from text fields are converted to numbers with the parseInt() global function.

LISTING 16-32

ScrollBy Controller

```
<html>
    <head>
        <title>
            ScrollBy Controller
        </title>

        <script type="text/javascript">
        function page(direction) {
            var pixFrame = parent.display;
            var deltaY = (pixFrame.innerHeight) ?
                pixFrame.innerHeight : pixFrame.document.body.scrollHeight;
            if (direction == "up") {
                deltaY = -deltaY;
            }
            parent.display.scrollBy(0, deltaY);
        }
        function customScroll(form) {
            parent.display.scrollBy(parseInt(form.x.value),
                parseInt(form.y.value));
        }
        </script>
    </head>
    <body>
```

continued

windowObject.setInterval()

LISTING 16-32 *(continued)*

```
   <b>ScrollBy Controller</b>
   <form name="custom">
      Enter an Horizontal increment <input type="text" name="x" value="0"
      size="4" /> and Vertical <input type="text" name="y" value="0"
      size="4" /> value.<br />
      Then <input type="button" value="click to scrollBy()"
      onclick="customScroll(this.form)" />
      <hr />
      <input type="button" value="PageDown" onclick="page('down')" /> <input
      type="button" value="PageUp" onclick="page('up')" />
   </form>
</body>
</html>
```

Related Items: `window.pageXOffset`, `window.pageYOffset` properties; `window.scroll()` method

scrollByLines(*intervalCount*)
scrollByPages(*intervalCount*)

Returns: Nothing
Compatibility: WinIE-, MacIE-, NN6+, Moz+, Safari-

The `window.scrollByLines()` and `window.scrollByPages()` methods scroll the document by a specified number of lines or pages, respectively. You can think of these methods as the script equivalents to clicking the arrow (`scrollByLines()`) and page (`scrollByPages()`) regions of the browser's vertical scroll bar. The argument to each method determines how many lines or pages to scroll, with positive values resulting in a downward scroll and negative values resulting in upward scrolling.

setInterval("*expr*", *msecDelay* [, *language*])
setInterval(funcRef, msecDelay [, funcarg1, ..., funcargn])

Returns: Interval ID integer
Compatibility: WinIE4+, MacIE4+, NN4+, Moz+, Safari+

It is important to understand the distinction between the `setInterval()` and `setTimeout()` methods. Before the `setInterval()` method was part of JavaScript, authors replicated the behavior with `setTimeout()`, but the task often required reworking scripts a bit.

Use `setInterval()` when your script needs to call a function or execute some expression repeatedly with a fixed time delay between calls to that function or expression. The delay is not at all like a wait state in some languages: Other processing does not halt while the delay is in effect. Typical applications include animation by moving an object around the page under controlled speed (instead of letting the JavaScript interpreter whiz the object through its path at CPU-dependent speeds). In a kiosk application, you can use `setInterval()` to advance slides that appear in other frames or as layers, perhaps changing the view every 10 seconds. Clock displays and countdown timers would also be suitable use of this method (even though you see examples in this book that use the old-fashioned `setTimeout()` way to perform timer and clock functions).

By contrast, `setTimeout()` is best suited for those times when you need to carry out a function or expression one time in the future — even if that future is only a second or two away. In other words, `setTimeout()` gives you a one-shot timer, whereas `setInterval()` gives you a recurring timer. See the discussion of the `setTimeout()` method later in this chapter for details on this application.

Although the primary functionality of the `setInterval()` method is the same in all browsers, NN/Moz and IE offer some extra possibilities depending on the way you use parameters to the method. For simple invocations of this method, the same parameters work in all browsers that support the method. First, I address the parameters that all browsers have in common.

The first parameter of the `setInterval()` method is the name of the function or expression to run after the interval elapses. This item must be a quoted string. If the parameter is a function, no function arguments are allowed inside the function's parentheses unless the arguments are literal strings (but see the next section, "Passing function parameters").

The second parameter of this method is the number of milliseconds (1,000 per second) that JavaScript should use as the interval between invocations of the function or expression. Even though the measure is in extremely small units, don't rely on 100 percent accuracy of the intervals. Various other internal processing delays may throw off the timing just a bit.

Just as with `setTimeout()`, `setInterval()` returns an integer value that is the ID for the interval process. That ID value lets you turn off the process with the `clearInterval()` method. That method takes the ID value as its sole parameter. This mechanism allows for the setting of multiple interval processes running and gives your scripts the power to stop individual processes at any time without interrupting the others.

IE4+ uses the optional third parameter to specify the scripting language of the statement or function being invoked in the first parameter. As long as you are scripting exclusively in JavaScript (the same as JScript), there is no need to include this parameter.

Passing function parameters

NN4+/Moz provides a mechanism for easily passing evaluated parameters to a function invoked by `setInterval()`. To use this mechanism, the first parameter of `setInterval()` must not be a string, but a reference to the function (no trailing parentheses). The second parameter remains the amount of delay. But beginning with the third parameter, you can include evaluated function arguments as a comma-delimited list:

```
intervalID = setInterval(cycleAnimation, 500, "figure1");
```

The function definition receives those parameters in the same form as any function:

```
function cycleAnimation(elemID) {...}
```

For use with a wider range of browsers, you can also cobble together the ability to pass parameters to a function invoked by `setInterval()`. Because the call to the other function is a string expression, you can use computed values as part of the strings via string concatenation. For example, if a function uses event handling to find the element that a user clicked (to initiate some animation sequence), that element's ID, referenced by a variable, can be passed to the function invoked by `setInterval()`:

```
function findAndCycle() {
   var elemID;
   // statements here that examine the event info
   // and extract the ID of the clicked element,
   // assigning that ID to the elemID variable
   intervalID = setInterval("cycleAnimation(" + elemID + ")", 500);
}
```

windowObject.setInterval()

If you need to pass ever-changing parameters with each invocation of the function from setInterval(), look instead to using setTimeout() at the end of a function to invoke that same function again.

Example

The demonstration of the setInterval() method entails a two-framed environment. The framesetting document is shown in Listing 16-33.

LISTING 16-33

SetInterval() Demonstration Frameset

```html
<html>
    <head>
        <title>setInterval() Method</title>
    </head>
    <frameset rows="50%,50%">
        <frame src="lst16-34.htm" name="control" />
        <frame src="bofright.htm" name="display" />
    </frameset>
</html>
```

In the top frame is a control panel with several buttons that control the automatic scrolling of the Bill of Rights text document in the bottom frame. Listing 16-34 shows the control-panel document. Many functions here control the interval, scrolling jump size, and direction, and they demonstrate several aspects of applying setInterval().

Notice that in the beginning the script establishes several global variables. Three of them are parameters that control the scrolling; the last one is for the ID value returned by the setInterval() method. The script needs that value to be a global value so that a separate function can halt the scrolling with the clearInterval() method.

All scrolling is performed by the autoScroll() function. For the sake of simplicity, all controlling parameters are global variables. In this application, placement of those values in global variables helps the page restart autoscrolling with the same parameters as it had when it last ran.

LISTING 16-34

SetInterval() Control Panel

```html
<html>
    <head>
        <title>ScrollBy Controller</title>
        <script type="text/javascript">
        var scrollSpeed = 500;
        var scrollJump = 1;
        var scrollDirection = "down";
        var intervalID;
```

```
    function autoScroll() {
        if (scrollDirection == "down") {
            scrollJump = Math.abs(scrollJump);
        } else if (scrollDirection == "up" && scrollJump > 0) {
            scrollJump = -scrollJump;
        }
        parent.display.scrollBy(0, scrollJump);
        if (parent.display.pageYOffset <= 0) {
            clearInterval(intervalID);
        }
    }

    function reduceInterval() {
        stopScroll();
        scrollSpeed -= 200;
        startScroll();
    }
    function increaseInterval() {
        stopScroll();
        scrollSpeed += 200;
        startScroll();
    }
    function reduceJump() {
        scrollJump -= 2;
    }
    function increaseJump() {
        scrollJump += 2;
    }
    function swapDirection() {
        scrollDirection = (scrollDirection == "down") ? "up" : "down";
    }
    function startScroll() {
        parent.display.scrollBy(0, scrollJump);
        if (intervalID) {
            clearInterval(intervalID);
        }
        intervalID = setInterval("autoScroll()",scrollSpeed);
    }
    function stopScroll() {
        clearInterval(intervalID);
    }
    </script>
</head>
<body onload="startScroll()">
    <b>AutoScroll by setInterval() Controller</b>
    <form name="custom">
        <input type="button" value="Start Scrolling"
        onclick="startScroll()" /> <input type="button" value="Stop Scrolling"
        onclick="stopScroll()" />
        <p><input type="button" value="Shorter Time Interval"
            onclick="reduceInterval()" /> <input type="button"
```

continued

449

LISTING 16-34 *(continued)*

```
            value="Longer Time Interval" onclick="increaseInterval()" /></p>
        <p><input type="button" value="Bigger Scroll Jumps"
            onclick="increaseJump()" /> <input type="button"
            value="Smaller Scroll Jumps" onclick="reduceJump()" /></p>
        <p><input type="button" value="Change Direction"
            onclick="swapDirection()" /></p>
    </form>
  </body>
</html>
```

The setInterval() method is invoked inside the startScroll() function. This function initially burps the page by one scrollJump interval so that the test in autoScroll() for the page being scrolled all the way to the top doesn't halt a page from scrolling before it gets started. Notice, too, that the function checks for the existence of an interval ID. If one is there, it is cleared before the new one is set. This is crucial within the design of the example page, because repeated clicking of the Start Scrolling button triggers multiple interval timers inside the browser. Only the most recent one's ID would be stored in intervalID, allowing no way to clear the older ones. But this little side trip makes sure that only one interval timer is running. One of the global variables, scrollSpeed, is used to fill the delay parameter for setInterval(). To change this value on the fly, the script must stop the current interval process, change the scrollSpeed value, and start a new process.

The intensely repetitive nature of this application is nicely handled by the setInterval() method.

Related Items: window.clearInterval(), window.setTimeout() methods

setTimeout("*expr*", *msecDelay* [, *language*])
setTimeout(*functionRef*, *msecDelay* [, *funcarg1*, ..., *funcargn*])

Returns: ID value for use with window.clearTimeout() method
Compatibility: WinIE3+, MacIE3+, NN2+, Moz+, Safari+

The name of this method may be misleading, especially if you have done other kinds of programming involving timeouts. In JavaScript, a *timeout* is an amount of time (in milliseconds) before a stated expression evaluates. A timeout is not a wait or script delay, but a way to tell JavaScript to hold off executing a statement or function for a desired amount of time. Other statements following the one containing setTimeout() execute immediately.

Suppose that you have a web page designed to enable users to interact with a variety of buttons or fields within a time limit (this is a web page running at a freestanding kiosk). You can turn on the timeout of the window so that if no interaction occurs with specific buttons or fields lower in the document after, say, 2 minutes (120,000 milliseconds), the window reverts to the top of the document or to a help screen. To tell the window to switch off the timeout after a user does navigate within the allotted time, you need to have any button that the user interacts with call the other side of a setTimeout() method — the clearTimeout() method — to cancel the current timer. (The clearTimeout() method is explained earlier in this chapter.) Multiple timers can run concurrently and are completely independent of one another.

Although the primary functionality of the setTimeout() method is the same in all browsers, NN/Moz and IE offer some extra possibilities depending on the way you use parameters to the method. For simple invocations of this method, the same parameters work in all browsers that support the method. I first address the parameters that all browsers have in common.

The expression that comprises the first parameter of the method window.setTimeout() is a quoted string that can contain either a call to any function or method or a stand-alone JavaScript statement. The expression evaluates after the time limit expires.

Understanding that this timeout does not halt script execution is very important. In fact, if you use a setTimeout() method in the middle of a script, the succeeding statements in the script execute immediately; after the delay time, the expression in the setTimeout() method executes. Therefore, I've found that the best way to design a timeout in a script is to plug it in as the last statement of a function: Let all other statements execute and then let the setTimeout() method appear to halt further execution until the timer goes off. In truth, however, although the timeout is holding, the user is not prevented from performing other tasks. And after a timeout timer is ticking, you cannot adjust its time. Instead, clear the timeout and start a new one.

If you need to use setTimeout() as a delay inside a function, break the function into two parts, using the setTimeout() method as a bridge between the two functions. You can see an example of this in Listing 16-25, where IE needs a little delay to finish opening a new window before content can be written for it. If it weren't for the required delay, the HTML assembly and writing would have been accomplished in the same function that opens the new window.

It is not uncommon for a setTimeout() method to invoke the very function in which it lives. For example, if you have written a Java applet to perform some extra work for your page, and you need to connect to it via the NPAPI, your scripts must wait for the applet to load and carry out its initializations. Although an onload event handler in the document ensures that the applet object is visible to scripts, it doesn't know whether the applet has finished its initializations. A JavaScript function that inspects the applet for a clue might need to poll the applet every 500 milliseconds until the applet sets some internal value indicating that all is ready, as shown here:

```
var t;
function autoReport() {
   if (!document.myApplet.done) {
      t = setTimeout("autoReport()",500);
   } else {
      clearTimeout(t);
      // more statements using applet data //
   }
}
```

JavaScript provides no built-in equivalent for a wait command. The worst alternative is to devise a looping function of your own to trap script execution for a fixed amount of time. Unfortunately, this approach prevents other processes from being carried out, so you should consider reworking your code to rely on a setTimeout() method instead.

NN4+/Moz provides a mechanism for passing parameters to functions invoked by setTimeout(). See the section "Passing function parameters" in the discussion of window.setInterval() for details on this topic and on passing parameters in other browser versions.

windowObject.setTimeout()

As a note to experienced programmers, neither setInterval() nor setTimeout() spawns new threads in which to run its invoked scripts. When the timer expires and invokes a function, the process gets at the end of the queue of any pending script processing in the JavaScript execution thread.

Example

When you load the HTML page in Listing 16-35, it triggers the updateTime() function, which displays the time (in hh:mm am/pm format) in the status bar. Instead of showing the seconds incrementing one by one (which may be distracting to someone trying to read the page), this function alternates the last character of the display between an asterisk and nothing, like a visual heartbeat.

LISTING 16-35

Display the Current Time

```html
<html>
    <head>
        <title>Status Bar Clock</title>
        <script type="text/javascript">
        var flasher = false;
        // calculate current time, determine flasher state,
        // and insert time into status bar every second
        function updateTime() {
            var now = new Date();
            var theHour = now.getHours();
            var theMin = now.getMinutes();
            var theTime = "" + ((theHour > 12) ? theHour - 12 : theHour);
            theTime += ((theMin < 10) ? ":0" : ":") + theMin;
            theTime += (theHour >= 12) ? " pm" : " am";
            theTime += ((flasher) ? " " : "*");
            flasher = !flasher;
            window.status = theTime;
            // recursively call this function every second to keep timer going
            timerID = setTimeout("updateTime()",1000);
        }
        </script>
    </head>
    <body onload="updateTime()">
    </body>
</html>
```

In this function, the setTimeout() method works in the following way: When the current time (including the flasher status) appears in the status bar, the function waits approximately 1 second (1,000 milliseconds) before calling the same function again. You don't have to clear the timerID value in this application because JavaScript does it for you every time the 1,000 milliseconds elapse.

A logical question to ask is whether this application should be using setInterval() instead of setTimeout(). This is a case in which either one does the job. Using setInterval() here would require that the interval process start outside the updateTime() function, because you need only one process running that repeatedly calls `updateTime()`. It would be a cleaner implementation instead of the tons of time-out processes spawned by Listing 16-35. On the other hand, the application would not run in legacy browsers, as Listing 16-35 does. That's likely not a problem at this point in time, but the example remains a decent example of the `setTimeout()` function.

To demonstrate passing parameters, you can modify the `updateTime()` function to add the number of times it gets invoked to the display in the status bar. For that to work, the function must have a parameter variable so that it can catch a new value each time it is invoked by `setTimeout()`'s expression. For all browsers, the function would be modified as follows (unchanged lines are represented by the ellipsis):

```
function updateTime(i) {
    ...
    window.status = theTime + "  (" + i + ")";
    // pass updated counter value with next call to this function
    timerID = setTimeout("updateTime(" + i+1 + ")",1000);
}
```

If you were running this exclusively in NN4+/Moz, you could use its more convenient way of passing parameters to the function:

```
timerID = setTimeout(updateTime,1000, i+1);
```

In either case, the `onload` event handler would also have to be modified to get the ball rolling with an initial parameter:

```
onload = "updateTime(0)";
```

Related Items: `window.clearTimeout()`, `window.setInterval()`, `window.clearInterval()` methods

showHelp("*URL*",["*contextID*"])

Returns: Nothing
Compatibility: WinIE4+, MacIE-, NN-, Moz-, Safari-

The IE-specific `showHelp()` method lets a script open a Winhelp window with a particular `.hlp` file. This method is specific to Win32 operating systems.

If your Winhelp file has context identifiers specified in various places, you can pass the ID as an optional second parameter. This lets the call to `showHelp()` navigate to a particular area of the `.hlp` file that applies to a specific element on the page.

See the Microsoft Visual Studio authoring environment for details on building Winhelp files.

showModalDialog("*URL*"[, *arguments*][, *features*])
showModelessDialog("*URL*"[, *arguments*][, *features*])

Returns: `returnValue` (modal) or `window` object (modeless)
Compatibility: WinIE4+, MacIE4+, NN-, Moz-, Safari 2.01+

IE4+ and Safari 2.01+ provide methods for opening a modal dialog-box window, which always stays in front of the main browser window while making the main window inaccessible to the user. In WinIE5, Microsoft added the modeless type of dialog box, which also stays in front but allows user access to whatever can be seen in the main window. You can load any HTML page or image that you like into the dialog-box window by providing a URL as the first parameter. Optional parameters let you pass data to a dialog box and give you considerable control over the look of the window. A similar type of dialog-box window is available in NN/Moz via the `window.openDialog()` method.

The windows generated by both methods are (almost) full-fledged `window` objects with some extra properties that are useful for what these windows are intended to do. Perhaps the most important property is the `window.dialogArgument` property. This property lets a script read the data that is passed to the window via the second parameter of both `showModalDialog()` and `showModelessDialog()`. Passed data can be in any valid JavaScript data type, including objects and arrays.

Displaying a modal dialog box has some ramifications for scripts. In particular, script execution in the main window halts at the statement that invokes the `showModalDialog()` method as long as the modal dialog box remains visible. Scripts are free to run in the dialog-box window during this time. The instant the user closes the dialog box, execution resumes in the main window. A call to show a modeless dialog box, on the other hand, does not halt processing because scripts in the main page or dialog-box window are allowed to communicate live with the other window.

Retrieving dialog-box data

To send data back to the main window's script from a modal dialog-box window, a script in the dialog-box window can set the `window.returnValue` property to any JavaScript value. It is this value that gets assigned to the variable receiving the returned value from the `setModelDialog()` method, as shown in the following example:

```
var specifications = window.showModalDialog("preferences.html");
```

The makeup and content of the returned data are in the hands of your scripts. No data is automatically returned for you.

Because a modeless dialog box coexists with your live main page window, returning data is not as straightforward as for a modal dialog box. The second parameter of the `showModelessDialog()` method takes on a special task that isn't exactly the same as passing parameters to the dialog box. Instead, if you define a global variable or a function in the main window's script, pass a reference to that variable or function as the second parameter to display the modeless dialog box. A script in the modeless dialog box can then point to that reference as the way to send data back to the main window before the dialog box closes (or when a user clicks something, such as an Apply button). This mechanism even allows for passing data back to a function in the main window. For example, say that the main window has a function defined as the following:

```
function receivePrefsDialogData(a, b, c) {
    // statements to process incoming values //
}
```

Then pass a reference to this function when opening the window:

```
dlog = showModelessDialog("prefs.html", receivePrefsDialogData);
```

A script statement in the dialog-box window's document can pick up that reference so that other statements can use it, such as a function for an Apply button's `onclick` event handler:

```
var returnFunc = window.dialogArguments;
...
function apply(form) {
    returnFunc(form.color.value, form.style.value, form.size.value);
}
```

Although this approach seems to block ways of getting parameters to the dialog box when it opens, you can always reference the dialog box in the main window's script and set form or variable values directly:

```
dlog = showModelessDialog("prefs.html", receivePrefsDialogData);
dlog.document.forms[0].userName.value = GetCookie("userName");
```

Be aware that a dialog-box window opened with either of these methods does not maintain a connection to the originating window via the `opener` property. The `opener` property for both dialog-box types is undefined.

Dialog-box window features

Both methods provide an optional third property that lets you specify visible features of the dialog-box window. Omitting the property sets all features to their default values. All parameters are to be contained by a single string, and each parameter's name–value pair is in the form of CSS `attribute:value` syntax. Table 16-4 lists all of the window features available for the two window styles. If you are designing for backward compatibility with IE4, you are restricted to the modal dialog box and a subset of features, as noted in the table. All values listed as Boolean take only the following four values: `yes`, `no`, `1`, and `0`.

TABLE 16-4

IE Dialog-Box Window Features

Feature	Type	Default	Description
	Boolean	yes	Whether to center dialog box (overridden by `dialogLeft` and/or `dialogTop`).
	Length	Varies	Outer height of the dialog-box window. IE4 default length unit is em; IE5+/Safari is pixel (px).
	Integer	Varies	Pixel offset of dialog box from left edge of screen.
	Integer	Varies	Pixel offset of dialog box from top edge of screen.
	Length	Varies	Outer width of the dialog-box window. IE4 default length unit is em; IE5+/Safari is pixel (px).
	String	raised | sunken	Border style.
help	Boolean	yes	Display Help icon in title bar.
resizable	Boolean	no	Dialog box is resizable (IE5+/Safari only).
status	Boolean	Varies	Display status bar at window bottom (IE5+/Safari only). Default is yes for untrusted dialog box, no for trusted dialog box.

type of syntax for these features lets you string multiple features together by separating each pair micolon within the string. For example:

```
r dlogData = showModalDialog("prefs.html", defaultData,
    "dialogHeight:300px; dialogWidth:460px; help:no");
```

they are not explicitly listed among the window features, scroll bars are normally displayed in the wind if the content exceeds the size assigned or available to the dialog box. If you don't want scroll bars to appear, have your dialog-box document's script set the `document.body.scroll` property to `false` as the page opens.

windowObject.**showModalDialog()**

Dialog-box cautions

A potential user problem to watch for is that typically, a dialog-box window does not open until the HTML file for the dialog box has loaded. Therefore, if there is substantial delay before a complex document loads, the user does not see any action indicating that something is happening. You may want to experiment with setting the `cursor` style sheet property and restoring it when the dialog box's document loads.

Example

To demonstrate the two styles of dialog boxes, I have implemented the same functionality (setting some session visual preferences) for both modal and modeless dialog boxes. This tactic shows you how to pass data back and forth between the main page and both styles of dialog-box windows.

The first example demonstrates how to use a modal dialog box. In the process, data is passed into the dialog-box window, and values are returned. Listing 16-36 is the HTML and scripting for the main page. A button's `onclick` event handler invokes a function that opens the modal dialog box. The dialog box's document (see Listing 16-37) contains several form elements for entering a user name and selecting a few color styles for the main page. Data from the dialog box is fashioned into an array to be sent back to the main window. That array is initially assigned to a local variable, `prefs`, as the dialog box closes. If the user cancels the dialog box, the returned value is an empty string, so nothing more in `getPrefsData()` executes. But when the user clicks OK, the array comes back. Each of the array items is read and assigned to its respective form value or style property. These values are also preserved in the global `currPrefs` array. This allows the settings to be sent to the modal dialog box (as the second parameter to `showModalDialog()`) the next time the dialog box is opened.

LISTING 16-36

Main Page for showModalDialog()

```
<html>
  <head>
    <title>window.setModalDialog() Method</title>
    <script type="text/javascript">
    var currPrefs = new Array();

    function getPrefsData() {
        var prefs = showModalDialog("lst16-40.htm", currPrefs,
          "dialogWidth:400px; dialogHeight:300px");
        if (prefs) {
            if (prefs["name"]) {
                document.all.firstName.innerText = prefs["name"];
                currPrefs["name"] = prefs["name"];
            }
            if (prefs["bgColor"]) {
                document.body.style.backgroundColor = prefs["bgColor"];
                currPrefs["bgColor"] = prefs["bgColor"];
            }
            if (prefs["textColor"]) {
                document.body.style.color = prefs["textColor"];
                currPrefs["textColor"] = prefs["textColor"];
            }
            if (prefs["h1Size"]) {
                document.all.welcomeHeader.style.fontSize = prefs["h1Size"];
```

```
            currPrefs["h1Size"] = prefs["h1Size"];
        }
    }
}
function init() {
    document.all.firstName.innerText = "friend";
}
</script>
</head>
<body bgcolor="#EEEEEE" style="margin:20px" onload="init()">
    <h1>window.setModalDialog() Method</h1>
    <hr />
    <h2 id="welcomeHeader">Welcome, <span id="firstName"> </span>!</h2>
    <hr />
    <p>Use this button to set style preferences for this page: <button
        id="prefsButton" onclick="getPrefsData()">Preferences</button></p>
</body>
</html>
```

The dialog box's document, shown in Listing 16-37, is responsible for reading the incoming data (and set-ting the form elements accordingly) and assembling form data for return to the main window's script. Notice when you load the example that the `title` element of the dialog box's document appears in the dia-log-box window's title bar.

When the page loads into the dialog-box window, the `init()` function examines the `window.dialogArguments` property. If it has any data, the data is used to preset the form elements to mir-ror the current settings of the main page. A utility function, `setSelected()`, preselects the option of a `select` element to match the current settings.

Buttons at the bottom of the page are explicitly positioned to be at the bottom-right corner of the window. Each button invokes a function to do what is needed to close the dialog box. In the case of the OK button, the `handleOK()` function sets the `window.returnValue` property to the data that comes back from the `getFormData()` function. This latter function reads the form element values and packages them in an array using the form elements' names as array indices. This helps keep everything straight back in the main win-dow's script, which uses the index names, and therefore is not dependent upon the precise sequence of the form elements in the dialog-box window.

LISTING 16-37

Document for the Modal Dialog Box

```
<html>
    <head>
        <title>User Preferences</title>
        <script type="text/javascript">
        // Close the dialog
        function closeme() {
            window.close();
        }
```

continued

LISTING 16-37 *(continued)*

```
// Handle click of OK button
function handleOK() {
   window.returnValue = getFormData();
   closeme();
}

// Handle click of Cancel button
function handleCancel() {
   window.returnValue = "";
   closeme();
}

// Generic function converts form element name-value pairs
// into an array
function getFormData() {
   var form = document.prefs;
   var returnedData = new Array();
   // Harvest values for each type of form element
   for (var i = 0; i < form.elements.length; i++) {
      if (form.elements[i].type == "text") {
         returnedData[form.elements[i].name] = form.elements[i].value;
      } else if (form.elements[i].type.indexOf("select") != -1) {
         returnedData[form.elements[i].name] = form.elements[i].
            options[form.elements[i].selectedIndex].value;
      } else if (form.elements[i].type == "radio") {
         returnedData[form.elements[i].name] = form.elements[i].value;
      } else if (form.elements[i].type == "checkbox") {
         returnedData[form.elements[i].name] = form.elements[i].value;
      } else
         continue;
   }
   return returnedData;
}

// Initialize by setting form elements from passed data
function init() {
   if (window.dialogArguments) {
      var args = window.dialogArguments;
      var form = document.prefs;
      if (args["name"]) {
         form.name.value = args["name"];
      }
      if (args["bgColor"]) {
         setSelected(form.bgColor, args["bgColor"]);
      }
      if (args["textColor"]) {
         setSelected(form.textColor, args["textColor"]);
      }
      if (args["h1Size"]) {
         setSelected(form.h1Size, args["h1Size"]);
      }
```

```
        }
    }

    // Utility function to set a SELECT element to one value
    function setSelected(select, value) {
        for (var i = 0; i < select.options.length; i++) {
            if (select.options[i].value == value) {
                select.selectedIndex = i;
                break;
            }
        }
        return;
    }

    // Utility function to accept a press of the
    // Enter key in the text field as a click of OK
    function checkEnter() {
        if (window.event.keyCode == 13) {
            handleOK();
        }
    }
    </script>
</head>
<body bgcolor="#EEEEEE" onload="init()">
    <h2>Web Site Preferences</h2>
    <hr />
    <form name="prefs" onsubmit="return false">
        <table>
            <tr>
                <td>Enter your first name:<input name="name" type="text"
                    value="" size="20" onkeydown="checkEnter()" /></td>
            </tr>
            <tr>
                <td>Select a background color: <select name="bgColor">
                        <option value="beige">Beige</option>
                        <option value="antiquewhite">Antique White</option>
                        <option value="goldenrod">Goldenrod</option>
                        <option value="lime">Lime</option>
                        <option value="powderblue">Powder Blue</option>
                        <option value="slategray">Slate Gray</option>
                    </select></td>
            </tr>
            <tr>
                <td>Select a text color: <select name="textColor">
                        <option value="black">Black</option>
                        <option value="white">White</option>
                        <option value="navy">Navy Blue</option>
                        <option value="darkorange">Dark Orange</option>
                        <option value="seagreen">Sea Green</option>
                        <option value="teal">Teal</option>
                    </select></td>
```

continued

459

LISTING 16-37   *(continued)*

```
        </tr>
        <tr>
          <td>Select "Welcome" heading font point size: <select
            name="h1Size">
              <option value="12">12</option>
              <option value="14">14</option>
              <option value="18">18</option>
              <option value="24">24</option>
              <option value="32">32</option>
              <option value="48">48</option>
          </select></td>
        </tr>
      </table>
    </form>
    <div style="position:absolute; left:200px; top:220px">
      <button style="width:80px"
      onclick="handleOK()">OK</button>   <button
      style="width:80px" onclick="handleCancel()">Cancel</button>
    </div>
  </body>
</html>
```

One last convenience feature of the dialog-box window is the `onkeypress` event handler in the text box. The function it invokes looks for the Enter key. If that key is pressed while the box has focus, the same `handleOK()` function is invoked, as though the user had clicked the OK button. This feature makes the dialog box behave as though the OK button is an automatic default, just as in real dialog boxes.

You should observe several important structural changes that were made to turn the modal approach into a modeless one. Listing 16-38 shows the version of the main window modified for use with a modeless dialog box. Another global variable, `prefsDlog`, is initialized to eventually store the reference to the modeless window returned by the `showModelessWindow()` method. The variable gets used to invoke the `init()` function inside the modeless dialog box, but also as conditions in an `if` construction surrounding the generation of the dialog box. The reason this is needed is to prevent multiple instances of the dialog box from being created (the button is still alive while the modeless window is showing). The dialog box won't be created again as long as there is a value in `prefsDlog` and the dialog-box window has not been closed (picking up the `window.closed` property of the dialog-box window).

The `showModelessDialog()` method's second parameter is a reference to the function in the main window that updates the main document. As you see in a moment, that function is invoked from the dialog box when the user clicks the OK or Apply button.

LISTING 16-38

Main Page for showModelessDialog()

```
<html>
  <head>
    <title>window.setModelessDialog() Method</title>
    <script type="text/javascript">
```

```
        var currPrefs = new Array();
        var prefsDlog;
        function getPrefsData() {
            if (!prefsDlog || prefsDlog.closed) {
                prefsDlog = showModelessDialog("lst16-42.htm", setPrefs,
                    "dialogWidth:400px; dialogHeight:300px");
                prefsDlog.init(currPrefs);
            }
        }

        function setPrefs(prefs) {
            if (prefs["bgColor"]) {
                document.body.style.backgroundColor = prefs["bgColor"];
                currPrefs["bgColor"] = prefs["bgColor"];
            }
            if (prefs["textColor"]) {
                document.body.style.color = prefs["textColor"];
                currPrefs["textColor"] = prefs["textColor"];
            }
            if (prefs["h1Size"]) {
                document.all.welcomeHeader.style.fontSize = prefs["h1Size"];
                currPrefs["h1Size"] = prefs["h1Size"];
            }
            if (prefs["name"]) {
                document.all.firstName.innerText = prefs["name"];
                currPrefs["name"] = prefs["name"];
            }
        }

        function init() {
            document.all.firstName.innerText = "friend";
        }
        </script>
    </head>
    <body bgcolor="#EEEEEE" style="margin:20px" onload="init()">
        <h1>window.setModelessDialog() Method</h1>
        <hr />
        <h2 id="welcomeHeader">Welcome, <span id="firstName"> </span>!</h2>
        <hr />
        <p>Use this button to set style preferences for this page: <button
            id="prefsButton" onclick="getPrefsData()">Preferences</button></p>
    </body>
</html>
```

Changes to the dialog-box window document for a modeless version (see Listing 16-39) are rather limited. A new button is added to the bottom of the screen for an Apply button. As in many dialog-box windows you see in Microsoft products, the Apply button lets current settings in dialog boxes be applied to the current document but without closing the dialog box. This approach makes experimenting with settings easier.

The Apply button invokes a handleApply() function, which works the same as handleOK() except that the dialog box is not closed. But these two functions communicate back to the main window differently from a modal dialog box. The main window's processing function is passed as the second parameter of

***windowObject*.showModalDialog()**

`showModelessDialog()` and is available as the `window.dialogArguments` property in the dialog-box window's script. That function reference is assigned to a local variable in both functions, and the remote function is invoked, passing the results of the `getFormData()` function as parameter values back to the main window.

LISTING 16-39

Document for the Modeless Dialog Box

```html
<html>
   <head>
      <title>User Preferences</title>
      <script type="text/javascript">
      // Close the dialog
      function closeme() {
         window.close();
      }

      // Handle click of OK button
      function handleOK() {
         var returnFunc = window.dialogArguments;
         returnFunc(getFormData());
         closeme();
      }

      // Handle click of Apply button
      function handleApply() {
         var returnFunc = window.dialogArguments;
         returnFunc(getFormData());
      }

      // Handle click of Cancel button
      function handleCancel() {
         window.returnValue = "";
         closeme();
      }

      // Generic function converts form element name-value pairs
      // into an array
      function getFormData() {
         var form = document.prefs;
         var returnedData = new Array();
         // Harvest values for each type of form element
         for (var i = 0; i < form.elements.length; i++) {
            if (form.elements[i].type == "text") {
               returnedData[form.elements[i].name] = form.elements[i].value;
            } else if (form.elements[i].type.indexOf("select") != -1) {
               returnedData[form.elements[i].name] = form.elements[i].
                  options[form.elements[i].selectedIndex].value;
            } else if (form.elements[i].type == "radio") {
               returnedData[form.elements[i].name] = form.elements[i].value;
            } else if (form.elements[i].type == "checkbox") {
```

```
                returnedData[form.elements[i].name] = form.elements[i].value;
            } else
                continue;
        }
        return returnedData;
    }

    // Initialize by setting form elements from passed data
    function init(currPrefs) {
        if (currPrefs) {
            var form = document.prefs;
            if (currPrefs["name"]) {
                form.name.value = currPrefs["name"];
            }
            if (currPrefs["bgColor"]) {
                setSelected(form.bgColor, currPrefs["bgColor"]);
            }
            if (currPrefs["textColor"]) {
                setSelected(form.textColor, currPrefs["textColor"]);
            }
            if (currPrefs["h1Size"]) {
                setSelected(form.h1Size, currPrefs["h1Size"]);
            }
        }
    }

    // Utility function to set a SELECT element to one value
    function setSelected(select, value) {
        for (var i = 0; i < select.options.length; i++) {
            if (select.options[i].value == value) {
                select.selectedIndex = i;
                break;
            }
        }
        return;
    }

    // Utility function to accept a press of the
    // Enter key in the text field as a click of OK
    function checkEnter() {
        if (window.event.keyCode == 13) {
            handleOK();
        }
    }
    </script>
</head>
<body bgcolor="#EEEEEE" onload="init()">
    <h2>Web Site Preferences</h2>
    <hr />
    <form name="prefs" onsubmit="return false">
        <table>
```

continued

LISTING 16-39 *(continued)*

```
      <tr>
        <td>Enter your first name:<input name="name" type="text"
          value="" size="20" onkeydown="checkEnter()" /></td>
      </tr>
      <tr>
        <td>Select a background color: <select name="bgColor">
            <option value="beige">Beige</option>
            <option value="antiquewhite">Antique White</option>
            <option value="goldenrod">Goldenrod</option>
            <option value="lime">Lime</option>
            <option value="powderblue">Powder Blue</option>
            <option value="slategray">Slate Gray</option>
          </select></td>
      </tr>
      <tr>
        <td>Select a text color: <select name="textColor">
            <option value="black">Black</option>
            <option value="white">White</option>
            <option value="navy">Navy Blue</option>
            <option value="darkorange">Dark Orange</option>
            <option value="seagreen">Sea Green</option>
            <option value="teal">Teal</option>
          </select></td>
      </tr>
      <tr>
        <td>Select "Welcome" heading font point size: <select
          name="h1Size">
            <option value="12">12</option>
            <option value="14">14</option>
            <option value="18">18</option>
            <option value="24">24</option>
            <option value="32">32</option>
            <option value="48">48</option>
          </select></td>
      </tr>
    </table>
  </form>
  <div style="position:absolute; left:120px; top:220px">
    <button style="width:80px"
    onclick="handleOK()">OK</button>   <button
    style="width:80px"
    onclick="handleCancel()">Cancel</button>   <button
    style="width:80px" onclick="handleApply()">Apply</button>
  </div>
</body>
</html>
```

The biggest design challenge you probably face with respect to these windows is deciding between a modal and modeless dialog-box style. Some designers insist that modality has no place in a graphical user interface; others say that there are times when you need to focus the user on a very specific task before any further processing can take place. That's where a modal dialog box makes perfect sense.

Related Item: `window.open()` method

sizeToContent()

Returns: Nothing
Compatibility: WinIE-, MacIE-, NN6+, Moz+, Safari-

The NN6+/Moz `window.sizeToContent()` method can be a valuable aid in making sure that a window (especially a subwindow) is sized for the optimum display of the window's content. But you must also be cautious with this method, or it will do more harm than good.

Invoking the `sizeToContent()` method resizes the window so that all content is visible. Concerns about variations in OS-specific rendering become a thing of the past. Naturally, you should perform this action only on a window whose content at the most occupies a space smaller than the smallest video monitor running your code (typically 640 × 480 pixels, but conceivably much smaller for future versions of the browser used on handheld computers).

You can get the user in trouble, however, if you invoke the method twice on the same window that contains the resizing script. This action can cause the window to expand to a size that may exceed the pixel size of the user's video monitor. Successive invocations fail to cinch up the window's size to its content again. Multiple invocations are safe, however, on subwindows when the resizing script statement is in the main window.

Example

Use The Evaluator (Chapter 13) in NN6+/Moz to try the `sizeToContent()` method. Assuming that you are running The Evaluator from the `Chap13` directory on the CD-ROM (or the directory copied as is to your hard disk), you can open a subwindow with one of the other files in the directory and then size the subwindow. Enter the following statements in the top text box:

```
a = window.open("lst13-02.htm","")
a.sizeToContent()
```

The resized subwindow is at the minimum recommended width for a browser window and at a height tall enough to display the little bit of content in the document.

As with any method that changes the size of the browser window, problems arise in browsers such as Firefox 2 that support tabbed browsing where multiple pages are opened as different tabs within the same browser instance. In a tabbed browser, it is impossible to resize the window of one page without altering all others. It's certainly still possible to open multiple browser instances to resolve this problem, but the default response to `window.open()` is to open a new tab, not a new browser window.

Related Item: `window.resizeTo()` method

stop()

Returns: Nothing
Compatibility: WinIE-, MacIE-, NN4+, Moz+, Safari-

The NN/Moz-specific stop() method offers a scripted equivalent of clicking the Stop button in the toolbar. The availability of this method allows you to create your own toolbar on your page and hide the toolbar (in the main window with signed scripts or in a subwindow). For example, if you have an image representing the Stop button in your page, you can surround it with a link whose action stops loading, as in the following:

```
<a href="javascript: void stop()"><img src="myStop.gif" border="0"></a>
```

A script cannot stop its own document from loading, but it can stop loading of another frame or window. Similarly, if the current document dynamically loads a new image or a multimedia MIME type file as a separate action, the stop() method can halt that process. Even though the stop() method is a window method, it is not tied to any specific window or frame: Stop means stop.

Related Items: window.back(), window.find(), window.forward(), window.home(), window.print() methods

Event handlers

onafterprint

onbeforeprint

Compatibility: WinIE5+, MacIE-, NN-, Moz-, Safari-

Each of these event handlers fires after the user has clicked the OK button in IE's Print dialog box. This goes for printing that is invoked manually (via menus and browser shortcut buttons) and the window.print() method.

Although printing is usually WYSIWYG, it is conceivable that you may want the printed version of a document to display more or less of the document than is showing at that instant. For example, you may have a special copyright notice that you want printed at the end of a page whenever it goes to the printer. In that case, the element with that content can have its display style sheet property set to none when the page loads. Before the document is sent to the printer, a script needs to adjust that style property to display the element as a block item; after printing, have your script revert the setting to none.

Immediately after the user clicks the OK button in the Print dialog box, the onbeforeprint event handler fires. As soon as the page(s) is sent to the printer or spooler, the onafterprint event handler fires.

Example

The following script fragment assumes that the page includes a div element whose style sheet includes a setting of display:none as the page loads. Somewhere in the Head, the print-related event handlers are set as properties:

```
function showPrintCopyright() {
    document.all.printCopyright.style.display = "block";
}
function hidePrintCopyright() {
    document.all.printCopyright.style.display = "none";
}
window.onbeforeprint = showPrintCopyright;
window.onafterprint = hidePrintCopyright;
```

onbeforeunload

Compatibility: WinIE4+, MacIE5+, NN-, Moz-, Safari-

Any user or scripted action that normally forces the current page to be unloaded or replaced causes the onbeforeunload event handler to fire. Unlike the onunload event handler, however, onbeforeunload is a bit better behaved when it comes to allowing complex scripts to finish before the actual unloading takes place. Moreover, you can assign a string value to the event.returnValue property in the event handler function. That string becomes part of a message in an alert window that gives the user a chance to stay on the page. If the user agrees to stay, the page does not unload, and any action that caused the potential replacement is canceled.

Example

The simple page in Listing 16-40 shows you how to give the user a chance to stay on the page.

LISTING 16-40

Using the onbeforeunload Event Handler

```html
<html>
   <head>
      <title>onbeforeunload Event Handler</title>
      <script type="text/javascript">
      function verifyClose() {
         event.returnValue =
            "We really like you and hope you will stay longer.";
      }

      window.onbeforeunload = verifyClose;
      </script>
   </head>
   <body>
      <h1>onbeforeunload Event Handler</h1>
      <hr />
      <p>Use this button to navigate to the previous page: <button id="go"
         onclick="history.back()">Go Back</button></p>
   </body>
</html>
```

Related Item: onunload event handler

onerror

Compatibility: WinIE4+, MacIE4+, NN3+, Moz+, Safari+

(See the discussion of the window.onerror property earlier in this chapter.)

onhelp

Compatibility: WinIE4+, MacIE4+, NN-, Moz-, Safari-

The generic onhelp event handler is discussed in Chapter 15, but it also fires when the user activates the context-sensitive help within a modal or modeless dialog box. In the latter case, a user can click the Help icon in the dialog box's title bar, at which time the cursor changes to a question mark. The user can then click any element in the window. At that second click, the onhelp event handler fires, and the event object contains information about the element clicked (the event.srcElement is a reference to the specific element), allowing a script to supply help about that element.

To prevent the browser's built-in help window from appearing, the event handler must evaluate to return false (IE4+) or set the event.returnValue property to false (IE5+).

Example

The following script fragment can be used to provide context-sensitive help within a dialog box. Help messages for only two form elements are shown here, but in a real application, you could easily add more messages.

```
function showHelp() {
    switch (event.srcElement.name) {
        case "bgColor" :
            alert("Choose a color for the main window\'s background.");
            break;
        case "name" :
            alert("Enter your first name for a friendly greeting.");
            break;
        default :
            alert("Make preference settings for the main page styles.");
    }
    event.returnValue = false;
}
window.onhelp = showHelp
```

Because this page's help focuses on form elements, the switch construction cases are based on the name properties of the form elements. For other kinds of pages, the id properties may be more appropriate.

Related Items: event object (Chapter 25); switch construction (Chapter 32)

onload

Compatibility: WinIE3+, MacIE3+, NN2+, Moz+, Safari+

The onload event handler fires in the current window at the end of the document loading process (after all text and image elements have been transferred from the source file server to the browser, and after all plug-ins and Java applets have loaded and started running). At that point, the browser's memory contains all the objects and script components in the document that the browser can possibly know about.

The onload handler is an attribute of a <body> tag for a single-frame document or of the <frameset> tag for the top window of a multiple-frame document. When the handler is an attribute of a <frameset> tag, the event triggers only after all frames defined by that frameset have completely loaded.

Use either of the following scenarios to insert an `onload` handler into a document:

```html
<html>
    <head>
    </head>
    <body [other attributes] onload="statementOrFunction">
        [body content]
    </body>
</html>

<html>
    <head>
    </head>
    <frameset [other attributes] onload="statementOrFunction">
        <frame [frame specification attributes] />
    </frameset>
</html>
```

This handler has a special capability when it's part of a frameset definition: The handler won't fire until the `onload` event handlers of all child frames in the frameset have fired. Therefore, if some initialization scripts depend on components existing in other frames, trigger them from the frameset's `onload` event handler. This brings up a good general rule of thumb for writing JavaScript: Scripts that execute during a document's loading should contribute to the process of generating the document and its objects. To act immediately on those objects, design additional functions that are called by the `onload` event handler for that window.

The type of operations suited for an `onload` event handler are those that can run quickly and without user intervention. Users shouldn't be penalized by having to wait for considerable postloading activity to finish before they can interact with your pages. At no time should you present a modal dialog box as part of an `onload` handler. Users who design macros on their machines to visit sites unattended may get hung up on a page that automatically displays an alert, confirm, or prompt dialog box. On the other hand, an operation such as setting the `window.defaultStatus` property is a perfect candidate for an `onload` event handler, as are initializing event handlers as properties of element objects in the page.

 Browsers equipped with pop-up window blockers ignore all `window.open()` method calls in `onload` event handler functions.

Related Items: `onunload` event handler; `window.defaultStatus` property

onresize

Compatibility: WinIE4+, MacIE4+, NN4+, Moz+, Safari-

If a user resizes a window, the action causes the `onresize` event handler to fire for the `window` object. When you assign a function to the event (for example, `window.onresize = handleResizes`), the NN/Moz event object conveys `width` and `height` properties that reveal the outer width and height of the entire window. A window resize should not reload the document such that an `onload` event handler fires (although some early Navigator versions did fire the extra event).

Related Item: `event` object (Chapter 25)

onscroll

Compatibility: WinIE4+, MacIE4+, NN7+, Moz+, Safari 1.3+

The onscroll event handler fires for the body element object as the result of manual scrolling of the document (via scroll bars or navigation keyboard keys) and scripted scrolling via the doScroll() method, via the scrollIntoView() method, or by adjusting the scrollTop and/or scrollLeft properties of the body element object. For manual scrolling and scrolling by doScroll(), the event seems to fire twice in succession. Moreover, the event.srcElement property is null even when the body element is handling the onscroll event handler.

Example

Listing 16-41 is a highly artificial demonstration of what can be a useful tool for some page designs. Consider a document that occupies a window or frame but that you don't want scrolled even by accident with one of the mouse wheels that are popular with Wintel PCs. If scrolling of the content would destroy the appearance or value of the content, you want to make sure that the page always zips back to the top. The onscroll event handler in Listing 16-41 does just that. Notice that the event handler is set as a property of the window object.

LISTING 16-41

Preventing a Page from Scrolling

```html
<html>
    <head>
        <title>onscroll Event Handler</title>
        <script type="text/javascript">
        window.onscroll = zipBack;
        function zipBack() {
            window.scroll(0,0);
        }
        </script>
    </head>
    <body>
        <h1>onscroll Event Handler</h1>
        <hr />
        This page always zips back to the top if you try to scroll it.
        <p><iframe frameborder="0" scrolling="no" height="1000"
            src="bofright.htm"></iframe></p>
    </body>
</html>
```

Related Items: scrollBy(), scrollByLines(), scrollByPages() methods

onunload

Compatibility: WinIE3+, MacIE3+, NN2+, Moz+, Safari+

An unload event reaches the current window just before a document is cleared from view. The most common ways windows are cleared are when new HTML documents are loaded into them or when a script begins writing new HTML on the fly for the window or frame.

Limit the extent of the `onunload` event handler to quick operations that do not inhibit the transition from one document to another. Do not invoke any methods that display dialog boxes. You specify `onunload` event handlers in the same places in an HTML document as the `onload` handlers: as a `<body>` tag attribute for a single-frame window or as a `<frameset>` tag attribute for a multiframe window. Both `onload` and `onunload` event handlers can appear in the same `<body>` or `<frameset>` tag without causing problems. The `onunload` event handler merely stays safely tucked away in the browser's memory, waiting for the `unload` event to arrive for processing as the document gets ready to clear the window.

Let me pass along one caution about the `onunload` event handler: Even though the event fires before the document goes away, don't burden the event handler with time-consuming tasks, such as generating new objects or submitting a form. The document will probably go away before the function completes, leaving the function looking for objects and values that no longer exist. The best defense is to keep your `onunload` event handler processing to a minimum.

 Browsers equipped with pop-up window blockers ignore all `window.open()` method calls in `onunload` **event handler functions.**

Related Item: `onload` event handler

frame Element Object

For HTML element properties, methods, and event handlers, see Chapter 15.

Properties	Methods	Event Handlers
allowTransparency		
borderColor		
contentDocument		
contentWindow		
frameBorder		
height		
longDesc		
marginHeight		
marginWidth		
name		
noResize		
scrolling		
src		
width		

Syntax

Accessing properties or methods of a frame element object from a frameset:

```
(IE4+)     document.all.frameID. property | method([parameters])
(IE5+/W3C) document.getElementById("frameID"). property | method([parameters])
```

Accessing properties or methods of a frame element from a frame document:

```
(IE4+)     parent.document.all.frameID. property | method([parameters])
(IE5+/W3C) parent.document.getElementById("frameID"). property |
           method([parameters])
```

Compatibility: WinIE4+, MacIE4+, NN6+, Moz+, Safari+

About this object

As noted in the opening section of this chapter, a frame element object is distinct from the frame object that acts as a window object in a document hierarchy. The frame element object is available to scripts only when all HTML elements are exposed in the object model, as in IE4+, NN6+, Mozilla, and Safari.

Because the frame element object is an HTML element, it shares the properties, methods, and event handlers of all HTML elements, as described in Chapter 15. By and large, you access the frame element object to set or modify an attribute value in the <frame> tag. If so, you simplify matters if you assign an identifier to the id attribute of the tag. Your tag still needs a name attribute if your scripts refer to frames through the original object model (a parent.frameName reference). Although there is no law against using the same identifier for both name and id attributes, using different names to prevent potential conflict with references in browsers that recognize both attributes is best.

To modify the dimensions of a frame, you must go the frameset element object that defines the cols and rows attributes for the frameset. These properties can be modified on the fly in modern browsers.

Properties

allowTransparency

Value: Boolean   Read/Write
Compatibility: WinIE6+, MacIE-, NN-, Moz-, Safari-

The allowTransparency property indicates whether the frame's background is transparent. This property applies primarily to the iframe object, because framesets don't have background colors or images to show through a transparent frame.

borderColor

Value: Hexadecimal triplet or color name string   Read/Write
Compatibility: WinIE4+, MacIE4+, NN-, Moz-, Safari-

If a frame displays a border (as determined by the frameborder attribute of the frame element or border attribute of the frameset element), it can have a color set separately from the rest of the frames. The initial color (if different from the rest of the frameset) is usually set by the bordercolor attribute of the <frame> tag. After that, scripts can modify settings as needed.

Modifying a single frame's border can be risky at times, depending on your color combinations. In practice, different browsers appear to follow different rules when it comes to negotiating conflicts or defining just how far a single frame's border extends into the border space. Color changes to individual frame borders do not always render. Verify your designs on as many browsers and operating system variations as you can to test your combinations.

Example

Although you may experience problems changing the color of a single frame border, the W3C DOM syntax would look like the following if the script were inside the framesetting document:

```
document.getElementById("contentsFrame").borderColor = "red";
```

The IE-only version would be

```
document.all["contentsFrame"].borderColor = "red";
```

These examples assume that the frame name arrives to a script function as a string. If the script is executing in one of the frames of the frameset, add a reference to `parent` in the preceding statements.

Related Items: `frame.frameBorder`, `frameset.frameBorder` properties

contentDocument

Value: document object reference   Read-Only
Compatibility: WinIE-, MacIE-, NN6+, Moz+, Safari+

The `contentDocument` property of a `frame` element object is nothing more than a reference to the document contained by that frame. This property bridges the gap between the `frame` element object and the `frame` object. Both of these objects contain the same `document` object, but from a scripting point of view, references most typically use the frame object to reach the document inside a frame, whereas the `frame` element is used to access properties equated with the `frame` tag's attributes. But if your script finds that it has a reference to the `frame` element object, you can use the `contentDocument` property to get a valid reference to the document and, therefore, any other content of the frame.

Example

A framesetting document script might be using the ID of a `frame` element to read or adjust one of the element properties and then need to perform some action on the content of the page through its `document` object. You can get the reference to the `document` object via a statement such as the following:

```
var doc = document.getElementById("Frame3").contentDocument;
```

Then your script can, for example, dive into a form in the document:

```
var val = doc.mainForm.entry.value;
```

Related Items: `contentWindow` property; `document` object

contentWindow

Value: document object reference   Read-Only
Compatibility: WinIE5.5+, MacIE-, NN7+, Moz1.0.1+, Safari-

The `contentWindow` property of a `frame` element object is simply a reference to the window generated by that frame. This property provides access to the frame's window, which can then be used to reach the document inside the frame.

frame.height

Example

You can get the reference to the window object associated with a frame via a statement such as the following:

```
var win = document.getElementById("Frame3").contentWindow;
```

Related Item: window object

frameBorder

Value: yes | no | 1 | 0 as strings   Read/Write
Compatibility: WinIE4+, MacIE4+, NN6+, Moz+, Safari+

The frameBorder property offers scripted access to a frame element object's frameborder attribute setting. IE does not respond well to modifying this property after the page has loaded.

Values for the frameBorder property are strings that substitute for Boolean values. Value yes or 1 means that the border is (supposed to be) turned on; no or 0 turns off the border.

Example

The default value for the frameBorder property is yes. You can use this setting to create a toggle script (which, unfortunately, does not change the appearance in IE). The W3C-compatible version looks like the following:

```
function toggleFrameScroll(frameID) {
    var theFrame = document.getElementById(frameID);
    if (theFrame.frameBorder == "yes") {
        theFrame.frameBorder = "no";
    } else {
        theFrame.frameBorder = "yes";
    }
}
```

Related Items: frameset.frameBorder properties.

height
width

Value: Integer   Read-Only
Compatibility: WinIE4+, MacIE4+, NN-, Moz-, Safari-

IE4+ lets you retrieve the height and width of a frame element object. These values are not necessarily the same as document.body.clientHeight and document.body.clientWidth, because the frame dimensions include chrome associated with the frame, such as scroll bars. These values are read-only. If you need to modify the dimensions of a frame, do so via the frameset element object's rows and/or cols properties. Reading integer values for a frame's height and width properties is much easier than trying to parse the rows and cols string properties.

Example

The following fragment assumes a frameset defined with two frames set up as two columns within the frameset. The statements here live in the framesetting document. They retrieve the current width of the left frame and increase the width of that frame by 10 percent. Syntax shown here is for the W3C DOM but can easily be adapted to IE-only terminology.

```
var frameWidth = document.getElementById("leftFrame").width;
document.getElementById("mainFrameset").cols =
    (Math.round(frameWidth * 1.1)) + ",*";
```

Notice that the numeric value of the existing frame width is first increased by 10 percent and then concatenated to the rest of the string property assigned to the frameset's cols property. The asterisk after the comma means that the browser should figure out the remaining width and assign it to the right frame.

Related Item: frameset object

longDesc

Value: URL string   Read/Write
Compatibility: WinIE6+, MacIE5+, NN6+, Moz+, Safari+

The longDesc property is the scripted equivalent of the longdesc attribute of the <frame> tag. This HTML 4 attribute is intended to provide browsers a URL to a document that contains a long description of the element. Future browsers can use this feature to provide information about the frame for visually impaired site visitors.

marginHeight
marginWidth

Value: Integer   Read/Write
Compatibility: WinIE6+, MacIE5+, NN6+, Moz+, Safari+

Browsers tend to insert content within a frame automatically by adding a margin between the content and the edge of the frame. These values are represented by the marginHeight (top and bottom edges) and marginWidth (left and right edges) properties. Although the properties are not read-only, changing the values after the frameset has loaded does not alter the appearance of the document in the frame. If you need to alter the margin(s) of a document inside a frame, adjust the document.body.style margin properties.

Also be aware that although the default values of these properties are empty (meaning when no marginheight or marginwidth attributes are set for the <frame> tag), margins are built into the page. The precise pixel count of those margins varies with operating system.

Related Item: style object (Chapter 26)

name

Value: String   Read/Write
Compatibility: WinIE4+, MacIE4+, NN6+, Moz+, Safari+

The name property is the identifier associated with the frame for use as a frame reference. Scripts can reference the frame through the name property (for example, top.frames["myFrame"]), which is typically assigned via the name attribute.

noResize

Value: Boolean   Read/Write
Compatibility: WinIE6+, MacIE5+, NN6+, Moz+, Safari+

Web designers commonly fix their framesets so that users cannot resize the frames (by dragging any divider border between frames). The `noResize` property lets you read and adjust that behavior of a frame after the page has loaded. For example, during some part of the interaction with a user on a page, you may allow the user to modify the frame size manually while in a certain mode. Or you may grant the user one chance to resize the frame. When the `onresize` event handler fires, a script sets the `noResize` property of the `frame` element to `false`. If you turn off resizing for a frame, all edges of the frame become nonresizable, regardless of the `noResize` value setting of adjacent frames. Turning off resizability has no effect on the ability of scripts to alter the sizes of frames via the `frameset` element object's `cols` or `rows` properties.

Example

The following statement turns off the ability for a frame to be resized:

```
parent.document.getElementById("myFrame1").noResize = true;
```

Because of the negative nature of the property name, it may be difficult to keep the logic straight (setting `noResize` to `true` means that resizability is turned off). Keep a watchful eye on your Boolean values.

Related Items: `frameset.cols`, `frameset.rows` properties

scrolling

Value: yes | no | 1 | 0 as strings   Read/Write
Compatibility: WinIE6+, MacIE5+, NN6+, Moz+, Safari+

The `scrolling` property lets scripts turn scroll bars on and off inside a single frame of a frameset. By default, scrolling is turned on unless overridden by the `scroll` attribute of the `<frame>` tag.

Values for the `scrolling` property are strings that substitute for Boolean values. Value `yes` or 1 means that scroll bars are visible (provided that there is more content than can be viewed without scrolling); `no` or 0 hides scroll bars in the frame. IE also recognizes (and sets as default) the `auto` value.

 **Although this property is read/write, changing its value by script does not alter a frame's appearance in WinIE, Mozilla browsers, or Safari.**

Example

Listing 16-42 produces a frameset consisting of eight frames. The content for the frames is generated by a script within the frameset (via the `fillFrame()` function). Event handlers (`onclick`) in the Body of each frame invoke the `toggleFrameScroll()` function. Both ways of referencing the `frame` element object are shown, with the IE-only version commented out.

In the `toggleFrameScroll()` function, the `if` condition checks whether the property is set to something other than `no`. This allows the condition to evaluate to `true` if the property is set to either `auto` (the first time) or `yes` (as set by the function). Note that the scroll bars don't disappear from the frames in IE, NN6+, Moz, or Safari.

LISTING 16-42

Controlling the frame.scrolling Property

```html
<html>
    <head>
        <title>frame.scrolling Property</title>
        <script type="text/javascript">
        function toggleFrameScroll(frameID) {
            // IE5+/W3C version
            var theFrame = document.getElementById(frameID);

            if (theFrame.scrolling != "no") {
                theFrame.scrolling = "no";
            } else {
                theFrame.scrolling = "yes";
            }
        }

        // generate content for each frame
        function fillFrame(frameID) {
            var page = "<html><body onclick='parent.toggleFrameScroll(\"" +
            frameID + "\")'><span style='font-size:24pt'>";
            page += "<p>This frame has the ID of:<\/p><p>" + frameID + ".<\/p>";
            page += "<\/span><\/body><\/html>";
            return page;
        }
        </script>
    </head>
    <frameset id="outerFrameset" cols="50%,50%">
        <frameset id="innerFrameset1" rows="25%,25%,25%,25%">
            <frame id="myFrame1" src="javascript:parent.fillFrame('myFrame1')" />
            <frame id="myFrame2" src="javascript:parent.fillFrame('myFrame2')" />
            <frame id="myFrame3" src="javascript:parent.fillFrame('myFrame3')" />
            <frame id="myFrame4" src="javascript:parent.fillFrame('myFrame4')" />
        </frameset>
        <frameset id="innerFrameset2" rows="25%,25%,25%,25%">
            <frame id="myFrame5" src="javascript:parent.fillFrame('myFrame5')" />
            <frame id="myFrame6" src="javascript:parent.fillFrame('myFrame6')" />
            <frame id="myFrame7" src="javascript:parent.fillFrame('myFrame7')" />
            <frame id="myFrame8" src="javascript:parent.fillFrame('myFrame8')" />
        </frameset>
    </frameset>
</html>
```

src

Value: URL string   Read/Write
Compatibility: WinIE6+, MacIE5+, NN6+, Moz+, Safari+

The src property of a frame element object offers an additional way of navigating to a different page within a frame (meaning other than assigning a new URL to the location.href property of the frame object). For backward compatibility with older browsers, however, continue using location.href for scripted navigation. Remember that the src property belongs to the frame element object, not the window object it represents. Therefore, references to the src property must be via the element's ID and/or node hierarchy.

Example

For best results, use fully formed URLs as value for the src property, as shown here:

```
parent.document.getElementById("mainFrame").src = "http://www.dannyg.com";
```

Relative URLs and javascript: pseudo-URLs will also work most of the time.

Related Item: location.href property

frameset Element Object

For HTML element properties, methods, and event handlers, see Chapter 15.

Properties	Methods	Event Handlers
border		
borderColor		
cols		
frameBorder		
frameSpacing		
rows		

Syntax

Accessing properties or methods of a frameset element object from a frameset:

```
(IE4+)    document.all.framesetID. property | method([parameters])
(IE5+/W3C) document.getElementById("framesetID"). property | method([parameters])
```

Accessing properties or methods of a frameset element from a frame document:

```
(IE4+)    parent.document.all.framesetID. property | method([parameters])
(IE5+/W3C) parent.document.getElementById("framesetID"). property |
          method([parameters])
```

Compatibility: WinIE4+, MacIE4+, NN6+, Moz+, Safari+

About this object

The `frameset` element object is the script-accessible equivalent of the element generated via the `<frameset>` tag. This element is different from the parent (window-type) object from the original object model. A `frameset` element object has properties and methods that impact the HTML element; by contrast, the `window` object referenced from documents inside frames via the `parent` or `top` window references contains a document and all the content that goes along with it.

When framesets are nested in one another, a node parent–child relationship exists between containing and contained framesets. For example, consider the following skeletal nested frameset structure:

```
<frameset id="outerFrameset" cols="30%, 70%">
   <frame id="frame1">
   <frameset id="innerFrameset" rows="50%,50%">
      <frame id="frame2">
      <frame id="frame3">
   </frameset>
</frameset>
```

When writing scripts for documents that go inside any of the frames of this structure, references to the framesetting window and frames are a flatter hierarchy than the HTML signifies. A script in any frame references the framesetting window via the `parent` reference; a script in any frame references another frame via the `parent.frameName` reference. In other words, the `window` objects of the frameset defined in a document are all siblings and have the same parent.

Such is not the case when viewing the preceding structure from the perspective of W3C node terminology. Parent–child relationships are governed by the nesting of HTML elements, irrespective of whatever windows get generated by the browser. Therefore, frame `frame2` has only one sibling: `frame3`. Both of those share one parent: `innerFrameset`. Both `innerFrameset` and `frame1` are children of `outerFrameset`. If your script were sitting on a reference to `frame2`, and you wanted to change the `cols` property of `outerFrameset`, you would have to traverse two generations of nodes:

```
frame2Ref.parentNode.parentNode.cols = "40%,60%";
```

What might confuse matters ever more in practice is that a script belonging to one of the frames must use window object terminology to jump out of the current `window` object to the frameset that generated the frame window for the document. In other words, there is no immediate way to jump directly from a document to the `frame` element object that defines the frame in which the document resides. The document's script accesses the node hierarchy of its frameset via the `parent.document` reference. But this reference is to the `document` object that contains the entire frameset structure. Fortunately, the W3C DOM provides the `getElementById()` method to extract a reference to any node nested within the document. Thus, a document inside one of the frames can access the `frame` element object just as though it were any element in a typical document (which it is):

```
parent.document.getElementById("frame2")
```

No reference to the containing `frameset` element object is necessary. Or to make that column width change from a script inside one of the frame windows, the statement would be

```
parent.document.getElementById("outerFrame").cols = "40%,60%";
```

The inner frameset is equally accessible by the same syntax.

479

Properties

border

Value: Integer   Read/Write
Compatibility: WinIE4+, MacIE4+, NN-, Moz-, Safari+

The border property of a frameset element object lets you read the thickness (in pixels) of the borders between frames of a frameset. If you do not specify a border attribute in the frameset's tag, the property is empty, rather than reflecting the actual border thickness applied by default.

Example

Even though the property is read/write, changing the value does not change the thickness of the border you see in the browser. If you need to find the thickness of the border, a script reference from one of the frame's documents would look like the following:

```
var thickness = parent.document.all.outerFrameset.border;
```

Related Item: frameset.frameBorder property

borderColor

Value: Hexadecimal triplet or color name string   Read/Write
Compatibility: WinIE4+, MacIE4+, NN-, Moz-, Safari-

The borderColor property lets you read the value of the color assigned to the bordercolor attribute of the frameset's tag. Although the property is read/write, changing the color by script does not alter the border colors rendered in the browser window. Attribute values set as color names are returned as hexadecimal triplets when you read the property value.

Example

To retrieve the current color setting in a frameset, a script reference from one of the frame's documents would look like the following:

```
var borderColor = parent.document.all.outerFrameset.borderColor;
```

Related Items: frame.borderColor, frameset.frameBorder properties

cols
rows

Value: String   Read/Write
Compatibility: WinIE4+, MacIE4+, NN6+, Moz+, Safari+

The cols and rows properties of a frameset element object let you read and modify the sizes of frames after the frameset has loaded. These two properties are defined in the W3C DOM. Values for both properties are strings, which may include percent symbols or asterisks. Therefore, if you are trying to increase or decrease the size of a frame column or row gradually, you must parse the string for the necessary original values before performing any math on them (or, in IE4+, use the frame element object's height and width properties to gauge the current frame size in pixels).

Adjusting these two properties lets you modify the frameset completely, including adding or removing columns or rows in the frameset grid. Because a change in the frameset structure could impact scripts by changing the size of the frames array associated with the parent window or unloading documents that contain needed data, be sure to test your scripts with both states of your frameset. If you want to remove a frame from a frameset view, you might be safer to specify the size of zero for that particular row or column in the frameset. Of course, a size of zero still leaves a 1-pixel frame, but it is essentially invisible if borders are not turned on and the 1-pixel frame has the same background color as the other frames. Another positive byproduct of this technique is that you can restore the other frame with its document state identical from when it was hidden.

When you have nested framesets defined in a single document, be sure to reference the desired frameset element object. One object may be specifying the columns, and another (nested) one specifies the rows for the grid. Assign a unique ID to each frameset element so that references can be reliably directed to the proper object.

Example

Listing 16-43, Listing 16-44, and Listing 16-45 show the HTML for a frameset and two of the three documents that go into the frameset. The final document is an HTML version of the U.S. Bill of Rights, which is serving here as a content frame for the demonstration.

The frameset listing (see Listing 16-43) shows a three-frame setup. Down the left column is a table of contents (see Listing 16-44). The right column is divided into two rows. In the top row is a simple control (see Listing 16-45) that hides and shows the table-of-contents frame. As the user clicks the hot text of the control (located inside a span element), the onclick event handler invokes the toggleTOC() function in the frameset.

LISTING 16-43

Frameset and Script for Hiding/Showing a Frame

```
<html>
    <head>
        <title>Hide/Show Frame Example</title>
        <script type="text/javascript">
        var origCols;
        function toggleTOC() {
            if (origCols) {
                showTOC();
            } else {
                hideTOC();
            }
        }
        function hideTOC() {
            var frameset = document.getElementById("outerFrameset");
            origCols = frameset.cols;
            frameset.cols = "0,*";
        }
        function showTOC() {
            if (origCols) {
                document.getElementById("outerFrameset").cols = origCols;
                origCols = null;
            }
```

continued

LISTING 16-43 *(continued)*

```
        }
      </script>
   </head>
   <frameset id="outerFrameset" frameborder="no" cols="150,*">
      <frame id="TOC" name="TOCFrame" src="lst16-44.htm" />
      <frameset id="innerFrameset1" rows="80,*">
         <frame id="controls" name="controlsFrame" src="lst16-45.htm" />
         <frame id="content" name="contentFrame" src="bofright.htm" />
      </frameset>
   </frameset>
</html>
```

When a user clicks the hotspot to hide the frame, the script copies the original `cols` property settings to a global variable. The variable is used in `showTOC()` to restore the frameset to its original proportions. This allows a designer to modify the HTML for the frameset without also having to dig into scripts to hard-wire the restored size.

LISTING 16-44

Table of Contents Frame Content

```
<html>
   <head>
      <title>Table of Contents</title>
   </head>
   <body bgcolor="#EEEEEE">
      <h3>
         Table of Contents
      </h3>
      <hr />
      <ul style="font-size:10pt">
         <li><a href="bofright.htm#article1" target="contentFrame">Article
            I</a></li>
         <li><a href="bofright.htm#article2" target="contentFrame">Article
            II</a></li>
         <li><a href="bofright.htm#article3" target="contentFrame">Article
            III</a></li>
         <li><a href="bofright.htm#article4" target="contentFrame">Article
            IV</a></li>
         <li><a href="bofright.htm#article5" target="contentFrame">Article
            V</a></li>
         <li><a href="bofright.htm#article6" target="contentFrame">Article
            VI</a></li>
         <li><a href="bofright.htm#article7" target="contentFrame">Article
            VII</a></li>
         <li><a href="bofright.htm#article8" target="contentFrame">Article
            VIII</a></li>
         <li><a href="bofright.htm#article9" target="contentFrame">Article
```

```
        IX</a></li>
      <li><a href="bofright.htm#article10" target="contentFrame">Article
         X</a></li>
   </ul>
   </body>
</html>
```

Control Panel Frame

```
<html>
   <head>
      <title>Control Panel</title>
   </head>
   <body>
      <p><span id="tocToggle" style="text-decoration:underline; cursor:pointer"
         onclick="parent.toggleTOC()">&lt;&lt;Hide/Show&gt;&gt;</span> Table of
         Contents</p>
   </body>
</html>
```

Related Item: frame object

frameBorder

Value: yes | no | 1 | 0 as strings   Read/Write
Compatibility: WinIE4+, MacIE4+, NN-, Moz-, Safari-

The frameBorder property offers scripted access to a frameset element object's frameborder attribute setting. IE4+ does not respond well to modifying this property after the page has loaded.

Values for the frameBorder property are strings that substitute for Boolean values. Value yes or 1 means that the border is (supposed to be) turned on; no or 0 turns off the border.

Example

The default value for the frameBorder property is yes. You can use this setting to create a toggle script (which, unfortunately, does not change the appearance in IE). The IE5+ version looks like the following:

```
function toggleFrameScroll(framesetID) {
   var theFrameset = document.getElementById(framesetID);
   if (theFrameset.frameBorder == "yes") {
      theFrameset.frameBorder = "no";
   } else {
      theFrameset.frameBorder = "yes";
   }
}
```

Related Item: frame.frameBorder property

frameSpacing

Value: Integer   Read/Write
Compatibility: WinIE4+, MacIE4+, NN-, Moz-, Safari-

The frameSpacing property of a frameset element object lets you read the spacing (in pixels) between frames of a frameset. If you do not specify a framespacing attribute in the frameset's tag, the property is empty, rather than reflecting the actual border thickness applied by default (usually 2).

Example

Even though the property is read/write in IE, changing the value does not change the thickness of the frame spacing you see in the browser. If you need to find the spacing as set by the tag's attribute, a script reference from one of the frame's documents would look like the following:

```
var spacing = document.getElementById("outerFrameset").frameSpacing;
```

Related Item: frameset.border property

iframe Element Object

For HTML element properties, methods, and event handlers, see Chapter 15.

Properties	Methods	Event Handlers
align		
allowTransparency		
contentDocument		
contentWindow		
frameBorder		
frameSpacing		
height		
hspace		
longDesc		
marginHeight		
marginWidth		
name		
noResize		
scrolling		
src		
vspace		
width		

Syntax

Accessing properties or methods of an iframe element object from a containing document:

```
(IE4+)      document.all.iframeID. property | method([parameters])
(IE4+/NN6)  window.frames["iframeName"]. property | method([parameters])
(IE5+/W3C)  document.getElementById("iframeID"). property | method([parameters])
```

Accessing properties of methods of an iframe element from a document inside the iframe element:

```
(IE4+)      parent.document.all.iframeID. property | method([parameters])
(IE5+/W3C)  parent.document.getElementById("iframeID"). property |
            method([parameters])
```

Compatibility: WinIE4+, MacIE4+, NN6+, Moz+, Safari+

About this object

An iframe element allows HTML content from a separate source to be loaded within the body of another document. In some respects, the NN4 layer element was a precursor to the iframe concept, but unlike the layer, an iframe element is not inherently positionable. It is positionable the same way as any other HTML element: by assigning positioning attributes to a style sheet associated with the iframe. Without explicit positioning, an iframe element appears in the body of a document in normal source-code order of elements. Unlike a frame of a frameset, an iframe can be placed arbitrarily in the middle of any document. If the frame changes size under script control, the surrounding content moves out of the way or cinches up.

What truly separates the iframe apart from other HTML elements is its ability to load and display external HTML files and, with the help of scripts, have different pages loaded into the iframe without disturbing the rest of the content of the main document. Pages loaded into the iframe can also have scripts and any other features that you may like to put into an HTML document (including XML in IE for Windows).

The iframe element has a rich set of attributes that let the HTML author control the look; size (height and width); and, to some degree, behavior of the frame. Most of those are accessible to scripts as properties of an iframe element object.

It is important to bear in mind that an iframe element is in many respects like a frame element, especially when it comes to window kinds of relationships. If you plant an iframe element in a document of the main window, that element shows up in the main window's object model as a frame, accessible via common frames terminology:

```
window.frames[i]
window.frames[frameName]
```

Within that iframe frame object is a document and all its contents. All references to the document objects inside the iframe must flow through the portal of the iframe frame.

Conversely, scripts in the document living inside an iframe can communicate with the main document via the parent reference. Of course, you cannot replace the content of the main window with another HTML document (using location.href, for instance) without destroying the iframe that was in the original document.

Properties
align
Value: String   Read/Write
Compatibility: WinIE4+, MacIE4+, NN6+, Moz+, Safari+

The align property governs how an iframe element aligns itself with respect to surrounding content on the page. Two of the possible values (left and right) position the iframe along the left and right edge (respectively) of the iframe's containing element (usually the body). Just as with an image, when an iframe is floated along the left and right edges of a container, other content wraps around the element. Table 16-5 shows all possible values and their meanings.

TABLE 16-5

Values of the align Property

Value	Description
absbottom	Aligns the bottom of the iframe with the imaginary line that extends along character descenders of surrounding text
absmiddle	Aligns the middle of the iframe with the center point between the surrounding text's top and absbottom
baseline	Aligns the bottom of the iframe with the baseline of surrounding text
bottom	Same as baseline in IE
left	Aligns the iframe flush with left edge of the containing element
middle	Aligns the imaginary vertical center line of surrounding text with the same for the iframe element
right	Aligns the iframe flush with the right edge of the containing element
texttop	Aligns the top of the iframe element with the imaginary line that extends along the tallest ascender of surrounding text
top	Aligns the top of the iframe element with the surrounding element's top

As your script changes the value of the align property, the page automatically reflows the content to suit the new alignment.

Example
The default setting for an iframe alignment is baseline. A script can shift the iframe to be flush with the right edge of the containing element as follows:

```
document.getElementById("iframe1").align = "right";
```

Related Items: iframe.hspace, iframe.vspace properties

allowTransparency

Value: Boolean

Read/Write

Compatibility: WinIE6+, MacIE-, NN-, Moz-, Safari-

The allowTransparency property indicates whether the frame's background is transparent. By setting this property to true, you allow a background color or image to show through the transparent frame.

contentDocument

Value: document object reference

Read-Only

Compatibility: WinIE-, MacIE-, NN6+, Moz+, Safari+

The contentDocument property of an iframe element object is nothing more than a reference to the document contained by that frame. If your script finds that it has a reference to an iframe element object, you can use the contentDocument property to get a valid reference to the document and, therefore, any other content of the frame.

Example

A document script might be using the ID of an iframe element to read or adjust one of the element properties; then it needs to perform some action on the content of the page through its document object. You can get the reference to the document object via a statement such as the following:

```
var doc = document.getElementById("Frame3").contentDocument;
```

Then your script can, for example, dive into a form in the document:

```
var val = doc.mainForm.entry.value;
```

Related Items: contentWindow property; document object

contentWindow

Value: document object reference

Read-Only

Compatibility: WinIE5.5+, MacIE-, NN7+, Moz1.0.1+, Safari-

The contentWindow property of an iframe element object serves as a reference to the window object generated by the frame. You can then use this window object as a means of accessing the document object and any document elements.

Related Items: contentDocument property; window object

frameBorder

(See frame.frameBorder() and frameset.frameBorder())

frameSpacing

Value: String

Read/Write

Compatibility: WinIE4+, MacIE4+, NN-, Moz-, Safari-

(See frameset.frameSpacing())

height
width

Value: Integer   Read/Write
Compatibility: WinIE4+, MacIE4+, NN6+, Moz+, Safari+

The height and width properties provide access to the height and width of the iframe object, and allow you to alter the size of the frame. Both properties are specified in pixels.

hspace
vspace

Value: Integer   Read/Write
Compatibility: WinIE4+, MacIE4+, NN-, Moz-, Safari-

These IE-specific properties allow for margins to be set around an iframe element. In general, hspace and vspace properties (and their HTML attributes) have been replaced by CSS margins and padding. These properties and their attributes are not recognized by any W3C standard (including HTML 4).

Values for these properties are integers representing the number of pixels of padding between the element and surrounding content. The hspace value assigns the same number of pixels to the left and right sides of the element; the vspace value is applied to both the top and bottom edges. Scripted changes to these values have no effect in WinIE5+.

Related Item: style.padding property

longDesc

Value: URL string   Read/Write
Compatibility: WinIE6+, MacIE5+, NN6+, Moz+, Safari+

The longDesc property is the scripted equivalent of the longdesc attribute of the <iframe> tag. This HTML 4 attribute is intended to provide browsers a URL to a document that contains a long description of the element. Future browsers can use this feature to provide information about the frame for visually impaired site visitors.

marginHeight
marginWidth

Value: Integer   Read/Write
Compatibility: WinIE4+, MacIE4+, NN6+, Moz+, Safari+

Browsers tend to insert content within a frame automatically by adding a margin between the content and the edge of the frame. These values are represented by the marginHeight (top and bottom edges) and marginWidth (left and right edges) properties. Although the properties are not read-only, changing the values after the frameset has loaded does not alter the appearance of the document in the frame. If you need to alter the margin(s) of a document inside a frame, adjust the document.body.style margin properties.

Also be aware that although the default values of these properties are empty (that is, when no marginheight or marginwidth attributes are set for the <iframe> tag), margins are built into the page. The precise pixel count of those margins varies with different operating systems.

Related Item: style object (Chapter 26)

name

Value: String Read/Write
Compatibility: WinIE4+, MacIE4+, NN6+, Moz+, Safari+

The name property is the identifier associated with the frame for use as a frame reference. Scripts can reference the frame through the name property (for example, `window.frames["myIframe"]`), which is typically assigned via the name attribute.

noResize

(See `frame.noResize()`)

scrolling

Value: yes | no | 1 | 0 as strings Read/Write
Compatibility: WinIE4+, MacIE4+, NN6+, Moz+, Safari+

The scrolling property lets scripts turn scroll bars on and off inside an iframe element. By default, scrolling is turned on unless overridden by the scroll attribute of the <iframe> tag.

Values for the scrolling property are strings that substitute for Boolean values. Value yes or 1 means that scroll bars are visible (provided that there is more content than can be viewed without scrolling); no or 0 hides scroll bars in the frame. IE4+ also recognizes (and sets as default) the auto value.

Example

The following toggleIFrameScroll() function accepts a string of the iframe element's ID as a parameter and switches between on and off scroll bars in the iframe. The if condition checks whether the property is set to something other than no. This test allows the condition to evaluate to true if the property is set to either auto (the first time) or yes (as set by the function).

```
function toggleFrameScroll(frameID) {
    // IE5 & NN6 version
    var theFrame = document.getElementById(frameID);

    if (theFrame.scrolling != "no") {
        theFrame.scrolling = "no";
    } else {
        theFrame.scrolling = "yes";
    }
}
```

Related Item: frame.scrolling property

src

Value: URL string Read/Write
Compatibility: WinIE4+, MacIE4+, NN6+, Moz+, Safari+

The src property of an iframe element object offers an additional way of navigating to a different page within an inline frame (that is, other than assigning a new URL to the location.href property of the frame object). Remember that the src property belongs to the iframe element object, not the window object it represents. Therefore, references to the src property must be via the element's ID and/or node hierarchy.

popup

Example

For best results, use fully formed URLs as value for the src property, as shown here:

```
document.getElementById("myIframe").src = "http://www.dannyg.com";
```

Relative URLs and javascript: pseudo-URLs also work most of the time.

Related Item: location.href property

popup Object

Properties	Methods	Event Handlers
document	hide()	
isOpen	show()	

Syntax

Creating a popup object:

```
var popupObj = window.createPopup()
```

Accessing properties or methods of a popup object from a document in the window that created the pop-up:

```
popupObj.property | method([parameters])
```

Compatibility: WinIE5.5+, MacIE-, NN-, Moz-, Safari-

About this object

A popup object is a chromeless window space that overlaps the window whose document generates the pop-up. A pop-up also appears in front of any dialog boxes. Unlike the dialog-box windows generated via IE's showModalDialog() and showModelessDialog() methods, your scripts must not only create the window, but also put content in it and then define where on the screen and how big it will be.

Because the pop-up window has no chrome (title bar, resize handles, and so on), you should populate its content with a border and/or background color so that it stands out from the main window's content. The following statements reflect a typical sequence of creating, populating, and showing a popup object:

```
var popup = window.createPopup();
var popupBody = popup.document.body;
popupBody.style.border = "solid 2px black";
popupBody.style.padding = "5px";
popupBody.innerHTML = "<p>Here is some text in a popup window</p>";
popup.show(200,100, 200, 50, document.body);
```

> **NOTE** As handy as it may be, in a strict W3C approach to JavaScript, you wouldn't use the innerHTML property because it isn't officially part of the W3C standard. However, it is often too powerful a convenience property to ignore, as much of the code throughout this book is a testament. The book does show the W3C node manipulation alternative to innerHTML in some examples. Refer to Chapter 18 for a thorough explanation and examples of the W3C alternative to innerHTML.

The pop-up window that IE creates is, in fact, a window, but only from the point of view of the document that it contains. In other words, although the number of properties and methods for the `popup` object is small, the `parentWindow` property of the document inside the pop-up points to a genuine `window` property. Even so, be aware that this pop-up does not appear as a distinct window among windows listed in the Windows Taskbar. If a user clicks outside the pop-up or switches to another application, the pop-up disappears, and you must reinvoke the `show()` method by script (complete with dimension and position parameters) to force the pop-up to reappear.

When you assign content to a pop-up, you are also responsible for making sure that the content fits the size of the pop-up you specify. If the content runs past the rectangular space (body text word wraps within the pop-up's rectangle), no scroll bars appear.

Properties

document

Value: `document` object reference   Read-Only
Compatibility: WinIE5.5+, MacIE-, NN-, Moz-, Safari-

Use the `document` property as a gateway to the content of a pop-up window. This property is the only access point available from the script that creates the pop-up to the pop-up itself. The most common application of this property is to set document properties governing the content of the pop-up window. For example, to give the pop-up a border (because the pop-up itself has no window chrome), the script that creates the window can assign values to the `style` property of the document in the pop-up window, as follows:

```
myPopup.document.body.style.border = "solid 3px gray";
```

Be aware that the `document` object of a pop-up window may not implement the full flexibility you know about primary window `document` objects. For example, you are not allowed to assign a URL to the `document.URL` property in a pop-up window.

Example

Use The Evaluator (Chapter 13) to experiment with the `popup` object and its properties. Enter the following statements in the top text box. The first statement creates a pop-up window whose reference is assigned to the `a` global variable. Next, a reference to the body of the pop-up's document is preserved in the `b` variable for the sake of convenience. Further statements work with these two variables.

```
a = window.createPopup()
b = a.document.body
b.style.border = "solid 2px black"
b.style.padding = "5px"
b.innerHTML = "<p>Here is some text in a popup window</p>"
a.show(200,100, 200, 50, document.body)
```

See the description of the `show()` method for details on the parameters.

Related Item: `document` object

isOpen

Value: Boolean   Read-Only
Compatibility: WinIE5.5+, MacIE-, NN-, Moz-, Safari-

While a pop-up window is visible, its `isOpen` property returns `true`; otherwise, the property returns `false`. Because any user action in the browser causes the pop-up to hide itself, the property is useful only for script statements that are running on their own after the pop-up is made visible.

popupObject.hide()

Example

Use The Evaluator (Chapter 13) to experiment with the isOpen property. Enter the following statements in the top text box. The sequence begins with a creation of a simple pop-up window, whose reference is assigned to the a global variable. Note that the final statement is actually two statements, designed so that the second statement executes while the pop-up window is still open.

```
a = window.createPopup();
a.document.body.innerHTML = "<p>Here is a popup window</p>";
a.show(200,100, 200, 50, document.body); alert("Popup is open:" + a.isOpen);
```

If you then click in the main window to hide the pop-up, you will see a different result if you enter the following statement in the top text box by itself:

```
alert("Popup is open:" + a.isOpen);
```

Related Item: popup.show() method

Methods
hide()
show(left, top, width, height[, positioningElementRef])
Returns: Nothing
Compatibility: WinIE5.5+, MacIE-, NN-, Moz-, Safari-

After you have created a popup object with the window.createPopup() method and populated it with content, you must explicitly show the window via the show() method. If the window is hidden because a user clicked the main browser window somewhere, the show() method (and all its parameters) must be invoked again. To have a script hide the window, invoke the hide() method for the popup object.

The first four parameters of the show() method are required; they define the pixel location and size of the pop-up window. By default, the coordinate space for the left and top parameters is the video display. Thus, a left and top setting of zero places the pop-up in the top-left corner of the video screen. But you can define a different coordinate space by adding an optional fifth parameter. This parameter must be a reference to an element on the page. To confine the coordinate space to the content region of the browser window, specify the document.body object as the positioning element reference.

Example

Listing 16-46 demonstrates the show() and hide() methods for a popup object. A click of the button on the page invokes the selfTimer() function, which acts as the main routine for this page. The goal is to produce a pop-up window that self-destructs 5 seconds after it appears. Along the way, a message in the pop-up counts down the seconds.

A reference to the pop-up window is preserved as a global variable called popup. After the popup object is created, the initContent() function stuffs the content into the pop-up by way of assigning style properties and some innerHTML for the body of the document that is automatically created when the pop-up is generated. A span element is defined so that another function later on can modify the content of just that segment of text in the pop-up. Notice that the assignment of content to the pop-up is predicated on the pop-up window's having been initialized (by virtue of the popup variable's having a value assigned to it) and that the pop-up window is not showing. Although invoking initContent() under any other circumstances is probably impossible, the validation of the desired conditions is good programming practice.

Back in `selfTimer()`, the `popup` object is displayed. Defining the desired size requires some trial and error to make sure that the pop-up window comfortably accommodates the text that is put into the pop-up in the `initContent()` function.

With the pop-up window showing, now is the time to invoke the `countDown()` function. Before the function performs any action, it validates that the pop-up has been initialized and is still visible. If a user clicks the main window while the counter is counting down, this changes the value of the `isOpen` property to `false`, and nothing inside the `if` condition executes.

This `countDown()` function grabs the inner text of the `span` and uses `paresInt()` to extract just the integer number (using base 10 numbering, because we're dealing with zero-leading numbers that can potentially be regarded as octal values). The condition of the `if` construction decreases the retrieved integer by one. If the decremented value is zero, the time is up, and the pop-up window is hidden with the `popup` global variable returned to its original, `null` value. But if the value is other than zero, the inner text of the `span` is set to the decremented value (with a leading zero), and the `setTimeout()` method is called upon to reinvoke the `countDown()` function in 1 second (1,000 milliseconds).

LISTING 16-46

Hiding and Showing a Pop-Up

```
<html>
    <head>
        <title>popup Object</title>
        <script type="text/javascript">
        var popup;
        function initContent() {
            if (popup && !popup.isOpen) {
                var popBody = popup.document.body;
                popBody.style.border = "solid 3px red";
                popBody.style.padding = "10px";
                popBody.style.fontSize = "24pt";
                popBody.style.textAlign = "center";
                var bodyText = "<P>This popup will self-destruct in ";
                bodyText += "<span id='counter'>05<\/span>";
                bodyText += " seconds...<\/P>";
                popBody.innerHTML = bodyText;
            }
        }
        function countDown() {
            if (popup && popup.isOpen) {
                var currCount = parseInt(popup.document.all.counter.innerText, 10);
                if (--currCount == 0) {
                    popup.hide();
                    popup = null;
                } else {
                    popup.document.all.counter.innerText = "0" + currCount;
                    setTimeout("countDown()", 1000);
                }
            }
        }
```

continued

popupObject.hide()

LISTING 16-46 *(continued)*

```
      function selfTimer() {
        popup = window.createPopup();
        initContent();
        popup.show(200,200,400,100,document.body);
        setTimeout("countDown()", 1000);
      }
      </script>
  </head>
  <body>
    <form>
      <input type="button" value="Impossible Mission"
      onclick="selfTimer()" />
    </form>
  </body>
</html>
```

The hide() method here is invoked by a script that is running while the pop-up window is showing. Because a pop-up window automatically goes away if a user clicks the main window, it is highly unlikely that the hide() method would ever be invoked by itself in response to user action in the main window. If you want a script in the pop-up window to close the pop-up, use parentWindow.close().

Related Items: popup.isOpen property, window.createPopup() method

Chapter 17

Location and History Objects

Not all objects in the document object model are things you can see in the content area of the browser window. Each browser window or frame maintains a bunch of other information about the page you are currently visiting and where you have been. The URL of the page you see in the window is called the *location,* and browsers store this information in the location object. As you surf the Web, the browser stores the URLs of your past pages in the history object. You can manually view what that object contains by looking in the browser menu that enables you to jump back to a previously visited page. This chapter is all about these two nearly invisible, but important, objects.

These objects are not only valuable to your browser, but also valuable to snoopers who might want to write scripts to see what URLs you're viewing in another frame or the URLs of other sites you've visited in the past dozen mouse clicks. As a result, security restrictions built into browsers limit access to some of these objects' properties (unless you use signed scripts in NN4+/Moz). For older browsers, these properties simply are not available from a script.

location Object

Properties	Methods	Event Handlers
hash	assign()	None
host	reload()	
hostname	replace()	
href		
pathname		
port		
protocol		
search		

Syntax

Loading a new document into the current window:

```
[window.]location.href = "URL";
```

Accessing location object properties or methods:

```
[window.]location.property | method([parameters])
```

About this object

In its place one level below window-style objects in the original document object hierarchy, the location object represents information about the URL of any currently open window or of a specific frame. To display the URL of the current web page, you can reference the location object like this:

```
document.write(location.href);
```

In this example, the href property evaluates to the URL, which is written to the current page in its entirety. The location object also allows you to access individual parts of the URL, as you see in a moment.

When you reference the location object in the framesetting document of a multiple-frame window, the location is given as the parent window's URL that appears in the Location (or Address) field of the browser. Each frame also has a location associated with it, although you may not see any overt reference to the frame's URL in the browser. To get URL information about a document located in another frame, the reference to the location object must include the window frame reference. For example, if you have a window consisting of two frames, Table 17-1 shows the possible references to the location objects for all frames comprising the web presentation.

NOTE Scripts cannot alter the URL displayed in the browser's Location/Address box. For security and privacy reasons, that text box cannot display anything other than the URL of a current page or URL in transit.

TABLE 17-1

Location Object References in a Two-Frame Browser Window

Reference	Description
location (or window.location)	URL of frame displaying the document that runs the script statement containing this reference
parent.location	URL information for parent window that defines the <frameset>
parent.frames[0].location	URL information for first visible frame
parent.frames[1].location	URL information for second visible frame
parent.otherFrameName.location	URL information for another named frame in the same frameset

Most properties of a location object deal with network-oriented information. This information involves various data about the physical location of the document on the network, including the host server, the protocol being used, and other components of the URL. Given a complete URL for a typical World Wide Web page, the window.location object assigns property names to various segments of the URL, as shown here:

```
http://www.example.com:80/promos/newproducts.html#giantGizmo
```

Property	Value
protocol	"http:"
hostname	"www.example.com"
port	"80"
host	"www.example.com:80"
pathname	"/promos/newproducts.html"
hash	"#giantGizmo"
href	"http://www.example.com:80/promos newproducts.html#giantGizmo"

The window.location object is handy when a script needs to extract information about the URL, perhaps to obtain a base reference on which to build URLs for other documents to be fetched as the result of user action. This object can eliminate a nuisance for web authors who develop sites on one machine and then upload them to a server (perhaps at an Internet service provider) with an entirely different directory structure. By building scripts to construct base references from the directory location of the current document, you can construct the complete URLs for loading documents. You don't have to change the base reference data manually in your documents as you shift the files from computer to computer or from directory to directory. To extract the segment of the URL and place it in the enclosing directory, use the following:

```
var baseRef = location.href.substring(0,location.href.lastIndexOf("/") + 1);
```

*windowObject.***location.hash**

> **CAUTION** Security alert: To allay fears of Internet security breaches and privacy invasions, scriptable browsers prevent your script in one frame from retrieving `location` object properties from other frames whose domain and server are not your own (unless you use signed scripts in NN4+/Moz or the user has set the IE browser to trust your site). This restriction puts a damper on many scripters' well-meaning designs and aids for web watchers and visitors. If you attempt such property accesses, however, you receive an "access denied" (or similar) security warning dialog box.

Setting the value of some `location` properties is the preferred way to control which document gets loaded into a window or frame. Though you may expect to find a method somewhere in JavaScript that contains a plain-language *Go* or *Open* word (to simulate what you see in the browser menu bar), you point your browser to another URL by setting the `window.location.href` property to that URL, as in:

```
window.location.href = "http://www.dannyg.com/";
```

The equals assignment operator (=) in this kind of statement is a powerful weapon. In fact, setting the `location.href` object to a URL of a different MIME type, such as one of the variety of sound and video formats, causes the browser to load those files into the plug-in or helper application designated in your browser's settings. The `location.assign()` method was originally intended for internal use by the browser, but it is available for scripters (although I don't recommend using it for navigation). Internet Explorer's object model includes a `window.navigate()` method that also loads a document into a window, but you can't use it for cross-browser applications.

Two other methods complement the `location` object's capability to control navigation. One method is the script equivalent of clicking Reload; the other method enables you to replace the current document's entry in the history with that of the next URL of your script's choice.

Properties

hash

Value: String   Read/Write
Compatibility: WinIE3+, MacIE3+, NN2+, Moz+, Safari+

The *hash mark* (#) is a URL convention that directs the browser to an anchor located in the document. Any name you assign to an anchor (with the `<a name="...">...</a>` tag pair) becomes part of the URL after the hash mark. A `location` object's `hash` property is the name of the anchor part of the current URL (which consists of the hash mark and the name).

If you have written HTML documents with anchors and directed links to navigate to those anchors, you have probably noticed that although the destination location shows the anchor as part of the URL (for example, in the Location field), the window's anchor value does not change as the user manually scrolls to positions in the document where other anchors are defined. An anchor appears in the URL only when the window has navigated there as part of a link or in response to a script that adjusts the URL.

Just as you can navigate to any URL by setting the `window.location.href` property, you can navigate to another hash in the same document by adjusting only the `hash` property of the location without the hash mark (as shown in the following example).

Listing 17-1 demonstrates how to use the `hash` property to access the anchor part of a URL. When you load the script in Listing 17-1, adjust the size of the browser window so that only one section is visible at a time. When you click a button, the script navigates to the next logical section in the progression and eventually takes you back to the top. The page won't scroll any farther than to the bottom of the document. Therefore, an anchor near the bottom of the page may not appear at the top of the browser window.

LISTING 17-1

A Document with Anchors

```html
<html>
    <head>
        <title>location.hash Property</title>
        <script type="text/javascript">
        function goNextAnchor(where) {
            window.location.hash = where;
        }
        </script>
    </head>
    <body>
        <h1><a id="start" name="start">Top</a></h1>
        <form>
            <input type="button" name="next" value="NEXT"
            onclick="goNextAnchor('sec1')" />
        </form>
        <hr /><br /><br /><br /><br /><br />
        <h1><a id="sec1" name="sec1">Section 1</a></h1>
        <form>
            <input type="button" name="next" value="NEXT"
            onclick="goNextAnchor('sec2')" />
        </form>
        <hr /><br /><br /><br /><br /><br />
        <h1><a id="sec2" name="sec2">Section 2</a></h1>
        <form>
            <input type="button" name="next" value="NEXT"
            onclick="goNextAnchor('sec3')" />
        </form>
        <hr /><br /><br /><br /><br /><br />
        <h1><a id="sec3" name="sec3">Section 3</a></h1>
        <form>
            <input type="button" name="next" value="BACK TO TOP"
            onclick="goNextAnchor('start')" />
        </form>
    </body>
</html>
```

NOTE   The property assignment event handling technique used in the previous example and through-out the chapter is a deliberate simplification to make the code more readable. It is generally better to use the more modern approach of binding events using the `addEventListener()` (NN6+/Moz/W3C) or `attachEvent()` (IE5+) methods. A modern cross-browser event handling technique is explained in detail in Chapter 25.

Anchor names are passed as parameters with each button's `onclick` event handler. Instead of going through the work of assembling a `window.location` value in the function by appending a literal hash mark and the value for the anchor, here I simply modify the `hash` property of the current window's location. This is the preferred, cleaner method.

If you attempt to read back the `window.location.hash` property in an added line of script, however, the window's actual URL probably will not have been updated yet, and the browser will appear to be giving your script false information. To prevent this problem in subsequent statements of the same function, construct the URLs of those statements from the same variable values you use to set the `window.location.hash` property; don't rely on the browser to give you the values you expect.

Related Item: `location.href` property

host

Value: String   Read/Write
Compatibility: WinIE3+, MacIE3+, NN2+, Moz+, Safari+

The `location.host` property describes both the hostname and port of a URL. The port is included in the value only when the port is an explicit part of the URL. If you navigate to a URL that does not display the port number in the Location field of the browser, the `location.host` property returns the same value as the `location.hostname` property.

Use the `location.host` property to extract the `hostname:port` part of the URL of any document loaded in the browser. This capability may be helpful for building a URL to a specific document that you want your script to access on the fly.

Use the documents in Listing 17-2, Listing 17-3, and Listing 17-4 as tools to help you learn the values that the various `window.location` properties return. In the browser, open the file for Listing 17-2. This file creates a two-frame window. The left frame contains a temporary placeholder (see Listing 17-4) that displays some instructions. The right frame has a document (see Listing 17-3) that enables you to load URLs into the left frame and get readings on three different windows available: the parent window (which creates the multiframe window), the left frame, and the right frame.

LISTING 17-2

Frameset for the Property Picker

```
<html>
   <head>
      <title>window.location Properties</title>
   </head>
   <frameset cols="50%,50%" border="1" bordercolor="black">
      <frame name="Frame1" src="lst17-04.htm" />
      <frame name="Frame2" src="lst17-03.htm" />
   </frameset>
</html>
```

LISTING 17-3

Property Picker

```
<html>
    <head>
        <title>Property Picker</title>
        <script type="text/javascript">
        var isNav = (typeof netscape != "undefined") ? true : false;

        function fillLeftFrame() {
            newURL = prompt("Enter the URL of a document to show in the left
                frame:","");
            if (newURL != null && newURL != "") {
                parent.frames[0].location = newURL;
            }
        }

        function showLocationData(form) {
            for (var i = 0; i <3; i++) {
                if (form.whichFrame[i].checked) {
                    var windName = form.whichFrame[i].value;
                    break;
                }
            }
            var theWind = "" + windName + ".location";
            if (isNav) {
                netscape.security.PrivilegeManager.enablePrivilege(
                    "UniversalBrowserRead");
            }
            var theObj = eval(theWind);
            form.windName.value = windName;
            form.windHash.value = theObj.hash;
            form.windHost.value = theObj.host;
            form.windHostname.value = theObj.hostname;
            form.windHref.value = theObj.href;
            form.windPath.value = theObj.pathname;
            form.windPort.value = theObj.port;
            form.windProtocol.value = theObj.protocol;
            form.windSearch.value = theObj.search;
            if (isNav) {
                netscape.security.PrivilegeManager.disablePrivilege(
                    "UniversalBrowserRead");
            }
        }
        </script>
    </head>
```

continued

LISTING 17-3 *(continued)*

```
<body>
    Click the "Open URL" button to enter the location of an HTML document to
    display in the left frame of this window.
    <form>
        <input type="button" name="opener" value="Open URL..."
        onclick="fillLeftFrame()" />
        <hr />
        <center>
            Select a window/frame. Then click the "Show Location Properties"
            button to view each window.location property value for the desired
            window.
            <p><input type="radio" name="whichFrame" value="parent"
                checked="checked" />Parent window <input type="radio"
                name="whichFrame" value="parent.frames[0]" />Left frame <input
                type="radio" name="whichFrame" value="parent.frames[1]" />This
                frame</p>
            <p><input type="button" name="getProperties"
                value="Show Location Properties"
                onclick="showLocationData(this.form)" /> <input type="reset"
                value="Clear" /></p>
            <table border="2">
                <tr>
                    <td align="right">Window:</td>
                    <td><input type="text" name="windName" size="30" /></td>
                </tr>
                <tr>
                    <td align="right">hash:</td>
                    <td><input type="text" name="windHash" size="30" /></td>
                </tr>
                <tr>
                    <td align="right">host:</td>
                    <td><input type="text" name="windHost" size="30" /></td>
                </tr>
                <tr>
                    <td align="right">hostname:</td>
                    <td><input type="text" name="windHostname" size="30" /></td>
                </tr>
                <tr>
                    <td align="right">href:</td>
                    <td><textarea name="windHref" rows="3" cols="30" wrap="soft">
                        </textarea></td>
                </tr>
                <tr>
                    <td align="right">pathname:</td>
                    <td><textarea name="windPath" rows="3" cols="30" wrap="soft">
                        </textarea></td>
                </tr>
                <tr>
                    <td align="right">port:</td>
                    <td><input type="text" name="windPort" size="30" /></td>
                </tr>
```

```
         <tr>
             <td align="right">protocol:</td>
             <td><input type="text" name="windProtocol" size="30" /></td>
         </tr>
         <tr>
             <td align="right">search:</td>
             <td><textarea name="windSearch" rows="3" cols="30"
                 wrap="soft"></textarea></td>
         </tr>
       </table>
     </center>
   </form>
 </body>
</html>
```

LISTING 17-4

Placeholder Document for Listing 17-2

```
<html>
   <head>
      <title>Opening Placeholder</title>
   </head>
   <body>
      Initial placeholder. Experiment with other URLs for this frame (see
      right).
   </body>
</html>
```

For the best results, open a URL to a web document on the network from the same domain and server from which you load the listings (perhaps your local hard disk). If possible, load a document that includes anchor points to navigate through a long document. Click the Left frame radio button and then click the button that shows all properties. This action fills the table in the right frame with all the available `location` properties for the selected window.

Related Items: `location.port`, `location.hostname` properties

hostname

Value: String   Read/Write
Compatibility: WinIE3+, MacIE3+, NN2+, Moz+, Safari+

The hostname of a typical URL is the name of the server on the network that stores the document you view in the browser. For most web sites, the server name includes not only the domain name, but also the `www.` prefix. The hostname does not, however, include the port number if the URL specifies such a number. Keep in mind that the `hostname` property will likely come up blank for pages that you open from your local hard drive (local host).

*windowObject***.location.href**

See Listing 17-2, Listing 17-3, and Listing 17-4 for a set of related pages to help you view the hostname data for a variety of other pages.

Related Items: `location.host`, `location.port` properties

href

Value: String   Read/Write
Compatibility: WinIE3+, MacIE3+, NN2+, Moz+, Safari+

Of all the `location` object properties, `href` (hypertext reference) is probably the one most often called upon in scripting. The `location.href` property supplies a string of the entire URL of the specified `window` object.

Using this property on the left side of an assignment statement is the JavaScript way of opening a URL for display in a window. Any of the following statements can load my web site's index page into a single-frame browser window:

```
window.location = "http://www.dannyg.com";
window.location.href = "http://www.dannyg.com";
```

At times, you may encounter difficulty by omitting a reference to a window. JavaScript may get confused and reference the `document.location` property. To prevent this confusion, the `document.location` property was deprecated (put on the no-no list) and replaced by the `document.URL` property. In the meantime, you can't go wrong by always specifying a window in the reference.

> **NOTE** You should be able to omit the `href` property name when assigning a new URL to the `location` object (for example, `location = "http://www.dannyg.com"`). Although this works in most browsers most of the time, some early browsers behave more reliably if you assign a URL explicitly to the `location.href` property. If you want to play it safe, use `location.href` at all times.

Sometimes, you must extract the name of the current directory in a script so that another statement can append a known document to the URL before loading it into the window. Although the other `location` object properties yield an assortment of a URL's segments, none of them provides the full URL to the current URL's directory. But you can use JavaScript string manipulation techniques to accomplish this task. Listing 17-5 shows such a possibility.

Depending on your browser, the values for the `location.href` property may be encoded with ASCII equivalents of nonalphanumeric characters. Such an ASCII value includes the % symbol and the ASCII numeric value. The most common encoded character in a URL is the space: %20. If you need to extract a URL and display that value as a string in your documents, you can safely pass all such potentially encoded strings through the JavaScript `unescape()` function. For example, if a URL is `http://www.example.com/product%20list`, you can convert it by passing it through the `unescape()` function, as in the following example.

```
var plainURL = unescape(window.location.href);
// result = "http://www.example.com/product list";
```

The inverse function, `escape()`, is available for sending encoded strings to server applications, such as CGI scripts. See Chapter 35 for more details on these functions.

Listing 17-5 shows how the `href` property can be used to view the directory URL of the current page. This example includes the `unescape()` function in front of the part of the script that captures the URL. This function serves cosmetic purposes by displaying the pathname in alert dialog boxes for browsers that normally display the ASCII-encoded version.

NOTE Although Listing 17-5 uses the unescape() global function for backward compatibility, that function (and its partner, escape()) have been removed from the ECMAScript standard as of version 3. These functions have been replaced by more modern versions, decodeURI() and encodeURI(). See Chapter 35 for details.

LISTING 17-5

Extracting the Directory of the Current Document

```
<html>
  <head>
    <title>Extract pathname</title>
    <script type="text/javascript">
    // general purpose function to extract URL of current directory
    function getDirPath(URL) {
        var result = unescape(URL.substring(0,(URL.lastIndexOf("/")) + 1));
        return result;
    }

    // handle button event, passing work onto general purpose function
    function showDirPath(URL) {
        alert(getDirPath(URL));
    }
    </script>
  </head>
  <body>
    <form>
        <input type="button" value="View directory URL"
        onclick="showDirPath(window.location.href)" />
    </form>
  </body>
</html>
```

Related Items: location.pathname, document.location properties; String object (Chapter 35)

pathname

Value: String   Read/Write
Compatibility: WinIE3+, MacIE3+, NN2+, Moz+, Safari+

The pathname component of a URL consists of the directory structure relative to the server's root volume. In other words, the root (the server name in an http: connection) is not part of the pathname. If the URI's path is to a file in the root directory, the location.pathname property is a single slash (/) character. Any other pathname starts with a slash character, indicating a directory nested within the root. The value of the location.pathname property also includes the document name.

See Listing 17-2, Listing 17-3, and Listing 17-4 earlier in this chapter for a multiple-frame example you can use to view the location.pathname property for a variety of URLs of your choice.

Related Item: location.href property

505

port

Value: String   Read/Write
Compatibility: WinIE3+, MacIE3+, NN2+, Moz+, Safari+

These days, few consumer-friendly web sites need to include the port number as part of their URLs. You see port numbers mostly in the less-popular protocols, in URLs to sites used for private development purposes, or in URLs to sites that have no assigned domain names. You can retrieve the value with the `location.port` property. If you extract the value from one URL and intend to build another URL with that component, be sure to include the colon delimiter between the server's IP address and port number.

If you have access to URLs containing port numbers, use the documents in Listing 17-2, Listing 17-3, and Listing 17-4 to experiment with the output of the `location.port` property.

Related Item: `location.host` property

protocol

Value: String   Read/Write
Compatibility: WinIE3+, MacIE3+, NN2+, Moz+, Safari+

The first component of any URL is the protocol used for the particular type of communication. For World Wide Web pages, the Hypertext Transfer Protocol (`http`) is the standard. Other common protocols you may see in your browser include HTTP-Secure (`https`), File Transfer Protocol (`ftp`), File (`file`), and Mail (`mailto`); web pages opened from your local hard drive use the `file` protocol. Values for the `location.protocol` property include not only the name of the protocol, but also the trailing colon delimiter. Thus, for a typical web-page URL, the `location.protocol` property is

```
http:
```

Notice that the usual slashes after the protocol in the URL are not part of the `location.protocol` value. Of all the `location` object properties, only the full URL (`location.href`) reveals the slash delimiters between the protocol and other components.

See Listing 17-2, Listing 17-3, and Listing 17-4 for a multiple-frame example you can use to view the `location.protocol` property for a variety of URLs. Notice that the protocol shows up initially as `file:` to indicate that the first page in the left frame is stored locally and accessed via the File protocol. Also try loading an FTP site to see the `location.protocol` value for that type of URL.

Related Item: `location.href` property

search

Value: String   Read/Write
Compatibility: WinIE3+, MacIE3+, NN2+, Moz+, Safari+

Perhaps you've noticed the long, cryptic URL that appears in the Location/Address field of your browser whenever you ask one of the World Wide Web search services to look up matches for items you enter in the keyword field. The URL starts the regular way — with protocol, host, and pathname values. But following the more traditional URL are search commands that are submitted to the search engine (typically, a CGI program running on the server). You can retrieve or set that trailing search query by using the `location.search` property.

Each search engine has its own formula for query submissions based on the designs of the HTML forms that obtain details from users. These search queries come in an encoded format that appears in anything but plain language. If you plan to script a search query, be sure you fully understand the search engine's format before you start assembling a string to assign to the `location.search` property of a window.

The most common format for search data is a series of name/value pairs. An equal symbol (=) separates a name and its value. Multiple name/value pairs have ampersands (&) between them. You should use the `escape()` function to convert the data to URL-friendly format, especially when the content includes spaces.

The `location.search` property also applies to any part of a URL after the filename, including parameters being sent to CGI programs on the server.

Passing data among pages via URLs

It is not uncommon to want to preserve some pieces of data that exist in one page so that a script in another page can pick up where the script processing left off in the first page. You can achieve persistence across page loads without any server programming through one of three techniques: the `document.cookie` (see Chapter 18), variables in framesetting documents, and the search string of a URL. That's really what happens when you visit search and e-commerce sites that return information to your browser. Rather than store, say, your search criteria on the server, they spit the criteria back to the browser as part of the URL. The next time you activate that URL, the values are sent to the server for processing (for example, to send you the next page of search results for a particular query).

Passing data among pages is not limited to client/server communication. You can use the search string strictly on the client side to pass data from one page to another. Unless some CGI process on the server is programmed to do something with the search string, a web server regurgitates the search string as part of the location data that comes back with a page. A script in the newly loaded page can inspect the search string (via the `location.search` property) and tear it apart to gather the data and put it into script variables. Take a look at Listing 17-6, Listing 17-7, and Listing 17-8 to see a powerful application of this technique.

As mentioned in the opening of Chapter 16 about frames, you can force a particular HTML page to open inside the frameset for which it is designed. But with the help of the search string, you can reuse the same framesetting document to accommodate any number of content pages that go into one of the frames (rather than specifying a separate frameset for each possible combination of pages in the frameset). The listings in this section create a simple example of how to force a page to load in a frameset by passing some information about the page to the frameset. Thus, if a user has a URL to one of the content frames (perhaps it has been bookmarked by right-clicking the frame, or it comes up as a search-engine result), the page appears in its designated frameset the next time the user visits the page.

The fundamental task going on in this scheme has two parts. The first is in each of the content pages, where a script checks whether the page is loaded inside a frameset. If the frameset is missing, a search string is composed and appended to the URL for the framesetting document. The framesetting document has its own short script that looks for the presence of the search string. If the string is there, the script extracts the search string data and uses it to load that specific page into the content frame of the frameset.

Listing 17-6 is the framesetting document. The `getSearchAsArray()` function is more complete than necessary for this simple example, but you can use it in other instances to convert any number of name/value pairs passed in the search string (in traditional format of `name1=value1&name2=value2&etc.`) into an array whose indexes are the names (making it easier for scripts to extract a specific piece of passed data).

LISTING 17-6

A Smart Frameset

```html
<html>
    <head>
        <title>Example Frameset</title>
        <script type="text/javascript">
        // Convert location.search into an array of values
        // indexed by name.
        function getSearchAsArray() {
            var results = new Array();
            var input = unescape(location.search.substr(1));
            if (input) {
                var srchArray = input.split("&");
                var tempArray = new Array();
                for (var i = 0; i < srchArray.length; i++) {
                    tempArray = srchArray[i].split("=");
                    results[tempArray[0]] = tempArray[1];
                }
            }
            return results;
        }

        function loadFrame() {
            if (location.search) {
                var srchArray = getSearchAsArray();
                if (srchArray["content"]) {
                    self.content.location.href = srchArray["content"];
                }
            }
        }
        </script>
    </head>
    <frameset cols="250,*" onload="loadFrame()">
        <frame name="toc" src="lst17-07.htm" />
        <frame name="content" src="lst17-08.htm" />
    </frameset>
</html>
```

Listing 17-7 is the HTML for the table-of-contents frame. Nothing elaborate goes on here, but you can see how normal navigation works for this simplified frameset. You can also see how this example could be easily built upon to provide a handy table-of-contents feature to a site with multiple sections or pages.

LISTING 17-7

The Table of Contents

```html
<html>
    <head>
        <title>Table of Contents</title>
    </head>
    <body bgcolor="#EEEEEE">
        <h3>Table of Contents</h3>
        <hr />
        <ul>
            <li><a href="lst17-08.htm" target="content">Page 1</a></li>
            <li><a href="lst17-08a.htm" target="content">Page 2</a></li>
            <li><a href="lst17-08b.htm" target="content">Page 3</a></li>
        </ul>
    </body>
</html>
```

Listing 17-8 shows one of the content pages. As the page loads, the checkFrameset() function is invoked. If the window does not load inside a frameset, the script navigates to the framesetting page, passing the current content URL as a search string. Notice that the loading of this page on its own does not get recorded to the browser's history and isn't accessed if the user clicks the Back button.

LISTING 17-8

A Content Page

```html
<html>
    <head>
        <title>Page 1</title>
        <script type="text/javascript">
        function checkFrameset() {
            if (parent == window) {
                // Use replace() to keep current page out of history
                location.replace("lst17-06.htm?content=" + escape(location.href));
            }
        }

        // Invoke the function
        checkFrameset();
        </script>
    </head>
    <body>
        <h1>Page 1</h1>
        <hr />
    </body>
</html>
```

windowObject.location.reload()

In practice, I recommend placing the code for the `checkFrameset()` function and call to it inside an external `.js` library and linking that library to each content document of the frameset. That's why the function assigns the generic `location.href` property to the search string: You can use it on any content page.

The code in Listing 17-6, Listing 17-7, and Listing 17-8 establishes a frameset containing two frames. In the left frame is a table of contents that allows you to navigate among three different pages, the first of which is initially displayed in the right frame. The interesting thing about the example is how you can specify a new page in the `content` parameter of the search property; then the page is opened within the frameset. For example, the following URL would result in the page hello.htm being opened in the right frame:

```
lst17-06.htm?content=hello.htm
```

In this example URL, the frameset page is first opened due to the inclusion of the file lst17-06.htm, whereas the hello.htm file is specified as the value of the `content` parameter.

Related Item: `location.href` property

Methods
assign("*URL*")

Returns: Nothing
Compatibility: WinIE3+, MacIE3+, NN2+, Moz+, Safari+

In earlier discussions about the `location` object, I said that you navigate to another page by assigning a new URL to the `location` object or `location.href` property. The `location.assign()` method does the same thing. In fact, when you set the `location` object to a URL, JavaScript silently applies the `assign()` method. No particular penalty or benefit comes from using the `assign()` method except perhaps making your code more understandable to others.

Related Item: `location.href` property

reload(*unconditionalGETBoolean*)

Returns: Nothing
Compatibility: WinIE4+, MacIE4+, NN3+, Moz+, Safari+

The `location.reload()` method may be named inappropriately because it makes you think of the Reload/Refresh button in the browser toolbar. The `reload()` method is actually more powerful than the Reload/Refresh button (a soft reload) in that it clears form control values that otherwise might survive the Reload/Refresh button. Note that MacIE and Safari do not preserve form control settings even with a soft reload.

Most form elements retain their screen states when you click Reload/Refresh. Text and `textarea` objects maintain whatever text is inside them; radio buttons and checkboxes maintain their checked status; `select` objects remember which item is selected. About the only items the Reload/Refresh button destroys are global variable values and any settable, but not visible, property (for example, the value of a `hidden input` object). I call this kind of reload a *soft reload*. A *hard reload*, on the other hand, should reset all data associated with a page, including default form selections.

Browsers are frustratingly irregular about the ways they reload a document in the memory cache. In theory, an application of the `location.reload()` method should retrieve the page from the cache if the page is still available there (and the `history.go(0)` method should be even gentler, preserving form element settings). Adding a `true` parameter to the method is supposed to force an *unconditional GET* to the server, ignoring the cached version of the page. Yet when it is crucial for your application to get a page from the cache (for speed) or from the server (to guarantee a fresh copy), the browser behaves just the opposite of the way you want it to behave. Meta tags supposedly designed to prevent caching of a page rarely, if ever, work. Some scripters have had success in reloading the page from the server by setting location.href to the URL of the page, plus a slightly different search string (for example, based on a string representation of the Date object) so that there is no match for the URL in the cache.

The bottom line is to be prepared to try different schemes to achieve the effect you want. Also be prepared not to get the results you need. In other words, learn to live with the fact that you don't really have exacting control over retrieving a fresh page.

Listing 17-9 provides a means of testing the different outcomes of a soft reload versus a hard reload. Open this example page in a browser, and click a radio button. Then enter some new text, and make a choice in the select object. Clicking the Soft Reload/Refresh button invokes a method that reloads the document as though you had clicked the browser's Reload/Refresh button. It also preserves the visible properties of form elements. The Hard Reload button invokes the location.reload() method, which resets all objects to their default settings.

LISTING 17-9

Hard versus Soft Reloading

```
<html>
    <head>
        <title>Reload Comparisons</title>
        <script type="text/javascript">
        function hardReload() {
            location.reload(true);
        }
        function softReload() {
            history.go(0);
        }
        </script>
    </head>
    <body>
        <form name="myForm">
            <input type="radio" name="rad1" value="1" />Radio 1<br />
            <input type="radio" name="rad1" value="2" />Radio 2<br />
            <input type="radio" name="rad1" value="3" />Radio 3
            <p><input type="text" name="entry" value="Original" /></p>
            <p><select name="theList">
                    <option>Red</option>
                    <option>Green</option>
                    <option>Blue</option>
                </select></p>
            <hr />
            <input type="button" value="Soft Reload" onclick="softReload()" />
            <input type="button" value="Hard Reload" onclick="hardReload()" />
        </form>
    </body>
</html>
```

Related Item: history.go() method

windowObject.location.replace()

replace("*URL*")

Returns: Nothing
Compatibility: WinIE4+, MacIE4+, NN3+, Moz+, Safari+

In a complex web site, you may have pages that you do not want to appear in the user's history list. For example, a registration sequence may lead the user to one or more intermediate HTML documents that won't make much sense to the user later. Or you may have a one-time introduction page that appears only the first time a user visits your site. You especially don't want users to see these pages again if they use the Back button to return to a previous URL. The location.replace() method navigates to another page, but it does not let the current page stay in the queue of pages accessible via the Back button.

Although you cannot prevent a document from appearing in the history list while the user views that page, you can instruct the browser to load another document into the window and replace the current history entry with the entry for the new document. This trick does not empty the history list but removes the current item from the list before the next URL is loaded. Removing the item from the history list prevents users from seeing the page again by clicking the Back button later.

Listing 17-10 shows how to use the replace() method to direct a web browser to a new URL. Calling the location.replace() method navigates to another URL similarly to assigning a URL to the location. The difference is that the document doing the calling doesn't appear in the history list after the new document loads. You can verify this by trying to click the Back button to return to the page after clicking Replace Me in Listing 17-10; the button is dimmed, because the page no longer exists in the browser history. Also check the history listing (in your browser's usual spot for this information) before and after clicking Replace Me.

LISTING 17-10

Invoking the location.replace() Method

```
<html>
   <head>
      <title>location.replace() Method</title>
      <script type="text/javascript">
      function doReplace() {
         location.replace("lst17-01.htm");
      }
      </script>
   </head>
   <body>
      <form name="myForm">
         <input type="button" value="Replace Me" onclick="doReplace()" />
      </form>
   </body>
</html>
```

Related Item: history object

history Object

Properties	Methods	Event Handler
current	back()	(None)
length	forward()	
next	go()	
previous		

Syntax

Accessing history object properties or methods:

> [window.]history.*property* | *method*([*parameters*])

About this object

As a user surfs the web, the browser maintains a list of URLs for the most recent stops. This list is represented in the scriptable object model by the history object. A script cannot surreptitiously extract actual URLs maintained in that list unless you use signed scripts (in NN4+/Moz; see Chapter 46 on the CD-ROM) and the user grants permission. Under unsigned conditions, a script can methodically navigate to each URL in the history (by relative number or by stepping back one URL at a time), in which case the user sees the browser navigating on its own as though possessed by a spirit. Good Netiquette dictates that you do not navigate a user outside your web site without the user's explicit permission.

One application for the history object and its back() or go() methods is to provide the equivalent of a Back button in your HTML documents. That button triggers a script that checks for any items in the history list and then goes back one page. Your document doesn't have to know anything about the URL from which the user lands at your page; it delegates the specifics of the navigation back to the browser.

The behavior of the Back and Forward buttons is also available through a pair of window methods: window.back() and window.forward(). The history object methods are not specific to a frame that is part of the reference. When the parent.frameName.history.back() method reaches the end of history for that frame, further invocations of that method are ignored.

IE's history mechanism is not localized to a particular frame of a frameset. Instead, the history.back() and history.forward() methods mimic the physical act of clicking the toolbar buttons. If you want to ensure cross-browser, if not cross-generational, behavior in a frameset, address references to the history.back() and history.forward() methods to the parent window.

You should use the history object and its methods with extreme care. Your design must be smart enough to watch what the user is doing with your pages (for example, by checking the current URL before navigating with these methods). Otherwise, you run the risk of confusing your user by navigating to unexpected places. Your script can also get into trouble because it cannot detect where the current document is in the Back–Forward sequence in history.

Properties
```
current
next
previous
```
Value: String   Read-Only
Compatibility: WinIE-, MacIE-, NN4+, Moz+, Safari-

To know where to go when you click the Back and Forward buttons, the browser maintains a list of URLs visited. To someone trying to invade your privacy and see what sites and pages you frequent, this information is valuable. That's why the three properties that expose the actual URLs in the history list are restricted to pages with signed scripts (NN4+/Moz) and whose visitors have given permission to read sensitive browser data (see Chapter 46 on the CD-ROM).

With signed scripts and permission, you can look through the entire array of history entries in any frame or window. Because the list is an array, you can extract individual items by index value. For example, if the array has 10 entries, you can see the fifth item by using normal array indexing methods:

```
var fifthEntry = window.history[4];
```

No property or method exists that directly reveals the index value of the currently loaded URL, but you can script an educated guess by comparing the values of the current, next, and previous properties of the `history` object against the entire list.

I personally don't like some unknown entity watching over my shoulder while I'm on the Net, so I respect that same feeling in others and therefore discourage the use of these powers unless the user is given adequate warning. The signed script permission dialog box does not offer enough detail about the consequences of revealing this level of information. This means that you should explicitly notify users of the fact that you are accessing their history, even when you have implicit permission via a signed script.

Related Item: `history.length` property

length
Value: Number   Read-Only
Compatibility: WinIE3+, MacIE3+, NN2+, Moz+, Safari+

Use the `history.length` property to count the items in the history list. Unfortunately, this nugget of information is not particularly helpful in scripting navigation relative to the current location because your script cannot extract anything from the place in the history queue where the current document is located. If the current document is at the top of the list (the most recently loaded), you can calculate relative to that location. But users can use the Go/View menu to jump around the history list as they like. The position of a listing in the history list does not change by virtue of navigating back to that document. A `history.length` of 1, however, indicates that the current document is the first one the user has loaded since starting the browser software.

Listing 17-11 shows how to use the `length` property to notify users of how many pages they've visited.

LISTING 17-11

A Browser History Count

```html
<html>
    <head>
        <title>History Object</title>
        <script type="text/javascript">
        function showCount() {
            var histCount = window.history.length;
            if (histCount > 5) {
                alert("My, my, you\'ve been busy. You have visited " + histCount +
                    " pages so far.");
            } else {
                alert("You have been to " + histCount + " Web pages this
                    session.");
            }
        }
        </script>
    </head>
    <body>
        <form>
            <input type="button" name="activity" value="My Activity"
            onclick="showCount()" />
        </form>
    </body>
</html>
```

Related Items: None

Methods
back()
forward()

Returns: Nothing
Compatibility: WinIE3+, MacIE3+, NN2+, Moz+, Safari+

Although the names might lead you to believe that these methods mimic the buttons on a browser's toolbar, they do not. The history.back() method is window/frame specific, meaning that if you direct successive back() methods to a frame within a frameset, the method is ignored when it reaches the first document to be loaded into that frame. The Back button and the window.back() method unload the frameset and continue taking you back through the browser's global history.

If you deliberately lead a user to a dead end in your web site, you should make sure that the HTML document provides a way to navigate back to a recognizable spot. Because you can easily create a new window that has no toolbar or menu bar (non-Macintosh browsers), you may end up stranding your users because they have no way of navigating out of a cul-de-sac in such a window. A button in your document should give the user a way back to the last location.

***windowObject*.history.back()**

Unless you need to perform some additional processing prior to navigating to the previous location, you can simply place this method as the parameter to the event handler attribute of a button definition. To guarantee compatibility across all browsers, direct this method at the parent document when used from within a frameset.

Less likely to be scripted than the `history.back()` action is the method that performs the opposite action: navigating forward one step in the browser's history list. The only time you can confidently use the `history.forward()` method is to balance the use of the `history.back()` method in the same script — where your script closely keeps track of how many steps the script heads in either direction. Use the `history.forward()` method with extreme caution and only after performing extensive user testing on your web pages to make sure that you've covered all user possibilities. Similar to navigating backward via `history.back()`, forward progress when using `history.forward()` extends only through the history listing for a given window or frame, not the entire browser history list.

Listing 17-12 and Listing 17-13 provide a little workshop in which you can test the behavior of a variety of forms of backward and forward navigation in different browsers.

LISTING 17-12

Navigation Lab Frameset

```
<html>
    <head>
        <title>Back and Forward</title>
    </head>
    <frameset cols="45%,55%">
        <frame name="controller" src="lst17-13.htm" />
        <frame name="display" src="lst17-01.htm" />
    </frameset>
</html>
```

LISTING 17-13

Navigation Lab Control Panel

```
<html>
    <head>
        <title>Lab Controls</title>
    </head>
    <body>
        <b>Load a series of documents into the right frame by clicking some of
        these links (make a note of the sequence you click on):</b>
        <p><a href="lst17-01.htm" target="display">Listing 17-1</a><br />
           <a href="lst17-05.htm" target="display">Listing 17-5</a><br />
           <a href="lst17-09.htm" target="display">Listing 17-9</a><br /></p>
        <hr />
        <form name="input">
            <b>Click on the various buttons below to see the results in this
            frameset:</b>
```

```
      <ul>
          <li><tt>history.back()</tt> and <tt>history.forward()</tt> for
              righthand frame:<input type="button" value="Back"
              onclick="parent.display.history.back()" /><input type="button"
              value="Forward" onclick="parent.display.history.forward()" />
              </li>
          <li><tt>history.back()</tt> for this frame:<input type="button"
              value="Back" onclick="history.back()" /></li>
          <li><tt>history.back()</tt> for parent:<input type="button"
              value="Back" onclick="parent.history.back()" /></li>
      </ul>
   </form>
 </body>
</html>
```

Related Items: `history.go()` method

go(*relativeNumber* | *"URLOrTitleSubstring"*)

Returns: Nothing
Compatibility: WinIE3+, MacIE3+, NN2+, Moz+, Safari+

Use the `history.go()` method to script navigation within the history list currently stored in the browser. If you elect to use a URL as a parameter, however, that precise URL must already exist in the history listing. Therefore, do not regard this method as an alternative to setting the `window.location` object to a brand-new URL.

For navigating n steps in either direction along the history list, use the `relativeNumber` parameter of the `history.go()` method. This number is an integer value that indicates which item in the list to use, relative to the current location. For example, if the current URL is at the top of the list (that is, the Forward button in the toolbar is dimmed), you need to use the following method to jump to the URL two items backward in the list:

```
    history.go(-2);
```

In other words, the current URL is the equivalent of `history.go(0)` (a method that reloads the window). A positive integer indicates a jump that many items forward in the history list. Thus, `history.go(-1)` is the same as `history.back()`, whereas `history.go(1)` is the same as `history.forward()`.

Alternatively, you can specify one of the URLs or document titles stored in the browser's history list (titles appear in the Go/View menu). As security and privacy concerns have increased over time, this variant of the `go()` method has been reined in. It's best not to use the string parameter in your scripting.

Like most other history methods, your script finds it difficult to manage the history list or the current URL's spot in the queue. That fact makes it even more difficult for your script to determine intelligently how far to navigate in either direction or to which specific URL or title matches it should jump. Use this method only for situations in which your web pages are in strict control of the user's activity (or for designing scripts for yourself that automatically crawl around sites according to a fixed regimen). When you give the user control over navigation, you have no guarantee that the history list will be what you expect, and any scripts you write that depend on a `history` object will likely break.

In practice, this method mostly performs a soft reload of the current window using the 0 parameter.

windowObject.history.go()

 If you are developing a page for all scriptable browsers, be aware that Internet Explorer's go() method behaves a little differently from Netscape's. In IE4+, the matching string must be part of the URL and not part of the document title, as in Navigator. This is another reason to steer clear of using the string approach to navigate via the history.go() method. Additionally, the reloading of a page with history.go(0) in IE often returns to the server to reload the page rather than reloading from the cache.

Listing 17-14 contains sample code that demonstrates how to navigate the history list via the go() method. Fill in either the number or text field of the page in Listing 17-14 and then click the associated button. The script passes the appropriate kind of data to the go() method. Be sure to use negative numbers for visiting a page earlier in the history.

NOTE Mozilla browsers respond only to the integer offset approach to using the history.go() method.

LISTING 17-14

Navigating to an Item in History

```
<html>
   <head>
      <title>history.go() Method</title>
      <script type="text/javascript">
      function doGoNum(form) {
         window.history.go(parseInt(form.histNum.value));
      }
      function doGoTxt(form) {
         window.history.go(form.histWord.value);
      }
      </script>
   </head>
   <body>
      <form>
         <b>Calling the history.go() method:</b>
         <hr />
         Enter a number (+/-):<input type="text" name="histNum" size="3"
         value="0" /> <input type="button" value="Go to Offset"
         onclick="doGoNum(this.form)" />
         <p>Enter a word in a title:<input type="text" name="histWord" />
            <input type="button" value="Go to Match"
            onclick="doGoTxt(this.form)" /></p>
      </form>
   </body>
</html>
```

Related Items: history.back(), history.forward(), location.reload() methods

Chapter 18

The Document and Body Objects

U ser interaction is a vital aspect of client-side JavaScript scripting, and most of the communication between script and user takes place by way of the document object and its components. Understanding the scope of the document object within each of the object models you support is key to implementing successful cross-browser applications.

Review the document object's place within the original object hierarchy. Figure 18-1 shows that the document object is a pivotal point for a large percentage of objects. In the W3C DOM, the document object plays an even more important role as the container of all element objects delivered with the page: The document object is the root of the entire document tree.

In fact, the document object and all that it contains is so big that I have divided its discussion into many chapters, each focusing on related object groups. This chapter looks at the document object and body object (which have conceptual relationships), whereas each of the succeeding chapters in this part of the book details objects contained by the document object.

Accessing arrays of objects contained by the document object

Writing new document content to a window or frame

Using the body element for IE window measurements

FIGURE 18-1

The basic document object model hierarchy.

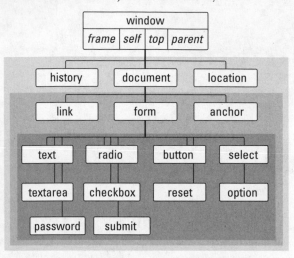

document Object

Compatibility: WinIE3+, MacIE3+, NN2+, Moz+, Safari+

Properties	Methods	Event Handlers
activeElement	attachEvent()†	onactivate†
alinkColor	captureEvents()	onbeforecut†
all†	clear()	onbeforedeactivate†
anchors[]	clearAttributes()†	onbeforeeditfocus†
applets[]	close()	onbeforepaste†
attributes†	createAttribute()	onclick†
baseURI	createCDATASection()	oncontextmenu†
bgColor	createComment()	oncontrolselect†
body	createDocumentFragment()	oncut†
charset	createElement()	ondblclick†
characterSet	createElementNS()	ondrag†
childNodes†	createEvent()	ondragend†
compatMode	createEventObject()	ondragenter†
contentType†	createNSResolver()	ondragleave†

Properties	Methods	Event Handlers
cookie	createRange()	ondragover†
defaultCharset	createStyleSheet()	ondragstart†
defaultView	createTextNode()	ondrop†
designMode	createTreeWalker()	onhelp†
doctype	detachEvent()†	onkeydown†
documentElement	elementFromPoint()	onkeypress†
documentURI	execCommand()	onkeyup†
domain	evaluate()	onmousedown†
embeds[]	focus()†	onmousemove†
expando	getElementById()	onmouseout†
fgColor	getElementsByName()	onmouseover†
fileCreatedDate	getElementsByTagName()†	onmouseup†
fileModifiedDate	getElementsByTagNameNS()†	onpaste†
fileSize	hasFocus()†	onpropertychange†
firstChild†	importNode()†	onreadyStatechange†
forms[]	mergeAttributes()†	onresizeend†
frames[]	open()	onresizestart†
height	queryCommandEnabled()	onselectionchange
ids[]	queryCommandIndterm()	onstop
images[]	queryCommandState()	
implementation†	queryCommandSupported()†	
inputEncoding	queryCommandText()	
lastChild†	queryCommandValue()	
lastModified	recalc()	
layers[]	releaseCapture()†	
linkColor	releaseEvents()	
links[]	routeEvent()	
location	setActive()†	
media†	write()	
mimeType	writeln()	
nameProp		
namespaces[]		
namespaceURI†		
nextSibling†		

continued

Properties	Methods	Event Handlers
nodeName†		
nodeType†		
ownerDocument†		
parentNode†		
parentWindow†		
plugins[]†		
previousSibling†		
protocol		
readyState†		
referrer		
scripts[]		
security		
selection		
strictErrorChecking		
styleSheets[]		
tags[]		
title		
uniqueID†		
URL		
URLUnencoded		
vlinkColor		
width		
xmlEncoding		
xmlStandalone		
xmlVersion		

†See Chapter 15.

Syntax

Accessing document object properties or methods:

        [window.]document.*property* | *method*([*parameters*])

About this object

A document object encompasses the totality of what exists inside the content region of a browser window or window frame (excluding toolbars, status lines, and so on). The document is a combination of the content and interface elements that make the web page worth visiting. In modern browsers the `document` object also serves as the root node of a page's hierarchical tree of nodes — that from which all other nodes grow.

Because the `document` object isn't explicitly represented in an HTML document by tags or any other notation, the original designers of JavaScript and object models decided to make the `document` object the portal to many settings that were represented in HTML as belonging to the `body` element. That element's tag contains attributes for document-wide attributes, such as background color (`bgcolor`) and link colors in various states (`alink`, `link`, and `vlink`). The `body` element also served as an HTML container for forms, links, and anchors. The `document` object, therefore, assumed a majority of the role of the `body` element. But even then, the `document` object became the most convenient place to bind some properties that extend beyond the `body` element, such as the `title` element and the URL of the link that referred the user to the page. When viewed within the context of the HTML source code, the original `document` object is somewhat schizophrenic. Even so, the `document` object has worked well as the basis for references to original object model objects, such as forms, images, and applets.

This, of course, was before every HTML element, including the `body` element, was exposed as an object through modern object models. Amazingly, even with the IE4+ object model and W3C DOM — both of which treat the `body` element as an object separate from the `document` object — script compatibility with the original object model is quite easily accomplished. The `document` object has assumed a new schizophrenia, splitting its personality between the original object model and the one that places the `document` object at the root of the hierarchy, quite separate from the `body` element object it contains. The object knows which face to put on based on the rest of the script syntax that follows it. This means that quite often there are multiple ways to achieve the same reference. For example, you can use the following statement in all scriptable browsers to get the number of form objects in a document:

```
document.forms.length
```

In IE4+, you can also use

```
document.tags["form"].length
```

And in the W3C DOM as implemented in IE5+ and NN6+/Moz/Cam/Safari, you can use

```
document.getElementsByTagName("form").length
```

Modern browsers provide a generic approach to accessing elements (`getElementsByTagName()` method in the W3C DOM) to meet the requirements of object models that expose every HTML (and XML) element as an object.

Promoting the `body` element to the ranks of exposed objects presented its own challenges to the new object model designers. The `body` element is the true owner of some properties that the original `document` object had to take on by default. Most properties that belonged to the original `document` object were renamed in their transfer to the `body` element. For example, the original `document.alinkColor` property is the `body.aLink` property in the modern model. But the `bgColor` property has not been renamed. For the sake of code compatibility, modern browsers recognize both properties, even though the W3C DOM has removed the old versions as properties of what it conceives as the `document` object. Considering the fact that modern browsers are now prevalent, you should be able to stick with the new properties from here on.

Properties
activeElement

Value: Object reference.   Read-Only
Compatibility: WinIE4+, MacIE4+, NN-, Moz-, Safari-

In IE4+, a script can examine the document.activeElement property to see which element currently has focus. The value returned is an element object reference. You can use any of the properties and methods listed in Chapter 15 to find out more about the object.

Although the element used to generate a mouse or keyboard event will most likely have focus, don't rely on the activeElement property to find out which element generated an event. The IE event.srcElement property is far more reliable.

Example

Use The Evaluator (see Chapter 13) with IE4+ to experiment with the activeElement property. Type the following statement into the top text box:

```
document.activeElement.value
```

After you press the Enter key, the Results box shows the value of the text box you just typed into (the very same expression you just typed). But if you then click the Evaluate button, you will see the value property of that button object appear in the Results box.

Related Items: event.srcElement property.

alinkColor
bgColor
fgColor
linkColor
vlinkColor

Value: Hexadecimal triplet or color name string.   Mostly Read/Write
Compatibility: WinIE3+, MacIE3+, NN2+, Moz+, Safari+

These five properties are the script equivalent of the <body> tag attributes of the same name (although the property names are case-sensitive). All five settings can be read via the document.body object in modern browsers. Values for all color properties can be either the common HTML hexadecimal triplet value (for example, "#00FF00") or any of the standard color names.

Example

I select some color values at random to plug into three settings of the ugly colors group for Listing 18-1. The smaller window displays a dummy button so that you can see how its display contrasts with color settings. Notice that the script sets the colors of the smaller window by rewriting the entire window's HTML code. After changing colors, the script displays the color values in the original window's textarea. Even though some colors are set with the color constant values, properties come back in the hexadecimal triplet values. You can experiment to your heart's content by changing color values in the listing. Every time you change the values in the script, save the HTML file and reload it in the browser.

LISTING 18-1

Tweaking the Color of Page Elements

```html
<html>
    <head>
        <title>Color Me</title>
        <script type="text/javascript">
        // may be blocked at load time by browser popup blockers
        var newWindow = window.open("","","height=150,width=300");

        function defaultColors() {
            return "bgcolor='#c0c0c0' vlink='#551a8b' link='#0000ff'";
        }

        function uglyColors() {
            return "bgcolor='yellow' vlink='pink' link='lawngreen'";
        }

        function showColorValues() {
            var result = "";
            result += "bgColor: " + newWindow.document.bgColor + "\n";
            result += "vlinkColor: " + newWindow.document.vlinkColor + "\n";
            result += "linkColor: " + newWindow.document.linkColor + "\n";
            document.forms[0].results.value = result;
        }

        // dynamically writes contents of another window
        function drawPage(colorStyle) {
            // work around popup blockers
            if (!newWindow || newWindow.closed) {
                newWindow = window.open("","","height=150,width=300");
            }
            var thePage = "";
            thePage += "<html><head><title>Color Sampler<\/title><\/head><body ";
            if (colorStyle == "default") {
                thePage += defaultColors();
            } else {
                thePage += uglyColors();
            }
            thePage += ">Just so you can see the variety of items and color, <a ";
            thePage += "href='http://www.nowhere.com'>here\'s a link<\/a>, and <a ";
            href='http://home.netscape.com'> here is another link <\/a> you can use
            on-line to visit and see how its color differs from the standard link.";
            thePage += "<form>";
            thePage += "<input type='button' name='sample' value='Just a Button'>";
            thePage += "<\/form><\/body><\/html>";
            newWindow.document.write(thePage);
            newWindow.document.close();
            showColorValues();
```

continued

LISTING 18-1 *(continued)*

```
        }

        // the following works properly only in Windows Navigator
        function setColors(colorStyle) {
            if (colorStyle == "default") {
                document.bgColor = "#c0c0c0";
            } else {
                document.bgColor = "yellow";
            }
        }

        // bind the event handlers
        function addEvent(elem, evtType, func) {
            if (elem.addEventListener) {
                elem.addEventListener(evtType, func, false);
            } else if (elem.attachEvent) {
                elem.attachEvent("on" + evtType, func);
            } else {
                elem["on" + evtType] = func;
            }
        }
        addEvent(window, "load", function() {
            addEvent(document.getElementById("default1"), "click",
                function(evt) {drawPage("default")});
            addEvent(document.getElementById("weird1"), "click",
                function(evt) {drawPage("ugly")});
            addEvent(document.getElementById("default2"), "click",
                function(evt) {setColors("default")});
            addEvent(document.getElementById("weird2"), "click",
                function(evt) {setColors("ugly")});
        });
        </script>
    </head>
    <body>
        Try the two color schemes on the document in the small window.
        <form>
            <input type="button" id="default1" name="default" value='Default Colors'
            /> <input type="button" id="weird1" name="weird" value="Ugly Colors" />
            <p><textarea name="results" rows="3" cols="20">
                </textarea></p>
            <hr />
            These buttons change the current document.
            <p><input type="button" id="default2" name="default"
                value='Default Colors' /> <input type="button" id="weird2"
                name="weird" value="Ugly Colors" /></p>
        </form>
    </body>
</html>
```

> **NOTE** The examples in this chapter take advantage of the modern approach to event handling, which involves the addEventListener() (NN6+/Moz/W3C) and attachEvent() (IE5+) methods. This event handling technique is explained in detail in Chapter 25.

Related Items: body.aLink, body.bgColor, body.link, body.text, body.vLink properties.

anchors[]

Value: Array of anchor objects.   Read-Only
Compatibility: WinIE3+, MacIE3+, NN2+, Moz+, Safari+

Anchor objects (described in Chapter 19) are points in an HTML document marked with `<a name="">` tags. Anchor objects are referenced in URLs by a hash value between the page URL and anchor name. Like other object properties that contain a list of nested objects, the document.anchors property delivers an indexed array of anchors in a document. Use the array references to pinpoint a specific anchor for retrieving any anchor property.

Anchor arrays begin their index counts with 0: The first anchor in a document, then, has the reference document.anchors[0]. And, as is true with any built-in array object, you can find out how many entries the array has by checking the length property. For example:

```
alert("This document has " + document.anchors.length + " anchors.");
```

The document.anchors property is read-only. To script navigation to a particular anchor, assign a value to the window.location or window.location.hash object, as described in the location object discussion in Chapter 17.

Example

In Listing 18-2, I append an extra script to Listing 17-1 to demonstrate how to extract the number of anchors in the document. The document dynamically writes the number of anchors found in the document. You will not likely ever need to reveal such information to users of your page, and the document.anchors property is not one that you will call frequently. The object model defines it automatically as a document property while defining actual anchor objects.

LISTING 18-2

Using Anchors to Navigate Through a Page

```html
<html>
  <head>
    <title>document.anchors Property</title>
    <script type="text/javascript">
    function goNextAnchor(where) {
      window.location.hash = where;
    }

    // bind the event handlers
    function addEvent(elem, evtType, func) {
      if (elem.addEventListener) {
        elem.addEventListener(evtType, func, false);
```

continued

LISTING 18-2 *(continued)*

```
        } else if (elem.attachEvent) {
            elem.attachEvent("on" + evtType, func);
        } else {
            elem["on" + evtType] = func;
        }
    }
    addEvent(window, "load", function() {
        addEvent(document.getElementById("next1"), "click",
            function(evt) {goNextAnchor("sec1")});
        addEvent(document.getElementById("next2"), "click",
            function(evt) {goNextAnchor("sec2")});
        addEvent(document.getElementById("next3"), "click",
            function(evt) {goNextAnchor("sec3")});
        addEvent(document.getElementById("next4"), "click",
            function(evt) {goNextAnchor("start")});
    });
    </script>
</head>
<body>
    <h1><a id="start" name="start">Top</a></h1>
    <form>
        <input type="button" id="next1" name="next" value="NEXT" />
    </form>
    <hr />
    <h1><a id="sec1" name="sec1">Section 1</a></h1>
    <form>
        <input type="button" id="next2" name="next" value="NEXT" />
    </form>
    <hr />
    <h1><a id="sec2" name="sec2">Section 2</a></h1>
    <form>
        <input type="button" id="next3" name="next" value="NEXT" />
    </form>
    <hr />
    <h1><a id="sec3" name="sec3">Section 3</a></h1>
    <form>
        <input type="button" id="next4" name="next" value="BACK TO TOP" />
    </form>
    <hr />
    <p>
        <script type="text/javascript">
        document.write("<i>There are " + document.anchors.length + " anchors
defined for this document<\/i>")
        </script>
    </p>
</body>
</html>
```

Related Items: anchor, location objects; document.links property.

applets[]

Value: Array of applet objects.   Read-Only
Compatibility: WinIE3+, MacIE3+, NN2+, Moz+, Safari+

The applets property refers to Java applets defined in a document by the <applet> tag. An applet is not officially an object in the document until the applet loads completely.

Most of the work you do with Java applets from JavaScript takes place through the methods and variables defined inside the applet. Although you can reference an applet according to its indexed array position within the applets array, you will more likely use the applet object's name in the reference to avoid any confusion.

Example

The document.applets property is defined automatically as the browser builds the object model for a document that contains applet objects. You will rarely access this property, except to determine how many applet objects a document has, as in this example:

```
var numApplets = document.applets.length;
```

Related Items: applet object.

baseURI

Value: String.   Read-Only
Compatibility: WinIE-, MacIE-, NN7+, Moz+, Safari-

The baseURI property reveals the absolute base URI of the document. You can check the base URI of a document in the Evaluator (see Chapter 13) by entering the following:

```
document.baseURI
```

Related Items: document.documentURI property.

bgColor

(See alinkColor)

body

Value: body element object.   Read/Write
Compatibility: WinIE4+, MacIE4+, NN6+, Moz+, Safari+

The document.body property is a shortcut reference to the body element object in modern object models. As you can see in the discussion of the body element object later in this chapter, that object has many key properties that govern the look of the entire page. Because the document object is the root of all references within any window or frame, the document.body property is easier to use to get to the body properties, rather than longer references normally used to access HTML element objects in both the IE4+ and W3C object models.

Example

Use The Evaluator (see Chapter 13) to examine properties of the body element object. First, to prove that the document.body is the same as the element object that comes back from longer references, enter the following statement into the top text box with either IE5+, NN6+/Moz, or some other W3C browser:

```
document.body == document.getElementsByTagName("body")[0]
```

Next, check out the body object's property listings later in this chapter and enter the listings into the top text box to review their results. For example:

```
document.body.bgColor
document.body.tagName
```

The main point to take from this example is that the document.body reference provides a simpler and more direct means of accessing a document's body object without having to use the getElementsByTagName() method.

Related Items: body element object.

charset

Value: String.   Read/Write
Compatibility: WinIE4+, MacIE4+, NN-, Moz-, Safari-

The charset property reveals the character set used by the browser (IE4+) to render the current document (the NN6+/Moz version of this property is called characterSet). You can find possible values for this property at

```
ftp://ftp.isi.edu/in-notes/iana/assignments/character-sets
```

Each browser and operating system has its own default character set. Values may also be set through a <meta> tag.

Example

Use The Evaluator (see Chapter 13) to experiment with the charset property. To see the default setting applied to the page, enter the following statement into the top text box:

```
document.charset
```

If you are running IE5+ for Windows and you enter the following statement, the browser will apply a different character set to the page:

```
document.charset = "iso-8859-2"
```

If your version of Windows does not have that character set installed in the system, the browser may ask permission to download and install the character set.

Related Items: characterSet, defaultCharset properties.

characterSet

Value: String.   Read/Write
Compatibility: WinIE-, MacIE-, NN6+, Moz+, Safari-

The `characterSet` property reveals the character set used by the browser to render the current document (the IE version of this property is called `charset`). You can find possible values for this property at

```
http://www.iana.org/assignments/character-sets
```

Each browser and operating system has its own default character set. Values may also be set through a `<meta>` tag.

Example

Use The Evaluator (see Chapter 13) to experiment with the `characterSet` property in NN6+/Moz. To see the default setting applied to the page, enter the following statement into the top text box:

```
document.charset
```

Related Items: `charset` property.

compatMode

Value: String.   Read-Only
Compatibility: WinIE6+, MacIE6+, NN7+, Moz+, Safari-

The `compatMode` property reveals the compatibility mode for the document, as determined by the `DOCTYPE` element's content. The value for this property can be one of the following string constants: `BackCompat` or `CSS1Compat`. The default setting for the `compatMode` property is `BackCompat`, which means that the document is not standards-compliant. By *standards-compliant* I'm referring to the CSS1 standard.

Example

You may find it useful to check the compatibility mode of a document in order to carry out processing specific to one of the modes. Following is an example of how you might branch to carry out processing for backward-compatible documents:

```
if (document.compatMode == "BackCompat") {
    // perform backward compatible processing
}
```

Related Items: *Standards Compatibility Modes* (see Chapter 13).

contentType

Value: String.   Read-Only
Compatibility: WinIE-, MacIE-, NN7+, Moz+, Safari-

The `contentType` property holds the content type (MIME type) of the document. For a normal HTML document, the value of this property is `text/html`.

cookie

Value: String.   Read/Write
Compatibility: WinIE3+, MacIE3+, NN2+, Moz+, Safari+

The cookie mechanism in a web browser lets you store small pieces of information on the client computer in a reasonably secure manner. In other words, when you need some tidbit of information to persist at the client level while either loading diverse HTML documents or moving from one session to another, the cookie mechanism saves the day. The cookie is commonly used as a means to store the username and password you enter into a password-protected web site. The first time you enter this information into a form, the server-side form processing program has the browser write the information back to a cookie on your hard disk (usually after encrypting the password). Rather than bothering you to enter the username and password the next time you access the site, the server searches the cookie data stored for that particular server and extracts the username and password for automatic validation processing behind the scenes.

Other applications of the cookie include storing user preferences and information about the user's previous visit to the site. Preferences may include font styles or sizes and whether the user prefers viewing content inside a frameset or not. As shown in Chapter 54 on the CD-ROM, a time stamp of the previous visit can allow a coded HTML page to display highlighted images next to content that has changed since the user's last visit, even if you have updated the page several times in the interim. Rather than hard-wiring New flags for *your* last visit, the scripts highlight what's new for the visitor.

The cookie file

Allowing some foreign server program to read from and write to your hard disk may give you pause, but browser cookie mechanisms don't just open up your drive's directory for the world to see (or corrupt). Instead, the cookie mechanism provides access to just one special text file (Navigator/Mozilla/Safari) or type of text file (Internet Explorer) located in a platform-specific spot on your drive.

In Mozilla-based browsers, for example, the cookie file is named `cookies.txt` and is located in a directory (whose name ends in `.slt`) within the browser's profile area. In Windows, that location is `C:\\Windows\Application Data\Mozilla\Profiles\[profilename]\`; in Mac OSX, the location is `[user]/Library/Mozilla/Profiles/[profilename]/`. Internet Explorer for Windows uses a different filing system: all cookies for each domain are saved in a domain-specific file inside the `C:\\Windows\Temporary Internet Files\` directory. Filenames begin with `Cookie:` and include the username and domain of the server that wrote the cookie. Safari cookies are recorded in an XML file named `Cookies.plist` within the `[user]/Library/Cookies/` directory.

A cookie file is a text file. If curiosity drives you to open a cookie file, I recommend you do so only with a copy saved in another directory or folder. Any alteration to the existing file can mess up whatever valuable cookies are stored there for sites you regularly visit. The data format for cookie files differs across browsers, in line with the different methodologies used for filing cookies. Inside the Mozilla file (after a few comment lines warning you not to manually alter the file) are lines of tab-delimited text. Each return-delimited line contains one cookie's information. The cookie file is just like a text listing of a database. In each of the IE cookie files, the same data points are stored for a cookie as for Mozilla, but the items are in a return-delimited list. The structure of these files is of no importance to scripting cookies, because all browsers utilize the same syntax for reading and writing cookies through the `document.cookie` property.

NOTE   As you experiment with browser's cookies, you will be tempted to look into the cookie file after a script writes some data to the cookie. The cookie file usually will not contain the newly written data, because in most browsers cookies are transferred to disk only when the user quits the browser; conversely, the cookie file is read into the browser's memory when it is launched. While you read, write, and delete cookies during a browser session, all activity is performed in memory (to speed up the process) to be saved later.

A cookie record

Among the fields of each cookie record are the following (not necessarily in this order):

- Domain of the server that created the cookie
- Information on whether you need a secure HTTP connection to access the cookie

- Pathname of URL(s) capable of accessing the cookie
- Expiration date of the cookie
- Name of the cookie entry
- String data associated with the cookie entry

Note that cookies are domain-specific. In other words, if one domain creates a cookie, another domain cannot access it through the browser's cookie mechanism behind your back. That reason is why it's generally safe to store what I call *throwaway passwords* (the username/password pairs required to access some free registration-required sites) in cookies. Moreover, sites that store passwords in a cookie usually do so as encrypted strings, making it more difficult for someone to hijack the cookie file from your unattended PC and figure out what your personal password scheme may be.

Cookies also have expiration dates. Because some browsers may allow no more than a fixed number of cookies (1000 in Firefox), the cookie file can get pretty full over the years. Therefore, if a cookie needs to persist past the current browser session, it should have an expiration date established by the cookie writer. Browsers automatically clean out any expired cookies.

Not all cookies have to last beyond the current session, however. In fact, a scenario in which you use cookies temporarily while working your way through a web site is quite typical. Many shopping sites employ one or more temporary cookie records to behave as the shopping cart for recording items you intend to purchase. These items are copied to the order form at checkout time. But after you submit the order form to the server, that client-side data has no particular value. As it turns out, if your script does not specify an expiration date, the browser keeps the cookie fresh in memory without writing it to the cookie file. When you quit the browser, that cookie data disappears as expected.

JavaScript access

Scripted access of cookies from JavaScript is limited to setting the cookie (with a number of optional parameters) and getting the cookie data (but with none of the parameters).

The original object model defines cookies as properties of documents, but this description is somewhat misleading. If you use the default path to set a cookie (that is, the current directory of the document whose script sets the cookie in the first place), all documents in that same server directory have read and write access to the cookie. A benefit of this arrangement is that if you have a scripted application that contains multiple documents, all documents served from the same directory can share the cookie data. Modern browsers, however, impose a limit of 20 named cookie entries (that is, one name/value pair) for any domain. If your cookie requirements are extensive, you need to fashion ways of concatenating cookie data (I do this in the Decision Helper application in Chapter 55 on the CD-ROM).

Saving cookies

To write cookie data to the cookie file, you use a simple JavaScript assignment operator with the `document.cookie` property. But the formatting of the data is crucial to achieving success. Here is the syntax for assigning a value to a cookie (optional items are in brackets; placeholders for data you supply are in italics):

```
document.cookie = "cookieName=cookieData
             [; expires=timeInGMTString]
             [; path=pathName]
             [; domain=domainName]
             [; secure]"
```

Let's examine each of the properties individually.

document.cookie

Name/Data

Each cookie must have a name and a string value (even if that value is an empty string). Such name/value pairs are fairly common in HTML, but they look odd in an assignment statement. For example, if you want to save the string "Fred" to a cookie named "userName," the JavaScript statement is

```
document.cookie = "userName=Fred";
```

If the browser sees no existing cookie in the current domain with this name, it automatically creates the cookie entry for you; if the named cookie already exists, the browser replaces the old data with the new data. Retrieving the document.cookie property at this point yields the following string:

```
userName=Fred
```

You can omit all the other cookie-setting properties, in which case the browser uses default values, as explained in a following section. For temporary cookies (those that don't have to persist beyond the current browser session), the name/value pair is usually all you need.

The entire name/value pair must be a single string with no semicolons, commas, or character spaces. To take care of spaces between words, preprocess the value with the JavaScript encodeURIComponent() function, which URI-encodes the spaces as %20 (and then be sure to convert the value to restore the human-readable spaces (through decodeURIComponent()) when you retrieve the cookie later).

You cannot save a JavaScript array or object to a cookie. But with the help of the Array.join() method, you can convert an array to a string; use String.split() to re-create the array after reading the cookie at a later time.

Expires

Expiration dates, when supplied, must be passed as Greenwich Mean Time (GMT) strings (see Chapter 30 about time data). To calculate an expiration date based on today's date, use the JavaScript Date object as follows:

```
var exp = new Date();
var oneYearFromNow = exp.getTime() + (365 * 24 * 60 * 60 * 1000);
exp.setTime(oneYearFromNow);
```

Since the getTime() and setTime() methods operate in milliseconds, the year you're adding to the current date must be converted to milliseconds. After making the calculation, the date is converted to the accepted GMT string format:

```
document.cookie = "userName=Fred; expires=" + exp.toGMTString();
```

In the cookie file, the expiration date and time is stored as a numeric value (in seconds) but, to set it, you need to supply the time in GMT format. You can delete a cookie before it expires by setting the named cookie's expiration date to a time and date earlier than the current time and date. The safest expiration parameter is

```
expires=Thu, 01-Jan-70 00:00:01 GMT
```

Omitting the expiration date signals the browser that this cookie is temporary. The browser never writes it to the cookie file and forgets it the next time you quit the browser.

Path

For client-side cookies, the default path setting (the current directory) is usually the best choice. You can, of course, create a duplicate copy of a cookie with a separate path (and domain) so that the same data is available to a document located in another area of your site (or the Web).

Domain

To help synchronize cookie data with a particular document (or group of documents), the browser matches the domain of the current document with the domain values of cookie entries in the cookie file. Therefore, if you were to display a list of all cookie data contained in a `document.cookie` property, you would get back all the name/value cookie pairs from the cookie file whose domain parameter matches that of the current document.

Unless you expect the document to be replicated in another server within your domain, you can usually omit the `domain` parameter when saving a cookie. Default behavior automatically supplies the domain of the current document to the cookie file entry. Be aware that a domain setting must have at least two periods, such as

```
.google.com
.hotwired.com
```

Or, you can write an entire URL to the domain, including the `http://` protocol.

SECURE

If you omit the `SECURE` parameter when saving a cookie, you imply that the cookie data is accessible to any document or server-side program from your site that meets the other domain- and path-matching properties. For client-side scripting of cookies, you should omit this parameter when saving a cookie.

Retrieving cookie data

Cookie data retrieved through JavaScript is contained in one string, which contains the whole name-data pair. Even though the cookie file stores other parameters for each cookie, you can retrieve only the name-data pairs through JavaScript. Moreover, when two or more (up to a maximum of 20) cookies meet the current domain criteria, these cookies are also lumped into that string, delimited by a semicolon and space. For example, a `document.cookie` string may look like this:

```
userName=Fred; password=NikL2sPacU
```

In other words, you cannot treat named cookies as objects. Instead, you must parse the entire cookie string, extracting the data from the desired name-data pair.

When you know that you're dealing with only one cookie (and that no more will ever be added to the domain), you can customize the extraction based on known data, such as the cookie name. For example, with a cookie name that is seven characters long, you can extract the data with a statement such as this:

```
var data = decodeURIComponent(document.cookie.substring(7,document
.cookie.length));
```

The first parameter of the `substring()` method includes the equal sign to separate the name from the data; this is where the 7 comes from in the code. This example works with single cookies only because it assumes that the cookie starts at the beginning of the cookie file, which may not be the case if there are multiple cookies.

document.cookie

A better approach to cookie extraction is to create a general-purpose function that can work with single- or multiple-entry cookies. Here is one I use in some of my pages:

```
function getCookieData(labelName) {
    var labelLen = labelName.length;
    // read cookie property only once for speed
    var cookieData = document.cookie;
    var cLen = cookieData.length;
    var i = 0;
    var cEnd;
    while (i < cLen) {
        var j = i + labelLen;
        if (cookieData.substring(i,j) == labelName) {
            cEnd = cookieData.indexOf(";",j);
            if (cEnd == -1) {
                cEnd = cookieData.length;
            }
            return decodeURIComponent(cookieData.substring(j+1, cEnd));
        }
        i++;
    }
    return "";
}
```

Calls to this function pass the label name of the desired cookie as a parameter. The function parses the entire cookie string, chipping away any mismatched entries (through the semicolons) until it finds the cookie name.

If all of this cookie code still makes your head hurt, you can turn to a set of functions devised by experienced JavaScripter and web site designer Bill Dortch of hIdaho Design. His cookie functions provide generic access to cookies that you can use in all of your cookie-related pages. Listing 18-3 shows Bill's cookie functions, which include a variety of safety nets for date calculation bugs that appeared in some legacy versions of Netscape Navigator. The code is updated with modern URL encoding and decoding methods. Don't be put off by the length of the listing: Most of the lines are comments.

LISTING 18-3

Bill Dortch's Cookie Functions

```
<html>
    <head>
        <title>Cookie Functions</title>
    </head>
    <body>
        <script type="text/javascript">
        //
        // Cookie Functions -- "Night of the Living Cookie" Version (25-Jul-96)
        //
        // Written by:  Bill Dortch, hIdaho Design
        // The following functions are released to the public domain.
```

```
//
//   This version takes a more aggressive approach to deleting
//   cookies.  Previous versions set the expiration date to one
//   millisecond prior to the current time; however, this method
//   did not work in Netscape 2.02 (though it does in earlier and
//   later versions), resulting in "zombie" cookies that would not
//   die.  DeleteCookie now sets the expiration date to the earliest
//   usable date (one second into 1970), and sets the cookie's value
//   to null for good measure.
//
//   Also, this version adds optional path and domain parameters to
//   the DeleteCookie function.  If you specify a path and/or domain
//   when creating (setting) a cookie**, you must specify the same
//   path/domain when deleting it, or deletion will not occur.
//
//   The FixCookieDate function must now be called explicitly to
//   correct for the 2.x Mac date bug.  This function should be
//   called *once* after a Date object is created and before it
//   is passed (as an expiration date) to SetCookie.  Because the
//   Mac date bug affects all dates, not just those passed to
//   SetCookie, you might want to make it a habit to call
//   FixCookieDate any time you create a new Date object:
//
//      var theDate = new Date();
//      FixCookieDate (theDate);
//
//   Calling FixCookieDate has no effect on platforms other than
//   the Mac, so there is no need to determine the user's platform
//   prior to calling it.
//
//   This version also incorporates several minor coding improvements.
//
//   **Note that it is possible to set multiple cookies with the same
//   name but different (nested) paths.  For example:
//
//      SetCookie ("color","red",null,"/outer");
//      SetCookie ("color","blue",null,"/outer/inner");
//
//   However, GetCookie cannot distinguish between these and will return
//   the first cookie that matches a given name.  It is therefore
//   recommended that you *not* use the same name for cookies with
//   different paths.  (Bear in mind that there is *always* a path
//   associated with a cookie; if you don't explicitly specify one,
//   the path of the setting document is used.)
//
//   Revision History:
//
//      "JavaScript Bible 6th Edition" Version (28-July-2006)
//        - Replaced deprecated escape()/unescape() functions with
//          encodeURI() and decodeURI() functions
```

continued

537

LISTING 18-3 *(continued)*

```
//
//     "Toss Your Cookies" Version (22-Mar-96)
//        - Added FixCookieDate() function to correct for Mac date bug
//
//     "Second Helping" Version (21-Jan-96)
//        - Added path, domain and secure parameters to SetCookie
//        - Replaced home-rolled encode/decode functions with
//          new (then) escape/unescape functions
//
//     "Free Cookies" Version (December 95)
//
//
//   For information on the significance of cookie parameters,
//   and on cookies in general, please refer to the official cookie
//   spec, at:
//
//       http://www.netscape.com/newsref/std/cookie_spec.html
//
//*****************************************************************
//
// "Internal" function to return the decoded value of a cookie
//
function getCookieVal (offset) {
   var endstr = document.cookie.indexOf (";", offset);
   if (endstr == -1) {
      endstr = document.cookie.length;
   }
   return decodeURIComponent(document.cookie.substring(offset, endstr));
}


//
//   Function to correct for 2.x Mac date bug.  Call this function to
//   fix a date object prior to passing it to SetCookie.
//   IMPORTANT:  This function should only be called *once* for
//   any given date object!  See example at the end of this document.
//
function FixCookieDate (date) {
   var base = new Date(0);
   var skew = base.getTime(); // dawn of (Unix) time - should be 0
   if (skew > 0) {  // Except on the Mac - ahead of its time
      date.setTime (date.getTime() - skew);
   }
}


//
//   Function to return the value of the cookie specified by "name".
//      name - String object containing the cookie name.
//      returns - String object containing the cookie value, or null if
//         the cookie does not exist.
//
function GetCookie (name) {
```

```
        var arg = name + "=";
        var alen = arg.length;
        var clen = document.cookie.length;
        var i = 0;
        while (i < clen) {
            var j = i + alen;
            if (document.cookie.substring(i, j) == arg) {
                return getCookieVal (j);
            }
            i = document.cookie.indexOf(" ", i) + 1;
            if (i == 0) {
                break;
            }
        }
        return null;
    }


    //
    //  Function to create or update a cookie.
    //    name - String object containing the cookie name.
    //    value - String object containing the cookie value.  May contain
    //      any valid string characters.
    //    [expires] - Date object containing the expiration data of the
    //      cookie.  If omitted or null, expires the cookie at the end of the
    //      current session.
    //    [path] - String object indicating the path for which the cookie is
    //      valid.
    //      If omitted or null, uses the path of the calling document.
    //    [domain] - String object indicating the domain for which the cookie
    //      is valid. If omitted or null, uses the domain of the calling
    //      document.
    //    [secure] - Boolean (true/false) value indicating whether cookie
    //      transmission requires a secure channel (HTTPS).
    //
    //  The first two parameters are required.  The others, if supplied, must
    //  be passed in the order listed above.  To omit an unused optional
    //  field, use null as a place holder.  For example, to call SetCookie
    //  using name, value and path, you would code:
    //
    //      SetCookie ("myCookieName", "myCookieValue", null, "/");
    //
    //  Note that trailing omitted parameters do not require a placeholder.
    //
    //  To set a secure cookie for path "/myPath", that expires after the
    //  current session, you might code:
    //
    //      SetCookie (myCookieVar, cookieValueVar, null, "/myPath", null,
    //         true);
    //
    function SetCookie (name,value,expires,path,domain,secure) {
```

continued

LISTING 18-3   *(continued)*

```
        document.cookie = name + "=" + encodeURIComponent (value) +
            ((expires) ? "; expires=" + expires.toGMTString() : "") +
            ((path) ? "; path=" + path : "") +
            ((domain) ? "; domain=" + domain : "") +
            ((secure) ? "; secure" : "");
    }


    //  Function to delete a cookie. (Sets expiration date to start of epoch)
    //    name -  String object containing the cookie name
    //    path -  String object containing the path of the cookie to delete.
    //            This MUST be the same as the path used to create the
    //            cookie, or null/omitted if
    //            no path was specified when creating the cookie.
    //    domain - String object containing the domain of the cookie to
    //            delete.  This MUST be the same as the domain used to
    //            create the cookie, or null/omitted if no domain was
    //            specified when creating the cookie.
    //
    function DeleteCookie (name,path,domain) {
        if (GetCookie(name)) {
            document.cookie = name + "=" +
                ((path) ? "; path=" + path : "") +
                ((domain) ? "; domain=" + domain : "") +
                "; expires=Thu, 01-Jan-70 00:00:01 GMT";
        }
    }


    //
    //  Examples
    //
    var expdate = new Date ();
    FixCookieDate (expdate); // Correct for Mac date bug (call only once)
    expdate.setTime (expdate.getTime() + (24 * 60 * 60 * 1000)); // 24 hrs
    SetCookie ("ccpath", "http://www.hidaho.com/colorcenter/", expdate);
    SetCookie ("ccname", "hIdaho Design ColorCenter", expdate);
    SetCookie ("tempvar", "This is a temporary cookie.");
    SetCookie ("ubiquitous", "This cookie will work anywhere in this
        domain",null,"/");
    SetCookie ("paranoid", "This cookie requires secure
        communications",expdate,"/",null,true);
    SetCookie ("goner", "This cookie must die!");
    document.write (document.cookie + "<br>");
    DeleteCookie ("goner");
    document.write (document.cookie + "<br>");
    document.write ("ccpath = " + GetCookie("ccpath") + "<br>");
    document.write ("ccname = " + GetCookie("ccname") + "<br>");
    document.write ("tempvar = " + GetCookie("tempvar") + "<br>");
    </script>
</body>
</html>
```

Extra batches

You may design a site that needs more than 20 cookies for a given domain. For example, in a shopping site, you never know how many items a customer may load into the shopping cart cookie.

Because each named cookie stores plain text, you can create your own text-based data structures to accommodate multiple pieces of information per cookie. (But also watch out for a practical limit of 2,000 characters per name/value pair within the 4,000 character maximum for any domain's combined cookies.) The trick is determining a delimiter character that won't be used by any of the data in the cookie. In Decision Helper (in Chapter 55 on the CD-ROM), for example, I use a period to separate multiple integers stored in a cookie.

With the delimiter character established, you must then write functions that concatenate these "subcookies" into single cookie strings and extract them on the other side. It's a bit more work, but well worth the effort to have the power of persistent data on the client.

Example

Experiment with the last group of statements in Listing 18-3 to create, retrieve, and delete cookies. You can also experiment with The Evaluator by assigning a name/value pair string to `document.cookie`, and then examining the value of the `cookie` property.

Related Items: `String` object methods (see Chapter 28).

defaultCharset

Value: String. Read/Write
Compatibility: WinIE4+, MacIE4+, NN-, Moz-, Safari-

The `defaultCharset` property reveals the character set used by the browser to render the current document. You can find possible values for this property at

```
http://www.iana.org/assignments/character-sets
```

Each browser and operating system has its own default character set. Values may also be set through a `<meta>` tag. The difference between the `defaultCharset` and `charset` properties is not clear, especially because both are read/write (although modifying the `defaultCharset` property has no visual effect on the page). However, if your scripts temporarily modify the `charset` property, you can use the `defaultCharset` property to return to the original character set:

```
document.charset = document.defaultCharset;
```

Example

Use The Evaluator (see Chapter 13) to experiment with the `defaultCharset` property. To see the default setting applied to the page, enter the following statement into the top text box:

```
document.defaultCharset
```

Related Items: `charset`, `characterSet` properties.

defaultView

Value: `window` or `frame` object reference. Read-Only
Compatibility: WinIE-, MacIE-, NN6+, Moz+, Safari-

document.doctype

The defaultView property returns a reference to the object serving as the viewer for the document. The viewer is responsible for rendering the document, and in Mozilla the object returned in the defaultView property is the window or frame object that contains the document. This W3C DOM Level 2 property provides access to computed CSS values being applied to any HTML element (through the document .defaultView.getComputedStyle() method).

Related Items: window and frame properties; window.getComputedStyle() method.

designMode

Value: String.   Read/Write
Compatibility: WinIE5+, MacIE-, NN7.1, Moz1.4+, Safari-

The designMode property is applicable only when WinIE5+ technology is being used as a component in another application. The property controls whether the browser module is being used for HTML editing. Modifying the property from within a typical HTML page in the IE5+ browser has no effect. But on the Mozilla side, the property can be used to turn an iframe element's document object into an HTML editable document. Visit http://www.mozilla.org/editor for current details and examples.

doctype

Value: DocumentType object reference.   Read-Only
Compatibility: WinIE-, MacIE5+, NN6+, Moz+, Safari-

The doctype property comes from the W3C Core DOM and returns a DocumentType object — a representation of the DTD information for the document. The DocumentType object (if one is explicitly defined in the source code) is the first child node of the root document node (and is thus a sibling to the HTML element).

Table 18-1 shows the typical DocumentType object property list and values for a generic HTML page. Future DOM specifications will allow these properties to be read/write.

TABLE 18-1

DocumentType Object in NN6+/Moz

Property	Value
entities	null
internalSubset	(empty)
name	html
notations	null
publicId	-//W3C//DTD XHTML 1.0 Transitional//EN
systemId	http://www.w3.org/TR/xhtml1/DTD/xhtml1-transitional.dtd

Related Items: Node object (Chapter 14).

Example

Take a look at the `document.doctype` object by entering the following line of code in the bottom text field of the Evaluator web page (see Chapter 13):

```
document.doctype
```

If you pay close attention you'll notice that the publicId property is actually set to `-//W3C//DTD HTML 4.01 Transitional//EN`, which is different from the value shown in Table 18-1. This reveals the fact that the Evaluator page declares itself as an HTML 4.01 document.

documentElement

Value: HTML or XML element object reference.   Read-Only
Compatibility: WinIE5+, MacIE5+, NN6+, Moz+, Safari+

The `documentElement` property returns a reference to the HTML (or XML) element object that contains all of the content of the current document. The naming of this property is a bit misleading, because the root document node is not an element, but its only child node is the HTML (or XML) element for the page. At best, you can think of this property as providing scripts with an *element face* to the `document` object and document node associated with the page currently loaded in the browser.

As compared to the `document.body` object, the `document.documentElement` object represents the `html` element for a page, whereas `docoument.body` represents the `body` element. This explains why `document.body` is a child of the `document.documentElement` object.

Example

Use The Evaluator (see Chapter 13) to examine the behavior of the `documentElement` property. In IE5+/W3C, enter the following statement into the top text field:

```
document.documentElement.tagName
```

The result is `HTML`, as expected.

Related Items: `ownerDocument` property (see Chapter 15).

documentURI

Value: String.   Read-Only
Compatibility: WinIE-, MacIE-, NN8+, Moz1.7+, Safari

The `documentURI` property contains the location of the document. This is the W3C DOM Level 3 equivalent of the non-W3C DOM `location.href` property. Use The Evaluator (see Chapter 13) to view the document URI by entering the following:

```
document.documentURI
```

Related Items: `document.baseURI` property.

domain

Value: String.   Read/Write
Compatibility: WinIE4+, MacIE4+, NN3+, Moz+, Safari+

document.expando

Security restrictions can get in the way of sites that have more than one server at their domain. Because some objects, especially the `location` object, prevent access to properties of other servers displayed in other frames, legitimate access to those properties are blocked. For example, it's not uncommon for popular sites to have their usual public access site on a server named something such as `www.popular.com`. If a page on that server includes a front end to a site search engine located at `search.popular.com`, visitors who use browsers with these security restrictions are denied access.

To guard against that eventuality, a script in documents from both servers can instruct the browser to think both servers are the same. In the preceding example, you would set the `document.domain` property in both documents to `popular.com`. Without specifically setting the property, the default value includes the server name as well, thus causing a mismatch between hostnames.

Before you start thinking that you can spoof your way into other servers, be aware that you can set the `document.domain` property only to servers with the same domain (following the two-dot rule) as the document doing the setting. Therefore, documents originating only from `xxx.popular.com` can set their `document.domain` properties to `popular.com` server.

Related Items: `window.open()` method; `window.location` object; security (see Chapter 46 on the CD-ROM).

embeds[]

Value: Array of embed element objects.   Read-Only
Compatibility: WinIE4+, MacIE4+, NN3+, Moz+, Safari+

Although now supplanted by the `<object>` tag, the `<embed>` tag used to be the markup that loaded data requiring a plug-in application to play or display. The `document.embeds` property is an array of embed element objects within the document:

```
var count = document.embeds.length;
```

Related Items: embed element object (see Chapter 41 on the CD-ROM).

expando

Value: Boolean.   Read/Write
Compatibility: WinIE4+, MacIE4+, NN-, Moz-, Safari-

Microsoft calls any custom property that is not a native property of the `document` object an *expando* property. By default, most objects in recent generations of browsers allow scripts to add new properties of objects as a way to temporarily store data without explicitly defining global variables. For example, if you want to maintain an independent counter of how often a function is invoked, you can create a custom property of the `document` object and use it as the storage facility:

```
document.counter = 0;
```

IE4+ enables you to control whether the `document` object is capable of accepting `expando` properties. The default value of the `document.expando` property is `true`, thus allowing custom properties. But the potential downside to this permissiveness, especially during the page construction phase, is that a misspelled native property name is gladly accepted by the `document` object. You may not be aware of why the title bar of the browser window doesn't change when you assign a new string to the `document.Title` property (which, in the case-sensitive world of JavaScript, is distinct from the native `document.title` property).

Example

Use The Evaluator (see Chapter 13) to experiment with the `document.expando` property in IE4+. Begin by proving that the `document` object can normally accept custom properties. Type the following statement into the top text field:

```
document.spooky = "Boo!"
```

This property is now set and stays that way until the page is either reloaded or unloaded.

Now freeze the `document` object's properties with the following statement:

```
document.expando = false
```

If you try to add a new property, such as the following, you receive an error:

```
document.happy = "tra la"
```

Interestingly, even though `document.expando` is turned off, the first custom property is still accessible and modifiable.

Related Items: `prototype` property of custom objects (Chapter 34).

fgColor

(See `alinkColor`)

fileCreatedDate
fileModifiedDate
fileSize

Value: String, Integer (fileSize).   Read-Only
Compatibility: WinIE4+, MacIE4+, NN-, Moz-, Safari-

These three IE-specific properties return information about the file that holds the current document. The first two properties (not implemented in MacIE) reveal the dates on which the current document's file was created and modified. For an unmodified file, its creation and modified dates are the same. The `fileSize` property reveals the number of bytes of the file.

Date values returned for the first two properties are in a format similar to mm/dd/yyyy. Note, however, that the values contain only the date and not the time. In any case, you can use the values as the parameter to a `new Date()` constructor function. You can then use date calculations for such information as the number of days between the current day and the most recent modification.

Not all servers may provide the proper date or size information about a file or in a format that IE can interpret. Test your implementation on the deployment server to ensure compatibility.

Also, be aware that these properties can be read only for a file that is loaded in the browser. JavaScript by itself cannot get this information about files that are on the server but not loaded in the browser.

Example

Listing 18-4 dynamically generates several pieces of content relating to the creation and modification dates of the file, as well as its size. More importantly, the listing demonstrates how to turn a value returned by the file date properties into a genuine date object that can be used for date calculations. In the case of Listing 18-4, the calculation is the number of full days between the creation date and the day someone views the file. Notice that the dynamically generated content is added very simply through the innerText properties of carefully located span elements in the body content.

LISTING 18-4

Displaying File Information for a Web Page

```html
<html>
   <head>
      <title>fileCreatedDate and fileModifiedDate Properties</title>
      <script type="text/javascript">
      function fillInBlanks() {
         var created = document.fileCreatedDate;
         var modified = document.fileModifiedDate;
         document.getElementById("created").innerText = created;
         document.getElementById("modified").innerText = modified;
         var createdDate = new Date(created).getTime();
         var today = new Date().getTime();
         var diff = Math.floor((today - createdDate) / (1000*60*60*24));
         document.getElementById("diff").innerText = diff;
         document.getElementById("size").innerText = document.fileSize;
      }

      // bind the event handlers
      function addEvent(elem, evtType, func) {
         if (elem.addEventListener) {
            elem.addEventListener(evtType, func, false);
         } else if (elem.attachEvent) {
            elem.attachEvent("on" + evtType, func);
         } else {
            elem["on" + evtType] = func;
         }
      }
      addEvent(window, "load", function() {
         fillInBlanks();
      });
      </script>
   </head>
   <body>
      <h1>fileCreatedDate and fileModifiedDate Properties</h1>
      <hr />
      <p>This file (<span id="size"> </span> bytes) was created on <span
         id="created"> </span> and most recently modified on <span
         id="modified"> </span>.</p>
      <p>It has been <span id="diff"> </span> days since this file was
         created.</p>
   </body>
</html>
```

Related Items: lastModified property.

forms[]

Value: Array.   Read-Only
Compatibility: WinIE3+, MacIE3+, NN2+, Moz+, Safari+

As I show in Chapter 21, which is dedicated to the form object, an HTML form (anything defined inside a `<form>...</form>` tag pair) is a JavaScript object unto itself. You can create a valid reference to a form according to its name (assigned through a form's name attribute). For example, if a document contains the following form definition:

```
<form name="phoneData">
    input item definitions
</form>
```

then your scripts can refer to the form object by name:

```
document.phoneData
```

However, a document object also tracks its forms in another way: as an array of form objects. The first item of a document.forms array is the form that loaded first (it was first from the top of the HTML code). If your document defines one form, the forms property is an array one entry in length; with three separate forms in the document, the array is three entries long.

Use standard array notation to reference a particular form from the document.forms array. For example, the first form in a document (the zeroth entry of the document.forms array) is referenced as

```
document.forms[0]
```

Any of the form object's properties or methods are available by appending the desired property or method name to the reference. For example, to retrieve the value of an input text field named homePhone from the second form of a document, the reference you use is

```
document.forms[1].homePhone.value
```

One advantage to using the document.forms property for addressing a form object or element instead of the actual form name is that you may be able to generate a library of generalizable scripts that know how to cycle through all available forms in a document and hunt for a form that has some special element and property. The following script fragment (part of a *repeat loop* described more fully in Chapter 32) uses a loop-counting variable (i) to help the script check all forms in a document:

```
for (var i = 0; i < document.forms.length; i++) {
    if (document.forms[i]. ... ) {
        statements
    }
}
```

One more variation on forms array references enables you to substitute the name of a form (as a string) for the forms array index. For example, the form named phoneData can be referenced as:

```
document.forms["phoneData"]
```

If you use a lot of care in assigning names to objects, you will likely prefer the document.formName style of referencing forms. In this book, you see both indexed array and form name style references. The advantage of using name references is that even if you redesign the page and change the order of forms in the document, references to the named forms will still be valid, whereas the index numbers of the forms will have changed. See also the discussion in Chapter 21 of the form object and how to pass a form's data to a function.

Example

The document in Listing 18-5 is set up to display an alert dialog box that simulates navigation to a particular music site, based on the selected status of the bluish check box. The user input here is divided into two forms: one form with the check box and the other form with the button that does the navigation. A block of copy fills the space in between. Clicking the bottom button (in the second form) triggers the function that fetches the checked property of the bluish check box by using the document.forms[i] array as part of the address.

LISTING 18-5

A Simple Form Example

```
<html>
  <head>
    <title>document.forms example</title>
    <script type="text/javascript">
    function goMusic() {
        if (document.forms[0].bluish.checked) {
            alert("Now going to the Blues music area...");
        } else {
            alert("Now going to Rock music area...");
        }
    }

    // bind the event handlers
    function addEvent(elem, evtType, func) {
        if (elem.addEventListener) {
            elem.addEventListener(evtType, func, false);
        } else if (elem.attachEvent) {
            elem.attachEvent("on" + evtType, func);
        } else {
            elem["on" + evtType] = func;
        }
    }
    addEvent(window, "load", function() {
        addEvent(document.getElementById("visit"), "click", goMusic);
    });
    </script>
  </head>
  <body>
    <form name="theBlues">
        <input type="checkbox" name="bluish" />Check here if you've got the
        blues.
    </form>
    <hr />
    M<br />
    o<br />
    r<br />
    e<br />
    <br />
```

```
        C<br />
        o<br />
        p<br />
        y<br />
        <hr />
        <form name="visit">
            <input type="button" id="visit" value="Visit music site" />
        </form>
    </body>
</html>
```

Related Items: `form` object (see Chapter 21).

frames[]

Value: Array.   Read-Only

Compatibility: WinIE4+, MacIE4+, NN-, Moz-, Safari-

The `document.frames` property is similar to the `window.frames` property, but its association with the `document` object may seem a bit illogical at times. The objects contained by the array returned from the property are window objects, which means they are the window objects of any `frame` elements (from a framesetting document) or `iframe` elements (from a plain HTML document) defined for the document. Distinguishing the window objects from the `iframe` element objects is important. Window objects have different properties and methods than the `frame` and `iframe` element objects. The latter's properties typically represent the attributes for those element's tags. If a document contains no `iframe` elements, the `document.frames` array length is zero.

Although you can access an individual frame object through the typical array syntax (for example, `document.frames[0]`), you can also use alternate syntax that Microsoft provides for collections of objects. The index number can also be placed inside parentheses, as in:

```
        document.frames(0)
```

Moreover, if the frames have values assigned to their `name` attributes, you can use the name (in string form) as a parameter:

```
        document.frames("contents")
```

And if the collection of frames has more than one frame with the same name, you must take special care. Using the duplicated name as a parameter forces the reference to return a collection of frame objects that share that name. Or, you can limit the returned value to a single instance of the duplicate-named frames by specifying an optional second parameter indicating the index. For example, if a document has two `iframe` elements with the name `contents`, a script could reference the second `window` object as:

```
        document.frames("contents", 1)
```

For the sake of cross-browser compatibility, my preference for referencing frame window objects is through the `window.frames` property.

Example

See Listings 16-7 and 16-8 for examples of using the `frames` property with window objects.

Related Items: `window.frames` property.

height
width

Value: Integer.   Read-Only
Compatibility: WinIE-, MacIE-, NN4+, Moz+, Safari+

The height and width properties provide the pixel dimensions of the content within the current window (or frame). If the document's content is smaller than the size of the browser's content region, the dimensions returned by these properties include the blank space to the right or bottom edges of the content area of the window. But if the content extends beyond the viewable edges of the content region, the dimensions include the unseen content as well. The corresponding measures in Internet Explorer are the document.body.scrollHeight and document.body.scrollWidth properties.

Example

Use The Evaluator (see Chapter 13) to examine the height and width properties of that document. Enter the following statement into the top text box and click the Evaluate button:

```
"height=" + document.height + "; width=" + document.width
```

Resize the window so that you see both vertical and horizontal scroll bars in the browser window and click the Evaluate button again. If either or both numbers get smaller, the values in the Results box are the exact size of the space occupied by the document. But if you expand the window to well beyond where the scroll bars are needed, the values extend to the number of pixels in each dimension of the window's content region.

Related Items: document.body.scrollHeight, document.body.scrollWidth properties.

images[]

Value: Array.   Read-Only
Compatibility: WinIE4+, MacIE3+, NN3+, Moz+, Safari+

With images treated as first-class objects beginning with NN3 and IE4, it's only natural for a document to maintain an array of all the image tags defined on the page (just as it does for links and anchors). The prime importance of having images as objects is that you can modify their content (the source file associated with the rectangular space of the image) on the fly. You can find details about the image object in Chapter 20.

Use image array references to pinpoint a specific image for retrieval of any image property or for assigning a new image file to its src property. Image arrays begin their index counts with 0: The first image in a document has the reference document.images[0]. And, as with any array object, you can find out how many images the array contains by checking the length property. For example:

```
var imageCount = document.images.length;
```

Images can also have names, so if you prefer, you can refer to the image object by its name, as in

```
var imageLoaded = document.imageName.complete;
```

or

```
var imageLoaded = document.images[imageName].complete;
```

The document.images array is a useful guide to knowing whether a browser supports swappable images. Any browser that treats an img element as an object always forms a document.images array in the page. If no images are defined in the page, the array is still there, but its length is zero. The array's existence, however, is the clue about image object compatibility. Because the `document.images` array evaluates to an array object when present, the expression can be used as a condition expression for branching to statements that involve image swapping:

```
if (document.images) {
    // image swapping or precaching here
}
```

Browsers that don't have this property (legacy and potentially mobile) evaluate `document.images` as `undefined` and thus the condition is treated as a `false` value.

Example

The `document.images` property is defined automatically as the browser builds the object model for a document that contains image objects. See the discussion about the `Image` object in Chapter 20 for reference examples.

Related Items: `Image` object (Chapter 20).

implementation

Value: Object.   Read-Only
Compatibility: WinIE6+, MacIE5+, NN6+, Moz+, Safari+

The Core W3C DOM defines the `document.implementation` property as an avenue to let scripts find out what DOM features (that is, modules of the DOM standard) are implemented for the current environment. Although the object returned by the property (a `DOMImplementation` object) has no properties, it has a method, `hasFeature()`, which lets scripts find out, for example, whether the environment supports HTML or just XML. The first parameter of the `hasFeature()` method is the feature in the form of a string. The second parameter is a string form of the version number. The method returns a Boolean value.

The "Conformance" section of the W3C DOM specification governs the module names (the standard also allows browser-specific features to be tested through the `hasFeature()` method). Module names include strings such as `HTML`, `XML`, `MouseEvents`, and so on.

Version numbering for W3C DOM modules corresponds to the W3C DOM level. Thus, the version for the XML DOM module in DOM Level 2 is known as `2.0`. Note that versions refer to DOM modules and not, for example, the separate HTML standard.

Example

Use The Evaluator (see Chapter 13) to experiment with the `document.implementation.hasFeature()` method. Enter the following statements one at a time into the top text field and examine the results:

```
document.implementation.hasFeature("HTML","1.0")
document.implementation.hasFeature("HTML","2.0")
document.implementation.hasFeature("HTML","3.0")
document.implementation.hasFeature("CSS","2.0")
document.implementation.hasFeature("CSS2","2.0")
```

Feel free to try other values. As of IE7, for some reason Internet Explorer returns false for some features that it indeed supports, such as CSS 2.0. In other words, it's probably not a good idea to place a lot of trust in the IE results of the `hasFeature()` method, at least for the time being.

inputEncoding

Value: String.
Compatibility: WinIE-, MacIE-, NN-, Moz1.8+, Safari-

Read-Only

The input encoding of a document is the character encoding that is in effect at the time when the document is parsed. For example, ISO-8859-1 is a common character encoding that you may see reported by the `inputEncoding` property.

lastModified

Value: Date string.
Compatibility: WinIE3+, MacIE3+, NN2+, Moz+, Safari+

Read-Only

Every disk file maintains a modified time stamp, and most (but not all) servers are configured to expose this information to a browser accessing a file. This information is available by reading the `document.lastModified` property. If your server supplies this information to the client, you can use the value of this property to present this information for readers of your web page. The script automatically updates the value for you, rather than requiring you to hand-code the HTML line every time you modify the home page.

If the value returned to you displays itself as a date in 1969, it means that you are positioned somewhere west of GMT, or Greenwich Mean Time (some number of time zones west of GMT at 1 January 1970), and the server is not providing the proper data when it serves the file. Sometimes server configuration can fix the problem, but not always.

The returned value is not a date object (see Chapter 30), but rather a straight string consisting of time and date, as recorded by the document's file system. The format of the string varies from browser to browser and version to version. You can, however, usually convert the date string to a JavaScript date object and use the date object's methods to extract selected elements for recompilation into readable form. Listing 18-6 shows an example.

Even local file systems don't necessarily provide the correct data for every browser to interpret. But put that same file on a UNIX or Windows web server, and the date appears correctly when accessed through the Net.

Example

Experiment with the `document.lastModified` property with Listing 18-6. But also be prepared for inaccurate readings if the file is located on some servers or local hard disks.

LISTING 18-6

Putting a Time Stamp on a Page

```
<html>
   <head>
      <title>Time Stamper</title>
   </head>
   <body>
      <center>
         <h1>GiantCo Home Page</h1>
```

```
      </center>
      <script type="text/javascript">
      update = new Date(document.lastModified);
      theMonth = update.getMonth() + 1;
      theDate = update.getDate();
      theYear = update.getFullYear();
      document.writeln("<I>Last updated:" + theMonth + "/" + theDate + "/" +
         theYear + "<\/I>");
      </script>
      <hr />
   </body>
</html>
```

As noted at great length in the Date object discussion in Chapter 30, you should be aware that date formats vary greatly from country to country. Some of these formats use a different order for date elements. When you hard-code a date format, it may take a form that is unfamiliar to other users of your page.

Related Items: Date object (see Chapter 30).

layers[]

Value: Array.   Read-Only
Compatibility: WinIE-, MacIE-, NN4, Moz-, Safari-

The layer object (see Chapter 40 on the CD-ROM) is the NN4 way of exposing positioned elements to the object model. Thus, the document.layers property is an array of positioned elements in the document. The Layer object and document.layers property are orphaned in NN4, and their importance is all but gone now that Mozilla has taken over. Chapter 40 on the CD-ROM includes several examples of how to carry out similar functionality as the document.layers property using the standard W3C DOM.

Related Items: layer object (see Chapter 40 on the CD-ROM).

linkColor

(See alinkColor)

links[]

Value: Array.   Read-Only
Compatibility: WinIE3+, MacIE3+, NN2+, Moz+, Safari+

The document.links property is similar to the document.anchors property, except that the objects maintained by the array are link objects — items created with <a href=""> tags. Use the array references to pinpoint a specific link for retrieving any link property, such as the target window specified in the link's HTML definition.

Link arrays begin their index counts with 0: The first link in a document has the reference document.links[0]. And, as with any array object, you can find out how many entries the array has by checking the length property. For example:

```
    var linkCount = document.links.length;
```

document.URL

Entries in the document.links property are full-fledged location objects, which means you have the same properties available to each member of the links[] array as you do in the location object.

Example

The document.links property is defined automatically as the browser builds the object model for a document that contains link objects. You rarely access this property, except to determine the number of link objects in the document.

Related Items: link object; document.anchors property.

URL

Value: String.   Read/Write and Read-Only (see text)
Compatibility: WinIE4+, MacIE4+, NN3+, Moz+, Safari+

The document.URL property is similar to the window.location property. A location object, you may recall from Chapter 17, consists of a number of properties about the document currently loaded in a window or frame. Assigning a new URL to the location object (or location.href property) tells the browser to load the page from that URL into the frame. The document.URL property, on the other hand, is simply a string (read-only in Navigator, Mozilla, and Safari) that reveals the URL of the current document. The value may be important to your script, but the property does not have the object power of the window.location object. You cannot change (assign another value to) this property value because a document has only one URL: its location on the Net (or your hard disk) where the file exists, and what protocol is required to get it.

This may seem like a fine distinction, and it is. The reference you use (window.location object or document.URL property) depends on what you are trying to accomplish specifically with the script. If the script is changing the content of a window by loading a new URL, you have no choice but to assign a value to the window.location object. Similarly, if the script is concerned with the component parts of a URL, the properties of the location object provide the simplest avenue to that information. To retrieve the URL of a document in string form (whether it is in the current window or in another frame), you can use either the document.URL property or the window.location.href property.

 The document.URL **property replaces the old** document.location **property, which is still supported in most browsers.**

Example

HTML documents in Listings 18-7 through 18-9 create a test lab that enables you to experiment with viewing the document.URL property for different windows and frames in a multiframe environment. Results are displayed in a table, with an additional listing of the document.title property to help you identify documents being referred to. The same security restrictions that apply to retrieving window.location object properties also apply to retrieving the document.URL property from another window or frame.

LISTING 18-7

A Simple Frameset for the URL Example

```
<html>
   <head>
      <title>document.URL Reader</title>
   </head>
```

```
    <frameset rows="60%,40%">
        <frame name="Frame1" src="lst18-09.htm" />
        <frame name="Frame2" src="lst18-08.htm" />
    </frameset>
</html>
```

LISTING 18-8

Showing Location Information for Different Contexts

```
<html>
    <head>
        <title>URL Property Reader</title>
        <script type="text/javascript">
        function fillTopFrame() {
            newURL=prompt("Enter the URL of a document to show in the top frame:","");
            if (newURL != null && newURL != "") {
                top.frames[0].location = newURL;
            }
        }

        function showLoc(item) {
            var windName = item.value;
            var theRef = windName + ".document";
            item.form.dLoc.value = decodeURIComponent(eval(theRef + ".URL"));
            item.form.dTitle.value = decodeURIComponent(eval(theRef + ".title"));
        }

        // bind the event handlers
        function addEvent(elem, evtType, func) {
            if (elem.addEventListener) {
                elem.addEventListener(evtType, func, false);
            } else if (elem.attachEvent) {
                elem.attachEvent("on" + evtType, func);
            } else {
                elem["on" + evtType] = func;
            }
        }
        addEvent(window, "load", function() {
            addEvent(document.getElementById("opener"), "click", fillTopFrame);
            addEvent(document.getElementById("parent"), "click",
                function(evt) {showLoc(document.getElementById("parent"));});
            addEvent(document.getElementById("upper"), "click",
                function(evt) {showLoc(document.getElementById("upper"));});
            addEvent(document.getElementById("this"), "click",
                function(evt) {showLoc(document.getElementById("this"));});
        });
        </script>
```

continued

LISTING 18-8   *(continued)*

```
    </head>
    <body>
        Click the "Open URL" button to enter the location of an HTML document to
        display in the upper frame of this window.
        <form>
            <input type="button" id="opener" name="opener" value="Open URL..." />
        </form>
        <hr />
        <form>
            Select a window or frame to view each document property values.
            <p><input type="radio" id="parent" name="whichFrame" value="parent"
                />Parent window <input type="radio" name="whichFrame" id="upper"
                value="top.frames[0]" />Upper frame <input type="radio"
                name="whichFrame" id="this" value="top.frames[1]" />This frame</p>
            <table border="2">
                <tr>
                    <td align="right">document.URL:</td>
                    <td><textarea name="dLoc" rows="3" cols="30" wrap="soft">
                        </textarea></td>
                </tr>
                <tr>
                    <td align="right">document.title:</td>
                    <td><textarea name="dTitle" rows="3" cols="30" wrap="soft">
                        </textarea></td>
                </tr>
            </table>
        </form>
    </body>
</html>
```

LISTING 18-9

A Placeholder Page for the URL Example

```
<html>
    <head>
        <title>Opening Placeholder</title>
    </head>
    <body>
        Initial place holder. Experiment with other URLs for this frame (see
        below).
    </body>
</html>
```

Related Items: location object; location.href, URLUnencoded properties.

media

Value: String.   Read/Write
Compatibility: WinIE5.5+, MacIE-, NN-, Moz-, Safari-

The document.media property indicates the output medium for which content is formatted. The property actually returns an empty string as of IE7, but the intention appears to be to provide a way to use scripting to set the equivalent of the CSS2 @media rule (one of the so-called *at* rules because of the at symbol). This style sheet rule allows browsers to assign separate styles for each type of output device on which the page is rendered (for example, perhaps a different font for a printer versus the screen). In practice, however, this property is not modifiable, at least through IE7.

Related Items: None.

mimeType

Value: String.   Read-Only
Compatibility: WinIE5+, MacIE-, NN-, Moz-, Safari-

Although this property is readable in WinIE5+, its value is not strictly speaking a MIME type, or at least not in traditional MIME format. Moreover, the results are inconsistent between IE versions 5, 6, and 7. Perhaps this property will be of more use in an XML, rather than HTML, document environment. In any case, this property in no way exposes supported MIME types in the current browser.

nameProp

Value: String.   Read-Only
Compatibility: WinIE6+, MacIE-, NN-, Moz-, Safari-

The nameProp property returns a string containing the title of the document, which is the same as document.title. If the document doesn't have a title, nameProp contains an empty string.

Related Items: title property.

namespaces[]

Value: Array of namespace objects.   Read-Only
Compatibility: WinIE5.5+, MacIE-, NN-, Moz-, Safari-

A namespace object can dynamically import an XML-based IE Element Behavior. The namespaces property returns an array of all namespace objects defined in the current document.

Related Items: None.

parentWindow

Value: window object reference.   Read-Only
Compatibility: WinIE4+, MacIE4+, NN-, Moz-, Safari-

The document.parentWindow property returns a reference to the window object containing the current document. The value is the same as any reference to the current window.

document.referrer

Example

To prove the `parentWindow` property points to the document's window, you can enter the following statement into the top text field of The Evaluator (see Chapter 13):

```
document.parentWindow == self
```

This expression evaluates to `true` only if both references are of the same object.

Related Items: `window` object.

plugins[]

Value: Array.   Read-Only
Compatibility: WinIE4+, MacIE4+, NN4+, Moz+, Safari+

The `document.plugins` property returns the same array of `embed` element objects that you get from the `document.embeds` property. This property has been deprecated in favor of `document.embeds`.

Related Items: `document.embeds` property.

protocol

Value: String.   Read/Write
Compatibility: WinIE4+, MacIE4+, NN-, Moz-, Safari-

The IE-specific `document.protocol` property returns the plain-language version of the protocol that was used to access the current document. For example, if the file is accessed from a web server, the property returns `Hypertext Transfer Protocol`. This property differs from the `location.protocol` property, which returns the portion of the URL that includes the often more cryptic protocol abbreviation (for example, `http:`). As a general rule, you want to hide all of this stuff from a web application user.

Example

If you use The Evaluator (Chapter 13) to test the `document.protocol` property, you will find that it displays `File Protocol` in the results because you are accessing the listing from a local hard disk or CD-ROM. However, if you upload the Evaluator web page to a web server and access it from the server, you will see the expected `Hypertext Transfer Protocol` result.

Related Items: `location.protocol` property.

referrer

Value: String.   Read-Only
Compatibility: WinIE3+, MacIE3+, NN2+, Moz+, Safari+

When a link from one document leads to another, the second document can, under JavaScript control, reveal the URL of the document containing the link. The `document.referrer` property contains a string of that URL. This feature can be a useful tool for customizing the content of pages based on the previous location the user was visiting within your site. A referrer contains a value only when the user reaches the current page through a link. Any other method of navigation (such as through the history, bookmarks, or by manually entering a URL) sets this property to an empty string.

 The `document.referrer` property usually returns an empty string unless the files are retrieved from a web server.

Example

This demonstration requires two documents (and for IE, you'll also need to access the documents from a web server). The first document, in Listing 18-10, simply contains one line of text as a link to the second document. In the second document, shown in Listing 18-11, a script verifies the document from which the user came through a link. If the script knows about that link, it displays a message relevant to the experience the user had at the first document. Also try opening Listing 18-11 in a new browser window from the Open File command in the File menu to see how the script won't recognize the referrer.

LISTING 18-10

An Example Referrer Page

```html
<html>
    <head>
        <title>document.referrer Property 1</title>
    </head>
    <body>
        <h1><a href="lst18-11.htm">Visit my sister document</a></h1>
    </body>
</html>
```

LISTING 18-11

Determining the Referrer when a Page Is Visited Through a Link

```html
<html>
    <head>
        <title>document.referrer Property 2</title>
    </head>
    <body>
        <h1>
            <script type="text/javascript">
            alert(document.referrer.length + "    :    " + document.referrer);
            if(document.referrer.length > 0 &&
                document.referrer.indexOf("lst18-10.htm") != -1) {
                document.write("How is my brother document?");
            } else {
                document.write("Hello, and thank you for stopping by.");
            }
            </script>
        </h1>
    </body>
</html>
```

Related Items: link object.

scripts[]

Value: Array.   Read-Only
Compatibility: WinIE4+, MacIE4+, NN-, Moz-, Safari-

The IE-specific document.scripts property returns an array of all script element objects in the current document. You can reference an individual script element object to read not only the properties it shares with all HTML element objects (see Chapter 15), but also script-specific properties, such as defer, src, and htmlFor. The actual scripting is accessible either through the innerText or text properties for any script element object.

Although the document.scripts array is read-only, many properties of individual script element objects are modifiable. Adding or removing script elements impacts the length of the document.scripts array. Don't forget, too, that if your scripts need to access a specific script element object, you can assign an id attribute to it and reference the element directly.

This property is an IE-specific convenience property that is the same as the W3C browser expression document.getElementsByTagName("script"), which returns an array of the same objects.

Example

You can experiment with the document.scripts array in The Evaluator (see Chapter 13). For example, you can see that only one script element object is in the Evaluator page if you enter the following statement into the top text field:

```
document.scripts.length
```

If you want to view all of the properties of that lone script element object, enter the following statement into the bottom text field:

```
document.scripts[0]
```

Among the properties are both innerText and text. If you assign an empty string to either property, the scripts are wiped out from the object model, but not from the browser. The scripts disappear because after the scripts loaded, they were cached outside of the object model. Therefore, if you enter the following statement into the top field:

```
document.scripts[0].text = ""
```

the script contents are gone from the object model, yet subsequent clicks of the Evaluate and List Properties buttons (which invoke functions of the script element object) still work.

Related Items: script element object (Chapter 37 on the CD-ROM).

security

Value: String.   Read-Only
Compatibility: WinIE5.5+, MacIE-, NN-, Moz-, Safari-

The security property reveals information about a security certificate, if one is associated with the current document.

selection

Value: Object.   Read-Only
Compatibility: WinIE4+, MacIE4+, NN-, Moz-, Safari-

The document.selection property returns a selection object whose content is represented in the browser window as a body text selection. That selection can be explicitly performed by the user (by clicking and dragging across some text) or created under script control through the WinIE TextRange object (see Chapter 36 on the CD-ROM). Because script action on a selection (for example, finding the next instance of selected text) is performed through the TextRange object, converting a selection to a TextRange object using the document.selection.createRange() method is common practice. See the selection object in Chapter 36 on the CD-ROM for more details.

Be aware that you cannot script interaction with text selections through user interface elements, such as buttons. Clicking a button gives focus to the button and deselects the selection. Use other events, such as document.onmouseup to trigger actions on a selection.

Example

See Listings 15-36 and 15-44 in Chapter 15 to see the document.selection property in action for script-controlled copying and pasting (WinIE only).

Related Items: selection, TextRange objects.

strictErrorChecking

Value: String.   Read-Only
Compatibility: WinIE-, MacIE-, NN-, Moz1.8+, Safari-

The strictErrorChecking property reveals the error-checking mode for the document. More specifically, if the property is set to true (the default), exceptions and errors related to DOM operations are reported. Otherwise, DOM-related exceptions may not be thrown, and errors may not be reported.

styleSheets[]

Value: Array.   Read-Only
Compatibility: WinIE4+, MacIE4+, NN6+, Moz+, Safari+

The document.styleSheets array consists of references to all style element objects in the document. Not included in this array are style sheets that are assigned to elements by way of the style attribute inside a tag or linked in through link elements. See Chapter 26 for details about the styleSheet object.

Related Items: styleSheet object (Chapter 26).

title

Value: String.   Read-Only and Read/Write
Compatibility: WinIE3+, MacIE3+, NN2+, Moz+, Safari+

A document's title is the text that appears between the <title>...</title> tag pair in an HTML document's Head portion. The title usually appears in the title bar of the browser window in a single-frame presentation, or in a tabbed pane within a multi-paned browser window. Only the title of the topmost framesetting document appears as the title of a multiframe window. Even so, the `title` property for an individual document within a frame is available through scripting. For example, if two frames are available (`UpperFrame` and `LowerFrame`), a script in the document occupying the `LowerFrame` frame can reference the `title` property of the other frame's document, such as this:

```
parent.UpperFrame.document.title
```

The `document.title` property is a holdover from the original document object model. HTML elements in recent browsers have an entirely different application of the `title` property (see Chapter 15). In modern browsers (IE4+/W3C/Moz/Safari), you should address the document's title by way of the `title` element object directly.

Related Items: `history` object.

URL

(See `location`)

URLUnencoded

Value: String.   Read-Only
Compatibility: WinIE5.5+, MacIE-, NN-, Moz-, Safari-

The `document.URL` property returns a URL-encoded string, meaning that non-alphanumeric characters in the URL are converted to URL-friendly characters (for example, a space becomes %20). You can always use the `decodeURI()` function on the value returned by the `document.URL` property, but the `URLUnencoded` property does that for you. If there are no URL-encoded characters in the URL, then both properties return identical strings.

Related Items: `document.URL` property.

vlinkColor

(See `alinkColor`)

width

(See `height`)

xmlEncoding
xmlStandalone
xmlVersion

Value: String.   Read-Only
Compatibility: WinIE-, MacIE-, NN-, Moz1.8+, Safari-

These three properties reveal information about the document as it pertains to XML. More specifically, they convey the XML encoding of the document, whether or not the document is a standalone XML document, and the XML version number of the document, respectively. If any of the property values cannot be determined, their values remain `null`.

Methods

captureEvents(*eventTypeList*)

Returns: Nothing.
Compatibility: WinIE-, MacIE-, NN4+, Moz-, Safari-

In Navigator 4 only, the natural propagation of an event is downward from the window object, through the document object, and eventually reaching its target. For example, if you click a button, the click event first reaches the window object; then it goes to the document object; if the button is defined within a layer, the event also filters through that layer; eventually (in a split second) the event reaches the button, where an onclick event handler is ready to act on that click.

Event capture with different syntax has been standardized in the W3C DOM and is implemented in W3C browsers, such as Firefox and Camino (Mozilla). More specifically, the W3C event capture model introduces the concept of an event listener, which enables you to bind an event handler function to an event. See the addEventListener() method in Chapter 15 for the W3C counterpart to the NN4 captureEvents() method. Also, see Chapter 25 for more details on the combination of event capture and event bubbling in the W3C DOM.

clear()

Returns: Nothing.
Compatibility: WinIE3+, MacIE3+, NN2+, Moz+, Safari+

Ever since NN2, the document.clear() method was intended to clear the current document from the browser window. This method is quite impractical, because you typically need some further scripts to execute after you clear the document, but if the scripts are gone, nothing else happens.

In practice, the document.clear() method never did what it was supposed to do (and in earlier browsers easily caused browser crashes). I recommend against using document.clear(), including in preparation for generating a new page's content with document.write(). The document.write() method clears the original document from the window before adding new content. If you truly want to empty a window or frame, then use document.write() to write a blank HTML document or to load an empty HTML document from the server.

Related Items: document.close(), document.write(), document.writeln() methods.

close()

Returns: Nothing.
Compatibility: WinIE3+, MacIE3+, NN2+, Moz+, Safari+

Whenever a layout stream is opened to a window through the document.open() method or either of the document writing methods (which also open the layout stream), you must close the stream after the document is written. This causes the Layout:Complete and Done messages to appear in the status line (although you may experience some bugs in the status message on some platforms). The document-closing step is very important to prepare the window for the next potential round of replenishment with new script-assembled HTML. If you don't close the document, subsequent writing is appended to the bottom of the document.

Some or all of the data specified for the window won't display properly until you invoke the document.close() method, especially when images are being drawn as part of the document stream. A common symptom is the momentary appearance and then disappearance of the document parts. If you see such behavior, look for a missing document.close() method after the last document.write() method.

Fixing the Sticky Wait Cursor

From time to time, various browsers fail to restore the cursor to normal after document.write() and document.close() (and some other content-modifying scripts). The cursor stubbornly remains in the wait mode or the progress bar keeps spinning when, in truth, all processing has been completed. One, albeit ugly, workaround that I have found effective is to force an extra document.close() via a javascript: pseudo-URL (just adding another document.close() to your script doesn't do the trick). For use within a frameset, the javascript: URL must be directed to the top of the frameset hierarchy, whereas the document.close() is aimed at the frame that had its content changed. For example, if the change is made to a frame named content, create a function, such as the following:

```
function recloseDoc() {
    top.location.href =
        "javascript:void (parent.content.document.close())";
}
```

If you place this function in the framesetting document, scripts that modify the content frame can invoke this script after any operation that prevents the normal cursor from appearing.

Example

Before you experiment with the document.close() method, be sure you understand the document.write() method described later in this chapter. After that, make a separate set of the three documents for that method's example (Listings 18-14 through 18-16 in a different directory or folder). In the takePulse() function listing, comment out the document.close() statement, as shown here:

```
msg += "<p>Make it a great day!</body></html>";
parent.frames[1].document.write(msg);
//parent.frames[1].document.close();
```

Now try the pages on your browser. You see that each click of the upper button appends text to the bottom frame, without first removing the previous text. The reason is that the previous layout stream was never closed. The document thinks that you're still writing to it. Also, without properly closing the stream, the last line of text may not appear in the most recently written batch.

Related Items: document.open(), document.clear(), document.write(), document.writeln() methods.

createAttribute("*attributeName*")

Returns: Attribute object reference.
Compatibility: WinIE6+, MacIE5+, NN6+, Moz+, Safari+

The document.createAttribute() method generates an attribute node object (formally known as an Attr object in W3C DOM terminology) and returns a reference to the newly created object. Invoking the method assigns only the name of the attribute, so it is up to your script to assign a value to the object's nodeValue property and then plug the new attribute into an existing element through that element's setAttributeNode() method (described in Chapter 15). The following sequence generates an attribute that becomes an attribute of a table element:

```
var newAttr = document.createAttribute("width");
newAttr.nodeValue = "80%";
document.getElementById("myTable").setAttributeNode(newAttr);
```

Attributes do not always have to be attributes known to the HTML standard, because the method also works for XML elements, which have custom attributes.

Example

To create an attribute and inspect its properties, enter the following text into the top text box of The Evaluator (see Chapter 13):

```
a = document.createAttribute("author")
```

Now enter a into the bottom text box to inspect the properties of an Attr object.

Related Items: setAttributeNode() method (Chapter 15).

createCDATASection("*data*")

Returns: CDATA section object reference.
Compatibility: WinIE-, MacIE5, NN7+, Moz+, Safari-

The document.createCDATASection() method generates a CDATA section node for whatever string you pass as the parameter. The value of the new node becomes the string that you pass.

createComment("*commentText*")

Returns: Comment object reference.
Compatibility: WinIE6+, MacIE5+, NN6+, Moz+, Safari+

The document.createComment() method creates an instance of a comment node. Upon creation, the node is in memory and available to be inserted into the document via any node's appendChild() or insertBefore() method.

Related Items: appendChild() and insertBefore() methods.

createDocumentFragment()

Returns: Document fragment object reference.
Compatibility: WinIE6+, MacIE5+, NN6+, Moz+, Safari+

The document.createDocumentFragment() method creates an instance of an empty document fragment node. This node serves as a holder that can be used to assemble a sequence of nodes in memory. After creating and assembling nodes into the document fragment, the entire fragment can be inserted into the document tree.

A document fragment is particularly helpful when your scripts assemble an arbitrary sequence of element and text nodes. By providing a parent node for all content within, the fragment node supplies the necessary parent node context for W3C DOM node methods, such as appendChild() during the content assembly process. If you then append or insert the document fragment node to an element in the rendered document tree, the fragment wrapper disappears, leaving just its content in the desired location in the document. Therefore, a typical usage pattern for a document fragment is to begin by creating an empty fragment node (through the createDocumentFragment() method), populate it at will with newly created element or text nodes or both, and then use the appropriate node method on a document tree's element to append, insert, or replace using the fragment node as the source material.

Related Items: None.

createElement("tagName")
createElementNS("namespaceURI", "tagName")

Returns: Element object reference.
Compatibility: WinIE4+, MacIE4+, NN6+, Moz+, Safari+

The document.createElement() and document.createElementNS() methods generate an element object for whatever HTML (or XML) tag name you pass as the parameter. An object created in this manner is not officially part of the current document node tree because it has not yet been placed into the document. But these methods are the way you begin assembling an element object that eventually gets inserted into the document. The createElementNS() method is identical to createElement() except the latter method accepts an extra parameter that you use to pass a namespace URI for the element. Additionally, the tag name that you specify when creating an element via createElementNS() must be a qualified name. Note, however, that createElementNS() is not supported in Internet Explorer through version 7.

The returned value is a reference to the object. Properties of that object include all properties (set to default values) that the browser's object model defines for that element object. Your scripts can then address the object through this reference to set the object's properties. Typically you do this before the object is inserted into the document, especially because otherwise read-only properties can be modified before the element is inserted into the document.

After the object is inserted into the document, the original reference (for example, a global variable used to store the value returned from the createElement() method) still points to the object, even while it is in the document and being displayed for the user. To demonstrate this effect, consider the following statements that create a simple paragraph element containing a text node:

```
var newText = document.createTextNode("Four score and seven years ago...");
var newElem = document.createElement("p");
newElem.id = "newestP";
newElem.appendChild(newText);
document.body.appendChild(newElem);
```

At this point, the new paragraph is visible in the document. But you can now modify, for example, the style of the paragraph by addressing either the element in the document object model or the variable that holds the reference to the object you created:

```
newElem.style.fontSize = "20pt";
```

or

```
document.getElementById("newestP").style.fontSize = "20pt";
```

The two references are inextricably connected and always point to the exact same object. Therefore, if you want to use a script to generate a series of similar elements (for example, a bunch of li list item elements), then you can use createElement() to make the first one and set all properties that the items have in common. Then use cloneNode() to make a new copy, which you can then treat as a separate element (and probably assign unique IDs to each one).

When scripting in the W3C DOM environment, you may rely on `document.createElement()` frequently to generate new content for a page or portion thereof (unless you prefer to use the convenience `innerHTML` property to add content in the form of strings of HTML). In a strict W3C DOM environment, creating new elements is not a matter of assembling HTML strings, but rather creating genuine element (and text node) objects.

Example

Chapter 15 contains numerous examples of the `document.createElement()` method in concert with methods that add or replace content to a document. See Listings 15-10, 15-21, 15-22, 15-28, 15-29, and 15-31.

Related Items: `document.createTextNode()` method.

createEvent("*eventType*")

Returns: Event object reference.
Compatibility: WinIE-, MacIE-, NN6+, Moz+, Safari+

The `document.createEvent()` method creates an instance of a W3C DOM `Event` object of the specified event category. Upon creation, the generic event must be initialized as a particular event type, and any other relevant properties set for the event. After successfully initializing the event, you can fire it through a call to the `dispatchEvent()` method.

Event types recognized by Mozilla are `KeyEvents`, `MouseEvents`, `MutationEvents`, and `UIEvents`. Beginning with Mozilla 1.7.5, the following additional types may also be used: `Event`, `KeyboardEvent`, `MouseEvent`, `MutationEvent`, `MutationNameEvent`, `TextEvent`, `UIEvent`. The process of initializing each of these event types requires its own series of parameters in the associated `initEvent()` method. See Chapter 25 for more details.

Example

Following is an example of how you might create an event, initialize it to a specific event type, and send it to a given element:

```
var evt = document.createEvent("MouseEvents");
evt.initEvent("mouseup", true, true);
document.getElementById("myButton").dispatchEvent(evt);
```

Related Items: `createEventObject()` method; W3C DOM event object (Chapter 25).

createEventObject([*eventObject*])

Returns: event object.
Compatibility: WinIE5.5+, MacIE-, NN-, Moz-, Safari-

The IE-specific `createEventObject()` method creates an `event` object, which can then be passed as a parameter to the `fireEvent()` method of any element object. The `event` object created by this event is just like an `event` object created by a user or system action.

An optional parameter enables you to base the new event on an existing `event` object. In other words, the properties of the newly created `event` object pick up all the properties of the `event` object passed as a parameter, which then enables you to modify properties of your choice. If you provide no parameter to the method, then you must fill the essential properties manually. For more about the properties of an `event` object, see Chapter 25.

Example

See the discussion of the fireEvent() method in Chapter 15 for an example of the sequence to follow when creating an event to fire on an element.

Related Items: createEvent() method; fireEvent() method (see Chapter 15); event object (see Chapter 25).

createNSResolver(*nodeResolver*)

Returns: XPath namespace resolver object reference.
Compatibility: WinIE-, MacIE-, NN7+, Moz+, Safari-

The createNSResolver() method is used in the context of XPath to alter a node so that it can resolve namespaces. This is necessary as part of the evaluation of an XPath expression. The only parameter is the node that is to serve as the basis for the namespace resolver.

Related Items: evaluate() method.

createRange()

Returns: Range object reference.
Compatibility: WinIE-, MacIE-, NN6+, Moz+, Safari-

The document.createRange() method creates an empty W3C DOM Range object with the boundary points of the range collapsed to the point before the first character of the rendered body text.

Related Items: Range object.

createStyleSheet(["*URL*"[, *index*]])

Returns: styleSheet object reference.
Compatibility: WinIE4+, MacIE4, NN-, Moz-, Safari-

The IE-specific createStyleSheet() method creates a styleSheet object, a type of object that includes style element objects as well as style sheets that are imported into a document through the link element. Thus you can dynamically load an external style sheet even after a page has loaded.

Unlike the other create methods entering W3C DOM usage, the createStyleSheet() method not only creates the style sheet, but it inserts the object into the document object model immediately. Thus, any style sheet rules that belong (or are assigned to) that object take effect on the page right away. If you'd rather create a style sheet and delay its deployment, you should use the createElement() method and element object assembly techniques.

If you don't specify any parameters to the method in WinIE, an empty styleSheet object is created. It is assumed that you will then use styleSheet object methods, such as addRule() to add the details to the style sheet. To link in an external style sheet file, assign the file's URL to the first parameter of the method. The newly imported style sheet is appended to the end of the document.styleSheets array of styleSheet objects. An optional second parameter lets you specify precisely where in the sequence of style sheet elements the newly linked style sheet should be inserted. A style sheet rule for any given selector is overridden by a style sheet for the same selector that appears later in the sequence of style sheets in a document.

Example

Listing 18-12 demonstrates adding an internal and external stylesheet to a document. For the internal addition, the addStyle1() function invokes document.createStyleSheet() and adds a rule governing the p elements of the page. In the addStyle2() function, an external file is loaded. That file contains the following two style rules:

```
h2 {font-size:20pt; color:blue}
p  {color:blue}
```

Notice that by specifying a position of zero for the imported stylesheet, the addition of the internal stylesheet always comes afterward in styleSheet object sequence. Thus, except when you deploy only the external style sheet, the red text color of the p elements override the blue color of the external style sheet. If you remove the second parameter of the createStyleSheet() method in addStyle2(), the external style sheet is appended to the end of the list. If it is the last style sheet to be added, the blue color prevails. Repeatedly clicking the buttons in this example continues to add the style sheets to the document.

LISTING 18-12

Creating and Applying Style Sheets

```html
<html>
   <head>
      <title>document.createStyleSheet() Method</title>
      <script type="text/javascript">
      function addStyle1() {
         var newStyle = document.createStyleSheet();
         newStyle.addRule("P", "font-size:16pt; color:red");
      }

      function addStyle2() {
         var newStyle = document.createStyleSheet("lst18-12.css",0);
      }

      // bind the event handlers
      function addEvent(elem, evtType, func) {
         if (elem.addEventListener) {
            elem.addEventListener(evtType, func, false);
         } else if (elem.attachEvent) {
            elem.attachEvent("on" + evtType, func);
         } else {
            elem["on" + evtType] = func;
         }
      }
      addEvent(window, "load", function() {
         addEvent(document.getElementById("addint"), "click", addStyle1);
         addEvent(document.getElementById("addext"), "click", addStyle2);
      });
      </script>
   </head>
```

continued

LISTING 18-12 *(continued)*

```
<body>
   <h1>document.createStyleSheet() Method</h1>
   <hr />
   <form>
      <input type="button" id="addint" value="Add Internal" />  <input
      type="button" id="addext" value="Add External" />
   </form>
   <h2>Section 1</h2>
   <p>Lorem ipsum dolor sit amet, consectetaur adipisicing elit, sed do
      eiusmod tempor incididunt ut labore et dolore magna aliqua. Ut enim
      adminim veniam, quis nostrud exercitation ullamco laboris nisi ut
      aliquip ex ea commodo consequat.</p>
   <h2>Section 2</h2>
   <p>Duis aute irure dolor in reprehenderit involuptate velit esse cillum
      dolore eu fugiat nulla pariatur. Excepteur sint occaecat cupidatat non
      proident, sunt in culpa qui officia deseruntmollit anim id est
      laborum.</p>
</body>
</html>
```

Related Items: styleSheet object (Chapter 26).

createTextNode("*text*")

Returns: Object.
Compatibility: WinIE5+, MacIE5+, NN6+, Moz+, Safari+

A text node is a W3C DOM object that contains body text without any HTML (or XML) tags, but is usually contained by (meaning, is a child of) an HTML (or XML) element. Without the IE innerText convenience property for modifying the text of an element, the W3C DOM relies on the node hierarchy of a document (Mozilla exceeds the W3C DOM by providing an innerHTML property, which you can use to replace text in an element). To insert or replace text inside an HTML element in the W3C DOM way, you create the text node and then use methods of the parent element (for example, appendChild(), insertBefore(), and replaceChild(), all described in Chapter 15) to modify the document's content. To generate a fresh text node, use document.createTextNode().

The sole parameter of the createTextNode() method is a string whose text becomes the nodeValue of the text node object returned by the method. You can also create an empty text node (passing an empty string) and assign a string to the nodeValue of the object later. As soon as the text node is present in the document object model, scripts can simply change the nodeValue property to modify text of an existing element. For more details on the role of text nodes in the W3C DOM, see Chapter 14.

Example

Although Chapters 14 and 15 (Listing 15-21, for instance) provide numerous examples of the createTextNode() method at work, using The Evaluator (see Chapter 13) is instructive to see just what the method generates in IE5+/W3C. You can use one of the built-in global variables of The Evaluator to hold a reference to a newly generated text node by entering the following statement into the top text field:

```
a = document.createTextNode("Hello")
```

The Results box shows that an object was created. Now, look at the properties of the object by entering a into the bottom text field. The precise listings of properties varies between IE5+ and W3C browsers, but the W3C DOM properties that they share in common indicate that the object is a node type 3 with a node name of #text. No parents, children, or siblings exist yet because the object created here is not part of the document hierarchy tree until it is explicitly added to the document.

To see how insertion works, enter the following statement into the top text field to append the text node to the myP paragraph:

```
document.getElementById("myP").appendChild(a)
```

The word *Hello* appears at the end of the simple paragraph lower on the page. Now you can modify the text of that node either through the reference from the point of view of the containing p element or through the global variable reference for the newly created node:

```
document.getElementById("myP").lastChild.nodeValue = "Howdy"
```

or

```
a.nodeValue = "Howdy"
```

Related Items: document.createElement() method.

createTreeWalker(*rootNode, whatToShow, filterFunction, entityRefExpansion*)

Returns: TreeWalker object reference.
Compatibility: WinIE-, MacIE-, NN7+, Moz1.4+, Safari-

The document.createTreeWalker() method creates an instance of a TreeWalker object that can be used to navigate the document tree. The first parameter to the method indicates the node in the document that is to serve as the root node of the tree. The second parameter is an integer constant that specifies one of several built-in filters for selecting nodes to be included in the tree. Following are the possible acceptable values for this parameter:

NodeFilter.SHOW_ALL	NodeFilter.SHOW_ATTRIBUTE
NodeFilter.SHOW_CDATA_SECTION	NodeFilter.SHOW_COMMENT
NodeFilter.SHOW_DOCUMENT	NodeFilter.SHOW_DOCUMENT_FRAGMENT
NodeFilter.SHOW_DOCUMENT_TYPE	NodeFilter.SHOW_ELEMENT
NodeFilter.SHOW_ENTITY	NodeFilter.SHOW_ENTITY_REFERENCE
NodeFilter.SHOW_NOTATION	NodeFilter.SHOW_PROCESSING_INSTRUCTION
NodeFilter.SHOW_TEXT	

The third parameter to the createNodeIterator() method is a reference to a filter function that can filter nodes even further than the *whatToShow* parameter. This function must accept a single node and return an integer value based upon one of the following constants: NodeFilter.FILTER_ACCEPT, NodeFilter.FILTER_REJECT, or NodeFilter.FILTER_SKIP. The idea is that you code the function to perform a test on each node and return an indicator value that lets the node iterator know whether or not to include the node in the tree. Your function doesn't loop through nodes. The TreeWalker object mechanism repetitively invokes the function as needed to look for the presence of whatever characteristic you wish to use as a filter.

document.elementFromPoint()

The final parameter to the method is a Boolean value that determines whether or not the content of entity reference nodes should be treated as hierarchical nodes. This parameter applies primarily to XML documents.

Related Items: TreeWalker object.

elementFromPoint(*x, y*)

Returns: Element object reference.
Compatibility: WinIE4+, MacIE4+, NN-, Moz-, Safari-

The IE-specific elementFromPoint() method returns a reference to whatever element object occupies the point whose integer coordinates are supplied as parameters to the method. The coordinate plane is that of the document, whose top-left corner is at point 0,0. This coordinate plane can be very helpful in interactive designs that need to calculate collision detection between positioned objects or mouse events.

When more than one object occupies the same point (for example, one element is positioned atop another), the element with the highest z-index value is returned. A positioned element always wins when placed atop a normal body-level element. And if multiple overlapping positioned elements have the same z-index value (or none by default), the element that comes last in the source code order is returned for the coordinate that they share in common.

Example

Listing 18-13 is a document that contains many different types of elements, each of which has an ID attribute assigned to it. The onmouseover event handler for the document object invokes a function that finds out which element the cursor is over when the event fires. Note that the event coordinates are event.clientX and event.clientY, which use the same coordinate plane as the page for their point of reference. As you roll the mouse over every element, its ID appears on the page. Some elements, such as br and tr, occupy no space in the document, so you cannot get their IDs to appear. On a typical browser screen size, a positioned element rests atop one of the paragraph elements so that you can see how the elementFromPoint() method handles overlapping elements. If you scroll the page, the coordinates for the event and the page's elements stay in sync.

LISTING 18-13

Tracking the Mouse as It Passes over Elements

```
<html>
    <head>
        <title>document.elementFromPoint() Method</title>
        <script type="text/javascript">
        function replaceHTML(elem, text) {
            while(elem.firstChild)
                elem.removeChild(elem.firstChild);
            elem.appendChild(document.createTextNode(text));
        }

        function showElemUnderneath() {
            var elem = document.elementFromPoint(event.clientX, event.clientY);
            replaceHTML(document.getElementById("mySpan"), elem.id);
        }

        // bind the event handlers
```

```
        function addEvent(elem, evtType, func) {
            if (elem.addEventListener) {
                elem.addEventListener(evtType, func, false);
            } else if (elem.attachEvent) {
                elem.attachEvent("on" + evtType, func);
            } else {
                elem["on" + evtType] = func;
            }
        }
        addEvent(window, "load", function() {
            addEvent(document, "mouseover", showElemUnderneath);
        });
        </script>
    </head>
    <body id="myBody">
        <h1 id="header">document.elementFromPoint() Method</h1>
        <hr id="myHR" />
        <p id="instructions">Roll the mouse around the page. The coordinates
            of the mouse pointer are currently atop an element<br id="myBR" />
            whose ID is:"<span id="mySpan" style="font-weight:bold"></span>".</p>
        <form id="myForm">
            <input id="myButton" type="button" value="Sample Button" /> 
        </form>
        <table border="1" id="myTable">
            <tr id="tr1">
                <td id="td_A1">Cell A1</td>
                <td id="td_B1">Cell B1</td>
            </tr>
            <tr id="tr2">
                <td id="td_A2">Cell A2</td>
                <td id="td_B2">Cell B2</td>
            </tr>
        </table>
        <h2 id="sec1">Section 1</h2>
        <p id="p1">Lorem ipsum dolor sit amet, consectetaur adipisicing elit, sed
            do eiusmod tempor incididunt ut labore et dolore magna aliqua. Ut enim
            adminim veniam, quis nostrud exercitation ullamco laboris nisi ut
            aliquip ex ea commodo consequat.</p>
        <h2 id="sec2">Section 2</h2>
        <p id="p2">Duis aute irure dolor in reprehenderit involuptate velit esse
            cillum dolore eu fugiat nulla pariatur. Excepteur sint occaecat
            cupidatat non proident, sunt in culpa qui officia deseruntmollit anim
            id est laborum.</p>
        <div id="myDIV"
        style="position:absolute; top:340; left:300; background-color:yellow">
            Here is a positioned element.
        </div>
    </body>
</html>
```

Related Items: event.clientX, event.clientY properties; positioned objects (Chapter 40 on the CD-ROM).

evaluate("expression", contextNode, resolver, type, result)

Returns: XPath result object reference.
Compatibility: WinIE-, MacIE-, NN7+, Moz+, Safari-

The document.evaluate() method evaluates an XPath expression and returns a result as an XPath result object (XPathResult). The most important parameter to this method is the first one, which contains the actual XPath expression as a string. The second parameter is the context node to which the expression applies, whereas the third parameter is the namespace resolver (see the createNSResolver() method). The resolver parameter can be specified as null as long as there aren't any namespace prefixes used within the expression.

The type parameter determines the type of the result of the expression and is specified as one of the XPath result types, such as 0 for any type, 1 for number, 2 for string, and so forth. Finally, a reusable result object can be specified in the last parameter, which will then be modified and returned from the method as the result of the expression.

Related Items: createNSResolver() method.

execCommand("*commandName*"[, *UIFlag*] [, *param*])

Returns: Boolean.
Compatibility: WinIE4+, MacIE-, NN7.1+, Moz1.3+, Safari1.3+

The execCommand() method is the JavaScript gateway to a set of commands that is outside of the methods defined for objects in the object model. A series of related methods (queryCommandEnable() and others) also facilitate management of these commands.

The syntax for the execCommand() method requires at least one parameter, a string version of the command name. Command names are not case-sensitive. An optional second parameter is a Boolean flag to instruct the command to display any user interface artifacts that may be associated with the command. The default is false. For the third parameter, some commands require that an attribute value be passed for the command to work. For example, to set the font size of a text range, the syntax is

```
myRange.execCommand("FontSize", true, 5);
```

The execCommand() method returns Boolean true if the command is successful; false if not successful. Some commands can return values (for example, finding out the font name of a selection), but those are accessed through the queryCommandValue() method.

In Internet Explorer, most of these commands operate on body text selections that are TextRange objects. As described in Chapter 36 on the CD-ROM, a TextRange object must be created under script control. But a TextRange object can be done in response to a user selecting some text in the document. Because a TextRange object is independent of the element hierarchy (indeed, a TextRange can spread across multiple nodes), it cannot respond to stylesheet specifications. Thus, many of the commands that can operate on a TextRange object have to do with formatting or modifying the text. For a list of commands that work exclusively on TextRange objects, see the TextRange.execCommand() method in Chapter 36 on the CD-ROM.

Although many of the commands intended for the TextRange also work when invoked from the document object, in this section the focus is on those commands that have scope over the entire document. Table 18-2 lists those few commands that work with the document. Also listed are many commands that work exclusively on text selections in the document, whether the selections are made manually by the user or with the help of the TextRange object (see Chapter 36 on the CD-ROM).

TABLE 18-2

document.execCommand() Commands

Command	Parameter	Description
BackColor	Color String	Encloses the current selection with a font element whose style attribute sets the background-color style to the parameter value.
CreateBookmark	Anchor String	Encloses the current selection (or text range) with an anchor element whose name attribute is set to the parameter value.
CreateLink	URL String	Encloses the current selection with an a element whose href attribute is set to the parameter value.
FontName	Font Face(s)	Encloses the current selection with a font element whose face attribute is set to the parameter value.
FontSize	Size String	Encloses the current selection with a font element whose size attribute is set to the parameter value.
FontColor	Color String	Encloses the current selection with a font element whose color attribute is set to the parameter value.
Indent	None	Indents the current selection.
JustifyCenter	None	Centers the current selection.
JustifyFull	None	Full-justifies the current selection.
JustifyLeft	None	Left-justifies the current selection.
JustifyRight	None	Right-justifies the current selection.
Outdent	None	Outdents the current selection.
Refresh	None	Reloads the page.
RemoveFormat	None	Removes formatting for the current selection.
SelectAll	None	Selects all text of the document.
UnBookmark	None	Removes anchor tags that surround the current selection.
Unlink	None	Removes link tags that surround the current selection.
Unselect	None	Deselects the current selection anywhere in the document.

Mozilla 1.4 and Safari 1.3 added a feature that allows scripts to turn an iframe element's document object into an HTML editable document. Here is an example of how to center the selected text in an iframe with an ID of msg:

```
document.getElementById("msg").contentDocument.execCommand("JustifyCenter");
```

Note that the contentDocument property is used to access the iframe as a document. Visit http://www.mozilla.org/editor for additional details and examples of the document.execCommand() method.

Example

You can find many examples of the execCommand() method for the TextRange object in Chapter 36 on the CD-ROM. But you can try out the document-specific commands in The Evaluator (see Chapter 13) in Internet Explorer if you like. Try each of the following statements in the top text box and click the Evaluate button:

```
document.execCommand("Refresh")
document.execCommand("SelectAll")
document.execCommand("Unselect")
```

All methods return true in the Results box.

Because any way you can evaluate a statement in The Evaluator forces a body selection to become deselected before the evaluation takes place, you can't experiment this way with the selection-oriented commands.

Related Items: queryCommandEnabled(), queryCommandIndterm(), queryCommandState(), queryCommandSupported(), queryCommandText(), queryCommandValue() methods.

getElementById("*elementID*")

Returns: Element object reference.
Compatibility: WinIE5+, MacIE5+, NN6+, Moz+, Safari+

The document.getElementById() method is the W3C DOM syntax for retrieving a reference to any element in a document that has a unique identifier assigned to its id attribute. If the document contains more than one instance of an ID, the method returns a reference to the first element in source code order with that ID. Because this method is such an important avenue to writing references to objects that are to be modified under script control, you can see how important it is to assign unique IDs to elements.

This method's name is quite a finger twister for scripters, especially compared to the IE4+ convention of letting a reference to any element begin simply with the object's ID. However, the getElementById() method is the modern way of acquiring an element's reference for W3C DOM-compatible browsers, including IE. When you type this method, be sure to use a lowercase d as the last character of the method name.

Unlike some other element-oriented methods (for example, getElementsByTagName()), which can be invoked on any element in a document, the getElementById() method works exclusively with the document object.

Example

You can find many examples of this method in use throughout this book, but you can take a closer look at how it works by experimenting in The Evaluator (see Chapter 13). A number of elements in The Evaluator have IDs assigned to them, so that you can use the method to inspect the objects and their properties. Enter the following statements into both the top and bottom text fields of The Evaluator. Results from the top field are references to the objects; results from the bottom field are lists of properties for the particular object.

```
document.getElementById("myP")
document.getElementById("myEM")
document.getElementById("myTitle")
document.getElementById("myScript")
```

Related Items: getElementsByTagName() method (Chapter 15).

getElementsByName("*elementName*")

Returns: Array.
Compatibility: WinIE5+, MacIE5+, NN6+, Moz+, Safari+

The document.getElementsByName() method returns an array of references to objects whose name attribute is assigned the element name passed as the method's attribute. Although NN6+/Moz recognizes name attributes even for elements that don't have them by default, IE does not. Therefore, for maximum cross-browser compatibility, use this method only to locate elements that have name attributes defined for them by default, such as form control elements. If the element does not exist in the document, the method returns an array of zero length.

For the most part, you are best served by using IDs on elements and the getElementById() method to unearth references to individual objects. But some elements, especially the input element of type radio, use the name attribute to group elements together. In that case, a call to getElementsByName() returns an array of all elements that share the name — facilitating perhaps a for loop that inspects the checked property of a radio button group. Thus, instead of using the old-fashioned approach by way of the containing form object:

```
var buttonGroup = document.forms[0].radioGroupName;
```

you can go more directly:

```
var buttonGroup = document.getElementsByName(radioGroupName);
```

In the latter case, you operate independently of the containing form object's index number or name. This assumes, of course, that a group name is not shared elsewhere on the page, which would certainly lead to confusion.

Example

Use The Evaluator (see Chapter 13) to test out the getElementsByName() method. All form elements in the upper part of the page have names associated with them. Enter the following statements into the top text field and observe the results:

```
document.getElementsByName("output")
document.getElementsByName("speed").length
document.getElementsByName("speed")[0].value
```

You can also explore all of the properties of the text field by typing the following expression into the bottom field:

```
document.getElementsByName("speed")[0]
```

Related Items: document.getElementById(), getElementsByTagName() methods.

importNode(node, deep)

Returns: Node object reference.
Compatibility: WinIE-, MacIE-, NN7+, Moz+, Safari-

The document.importNode() method imports a node from another document object into the current document object. A copy of the original node is made when the node is imported, meaning that the original node remains unchanged. The second parameter to the method is a Boolean value that determines whether or not the node's entire subtree is imported (true) or just the node itself (false).

open(["*mimeType*"] [,"*replace*"])

Returns: Nothing.
Compatibility: WinIE3+, MacIE3+, NN2+, Moz+, Safari+

Opening a document is different from opening a window. In the case of a window, you're creating a new object, both on the screen and in the browser's memory. Opening a document, on the other hand, tells the browser to get ready to accept some data for display in the window named or implied in the reference to the document.open() method. (For example, parent.frames[1].document.open() may refer to a different frame in a frameset, whereas document.open() implies the current window or frame.) Therefore, the method name may mislead newcomers because the document.open() method has nothing to do with loading documents from the web server or hard disk. Rather, this method is a prelude to sending data to a window through the document.write() or document.writeln() methods. In a sense, the document.open() method merely opens the valve of a pipe; the other methods send the data down the pipe like a stream, and the document.close() method closes that valve as soon as the page's data has been sent in full.

The document.open() method is optional because a document.write() method that attempts to write to a closed document automatically clears the old document and opens the stream for a new one. Whether or not you use the document.open() method, be sure to use the document.close() method after all the writing has taken place.

An optional parameter to the document.open() method enables you to specify the nature of the data being sent to the window. A MIME (Multipurpose Internet Mail Extension) type is a specification for transferring and representing multimedia data on the Internet (originally for mail transmission, but now applicable to all Internet data exchanges). You've seen MIME depictions in the list of helper applications in your browser's preferences settings. A pair of data type names separated by a slash represents a MIME type (such as text/html and image/gif). When you specify a MIME type as a parameter to the document.open() method, you're instructing the browser about the kind of data it is about to receive, so that it knows how to render the data. Common values that most browsers accept are:

```
text/html
text/plain
image/gif
image/jpeg
image/xbm
```

If you omit the parameter, JavaScript assumes the most popular type, text/html — the kind of data you typically assemble in a script prior to writing to the window. The text/html type includes any images that the HTML references. Specifying any of the image types means that you have the raw binary representation of the image that you want to appear in the new document — possible, but unlikely.

Another possibility is to direct the output of a write() method to a plug-in. For the mimeType parameter, specify the plug-in's MIME type (for example, application/x-director for Shockwave). Again, the data you write to a plug-in must be in a form that it knows how to handle. The same mechanism also works for writing data directly to a helper application.

 IE accepts only the text/html MIME type parameter.

Modern browsers include a second, optional parameter to the method: replace. This parameter does for the document.open() method what the replace() method does for the location object. For document.open(), it means that the new document you are about to write replaces the previous document in the window or frame from being recorded to that window or frame's history.

Example

You can see an example of where the document.open() method fits in the scheme of dynamically creating content for another frame in the discussion of the document.write() method later in this chapter.

Related Items: document.close(), document.clear(), document.write(), document.writeln() methods.

queryCommandEnabled("*commandName*")
queryCommandIndterm("*commandName*")
queryCommandCommandState("*commandName*")
queryCommandSupported("*commandName*")
queryCommandText("*commandName*")
queryCommandValue("*commandName*")

Returns: Various values.
Compatibility: WinIE4+, MacIE-, NN7.1, Moz1.3+, Safari-

These six methods lend further support to the execCommand() method for document and TextRange objects in WinIE. If you choose to use the execCommand() method to achieve some stylistic change on a text selection, you can use some of these query methods to make sure the browser supports the desired command and to retrieve any returned values. Table 18-3 summarizes the purpose and returned values for each of the query methods.

TABLE 18-3

IE Query Commands

queryCommand	Returns	Description
Enabled	Boolean	Reveals whether the document or TextRange object is in a suitable state to be invoked.
Indterm	Boolean	Reveals whether the command is in an indeterminate state.
CommandState	Boolean | null	Reveals whether the command has been completed (true), is still working (false), or is in an indeterminate state (null).
Supported	Boolean	Reveals whether the command is supported in the current browser.
Text	String	Returns any text that may be returned by a command.
Value	Varies	Returns whatever value (if any) is returned by a command.

document.write()

Because the execCommand() method cannot be invoked on a page while it is still loading, any such invocations that may collide with the loading of a page should check with queryCommandEnabled() prior to invoking the command. Validating that the browser version running the script supports the desired command is also a good idea. Therefore, you may want to wrap any command call with the following conditional structure:

```
if (document.queryCommandEnabled(commandName) &&
    document.queryCommandSupported(commandName)) {
    ...
}
```

When using a command to read information about a selection, use the queryCommandText() or queryCommandValue() methods to catch that information (recall that the execCommand() method itself returns a Boolean value regardless of the specific command invoked).

Example

See the examples for these methods covered under the TextRange object in Chapter 36 on the CD-ROM.

Related Items: TextRange object (see Chapter 36 on the CD-ROM); execCommand() method.

recalc([allFlag])

Returns: Nothing.
Compatibility: WinIE5+, MacIE-, NN-, Moz-, Safari-

IE5 introduced the concept of dynamic properties. With the help of the setExpression() method of all elements and the expression() style sheet value, you can establish dependencies between object properties and potentially dynamic properties, such as a window's size or a draggable element's location. After those dependencies are established, the document.recalc() method causes those dependencies to be recalculated — usually in response to some user action, such as resizing a window or dragging an element.

The optional parameter is a Boolean value. The default value, false, means that the recalculations are performed only on expressions for which the browser has detected any change since the last recalculation. If you specify true, however, all expressions are recalculated whether they have changed or not.

Mozilla 1.4 includes a feature that allows scripts to turn an iframe element's document object into an HTML editable document. Part of the scripting incorporates the document.execCommand() and related methods. Visit http://www.mozilla.org/editor for current details and examples.

Example

You can see an example of recalc() in Listing 15-32 for the setExpression() method. In that example, the dependencies are between the current time and properties of standard element objects.

Related Items: getExpression(), removeExpression(), setExpression() methods (Chapter 15).

write("string1" [,"string2" ... [, "stringn"]])
writeln("string1" [,"string2" ... [, "stringn"]])

Returns: Boolean true if successful.
Compatibility: WinIE3+, MacIE3+, NN2+, Moz+, Safari+

Both of these methods send text to a document for display in its window. The only difference between the two methods is that `document.writeln()` appends a carriage return to the end of the string it sends to the document. This carriage return is helpful for formatting source code when viewed through the browser's source view window. For new lines in rendered HTML that is generated by these methods, you must still write a `<br>` to insert a line break.

A common, incorrect conclusion that many JavaScript newcomers make is that these methods enable a script to modify the contents of an existing document, which is not true. As soon as a document has loaded into a window (or frame), the only fully backward-compatible text that you can modify without reloading or rewriting the entire page is the content of text and `textarea` objects. In IE4+, you can modify HTML and text through the `innerHTML`, `innerText`, `outerHTML`, and `outerText` properties of any element. For W3C DOM–compatible browsers, you can modify an element's text by setting its `nodeValue` or `innerHTML` properties. The preferred approach for modifying the content of a node involves strict adherence to the W3C DOM, which requires creating and inserting or replacing new elements, as described in Chapter 15 and demonstrated in examples throughout this chapter and the rest of the book.

The two safest ways to use the `document.write()` and `document.writeln()` methods are to:

- Write some or all of the page's content by way of scripts embedded in the document
- Send HTML code either to a new window or to a separate frame in a multiframe window

For the first case, you essentially interlace script segments within your HTML. The scripts run as the document loads, writing whatever scripted HTML content you like. This task is exactly what you did in `script1.htm` in Chapter 3. This task is also how you can have one page generate browser-specific HTML when a particular class of browser requires unique syntax.

In the latter case, a script can gather input from the user in one frame and then algorithmically determine the layout and content destined for another frame. The script assembles the HTML code for the other frame as a string variable (including all necessary HTML tags). Before the script can write anything to the frame, it can optionally open the layout stream (to close the current document in that frame) with the `parent.frameName.document.open()` method. In the next step, a `parent.frameName.document.write()` method pours the entire string into the other frame. Finally, a `parent.frameName.document.close()` method ensures that the total data stream is written to the window. Such a frame looks just the same as if it were created by a source document on the server rather than on the fly in memory. The `document` object of that window or frame is a full citizen as a standard `document` object. You can, therefore, even include scripts as part of the HTML specification for one of these temporary HTML pages.

After an HTML document (containing a script that is going to write via the `write()` or `writeln()` methods) loads completely, the page's incoming stream closes automatically. If you then attempt to apply a series of `document.write()` statements, the first `document.write()` method completely removes all vestiges of the original document. That includes all of its objects and scripted variable values. Therefore, if you try to assemble a new page with a series of `document.write()` statements, the script and variables from the original page will be gone before the second `document.write()` statement executes. To get around this potential problem, assemble the content for the new screen of content as one string variable and then pass that variable as the parameter to a single `document.write()` statement. Also be sure to include a `document.close()` statement in the next line of script.

Assembling HTML in a script to be written via the `document.write()` method often requires skill in concatenating string values and nesting strings. A number of JavaScript `String` object shortcuts facilitate the formatting of text with HTML tags (see Chapter 28 for details).

document.write()

If you are writing to a different frame or window, you are free to use multiple `document.write()` statements if you like. Whether your script sends lots of small strings via multiple `document.write()` methods or assembles a larger string to be sent through one `document.write()` method depends partly on the situation and partly on your own scripting style. From a performance standpoint, a fairly standard procedure is to do more preliminary work in memory and place as few I/O (input/output) calls as possible. On the other hand, making a difficult-to-track mistake is easier in string concatenation when you assemble longer strings. My personal preference is to assemble longer strings, but you should use the system that's most comfortable for you.

You may see another little-known way of passing parameters to these methods. Instead of concatenating string values with the plus (+) operator, you can also bring string values together by separating them with commas, in which case the strings appear to be arguments to the `document.write()` method. For example, the following two statements produce the same results:

```
document.write("Today is " + new Date());
document.write("Today is ",new Date());
```

Neither form is better than the other, so use the one that feels more comfortable to your existing programming style.

> **NOTE** Dynamically generating scripts requires an extra trick, especially in NN. The root of the problem is that if you try code, such as `document.write("<script></script>")`, the browser interprets the end script tag as the end of the script that is doing the writing. You have to trick the browser by separating the end tag into a couple of components. Escaping the forward slash also helps. For example, if you want to load a different `.js` file for each class of browser, the code looks similar to the following:

```
// variable 'browserVer' is a browser-specific string
// and 'page' is the HTML your script is accumulating
// for document.write()
page += "<script type='text/javascript' src='" +
   browseVer + ".js'><" + "\/script>";
```

Using the `document.open()`, `document.write()`, and `document.close()` methods to display images in a document requires some small extra steps. First, any URL assignments that you write via `document.write()` must be complete (not relative) URL references. Alternatively, you can write the `<base>` tag for the dynamically generated page so that its `href` attribute value matches that of the file that is writing the page.

The other image trick is to be sure to specify `height` and `width` attributes for every image, scripted or otherwise. Document-rendering performance is improved on all platforms, because the values help the browser lay out elements even before their details are loaded.

In addition to the `document.write()` example that follows (see Listings 18-14 through 18-16), you can find fuller implementations that use this method to assemble images and bar charts in many of the applications in Chapters 49 through 58 on the CD-ROM. Because you can assemble any valid HTML as a string to be written to a window or frame, a customized, on-the-fly document can be as elaborate as the most complex HTML document that you can imagine.

Example

The example in Listings 18-14 through 18-16 demonstrates several important points about using the `document.write()` or `document.writeln()` methods for writing to another frame. First is the fact that you can write any HTML code to a frame, and the browser accepts it as if the source code came from an HTML file somewhere. In the example, I assemble a complete HTML document, including basic HTML tags for completeness.

LISTING 18-14

A Frameset for the Document Writing Example

```html
<html>
    <head>
        <title>Writin' to the doc</title>
    </head>
    <frameset rows="50%,50%">
        <frame name="Frame1" src="lst18-15.htm" />
        <frame name="Frame2" src="lst18-16.htm" />
    </frameset>
</html>
```

LISTING 18-15

Writing a Document Based upon User Input

```html
<html>
    <head>
        <title>Document Write Controller</title>
        <script type="text/javascript">
        function takePulse(form) {
            var msg = "<html><head><title>On The Fly with " +
                form.yourName.value + "<\/title><\/head>";
            msg += "<body bgcolor='salmon'><h1>Good Day " + form.yourName.value +
                "!<\/h1><hr />";
            for (var i = 0; i < form.how.length; i++) {
                if (form.how[i].checked) {
                    msg += form.how[i].value;
                    break;
                }
            }
            msg += "<br />Make it a great day!<\/body><\/html>";
            parent.Frame2.document.write(msg);
            parent.Frame2.document.close();
        }

        function getTitle() {
            alert("Lower frame document.title is now:" +
                parent.Frame2.document.title);
        }

        // bind the event handlers
        function addEvent(elem, evtType, func) {
            if (elem.addEventListener) {
                elem.addEventListener(evtType, func, false);
            } else if (elem.attachEvent) {
```

continued

583

LISTING 18-15 *(continued)*

```
            elem.attachEvent("on" + evtType, func);
        } else {
            elem["on" + evtType] = func;
        }
    }
    addEvent(window, "load", function() {
        addEvent(document.getElementById("enter"), "click",
            function(evt) {takePulse(document.getElementById("enter").form)});
        addEvent(document.getElementById("peek"), "click", getTitle);
    });
    </script>
</head>
<body>
    Fill in a name, and select how that person feels today. Then click "Write
    To Below" to see the results in the bottom frame.
    <form>
        Enter your first name:<input type="text" name="yourName"
        value="Dave" />
        <p>How are you today? <input type="radio" name="how"
            value="I hope that feeling continues forever."
            checked="checked" />Swell <input type="radio" name="how"
            value="You may be on your way to feeling Swell" />Pretty Good
            <input type="radio" name="how"
            value="Things can only get better from here." />So-So</p>
        <p><input type="button" id="enter" name="enter"
            value="Write To Below" /></p>
        <hr />
        <input type="button" id="peek" name="peek"
            value="Check Lower Frame Title" />
    </form>
</body>
</html>
```

LISTING 18-16

A Placeholder Page for the Document Writing Example

```
<html>
    <head>
        <title>Placeholder</title>
    </head>
    <body>
    </body>
</html>
```

It is important to note that this example customizes the content of the document based on user input. This customization makes the experience of working with your web page feel far more interactive to the user — yet you're doing it without any server-side programs.

The second point I want to bring home is that the document created in the separate frame by the `document.write()` method is a genuine `document` object. In this example, the `<title>` tag of the written document changes if you redraw the lower frame after changing the entry of the name field in the upper frame. If you click the lower button after updating the bottom frame, you see that the `document.title` property has, indeed, changed to reflect the `<title>` tag written to the browser in the course of displaying the frame's page. The fact that you can artificially create full-fledged, JavaScript `document` objects on the fly represents one of the most important powers of serverless CGI scripting (for information delivery to the user) with JavaScript. You have much to take advantage of here if your imagination is up to the task.

Note that you can easily modify Listing 18-15 to write the results to the same frame as the document containing the field and buttons. Instead of specifying the lower frame:

```
parent.frames[1].document.open()
parent.frames[1].document.write(msg)
parent.frames[1].document.close()
```

The code simply can use:

```
document.open()
document.write(msg)
document.close()
```

This code would replace the form document with the results and not require any frames in the first place. Because the code assembles all of the content for the new document into one variable value, that data survive the one `document.write()` method.

The frameset document (see Listing 18-14) creates a blank frame by loading a blank document (see Listing 18-16). An alternative I highly recommend is to have the framesetting document fill the frame with a blank document of its own creation. See the section "Blank frames" in Chapter 16 for further details about this technique.

Related Items: `document.open()`; `document.close()`; `document.clear()` methods.

Event handlers

onselectionchange

Compatibility: WinIE5.5+, MacIE-, NN-, Moz-, Safari-

The `onselectionchange` event can be triggered by numerous user actions, although all of those actions occur on elements that are under the influence of the WinIE5.5+ edit mode.

Related Items: `oncontrolselect` event handler.

onstop

Compatibility: WinIE5+, MacIE-, NN-, Moz-, Safari-

The `onstop` event fires in WinIE5+ when the user clicks the browser's Stop button. Use this event handler to stop potentially runaway script execution on a page, because the Stop button does not otherwise control scripts after a page has loaded. If you are having a problem with a runaway repeat loop during development, you can temporarily use this event handler to let you stop the script for debugging.

document.onstop

Example

Listing 18-17 provides a simple example of an intentional infinitely looping script. In case you load this page into a browser other than IE5+, you can click the Halt Counter button to stop the looping. The Halt Counter button as well as the `onstop` event handler invokes the same function.

LISTING 18-17

Stopping a Script Using the onstop Event Handler

```html
<html>
    <head>
        <title>onStop Event Handler</title>
        <script type="text/javascript">
        var counter = 0;
        var timerID;
        function startCounter() {
            document.forms[0].display.value = ++counter;
            //clearTimeout(timerID)
            timerID = setTimeout("startCounter()", 10);
        }
        function haltCounter() {
            clearTimeout(timerID);
            counter = 0;
        }

        // bind the event handlers
        function addEvent(elem, evtType, func) {
            if (elem.addEventListener) {
              elem.addEventListener(evtType, func, false);
            } else if (elem.attachEvent) {
              elem.attachEvent("on" + evtType, func);
            } else {
              elem["on" + evtType] = func;
            }
        }
        addEvent(window, "load", function() {
            addEvent(document, "stop", haltCounter);
            addEvent(document.getElementById("start"), "click", startCounter);
            addEvent(document.getElementById("halt"), "click", haltCounter);
        });
        </script>
    </head>
    <body>
        <h1>onStop Event Handler</h1>
        <hr />
        <p>Click the browser's Stop button (in IE) to stop the script counter.</p>
        <form>
            <p><input type="text" name="display" /></p>
            <input type="button" id="start" value="Start Counter" />
            <input type="button" id="halt" value="Halt Counter" />
```

```
      </form>
    </body>
  </html>
```

Related Items: Repeat loops (Chapter 32).

body Element Object

Compatibility: WinIE4+, MacIE4+, NN6+, Moz+, Safari+

For HTML element properties, methods, and event handlers, see Chapter 15.

Properties	Methods	Event Handlers
alink	createControlRange()	onafterprint
background	createTextRange()	onbeforeprint
bgColor	doScroll()	onscroll
bgProperties		
bottomMargin		
leftMargin		
link		
noWrap		
rightMargin		
scroll		
scrollLeft		
scrollTop		
text		
topMargin		
vLink		

Syntax

Accessing body element object properties or methods:

    [window.] document.body.property | method([parameters])

About this object

In object models that reveal HTML element objects, the body element object is the primary container of the content that visitors see on the page. The body contains all rendered HTML. This special place in the node hierarchy gives the body object some special powers, especially in the IE object model.

As if to signify the special relationship, both the IE and W3C object models provide the same shortcut reference to the body element: document.body. As a first-class HTML element object (as evidenced by the long lists of properties, methods, and event handlers covered in Chapter 15), you are also free to use other syntaxes to reach the body element.

You are certainly familiar with several body element attributes that govern body-wide content appearance, such as link colors (in three states) and background (color or image). But IE and NN/Mozilla (and the W3C so far) have some very different ideas about the body element's role in scripting documents. Many methods and properties that NN/Mozilla considers to be the domain of the window (for example, scrolling, inside window dimensions, and so forth), IE puts into the hands of the body element object. Therefore, whereas NN/Mozilla scrolls the window (and whatever it may contain), IE scrolls the body (inside whatever window it lives). And because the body element fills the entire viewable area of a browser window or frame, that viewable rectangle is determined in IE by the body's scrollHeight and scrollWidth properties, whereas NN4+/Moz features window.innerHeight and window.innerWidth properties. This distinction is important to point out because when you are scripting window- or document-wide appearance factors, you may have to look for properties and methods for the window or body element object, depending on your target browser(s).

NOTE   Use caution when referencing the document.body object while the page is loading. The object may not officially exist until the page has completely loaded. If you need to set some initial properties through scripting, do so in response to the onload event handler located in the <body> tag. Attempts at setting body element object properties in immediate scripts inside the head element may result in error messages about the object not being found.

Properties
aLink
bgColor
link
text
vLink

Value: Hexadecimal triplet or color name string.   Read/Write
Compatibility: WinIE4+, MacIE4+, NN6+, Moz+, Safari+

The aLink, link, and vLink properties replaced the ancient document properties alinkColor, linkColor, and vlinkColor. The bgColor property is the same as the old document.bgColor property, while the text property replaced the document.fgColor property. These properties serve as the scripted equivalents of the HTML attributes for the body element — the property names more closely align themselves with the HTML attributes than the old property names.

I use past tense when referring to these properties because CSS has largely made them obsolete. Granted, they still work but will likely fall into disuse as web developers continue to embrace style sheets as the preferred means of altering color in web pages. Link colors that are set through pseudo-class selectors in style sheets (as style attributes of the body element) must be accessed through the style property for the body object.

background

Value: URL string.   Read/Write
Compatibility: WinIE4+, MacIE4+, NN6+, Moz+, Safari+

The `background` property enables you to set or get the URL for the background image (if any) assigned to the `body` element. A `body` element's background image overlays the background color in case both attributes or properties are set. To remove an image from the document's background, set the `document.body.background` property to an empty string.

Similar to the properties that provide access to colors on the page, the background image in modern web pages should be set through style sheets, as opposed to the `body.background` property. In that case, you access the background programmatically through the `style` property of the `body` object.

bgColor

(See `aLink`)

bgProperties

Value: String constant.   Read/Write
Compatibility: WinIE4+, MacIE4+, NN-, Moz-, Safari-

The IE-specific `bgProperties` property is an alternative way of adjusting whether the background image should remain fixed when the user scrolls the document or if it should scroll with the document. Initial settings for this behavior should be done through the `background-attachment` CSS attribute and modified under script control by way of the `body` element's `style.backgroundAttachment` property.

No matter which way you reference this property, the only allowable values are string constants `scroll` (the default) or `fixed`.

Example

Both of the following statements change the default behavior of background image scrolling in IE4+:

```
document.body.bgProperties = "fixed";
```

or

```
document.body.style.backgroundAttachment = "fixed";
```

The added benefit of using the style sheet version is that it also works in NN6+/Moz.

Related Items: `body.background` property.

bottomMargin
leftMargin
rightMargin
topMargin

Value: Integer.   Read/Write
Compatibility: WinIE4+, MacIE4+, NN-, Moz-, Safari-

document.body.rightMargin

The four IE-specific margin properties are alternatives to setting the corresponding four margin style sheet attributes for the body element (body.style.marginBottom, and so on). Style sheet margins represent blank space between the edge of an element's content and its next outermost container. In the case of the body element, that container is an invisible document container.

Of the four properties, only the one for the bottom margin may be confusing if the content does not fill the vertical space of a window or frame. The margin value is not automatically increased to accommodate the extra blank space.

Example

Both of the following statements change the default left margin in IE4+:

```
document.body.leftMargin = 30;
```

or

```
document.body.style.marginLeft = 30;
```

Related Items: style object.

leftMargin

(See bottomMargin)

link

(See aLink)

noWrap

Value: Boolean.   Read/Write
Compatibility: WinIE4+, MacIE4+, NN-, Moz-, Safari-

The noWrap property enables you to modify the body element behavior normally set through the nowrap attribute. Because the property name is a negative, the Boolean logic needed to control it can get confusing.

The default behavior for a body element is for text to wrap within the width of the window or frame. This behavior occurs when the value of noWrap is its default value of false. By turning noWrap to true, a line of text continues to render past the right edge of the window or frame until the HTML contains a line break (or end of paragraph). If the text continues on past the right edge of the window, the window (or frame) gains a horizontal scroll bar (of course, not if a frame is set to not scroll).

By and large, users don't like to scroll in any direction if they don't have to. Unless you have a special need to keep single lines intact, let the default behavior rule the day.

Example

To change the word-wrapping behavior from the default, the statement is:

```
document.body.noWrap = true;
```

Related Items: None.

rightMargin

(See bottomMargin)

scroll

Value: Constant string.   Read/Write
Compatibility: WinIE4+, MacIE4+, NN-, Moz-, Safari-

The IE-specific `scroll` property provides scripted access to the IE-specific `scroll` attribute of a `body` element. By default, an IE `body` element displays a vertical scroll bar even if the height of the content does not warrant it; a horizontal scroll bar appears only when the content is forced to be wider than the window or frame. You can make sure that both scroll bars are hidden by setting the `scroll` attribute to `no` or changing it through a script. Possible values for this property are the constant strings `yes` and `no`.

Other than `frame` attributes and NN4+/Moz-signed scripts, other browsers do not provide facilities for turning off scroll bars under script control. You can generate a new window (via the `window.open()` method) and specify that its scroll bars be hidden.

Example

To change the scroll bar appearance from the default, the statement is:

```
document.body.scroll = "no";
```

Related Items: `window.scrollbars` property; `window.open()` method.

scrollLeft
scrollTop

Value: Integer.   Read/Write
Compatibility: WinIE4+, MacIE4+, NN7+, Moz+, Safari-

Even though the `scrollLeft` and `scrollTop` properties of the `body` object are the same as those for generic HTML element objects, they play an important role in determining the position of positioned elements (described more fully in Chapter 40 on the CD-ROM). Because the mouse event and element position properties tend to be relative to the visible content region of the browser window, you must take the scrolling values of the `document.body` object into account when assigning an absolute position. Values for both of these properties are integers representing pixels.

Example

Listing 18-18 is an unusual construction that creates a frameset and creates the content for each of the two frames all within a single HTML document. In the left frame of the frameset are two fields that are ready to show the pixel values of the right frame's `xOffset` and `yOffset` properties. The content of the right frame is a 30-row table of fixed width (800 pixels). Mouse-click events are captured by the document level (see Chapter 25), allowing you to click any table or cell border or outside the table to trigger the `showOffsets()` function in the right frame. That function is a simple script that displays the page offset values in their respective fields in the left frame.

LISTING 18-18

Determining Scroll Values

```
<html>
  <head>
    <title>Master of all Windows</title>
```

continued

591

LISTING 18-18 *(continued)*

```
<script type="text/javascript">
function leftFrame() {
    var output = "<html><body><h3>Body Scroll Values<\/h3><hr />\n";
    output += "<form>body.scrollLeft:<input type='text' name='xOffset'
        size=4 /><br />\n";
    output += "body.scrollTop:<input type='text' name='yOffset'
        size=4 /><br />\n";
    output += "<\/form><\/body><\/html>";
    return output;
}

function rightFrame() {
    var output = "<html><head><script type='text/javascript'>\n";
    output += "function showOffsets() {\n";
    output += "parent.readout.document.forms[0].xOffset.value =
        document.body.scrollLeft\n";
    output += "parent.readout.document.forms[0].yOffset.value =
        document.body.scrollTop\n}\n";
    output += "document.onclick = showOffsets\n";
    output += "<\/script><\/head><body><h3>Content Page<\/h3>\n";
    output += "Scroll this frame and click on a table border to view page
        offset values.<br /><hr />\n";
    output += "<table border=5 width=800>";
    var oneRow = "<td>Cell 1<\/td><td>Cell 2<\/td><td>Cell 3<\/td><td>Cell
        4<\/td><td>Cell 5<\/td>";
    for (var i = 1; i <= 30; i++) {
        output += "<tr><td><b>Row " + i + "<\/b><\/td>" + oneRow +
            "<\/tr>";
    }
    output += "<\/table><\/body><\/html>";
    return output;
}
</script>
</head>
<frameset cols="30%,70%">
    <frame name="readout" src="javascript:parent.leftFrame()" />
    <frame name="display" src="javascript:parent.rightFrame()" />
</frameset>
</html>
```

Related Items: window.pageXOffset, window.pageYOffset properties.

text

(See aLink)

topMargin

(See bottomMargin)

vLink

(See aLink)

Methods

createControlRange()

Returns: Array.
Compatibility: WinIE5+, MacIE-, NN-, Moz-, Safari-

This method creates a control range in WinIE5+ browsers. Control ranges are used for control-based selection, as opposed to text-based selection made possible by text ranges. The method only applies to documents in edit mode. In regular document view mode, the createControlRange() method returns an empty array.

createTextRange()

Returns: Object.
Compatibility: WinIE4+, MacIE-, NN-, Moz-, Safari-

The body element object is the most common object to use to generate a TextRange object in IE4+, especially when the text you are about to manipulate is part of the document's body text. The initial TextRange object returned from the createTextRange() method encompasses the entire body element's HTML and body text. Further action on the returned object is required to set the start and end point of the range. See Chapter 36's discussion of the TextRange object for more details (located on the CD-ROM).

Example

See Listing 36-10 (on the CD-ROM) for an example of the createTextRange() method in action.

Related Items: TextRange object (Chapter 36 on the CD-ROM).

doScroll(["scrollAction"])

Returns: Nothing.
Compatibility: WinIE5+, MacIE-, NN-, Moz-, Safari-

Use the doScroll() method to simulate user action on the scroll bars inside a window or frame that holds the current document. This method comes in handy if you are creating your own scroll bars in place of the standard system scroll bars. Scrolling is instantaneous, however, rather than with animation even if the Display control panel is set for animated scrolling. The parameter for this method is one of the string constant values shown in Table 18-4. In practice, occasionally the longer scroll action names more closely simulate an actual click on the scroll bar component, whereas the shortcut versions may scroll at a slightly different increment.

TABLE 18-4

document.body.doScroll() Parameters

Long Parameter	Short Parameter	Scroll Action Simulates
scrollbarDown	down	Clicking the down arrow.
scrollbarHThumb	n/a	Clicking the horizontal scroll bar thumb (no scrolling action).
scrollbarLeft	left	Clicking the left arrow.
scrollbarPageDown	pageDown	Clicking the page down area or pressing PgDn (default).
scrollbarPageLeft	pageLeft	Clicking the page left area.
scrollbarPageRight	pageRight	Clicking the page right area.
scrollbarPageUp	pageUp	Clicking the page up area or pressing PgUp.
scrollbarVThumb	n/a	Clicking the vertical scroll bar thumb (no scrolling action).

Unlike scrolling to a specific pixel location (by setting the body element's scrollTop and scrollLeft properties), the doScroll() method depends entirely on the spatial relationship between the body content and the window or frame size. Also, the doScroll() method triggers the onscroll event handler for the body element object.

Be aware that scripted modifications to body content can alter these spatial relationships. IE is prone to being sluggish in updating all of its internal dimensions after content has been altered. Should you attempt to invoke the doScroll() method after such a layout modification, the scroll may not be performed as expected. You may find the common trick of using setTimeout() to delay the invocation of the doScroll() method by a fraction of a second.

Example

Use The Evaluator (see Chapter 13) to experiment with the doScroll() method in IE5+. Size the browser window so that at least the vertical scroll bar is active (meaning it has a thumb region). Enter the following statement into the top text field and press Enter a few times to simulate clicking the PgDn key:

```
document.body.doScroll()
```

Return to the top of the page and now do the same for scrolling by the increment of the scroll bar down arrow:

```
document.body.doScroll("down")
```

You can also experiment with upward scrolling. Enter the desired statement in the top text field and leave the text cursor in the field. Manually scroll to the bottom of the page and then press Enter to activate the command.

Related Items: body.scroll, body.scrollTop, body.scrollLeft properties; window.scroll(), window.scrollBy(), window.scrollTo() methods.

Event handlers
onafterprint
onbeforeprint
(See the onafterprint event handler for the window object, Chapter 16)

TreeWalker Object

Property	Method	Event Handler
currentNode	firstChild()	(None)
expandEntityReference	lastChild()	
filter	nextNode()	
root	nextSibling()	
whatToShow	parentNode()	
	previousNode()	
	previousSibling()	

Syntax
Creating a TreeWalker object:

```
var treewalk = document.createTreeWalker(document, whatToShow, filterFunction,
entityRefExpansion);
```

Accessing TreeWalker object properties and methods:

```
TreeWalker.property | method([parameters])
```

Compatibility: WinIE-, MacIE-, NN7+, Moz+, Safari-

About this object
The TreeWalker object serves as a container for a list of nodes that meet the criteria defined by the document.createTreeWalker() method, which is used to create the object. The list of nodes contained by a TreeWalker object conforms to the same hierarchical structure of the document from which they are referenced. The TreeWalker object provides a means of navigating through this list of nodes based upon their inherent tree-like structure.

You can think of the TreeWalker object as somewhat of an iterator object since its main purpose is to provide a means of stepping through nodes in a list. However, in this case the list is a hierarchical tree, as opposed to a linear list. The TreeWalker object maintains a pointer inside the list of nodes that always points to the current node. Whenever you navigate through the list using the TreeWalker object, the navigation is always relative to the pointer. For example, referencing the previous or next node through calls to the previousNode() or nextNode() methods depends upon the current position of the node pointer in the tree.

TreeWalker.currentNode

Use the `document.createTreeWalker()` method to create a `TreeWalker` object for a particular document. This method requires a user function that serves as a filter for nodes selected to be part of the tree. A reference to the function is the third parameter of the method call. The return value of this user function can be one of three constant values, which indicate the status of the current node: `NodeFilter.FILTER_ACCEPT`, `NodeFilter.FILTER_REJECT`, or `NodeFilter.FILTER_SKIP`. The difference between `NodeFilter.FILTER_REJECT` and `NodeFilter.FILTER_SKIP` is that descendents of skipped nodes may still qualify as part of the tree, whereas rejected nodes and their descendents are excluded altogether. Following is an example of a user function you could use to create a `TreeWalker` object:

```
function ratingAttrFilter(node) {
    if (node.hasAttribute("rating")) {
        return NodeFilter.FILTER_ACCEPT;
    }
    return NodeFilter.FILTER_REJECT;
}
```

In this example function, only nodes containing an attribute named `rating` are allowed through the filter, which means only those nodes will get added to the list (tree). With this function in place, you then call the `document.createTreeWalker()` method to create the `TreeWalker` object:

```
var myTreeWalker = document.createTreeWalker(document, NodeFilter.SHOW_ELEMENT,
    ratingAttrFilter, false);
```

Now that the `TreeWalker` object is created, you can use its properties and methods to access individual nodes and navigate through the list.

Properties

currentNode

Value: Node reference.   Read/Write
Compatibility: WinIE-, MacIE-, NN7+, Moz+, Safari-

The `currentNode` property returns a reference to the current node, which sits at the location of the tree's node pointer. Although you can use the `currentNode` property to access the current node, you can also use it to set the current node.

Example

To assign a node to the current position in the tree, just create an assignment statement using the `currentNode` property:

```
myTreeWalker.currentNode = document.getElementById("info");
```

Related Item: `root` property.

```
expandEntityReference
filter
root
whatToShow
```
Value: See text.   Read-Only
Compatibility: WinIE-, MacIE-, NN7+, Moz+, Safari-

These properties reflect the parameter values passed into the `document.createTreeWalker()` method upon the creation of the `TreeWalker` object.

Related Item: `document.createTreeWalker()` method.

Methods
```
firstChild()
lastChild()
nextSibling()
parentNode()
previousSibling()
```
Returns: Node reference.
Compatibility: WinIE-, MacIE-, NN7+, Moz+, Safari-

These methods return references to nodes within the hierarchy of the tree-like list of nodes contained by the `TreeWalker` object. There is a parent-child relationship among all of the nodes in the tree, and these functions are used to obtain node references based upon this relationship. The node pointer within the tree moves to the new node whenever you use one of these methods to navigate to a given node. This means you can access the new node as the current node after calling one of these navigation methods.

Example
The following code shows how to obtain the tag name of the parent node of the current node in the `TreeWalker` object:

```
if (myTreeWalker.parentNode()) {
    var parentTag = myTreeWalker.currentNode.tagName;
}
```

Related Items: `nextNode()`, `previousNode()` methods.

```
nextNode()
previousNode()
```
Returns: Node reference.
Compatibility: WinIE-, MacIE-, NN7+, Moz+, Safari-

The `nextNode()` and `previousNode()` methods navigate back and forth in the list of nodes contained by the `TreeWalker` object. It's important to note that these methods operate on the node list as if it has been flattened from a tree into a linear sequence of nodes. Both methods move the internal node pointer to the next or previous node, respectively.

Running Subhead

Example

The following code demonstrates both the node filter function and a typical function you could use to display (in a series of alert windows, perhaps for debugging purposes) the IDs of all elements inside the body that have id attributes assigned. The nextNode() method is called first to advance the TreeWalker's node pointer to the first node of the collection, and then iteratively (inside a do-while construction) to obtain the next node that passes the node filter's test.

```
function idFilter(node) {
    if (node.hasAttribute("id")) {
        return NodeFilter.FILTER_ACCEPT;
    }
    return NodeFilter.FILTER_SKIP;
}

function showIds() {
    var tw =
    document.createTreeWalker(document.body, NodeFilter.SHOW_ELEMENT, idFilter,
false);
    // make sure TreeWalker contains at least one node, and go to it if true
    if (tw.nextNode()) {
        do {
            alert(tw.currentNode.id);
        } while (tw.nextNode());
    }
}
```

Related Items: parentNode() method.

Chapter 19

Link and Anchor Objects

T he Web is based on the notion that the world's information can be strung together by way of the *hyperlink* — the clickable hunk of text or image that enables an inquisitive reader to navigate to a further explanation or related material. Of all the document objects you work with in JavaScript, the link is the one that makes that connection. Anchors also provide guideposts to specific locations within documents.

As scriptable objects going back to the first scriptable browsers, links and anchors are comparatively simple devices. But this simplicity belies their significance in the entire scheme of the Web. Under script control, links can be far more powerful than mere tethers to locations on the Web.

In modern browsers, the notion of separating links and anchors as similar yet distinctly different objects begins to fade. The association of the word *link* with objects is potentially confused by the newer browsers' recognition of the link element (see Chapter 37 on the CD-ROM), which has an entirely different purpose, as a scriptable object. Taking the place of the anchor and link objects is an HTML element object representing the element created by the `<a>` tag. As an element object, the a element assumes all of the properties, methods, and event handlers that accrue to all HTML element objects in modern object models. To begin making that transition, this chapter treats all three types of objects at the same time.

Anchor, Link, and a Element Objects

For HTML element properties, methods, and event handlers, see Chapter 15.

Properties	Methods	Event Handlers
charset		
coords		
hash		
host		
hostname		
href		
hreflang		
Methods		
mimeType		
name		
nameProp		
pathname		
port		
protocol		
rel		
rev		
search		
shape		
target		
type		
urn		

Syntax

Accessing link object properties:

```
(all)      [window.]document.links[index].property
```

Accessing a element object properties:

```
(IE4+)     [window.]document.all.elemID.property | method([parameters])
(IE5+/W3C) [window.]document.getElementById("elemID").property |
           method([parameters])
```

Compatibility: WinIE4+, MacIE4+, NN6+, Moz+, Safari+

About this object

A little scripting history can help you understand where the link and anchor objects came from and how the a element object evolved from them.

Using the terminology of the original object model, the anchor and link objects are both created in the object model from the `<a>` tag. What distinguishes a link from an anchor is the presence of the `href` attribute in the tag. Without an `href` attribute, the element is an anchor object, which has only a single property (`name`) in modern browsers. A link, on the other hand, is much more alive as an object — all because of the inclusion of an `href` attribute, which usually points to a URL to load into a window or frame.

When object models treat HTML elements as objects, both the anchor and link objects are subsumed by the a element object. Even so, one important characteristic from the original object holds true: All a element objects that behave as link objects (by virtue of the presence of an `href` attribute) are members of the `document.links` property array. Therefore, if your scripts need to inspect or modify properties of all link objects on a page, they can do so by way of a `for` loop through the array of link objects. This is true even if you script solely for modern browsers and want to, say, change a style attribute of all links (for example, change their `style.textDecoration` property from `none` to `underline`). The fact that the same element can have different behaviors depending on the existence of one attribute makes me think of the a element object as potentially two different animals. Thus, you see references to link and anchor objects throughout this book when the distinction between the two is important.

Scripting newcomers are often confused about the purpose of the `target` attribute of an a element when they want a scripted link to act on a different frame or window. Under plain HTML, the `target` attribute points to the frame or window into which the new document (the one assigned to the `href` attribute) is to load, leaving the current window or frame intact. But if you intend to use event handlers to navigate (by setting the `location.href` property), the `target` attribute does not apply to the scripted action. Instead, assign the new URL to the `location.href` property of the desired frame or window. For example, if one frame contains a table of contents consisting entirely of links, the `onclick` event handlers of those links can load other pages into the `main` frame by assigning the URL to the `parent.main.location.href` property. You must also cancel the default behavior of any link, as described in the discussion of the generic `onclick` event handler in Chapter 15.

When you want a click of the link (whether the link consists of text or an image) to initiate an action without actually navigating to another URL, you can use a special technique — the `javascript:` pseudo-URL — to direct the URL to a JavaScript function. The URL `javascript:functionName()` is a valid parameter for the `href` attribute (and not just in the link object). You can also add a special `void` operator that guarantees that the called function does not trigger any true linking action (`href="javascript: void someFunction()"`). Specifying an empty string for the `href` attribute yields an FTP-like file listing for the client computer — an undesirable artifact. Don't forget, too, that if the URL leads to a type of file that initiates a browser helper application (for example, to play a QuickTime movie), the helper app or plug-in loads and plays without changing the page in the browser window.

NOTE Usage of the `javascript:` pseudo-URL is controversial. There is no published industry standard that supports it, even though most browsers do. It is also unfriendly to users who visit the page with scripting disabled or unavailable (for example, browsers designed for visually impaired users) because the links won't do anything, leading to frustration. You should also be aware that search engines won't follow these types of links when they work their way through a site.

a.charset

A single link can change the content of more than one frame at the same time with the help of JavaScript. If you want only JavaScript-enabled browsers to act on such links, one approach is to use a `javascript:` pseudo-URL to invoke a function that changes the `location.href` properties of multiple frames. For example, consider the following function, which changes the content of two frames:

```
function navFrames(url1, url2) {
    parent.product.location.href = url1;
    parent.accessories.location.href = url2;
}
```

Then you can have a `javascript:` pseudo-URL invoke this multipurpose function and pass the specifics for the link as parameters:

```
<a href="javascript: void navFrames('products/gizmo344.html',
'access/access344.html')">Deluxe Super Gizmo</a>
```

Or if you want one link to do something for everyone, but something extra for JavaScript-enabled browsers (an approach that is desirable when designing a page for accessibility), you can combine the standard link behavior with an `onclick` event handler to take care of both situations:

```
function setAccessFrame(url) {
    parent.accessories.location.href = url;
}
...
<a href="products/gizmo344.html" target="product"
onclick="setAccessFrame('access/access344.html')">Deluxe Super Gizmo</a>
```

> **NOTE** The property assignment event handling technique in the previous example is a deliberate simplification to make the code more readable. It is generally better to use the more modern approach of binding events using the `addEventListener()` (NN6+/Moz/W3C) or `attachEvent()` (IE5+) method. A modern cross-browser event handling technique is explained in detail in Chapter 25.

Notice here that the `target` attribute is necessary for the standard link behavior, whereas the script assigns a URL to a frame's `location.href` property.

One additional technique allows a single link tag to operate for both scriptable and nonscriptable browsers. For nonscriptable browsers, establish a genuine URL to navigate from the link. Then make sure that the link's `onclick` event handler evaluates to `return false` or cancels the default action. At click time, a scriptable browser executes the event handler and ignores the `href` attribute; a nonscriptable browser ignores the event handler and follows the link. See the discussion of the generic `onclick` event handler in Chapter 15 for more details.

Properties

charset

Value: String   Read/Write
Compatibility: WinIE6+, MacIE6+, NN6+, Moz+, Safari+

The `charset` property represents the HTML 4 `charset` attribute of an a element. It advises the browser of the character set used by the document to which the `href` attribute points. The value is a string of one of the character set codes from the registry at `http://www.iana.org/assignments/character-sets`. The most commonly used character set on the Web is called `ISO-8859-5`.

coords
shape

Value: Strings   Read/Write
Compatibility: WinIE6+, MacIE6+, NN6+, Moz+, Safari+

HTML 4 provides specifications for a elements that accommodate different shapes (rect, circle, and poly) and coordinates when the link surrounds an image. Although the coords and shape properties are present for a element objects in all W3C DOM–compatible browsers, active support for the feature is not present in NN6.

hash
host
hostname
pathname
port
protocol
search

Value: Strings   Read/Write
Compatibility: WinIE3+, MacIE3+, NN2+, Moz+, Safari+

This large set of properties is identical to the same-named properties of the location object (see Chapter 17). All properties are components of the URL that is assigned to the link object's href attribute. Although none of these properties appears in the W3C DOM specification for the a element object, the properties survive in modern browsers for backward compatibility. If you want to script the change of the destination for a link, try modifying the value of the object's href property rather than individual components of the URL.

Related Item: location object

href

Value: String   Read/Write
Compatibility: WinIE3+, MacIE3+, NN2+, Moz+, Safari+

The href property (included in the W3C DOM) is the URL of the destination of an a element equipped to act as a link. URLs can be relative or absolute.

In W3C DOM–compatible browsers, you can turn an anchor object into a link object by assigning a value to the href property even if the a element has no href attribute in the HTML that loads from the server. Naturally, this conversion is temporary, and it lasts only as long as the page is loaded in the browser. When you assign a value to the href property of an a element that surrounds text, the text assumes the appearance of a link (either the default appearance or whatever style you assign to links).

Related Item: location object

a.name

hreflang

Value: String   Read/Write
Compatibility: WinIE6+, MacIE6+, NN6+, Moz+, Safari+

The hreflang property advises the browser (if the browser takes advantage of it) about the written language used for the content to which the a element's href attribute points. Values for this property must be in the form of the standard language codes (for example, en-us for U.S. English).

Methods

Value: String   Read/Write
Compatibility: WinIE4+, MacIE4+, NN-, Moz-, Safari-

The Methods property (note the uppercase M) represents the HTML 4 methods attribute for an a element. Values for this attribute and property serve as advisory instructions to the browser about which HTTP method(s) to use for accessing the destination document. This is a rare case in which an HTML 4 attribute is not echoed in the W3C DOM. In any case, although IE4+ supports the property, the IE browsers do nothing special with the information.

mimeType

Value: String   Read-Only
Compatibility: WinIE4+, MacIE-, NN-, Moz-, Safari-

This property is used to obtain the MIME type of the document linked to by the a element. The HTML 4 and W3C DOM specifications define a type attribute and type property instead of mimeType. The property is a read-only property and, therefore, has no control over the MIME type of the destination document.

Related Item: a.type property

name

Value: String   Read/Write
Compatibility: WinIE3+, MacIE3+, NN2+, Moz+, Safari+

Although a name attribute is optional for an a element serving solely as a link object, it is required for an anchor object. This value is exposed to scripting via the name property. Although it is unlikely that you will need to change the value by scripting, you can use this property as a way to identify a link object from among the document.links arrays in a repeat loop. For example:

```
for (var i = 0; i < document.links.length; i++) {
    if (document.links[i].name == "bottom" {
        // statements dealing with the link named "bottom"
    }
}
```

If this code makes it inside the if clause, you know you've found a link with the name bottom.

nameProp

Value: String   Read-Only
Compatibility: WinIE4+, MacIE4+, NN-, Moz-, Safari-

The IE-specific nameProp property is a convenience property that retrieves the segment of the href to the right of the rightmost forward slash character of the URL. Most typically, this value is the name of the file from a URL. But if the URL also includes a port number, that number is returned as part of the nameProp value.

rel
rev

Value: String   Read/Write
Compatibility: WinIE4+, MacIE4+, NN6+, Moz+, Safari+

The rel and rev properties define relationships in the forward and back directions with respect to the destination document of the a element. In other words, you're describing how a link relates to the document to which it points, as well as how the document relates back. For example, in a table-of-contents page, each link to a chapter might have its rel attribute set to chapter, whereas its rev attribute might be set to contents. Browsers have yet to exploit most of the potential of these attributes and properties.

A long list of values is predefined for these properties, based on the corresponding attribute values specified in HTML 4. If the browser does nothing with a particular value, the value is ignored. You can string together multiple values in a space-delimited list inside a single string. Accepted values are as follows:

alternate	contents	index	start
appendix	copyright	next	stylesheet
bookmark	glossary	prev	subsection
chapter	help	section	

target

Value: String   Read/Write
Compatibility: WinIE3+, MacIE3+, NN2+, Moz+, Safari+

An important property of the link object is the target. This value reflects the window name supplied to the target attribute in the a element.

You can temporarily change the target for a link. But as with most transient object properties, the setting does not survive soft reloads. Rather than alter the target this way, you can safely force the target change by letting the href attribute call a javascript:functionName() psuedo-URL in which the function assigns a document to the desired window.location. If you have done extensive HTML authoring before, you will find it hard to break the habit of relying on the target attribute.

Another drawback to the target attribute is the fact that it isn't supported by the strict XHTML DTD. So if you develop XHTML pages that must validate with the strict DTD, you will not be able to include a target attribute in your <a> tags. Instead, use the page's onload event handler or the a element's onclick event

a.urn

handler to invoke a function that assigns the desired value to the `target` property. In this case, you are using a JavaScript property to sidestep a limitation associated with an HTML attribute.

Related Item: `document.links` property

type

Value: String   Read/Write
Compatibility: WinIE6+, MacIE6+, NN6+, Moz+, Safari+

The `type` property represents the HTML 4 `type` attribute, which specifies the MIME type for the content of the destination document to which the element's `href` attribute points. This is primarily an advisory property for browsers that wish to, say, display different cursor styles based on the anticipated type of content at the other end of the link. Thus far, browsers do not take advantage of this feature. However, you can assign MIME type values to the attribute (for example, `video/mpeg`) and let scripts read those values for making style changes to the link text after the page loads. IE4+ also implements a similar property in the `mimeType` property.

Related Item: `a.mimeType` property

urn

Value: String   Read/Write
Compatibility: WinIE4+, MacIE4+, NN-, Moz-, Safari-

The `urn` property represents the IE-specific `URN` attribute, which enables authors to use a URN (Uniform Resource Name) for the destination of the a element. (See `http://www.ietf.org/rfc/rfc2141.txt` for information about URNs.) This property is not in common use.

Chapter 20

Image, Area, Map, and Canvas Objects

For modern web browsers, images and areas — those items created by the `<img>` and `<area>` tags — are first-class objects that you can script for enhanced interactivity. You can swap the image displayed in an `<img>` tag with other images, perhaps to show the highlighting of an icon button when the cursor rolls atop it. And with scriptable client-side area maps, pages can be smarter about how they respond to users' clicks on image regions.

One further benefit afforded scripters is that they can preload images into the browser's image cache as the page loads. With cached images, the user experiences no delay when the first swap occurs. The need for this capability has diminished slightly with higher bandwidth connections, but it still isn't a bad idea for those users who still rely on connections with speed limitations.

New on the graphical JavaScript scene is the notion of a canvas, which is a graphical region that you can use to carry out graphics operations via JavaScript code. A few browsers already support canvases, so you can get started tinkering with them now.

Image and img Element Objects

For HTML element properties, methods, and event handlers, see Chapter 15.

img

Properties	Methods	Event Handlers
align		onabort
alt		onerror
border		onload
complete		
dynsrc		
fileCreatedDate		
fileModifiedDate		
fileSize		
fileUpdatedDate		
height		
href		
hspace		
isMap		
loop		
longDesc		
lowsrc		
mimeType		
name		
nameProp		
naturalHeight		
naturalWidth		
protocol		
src		
start		
useMap		
vspace		
width		
x		
y		

Syntax

Creating an Image object:

```
imageObject = new Image([pixelWidth, pixelHeight]);
```

Accessing img element and image object properties or methods:

```
(NN3+/IE4+)   [window.]document.imageName. property | method([parameters])
(NN3+/IE4+)   [window.]document.images[index]. property | method([parameters])
(NN3+/IE4+)   [window.]document.images["imageName"]. property |
              method([parameters])
(IE4+)        [window.]document.all.elemID.property | method([parameters])
(IE5+/W3C)    [window.]document.getElementById("elemID").property |
              method([parameters])
```

Compatibility: WinIE4+, MacIE4+, NN3+, Moz+, Safari+

About this object

Before getting into detail about images as objects, it's important to understand the distinction between instances of the static Image object and img element objects. The former exist only in the browser's memory without showing anything to the user; the latter are the elements on the page generated via the <img> (or nonsanctioned, but accepted, <image>) tag. Scripts use instances of the Image object to precache images for a page, but Image object instances obviously have fewer applicable properties, methods, and event handlers because they are neither visible on the page nor influenced by tag attributes.

The primary advantage of treating img elements as objects is that scripts can change the image that occupies the img object's space on the page, even after the document has loaded and displayed an initial image. The key to this scriptability is the src property of an image.

In a typical scenario, a page loads with an initial image. That image's tags specify any of the extra attributes, such as height and width (which help speed the rendering of the page), and specify whether the image uses a client-side image map to make it interactive. (See the area object later in this chapter.) As the user spends time on the page, the image can then change (perhaps in response to user action or some timed event in the script), replacing the original image with a new one in the same space. In legacy browsers that support the img element object, the height and width of the initial image that loads into the element establishes a fixed-sized rectangular space for the image. Attempts to fit an image of another size into that space forces the image to scale (up or down, as the case may be) to fit the rectangle. But in modern browsers (IE4+/Moz/W3C), a change in the image's size is reflected by an automatic reflow of the page content around the different size.

The benefit of separate instances of the Image object is that a script can create a virtual image to hold a preloaded image. (The image is loaded into the image cache but the browser does not display the image.) The hope is that one or more unseen images will load into memory while the user is busy reading the page or waiting for the page to download. Then, in response to user action on the page, an image can change instantaneously rather than forcing the user to wait for the image to load on demand.

To preload an image, begin by assigning a new, empty image object to a global variable. The new image is created via the constructor function available to the Image object:

```
var imageVariable = new Image(width, height);
```

You help the browser allocate memory for the image if you provide the pixel height and width of the precached image as parameters to the constructor function. All that this statement does is create an object in memory whose properties are all empty. To force the browser to load the image into the cache, assign an image file URL to the object's src property:

```
var oneImage = new Image(55,68);
oneImage.src = "neatImage.gif";
```

As this image loads, you see the progress in the status bar just like any image. Later, assign the src property of this stored image to the src property of the img element object that appears on the page:

```
document.images["someImage"].src = oneImage.src;
```

Depending on the type and size of image, you will be amazed at the speedy response of this kind of loading. With small-palette graphics, the image displays instantaneously.

A popular user-interface technique is to change the appearance of an image that represents a clickable button when the user rolls the mouse pointer atop that art. This action assumes that a mouse event fires on an element associated with the object. Image rollovers are most commonly accomplished in two different image states: normal and highlighted. But you may want to increase the number of states to more closely simulate the way clickable buttons work in application programs. In some instances, a third state signifies that the button is switched on. For example, if you use rollovers in a frame for navigational purposes and the user clicks a button to navigate to the Products area, that button stays selected but in a different style than the rollover highlights. Some designers go one step further by providing a fourth state that appears briefly when the user mouses down an image. Each one of these states requires the download of yet another image, so you have to gauge the effect of the results against the delay in loading the page.

The speed with which image swapping takes place may lead you to consider using this approach for animation. Though this approach may be practical for brief bursts of animation, the many other ways of introducing animation to your web page (such as via GIF89a-standard images, Flash animations, Java applets, and a variety of plug-ins) produce animation that offers better speed control. In fact, swapping preloaded JavaScript image objects for some cartoon-like animations may be too fast. You can build a delay mechanism around the setInterval() method, but the precise timing between frames varies with client processor performance.

All browsers that implement the img element object also implement the document.images array. You can (and probably should) use the availability of this array as a conditional switch before any script statements that work with the img element or Image object. The construction to use is as follows:

```
if (document.images) {
    // statements working with images as objects
}
```

Earlier browsers treat the absence of this array as the equivalent of false in the if clause's conditional statement.

Most of the properties discussed here mirror attributes of the img HTML element. For more details on the meanings and implications of attribute values on the rendered content, consult the HTML 4.01 specification (http://www.w3.org/TR/REC-html401) and Microsoft's extensions for IE (http://msdn.microsoft.com/workshop/author/dhtml/reference/objects/img.asp).

Properties

align

Value: String.   Read/Write
Compatibility: WinIE4+, MacIE4+, NN6+, Moz+, Safari+

The align property defines how the image is oriented in relation to surrounding text content. It is a double-duty property because you can use it to control the vertical or horizontal alignment depending on the value (and whether the image is influenced by a float style attribute). Values are string constants, as follows:

```
absbottom    middle
absmiddle    right
baseline     texttop
```

```
bottom          top
left
```

The default alignment for an image is `bottom`. Increasingly, element alignment is handed over to stylesheet control. In modern web pages, designers are encouraged to use stylesheets as opposed to element attributes for presentation details such as alignment.

Listing 20-1 enables you to choose from the different `align` property values as they influence the layout of an image whose HTML is embedded inline with some other text. Resize the window to see different perspectives on word-wrapping on a page and their effects on the alignment choices. Not all browsers provide distinctive alignments for each choice, so experiment in multiple supported browsers.

LISTING 20-1

Testing an Image's align Property

```html
<html>
    <head>
        <title>img align Property</title>
        <script type="text/javascript">
        function setAlignment(sel) {
            document.getElementById("myIMG").align =
                sel.options[sel.selectedIndex].value;
        }
        </script>
    </head>
    <body>
        <h1>img align Property</h1>
        <hr />
        <form>
            Choose the image alignment: <select onchange="setAlignment(this)">
                <option value="absbottom">absbottom</option>
                <option value="absmiddle">absmiddle</option>
                <option value="baseline">baseline</option>
                <option value="bottom" selected="selected">bottom</option>
                <option value="left">left</option>
                <option value="middle">middle</option>
                <option value="right">right</option>
                <option value="texttop">texttop</option>
                <option value="top">top</option>
            </select>
        </form>
        <hr />
        <p>Lorem ipsum dolor sit amet, consectetaur adipisicing elit, sed do
            eiusmod tempor incididunt ut labore et dolore magna aliqua. <img
            alt="image" id="myIMG" src="desk1.gif" height="90" width="120" /> Ut
            enim adminim veniam, quis nostrud exercitation ullamco laboris nisi ut
            aliquip ex ea commodo consequat.</p>
    </body>
</html>
```

Related Items: `text-align`, `float` stylesheet attributes.

alt

Value: String.   Read/Write
Compatibility: WinIE4+, MacIE4+, NN6+, Moz+, Safari+

The alt property enables you to set or modify the text that the browser displays in the image's rectangular space (if height and width are specified in the tag) before the image downloads to the client. Also, if a browser has images turned off (or is incapable of displaying images), the alt text helps users identify what is normally displayed in that space. You can modify this alt text even after the page loads.

Example

Use The Evaluator (Chapter 13) to assign a string to the alt property of the document.myIMG image on the page. First, assign a nonexistent image to the src property to remove the existing image:

```
document.myIMG.src = "fred.gif"
```

Scroll down to the image, and you can see a space for the image. Now, assign a string to the alt property:

```
document.myIMG.alt = "Fred\'s face"
```

The extra backslash is required to escape the apostrophe inside the string. Scroll down to see the new alt text in the image space.

Related Item: title property.

border

Value: Integer.   Read/Write
Compatibility: WinIE4+, MacIE4+, NN3+, Moz+, Safari+

The border property defines the thickness in pixels of a border around an image. Remember that if you wrap an image inside an a element to make use of the mouse events (for rollovers and such), be sure to set the border=0 attribute of the <img> tag to prevent the browser from generating the usual link kind of border around the image. Even though the default value of the attribute is zero, surrounding the image with an a element or attaching the image to a client-side image map puts a border around the image.

Example

Feel free to experiment with the document.myIMG.border property for the image in The Evaluator (Chapter 13) by assigning different integer values to the property.

Related Items: isMap, useMap properties.

complete

Value: Boolean.   Read-Only
Compatibility: WinIE4+, MacIE4+, NN3+, Moz+, Safari-

Sometimes you may want to make sure that an image is not still in the process of loading before allowing another process to take place. This situation is different from waiting for an image to load before triggering some other process (which you can do via the image object's onload event handler). To verify that the img object displays a completed image, check for the Boolean value of the complete property. To verify that a particular image file has loaded, first find out whether the complete property is true; then compare the src property against the desired filename.

An image's `complete` property switches to `true` even if only the specified `lowsrc` image has finished loading. Do not rely on this property alone for determining whether the `src` image has loaded if both `src` and `lowsrc` attributes are specified in the `<img>` tag.

One of the best ways to use this property is in an `if` construction's conditional statement:

```
if (document.myImage.complete) {
    // statements that work with document.myImage
}
```

To experiment with the `image.complete` property, quit and relaunch your browser before loading Listing 20-2 (in case the images are in memory cache). As each image loads, click the "Is it loaded yet?" button to see the status of the `complete` property for the `image` object. The value is `false` until the loading finishes; then, the value becomes `true`. The arch image is the bigger of the two image files. You may have to quit and relaunch your browser between trials to clear the arch image from the cache (or empty the browser's memory cache). If you experience difficulty with this property in your scripts, try adding an `onload` event handler (even if it is empty, as in Listing 20-2) to your `<img>` tag.

LISTING 20-2

Scripting image.complete

```html
<html>
    <head>
        <title></title>
        <script type="text/javascript">
        function loadIt(theImage,form) {
            form.result.value = "";
            document.images[0].src = theImage;
        }
        function checkLoad(form) {
            form.result.value = document.images[0].complete;
        }
        </script>
    </head>
    <body>
        <img alt="image" src="cpu2.gif" width="120" height="90" onload="" />
        <form>
            <input type="button" value="Load keyboard"
            onclick="loadIt('cpu2.gif',this.form)" /> <input type="button"
            value="Load arch" onclick="loadIt('arch.gif',this.form)" />
            <p><input type="button" value="Is it loaded yet?"
                onclick="checkLoad(this.form)" /> <input type="text"
                name="result" /></p>
        </form>
    </body>
</html>
```

> **NOTE**   The property assignment event handling technique in the previous example is a deliberate simplification to make the code more readable. It is generally better to use the more modern approach of binding events using the addEventListener() (NN6+/Moz/W3C) or attachEvent() (IE5+) methods. A modern cross-browser event handling technique is explained in detail in Chapter 25.

Related Items: img.src, img.lowsrc, img.readyState properties; onload event handler.

dynsrc

Value: URL string.   Read/Write
Compatibility: WinIE4-6, MacIE4+, NN-, Moz-, Safari-

The dynsrc property is a URL to a video source file, which (in IE) you can play through an img element. You can turn a space devoted to a static image into a video viewer by assigning a URL of a valid video source (for example, an .avi or .mpg file) to the dynsrc property of the image element object. Unlike the src property of image objects, assigning a URL to the dynsrc property does not precache the video.

You may experience buggy behavior in various IE versions when you assign a value to an image's dynsrc property after the img element renders a .gif or .jpg image. In WinIE5, the status bar indicates that the video file is still downloading, even though the download is complete. Clicking the Stop button has no effect. WinIE5.5+ may not even load the video file, leaving a blank space on the page. MacIE5 changes between static and motion images with no problems, but playing the video file multiple times causes the img element to display black space beyond the element's rectangle.

Related Items: img.loop, img.start properties.

fileCreatedDate
fileModifiedDate
fileUpdatedDate
fileSize

Value: String, Integer (fileSize).   Read-Only
Compatibility: WinIE4+, MacIE5+, NN-, Moz-, Safari-

These four IE-specific properties return information about the file displayed in the img element (whether still or motion image). Three of the properties reveal the dates on which the current image's file was created, modified, and updated. For an unmodified file, its creation and modified dates are the same. The updated date of an image is the date on which the image file was last uploaded to the server; the fileUpdatedDate property is only supported on WinIE5.5+ and MacIE5. The fileSize property reveals the number of bytes of the file.

Date values returned for the first two properties are formatted differently between IE4 and IE5. The former provides a full readout of the day and date; the latter returns a format similar to mm/dd/yyyy. Note, however, that the values contain only the date and not the time. In any case, you can use the values as the parameter to a new Date() constructor function. This enables you to then use date calculations for such information as the number of days between the current day and the most recent modification.

Not all servers provide the proper date or size information about a file or in a format that IE can interpret. Test your implementation on the deployment server to ensure compatibility.

Also, be aware that these properties can be read-only for a file that is loaded in the browser. JavaScript by itself cannot get this information about files on the server that are not loaded in the browser.

 All of these file-related properties are present in the Mac version of IE, but the values are empty.

Example

These properties are similar to the same-named properties of the document object. You can see these properties in action in Listing 18-4. Make a copy of that listing, and supply an image before modifying the references from the document object to the image object to see how these properties work with the img element object.

Or just test them out one at a time using an existing image in the Evaluator (Chapter 13):

```
document.getElementById("myIMG").fileSize
```

Related Items: None.

height
width

Value: Integer.   Read/Write (see text)
Compatibility: WinIE4+, MacIE4+, NN3+, Moz+, Safari+

The height and width properties return and control the pixel height and width of an image object. The property is read/write in all modern browsers that support the img element object. However, the net effect of changing these properties varies from browser to browser. For example, if you adjust the height property of an image in Mozilla, the browser automatically scales the image within the same proportions as the original. But adjusting the width property has no effect on the height property. In IE7, the opposite effect is true in regard to width and height. Any time an image is scaled dynamically, unwanted pixelation can occur in the image, so modify an image's size with extreme care.

Example

Use The Evaluator (Chapter 13) to experiment with the height and width properties. Begin retrieving the default values by entering the following two statements into the top text box:

```
document.myIMG.height
document.myIMG.width
```

Increase the height of the image from its default 90 to 180:

```
document.myIMG.height = 180
```

Next, exaggerate the width:

```
document.myIMG.width = 400
```

View the resulting image.

Related Items: hspace, vspace properties.

href

(See src property)

img.longDesc

hspace
vspace

Value: Integer.   Read/Write
Compatibility: WinIE4+, MacIE4+, NN3+, Moz+, Safari+

The hspace and vspace properties control the pixel width of a transparent margin surrounding an image. Specifically, hspace controls the margins at the left and right of the image; vspace controls the top and bottom margins. Images, by default, have margins of zero pixels.

Example

Use The Evaluator (Chapter 13) to experiment with the hspace and vspace properties. Begin by noticing that the image near the bottom of the page has no margins specified for it and is flush left with the page. Now assign a horizontal margin spacing of 30 pixels:

```
document.myIMG.hspace = 30
```

The image has shifted to the right by 30 pixels. An invisible margin also exists to the right of the image.

Related Items: height, width properties.

isMap

Value: Boolean.   Read/Write
Compatibility: WinIE4+, MacIE4+, NN6+, Moz+, Safari+

The isMap property enables you to set whether the image should act as a server-side image map. When set as a server-side image map, pixel coordinates of the click are passed as parameters to whatever link href surrounds the image. For client-side image maps, see the useMap property later in this chapter.

Example

The image in The Evaluator page is not defined as an image map. Thus, if you type the following statement into the top text box, the property returns false:

```
document.myIMG.isMap
```

Related Item: img.useMap property.

longDesc

Value: URL string.   Read/Write
Compatibility: WinIE6+, MacIE5+, NN6+, Moz+, Safari+

The longDesc property is a URL of a file that is intended to provide a detailed description of the image associated with the img element. Current browsers recognize this property, but do not do anything special with the information — whether specified by script or the longdesc attribute.

Related Item: alt property.

loop

Value: Integer.   Read/Write
Compatibility: WinIE4-6, MacIE4+, NN-, Moz-, Safari-

The loop property represents the number of times a video clip playing through the img element object should run. After the video plays that number of times, only the first frame of the video appears in the image area. The default value is 1; but if you set the value to -1, the video plays continuously. Unfortunately, setting the property to 0 prior to assigning a URL to the dynsrc property does not prevent the movie from playing at least once (except on the Mac, as noted in the dynsrc property discussion earlier in this chapter).

Related Item: dynsrc property.

lowsrc
lowSrc
Value: URL string.   Read/Write
Compatibility: WinIE4+, MacIE4+, NN3+, Moz+, Safari-

For image files that take several seconds to load, modern browsers enable you to specify a lower-resolution image or some other quick-loading placeholder to stand in while the big image crawls to the browser. You assign this alternate image via the lowsrc attribute in the <img> tag. The attribute is reflected in the lowsrc property of an image object.

All compatible browsers recognize the all-lowercase version of this property. NN6 also recognizes an interCap "S" version of the property, lowSrc.

Be aware that if you assign a URL to the lowsrc attribute, the complete property switches to true and the onLoad event handler fires when the alternate file finishes loading: The browser does not wait for the main src file to load.

Example
See Listing 20-4 for the image object's onload event handler to see how the source-related properties affect event processing.

Related Items: img.src, img.complete properties.

mimeType
Value: String.   Read-Only
Compatibility: WinIE6+, MacIE-, NN-, Moz-, Safari-

The mimeType property returns a plain-language description of the MIME type for the image, such as JPEG Image or GIF Image.

Example
You can use the mimeType property in Internet Explorer to determine the format of an image, as the following example demonstrates:

```
if (document.myIMG.mimeType.indexOf("JPEG") != -1) {
    // Carry out JPEG-specific processing
}
```

In this example, the indexOf() method is used to check for the presence of the phrase "JPEG" anywhere in the MIME type string. This works because the string returned in the mimeType property for JPEG images is "JPEG Image".

Related Items: None.

name

Value: Identifier string.   Read/Write
Compatibility: WinIE3+, MacIE3+, NN2+, Moz+, Safari+

The name property returns the value assigned to the name attribute of an img element. Modern browsers allow you to use the ID of the element (id attribute) to reference the img element object via document.all (IE) and document.getElementById(). But references in the form of document.imageName and document.images[imageName] must use only the value assigned to the name attribute.

In some designs, it may be convenient to assign numerically sequenced names to img elements, such as img1, img2, and so on. As with any scriptable identifier, the name cannot begin with a numeric character. Rarely, if ever, will you need to change the name of an img element object.

Example

You can use The Evaluator (Chapter 13) to examine the value returned by the name property of the image on that page. Enter the following statement into the top text box:

```
document.myIMG.name
```

Of course, this is redundant because the name is part of the reference to the object.

Related Item: id property.

nameProp

Value: Filename string.   Read-Only
Compatibility: WinIE5+, MacIE-, NN-, Moz-, Safari-

Unlike the src property, which returns a complete URL in IE, the IE nameProp property returns only the filename exclusive of protocol and path. If your image-swapping script needs to read the name of the file currently assigned to the image (to determine which image to show next), the nameProp property makes it easier to get the actual filename without having to perform extensive parsing of the URL.

Example

You can use The Evaluator Sr. (Chapter 13) to compare the results of the src and nameProp properties in WinIE5+. Enter each of the following statements into the top text box:

```
document.myIMG.src
document.myIMG.nameProp
```

Related Item: img.src property.

naturalHeight
naturalWidth

Value: Integer.   Read-Only
Compatibility: WinIE-, MacIE-, NN6+, Moz+, Safari-

The naturalHeight and naturalWidth properties return the unscaled height and width of the image, in pixels. These properties are useful in situations where script code or img element attributes have scaled an image and you wish to know the image's original size.

Example

Use The Evaluator (Chapter 13) to experiment with the `naturalHeight` and `naturalWidth` properties in a Mozilla-based browser. Begin retrieving the default values by entering the following statement into the top text box:

    document.myIMG.width

Increase the width of the image from its default 120 to 200:

    document.myIMG.width = 200

If you scroll down to the image, you see that the image has scaled in proportion. You can now find out the natural width of the original image by taking a look at the `naturalWidth` property:

    document.myIMG.naturalWidth

The Evaluator will reveal 120 as the natural image width even though the image is currently scaled to 200.

Related Items: `img.height`, `img.width` properties.

protocol

Value: String.　　　　　　　　　　　　　　　　　　　　　　　　　　　　　Read-Only
Compatibility: WinIE4+, MacIE5+, NN-, Moz-, Safari-

The IE `protocol` property returns only the protocol portion of the complete URL returned by the `src` property. This allows your script, for example, to see if the image is sourced from a local hard drive or a web server. Values returned are not the actual protocol strings; rather, they are descriptions thereof: `HyperText Transfer Protocol` or `File Protocol`.

Example

You can use The Evaluator Sr. (Chapter 13) to examine the `protocol` property of the image on the page. Enter the following statement into the top text box:

    document.myIMG.protocol

Related Items: `img.src`, `img.nameProp` properties.

src

Value: URL string.　　　　　　　　　　　　　　　　　　　　　　　　　　　Read/Write
Compatibility: WinIE4+, MacIE4+, NN3+, Moz+, Safari+

The `src` property is the gateway to precaching images (in instances of the `Image` object that are stored in memory) and performing image swapping (in `img` element objects). Assigning a URL to the `src` property of an image object in memory causes the browser to load the image into the browser's cache (provided the user has the cache turned on). Assigning a URL to the `src` property of an `img` element object causes the element to display the new image. To take advantage of this powerful combination, you preload alternate versions of swappable images into image objects in memory and then assign the `src` property of the image object to the `src` property of the desired `img` element object.

In legacy browsers, the size of the image defined by the original `img` element governs the rectangular space devoted to that image. An attempt to assign an image of a different size to that `img` element object causes the image to rescale to fit the rectangle (usually resulting in a distorted image). In all modern browsers,

img.src

however, the `img` element object resizes itself to accommodate the image, and the page content reflows around the new size.

Note that when you read the `src` property, it returns a fully formed URL of the image file including protocol and path. This often makes it inconvenient to let the name of the file guide your script to swap images with another image in a sequence of your choice. Some other mechanism (such as storing the current filename in a global variable) may be easier to work with (and see the WinIE5+ `nameProp` property).

Example

In the following example (see Listing 20-3), you see a few applications of image objects. Of prime importance is a comparison of how precached and regular images feel to the user. As a bonus, you see an example of how to set a timer to automatically change the images displayed in an image object. This feature is a popular request among sites that display advertising banners or slide shows.

As the page loads, a global variable is handed an array of image objects. Entries of the array are assigned string names as index values ("desk1", "desk2", and so on). The intention is that these names ultimately will be used as addresses to the array entries. Each image object in the array has a URL assigned to it, which precaches the image.

The page (see Figure 20-1) includes two `img` elements: one that displays noncached images and one that displays cached images. Under each image is a `select` element that you can use to select one of four possible image files for each element. The `onchange` event handler for each `select` list invokes a different function to change the noncached (`loadIndividual()`) or cached (`loadCached()`) images. Both of these functions take as their single parameter a reference to the form that contains the `select` elements.

To cycle through images at five-second intervals, the `checkTimer()` function looks to see if the timer check box is selected. If so, the `selectedIndex` property of the cached image `select` control is copied and incremented (or reset to zero if the index is at the maximum value). The `select` element is adjusted, so you can now invoke the `loadCached()` function to read the currently selected item and set the image accordingly.

For some extra style points, the `<body>` tag includes an `onunload` event handler that invokes the `resetSelects()` function. This general-purpose function loops through all forms on the page and all elements within each form. For every `select` element, the `selectedIndex` property is reset to zero. Thus, if a user reloads the page, or returns to the page via the Back button, the images start in their original sequence. An `onload` event handler makes sure that the images are in sync with the `select` choices and the `checkTimer()` function is invoked with a five-second delay. Unless the timer check box is checked, however, the cached images don't cycle.

LISTING 20-3

A Scripted Image Object and Rotating Images

```
<html>
   <head>
      <title>Image Object</title>
      <script type="text/javascript">
      // global declaration for 'desk' images array
      var imageDB;
      // pre-cache the 'desk' images
      if (document.images) {
```

```
        // list array index names for convenience
        var deskImages = new Array("desk1", "desk2", "desk3", "desk4");
        // build image array and pre-cache them
        imageDB = new Array(4);
        for (var i = 0; i < imageDB.length ; i++) {
            imageDB[deskImages[i]] = new Image(120,90);
            imageDB[deskImages[i]].src = deskImages[i] + ".gif";
        }
    }
// change image of 'individual' image
function loadIndividual(form) {
    if (document.images) {
        var gifName =
            form.individual.options[form.individual.selectedIndex].value;
        document.getElementById("thumbnail1").src = gifName + ".gif";
    }
}
// change image of 'cached' image
function loadCached(form) {
    if (document.images) {
        var gifIndex =
            form.cached.options[form.cached.selectedIndex].value;
        document.getElementById("thumbnail2").src = imageDB[gifIndex].src;
    }
}
// if switched on, cycle 'cached' image to next in queue
function checkTimer() {
    if (document.images && document.Timer.timerBox.checked) {
        var gifIndex = document.selections.cached.selectedIndex;
        if (++gifIndex > imageDB.length - 1) {
            gifIndex = 0;
        }
        document.selections.cached.selectedIndex = gifIndex;
        loadCached(document.selections);
        var timeoutID = setTimeout("checkTimer()",5000);
    }
}
// reset form controls to defaults on unload
function resetSelects() {
    for (var i = 0; i < document.forms.length; i++) {
        for (var j = 0; j < document.forms[i].elements.length; j++) {
            if (document.forms[i].elements[j].type == "select-one") {
                document.forms[i].elements[j].selectedIndex = 0;
            }
        }
    }
}
// get things rolling
function init() {
    loadIndividual(document.selections);
```

continued

LISTING 20-3   *(continued)*

```
                loadCached(document.selections);
                setTimeout("checkTimer()",5000);
            }
        </script>
    </head>
    <body onload="init()" onunload="resetSelects ()">
        <h1>Image Object</h1>
        <hr />
        <center>
            <table border="3" cellpadding="3">
                <tr>
                    <th></th>
                    <th>Individually Loaded</th>
                    <th>Pre-cached</th>
                </tr>
                <tr>
                    <td align="right"><b>Image:</b></td>
                    <td><img alt="image" src="cpu1.gif" id="thumbnail1"
                        height="90" width="120" /></td>
                    <td><img alt="image" src="desk1.gif" id="thumbnail2"
                        height="90" width="120" /></td>
                </tr>
                <tr>
                    <td align="right"><b>Select image:</b></td>
                    <form name="selections">
                    <td><select name="individual"
                        onchange="loadIndividual(this.form)">
                            <option value="cpu1">Wires</option>
                            <option value="cpu2">Keyboard</option>
                            <option value="cpu3">Disks</option>
                            <option value="cpu4">Cables</option>
                        </select></td>
                    <td><select name="cached" onchange="loadCached(this.form)">
                        <option value="desk1">Bands</option>
                        <option value="desk2">Clips</option>
                        <option value="desk3">Lamp</option>
                        <option value="desk4">Erasers</option>
                    </select></td>
                    </form>
                </tr>
            </table>
            <form name="Timer">
                <input type="checkbox" name="timerBox"
                onclick="checkTimer()" />Auto-cycle through pre-cached images
            </form>
        </center>
    </body>
</html>
```

FIGURE 20-1

The image object demonstration page.

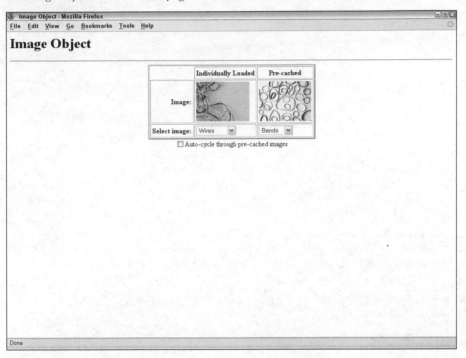

Related Items: `img.lowsrc`, `img.nameProp` properties.

start

Value: String.   Read/Write
Compatibility: WinIE4-6, MacIE4+, NN-, Moz-, Safari-

The `start` property works in conjunction with video clips viewed through the `img` element in IE4+. By default, a clip starts playing (except on the Macintosh) when the image file opens. This follows the default setting of the `start` property: `"fileopen"`. Another recognized value is `"mouseover"`, which prevents the clip from running until the user rolls the mouse pointer atop the image.

Related Items: `img.dynsrc`, `img.loop` properties.

useMap

Value: Identifier string.   Read/Write
Compatibility: WinIE4+, MacIE4+, NN6+, Moz+, Safari+

The `useMap` property represents the `usemap` attribute of an `img` element, pointing to the name assigned to the `map` element in the page (see Listing 20-6). This `map` element contains the details about the client-side image map (described later in this chapter). The value for the `useMap` property must include the hash mark

img.onabort

that defines an internal HTML reference on the page. If you need to switch among two or more image maps for the same `img` element (for example, you swap images or the user is in a different mode), you can define multiple `map` elements each with a different name. Then change the value of the `useMap` property for the `img` element object to associate a different map with the image.

Related Item: `isMap` property.

vspace

(See `hspace`)

width

(See `height`)

x
y

Value: Integer.   Read-Only
Compatibility: WinIE-, MacIE-, NN4, Moz1+, Safari1+

A script can retrieve the x and y coordinates of an `img` element (the top-left corner of the rectangular space occupied by the image) via the x and y properties. These properties are read-only. These properties are generally not used in favor of the `offsetLeft` and `offsetTop` properties of any element, which are also supported in IE.

Related Items: `img.offsetLeft`, `img.offsetTop` properties; `img.scrollIntoView()`, `window.scrollTo()` methods.

Event handlers

onabort
onerror

Compatibility: WinIE4+, MacIE4+, NN3+, Moz+, Safari+

Your scripts may need to be proactive when a user clicks the Stop button while an image loads or when a network or server problem causes the image transfer to fail. Use the `onabort` event handler to activate a function in the event of a user clicking the Stop button; use the `onerror` event handler for the unexpected transfer snafu.

In practice, these event handlers don't supply all the information you may like to have in a script, such as the filename of the image loading at the time. If such information is critical to your scripts, the scripts need to store the name of a currently loading image to a variable before they set the image's `src` property. You also don't know the nature of the error that triggers an error event. You can treat such problems by forcing a scripted page to reload or by navigating to an entirely different spot in your web site.

Example

Listing 20-4 includes an `onabort` event handler. If the images already exist in the cache, you must quit and relaunch the browser to try to stop the image from loading. In that example, I provide a reload option for the entire page. How you handle the exception depends a great deal on your page design. Do your best to smooth over any difficulties that users may encounter.

onload

Compatibility: WinIE3+, MacIE3+, NN2+, Moz+, Safari+

An img object's onload event handler fires when one of three actions occurs: an image's lowsrc image finishes loading; in the absence of a lowsrc image specification, the src image finishes loading; or when each frame of an animated GIF (GIF89a format) appears.

It's important to understand that if you define a lowsrc file inside an <img> tag, the img object receives no further word about the src image having completed its loading. If this information is critical to your script, verify the current image file by checking the src property of the image object.

Be aware, too, that an img element's onload event handler may fire before the other elements on the page have completed loading. If the event handler function refers to other elements on the page, the function should verify the existence of other elements prior to addressing them.

Quit and restart your browser to get the most from Listing 20-4. As the document first loads, the lowsrc image file (the picture of pencil erasers) loads ahead of the computer keyboard image. When the erasers are loaded, the onload event handler writes "done" to the text field even though the main image is not loaded yet. You can experiment further by loading the arch image. This image takes longer to load, so the lowsrc image (set on the fly, in this case) loads way ahead of it.

LISTING 20-4

The Image onload Event Handler

```
<html>
   <head>
      <title></title>
      <script type="text/javascript">
      function loadIt(theImage,form) {
         if (document.images) {
            form.result.value = "";
            document.images[0].lowsrc = "desk1.gif";
            document.images[0].src = theImage;
         }
      }
      function checkLoad(form) {
         if (document.images) {
            form.result.value = document.images[0].complete;
         }
      }
      function signal() {
         if(confirm("You have stopped the image from loading. Do you want to
            try again?")) {
            location.reload();
         }
      }
      </script>
   </head>
```

continued

LISTING 20-4 *(continued)*

```
<body>
    <img alt="image" src="cpu2.gif" lowsrc="desk4.gif" width="120"
    height="90" onload="if (document.forms[0].result)
    document.forms[0].result.value='done'" onabort="signal()" />
    <form>
        <input type="button" value="Load keyboard"
        onclick="loadIt('cpu2.gif',this.form)" /> <input type="button"
        value="Load arch" onclick="loadIt('arch.gif',this.form)" />
        <p><input type="button" value="Is it loaded yet?"
            onclick="checkLoad(this.form)" /> <input type="text"
            name="result" /> <input type="hidden" /></p>
    </form>
</body>
</html>
```

Related Items: `img.src`, `img.lowsrc` properties.

area Element Object

For HTML element properties, methods, and event handlers, see Chapter 15.

Properties	Methods	Event Handlers
alt		
coords		
hash		
host		
hostname		
href		
noHref		
pathname		
port		
protocol		
search		
shape		
target		

Syntax

Accessing `area` element object properties:

```
(NN3+/IE4+)    [window.]document.links[index].property
(IE4+)         [window.]document.all.elemID.property | method([parameters])
(IE4+)         [window.]document.all.MAPElemID.areas[index].property |
               method([parameters])
(IE5+/W3C)     [window.]document.getElementById("MAPElemID).areas[index].property |
               method([parameters])
(IE5+/W3C)     [window.]document.getElementById("elemID").property |
               method([parameters])
```

Compatibility: WinIE4+, MacIE4+, NN3+, Moz+, Safari+

About this object

Document object models treat an image map area object as one of the link (a element) objects in a document (see the anchor object in Chapter 19). When you think about it, such treatment is not illogical at all because clicking a map area generally leads the user to another document or anchor location in the same document — a hyperlinked reference.

Although the HTML definitions of links and map areas differ greatly, the earliest scriptable implementations of both kinds of objects had nearly the same properties and event handlers. Starting with IE4, NN6/Moz, and W3C-compatible browsers, all `area` element attributes are accessible as scriptable properties. Moreover, you can change the makeup of client-side image map areas by way of the `map` element object. The `map` element object contains an array of `area` element objects nested inside. You can remove, modify, or add to the `area` elements inside the `map` element.

Client-side image maps are fun to work with, and they have been well documented in HTML references since Netscape Navigator 2 introduced the feature. Essentially, you define any number of areas within the image based on shape and coordinates. Many graphics tools can help you capture the coordinates of images that you need to enter into the `coords` attribute of the `<area>` tag.

TIP If one gotcha exists that trips up most HTML authors, it's the tricky link between the `<img>` and `<map>` tags. You must assign a name to the `<map>`; in the `<img>` tag, the `usemap` attribute requires a hash symbol (#) and the map name. If you forget the hash symbol, you can't create a connection between the image and its map.

Listing 20-5 contains an example of a client-side image map that allows you to navigate through different geographical features of the Middle East. As you drag the mouse around an aerial image, certain regions cause the mouse pointer to change, indicating that there is a link associated with the region. Clicking a region results in an alert box indicating which region you clicked.

LISTING 20-5

A Simple Client-Side Image Map

```html
<html>
   <head>
      <title></title>
      <script type="text/javascript">
      function show(msg) {
         window.status = msg;
         return true;
      }
      function go(where) {
         alert("We're going to " + where + "!");
      }
      function clearIt() {
         window.status = "";
         return true;
      }
      </script>
   </head>
   <body>
      <h1>Sinai and Vicinity</h1>
      <img alt="image" src="nile.gif" width="320" height="240"
      usemap="#sinai" />
      <map id="sinai" name="sinai">
         <area href="javascript:go('Cairo')" coords="12,152,26,161"
         shape="rect" onmouseover="return show('Cairo')"
         onmouseout="return clearIt()" />
         <area href="javascript:go('the Nile River')"
         coords="1,155,6,162,0,175,3,201,61,232,109,227,167,238,274,239,292,
         220,307,220,319,230,319,217,298,213,282,217,267,233,198,228,154,227,
         107,221,71,225,21,199,19,165,0,149"
         shape="poly" onmouseover="return show('Nile River')"
         onmouseout="return clearIt()" />
         <area href="javascript:go('Israel')" coords="95,69,201,91"
         shape="rect" onmouseover="return show('Israel')"
         onmouseout="return clearIt()" />
         <area href="javascript:go('Saudi Arabia')" coords="256,57,319,121"
         shape="rect" onmouseover="return show('Saudi Arabia')"
         onmouseout="return clearIt()" />
         <area href="javascript:go('the Mediterranean Sea')"
         coords="1,55,26,123" shape="rect"
         onmouseover="return show('Mediterranean Sea')"
         onmouseout="return clearIt()" />
         <area href="javascript:go('the Mediterranean Sea')"
         coords="27,56,104,103" shape="rect"
         onmouseover="return show('Mediterranean Sea')"
         onmouseout="return clearIt()" />
      </map>
   </body>
</html>
```

Properties
alt

Value: String.   Read/Write
Compatibility: WinIE4+, MacIE4+, NN6+, Moz+, Safari+

The alt property represents the alt attribute of an area. Internet Explorer displays the alt text in a tiny pop-up window (tool tip) above an area when you pause (hover) the mouse pointer over it. There is debate among web developers about Microsoft's usage of tool tips for alt text, both in image maps and regular images.

Future browsers may implement this attribute to provide additional information about the link associated with the area element. For the time being, Internet Explorer is the only mainstream browser to use the alt property in any noticeable way.

Related Item: title property.

coords
shape

Value: String.   Read/Write
Compatibility: WinIE4+, MacIE4+, NN6+, Moz+, Safari+

The coords and shape properties control the location, size, and shape of the image hot spot governed by the area element. Shape values that you can use for this property control the format of the coords property values, as follows:

Shape	Coordinates	Example
circ	center-x, center-y, radius	"30, 30, 20"
circle	center-x, center-y, radius	"30, 30, 20"
poly	x1, y1, x2, y2,...	"0, 0, 0, 30, 15, 30, 0, 0"
polygon	x1, y1, x2, y2,...	"0, 0, 0, 30, 15, 30, 0, 0"
rect	left, top, right, bottom	"10, 20, 60, 40"
rectangle	left, top, right, bottom	"10, 20, 60, 40"

The default shape for an area is a rectangle.

Related Items: None.

map

```
hash
host
hostname
href
pathname
port
protocol
search
target
```

(See corresponding properties of the link object in Chapter 19)

noHref

Value: Boolean.   Read/Write
Compatibility: WinIE4+, MacIE4+, NN6+, Moz+, Safari+

The noHref property is used to enable or disable a particular area within a map. The property is true by default, which means an area is enabled. Set the property to false to prevent the area from serving as a link within the map.

shape

(See coords)

map Element Object

For HTML element properties, methods, and event handlers, see Chapter 15.

Properties	Methods	Event Handlers
areas[]		onscroll
name		

Syntax

Accessing map element object properties:

```
(IE4+)       [window.]document.all.elemID.property | method([parameters])
(IE5+/W3C)   [window.]document.getElementById("elemID").property |
             method([parameters])
```

Compatibility: WinIE4+, MacIE4+, NN6+, Moz+, Safari+

About this object

The map element object is an invisible HTML container for all area elements, each of which defines a "hot" region for an image. Client-side image maps associate links (and targets) to rectangular, circular, or polygonal regions of the image.

By far, the most important properties of a map element object are the areas array and, to a lesser extent, its name. It is unlikely that you will change the name of a map. (It is better to define multiple map elements with different names, and then assign the desired name to an img element object's useMap property.) But you can use the areas array to change the makeup of the area objects inside a given client-side map.

Properties

areas[]

Value: Array of area element objects.   Read/Write
Compatibility: WinIE4+, MacIE4+, NN6+, Moz+, Safari+

Use the areas array to iterate through all area element objects within a map element. Whereas Mozilla adheres closely to the document node structure of the W3C DOM, IE4+ provides more direct access to the area element objects nested inside a map. If you want to rewrite the area elements inside a map, you can clear out the old ones by setting the length property of the areas array to zero. Then assign area element objects to slots in the array to build that array.

Listing 20-6 demonstrates how to use scripting to replace the area element objects inside a map element. The scenario is that the page loads with one image of a computer keyboard. This image is linked to the keyboardMap client-side image map, which specifies details for three hot spots on the image. If you then switch the image displayed in that img element, scripts change the useMap property of the img element object to point to a second map that has specifications more suited to the desk lamp in the second image. Roll the mouse pointer atop the images, and view the URLs associated with each area in the status bar (for this example, the URLs do not lead to other pages).

Another button on the page, however, invokes the makeAreas() function (not working in MacIE5), which creates four new area element objects and (through DOM-specific pathways) adds those new area specifications to the image. If you roll the mouse atop the image after the function executes, you can see that the URLs now reflect those of the new areas. Also note the addition of a fourth area, whose status bar message appears in Figure 20-2.

LISTING 20-6

Modifying area Elements on the Fly

```
<html>
   <head>
      <title>map Element Object</title>
      <script type="text/javascript">
      // generate area elements on the fly
      function makeAreas() {
         document.getElementById("myIMG").src = "desk3.gif";
         // build area element objects
```

continued

LISTING 20-6   *(continued)*

```
        var area1 = document.createElement("area");
        area1.href = "Script-Made-Shade.html";
        area1.shape = "polygon";
        area1.coords = "52,28,108,35,119,29,119,8,63,0,52,28";
        var area2 = document.createElement("area");
        area2.href = "Script-Made-Base.html";
        area2.shape = "rect";
        area2.coords = "75,65,117,87";
        var area3 = document.createElement("area");
        area3.href = "Script-Made-Chain.html";
        area3.shape = "polygon";
        area3.coords = "68,51,73,51,69,32,68,51";
        var area4 = document.createElement("area");
        area4.href = "Script-Made-Emptyness.html";
        area4.shape = "rect";
        area4.coords = "0,0,50,120";
        // stuff new elements into MAP child nodes
        var mapObj = document.getElementById("lamp_map");
        while (mapObj.childNodes.length) {
            mapObj.removeChild(mapObj.firstChild);
        }
        mapObj.appendChild(area1);
        mapObj.appendChild(area2);
        mapObj.appendChild(area3);
        mapObj.appendChild(area4);
        // workaround NN6 display bug
        document.getElementById("myIMG").style.display = "inline";
    }

    function changeToKeyboard() {
        document.getElementById("myIMG").src = "cpu2.gif";
        document.getElementById("myIMG").useMap = "#keyboardMap";
    }

    function changeToLamp() {
        document.getElementById("myIMG").src = "desk3.gif";
        document.getElementById("myIMG").useMap = "#lampMap";
    }
    </script>
</head>
<body>
    <h1>map Element Object</h1>
    <hr />
    <img alt="image" id="myIMG" src="cpu2.gif" width="120" height="90"
    usemap="#keyboardMap" />
    <map id="keyboardMap" name="keyboardMap">
        <area href="AlpaKeys.htm" shape="rect" coords="0,0,26,42" />
        <area href="ArrowKeys.htm" shape="polygon"
        coords="48,89,57,77,69,82,77,70,89,78,84,89,48,89" />
        <area href="PageKeys.htm" shape="circle" coords="104,51,14" />
```

```
        </map>
        <map name="lampMap" id="lamp_map">
           <area href="Shade.htm" shape="polygon"
           coords="52,28,108,35,119,29,119,8,63,0,52,28" />
           <area href="Base.htm" shape="rect" coords="75,65,117,87" />
           <area href="Chain.htm" shape="polygon"
           coords="68,51,73,51,69,32,68,51" />
        </map>
        <form>
           <p><input type="button" value="Load Lamp Image"
              onclick="changeToLamp()" /> <input type="button"
              value="Write Map on the Fly" onclick="makeAreas()" /></p>
           <p><input type="button" value="Load Keyboard Image"
              onclick="changeToKeyboard()" /></p>
        </form>
    </body>
</html>
```

FIGURE 20-2

Scripts created a special client-side image map for the image.

Related Items: area element object.

canvas Element Object

For HTML element properties, methods, and event handlers, see Chapter 15.

Properties	Methods	Event Handlers
fillStyle	arc()	
globalAlpha	arcTo()	
globalCompositeOperation	bezierCurveTo()	
lineCap	beginPath()	
lineJoin	clearRect()	
lineWidth	clip()	
miterLimit	closePath()	
shadowBlur	createLinearGradient()	
shadowColor	createPattern()	
shadowOffsetX	createRadialGradient()	
shadowOffsetY	drawImage()	
strokeStyle	fill()	
target	fillRect()	
	getContext()	
	lineTo()	
	moveTo()	
	quadraticCurveTo()	
	rect()	
	restore()	
	rotate()	
	save()	
	scale()	
	stroke()	
	strokeRect()	
	translate()	

Syntax

Accessing canvas element object properties:

```
(W3C)       [window.]document.getElementById("canvasID").property |
                method([parameters])
```

Compatibility: WinIE-, MacIE-, NN-, Moz1.8+, Safari1.3+

About this object

A *canvas* is a relatively new construct that enables you to create a rectangular region on a page that can be drawn to programmatically through JavaScript. Relative to a web page, a canvas appears as an image since it occupies a rectangular space. Unlike images, however, canvas content is generated programmatically using a series of methods defined on the canvas object. Support for canvases first appeared in the Safari browser in version 1.3, and then spread to Mozilla browsers in Mozilla version 1.8, which corresponds to Firefox 1.5.

Canvas objects are created and positioned on the page using the <canvas> tag, which supports only two unique attributes: width and height. After the canvas is created, the remainder of the work associated with creating a canvas graphic falls to JavaScript code. You'll typically want to create a special draw function that takes on the task of drawing to the canvas upon the page loading. The job of the draw function is to use the methods of the canvas object to render the canvas graphic.

Listing 20-7 contains a skeletal page for placing a basic canvas with a border. Notice that there is a draw() function that is ready to receive code that renders the canvas graphic.

LISTING 20-7

A Skeletal Canvas

```
<html>
    <head>
        <title>canvas Object</title>
        <script type="text/javascript">
        function draw() {
            // Draw some stuff
        }
        </script>
        <style type="text/css">
            canvas { border: 1px solid black; }
        </style>
    </head>
    <body onload="draw();">
        <h1>canvas Object</h1>
        <hr />
        <canvas width="350" height="250"></canvas>
    </body>
</html>
```

Listing 20-8 contains a more interesting canvas example that builds on the skeletal page by adding some actual canvas drawing code. The properties and methods in the canvas object provide you with the capability to do some amazing things, so consider this example a rudimentary scratching of the canvas surface.

LISTING 20-8

A Canvas Containing a Simple Chart

```html
<html>
    <head>
        <title>canvas Object</title>
        <script type="text/javascript">
        function draw() {
            var canvas = document.getElementById("chart");
            if (canvas.getContext) {
                var context = canvas.getContext("2d");
                context.lineWidth = 20;

                // First bar
                context.strokeStyle = "red";
                context.beginPath();
                context.moveTo(20, 90);
                context.lineTo(20, 10);
                context.stroke();

                // Second bar
                context.strokeStyle = "green";
                context.beginPath();
                context.moveTo(50, 90);
                context.lineTo(50, 50);
                context.stroke();

                // Third bar
                context.strokeStyle = "yellow";
                context.beginPath();
                context.moveTo(80, 90);
                context.lineTo(80, 25);
                context.stroke();

                // Fourth bar
                context.strokeStyle = "blue";
                context.beginPath();
                context.moveTo(110, 90);
                context.lineTo(110, 75);
                context.stroke();
            }
        }
        </script>
        <style type="text/css">
            canvas { border: 1px solid black; }
        </style>
    </head>
    <body onload="draw();">
        <h1>canvas Object</h1>
        <hr />
```

```
      <canvas id="chart" width="130" height="100"></canvas>
   </body>
</html>
```

Figure 20-3 shows this canvas example in action, which involves the display of a simple bar chart. The thing to keep in mind is that this bar chart is being rendered programmatically using vector graphics, which is quite powerful.

This example reveals a few more details about how canvases work. First off, notice that you must first obtain a context in order to perform operations on the canvas. In reality, you perform graphics operations on a canvas context, not the canvas element itself. The job of a context is to provide you with a virtual surface on which to draw. You obtain a canvas context by calling the getContext() method on the canvas object and specifying the type of context; currently, only the 2d (two-dimensional) context is supported in browsers.

When you have a context, canvas drawing operations are carried out relative to the context. You are then free to tinker with stroke and fill colors, create paths and fills, and do most of the familiar graphical things that go along with vector drawing.

You can find a more complete tutorial and examples dedicated to drawing with the canvas element at http://developer.mozilla.org/en/docs/Canvas_tutorial.

FIGURE 20-3

A simple bar chart created using a vector canvas.

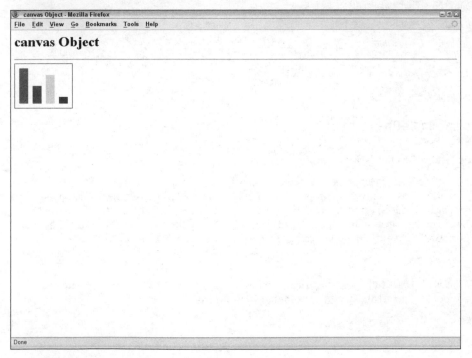

contextObject.fillStyle

Properties
fillStyle

Value: String.   Read/Write
Compatibility: WinIE-, MacIE-, NN-, Moz1.8+, Safari1.3+

The fillStyle property is used to set the brush used in fill operations when a region of a canvas is filled with a color or pattern. Although you can create gradients and other interesting patterns for use in filling shapes, the most basic usage of the fillStyle property is to create a solid color fill by setting the property to an HTML-style color (#RRGGBB). All fill operations that follow the fillStyle setting will use the new fill style.

Example

Setting a fill color simply involves assigning an HTML-style color to the fillStyle property:

```
context.fillStyle = "#FF00FF";
```

Related Item: strokeStyle property.

globalAlpha

Value: Float.   Read/Write
Compatibility: WinIE-, MacIE-, NN-, Moz1.8+, Safari1.3+

The globalAlpha property is a floating-point property that establishes the transparency (or opacity, depending on how you think about it) of the content drawn on a canvas. Acceptable values for this property range from 0.0 (fully transparent) to 1.0 (fully opaque). The default setting is 1.0, which means that all canvases have no transparency initially.

Example

To set the transparency of a canvas to 50 percent transparency, set the globalAlpha property to 0.5:

```
context.globalAlpha = 0.5;
```

Related Item: None.

globalCompositeOperation

Value: String.   Read/Write
Compatibility: WinIE-, MacIE-, NN-, Moz1.8+, Safari1.3+

The globalCompositeOperation property determines how the canvas appears in relation to background content on a web page. This is a powerful property because it can dramatically affect the manner in which canvas content appears with respect to any underlying web page content. The default setting is source-over, which means opaque areas of the canvas are displayed but transparent areas are not. Other popular settings include copy, lighter, and darker, among others.

Example

If you want a canvas to always fully cover the background web page regardless of any transparent areas it may have, you should set the globalCompositeOperation property to copy:

```
context.globalCompositeOperation = "copy";
```

Related Item: None.

lineCap
lineJoin
lineWidth

Value: String, Float (lineWidth).   Read/Write
Compatibility: WinIE-, MacIE-, NN-, Moz1.8+, Safari1.3+

These properties all impact the manner in which lines are drawn on a canvas. The lineCap property determines the appearance of line end points (butt, round, or square). Similar to lineCap is the lineJoin property, which determines how lines are joined to each other (bevel, miter, or round). By default, lines terminate with no special end point (butt) and are joined cleanly with no special joint graphic (miter).

The lineWidth property establishes the width of lines and is expressed as an integer value greater than 0 in the canvas coordinate space. When a line is drawn, its width appears centered over the line coordinates.

Example

You'll often want to change the lineWidth property to get different effects when assembling a canvas graphic. Here's an example of setting a wider line width (10 in this case):

```
context.lineWidth = 10;
```

Related Items: miterLimit, strokeStyle properties.

miterLimit

Value: Float.   Read/Write
Compatibility: WinIE-, MacIE-, NN-, Moz1.8+, Safari1.3+

The miterLimit property is a floating-point value that determines more specifically how lines are joined together. The miterLimit property works in conjunction with the lineJoin property to cleanly and consistently join lines in a path.

Related Item: lineJoin property.

shadowBlur
shadowColor
shadowOffsetX
shadowOffsetY

Value: Integer, String (shadowColor).   Read/Write
Compatibility: WinIE-, MacIE-, NN-, Moz1.8+, Safari1.3+

These properties all work in conjunction to establish a shadow around canvas content. The shadowBlur property determines the width of the shadow itself, whereas shadowColor sets the color of the shadow as an HTML-style RGB value (#RRGGBB). Finally, the shadowOffsetX and shadowOffsetY properties specify exactly how far the shadow is offset from a graphic. The shadowBlur, shadowOffsetX, and shadowOffsetY properties are all expressed in units of the canvas coordinate space.

Example

The following code creates a shadow that is 5 units wide, light gray in color (#BBBBBB), and offset 3 units in both the X and Y directions:

contextObject.arc()

```
context.shadowBlur = 5;
context.shadowColor = "#BBBBBB";
context.shadowOffsetX = 3;
context.shadowOffsetY = 3;
```

Related Item: None.

strokeStyle

Value: String.   Read/Write
Compatibility: WinIE-, MacIE-, NN-, Moz1.8+, Safari1.3+

The strokeStyle property controls the style of strokes used to draw on the canvas. You are free to set the stroke style to a gradient or pattern using more advanced canvas features, but the simpler approach is to just set a solid colored stroke as an HTML-style color value (#RRGGBB). The default stroke style is a solid black stroke.

Example

To change the stroke style to a solid green brush, set the strokeStyle property to the color green:

```
context.strokeStyle = "#00FF00";
```

Related Item: fillStyle property.

Methods

arc(*x, y, radius, startAngle, endAngle, clockwise*)
arcTo(*x1, y1, x2, y2, radius*)
bezierCurveTo(*cp1x, cp1y, cp2x, cp2y, x, y*)
quadraticCurveTo(*cpx, cpy, x, y*)

Returns: Nothing.
Compatibility: WinIE-, MacIE-, NN-, Moz1.8+, Safari1.3+

These methods are all responsible for drawing curves in one way or another. If you have any experience with drawing vector graphics, then you're probably familiar with the difference between arcs, Bezier curves, and quadratic curves.

The arc() method draws a curved line based upon a center point, a radius, and start and end angles. You can think of this method as tracing the curve of a circle from one angle to another. The angles are expressed in radians, not degrees, so you'll probably need to convert degrees to radians:

```
var radians = (Math.PI / 180) * degrees;
```

The last argument to arc() is a Boolean value that determines whether or not the arc is drawn in the clockwise (true) or counterclockwise (false) direction.

The arcTo() method draws an arc along a curve based upon tangent lines of a circle. This method is not implemented in Mozilla until version 1.8.1.

Finally, the bezierCurveTo() and quadraticCurveTo() methods draw a curved line based upon arguments relating to Bezier and quadratic curves, respectively, which are a bit beyond this discussion. To learn more about Bezier and quadratic curves, check out en.wikipedia.org/wiki/Bézier_curve.

beginPath()
closePath()

Returns: Nothing.
Compatibility: WinIE-, MacIE-, NN-, Moz1.8+, Safari1.3+

These two methods are used to manage paths. Call the `beginPath()` method to start a new path, into which you can then add shapes. When you're finished, call `closePath()` to close up the path. The only purpose of `closePath()` is to close a subpath that is still open, meaning that you want to finish connecting an open shape back to its start. If you've created a path that is already closed, there is no need to call the `closePath()` method. Listing 20-8 contains a good example of where the `closePath()` method is unnecessary because the bar shapes don't need to be closed.

clip()

Returns: Nothing.
Compatibility: WinIE-, MacIE-, NN-, Moz1.8+, Safari1.3+

The `clip()` method recalculates the clipping path based upon the current path and the clipping path that already exists. Subsequent drawing operations rely on the newly calculated clipping path.

createLinearGradient(*x1, y1, x2, y2*)
createRadialGradient(*x1, y1, radius1, x2, y2, radius2*)
createPattern(*image, repetition*)

Returns: Gradient object reference, pattern object reference (`createPattern()`).
Compatibility: WinIE-, MacIE-, NN-, Moz1.8+, Safari1.3+

These methods are used to create special patterns and gradients for fill operations. A linear gradient is specified as a smooth color transition between two coordinates, whereas a radial gradient is specified based upon two circles with similar radii. You set the actual color range of a gradient by calling the `addColorStop()` method on the gradient object returned from the `createLinearGradient()` and `createRadialGradient()` methods. The `addColorStop()` method accepts a floating-point offset and a string color value as its only two arguments.

The `createPattern()` method is used to create a fill pattern based upon an image. You provide an image object and a repetition argument for how the image is tiled when filling a region. Repetition options include `repeat`, `repeat-x`, `repeat-y`, and `no-repeat`.

drawImage(*image, x, y*)
drawImage(*image, x, y, width, height*)
drawImage(*image, srcX, srcY, srcWidth, srcHeight, destX, destY, destWidth, destHeight*)

Returns: Nothing.
Compatibility: WinIE-, MacIE-, NN-, Moz1.8+, Safari1.3+

These `drawImage()` methods all draw an image to the context. The difference between them has to do with if and how the image is scaled as it is drawn. The first version draws the image at a coordinate with no scaling, whereas the second version scales the image to the specified target width and height. Finally, the third version enables you to draw a portion of the image to a target location with a scaled width and height.

contextObject.arc()

```
fill()
fillRect(x, y, width, height)
clearRect(x, y, width, height)
```
Returns: Nothing.
Compatibility: WinIE-, MacIE-, NN-, Moz1.8+, Safari1.3+

These methods are used to fill and clear areas. The `fill()` method fills the area within the current path, whereas the `fillRect()` method fills a specified rectangle independent of the current path. The `clearRect()` method is used to clear (erase) a rectangle.

getContext(*contextID*)

Returns: Context object reference.
Compatibility: WinIE-, MacIE-, NN-, Moz1.8+, Safari1.3+

The `getContext()` method operates on a canvas element object, not a context, and is used to obtain a context for further graphical operations. You must call this method to obtain a context before you can draw to a canvas since all of the canvas drawing methods are actually called relative to a context, not a canvas. For the standard two-dimensional canvas context, specify `"2d"` as the sole parameter to the method.

```
lineTo(x, y)
moveTo(x, y)
```
Returns: Nothing.
Compatibility: WinIE-, MacIE-, NN-, Moz1.8+, Safari1.3+

These two methods are used to draw lines and adjust the stroke location. The `moveTo()` method simply moves the current stroke location without adding anything to the path. The `lineTo()` method, on the other hand, draws a line from the current stroke location to the specified point. It's worth pointing out that drawing a line with the `lineTo()` method only adds a line to the current path; the line doesn't actually appear on the canvas until you call the `stroke()` method to carry out the actual drawing of the path.

rect(x, y, width, height)

Returns: Nothing.
Compatibility: WinIE-, MacIE-, NN-, Moz1.8+, Safari1.3+

The `rect()` method adds a rectangle to the current path. Similar to other drawing methods, the rectangle is actually just added to the current path, which isn't truly visible until you render it using the `stroke()` method.

```
restore()
save()
```
Returns: Nothing.
Compatibility: WinIE-, MacIE-, NN-, Moz1.8+, Safari1.3+

It's possible to save and restore the state of the graphic context, in which case you can make changes and then return to a desired state. The context state includes information such as the clip region, line width, fill color, and so forth. Call the `save()` and `restore()` methods to save and restore the context state.

rotate(*angle*)
scale(*x, y*)
translate(*x, y*)

Returns: Nothing.
Compatibility: WinIE-, MacIE-, NN-, Moz1.8+, Safari1.3+

All of the drawing operations that you perform on a canvas are expressed in units relative to the coordinate system of the canvas. These three methods enable you to alter the canvas coordinate system by rotating, scaling, or translating its origin. Rotating the coordinate system affects how angles are expressed in drawing operations that involve angles. Scaling the coordinate system impacts the relative size of units expressed in the system. And finally, translating the coordinate system alters the location of the origin, which affects where positive and negative values intersect on the drawing surface.

stroke()
strokeRect(*x, y, width, height*)

Returns: Nothing.
Compatibility: WinIE-, MacIE-, NN-, Moz1.8+, Safari1.3+

Most of the drawing operations on a canvas impact the current path, which you can think of as a drawing you've committed to memory but have yet to put on paper. You render a path to the canvas by calling the `stroke()` method. If you want to draw a rectangle to the canvas without dealing with the current path, call the `strokeRect()` method.

Chapter 21

The Form and Related Objects

Prior to the advent of dynamic object models and automatic page reflow, the majority of scripting in an HTML document took place in and around forms. Even with all the modern DHTML powers, forms remain the primary user interface elements of HTML documents because they enable users to input information and make choices in very familiar user interface elements, such as buttons, option lists, and so on.

Expanded object models of W3C-compatible browsers include scriptable access to form-related elements that are part of the HTML 4.0 specification. One pair of elements, `fieldset` and `legend`, provides both contextual and visual containment of form controls in a document. Another element, `label`, provides context for text labels that usually appear adjacent to form controls. Although there is generally little reason to script these objects, the browsers give you access to them just as they do for virtually every HTML element supported by the browser.

An interesting new twist in the form equation is Web Forms 2.0, which is a dramatically improved form technology based upon the original form features in HTML 4.0. Web Forms 2.0 establishes a powerful and consistent set of form controls that include built-in validation and much needed standard controls such as an interactive date picker, among other things. Only Opera 9 supports the new features, but other browsers will likely adopt them in the future.

The Form in the Object Hierarchy

Take another look at the JavaScript object hierarchy in the lowest common denominator object model (refer to Figure 14-1). The `form` element object can contain a wide variety of form element objects (sometimes called *form controls*), which I cover in Chapters 22 through 24. In this chapter, however, I focus primarily on the container.

The good news on the compatibility front is that much of the client-side scripting works on all scriptable browsers. Although you are free to use the newer getElementById() approach of addressing forms and their nested elements when your audience exclusively uses newer browsers, it can serve you well to be comfortable with the old-fashioned reference syntax. In fact, one of the older approaches to form referencing is still endorsed by the W3C, so you can use it without worrying about your code being antiquated for the sake of compatibility. Knowing this, almost all example code in this and the next three chapters uses syntax that is compatible across all browsers, including the earliest scriptable browsers.

form Object

For HTML element properties, methods, and event handlers, see Chapter 15.

Properties	Methods	Event Handlers
acceptCharset	handleEvent()	onreset
action	reset()	onsubmit
autocomplete	submit()	
elements[]		
encoding		
enctype		
length		
method		
name		
target		

Syntax

Accessing form object properties or methods:

```
(All)        [window.]document.formName. property | method([parameters])
(All)        [window.]document.forms[index]. property | method([parameters])
(IE4+)       [window.]document.all.elemID.property | method([parameters])
(All/W3C)    [window.]document.forms["formName"]. property | method([parameters])
(All/W3C)    [window.]document.forms["formName"].elements["property"] |
             method([parameters])
(IE5+/W3C)   [window.]document.getElementById("elemID").property |
             method([parameters])
```

Compatibility: WinIE3+, MacIE3+, NN2+, Moz+, Safari+

About this object

Forms and their elements are the most common two-way gateways between users and JavaScript scripts. A form control element provides the only way that users can enter textual information across all browsers.

Form controls also provide somewhat standardized and recognizable user interface elements for the user to make a selection from a predetermined set of choices. Sometimes those choices appear in the form of an on/off check box, in a set of mutually exclusive radio buttons, or as a selection from a list.

As you have seen in many web sites, the form is the avenue for the user to enter information that is sent to the server housing the web files. Just what the server does with this information depends on the programs running on the server. If your web site runs on a server directly under your control (that is, it is *in-house* or *hosted* by a service), you have the freedom to set up all kinds of data-gathering or database search programs to interact with the user. But with some of the more consumer-oriented Internet service providers (ISPs), you may have no server-side application support available — or, at best, a limited set of popular but inflexible CGI (Common Gateway Interface) programs available to all customers of the service. Custom databases or transactional services are rarely provided for this kind of Internet service.

Regardless of your Internet server status, you can find plenty of uses for JavaScript scripts in forms. For instance, rather than using data exchanges (and Internet bandwidth) to gather raw user input and report any input errors, a JavaScript-enhanced document can preprocess the information to make sure that it employs the format that your back-end database or other programs most easily process. All corrective interaction takes place in the browser, without one extra bit flowing across the Net. I devote all of Chapter 43 (on the CD-ROM) to these kinds of form data-validation techniques. Additionally, Web Forms 2.0, which you meet later in this chapter, includes built-in support for many of the common validation tasks that are typically solved via JavaScript.

How you define a `form` element (independent of the user interface elements described in subsequent chapters) depends a great deal on how you plan to use the information from the form's controls. If you intend to use the form exclusively for JavaScript purposes (that is, no queries or postings going to the server), you do not need to use the `action`, `target`, and `method` attributes. But if your web page will be feeding information or queries back to a server, you need to specify at least the `action` and `method` attributes. You need to also specify the `target` attribute if the resulting data from the server is to be displayed in a window other than the calling window and the `enctype` attribute if your form's scripts fashion the server-bound data in a MIME type other than in a plain ASCII stream.

References to form control elements

For most client-side scripting, user interaction comes from the elements within a form; the `form` element object is merely a container for the various control elements. If your scripts perform any data validation checks on user entries prior to submission or other calculations, many statements have the `form` object as part of the reference to the element.

A complex HTML document can have multiple `form` objects. Each `<form>...</form>` tag pair defines one form. You don't receive any penalties (except for potential confusion on the part of someone reading your script) if you reuse a name for an element in each of a document's forms. For example, if each of three forms has a grouping of radio buttons with the name "choice," the object reference to each button ensures that JavaScript doesn't confuse them. The reference to the first button of each of those button groups is as follows:

```
document.forms[0].choice[0]
document.forms[1].choice[0]
document.forms[2].choice[0]
```

If you assign identifiers to `id` attributes, however, you should not reuse an identifier on the same page.

Passing forms and elements to functions

When a form or form element contains an event handler that calls a function defined elsewhere in the document, you can use a couple of shortcuts to simplify the task of addressing the objects while the function does its work. Failure to grasp this concept not only causes you to write more code than you have to, but it also hopelessly loses you when you try to trace somebody else's code in his or her JavaScripted document. The watchword in event handler parameters is

    this

which represents a reference to the current object that contains the event handler attribute. For example, consider the function and form definition in Listing 21-1. The entire user interface for this listing consists of form elements, as shown in Figure 21-1.

LISTING 21-1

Passing the form Object as a Parameter

```
<html>
    <head>
        <title>Beatle Picker</title>
        <script type="text/javascript">
        function processData(form) {
            for (var i = 0; i < form.Beatles.length; i++) {
                if (form.Beatles[i].checked) {
                    break;
                }
            }
            var chosenBeatle = form.Beatles[i].value;
            var chosenSong = form.song.value;
            alert("Looking to see if " + chosenSong + " was written by " +
                chosenBeatle + "...");
        }

        function checkSong(songTitle) {
            var enteredSong = songTitle.value;
            alert("Making sure that " + enteredSong +
                " was recorded by the Beatles.");
        }
        </script>
    </head>
    <body>
        <form name="Abbey Road">
            Choose your favorite Beatle:
            <input type="radio" name="Beatles" id="Beatles1"
                value="John Lennon" checked="true" />John
            <input type="radio" name="Beatles" id="Beatles2"
                value="Paul McCartney" />Paul
            <input type="radio" name="Beatles" id="Beatles3"
                value="George Harrison" />George
```

```
        <input type="radio" name="Beatles" id="Beatles4"
            value="Ringo Starr" />Ringo
        <p>Enter the name of your favorite Beatles song:<br />
        <input type="text" name="song" id="song" value="Eleanor Rigby"
            onchange="checkSong(this)" /></p>
        <p><input type="button" name="process" id="process"
            value="Process Request..." onclick="processData(this.form)" /></p>
    </form>
  </body>
</html>
```

> **NOTE** The property assignment event handling technique in the previous example is a deliberate simplification to make the code more readable. It is generally better to use the more modern approach of binding events using the addEventListener() (NN6+/Moz/W3C) or attachEvent() (IE5+) methods. A modern cross-browser event handling technique is explained in detail in Chapter 25.

FIGURE 21-1

Controls pass different object references to functions in Listing 21-1.

form

The processData() function, which needs to read and write properties of multiple form control elements, can reference the controls in two ways. One way is to have the onclick event handler (in the button element at the bottom of the document) call the processData() function and not pass any parameters. Inside the function, all references to objects (such as the radio buttons or the song field) must be complete references, such as

```
document.forms[0].song.value
```

to retrieve the value entered into the song field.

A more efficient way is to send a reference to the form object as a parameter with the call to the function (as shown in Listing 21-1). By specifying this.form as the parameter, you tell JavaScript to send along everything it knows about the form from which the function is called. This works because form is a property of every form control element; the property is a reference to the form that contains the control. Therefore, this.form passes the value of the form property of the control.

At the function, the reference to the form object is assigned to a variable name (arbitrarily set to form here) that appears in parentheses after the function name. I use the parameter variable name form here because it represents an entire form. But you can use any valid variable name you like.

The reference to the form contains everything the browser needs to know to find that form within the document. Any statements in the function can therefore use the parameter value in place of the longer, more cumbersome reference to the form. Thus, here I can use form to take the place of document.forms[0] or document.forms["Beatles"] in any address. To get the value of the song field, the reference is:

```
form.song.value
```

Had I assigned the form object to a parameter variable called sylvester, the reference would have been:

```
sylvester.song.value
```

When a function parameter is a reference to an object, statements in the function can retrieve or set properties of that object as well as invoke the object's methods.

Another version of the this parameter passing style simply uses the word this as the parameter. Unlike this.form, which passes a reference to the entire form connected to a particular element, this passes a reference only to that one element. In Listing 21-1, you can add an event handler to the song field to do some validation of the entry (to make sure that the entry appears in a database array of Beatles' songs created elsewhere in the document). Therefore, you want to send only the field object to the function for analysis:

```
<input type="text" name="song" id="song" onchange="checkSong(this)" />
```

You then have to create a function to catch this call:

```
function checkSong(songTitle) {
    var enteredSong = songTitle.value;
    alert("Making sure that " + enteredSong + " was recorded by the Beatles.");
}
```

Within this function, you can go straight to the heart — the value property of the field element — without a long reference.

One further extension of this methodology passes only a single property of a form control element as a parameter. In the last example, the checkSong() function needs only the value property of the field, so the event handler can pass `this.value` as a parameter. Because `this` refers to the very object in which the event handler appears, the `this.propertyName` syntax enables you to extract and pass along a single property:

```
<input type="text" name="song" id="song" onchange="checkSong(this.value)" />
```

A benefit of this way of passing form element data is that the function doesn't have to do as much work:

```
function checkSong(songTitle) {
    alert("Making sure that " + songTitle + " was recorded by the Beatles.");
}
```

Unlike passing object references (like the form and text field objects above), when you pass a property value (for example, `this.value`), the property's value is passed with no reference to the object from which it came. This suffices when the function just needs the value to do its job. However, if part of that job is to modify the object's property (for example, converting all text from a field to uppercase and redisplaying the converted text), the value passed to the function does not maintain a "live" connection with its object. To modify a property of the object that invokes an event handler function, you need to pass some object reference so that the function knows where to go to work on the object.

> **TIP** Many programmers with experience in other languages expect parameters to be passed either by reference or by value, but not both ways. The rule of thumb in JavaScript, however, is fairly simple: object references are passed by reference; property values are passed by value.

Here are some guidelines to follow when deciding what kind of value to pass to an event handler function:

- Pass the entire form control object (`this`) when the function needs to make subsequent access to that same element (perhaps reading an object's `value` property, converting the value to all uppercase letters, and then writing the result back to the same object's `value` property).

- Pass only one property (`this.propertyName`) when the function needs read-only access to that property.

- Pass the entire `form` element object (`this.form`) for the function to access multiple elements inside a form (for example, a button click means that the function must retrieve a field's content). Remember, too, that control objects all have a `form` property, which is a reference to the containing `form` object. Therefore, if you pass only `this`, the function can still obtain the form reference.

Also be aware that you can submit multiple parameters (for example, `onclick="someFunction (this.form, this.name)"`) or even an entirely different object from the same form (for example, `onclick="someFunction(this.form.emailAddr.value)"`). Simply adjust your function's incoming parameters accordingly. (See Chapter 34 for more details about custom functions.)

E-mailing forms

A common request among scripters is how to send a form via e-mail to the page's author. This includes the occasional desire to send "secret" e-mail to the author whenever someone visits the web site. Let me address the privacy issue first.

A site visitor's e-mail address is valuable personal information that you should not retrieve without the visitor's permission or knowledge. Early browser versions employed various approaches to help safeguard e-mail addresses. Some were more effective than others. Due to the unreliable nature and occasionally awkward user interface of mailing a form via the `mailto:` URL, I do not recommend its use.

form

Many ISPs that host web sites provide standard CGIs for forwarding forms to an e-mail address of your choice. Search the Web for "formmail service" to locate third-party suppliers of this feature if you don't have access to server programming for yourself.

The remaining discussion about mailing forms focuses primarily on modern browsers and assumes an ideally configured e-mail program is installed. You should be aware that mailing forms in the following ways is controversial in some web standards circles since making an assumption about what the user has installed is somewhat of a leap of faith. Consequently, the W3C HTML specification does not endorse these techniques specifically. Use these facilities judiciously and only after extensive testing on the client browsers you intend to support.

If you want to have forms submitted as e-mail messages, you must attend to three `<form>` tag attributes. The first is the `method` attribute. You must set it to `POST`. Next comes `enctype`. If you omit this attribute, the e-mail client sends the form data as an attachment consisting of escaped name-value pairs, as in this example:

```
name=Danny+Goodman&rank=Scripter+First+Class&serialNumber=042
```

But if you set the `enctype` attribute to text/plain, the form name-value pairs are placed in the body of the mail message in a more human-readable format:

```
name=Danny Goodman
rank=Scripter First Class
serialNumber=042
```

The last attribute of note is the `action` attribute, which is normally the spot to place a URL to another file or server CGI. Substitute the URL with the special `mailto:` URL followed by an optional parameter for the subject. Here is an example:

```
action="mailto:prez@whitehouse.gov?subject=Opinion%20Poll"
```

To sum up, the following example shows the complete `<form>` tag for e-mailing the form:

```
<form name="entry"
    method="POST"
    enctype="text/plain"
    action="mailto:prez@whitehouse.gov?subject=Opinion Poll">
```

None of this requires any JavaScript at all. But seeing how you can use the attributes — and the fact that these attributes are exposed as properties of the `form` element object — you might see some extended possibilities for script control over forms.

Changing form attributes

All modern browsers expose `form` element attributes as modifiable properties. Therefore, you can change, say, the action of a form via a script in response to user interaction on your page. For example, you can have two different CGI programs invoked on your server depending on whether a form's check box is checked.

TIP The best opportunity to change the properties of a `form` element object is in a function invoked by the form's `onsubmit` event handler. The modifications are performed at the last instant prior to actual submission, leaving no room for user-induced glitches to get in the way.

Buttons in forms

A common mistake that newcomers to scripting make is defining all clickable buttons as the submit type of input object (`<input type="submit">`). The Submit button does exactly what it says — it submits the form. If you don't set any `method` or `action` attributes of the `<form>` tag, the browser inserts its default values for you: `method=GET` and `action=pageURL`. When you submit a form with these attributes, the page reloads itself and resets all field values to their initial values.

Use a Submit button only when you want the button to actually submit the form. If you want a button for other types of action, use the button style (`<input type="button">`). A regular button can invoke a function that performs some internal actions and then invokes the `form` element object's `submit()` method to submit the form under script control.

Redirection after submission

Undoubtedly, you have submitted a form to a site and seen a "Thank You" page come back from the server to verify that your submission was accepted. This is warm and fuzzy, if not logical, feedback for the submission action. It is not surprising that you would want to re-create that effect even if the submission is to a `mailto:` URL. Unfortunately, a problem gets in the way.

A common sense approach to the situation calls for a script to perform the submission (via the `form` `.submit()` method) and then navigate to another page that does the "Thank You." Here is such a scenario from inside a function triggered by a click of a link surrounding a nice, graphical Submit button:

```
function doSubmit() {
    document.forms[0].submit();
    location.href = "thanks.html";
}
```

The problem is that when another statement executes immediately after the `form.submit()` method, the submission is canceled. In other words, the script does not wait for the submission to complete itself and verify to the browser that all is well (even though the browser appears to know how to track that information given the status bar feedback during submission). The point is, because JavaScript does not provide an event that is triggered by a successful submission, there is no sure-fire way to display your own "Thank You" page.

Don't be tempted by the `window.setTimeout()` method to change the location after some number of milliseconds following the `form.submit()` method. You cannot predict how fast the network and/or server is for every visitor. If the submission does not complete before the timeout ends, the submission is still canceled — even if it is partially complete.

Form element arrays

Document object models provide a feature that is beneficial to a lot of scripters. If you create a series of like-named objects, they automatically become an array of objects accessible via array syntax (see Chapter 7). This is particularly helpful when you create forms with columns and rows of fields, such as in an order form. By assigning the same name to all fields in a column, you can employ `for` loops to cycle through each row using the loop index as an array index.

As an example, the following code shows a typical function that calculates the total for an order form row (and calls another custom function to format the value):

```
function extendRows(form) {
    for (var i = 0; i < Qty.length; i++) {
        var rowSum = form.Qty[i].value * form.Price[i].value;
        form.Total[i].value = formatNum(rowSum,2);
    }
}
```

All fields in the Qty column are named `Qty`. The item in the first row has an array index value of zero and is addressed as `form.Qty[i]`.

About <input> element objects

Whereas this chapter focuses strictly on the `form` element as a container of controls, the next three chapters discuss different types of controls that nest inside a form. Many of these controls share the same HTML tag: `<input>`. Only the `type` attribute of the `<input>` tag determines whether the browser shows you a clickable button, a check box, a text field, or so on. The fact that one element has so many guises makes the system seem illogical at times to scripters.

An `input` element has some attributes (and corresponding scriptable object properties) that simply don't apply to every type of form control. For example, although the `maxLength` property of a text box makes perfect sense in limiting the number of characters that a user can type into it, the property has no bearing whatsoever on form controls that act as clickable buttons. Similarly, you can switch a radio button or check box on or off by adjusting the `checked` property; however, that property simply doesn't apply to a text box.

As the document object models have evolved, they have done so in an increasingly object-oriented way. The result in this form-oriented corner of the model is that all elements created via the `<input>` tag have a long list of characteristics that they all share by virtue of being types of `input` elements—they inherit the properties and methods that are defined for any `input` element. To try to limit the confusion, I divide the chapters in this book that deal with `input` elements along functional lines (clickable buttons in one chapter, text fields in the other), and only list and discuss those `input` element properties and methods that apply to the specific control type.

In the meantime, this chapter continues with details of the `form` element object.

Properties
acceptCharset
Value: String.   Read/Write
Compatibility: WinIE5+, MacIE5+, NN6+, Moz+, Safari+

The `acceptCharset` property represents the `acceptcharset` attribute of the `form` element in HTML 4.0. The value is a list of one or more recognized character sets that the server receiving the form must support. For a list of registered character set names, see `http://www.iana.org/assignments/character-sets`.

Related Items: None.

action

Value: URL string.   Read/Write (see text)
Compatibility: WinIE3+, MacIE3+, NN2+, Moz+, Safari+

The `action` property (along with the `method` and `target` properties) primarily functions for HTML authors whose pages communicate with server-based CGI scripts. This property is the same as the value you assign to the `action` attribute of a `<form>` tag. The value is typically a URL on the server where queries or postings are sent for submission.

User input may affect how you want your page to access a server. For example, a checked box in your document may set a form's `action` property so that a CGI script on one server handles all the input, whereas an unchecked box means the form data goes to a different CGI script or a CGI script on an entirely different server. Or, one setting may direct the action to one `mailto:` address, whereas another setting sets the `action` property to a different `mailto:` address.

Although the specifications for all three related properties indicate that you can set them on the fly, such changes are ephemeral. A soft reload eradicates any settings you make to these properties, so you should make changes to these properties only in the same script function that submits the form (see `form.submit()` later in this chapter).

Related Items: `form.method`, `form.target`, `form.encoding` properties.

autocomplete

Value: String.   Read/Write
Compatibility: WinIE5+, MacIE-, NN-, Moz-, Safari-

Microsoft added a feature to forms starting with WinIE5 that allows the browser to supply hints for filling out form controls if the controls' names map to a set of single-line text controls defined via some additional attributes linked to the vCard XML schema. For details on implementing this browser feature, see `http://msdn.microsoft.com/library/default.asp?url=/workshop/author/dhtml/reference/properties/autocomplete.asp`. Values for the `autoComplete` property are your choice of two strings: `on` or `off`. In either case, the `form` element object does not report knowing about this property unless you set the `autocomplete` attribute in the form's tag.

Related Items: None.

elements[]

Value: Array of form control elements.   Read-Only
Compatibility: WinIE3+, MacIE3+, NN2+, Moz+, Safari+

Elements include all the user interface elements defined for a form: text fields, buttons, radio buttons, check boxes, selection lists, and more. The `elements` property is an array of all form control items defined within the current form. For example, if a form defines three `<input>` items, the `elements` property for that form is an array consisting of three entries (one for each item in source code order). Each entry is a valid reference to that element; so, to extract properties or call methods for those elements, your script must dig deeper in the reference. Therefore, if the first element of a form is a text field and you want to extract the string currently showing in the field (a text element's `value` property), the reference looks like this:

```
document.forms[0].elements[0].value
```

form.elements

Notice that this reference summons two array-oriented properties along the way: one for the document's `forms` property and one for the form's `elements` property.

In practice, I suggest you refer to form controls (and forms) by their names (or IDs if you prefer to use `document.getElementById()`). This allows you the flexibility to move controls around the page as you fine-tune the design, and you don't have to worry about the source code order of the controls. The `elements` array comes in handy when you need to iterate through all of the controls within a form. If your script needs to loop through all elements of a form in search of particular kinds of elements, use the `type` property of every `form` control object to identify which kind of object it is. The `type` property consists of the same string used in the `type` attribute of an `<input>` tag.

Overall, I prefer to generate meaningful names for each form control element and use those names in references throughout my scripts. The `elements` array helps with form control names, as well. Instead of a numeric index to the `elements` array, you can use the string name of the control element as the index. Thus, you can create a generic function that processes any number of form control elements, and simply pass the string name of the control as a parameter to the function. Then use that parameter as the `elements` array index value. For example:

```
function putVal(controlName, val) {
    document.forms[0].elements[controlName].value = val;
}
```

If you want to modify the number of controls within a form, you should use the element and/or node management facilities of the browser(s) of your choice. For example, in modern browsers you can assemble the HTML string for an entirely new set of form controls and then assign that string to the `innerHTML` property of the `form` element object.

> **NOTE** As handy as it may be, in a strict W3C approach to JavaScript, you wouldn't use the `innerHTML` property since it isn't officially part of the W3C standard. However, it is often too powerful a convenience property to ignore, as much of the code throughout this book is a testament. The book does show the W3C node manipulation alternative to `innerHTML` in some examples. Refer to Chapter 18 for a thorough explanation and examples of the W3C alternative to `innerHTML`.

The document in Listing 21-2 demonstrates a practical use of the `elements` property. A form contains four fields and some other elements mixed in between (see Figure 21-2). The first part of the function that acts on these items repeats through all the elements in the form to find out which ones are text box objects and which text box objects are empty. Notice how I use the `type` property to separate text box objects from the rest, even when radio buttons appear amid the fields. If one field has nothing in it, I alert the user and use that same index value to place the insertion point at the field with the field's `focus()` method.

LISTING 21-2

Using the form.elements Array

```html
<html>
    <head>
        <title>Elements Array</title>
        <script type="text/javascript">
        function verifyIt() {
            var form = document.forms[0];
            for (i = 0; i < form.elements.length; i++) {
                if (form.elements[i].type == "text" &&
                    form.elements[i].value == "") {
                    alert("Please fill out all fields.");
                    form.elements[i].focus();
                    break;
                }
                // more tests
            }
            // more statements
        }
        </script>
    </head>
    <body>
        <form>
            Enter your first name:<input type="text" name="firstName"
                id="firstName" />
            <p>Enter your last name:<input type="text" name="lastName"
                id="lastName" /></p>
            <p><input type="radio" name="gender" id="gender1" />Male
                <input type="radio" name="gender" id="gender2" />Female</p>
            <p>Enter your address:<input type="text" name="address" id="address"
                /></p>
            <p>Enter your city:<input type="text" name="city" id="city" /></p>
            <p><input type="checkbox" name="retired" id="retired" />I am
                retired</p>
        </form>
        <form>
            <input type="button" name="act" id="act" value="Verify"
                onclick="verifyIt()" />
        </form>
    </body>
</html>
```

FIGURE 21-2

The elements array helps find text fields for validation.

Related Items: text, textarea, button, radio, checkbox, select objects.

encoding
enctype

Value: MIME type string.   Read/Write (see text)
Compatibility: WinIE6+, MacIE5+, NN6+, Moz+, Safari+

You can define a form to alert a server when the data you submit is in a MIME type. The encoding property reflects the setting of the enctype attribute in the form definition. The enctype property name is defined for form element objects in the W3C DOM (with encoding removed), but NN6+ provides both properties for backward and forward compatibility.

For mailto: URLs, I recommend setting this value (in the tag or via script) to "text/plain" to have the form contents placed in the mail message body. If the definition does not have an enctype attribute, this property is an empty string.

Related Items: form.action, form.method properties.

length

Value: Integer.   Read-Only
Compatibility: WinIE3+, MacIE3+, NN2+, Moz+, Safari+

The length property of a form element object provides the same information as the length property of the form's elements array. The property provides a convenient, if not entirely logical, shortcut to retrieving the number of controls in a form.

Related Items: form.elements property.

method

Value: String (GET or POST).   Read/Write (see text)
Compatibility: WinIE3+, MacIE3+, NN2+, Moz+, Safari+

A form's method property is either the GET or POST value (not case-sensitive) assigned to the method attribute in a <form> definition. Terminology overlaps here a bit, so be careful to distinguish a form's method of transferring its data to a server from the object-oriented method (action or function) that all JavaScript forms have.

The method property is of primary importance to HTML documents that submit a form's data to a server-based CGI script because it determines the format used to convey this information. For example, to submit a form to a mailto: URL, the method property must be POST. Details of forms posting and CGI processing are beyond the scope of this book. Consult HTML or CGI documentation to determine which is the appropriate setting for this attribute in your web server environment. If a form does not have a method attribute explicitly defined for it, the default value is GET.

Related Items: form.action, form.target, form.encoding properties.

name

Value: Identifier string.   Read/Write
Compatibility: WinIE3+, MacIE3+, NN2+, Moz+, Safari+

Assigning a name to a form via the name attribute is optional but highly recommended when your scripts need to reference a form or its elements. This attribute's value is retrievable as the name property of a form. You don't have much need to read this property unless you inspect another source's document for its form construction, as in:

```
var formName = parent.frameName.document.forms[0].name;
```

Moreover, because server-side CGI programs frequently rely on the name of the form for validation purposes, it is unlikely you will need to change this property.

target

Value: Identifier string.   Read/Write (see text)
Compatibility: WinIE3+, MacIE3+, NN2+, Moz+, Safari+

Whenever an HTML document submits a query to a server for processing, the server typically sends back an HTML page — whether it is a canned response or, more likely, a customized page based on the input provided by the user. You see this situation all the time when you perform a search at web sites. In a multi-frame or multiwindow environment, you may want to keep the form part of this transaction in view for the

form.reset()

user but leave the responding page in a separate frame or window for viewing. The purpose of the `target` attribute of a `<form>` definition is to enable you to specify where the output from the server's query should be displayed.

The value of the `target` property is the name of the window or frame. For instance, if you define a frameset with three frames and assign the names `Frame1`, `Frame2`, and `Frame3` to them, you need to supply one of these names (as a quoted string) as the parameter of the `target` attribute of the `<form>` definition. Browsers also observe four special window names that you can use in the `<form>` definition: `_top`, `_parent`, `_self`, and `_blank`. To set the target as a separate subwindow opened via a script, use the window name from the `window.open()` method's second parameter and not the window object reference that the method returns.

If you code your page to validate according to strict XHTML, you won't be able to include a `target` attribute for a form. But you can still use a script to assign a value to the property without interfering with the validation.

Related Items: form.action, form.method, form.encoding properties.

Methods
reset()
Returns: Nothing.
Compatibility: WinIE4+, MacIE4+, NN3+, Moz+, Safari+

A common practice, especially with a long form, is to provide a button that enables the user to return all the form elements to their default settings. The standard Reset button (a separate object type described in Chapter 22) does that task just fine. But if you want to clear the form using script control, you must do so by invoking the `reset()` method for the form. More than likely, such a call is initiated from outside the form, perhaps from a function or graphical button. In such cases, make sure that the reference to the `reset()` method includes the complete reference to the form you want to reset—even if the page only has one form defined for it.

In Listing 21-3, I assign the act of resetting the form to the `href` attribute of a link object (that is attached to a graphic called `reset.jpg`). I use the `javascript:` URL to invoke the `reset()` method for the form directly (in other words, without doing it via function). Note that the form's action in this example is to a nonexistent URL. If you click the Submit icon, you receive an "unable to locate" error from the browser.

LISTING 21-3

form.reset() and form.submit() Methods

```
<html>
  <head>
    <title>Registration Form</title>
  </head>
  <body>
    <form name="entries" method="POST"
    action="http://www.u.edu/pub/cgi-bin/register">
        Enter your first name:<input type="text" name="firstName"
          id="firstName" />
        <p>Enter your last name:<input type="text" name="lastName"
          id="lastName" /></p>
        <p>Enter your address:<input type="text" name="address"
```

```
        id="address" /></p>
      <p>Enter your city:<input type="text" name="city" id="city" /></p>
      <p><input type="radio" name="gender" id="gender1" checked="checked"
        />Male <input type="radio" name="gender" id="gender2" />Female</p>
      <p><input type="checkbox" name="retired" id="retired" />I am
        retired</p>
   </form>
   <p><a href="javascript:document.forms[0].submit()"><img alt="image"
      src="submit.jpg" height="25" width="100" border="0" /></a> <a
      href="javascript:document.forms[0].reset()"><img alt="image"
      src="reset.jpg" height="25" width="100" border="0" /></a></p>
</body>
</html>
```

Related Items: `onreset` event handler; `reset` object.

submit()

Returns: Nothing.
Compatibility: WinIE3+, MacIE3+, NN2+, Moz+, Safari+

The most common way to send a form's data to a server's CGI program for processing is to have a user click a Submit button. The standard HTML Submit button is designed to send data from all named elements of a form according to the specifications listed in the `<form>` definition's attributes. But if you want to submit a form's data to a server automatically for a user, or want to use a graphical button for submission, you can accomplish the submission with the `form.submit()` method.

Invoking this method is almost the same as a user clicking a form's Submit button (except that the `onsubmit` event handler is not triggered). Therefore, you may have an image on your page that is a graphical submission button. If that image is surrounded by a link object, you can capture a mouse click on that image and trigger a function whose content includes a call to a form's `submit()` method (see Listing 21-3).

In a multiple-form HTML document, however, you must reference the proper form either by name or according to its position in a `document.forms` array. Always make sure that the reference you specify in your script points to the desired form before you submit any data to a server.

As a security and privacy precaution for people visiting your site, JavaScript ignores all `submit()` methods whose associated form actions are set to a `mailto:` URL. Many web page designers would love to have secret e-mail addresses captured from visitors. Because such a capture can be considered an invasion of privacy, the power has been disabled since early browser versions. You can, however, still use an explicit Submit button object to mail a form to you from browsers. (See the section "E-mailing forms" earlier in this chapter.)

Because the `form.submit()` method does not trigger the form's `onsubmit` event handler, you must perform any presubmission processing and forms validation in the same script that ends with the `form.submit()` statement. You also do not want to interrupt the submission process after the script invokes the `form.submit()` method. Script statements inserted after one that invokes `form.submit()` — especially those that navigate to other pages or attempt a second submission — cause the first submission to cancel itself.

Related Item: `onsubmit` event handler.

Event handlers

onreset

Compatibility: WinIE4+, MacIE4+, NN3+, Moz+, Safari+

Immediately before a Reset button returns a form to its default settings, JavaScript sends a reset event to the form. By including an onreset event handler in the form definition, you can trap that event before the reset takes place.

A friendly way of using this feature is to provide a safety net for a user who accidentally clicks the Reset button after filling out a form. The event handler can run a function that asks the user to confirm the action.

The onreset event handler must evaluate to return true for the event to continue to the browser. This may remind you of the way onmouseover and onmouseout event handlers work for links and image areas. This requirement is far more useful here because your function can control whether the reset operation ultimately proceeds to conclusion.

Listing 21-4 demonstrates one way to prevent accidental form resets or submissions. Using standard Reset and Submit buttons as interface elements, the <form> object definition includes both event handlers. Each event handler calls its own function that offers a choice for users. Notice how each event handler includes the word return and takes advantage of the Boolean values that come back from the confirm() method dialog boxes in both functions.

LISTING 21-4

The onreset and onsubmit Event Handlers

```
<html>
   <head>
      <title>Submit and Reset Confirmation</title>
      <script type="text/javascript">
      function allowReset() {
         return window.confirm("Go ahead and clear the form?");
      }
      function allowSend() {
         return window.confirm("Go ahead and mail this info?");
      }
      </script>
   </head>
   <body>
      <form method="POST" enctype="text/plain"
      action="mailto:trash4@dannyg.com" onreset="return allowReset()"
      onsubmit="return allowSend()">
         Enter your first name:<input type="text" name="firstName"
            id="firstName" />
         <p>Enter your last name:<input type="text" name="lastName"
            id="lastName" /></p>
         <p>Enter your address:<input type="text" name="address"
            id="address" /></p>
```

```
        <p>Enter your city:<input type="text" name="city" id="city" /></p>
        <p><input type="radio" name="gender" id="gender1" checked="checked"
            />Male <input type="radio" name="gender" id="gender2" />Female</p>
        <p><input type="checkbox" name="retired" id="retired" />I am retired</p>
        <p><input type="reset" /> <input type="submit" /></p>
      </form>
    </body>
  </html>
```

onsubmit

Compatibility: WinIE3+, MacIE3+, NN2+, Moz+, Safari+

No matter how a form's data is actually submitted (by a user clicking a Submit button or by a script invoking the form.submit() method), you may want your JavaScript-enabled HTML document to perform some data validation on the user input, especially with text fields, before the submission heads for the server. You have the option of doing such validation while the user enters data (see Chapter 43 on the CD-ROM) or in batch mode before sending the data to the server (or both). The place to trigger this last-ditch data validation is the form's onsubmit event handler. Note, however, that this event fires only from a genuine Submit type <input> element and not from the form's submit() method.

When you define an onsubmit handler as an attribute of a <form> definition, JavaScript sends the submit event to the form just before it dashes off the data to the server. Therefore, any script or function that is the parameter of the onsubmit attribute executes before the data is actually submitted. Note that this event handler fires only in response to a genuine Submit-style button and not from a form.submit() method.

Any code executed for the onsubmit event handler must evaluate to an expression consisting of the word return plus a Boolean value. If the Boolean value is true, the submission executes as usual; if the value is false, no submission is made. Therefore, if your script performs some validation prior to submitting data, make sure that the event handler calls that validation function as part of a return statement (as shown in Listing 21-4).

Even after your onsubmit event handler traps a submission, JavaScript's security mechanism can present additional alerts to the user depending on the server location of the HTML document and the destination of the submission.

fieldset and legend Element Objects

For HTML element properties, methods, and event handlers, see Chapter 15.

Properties	Methods	Event Handlers
align		
form		

fieldset

Syntax

Accessing `fieldset` or `legend` element object properties or methods:

```
(IE4+)        [window.]document.all.elemID.property | method([parameters])
(IE5+/W3C)    [window.]document.getElementById("elemID").property |
              method([parameters])
```

Compatibility: WinIE4+, MacIE4+, NN6+, Moz+, Safari+

About these objects

The `fieldset` and `legend` elements go hand in hand to provide some visual context to a series of form controls within a form. Browsers that implement the `fieldset` element draw a rectangle around the document space occupied by the form controls nested inside the `fieldset` element. The rectangle renders the full width of the body, unless its width is controlled by appropriate stylesheet properties (for example, `width`). To that rectangle is added a text label that is assigned via the `legend` element nested inside the `fieldset` element. None of this HTML-controlled grouping is necessary if you design a page layout that already provides graphical elements to group the form controls together.

Nesting the elements properly is essential to obtaining the desired browser rendering. A typical HTML sequence looks like the following:

```
<form>
<fieldset>
<legend>Legend Text</legend>
All your form controls and their labels go here.
</fieldset>
</form>
```

You can have more than one `fieldset` element inside a form. Each set has a rectangle drawn around it. This can help organize a long form into more easily digestible blocks of controls for users — yet the single form retains its integrity for submission to the server.

A `fieldset` element acts like any HTML container with respect to stylesheets and the inheritance thereof. For example, if you set the `color` style property of a `fieldset` element, the color affects the text of elements nested within; however, the color of the border drawn by the browser is unaffected. Assigning a color to the `fieldset` style's `border-color` property colors just the border and not the textual content of nested elements.

Note that the content of the `legend` element can be any HTML. Alternatively, you can assign a distinctive stylesheet rule to the `legend` element. If your scripts need to modify the text of the legend, you can accomplish this in modern browsers with the `nodeValue` properties of HTML element objects.

Only two element-specific properties are assigned to this object pair. The first is the `align` property of the `legend` object. This property matches the capabilities of the `align` attribute for the element as specified in the HTML 4.0 recommendation (albeit the property is deprecated in favor of stylesheet rules). MacIE5+ and WinIE5.5+ enable you to adjust this property on the fly (generally between your choices of "right" and "left") to alter the location of the legend at the top of the fieldset rectangle.

Because these elements are children of a `form` element, it makes sense that the DOM Level 2 specification supplies the read-only `form` property to both of these objects. That property returns a reference to the `form` element object that encloses either element. The `form` property for the `fieldset` and `legend` objects is implemented in modern browsers.

label Element Object

For HTML element properties, methods, and event handlers, see Chapter 15.

Properties	Methods	Event Handlers
form		
htmlFor		

Syntax

Accessing label element object properties or methods:

```
(IE4+)       [window.]document.all.elemID.property | method([parameters])
(IE5+/W3C)   [window.]document.getElementById("elemID").property |
             method([parameters])
```

Compatibility: WinIE4+, MacIE4+, NN6+, Moz+, Safari+

About this object

With the push in the HTML 4.0 specification to provide context-oriented tags for just about every bit of content on the page, the W3C HTML working group filled a gap with respect to text that usually hangs in front of or immediately after input, select, and textarea form control elements. You use these text chunks as labels for the items to describe the purpose of the control. The only input element that had an attribute for its label was the button input type. But even the newer button element did away with that.

A label element enables you to surround a control's label text with a contextual tag. In addition, one of the element's attributes — for — enables you to associate the label with a particular form control element. In the HTML, the for attribute is assigned the ID of the control with which the label is associated. A label element can be associated with a form control if the form control's tag is contained between the label element's start and end tags.

At first glance, browsers do nothing special (from a rendering point of view) for a label element. But for some kinds of elements, especially check box and radio input type elements, browsers help restore to users a vital user-interface convention: clicking the label is the same as clicking the control. For text elements, focus events are passed to the text input element associated with the label. In fact, all events that are directed at a label bubble upward to the form control associated with it. The following page fragment demonstrates how fieldset, legend, and label elements look in a form consisting of two radio buttons:

```
<form ...>
<fieldset id="form1set1">
<legend id="form1set1legend">Choose the Desired Performance</legend>
<input type="radio" name="speed" id="speed1" />
   <label for="speed1">Fastest (lower quality)</label><br />
<input type="radio" name="speed" id="speed2" />
   <label for="speed2">Slower (best quality)</label>
</fieldset>
</form>
```

665

Even so, a `label` and its associated form control element do not have to be adjacent to each other in the source code. For example, you can have a label in one cell of a table row with the form control in another cell (in the same or different row).

Properties
htmlFor

Value: Element object reference. Read/Write
Compatibility: WinIE4+, MacIE4+, NN6+, Moz+, Safari+

The `htmlFor` property is the scripted equivalent of the `for` attribute of the `label` element. An acceptable value is a full reference to a form control element (`input`, `textarea`, or `select` element objects). It is highly unlikely that you would modify this property for an existing `label` element. However, if your script is creating a new `label` element (perhaps a replacement form), use this property to associate the label with a form control.

Scripting and Web Forms 2.0

Standard HTML forms have been with us for some time, which means it shouldn't necessarily come as a surprise that there is an effort to revamp the handling of forms on the Web. Although there are several from technologies vying for the limelight, Web Forms 2.0 is the one with the most momentum, at least for now.

It's difficult to mention Web Forms 2.0 without also mentioning XForms, which is in many ways a competing form technology. Unlike Web Forms 2.0, which is based on traditional HTML code and scripting, XForms relies on a specialized XML syntax to describe form components. This doesn't necessarily make either technology better or worse than the other, except for the fact that Web Forms 2.0 is already supported by a production web browser (Opera 9). And as history has shown, early adoption is one of the best ways for an emerging technology to take hold.

Speaking of browsers and forms, it's worth noting that Microsoft doesn't appear to be very eager to back either Web Forms 2.0 or XForms. They have their own XML-based form technology known as XAML that has ties to the next generation Windows operating system. The Mozilla Foundation was involved in developing the Web Forms 2.0 specification and has stated a commitment to supporting it natively in the Gecko browser engine that forms the core of Mozilla-based browsers. The same goes for Apple and their desire to support Web Forms 2.0 in their Safari browser. So expect to see much broader support for Web Forms 2.0 in the very near future, and in the meantime there are plug-ins available for several major browsers.

What is Web Forms 2.0?

Like HTML and JavaScript, Web Forms 2.0 is a specification that describes how a technology is supposed to work. In this case, the specification describes a set of rich user interface components that carry out common information gathering tasks such as allowing the user to select a date or enter text. Traditional HTML supports such tasks via forms as well, but those forms are fairly limited and require a decent amount of scripting in order to provide any significant degree of user friendliness. Thanks to modern user interface design, web users have to expect form validation, an auto-completion feature for frequently entered text, and visual user interfaces for common data entry tasks such as the selection of a date.

Web Forms 2.0 addresses the limitations of HTML forms by offering advanced form validation without scripting, auto-completion, careful control over the input focus, and a host of new form control types such as specialized date/time and URL input controls, among others. You can begin using Web Forms 2.0 right away in the Opera browser (as of version 9), although there are browser add-ons that support it in other major browsers.

Web Forms 2.0 and JavaScript

Scripting's role in Web Forms 2.0 is primarily that as a programmatic equivalent to operations and behaviors that are built into any browser that supports the standard. For example, Web Forms 2.0 includes a facility known as *repetition blocks*, whereby a form can grow or shrink as needed, such as a tabular order form whose rows of input elements grow as the user adds new items to the order. The Web Forms mechanism takes care of adding repeated rows of form controls and assigning names to elements indicating row numbers (there is a special button type whose tag attributes link it to the template that is repeated). The DOM interface provided with Web Forms allows script access to adding and subtracting rows if the page design requires it.

If it sounds as though Web Forms 2.0 is trying to displace JavaScript, in a way that's true. The purpose is to rely less on scripting for form validation and other Dynamic HTML surrounding forms, offering page authors a more standardized way of handling these common tasks. But the creators of Web Forms 2.0 also know that scripters will want to get their hands on the new forms "stuff," and therefore provide ample script access.

For more information about Web Forms 2.0, visit `http://www.whatwg.org/specs/web-forms/current-work`.

Chapter 22

Button Objects

This chapter is devoted to those lovable buttons that invite users to initiate action and make choices with a single click of the mouse button. In this category fall the standard system-looking buttons with labels on them, as well as radio buttons and checkboxes. For such workhorses of the HTML form, these objects have a limited vocabulary of object-specific properties, methods, and event handlers.

I group together the button, submit, and reset objects for an important reason: They look alike yet they are intended for very different purposes. Knowing when to use which button is important — especially when to differentiate between the button and submit objects. Many a newcomer gets the two confused and winds up with scripting error headaches. That confusion won't happen to you by the time you finish this chapter.

IN THIS CHAPTER

Triggering action from a user's click of a button

Assigning hidden values to radio and checkbox buttons

Distinguishing between radio button families and their individual buttons

The button Element Object, and the Button, Submit, and Reset Input Objects

For HTML element properties, methods, and event handlers, see Chapter 15.

Properties	Methods	Event Handlers
form	click()	onclick
name		onmousedown
type		onmouseup
value		

document.*formObject.buttonObject*

Syntax

Accessing button object properties or methods:

```
(All)      [window.]document.formName.buttonName.property | method([parameters])
(All)      [window.]document.formName.elements[index].property |
           method([parameters])
(All)      [window.]document.forms[index].buttonName.property |
           method([parameters])
(All)      [window.]document.forms["formName"].buttonName.property |
           method([parameters])
(All)      [window.]document.forms["formName"].elements[index].property |
           method([parameters])
(IE4+)     [window.]document.all.elemID.property | method([parameters])
(IE5+/W3C) [window.]document.getElementById("elemID").property |
           method([parameters])
```

Compatibility: WinIE4+, MacIE4+, NN6+, Moz+, Safari+

About these objects

Button objects generate standard, pushbutton-style user interface elements on the page, depending on the operating system on which the particular browser runs. In the early days, the browsers called upon the operating systems to generate these standard interface elements. In more recent versions, the browsers define their own look, albeit frequently still different for each operating system. More recently, the appearance of a button may also be influenced by browser-specific customizations that browser makers put into their products. Even so, any computer user will recognize a button when the browser produces it on the page.

There are two ways to put standard buttons into a page. The first, and completely backward-compatible way, is to use input elements nested inside a form container. The modern approach involves the button HTML element, which provides a slightly different way of specifying a button in a page, including the option of putting a button outside of a form (presumably for some client-side script execution, independent of form submission). From an HTML point of view, the difference between the two concerns itself with the way the label of the button is specified. With an input element, the string assigned to the value attribute becomes the label of the button; but a button element is a container (meaning with an end tag), whose content becomes the button's label. You can still assign a value to the value attribute, which, if a form contains the button, gets submitted to the server, independent of the label text.

Always give careful thought to the label that you assign to a button. Because a button initiates some action, make sure that the verb in the label clearly defines what happens after you click it. Also, take cues from experienced user interface designers who craft operating system and commercial software buttons: Be concise. If you find your button labels going longer than two or three words, reconsider the design of your page so that the user can clearly understand the purpose of any button from a shorter label.

Browsers automatically display a button sized to accommodate the label text. But only modern browsers (IE4+/Moz+/W3C) allow you to control more visual aspects of the button, such as size, label font, and coloration. And, as for the position of the button on the page, buttons, as in all in-line elements, appear where they occur in the source code. You can, of course, use element positioning (Chapter 40 on the CD-ROM) to make a button appear wherever you want it. But if your pages run on multiple operating systems and generations of browsers, be aware that the appearance (and size) of a button will not be identical on all screens. Check out the results on as many platforms as possible.

Buttons in the Windows environment follow their normal behavior in that they indicate the focus with highlighted button-label text (usually with a dotted rectangle). Some newer browsers running on other operating systems offer this kind of highlighting and selection as a user option. IE5+ provides additional input element features that prevent buttons from receiving this kind of visible focus.

The lone button object event handler that works on all browser versions is one that responds to a user clicking the pointer atop the button: the onclick event handler. Virtually all action surrounding a button object comes from this event handler. You rarely need to extract property values or invoke the click() method. Modern browsers include support for the individual component events of a click: mousedown and mouseup; there's also a plethora of user-initiated events for buttons that you can use.

Two special variants of the button input object are the *submit* and *reset* input objects. With their heritages going back to early incarnations of HTML, these two button types perform special operations on their own. The submit-style button automatically sends the data within the same form object to the URL listed in the action attribute of the <form> definition. The method attribute dictates the format in which the button sends the data. Therefore, you don't have to script this action if your HTML page is communicating with a program (often a CGI script) on the server.

If the form's action attribute is set to a mailto: URL, you must provide the page visitor with a Submit button to carry out the action. Setting the form's enctype attribute to text/plain is also helpful so that the form data arrives in a more readable form than the normal encoded name-value pairs. See "E-mailing forms" in Chapter 21 for details about submitting form content via e-mail.

The partner of the Submit button is the Reset button. This button, too, has special powers. A click of this button type restores all elements within the form to their default values. That goes for text objects, radio button groups, checkboxes, and selection lists. The most common application of the button is to clear entry fields of the last data entered by the user.

All that distinguishes these three types of buttons from each other in the <input> tag or <button> tag is the parameter of the type attribute. For buttons not intended to send data to a server, use the "button" style (this is the default value for the button element). You should reserve "submit" and "reset" for their special powers.

If you want an image to behave like a button in all scriptable browsers, consider either associating a link with an image (see the discussion on the link object in Chapter 19) or creating a client-side image map (see the area object discussion in Chapter 20). An even better idea that applies solely to modern browsers is to use the input element with a type attribute set to image (discussed later in this chapter).

Probably the biggest mistake scripters make with these buttons is using a Submit button to do the work of a plain button. Because these two buttons look alike, and the submit type of input element has a longer tradition than the button, confusing the two is easy. But if all you want is to display a button that initiates client-side script execution, use a plain button. The Submit button attempts to submit the form. If no action attribute is set, then the page reloads, and all previous processing and field entries are erased. The plain button does its job quietly without reloading the page (unless the script intentionally does so).

Properties

form

Value: Form object reference. Read-Only
Compatibility: WinIE4+, MacIE4+, NN6+, Moz+, Safari+

document.*formObject.buttonObject*.value

A property of every `input` element object is a reference to the `form` element that contains the control. This property can be very convenient in a script when you are dealing with one form control that is passed as a parameter to the function and you want to either access another control in the same form or invoke a method of the form. An event handler of any `input` element can pass `this` as the parameter, and the function can still get access to the form without having to hard-wire the script to a particular form name or document layout.

Related Items: `form` object.

name

Value: Identifier string.   Read/Write (see text)
Compatibility: WinIE4+, MacIE4+, NN6+, Moz+, Safari+

A button's name is fixed in the `input` or `button` element's `name` attribute and can be adjusted via scripting in modern browsers. You may need to retrieve this property in a general-purpose function handler called by multiple buttons in a document. The function can test for a button name and perform the necessary statements for that button:

```
if (button.name == "Calculate") {
    // Perform calculation
}
```

If you change the name of the object, even a soft reload or window resize restores its original name.

Related Items: `name` property of all `form` elements.

type

Value: String.   Read-Only
Compatibility: WinIE4+, MacIE4+, NN6+, Moz+, Safari+

The precise value of the `type` property echoes the setting of the `type` attribute of the `<input>` or `<button>` tag that defines the object: `button`; `submit`; or `reset`.

value

Value: String.   Read/Write (see text)
Compatibility: WinIE4+, MacIE4+, NN6+, Moz+, Safari+

Both `input` and `button` elements have the `value` attribute, which is represented by the `value` property in the object model. But the purpose of the attribute/property in the two elements differs. For the `input` element, the `value` property represents the label displayed on the button. For a `button` element, however, the label text is created by the HTML text between the start and end tags for the `button` element. When the `input` element has a `name` value associated with it, the name-value pair is submitted along with the form.

If you do not assign a `value` attribute to a reset or submit style button, the browsers automatically assign the labels `Reset` and `Submit` without assigning a value. A value property can be any string, including multiple words.

You can modify this text on the fly in a script. Modern browsers are smart enough to resize the button and reflow the page to meet the new space needs; the new label survives a window resizing, but not a soft reload of the page.

Related Items: `value` property of text object.

Methods
click()

Returns: Nothing.
Compatibility: WinIE4+, MacIE4+, NN6+, Moz+, Safari+

A button's `click()` method simulates, via scripting, the human action of clicking that button, resulting in a triggering of a `click` event.

Related Items: `onclick` event handler.

Event handlers
onclick

Compatibility: WinIE3+, MacIE3+, NN2+, Moz+, Safari+

Virtually all button action takes place in response to the `onclick` event handler. A *click* is defined as a press and release of the mouse button while the screen pointer rests atop the button. The event goes to the button only after the user releases the mouse button.

For a Submit button, you should probably omit the `onclick` event handler and allow the form's `onsubmit` event handler to take care of last-minute data entry validation before sending the form. By triggering validation with the `onsubmit` event handler, your scripts can cancel the submission if something is not right (see the `form` object discussion in Chapter 21).

Listing 22-1 demonstrates not only the `onclick` event handler of a button but also how you may need to extract a particular button's `name` or `value` properties from a general-purpose function that services multiple buttons. In this case, each button passes its own object as a parameter to the `displayTeam()` function. The function then displays the results in an alert dialog box. A real-world application would probably perform more sophisticated actions based on the button clicked.

LISTING 22-1

Three Buttons Sharing One Function

```
<html>
  <head>
    <title>Button Click</title>
    <script type="text/javascript">
    function displayTeam(btn) {
      switch (btn.value) {
      case "Starsky":
        alert("Starsky & Hutch");
        break;
      case "Tango":
        alert("Tango & Cash");
        break;
```

continued

LISTING 22-1 *(continued)*

```
        case "Turner":
            alert("Turner & Hooch");
            break;
        }
    }
    </script>
</head>
<body>
    Click on your favorite half of a popular crime fighting team:
    <form>
        <input type="button" value="Starsky" onclick="displayTeam(this)" />
        <input type="button" value="Tango" onclick="displayTeam(this)" />
        <input type="button" value="Turner" onclick="displayTeam(this)" />
    </form>
</body>
</html>
```

> **NOTE**   The property assignment event handling technique used in the previous example and through-out the chapter is a deliberate simplification to make the code more readable. It is generally better to use the more modern approach of binding events using the addEventListener() (NN6+/Moz/W3C) or attachEvent() (IE5+) methods. A modern cross-browser event handling technique is explained in detail in Chapter 25.

Related Items: button.onmousedown, button.onmouseup, form.onsubmit event handlers.

onmousedown
onmouseup

Compatibility: WinIE4+, MacIE4+, NN4+, Moz+, Safari+

Modern browsers have event handlers for the components of a click event: the onmousedown and onmouseup event handlers. These events fire in addition to the onclick event handler.

The system-level buttons provided by the operating system perform their change of appearance while a button is being pressed. Therefore, trapping for the components of a click action won't help you in changing the button's appearance via scripting. Remember that a user can roll the cursor off the button while the button is still down. When the cursor leaves the region of the button, the button's appearance returns to its unpressed look, but any setting you make with the onmousedown event handler won't undo itself with an onmouseup counterpart, even after the user releases the mouse button elsewhere. On the other hand, if you can precache a click-on and click-off sound, you can use these events to fire the respective sounds in response to the mouse button action.

Related Items: button.onclick event handler.

checkbox Input Object

For HTML element properties, methods, and event handlers, see Chapter 15.

Properties	Methods	Event Handlers
checked	click()†	onclick†
form†		
name†		
type		
value		

† See Button object.

Syntax

Accessing checkbox properties or methods:

```
(All)      [window.]document.formName.boxName.property | method([parameters])
(All)      [window.]document.formName.elements[index].property |
           method([parameters])
(All)      [window.]document.forms[index].boxName.property | method([parameters])
(All)      [window.]document.forms["formName"].boxName.property |
           method([parameters])
(All)      [window.]document.forms["formName"].elements[index].property |
           method([parameters])
(IE4+)     [window.]document.all.elemID.property | method([parameters])
(IE5+/W3C) [window.]document.getElementById("elemID").property |
           method([parameters])
```

Compatibility: WinIE3+, MacIE3+, NN2+, Moz+, Safari+

About this object

Checkboxes have a very specific purpose in modern graphical user interfaces: to toggle between "on" and "off" settings. As with a checkbox on a printed form, a mark in the box indicates that the label text is true or should be included for the individual who made that mark. When the box is unchecked or empty, the text is false or should not be included. If two or more checkboxes are physically grouped together, they should have no interaction: Each is an independent setting (see the discussion on the radio object for interrelated buttons).

I make these user interface points at the outset because, in order to present a user interface in your HTML pages consistent with the user's expectations based on exposure to other programs, you must use checkbox objects only for on/off choices that the user makes. Using a checkbox as an action button that, for example, navigates to another URL is not good form. Just as they do in a Windows or Mac dialog box, users make settings with checkboxes and radio buttons and initiate action by clicking a standard button or image map.

document.*formObject.checkboxObject*.checked

That's not to say that a checkbox object cannot perform some limited action in response to a user's click, but such actions are typically related to the context of the checkbox button's label text. For example, in some Windows and Macintosh dialog boxes, turning on a checkbox may activate a bunch of otherwise inactive settings elsewhere in the same dialog box. Modern browsers allow disabling (dimming) or hiding form elements, so a checkbox may control those visible attributes of related controls. Or, in a two-frame window, a checkbox in one frame may control whether the viewer is an advanced user. If so, the content in the other frame may be more detailed. Toggling the checkbox changes the complexity level of a document showing in the other frame (using different URLs for each level). The bottom line, then, is that you should use checkboxes for toggling between on/off settings. Provide regular buttons for users to initiate processing.

In the `<input>` tag for a checkbox, you can preset the checkbox to be checked when the page appears by adding the constant `checked` attribute to the definition. If you omit this attribute, the button takes on its default, unchecked appearance. As for the checkbox label text, its definition lies outside the `<input>` tag, usually as text that appears next to the tag. If you look at the way checkboxes behave in HTML browsers, this location makes sense: The label is not an active part of the checkbox (as it typically is in Windows and Macintosh user interfaces, where clicking the label is the same as clicking the box).

Naming a checkbox can be an important part of the object definition, depending on how you plan to use the information in your script or document. For forms whose content goes to a program running on the server, you must word the box name as needed for use by the server program so that the program can parse the form data and extract the setting of the checkbox. For JavaScript client-side use, you can assign not only a name that describes the button, but also a value useful to your script for making `if...else` decisions or for assembling strings that are eventually displayed in a window or frame.

Properties

checked

Value: Boolean.   Read/Write
Compatibility: WinIE3+, MacIE3+, NN2+, Moz+, Safari+

The simplest property of a checkbox reveals (or lets you set) whether or not a checkbox is checked. The value is `true` for a checked box and `false` for an unchecked box. To check a box via a script, simply assign `true` to the checkbox's `checked` property:

```
document.forms[0].boxName.checked = true;
```

Setting the `checked` property from a script does not trigger a `click` event for the checkbox object. So, the `onclick` event handler won't get called in response to a checkbox being checked via the `checked` property.

You may need an instance in which one checkbox automatically checks or unchecks another checkbox elsewhere in the same or other form of the document. To accomplish this task, create an `onclick` event handler for the one checkbox and build a statement similar to the preceding one to set the other related checkbox to `true`. Don't get too carried away with this feature, however: For a group of interrelated, mutually exclusive choices, use a group of radio buttons instead.

If your page design requires that a checkbox be checked after the page loads, don't bother trying to script this checking action. Simply add the one-word `checked` attribute to the `<input>` tag. Because the `checked` property is a Boolean value, you can use its results as an argument for an `if` clause, as shown in the next example.

The simple example in Listing 22-2 passes a form object reference to the JavaScript function. The function, in turn, reads the `checked` value of the form's checkbox object (`checkThis.checked`) and uses its Boolean value as the test result for the `if...else` construction.

The checked Property as a Conditional

```
<html>
    <head>
        <title>Checkbox Inspector</title>
        <script type="text/javascript">
        function inspectBox(form) {
            if (form.checkThis.checked) {
                alert("The box is checked.");
            } else {
                alert("The box is not checked at the moment.");
            }
        }
        </script>
    </head>
    <body>
        <form>
            <input type="checkbox" name="checkThis" />Check here
            <p><input type="button" name="boxChecker" value="Inspect Box"
                onclick="inspectBox(this.form)" /></p>
        </form>
    </body>
</html>
```

Related Items: defaultChecked, value properties.

defaultChecked

Value: Boolean. Read-Only
Compatibility: WinIE3+, MacIE3+, NN2+, Moz+, Safari+

Sometimes you may find it beneficial to know if the initial setting of a checkbox has changed. The checked property alone can't tell you this because it reflects only the current state of a checkbox. Another property, defaultChecked, keeps up with the initial state of a checkbox.

If you add the checked attribute to the <input> definition for a checkbox, the defaultChecked property for that object is true; otherwise, the property is false. Having access to this property enables your scripts to examine checkboxes to see if they have been adjusted (presumably by the user, if your script does not set properties).

The following function is designed to compare the current setting of a checkbox against its default value:

```
function compareBrowser(thisBox) {
    if (thisBox.checked != thisBox.defaultChecked) {
        // statements about using a different set of HTML pages
    }
}
```

document.*formObject.checkboxObject*.value

The if construction compares the current status of the box against its default status. Both are Boolean values, so they can be compared against each other. If the current and default settings don't match, the function goes on to handle the case in which the current setting is other than the default.

Related Items: checked, value properties.

type

Value: String (checkbox).   Read-Only
Compatibility: WinIE4+, MacIE4+, NN3+, Moz+, Safari+

Use the type property to help you identify a checkbox object from an unknown group of form elements. Just look for the string checkbox as the type of a form element to know if it is indeed a checkbox.

Related Items: form.elements property.

value

Value: String.   Read/Write
Compatibility: WinIE3+, MacIE3+, NN2+, Moz+, Safari+

A checkbox object's value property is a string of any text that you want to associate with the box. Note that the checkbox's value property is not the label, as it is for a regular button, but hidden text associated with the checkbox. For instance, the label that you attach to a checkbox may not be worded in a way that is useful to your script. But if you place that useful wording in the value attribute of the checkbox tag, you can extract that string via the value property.

When a checkbox object's data is submitted to a CGI program, the value property is sent as part of the name-value pair if the box is checked (nothing about the checkbox is sent if the box is unchecked). If you omit the value attribute in your definition, the property always yields the string "on," which is submitted to a CGI program when the box is checked. From the JavaScript side, don't confuse this string with the on and off settings of the checkbox: Use the checked property to determine a checkbox's status.

The scenario for the skeleton HTML page in Listing 22-3 is a form with a checkbox whose selection determines which of two actions to follow for submission to the server. After the user clicks the Submit button, a JavaScript function examines the checkbox's checked property. If the property is true (the button is checked), the script sets the action property for the entire form to the content of the value property—thus influencing where the form goes on the server side. If you try this listing on your computer, the result you see varies widely with the browser version you use. For most browsers, you see some indication (an error alert or other screen notation) that a file with the name primaryURL or alternateURL doesn't exist. The names and the error message come from the submission process for this demonstration.

LISTING 22-3

Adjusting a Server Submission Action

```
<html>
  <head>
    <title>Checkbox Submission</title>
    <script type="text/javascript">
    function setAction(form) {
        if (form.checkThis.checked) {
```

```
            form.action = form.checkThis.value;
        } else {
            form.action = "file://primaryURL";
        }
        return true;
    }
    </script>
</head>
<body>
    <form method="POST" action="">
        <input type="checkbox" name="checkThis"
        value="file://alternateURL" />Use alternate
        <p><input type="submit" name="boxChecker"
            onclick="return setAction(this.form)" /></p>
    </form>
</body>
</html>
```

Related Items: checked property.

Methods
click()

Returns: Nothing.
Compatibility: WinIE3+, MacIE3+, NN2+, Moz+, Safari+

The intention of the click() method is to enact, via script, the physical act of clicking a checkbox (but without triggering the onclick event handler). However, your scripts are better served by setting the checked property so that you know exactly what the setting of the box is at any time.

Related Items: checked property; onclick event handler.

Event handlers
onclick

Compatibility: WinIE3+, MacIE3+, NN2+, Moz+, Safari+

Because users regularly click checkboxes, the objects have an event handler for the click event. Use this event handler only if you want your page (or variable values hidden from view) to respond in some way to the action of clicking a checkbox. Most user actions, as mentioned earlier, are initiated by clicking standard buttons rather than checkboxes, so be careful not to overuse event handlers in checkboxes.

The page in Listing 22-4 shows how to trap the click event in one checkbox to influence the visibility and display of other form controls. After you turn on the Monitor checkbox, a list of radio buttons for monitor sizes appears. Similarly, engaging the Communications checkbox makes two radio buttons visible. Your choice of radio button brings up one of two further choices within the same table cell (see Figure 22-1).

Notice how the toggle() function was written as a generalizable function. This function can accept a reference to any checkbox object and any related span. If five more groups like this were added to the table, no additional functions would be needed.

FIGURE 22-1

Clicking each checkbox reveals additional relevant choices.

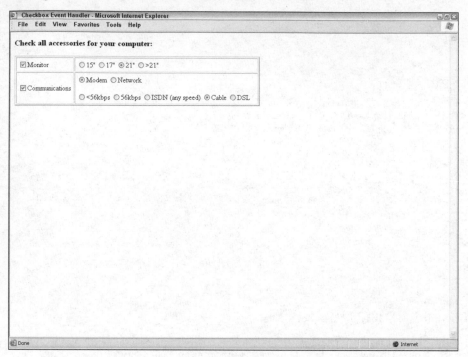

In the swap() function, an application of a nested if...else shortcut construction is used to convert the Boolean values of the checked property to the strings needed for the display style property. The nesting is used to allow a single statement to take care of two conditions: the group of buttons to be controlled and the checked property of the button invoking the function. This function is not generalizable, because it contains explicit references to objects in the document. The swap() function can be made generalizable, but due to the special relationships between pairs of span elements (meaning one has to be hidden while the other is displayed in its place), the function would require more parameters to fill in the blanks where explicit references are needed.

LISTING 22-4

A Checkbox and an onclick Event Handler

```html
<html>
    <head>
        <title>Checkbox Event Handler</title>
        <style type="text/css">
        #monGroup {visibility:hidden}
        #comGroup {visibility:hidden}
        </style>
        <script type="text/javascript">
```

```
        // toggle visibility of a main group spans
        function toggle(chkbox, group) {
            var visSetting = (chkbox.checked) ? "visible" : "hidden";
            document.getElementById(group).style.visibility = visSetting;
        }
        // swap display of communications sub group spans
        function swap(radBtn, group) {
            var modemsVisSetting = (group == "modems") ? ((radBtn.checked) ?
                "" : "none") : "none";
            var netwksVisSetting = (group == "netwks") ? ((radBtn.checked) ?
                "" : "none") : "none";
            document.getElementById("modems").style.display = modemsVisSetting;
            document.getElementById("netwks").style.display = netwksVisSetting;
        }
    </script>
</head>
<body>
    <form>
        <h3>Check all accessories for your computer:</h3>
        <table border="2" cellpadding="5">
            <tr>
                <td><input type="checkbox" name="monitor"
                    onclick="toggle(this, 'monGroup')" />Monitor</td>
                <td><span id="monGroup"><input type="radio"
                    name="monitorType" />15" <input type="radio"
                    name="monitorType" />17" <input type="radio"
                    name="monitorType" />21" <input type="radio"
                    name="monitorType" />&gt;21"</span></td>
            </tr>
            <tr>
                <td><input type="checkbox" name="comms"
                    onclick="toggle(this, 'comGroup')" />Communications</td>
                <td><span id="comGroup"><p><input type="radio" name="commType"
                    onclick="swap(this, 'modems')" />Modem <input type="radio"
                    name="commType" onclick="swap(this, 'netwks')" />Network</p>
                    <p><span id="modems" style="display:none"><input type="radio"
                    name="modemType" />&lt;56kbps <input type="radio"
                    name="modemType" />56kbps <input type="radio"
                    name="modemType" />ISDN (any speed) <input type="radio"
                    name="modemType" />Cable <input type="radio"
                    name="modemType" />DSL</span> <span id="netwks"
                    style="display:none"><input type="radio"
                    name="netwkType" />Ethernet 10Mbps (10-Base T) <input
                    type="radio" name="netwkType" />Ethernet 100Mbps (10/100)
                    <input type="radio" name="netwkType" />T1 or
                    greater</span>  </p></span></td>
            </tr>
        </table>
    </form>
</body>
</html>
```

Related Items: checkbox mouse-related event handler.

radio Input Object

Properties	Methods	Event Handlers
See `checkbox` object.		

Syntax

Accessing radio object properties or methods:

```
(All)      [window.]document.formName.buttonGroupName[index].property |
           method([parameters])
(All)      [window.]document.formName.elements[index] [index].property |
           method([parameters])
(All)      [window.]document.forms[index]. buttonGroupName[index].property |
           method([parameters])
(All)      [window.]document.forms["formName"]. buttonGroupName[index].property |
           method([parameters])
(All)      [window.]document.forms["formName"].elements[index].property |
           method([parameters])
(IE4+)     [window.]document.all.elemID[index].property | method([parameters])
(IE5+/W3C) [window.]document.getElementById("elemID")[index].property |
           method([parameters])
```

Compatibility: WinIE3+, MacIE3+, NN2+, Moz+, Safari+

About this object

A radio button object is an unusual one within the body of JavaScript applications. In every other case of form control elements, one object equals one visual element on the screen. But a radio object actually consists of a group of radio buttons. Because of the nature of radio buttons — a mutually exclusive choice among two or more selections — a group always has multiple visual elements. All buttons in the group share the same name — which is how the browser knows to group buttons together and to let the clicking of a button deselect any other selected button within the group. Beyond that, however, each button can have unique properties, such as its `value` or `checked` property.

Use JavaScript array syntax to access information about an individual button within the button group. Look at the following example of defining a button group and see how to reference each button. This button group lets the user select an image size from a group of standard sizes, which includes the number of megapixels used by that size as the value:

```
<form>
<b>Select your desired image size:</b><br />
<input type="radio" name="sizes" value="0.073" checked="checked" />320x240
<input type="radio" name="sizes" value="0.293" />640x480
<input type="radio" name="sizes" value="0.75" />1024x768
<input type="radio" name="sizes" value="1.25" />1280x1024
</form>
```

After this group displays on the page, the first radio button is preselected for the user. Only one property of a radio button object (length) applies to all members of the group. However, the other properties apply to individual buttons within the group. To access any button, use an array index value as part of the button group name. For example:

```
firstBtnValue = document.forms[0].sizes[0].value;  // "0.073"
secondBtnValue = document.forms[0].sizes[1].value; // "0.293"
```

Any time you access the checked, defaultChecked, type, or value property, you must point to a specific button within the group according to its order in the array (or each button can also have a unique ID). The order of buttons in the group depends on the sequence in which the individual buttons are defined in the HTML document. In other words, to uncover the currently selected radio button, your script has to iterate through all radio buttons in the radio group. Examples of this come later in the discussion of this object.

Supplying a value attribute to a radio button can be very important in your script. Although the text label for a button is defined outside the <input> tag, the value attribute lets you store any string in the button's hip pocket. In the earlier example, the radio button labels were just first names, whereas the value properties were set in the definition to the full names of the actors. The values could have been anything that the script needed, such as birth dates, shoe sizes, URLs, or the first names again (because a script has no way to retrieve the labels except through innerHTML or node property access in more modern browsers). The point is that the value attribute should contain whatever string the script needs to derive from the selection made by the user. The value attribute contents are also what is sent to a server-side program in a submit action for the form.

How you decide to orient a group of buttons on the screen is entirely up to your design and the real estate available within your document. You can string them in a horizontal row (as shown earlier), place <br /> tags after each one to form a column, or do so after every other button to form a double column. Numeric order within the array is determined only by the order in which the buttons are defined in the source code, not by where they appear. To determine which radio button of a group is checked before doing processing based on that choice, you need to construct a repeat loop to cycle through the buttons in the group (shown in the next example). For each button, your script examines the checked property.

Properties

checked

Value: Boolean.   Read/Write
Compatibility: WinIE3+, MacIE3+, NN2+, Moz+, Safari+

Only one radio button in a group can be highlighted (checked) at a time (the browser takes care of highlighting and unhighlighting buttons in a group for you). That one button's checked property is set to true, whereas all others in the group are set to false. By setting the checked property of one button in a group to true, all other buttons automatically uncheck themselves.

Listing 22-5 uses a repeat loop in a function to look through all buttons in a group of image sizes in search of the checked button. After the loop finds the one whose checked property is true, it returns the value of the index. In one instance, that index value is used to extract the value property for display in the alert dialog box; in the other instance, the value helps determine which button in the group is next in line to have its checked property set to true.

LISTING 22-5

Finding the Selected Button in a Radio Group

```html
<html>
    <head>
        <title>Extracting Highlighted Radio Button</title>
        <script type="text/javascript">
        function getSelectedButton(buttonGroup){
            for (var i = 0; i < buttonGroup.length; i++) {
                if (buttonGroup[i].checked) {
                    return i;
                }
            }
            return 0;
        }
        function showMegapixels(form) {
            var i = getSelectedButton(form.sizes);
            alert("That image size requires " + form.sizes[i].value + " megapixels.");
        }
        function cycle(form) {
            var i = getSelectedButton(form.sizes);
            if (i+1 == form.sizes.length) {
                form.sizes[0].checked = true;
            } else {
                form.sizes[i+1].checked = true;
            }
        }
        </script>
    </head>
    <body>
        <form>
            <b>Select your desired image size:</b>
            <p><input type="radio" name="sizes" value="0.073"
                checked="checked" />320x240 <input type="radio" name="sizes"
                value="0.293" />640x480 <input type="radio" name="sizes"
                value="0.75" />1024x768 <input type="radio" name="sizes"
                value="1.25" />1280x1024 </p>
            <p><input type="button" name="Viewer" value="View Megapixels..."
                onclick="showMegapixels(this.form)" /></p>
            <p><input type="button" name="Cycler" value="Cycle Buttons"
                onclick="cycle(this.form)" /></p>
        </form>
    </body>
</html>
```

Related Items: defaultChecked property.

defaultChecked

Value: Boolean. Read-Only
Compatibility: WinIE3+, MacIE3+, NN2+, Moz+, Safari+

If you add the `checked` attribute to the `<input>` definition for a radio button, the `defaultChecked` property for that object is `true`; otherwise, the property is `false`. Having access to this property enables your scripts to examine individual radio buttons to see if they have been adjusted (presumably by the user, if your script does not perform automatic clicking).

In the following script fragment, a function is passed a reference to a form containing the image sizes radio buttons:

```
function groupChanged(form) {
    for (var i = 0; i < form.sizes.length; i++) {
        if (form.sizes[i].defaultChecked) {
            if (!form.sizes[i].checked) {
                alert("This radio group has been changed.");
            }
        }
    }
}
```

The goal in this code is to see, in as general a way as possible (supplying the radio group name where needed), if the user changed the default setting. Looping through each of the radio buttons, you look for the one whose `checked` attribute is set in the `<input>` definition. With that index value (`i`) in hand, you then look to see if that entry is still checked. If not (notice the `!` negation operator), you display an alert dialog box about the change.

Related Items: `checked`, `value` properties.

length

Value: Integer. Read-Only
Compatibility: WinIE3+, MacIE3+, NN2+, Moz+, Safari+

A radio button group has *length* — the number of individual radio buttons defined for that group. Attempting to retrieve the length of an individual button yields a `null` value. The `length` property is valuable for establishing the maximum range of values in a repeat loop that must cycle through every button within that group. If you specify the `length` property to fill that value (rather than hard-wiring the value), the loop construction will be easier to maintain — as you make changes to the number of buttons in the group during page construction, the loop adjusts to the changes automatically.

Related Items: None.

name

Value: Identifier string. Read-Only
Compatibility: WinIE3+, MacIE3+, NN2+, Moz+, Safari+

The `name` property, although associated with an entire radio button group, can be read only from individual buttons in the group, such as

```
btnGroupName = document.forms[0].groupName[2].name;
```

document.*formObject.radioObject*.onclick

In that sense, each radio button element in a group inherits the name of the group. Your scripts have little need to extract the name property of a button or group. More often than not, you will hard-wire a button group's name into your script to extract other properties of individual buttons. Getting the name property of an object whose name you know is obviously redundant. But understanding the place of radio button group names in the scheme of JavaScript objects is important for all scripters.

Related Items: value property.

type

Value: String (radio).   Read-Only
Compatibility: WinIE4+, MacIE4+, NN3+, Moz+, Safari+

Use the type property to help identify a radio object from an unknown group of form elements. To find out if a form element is a radio object, just look for the string radio as the type of the element.

Related Items: form.elements property.

value

Value: String.   Read/Write
Compatibility: WinIE3+, MacIE3+, NN2+, Moz+, Safari+

As described earlier in this chapter for the checkbox object, the value property contains arbitrary information that you assign when mapping out the <input> definition for an individual radio button. Using this property is a handy shortcut to correlating a radio button label with detailed or related information of interest to your script or server-side application. If you like, the value property can contain the same text as the label.

Related Items: name property.

Methods
click()

Returns: Nothing.
Compatibility: WinIE3+, MacIE3+, NN2+, Moz+, Safari+

The intention of the click() method is to enact, via a script, the physical act of clicking a radio button. However, you better serve your scripts by setting the checked properties of all buttons in a group so that you know exactly what the setting of the group is at any time.

Related Items: checked property; onclick event handler.

Event handlers
onclick

Compatibility: WinIE3+, MacIE3+, NN2+, Moz+, Safari+

Radio buttons, more than any user interface element available in HTML, are intended for use in making choices that other objects, such as submit or standard buttons, act upon later. You may see cases in Windows or Mac programs in which highlighting a radio button — at most — activates or brings into view additional, related settings (see Listing 22-4).

I strongly advise you not to use scripting handlers that perform significant actions at the click of any radio button. At best, you may want to use knowledge about a user's clicking of a radio button to adjust a global variable or document.cookie setting that influences subsequent processing. Be aware, however, that if you script such a hidden action for one radio button in a group, you must also script similar actions for others in the same group. That way, if a user changes the setting back to a previous condition, the global variable is reset to the way it was. JavaScript, however, tends to run fast enough so that a batch operation can make such adjustments after the user clicks a more action-oriented button.

Every time a user clicks one of the radio buttons in Listing 22-6, he or she sets a global variable to true or false, depending on whether the person chose the smallest image size. This action is independent of the action that is taking place if the user clicks on the View Megapixels action button. An onunload event handler in the <body> definition triggers a function that displays an informational warning message just before the page clears (click the browser's Reload button to leave the current page prior to reloading). Here I use an initialize function triggered by onload so that the current radio button selection sets the global value upon a reload.

LISTING 22-6

An onclick Event Handler for Radio Buttons

```
<html>
    <head>
        <title>Radio Button onClick Handler</title>
        <script type="text/javascript">
        var LoRes = false
        function initValue() {
            LoRes = document.forms[0].sizes[0].checked;
        }
        function showMegapixels(form) {
            for (var i = 0; i < form.sizes.length; i++) {
                if (form.sizes[i].checked) {
                    break;
                }
            }
            alert("That image size requires " + form.sizes[i].value + " megapixels.");
        }
        function setLoRes(setting) {
            LoRes = setting;
        }
        function exitMsg() {
            if (LoRes) {
                alert("You should probably use a higher resolution image.");
            }
        }
        </script>
    </head>
    <body onload="initValue()" onunload="exitMsg()">
        <form>
            <b>Select your desired image size:</b>
```

continued

687

LISTING 22-6   *(continued)*

```
        <p><input type="radio" name="sizes" value="0.073"
           checked="checked" onclick="setLoRes(true)" />320x240 <input
           type="radio" name="sizes" value="0.293"
           onclick="setLoRes(false)" />640x480 <input type="radio"
           name="sizes" value="0.75"
           onclick="setLoRes(false)" />1024x768 <input type="radio"
           name="sizes" value="1.25"
           onclick="setLoRes(false)" />1280x1024 </p>
        <p><input type="button" name="Viewer" value="View Megapixels..."
           onclick="showMegapixels(this.form)" /></p>
    </form>
  </body>
</html>
```

---

image Input Object

For HTML element properties, methods, and event handlers, see Chapter 15.

Properties	Methods	Event Handlers
complete		
form†		
name†		
src		
type		

† See Button object.

Syntax

Accessing image input object properties or methods:

(All)	[window.]document.*formName.imageName.property* | *method*([*parameters*])
(All)	[window.]document.*formName*.elements[*index*].*property* | *method*([*parameters*])
(All)	[window.]document.forms[*index*].*imageName.property* | *method*([*parameters*])
(All)	[window.]document.forms["*formName*"].*imageName.property* | *method*([*parameters*])
(All)	[window.]document.forms["*formName*"].elements[*index*].*property* | *method*([*parameters*])
(IE4+)	[window.]document.all.*elemID.property* | *method*([*parameters*])
(IE5+/W3C)	[window.]document.getElementById("*elemID*").*property* | *method*([*parameters*])

Compatibility: WinIE4+, MacIE4+, NN6+, Moz+, Safari+

About this object

Modern browsers support the image input element among scriptable objects. The image input object most closely resembles the button input object but replaces the value property (which defines the label for the button) with the src property, which defines the URL for the image that is to be displayed in the form control. This is a much simpler way to define a clickable image icon, for example, than the way required for compatibility with older browsers: wrapping an img element inside an a element so that you can use the a element's event handlers.

Although this element loads a regular Web image in the document, you have virtually no control over the image, which the img element provides. Be sure the rendering is as you predict.

Properties

complete

Value: Boolean.   Read-Only
Compatibility: WinIE4+, MacIE4+, NN-, Moz-, Safari-

The complete property works as it does for an img element, reporting true if the image has finished loading. Otherwise the property returns false. Interestingly, there is no onload event handler for this object.

Related Items: image.complete property.

src

Value: URL string.   Read/Write
Compatibility: WinIE4+, MacIE4+, NN6+, Moz+, Safari+

Like the img element object, the image input element's src property controls the URL of the image being displayed in the element. The property can be used for image swapping in a form control, just as it is for a regular img element. Because the image input element has all necessary mouse event handlers available (for example, onmouseover, onmouseout, onmousedown) you can script rollovers, click-downs, or any other user interface technique that you feel is appropriate for your buttons and images. To adapt code written for link-wrapped images, move the event handlers from the a element to the image input element, and make sure the name of the image input element is the same as your old img element.

Older browsers load images into an image input element, but no event handlers are recognized.

Related Items: image.src property.

type

Value: String (image).   Read-Only
Compatibility: WinIE4+, MacIE4+, NN6+, Moz+, Safari+

Use the type property to help you identify an image input object from an unknown group of form elements. Just look for the string image as the type of a form element to know if it is indeed an image input object.

Related Items: form.elements property.

Chapter 23

Text-Related Form Objects

T he document object model for forms includes four text-related user interface objects — text, password, and hidden input element objects, plus
the textarea element object. All four of these objects are used for entry,
display, or temporary storage of text data. Although all of these objects can have
text placed in them by default as the page loads, scripts can also modify the contents of these objects. Importantly, all but the hidden objects retain their user- or
script-modified content during a soft reload (for example, clicking the Reload
button) in Mozilla and Internet Explorer; hidden objects revert to their default
values on all reloads.

A more obvious difference between the hidden object and the rest is that its
invisibility removes it from the realm of user events and actions. Therefore, the
range of scripted possibilities is much smaller for the hidden object.

The persistence of text and textarea object data through reloads (and window
resizes), however, is not reliable enough, nor consistent enough across all modern browsers to be used in lieu of a temporary cookie. This is a change from past
implementations.

IN THIS CHAPTER

Capturing and modifying text field contents

Triggering action by entering text

Capturing individual keystroke events

Text Input Object

For HTML element properties, methods, and event handlers, see Chapter 15.

document.*formObject.textObject*

Properties	Methods	Event Handlers
defaultValue	select()	onafterupdate
form		onbeforeupdate
maxLength		onchange
name		onerrorupdate
readOnly		onselect
size		
type		
value		

Syntax

Accessing text `input` object properties or methods:

(All)	`[window.]document.`*formName*`.`*fieldName*`.`*property* | *method*`([`*parameters*`])`
(All)	`[window.]document.`*formName*`.elements[`*index*`].`*property* | *method*`([`*parameters*`])`
(All)	`[window.]document.forms[`*index*`].`*fieldName*`.`*property* | *method*`([`*parameters*`])`
(All)	`[window.]document.forms["`*formName*`"].`*fieldName*`.`*property* | *method*`([`*parameters*`])`
(All)	`[window.]document.forms["`*formName*`"].elements[`*index*`].`*property* | *method*`([`*parameters*`])`
(IE4+)	`[window.]document.all.`*elemID*`.`*property* | *method*`([`*parameters*`])`
(IE5+/W3C)	`[window.]document.getElementById("`*elemID*`").`*property* | *method*`([`*parameters*`])`

Compatibility: WinIE3+, MacIE3+, NN2+, Moz+, Safari+

About this object

The text `input` object is the primary medium for capturing single-line, user-entered text. By default, browsers tend to display entered text in a monospaced font (usually Courier or a derivative) so that you can easily specify the width (`size`) of a field based on the anticipated number of characters that a user may put into the field. Until you get to modern (IE4+ and W3C) browsers, the font is a fixed size and always is left-aligned in the field. In those later browsers, stylesheets can control the font characteristics of a text field. If your design requires multiple lines of text, use the `textarea` object that comes later in this chapter.

Text object methods and event handlers use terminology that may be known to Windows users but not to Macintosh users. A field is said to have *focus* whenever the user clicks or tabs into the field. When a field has focus, either the text insertion pointer flashes, or any text in the field may be selected. Only one text object on a page can have focus at a time. The inverse user action—clicking or tabbing away from a text object—is called a *blur*. Clicking another object, whether it is another field or a button of any kind, causes a field that currently has focus to blur.

If you don't want the contents of a field to be changed by the user, you have three possibilities — depending on the vintage of browsers you need to support: forcing the field to lose focus; disabling the field; or setting the field's readOnly property.

The tactic that is completely backward compatible uses the following event handler in a field you want to protect:

```
onfocus="this.blur()"
```

Starting with IE4 and NN6/Moz1, the object model provides a disabled property for form controls. Setting the property to true leaves the element visible on the page, but the user cannot access the control. The same browsers provide a readOnly property, which doesn't dim the field, but prevents typing in the field.

Text fields and events

Focus and blur also interact with other possible user actions to a text object: selecting and changing. *Selecting* occurs when the user clicks and drags across any text in the field; *changing* occurs when the user makes any alteration to the content of the field and then either tabs or clicks away from that field.

When you design event handlers for fields, be aware that a user's interaction with a field may trigger more than one event with a single action. For instance, clicking a field to select text may trigger both a focus and select event. If you have conflicting actions in the onfocus and onselect event handlers, your scripts can do some weird things to the user's experience with your page. Displaying alert dialog boxes, for instance, also triggers blur events, so a field that has both an onselect handler (which displays the alert) and an onblur handler gets a nasty interaction from the two.

As a result, be very judicious with the number of event handlers you specify in any text object definition. If possible, pick one user action that you want to use to initiate some JavaScript code execution and deploy it consistently on the page. Not all fields require event handlers — only those you want to perform some action as the result of user activity in that field.

Many newcomers also become confused by the behavior of the change event. To prevent this event from being sent to the field for every character the user types, any change to a field is determined only *after* the field loses focus by the user's clicking or tabbing away from it. At that point, instead of a blur event being sent to the field, only a change event is sent, triggering an onchange event handler if one is defined for the field. This extra burden of having to click or tab away from a field may entice you to shift any onchange event handler tasks to a separate button that the user must click to initiate action on the field contents.

Starting with version 4 browsers, text fields also have event handlers for keyboard actions, namely onkeydown, onkeypress, and onkeyup. With these event handlers, you can intercept keystrokes before the characters reach the text field. Thus, you can use keyboard events to prevent anything but numbers from being entered into a text box while the user types the characters.

To extract the current content of a text object, summon the property document.formName.fieldName.value. After you have the string value, you can use JavaScript's string object methods to parse or otherwise massage that text as needed for your script. If the field entry is a number and you need to pass that value to methods requiring numbers, you have to convert the text to a number with the help of the parseInt() or parseFloat() global functions.

Text Boxes and the Enter/Return Key

Early browsers established a convention that continues to this day. When a form consists of only one text box, a press of the Enter/Return key acts the same as clicking a Submit button for the form. You have probably experienced this many times when entering a value into a single search field of a form. Press the Enter/Return key, and the search request goes off to the server.

The flip side is that if the form contains more than one text box, the Enter/Return key does no submission from any of the text boxes (IE for the Mac and Safari are exceptions: they submit no matter how many text boxes there are). But with the advent of keyboard events, you can script this action (or the invocation of a client-side script) into any text boxes of the form you like. To make it work with all flavors of browsers capable of keyboard events requires a small conversion function that extracts the DOM-specific desired code from the keystroke. The following listing shows a sample page that demonstrates how to implement a function that inspects each keystroke from a text field and initiates processing if the key pressed is the Enter/Return key:

```
<html>
  <head>
    <title>Enter/Return Event Trigger</title>
    <script type="text/javascript">
    // Event object processor
    function isEnterKey(evt) {
        evt = (evt) ? evt : ((window.event) ? window.event : null);
        var keyCode;
        if (evt) {
            keyCode = (evt.keyCode) ? evt.keyCode : evt.which;
        }
        return (keyCode == 13);
    }

    function processOnEnter(fld, evt) {
        if (isEnterKey(evt)) {
            alert("Ready to do some work with the form.");
            return false;
        }
        return true;
    }
    </script>
  </head>
  <body>
    <h1>Enter/Return Event Trigger</h1>
    <hr />
    <form onsubmit="return false">
        Field 1: <input type="text" name="field1"
        onkeydown="processOnEnter(this, event)" />
        Field 2: <input type="text" name="field2"
        onkeydown="processOnEnter(this, event)" />
        Field 3: <input type="text" name="field3"
        onkeydown="processOnEnter(this, event)" />
    </form>
  </body>
</html>
```

Properties
defaultValue

Value: String.   Read-Only
Compatibility: WinIE3+, MacIE3+, NN2+, Moz+, Safari+

Though your users and your scripts are free to muck with the contents of a text object by assigning strings to the value property, you can always extract (and thus restore, if necessary) the string assigned to the text object in its <input> definition. The defaultValue property yields the string parameter of the value attribute.

> **NOTE** Listings 23-1, 23-2, and 23-3 feature a form with only one text input element. The rules of HTML forms say that such a form submits itself if the user presses the Enter key whenever the field has focus. Such a submission to a form whose action is undefined causes the page to reload, thus stopping any scripts that are running at the time. form elements for these example listings contain an onsubmit event handler that both blocks the submission and attempts to trigger the text box onchange event handler to run the demonstration script. In some browsers, such as MacIE5, you may have to press the Tab key or click outside of the text box to trigger the onchange event handler after you enter a new value.

Listing 23-1 has a simple form with a single field that has a default value set in its tag. A function (resetField()) restores the contents of the page's lone field to the value assigned to it in the <input> definition. For a single-field page such as this, defining a type="reset" button or calling form.reset() works the same way because such buttons reestablish default values of all elements of a form. But if you want to reset only a subset of fields in a form, follow the example button and function in Listing 23-1.

LISTING 23-1

Resetting a Text Object to Default Value

```
<html>
  <head>
    <title>Text Object DefaultValue</title>
    <script type="text/javascript">
    function upperMe(field) {
      field.value = field.value.toUpperCase();
    }
    function resetField(form) {
      form.converter.value = form.converter.defaultValue;
    }
    </script>
  </head>
  <body>
    <form onsubmit="window.focus(); return false">
      Enter lowercase letters for conversion to uppercase: <input
      type="text" id="convert" name="converter" value="sample"
      onchange="upperMe(this)" /> <input type="button" id="reset"
      value="Reset Field" onclick="resetField(this.form)" />
    </form>
  </body>
</html>
```

> **NOTE**   The property assignment event handling technique used in this example and throughout the chapter is a deliberate simplification to make the code more readable. It is generally better to use the more modern approach of binding events using the addEventListener() (NN6+/Moz/W3C) or attachEvent() (IE5+) methods. A modern cross-browser event handling technique is explained in detail in Chapter 25.

Related Items: value property.

form

Value: Form object reference.   Read-Only
Compatibility: WinIE3+, MacIE3+, NN2+, Moz+, Safari+

A property of every input element object is a reference to the form element that contains the control. This property can be very convenient in a script when you are dealing with one form control that is passed as a parameter to the function and you want to either access another control in the same form or invoke a method of the form. An event handler of any input element can pass this as the parameter, and the function can still get access to the form without having to hard-wire the script to a particular form name or document layout.

The following function fragment receives a reference to a text element as the parameter. The text element reference is needed to decide which branch to follow; then the form is submitted.

```
function setAction(fld) {
    if (fld.value.indexOf("@") != -1) {
        fld.form.action = "mailto:" + fld.value;
    } else {
        fld.form.action = "cgi-bin/normal.pl";
    }
    fld.form.submit();
}
```

Notice how this function doesn't have to worry about the form reference, because its job is to work with whatever form encloses the text field that triggers this function.

Related Items: form object.

maxLength

Value: Integer.   Read/Write
Compatibility: WinIE4+, MacIE4+, NN6+, Moz+, Safari+

The maxLength property controls the maximum number of characters allowed to be typed into the field. There is no interaction between the maxLength and size properties. This value is normally set initially via the maxlength attribute of the input element.

Use The Evaluator (Chapter 13) to experiment with the maxLength property. The top text field has no default value, but you can temporarily set it to only a few characters and see how it affects entering new values:

```
document.forms[0].input.maxLength = 3;
```

Try typing this into the field to see the results of the change. To restore the default value, reload the page.

Related Items: size property.

name

Value: Identifier string.   Read/Write
Compatibility: WinIE3+, MacIE3+, NN2+, Moz+, Safari+

Text object names are important for two reasons. First, if your HTML page submits information to a CGI script or server application, the input device passes the name of the text object along with the data to help the server program identify the data being supplied by the form. Second, you can use a text object's name in its reference within JavaScript coding. If you assign distinctive, meaningful names to your fields, these names will help you read and debug your JavaScript listings (and will help others follow your scripting tactics).

Be as descriptive about your text object names as you can. Borrowing text from the field's on-page label may help you mentally map a scripted reference to a physical field on the page. Like all JavaScript object names, text object names must begin with a letter and be followed by any number of letters or numbers. Avoid punctuation symbols with the exception of the very safe underscore character.

Although I urge you to use distinctive names for all objects you define in a document, you can make a case for assigning the same name to a series of interrelated fields — and JavaScript is ready to help. Within a single form, any reused name for the same object type is placed in an indexed array for that name. For example, if you define three fields with the name `entry`, the following statements retrieve the `value` property for each field:

```
data = document.forms[0].entry[0].value;
data = document.forms[0].entry[1].value;
data = document.forms[0].entry[2].value;
```

This construction may be useful if you want to cycle through all of a form's related fields to determine which ones are blank. Elsewhere, your script probably needs to know what kind of information each field is supposed to receive, so that it can process the data intelligently. I don't often recommend reusing object names, but you should be aware of how the object model handles them in case you need this construction. See Chapter 21 for more details.

Consult Listing 23-2 later in this chapter, where I use the text object's name, `convertor`, as part of the reference when assigning a value to the field. To extract the name of a text object, you can use the property reference. Therefore, assuming that your script doesn't know the name of the first object in the first form of a document, the statement is

```
var objectName = document.forms[0].elements[0].name;
```

Related Items: `form.elements` property; all other `form` element objects' `name` property.

readOnly

Value: Boolean.   Read/Write
Compatibility: WinIE4+, MacIE4+, NN6+, Moz+, Safari+

To display text in a text field yet prevent users from modifying it, newer browsers offer the `readOnly` property (and tag attribute). When set to `true`, the property prevents users from changing or removing the content of the text field. Unlike a disabled text field, a read-only text field looks just like an editable one.

Use The Evaluator (Chapter 13) to set the bottom text box to be read-only. Begin by typing anything you want in the bottom text box. Then enter the following statement into the top text box:

```
document.forms[0].inspector.readOnly = true;
```

document.*formObject.textObject*.value

Although existing text in the box is selectable (and therefore can be copied into the clipboard), it cannot be modified or removed.

Related Items: disabled property.

size

Value: Integer.   Read/Write
Compatibility: WinIE4+, MacIE4+, NN6+, Moz+, Safari+

Unless otherwise directed, a text box is rendered to accommodate approximately 20 characters of text for the font family and size assigned to the element's stylesheet. You can adjust this under script control (in case the size attribute of the tag wasn't enough) via the size property, whose value is measured in characters (not pixels). Be forewarned, however, that browsers don't always make completely accurate estimates of the space required to display a set number of characters. If you are setting the maxlength attribute of a text box, making the size one or two characters larger is often a safe bet.

Resize the bottom text box of The Evaluator (Chapter 13) by entering the following statements into the top text box:

```
document.forms[0].inspector.size = 20;
document.forms[0].inspector.size = 400;
```

Reload the page to return the size back to normal (or set the value to 80).

Related Items: maxLength property.

type

Value: String (text).   Read-Only
Compatibility: WinIE4+, MacIE4+, NN3+, Moz+, Safari+

Use the type property to help you identify a text input object from an unknown group of form elements.

Related Items: form.elements property.

value

Value: String.   Read/Write
Compatibility: WinIE3+, MacIE3+, NN2+, Moz+, Safari+

A text object's value property is the two-way gateway to the content of the field. A reference to an object's value property returns the string currently showing in the field. Note that all values coming from a text object are string values. If your field prompts a user to enter a number, your script may have to perform data conversion to the number-as-string value ("42" instead of plain, old 42) before a script can perform math operations on it. JavaScript tries to be as automatic about this data conversion as possible and follows some rules about it (see Chapter 28). If you see an error message that says a value is not a number (for a math operation), the value is still a string.

Your script places text of its own into a field for display to the user by assigning a string to the value property of a text object. Use the simple assignment operator. For example:

```
document.forms[0].ZIP.value = "90210";
```

JavaScript is more forgiving about data types when assigning values to a text object. JavaScript does its best to convert a value to a string on its way to a text object display. Even Boolean values get converted to their string equivalents `true` or `false`. Scripts can place numeric values into fields without a hitch. But remember that if a script later retrieves these values from the text object, they will come back as strings. About the only values that don't get converted are objects. They typically show up in text boxes as `[object]` or, in some browsers, a more descriptive label for the object.

Storing arrays in a field requires special processing. You need to use the `array.join()` method to convert an array into a string. Each array entry is delimited by a character you establish in the `array.join()` method. Later you can use the `string.split()` method to turn this delimited string into an array.

As a demonstration of how to retrieve and assign values to a text object, Listing 23-2 shows how the action in an `onchange` event handler is triggered. Enter any lowercase letters into the field and click out of the field. I pass a reference to the entire form object as a parameter to the event handler. The function extracts the value, converts it to uppercase (using one of the JavaScript string object methods), and assigns it back to the same field in that form.

LISTING 23-2

Getting and Setting a Text Object's Value

```html
<html>
    <head>
        <title>Text Object Value</title>
        <script type="text/javascript">
        function upperMe(form) {
            inputStr = form.converter.value;
            form.converter.value = inputStr.toUpperCase();
        }
        </script>
    </head>
    <body>
        <form onsubmit="window.focus(); return false">
            Enter lowercase letters for conversion to uppercase: <input
            type="text" name="converter" value="sample"
            onchange="upperMe(this.form)" />
        </form>
    </body>
</html>
```

I also show two other ways to accomplish the same task, each one more efficient than the previous example. Both utilize the shortcut object reference to get at the heart of the text object. Listing 23-3 passes the text object — contained in the `this` reference — to the function handler. Because that text object contains a complete reference to it (out of sight, but there just the same), you can access the `value` property of that object and assign a string to that object's `value` property in a simple assignment statement.

document.*formObject.textObject*.value

LISTING 23-3

Passing a Text Object (as this) to the Function

```html
<html>
    <head>
        <title>Text Object Value</title>
        <script type="text/javascript">
        function upperMe(field) {
            field.value = field.value.toUpperCase();
        }
        </script>
    </head>
    <body>
        <form onsubmit="window.focus(); return false">
            Enter lowercase letters for conversion to uppercase: <input
            type="text" name="converter" value="sample"
            onchange="upperMe(this)" />
        </form>
    </body>
</html>
```

Yet another way is to deal with the field values directly in an embedded event handler — instead of calling an external function (which is possibly a little cleaner since there is just a single line of code in the function anyway). With the upperMe() function removed from the document, the event handler attribute of the <input> tag changes to do all the work:

```html
<input type="text" name="converter" value="sample"
    onchange="this.value = this.value.toUpperCase()" />
```

The right-hand side of the assignment expression extracts the current contents of the field and (with the help of the toUpperCase() method of the string object) converts the original string to all uppercase letters. The result of this operation is assigned to the value property of the field.

The application of the this keyword in the previous examples may be confusing at first, but these examples represent the range of ways in which you can use such references effectively. Using this by itself as a parameter to an object's event handler refers only to that single object — a text object in Listing 23-3. If you want to pass along a broader scope of objects that contain the current object, use the this keyword along with the outer object layer that you want. In Listing 23-2, I sent a reference to the entire form along by specifying this.form — meaning the form that contains "this" object, which is being defined in the line of HTML code.

At the other end of the scale, you can use similar-looking syntax to specify a particular property of the this object. Thus, in the last example, I zeroed in on just the value property of the current object being defined — this.value. Although the formats of this.form and this.value appear the same, the fact that one is a reference to an object and the other just a value can influence the way your functions work. When you pass a reference to an object, the function can read and modify properties of that object (as well as invoke its functions); but when the parameter passed to a function is just a property value, you cannot modify that value without building a complete reference to the object and its value.

Related Items: form.defaultValue property.

Methods
blur()

Returns: Nothing.
Compatibility: WinIE3+, MacIE3+, NN2+, Moz+, Safari+

Just as a camera lens blurs when it goes out of focus, a text object blurs when it loses focus — when someone clicks or tabs out of the field. Under script control, blur() deselects whatever may be selected in the field, and the text insertion pointer leaves the field. The pointer does not proceed to the next field in tabbing order, as it does if you perform a blur by tabbing out of the field manually.

The following statement invokes the blur() method on a text box named vanishText:

    document.forms[0].vanishText.blur();

Related Items: focus() method; onblur event handler.

focus()

Returns: Nothing.
Compatibility: WinIE3+, MacIE3+, NN2+, Moz+, Safari+

For a text object, having focus means that the text insertion pointer is flashing in that text object's field (having focus means something different for buttons in a Windows environment). Giving a field focus is like opening it up for human editing.

Setting the focus of a field containing text does not let you place the cursor at any specified location in the field. The cursor usually appears at the beginning of the text (although in WinIE4+, you can use the TextRange object to position the cursor wherever you want in the field, as shown in Chapter 36 on the CD-ROM). To prepare a field for entry to remove the existing text, use both the focus() and select() methods.

See Listing 23-4 for an example of an application of the focus() method in concert with the select() method.

Related Items: select() method; onfocus event handler.

select()

Returns: Nothing.
Compatibility: WinIE3+, MacIE3+, NN2+, Moz+, Safari+

Selecting a field under script control means selecting all text within the text object. A typical application is one in which an entry validation script detects a mistake on the part of the user. After alerting the user to the mistake (via a window.alert() dialog box), the script finishes its task by selecting the text of the field in question. Not only does this action draw the user's eye to the field needing attention (especially important if the validation code is checking multiple fields), but it also keeps the old text there for the user to examine for potential problems. With the text selected, the next key the user presses erases the former entry.

Trying to select a text object's contents with a click of a button is problematic. One problem is that a click of the button brings the document's focus to the button, which disrupts the selection process. For more ensured selection, the script should invoke both the focus() and the select() methods for the field, in that order. No penalty exists for issuing both methods, and the extra insurance of the second method provides a more consistent user experience with the page.

document.*formObject.textObject*.select()

Some versions of WinIE are known to exhibit anomalous (meaning buggy) behavior when using the technique of focusing and selecting a text field after the appearance of an alert dialog box. The fix is not elegant, but it works: inserting an artificial delay via the `setTimeout()` method before invoking a separate function that focuses and selects the field. Better-behaved browsers accept the workaround with no penalty.

Selecting a text object via script does *not* trigger the same `onselect` event handler for that object as the one that triggers if a user manually selects text in the field. Therefore, no event handler script is executed when a user invokes the `select()` method.

A click of the Verify button in Listing 23-4 performs a validation on the contents of the text box, making sure the entry consists of all numbers. All work is controlled by the `checkNumeric()` function, which receives a reference to the field needing inspection as a parameter. Because of the way the delayed call to the `doSelection()` function has to be configured, various parts of what will become a valid reference to the form are extracted from the field's and form's properties. If the validation (performed in the `isNumber()` function) fails, the `setSelection()` method is invoked after an artificial delay of zero milliseconds. As goofy as this sounds, this method is all that IE needs to recover from the display and closure of the alert dialog box. Because the first parameter of the `setTimeout()` method must be a string, the example assembles a string invocation of the `setSelection()` function via string versions of the form and field names. All that the `setSelection()` function does is focus and select the field whose reference is passed as a parameter. This function is now generalizable to work with multiple text boxes in a more complex form.

LISTING 23-4

Selecting a Field

```
<html>
  <head>
    <title>Text Object Select/Focus</title>
    <script type="text/javascript">
    // general purpose function to see if a suspected numeric input is a number
    function isNumber(inputStr) {
        for (var i = 0; i < inputStr.length; i++) {
            var oneChar = inputStr.charAt(i);
            if (oneChar < "0" || oneChar > "9") {
                alert("Please make sure entries are numbers only.");
                return false;
            }
        }
        return true;
    }

    function checkNumeric(fld) {
        var inputStr = fld.value;
        var fldName = fld.name;
        var formName = fld.form.name;
        if (isNumber(inputStr)) {
            // statements if true
        } else {
            setTimeout("doSelection(document." + formName + "." + fldName +
                ")", 0);
        }
```

```
    }

    function doSelection(fld) {
        fld.focus();
        fld.select();
    }

    </script>
</head>
<body>
    <form name="entryForm" onsubmit="return false">
        Enter any positive integer: <input type="text" name="numeric" />
        <p><input type="button" value="Verify"
            onclick="checkNumeric(this.form.numeric)" /></p>
    </form>
</body>
</html>
```

Related Items: focus() method; onselect event handler.

Event handlers
onafterupdate
onbeforeupdate
onerrorupdate

Compatibility: WinIE4+, MacIE-, NN-, Moz-, Safari-

If you are using WinIE data binding on a text element, the element is subject to three possible events in the course of retrieving updated data. The onbeforeupdate and onafterupdate events fire immediately before and after (respectively) the update takes place. If an error occurs in the retrieval of data from the database, the onerrorupdate event fires.

All three events may be used for advisory purposes. For example, an onafterupdate event handler may temporarily change the font characteristics of the element to signify the arrival of fresh data. Or an onerrorupdate event handler may fill the field with hyphens because no valid data exists for the field. These events apply only to input elements of type text (meaning not password or hidden types).

Related Items: dataFld, dataSrc properties (Chapter 15).

onblur
onfocus
onselect

Compatibility: WinIE3+, MacIE3+, NN2+, Moz+, Safari+

All three of these event handlers should be used only after you have a firm understanding of the interrelationships of the events that reach text objects. You must use extreme care and conduct lots of user testing before including more than one of these three event handlers in a text object. Because some events cannot occur without triggering others either immediately before or after (for example, an onfocus occurs immediately before an onselect if the field did not have focus before), whatever actions you script for these events should be as distinct as possible to avoid interference or overlap.

In particular, be careful about displaying modal dialog boxes (for example, window.alert() dialog boxes) in response to the onfocus event handler. Because the text field loses focus when the alert displays and then regains focus after the alert is closed, you can get yourself into a loop that is difficult to break out of. If you get trapped in this manner, try the keyboard shortcut for reloading the page (Ctrl+R or ⌘-R) repeatedly as you keep closing the dialog box window.

A question often arises about whether data-entry validation should be triggered by the onblur or onchange event handler. An onblur validation cannot be fooled, whereas an onchange one can be (the user simply doesn't change the bad entry as he or she tabs out of the field). What I don't like about the onblur way is it can cause a frustrating experience for a user who wants to tab through a field now and come back to it later (assuming your validation requires data be entered into the field before submission). As in Chapter 43's discussion (on the CD-ROM) about form data validation, I recommend using onchange event handlers to trigger immediate data checking and then using another last-minute check in a function called by the form's onsubmit event handler.

To demonstrate one of these event handlers, Listing 23-5 shows how you may use the window's status bar as a prompt message area after a user activates any field of a form. When the user tabs to or clicks on a field, the prompt message associated with that field appears in the status bar. In Figure 23-1, the user has tabbed to the second text box, which caused the status bar message to display a prompt for the field.

NOTE Some people frown upon the idea of using the browser's status bar to convey information via JavaScript, with the logic being that you shouldn't tamper with its built-in purpose of displaying status messages directly from the browser itself. In fact, Mozilla browsers by default prevent you from altering the status text. You can easily change this setting by navigating to the about:config URL in your Mozilla-based browser, and then changing the dom.disable_window_status_change preference to false; just double-click a preference to change its value.

LISTING 23-5

The onfocus Event Handler

```
<html>
  <head>
    <title>Elements Array</title>
    <script type="text/javascript">
    function prompt(msg) {
       window.status = "Please enter your " + msg + ".";
    }
    </script>
  </head>
  <body>
    <form>
      Enter your first name:<input type="text" name="firstName"
      onfocus="prompt('first name')" />
      <p>Enter your last name:<input type="text" name="lastName"
      onfocus="prompt('last name')" /></p>
      <p>Enter your address:<input type="text" name="address"
```

```
         onfocus="prompt('address')" /></p>
         <p>Enter your city:<input type="text" name="city"
         onfocus="prompt('city')" /></p>
      </form>
   </body>
</html>
```

FIGURE 23-1

An onfocus event handler triggers a status bar display.

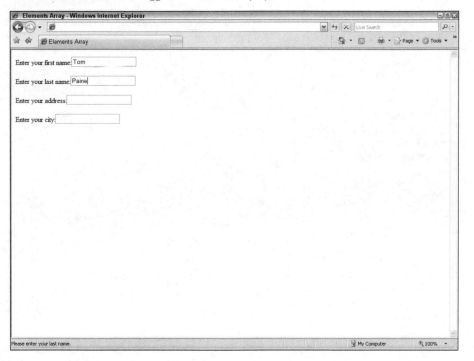

onchange

Compatibility: WinIE3+, MacIE3+, NN2+, Moz+, Safari+

Of all the event handlers for a text object, you will probably use the `onchange` handler the most in your forms (see Listing 23-6). This event is the one I prefer for triggering the validation of whatever entry the user just typed in the field. The potential hazard of trying to do only a batch-mode data validation of all entries before submitting an entire form is that the user's mental focus is away from the entry of a given field as well. When you immediately validate an entry, the user is already thinking about the information category in question. See Chapter 43 on the CD-ROM for more about data-entry validation, including a technique that validates user input in real time as a user types each character.

LISTING 23-6

Data Validation via an onchange Event Handler

```html
<html>
    <head>
        <title>Text Object Select/Focus</title>
        <script type="text/javascript">
        // general purpose function to see if a suspected numeric input is a number
        function isNumber(inputStr) {
            for (var i = 0; i < inputStr.length; i++) {
                var oneChar = inputStr.substring(i, i + 1);
                if (oneChar < "0" || oneChar > "9") {
                    alert("Please make sure entries are numbers only.");
                    return false;
                }
            }
            return true;
        }

        function checkIt(form) {
            inputStr = form.numeric.value;
            if (isNumber(inputStr)) {
                // statements if true
            } else {
                form.numeric.focus();
                form.numeric.select();
            }
        }
        </script>
    </head>
    <body>
        <form name="entryForm" onsubmit="checkIt(this); return false">
            Enter any positive integer: <input type="text" name="numeric"
            onchange="checkIt(this.form)" />
        </form>
    </body>
</html>
```

password Input Object

Properties	Methods	Event Handlers
See "Text Input Object" section earlier in this chapter.		

Syntax

See "Text Input Object" section earlier in this chapter.

Compatibility: WinIE3+, MacIE3+, NN2+, Moz+, Safari+

About this object

A password-style field looks like a text object, but when the user types something into the field, only asterisks or bullets (depending on your operating system) appear in the field. For the sake of security, any password exchanges should be handled by a server-side program (CGI, Java servlet, and so on).

Scripts can treat a password object exactly like a text `input` object. This may lead a scripter to capture a user's Web site password for storage in the `document.cookie` of the client machine. A password object value property is returned in plain language, so that such a captured password would be stored in the cookie file the same way. Because a client machine's cookie file can be examined on the local computer (perhaps by a snoop during lunch hour), plain-language storage of passwords is a potential security risk. Instead, develop a scripted encryption algorithm for your page for reading and writing the password in the cookie. Most password-protected sites, however, usually have a server program (CGI, for example) encrypt the password prior to sending it back to the cookie.

See the text object discussion for the behavior of password object's properties, methods, and event handlers. The `type` property for this object returns `password`.

hidden Input Object

Properties	Methods	Event Handlers
See "Text Input Object" section earlier in the chapter.		

Syntax

See "Text Input Object" section earlier in the chapter.

Compatibility: WinIE4+, MacIE4+, NN3+, Moz+, Safari+

About this object

A hidden object is a simple string holder within a form object whose contents are not visible to the user of your Web page. Despite the long list of properties, methods, and event handlers that this input element type inherits by virtue of being an input element, you will be doing little with a `hidden` element beyond reading and writing its `value` property.

The `hidden` object plays a vital role in applications that rely on CGI programs on the server. Very often, the server has data that it needs to convey to itself the next time the client makes a submission (for example, a user ID captured at the application's login page). A CGI program can generate an HTML page with the necessary data hidden from the user but located in a field transmitted to the server at submit time.

Along the same lines, a page for a server application may present a user-friendly interface that makes data-entry easy for the user. But on the server end, the database or other application requires that the data be in a more esoteric format. A script located in the page generated for the user can use the onsubmit event handler to perform the last-minute assembly of user-friendly data into database-friendly data in a hidden field. When the CGI program receives the request from the client, it passes along the hidden field value to the database.

I am not a fan of the hidden object for use on client-side-only JavaScript applications. If I want to deliver with my JavaScript-enabled pages some default data collections or values, I do so in JavaScript variables and arrays as part of the script.

Because scripted changes to the contents of a hidden field are fragile (for example, a soft reload erases the changes), the only place you should consider making such changes is in the same script that submits a form to a CGI program or in a function triggered by an onsubmit event handler. In effect, you're just using the hidden fields as holding pens for the scripted data to be submitted. For more persistent storage, use the document.cookie property or genuine text fields in hidden frames, even if just for the duration of the visit to the page.

For information about the properties of the hidden object, consult the earlier listing for the text input object. The type property for this object returns hidden.

textarea Element Object

For HTML element properties, methods, and event handlers, see Chapter 15.

Properties	Methods	Event Handlers
cols	createTextRange()	onafterupdate†
form†	select()†	onbeforeupdate†
name†		onchange
readOnly†		onerrorupdate†
rows		
type†		
wrap		

† See "Text Input Object" section earlier in the chapter

Syntax

Accessing textarea element object properties or methods:

```
(All)        [window.]document.formName.textareaName.property |
             method([parameters])
(All)        [window.]document.formName.elements[index].property |
             method([parameters])
(All)        [window.]document.forms[index].textareaName.property |
             method([parameters])
```

```
(All)        [window.]document.forms["formName"].textareaName.property |
             method([parameters])
(All)        [window.]document.forms["formName"].elements[index].property |
             method([parameters])
(IE4+)       [window.]document.all.elemID.property | method([parameters])
(IE5+/W3C)   [window.]document.getElementById("elemID").property |
             method([parameters])
```

Compatibility: WinIE3+, MacIE3+, NN2+, Moz+, Safari+

About this object

Although not in the same HTML syntax family as other `<input>` elements of a form, a `textarea` object is indeed a form input element, providing multiple-line text input facilities. Although some browsers let you put a `textarea` element anywhere in a document, it really should be contained by a `form` element.

A `textarea` object closely resembles a text object, except for attributes that define its physical appearance on the page. Because the intended use of a `textarea` object is for multiple-line text input, the attributes include specifications for height (number of rows) and width (number of columns in the monospaced font). No matter what size you specify, the browser displays a textarea with horizontal and vertical scrollbars in older browsers; more recent browsers tend to be smarter about displaying scrollbars only when needed (although there are exceptions). Text entered in the textarea wraps by default in all modern browsers, although the wrapping can be adjusted via the `wrap` attribute in IE. The `wrap` attribute can be set to `soft` (the default), `hard`, or `off` in IE. The `soft` and `hard` settings result in word wrapping, whereas the `off` setting causes text to scroll for a significant distance horizontally (the horizontal scrollbar appears automatically). This field is, indeed, a primitive text field by GUI computing standards in that font specifications made possible in newer browsers by way of stylesheets apply to all text in the box.

Use The Evaluator Sr. (Chapter 13) to play with the `cols` and `rows` property settings for the Results textarea on that page. Shrink the width of the textarea by entering the following statement into the top text box:

```
document.forms[0].output.cols = 30;
```

And make the textarea one row deeper:

```
document.forms[0].output.rows++;
```

All properties, methods, and event handlers of text objects apply to the `textarea` object. They all behave exactly the same way (except, of course, for the `type` property, which is `textarea`). Therefore, refer to the previous listings for the text object for scripting details for those items. Some additional properties that are unique to the `textarea` object are discussed next.

Carriage returns inside textareas

The three classes of operating systems supported by modern browsers — Windows, Macintosh, and UNIX — do not agree about what constitutes a carriage return character in a text string. This discrepancy carries over to the `textarea` object and its contents on these platforms.

After a user enters text and uses Enter/Return on the keyboard, one or more unseen characters are inserted into the string. In the parlance of JavaScript's literal string characters, the carriage return consists of some combination of the newline (\n) and return (\r) character. The following table shows the characters inserted into the string for each operating system category.

textarea.wrap

Operating System	Character String
Windows	\r\n
Macintosh	\r
UNIX	\n

This tidbit is valuable if you need to remove carriage returns from a textarea for processing in a CGI or local script. The problem is that you obviously need to perform platform-specific operations on each. For the situation in which you must preserve the carriage return locations, but your server-side database cannot accept the carriage return values, I suggest you use the string.escape() method to URL-encode the string. The return character is converted to %0D and the newline character is converted to %0A. Of course these characters occupy extra character spaces in your database, so these additions must be accounted for in your database design.

As far as writing carriage returns into textareas, the situation is a bit easier. From NN3 and IE4 onward, if you specify any one of the combinations in the preceding table, all platforms know how to automatically convert the data to the form native to the operating system. Therefore, you can set the value of a textarea object to 1\r\n2\r\n3 in all platforms, and a columnar list of the numbers 1, 2, and 3 will appear in those fields. Or, if you URL-encoded the text for saving to a database, you can unescape that character string before setting the textarea value, and no matter what platform the visitor has, the carriage returns are rendered correctly. Upon reading those values again by script, you can see that the carriage returns are in the form of the platform (shown in the previous table).

Properties

cols
rows

Value: Integer.   Read/Write
Compatibility: WinIE4+, MacIE4+, NN6+, Moz+, Safari+

The displayed size of a textarea element is defined by its cols and rows attributes, which are represented in the object model by the cols and rows properties, respectively. Values for these properties are integers. For cols, the number represents the number of characters that can be displayed without horizontal scrolling of the textarea; for rows, the number is the number of lines of text that can be displayed without vertical scrolling.

Related Items: wrap property.

wrap

Value: String.   Read/Write
Compatibility: WinIE4+, MacIE4+, NN-, Moz-, Safari-

The wrap property represents the wrap attribute, which, surprisingly, is not a W3C-sanctioned attribute as of HTML 4.01. In any case, IE4+ lets you adjust the property by scripting. Allowable string values are soft, hard, and off. The browser adds soft returns (the default in IE) to word-wrap the content, but no carriage return characters are actually inserted into the text. A setting for hard returns means that carriage return characters are added to the text (and would be submitted with the value to a server application). With wrap set to off, text continues to extend beyond the right edge of the textarea until the user manually presses the Enter/Return key.

Related Items: cols property.

Methods

createTextRange()

Returns: TextRange object.
Compatibility: WinIE4+, MacIE-, NN-, Moz-, Safari-

The createTextRange() method for a textarea operates just as the document.createTextRange() method, except that the range consists of text inside the textarea element, apart from the regular body content. This version of the TextRange object comes in handy when you want a script to control the location of the text insertion pointer inside a textarea element for the user.

See the example for the TextRange.move() method in Chapter 36 on the CD-ROM to see how to control the text insertion pointer inside a textarea element.

Related Items: TextRange object (Chapter 36 on the CD-ROM).

Chapter 24

Select, Option, and FileUpload Objects

*S*election lists — whether in the form of pop-up menus or scrolling lists — are space-saving form elements in HTML pages. They enable designers to present a lot of information in a comparatively small space. At the same time, users are familiar with the interface elements from working in their own operating systems' preference dialog boxes and application windows.

However, selection lists are more difficult to script, especially in older browsers, because the objects themselves are complicated entities. Scripts find all the real data associated with the form control in option elements that are nested inside select elements. As you can see throughout this chapter, backward-compatible references necessary to extract information from a select element object and its option objects can get pretty long. On the upside, the most painful backward compatibility efforts are all but unnecessary given the proliferation of modern browsers.

The other object covered in this chapter, the fileUpload input object, is frequently misunderstood as being more powerful than it actually is. It is, alas, not the great file transfer elixir desired by many page authors.

IN THIS CHAPTER

Triggering action based on a user's selection in a pop-up or select list

Modifying the contents of select objects

Using the fileUpload object

select Element Object

For HTML element properties, methods, and event handlers, see Chapter 15.

Properties	Methods	Event Handlers
form†	add()	onchange
length	options[i].add()	
multiple	item()	
name†	namedItem()	
options[]	remove()	
selectedIndex	options[i].remove()	
size		
type		
value		

†See "Text Input Object" (Chapter 23).

Syntax

Accessing select element object properties:

```
(All)       [window.]document.formName.selectName.property | method([parameters])
(All)       [window.]document.formName.elements[index].property |
            method([parameters])
(All)       [window.]document.forms[index].selectName.property |
            method([parameters])
(All)       [window.]document.forms["formName"].selectName.property |
            method([parameters])
(All)       [window.]document.forms["formName"].elements[index].property |
            method([parameters])
(IE4+)      [window.]document.all.elemID.property | method([parameters])
(IE5+/W3C)  [window.]document.getElementById("elemID").property |
            method([parameters])
```

Compatibility: WinIE3+, MacIE3+, NN2+, Moz+, Safari+

About this object

select element objects are perhaps the most visually interesting user interface elements among the standard built-in objects. In one format, they appear on the page as pop-up lists; in another format, they appear as scrolling list boxes. Pop-up lists, in particular, offer efficient use of page real estate for presenting a list of choices for the user. Moreover, only the choice selected by the user shows on the page, minimizing the clutter of unneeded verbiage.

Compared with other JavaScript objects, select objects are difficult to script — mostly because of the complexity of data that goes into a list of items. What the user sees as a select element on the page consists of both that element and option elements that contain the actual choices from which the user makes a selection. Some properties that are of value to scripters belong to the select object, whereas others belong to the nested option objects. For example, you can extract the number (index) of the currently selected option in the list — a property of the entire select object. To get the displayed text of the selected option, however, you must zero in further to extract the text property of a single option among all options defined for the object.

When you define a select object within a form, the construction of the `<select>...</select>` tag pair is easy to inadvertently mess up. First, most attributes that define the entire object — such as name, size, and event handlers — are attributes of the opening `<select>` tag. Between the end of the opening tag and the closing `</select>` tag are additional tags for each option to be displayed in the list. The following object definition creates a selection pop-up list containing three color choices:

```
<form>
<select name="RGBColors" onchange="changeColor(this)">
    <option selected="selected">Red</option>
    <option>Green</option>
    <option>Blue</option>
</select>
</form>
```

The indented formatting of the tags in the HTML document is not critical. I indent the lines of options merely for the sake of readability, which is still a worthy cause even if it isn't technically necessary.

By default, a select element is rendered as a pop-up list. To make it appear as a scrolled list, assign an integer value greater than 1 to the size attribute to specify how many options should be visible in the list without scrolling — how tall the list's box should be, measured in lines. Because scrollbars in GUI environments tend to require a fair amount of space to display a minimum set of clickable areas (including sliding "thumbs"), you should set list-box style sizes to no less than 4. If that makes the list box too tall for your page design, consider using a pop-up menu instead.

Significant differences exist in the way each GUI platform presents pop-up menus. Because each browser sometimes relies on the operating system to display its native pop-up menu style (and sometimes the browser designers go their own way), considerable differences exist among the OS and browser platforms in the size of a given pop-up menu. What fits nicely within a standard window width of one OS may not fit in the window of another OS in a different browser. In other words, you cannot rely on any select object having a precise dimension on a page (in case you're trying to align a select object with an image).

In list-box form, you can set a select object to accept multiple, noncontiguous selections. Users typically accomplish such selections by holding down a modifier key (the Shift, Ctrl, or ⌘ key, depending on the operating system) while clicking additional options. To switch on this capability for a select object, include the multiple attribute constant in the definition.

For each entry in a list, your `<select>` tag definition must include an `<option>` tag plus the text as you want it to appear in the list. If you want a pop-up list to show a default selection when the page loads, you must attach a selected attribute to that item's `<option>` tag. Without this attribute, the default item may be empty or the first item, depending on the browser. (I go more in depth about this in the option object discussion later in this chapter.) You can also assign a string to each option's value attribute. As with radio buttons, this value can be text other than the wording displayed in the list. In essence, your script can act on that "hidden" value rather than on the displayed text, such as letting a plain-language select listing actually refer to a complex URL. This string value is also the value sent to a CGI program (as part of the name-value pair) when the user submits the select object's form.

One behavioral aspect of the select object may influence your page design. The onchange event handler triggers immediately when a user makes a new selection in a pop-up list. If you prefer to delay any action until the user makes other settings in the form, omit an onchange event handler in the select object — but be sure to create a button that enables users to initiate an action governed by those user settings.

Modifying select options (NN3+, IE4+)

Script control gives you considerable flexibility in modifying the contents and selection of a `select` object. There are several techniques at your disposal when it comes to working with the `select` object, including some whose support dates back to NN3 and IE4. I quickly show you how to approach the `select` object from this backward-compatible perspective, and then move on to revealing a W3C standard approach a bit later in the chapter. Some aspects of manipulating the `select` object are rather straightforward, such as changing the `selectObj.options[i].text` property to alter the display of a single-option entry. The situation gets tricky, though, when the number of options in the `select` object changes. Your choices include

- Removing an individual option (and thus collapsing the list)
- Reducing an existing list to a fewer number of options
- Removing all options
- Adding new options to a `select` object

To remove an option from the list, set the specific option to `null`. For example, if a list contains five items and you want to eliminate the third item altogether (reducing the list to four items), the syntax (from the `select` object reference) for doing that task is this:

```
selectObj.options[2] = null;
```

After this statement, `selectObj.options.length` equals 4.

In another scenario, suppose that a `select` object has five options in it and you want to replace it with one having only three options. You first must hard-code the `length` property to 3:

```
selectObj.options.length = 3;
```

Then, set individual `text` and `value` properties for index values 0 through 2.

Perhaps you want to start building a new list of contents by completely deleting the original list (without harming the `select` object). To accomplish this, set the `length` to 0:

```
selectObj.options.length = 0;
```

From here, you have to create new options (as you do when you want to expand a list from, say, three to seven options). The mechanism for creating a new option involves an object constructor: `new Option()`. This constructor accepts up to four parameters, which enable you to specify the equivalent of an `<option>` tag's attributes:

- Text to be displayed in the option
- Contents of the option's `value` property
- Whether the item is the `defaultSelected` option (Boolean)
- Whether the item is selected (Boolean)

You can set any (or none) of these items as part of the constructor and return to other statements to set their properties. I suggest setting the first two parameters (leave the others blank) and then setting the `selected` property separately. The following is an example of a statement that creates a new, fifth entry, in a `select` object and sets both its displayed `text` and `value` properties:

```
selectObj.options[4] = new Option("Yahoo","http://www.yahoo.com");
```

To demonstrate all of these techniques, Listing 24-1 enables you to change the text of a `select` object — first by adjusting the text properties in the same number of options and then by creating an entirely new set of options. Radio button `onclick` event handlers trigger functions for making these changes — rare examples of when radio buttons can logically initiate visible action.

LISTING 24-1

Modifying select Options

```html
<html>
  <head>
    <title>Changing Options On The Fly</title>
    <script type="text/javascript" language="JavaScript">
    // flag to reload page for older NNs
    var isPreNN6 = (navigator.appName == "Netscape" &&
        parseInt(navigator.appVersion) <= 4);

    // initialize color list arrays
    plainList = new Array(6);
    hardList = new Array(6);
    plainList[0] = "cyan";
    hardList[0] = "#00FFFF";
    plainList[1] = "magenta";
    hardList[1] = "#FF00FF";
    plainList[2] = "yellow";
    hardList[2] = "#FFFF00";
    plainList[3] = "lightgoldenrodyellow";
    hardList[3] = "#FAFAD2";
    plainList[4] = "salmon";
    hardList[4] = "#FA8072";
    plainList[5] = "dodgerblue";
    hardList[5] = "#1E90FF";

    // change color language set
    function setLang(which) {
        var listObj = document.forms[0].colors;
        // filter out old browsers
        if (listObj.type) {
            // find out if it's 3 or 6 entries
            var listLength = listObj.length;
            // save selected index
            var currSelected = listObj.selectedIndex;
            // replace individual existing entries
            for (var i = 0; i < listLength; i++) {
                if (which == "plain") {
                    listObj.options[i].text = plainList[i];
                } else {
                    listObj.options[i].text = hardList[i];
                }
```

continued

LISTING 24-1 *(continued)*

```
        }
        if (isPreNN6) {
            history.go(0);
        } else {
            listObj.selectedIndex = currSelected;
        }
    }
}

// create entirely new options list
function setCount(choice) {
    var listObj = document.forms[0].colors;
    // filter out old browsers
    if (listObj.type) {
        // get language setting
        var lang = (document.forms[0].geekLevel[0].checked) ?
            "plain" : "hard";
        // empty options from list
        listObj.length = 0;
        // create new option object for each entry
        for (var i = 0; i < choice.value; i++) {
            if (lang == "plain") {
                listObj.options[i] = new Option(plainList[i]);
            } else {
                listObj.options[i] = new Option(hardList[i]);
            }
        }
        listObj.options[0].selected = true;
        if (isPreNN6) {
            history.go(0);
        }
    }
}
</script>
</head>
<body>
    <h1>Flying Select Options</h1>
    <form>
        Choose a palette size: <input type="radio" name="paletteSize"
        value="3" onclick="setCount(this)" checked="checked" />Three <input
        type="radio" name="paletteSize" value="6"
        onclick="setCount(this)" />Six
        <p>Choose geek level: <input type="radio" name="geekLevel" value=""
            onclick="setLang('plain')" checked="checked" />Plain-language
            <input type="radio" name="geekLevel" value=""
            onclick="setLang('hard')" />Gimme hex-triplets!</p>
        <p>Select a color: <select name="colors">
            <option selected="selected">cyan</option>
            <option>magenta</option>
            <option>yellow</option>
```

```
            </select></p>
        </form>
    </body>
</html>
```

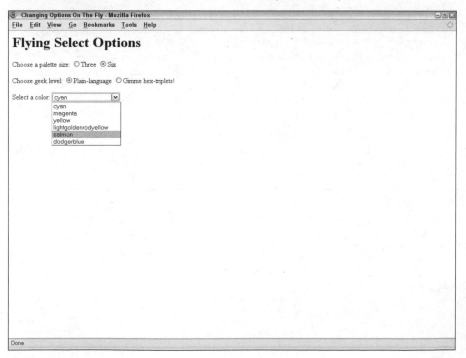

> **NOTE** The property assignment event handling technique used in this example and throughout the chapter is a deliberate simplification to make the code more readable. It is generally better to use the more modern approach of binding events using the addEventListener() (NN6+/Moz/W3C) or attachEvent() (IE5+) methods. A modern cross-browser event handling technique is explained in detail in Chapter 25.

In an effort to make this code easily maintainable, the color choice lists (one in plain language, the other in hexadecimal triplet color specifications) are established as two separate arrays. Repeat loops in both large functions can work with these arrays no matter how big they get.

The first two radio buttons (see Figure 24-1) trigger the setLang() function. This function's first task is to extract a reference to the select object to make additional references shorter (just listObj). Then by way of the length property, you find out how many items are currently displayed in the list because you just want to replace as many items as are already there. In the repeat loop, you set the text property of the existing select options to corresponding entries in either of the two array listings.

FIGURE 24-1

Radio button choices alter the contents of the select object on the fly.

select

In the second pair of radio buttons, each button stores a value indicating how many items should be displayed when the user clicks the button. This number is picked up by the setCount() function and is used in the repeat loop as a maximum counting point. In the meantime, the function finds the selected language radio button and zeros out the select object entirely. Options are rebuilt from scratch using the new Option() constructor for each option. The parameters are the corresponding display text entries from the arrays. Because none of these new options have other properties set (such as which one should be selected by default), the function sets that property of the first item in the list.

Notice that both functions call history.go(0) for legacy browsers after setting up their select objects. The purpose of this call is to give these earlier Navigator versions an opportunity to resize the select object to accommodate the contents of the list. The difference in size here is especially noticeable when you switch from the six-color, plain-language list to any other list. Without resizing, some long items are not readable. IE4+ and NN6+/Moz, on the other hand, automatically redraw the page to the newly sized form element.

Modifying select options (IE4+)

Microsoft offers another way to modify select element options for IE4+, but the technique involves two proprietary methods of the options array property of the select object. Because I cover all other ways of modifying the select element in this section, I cover the IE way of doing things here as well.

The two options array methods are add() and remove(). The add() method takes one required parameter and one optional parameter. The required parameter is a reference to an option element object that your script creates in another statement (using the document.createElement() method). If you omit the second parameter to add(), the new option element is appended to the current collection of items. But you can also specify an index value as the second parameter. The index points to the position in the options array where the new item is to be inserted.

Listing 24-2 shows how to modify the two main functions from Listing 24-1 using the IE approach exclusively (changes and additions appear in bold). The script assumes that only IE browsers ever load the page (in other words, there is no filtering for browser brand here). When replacing one set of options with another, there are two approaches demonstrated. In the first (the setLang() function), the replacements have the same number of items, so the length of existing options provides a counter and index value for the remove() and add() methods. But when the number of items may change (as in the setCount() function), a tight loop removes all items before they are added back via the add() method without a second parameter (items are appended to the list). The approach shown in Listing 24-2 has no specific benefit over that of Listing 24-1.

LISTING 24-2

Modifying select Options (IE4+)

```
// change color language set
function setLang(which) {
   var listObj = document.forms[0].colors;
   var newOpt;
   // filter out old IE browsers
   if (listObj.type) {
      // find out if it's 3 or 6 entries
```

```
        var listLength = listObj.length;
        // save selected index
        var currSelected = listObj.selectedIndex;
        // replace individual existing entries
        for (var i = 0; i < listLength; i++) {
            newOpt = document.createElement("option");
            newOpt.text = (which == "plain") ? plainList[i] : hardList[i];
            listObj.options.remove(i);
            listObj.options.add(newOpt, i);
        }
        listObj.selectedIndex = currSelected;
    }
}

// create entirely new options list
function setCount(choice) {
    var listObj = document.forms[0].colors;
    var newOpt;
    // filter out old browsers
    if (listObj.type) {
        // get language setting
        var lang = (document.forms[0].geekLevel[0].checked) ? "plain" : "hard";
        // empty options from list
        while (listObj.options.length) {
            listObj.options.remove(0);
        }
        // create new option object for each entry
        for (var i = 0; i < choice.value; i++) {
            newOpt = document.createElement("option");
            newOpt.text = (lang == "plain") ? plainList[i] : hardList[i];
            listObj.options.add(newOpt);
        }
        listObj.options[0].selected = true;
    }
}
```

Modifying select options (W3C DOM)

Yet another approach is possible in browsers that closely adhere to the W3C DOM Level 2 standard. In NN6+, Mozilla, and Safari, for example, you can use the add() and remove() methods of the select element object. They work very much like the same-named methods for the options array in IE4+, but these are methods of the select element object itself. The other main difference between the two syntaxes is that the add() method does not use the index value as the second parameter but rather a reference to the option element object before which the new option is inserted. The second parameter is required, so to simply append the new item at the end of the current list, supply null as the parameter. Listing 24-3 shows the W3C-compatible version of the select element modification scripts shown in Listings 24-1 and 24-2. I highlight source code lines in bold that exhibit differences between the IE4+ and W3C DOM versions.

LISTING 24-3

Modifying select Options (W3C)

```
// change color language set
function setLang(which) {
    var listObj = document.forms[0].colors;
    var newOpt;
    // filter out old IE browsers
    if (listObj.type) {
        // find out if it's 3 or 6 entries
        var listLength = listObj.length;
        // save selected index
        var currSelected = listObj.selectedIndex;
        // replace individual existing entries
        for (var i = 0; i < listLength; i++) {
            newOpt = document.createElement("option");
            newOpt.text = (which == "plain") ? plainList[i] : hardList[i];
            listObj.remove(i);
            listObj.add(newOpt, listObj.options[i]);
        }
        listObj.selectedIndex = currSelected;
    }
}

// create entirely new options list
function setCount(choice) {
    var listObj = document.forms[0].colors;
    var newOpt;
    // filter out old browsers
    if (listObj.type) {
        // get language setting
        var lang = (document.forms[0].geekLevel[0].checked) ? "plain" : "hard";
        // empty options from list
        while (listObj.options.length) {
            listObj.remove(0);
        }
        // create new option object for each entry
        for (var i = 0; i < choice.value; i++) {
            newOpt = document.createElement("option");
            newOpt.text = (lang == "plain") ? plainList[i] : hardList[i];
            listObj.add(newOpt, null);
        }
        listObj.options[0].selected = true;
    }
}
```

As with the IE4 version, the W3C version offers no specific benefit over the original, backward-compatible approach. Choose the most modern one that fits the types of browsers you need to support with your page.

Properties

length

Value: Integer.   Read/Write (see text)
Compatibility: WinIE3+, MacIE3+, NN2+, Moz+, Safari+

Like all JavaScript arrays, the options array has a length property of its own. But rather than having to reference the options array to determine its length, the select object has its own length property that you use to find out how many items are in the list. This value is the number of options in the object. A select object with three choices in it has a length property value of 3.

In browsers dating back to NN3 and IE4 you can adjust this value downward after the document loads. This is one way to decrease the number of options in a list. Setting the value to 0 causes the select object to empty but not disappear.

See Listing 24-1 for an illustration of the way you use the length property to help determine how often to cycle through the repeat loop in search of selected items. Because the loop counter, i, must start at 0, the counting continues until the loop counter is one less than the actual length value (which starts its count with 1).

Related Item: options property.

multiple

Value: Boolean.   Read/Write
Compatibility: WinIE4+, MacIE4+, NN6+, Moz+, Safari+

The multiple property represents the multiple attribute setting for a select element object. If the value is true, the element accepts multiple selections by the user (for example, Ctrl+clicking in Windows). If you want to convert a pop-up list into a multiple select pick list, you must also adjust the size property to direct the browser to render a set number of visible choices in the list.

The following statement toggles between single and multiple selections on a select element object whose size attribute is set to a value greater than 1:

```
document.forms[0].mySelect.multiple = !document.forms[0].mySelect.multiple;
```

Related Item: size property.

options[*index*]

Value: Array of option element objects.   Read-Only
Compatibility: WinIE3+, MacIE3+, NN2+, Moz+, Safari+

You typically don't summon this property by itself. Rather, it is part of a reference to a specific option's properties (or methods in later browsers) within the entire select object. In other words, the options property is a kind of gateway to more specific properties, such as the value assigned to a single option within the list.

In modern browsers (IE4+ and W3C), you can reference individual options as separate HTML element objects. These references do not require the reference to the containing form or select element objects. If backward compatibility is a priority, however, I recommend you stick with the long references through the select objects.

select.options[*index*].selected

I list the next several properties here in the select object discussion because they are backward-compatible with all browsers, including browsers that don't treat the option element as a distinct object. Be aware that all properties shown here that include options[index] as part of their references are also properties of the option element object in IE4+ and W3C browsers.

See Listings 24-1 through 24-3 for examples of how the options array references information about the options inside a select element.

Related Items: All options[index].property items.

options[*index*].defaultSelected

Value: Boolean.   Read-Only
Compatibility: WinIE3+, MacIE3+, NN2+, Moz+, Safari+

If your select object definition includes one option that features the selected attribute, that option's defaultSelected property is set to true. The defaultSelected property for all other options is false. If you define a select object that allows multiple selections (and whose size attribute is greater than 1), however, you can define the selected attribute for more than one option definition. When the page loads, all items with that attribute are preselected for the user (even in noncontiguous groups).

The following statement preserves a Boolean value if the first option of the select list is the default selected item:

```
var zeroIsDefault = document.forms[0].listName.options[0].defaultSelected;
```

Related Item: options[index].selected property.

options[*index*].index

Value: Integer.   Read-Only
Compatibility: WinIE3+, MacIE3+, NN6+, Moz+, Safari+

The index value of any single option in a select object likely is a redundant value in your scripting. Because you cannot access the option without knowing the index anyway (in brackets as part of the options[index] array reference), you have little need to extract the index value. The value is a property of the item just the same.

The following statement assigns the index integer of the first option of a select element named listName to a variable named itemIndex.

```
var itemIndex = document.forms[0].listName.options[0].index;
```

Related Item: options property.

options[*index*].selected

Value: Boolean.   Read/Write
Compatibility: WinIE3+, MacIE3+, NN2+, Moz+, Safari+

As mentioned earlier in the discussion of this object, better ways exist for determining which option a user selects from a list than looping through all options and examining the selected property. An exception to that "rule" occurs when you set up a list box to enable multiple selections. In this situation, the selectedIndex property returns an integer of only the topmost item selected. Therefore, your script needs to look at the true or false values of the selected property for each option in the list and determine what to do with the text or value data.

To accumulate a list of all items selected by the user, the `seeList()` function in Listing 24-4 systematically examines the `options[index].selected` property of each item in the list. The text of each item whose `selected` property is `true` is appended to the list. I add the "\n" inline carriage returns and spaces to make the list in the alert dialog box look nice and indented. If you assign other values to the `value` attributes of each option, the script can extract the `options[index].value` property to collect those values instead.

LISTING 24-4

Cycling through a Multiple-Selection List

```html
<html>
    <head>
        <title>Accessories List</title>
        <script type="text/javascript">
        function seeList(form) {
            var result = "";
            for (var i = 0; i < form.accList.length; i++) {
                if (form.accList.options[i].selected) {
                    result += "\n   " + form.accList.options[i].text;
                }
            }
            alert("You have selected:" + result);
        }
        </script>
    </head>
    <body>
        <form>
            <p>Control/Command-click on all accessories you use: <select
                name="accList" size="9" multiple="multiple">
                    <option selected="selected">Color Monitor</option>
                    <option>Modem</option>
                    <option>Scanner</option>
                    <option>Laser Printer</option>
                    <option>Tape Backup</option>
                    <option>MO Drive</option>
                    <option>Video Camera</option>
                </select></p>
            <p><input type="button" value="View Summary..."
                onclick="seeList(this.form)" />
            </p>
        </form>
    </body>
</html>
```

Related Items: `options[index].text`, `options[index].value`, `selectedIndex` properties.

options[*index*].text

Value: String.   Read/Write
Compatibility: WinIE3+, MacIE3+, NN2+, Moz+, Safari+

The text property of an option is the text of the item as it appears in the list. If you can pass that wording along with your script to perform appropriate tasks, this property is the one you want to extract for further processing. But if your processing requires other strings associated with each option, assign a value attribute in the definition and extract the options[index].value property (see Listing 24-6).

To demonstrate the text property of an option, Listing 24-5 applies the text from a selected option to the document.bgColor property of a document in the current window. The color names are part of the collection built into all scriptable browsers; fortunately, the values are case-insensitive so that you can capitalize the color names displayed and assign them to the property.

LISTING 24-5

Using the options[*index*].text Property

```html
<html>
   <head>
      <title>Color Changer 1</title>
      <script type="text/javascript">
      function seeColor(form) {
         var newColor =
            (form.colorsList.options[form.colorsList.selectedIndex].text);
         document.bgColor = newColor;
      }
      </script>
   </head>
   <body>
      <form>
         <p>Choose a background color: <select name="colorsList">
               <option selected="selected">Gray</option>
               <option>Lime</option>
               <option>Ivory</option>
               <option>Red</option>
            </select></p>
         <p><input type="button" value="Change It"
            onclick="seeColor(this.form)" /></p>
      </form>
   </body>
</html>
```

Related Item: options[index].value property.

options[*index*].value

Value: String.   Read/Write
Compatibility: WinIE4+, MacIE4+, NN4+, Moz+, Safari+

In many instances, the words in the options list appear in a form that is convenient for the document's users but inconvenient for the scripts behind the page. Rather than set up an elaborate lookup routine to match the selectedIndex or options[index].text values with the values your script needs, you can easily store those values in the value attribute of each <option> definition of the select object. You can then extract those values as needed.

You can store any string expression in the value attributes. That includes URLs, object properties, or even entire page descriptions that you want to send to a parent.frames[index].document.write() method.

Starting with IE4 and W3C browsers, the select element object itself has a value property that returns the value property of the selected option. But for backward compatibility, use the longer approach shown in the example in Listing 24-6.

Listing 24-6 requires the option text that the user sees to be in familiar, multiple-word form. But to set the color using the browser's built-in color palette, you must use the one-word form. Those one-word values are stored in the value attributes of each <option> definition. The function then reads the value property, assigning it to the bgColor of the current document. If you prefer to use the hexadecimal triplet form of color specifications, those values are assigned to the value attributes (<option value="#e9967a">Dark Salmon).

LISTING 24-6

Using the options[*index*].value Property

```
<html>
   <head>
      <title>Color Changer 2</title>
      <script type="text/javascript">
      function seeColor(form) {
         var newColor =
            (form.colorsList.options[form.colorsList.selectedIndex].value);
         document.bgColor = newColor;
      }
      </script>
   </head>
   <body>
      <form>
         <p>Choose a background color: <select name="colorsList">
            <option selected="selected" value="cornflowerblue">
            Cornflower Blue</option>
            <option value="darksalmon">Dark Salmon</option>
            <option value="lightgoldenrodyellow">
            Light Goldenrod Yellow</option>
            <option value="seagreen">Sea Green</option>
            </select></p>
         <p><input type="button" value="Change It"
            onclick="seeColor(this.form)" /></p>
      </form>
   </body>
</html>
```

Related Item: options[index].text property.

selectedIndex

Value: Integer.   Read/Write
Compatibility: WinIE3+, MacIE3+, NN2+, Moz+, Safari+

When a user clicks a choice in a selection list, the selectedIndex property changes to a zero-based number corresponding to that item in the list. The first item has a value of 0. This information is valuable to a script that needs to extract the value or text of a selected item for further processing.

You can use this information as a shortcut to getting at a selected option's properties. To examine a select object's selected property, rather than cycling through every option in a repeat loop, use the object's selectedIndex property to fill in the index value for the reference to the selected item. The wording gets kind of long; but from an execution standpoint, this methodology is much more efficient. Note, however, that when the select object is a multiple-style, the selectedIndex property value reflects the index of only the topmost item selected in the list.

To script the selection of a particular item, assign an integer value to the select element object's selectedIndex property, as shown in Listings 24-1 through 24-3.

In the inspect() function of Listing 24-7, notice that the value inside the options property index brackets is a reference to the object's selectedIndex property. Because this property always returns an integer value, it fulfills the needs of the index value for the options property. Therefore, if you select Green in the pop-up menu, form.colorsList.selectedIndex returns a value of 1; that reduces the rest of the reference to form.colorsList.options[1].text, which equals "Green."

LISTING 24-7

Using the selectedIndex Property

```html
<html>
   <head>
      <title>Select Inspector</title>
      <script type="text/javascript">
      function inspect(form) {
         alert(form.colorsList.options[form.colorsList.selectedIndex].text);
      }
      </script>
   </head>
   <body>
      <form>
         <p><select name="colorsList">
               <option selected="selected">Red</option>
               <option value="Plants">Green</option>
               <option>Blue</option>
            </select></p>
         <p><input type="button" value="Show Selection"
            onclick="inspect(this.form)" /></p>
      </form>
   </body>
</html>
```

Related Item: options property.

size

Value: Integer.   Read/Write
Compatibility: WinIE4+, MacIE4+, NN6+, Moz+, Safari+

The size property represents the size attribute setting for a select element object. You can modify the integer value of this property to change the number of options that are visible in a pick list without having to scroll.

The following statement uses the size property to set the number of visible items to 5:

```
document.forms[0].mySelect.size = 5;
```

Related Item: multiple property.

type

Value: String.   Read-Only
Compatibility: WinIE4+, MacIE4+, NN3+, Moz+, Safari+

Use the type property to help you identify a select object from an unknown group of form elements. The precise string returned for this property depends on whether the select object is defined as a single- (select-one) or multiple- (select-multiple) type.

Related Item: form.elements property.

value

Value: String.   Read/Write (see text)
Compatibility: WinIE4+, MacIE4+, NN6+, Moz+, Safari+

The more recent browsers (and the W3C DOM) provide a value property for the select element object. This property returns the string assigned to the value attribute (or value property) of the currently selected option element. If you do not assign a string to the attribute or property, the value property returns an empty string. For these browser generations, you can use this shortcut reference to the select element object's value property instead of the longer version that requires a reference to the selectedIndex property and the options array of the element object.

The seeColor() function in Listing 24-6 that accesses the chosen value the long way can be simplified for newer browsers only with the following construction:

```
function seeColor(form) {
    document.bgColor = form.colorsList.value;
}
```

Related Item: options[index].value property.

Methods

```
add(newOptionElementRef[, index])
add(newOptionElementRef, optionElementRef)
remove(index)
```
Returns: Nothing.
Compatibility: WinIE5+, MacIE5+, NN6+, Moz+, Safari+

These methods represent the W3C approach to adding and removing option elements from a selection. The first parameter to each of the add() methods is the new option element object to be added to the selection. The second parameters differ due to variances in IE and other W3C browsers. The first version of add() is the IE version, which allows you to specify an optional index position for the new option; the option is placed just before the index position or it is appended to the end of the selection list if no index is provided. The W3C approach is represented by the second add() method, which requires an option object reference as the second parameter. This reference is to an option already in the selection list; the new option is added just before the option or it is appended to the end of the selection list if null is passed as the second parameter.

The remove() method requires the index of the option to be removed, and simply removes the option from the selection list.

```
options.add(elementRef[, index])
options.remove()
```
Returns: Nothing.
Compatibility: WinIE4+, MacIE4+, NN-, Moz-, Safari-

These two IE-specific methods belong to the options array property of a select element object. See the discussion at the opening of the select element object earlier in this chapter to see how to use these methods and their counterparts in other browser versions and object models.

```
item(index)
namedItem("optionID")
```
Returns: option element reference.
Compatibility: WinIE5+, MacIE5+, NN-, Moz-, Safari-

The item() and namedItem() methods are IE-specific convenience methods that access option element objects nested inside a select object. In a sense, they provide shortcuts to referencing nested options without having to use the options array property and the indexing within that array.

The parameter for the item() method is an index integer value. For example, the following two statements refer to the same option element object:

```
document.forms[0].mySelect.options[2]
document.forms[0].mySelect.item(2)
```

If your script knows the ID of an option element, it can use the namedItem() method, supplying the string version of the ID as the parameter, to return a reference to that option element.

The following statement assigns an option element reference to a variable:

```
var oneOption = document.forms[0].mySelect.namedItem("option3_2");
```

Related Item: options property.

Event handlers

onchange

Compatibility: WinIE3+, MacIE3+, NN2+, Moz+, Safari+

As a user clicks a new choice in a select object, the object receives a change event that the onchange event handler can capture. In examples earlier in this section (Listings 24-6 and 24-7, for example), the action is handed over to a separate button. This design may make sense in some circumstances, especially when you use multiple select lists or any list box. (Typically, clicking a list box item does not trigger any action that the user sees.) There are also accessibility concerns for users who do not have JavaScript enabled. Restricting action to scripted events (without a corresponding "Go" or similar explicit button adjacent to the select element) may mean that choosing an item in the list would have no effect. Therefore, consider your users carefully before implementing actions exclusively via the change event.

To bring a pop-up menu to life, bind an onchange event handler to the <select> definition. If the user makes the same choice as previously selected, the onchange event handler is not triggered. In this case, you can still trigger an action via the onclick event handler; but this event works for the select object only in modern browsers.

Listing 24-8 is a version of Listing 24-6 that invokes all action as the result of a user making a selection from the pop-up menu. The onchange event handler for the <select> tag replaces the action button. For this application — when you desire a direct response to user input — an appropriate method is to have the action triggered from the pop-up menu rather than by a separate action button.

Notice two other important changes. First, the select element now contains a blank first option. When a user visits the page, nothing is selected yet, so you should present a blank option to encourage the user to make a selection. The function also makes sure that the user selects one of the color-valued items before it attempts to change the background color.

Second, the onload event handler invokes the seeColor() method, passing as a parameter a reference to the select element. This forces any color selection to be carried out when the page is initially loaded. As an example, this might take place if you navigate to another page and then use the browser's Back button to return to the color page. Thus, if the select element choice persists, the background color is adjusted accordingly after the page loads.

LISTING 24-8

Triggering a Color Change from a Pop-Up Menu

```html
<html>
   <head>
      <title>Color Changer 2</title>
      <script type="text/javascript">
```

continued

LISTING 24-8   *(continued)*

```
    function seeColor(list) {
        var newColor = (list.options[list.selectedIndex].value);
        if (newColor) {
            document.bgColor = newColor;
        }
    }
    </script>
</head>
<body onload="seeColor(document.getElementById('colorsList'))">
    <form>
        <p>Choose a background color: <select name="colorsList"
            id="colorsList" onchange="seeColor(this)">
            <option selected="selected" value=""></option>
            <option value="cornflowerblue">Cornflower Blue</option>
            <option value="darksalmon">Dark Salmon</option>
            <option value="lightgoldenrodyellow">
            Light Goldenrod Yellow</option>
            <option value="seagreen">Sea Green</option>
        </select></p>
    </form>
</body>
</html>
```

option Element Object

For HTML element properties, methods, and event handlers, see Chapter 15.

Properties	Methods	Event Handlers
defaultSelected		
form†		
label		
selected		
text		
value		

†See "Text Input Object" (Chapter 23).

Syntax

Accessing option object properties:

(All)   [window.]document.*formName*.*selectName*.options[*index*].*property* | *method*([*parameters*])

(All)	[window.]document.*formName*.elements[*index*].options[*index*].*property* | method([*parameters*])
(All)	[window.]document.forms[*index*].*selectName*.options[*index*].*property* | method([*parameters*])
(All)	[window.]document.forms["*formName*"].*selectName*.options[*index*]. *property* | method([*parameters*])
(All)	[window.]document.forms["*formName*"].elements[*index*].options[*index*]. *property* | method([*parameters*])
(IE4+)	[window.]document.all.*elemID*.*property* | method([*parameters*])
(IE5+/W3C)	[window.]document.getElementById("*elemID*").*property* | method([*parameters*])
(W3C)	[window.]document.forms[*index*].*selectName*.item(*index*).*property* | method([*parameters*])
(W3C)	[window.]document.forms["*formName*"].*selectName*.namedItem(*elemID*). property | method([parameters])

Compatibility: WinIE3+, MacIE3+, NN2+, Moz+, Safari+

About this object

option elements are nested inside select elements. Each option represents an item in the list of choices presented by the select element. Properties of the option element object let scripts inspect whether a particular option is currently selected or is the default selection. Other properties enable you to get or set the hidden value associated with the option as well as the visible text. For more details about the interaction between the select and option element objects, see the discussion about the select object earlier in this chapter as well as the discussion of the properties and methods associated with the options array returned by the select object's options property.

I discuss all backward-compatible option object properties (defaultSelected, selected, text, and value) among the options property descriptions in the select object section. The only items listed in this section are those that are unique to the option element object defined in newer browsers.

In all browsers dating back to NN3 and IE4, there is a provision for creating a new option object via an Option object constructor function. The syntax is as follows:

```
var newOption = new Option("text","value");
```

Here, *text* is the string that is displayed for the item in the list, and *value* is the string assigned to the value property of the new option. This new option object is not added to a select object until you assign it to a slot in the options array of the select object. You can see an example of this approach to modifying options in Listing 24-1.

Properties
label

Value: String.   Read/Write
Compatibility: WinIE6+, MacIE5+, NN6+, Moz+, Safari+

The label property corresponds to the HTML 4.01 label attribute of an option element. This attribute (and property) enables you to assign alternate text for an option. In MacIE5, any string assigned to the label attribute or corresponding property overrides the display of text found between the start and end tags of the option element. Therefore, you can assign content to both the attribute and tag, but only browsers adhering to the HTML 4.01 standard for this element display the value assigned to the label. Although the label property is implemented in NN6, the browser does not modify the option item's text to reflect the property's setting. This problem is resolved in Moz+ browsers.

The following statement modifies the text that appears as the selected text in a pop-up list:

```
document.forms[0].mySelect.options[3].label = "Widget 9000";
```

If this option is the currently selected one, the text on the pop-up list at rest changes to the new label.

Related Item: text property.

optgroup Element Object

For HTML element properties, methods, and event handlers, see Chapter 15.

Properties	Methods	Event Handlers
form†		
label		

†See "Text Input Object" (Chapter 23).

Syntax

Accessing optgroup object properties:

```
(IE)      [window.]document.all.elemID".property | method([parameters])
(W3C)     [window.]document.getElementById("elemID").property |
          method([parameters])
```

Compatibility: WinIE6+, MacIE5+, NN6+, Moz+, Safari+

About this object

An optgroup element in the HTML 4.01 specification enables authors to group options into subgroups within a select list. The label assigned to the optgroup element is rendered in the list as a non-selectable item, usually differentiated from the selectable items by some alternate display. In W3C browsers, optgroup items by default are shown in bold italic, whereas all option elements nested within an optgroup are indented but with normal font characteristics.

Browsers not recognizing this element ignore it. All options are presented as if the optgroup elements are not there.

Properties
label

Value: String.   Read/Write
Compatibility: WinIE6+, MacIE5+, NN6+, Moz+, Safari+

The `label` property corresponds to the HTML 4.01 `label` attribute of an `optgroup` element. This attribute (and property) enables you to assign text to the label that encompasses a group of nested `option` elements in the pop-up list display.

 **MacIE5 exhibits a bug that prevents scripts from assigning values to the last `optgroup` element inside a `select` element.**

Listing 24-9 demonstrates how a script can alter the text of option group labels. This page is an enhanced version of the background color setters used in other examples of this chapter. Be aware that several versions of IE prior to IE7 do not alter the last `optgroup` element's label, and NN6+ achieves only a partial change to the text displayed in the `select` element. Newer Mozilla-based browsers such as Firefox 1.5 and 2.0 have no problems with the task.

LISTING 24-9

Modifying optgroup Element Labels

```html
<html>
    <head>
        <title>Color Changer 3</title>
        <script type="text/javascript">
        var regularLabels = ["Reds","Greens","Blues"];
        var naturalLabels = ["Apples","Leaves","Sea"];
        function setRegularLabels(list) {
            var optGrps = list.getElementsByTagName("optgroup");
            for (var i = 0; i < optGrps.length; i++) {
                optGrps[i].label = regularLabels[i];
            }
        }
        function setNaturalLabels(list) {
            var optGrps = list.getElementsByTagName("optgroup");
            for (var i = 0; i < optGrps.length; i++) {
                optGrps[i].label = naturalLabels[i];
            }
        }
        function seeColor(list) {
            var newColor = (list.options[list.selectedIndex].value);
            if (newColor) {
                document.bgColor = newColor;
            }
        }
        </script>
    </head>
    <body onload="seeColor(document.getElementById('colorsList'))">
        <form>
            <p>Choose a background color: <select name="colorsList"
                id="colorsList" onchange="seeColor(this)">
                    <optgroup id="optGrp1" label="Reds">
                        <option value="#ff9999">Light Red</option>
                        <option value="#ff3366">Medium Red</option>
```

continued

LISTING 24-9   *(continued)*

```
                <option value="#ff0000">Bright Red</option>
                <option value="#660000">Dark Red</option>
              </optgroup>
              <optgroup id="optGrp2" label="Greens">
                <option value="#ccff66">Light Green</option>
                <option value="#99ff33">Medium Green</option>
                <option value="#00ff00">Bright Green</option>
                <option value="#006600">Dark Green</option>
              </optgroup>
              <optgroup id="optGrp3" label="Blues">
                <option value="#ccffff">Light Blue</option>
                <option value="#66ccff">Medium Blue</option>
                <option value="#0000ff">Bright Blue</option>
                <option value="#000066">Dark Blue</option>
              </optgroup>
          </select></p>
        <p><input type="radio" name="labels" checked="checked"
          onclick="setRegularLabels(this.form.colorsList)" />Regular Label
          Names <input type="radio" name="labels"
          onclick="setNaturalLabels(this.form.colorsList)" />Label Names from
          Nature</p>
      </form>
    </body>
</html>
```

Related Item: option.label property.

file Input Element Object

For HTML element properties, methods, and event handlers, see Chapter 15.

Properties	Methods	Event Handlers
defaultValue†	select()†	onchange†
form†		
name†		
readOnly†		
size†		
type†		
value†		

†See "Text Input Object" (Chapter 23).

Syntax

Accessing `file` input element object properties:

```
(NN3+/IE4+)      [window.]document.formName.inputName.property |
                 method([parameters])
(NN3+/IE4+)      [window.]document.formName.elements[index].property |
                 method([parameters])
(NN3+/IE4+)      [window.]document.forms[index].inputName.property |
                 method([parameters])
(NN3+/IE4+)      [window.]document.forms["formName"].inputName.property |
                 method([parameters])
(NN3+/IE4+)      [window.]document.forms["formName"].elements[index].property |
                 method([parameters])
(IE4+)           [window.]document.all.elemID.property | method([parameters])
(IE5+/W3C)       [window.]document.getElementById("elemID").property |
                 method([parameters])
```

Compatibility: WinIE4+, MacIE4+, NN3+, Moz+, Safari+

About this object

Some Web sites enable you to upload files from the client to the server, typically by using a form-style sub-mission to a CGI program on the server. The `input` element whose type is set to `"file"` (also known as a `fileUpload` object) is merely a user interface that enables users to specify which file on their PC they want to upload. Without a server process capable of receiving the file, the `file` input element does nothing. Moreover, you must also set two `form` element attributes as follows:

```
method="POST"
enctype="multipart/form-data"
```

This element displays a field and a Browse button. The Browse button leads to an Open File dialog box (in the local operating system's interface vernacular) where a user can select a file. After you make a selection, the filename (or pathname, depending on the operating system) appears in the `file` input element's field. The `value` property of the object returns the filename.

You do not have to script much for this object on the client side. The `value` property, for example, is read-only in earlier browsers; in addition, a form cannot surreptitiously upload a file to the server without the user's knowledge or consent.

Listing 24-10 helps you see what the `file` input element looks like in an example page.

LISTING 24-10

file Input Element

```
<html>
    <head>
        <title>FileUpload Object</title>
    </head>
    <body>
        <form method="POST" action="yourCGIURL" enctype="multipart/form-data">
            File to be uploaded: <input type="file" size="40" name="fileToGo" />
            <p><input type="button" value="View Value"
                onclick="alert(this.form.fileToGo.value)" /></p>
        </form>
    </body>
</html>
```

In a true production environment, a Submit button and a URL to your CGI process are specified for the action attribute of the `<form>` tag. You would also likely use the more modern (but more code intensive) event binding approach to handle the onclick event, as you've seen in other examples in this chapter — here it was more concise to stick with the simple attribute assignment technique.

Chapter 25

Event Objects

P rior to version 4 browsers, user and system actions — events — were captured predominantly by event handlers defined as attributes inside HTML
tags. For instance, when a user clicked a button, the `click` event triggered
the `onclick` event handler in the tag. That handler may invoke a separate function or perform some inline JavaScript script. Even so, the events themselves
were rather dumb: Either an event occurred or it didn't. Where an event
occurred (that is, the screen coordinates of the pointer at the moment the mouse
button was clicked) and other pertinent event tidbits (for example, whether a
keyboard modifier key was pressed at the same time) were not part of the equation. Until version 4 browsers, that is.

While remaining fully backward-compatible with the event handler mechanism
of old, version 4 browsers had the first event model that turned events into first-
class objects whose properties automatically carry a lot of relevant information
about the event when it occurs. These properties are fully exposed to scripts,
allowing pages to respond more intelligently about what the user does with the
page and its elements.

Another new aspect of version 4 event models was the notion of "event propagation." It was possible to have an event processed by an object higher up the element containment hierarchy whenever it made sense to have multiple objects share
one event handler. That the event being processed carried along with it information
about the intended target, plus other golden information nuggets, made it possible
for event handler functions to be smart about processing the event without requiring an event handler call to pass all kinds of target-specific information.

Unfortunately, the joy of this newly found power is tempered by the forces of
object model incompatibility. Event object models are clearly divided along two
fronts: the IE4+ model and the model adopted by the W3C DOM Level 2 as
implemented in NN6+/Moz/Safari. Many of these distinctions are addressed in
the overviews of the object models in Chapter 15. In this chapter, you find out
more about the actual event objects that contain all the "goodies." Where possible, cross-browser concerns are addressed.

IN THIS CHAPTER

The "life" of an event object

Event support in different
browser generations

Retrieving information from an
event

Why "Events"?

Graphical user interfaces are more difficult to program than the "old-fashioned" command-line interface. With a command-line or menu-driven system, users were intentionally restricted in the types of actions they could take at any given moment. The world was very modal, primarily as a convenience to programmers who led users through rigid program structures.

That all changed in a graphical user interface, such as Windows, MacOS, XWindow System, and all others derived from the pioneering work of the Xerox Star system. The challenge for programmers is that a good user interface in this realm must make it possible for users to perform all kinds of actions at any given moment: roll the mouse, click a button, type a key, select text, choose a pull-down menu item, and so on. To accommodate this, a program (or, better yet, the operating system) must be on the lookout for any possible activity coming from all input ports, whether it be the mouse, keyboard, or network connection.

A common methodology to accomplish this at the operating system level is to look for any kind of event, whether it comes from user action or some machine-generated activity. The operating system or program then looks up how it should process each kind of event. Such events, however, must have some smarts about them so that the program knows what and where on the screen the event is.

What an event knows (and when it knows it)

Although the way to reference an event object varies a bit among the three event models, the one concept they all share is that an event object is created the instant the event action occurs. For instance, if you click a button, an event object is created in the browser's memory. As the object is created, the browser assigns values to the object's properties — properties that reflect numerous characteristics of that specific event. For a `click` event, that information includes the coordinates of the click and which mouse button was used to generate the event. To be even more helpful, the browser does some quick calculations to determine that the coordinates of the `click` event coincide with the rectangular space of a button element on the screen. Therefore, the event object has as one of its properties a reference to the "screen thing" that you clicked on.

Most event object properties (all of them in some event models) are read-only, because an event object is like a snapshot of an event action. If the event model were to allow modification of event properties, performing both potentially useful and potentially unfriendly actions would be possible. For example, how frustrating would it be to a user to attempt to type into a text box only to have a keystroke modified after the actual key press and then have a totally different character appear in the text box? On the other hand, perhaps it may be useful in some situations to make sure that anything typed into a text box is converted to uppercase characters, no matter what is typed. Each event model brings its own philosophy to the table in this regard. For example, the IE4+ event model allows keyboard character events to be modified by script; the W3C DOM event model does not.

Perhaps the most important aspect of an event object to keep in mind is that it exists only as long as scripts process the event. An event can trigger an event handler — usually a function. That function, of course, can invoke other functions. As long as statements are still executing in response to the event handler, the event object and all its properties are still "alive" and available to your scripts. But after the last script statement runs, the event object reverts to an empty object.

The reason an event object has such a brief life is that there can be only one event object at a time. In other words, no matter how complex your event handler functions are or how rapidly events fire, they are executed serially (for experienced programmers: there is one execution thread). The operating system buffers events that start to bunch up on each other. Except in rare cases in which the buffer gets full and events are not recorded, event handlers are executed in the order in which the events occur.

The static Event object

Up to this point, the discussion has been about the event object (with a lowercase "e"), which is one instance of an event, with all the properties associated with that specific event action. In the W3C DOM event model, there is also a static Event object (with an uppercase "E") that includes additional subcategories within. These subcategories are all covered later in this chapter, but they are introduced here to draw the contrast between the event and Event objects. The former, as you've seen, is a transient object with details about a specific event action; the latter serves primarily as a holder of event-related constant values that scripts can use. The static Event object is always available to scripts inside any window or frame. If you want to see a list of all Event object properties in NN6+/Moz, use The Evaluator (Chapter 13): enter Event into the bottom text box (also check out the KeyEvent object in NN6+/Moz).

The static Event object also turns out to be the object from which event objects are cloned. Thus, the static Event object has a number of properties and methods that apply to (are inherited by) the event objects created by event actions. These relationships are more important in the W3C DOM event model, which builds upon the DOM's object-oriented tendencies to implement the event model.

Event Propagation

Prior to version 4 browsers, an event fired on an object. If an event handler was defined for that event and that object, the handler executed; if there was no event handler, the event just disappeared into the ether. Newer browsers, however, send events on a longer ride, causing them to propagate through the document object models. As you know by now, two propagation models exist, one for each of the event models in use today: IE4+ and W3C DOM as implemented in NN6+/Moz/Safari. It's also worth mentioning the event model that is unique to NN4, which served as a third model prior to NN4 succumbing to modern browsers. The NN4 event model has historical relevance because it aids in understanding the latter two models. Conceptually, the NN4 and IE4+ propagation models are diametrically opposite each other — any NN4 event propagates inward toward the target, whereas an IE event starts at the target and propagates outward. But the W3C DOM model manages to implement both models simultaneously, albeit with all new syntax so as not to step on the older models.

At the root of all three models is the notion that every event has a target. For user-initiated actions, this is fairly obvious. If you click a button or type in a text box, that button is the target of your mouse-related event; the text box is the target of your keyboard event. System-generated events are not so obvious, such as the onload event after a page finishes loading. In all event models, this event fires on the window object. What distinguishes the event propagation models is how an event reaches its target, and what, if anything, happens to the event after it finishes executing the event handler associated with the target.

NN4-only event propagation

Although NN4 has given way to newer browsers, its propagation model initiated some concepts that are found in the modern W3C DOM event propagation model. The name for the NN4 model is *event capture*.

In NN4, all events propagate from the top of the document object hierarchy (starting with the window object) downward to the target object. For example, if you click a button in a form, the click event passes through the window and document (and, if available, layer) objects before reaching the button (the form object is not part of the propagation path). This propagation happens instantaneously, so that there is no performance penalty by this extra journey.

The event that passes through the `window`, `document`, and `layer` objects is a fully formed event object, complete with all properties relevant to that event action. Therefore, if the event were processed at the window level, one of the event object's properties is a reference to the target object, so that the event handler scripts at the window level can find out information, such as the name of the button, and even get a reference to its enclosing form.

By default, event capture is turned off. To instruct the `window`, `document`, or `layer` object levels to process that passing click object requires turning on event capture for the `window`, `document`, and/or `layer` object.

Enabling NN4 event capture

All three objects just mentioned — `window`, `document`, and `layer` — have a `captureEvents()` method. You use this method to enable event capture at any of those object levels. The method requires one or more parameters, which are the event types (as supplied by `Event` object constants) that the object should capture, while letting all others pass untouched. For example, if you want the `window` object to capture all `keypress` events, you include the following statement in a script that executes as the page loads:

```
window.captureEvents(Event.KEYPRESS);
```

Defining event handlers in the intended targets is also a good idea, even if they are empty (for example, `onkeypress=""`) to help NN4 generate the event in the first place. If you want the window to capture multiple event types, string the event type constants together, separated by the pipe character:

```
window.captureEvents(Event.KEYPRESS | Event.CLICK);
```

Now you must assign an action to the event at the window's level for each event type. More than likely, you have defined functions to execute for the event. Assign a function reference to the event handler by setting the handler property of the `window` object:

```
window.onkeypress = processKeyEvent;
window.onclick = processClickEvent;
```

Hereafter, if a user clicks a button or types into a field inside that window, the events are processed by their respective window-level event handler functions.

Turning off event capture

As soon as you enable event capture for a particular event type in a document, that capture remains in effect until the page unloads or you specifically disable the capture. You can turn off event capture for each event via the `window`, `document`, or `layer` `releaseEvents()` method. The `releaseEvents()` method takes the same kind of parameters — `Event` object type constants — as the `captureEvents()` method.

The act of releasing an event type simply means that events go directly to their intended targets without stopping elsewhere for processing, even if an event handler for the higher-level object is still defined. And because you can release individual event types based on parameters set for the `releaseEvents()` method, other events being captured are not affected by the release of others.

Passing events toward their targets

If you capture a particular event type in NN4, your script may need to perform some limited processing on that event before letting it reach its intended target. For example, perhaps you want to do something special if a user clicks an element with the Shift meta key pressed. In that case, the function that handles the event at the document level inspects the event's `modifiers` property to determine if the Shift key was pressed at the time of the event. If the Shift key was not pressed, you want the event to continue on its way to the element that the user clicked.

To let an event pass through the object hierarchy to its target, you use the `routeEvent()` method, passing as a parameter the event object being handled in the current function. A `routeEvent()` method does not guarantee that the event will reach its intended destination, because another object in between may have event capturing for that event type turned on and will intercept the event. That object, too, can let the event pass through with its own `routeEvent()` method.

In some cases, your scripts need to know if an event that is passed onward by the `routeEvent()` method activated a function that returns a value. This knowledge is especially valuable if your event must return a `true` or `false` value to let an object know if it should proceed with its default behavior (for example, whether a link should activate its `href` attribute URL or cancel after the event handler evaluates to `return true` or `return false`). When a function is invoked by the action of a `routeEvent()` method, the return value of the destination function is passed back to the `routeEvent()` method. That value, in turn, can be returned to the object that originally captured the event.

Event traffic cop

The last scenario is one in which a higher-level object captures an event and directs the event to a particular object elsewhere in the hierarchy. For example, you could have a document-level event handler function direct every `click` event whose `modifiers` property indicates that the Alt key was pressed to a Help button object whose own `onclick` event handler displays a help panel (perhaps shows an otherwise hidden layer).

You can redirect an event to any object via the `handleEvent()` method. This method works differently from the others described in this chapter, because the object reference of this method is the reference of the object to handle the event (with the event object being passed as a parameter, such as the other methods). As long as the target object has an event handler defined for that event, it will process the event as if it had received the event directly from the system (even though the event object's target property may be some other object entirely).

IE4+ event propagation

IE's event propagation model is called *event bubbling*, in which events "bubble" upward from the target object through the HTML element containment hierarchy. It's important to distinguish between the old-fashioned document object hierarchy (followed in the NN4 event capture model) and the more modern notion of HTML element containment — a concept that carries over to the W3C DOM as well.

A good way to demonstrate the effect of event bubbling — a behavior that is turned on by default — is to populate a simple document with lots of event handlers to see which ones fire and in what order. Listing 25-1 has `onclick` event handlers defined for a button inside a form, the form itself, and other elements and objects all the way up the hierarchy out to the window.

LISTING 25-1

Event Bubbling Demonstration

```
<html onclick="alert('Event is now at the HTML element.')">
    <head>
        <title>Event Bubbles</title>
        <script type="text/javascript">
        function init() {
```

continued

LISTING 25-1 *(continued)*

```
        window.onclick = winEvent
        document.onclick = docEvent;
        document.body.onclick = docBodEvent;
    }
    function winEvent() {
        alert("Event is now at the window object level.");
    }
    function docEvent() {
        alert("Event is now at the document object level.");
    }
    function docBodEvent() {
        alert("Event is now at the BODY element.");
    }
    </script>
</head>
<body onload="init()">
    <h1>Event Bubbles</h1>
    <hr />
    <form onclick="alert('Event is now at the FORM element.')">
        <input type="button" value="Button 'main1'" name="main1"
        onclick="alert('Event started at Button: ' + this.name)" />
    </form>
</body>
</html>
```

You can try this listing in IE4+ and even NN6+/Moz or Safari, because W3C DOM browsers also observe event bubbling. But you will notice differences in the precise propagation among WinIE4+, MacIE4+, and W3C DOM browsers. But first, notice that after you click the button in Listing 25-1, the event first fires at the target: the button. Then the event bubbles upward through the HTML containment to fire at the enclosing form element; next to the enclosing body element; and so on. Where the differences occur are after the body element. Table 25-1 shows the objects for which event handlers are defined in Listing 25-1 and which objects have the click event bubble to them in the three classes of browsers.

TABLE 25-1

Event Bubbling Variations for Listing 25-1

Event Handler Location	WinIE4+	MacIE4+	NN6+/Moz/Safari
button	Yes	Yes	Yes
form	Yes	Yes	Yes
body	Yes	Yes	Yes
HTML	Yes	No	Yes
document	Yes	Yes	Yes
window	No	No	Yes

Despite the discrepancies in Table 25-1, events do bubble through the most likely HTML containers that come to mind. The object level with the most global scope and that works in all browser categories shown in the table is the document object.

Preventing IE event bubbling

Because bubbling occurs by default, there are times when you may prefer to prevent an event from bubbling up the hierarchy. For example, if you have one handler at the document level whose job is to deal with the click event from a related series of buttons, any other object that receives click events will allow those events to bubble upward to the document level unless the bubbling is cancelled. Having the event bubble up could conflict with the document-level event handler.

Each event object in IE has a property called cancelBubble. The default value of this property is false, which means that the event bubbles to the next outermost container that has an event handler for that event. But if, in the execution of an event handler, that property is set to true, the processing of that handler finishes its job, but the event does not bubble up any higher. Therefore, to stop an event from bubbling beyond the current event handler, include the following statement somewhere in the handler function:

```
event.cancelBubble = true;
```

You can prove this to yourself by modifying the page in Listing 25-1 to cancel bubbling at any level. For example, if you change the event handler of the form element to include a statement that cancels bubbling, the event goes no further than the form in IE (the syntax is different for NN6+/Moz, as discussed later in this chapter):

```
<form onclick="alert('Event is now at the form element.');
    event.cancelBubble=true">
```

Preventing IE event default action

In the days when events were almost always bound to elements by way of attributes in tags, the technique to block the event's default action was to make sure the event handler evaluated to return false. This is how, for instance, a form element's onsubmit event handler could prevent the form from carrying out the submission if client-side form validation failed.

To enhance that capability — especially when events are bound by other means, such as object element properties — IE's event object includes a returnValue property. Assign false to this property in the event handler function to block the element's default action to the event:

```
event.returnValue = false;
```

This way of blocking default actions in IE is often more effective than the old return false technique.

Redirecting events

Starting with IE5.5, you can redirect an event to another element, but with some limitations. The mechanism that makes this possible is the fireEvent() method of all HTML element objects (see Chapter 15). This method isn't so much redirecting an event as causing a brand-new event to be fired. But you can pass most of the properties of the original event object with the new event by specifying a reference to the old event object as the optional second parameter to the fireEvent() method.

The big limitation in this technique, however, is that the reference to the target element gets lost in this hand-off to the new event. The srcElement property of the old event gets overwritten with a reference to the object that is the target of the call to fireEvent(). For example, consider the following onclick event handler function for a button inside a form element:

```
function buttonEvent() {
    event.cancelBubble = true;
    document.body.fireEvent("onclick", event);
}
```

By cancelling event bubbling, the event does not propagate upward to the enclosing form element. Instead, the event is explicitly redirected to the body element, passing the current event object as the second parameter. When the event handler function for the body element runs, its event object has information about the original event, such as the mouse button used for the click and the coordinates. But the event.srcElement property points to the document.body object. As the event bubbles upward from the body element, the srcElement property continues to point to the document.body object. You can see this at work in Listing 25-2 for IE5.5+.

LISTING 25-2

Cancelling and Redirecting Events in IE5.5+

```
<html onclick="revealEvent('HTML', event)">
  <head>
    <title>Event Cancelling & Redirecting</title>
    <script type="text/javascript">
    // display alert with event object info
    function revealEvent(elem, evt) {
        var msg = "Event (from " + evt.srcElement.tagName + " at ";
        msg += event.clientX + "," + event.clientY + ") is now at the ";
        msg += elem + " element.";
        alert(msg);
    }
    function init() {
        document.onclick = docEvent;
        document.body.onclick = docBodEvent;
    }
    function docEvent() {
        revealEvent("document", event);
    }
    function docBodEvent() {
        revealEvent("BODY", event);
    }
    function buttonEvent(form) {
        revealEvent("BUTTON", event);
        // cancel if checked (IE4+)
        event.cancelBubble = form.bubbleCancelState.checked;
        // redirect if checked (IE5.5+)
        if (form.redirect.checked) {
            document.body.fireEvent("onclick", event);
        }
    }
```

```
        </script>
    </head>
    <body onload="init()">
        <h1>Event Cancelling &amp; Redirecting</h1>
        <hr />
        <form onclick="revealEvent('FORM', event)">
            <p><button name="main1" onclick="buttonEvent(this.form)">Button
                'main1'</button></p>
            <p><input type="checkbox" name="bubbleCancelState"
                onclick="event.cancelBubble=true" />Cancel Bubbling at BUTTON<br />
                <input type="checkbox" name="redirect"
                onclick="event.cancelBubble=true" /> Redirect Event to BODY</p>
        </form>
    </body>
</html>
```

Listing 25-2 is a modified version of Listing 25-1. Major additions are enhanced event handlers at each level so that you can see the tag name of the event that is regarded as the srcElement of the event as well as the coordinates of the click event. With both check boxes unchecked, events bubble upward from the button, and the button element is then shown to be the original target all the way up the bubble hierarchy. If you check the Cancel Bubbling check box, the event goes no further than the button element, because that's where event bubbling is turned off. If you then check the Redirect Event to body check box, the original event is cancelled at the button level, but a new event is fired at the body element. But notice that by passing the old event object as the second parameter, the click location properties of the old event are applied to the new event directed at the body. This event then continues to bubble upward from the body.

As a side note, if you uncheck the Cancel Bubbling check box but leave the Redirect Event box checked, you can see how the redirection is observed at the end of the button's event handler, and something special goes on. The original event is held aside by the browser while the redirected event bubbles upward. As soon as that event-processing branch finishes, the original bubbling propagation carries on with the form. Notice, though, that the event object still knows that it was targeted at the button element, and the other properties are intact. This means that for a time, two event objects were in the browser's memory, but only one is "active" at a time. While the redirected event is propagating, the window.event object refers to that event object only.

Applying event capture

WinIE 5 and later also provide a kind of event capture, which overrides all other event propagation. Intended primarily for temporary capture of mouse events, it is controlled not through the event object but via the setCapture() and releaseCapture() methods of all HTML element objects (described in Chapter 15).

When you engage capture mode, all mouse events are directed to the element object that invoked the setCapture() method, regardless of the actual target of the event. This action facilitates such activities as element dragging so that mouse events that might fire outside of the intended target (for example, when dragging the cursor too fast for the animation to track) continue to go to the target. When the drag mode is no longer needed, invoke the releaseCapture() method to allow mouse events to propagate normally.

W3C event propagation

Yielding to arguments in favor of both NN4's event capture and IE's event bubbling, the W3C DOM group managed to assemble an event model that employs both propagation systems. Although forced to use new syntax so as not to conflict with older browsers, the W3C DOM propagation model works like the NN4 one for capture and like IE4+ for bubbling. In other words, an event bubbles by default, but you can also turn on event capture if you want. Thus, an event first trickles down the element containment hierarchy to the target; then it bubbles up through the reverse path.

Event bubbling is on by default, just as in IE4+. To enable capture, you must apply a W3C DOM event listener to an object at some higher container. Use the addEventListener() method (see Chapter 15) for any visible HTML element or node. One of the parameters of the addEventListener() method determines whether the event listener function should be triggered while the event is bubbling or is captured.

Listing 25-3 is a simplified example for NN6+/Moz/W3C that demonstrates how a click event aimed at a button can be both captured and allowed to bubble. Most event handling functions are assigned inside the init() function. Borrowing code from Listing 25-1, event handlers are assigned to the window, document, and body objects as property assignments. These are automatically treated as bubble-type event listeners. Next, two objects — the document and a form — are given capture-type event listeners for the click event. The document object event listener invokes the same function as the bubble-type event handler (the alert text includes some asterisks to remind you that it is the same alert being displayed in both the capture and bubble phases of the event). For the form object, however, the capture-type event listener is directed to one function, while a bubble-type listener for the same object is directed at a separate function. In other words, the form object invokes one function as the event trickles down to the target and another function when the event starts bubbling back up. Many of the event handler functions dynamically read the eventPhase property of the event object to reveal which phase of event propagation is in force at the instance the event handler is invoked (although an apparent bug reports the incorrect phase at the document object during event capture).

LISTING 25-3

W3C Event Capture and Bubble

```html
<html>
    <head>
        <title>W3C DOM Event Propagation</title>
        <script type="text/javascript">
        function init() {
            // using old syntax to assign bubble-type event handlers
            window.onclick = winEvent;
            document.onclick = docEvent;
            document.body.onclick = docBodEvent;
            // turn on click event capture for document and form objects
            document.addEventListener("click", docEvent, true);
            document.forms[0].addEventListener("click", formCaptureEvent, true);
            // set event listener for bubble
            document.forms[0].addEventListener("click", formBubbleEvent, false);
        }
        function winEvent(evt) {
            alert("Event is now at the window object level (" +
```

```
        getPhase(evt) + ").");
    }
    function docEvent(evt) {
        alert("Event is now at the **document** object level (" +
            getPhase(evt) + ").");
    }
    function docBodEvent(evt) {
        alert("Event is now at the BODY level (" + getPhase(evt) + ").");
    }
    function formCaptureEvent(evt) {
        alert("This alert triggered by FORM only on CAPTURE.");
    }
    function formBubbleEvent(evt) {
        alert("This alert triggered by FORM only on BUBBLE.");
    }
    // reveal event phase of current event object
    function getPhase(evt) {
        switch (evt.eventPhase) {
        case 1:
            return "CAPTURING";
            break;
        case 2:
            return "AT TARGET";
            break;
        case 3:
            return "BUBBLING";
            break;
        default:
            return "";
        }
    }
    </script>
</head>
<body onload="init()">
    <h1>W3C DOM Event Propagation</h1>
    <hr />
    <form>
        <input type="button" value="Button 'main1'" name="main1"
        onclick="alert('Event is now at the button object level (' +
        getPhase(event) + ').')" />
    </form>
</body>
</html>
```

If you want to remove event capture after it has been enabled, use the removeEventListener() method on the same object as the event listener that was originally added (see Chapter 15). And, because multiple event listeners can be attached to the same object, specify the exact same three parameters to the removeEventListener() method as applied to the addEventListener() method.

Preventing W3C event bubbling or capture

Corresponding to the `cancelBubble` property of the IE4+ `event` object is an event object method in the W3C DOM. The method that prevents propagation in any event phase is the `stopPropagation()` method. Invoke this method anywhere within an event listener function. The current function executes to completion, but the event propagates no further.

Listing 25-4 extends the example of Listing 25-3 to include two check boxes that let you stop propagation type at the `form` element in your choice of the capture or bubble phase.

LISTING 25-4

Preventing Bubble and Capture

```html
<html>
    <head>
        <title>W3C DOM Event Propagation</title>
        <script type="text/javascript">
        function init() {
            // using old syntax to assign bubble-type event handlers
            window.onclick = winEvent;
            document.onclick = docEvent;
            document.body.onclick = docBodEvent;
            // turn on click event capture for two objects
            document.addEventListener("click", docEvent, true);
            document.forms[0].addEventListener("click", formCaptureEvent, true);
            // set event listener for bubble
            document.forms[0].addEventListener("click", formBubbleEvent, false);
        }
        function winEvent(evt) {
            if (evt.target.type == "button") {
                alert("Event is now at the window object level (" +
                    getPhase(evt) + ").");
            }
        }
        function docEvent(evt) {
            if (evt.target.type == "button") {
                alert("Event is now at the **document** object level (" +
                    getPhase(evt) + ").");
            }
        }
        function docBodEvent(evt) {
            if (evt.target.type == "button") {
                alert("Event is now at the BODY level (" + getPhase(evt) + ").");
            }
        }
        function formCaptureEvent(evt) {
            if (evt.target.type == "button") {
                alert("This alert triggered by FORM only on CAPTURE.");
                if (document.forms[0].stopAllProp.checked) {
```

```
                evt.stopPropagation();
            }
        }
    }
    function formBubbleEvent(evt) {
        if (evt.target.type == "button") {
            alert("This alert triggered by FORM only on BUBBLE.");
            if (document.forms[0].stopDuringBubble.checked) {
                evt.preventBubble();
            }
        }
    }
    // reveal event phase of current event object
    function getPhase(evt) {
        switch (evt.eventPhase) {
        case 1:
            return "CAPTURING";
            break;
        case 2:
            return "AT TARGET";
            break;
        case 3:
            return "BUBBLING";
            break;
        default:
            return "";
        }
    }
    </script>
</head>
<body onload="init()">
    <h1>W3C DOM Event Propagation</h1>
    <hr />
    <form>
        <input type="checkbox" name="stopAllProp" />Stop all propagation at
        FORM<br />
        <input type="checkbox" name="stopDuringBubble" />Prevent bubbling past
        FORM
        <hr />
        <input type="button" value="Button 'main1'" name="main1"
        onclick="alert('Event is now at the button object level (' +
        getPhase(event) + ').')" />
    </form>
</body>
</html>
```

In addition to the W3C DOM stopPropagation() method, NN6+, Moz, and Safari also support IE's cancelBubble property for syntactical convenience.

Preventing W3C event default action

The W3C DOM counterpart to IE's returnValue property is the event object's preventDefault() method. Invoke this method in an event handler function when you wish to block the element's default action to the event:

```
evt.preventDefault();
```

Redirecting W3C DOM events

The mechanism for sending an event to an object outside the normal propagation pattern in W3C is similar to that of IE4+, although with different syntax and an important requirement. In place of the IE4+ fireEvent() method, NN6+/Moz/Safari uses the W3C DOM dispatchEvent() method. The sole parameter of the method is an event object, but it cannot be an event object that is already propagating through the element hierarchy. Instead, you must create a new event object via a W3C DOM event object constructor (described later in this chapter). Listing 25-5 is the same as the IE4+ Listing 25-2, but with just a few modifications to run in the W3C event model. Notice that the dispatchEvent() method passes a newly created event object as its sole parameter.

LISTING 25-5

Cancelling and Redirecting Events in the W3C DOM

```
<html onclick="revealEvent('HTML', event)">
  <head>
    <title>Event Cancelling & Redirecting</title>
    <script type="text/javascript">
    // display alert with event object info
    function revealEvent(elem, evt) {
       var msg = "Event (from " + evt.target.tagName + " at ";
       msg += evt.clientX + "," + evt.clientY + ") is now at the ";
       msg += elem + " element.";
       alert(msg);
    }
    function init() {
       document.onclick = docEvent;
       document.body.onclick = docBodEvent;
    }
    function docEvent(evt) {
       revealEvent("document", evt);
    }
    function docBodEvent(evt) {
       revealEvent("BODY", evt);
    }
    function buttonEvent(form, evt) {
       revealEvent("BUTTON", evt);
       // redirect if checked
       if (form.redirect.checked) {
          var newEvt = document.createEvent("MouseEvents");
          newEvt.initMouseEvent("click", true, true, window, 0, 0, 0, 0,
             0, false, false, false, false, 0, null);
```

```
        document.body.dispatchEvent(newEvt);
      }
      // cancel if checked
      if (form.bubbleCancelState.checked) {
        evt.stopPropagation();
      }
    }
  </script>
</head>
<body onload="init()">
  <h1>Event Cancelling & Redirecting</h1>
  <hr />
  <form onclick="revealEvent('FORM', event)">
    <p><button name="main1" onclick="buttonEvent(this.form, event)">Button
      'main1'</button></p>
    <p><input type="checkbox" name="bubbleCancelState"
      onclick="event.stopPropagation()" />Cancel Bubbling at BUTTON<br />
      <input type="checkbox" name="redirect"
      onclick="event.stopPropagation()" /> Redirect Event to BODY</p>
  </form>
</body>
</html>
```

Referencing the event object

Just as there are two different event object models in today's browsers, the way your scripts access those objects is divided into two camps: the IE way and the W3C (NN4+/Moz/Safari) way. I start with the simpler, IE way.

In IE4+, the `event` object is accessible as a property of the `window` object:

```
window.event
```

But, as you are well aware, the `window` part of references is optional, so your scripts can treat the `event` object as if it were a global reference:

```
event.propertyName
```

Thus, any statement in an event handler function can access the `event` object without any special preparation or initializations.

The situation is a bit more complicated in the W3C event model. In some cases you must explicitly pass the event object as a parameter to an event handler function, whereas in other cases, the event object is delivered as a parameter automatically. The difference depends on how the event handler function is bound to the object.

Binding Events

Perhaps the most important facet of event handling in any script is binding an event to an element on the page. There are several different ways that you can carry out this event binding, and as you might expect, they aren't all compatible across different browsers. Furthermore, some of the techniques are considered passé in the sense that they have been improved upon by more modern approaches. Following are the four main techniques that can be used to bind events to elements:

- Assignment through tag attributes
- Assignment through object properties
- Attachment in IE
- Event listeners in NN/Moz/W3C

The following sections explore these event binding options in more detail, with an emphasis on showing you how to craft a modern, cross-browser event binding function based upon the last two techniques listed.

Binding events through tag attributes

Dating back to some of the earliest JavaScript-powered browsers, the original way of binding event handlers to objects is through an attribute in the element's tag. To bind an event in this manner, you simply assign inline JavaScript code in the attribute of an element, as in the following:

```
<input type="button" value="Click Me" onclick="handleClick();" />
```

The attribute name is the name of the event being handled, and its value is inline JavaScript code that is executed upon the event firing. You can include multiple statements in the event attribute, as this code reveals:

```
<input type="button" value="Click Me"
onclick="doSomething(this); doSomethingElse(this.form);" />
```

For modern browsers that support the W3C event model (NN6+/Moz/Safari/Opera), if you intend to inspect properties of the event within the event handler function, you must specify the event object as a parameter by passing `event` as a parameter, as in:

```
<input type="button" value="Click Me" onclick="handleClick(event);" />
```

This is the only time in the W3C model that you see an explicit reference to the `event` (lowercase e) object as if it were a global reference. This reference does not work in any other context — only as a parameter to an event handler function. If you have multiple parameters, the `event` reference can go in any order, but I tend to put it last:

```
<input type="button" value="Click Me" onclick="doSomething(this, event);" />
```

The function definition that is bound to the element should therefore have a parameter variable in place to catch the event object parameter:

```
function doSomething(widget, evt) {...}
```

You have no restrictions on how you name this parameter variable. In some examples of this book, you may see the variable assigned as `event` or, more commonly, `evt`. When working with cross-browser scripts, avoid using `event` as a parameter variable name so as not to interfere with the Internet Explorer `window.event` property.

The good news is that binding an event through an event tag attribute works well across all browsers. The bad news is that it goes against the prevailing trend in web design, which is to separate HTML content from the code that makes it interactive. In other words, there is a concerted effort among web developers to clearly delineate JavaScript code from HTML code.

This concept is closely related to the notion of separating content from presentation, which is afforded by style sheets. In this way, you could think of a web page as having three distinct components: HTML content, CSS, and JavaScript code. Keeping these three components as compartmentalized as possible results in cleaner, more manageable code.

 You see many examples of event tag attribute binding throughout this book while demonstrating various objects, properties, and methods. The usage is intentional because it is generally easier to understand the concepts under discussion when the events are bound closely to the elements.

The trick to maintaining a clean separation between JavaScript event binding and HTML code is to bind the events purely within script code as opposed to within attributes of HTML elements. The latter three event binding approaches mentioned earlier all offer this separation.

Binding events through object properties

Dating back as far as NN3 and IE4, element objects have event properties that can be used to bind events by assignment. For every event that an element is capable of receiving and responding to, there is a suitably named property, in all lowercase. For example, the `button` element object has a property named `onclick` that corresponds to the `onclick` event. You can bind an event handler to a `button` element by assigning a function reference to the `onclick` property:

```
document.forms[0].myButton.onclick = handleClick;
```

NOTE **Although event properties should be specified in all lowercase (`onclick`), some browsers also recognize mixed case event names (`onClick`).**

One catch to binding events as object properties is that at first glance it doesn't appear to be possible to pass your own parameters to the invoked handler functions. W3C browsers pass an event object as the only parameter to event handler functions, but this doesn't exactly leave room for you to include your own parameters. Without any further trickery, this means that your functions should receive the passed event object in a parameter variable:

```
function doSomething(evt) {...}
```

Recall that the `event` object contains a reference to the object that was the target of the event. From that, you can access any properties of that object, such as the `form` object that contains a form control object.

It is in fact perfectly possible to pass along your own parameters; it just takes an intermediary anonymous function to do the go-between work. For example, the following code demonstrates how to pass a single custom parameter along with the standard `event` object:

```
document.forms[0].myButton.onclick =
    function(evt) {doSomething("Cornelius", evt);};
```

In this example, a name string is passed along as the first parameter to the event handler, whereas the `event` object (automatically passed to the anonymous function as its sole parameter, and assigned to the parameter variable `evt`) is routed along as the second parameter. The actual handler code would look something like this:

```
function doSomething(firstName, evt) {...}
```

The evt parameter variable in the doSomething() event handler function acts as a reference to the event object for statements within the function. If you need to invoke other functions from there, you can pass the event object reference further along as needed. The event object retains its properties as long as the chain of execution triggered by the event action continues.

Binding events through IE attachments

In IE5 Microsoft set out to establish a new means of binding events to elements through attachments, which were originally intended for use with IE behaviors (see Chapter 48 on the CD-ROM). Eventually, the attachment approach to event binding expanded beyond behaviors and became the de facto IE standard for event binding. Seeing as how IE (as of version 7) still does not support the W3C approach to binding events, which you see in the next section, you should consider attachments the preferred way of handling events in IE for the foreseeable future.

IE event attachments are managed through the attachEvent() and detachEvent() methods, which are supported by all element objects that are capable of receiving events. By using both of these methods, you can bind and unbind events throughout the course of an application as needed.

The attachEvent() method takes the following form:

```
elementReference.attachEvent("event", functionReference);
```

To put this form in perspective, the following is an example of binding an event using the attachEvent() method in IE:

```
document.getElementById("myButton").attachEvent("onclick", doSomething);
```

The first parameter to the attachEvent() is the string name of the event, including the "on" prefix, as in "onclick". The second parameter is a reference to the event handler function for the event.

One new power afforded by IE event attachment is the ability to attach the same event to the same element multiple times (presumably pointing to different event handler functions). Just remember that if you choose to bind multiple events of the same type to the same element, they will be processed in the reverse order that they were assigned. This means the first event added is processed last.

Since the IE event model is predicated on the event object, which is a property of the window object, there is no event object passed into the event handler function. To access event properties, you just access the window's event object using either window.event or just event. The latter approach works because the window object is always assumed in client-side scripting. The upcoming section "event Object Compatibility" shows how to reconcile the IE window.event property and the W3C event event handler parameter.

The IE event binding approach also offers the ability to unbind an event, which means the targeted element will no longer receive event notifications. You unbind an IE event by calling the detachEvent() method on the element, like this:

```
document.getElementById("myButton").detachEvent("onclick", doSomething);
```

This example reveals how the detachEvent() method relies on the exact same syntax as attachEvent().

Binding events through W3C listeners

The W3C approach to binding events is logically similar to IE event attachment in that it revolves around two methods: addEventListener() and removeEventListener(). These two methods give elements the ability to listen for events and then respond accordingly. Also similarly to the IE `attachEvent()` and `detachEvent()` methods, `addEventListener()` and `removeEventListener()` work as a pair for adding and removing event listeners, respectively.

The `addEventListener()` method takes the following form:

```
elementReference.addEventListener("eventType", functionReference,
    captureSwitch);
```

The following example should help to reveal the practical usage of the method:

```
document.getElementById("myButton").addEventListener("click", doSomething,
    false);
```

Note how the event name is specified without the `on` prefix, which is different from the name used in IE event attachments. The other notable difference in W3C event listeners as compared to IE event attachments involves the third parameter to `addEventListener()`, `captureSwitch`, which determines whether the element should listen for the event during the capture phase of event propagation. Later in the chapter you learn about event propagation and how this parameter might be used to tweak the propagation of an event. For now, just know that the parameter is typically set to `false`.

Similar to IE event attachments, you can add the same event listener to the same element multiple times. Unlike the IE approach, however, is the fact that W3C events added in this manner are processed in the same order that they were assigned. This means the first event added is processed first.

Another similarity the W3C event model has to IE event handling is the ability to unbind an event from an element. The W3C version of event unbinding involves the `removeEventListener()` method, which is demonstrated in this example:

```
document.getElementById("myButton").removeEventListener("click", doSomething,
    false);
```

This example shows how the `removeEventListener()` method accepts the same parameters as `addEventListener()`.

A cross-browser event binding solution

Pulling together what you've learned about modern event handling, you know it must be possible to reconcile the IE and W3C approaches to event binding. In fact, it doesn't take all that much extra code to bind events in a manner that cleanly attempts to use the latest event binding techniques while still gracefully falling back on an older technique (object properties) for legacy browsers.

Following is a cross-browser function you can use to add an event binding to an element:

```
function addEvent(elem, evtType, func) {
    if (elem.addEventListener) {
        elem.addEventListener(evtType, func, false);
    } else if (elem.attachEvent) {
        elem.attachEvent("on" + evtType, func);
    } else {
        elem["on" + evtType] = func;
    }
}
```

Parameters for the function are a reference to the element, a string of the event type (that is, the version without the on prefix), and a reference to the function to be invoked when the event fires on the element. The addEvent() function first attempts to use the addEventListener() method on the supplied element, which satisfies modern W3C browsers (NN6+/Mozilla/Safari/Opera). If that fails, attachEvent() is tried, which accommodates modern IE browsers (IE5+). If that's a bust, the function falls back on simply assigning the event handler function to the event object property, which works on the vast majority of browsers.

> **NOTE** You could easily extend the addEvent() function to allow for the captureSwitch parameter of the addEventListener() method by adding a fourth parameter and passing it to addEventListener() instead of passing false.

Of course, the addEvent() function has to get called in order to bind events for a page. The onload event provides a great opportunity for binding events but, as you know, it's not a good idea to just call the addEvent() function in the onload HTML attribute. That would go against everything you've just learned. The trick is to first add an anonymous event handler for the onload event, and then carry out your other event bindings within that function. Here's an example of how you might do this:

```
addEvent(window, "load", function() {
    addEvent(document.getElementById("myButton"), "click", handleClick);
    addEvent(document.body, "mouseup",
        function(evt) {handleClick(evt);});
});
```

In case you need to unbind an event, here is a suitable cross-browser function for unbinding events:

```
function removeEvent(elem, evtType, func) {
    if (elem.removeEventListener) {
        elem.removeEventListener(evtType, func, false);
    } else if (elem.detachEvent) {
        elem.detachEvent("on" + evtType, func);
    } else {
        elem["on" + evtType] = null;
    }
}
```

event Object Compatibility

Despite the incompatible ways that W3C DOM and IE event objects arrive at an event handler function, you can easily stuff the object into one variable that both browser types can use. For example, the following function fragment receives a W3C DOM event object but also accommodates the IE event object:

```
function doSomething(evt) {
    evt = (evt) ? evt : ((window.event) ? window.event : null);
    if (evt) {
        // browser has an event to process
        ...
    }
}
```

If an event object arrives as a parameter, it continues to be available as evt; but if not, the function makes sure that a window.event object is available and assigns it to the evt variable; finally, if the browser doesn't know about an event object, the evt variable is made null. Processing continues only if evt contains an event object.

That's the easy part. The madness comes in the details: reading properties of the event object when the property names can vary widely across the two event object models. Sections later in this chapter provide details of each property and method of both event object models, but seeing an overview of the property terminology on a comparative basis is helpful. Table 25-2 lists the common information bits and actions you are likely to want from an event object and the property or method names used in the event object models.

TABLE 25-2

Common event Object Properties and Methods

Property/Action	IE4+	W3C DOM
Target element	srcElement	target
Event type	type	type
X coordinate in element	offsetX	n/a†
Y coordinate in element	offsetY	n/a†
X coordinate on page	n/a†	pageX††
Y coordinate on page	n/a†	pageY††
X coordinate in window	clientX	clientX
Y coordinate in window	clientY	clientY
X coordinate on screen	screenX	screenX
Y coordinate on screen	screenY	screenY
Mouse button	button	button
Keyboard key	keyCode	keyCode††
Shift key pressed	shiftKey	shiftKey
Alt key pressed	altKey	altKey
Ctrl key pressed	ctrlKey	ctrlKey
Previous Element	fromElement	relatedTarget
Next Element	toElement	relatedTarget
Cancel bubbling	cancelBubble	preventBubble()
Prevent default action	returnValue	preventDefault()

†Value can be derived through calculations with other properties.

††Not an official W3C DOM property, but is supported in Mozilla, Safari, and Opera.

As you can see in Table 25-2, properties for the IE4+ and W3C event objects have a lot in common. Perhaps the most important incompatibility to overcome is referencing the element that is the intended target of the event. This, too, can be branched in your code to achieve a common variable that references the element. For example, embedded within the previous function fragment can be a statement, such as the following:

```
var elem = (evt.target) ? evt.target : ((evt.srcElement) ?
    evt.srcElement : null);
```

Each event model has additional properties that are not shared by the other. Details about these are covered in the rest of this chapter.

Dueling Event Models

Despite the sometimes widely divergent ways event object models treat their properties, accommodating a wide range of browsers for event manipulation is not difficult. In this section, you see two scripts that examine important event properties. The first script reveals which, if any, modifier keys are held down during an event; the second script extracts the codes for both mouse buttons and keyboard keys. Both scripts work with all modern browsers that have event objects.

Cross-platform modifier key check

Listing 25-6 demonstrates branching techniques for examining the modifier key(s) being held down while an event fires. You can find details of the event object properties, such as `modifiers` and `altKey`, later in this chapter. To see the page in action, click a link, type into a text box, and click a button while holding down any combination of modifier keys. A series of four check boxes representing the four modifier keys is at the bottom. As you click or type, the check box(es) of the pressed modifier key(s) become checked.

LISTING 25-6

Checking Events for Modifier Keys

```
<html>
    <head>
        <title>Event Modifiers</title>
        <script type="text/javascript">
        function checkMods(evt) {
            evt = (evt) ? evt : ((window.event) ? window.event : null);
            if (evt) {
                var elem = (evt.target) ? evt.target : evt.srcElement;
                var form = document.output;
                form.modifier[0].checked = evt.altKey;
                form.modifier[1].checked = evt.ctrlKey;
                form.modifier[2].checked = evt.shiftKey;
                form.modifier[3].checked = false;
            }
            return false;
        }

        // bind the event handlers
```

```
        function addEvent(elem, evtType, func) {
            if (elem.addEventListener) {
                elem.addEventListener(evtType, func, false);
            } else if (elem.attachEvent) {
                elem.attachEvent("on" + evtType, func);
            } else {
                elem["on" + evtType] = func;
            }
        }
        addEvent(window, "load", function() {
            addEvent(document.getElementById("link"), "mousedown",
                function(evt) {return checkMods(evt);});
            addEvent(document.getElementById("text"), "keyup",
                function(evt) {checkMods(evt);});
            addEvent(document.getElementById("button"), "click",
                function(evt) {checkMods(evt);});
        });
        </script>
    </head>
    <body>
        <h1>Event Modifiers</h1>
        <hr />
        <p>Hold one or more modifier keys and click on <a
            id="link" href="javascript:void(0)">this link</a> to see which
            keys you are holding.</p>
        <form name="output">
            <p>Enter some text with uppercase and lowercase letters: <input
                id="text" type="text" size="40" /></p>
            <p><input id="button" type="button" value="Click Here With Modifier Keys"
                /></p>
            <p><input type="checkbox" name="modifier" />Alt <input type="checkbox"
                name="modifier" />Control <input type="checkbox"
                name="modifier" />Shift <input type="checkbox"
                name="modifier" />Meta</p>
        </form>
    </body>
</html>
```

The script checks the event object property for each of three modifiers to determine which, if any, modifier keys are being pressed.

Cross-platform key capture

To demonstrate keyboard events in both event capture models, Listing 25-7 captures the key character being typed into a text box, as well as the mouse button used to click a button.

LISTING 25-7

Checking Events for Key and Mouse Button Pressed

```html
<html>
    <head>
        <title>Button and Key Properties</title>
        <script type="text/javascript">
        function checkWhich(evt) {
            evt = (evt) ? evt : ((event) ? event : null);
            if (evt) {
                var thingPressed = "";
                var elem = (evt.target) ? evt.target : evt.srcElement;
                if (elem.type == "textarea") {
                    thingPressed = (evt.charCode) ? evt.charCode : evt.keyCode;
                } else if (elem.type == "button") {
                    thingPressed = (typeof evt.button != "undefined") ? evt.button :
"n/a";
                }
                window.status = thingPressed;
            }
            return false;
        }

        // bind the event handlers
        function addEvent(elem, evtType, func) {
            if (elem.addEventListener) {
                elem.addEventListener(evtType, func, false);
            } else if (elem.attachEvent) {
                elem.attachEvent("on" + evtType, func);
            } else {
                elem["on" + evtType] = func;
            }
        }
        addEvent(window, "load", function() {
            addEvent(document.getElementById("button"), "mousedown",
                function(evt) {checkWhich(evt);});
            addEvent(document.getElementById("text"), "keypress",
                function(evt) {checkWhich(evt);});
        });
        </script>
    </head>
    <body>
        <h1>Button and Key Properties</h1>
        (results in the status bar)
        <hr />
        <form>
            <p>Mouse down atop this <input id="button" type="button" value="Button"
                /> with either mouse button (if you have more than one).</p>
            <p>Enter some text with uppercase and lowercase letters: <textarea
                id="text" cols="40" rows="4" wrap="virtual"></textarea>
```

```
            </p>
        </form>
    </body>
</html>
```

The codes displayed for the keyboard event are equivalent to the ASCII values of character keys. If you need the codes of other keys, the `onkeydown` and `onkeyup` event handlers provide Unicode values for any key that you press on the keyboard. See the `charCode` and `keyCode` property listings for event objects later in this chapter for more details.

Event Types

Although browsers prior to version 4 did not have an accessible event object, this is a good time to summarize the evolution of what in today's browsers is known as the `type` property. The `type` property reveals the kind of event that generates an event object (the event handler name minus the "on"). Object models in IE4+ and NN6+/W3C provide event handlers for virtually every HTML element, so that it's possible, for example, to define an `onclick` event handler for not only a clickable button but also a p or even an arbitrary `span` element.

Older Browsers

Earlier browsers tended to limit the number of event handlers for any particular element to just those that made sense for the kind of element it was. Even so, many scripters wanted more event handlers on more objects. But until that became a reality in IE4+ and NN6+/W3C, authors had to know the limits of the object models. Table 25-3 shows the event handlers available for objects within three generations of early browsers. Each column represents the version in which the event type was introduced. For example, the `window` object started out with four event types and gained three more when NN4 was released. In contrast, the `area` object was exposed as an object for the first time in NN3, which is where the first event types for that object are listed.

With the exception of the NN4 `layer` object, all objects shown in Table 25-3 have survived into the newer browsers, so that you can use these event handlers with confidence. Again, keep in mind that of the browsers listed in Table 25-3, only NN4 has an `event` object of any kind exposed to scripts.

TABLE 25-3

Event Types through the Early Ages

Object	NN2/IE3	NN3	NN4
window	blur		dragdrop
	focus		move
	load		resize

continued

continued

TABLE 25-3	*(continued)*		
Object	**NN2/IE3**	**NN3**	**NN4**
	unload		
layer			blur
			focus
			load
			mouseout
			mouseover
			mouseup
link	click	mouseout	dblclick
	mouseover		mousedown
			onmouseup
area		mouseout	click
		mouseover	
image		abort	
		error	
		load	
Form	submit	reset	
text, textarea, password			
	blur		keydown
	change		keypress
	focus		keyup
	select		
all buttons	click		mousedown
			mouseup
select	blur		
	change		
	focus		
fileUpload		blur	
		focus	
		select	

Event types in IE4+ and NN6+/W3C

By now you should have at least scanned the list of event handlers defined for elements in common, as shown in Chapter 15. This list of event types is enormous. A sizable number of the event types are unique to IE4, IE5, and IE5.5+, and in some cases, just the Windows version at that.

If you compose pages for both IE4+ and NN6+/W3C, however, you need to know which event types these browser families and generations have in common. Event types for NN6+/Moz/Safari are based primarily on the W3C DOM Level 2 specification, although they also include keyboard events, whose formal standards are still under development for DOM Level 3. Table 25-4 lists a common denominator of event types for modern browsers and the objects that support them. Although not as long as the IE event list, the event types in Table 25-4 are the basic set you should get to know for all browsers.

TABLE 25-4

IE4+ and W3C DOM Event Types in Common

Event type	Applicable Elements
abort	object
blur	window, button, text, password, label, select, textarea
change	text, password, textarea, select
click	All elements
error	window, frameset, object
focus	window, button, text, password, label, select, textarea
keydown	text, password, textarea
keypress	text, password, textarea
keyup	text, password, textarea
load	window, frameset, object
mousedown	All elements
mousemove	All elements
mouseout	All elements
mouseover	All elements
mouseup	All elements
reset	form
resize	window
scroll	window
select	text, password, textarea
submit	form
unload	window, frameset

IE4+ event Object

Properties	Methods	Event Handlers
altKey		
altLeft		
behaviorCookie		
behaviorPart		
bookmarks		
boundElements		
button		
cancelBubble		
clientX		
clientY		
contentOverflow		
ctrlKey		
ctrlLeft		
dataFld		
dataTransfer		
fromElement		
keyCode		
nextPage		
offsetX		
offsetY		
propertyName		
qualifier		
reason		
recordset		
repeat		
returnValue		
saveType		
screenX		
screenY		
shiftKey		
shiftLeft		
srcElement		
srcFilter		

Properties	Methods	Event Handlers
srcUrn		
toElement		
type		
wheelData		
x		
y		

Syntax

Accessing IE4+ event object properties:

> [window.]event.*property*

Compatibility: WinIE4+, MacIE4+, NN-, Moz-, Safari-

About this object

The IE4+ event object is a property of the window object. Its basic operation is covered earlier in this chapter.

You can see a little of what the event object is about with the help of The Evaluator (see Chapter 13). If you type event into the bottom text box, you can examine the properties of the event object for the event that triggers the function that displays the event object properties. If you press the Enter key in the text box, you see properties of the keypress event that caused the internal script to run; click the List Properties button to see the properties of the click event fired at the button. Hold down some of the modifier keys while clicking to see how this affects some of the properties.

As you review the properties for the event object, make special note of the compatibility rating for each property. The list of properties for this object has grown over the evolution of the IE4+ event object model. Also, most properties are listed here as being read-only, which they were in IE4. But for IE5+, these properties are also Read/Write if the event is created artificially via methods, such as IE5.5+'s document .createEventObject() method. Event objects that are created by user or system action have very few properties that can be modified on the fly (to prevent your scripts from altering user actions). Notice, too, that some properties are the same as for the W3C DOM event object, as revealed in the compatibility ratings.

Properties

altKey
ctrlKey
shiftKey

Value: Boolean.   Read-Only
Compatibility: WinIE4+, MacIE4+, NN6+, Moz+, Safari+

(IE) event.behaviorCookie

When an `event` object is created in response to a user or system action, these three properties are set based on whether their corresponding keys were being held down at the time — a Shift-click, for example. If the key was held down, the property is assigned a value of `true`; otherwise the value is `false`.

Most commonly, you use expressions consisting of this property as `if` construction condition statements. Because these are Boolean values, you can combine multiple properties in a single condition. For example, if you have a branch of a function that is to execute only if the event occurred with both the Shift and Control keys held down, the condition looks as the following:

```
if (event.shiftKey && event.ctrlKey) {
    // statements to execute
}
```

Conversely, you can take a more user-friendly approach to provide special processing if the user holds down any one of the three modifier keys:

```
if (event.shiftKey || event.ctrlKey || event.altKey) {
    // statements to execute
}
```

The rationale behind this approach is to offer perhaps some shortcut operation for users, but not force them to memorize a specific modifier key combination.

Example

See Listing 25-6, where the values of these three properties are used to set the `checked` properties of corresponding check boxes for a variety of event types.

Related Items: `altLeft`, `ctrlLeft`, `shiftLeft` properties.

altLeft
ctrlLeft
shiftLeft

Value: Boolean.　　　　　　　　　　　　　　　　　　　　　　　　　　　　　Read-Only
Compatibility: WinIE5.5+, MacIE-, NN-, Moz-, Safari-

Some versions of Windows allow events to be modified by only the left-hand Alt, Ctrl, and Shift keys when using IE5.5+. For these modifiers to be recorded by the `event` object, focus must be on the document (body), and not in any form control. If the left-key version is `false` and the regular version is `true`, then your script knows that the right-hand key had been held down during the event.

Related Items: `altKey`, `ctrlKey`, `shiftKey` properties.

behaviorCookie
behaviorPart

Value: Integer.　　　　　　　　　　　　　　　　　　　　　　　　　　　　　　Read-Only
Compatibility: WinIE6+, MacIE-, NN-, Moz-, Safari-

These two properties are related to a Windows technology that Microsoft calls *rendering behaviors*. Unlike the behaviors discussed under the `addBehavior()` method in Chapter 15, rendering behaviors are written in C++ and provide services for custom drawing on your web page. For more details, consult the document "Implementing Rendering Behaviors" at `http://msdn.microsoft.com/workshop/browser/editing/imprendbehav.asp`.

```
bookmarks
boundElements
dataFld
qualifier
reason
recordset
```

Value: See text.   Read-Only
Compatibility: WinIE6+, MacIE-, NN-, Moz-, Safari-

This group of event object properties is tied to using Data Binding in Windows versions of IE4+. Extensive details of Data Binding lie outside the scope of this book, but Table 25-5 provides a summary of these event object properties within that context (much of the terminology is used in Data Binding, but doesn't affect other scripting). For more details, search for ActiveX Data Objects (ADO) at http://msdn.microsoft.com/workshop/.

> **NOTE** Although still supported in IE, Microsoft's original ADO technology has given way to ADO.NET, which is designed for tighter integration with Microsoft's .NET architecture. To learn more about the differences between the two technologies, visit http://msdn.microsoft.com/library/en-us/dndotnet/html/adonetprogmsdn.asp.

TABLE 25-5

ADO-Related event Object Properties

Property	Value	First Implemented	Description
bookmarks	Array	IE4	Array of ADO bookmarks (saved positions) for records within a recordset associated with the object that received the event.
boundElements	Array	IE5	Array of element references for all elements bound to the same data set that was touched by the current event.
dataFld	String	IE5	Name of the data source column that is bound to a table cell that receives a cellchange event.
qualifier	String	IE5	Name of the data member associated with a data source that receives a data-related event. Available only if the data source object (DSO) allows multiple-named data members or a qualifier has been explicitly set via the datasrc attribute of the bound element. Read-write in IE5+.
reason	Integer	IE4	Set only from onDataSetComplete event, provides the result code of the data set loading (0=successful; 1=transfer aborted; 2=other error).
recordset	Object	IE4	Reference to the current recordset in a data source object.

button

Value: Integer.   Read-Only
Compatibility: WinIE4+, MacIE4+, NN6+, Moz+, Safari+

The button property reveals which button or buttons were pressed to activate a mouse event. If no mouse button is pressed to generate an event, this property is zero in IE. But integers 1 through 7 reveal single and multiple button presses, including three-button mice when they are recognized by the operating system. Integer values in IE correspond to buttons according to the following scheme:

Value	Description
0	No button
1	Left (primary) button
2	Right button
3	Left and right buttons together
4	Middle button
5	Left and middle buttons together
6	Right and middle buttons together
7	Left, middle, and right buttons together

Mouse buttons other than the primary one are easier to look for in mousedown or mouseup events rather than onclick events. Be aware that as the user works toward pressing multiple buttons, each press fires a mousedown event. Therefore, if the user presses the left button first, the mousedown event fires, with the event.button property bearing the 1 value; as soon as the right button is pressed, the mousedown event fires again, but this time with an event.button value of 3. If your script intends to perform special action with both buttons pressed, it should ignore and not perform any action for a single mouse button, because that one-button event will very likely fire in the process, disturbing the intended action.

Exercise caution when scripting the event.button property for both IE4+ and NN6+/Moz/W3C. The W3C DOM event model defines different button values for mouse buttons (0, 1, and 2 for left, middle, and right) and no values for multiple buttons.

Example

See Listing 25-7, where the event.button property is revealed in the status bar. Try pressing individual mouse buttons on, for example, the screen button. Then try combinations, watching the results very closely in the status bar.

Related Items: None.

cancelBubble

Value: Boolean.   Read/Write
Compatibility: WinIE4+, MacIE4+, NN6+, Moz+, Safari+

The cancelBubble property (which sounds more as if it should be a method name) determines whether the current event object bubbles up any higher in the element containment hierarchy of the document. By default, this property is false, meaning that if the event is supposed to bubble, it will do so automatically.

To prevent event bubbling for the current event, set the property to `true` anywhere within the event handler function. As an alternative, you can cancel bubbling directly in an element's event handler attribute, as in the following:

```
onclick="doButtonClick(this); event.cancelBubble = true"
```

Cancelling event bubbling works only for the current event. The very next event to fire will have bubbling enabled (provided the event bubbles).

Example

See Listing 25-2 to see the `cancelBubble` property in action. Even though that listing has some features that apply to IE5.5+, the bubble cancelling demonstration works all the way back to IE4.

Related Items: `returnValue` property.

clientX
clientY
offsetX
offsetY
screenX
screenY
x
y

Value: Integer. Read/Write
Compatibility: WinIE4+, MacIE4+, NN6+, Moz+, Safari+

An IE `event` object provides coordinates for an event in as many as four coordinate spaces: the element itself, the parent element of the event's target, the viewable area of the browser window, and the entire video screen. Unfortunately, misleading values can be returned by some of the properties that correspond to these coordinate spaces, as discussed in this section. Note that no properties provide the explicit position of an event relative to the entire page, in case the user has scrolled the window.

Starting with the innermost space — that of the element that is the target of the event — the `offsetX` and `offsetY` properties should provide pixel coordinates within the target element. This is how, for example, you could determine the click point on an image, regardless of whether the image is embedded in the `body` or floating around in a positioned `div`. Windows versions through IE7 produce the correct values in most cases. But for some elements that are child elements of the `body` element, the vertical (y) value may be relative to the viewable window, rather than just the element itself. You can see an example of this when you work with Listing 25-8 and click the `h1` or `p` elements near the top of the page. This problem does not affect MacIE, but there is another problem on Mac versions: If the page is scrolled away from its normal original position, the scrolled values are subtracted from the `clientX` and `clientY` values. This is an incompatibility bug, and you must take this error into account if you need click coordinates inside an element for a potentially scrolled page. This error correction must be done only for the Mac, because Windows works okay.

Extending scope to the offset parent element of the event's target, the `x` and `y` properties in IE5+ for Windows should return the coordinates for the event relative to the target's offset parent element (the element that can be found via the `offsetParent` property). For most non-positioned elements, these values are the same as the `clientX` and `clientY` properties because, as discussed in a moment, the offset parent element has a zero offset with *its* parent, the body. Observe an important caution about the x and y properties: In WinIE4 and through MacIE5, the properties do not take into account any offset parent locations other than the body. Even in WinIE5+, this property can give false readings in some circumstances. By and large, these two properties should not be used.

The next set of coordinates, clientX and clientY, are relative to the visible document area of the browser window. When the document is scrolled all the way to the top (or the document doesn't scroll at all), these coordinates are the same as the coordinates on the entire page. But because the page can scroll "underneath" the viewable window, the coordinates on the page can change if the page scrolls. Also, in the Windows versions of IE, you can actually register mouse events that are up to 2 pixels outside of the body element, which seems weird, but true. Therefore, in WinIE, if you click the background of the body, the event fires on the body element, but the clientX/clientY values will be 2 pixels greater than offsetX/offsetY (they're equal in MacIE). Despite this slight discrepancy, you should rely on the clientX and clientY properties if you are trying to get the coordinates of an event that may be in a positioned element, but have those coordinates relative to the entire viewable window, rather than just the positioning context.

Taking the page's scrolling into account for an event coordinate is often important. After all, unless you generate a fixed-size window for a user, you don't know how the browser window will be oriented. If you're looking for a click within a specific region of the page, you must take page scrolling into account. The scrolling factor can be retrieved from the document.body.scrollLeft and document.body.scrollTop properties. When reading the clientX and clientY properties, be sure to add the corresponding scroll properties to get the position on the page:

```
var coordX = event.clientX + document.body.scrollLeft;
var coordY = event.clientY + document.body.scrollTop;
```

Do this in your production work without fail.

Finally, the screenX and screenY properties return the pixel coordinates of the event on the entire video screen. These properties may be more useful if IE provided more window dimension properties. In any case, because mouse events fire only when the cursor is somewhere in the content region of the browser window, don't expect to get screen values of anywhere outside this region.

If these descriptions seem confusing to you, you are not alone. Throw in a few bugs, and it may seem like quite a mess. But think how you may use event coordinates in scripts. By and large, you want to know one of two types of mouse event coordinates: within the element itself and within the page. Use the offsetX/offsetY properties for the former; use clientX/clientY (plus the scroll property values) for the latter.

Although the coordinate properties are used primarily for mouse events, there is a little quirk that may let you determine if the user has resized the window via the maximize icon in the title bar (on the Mac, this is called the zoom box) or the resize handle at the bottom-right corner of the screen. Mouse event coordinates are recorded in the event object for a resize event. In the case of the maximize icon, the clientY coordinate is a negative value (above the client space) and the clientX coordinate is within about 45 pixels of the previous width of the window (document.body.clientWidth). This, of course, happens after the window has resized, so it is not a way to prevent window resizing.

Example

Listing 25-8 provides readings of all event coordinate properties in an interactive way. An onmousedown event handler triggers all event handling, and you can click the mouse anywhere on the page to see what happens. You see the tag of the element targeted by the mouse event to help you visualize how some of the coordinate properties are determined. An image is encased inside a positioned div element to help you see what happens to some of the properties when the event is targeted inside a positioned element.

LISTING 25-8

IE4+ Event Coordinate Properties

```html
<html>
    <head>
        <title>X and Y Event Properties (IE4+ Syntax)</title>
        <script type="text/javascript">
        function checkCoords(evt) {
            evt = (evt) ? evt : ((window.event) ? window.event : null);
            if (evt) {
                var elem = (evt.target) ? evt.target : evt.srcElement;
                var form = document.forms[0];
                form.srcElemTag.value = "<" + elem.tagName + ">";
                form.clientCoords.value = evt.clientX + "," + evt.clientY;
                if (typeof document.body.scrollLeft != "undefined") {
                    form.pageCoords.value = (evt.clientX + document.body.scrollLeft) +
                        "," + (evt.clientY + document.body.scrollTop);
                }
                form.offsetCoords.value = evt.offsetX + "," + evt.offsetY;
                form.screenCoords.value = evt.screenX + "," + evt.screenY;
                form.xyCoords.value = evt.x + "," + evt.y;
                if (elem.offsetParent) {
                    form.parElem.value = "<" + elem.offsetParent.tagName + ">";
                }
                return false;
            }
        }
        function handleSize(evt) {
            evt = (evt) ? evt : ((window.event) ? window.event : null);
            if (evt) {
                document.forms[0].resizeCoords.value = evt.clientX + "," + evt.clientY;
            }
        }

        // bind the event handlers
        function addEvent(elem, evtType, func) {
            if (elem.addEventListener) {
                elem.addEventListener(evtType, func, false);
            } else if (elem.attachEvent) {
                elem.attachEvent("on" + evtType, func);
            } else {
                elem["on" + evtType] = func;
            }
        }
        addEvent(window, "load", function() {
            addEvent(document.body, "mousedown",
                function(evt) {checkCoords(evt);});
            addEvent(document.body, "resize",
                function(evt) {handleSize(evt);});
        });
```

continued

LISTING 25-8 *(continued)*

```
        </script>
</head>
<body>
    <h1>X and Y Event Properties (IE4+ Syntax)</h1>
    <hr />
    <p>Click on any element to see the coordinate values
        for the event object.</p>
    <form name="output">
        <table>
            <tr>
                <td colspan="2">IE Mouse Event Coordinates:</td>
            </tr>
            <tr>
                <td align="right">srcElement:</td>
                <td><input type="text" name="srcElemTag" size="10" /></td>
            </tr>
            <tr>
                <td align="right">clientX, clientY:</td>
                <td><input type="text" name="clientCoords" size="10" /></td>
                <td align="right">...With scrolling:</td>
                <td><input type="text" name="pageCoords" size="10" /></td>
            </tr>
            <tr>
                <td align="right">offsetX, offsetY:</td>
                <td><input type="text" name="offsetCoords" size="10" /></td>
            </tr>
            <tr>
                <td align="right">screenX, screenY:</td>
                <td><input type="text" name="screenCoords" size="10" /></td>
            </tr>
            <tr>
                <td align="right">x, y:</td>
                <td><input type="text" name="xyCoords" size="10" /></td>
                <td align="right">...Relative to:</td>
                <td><input type="text" name="parElem" size="10" /></td>
            </tr>
            <tr>
                <td align="right"><input type="button" value="Click Here" /></td>
            </tr>
            <tr>
                <td colspan="2"><hr /></td>
            </tr>
            <tr>
                <td colspan="2">Window Resize Coordinates:</td>
            </tr>
            <tr>
                <td align="right">clientX, clientY:</td>
                <td><input type="text" name="resizeCoords" size="10" /></td>
            </tr>
```

```
        </table>
      </form>
      <div id="display" style="position:relative; left:100">
         <img alt="image" src="nile.gif" width="320" height="240" border="0" />
      </div>
    </body>
</html>
```

Here are some tasks to try in IE with the page that loads from Listing 25-8 to help you understand the relationships among the various pairs of coordinate properties:

1. Click the dot above the "i" on the "Click Here" button label. The target element is the button (input) element, whose offsetParent is a table cell element. The offsetY value is very low because you are near the top of the element's own coordinate space. The client coordinates (and x and y), however, are relative to the viewable area in the window. If your browser window is maximized in Windows, the screenX and clientX values will be the same; the difference between screenY and clientY is the height of all the window chrome above the content region. With the window not scrolled at all, the client coordinates are the same with and without scrolling taken into account.

2. Jot down the various coordinate values and then scroll the page down slightly (clicking the scrollbar fires an event) and click the dot on the button again. The clientY value shrinks because the page has moved upward relative to the viewable area, making the measure between the top of the area smaller with respect to the button. The Windows version does the right thing with the offset properties, by continuing to return values relative to the element's own coordinate space; the Mac, unfortunately, subtracts the scrolled amount from the offset properties.

3. Click the large image. The client properties perform as expected for both Windows and Mac, as do the screen properties. For Windows, the x and y properties correctly return the event coordinates relative to the img element's offsetParent, which is the div element that surrounds it. Note, however, that the browser "sees" the div as starting 10 pixels to the left of the image. In WinIE5.5+, you can click within those 10 transparent pixels to the left of the image to click the div element. This padding is inserted automatically and impacts the coordinates of the x and y properties. A more reliable measure of the event inside the image is the offset properties. The same is true in the Macintosh version, as long as the page isn't scrolled, in which case the scroll, just as in Step 2, affects the values above.

4. Click the top hr element under the heading. It may take a couple of tries to actually hit the element (you've made it when the hr element shows up in the srcElement box). This is to reinforce the way the client properties provide coordinates within the element itself (again, except on the Mac when the page is scrolled). Clicking at the very left end of the rule, you eventually find the 0,0 coordinate.

Finally, if you are a Windows user, here are two examples to try to see some of the unexpected behavior of coordinate properties.

1. With the page not scrolled, click anywhere along the right side of the page, away from any text so that the body element is srcElement. Because the body element theoretically fills the entire content region of the browser window, all coordinate pairs except for the screen coordinates should be the same. But offset properties are 2 pixels less than all the others. By and large, this difference won't matter in your scripts, but you should be aware of this potential discrepancy if precise

positioning is important. For inexplicable reasons, the offset properties are measured in a space that is inset 2 pixels from the left and top of the window. This is not the case in the Macintosh version, where all value pairs are the same from the body perspective.

2. Click the text of the h1 or p elements (just above and below the long horizontal rule at the top of the page). In theory, the offset properties should be relative to the rectangles occupied by these elements (they're block elements, after all). But instead, they're measured in the same space as the client properties (plus the 2 pixels). This unexpected behavior doesn't have anything to do with the cursor being a text cursor, because if you click inside any of the text box elements, their offset properties are properly relative to their own rectangles. This problem does not afflict the Macintosh version.

Many of these properties are also in the W3C DOM and are therefore supported in W3C DOM browsers. Unsupported properties display their values as undefined when you run Listing 25-8 in those browsers.

You can see further examples of important event coordinate properties in action in the discussion of dragging elements around the IE page in Chapter 40 on the CD-ROM.

Related Items: fromElement, toElement properties.

dataTransfer

Value: Object.   Read-Only
Compatibility: WinIE5+, MacIE-, NN-, Moz-, Safari2+

The dataTransfer property is a reference to the dataTransfer object. Use this object in drag-and-drop operations (that is, with drag-and-drop-related events) to control not only the data that gets transferred from the source to the target but also to control the look of the cursor along the way.

Table 25-6 lists the properties and methods of the dataTransfer object.

TABLE 25-6

dataTransfer object Properties and Methods

Property/Method	Returns	Description
dropEffect	String	An element that is a potential recipient of a drop action can use the ondragenter, ondragover, or ondrop event handler to set the cursor style to be displayed when the cursor is atop the element. Before this can work, the source element's ondragstart event handler must assign a value to the event.effectAllowed property. Possible string values for both properties are copy, link, move, or none. These properties correspond to the Windows system cursors for the operations users typically do with files and in other documents. You must also cancel the default action (meaning set event.returnValue to false) for all of these drop element event handlers: ondragenter, ondragover, and ondrop.

Property/Method	Returns	Description
effectAllowed	String	Set in response to an `ondragstart` event of the source element, this property determines which kind of drag-and-drop action will be taking place. Possible string values are `copy`, `link`, `move`, or `none`. This property value must match the `dropEffect` property value for the target element's event object. Also, cancel the default action (meaning, set `event.returnValue` to `false`) in the `ondragstart` event handler.
clearData([format])	Nothing	Removes data in the clipboard. If no format parameters are supplied, all data are cleared. Data formats can be one or more of the following strings: `Text`, `URL`, `File`, `HTML`, `Image`.
getData(format)	String	Retrieves data of the specified format from the clipboard. The format is one of the following strings: `Text`, `URL`, `File`, `HTML`, `Image`. The clipboard is not emptied after you get the data, so that it can be retrieved in several sequential operations.
setData(format, data)	Boolean	Stores string data in the clipboard. The format is one of the following strings: `Text`, `URL`, `File`, `HTML`, `Image`. For non-text data formats, the data must be a string that specifies the path or URL to the content. Returns `true` if the transfer to the clipboard is successful.

The `dataTransfer` object acts as a conduit and controller of data that your scripts need to transfer from one element to another in response to a user's drag-and-drop action. You need to adhere to a well-defined sequence of actions triggered by a handful of event handlers. This means that the object is invoked on different instances of the `event` object as different events fire in the process of dragging and dropping.

The sequence begins at the source element, where an `ondragstart` event handler typically assigns a value to the `dropEffect` property and uses the `getData()` method to explicitly capture whatever data it is about the source object that gets transferred to the eventual target. For example, if you drag an image, the information being transferred may simply be the URL of the image — data that is extractable from the `event.srcElement.src` property of that event (the `src` property of the image, that is).

At the target element(s), three event handlers must be defined: `ondragenter`, `ondragover`, and `ondrop`. Most commonly, the first two event handlers do nothing more than mark the element for a particular `dropEffect` (which must match the `effectAllowed` set at the source during the drag's start) and set `event.returnValue` to false so that the cursor displays the desired cursor. These actions are also carried out in the `ondrop` event handler, but that is also the handler that does the processing of the destination action at the target element. This is when the `dataTransfer` object's `getData()` method is invoked to pick up the data that has been "stored" away by `getData()` at the start of the drag. If you also want to make sure that the data is not picked up accidentally by another event, invoke the `clearData()` method to remove that data from memory.

Note that the style of dragging being discussed here is not the kind in which you see the source element actually moving on the screen (although you could script it that way). The intention is to treat drag-and-drop operations just as Windows does in, say, the Windows Explorer window or on the Desktop. To the user, the draggable component becomes encapsulated in the cursor. That's why the properties of the `dataTransfer` object control the appearance of the cursor at the drop point as a way of conveying to the user the type of action that will occur with the impending drop. Apple implements the same behavior in Safari 2.

Example

An extensive example of the `dataTransfer` property in action can be found in Listing 15-37 in the section for the `ondrag` event handler.

Related Items: `ondragend`, `ondragenter`, `ondragleave`, `ondragover`, `ondragstart`, `ondrop` event handlers.

fromElement
toElement

Value: Element object.   Read-Only
Compatibility: WinIE4+, MacIE4+, NN-, Moz-, Safari-

The `fromElement` and `toElement` properties allow an element to uncover where the cursor rolled in from or has rolled out to. These properties extend the power of the `onmouseover` and `onmouseout` event handlers by expanding their scope to outside the current element (usually to an adjacent element).

When the `onmouseover` event fires on an element, the cursor had to be over some other element just beforehand. The `fromElement` property holds a reference to that element. Conversely, when the `onmouseout` event fires, the cursor is already over some other element. The `toElement` property holds a reference to that element.

Example

Listing 25-9 provides an example of how the `fromElement` and `toElement` properties can reveal the life of the cursor action before and after it rolls into an element. When you roll the cursor to the center box (a table cell), its `onmouseover` event handler displays the text from the table cell from which the cursor arrived.

LISTING 25-9

Using the toElement and fromElement Properties

```
<html>
   <head>
      <title>fromElement and toElement Properties</title>
      <style type="text/css">
      .direction {background-color:#00FFFF; width:100; height:50;
      text-align:center}
      #main {background-color:#FF6666; text-align:center}
      </style>
      <script type="text/javascript">
      function showArrival() {
         var direction = (event.fromElement.innerText) ?
            event.fromElement.innerText : "parts unknown";
         status = "Arrived from: " + direction;
      }
      function showDeparture() {
         var direction = (event.toElement.innerText) ?
            event.toElement.innerText : "parts unknown";
         status = "Departed to: " + direction;
      }
```

```
        </script>
    </head>
    <body>
        <h1>fromElement and toElement Properties</h1>
        <hr />
        <p>Roll the mouse to the center box and look for arrival information in
            the status bar. Roll the mouse away from the center box and look for
            departure information in the status bar.</p>
        <table cellspacing="0" cellpadding="5">
            <tr>
                <td></td>
                <td class="direction">North</td>
                <td></td></tr>
            <tr>
                <td class="direction">West</td>
                <td id="main" onmouseover="showArrival()"
                onmouseout="showDeparture()">Roll</td>
                <td class="direction">East</td>
            </tr>
            <tr>
                <td></td>
                <td class="direction">South</td>
                <td></td>
            </tr>
        </table>
    </body>
</html>
```

This is a good example to experiment with in the browser, because it also reveals a potential limitation. The element registered as the toElement or fromElement must fire a mouse event to register itself with the browser. If not, the next element in the sequence that registers itself is the one acknowledged by these properties. For example, if you roll the mouse into the center box and then extremely quickly roll the cursor to the bottom of the page, you may bypass the South box entirely. The text that appears in the status bar is actually the inner text of the body element, which is the element that caught the first mouse event to register itself as the toElement for the center table cell.

Related Items: srcElement property.

keyCode

Value: Integer.   Read-Only
Compatibility: WinIE4+, MacIE4+, NN6+, Moz+, Safari+

For keyboard events, the keyCode property returns an integer corresponding to the Unicode value of the character (for onkeypress events) or the keyboard character key (for onkeydown and onkeyup events). There is a significant distinction between these numbering code systems.

If you want the Unicode values (the same as ASCII values for the Latin character set) for the key that a user pressed, get the keyCode property from the onkeypress event handler. For example, a lowercase "a" returns 97, while an uppercase "A" returns 65. Non-character keys, such as arrows, page navigation, and function keys, return a null value for the keyCode property during onkeypress events. In other words, the keyCode property for onkeypress events is more like a character code than a key code.

779

(IE) event.keyCode

To capture the exact keyboard key that the user presses, use either the `onkeydown` or `onkeyup` event handler. For these events, the `event` object captures a numeric code associated with a particular key on the keyboard. For the character keys, this varies with the language assigned as the system language. Importantly, there is no distinction between uppercase or lowercase: The "A" key on the Latin keyboard returns a value of 65, regardless of the state of the Shift key. At the same time, however, the press of the Shift key fired its own `onkeydown` and `onkeyup` events, setting the `keyCode` value to 16. Other non-character keys — arrows, page navigation, function, and similar — have their own codes as well. This gets very detailed, including special key codes for the numeric keyboard keys that are different from their corresponding numbers along the top row of the alphanumeric keyboard.

Be sure to see the extensive section on keyboard events in Chapter 15 for examples of how to apply the `keyCode` property in applications.

Example

Listing 25-10 provides an additional play area to view the `keyCode` property for all three keyboard events while you type into a `textarea`. You can use this page later as an authoring tool to grab the precise codes for keyboard keys you may not be familiar with.

LISTING 25-10

Displaying keyCode Property Values

```
<html>
    <head>
        <title>keyCode Property</title>
        <style type="text/css">
        td {text-align:center}
        </style>
        <script type="text/javascript">
        function showCode(which, evt) {
            evt = (evt) ? evt : ((event) ? event : null);
            if (evt) {
                document.forms[0].elements[which].value = evt.keyCode;
            }
        }

        function clearEm() {
            for (var i = 1; i < document.forms[0].elements.length; i++) {
                document.forms[0].elements[i].value = "";
            }
        }

        // bind the event handlers
        function addEvent(elem, evtType, func) {
            if (elem.addEventListener) {
                elem.addEventListener(evtType, func, false);
            } else if (elem.attachEvent) {
                elem.attachEvent("on" + evtType, func);
            } else {
                elem["on" + evtType] = func;
```

```
            }
        }
        addEvent(window, "load", function() {
            addEvent(document.getElementById("scratchpad"), "keydown",
                function(evt) {clearEm(); showCode("down", evt);});
            addEvent(document.getElementById("scratchpad"), "keypress",
                function(evt) {showCode("press", evt);});
            addEvent(document.getElementById("scratchpad"), "keyup",
                function(evt) {showCode("up", evt);});
        });
    </script>
</head>
<body>
    <h1>keyCode Property</h1>
    <hr />
    <form>
        <p><textarea id="scratchpad" name="scratchpad" cols="40" rows="5"
        wrap="hard"></textarea></p>
        <table cellpadding="5">
            <tr>
                <th>Event</th>
                <th>event.keyCode</th>
            </tr>
            <tr>
                <td>onKeyDown:</td>
                <td><input type="text" name="down" size="3" /></td>
            </tr>
            <tr>
                <td>onKeyPress:</td>
                <td><input type="text" name="press" size="3" /></td>
            </tr>
            <tr>
                <td>onKeyUp:</td>
                <td><input type="text" name="up" size="3" /></td>
            </tr>
        </table>
    </form>
</body>
</html>
```

The following are some specific tasks to try with the page to examine key codes (if you are not using a browser set for English and a Latin-based keyboard, your results may vary):

1. Enter a lowercase "a". Notice how the onkeypress event handler shows the code to be 97, which is the Unicode (and ASCII) value for the first of the lowercase letters of the Latin alphabet. But the other two events record just the key's code: 65.

2. Type an uppercase "A" via the Shift key. If you watch closely, you see that the Shift key, itself, generates the code 16 for the onkeydown and onkeyup events. But the character key then shows the value 65 for all three events, because the ASCII value of the uppercase letter happens to match the keyboard key code for that letter.

3. Press and release the Down Arrow key (be sure the cursor still flashes in the textarea, because that's where the keyboard events are being monitored). As a non-character key, it does not fire an onkeypress event. But it does fire the other events, and assigns 40 as the code for this key.

4. Poke around with other non-character keys. Some may produce dialog boxes or menus, but their key codes are recorded nonetheless. Note that not all keys on a Macintosh keyboard register with MacIE.

Notice also that the keyCode property doesn't work properly for the onkeypress event in Mozilla-based browsers. This is because Mozilla uses the charCode property for the onkeypress event instead of keyCode. You could make the code in the listing work for all modern browsers with the following modification in the showCode() function:

```
if (evt) {
    var charCode = (evt.charCode) ? evt.charCode : evt.keyCode;
    document.forms[0].elements[which].value = charCode;
}
```

Related Items: onkeydown, onkeypress, onkeyup event handlers.

nextPage

Value: String.   Read-Only
Compatibility: WinIE5.5+, MacIE-, NN-, Moz-, Safari-

The nextPage property is applicable only if your WinIE5.5+ page uses a TemplatePrinter behavior. Values of this property are one of the following strings: left, right, or an empty string. For more information about the TemplatePrinter behavior for WinIE5.5+, see the following:

```
http://msdn.microsoft.com/workshop/browser/hosting/printpreview/reference/behavior
    s/TemplatePrinter.asp
```

propertyName

Value: String.   Read-Only
Compatibility: WinIE5+, MacIE-, NN-, Moz-, Safari-

The propertyName property is filled only after an onpropertychange event fires.

If a script modifies a property, the onpropertychange event handler fires, and the string name of the property is stuffed into the event.propertyName property. If the property happens to be a property of the style object associated with the element, the propertyName is the full property reference, as in style.backgroundColor.

Example

See Listing 15-45 in the section about the onpropertychange event handler for an example of the values returned by this property.

Related Items: onpropertychange event handler (Chapter 15).

repeat

Value: Boolean.   Read-Only
Compatibility: WinIE5+, MacIE-, NN-, Moz-, Safari-

The `repeat` property reveals for `onkeydown` events only whether the key is in repeat mode (as determined by the Keyboard control panel settings in the system). With this information, you can prevent the automatic triggering of repeat mode from causing multiple characters from being recognized by the browser. This property can come in handy if users may be physically challenged and may occasionally and accidentally hold down a key too long. The following script fragment in an `onkeydown` event handler for a text box or `textarea` prevents multiple characters from appearing even if the system goes into repeat mode:

```
if (event.repeat) {
    event.returnValue = false;
}
```

By disabling the default action while in repeat mode, no further characters reach the text box until repeat mode goes away (meaning, with the press of another key).

Related Items: `onkeydown` event handler.

returnValue

Value: Boolean.   Read-Only
Compatibility: WinIE4+, MacIE4+, NN-, Moz-, Safari1.2+

While IE4+ continues to honor the original way of preventing default action for an event handler (that is, having the last statement of the event handler evaluate to `return false`), the IE4+ event model provides a property that lets the cancellation of default action take place entirely within a function invoked by an event handler. By default, the `returnValue` property of the `event` object is `true`, meaning that the element processes the event after the scripted handler completes its job, just as if the script weren't there. Normal processing, for example, is displaying a typed character, navigating to a link's `href` URL upon being clicked, or submitting a form after the Submit button is clicked.

But you don't always want the default action to occur. For example, consider a text box that is supposed to allow only numbers to be typed in it. The `onkeypress` event handler can invoke a function that inspects each typed character. If the character is not a numeric character, it should not reach the text box for display. The following validation function may be invoked from the `onkeypress` event handler of just such a text box:

```
function checkIt() {
    var charCode = event.keyCode;
    if (charCode < 48 || charCode > 57) {
        alert("Please make sure entries are numerals only.");
        event.returnValue = false;
    }
}
```

By using this event handler, the errant character won't appear in the text box.

Note that this property is not a substitute for the `return` statement of a function. If you need a value to be returned to the invoking statement, you can use a `return` statement in addition to setting the `event` `.returnValue` property.

Example

You can find several examples of the returnValue property at work in Chapter 15 and Chapter 1. Look at Listings 15-30, 15-33, 15-36, 15-37, 15-38, and 15-44. Moreover, many of the other examples in Chapter 15 can substitute the returnValue property way of cancelling the default action if the scripts were to be run exclusively on IE4+.

Related Items: return statement (Chapter 34).

saveType

Value: String.   Read-Only
Compatibility: WinIE5.5+, MacIE-, NN-, Moz-, Safari-

The saveType property is assigned a value only when an oncontentsave event is bound to a WinIE DHTML behavior (.htc). For more information about behaviors, see the following:

> http://msdn.microsoft.com/workshop/author/behaviors/overview.asp

Related Items: addBehavior() method.

srcElement

Value: Element object reference.   Read-Only
Compatibility: WinIE4+, MacIE4+, NN-, Moz-, Safari1.2+

The srcElement property is a reference to the HTML element object that is the original target of the event. Because an event may bubble up through the element containment hierarchy and be processed at any level along the way, having a property that points back to the element from which the event originated is comforting. After you have a reference to that element, you can read or write any properties that belong to that element or invoke any of its methods.

Example

As a simplified demonstration of the power of the srcElement property, Listing 25-11 has but two event handlers defined for the body element, each invoking a single function. The idea is that the onmousedown and onmouseup events will bubble up from whatever their targets are, and the event handler functions will find out which element is the target and modify the color style of that element.

An extra flair is added to the script in that each function also checks the className property of the target element. If the className is bold — a class name shared by three span elements in the paragraph — the stylesheet rule for that class is modified so that all items share the same color. Your scripts can do even more in the way of filtering objects that arrive at the functions to perform special operations on certain objects or groups of objects.

Notice that the scripts don't have to know anything about the objects on the page to address each clicked one individually. That's because the srcElement property provides all of the specificity needed for acting on the target element.

LISTING 25-11

Using the srcElement Property

```html
<html>
   <head>
      <title>srcElement Property</title>
      <style type="text/css">
      .bold {font-weight:bold}
      .ital {font-style:italic}
      </style>
      <script type="text/javascript">
      function highlight() {
         var elem = event.srcElement;
         if (elem.className == "bold") {
            document.styleSheets[0].rules[0].style.color = "red";
         } else {
            elem.style.color = "#FFCC00";
         }
      }
      function restore() {
         var elem = event.srcElement;
         if (elem.className == "bold") {
            document.styleSheets[0].rules[0].style.color = "";
         } else {
            elem.style.color = "";
         }
      }

      // bind the event handlers
      function addEvent(elem, evtType, func) {
         if (elem.addEventListener) {
            elem.addEventListener(evtType, func, false);
         } else if (elem.attachEvent) {
            elem.attachEvent("on" + evtType, func);
         } else {
            elem["on" + evtType] = func;
         }
      }
      addEvent(window, "load", function() {
         addEvent(document.body, "mousedown", highlight);
         addEvent(document.body, "mouseup", restore);
      });
      </script>
   </head>
   <body>
      <h1>srcElement Property</h1>
      <hr />
      <p>One event handler...</p>
```

continued

785

LISTING 25-11 *(continued)*

```
<ul>
    <li>Can</li>
    <li>Cover</li>
    <li>Many</li>
    <li>Objects</li>
</ul>
<p>Lorem ipsum dolor sit amet, consectetaur adipisicing elit, <span
    class="bold">sed do</span> eiusmod tempor incididunt <span
    class="ital">ut labore et</span> dolore magna aliqua. Ut enim adminim
    veniam, <span class="bold">quis nostrud exercitation</span> ullamco
    laboris nisi ut aliquip ex ea <span class="bold">commodo
    consequat</span>.</p>
</body>
</html>
```

Related Items: `fromElement`, `toElement` properties.

srcFilter

Value: String.   Read-Only
Compatibility: WinIE4+, MacIE-, NN-, Moz-, Safari-

According to Microsoft, the `srcFilter` property should return a string of the name of the filter that was applied to trigger an `onfilterchange` event handler. While the property exists in the `event` object, its value is always `null`, at least through WinIE7.

Related Items: `onfilterchange` event handler; `style.filter` object.

srcUrn

Value: String.   Read-Only
Compatibility: WinIE5+, MacIE-, NN-, Moz-, Safari-

If an event is fired in a WinIE behavior attached to an element, and the behavior has a URN identifier defined for it, the `srcUrn` property returns the string from the URN identifier. For more information about behaviors, see

> http://msdn.microsoft.com/workshop/author/behaviors/overview.asp

Related Items: `addBehavior()` method.

toElement

(See `fromElement`)

type

Value: String.   Read-Only
Compatibility: WinIE4+, MacIE4+, NN4+, Moz+, Safari+

You can find out what kind of event fired to create the current event object by way of the type property. The value is a string version of the event name — just the name of the event without the "on" prefix that is normally associated with event names in IE. This property can be helpful when you designate one event handler function to process different kinds of events. For example, both the onmousedown and onclick event handlers for an object can invoke one function. Inside the function, a branch is written for whether the type comes in as mousedown or click, with different processing for each event type. That is not to endorse such event handler function sharing, but for you to be aware of this power should your script constructions find the property helpful.

This property and its values are fully compatible with the NN6+/Moz/W3C event models.

Example

Use The Evaluator (Chapter 13) to see values returned by the type property. Enter the following object name into the bottom text box and press Enter/Return:

    event

If necessary, scroll the Results box to view the type property, which should read keypress. Now click the List Properties button. The type changes to click. The reason for these types is that the event object whose properties are being shown here is the event that triggers the function to show the properties. From the text box, an onkeypress event handler triggers that process; from the button, an onclick event handler does the job.

Related Items: All event handlers (Chapter 15).

wheelData

Value: Integer.   Read-Only
Compatibility: WinIE5.5+, MacIE-, NN-, Moz-, Safari-

The wheelData property returns an integer indicating which direction the mouse wheel was rolled for an onmousewheel event. The values returned are typically either 120 or –120, with a positive value indicating that the mouse wheel was rolled toward the screen and a negative value indicating that the wheel was rolled the opposite direction.

NN6+/Moz/Safari event Object

Properties	Methods	Event Handlers
altKey	initEvent()	
bubbles	initKeyEvent()	
button	initMouseEvent()	
cancelBubble	initMutationEvent()	
cancelable	initUIEvent()	
charCode	preventDefault()	
clientX	stopPropagation()	

continued

Properties	Methods	Event Handlers
clientY		
ctrlKey		
currentTarget		
detail		
eventPhase		
isChar		
keyCode		
layerX		
layerY		
metaKey		
originalTarget		
pageX		
pageY		
relatedTarget		
screenX		
screenY		
shiftKey		
target		
timeStamp		
type		
view		

Syntax

Accessing NN6+/Moz event object properties and methods:

eventObject.property | *method([parameters])*

Compatibility: WinIE-, MacIE-, NN6+, Moz+, Safari+

About this object

Although it is based largely on the event object as defined by the W3C DOM Level 2, the NN6+/Moz event object also carries forward several characteristics from the NN4 event object. A few properties are continued primarily for backward compatibility. But because future Mozilla development will likely forego the peculiarities of the NN4 DOM and event models, you should ignore these items (as highlighted below). Wherever possible, look forward and embrace the W3C DOM aspects of the event model. Safari, for example, implements a lot of the W3C DOM event model, but excludes all old NN4 properties.

Although the NN6+/Moz event model provides a bubbling event propagation model just as IE4+, the incompatibility of referencing event objects between the event models is still there. In the W3C DOM (as in

NN4), an event object is explicitly passed as a parameter to event handler (or, rather, event listener) functions. But after you have a browser-specific event object assigned to a variable inside a function, a few important properties have the same names between the IE4+ and W3C DOM event models. If Microsoft adopts more of the W3C DOM event model in future versions of IE, the compatibility situation should improve.

The event object discussed in this section is the instance of an event that is created as the result of a user or system event action. The W3C DOM includes an additional static Event object. Many of the properties of the static Event object are inherited by the event instances, so the detailed coverage of those shared properties is in this section because it is the event object you'll be scripting for the most part.

In many code fragments in the following detail sections, you will see references that begin with the evt reference. This assumes that the statement(s) resides inside a function that has assigned the incoming event object to the evt parameter variable:

```
function myFunction(evt) {...}
```

As shown earlier in this chapter, you can equalize W3C DOM and IE4+ event object references when it is practical to do so because the scripts work on identical (or similar) event object properties. The results of this equalization are typically stored in the evt variable.

Properties
altKey
ctrlKey
metaKey
shiftKey

Value: Boolean.   Read-Only
Compatibility: WinIE4+, MacIE4+, NN6+, Moz+, Safari+

When an event object is created in response to a user or system action, these four properties are set based on whether their corresponding keys were being held down at the time — a Shift-click, for example. If the key was held down, the property is assigned a value of true; otherwise the value is false. The metaKey property corresponds to the Command key on the Macintosh keyboard but does not register for the Windows key on Wintel computers.

Most commonly, you use expressions consisting of this property as if construction condition statements. Because these are Boolean values, you can combine multiple properties in a single condition. For example, if you have a branch of a function that is to execute only if the event occurred with both the Shift and Control keys held down, the condition looks as the following:

```
if (evt.shiftKey && evt.ctrlKey) {
   // statements to execute
}
```

Conversely, you can take a more user-friendly approach to provide special processing if the user holds down any one of the four modifier keys:

```
if (evt.shiftKey || evt.ctrlKey || evt.metaKey || evt.altKey) {
   // statements to execute
}
```

The rationale behind this approach is to offer perhaps some shortcut operation for users, but not force them to memorize a specific modifier key combination.

Example

See Listing 25-6, where the values of these properties are used to set the checked properties of corresponding check boxes for a variety of event types.

Related Items: None.

bubbles

Value: Boolean.   Read-Only
Compatibility: WinIE-, MacIE-, NN6+, Moz+, Safari+

Not every event bubbles. For example, an onsubmit event propagates no further than the form object with which the event is associated. Events that do not bubble have their event object's bubbles property set to false; all others have the property set to true. You use this property in the rare circumstance of a single event handler function processing a wide variety of events. You may want to perform special operations only on events that can bubble and handle the others without special treatment. For this branch, you can use the property in an if condition statement:

```
if (evt.bubbles) {
    // special processing for bubble-able events
}
```

You do not have to branch, however, just to cancel bubbling. A non-propagating event doesn't mind if you tell it not to propagate.

Related Items: cancelBubble property.

button

Value: Integer.   Read-Only
Compatibility: WinIE4+, MacIE4+, NN6+, Moz+, Safari+

The button property reveals the button that was pressed to activate the mouse event. In the W3C DOM, the left (primary) button returns a value of 0. If the mouse is a three-button mouse, the middle button returns 1. The right button (on any multibutton mouse) returns a value of 2.

Mouse buttons other than the primary one are easier to look for in mousedown or mouseup events, rather than onclick events. In the case of a user pressing multiple buttons, only the most recent button is registered.

Exercise caution when scripting the button property across browsers. The respective event models define different button values for mouse buttons.

Example

See Listing 25-7, where the button property is revealed in the status bar. Try pressing individual mouse buttons on, say, the screen button.

Related Items: None.

cancelable

Value: Boolean.   Read-Only
Compatibility: WinIE-, MacIE-, NN6+, Moz+, Safari+

If an event is cancelable, then its default action can be prevented from occurring with the help of a script. Although most events are cancelable, some are not. The cancelable property lets you inquire about a particular event object to see if its event type is cancelable. Values for the property are Booleans. You may want to perform special operations only on events that are cancelable and handle the others without special treatment. For this branch, you can use the property in an if condition statement:

```
if (evt.cancelable) {
    // special processing for cancelable events
}
```

You do not have to branch, however, just to prevent an event's default action. A non-cancelable event doesn't mind if you tell it to prevent the default action.

Related Items: preventDefault() method.

cancelBubble

Value: Boolean.   Read/Write
Compatibility: WinIE4+, MacIE4+, NN6+, Moz+, Safari+

The cancelBubble property is a rare instance of an IE4+ event property being implemented in NN6+/Moz/Safari even though the property is not defined in the W3C DOM. The property operates the same as in IE4+ in that it determines whether the current event object bubbles up any higher in the element containment hierarchy of the document. By default, this property is false, meaning that if the event is supposed to bubble, it will do so automatically.

To prevent event bubbling for the current event, set the property to true anywhere within the event handler function. Cancelling event bubbling works only for the current event. The very next event to fire will have bubbling enabled (provided the event bubbles).

If you are trying to migrate your code as much as possible to the W3C DOM, use the stopPropagation() method instead of cancelBubble. For cross-browser compatibility, however, cancelBubble is a safe bet.

Example

See Listing 25-2 to see the cancelBubble property in action in an IE environment. Even though that listing has some features that apply to WinIE5.5+, the bubble cancelling demonstration works all the way back to IE4.

Related Items: stopPropagation() method.

charCode
keyCode

Value: Integer.   Read-Only
Compatibility: WinIE-, MacIE-, NN6+, Moz+, Safari+

The W3C DOM event object model clearly distinguishes between the Unicode character attached to the alphanumeric keys of the keyboard and the code attached to each of the keyboard keys (regardless of its character). To inspect the character of a key, use the onkeypress event to create the event object, and then look at the `event` object's `charCode` property. This is the property that returns 97 for "a" and 65 for "A" because it's concerned with the character associated with the key action. This property's value is zero for `onkeydown` and `onkeyup` events.

In contrast, the `keyCode` property is filled with a non-zero value only from `onkeydown` and `onkeyup` events (`onkeypress` sets the property to zero) when alphanumeric keys are pressed; for most other non-character keys, all three events fill the `keyCode` property. Through this property you can look for non-character keys, such as arrows, page navigation, and function keys. For the character keys, there is no distinction between uppercase or lowercase: The "A" key on the Latin keyboard returns a value of 65, regardless of the state of the Shift key. At the same time, however, the press of the Shift key fires its own `onkeydown` and `onkeyup` events, setting the `keyCode` value to 16 (except in Safari, which does not register modifier keys in this way). Other non-character keys — arrows, page navigation, function, and similar — have their own codes as well. This gets very detailed, including special key codes for the numeric keyboard keys that are different from their corresponding numbers along the top row of the alphanumeric keyboard.

Be sure to see the extensive section on keyboard events in Chapter 15 for examples of how to apply the `keyCode` property in applications.

Example

Listing 25-12 provides a play area to view the `charCode` and `keyCode` properties for all three keyboard events while you type into a `textarea`. You can use this later as an authoring tool to grab the precise codes for keyboard keys you may not be familiar with.

LISTING 25-12

Displaying charCode and keyCode Property Values

```
<html>
  <head>
    <title>charCode and keyCode Properties</title>
    <style type="text/css">
    td {text-align:center}
    </style>
    <script type="text/javascript">
    function showCode(which, evt) {
       document.forms[0].elements[which + "Char"].value = evt.charCode;
       document.forms[0].elements[which + "Key"].value = evt.keyCode;
    }
    function clearEm() {
       for (var i = 1; i < document.forms[0].elements.length; i++) {
          document.forms[0].elements[i].value = "";
       }
    }

    // bind the event handlers
    function addEvent(elem, evtType, func) {
       if (elem.addEventListener) {
          elem.addEventListener(evtType, func, false);
       } else if (elem.attachEvent) {
          elem.attachEvent("on" + evtType, func);
       } else {
          elem["on" + evtType] = func;
```

```
            }
        }
        addEvent(window, "load", function() {
            addEvent(document.getElementById("scratchpad"), "keydown",
                function(evt) {clearEm(); showCode("down", evt);});
            addEvent(document.getElementById("scratchpad"), "keypress",
                function(evt) {showCode("press", evt);});
            addEvent(document.getElementById("scratchpad"), "keyup",
                function(evt) {showCode("up", evt);});
        });
    </script>
</head>
<body>
    <h1>charCode and keyCode Properties</h1>
    <hr />
    <form>
        <p><textarea id="scratchpad" name="scratchpad" cols="40" rows="5"
        wrap="hard"></textarea></p>
        <table cellpadding="5">
            <tr>
                <th>Event</th>
                <th>event.charCode</th>
                <th>event.keyCode</th>
            </tr>
            <tr>
                <td>onKeyDown:</td>
                <td><input type="text" name="downChar" size="3" /></td>
                <td><input type="text" name="downKey" size="3" /></td>
            </tr>
            <tr>
                <td>onKeyPress:</td>
                <td><input type="text" name="pressChar" size="3" /></td>
                <td><input type="text" name="pressKey" size="3" /></td>
            </tr>
            <tr>
                <td>onKeyUp:</td>
                <td><input type="text" name="upChar" size="3" /></td>
                <td><input type="text" name="upKey" size="3" /></td>
            </tr>
        </table>
    </form>
</body>
</html>
```

Here are some specific tasks to try with the page in NN6+/Moz to examine key codes (if you are not using a browser set for English and a Latin-based keyboard, your results may vary):

1. Enter a lowercase "a". Notice how the onkeypress·event handler shows the charCode to be 97, which is the Unicode (and ASCII) value for the first of the lowercase letters of the Latin alphabet. But the other two event types record just the key's code: 65.

793

2. Type an uppercase "A" via the Shift key. If you watch closely, you see that the Shift key, itself, generates the key code 16 for the `onkeydown` and `onkeyup` events. But the character key then shows the value 65 for all three events (until you release the Shift key), because the ASCII value of the uppercase letter happens to match the keyboard key code for that letter.

3. Press and release the Down Arrow key (be sure the cursor still flashes in the `textarea`, because that's where the keyboard events are being monitored). As a non-character key, all three events stuff a value into the `keyCode` property, but zero into `charCode`. The `keyCode` value for this key is 40.

4. Poke around with other non-character keys. Some may produce dialog boxes or menus, but their key codes are recorded nonetheless.

Related Items: `onkeydown`, `onkeypress`, `onkeyup` event handlers.

clientX
clientY
layerX
layerY
pageX
pageY
screenX
screenY

Value: Integer.   Read-Only
Compatibility: WinIE4+, MacIE4+, NN6+, Moz+, Safari+

The W3C DOM `event` object borrows mouse coordinate properties from both the NN4 and IE4+ event models. If you have worked with event coordinates in these other browsers, you have nothing new to learn for W3C DOM-compatible browsers.

Like the IE4+ `event` object, the W3C DOM `event` object's `clientX` and `clientY` properties are the coordinates within the viewable content region of the window. These values are relative to the window space, not the document. But unlike IE4+, you don't have to calculate the position of the coordinates within the document because another pair of NN/Moz/Safari properties, `pageX` and `pageY`, provide that information automatically. If the page has not scrolled, the values of the client and page coordinates are the same. Because it is usually more important to know an event's coordinates with respect to the document than the window, the `pageX` and `pageY` properties are used most often.

Another NN/Moz/Safari property pair, `layerX` and `layerY`, borrow terminology from the now defunct layer schemes of NN4, but the properties can still be quite valuable nonetheless. These coordinates are measured relative to the positioning context of the element that received the event. For regular, unpositioned elements in the `body` part of a document, that positioning context is the `body` element. Thus, for those elements, the values of the page and layer coordinates will be the same. But if you create a positioned element, the coordinate space is measured from the top-left corner of that space. Thus, if you are using the coordinates to assist in scripted dragging of positioned elements, you can confine your scope to just the positioned element.

One coordinate system missing from the NN6+/Moz repertoire, but present in Safari, is that of the target element itself (comparable to the `offsetX` and `offsetY` properties of IE4+). These values, however, can be calculated in NN/Moz by subtracting from the page coordinate properties the `offsetLeft` and `offsetTop` properties of both the target element and its positioning context. For example, if you want to get the coordinates of a mouse event inside an image, the event handler can calculate those values as follows:

```
var clickOffsetX = evt.pageX - evt.target.offsetLeft -
    document.body.offsetLeft;
var clickOffsetY = evt.pageY - evt.target.offsetTop -
    document.body.offsetTop;
```

The last set of coordinate properties, screenX and screenY, provide values relative to the entire video display. Of all these properties, only the client and screen coordinates are defined in the W3C DOM Level 2 standard.

Keep in mind that in most W3C DOM–compatible browsers, event targets include text nodes inside elements. Because nodes do not have all the properties of elements (for example, they have no offset properties signifying their location in the document), you may sometimes have to go to the target node's parent node to get an element object whose offset properties provide the necessary page geography. This matters, of course, only if your scripts need to concern themselves with mouse events on text.

Example

You can see the effects of the coordinate systems and associated NN6+/Moz properties with the page in Listing 25-13. You can view coordinate values for all four measuring systems, as well as some calculated value. Two clickable objects are provided so that you can see the differences between an object not in any layer and an object residing within a layer (although anything you see is clickable, including text nodes). Figure 25-1 shows the results of a click inside the positioned layer.

FIGURE 25-1

NN6+/Moz event coordinates for a click inside a positioned element.

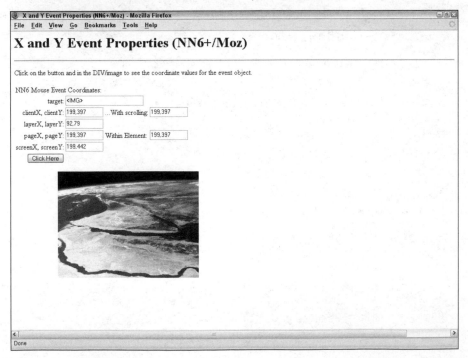

One of the calculated fields applies window scrolling values to the client coordinates. But, as you will see, these calculated values are the same as the more convenient page coordinates. The other calculated field shows the coordinates relative to the rectangular space of the target element. Notice in the code that if the nodeType of the target indicates a text node, that node's parent node (an element) is used for the calculation.

LISTING 25-13

NN6+/Moz/Safari Event Coordinate Properties

```html
<html>
  <head>
    <title>X and Y Event Properties (NN6+/Moz)</title>
    <script type="text/javascript">
    function checkCoords(evt) {
        var form = document.forms["output"];
        var targText, targElem;
        if (evt.target.nodeType == 3) {
            targText = "[textnode] inside <" + evt.target.parentNode.tagName + ">";
            targElem = evt.target.parentNode;
        } else {
            targText = "<" + evt.target.tagName + ">";
            targElem = evt.target;
        }
        form.srcElemTag.value = targText;
        form.clientCoords.value = evt.clientX + "," + evt.clientY;
        form.clientScrollCoords.value = (evt.clientX + window.scrollX) +
            "," + (evt.clientY + window.scrollY);
        form.layerCoords.value = evt.layerX + "," + evt.layerY;
        form.pageCoords.value = evt.pageX + "," + evt.pageY;
        form.inElemCoords.value =
            (evt.pageX - targElem.offsetLeft - document.body.offsetLeft) +
            "," + (evt.pageY - targElem.offsetTop - document.body.offsetTop);
        form.screenCoords.value = evt.screenX + "," + evt.screenY;
        return false;
    }

    // bind the event handler
    function addEvent(elem, evtType, func) {
      if (elem.addEventListener) {
          elem.addEventListener(evtType, func, false);
      } else if (elem.attachEvent) {
          elem.attachEvent("on" + evtType, func);
      } else {
          elem["on" + evtType] = func;
      }
    }
    addEvent(window, "load", function() {
      addEvent(document.body, "mousedown",
          function(evt) {checkCoords(evt);});
```

```
      });
    </script>
  </head>
  <body>
    <h1>X and Y Event Properties (NN6+/Moz)</h1>
    <hr />
    <p>Click on the button and in the DIV/image to see the coordinate values
       for the event object.</p>
    <form name="output">
      <table>
        <tr>
          <td colspan="2">NN6 Mouse Event Coordinates:</td>
        </tr>
        <tr>
          <td align="right">target:</td>
          <td colspan="3"><input type="text" name="srcElemTag" size-"25"
          /></td>
        </tr>
        <tr>
          <td align="right">clientX, clientY:</td>
          <td><input type="text" name="clientCoords" size="10" /></td>
          <td align="right">...With scrolling:</td>
          <td><input type="text" name="clientScrollCoords" size="10" /></td>
        </tr>
        <tr>
          <td align="right">layerX, layerY:</td>
          <td><input type="text" name="layerCoords" size="10" /></td>
        </tr>
        <tr>
          <td align="right">pageX, pageY:</td>
          <td><input type="text" name="pageCoords" size="10" /></td>
          <td aligh="right">Within Element:</td>
          <td><input type="text" name="inElemCoords" size="10" /></td>
        </tr>
        <tr>
          <td align="right">screenX, screenY:</td>
          <td><input type="text" name="screenCoords" size="10" /></td>
        </tr>
        <tr>
          <td align="right"><input type="button" value="Click Here" /></td>
        </tr>
      </table>
    </form>
    <div id="display" style="position:relative; left:100">
      <img alt="image" src="nile.gif" width="320" height="240" border="0" />
    </div>
  </body>
</html>
```

Related Items: target property.

currentTarget

Value: Element object reference.   Read-Only
Compatibility: WinIE-, MacIE-, NN6+, Moz+, Safari+

As an event courses its way through its propagation paths, an event listener may process that event along the way. Though the event knows what the target is, it can also be helpful for the event listener function to know which element's event listener is now processing the event. The `currentTarget` property provides a reference to the element object whose event listener is processing the event. This allows one listener function to potentially process the event from different levels, branching the code to accommodate different element levels that process the event.

A valuable companion piece of information about the event is the `eventPhase` property, which helps your event listener function determine if the event is in capture mode, bubble mode, or is at the target. This property is demonstrated in the next section.

Example

Listing 25-14 shows the power of the `currentTarget` property in revealing the element that is processing an event during event propagation. Similar to the code in Listing 25-3, this example is made simpler because it lets the event object's properties do more of the work to reveal the identity of each element that processes the event. Event listeners assigned for various propagation modes are assigned to a variety of nodes in the document. After you click the button, each listener in the propagation chain fires in sequence. The alert dialog box shows which node is processing the event. And, as in Listing 25-3, the `eventPhase` property is used to help display the propagation mode in force at the time the event is processed by each node.

LISTING 25-14

currentTarget and eventPhase Properties

```
<html>
   <head>
      <title>currentTarget and eventPhase Properties</title>
      <script type="text/javascript">
      function processEvent(evt) {
         var currTargTag, msg;
         if (evt.currentTarget.nodeType == 1) {
            currTargTag = "<" + evt.currentTarget.tagName + ">";
         } else {
            currTargTag = evt.currentTarget.nodeName;
         }
         msg = "Event is now at the " + currTargTag + " level ";
         msg += "(" + getPhase(evt) + ").";
         alert(msg);
      }
      // reveal event phase of current event object
      function getPhase(evt) {
         switch (evt.eventPhase) {
         case 1:
            return "CAPTURING";
            break;
```

```
            case 2:
                return "AT TARGET";
                break;
            case 3:
                return "BUBBLING";
                break;
            default:
                return "";
            }
        }

    // bind the event handlers
    function addEvent(elem, evtType, func) {
        if (elem.addEventListener) {
            elem.addEventListener(evtType, func, false);
        } else if (elem.attachEvent) {
            elem.attachEvent("on" + evtType, func);
        } else {
            elem["on" + evtType] = func;
        }
    }
    addEvent(window, "load", function() {
        // using old syntax to assign bubble-type event handlers
        document.onclick = processEvent;
        document.body.onclick = processEvent;
        // turn on click event capture for document and form
        document.addEventListener("click", processEvent, true);
        document.forms[0].addEventListener("click", processEvent, true);
        // set bubble event listener for form
        document.forms[0].addEventListener("click", processEvent, false);
        // turn on event capture for the button
        document.getElementById("main1").addEventListener("click",
            processEvent, true);
    });
    </script>
</head>
<body>
    <h1>currentTarget and eventPhase Properties</h1>
    <hr />
    <form>
        <input type="button" value="A Button" id="main1" name="main1" />
    </form>
</body>
</html>
```

You can also click other places on the page. For example, if you click to the right of the button, you will be clicking the `form` element. Event propagation and processing adjusts accordingly. Similarly, if you click the header text, the only event listeners that see the event are in the document and `body` levels.

Related Items: `eventPhase` property.

detail

Value: Integer.   Read-Only
Compatibility: WinIE-, MacIE-, NN6+, Moz+, Safari2+

The detail property is included in the W3C DOM specification as an extra property whose purpose can be determined by the browser maker. Mozilla-based browsers and Safari 2 increment a numeric value for rapid instances of click events on an object.

Related Items: None.

eventPhase

Value: Integer.   Read-Only
Compatibility: WinIE-, MacIE-, NN6+, Moz+, Safari+

An event fires in one of three possible event phases: event capture, at the target, or bubbling. Because the same event listener function may be processing an event in multiple phases, it can inspect the value of the eventPhase property of the event object to see in which phase the event was when the function was invoked. Values for this property are integers 1 (capture), 2 (at target), or 3 (bubbling).

Example

See Listing 25-14 earlier in this chapter for an example of how you can use a switch construction to branch function processing based on the event phase of the current event object.

Related Items: currentTarget property.

isChar

Value: Boolean.   Read-Only
Compatibility: WinIE-, MacIE-, NN6+, Moz+, Safari-

You can find out from each keyboard event whether the key being pressed is a character key by examining the isChar property. Most typically, however, you are already filtering for character or non-character keys by virtue of the event handlers used to capture keyboard actions: onkeypress for character keys; onkeydown or onkeyup for non-character keys. Be aware that the isChar property returns inconsistent values (even for the same key) in the first release of NN6.

Related Items: charCode, keyCode properties.

isTrusted

Value: Boolean.   Read-Only
Compatibility: WinIE-, MacIE-, NN8+, Moz1.7.5+, Safari-

Because an event can be generated by user action or script, the isTrusted property enables you to determine how the event was created. Any event triggered by user action is considered to be trusted from a security point of view. Therefore, when this property returns true, it means that the event came to life as the result of user activity (clicking, keyboarding, and so on).

originalTarget

Value: Node object reference. Read-Only
Compatibility: WinIE-, MacIE-, NN6+, Moz+, Safari-

The originalTarget property provides a reference to the node object that serves as the genuine first target of the event. This information is typically associated with the internal construction of certain elements, which makes it less useful for scripting purposes. Additionally, in many cases the originalTarget property holds the same value as the target property.

relatedTarget

Value: Element object. Read-Only
Compatibility: WinIE-, MacIE-, NN6+, Moz+, Safari+

The relatedTarget property allows an element to uncover where the cursor rolled in from or has rolled out to. This property extends the power of the onmouseover and onmouseout event handlers by expanding their scope to outside the current element (usually to an adjacent element). This one W3C DOM property does the same duty as the fromElement and toElement properties of the IE4+ event object.

When the onmouseover event fires on an element, the cursor had to be over some other element just beforehand. The relatedTarget property holds a reference to that element. Conversely, when the onmouseout event fires, the cursor is already over some other element. The relatedTarget property holds a reference to that element.

Example

Listing 25-15 provides an example of how the relatedTarget property can reveal the life of the cursor action before and after it rolls into an element. When you roll the cursor to the center box (a table cell), its onmouseover event handler displays the text from the table cell from which the cursor arrived (the nodeValue of the text node inside the table cell). If the cursor comes in from one of the corners (not easy to do), a different message is displayed.

The two functions that report the results employ a bit of filtering to make sure that they process the event object only if the event occurs on an element and if the relatedTarget element is anything other than a nested text node of the central table cell element. Because nodes respond to events in W3C DOM browsers, this extra filtering prevents processing whenever the cursor makes the transition from the central td element to its nested text node.

LISTING 25-15

Using the relatedTarget Property

```
<html>
   <head>
      <title>relatedTarget Properties</title>
      <style type="text/css">
      .direction {background-color:#00FFFF; width:100; height:50;
      text-align:center}
      #main {background-color:#FF6666; text-align:center}
      </style>
```

continued

LISTING 25-15 *(continued)*

```
<script type="text/javascript">
function showArrival(evt) {
   if (evt.target.nodeType == 1) {
      if (evt.relatedTarget != evt.target.firstChild) {
         var direction = (evt.relatedTarget.firstChild) ?
            evt.relatedTarget.firstChild.nodeValue : "parts unknown";
         window.status = "Arrived from: " + direction;
      }
   }
}
function showDeparture(evt) {
   if (evt.target.nodeType == 1) {
      if (evt.relatedTarget != evt.target.firstChild) {
         var direction = (evt.relatedTarget.firstChild) ?
            evt.relatedTarget.firstChild.nodeValue : "parts unknown";
         window.status = "Departed to: " + direction;
      }
   }
}

// bind the event handlers
function addEvent(elem, evtType, func) {
   if (elem.addEventListener) {
      elem.addEventListener(evtType, func, false);
   } else if (elem.attachEvent) {
      elem.attachEvent("on" + evtType, func);
   } else {
      elem["on" + evtType] = func;
   }
}
addEvent(window, "load", function() {
   addEvent(document.getElementById("main"), "mouseover",
      function(evt) {showArrival(evt);});
   addEvent(document.getElementById("main"), "mouseout",
      function(evt) {showDeparture(evt);});
});
</script>
</head>
<body>
   <h1>relatedTarget Properties</h1>
   <hr />
   <p>Roll the mouse to the center box and look for arrival information in
      the status bar. Roll the mouse away from the center box and look for
      departure information in the status bar.</p>
   <table cellspacing="0" cellpadding="5">
```

```
      <tr>
          <td></td>
          <td class="direction">North</td>
          <td></td>
      </tr>
      <tr>
          <td class="direction">West</td>
          <td id="main">Roll</td>
          <td class="direction">East</td>
      </tr>
      <tr>
          <td></td>
          <td class="direction">South</td>
          <td></td>
      </tr>
    </table>
  </body>
</html>
```

Related Items: target property.

target

Value: Element object reference. Read-Only
Compatibility: WinIE-, MacIE-, NN6+, Moz+, Safari+

The target property is a reference to the HTML element object that is the original target of the event. Because an event may trickle down and bubble up through the element containment hierarchy and be processed at any level along the way, having a property that points back to the element from which the event originated is comforting. As soon as you have a reference to that element, you can read or write any properties that belong to that element or invoke any of its methods.

Example

As a simplified demonstration of the power of the target property, Listing 25-16 has but two event handlers defined for the body element, each invoking a single function. The idea is that the onmousedown and onmouseup events will bubble up from whatever their targets are, and the event handler functions will find out which element is the target and modify the color style of that element.

An extra flair is added to the script in that each function also checks the className property of the target element. If the className is bold — a class name shared by three span elements in the paragraph — the stylesheet rule for that class is modified so that all items share the same color. Your scripts can do even more in the way of filtering objects that arrive at the functions to perform special operations on certain objects or groups of objects.

Notice that the scripts don't have to know anything about the objects on the page to address each clicked one individually. That's because the target property provides all of the specificity needed for acting on the target element.

LISTING 25-16

Using the target Property

```html
<html>
    <head>
        <title>target Property</title>
        <style type="text/css">
        .bold {font-weight:bold}
        .ital {font-style:italic}
        </style>
        <script type="text/javascript">
        function highlight(evt) {
            var elem = (evt.target.nodeType == 3) ? evt.target.parentNode :
                evt.target;
            if (elem.className == "bold") {
                document.styleSheets[0].cssRules[0].style.color = "red";
            } else {
                elem.style.color = "#FFCC00";
            }
        }
        function restore(evt) {
            var elem = (evt.target.nodeType == 3) ? evt.target.parentNode :
                evt.target;
            if (elem.className == "bold") {
                document.styleSheets[0].cssRules[0].style.color = "black";
            } else {
                elem.style.color = "black";
            }
        }

        // bind the event handlers
        function addEvent(elem, evtType, func) {
            if (elem.addEventListener) {
                elem.addEventListener(evtType, func, false);
            } else if (elem.attachEvent) {
                elem.attachEvent("on" + evtType, func);
            } else {
                elem["on" + evtType] = func;
            }
        }
        addEvent(window, "load", function() {
            addEvent(document.body, "mousedown",
                function(evt) {highlight(evt);});
            addEvent(document.body, "mouseup",
                function(evt) {restore(evt);});
        });
        </script>
    </head>
    <body>
        <h1>target Property</h1>
```

```
      <hr />
      <p>One event handler...</p>
      <ul>
         <li>Can</li>
         <li>Cover</li>
         <li>Many</li>
         <li>Objects</li>
      </ul>
      <p>Lorem ipsum dolor sit amet, consectetaur adipisicing elit, <span
         class="bold">sed do</span> eiusmod tempor incididunt <span
         class="ital">ut labore et</span> dolore magna aliqua. Ut enim adminim
         veniam, <span class="bold">quis nostrud exercitation</span> ullamco
         laboris nisi ut aliquip ex ea <span class="bold">commodo
         consequat</span>.</p>
   </body>
</html>
```

Related Items: relatedTarget property.

timeStamp

Value: Integer.   Read-Only
Compatibility: WinIE-, MacIE-, NN6+, Moz+, Safari+

Each event receives a time stamp in milliseconds, based on the same date epoch as the Date object (1 January 1970). Just as with the Date object, accuracy is wholly dependent on the accuracy of the system clock of the client computer.

Although the precise time of an event may be of value in only some situations, the time between events can be useful for applications, such as timed exercises or action games. You can preserve the time of the most recent event in a global variable, and compare the time of the current time stamp against the stored value to determine the elapsed time between events.

Example

Listing 25-17 uses the timeStamp property to calculate the instantaneous typing speed when you type into a textarea. The calculations are pretty raw, and work only on intra-keystroke times without any averaging or smoothing that a more sophisticated typing tutor might perform. Calculated values are rounded to the nearest integer.

LISTING 25-17

Using the timeStamp Property

```
<html>
   <head>
      <title>timeStamp Property</title>
      <script type="text/javascript">
      var stamp;
```

continued

LISTING 25-17 *(continued)*

```
function calcSpeed(evt) {
    if (stamp) {
        var gross = evt.timeStamp - stamp;
        var wpm = Math.round(6000/gross);
        document.getElementById("wpm").firstChild.nodeValue = wpm + " wpm.";
    }
    stamp = evt.timeStamp;
}

// bind the event handlers
function addEvent(elem, evtType, func) {
    if (elem.addEventListener) {
        elem.addEventListener(evtType, func, false);
    } else if (elem.attachEvent) {
        elem.attachEvent("on" + evtType, func);
    } else {
        elem["on" + evtType] = func;
    }
}
addEvent(window, "load", function() {
    addEvent(document.getElementById("scratchpad"), "keypress",
        function(evt) {calcSpeed(evt);});
    addEvent(document.body, "mouseup",
        function(evt) {restore(evt);});
});
</script>
</head>
<body>
    <h1>timeStamp Property</h1>
    <hr />
    <p>Start typing, and watch your instantaneous typing speed below:</p>
    <p><textarea id="scratchpad" cols="60" rows="10" wrap="hard"></textarea></p>
    <p>Typing Speed: <span id="wpm"> </span></p>
</body>
</html>
```

Related Items: Date object.

type

Value: String. Read-Only
Compatibility: WinIE4+, MacIE4+, NN6+, Moz+, Safari+

You can find out what kind of event fired to create the current event object by way of the type property. The value is a string version of the event name — just the name of the event without the "on" prefix that is normally associated with event listener names in NN6+/Moz/W3C. This property can be helpful when you designate one event handler function to process different kinds of events. For example, both the onmousedown and onclick event listeners for an object can invoke one function. Inside the function, a branch is written for whether the type comes in as mousedown or click, with different processing for each event type. That is not to endorse such event handler function sharing, but be aware of this power should your script constructions find the property helpful.

This property and its values are fully compatible with the NN4 and IE4+ event models.

CAUTION Keyboard events in Safari report their types as khtml_keydown, khtml_keypress, and khtml_keyup, using the prefix referring to the name of the rendering engine on which Safari is built. This is probably to avoid committing to an unfinished W3C DOM Level 3 keyboard event specification.

Related Items: All event handlers (Chapter 15).

view
Value: Window object reference.   Read-Only
Compatibility: WinIE-, MacIE-, NN6+, Moz+, Safari+

The closest that the W3C DOM Level 2 specification comes to acknowledging the browser window is an abstract object called an *abstract view* (AbstractView class). The object's only property is a reference to the document that it contains — the root document node that you've come to know and love. User events always occur within the confines of one of these views, and this is reflected in the event object's view property. This property holds a reference to the window object (which can be a frame) in which the event occurs. This reference allows an event object to be passed to scripts in other frames and those scripts can then gain access to the document object of the target element's window.

Related Items: window object.

Methods
```
initEvent("eventType", bubblesFlag, cancelableFlag)
initKeyEvent("eventType", bubblesFlag, cancelableFlag,
view, ctrlKeyFlag, altKeyFlag, shiftKeyFlag, metaKeyFlag,
keyCode, charCode)
initMouseEvent("eventType", bubblesFlag, cancelableFlag,
view, detailVal, screenX, screenY, clientX, clientY,
ctrlKeyFlag, altKeyFlag, shiftKeyFlag, metaKeyFlag,
buttonCode, relatedTargetNodeRef)
initMutationEvent("eventType", bubblesFlag, cancelableFlag,
relatedNodeRef, prevValue, newValue, attrName,
attrChangeCode)
initUIEvent("eventType", bubblesFlag, cancelableFlag, view,
detailVal)
```
Returns: Nothing.
Compatibility: WinIE-, MacIE-, NN6+, Moz+, Safari+

The W3C DOM event object initialization methods provide a means of initializing a newly created event with a complete set of property values associated with that particular event. The parameters to each of the initialization methods vary according to the type of event being initialized. However, all of the initialization methods share the first three parameters: eventType, bubblesFlag, and cancelableFlag. The eventType parameter is a string identifier for the event's type, such as "mousedown" or "keypress". The bubblesFlag parameter is a Boolean value that specifies whether the event's default propagation behavior is to bubble (true) or not (false). The cancelableFlag parameter is also a Boolean value, and its job is to specify if the event's default action may be prevented with a call to the preventDefault() method (true) or not (false).

A few of the methods also include view and detailVal parameters, which correspond to the window or frame in which the event occurred and the integer code of detail data associated with the event, respectively. Additional parameters are specified for some of the methods, and are unique to the event being initialized.

You don't have to use the more detailed methods if you need a simple event. For example, if you want a simple mouseup event, you can initialize a generic event with initEvent(), and dispatch the event to the desired element, without having to fill in all of the coordinate, button, and other parameters of the initMouseEvent() method:

```
var evt = document.createEvent("MouseEvents");
evt.initEvent("mouseup", true, true);
document.getElementById("myButton").dispatchEvent(evt);
```

For more details about W3C DOM event types and the values expected for each of the more complex initialization methods, visit http://www.w3.org/TR/DOM-Level-2-Events/events.html#Events-eventgroupings.

Related Items: document.createEvent() method.

preventDefault()

Returns: Nothing.
Compatibility: WinIE-, MacIE-, NN6+, Moz+, Safari+

While NN6+ continues to honor the original way of preventing default action for an event handler (that is, having the last statement of the event handler evaluate to return false), the W3C DOM event model provides a method that lets the cancellation of default action take place entirely within a function invoked by an event handler. For example, consider a text box that is supposed to allow only numbers to be typed in it. The onkeypress event handler can invoke a function that inspects each typed character. If the character is not a numeric character, it does not reach the text box for display. The following validation function may be invoked from the onkeypress event handler of just such a text box:

```
function checkIt(evt) {
    var charCode = evt.charCode;
    if (charCode < 48 || charCode > 57) {
        alert("Please make sure entries are numbers only.");
        evt.preventDefault();
    }
}
```

This way, the errant character won't appear in the text box.

Invoking the preventDefault() method in NN6+/Moz/Safari is the equivalent of assigning true to event.returnValue in IE5+.

Related Items: cancelable property.

stopPropagation()

Returns: Nothing.
Compatibility: WinIE-, MacIE-, NN6+, Moz+, Safari+

Use the stopPropagation() method to stop events from trickling down or bubbling up further through the element containment hierarchy. A statement in the event listener function that invokes

```
evt.stopPropagation();
```

is all that is needed. As an alternative, you can cancel bubbling directly in an element's event handler attribute, as in the following:

```
onclick="doButtonClick(this); event.stopPropagation()"
```

If you are writing cross-browser scripts, you also have the option of using the cancelBubble property, which is compatible with IE4+.

Related Items: bubbles, cancelBubble properties.

Chapter 26

Style Sheet and Style Objects

IN THIS CHAPTER

Managing stylesheets by script

Changing element styles on the fly

Distinguishing among `style`, `styleSheet`, **and style objects**

S tylesheets promote a concept that makes excellent sense in the fast-paced, high-volume content creation environment that is today's World Wide Web: separating content from the rendering details of the content. Textual content may come from any number of electronic sources, but it may need to be dropped into different contexts—just like an online news feed that becomes amalgamated into dozens of web portal sites, each with its own look and feel. All the content author cares about is the text and its meaning; the web page designer then decides how that content should be rendered on the page.

The stylesheet concept has other advantages. Consider the large corporate web site that wants to promote its identity through a distinct style. A family of stylesheets can dictate the font face, font size, the look of emphasized text, and the margin width of all body text. To apply these styles on an element-by-element basis would not only be a tedious page-authoring task, it is fraught with peril. If the style is omitted from the tags of one page, the uniformity of the look is destroyed. Worse yet, if the corporate design changes to use a different font face, the task of changing every style in every tag—even with a highly powered search-and-replace operation—is risky. But if a single external stylesheet file dictates the styles, then the designer need make only one change in that one file to cause the new look to ripple through the entire web site.

Learning how to create and apply stylesheets is beyond the scope of this book, and this chapter assumes you already are familiar with stylesheet terminology, such as a stylesheet rule and a selector. If these terms are not in your vocabulary, you can find numerous tutorials on the subject both online and in books. Although IE, Firefox, Camino, Safari, and other recent browsers adhere fairly closely to W3C standards for stylesheets (called Cascading Style Sheets, or CSS for short), your first learning experience should come from sources that focus on standards, rather than browser-specific features. Microsoft includes some extras in the stylesheet vocabulary that work only on IE4+ for Windows; Firefox and other Mozilla-based browsers have specially named, preliminary properties that offer future CSS3 capabilities in advance of the final standards. Unless you develop for a single target browser brand and client operating system, learning the common denominator of stylesheet features is the right way to go. Details in this chapter cover all versions, so pay close attention to compatibility listings for each item.

Making Sense of the Object Names

The first task in this chapter is to clarify the seemingly overlapping terminology for the stylesheet-related objects that you will be scripting. Some objects are more abstract than others, but they are all important. The objects in question are

- style element object
- styleSheet object (a member of the styleSheets array)
- rule or cssRule object (a member of the rules or cssRules array)
- style object

A style element object is the object that represents the <style> tag in your document. Most of its properties are inherited from the basic HTML element objects you see detailed in Chapter 15. By and large, you won't be reading or writing stylesheet properties via the style element object.

A stylesheet can be embedded in a document via the <style> tag or it may be linked in via a <link> tag. One property of the document object, the styleSheets property, returns an array (collection) of all styleSheet objects that are currently "visible" to the document, whether or not they are disabled. Included in the collection are stylesheets defined by a <style> tag or linked in via a <link> tag. Even though the <style> tag, for example, contains lines of code that make up the rules for a stylesheet, the style element object is not the path to reach the individual rules. The styleSheet object is. It is through the styleSheet object that you can enable or disable an entire sheet, access individual rules (via the rules or cssRules property array), and add or delete rules for that stylesheet.

The meat of any stylesheet is the rules that define how elements are to be rendered. At this object level, the terminology forks in IE4 and NN6/Moz. The IE4+ object model calls each stylesheet rule a rule object; the W3C DOM Level 2 model (in NN6+/Moz), calls each rule a cssRule object. MacIE5 and Safari support both references to the same object. Despite the incompatible object names, the two objects share key property names. Assembling a reference to a rule requires array references. For example, the reference to the first rule of the first styleSheet object in the document is as follows for various browsers:

```
var oneRule = document.styleSheets[0].rules[0];        // IE4+, MacIE5, Safari
var oneRule = document.styleSheets[0].cssRules[0];     // NN6+/Moz, MacIE5, Safari
```

The last object of this quartet of style-related objects is the style object. This object is the mother lode, where actual style definitions take place. In earlier chapters, you have seen countless examples of modifying one or more style properties of an element. Most typically, this modification is accomplished through the style property of the HTML element. For example, you would set the font color of a span element whose ID is "hot" as follows:

```
document.getElementById("hot").style.color = "red";
```

The style object is also a property of a rule/cssRule object. Thus, if you need to modify the style of elements affected by an existing stylesheet rule, you approach the style object through a different reference path, but the style object is treated just as it is for elements:

```
document.styleSheets[0].rules[0].style.color = "red";      // IE4+, MacIE5, Safari
document.styleSheets[0].cssRules[0].style.color = "red";   // NN6+/Moz, MacIE5, Safari
```

Many scripters concern themselves solely with the style object, and at that, a style object associated with a particular element object. Rare are instances that require manipulation of styleSheet objects beyond perhaps enabling and disabling them under script control. Therefore, if you are learning about these objects for the first time, pay closest attention to the style object details rather than to the other related objects.

Imported Stylesheets

Stylesheets embedded in a document via the style element can import additional stylesheets via the @import selector:

```
<style type="text/css">
@import url(externalStyle.css);
p {font-size:16pt}
</style>
```

In this example scenario, the document sees just one styleSheet object. But that object has a stylesheet nested inside — the stylesheet defined by the external file. IE4+ calls one of these imported stylesheets an import object. An import object has all the properties of any styleSheet object, but its parentStyle property is a reference to the styleSheet that "owns" the @import rule. In fact, the @import statement does not even appear among the rules collection of the IE styleSheet object. Therefore, to access the first rule of the imported stylesheet, the reference is as the following:

```
document.styleSheets[0].imports[0].rules[0]
```

The W3C DOM and NN6+/Moz treat import rule objects differently from the IE model. To the W3C DOM, even an at-rule is considered one of the cssRules collections of a styleSheet object. One of the properties of a cssRule object is type, which conveys an integer code value revealing whether the rule is a plain CSS rule or one of several other types, including an import rule. Of course, an imported rule object then has as one of its properties the styleSheet object that, in turn, contains the rules defined in the external stylesheet file. The parent-child relationship exists here, as well, whereby the stylesheet that contains the @import rule is referenced by the imported styleSheet object's parentStyle property (just as in IE4+).

Reading Style Properties

Both the IE4+ and W3C object models exhibit a behavior that at first glance may seem disconcerting. On the one hand, the W3C and good HTML practice encourage defining styles remotely (that is, embedded via <style> or <link> tags) rather than as values assigned to the style attribute of individual element tags throughout the document. This more closely adheres to the notion of separating style from content.

On the other hand, object models can be very literal beasts. Strictly speaking, if an element object presents a scriptable property that reflects an attribute for that element's tag, the first time a script tries to read that property, a value will be associated with that property *only* if the attribute is explicitly assigned in the HTML code. But if you assign stylesheet settings via remote stylesheets, the values are not explicitly set in the tag. Therefore, the style property of such an element comes up empty, even though the element is under the stylistic control of the remote stylesheet. If all you want to do is assign a new value to a style property, that's not a problem, because your assignment to the element object's style property overrides whatever style is assigned to that property in the remote stylesheet (and then that new value is subsequently readable from the style property). But if you want to see what the current setting is, the initial value won't be in the element's style object.

style

Microsoft (in IE5+) and the W3C DOM provide competing (and incompatible) solutions so this problem.

IE5+ provides an extra, read-only property — currentStyle — that reveals the stylesheet values that are currently being applied to the element, regardless of where the stylesheet definitions are. The currentStyle property returns an object that is in the same format and has most of the same properties as the regular style property. If your audience runs browsers no earlier than IE5, you should make a habit of reading styles for an element via its currentStyle property. If you want a change to a style object's property to apply to only one element, use the element's style property to set that value; but if the change is to apply to all elements covered by the same remote stylesheet rule, modify the style property of the rule object.

The W3C DOM solution is the getComputedStyle() method. Although the W3C DOM doesn't (yet) talk about a window object, it does describe an object (called the defaultView) which Mozilla-based browsers channel through the window object. The truly W3C standard way to access this method (supported by both Mozilla-based browsers and Safari 1.3+) is via the document.defaultView object. To read the value of a particular style property being applied to an element, you first retrieve a *computed style* value for the element, and then read the desired CSS style property. For example, to read the font-family currently applied to an element whose ID is myP, use the following sequence:

```
var elem = document.getElementById("myP");
var computedStyle = document.defaultView.getComputedStyle(elem, "");
var fontFam = computedStyle.getPropertyValue("font-family");
```

Note that you must use the CSS property name (for example, font-family) and not the scripted equivalent of that property (for example, fontFamily).

style Element Object

See Chapter 15 for items shared by all HTML elements.

Properties	Methods	Event Handlers
media		
type		

Syntax

Accessing style element object properties and methods:

```
(IE4+)       document.all.objectID.property | method([parameters])
(IE5+/W3C)   document.getElementById(objectID).property | method([parameters])
```

Compatibility: WinIE4+, MacIE4+, NN6+, Moz+, Safari+

About this object

The `style` element is among the classification of HTML directive elements (see Chapter 37 on the CD-ROM) in that it goes in the `head` portion of a document and does not have any of its own content rendered in the page. But the contents obviously have a great amount of control over the rendering of other elements. Most of the properties, methods, and event handlers that the `style` element inherits from all HTML elements are irrelevant.

One exception is the Boolean `disabled` property. Although there are additional ways to disable a stylesheet (the `disabled` property of the `styleSheet` object), it may be easier to disable or enable a stylesheet by way of the `style` element object. Because you can assign an ID to this element and reference it explicitly, doing so may be more convenient than trying to identify which `styleSheet` object among the document's `styleSheets` collection you intend to enable or disable.

Properties

media

Value: String.   Read/Write
Compatibility: WinIE4+, MacIE4+, NN6+, Moz+, Safari+

The `media` property represents the `media` attribute of a `style` element. This attribute can define what kind of output device is governed by the stylesheet. The HTML 4.0 specification has lofty goals for this attribute, but most browsers are limited to the following values: `screen`, `print`, and `all`. Thus, you can design one set of styles to apply when the page is viewed on the computer screen and a different set for when it's printed.

Other types that may eventually enter the picture with the `media` property include `braille`, `embossed`, `handheld`, `projection`, `speech`, `tty`, and `tv`. Web development tools have already begun offering support for these property values. For example, Dreamweaver 8 has a special toolbar that allows you to access all of the previously listed `media` types except for `aural`, `braille`, and `embossed`. Opera is currently the only browser to support `media` property settings beyond `screen`, `print`, and `all`. In Opera, you can also specify `projection`, `handheld`, `speech`, and `tv`.

type

Value: String.   Read/Write
Compatibility: WinIE4+, MacIE4+, NN6+, Moz+ , Safari+

The `type` property represents the `type` attribute of the `style` element. For Cascading Style Sheets, this property is always set to `text/css`. If your scripts assign some other value to this property and the browser does not support that stylesheet type, the stylesheet no longer functions as a Cascading Style Sheet, and any styles it controls revert to their default styles.

styleSheet Object

Properties	Methods	Event Handlers
cssRules	addImport()	
cssText	addRule()	
disabled	deleteRule()	
href	insertRule()	
id	removeRule()	
imports		
media		
ownerNode		
ownerRule		
owningElement		
pages		
parentStyleSheet		
readOnly		
rules		
title		
type		

Syntax

Accessing styleSheet object properties and methods:

>   (IE4+/W3C)   document.styleSheets[*index*].*property* | *method*([*parameters*])

Compatibility: WinIE4+, MacIE4+, NN6+, Moz+, Safari+

About this object

If the style element object is the concrete incarnation of a stylesheet, then the styleSheet object is its abstract equivalent. A styleSheet object exists by virtue of a stylesheet definition being embedded in the current document either by way of the <style> tag or linked in from an external file via the <link> tag. Each element that introduces a stylesheet into a document creates a separate styleSheet object. Access to a styleSheet object is via the document.styleSheets array. If the document contains no stylesheet definitions, then the array has a length of zero. Styles that are introduced into a document by way of an element's style attribute are not considered styleSheet objects.

Although both IE4+ and W3C DOM browsers present styleSheet objects — and the object represents the same "thing" in both browser families — the set of properties and methods diverges widely between browsers. In many cases, the object provides the same information but through differently named properties in the two families. Interestingly, on some important properties, such as the ones that return the array of style rules and a reference to the HTML element that is responsible for the stylesheet's being in the document, MacIE5 and Safari provide both the Microsoft and W3C terminology. Methods for this object focus on adding rules to and deleting rules from the stylesheet. For the most part, however, your use of the `styleSheet` object will be as a reference gateway to individual rules (via the `rules` or `cssRules` array).

Properties

cssRules

Value: Array of rule objects.   Read-Only
Compatibility: WinIE-, MacIE5, NN6+, Moz+, Safari+

The `cssRules` property returns an array of stylesheet rule objects. Strictly speaking, the objects are called `cssRule` objects in the W3C DOM terminology. This property is implemented in MacIE5, but not in the Windows version as of IE7. The list of rule objects is in source code order. The corresponding WinIE4+ property is `rules`.

Example

Use The Evaluator (Chapter 13) to look at the `cssRules` property in W3C/Moz browsers or MacIE5. First, view how many rules are in the first `styleSheet` object of the page by entering the following statement into the top text box:

```
document.styleSheets[0].cssRules.length
```

Now use the array with an index value to access one of the rule objects to view the rule object's properties list. Enter the following statement into the bottom text box:

```
document.styleSheets[0].cssRules[1]
```

You use this syntax to modify the style details of an individual rule belonging to the `styleSheet` object.

Keep in mind that you can access the same information in WinIE by changing the example code to use the `rules` property instead of `cssRules`.

Related Items: `rules` property, `cssRule`, `rule` objects.

cssText

Value: String.   Read/Write
Compatibility: WinIE5+, MacIE5, NN-, Moz-, Safari-

The `cssText` property contains a string of all stylesheet rules contained by the `styleSheet` object. Parsing this text in search of particular strings is not wise because the text returned by this property can have carriage returns and other formatting that is not obvious from the text that is assigned to the rules in the stylesheet. But you can use this property as a way to completely rewrite the rules of a stylesheet in a rather brute-force manner: Assemble a string consisting of all the new rules and assign that string to the `cssText` property. The more formal way of modifying rules (adding and removing them) is perhaps better form, but there is no penalty for using the `cssText` property if your audience is strictly IE5+.

Example

Use The Evaluator (Chapter 13) in WinIE to replace the style rules in one blast via the `cssText` property. Begin by examining the value returned from the property for the initially disabled stylesheet by entering the following statement into the top text box:

```
document.styleSheets[0].cssText
```

Next, enable the stylesheet so that its rules are applied to the document:

```
document.styleSheets[0].disabled = false
```

Finally, enter the following statement into the top text box to overwrite the stylesheet with entirely new rules.

```
document.styleSheets[0].cssText = "p {color:red}"
```

Reload the page after you are finished to restore the original state.

Related Items: addRule(), deleteRule(), insertRule(), removeRule() methods.

disabled

Value: Boolean.   Read/Write
Compatibility: WinIE4+, MacIE4+, NN6+, Moz+, Safari+

While the disabled property of the style element object works with that element only, the styleSheet object's disabled property works with a styleSheet object that comes into the document by a link element as well.

Enabling and disabling stylesheets is one way to swap different appearance styles for a page, allowing the user to select the preferred style. The page can contain multiple stylesheets that control the same selectors, but your script can enable one and disable another to change the overall style. You can even perform this action via the onload event handler. For example, if you have separate stylesheets for Windows and Mac browsers, you can put both of them in the document, initially both disabled. An onload event handler determines the operating system and enables the stylesheet tailored for that OS. Unless your stylesheets are very extensive, there is little download performance penalty for having both stylesheets in the document.

Example

Use The Evaluator (Chapter 13) to toggle between the enabled and disabled state of the first styleSheet object on the page. Enter the following statement into the top text box:

```
document.styleSheets[0].disabled = (!document.styleSheets[0].disabled)
```

The inclusion of the NOT operator (!) forces the state to change from true to false or false to true with each click of the Evaluate button.

Related Items: disabled property of the style element object.

href

Value: String.   Read/Write (See Text)
Compatibility: WinIE4+, MacIE4+, NN6+, Moz+, Safari+

When a stylesheet is linked into a document via a link element, the href property of the styleSheet object contains a string with the URL to that file. Essentially, the href property of the link element is passed along to the styleSheet object that loads as a result. In WinIE4+ only, this property is read/write, allowing you to dynamically link in an external stylesheet file after the page has loaded. In MacIE and NN6+/Moz, this property is read-only.

Related Items: link element object.

id

Value: String.   Read-Only
Compatibility: WinIE4+, MacIE4+, NN-, Moz-, Safari-

The id property of a styleSheet object inherits the id property of its containing element (style or link element). This can get confusing, because it may appear as though two objects in the document have the same ID. The id string, however, can be used as an index to the document.styleSheets array in IE4+ (for example, document.styleSheets["myStyle"]). NN/Moz does not provide a comparable identifier associated with a styleSheet object.

Related Items: id property of all element objects.

imports

Value: Array of styleSheet objects.   Read-Only
Compatibility: WinIE4+, MacIE4+, NN-, Moz-, Safari-

A stylesheet can contain one or more @import rules to import an external stylesheet file into the document. Each imported styleSheet object is treated as an import object. The imports property is a collection of all imported styleSheet objects that belong to the current styleSheet object. Imported stylesheets are not added to the document.styleSheets collection, so that references to an imported styleSheet object must be through the document.styleSheets[i].imports[i] array.

An import object is, itself, a styleSheet object. All properties and methods applicable to a styleSheet object also apply to an import object. Therefore, if you want to load a different external stylesheet into the page, you can assign the new URL to the imported styleSheet object's href property:

```
document.styleSheets[0].imports[0].href = "alternate.css";
```

Modifications of this nature work in IE for Windows, but not in MacIE.

Related Items: styleSheet object.

media

Value: See text.   Read/Write
Compatibility: WinIE4+, MacIE4+, NN6+, Moz+, Safari+

Cascading Style Sheets can be defined to apply to specific output media, such as the video display screen, printer, and, in the future, devices such as speech synthesizers or Braille generators. A stylesheet gets this direction from the media attribute of a style or link element. That value is represented in the media property of the styleSheet object.

In IE4+, the media property value is a string with one of three possible values: screen, printer, all. The W3C DOM and NN6+ take this one step further by allowing for potentially multiple values being assigned to the media attribute. The NN6+/Moz/Safari value is an array of string media names (returned in an object called a mediaList).

Related Items: type property of the style element object.

ownerNode

Value: Node reference. Read-Only
Compatibility: WinIE-, MacIE-, NN6+, Moz+, Safari+

The `ownerNode` property is a reference to the document node in which the `styleSheet` object is defined. For `styleSheet` objects defined inside `style` and `link` elements, the `ownerNode` property is a reference to that element. The corresponding property in IE4+ is `owningElement`. Oddly, MacIE5 has an additional, misnamed property called `owningNode`, whose value equals that of the `owningElement` property.

Example

Use The Evaluator (Chapter 13) with NN6+/Moz/Safari to inspect the `ownerNode` of the first `styleSheet` object in the document. Enter the following statement into the top text box:

```
document.styleSheets[0].ownerNode.tagName
```

The returned value is the `style` element tag name.

Related Items: `ownerRule`, `owningElement` property.

ownerRule

Value: `cssRule` object. Read-Only
Compatibility: WinIE-, MacIE-, NN6+, Moz+, Safari+

The `ownerRule` property applies to a `styleSheet` object that has been imported into a document via the `@import` rule. The property returns a reference to the `@import` rule responsible for loading the external stylesheet. There is an interaction between the `ownerRule` and `ownerNode` properties in that an imported rule has an `ownerRule` but its `ownerNode` property is `null`; conversely, a regular `styleSheet` has an `ownerNode`, but its `ownerRule` property is `null`.

Related Items: `ownerNode` property.

owningElement

Value: Element reference. Read-Only
Compatibility: WinIE4+, MacIE4+, NN-, Moz-, Safari-

The `owningElement` property is a reference to the element object in which the `styleSheet` object is defined. For `styleSheet` objects defined inside `style` and `link` elements, the `owningElement` property is a reference to that element. The corresponding property in NN6+/Moz is `ownerNode`. Oddly, MacIE5 has an additional, misnamed property called `owningNode`, whose value equals that of the `owningElement` property.

Example

Use The Evaluator (Chapter 13) with IE4+ to inspect the `owningElement` of the first `styleSheet` object in the document. Enter the following statement into the top text box:

```
document.styleSheets[0].owningElement.tagName
```

The returned value is the `style` element tag name.

Related Items: `ownerNode` property.

pages

Value: Array of @page rules.   Read-Only
Compatibility: WinIE5.5+, MacIE-, NN-, Moz-, Safari-

An @page style rule defines the dimensions and margins for printed versions of a web page. The pages property returns a collection of @page rules contained by the current styleSheet object. If no @page rules are defined in the stylesheet, the array has a length of zero.

While an @page rule has the same properties as any rule object, it has one more read-only property, the pseudoClass property, which returns any pseudo-class definitions in the rule. For example, the following @page rules define different rectangle specifications for the left and right printed pages:

```
@page :left {margin-left:4cm; margin-right:3cm;}
@page :right {margin-left:3cm; margin-right:4cm;}
```

Values for the pseudoClass property of these two page rules are :left and :right, respectively.

To the W3C DOM, an @page rule is just another rule object, but one whose type property returns page.

For more information about the paged media specification, see http://www.w3.org/TR/REC-CSS2/page.html.

Related Items: None.

parentStyleSheet

Value: styleSheet object.   Read-Only
Compatibility: WinIE4+, MacIE4+, NN6+, Moz+, Safari+

An imported stylesheet is present thanks to the hosting of a styleSheet object created by a style or link element. That host styleSheet object is referenced by the parentStyleSheet property. For most styleSheet objects (that is, those not imported via the @import rule), the parentStyleSheet property is null. Take note of the distinction between the parentStyleSheet property, which points to a styleSheet object, and the various properties that refer to the HTML element that "owns" the styleSheet object.

Related Items: None.

readOnly

Value: Boolean.   Read-Only
Compatibility: WinIE4+, MacIE4+, NN-, Moz-, Safari-

The readOnly property's name is a bit misleading. Its Boolean value lets your script know whether the current stylesheet was embedded in the document by way of the style element or brought in from an external file via the link element or @import rule. When embedded by a style element, the readOnly property is false; for stylesheets defined outside the page, the property is true. But a value of true doesn't mean that your scripts cannot modify the style properties. Style properties can still be modified on the fly, but of course the changes will not be reflected in the external file from which the initial settings came.

Related Items: owningElement property.

rules

Value: Array of `rule` objects.   Read-Only
Compatibility: WinIE4+, MacIE4+, NN-, Moz-, Safari+

The `rules` property returns an array of all rule objects (other than @ rules) defined in the current stylesheet. The order of rule objects in the array is based on source code order of the rules defined in the `style` element or in the external file.

Use the `rules` array as the primary way to reference an individual rule inside a stylesheet. If you use a `for` loop to iterate through all rules in search of a particular rule, you will most likely be looking for a match of the rule object's `selectorText` property. This assumes, of course, that each selector is unique within the stylesheet. Using unique selectors is good practice, but no restrictions prevent you from reusing a selector name in a stylesheet for additional style information applied to the same selector elements.

The corresponding property name for NN6+/Moz is `cssRules`. MacIE5 and Safari respond to both the `rules` and `cssRules` properties.

Example

Use The Evaluator (Chapter 13) with IE4+ to examine the `rules` property of the first `styleSheet` object in the page. First, find out how many rules are in the first `styleSheet` object by entering the following statement into the top text box:

```
document.styleSheets[0].rules.length
```

Next, examine the properties of one of the rules by entering the following statement into the bottom text box:

```
document.styleSheets[0].rules[1]
```

You now see all the properties that IE4+ exposes for a rule object.

Related Items: `rule` object; `cssRules` property.

title

Value: String.   Read/Write
Compatibility: WinIE4+, MacIE4+, NN6+, Moz+, Safari+

If you assign a value to the `title` attribute of a `style` element or a `link` element that loads a stylesheet, that string value filters down to the `title` property of the `styleSheet` object. You can use the string value as a kind of identifier, but it is not usable as a true identifier that you can use as an index to the `styleSheets` array. In visible HTML elements, the `title` attribute usually sets the text that displays with the tooltip over the element. But for the unseen `style` and `link` elements, the attribute has no impact on the rendered display of the page. Therefore, you can use this attribute and corresponding property to convey any string value you want.

Related Items: `title` property of all HTML elements.

type

Value: String.   Read/Write
Compatibility: WinIE4+, MacIE4+, NN6+, Moz+, Safari+

The `type` property of a `styleSheet` object picks up the `type` attribute of the `style` or `link` element that embeds a stylesheet into the page. Unless you are experimenting with some new types of stylesheet language (assuming it is even supported in the browser), the value of the type property is `text/css`.

Related Items: None.

Methods
addImport("*URL*"[, *index*])
Returns: Integer.
Compatibility: WinIE4+, MacIE4+, NN-, Moz-, Safari-

The addImport() method lets you add an @import rule to a styleSheet object. A required first parameter is the URL of the external .css file that contains one or more stylesheet rules. If you omit the second parameter, the @import rule is appended to the end of rules in the styleSheet object. Or you can specify an integer as the index of the position within the rules collection where the rule should be inserted. The order of rules in a styleSheet object can influence the cascading order of overlapping stylesheet rules (that is, multiple rules that apply to the same elements).

The value returned by the method is an integer representing the index position of the new rule within the rules collection of the styleSheet. If you need subsequent access to the new rule, you can preserve the value returned by the addImport() method and use it as the index to the rules collection.

Related Items: addRule() method.

addRule("*selector*", "*styleSpec*"[, *index*])
removeRule(*index*)
Returns: Integer (for addRule()).
Compatibility: WinIE4+, MacIE4+, NN-, Moz-, Safari-

The addRule() method appends or inserts a stylesheet rule into the current styleSheet object. The first two parameters are strings for the two components of every rule: the selector and the style specification. Any valid selector, including multiple, space-delimited selectors, is permitted. For the style specification, the string should contain the semicolon-delimited list of style attribute:value pairs, but without the curly braces that surround the specification in a regular stylesheet rule.

If you omit the last parameter, the rule is appended to the end of the rules collection for the stylesheet. Or, you can specify an integer index value signifying the position within the rules collection where the new rule should go. The order of rules in a styleSheet object can influence the cascading order of overlapping stylesheet rules (meaning multiple rules that apply to the same elements).

The return value conveys no meaningful information.

To remove a rule from a styleSheet object's rules collection, invoke the removeRule() method. Exercise some care here, because you must have the correct index value for the rule that you want to remove. Your script can use a for loop to iterate through the rules collection, looking for a match of the selectorText property (assuming that you have unique selectors). The index for the matching rule can then be used as the parameter to removeRule(). This method returns no value.

For NN6+/Moz, the corresponding methods are called insertRule() and deleteRule().

Example
Use The Evaluator (Chapter 13) with IE4+ to add a stylesheet rule to the first styleSheet object of the page. First, make sure the stylesheet is enabled by entering the following statement into the top text box:

```
document.styleSheets[0].disabled = false
```

Next, append a style that sets the color of the textarea element:

```
document.styleSheets[0].addRule("textarea", "color:red")
```

Enter any valid object (such as document.body) into the bottom text box to see how the style has been applied to the textarea element on the page.

Now remove the style, using the index of the last item of the rules collection as the index:

```
document.styleSheets[0].removeRule(document.styleSheets[0].rules.length - 1)
```

The text in the textarea returns to its default color.

Related Items: deleteRule(), insertRule() methods.

deleteRule(*index*)
insertRule("*rule*", *index*)

Returns: Integer (for insertRule()).
Compatibility: WinIE-, MacIE5, NN6+, Moz+, Safari+

The insertRule() method appends or inserts a stylesheet rule into the current styleSheet object. The first parameter is a string containing the style rule as it would normally appear in a stylesheet, including the selector and curly braces surrounding the semicolon-delimited list of style attribute:value pairs.

You must supply an index location within the cssRules array where the new rule is to be inserted. If you want to append the rule to the end of the list, use the length property of the cssRules collection for the parameter. The order of rules in a styleSheet object can influence the cascading order of overlapping stylesheet rules (meaning multiple rules that apply to the same elements).

The return value is an index for the position of the inserted rule.

To remove a rule from a styleSheet object's cssRules collection, invoke the deleteRule() method. Exercise some care here, because you must have the correct index value for the rule that you want to remove. Your script could use a for loop to iterate through the cssRules collection, looking for a match of the selectorText property (assuming that you have unique selectors). The index for the matching rule can then be used as the parameter to deleteRule(). This method returns no value.

For IE4+, the corresponding methods are called addRule() and removeRule().

Example

Use The Evaluator (Chapter 13) with NN6+/Moz to add a stylesheet rule to the first styleSheet object of the page. First, make sure the stylesheet is enabled by entering the following statement into the top text box:

```
document.styleSheets[0].disabled = false
```

Next, append a style that sets the color of the textarea element:

```
document.styleSheets[0].insertRule("textarea {color:red}",
document.styleSheets[0].cssRules.length)
```

Enter any valid object (such as document.body) into the bottom text box to see how the style has been applied to the textarea element on the page.

Now remove the style, using the index of the last item of the rules collection as the index:

```
document.styleSheets[0].deleteRule(document.styleSheets[0].cssRules.length - 1)
```

Related Items: addRule(), removeRule() methods.

cssRule and rule Objects

Properties	Methods	Event Handlers
cssText		
parentStyleSheet		
readOnly		
selectorText		
style		
type		

Syntax

Accessing rule or cssRule object properties:

```
(IE4+)         document.styleSheets[index].rules[index].property
(MacIE5/W3C)   document.styleSheets[index].cssRules[index].property
```

About these objects

The rule and cssRule objects are different object model names for the same objects. For IE4+, the object is known as a *rule* (and a collection of them the rules collection); for NN6+/Moz/Safari (and MacIE5), the object follows the W3C DOM recommendation, calling the object a *cssRule* (and a collection of them the cssRules collection). For the remainder of this section, they will be referred to generically as the rule object.

A rule object has two major components. The first is the selector text, which governs which element(s) are to be influenced by the style rule. The second component is the style definition, with its set of semicolon-delimited attribute:value pairs. In both the IE4+ and NN6+/Moz/W3C object models, the style definition is treated as an object: the style object, which has tons of properties representing the style attributes available in the browser. The style object that belongs to a rule object is precisely the same style object that is associated with every HTML element object. Accessing style properties of a stylesheet rule requires a fairly long reference, as in

```
document.styleSheets[0].rules[0].style.color = "red";
```

but the format follows the logic of JavaScript's dot-syntax to the letter.

Properties

cssText

Value: String.   Read/Write
Compatibility: WinIE-, MacIE5, NN6+, Moz+, Safari+

The cssText property returns the full text of the current cssRule object. While the text returned from this property can be parsed to locate particular strings, it is easier and more reliable to access individual style properties and their values via the style property of a cssRule object.

Related Items: style property.

parentStyleSheet

Value: styleSheet object.   Read-Only
Compatibility: WinIE-, MacIE5, NN6+, Moz+, Safari+

The parentStyleSheet property is a reference to the styleSheet object that contains the current cssRule object. The return value is a reference to a styleSheet object, from which scripts can read and write properties related to the entire stylesheet.

Related Items: parentRule property.

readOnly

Value: Boolean.   Read-Only
Compatibility: WinIE5+, MacIE5, NN-, Moz-, Safari-

The readOnly property's name is a bit misleading. Its Boolean value lets your script know whether the current rule's styleSheet was embedded in the document by way of the style element or brought in from an external file via the link element or @import rule. When embedded by a style element, the readOnly property is false; for stylesheets defined outside the page, the property is true. But a value of true doesn't mean that your scripts cannot modify the style properties. Style properties can still be modified on the fly, but of course the changes are not reflected in the external file from which the initial settings came.

Related Items: styleSheet.readOnly property.

selectorText

Value: String.   Read-Only
Compatibility: WinIE5+, MacIE5, NN6+, Moz+, Safari+

The selectorText property returns only the selector portion of a stylesheet rule. The value is a string, and if the selector contains multiple, space-delimited items, the selectorText value returns the same space-delimited string. For selectors that are applied to classes (preceded by a period) or ids (preceded by a crosshatch), those leading characters are returned as part of the string as well.

If you want to change the selector for a rule, removing the original rule and adding a new one in its place is better. You can always preserve the style property of the original rule and assign the style to the new rule.

Example

Use The Evaluator (Chapter 13) to examine the selectorText property of rules in the first styleSheet object of the page. Enter each of the following statements in the top text box:

```
document.styleSheets[0].rules[0].selectorText
document.styleSheets[0].rules[1].selectorText
```

Compare these values against the source code view for the style element in the page.

Related Items: style property.

style

Value: style object.   Read/Write
Compatibility: WinIE5+, MacIE5, NN6+, Moz+, Safari+

The `style` property of a rule (or `cssRule`) is, itself, an object whose properties consist of the CSS style properties supported by the browser. Modifying a property of the `style` object requires a fairly long reference, as in

```
document.styleSheets[0].rules[0].style.color = "red";
```

Any change you make to the rule's `style` properties is reflected in the rendered style of whatever elements are denoted by the rule's selector. If you want to change the style of just one element, access the `style` property of just that element. Style values applied directly to an element override whatever stylesheet style values are associated with the element.

Example

Use The Evaluator (Chapter 13) to modify a `style` property of one of the `styleSheet` rules in the page. The syntax shown here is for IE4+, but you can substitute the `cssRules` reference for the `rules` collection reference in NN6+/Moz, MacIE5, and W3C browsers if you like.

Begin by reloading the page and making sure the stylesheet is enabled. Enter the following statement into the top text box:

```
document.styleSheets[0].disabled = false
```

The first rule is for the `myP` element on the page. Change the rule's `font-size` style:

```
document.styleSheets[0].rules[0].style.fontSize = "20pt"
```

Look over the `style` object properties in the discussion of the `style` object later in this chapter and have fun experimenting with different style properties. After you are finished, reload the page to restore the styles to their default states.

Related Items: `style` object.

type

Value: Integer.   Read-Only
Compatibility: WinIE-, MacIE-, NN6+, Moz+, Safari+

The W3C DOM defines several classes of stylesheet rules. To make it easier for a script to identify the kind of `cssRule` it is working with, the `type` property returns an integer whose value is associated with one of the known `cssRule` types. While not all of these rule types may be implemented in current browsers, the complete W3C DOM list is as follows:

Type	Description
0	Unknown type
1	Regular style rule
2	@charset rule
3	@import rule
4	@media rule
5	@font-face rule
6	@page rule

Most of the stylesheet rules you work with are type 1. To learn more about these rule types, consult the W3C specification for CSS at http://www.w3.org/TR/REC-CSS2.

Related Items: None.

currentStyle, runtimeStyle, and style Objects

Properties	Methods	Event Handlers
(See the following text)		

Syntax

Accessing currentStyle, runtimeStyle, or style object properties:

(IE4+/W3C)	*elementReference*.style.*property*
(IE4+/W3C)	document.styleSheets[*index*].style.*property*
(IE5+)	*elementReference*.currentStyle.*property*
(IE5.5+)	*elementReference*.runtimeStyle.*property*

About these objects

All three of these objects — currentStyle, runtimeStyle, and style — return an object that contains dozens of properties related to stylesheet specifications associated either with a styleSheet object (for the style object only) or any rendered HTML element object. With the browser page reflow facilities of modern browsers, changes made to the properties of the style and IE-specific runtimeStyle objects are reflected immediately by the rendered content on the page.

The primary object, the style object, is accessed as a property of an HTML element object. It is vital to remember that style properties of an HTML element are reflected by the style object only if the specifications are made via the style attribute inside the element's tag. If your coding style requires that stylesheets be applied via style or link tags, and if your scripts need to access the style property values as set by those stylesheets, then you must read the properties of the effective stylesheet through the read-only currentStyle property (available in IE5+) or the W3C DOM window.getComputedStyle() method (NN6+/Moz).

IE's currentStyle object does not have precisely the same properties as its style object. Missing from the currentStyle object are the properties that contain combination values, such as border or borderBottom. On the other hand, currentStyle provides separate properties for each of the sides of a clipping rectangle (clipTop, clipRight, clipBottom, and clipLeft), which the clip property does not provide.

Microsoft introduced one more flavor of style object — the runtimeStyle object — in IE5.5. This object lets scripts override any style property that is set in a stylesheet or via the style attribute. In other words, the runtimeStyle object is like a read/write version of currentStyle except that assigning a new value to one of its properties does not modify the stylesheet definition or the value assigned in a style attribute. By and large, however, your scripts will modify the style property of an element to make changes, unless you modify styles by enabling and disabling stylesheets (or changing the className property of an element so that it is under the control of a different selector).

Style properties

If you add up all the style object properties available in browsers starting with IE4 and NN6/Moz, you have a list approximately 180 properties long. A sizable percentage are in common among all browsers and are scriptable versions of W3C Cascading Style Sheet properties. The actual CSS property names are frequently script-unfriendly in that multiple-worded properties have hyphens in them, such as font-size. JavaScript identifiers do not allow hyphens, so multiple-worded properties are converted to interCap versions, such as fontSize.

Not all style properties are supported by all browsers that have the style object in their object models. Microsoft, in particular, has added many properties that are sometimes unique to IE and sometimes unique to just IE for Windows. On the Mozilla side, you find some properties that appear to be supported by the style object, but the browser doesn't genuinely support the attributes. For example, the CSS specification defines several attributes that enhance the delivery of content that is rendered through a speech synthesizer. Although Firefox doesn't qualify, the Gecko browser engine at its core could be adapted to such a browser. Therefore, if you see a property in the following listings that doesn't make sense to you, test it out in the compatible browsers to verify that it works as you need it. You will also find some properties that are proprietary to Mozilla-based browsers — properties that begin with moz. These properties are preliminary implementations of as yet unreleased CSS Level 3 properties. The moz prefix lets you use these properties today without conflicting with future, sanctioned implementations of the properties (which won't have the moz prefix). When specifying these properties in CSS syntax for your stylesheets, the properties begin with the special prefix -moz-, as in -moz-opacity (and the scripted equivalent, mozOpacity).

Some browsers also expose advanced style object properties to scripters, when, in fact, they are not genuinely supported in the browser. For example, an inspection of the style object for MacIE5 and NN6+/Moz shows a quotes property, which matches the quotes style property in the W3C CSS2 specification. But in truth, the quotes style property cannot be set by script in these browsers. When you see that a property is supported by MacIE5 and NN6+/Moz but not others, testing out the style property (and the stylesheet attribute as well) in The Evaluator is a good idea before attempting to employ the property in your application.

With so many properties associated with an object, it may be difficult to locate the specific property you need for a particular style effect. To help you locate properties, the listings that follow are divided into functional categories, ordered by popularity:

Category	Description
Text & Fonts	Font specifications, text rendering, text alignment
Inline Display & Layout	Element flow, alignment, and display
Positioning	Explicit positioning of "layers"
Background	Background images and colors
Borders & Edges	Borders, padding, and margins around elements
Lists	Details for ul and ol elements
Scroll bars	Scroll bar colors (WinIE5.5+ only)
Tables	Details for table elements and components
Printing	Page breaks and alignment for printed pages
Miscellaneous	Odds and ends
Aural	For rendering via speech-synthesis

Property values

All `style` object property values are strings. Moreover, many groups of style properties share the same format for their values. Knowing the formats for the frequently used values is helpful. The purpose of this chapter is not to teach you about stylesheets but to show you how to script them. Therefore, if you see unfamiliar terminology here, consult online or print instructional material about Cascading Style Sheets.

Length

Values for length cover a wide range, but they all define an amount of physical space in the document. Because content can be displayed on a video monitor or printed on a sheet of paper, any kind of length value should include a unit of measure as well as the quantity. One group of units (px, em, ex) are considered *relative* units, because the precise size depends on factors beyond the control of the stylesheet (for example, the pixel density of the display) or units set by elements with more global scope (for example, a p element's margin em length dependent upon the body element's font-size setting). *Absolute* units (in, cm, mm, pi, pt) are more appropriate for printed output. Length units are referred in script according to the following table:

Unit	Script Version	Example
pixel	px	14px
em	em	1.5em
ex	ex	1.5ex
inch	in	3.0in
centimeter	cm	4.0cm
millimeter	mm	40mm
pica	pi	72pi
point	pt	14pt

A length value can also be represented by a percentage as a string. For example, the `lineHeight` style for a paragraph would be set to 120% of the font size established for the paragraph by the following statement:

```
document.getElementById("myP").style.lineHeight = "120%";
```

Style inheritance — an important CSS concept — often has significant impact on style properties whose values are lengths.

Color

Values for colors can be one of three types:

■ RGB values (in a few different formats)
■ plain-language versions of the color names
■ plain-language names of system user interface items

RGB values can be expressed as hexadecimal values. The most common way is with a crosshatch character followed by six hex numbers, as in #ff00ff (letters can be uppercase or lowercase). A special shortcut is also available to let you specify three numbers with the assumption that they will be expanded to pairs of numbers. For example, a color of #f0f is expanded internally to be #ff00ff.

An alternative RGB expression is with the `rgb()` prefix and three numbers (from 0 to 255) or percentages corresponding to the red, green, and blue components of the color. Here are a couple of examples:

```
document.styleSheets[0].rules[0].style.color = "rgb(0, 255, 0)";
document.styleSheets[0].rules[0].style.color = "rgb(0%, 100%, 0%)";
```

Browsers also respond to a long list of plain-language color names originally adopted from the X Window System palette by Netscape and now known as X11 colors. You can see the list with sample colors at `http://en.wikipedia.org/wiki/X11_color_names`. Not all of those colors are necessarily part of what are known as "web safe" colors. For a demonstration of web safe colors, visit `http://www.lynda.com/hexh.html`. Of course, it's worth noting that "web safe" colors only enter the picture when a user is limited to an 8-bit (256) color display, which is rare these days.

The last category of color values references user interface pieces, many of which are determined by the user's control panel for video display. The string values correspond to recognizable UI components (also called system colors), as follows:

`activeborder`	`highlight`	`threeddarkshadow`
`activecaption`	`highlighttext`	`threedface`
`appworkspace`	`inactiveborder`	`threedhighlight`
`background`	`inactivecaption`	`threedlightshadow`
`buttonface`	`inactivecaptiontext`	`threedshadow`
`buttonhighlight`	`infobackground`	`window`
`buttonshadow`	`infotext`	`windowframe`
`buttontext`	`menu`	`windowtext`
`captiontext`	`menutext`	
`graytext`	`scrollbar`	

Using these color settings may be risky for public sites, because you are at the mercy of the color settings the user has chosen. For a corporate environment where system installations and preferences are strictly controlled, these values could help define a safe color scheme for your pages.

Rectangle sides

Many style properties control the look of sides of rectangles (for example, thickness of a border around a block element). In most cases, the style values can be applied to individual sides or combinations of sides, depending on the number of values supplied to the property. The number of values affects the four sides of the rectangle according to the following matrix:

Number of Values	Impact
1	All four sides set to the one value
2	Top and bottom sides set to first value; left and right sides set to second value
3	Top side set to first value; left and right sides set to second value; bottom side set to third value
4	Top, right, bottom, and left sides set to individual values in that order

elementRef.style

For example, to set the border color of an element so that all sides are red, the syntax is

```
elementRef.style.borderColor = "red";
```

To set the top and bottom to red but the left and right to green, the syntax is

```
elementRef.style.borderColor = "red green";
```

Properties that accept these multiple values cover a wide range of styles. Values may be colors, lengths, or selections from a fixed list of possible values.

Combination values

Another category of style values includes properties that act as shortcuts for several related properties. For example, the border property encompasses the borderWidth, borderStyle, and borderColor properties. This is possible because very different classes of values represent the three component properties: borderWidth is a length; borderStyle is based on a fixed list of values; and borderColor is a color value. Therefore, you can specify one or more of these property values (in any order), and the browser knows how to apply the values to the detailed subproperty. Only one value is permitted for any one of these subproperties, which means that if the property is one of the four-sided styles described in the previous section, the value is applied to all four sides equally.

For example, setting the border property to a single value, as in

```
elementRef.style.border = "blue";
```

is the same as setting

```
elementRef.style.borderColor = "blue";
```

But if you set multiple items, as in

```
elementRef.style.border = "groove blue 3px";
```

then you have set the equivalent of the following three statements:

```
elementRef.style.borderStyle = "groove"
elementRef.style.borderColor = "blue";
elementRef.style.borderWidth = "3px";
```

In the property descriptions that follow, these combination values are denoted by their scripted property names and the OR (||) operator, as in

```
border = "borderStyle || borderColor || borderWidth";
```

URLs

Unlike other property values containing URLs, a style property requires a slightly different format. This format includes the url() prefix, with the actual URL (relative or absolute) located inside the parentheses. The URL itself is not quoted, but the entire property value is, as in

```
elementRef.style.backgroundImage = "url(chainlink.jpg)";
```

URLs should not have any spaces in them, but if they do, use the URL-encoded version for the file specification: convert spaces to %20. This format distinguishes a URL value from some other string value for shortcut properties.

Text and font properties
color
Compatibility: WinIE4+, MacIE4+, NN6+, Moz+, Safari+
Controls: Foreground color of an element, primarily used to assign color to text. May also affect edges and highlights of other elements in some browsers.
Value: Color specification.
Example: `elementRef.style.color = "rgb(#22FF00)";`

font
Compatibility: WinIE4+, MacIE4+, NN6+, Moz+, Safari+
Controls: Up to six font-related style properties.
Value: Combination values: `fontStyle || fontVariant || fontWeight || fontSize || lineHeight || fontFamily`. See individual properties for their value formats.
Example: `elementRef.style.font = "bold sans-serif 16px";`

fontFamily
Compatibility: WinIE4+, MacIE4+, NN6+, Moz+, Safari+
Controls: Font family to be applied to an element in order of priority.
Value: Comma-delimited list of font families to be applied to element, starting with the most preferred font family name. You can also use one of several generic family names that rely on the browser to choose the optimal font to match the class: `serif | sans-serif | cursive | fantasy | monospace`. Not all browsers support all constants, but `serif`, `sans-serif`, and `monospace` are commonly implemented.
Example: `elementRef.style.fontFamily = "Bauhaus 93, Arial, monospace";`

fontSize
Compatibility: WinIE4+, MacIE4+, NN6+, Moz+, Safari+
Controls: Size of the characters of the current font family.
Value: Lengths (generally px or pt values); relative size constants: `larger | smaller`; absolute size constants: `xx-small | x-small | small | medium | large | x-large | xx-large`
Examples: `elementRef.style.fontSize = "16px"; elementRef.style.fontSize = "small";`

fontSizeAdjust
Compatibility: WinIE-, MacIE5, NN6+, Moz+, Safari-
Controls: Aspect value of a secondary font family so that it maintains a similar character height as the primary font family.
Value: Number (including floating-point value) or `none`
Example: `elementRef.style.fontSizeAdjust = "1.05";`

fontStretch
Compatibility: WinIE-, MacIE5, NN6+, Moz+, Safari-
Controls: Rendered width of a font's characters.
Value: Constant `ultra-condensed | extra-condensed | condensed | semi-condensed | semi-expanded | expanded | extra-expanded | ultra-expanded` or `wider | narrower | inherit | normal`
Example: `elementRef.style.fontStretch = "expanded";`

fontStyle

Compatibility: WinIE4+, MacIE4+, NN6+, Moz+, Safari+
Controls: Italic style of characters.
Value: Constant normal | italic | oblique | inherit
Example: elementRef.style.fontStyle = "italic";

fontVariant

Compatibility: WinIE4+, MacIE4+, NN6+, Moz+, Safari1.3+
Controls: Rendering characters as small caps.
Value: Constant normal | small-caps | inherit
Example: elementRef.style.fontVariant = "small-caps";

fontWeight

Compatibility: WinIE4+, MacIE4+, NN6+, Moz+, Safari+
Controls: Rendering characters in bold or light weights. Fonts that support numbered gradations can be controlled by those numbers. Normal = 400; Bold = 700.
Value: Constant bold | bolder | lighter | normal | 100 | 200 | 300 | 400 | 500 | 600 | 700 | 800 | inherit
Example: elementRef.style.fontWeight = "bold";

letterSpacing

Compatibility: WinIE4+, MacIE4+, NN6+, Moz+, Safari+
Controls: Spacing between characters. Used to override a font family's own characteristics.
Value: Length (usually em units, relative to current font size); Constant normal | inherit
Example: elementRef.style.letterSpacing = "1.2em";

lineBreak

Compatibility: WinIE5+, MacIE-, NN-, Moz-, Safari-
Controls: Line-break rules for Japanese text content.
Value: Constant normal | strict
Example: elementRef.style.lineBreak = "strict";

lineHeight

Compatibility: WinIE4+, MacIE4+, NN6+, Moz+, Safari+
Controls: Height of the rectangular space that holds a line of text characters.
Value: Length (usually em units, relative to current font size); number (a multiplier on the inherited line height); percentage (relative to inherited line height); constant normal | inherit
Example: elementRef.style.lineHeight = "1.1";

quotes

Compatibility: WinIE-, MacIE5, NN6+, Moz+, Safari-
Controls: Characters to be used for quotation marks.
Value: Space-delimited pairs of open and close quotation symbols; Constant none | inherit
Example: elementRef.style.quotes = "« »";

rubyAlign

Compatibility: WinIE5+, MacIE5, NN-, Moz-, Safari-
Controls: Alignment of ruby text within a ruby element.
Value: Constant auto | left | center | right | distribute-letter | distribute-space | line-edge
Example: RUBYelementRef.style.rubyAlign = "distribute=letter";

rubyOverhang

Compatibility: WinIE5+, MacIE5, NN-, Moz-, Safari-
Controls: Overhang of ruby text within a ruby element.
Value: Constant auto | whitespace | none
Example: RUBYelementRef.style.rubyOverhang = "whitespace";

rubyPosition

Compatibility: WinIE5+, MacIE5, NN-, Moz-, Safari-
Controls: Placement of ruby text with respect to the ruby element's base text.
Value: Constant above | inline
Example: RUBYelementRef.style.rubyPosition = "inline";

textAlign

Compatibility: WinIE4+, MacIE4+, NN6+, Moz+, Safari+
Controls: Horizontal alignment of text with respect to its containing element.
Value: Constant center | justify | left | right
Example: elementRef.style.textAlign = "center";

textAlignLast

Compatibility: WinIE5.5+, MacIE-, NN-, Moz-, Safari-
Controls: Horizontal alignment of last line of text in a paragraph.
Value: Constant auto | center | justify | left | right
Example: elementRef.style.textAlignLast = "justify";

textAutospace

Compatibility: WinIE5+, MacIE-, NN-, Moz-, Safari-
Controls: Extra spacing between ideographic and non-ideographic text.
Value: Constant none | ideograph-alpha | ideograph-numeric | ideograph-parenthesis | ideograph-space
Example: elementRef.style.textAutospace = "ideograph=alpha";

textDecoration

Compatibility: WinIE4+, MacIE4+, NN6+, Moz+, Safari+
Controls: Display of underline, overline, or line-through with text.
Value: Constant none | blink | line-through | overline | underline
Example: elementRef.style.textDecoration = "underline";

textDecorationBlink
textDecorationLineThrough
textDecorationNone
textDecorationOverline
textDecorationUnderline

Compatibility: WinIE4+, MacIE4+, NN-, Moz-, Safari-
Controls: Individual text decoration characteristics for text, allowing for multiple decorations to be applied to the same text.
Value: Boolean (not strings) true | false
Example: elementRef.style.textDecorationUnderline = true;

textIndent

Compatibility: WinIE4+, MacIE4+, NN6+, Moz+, Safari+
Controls: Amount of indentation for the first line of a block text element (for example, p).
Value: Length (negative values for outdenting); percentage (relative to inherited value)
Example: elementRef.style.textIndent = "2.5em";

textJustify

Compatibility: WinIE5+, MacIE5, NN-, Moz-, Safari-
Controls: Additional detailed specifications for an element whose textAlign property is set to justify.
Value: Constant auto | distribute | distribute-all-lines | distribute-center-last | inter-cluster | inter-ideograph | inter-word | kashida | newspaper
Example: elementRef.style.textJustify = "distribute";

textJustifyTrim

Compatibility: WinIE5+, MacIE5, NN-, Moz-, Safari-
Reserved for future use.

textKashidaSpace

Compatibility: WinIE5.5+, MacIE-, NN-, Moz-, Safari-
Controls: Ratio of kashida expansion to white space expansion for Arabic writing systems.
Value: Percentage
Example: elementRef.style.textKashidaSpace = "90%";

textOverflow

Compatibility: WinIE6+, MacIE-, NN-, Moz-, Safari1.3+
Controls: Whether an ellipsis (. . .) is displayed at the end of a line of overflowed text to indicate that more text is available.
Value: Constant clip | ellipsis

textShadow

Compatibility: WinIE-, MacIE5, NN6+, Moz+, Safari1.2+
Controls: Shadow rendering around text characters. Note: The `style` attribute for this property is not implemented in MacIE5 or NN6+/Moz, but the property is listed as valid for a `style` object.
Value: Each shadow specification consists of an optional color and three space-delimited length values (horizontal shadow offset, vertical shadow offset, blur radius length). Multiple shadow specifications are comma-delimited.

textTransform

Compatibility: WinIE4+, MacIE4+, NN6+, Moz+, Safari+
Controls: Case rendering of the text (meaning without altering the case of the original text).
Value: Constant `none | capitalize | lowercase | uppercase`
Example: `elementRef.style.textTransform = "uppercase";`

textUnderlinePosition

Compatibility: WinIE5.5+, MacIE-, NN-, Moz-, Safari-
Controls: Whether an underline text decoration is displayed above or below the text. Seems redundant with `textDecorationUnderline` and `textDecorationOverline`.
Value: Constant `above | below`
Example: `elementRef.style.textUnderlinePosition = "above";`

unicodeBidi

Compatibility: WinIE5+, MacIE5, NN6+, Moz+, Safari+
Controls: Within bidirectional text (for example, English and Arabic), to what extent an alternate direction text block is embedded within the outer element.
Value: Constant `normal | embed | bidi-override`
Example: `elementRef.style.unicodeBidi = "embed";`

whiteSpace

Compatibility: WinIE5.5+, MacIE5, NN6+, Moz+, Safari+
Controls: Treatment of white space characters within an element's source code.
Value: Constant `normal | nowrap | pre`
Example: `elementRef.style.whiteSpace = "nowrap";`

wordBreak

Compatibility: WinIE5+, MacIE-, NN-, Moz-, Safari-
Controls: Word breaking characteristics, primarily for Asian-language text or text containing a mixture of Asian and Latin characters.
Value: Constant `normal | break-all | keep-all`
Example: `elementRef.style.wordBreak = "break-all";`

wordSpacing

Compatibility: WinIE6+, MacIE4+, NN6+, Moz+, Safari+
Controls: Spacing between words.
Value: Length (usually in em units); Constant normal
Example: elementRef.style.wordSpacing = "1em";

wordWrap

Compatibility: WinIE5.5+, MacIE-, NN-, Moz-, Safari1.3+
Controls: Word wrapping characteristics of text in a block element, explicitly sized inline element, or positioned element.
Value: Constant normal | break-word
Example: elementRef.style.wordWrap = "break-word";

writingMode

Compatibility: WinIE5.5+, MacIE-, NN-, Moz-, Safari-
Controls: Direction of content flow (left-to-right/top-to-bottom or top-to-bottom/right-to-left, as in some Asian languages).
Value: Constant lr-tb | tb-rl
Example: elementRef.style.writingMode = "tb-rl";

Inline display and layout properties

clear

Compatibility: WinIE4+, MacIE4+, NN6+, Moz+, Safari+
Controls: Layout orientation of an element with respect to a neighboring floating element.
Value: Constant both | left | none | right
Example: elementRef.style.clear = "right";

clip

Compatibility: WinIE4+, MacIE4+, NN6+, Moz+, Safari+
Controls: The clipping rectangle of an element (that is, the position of the rectangle through which the user sees an element's content).
Value: rect(topLength, rightLength, bottomLength, leftLength) | auto
Example: elementRef.style.clip = "rect(10px, 300px, 200px, 0px)";

clipBottom
clipLeft
clipRight
clipTop

Compatibility: WinIE5+, MacIE-, NN-, Moz-, Safari-
Controls: Individual edges of the clipping rectangle of an element. These properties are read-only properties of the currentStyle object.
Value: Length | auto
Example: var leftEdge = *elementRef*.currentStyle.clipLeft;

content

Compatibility: WinIE-, MacIE5, NN6+, Moz+, Safari1.3+

Controls: The content rendered in addition to the element, usually to be applied with a `:before` or `:after` pseudo-class. This feature will become more useful when CSS counters are implemented in browsers. They'll provide automatic section or paragraph numbering. While the CSS equivalent is implemented in NN7/Moz/Safari, changes to the scripted property are not rendered.

Value: See `http://www.w3.org/TR/REC-CSS2/generate.html#propdef-content`.

counterIncrement

Compatibility: WinIE-, MacIE5, NN6+, Moz1.8+, Safari-

Controls: The jumps in counter values to be displayed via the `content` style property.

Value: One or more pairs of counter identifier and integers.

counterReset

Compatibility: WinIE-, MacIE5, NN6+, Moz1.8+, Safari-

Controls: Resets a named counter for content to be displayed via the `content` style property.

Value: One or more pairs of counter identifier and integers.

cssFloat

Compatibility: WinIE-, MacIE5, NN6+, Moz+, Safari+

Controls: Horizontal alignment of an element that allows other content to wrap around the element (usually text wrapping around an image). Corresponds to the CSS `float` style attribute. See also the `floatStyle` property, later in this chapter. Floating (non-positioned) elements follow a long sequence of rules for their behavior, detailed at `http://www.w3.org/TR/REC-CSS2/visuren.html#propdef-float`.

Value: Constant `left` | `right` | `none`

Example: `elementRef.style.cssFloat = "right";`

cursor

Compatibility: WinIE4+, MacIE4+, NN6+, Moz+, Safari1.3+

Controls: The icon used for the cursor on the screen from a library of system-generated cursors. The CSS2 specification defines syntax for downloadable cursors, but this feature is not implemented in NN6+/Moz. You can change this style property only if a `:hover` pseudo-class is initially defined for the element.

Value: Constant `auto` | `crosshair` | `default` | `e-resize` | `help` | `move` | `n-resize` | `ne-resize` | `nw-resize` | `pointer` | `s-resize` | `se-resize` | `sw-resize` | `text` | `w-resize` | `wait`. New values for IE6 are: `all-scroll` | `col-resize` | `no-drop` | `not-allowed` | `progress` | `row-resize` | `url` | `vertical-text`. Mozilla-based browsers include: `alias` | `cell` | `context-menu` | `copy` | `count-down` | `count-up` | `count-up-down` | `grab` | `grabbing` | `spinning`.

Example: `elementRef.style.cursor = "hand";`

elementRef.style.layoutGridChar

direction

Compatibility: WinIE5+, MacIE5, NN6+, Moz+, Safari+
Controls: Layout direction (left-to-right or right-to-left) of inline text (same as `dir` attribute of an element).
Value: Constant `ltr | rtl`
Example: `elementRef.style.direction = "rtl";`

display

Compatibility: WinIE4+, MacIE4+, NN6+, Moz+, Safari+
Controls: Whether an element is displayed on the page and in which display mode. Content surrounding an undisplayed element cinches up to occupy the undisplayed element's space — as if the element didn't exist for rendering purposes (see the `visibility` property for a different approach). Commonly used to hide or show segments of a graphical tree structure. Also used to direct the browser to display an element as inline or block-level element. Some special-purpose values are associated with specific element types (for example, lists, table cells, and so on).
Value: Constant `block | compact | inline | inline-table | list-item | none | run-in | table | table-caption | table-cell | table-column-group | table-footer-group | table-header-group | table-row | table-row-group`
Example: `elementRef.style.display = "none"; // removes element from page`

filter

Compatibility: WinIE4+, MacIE-, NN-, Moz-, Safari-
Controls: Rendering effects on static content and on transitions between hiding and showing elements. Microsoft made a massive overhaul of the `filter` stylesheet syntax in WinIE5.5 (using the `DXImageTransform` ActiveX control). Scripting transitions require several steps to load the transition and actions before playing the transition. Use `style.filter` to read or write the entire filter specification string; use the `elem.styles[i]` object to access individual filter properties. See the discussion of the `filter` object later in this chapter.
Value: Filter specification as string.
Example: `var filterSpec = elementRef.style.filter = "alpha(opacity=50) flipH()";`

layoutGrid

Compatibility: WinIE5+, MacIE-, NN-, Moz-, Safari-
Controls: Page grid properties (primarily for Asian-language pages).
Value: Combination values: `layoutGridMode || layoutGridType || layoutGridLine || layoutGridChar`. See individual properties for their value formats.
Example: `elementRef.style.layoutGrid = "2em fixed";`

layoutGridChar

Compatibility: WinIE5+, MacIE-, NN-, Moz-, Safari-
Controls: Size of the character grid (Asian languages).
Value: Length; Percentage; Constant `none | auto`
Example: `elementRef.style.layoutGridChar = "2em";`

layoutGridLine

Compatibility: WinIE5+, MacIE-, NN-, Moz-, Safari-
Controls: Line height of the grid (Asian languages).
Value: Length; Percentage; Constant `none` | `auto`
Example: `elementRef.style.layoutGridLine = "110%";`

layoutGridMode

Compatibility: WinIE5+, MacIE-, NN-, Moz-, Safari-
Controls: One- or two-dimensional grid (Asian languages).
Value: Constant `both` | `none` | `line` | `char`
Example: `elementRef.style.layoutGridMode = "both";`

layoutGridType

Compatibility: WinIE5+, MacIE-, NN-, Moz-, Safari-
Controls: Type of grid for text content (Asian languages).
Value: Constant `loose` | `strict` | `fixed`
Example: `elementRef.style.layoutGridType = "strict";`

markerOffset

Compatibility: WinIE-, MacIE-, NN6+, Moz+, Safari-
Controls: Distance between the edges of a marker box (content whose display is of a marker type) and a block-level element's box. Note: The CSS property is not implemented in MacIE5 or NN6+/Moz, but the property is listed as valid for a `style` object.
Value: Length; Constant `auto`
Example: `elementRef.style.markerOffset = "2em";`

marks

Compatibility: WinIE-, MacIE5, NN6+, Moz+, Safari-
Controls: Rendering of crop marks and the like on the printed page. Note: The CSS property is not implemented in MacIE5 or NN6+/Moz, but the property is listed valid for a `style` object.
Value: Constant `crop` || `cross` | `none`
Example: `elementRef.style.marks = "crop";`

maxHeight
maxWidth
minHeight
minWidth

Compatibility: WinIE (see text), MacIE-, NN6+, Moz+, Safari1+
Controls: Maximum or minimum height or width of an element. Microsoft supports `maxHeight` only starting with IE7.
Value: Length; Percentage; Constant (for max properties only) `none`
Example: `elementRef.style.maxWidth = "300px";`

elementRef.style.styleFloat

mozOpacity

Compatibility: WinIE-, MacIE-, NN7+, Moz+, Safari-
Controls: The level of opacity (transparency) of the element as a percentage; the lower the value, the more transparent the element becomes (0% or 0.0 is completely transparent, while 100% or 1.0 is completely opaque).
Value: Percentage, or numeric value between 0.0 and 1.0.
Example: `elementRef.style.mozOpacity = "75%";`

opacity

Compatibility: WinIE-, MacIE-, NN-, Moz1.7.2+, Safari1.2+
Controls: The level of opacity (transparency) of the element as a percentage; the lower the value, the more transparent the element becomes (0% or 0.0 is completely transparent, while 100% or 1.0 is completely opaque). Unlike `mozOpacity`, which is unique to Mozilla, `opacity` is the official W3C standard for opacity.
Value: Percentage, or numeric value between 0.0 and 1.0.
Example: `elementRef.style.opacity = "25%";`

overflow

Compatibility: WinIE4+, MacIE4+, NN6+, Moz+, Safari+
Controls: The rendering of a block-level element's content when its native rectangle exceeds that of its next outermost rectangular space. A `hidden` overflow clips the block-level content; a `scrolled` overflow forces the outermost rectangle to display scroll bars so that users can scroll around the block-level element's content; a `visible` overflow causes the block-level element to extend beyond the outermost container's rectangle (indeed, "overflowing" the container).
Value: Constant `auto | hidden | scroll | visible`
Example: `elementRef.style.overflow = "scroll";`

overflowX
overflowY

Compatibility: WinIE5+, MacIE-, NN-, Moz1.8+, Safari1.2
Controls: The rendering of a block-level element's content when its native rectangle exceeds the width (`overflowX`) or height (`overflowY`) of its next outermost rectangular space. A hidden overflow clips the block-level content; a scrolled overflow forces the outermost rectangle to display scroll bars so that users can scroll around the block-level element's content; a visible overflow causes the block-level element to extend beyond the outermost container's rectangle (indeed, "overflowing" the container).
Value: Constant `auto | hidden | scroll | visible`
Example: `elementRef.style.overflowX = "scroll";`

styleFloat

Compatibility: WinIE4+, MacIE4+, NN-, Moz-, Safari-
Controls: Horizontal alignment of an element that allows other content to wrap around the element (usually text wrapping around an image). Corresponds to the CSS `float` style attribute. See also the `cssFloat` property, earlier in the chapter. Floating (non-positioned) elements follow a long sequence of rules for their behavior, detailed at `http://www.w3.org/TR/REC-CSS2/visuren.html#propdef-float`.
Value: Constant `left | right | none`
Example: `elementRef.style.styleFloat = "right";`

verticalAlign

Compatibility: WinIE4+, MacIE4+, NN6+, Moz+, Safari1.2+
Controls: How inline and table cell content aligns vertically with surrounding content. Not all constant values are supported by all browsers.
Value: Constant baseline | bottom | middle | sub | super | text-bottom | text-top | top; Length; Percentage.
Example: elementRef.style.verticalAlign = "baseline";

visibility

Compatibility: WinIE4+, MacIE4+, NN6+, Moz+, Safari+
Controls: Whether an element is displayed on the page. The element's space is preserved as empty space when the element is hidden. To cinch up surrounding content, see the display property. This property is used frequently for hiding and showing positioned element under script control.
Value: Constant collapse | hidden | visible
Example: elementRef.style.visibility = "hidden";

width

Compatibility: WinIE4+, MacIE4+, NN6+, Moz+, Safari+
Controls: Horizontal dimension of a block-level element. Earlier browsers exhibit unexpected behavior when nesting elements that have their width style properties set.
Value: Length; Percentage; Constant auto
Example: elementRef.style.width = "200px";

zoom

Compatibility: WinIE5.5+, MacIE-, NN-, Moz-, Safari-
Controls: Magnification factor of a rendered element.
Value: Constant normal; Percentage (where 100% is normal); floating-point number (scale multiplier, where 1.0 is normal)
Example: elementRef.style.zoom = ".9";

Positioning properties

See Chapter 40 on the CD-ROM for coding examples of positioned elements and their style properties.

bottom
right

Compatibility: WinIE5+, MacIE5, NN6+, Moz+, Safari+
Controls: The offset measure of a positioned element from its containing rectangle's bottom and right edges, respectively. In practice, you should adjust the size of a positioned element via the style's height and width properties.
Value: Length; Percentage; Constant auto
Example: elementRef.style.bottom = "20px";

left
top

Compatibility: WinIE4+, MacIE4+, NN6+, Moz+, Safari+

Controls: The offset measure of a positioned element from its containing rectangle's left and top edges, respectively. In practice, use these properties to position an element under script control. To position an absolute-positioned element atop an inline element, calculate the position of the inline element via the `offsetTop` and `offsetLeft` properties with some browser-specific adjustments, as shown in Chapter 40 on the CD-ROM.

Value: Length; Percentage; Constant `auto`

Example: `elementRef.style.top = "250px";`

height
width

Compatibility: WinIE4+, MacIE4+, NN6+, Moz+, Safari+

Controls: Height and width of a block-level element's box. Used most commonly to adjust the dimensions of a positioned element (Chapter 40 on the CD-ROM).

Value: Length; Percentage; Constant `auto`

Example: `elementRef.style.height = "300px";`

pixelBottom
pixelHeight
pixelLeft
pixelRight
pixelTop
pixelWidth

Compatibility: WinIE4+, MacIE4+, NN-, Moz-, Safari+

Controls: Integer pixel values for (primarily positioned) elements. Because the non-pixel versions of these properties return strings that also contain the unit measure (for example, `30px`), these properties let you work exclusively in integers for pixel units. The same can be done cross-platform by using `parseInt()` on the non-pixel versions of these properties. The `pixelBottom` and `pixelRight` properties are not in MacIE4.

Value: Integer

Example: `elementRef.style.pixelTop = elementRef.style.pixelTop + 20;`

posBottom
posHeight
posLeft
posRight
posTop
posWidth

Compatibility: WinIE4+, MacIE4+, NN-, Moz-, Safari-

Controls: Numeric values for (primarily positioned) elements in whatever unit was specified by the corresponding `style` attribute. Because the non-pos versions of these properties return strings that also contain the unit measure (for example, `1.2em`), these properties let you work exclusively in numbers in the same units as the style was originally defined. The same can be done cross-platform by using `parseFloat()` on the non-pixel versions of these properties.

Value: Integer

Example: `elementRef.style.posTop = elementRef.style.posTop + 0.5;`

position

Compatibility: WinIE4+, MacIE4+, NN6+, Moz+, Safari+

Controls: The type of positioning to be applied to the element. An element that is not explicitly positioned is said to be *static*. A relative-positioned element appears in its normal page flow location but can be explicitly positioned relative to that location. An absolute-positioned element must have its `top` and `left` style attributes set to give the element a set of coordinates for its location. MacIE5 and NN6+/Moz/Safari also allow for a fixed positioned element, which remains at its designated position in the browser window, even if the page scrolls (for example, for a watermark effect). You cannot use scripts to change between positioned and non-positioned style settings. See Chapter 40 on the CD-ROM for more information on positioned elements.

Value: Constant `absolute | fixed | relative | static`

Example: `elementRef.style.position = "absolute";`

zIndex

Compatibility: WinIE4+, MacIE4+, NN6+, Moz+, Safari+

Controls: Front-to-back layering of positioned elements. Multiple items with the same `zIndex` value are layered in source code order (earliest item at the bottom). The higher the value, the closer to the user's eye the element is.

Value: Integer number; Constant `auto`

Example: `elementRef.style.zIndex = "3";`

Background properties

background

Compatibility: WinIE4+, MacIE4+, NN6+, Moz+, Safari+

Controls: Up to five background style properties for an element.

Value: Combination values: `backgroundAttachment || backgroundColor || backgroundImage || backgroundPosition || backgroundRepeat`

Example: `elementRef.style.background = "scroll url(bricks.jpg) repeat-x";`

backgroundAttachment

Compatibility: WinIE4+, MacIE4+, NN6+, Moz+, Safari1.2+

Controls: Whether the background image remains fixed or scrolls with the content. Default is `scroll`.

Value: Constant `fixed | scroll`

Example: `elementRef.style.backgroundAttachment = "fixed";`

backgroundColor

Compatibility: WinIE4+, MacIE4+, NN6+, Moz+, Safari+
Controls: Solid, opaque color for the background, or completely transparent. If you assign a background image, the color is layered behind the image so that any transparent spots of the image show the background color.
Value: Color value; Constant transparent
Example: elementRef.style.backgroundColor = "salmon";

backgroundImage

Compatibility: WinIE4+, MacIE4+, NN6+, Moz+, Safari+
Controls: The URL (if any) of an image to be used for the background for the element.
Value: URL value; Constant none
Example: elementRef.style.backgroundImage = "url(bricks.jpg)";

backgroundPosition

Compatibility: WinIE4+, MacIE4+, NN6+, Moz+, Safari+
Controls: The left-top location of the background image. Any offset from the left-top corner (default value "0% 0%") allows background color to show through along left and top edges of the element.
Value: Length values; Percentages; Constant left | center | right || top | center | bottom. While single values are accepted, their behavior may not be as expected. Providing space-delimited pairs of values is more reliable.
Example: elementRef.style.backgroundPosition = "left top";

backgroundPositionX
backgroundPositionY

Compatibility: WinIE4+, MacIE4+, NN-, Moz-, Safari1.3+
Controls: The left (backgroundPositionX) and top (backgroundPositionY) locations of the background image. Any offset from the left-top corner (default value "0%") allows background color to show through along left and top edges of the element.
Value: Length value; Percentage; Constant left | center | right (for backgroundPositionX); Constant top | center | bottom (for backgroundPositionY).
Example: elementRef.style.backgroundPositionX = "5px";

backgroundRepeat

Compatibility: WinIE4+, MacIE4+, NN6+, Moz+, Safari+
Controls: Image repetition characteristics of a background image. You can force the image to repeat along a single axis, if you want.
Value: Constant repeat | repeat-x | repeat-y | no-repeat
Example: elementRef.style.backgroundRepeat = "repeat-y";

Border and edge properties

border

Compatibility: WinIE4+, MacIE4+, NN6+, Moz+, Safari+
Controls: Up to three border characteristics (color, style, and width) for all four edges of an element.
Value: Combination values `borderColor` || `borderStyle` || `borderWidth`
Example: `elementRef.style.border = "green groove 2px";`

borderBottom
borderLeft
borderRight
borderTop

Compatibility: WinIE4+, MacIE4+, NN6+, Moz+, Safari+
Controls: Up to three border characteristics (color, style, and width) for a single edge of an element.
Value: Combination values
      (for `borderBottom`) `borderBottomColor` || `borderBottomStyle` || `borderBottomWidth`
      (for `borderLeft`) `borderLeftColor` || `borderLeftStyle` || `borderLeftWidth`
      (for `borderRight`) `borderRightColor` || `borderRightStyle` || `borderRightWidth`
      (for `borderTop`) `borderTopColor` || `borderTopStyle` || `borderTopWidth`
Example: `elementRef.style.borderLeft = "#3300ff solid 2px";`

borderBottomColor
borderLeftColor
borderRightColor
borderTopColor

Compatibility: WinIE4+, MacIE4+, NN6+, Moz+, Safari+
Controls: Color for a single border edge of an element.
Value: Color values; Constant `transparent`
Example: `elementRef.style.borderTopColor = "rgb(30%, 50%, 0%)";`

borderBottomStyle
borderLeftStyle
borderRightStyle
borderTopStyle

Compatibility: WinIE4+, MacIE4+, NN6+, Moz+, Safari+
Controls: Rendered style for a border edge of an element.
Value: Constant `none` | `hidden` | `dotted` | `dashed` | `solid` | `double` | `groove` | `ridge` | `inset` | `outset`.
WinIE versions prior to IE5.5 do not respond to the `dotted` or `dashed` types; MacIE does not respond to the `hidden` type.
Example: `elementRef.style.borderRightStyle = "double";`

borderBottomWidth
borderLeftWidth
borderRightWidth
borderTopWidth

Compatibility: WinIE4+, MacIE4+, NN6+, Moz+, Safari+
Controls: Thickness of a border edge of an element.
Value: Length value; Constant thin | medium | thick (precise measure is at browser's discretion).
Example: elementRef.style.borderBottomWidth = "5px";

borderColor

Compatibility: WinIE4+, MacIE4+, NN6+, Moz+, Safari+
Controls: Rendered color for one to four sides of an element.
Value: Color values for one to four rectangle sides.
Example: elementRef.style.borderColor = "green black";

borderStyle

Compatibility: WinIE4+, MacIE4+, NN6+, Moz+, Safari+
Controls: Rendered style for one to four sides of an element.
Value: One to four rectangle side constants none | hidden | dotted | dashed | solid | double | groove | ridge | inset | outset. WinIE versions prior to IE5.5 do not respond to the dotted or dashed types; MacIE does not respond to the hidden type.
Example: elementRef.style.borderStyle = "ridge";

borderWidth

Compatibility: WinIE4+, MacIE4+, NN6+, Moz+, Safari+
Controls: Thickness of border for one to four sides of an element.
Value: One to four rectangle side length value or constants thin | medium | thick (precise dimension is at browser's discretion).
Example: elementRef.style.borderWidth = "5px 4px 5px 3px";

margin

Compatibility: WinIE4+, MacIE4+, NN6+, Moz+, Safari+
Controls: Thickness of transparent margin space outside the element's borders for one to four edges.
Value: One to four rectangle side length values.
Example: elementRef.style.margin = "10px 5px";

marginBottom
marginLeft
marginRight
marginTop

Compatibility: WinIE4+, MacIE4+, NN6+, Moz+, Safari+
Controls: Thickness of transparent margin space outside the element's borders for a single border edge.

Value: Length value
Example: elementRef.style.marginBottom = "50px";

mozBorderRadius
mozBorderRadiusBottomLeft
mozBorderRadiusBottomRight
mozBorderRadiusTopLeft
mozBorderRadiusTopRight

Compatibility: WinIE-, MacIE-, NN7+, Moz+, Safari-
Controls: Radius of the border around the element. You can specify each radius corner as a series of values in the mozBorderRadius style (one value for all four corners; two values for top-left/bottom-right and top-right/bottom-left; three values for top-left, top-right/bottom-left, and bottom-right; four values for top-left, top-right, bottom-right, bottom-left), or set each corner radius individually with its own property.
Value: Radius length value
Example: elementRef.style.mozBorderRadius = "20px 10px 20px 10px";

outline

Compatibility: WinIE-, MacIE5, NN-, Moz1.8.1+, Safari1.2+
Controls: Up to three characteristics of an outline surrounding an element (similar to a border, but not shifting the location of internal content).
Value: Combination values: outlineColor || outlineStyle || outlineWidth
Example: elementRef.style.outline = "red groove 2px";

outlineColor

Compatibility: WinIE-, MacIE5, NN-, Moz1.8.1+, Safari1.2+
Controls: Color of all four edges of an outline.
Value: Color values; Constant invert
Example: elementRef.style.outlineColor = "cornflowerblue";

outlineOffset

Compatibility: WinIE-, MacIE5, NN-, Moz1.8.1+, Safari1.2+
Controls: The space between an outline surrounding an element and the border of the element.
Value: Length value
Example: elementRef.style.outlineOffset = "3px";

outlineStyle

Compatibility: WinIE-, MacIE5, NN-, Moz1.8.1+, Safari1.2+
Controls: Rendered style for all four sides of an element outline.
Value: Constant none | hidden | dotted | dashed | solid | double | groove | ridge | inset | outset
Example: elementRef.style.outlineStyle = "ridge";

outlineWidth

Compatibility: WinIE-, MacIE5, NN-, Moz1.8.1+, Safari1.2+
Controls: Thickness of all four sides of an element outline.
Value: Length value or constant thin | medium | thick (precise dimension is at browser's discretion)
Example: elementRef.style.outlineWidth = "4px";

padding

Compatibility: WinIE4+, MacIE4+, NN6+, Moz+, Safari+
Controls: Thickness of space between an element's content and its borders for one to four edges.
Value: One to four rectangle side length values.
Example: elementRef.style.padding = "5px";

paddingBottom
paddingLeft
paddingRight
paddingTop

Compatibility: WinIE4+, MacIE4+, NN6+, Moz+, Safari+
Controls: Thickness of space between an element's content and its borders for a single edge.
Value: Length value
Example: elementRef.style.paddingBottom = "20px";

List properties

listStyle

Compatibility: WinIE4+, MacIE4+, NN6+, Moz+, Safari+
Controls: Up to three characteristics of a list (ol or ul) presentation. Also applies to dd, dt, and li elements.
Value: Combination values listStyleImage || listStylePosition || listStyleType
Example: elementRef.style.listStyle = "none inside lower-alpha";

listStyleImage

Compatibility: WinIE4+, MacIE4+, NN6+, Moz+, Safari+
Controls: URL of the image to be used as a marker for a list item.
Value: URL value; Constant none
Example: elementRef.style.listStyleImage = "url(custombullet.jpg)";

listStylePosition

Compatibility: WinIE4+, MacIE4+, NN6+, Moz+, Safari+
Controls: Whether the marker should be formatted inside the wrapped text of its content or dangle outside the wrapped text (default).
Value: Constant inside | outside
Example: elementRef.style.listStylePosition = "inside";

listStyleType

Compatibility: WinIE4+, MacIE4+, NN6+, Moz+, Safari+
Controls: Which of the standard marker sets should be used for items in the list. A change to this property for a single li element causes succeeding items to be in the same style.
Value: For ul elements, constant circle | disc | square
For ol elements, constant decimal | decimal-leading-zero | lower-alpha | lower-greek | lower-latin | lower-roman | upper-alpha | upper-greek | upper-latin | upper-roman, and non-Roman formats when supported by the operating system (as in Mozilla for MacOS X): armenian | georgian | hebrew | cjk-ideographic | hiragana | hiragana-iroha | katakana | katakana-iroha.
Example: elementRef.style.listStyleType = "upper-roman";

Scroll bar properties

scrollbar3dLightColor
scrollbarArrowColor
scrollbarBaseColor
scrollbarDarkShadowColor
scrollbarFaceColor
scrollbarHighlightColor
scrollbarShadowColor
scrollbarTrackColor

Compatibility: WinIE5.5, Mac-, NN-, Moz-, Safari-
Controls: Colors of individual components of scroll bars when they are displayed for applet, body, div, embed, object, or textarea elements. To experiment with how different colors can affect the individual components, visit http://msdn.microsoft.com/workshop/samples/author/dhtml/refs/ scrollbarColor.htm.
Value: Color values; Constant none
Example: elementRef.style.scrollbarTrackColor = "hotpink";

Table properties

borderCollapse

Compatibility: WinIE5+, MacIE5, NN6+, Moz+, Safari1.3+
Controls: Whether a table element adheres to the CSS2 separated borders model or the collapsed borders model. Style is not fully supported in MacIE5.
Value: Constant collapse | separate
Example: elementRef.style.borderCollapse = "separate";

borderSpacing

Compatibility: WinIE5+, MacIE5, NN6+, Moz+, Safari+
Controls: For a table following the separated borders model, the thickness of the spacing between cell rectangles (akin to the cellspacing attribute of table elements). Style is not fully supported in MacIE5.
Value: One length value (for horizontal and vertical spacing) or comma-delimited list of two length values (the first for horizontal; the second for vertical).
Example: elementRef.style.borderSpacing = "10px";

*elementRef.*style.pageBreakAfter

captionSide

Compatibility: WinIE-, MacIE5, NN6+, Moz+, Safari+
Controls: Position of the `caption` element inside a `table` element. Style is not implemented in MacIE5 and is only partially implemented in Safari.
Value: Constant `top | right | bottom | left`
Example: `elementRef.style.captionSide = "bottom";`

emptyCells

Compatibility: WinIE-, MacIE5, NN6+, Moz+, Safari1.3+
Controls: Rendering of cells and their borders when the cells have no content. Default behavior is to not render borders around empty cells. Style is not implemented in MacIE5.
Value: Constant `show | hide`
Example: `elementRef.style.emptyCells = "show";`

tableLayout

Compatibility: WinIE5+, MacIE5, NN6+, Moz+, Safari+
Controls: Whether table is rendered progressively based on fixed width settings of the first row of cells or is rendered after the widths of all row content can be determined. Modifying this property after a table loads has no effect on the table.
Value: Constant `auto | fixed`
Example: `elementRef.style.tableLayout = "auto";`

Page and printing properties

orphans
widows

Compatibility: WinIE-, MacIE5, NN6+, Moz+, Safari-
Controls: The minimum number of lines of a paragraph to be displayed at the bottom of a page (orphans) or top of a page (widows) when a page break occurs.
Value: Integer
Example: `elementRef.style.orphans = "4";`

page

Compatibility: WinIE-, MacIE5, NN6+, Moz+, Safari-
Controls: The page (defined in an `@page` rule) with which the current element should be associated for printing.
Value: Identifier assigned to an existing `@page` rule
Example: `elementRef.style.page = "landscape";`

pageBreakAfter
pageBreakBefore

Compatibility: WinIE4+, MacIE4+, NN6+, Moz+, Safari1.3+
Controls: Whether a printed page break should be before or after the current element and the page break type.

Value: Constant `auto | always | avoid | left | right`
Example: `elementRef.style.pageBreakBefore = "always";`

pageBreakInside

Compatibility: WinIE-, MacIE5, NN6+, Moz+, Safari-
Controls: Whether a printed page break is allowed inside an element.
Value: Constant `auto | avoid`
Example: `elementRef.style.pageBreakInside = "avoid";`

size

Compatibility: WinIE-, MacIE-, NN6+, Moz+, Safari-
Controls: The size or orientation of the page box (linked to the style rule via the page property) used to determine printed pages.
Value: One (same value for width and height) or two space-delimited (width and height) length values; constant `auto | portrait | landscape`
Example: `elementRef.style.size = "portrait";`

Miscellaneous properties

accelerator

Compatibility: WinIE5+, MacIE-, NN-, Moz-, Safari-
Controls: Whether an accelerator key is defined for an element.
Value: Boolean
Example: `elementRef.style.accelerator = "true";`

behavior

Compatibility: WinIE5+, MacIE-, NN-, Moz-, Safari-
Controls: The external behavior to be applied to the current element.
Value: Space-delimited list of URL values. URLs can be a file location, an `object` element ID, or one of the built-in (default) behaviors.
Example: `elementRef.style.behavior = "url(#default#anchorClick)";`

cssText

Compatibility: WinIE4+, MacIE4+, NN6+, Moz+, Safari1.3+
Controls: Actual CSS rule text (read-only). This property exists by virtue of the browser's object model and is not part of the CSS specification. There is no corresponding CSS attribute.
Value: String
Example: `var cssRuleText = elementRef.style.cssText;`

imeMode

Compatibility: WinIE5+, MacIE-, NN-, Moz-, Safari-
Controls: Whether text is entered into a text `input` or `textarea` element through the Input Method Editor (for languages, such as Chinese, Japanese, or Korean).
Value: Constant `auto | active | inactive | disabled`
Example: `elementRef.style.imeMode = "active";`

elementRef.style.*filterObject*

Aural properties

Although these properties are defined in the CSS2 specification and placeholders exist for them in Mozilla-based browsers, the styles are not implemented. The script equivalent properties are listed here for the sake of completeness only.

```
azimuth
cue
cueAfter
cueBefore
elevation
pause
pauseAfter
pauseBefore
pitch
pitchRange
playDuring
richness
speak
speakHeader
speakNumeral
speakPunctuation
speechRate
stress
voiceFamily
volume
```

Compatibility: WinIE-, MacIE-, NN6+, Moz+, Safari-
Controls: A variety of styles primarily for browsers that support speech synthesis output.
Value: Consult `http://www.w3.org/TR/REC-CSS2/aural.html` for details on aural stylesheets.

filter Object

Properties	Methods	Event Handlers
See text		

Syntax

Accessing `filter` object properties and methods:

```
(IE4+)    document.all.objectID.filters[i].property | method([parameters])
(IE5.5+)  document.all.objectID.filters[filterName].property |
          method([parameters])
```

Compatibility: WinIE4+, MacIE-, NN-, Moz-, Safari-

About this object

Earlier in this chapter, the `style.filter` property was shown to allow reading and writing of the string value that is assigned to an element's `style.filter` property. Filters are available in WinIE only, even though MacIE5 returns the `style.filter` property value. The purpose of this section is to teach you not how to use filters but rather, how to script them.

Multiple filters are merely part of the space-delimited list of filters. Some filter types have additional specifications. For example, the `glow()` filter has three properties that more clearly define how the element should be rendered with a glow effect. The stylesheet rule for an element whose ID is `glower` looks like the following:

```
#glower {filter:glow(color=yellow, strength=5, enabled=true)}
```

Accessing the `currentStyle.filter` property for that element yields the string value:

```
glow(color=yellow, strength=5, enabled=true)
```

Attempting to modify a single subproperty of the `glow()` filter by way of string parsing would be cumbersome and hazardous at best. For example, imagine trying to increment the glow filter's `strength` property by 5.

Reading and writing subproperties

A cleaner way to work with individual properties of a filter is to access the filter as an object belonging to the element affected by the filter. Each type of filter object has as its properties the individual sub-properties that you set in the stylesheet. Continuing with the `glow()` filter example, you could access just the `color` property of the filter as follows:

```
var currColor = document.all.glower.filters["glow"].color;
```

To modify the color, assign a new value to the `filter` object's property:

```
document.all.glower.filters["glow"].color = "green";
```

To increment a numeric value, such as increasing the `glow()` filter's `strength` property by 5, use a construction such as the following (long-winded though it may be):

```
document.all.glower.filters["glow"].strength =
document.all.glower.filters["glow"].strength + 5;
```

Table 26-1 lists the filter object names that work all the way back to IE4 and the properties associated with each filter type.

TABLE 26-1

IE4-Compatible Static Filter Types

Filter Name	Description and Properties		
alpha()	Transparency level		
	Properties:	opacity	(0 to 100)
		finishopacity	(0 to 100)
		style	(gradient shape 0 to 3)
		startX	(coordinate integer)
		startY	(coordinate integer)
		finishX	(coordinate integer)
		finishY	(coordinate integer)
blur()	Simulating blurred motion		
	Properties:	add	(1 or 0)
		direction	(0, 45, 90, 135, 180, 225, 270, 315)
		strength	(pixel count)
chroma()	Color transparency		
	Properties:	color	(color value)
dropShadow()	Shadow effect		
	Properties:	color	(color value)
		offx	(horizontal offset pixels)
		offy	(vertical offset pixels)
		positive	(1 or 0)
flipH()	Horizontally mirrored image		
	Properties:	None	
flipV()	Vertically mirrored image		
	Properties:	None	
glow()	Outer edge radiance		
	Properties:	color	(color value)
		strength	(intensity 1 to 255)
gray()	Eliminate color		
	Properties:	None	
invert()	Opposite hue, saturation, brightness levels		
	Properties:	None	

Filter Name	Description and Properties		
light()	Add light source (controlled by methods)		
	Properties:	None	
mask()	Overlay transparent mask		
	Properties:	color	(color value)
shadow()	Render as silhouette		
	Properties:	color	(color value)
		direction	(0, 45, 90, 135, 180, 225, 270, 315)
wave()	Add sine-wave distortion		
	Properties:	add	(1 or 0)
		freq	(integer number of waves)
		light	(strength 0 to 100)
		phase	(percentage offset 0 to 100)
		strength	(intensity 0 to 255)
xRay()	Render edges only		
	Properties:	None	

In addition to the static filter types, which are applied to content and sit there unless modified by script, the IE4+ filter object also provides types for blends and reveals for transitions between visible and invisible elements. Scripting transitions to act when a script hides or shows an element requires a few lines of code, including calls to some of the filter object's methods. First, Table 26-2 shows the IE4+ syntax for transition filters.

TABLE 26-2

IE4+ Transition Filters

Filter Name	Description and Properties		
blendTrans()	Fades out old element, fades in new element		
	Properties:	duration	(floating-point number of seconds)
	Methods:	apply()	(freezes current display)
		play()	(plays the transition)
		stop()	(stops transition mid-stream)

continued

TABLE 26-2 *(continued)*			
Filter Name	**Description and Properties**		
revealTrans()	Reveals element to be shown through an effect		
	Properties:	duration	(floating-point number of seconds)
		transition	(code number for effect)
			0 Box in
			1 Box out
			2 Circle in
			3 Circle out
			4 Wipe up
			5 Wipe down
			6 Wipe right
			7 Wipe left
			8 Vertical blinds
			9 Horizontal blinds
			10 Checkerboard across
			11 Checkerboard down
			12 Random dissolve
			13 Split vertical in
			14 Split vertical out
			15 Split horizontal in
			16 Split horizontal out
			17 Strips left down
			18 Strips left up
			19 Strips right down
			20 Strips right up
			21 Random bars horizontally
			22 Random bars vertically
			23 Random effect
	Methods:	apply()	(freezes current display)
		play()	(plays the transition)
		stop()	(stops transition mid-stream)

To make a transition work under script control, a filter must be applied to the element that you want the transition to work on. That can be done by script or by assigning a filter style to the element. As for the scripting, you begin by invoking the apply() method of the desired filter object. Next, script the change, such as assigning a new URL to the src property of an img element. While you do this, the apply() method freezes the image until you invoke the play() method on the filter. Listing 26-1 effects a checkerboard transition between two images after you click the image.

LISTING 26-1

A Reveal Transition Between Images

```
<html>
  <head>
    <title>IE Transition</title>
    <style type="Lext/css">
    img {filter:revealTrans(transition=10)}
    </style>
    <script type="text/javascript">
    function doReveal() {
        document.getElementById("myIMG").filters["revealTrans"].apply();
        if (document.getElementById("myIMG").src.indexOf("desk1") != -1) {
            document.getElementById("myIMG").src = "desk3.gif";
        } else {
            document.getElementById("myIMG").src = "desk1.gif";
        }
        document.getElementById("myIMG").filters["revealTrans"].play();
    }
    </script>
  </head>
  <body>
    <h1>IE Transition</h1>
    <hr />
    <p>Click on the image to cause a reveal transition.</p>
    <img id="myIMG" alt="image" src="desk1.gif" height="90" width="120"
    onclick="doReveal()" />
  </body>
</html>
```

> **NOTE** The property assignment event handling technique used in this example and the next is a deliberate simplification to make the code more readable. It is generally better to use the more modern approach of binding events using the addEventListener() (NN6+/Moz/W3C) or attachEvent() (IE5+) methods. A modern cross-browser event handling technique is explained in detail in Chapter 25.

Building on the example in Listing 26-1, the next example in Listing 26-2 demonstrates how a script can also modify a filter object's property, including a transition filter. Before the transition filter has its apply() method invoked, the script sets the transition type based on a user choice in a select list.

LISTING 26-2

Choosing Reveal Transitions Between Images

```html
<html>
    <head>
        <title>IE Transition and Choices</title>
        <style type="text/css">
        img {filter:revealTrans(transition=10)}
        </style>
        <script type="text/javascript">
        function doReveal() {
            document.getElementById("myIMG").filters["revealTrans"].transition =
                document.forms[0].transChoice.value;
            document.getElementById("myIMG").filters["revealTrans"].apply();
            if (document.getElementById("myIMG").src.indexOf("desk1") != -1) {
                document.getElementById("myIMG").src = "desk3.gif";
            } else {
                document.getElementById("myIMG").src = "desk1.gif";
            }
            document.getElementById("myIMG").filters["revealTrans"].play();
        }
        </script>
    </head>
    <body>
        <h1>IE Transition and Choices</h1>
        <hr />
        <form>
            <p>Choose the desired transition type: <select name="transChoice">
                <option value="0">Box in</option>
                <option value="1">Box out</option>
                <option value="2">Circle in</option>
                <option value="3">Circle out</option>
                <option value="4">Wipe up</option>
                <option value="5">Wipe down</option>
                <option value="6">Wipe right</option>
                <option value="7">Wipe left</option>
                <option value="8">Vertical blinds</option>
                <option value="9">Horizontal blinds</option>
                <option value="10">Checkerboard across</option>
                <option value="11">Checkerboard down</option>
                <option value="12">Random dissolve</option>
                <option value="13">Split vertical in</option>
                <option value="14">Split vertical out</option>
                <option value="15">Split horizontal in</option>
                <option value="16">Split horizontal out</option>
                <option value="17">Strips left down</option>
```

```
            <option value="18">Strips left up</option>
            <option value="19">Strips right down</option>
            <option value="20">Strips right up</option>
            <option value="21">Random bars horizontally</option>
            <option value="22">Random bars vertically</option>
            <option value="23">Random effect</option>
        </select></p>
    </form>
    <p>Click on the image to cause a reveal transition.</p>
    <img alt="image" id="myIMG" src="desk1.gif" height="90" width="120"
    onclick="doReveal()" />
    </body>
</html>
```

WinIE5.5+ filter syntax changes

While WinIE5.5+ still supports the original IE4 way of controlling filters, the browser also implements a new filter component, which Microsoft strongly encourages authors to use (as evidenced by the difficulty in finding documentation for the IE4 syntax at its developer web site). In the process of implementing this new filter component, the names of many filters change, as do their individual properties. Moreover, the way the filter component is invoked in the stylesheet is also quite different from the original component.

The stylesheet syntax requires a reference to the new component as well as the filter name. Here is the old way:

```
#glower {filter:glow(color=yellow, strength=5, enabled=true)}
```

And here is the new way:

```
#glower {filter:progid:DXImageTransform.Microsoft.Glow(color=yellow,
    strength=5, enabled=true)}
```

Don't overlook the extra `progid:` pointer in the reference. This program identifier becomes part of the filter name that your scripts use to reference the filter:

```
document.getElementById("glower").filters[
    "DXImageTransform.Microsoft.Glow"].color = "green";
```

While some of the filter names and properties stay the same (except for the huge prefix), several older properties are subsumed by new filters whose properties help identify the specific effect. The former `revealTrans()` filter is now divided among several new filters dedicated to transition effects. Table 26-3 shows the IE5.5+ syntax.

NOTE Using the filter syntax introduced in IE5.5+ can cause frequent crashes of the browser (at least early released versions), especially transition filters. If you implement the new syntax, be sure to torture-test your pages extensively. Ideally, you should encourage users of these pages to run IE6+.

elementRef.style.*filterObject*

TABLE 26-3

IE5.5 DXImageTransform.Microsoft Filter Names

Filter Name	Description and Properties		
Alpha()	Transparency level		
	Properties:	opacity	(0 to 100)
		finishopacity	(0 to 100)
		style	(gradient shape 0 to 3)
		startX	(coordinate integer)
		startY	(coordinate integer)
		finishX	(coordinate integer)
		finishY	(coordinate integer)
Barn()	Barn-door style transition		
	Properties:	duration	(floating-point number of seconds)
		motion	(in or out)
		orientation	(horizontal or vertical)
		percent	(0 to 100)
		status	0 (stopped), 1 (applied), 2 (playing)
	Methods:	apply()	(freezes current display)
		play()	(plays the transition)
		stop()	(stops transition mid-stream)
BasicImage()	Element rotation, flip, color effects, and opacity		
	Properties:	grayScale	(1 or 0)
		invert	(1 or 0)
		mask	(1 or 0)
		maskColor	(color value)
		mirror	(1 or 0)
		opacity	(0.0 to 1.0)
		rotation	0 (no rotation), 1 (90°), 2 (180°), 3 (270°)
		xRay	(1 or 0)

Filter Name	Description and Properties		
Blinds()	Action transition with Venetian blind effect		
	Properties:	direction	(up, down, right, left)
		squaresX	(integer column count)
		squaresY	(integer row count)
		status	0 (stopped), 1 (applied), 2 (playing)
	Methods:	apply()	(freezes current display)
		play()	(plays the transition)
		stop()	(stops transition mid-stream)
Checkerboard()	Action transition with checkerboard effect		
	Properties:	bands	(1 to 100)
		direction	(up, down, right, left)
		duration	(floating-point number of seconds)
		percent	(0 to 100)
		slideStyle	(HIDE, PUSH, SWAP)
		status	0 (stopped), 1 (applied), 2 (playing)
	Methods:	apply()	(freezes current display)
		play()	(plays the transition)
		stop()	(stops transition mid-stream)
Chroma()	Color transparency		
	Properties:	color	(color value)
DropShadow()	Shadow effect		
	Properties:	color	(color value)
		offx	(horizontal offset pixels)
		offy	(vertical offset pixels)
		positive	(1 or 0)
Fade()	Blend transition		
	Properties:	duration	(floating-point number of seconds)
		overlap	(0.0 to 1.0 seconds)
		percent	(0 to 100)
		status	0 (stopped), 1 (applied), 2 (playing)
	Methods:	apply()	(freezes current display)
		play()	(plays the transition)
		stop()	(stops transition mid-stream)

continued

TABLE 26-3 *(continued)*			
Filter Name	**Description and Properties**		
`Glow()`	Outer edge radiance		
	Properties:	`color`	(color value)
		`strength`	(intensity 1 to 255)
`Iris()`	Action transition with zoom effect		
	Properties:	`duration`	(floating-point number of seconds)
		`irisStyle`	(CIRCLE, CROSS, DIAMOND, PLUS, SQUARE, STAR)
		`motion`	(in or out)
		`percent`	(0 to 100)
		`status`	0 (stopped), 1 (applied), 2 (playing)
	Methods:	`apply()`	(freezes current display)
		`play()`	(plays the transition)
		`stop()`	(stops transition mid-stream)
`Light()`	Add light source (controlled by methods)		
	Properties:	None	
	Methods:	`addAmbient (red, green, blue, strength)`	
		`addCone (sourceLeft, sourceTop, sourceZAxis, targetLeft, targetTop, red, green, blue, strength, spreadAngle)`	
		`addPoint (sourceLeft, sourceTop, sourceZAxis, red, green, blue, strength)`	
		`changeColor (lightID, red, green, blue, absoluteColorFlag)`	
		`changeStrength (lightID, strength, absoluteIntensityFlag)`	
		`clear()`	
		`moveLight (lightID, sourceLeft, sourceTop, sourceZAxis, absoluteMovementFlag)`	
`MaskFilter()`	Overlay transparent mask		
	Properties:	`color`	(color value)
`MotionBlur()`	Simulating blurred motion		
	Properties:	`add`	(1 or 0)
		`direction`	(0, 45, 90, 135, 180, 225, 270, 315)
		`strength`	(pixel count)

Filter Name	Description and Properties		
RandomDissolve()	Pixelated dissolve transition		
	Properties:	duration	(floating-point number of seconds)
		percent	(0 to 100)
		status	0 (stopped), 1 (applied), 2 (playing)
	Methods:	apply()	(freezes current display)
		play()	(plays the transition)
		stop()	(stops transition mid-stream)
RandomBars()	Bar style transition		
	Properties:	duration	(floating-point number of seconds)
		orientation	(horizontal or vertical)
		percent	(0 to 100)
		status	0 (stopped), 1 (applied), 2 (playing)
	Methods:	apply()	(freezes current display)
		play()	(plays the transition)
		stop()	(stops transition mid-stream)
Shadow()	Render as silhouette		
	Properties:	color	(color value)
		direction	(0, 45, 90, 135, 180, 225, 270, 315)
Stripes()	Striped style transition		
	Properties:	duration	(floating-point number of seconds)
		motion	(in or out)
		percent	(0 to 100)
		status	0 (stopped), 1 (applied), 2 (playing)
	Methods:	apply()	(freezes current display)
		play()	(plays the transition)
		stop()	(stops transition mid-stream)
Wave()	Add sine-wave distortion		
	Properties:	add	(1 or 0)
		freq	(integer number of waves)
		light	(strength 0 to 100)
		phase	(percentage offset 0 to 100)
		strength	(intensity 0 to 255)
xRay()	Render edges only		
	Properties:	None	

elementRef.style.*filterObject*

For more details on deploying filters in IE for Windows, visit `http://msdn.microsoft.com/library/` `default.asp?url=/workshop/author/filter/filters.asp`. Because most of the live examples require WinIE5.5+, be sure to use that version for the best experience at that page.

Chapter 27

Ajax and XML

XML (eXtensible Markup Language) is an undeniably hot topic in the Internet world, and has been for the past few years. Not only has the W3C organization formed multiple working groups and recommendations for XML and its offshoots, but the W3C DOM recommendation also has XML in mind when it comes to defining how elements, attributes, and data of any kind — not just the HTML vocabulary — are exposed to browsers as an object model. Most of the arcana of the W3C DOM Core specification — especially the structure based on the node — are in direct response to the XML possibilities of documents that are beginning to travel the Internet.

During its early explorations into XML and browsers, Microsoft devised a custom HTML element — the `<xml>` tag — that allowed authors to embed XML data into an HTML document. These tags created what were called XML *data islands*. A more practical solution came slightly later with the creation of an ActiveX control that could retrieve XML data (from either a static `.xml` file or a web service that returns XML-structured data) into a web page without disturbing the HTML portion. Scripts could then use W3C DOM methods and properties to read the node tree as needed. Mozilla, Opera, and Safari browsers emulate the behavior of this `XMLHttpRequest` control in a native object so that modern web applications can load external XML data into a page for script inspection and manipulation. In an unusual turn of events, Microsoft has also now implemented the native `XMLHttpRequest` object in IE7 to match the implementation of other browsers

The functionality made possible by the `XMLHttpRequest` object encapsulates the much-hyped buzzword Ajax, which stands for Asynchronous JavaScript And XML. This chapter covers both WinIE XML data islands and the client-side aspects of Ajax (the `XMLHttpRequest` object). Out of necessity, this book assumes that you are already familiar with XML such that your server-based applications serve up XML data exclusively, embed XML islands into HTML documents, or convert database data into XML. The focus of this chapter, and application examples in Chapters 52 and 57, is how to access XML data and apply that data to rendered HTML content.

867

Elements and Nodes

When you leave the specialized DOM vocabulary of HTML elements, the world can appear rather primitive — a highly granular world of node hierarchies, elements, element attributes, and node data. This granularity is a necessity in an environment in which the elements are far from generic and the structure of data in a document does not have to follow a format handed down from above. One web application can describe an individual's contact information with one set of elements, whereas another application uses a completely different approach to element names, element nesting, and their sequence.

Fortunately, most, if not all, scripting you do on XML data is on data served up by your own applications. Therefore, you know what the structure of the data is — or you know enough of it to let your scripts access the data.

The discussion of the W3C DOM in Chapter 14 should serve as a good introduction to the way you need to think about elements and their content. All relevant properties and methods are listed among the items shared by all elements in Chapter 15.

XML data, whether delivered raw or embedded in a WinIE HTML document as a *data island* is a hierarchy of nodes. Typically, the outermost nodes are elements. Some elements have attributes, each of which is a typical name/value pair. Some elements have data that goes between the start and end tags of the element (such data is a text node nested inside the element node). And some elements can have both attributes and data. When an XML data collection contains the equivalent of multiple database records, an element container whose tag name is the same as each of the other records surrounds each record. Thus, the getElementsByTagName() method frequently accesses a collection of like-named elements.

When you have a reference to an element node, you can reference that element's attributes as properties; however, a more formal access route is through the getAttribute() method of the element. If the element has text data between its start and end tags, you can access that data from the element's reference by calling the firstChild.nodeValue property (although you may want to verify that the element has a child node of the text type before committing to retrieving the data).

Of course, your specific approach to xml elements and their data varies with what you intend to script with the data. For example, you may wish to do nothing more with scripting than enable a different style sheet for the data based on a user choice. The XSL (eXtensible Stylesheet Language) standard is a kind of (non-JavaScript) scripting language for transforming raw xml data into a variety of presentations. But you can still use JavaScript to connect user-interface elements that control which of several style sheets renders the data. Or, as demonstrated in Chapters 52 and 57, you may want to use JavaScript for more explicit control over the data and its rendering, taking advantage of JavaScript sorting and data manipulation facilities along the way.

Table 27-1 summarizes the W3C DOM Core objects, properties, and methods that you are most likely to use in extracting data from xml elements. You can find details of all of these items in Chapter 15.

TABLE 27-1

Properties and Methods for XML Element Reading

Property or Method	Description
Node.nodeValue	Data of a text node
Node.nodeType	Which node type

Property or Method	Description
Node.parentNode	Reference to parent node
Node.childNodes	Array of child nodes
Node.firstChild	First of all child nodes
Node.lastChild	Last of all child nodes
Node.previousSibling	Previous node at same level
Node.nextSibling	Next node at same level
Element.parentNode	Reference to parent node
Element.childNodes	Array of child nodes
Element.firstChild	First of all child nodes
Element.lastChild	Last of all child nodes
Element.previousSibling	Previous node at same level
Element.nextSibling	Next node at same level
Element.tagName	Tag name
Element.getAttribute(name)	Retrieves attribute (Attr) object
Element.getElementsByTagName(name)	Array of nested, named elements
Attr.name	Name part of attribute object's name/value pair
Attr.value	Value part of attribute object's name/value pair

xml Element Object

For HTML element properties, methods, and event handlers, see Chapter 15.

Properties	Methods	Event Handlers
src		
XMLDocument		

Syntax

Accessing xml element object properties or methods:

(IE5+)   [window.]document.all.*elementID.property* | *method([parameters])*

Compatibility: WinIE5+, MacIE-, NN-, Moz-, Safari-

About this object

The xml element object is the primary container of an xml data island within an HTML page. If your scripts intend to traverse the node hierarchy within the element, or simply access properties of nested elements,

869

you should assign an identifier to the id attribute of the XML element. For example, if the XML data contains results from a database query for music recordings that match some user-entered criteria, each returned record might be denoted as a recording element as follows:

```
<xml id="results">
    <searchresults>
        <recording>
            ...elements with details...
        </recording>
        <recording>
            ...elements with details...
        </recording>
        <recording>
            ...elements with details...
        </recording>
    </searchresults>
</xml>
```

Your script can now obtain an array of references to recording elements as follows:

```
var recs =
    document.getElementById("results").getElementsByTagName("recording");
```

Although it is also true that there is no known HTML element with the tag name recording (which enables you to use document.getElementsByTagName("recording")), the unpredictability of xml data element names is reason enough to limit the scope of the getElementsByTagName() method to the xml data island.

The W3C DOM Level 2 does not define an xml element object within the HTML section. However, you can embed an XML document inside an HTML document in Mozilla even though the standards clearly indicate that a document can be one or the other, but not both. Of course, the browser understandably gets confused when custom elements have tag names that already belong to the HTML DTD. Therefore, I do not recommend attempting to embed custom elements into an HTML document for NN6+/Moz unless you are very careful to use entirely unique tag names that don't clash in any way with HTML or know how to use XML namespaces within an XHTML document.

Properties

src

Value: String.   Read/Write
Compatibility: WinIE5+, MacIE-, NN-, Moz-, Safari-

The src property represents the src attribute of the xml element. The attribute points to the URL of an external xml document whose data is embedded within the current HTML document.

XMLDocument

Value: Object reference.   Read-Only
Compatibility: WinIE5+, MacIE-, NN-, Moz-, Safari-

The XMLDocument property returns a reference to Microsoft's proprietary XML document object and the object model associated with it (the so-called XML DOM). A lot of this object model is patterned after the W3C DOM model, but access to these properties is through a rather roundabout way. For more details, visit

```
http://msdn.microsoft.com/library/default.asp?url=/workshop/author/dhtml/reference
/objects/xml.asp
```

XMLHttpRequest Object

Properties	Methods	Event Handlers
readyState	abort()	onreadystatechange
responseText	getAllResponseHeaders()	
responseXML	getResponseHeader()	
status	open()	
statusText	send()	
	setRequestHeader()	

Syntax

Accessing XMLHttpRequest object properties or methods:

(IE5+/Moz)   XMLHttpRequestObjectRef.*property* | *method*([*parameters*])

Compatibility: WinIE5+, MacIE-, NN7+, Moz+, Safari1.2+

About this object

The XMLHttpRequest object is an abstract object that lets your scripts retrieve XML data from, or send XML data to, any URL designed for that purpose. All of the action occurs invisibly to the user, and it is the responsibility of your scripts to make the connection with the server and process the XML data either after retrieval or prior to submission. This object was originally designed by Microsoft as part of its XML Core Services (MSXML), as first released as part of Internet Explorer 5 for Windows. Mozilla engineers implemented much of the same functionality in Mozilla browsers, with almost identical syntax. Similar functionality entered the Safari equation in Safari 1.2, not to mention the Opera browser in Opera 8. These latter implementations follow very closely to the Mozilla XMLHttpRequest implementation.

Where the IE and Mozilla variations differ is how you create the object to begin. Because the IE version is an ActiveX control, you create the object using the ActiveXObject constructor function. At least that's the case with versions of IE prior to version 7. In IE7, Microsoft finally got around to supporting the Mozilla object creation approach, which involves using a constructor for the XMLHttpRequest object. If you plan on using the XMLHttpRequest object in versions of IE prior to version 7, which is likely, you must equalize the creation of the two object versions in a single document and branch your code accordingly. Use object detection to handle the branching most effectively:

```
var req = null;
// branch for native XMLHttpRequest object
```

XMLHttpRequest

```
if (window.XMLHttpRequest) {
   try {
      req = new XMLHttpRequest();
   } catch(e) {
      req = null;
   }
// branch for IE/Windows ActiveX version
} else if (window.ActiveXObject) {
   try {
      req = new ActiveXObject("Msxml2.XMLHTTP");
   } catch(e) {
      try {
         req = new ActiveXObject("Microsoft.XMLHTTP");
      } catch(e) {
         req = null;
      }
   }
}
```

Notice in the code how there are actually two different ActiveX objects that support the XMLHttpRequest functionality in IE. The first ActiveX object, Microsoft.XMLHTTP, represents the first incarnation of XMLHttpRequest as found in IE5. IE5.5 supplanted this ActiveX object with a newer one called Msxml2.XMLHTTP, which continued to be the IE-preferred means of accessing XMLHttpRequest through IE6. IE7 added support for the Mozilla-style approach of instantiating an actual XMLHttpRequest object without ActiveX. The example code, therefore, demonstrates how to gracefully create an XMLHttpRequest object while taking into consideration the various browser inconsistencies dating back to IE5/NN6/Moz1/Safari1.2/Opera8.

After the object is created, the basic syntax for opening a connection, sending the request, and retrieving the response data is the same for both WinIE and other browsers. To retrieve an XML document (node tree) from a URL source, the basic conceptual sequence is as follows:

1. Open the request object, specifying the request type and URL.
2. Bind an event handler function to the request object; this function is called when the request finishes.
3. Send the request.
4. Process the results of the request.

Let's take a look at each of these steps and the JavaScript code involved. Following is the code required to open the request object:

```
req.open("GET", "sourceURL", true);
```

This line of code opens the request object by passing along the GET request type, the URL of the data source, and whether or not the request is synchronous or asynchronous. The last argument is undoubtedly the most important because it directly controls whether or not the request is allowed to place in the background (asynchronously) or if the script should wait on the request (synchronously). Seeing as how the word *asynchronous* is in the acronym Ajax, it stands to reason that all Ajax requests pass true as the third parameter to the open() method. The asynchronous nature of Ajax is what gives Ajax applications such a unique feel in that work can be carried out on the server and dynamically reflected on the client as it finishes.

The event handler binding in Step 2 of the previous list involves setting a function reference to the `onreadystatechange` property:

```
req.onreadystatechange = processRequest;
```

The function you assign here is called when the status of the request changes. You will typically only be concerned with the status changing to "complete."

An intermediate step that isn't strictly required involves setting the content type of the request header. The `XMLHttpRequest` object isn't limited to opening XML documents. Because of this, you may want to explicitly set the header type to `text/xml` just to make sure there is no confusion when you are opening XML data; some browsers act very strict with respect to the content type of the header. Following is the code that sets the header's content type:

```
req.setRequestHeader("Content-Type", "text/xml");
```

Step 3, sending the request, is perhaps the simplest step in performing an Ajax request:

```
req.send("");
```

At this point, the request has been issued and you can begin to check and see if it has completed. Control has returned to the browser thanks to the asynchronous nature of the request. The job of checking the status of the request and processing any results falls to the `processRequest()` handler function that was set a moment ago.

The request handler function is automatically called when a change occurs in the state of the request. It is possible for the request to cycle through any of the following states:

- Uninitialized (0)
- Loading (1)
- Loaded (2)
- Interactive (3)
- Complete (4)

The number beside each of the states corresponds to possible values for the `readyState` property of the request object. This is the property you use to find out if the request has finished and is ready for processing. There is one other property, however, that is important before charging into the XML processing. I'm referring to the `status` property, which really has only one value of concern to you, `200`, which means the request was successful.

Pulling this information together enables you to assemble a skeletal request event handling function:

```
function processRequest(req) {
    if (req.readyState == 4 && req.status == 200) {
        var xmlDoc = req.responseXML;
        // further processing of document here
    }
}
```

At this point, scripts can inspect the contents of the `xmlDoc` value by way of W3C DOM node properties and methods.

NOTE   The `XMLHttpRequest` object in some browsers must reference pages served from a web server, and not a local file. You can experiment successfully from a personal web server running on your PC, but not with files accessed through the `file:` protocol.

XMLHttpRequest

Listing 27-1 shows a utility script that retrieves XML content from a URL (passed as a parameter to the `loadXML()` function) in a cross-browser manner. Additional error checking verifies that the retrieval is successful before moving forward. Notice that this code is more of an Ajax template than a functioning example. You have to plug in your own code inside the `processRequest()` function once the `xmlDoc` variable is set.

LISTING 27-1

Utility XML Data Reading Script

```
var req = null;

// retrieve XML document as document object
function loadXMLDoc(url) {
    // branch for native XMLHttpRequest object
    if (window.XMLHttpRequest) {
        try {
            req = new XMLHttpRequest();
        } catch(e) {
            req = null;
        }
    // branch for IE/Windows ActiveX version
    } else if (window.ActiveXObject) {
        try {
            req = new ActiveXObject("Msxml2.XMLHTTP");
        } catch(e) {
            try {
                req = new ActiveXObject("Microsoft.XMLHTTP");
            } catch(e) {
                req = null;
            }
        }
    }

    if (req) {
        req.open("GET", url, true);
        req.onreadystatechange = processRequest;
        req.setRequestHeader("Content-Type", "text/xml");
        req.send("");
    }
}

function processRequest() {
    if (req.readyState == 4 && req.status == 200) {
        var xmlDoc = req.responseXML;
        if (xmlDoc) {
            // get busy processing XML
        }
    }
}
```

Properties and methods described in this chapter are those that the object has in common for both WinIE and Mozilla browsers, as well as Safari and Opera. You can see examples of this object and the template in Listing 27-1 within the applications of Chapters 52 and 57.

Properties

readyState

Value: Integer.   Read-Only
Compatibility: WinIE5+, MacIE-, NN7+, Moz+, Safari1.2+

Your scripts can read the value of the readyState property to determine the state of the XMLHttpRequest object, particularly while it is operating during its initialization or data transfer. Values are the same as for other objects that offer this property. See the bulleted list earlier in this chapter as well as Table 15-6 for integer values and their meanings. When carrying out asynchronous (Ajax) requests, you assign an onreadystatechange event handler to the XMLHttpRequest object, the event function then inspects the readyState property for further processing.

Related Items: status property.

responseText

Value: String.   Read-Only
Compatibility: WinIE5+, MacIE-, NN7+, Moz+, Safari1.2+

After the send() method executes, and if the server returns any data (as it will with a GET operation), you can access a string version of the returned data through the responseText property. If the returned data is an XML document, this property provides a string-only version of the entire content.

Related Items: responseXML property.

responseXML

Value: XML document object.   Read-Only
Compatibility: WinIE5+, MacIE-, NN7+, Moz+, Safari1.2+

After the send() method executes, and if the server returns any data (as it will with a GET operation), you can access the returned W3C DOM—compliant document object through the responseXML property. The object to which this property points is a genuine document node (nodeType of 9), which gives your scripts the power to walk the node tree, and retrieve tags, attributes, and text nodes inside elements, as you would with any DOM document.

As the examples in Chapters 52 and 57 demonstrate, you can use the data from the XML document to build HTML that displays the XML content in the format of your choice (using JavaScript as a more flexible alternative to XSL). If your page is interactive to the extent that users can modify the content, you may then modify the document tree stored in your script variable and send the revised XML back to the server by opening a new XMLHttpRequest connection pointing to the URL that accepts the posted data.

Related Items: responseText property; open() method.

status

Value: Integer.   Read-Only
Compatibility: WinIE5+, MacIE-, NN7+, Moz+, Safari1.2+

After the `send()` method executes, you can read the status of the transaction through the `status` property. The value is an integer corresponding to the response issued by the server at the end of the transaction. A successful transaction value is 200 (corresponding to the OK `statusText` property value). Perhaps the other most common status value is 404, which occurs if the URL you supply to the `open()` method points to a file or source not found on the server. As shown in Listing 27-1, you can use the 200 value as the key to determining if the transaction is a success. You might consider reporting any other value to the user (although inexperienced users may not understand the meaning of the status text).

A complete list of status values and related descriptions (status text) is shown in Table 27-2. Keep in mind that the vast majority of the time you will be concerned only with whether or not the status code is 200 (OK).

TABLE 27-2

HTTP Status Codes for the status Property

Status Code	Status Text
100	Continue
101	Switching Protocols
200	OK
201	Created
202	Accepted
203	Non-Authoritative Information
204	No Content
205	Reset Content
206	Partial Content
300	Multiple Choices
301	Moved Permanently
302	Found
303	See Other
304	Not Modified
305	Use Proxy
307	Temporary Redirect
400	Bad Request
401	Unauthorized
402	Payment Required
403	Forbidden

Status Code	Status Text
404	Not Found
405	Method Not Allowed
406	Not Acceptable
407	Proxy Authentication Required
408	Request Timeout
409	Conflict
410	Gone
411	Length Required
412	Precondition Failed
413	Request Entity Too Large
414	Request-URI Too Long
415	Unsupported Media Type
416	Requested Range Not Suitable
417	Expectation Failed
500	Internal Server Error
501	Not Implemented
502	Bad Gateway
503	Service Unavailable
504	Gateway Timeout
505	HTTP Version Not Supported

Related Items: statusText property.

statusText

Value: String.   Read-Only
Compatibility: WinIE5+, MacIE-, NN7+, Moz+, Safari1.2+

After the send() method executes, you can read the plain-language status of the transaction through the statusText property. The value is a string corresponding to the response integer by the server at the end of the transaction. A successful transaction value is OK (corresponding to the 200 status property value). Use the status property for testing the results in your script, and the statusText property to report errors to users. Table 27-2 contains a list of the possible status text values that may be stored in the statusText property. See Listing 27-1.

Related Items: status property.

Methods

abort()

Returns: Nothing.
Compatibility: WinIE5+, MacIE-, NN7+, Moz+, Safari1.2+

The abort() method stops any transaction currently in progress. This method is the scripted equivalent of clicking a browser's Stop button while it retrieves contents of a web page.

Related Items: readyState property; send() method.

getAllResponseHeaders()
getResponseHeader("*headerName*")

Returns: String.
Compatibility: WinIE5+, MacIE-, NN7+, Moz+, Safari1.2+

For each transaction, the server transmits a series of name/value pairs as a header to the actual data. The getAllResponseHeaders() method returns the complete set as received by the XMLHttpRequest object. Such a header set may look like the following:

```
Date: Mon, 12 Feb 2007 03:12:59 GMT
Server: Apache/1.3.27 (Darwin)
Last-Modified: Sun, 28 Jan 2007 22:13:04 GMT
Etag: "12babe-3a2-3f809770"
Accept-Ranges: bytes
Content-Length: 930
Keep-Alive: timeout=15, max=100
Connection: Keep-Alive
Content-Type: text/xml
```

If you want to retrieve the value of just one of the headers, use the getResponseHeader() method and pass as a parameter a string with only the name portion of one of the headers. For example:

```
var size = req.getResponseHeader("Content-Length");
```

The parameter is not case-sensitive, but the spelling (along with any hyphen in the name) is critical.

Related Items: readyState property; send() method.

open("*method*", "URL"[, *asyncFlag*[, "*userName*"[, "*password*"]]])

Returns: Nothing.
Compatibility: WinIE5+, MacIE-, NN7+, Moz+, Safari1.2+

Use the open() method to specify the transaction type and URL of the destination of the request. The *method* parameter may be either GET (for retrieving data from a server) or POST (for sending XML to a server). The *URL* may be either relative to the current page, or a complete http: URL.

Three additional parameters are optional. The first is a Boolean value for whether the request should be asynchronous. If true (the default), the XMLHttpRequest object does not wait for a response (after the send() method) before continuing with script processing. By setting this parameter to false, you ensure that processing continues only after the transaction has completed or timed out. Of course, this also ensures that the user can't do anything while you wait for the server to process your request and may feel as though the browser has frozen. The preferred approach is to set the parameter to `true` and carry out all requests asynchronously. All of the `XMLHttpRequest` examples in this book (Chapters 52 and 57 primarily) utilize this latter asynchronous (Ajax) approach.

The other optional parameters are strings for a username and password if one is needed to access the URL.

Note that the `open()` method merely fills various properties of the request, and that the request does not occur until the `send()` method is invoked.

Related Items: `open()` method.

send(*content*)

Returns: Nothing.
Compatibility: WinIE5+, MacIE-, NN7+, Moz+, Safari1.2+

After setting the characteristics of the request through the `open()` method and its parameters, invoke the `send()` method to trigger the actual request over the network. For a GET operation, specify `""` or `null` as the parameter. But for a POST operation, the parameter should be a reference to a DOM document that has been assembled in script. You may also specify a string as the value being posted to the request's URL.

Related Items: `open()` method.

setRequestHeader("*name*", "*value*")

Returns: Nothing.
Compatibility: WinIE5+, MacIE-, NN7+, Moz+, Safari1.2+

The `setRequestHeader()` method enables you to specify a name/value pair for the header being sent with the HTTP request. For this method to succeed, it must be called only when `readyState` is set to 1 (Loading); see Table 15-6 for more details. In practical coding terms, this equates to you setting the request header after the call to `open()` but before the call to `send()`.

Related Items: `readyState` property.

Part IV

JavaScript Core Language Reference

Chapter 28

The String Object

Chapter 6's tutorial introduced you to the concepts of values and the types of values that JavaScript works with — features, such as strings, numbers, and Boolean values. In this chapter, you look more closely at the very important String data type, as well as its relationship to the Number data type. Along the way, you encounter the many ways in which JavaScript enables scripters to manipulate strings.

NOTE Much of the syntax that you see in this chapter is identical to that of the Java programming language. Because the scope of JavaScript activity is much narrower than that of Java, you don't have nearly as much to learn for JavaScript as for Java.

IN THIS CHAPTER

How to parse and work with text

Performing search-and-replace operations

Scripted alternatives to text formatting

String and Number Data Types

Although JavaScript is what is known as a "loosely typed" language, you still need to be aware of several data types because of their impact on the way you work with the information in those forms. In this section, I focus on strings and two types of numbers.

Simple strings

A *string* consists of one or more standard text characters placed between matching quote marks. JavaScript is forgiving in one regard: You can use single or double quotes, as long as you match two single quotes or two double quotes around a string. A major benefit of this scheme becomes apparent when you try to include quoted text inside a string. For example, say that you're assembling a line of HTML code in a variable that you will eventually write to a new window completely controlled by JavaScript. The line of text that you want to assign to a variable is the following:

```
<input type="checkbox" name="candy" />Chocolate
```

To assign this entire line of text to a variable, you have to surround the line in quotes. But because quotes appear inside the string, JavaScript (or any language) has problems deciphering where the string begins or ends. By carefully placing the other kind of quote pairs, however, you can make the assignment work. Here are two equally valid ways:

```
result = '<input type="checkbox" name="candy" />Chocolate';
result = "<input type='checkbox' name='candy' />Chocolate";
```

Notice that in both cases, the same unique pair of quotes surrounds the entire string. Inside the string, two quoted strings appear that are treated as such by JavaScript. It is helpful stylistically if you settle on one form or the other, and then use that form consistently throughout your scripts.

Building long string variables

The act of joining strings together — concatenation — enables you to assemble long strings out of several little pieces. This feature is very important for some scripting — for example, when you need to build an HTML page's specifications entirely within a variable before writing the page to another frame with one `document.write()` statement. It is often unwieldy and impractical to include such lengthy information in a single string on one line of code, which is why you will likely need to build the large string out of substrings.

One tactic that I use keeps the length of each statement in this building process short enough so that it's easily readable in your text editor. This method uses the add-by-value assignment operator (+=) that appends the right-hand side of the equation to the left-hand side. Here is a simple example, which begins by initializing a variable, `newDocument`, as an empty string:

```
var newDocument = "";
newDocument += "<html><head><title>Glory Enough for All</title></head>";
newDocument += "<body><h1>The Battle of the Crater</h1>";
newDocument += "by Duane Schultz<hr />";
```

Starting with the second line, each statement adds more data to the string being stored in `newDocument`. You can continue appending string data until the entire page's specification is contained in the `newDocument` variable.

> **NOTE** Excessive use of the add-by-value operator involving large quantities of text can become inefficient. If you are experiencing slow performance when accumulating large strings, try pushing your string segments into items of an array (see Chapter 31). Then use the array's `join()` method to generate the resulting large string value.

Joining string literals and variables

In some cases, you need to create a string out of literal strings (characters with quote marks around them) and string variable values. The methodology for concatenating these types of strings is no different from that of multiple string literals. The plus-sign operator does the job. Therefore, in the following example, a variable contains a name. That variable value is made a part of a larger string whose other parts are string literals:

```
teamName = prompt("Please enter your favorite team:","");
var msg = "The " + teamName + "are victorious!";
alert(msg);
```

Some common problems that you may encounter while attempting this kind of concatenation include the following:

- Accidentally omitting one of the quotes around a literal string
- Failing to insert blank spaces in the string literals to accommodate word spacing
- Forgetting to concatenate punctuation after a variable value

Also, don't forget that what I show here as variable values can be any expression that evaluates to a string, including property references and the results of some methods. For example:

```
var msg = "The name of this document is " + document.title + ".";
alert(msg);
```

Special inline characters

The way string literals are created in JavaScript makes adding certain characters to strings difficult. I'm talking primarily about adding quotes, carriage returns, apostrophes, and tab characters to strings. Fortunately, JavaScript provides a mechanism for entering such characters into string literals. A backslash symbol, followed by the character that you want to appear as inline, makes that task happen. For the "invisible" characters, a special set of letters following the backslash tells JavaScript what to do.

The most common backslash pairs are as follows:

- \\"   Double quote
- \\'   Single quote (apostrophe)
- \\\\   Backslash
- \\b   Backspace
- \\t   Tab
- \\n   New line
- \\r   Carriage return
- \\f   Form feed

Use these "inline characters" (also known as "escaped characters," but this terminology has a different connotation for Internet strings) inside quoted string literals to make JavaScript recognize them. When assembling a block of text that needs a new paragraph, insert the \n character pair. Here are some examples of syntax using these special characters:

```
msg = "You\'re doing fine.";
msg = "This is the first line.\nThis is the second line.";
msg = document.title + "\n" + document.links.length + " links present.";
```

Technically speaking, a complete carriage return, as known from typewriting days, is both a line feed (advance the line by one) and a carriage return (move the carriage all the way to the left margin). Although JavaScript strings treat a line feed (\n new line) as a full carriage return, you may have to construct \r\n breaks when assembling strings that go back to a cgi script on a server. The format that you use all depends on the string-parsing capabilities of the cgi program. (Also see the special requirements for the textarea object in Chapter 20.)

Confusing the strings assembled for display in textarea objects or alert boxes with strings to be written as HTML is easy. For HTML strings, make sure that you use the standard HTML tags for line-breaks (<br>) and paragraph breaks (<p>) rather than the inline return or line feed symbols.

String Object

Properties	Methods
constructor	anchor()
length	big()
prototype†	blink()
	bold()
	charAt()
	charCodeAt()
	concat()
	fixed()
	fontcolor()
	fontsize()
	fromCharCode()†
	indexOf()
	italics()
	lastIndexOf()
	link()
	localeCompare()
	match()
	replace()
	search()
	slice()
	small()
	split()
	strike()
	sub()
	substr()
	substring()
	sup()
	toLocaleLowerCase()
	toLocaleUpperCase()
	toLowerCase()
	toString()
	toUpperCase()
	valueOf()

†Member of the static String object

Syntax

Creating a string object:

```
var myString = new String("characters");
```

Creating a string value:

```
var myString = "characters";
```

Accessing static `String` object properties and methods:

```
String.property | method([parameters])
```

Accessing string object properties and methods:

```
string.property | method([parameters])
```

Compatibility: WinIE3+, MacIE3+, NN2+, Moz+, Safari+

About this object

JavaScript draws a fine line between a string value and a string object. Both let you use the same methods on their contents, so that by and large, you do not have to create a string object (with the `new String()` constructor) every time you want to assign a string value to a variable. A simple assignment operation (`var myString = "fred"`) is all you need to create a string value that behaves on the surface very much like a full-fledged string object.

Where the difference comes into play is when you want to exploit the "object-ness" of a genuine string object, which I explain further in the discussion of the `string.prototype` property later in this chapter. You may also encounter the need to use a full-fledged string object when passing string data to Java applets. If you find that your applet doesn't receive a string value as a Java `String` data type, then create a new string object via the JavaScript constructor function before passing the value onto the applet.

With string data often comes the need to massage that text in scripts. In addition to concatenating strings, you at times need to extract segments of strings, delete parts of strings, and replace one part of a string with some other text. Unlike many plain-language scripting languages, JavaScript is fairly low-level in its built-in facilities for string manipulation. This characteristic means that unless you can take advantage of the regular expression powers of IE4+/Moz1+ or advanced array techniques, you must fashion your own string handling routines out of very elemental powers built into JavaScript. Later in this chapter, I provide several functions that you can use in your own scripts for common string handling in a manner fully compatible with older browsers.

As you work with string values, visualize every string value as an object with properties and methods like other JavaScript objects. JavaScript defines a few properties and a slew of methods for any string value (and one extra property for the static `String` object that is always present in the context of the browser window). The syntax is the same for string methods as it is for any other object method:

```
stringObject.method()
```

What may seem odd at first is that the `stringObject` part of this reference can be any expression that evaluates to a string, including string literals, variables containing strings, methods or functions that return strings, or other object properties. Therefore, the following examples of calling the `toUpperCase()` method are all valid:

```
"blah blah blah".toUpperCase()
yourName.toUpperCase() // yourName is a variable containing a string
window.prompt("Enter your name","").toUpperCase()
document.forms[0].entry.value.toUpperCase() // entry is a text field object
```

stringObject.length

A very important (and often misunderstood) concept to remember is that invoking a string method does not change the string object that is part of the reference. Rather, the method returns a string value, which can be used as a parameter to another method or function call, or assigned to a variable.

Therefore, to change the contents of a string variable to the results of a method, you must use an assignment operator, as in:

```
yourName = yourName.toUpperCase(); // variable is now all uppercase
```

Properties

constructor

Value: Function reference.   Read/Write
Compatibility: WinIE4+, MacIE4+, NN4+, Moz+, Safari+

The `constructor` property is a reference to the function that was invoked to create the current string. For a native JavaScript string object, the constructor function is the built-in `String()` constructor.

When you use the `new String()` constructor to create a string object, the type of the value returned by the constructor is `object` (meaning the `typeof` operator returns `object`). Therefore, you can use the `constructor` property on an object value to see if it is a string object:

```
if (typeof someValue == "object" ) {
    if (someValue.constructor == String) {
        // statements to deal with string object
    }
}
```

Although the property is read/write, and you can assign a different constructor to the `String.prototype`, the native behavior of a `String` object persists through the new constructor.

Example

Use The Evaluator (Chapter 13) to test the value of the `constructor` property. One line at a time, enter and evaluate the following statements into the top text box:

```
a = new String("abcd")
a.constructor == String
a.constructor == Number
```

Related Items: `prototype` property.

length

Value: Integer.   Read-Only
Compatibility: WinIE3+, MacIE3+, NN2+, Moz+, Safari+

The most frequently used property of a string is `length`. To derive the length of a string, read its property as you would read the `length` property of any object:

```
string.length
```

The length value represents an integer count of the number of characters within the string. Spaces and punctuation symbols count as characters. Any backslash special characters embedded in a string count as one character, including such characters as newline and tab. Here are some examples:

```
"Lincoln".length // result = 7
"Four score".length // result = 10
"One\ntwo".length // result = 7
"".length // result = 0
```

The length property is commonly summoned when dealing with detailed string manipulation in repeat loops. For example, if you want to iterate through every character in a string and somehow examine or modify each character, you would use the string's length as the basis for the loop counter.

prototype

Value: String object.   Read/Write
Compatibility: WinIE4+, MacIE4+, NN3+, Moz+, Safari+

String objects defined with the new String("stringValue") constructor are robust objects compared to run-of-the-mill variables that are assigned string values. You certainly don't have to create this kind of string object for every string in your scripts, but these objects do come in handy if you find that strings in variables go awry. This happens occasionally while trying to preserve string information as script variables in other frames or windows. By using the string object constructor, you can be relatively assured that the string value will be available in the distant frame when needed.

Another benefit to using true string objects is that you can assign prototype properties and methods to all string objects in the document. A *prototype* is a property or method that becomes a part of every new object created after the prototype items are added. For strings, as an example, you may want to define a new method for converting a string into styled HTML content that isn't already defined by the JavaScript string object. Listing 28-1 shows how to create and use such a prototype.

LISTING 28-1

A String Object Prototype

```
<html>
  <head>
    <title>String Object Prototype</title>
    <script type="text/javascript">
    function makeItHot() {
      return "<span style='color:red'>" + this.toString() + "<\/span>";
    }
    String.prototype.hot = makeItHot;
    </script>
  </head>
  <body>
    <script type="text/javascript">
    document.write("<h1>This site is on " + "FIRE".hot() + "!!<\/h1>");
    </script>
  </body>
</html>
```

A function definition (makeItHot()) accumulates string data to be returned to the object when the function is invoked as the object's method. The this keyword refers to the object making the call, which you convert to a string for concatenation with the rest of the strings to be returned. In the page's Body, that prototype method is invoked in the same way one invokes existing String methods that turn strings into HTML tags (discussed later in this chapter).

In the next sections, I divide string object methods into two distinct categories. The first, parsing methods, focuses on string analysis and character manipulation within strings. The second group, formatting methods, is devoted entirely to assembling strings in HTML syntax for those scripts that assemble the text to be written into new documents or other frames.

Parsing methods

string.charAt(*index*)

Returns: One-character string.
Compatibility: WinIE3+, MacIE3+, NN2+, Moz+, Safari+

Use the string.charAt() method to read a single character from a string when you know the position of that character. For this method, you specify an index value in the string as a parameter to the method. The index value of the first character of the string is 0. To grab the last character of a string, mix string methods:

```
myString.charAt(myString.length - 1)
```

If your script needs to get a range of characters, use the string.substring() method. Using string.substring() to extract a character from inside a string is a common mistake — the string.charAt() method is more efficient.

Example

Enter each of the following statements into the top text box of The Evaluator:

```
a = "banana daiquiri"
a.charAt(0)
a.charAt(5)
a.charAt(6)
a.charAt(20)
```

Results from each of the charAt() methods should be b, a (the third "a" in "banana"), a space character, and an empty string, respectively.

Related Items: string.lastIndexOf(), string.indexOf(), string.substring() methods.

string.charCodeAt([*index*])
String.fromCharCode(*num1* [, *num2* [, ... *numn*]])

Returns: Integer code number for a character; concatenated string value of code numbers supplied as parameters.
Compatibility: WinIE4+, MacIE4+, NN4+, Moz+, Safari+

Conversions from plain language characters to their numeric equivalents have a long tradition in computer programming. For a long time, the most common numbering scheme was the ASCII standard, which covers the basic English, alphanumeric characters and punctuation within 128 values (numbered 0 through 127).

An extended version with a total of 256 characters, with some variations depending on the operating system, accounts for other roman characters in other languages, particularly vowels with umlauts and other pronunciation marks. To bring all languages, including pictographic languages and other non-Roman alphabets, into the computer age, a world standard called Unicode provides space for thousands of characters. All modern browsers work with the Unicode system.

In JavaScript, character conversions are handled by string methods. The two methods that perform character conversions work in very different ways syntactically. The first, `string.charCodeAt()`, converts a single string character to its numerical equivalent. The string being converted is the one to the left of the method name — and the string may be a literal string or any other expression that evaluates to a string value. If no parameter is passed, the character being converted is by default the first character of the string. However, you can also specify a different character as an index value into the string (first character is 0), as demonstrated here:

```
"abc".charCodeAt()   // result = 97
"abc".charCodeAt(0)  // result = 97
"abc".charCodeAt(1)  // result = 98
```

If the string value is an empty string or the index value is beyond the last character, the result is `NaN`.

To convert numeric values to their characters, use the `String.fromCharCode()` method. Notice that the object beginning the method call is the static `String` object, not a string value. Then, as parameters, you can include one or more integers separated by commas. In the conversion process, the method combines the characters for all of the parameters into one string, an example of which is shown here:

```
String.fromCharCode(97, 98, 99)  // result "abc"
```

NOTE Although most modern browsers support character values across the entire Unicode range, the browser won't render characters above 255 unless the computer is equipped with language and font support for the designated language.

Example

Listing 28-2 provides examples of both methods on one page. Moreover, because one of the demonstrations relies on the automatic capture of selected text on the page, the scripts include code to accommodate the different handling of selection events and capture of the selected text in a variety of browsers.

After you load the page, select part of the body text anywhere on the page. If you start the selection with the lowercase letter "a," the character code displays as 97. If you select no text, the result is `NaN`.

Try entering numeric values in the three fields at the bottom of the page. Values below 32 are ASCII control characters that most fonts represent as hollow squares. But try all other values to see what you get. Notice that the script passes all three values as a group to the `String.fromCharCode()` method, and the result is a combined string. Thus, Figure 28-1 shows what happens when you enter the uppercase ASCII values for a three-letter animal name.

NOTE The property assignment event handling technique employed throughout the code in this chapter and much of the book is a deliberate simplification to make the code more readable. It is generally better to use the more modern approach of binding events using the `addEventListener()` (NN6+/Moz/W3C) or `attachEvent()` (IE5+) methods. A modern cross-browser event handling technique is explained in detail in Chapter 25.

stringObject.charCodeAt()

LISTING 28-2

Character Conversions

```html
<html>
    <head>
        <title>Character Codes</title>
        <script type="text/javascript">
        function showCharCode() {
            var theText = "";
            if (window.getSelection) {
                theText = window.getSelection().toString();
            } else if (document.getSelection) {
                theText = document.getSelection();
            } else if (document.selection && document.selection.createRange) {
                theText = document.selection.createRange().text;
            }
            if (theText) {
                document.forms[0].charCodeDisplay.value = theText.charCodeAt();
            } else {
                document.forms[0].charCodeDisplay.value = " ";
            }
        }
        function showString(form) {
            form.result.value = String.fromCharCode(
                form.entry1.value,form.entry2.value,form.entry3.value);
        }
        document.onmouseup = showCharCode;
        </script>
    </head>
    <body onmouseup="showCharCode()">
        <b>Capturing Character Codes</b>
        <form>
            Select any of this text, and see the character code of the first
            character.
            <p>Character Code:<input type="text" name="charCodeDisplay"
                size="3" /><br /></p>
            <hr />
            <b>Converting Codes to Characters</b><br />
            Enter a value 0-255:<input type="text" name="entry1" size="6" /><br />
            Enter a value 0-255:<input type="text" name="entry2" size="6" /><br />
            Enter a value 0-255:<input type="text" name="entry3" size="6" /><br />
            <input type="button" id="showstr" value="Show String"
            onclick="showString(this.form)" /> Result:<input type="text"
            name="result" size="5" />
        </form>
    </body>
</html>
```

FIGURE 28-1

Conversions from text characters to ASCII values and vice versa.

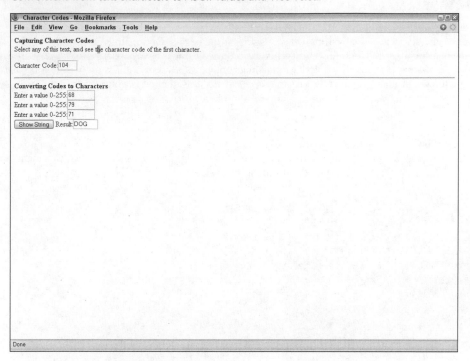

Related Items: None.

string.concat(*string2*)

Returns: Combined string.
Compatibility: WinIE4+, MacIE4+, NN4+, Moz+, Safari+

JavaScript's add-by-value operator (+=) provides a convenient way to concatenate strings. Most browsers, however, include a string object method that performs the same task. The base string to which more text is appended is the object or value to the left of the period. The string to be appended is the parameter of the method, as the following example demonstrates:

```
"abc".concat("def")  // result: "abcdef"
```

As with the add-by-value operator, the concat() method doesn't know about word spacing. You are responsible for including the necessary space between words if the two strings require a space between them in the result.

Related Items: Add-by-value (+=) operator.

`string.indexOf(searchString [, startIndex])`

Returns: Index value of the character within *string* where *searchString* begins.
Compatibility: WinIE3+, MacIE3+, NN2+, Moz+, Safari+

Like some languages' offset string function, JavaScript's `indexOf()` method enables your script to obtain the number of the character in the main string where a search string begins. Optionally, you can specify where in the main string the search should begin — but the returned value is always relative to the very first character of the main string. Such as all string object methods, index values start their count with 0. If no match occurs within the main string, the returned value is -1. Thus, this method is a convenient way to determine whether one string contains another, regardless of position.

Example

Enter each of the following statements (up to but not including the "//" comment symbols) into the top text box of The Evaluator (you can simply replace the parameters of the `indexOf()` method for each statement after the first one). Compare your results with the results shown below.

```
a = "bananas"
a.indexOf("b")      // result = 0 (index of 1st letter is zero)
a.indexOf("a")      // result = 1
a.indexOf("a",1)    // result = 1 (start from 2nd letter)
a.indexOf("a",2)    // result = 3 (start from 3rd letter)
a.indexOf("a",4)    // result = 5 (start from 5th letter)
a.indexOf("nan")    // result = 2
a.indexOf("nas")    // result = 4
a.indexOf("s")      // result = 6
a.indexOf("z")      // result = -1 (no "z" in string)
```

Related Items: `string.lastIndexOf()`, `string.charAt()`, `string.substring()` methods.

`string.lastIndexOf(searchString[, startIndex])`

Returns: Index value of the last character within string where *searchString* begins.
Compatibility: WinIE3+, MacIE3+, NN2+, Moz+, Safari+

The `string.lastIndexOf()` method is closely related to the method `string.indexOf()`. The only difference is that this method starts its search for a match from the end of the string (`string.length - 1`) and works its way backward through the string. All index values are still counted, starting with 0, from the front of the string. The examples that follow use the same values as in the examples for `string.indexOf()` so that you can compare the results. In cases where only one instance of the search string is found, the results are the same; but when multiple instances of the search string exist, the results can vary widely — hence the need for this method.

Example

Enter each of the following statements (up to, but not including the "//" comment symbols) into the top text box of The Evaluator (you can simply replace the parameters of the `lastIndexOf()` method for each statement after the first one). Compare your results with the results shown below.

```
a = "bananas"
a.lastIndexOf("b")    // result = 0 (index of 1st letter is zero)
a.lastIndexOf("a")    // result = 5
a.lastIndexOf("a",1)  // result = 1 (from 2nd letter toward the front)
```

```
a.lastIndexOf("a",2)   // result = 1 (start from 3rd letter working toward front)
a.lastIndexOf("a",4)   // result = 3 (start from 5th letter)
a.lastIndexOf("nan")   // result = 2 [except for -1 Nav 2.0 bug]
a.lastIndexOf("nas")   // result = 4
a.lastIndexOf("s")     // result = 6
a.lastIndexOf("z")     // result = -1 (no "z" in string)
```

Related Items: `string.lastIndexOf()`, `string.charAt()`, `string.substring()` methods.

string.`localeCompare(`*string2*`)`

Returns: Integer.
Compatibility: WinIE5.5+, MacIE-, NN6+, Moz+, Safari+

The `localeCompare()` method lets a script compare the cumulative Unicode values of two strings, taking into account the language system for the browser. The need for this method affects only some language systems (Turkish is said to be one). If the two strings, adjusted for the language system, are equal, the value returned is zero. If the string value on which the method is invoked (meaning the string to the left of the period) sorts ahead of the parameter string, the value returned is a negative integer; otherwise the returned value is a positive integer.

The ECMA standard for this method leaves the precise positive or negative values up to the browser designer. NN6+ calculates the cumulative Unicode values for both strings and subtracts the string parameter's sum from the string value's sum. IE5.5+ and FF1+, on the other hand, return -1 or 1 if the strings are not colloquially equal.

Related Items: `string.toLocaleLowerCase()`, `string.toLocaleUpperCase()` methods.

string.`match(`*regExpression*`)`

Returns: Array of matching strings.
Compatibility: WinIE4+, MacIE4+, NN4+, Moz+, Safari+

The `string.match()` method relies on the `RegExp` (regular expression) object to carry out a match within a string. The string value under scrutiny is to the left of the dot, whereas the regular expression to be used by the method is passed as a parameter. The parameter must be a regular expression object, created according to the two ways these objects can be generated.

This method returns an array value when at least one match turns up; otherwise the returned value is `null`. Each entry in the array is a copy of the string segment that matches the specifications of the regular expression. You can use this method to uncover how many times a substring or sequence of characters appears in a larger string. Finding the offset locations of the matches requires other string parsing.

Example

To help you understand the `string.match()` method, Listing 28-3 provides a workshop area for experimentation. Two fields occur for data entry: the first is for the long string to be examined by the method; the second is for a regular expression. Some default values are provided in case you're not yet familiar with the syntax of regular expressions (see Chapter 42 on the CD-ROM). A checkbox lets you specify whether the search through the string for matches should be case-sensitive. After you click the "Execute match()" button, the script creates a regular expression object out of your input, performs the `string.match()` method on the big string, and reports two kinds of results to the page. The primary result is a string version of the array returned by the method; the other is a count of items returned.

LISTING 28-3

Regular Expression Match Workshop

```html
<html>
    <head>
        <title>Regular Expression Match</title>
        <script type="text/javascript">
        function doMatch(form) {
            var str = form.entry.value;
            var delim = (form.caseSens.checked) ? "/g" : "/gi";
            var regexp = eval("/" + form.regexp.value + delim);
            var resultArray = str.match(regexp);
            if (resultArray) {
                form.result.value = resultArray.toString();
                form.count.value = resultArray.length;
            } else {
                form.result.value = "<no matches>";
                form.count.value = "";
            }
        }
        </script>
    </head>
    <body>
        <b>String Match with Regular Expressions</b>
        <hr />
        <form>
            Enter a main string:<input type="text" name="entry" size="60"
            value="Many a maN and womAN have meant to visit GerMAny." /><br />
            Enter a regular expression to match:<input type="text" name="regexp"
            size="25" value="\wa\w" /> <input type="checkbox"
            name="caseSens" />Case-sensitive
            <p><input type="button" value="Execute match()"
                onclick="doMatch(this.form)" /> <input type="reset" /></p>
            <p>Result:<input type="text" name="result" size="40" /><br />
                Count:<input type="text" name="count" size="3" /><br /></p>
        </form>
    </body>
</html>
```

The default value for the main string has unusual capitalization intentionally. The capitalization lets you see more clearly where some of the matches come from. For example, the default regular expression looks for any three-character string that has the letter "a" in the middle. Six string segments match that expression. With the help of capitalization, you can see where each of the four strings containing "man" is extracted from the main string. The following table lists some other regular expressions to try with the default main string.

stringObject.replace()

RegExp	Description
man	Both case-sensitive and not
man\b	Where "man" is at the end of a word
\bman	Where "man" is at the start of a word
me*an	Where zero or more "e" letters occur between "m" and "a"
.a.	Where "a" is surrounded by any one character (including space)
\sa\s	Where "a" is surrounded by a space on both sides
z	Where a "z" occurs (none in the default string)

In the scripts for Listing 28-3, if the `string.match()` method returns `null`, you are informed politely, and the count field is emptied.

Related Items: `RegExp` object (Chapter 42 on the CD-ROM).

string.replace(regExpression, replaceString)

Returns: Changed string.
Compatibility: WinIE4+, MacIE4+, NN4+, Moz+, Safari+

Regular expressions are commonly used to perform search-and-replace operations. In conjunction with the `string.search()` method, JavaScript's `string.replace()` method provides a simple framework in which to perform this kind of operation on any string.

Searching and replacing requires three components. The first is the main string that is the target of the operation. Second is the regular expression to search for. And third is the string to replace each instance of the text found by the operation. For the `string.replace()` method, the main string is the string value or object referenced to the left of the period. This string can also be a literal string (that is, text surrounded by quotes). The regular expression to search for is the first parameter, whereas the replacement string is the second parameter.

The regular expression definition determines whether the replacement is of just the first match encountered in the main string or all matches in the string. If you add the g parameter to the end of the regular expression, then one invocation of the `replace()` method performs global search-and-replace through the entire main string.

As long as you know how to generate a regular expression, you don't have to be a whiz to use the `string.replace()` method to perform simple replacement operations. But using regular expressions can make the operation more powerful. Consider these soliloquy lines by Hamlet:

```
To be, or not to be: that is the question:
Whether 'tis nobler in the mind to suffer
```

If you wanted to replace both instances of "be" with "exist," you can do it in this case by specifying

```
var regexp = /be/g;
soliloquy.replace(regexp, "exist");
```

But you can't always be assured that the letters "b" and "e" will be standing alone as a word. What happens if the main string contains the word "being" or "saber"? The above example replaces the "be" letters in them as well.

The regular expression help comes from the special characters to better define what to search for. In the example here, the search is for the word "be." Therefore, the regular expression surrounds the search text with word boundaries (the \b special character), as in *stringObject*.**replace()**

```
var regexp = /\bbe\b/g;
soliloquy.replace(regexp, "exist");
```

This syntax also takes care of the fact that the first two "be" words are followed by punctuation, rather than a space, as you may expect for a freestanding word. For more about regular expression syntax, see Chapter 42 on the CD-ROM.

Example

The page in Listing 28-4 lets you practice with the `string.replace()` and `string.search()` methods and regular expressions in a friendly environment. The source text is a five-line excerpt from *Hamlet*. You can enter the regular expression to search for, and the replacement text as well. Note that the script completes the job of creating the regular expression object, so that you can focus on the other special characters used to define the matching string. All replacement activities act globally, because the g parameter is automatically appended to any expression you enter.

Default values in the fields replace the contraction 'tis with "it is" after you click the "Execute replace()" button (see Figure 28-2). Notice that the backslash character in front of the apostrophe of 'tis (in the string assembled in `mainString`) makes the apostophe a non-word boundary, and thus allows the `\B't` regular expression to find a match there. As described in the section on the `string.search()` method, the button connected to that method returns the offset character number of the matching string (or `-1` if no match occurs).

FIGURE 28-2

Using the default replacement regular expression.

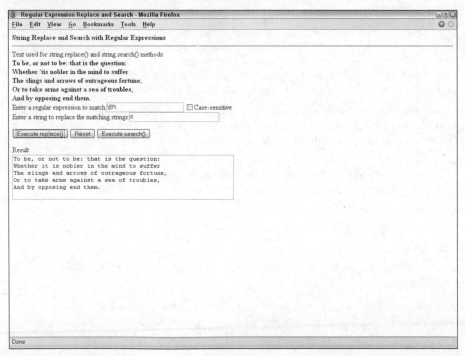

You could modify the listing so that it actually replaces text in the HTML paragraph for modern browsers. The steps include wrapping the paragraph in its own element (for example, a `span`) and invoking the `replace()` method on the `innerHTML` of that element. Assign the results to the `innerHTML` property of that element to complete the job.

LISTING 28-4

Lab for string.replace() and string.search()

```
<html>
   <head>
      <title>Regular Expression Replace and Search</title>
      <script type="text/javascript">
      var mainString = "To be, or not to be: that is the question:\n";
      mainString += "Whether \'tis nobler in the mind to suffer\n";
      mainString += "The slings and arrows of outrageous fortune,\n";
      mainString += "Or to take arms against a sea of troubles,\n";
      mainString += "And by opposing end them.";

      function doReplace(form) {
         var replaceStr = form.replaceEntry.value;
         var delim = (form.caseSens.checked) ? "/g" : "/gi";
         var regexp = eval("/" + form.regexp.value + delim);
         form.result.value = mainString.replace(regexp, replaceStr);
      }
      function doSearch(form) {
         var replaceStr = form.replaceEntry.value;
         var delim = (form.caseSens.checked) ? "/g" : "/gi";
         var regexp = eval("/" + form.regexp.value + delim);
         form.result.value = mainString.search(regexp);
      }
      </script>
   </head>
   <body>
      <b>String Replace and Search with Regular Expressions</b>
      <hr />
      Text used for string.replace() and string.search() methods:<br />
      <b>To be, or not to be: that is the question:<br />
      Whether 'tis nobler in the mind to suffer<br />
      The slings and arrows of outrageous fortune,<br />
      Or to take arms against a sea of troubles,<br />
      And by opposing end them.</b>
      <form>
         Enter a regular expression to match:<input type="text" name="regexp"
         size="25" value="\B't" /> <input type="checkbox"
         name="caseSens" />Case-sensitive<br />
         Enter a string to replace the matching strings:<input type="text"
         name="replaceEntry" size="30" value="it " />
```

continued

LISTING 28-4 *(continued)*

```
        <p><input type="button" value="Execute replace()"
            onclick="doReplace(this.form)" /> <input type="reset" /> <input
            type="button" value="Execute search()"
            onclick="doSearch(this.form)" /></p>
        <p>Result:<br />
            <textarea name="result" cols="60" rows="5" wrap="virtual">
            </textarea></p>
    </form>
  </body>
</html>
```

Related Items: `string.match()` method; RegExp object.

string.search(*regExpression*)

Returns: Offset integer.
Compatibility: WinIE4+, MacIE4+, NN4+, Moz+, Safari+

The results of the `string.search()` method may remind you of the `string.indexOf()` method. In both cases, the returned value is the character number where the matching string first appears in the main string, or -1 if no match occurs. The big difference, of course, is that the matching string for `string.search()` is a regular expression.

Example

Listing 28-4, for the `string.replace()` method, also provides a laboratory to experiment with the `string.search()` method.

Related Items: `string.match()` method; RegExp object.

string.slice(*startIndex* [, *endIndex*])

Returns: String.
Compatibility: WinIE4+, MacIE4+, NN4+, Moz+, Safari+

The `string.slice()` method resembles the method `string.substring()` in that both let you extract a portion of one string and create a new string as a result (without modifying the original string). A helpful improvement in `string.slice()`, however, is that specifying an ending index value relative to the end of the main string is easier.

Using `string.substring()` to extract a substring that ends before the end of the string requires machinations, such as the following:

```
string.substring(4, (string.length-2))
```

Instead, you can assign a negative number to the second parameter of `string.slice()` to indicate an offset from the end of the string:

```
string.slice(4, -2)
```

The second parameter is optional. If you omit the second parameter, the returned value is a string from the starting offset to the end of the main string.

Example

With Listing 28-5, you can try several combinations of parameters with the `string.slice()` method (see Figure 28-3). A base string is provided (along with character measurements). Select from the different choices available for parameters and study the outcome of the slice.

LISTING 28-5

Slicing a String

```html
<html>
    <head>
        <title>String Slicing and Dicing, Part I</title>
        <script type="text/javascript">
        var mainString = "Electroencephalograph";
        function showResults() {
            var form - document.forms[0];
            var param1 =
                parseInt(form.param1.options[form.param1.selectedIndex].value);
            var param2 =
                parseInt(form.param2.options[form.param2.selectedIndex].value);
            if (!param2) {
                form.result1.value = mainString.slice(param1);
            } else {
                form.result1.value = mainString.slice(param1, param2);
            }
        }
        </script>
    </head>
    <body>
    <b>String slice() Method</b>
    <hr />
    Text used for the methods:<br />
    <span style="font-size:larger"><tt><b>Electroencephalograph<br />
    ----5----5----5----5-</b></tt></span>
    <form>
        <table>
            <tr>
                <th>String Method</th>
                <th>Method Parameters</th>
                <th>Results</th>
            </tr>
            <tr>
                <td>string.slice()</td>
                <td rowspan="3" valign="middle">
                ( <select name="param1" onchange="showResults()">
                    <option value="0">0</option>
                    <option value="1">1</option>
                    <option value="2">2</option>
                    <option value="3">3</option>
                    <option value="5">5</option>
```

continued

901

stringObject.slice()

LISTING 28-5   (continued)

```
            </select>, <select name="param2" onchange="showResults()">
                <option>(None)</option>
                <option value="5">5</option>
                <option value="10">10</option>
                <option value="-1">-1</option>
                <option value="-5">-5</option>
                <option value="-10">-10</option>
            </select> )
            </td>
            <td><input type="text" name="result1" size="25" /></td>
        </tr>
        </table>
    </form>
    </body>
</html>
```

FIGURE 28-3

Lab for exploring the string.slice() method.

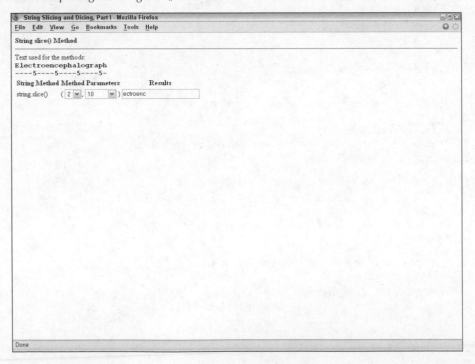

Related Items: `string.substr()`, `string.substring()` methods.

string.split("*delimiterCharacter*" [, *limitInteger*])

Returns: Array of delimited items.
Compatibility: WinIE4+, MacIE4+, NN3+, Moz+, Safari+

The split() method is the functional opposite of the array.join() method (see Chapter 31). From the string object point of view, JavaScript splits a long string into pieces delimited by a specific character and then creates a dense array with those pieces. You do not need to initialize the array via the new Array() constructor. Given the powers of array object methods, such as array.sort(), you may want to convert a series of string items to an array to take advantage of those powers. Also, if your goal is to divide a string into an array of single characters, you can still use the split() method, but specify an empty string as a parameter. For some older browsers such as NN3 and IE4, only the first parameter is observed.

In modern browsers, you can use a regular expression object for the first parameter, enhancing the powers of finding delimiters in strings. For example, consider the following string:

```
var nameList = "1.Fred,2.Jane,3.Steve";
```

To convert that string into a three-element array of only the names takes a lot of parsing without regular expressions before you can even use string.split(). However, with a regular expression as a parameter,

```
var regexp = /,*\d.\b/;
var newArray = nameList.split(regexp);
    // result = an array "Fred", "Jane", "Steve"
```

the new array entries hold only the names and not the leading numbers or periods. A second addition is an optional second parameter. This integer value allows you to specify a limit to the number of array elements generated by the method.

Example

Use The Evaluator (Chapter 13) to see how the string.split() method works. Begin by assigning a comma-delimited string to a variable:

```
a = "Anderson,Smith,Johnson,Washington"
```

Now split the string at comma positions so that the string pieces become items in an array, saved as b:

```
b = a.split(",")
```

To prove that the array contains four items, inspect the array's length property:

```
b.length    // result: 4
```

Related Items: array.join() method.

string.substr(*start* [, *length*])

Returns: String.
Compatibility: WinIE4+, MacIE4+, NN4+, Moz+, Safari+

The string.substr() method offers a variation of the string.substring() method that has been in the JavaScript language since the beginning. The distinction is that the string.substr() method's parameters specify the starting index and a number of characters to be included from that start point. In contrast, the string.substring() method parameters specify index points for the start and end characters within the main string.

stringObject.substr()

As with all string methods requiring an index value, the `string.substr()` first parameter is zero-based. If you do not specify a second parameter, the returned substring starts at the indexed point and extends to the end of the string. A second parameter value that exceeds the end point of the string means that the method returns a substring to the end of the string.

Even though this method is newer than its partner, it is not part of the ECMA standard as of Edition 3 of the language spec. But because the method is so widely used, the standard does acknowledge it so that other scripting contexts can implement the method consistent with browser practice.

Example

Listing 28-6 lets you experiment with a variety of values to see how the `string.substr()` method works.

LISTING 28-6

Reading a Portion of a String

```
<html>
    <head>
        <title>String Slicing and Dicing, Part II</title>
        <script type="text/javascript">
        var mainString = "Electroencephalograph";
        function showResults() {
            var form = document.forms[0];
            var param1 =
                parseInt(form.param1.options[form.param1.selectedIndex].value);
            var param2 =
                parseInt(form.param2.options[form.param2.selectedIndex].value);
            if (!param2) {
                form.result1.value = mainString.substr(param1);
            } else {
                form.result1.value = mainString.substr(param1, param2);
            }
        }
        </script>
    </head>
<body>
    <b>String substr() Method</b>
    <hr />
    Text used for the methods:<br />
    <span style="font-size:larger"><tt><b>Electroencephalograph<br />
    ----5----5----5----5-</b></tt></span>
    <form>
        <table>
            <tr>
                <th>String Method</th>
                <th>Method Parameters</th>
                <th>Results</th>
```

```
        </tr>
        <tr>
            <td>string.substr()</td>
            <td rowspan="3" valign="middle">
            ( <select name="param1" onchange="showResults()">
                <option value="0">0</option>
                <option value="1">1</option>
                <option value="2">2</option>
                <option value="3">3</option>
                <option value="5">5</option>
            </select>, <select name="param2" onchange="showResults()">
                <option>(None)</option>
                <option value="5">5</option>
                <option value="10">10</option>
                <option value="20">20</option>
            </select> )
            </td>
            <td><input type="text" name="result1" size="25" /></t.d>
        </tr>
    </table>
  </form>
</body>
</html>
```

Related Items: `string.substring()` method.

string.substring(*indexA, indexB*)

Returns: String of characters between index values *indexA* and *indexB*.
Compatibility: WinIE3+, MacIE3+, NN2+, Moz+, Safari+

The `string.substring()` method enables your scripts to extract a copy of a contiguous range of characters from any string. The parameters to this method are the starting and ending index values (first character of the string object is index value 0) of the main string from which the excerpt should be taken. An important item to note is that the excerpt goes up to, but does not include, the character pointed to by the higher index value.

It makes no difference which index value in the parameters is larger than the other: The method starts the excerpt from the lowest value and continues to (but does not include) the highest value. If both index values are the same, the method returns an empty string; and if you omit the second parameter, the end of the string is assumed to be the endpoint.

Example

Listing 28-7 lets you experiment with a variety of values to see how the `string.substring()` method works.

stringObject.substring()

LISTING 28-7

Reading a Portion of a String

```html
<html>
    <head>
        <title>String Slicing and Dicing, Part III</title>
        <script type="text/javascript">
        var mainString = "Electroencephalograph";
        function showResults() {
            var form = document.forms[0];
            var param1 =
                parseInt(form.param1.options[form.param1.selectedIndex].value);
            var param2 =
                parseInt(form.param2.options[form.param2.selectedIndex].value);
            if (!param2) {
                form.result1.value = mainString.substring(param1);
            } else {
                form.result1.value = mainString.substring(param1, param2);
            }
        }
        </script>
    </head>
    <body>
        <b>String substr() Method</b>
        <hr />
        Text used for the methods:<br />
        <span style="font-size:larger"><tt><b>Electroencephalograph<br />
        ----5----5----5----5-</b></tt></span>
        <form>
            <table>
                <tr>
                    <th>String Method</th>
                    <th>Method Parameters</th>
                    <th>Results</th>
                </tr>
                <tr>
                    <td>string.substring()</td>
                    <td>( <select name="param1" onchange="showResults()">
                        <option value="0">0</option>
                        <option value="1">1</option>
                        <option value="2">2</option>
                        <option value="3">3</option>
                        <option value="5">5</option>
                    </select>, <select name="param2" onchange="showResults()">
                        <option>(None)</option>
                        <option value="3">3</option>
                        <option value="5">5</option>
                        <option value="10">10</option>
                    </select> )
```

```
            </td>
            <td><input type="text" name="result1" size="25" /></td>
        </tr>
    </table>
  </form>
 </body>
</html>
```

Related Items: `string.substr()`, `string.slice()` methods.

string.`toLocaleLowerCase()`
string.`toLocaleUpperCase()`

Returns: String.
Compatibility: WinIE5.5+, MacIE-, NN6+, Moz+, Safari-

These two methods are variations on the standard methods for changing the case of a string. They take into account some language systems whose cases for a particular character don't necessarily map to the Latin alphabet character mappings.

Related Items: `string.toLowerCase()`, `string.toUpperCase()` methods.

string.`toLowerCase()`
string.`toUpperCase()`

Returns: The string in all lower- or uppercase, depending on which method you invoke.
Compatibility: WinIE3+, MacIE3+, NN2+, Moz+, Safari+

A great deal of what takes place on the Internet (and in JavaScript) is case-sensitive. URLs on some servers, for instance, are case-sensitive for directory names and filenames. These two methods, the simplest of the string methods, return a copy of a string converted to either all lowercase or all uppercase. Any mixed-case strings get converted to a uniform case. If you want to compare user input from a field against some coded string without worrying about matching case, you can convert both strings to the same case for the comparison.

Example

You can use the `toLowerCase()` and `toUpperCase()` methods on literal strings, as follows:

```
var newString = "HTTP://www.Netscape.COM".toLowerCase();
    // result = "http://www.netscape.com"
```

The methods are also helpful in comparing strings when case is not important, as follows:

```
if (guess.toUpperCase() == answer.toUpperCase()) {...}
    // comparing strings without case sensitivity
```

Related Items: `string.toLocaleLowerCase()`, `string.toLocaleUpperCase()` methods.

stringObject.toString()

string.`toString()`
string.`valueOf()`

Returns: String value.
Compatibility: WinIE4+, MacIE4+, NN4+, Moz+, Safari+

Both of these methods return string values (as opposed to full-fledged string objects). If you have created a string object via the `new String()` constructor, the type of that item is object. Therefore, if you want to examine more precisely what kind of value is held by the object, you can use the `valueOf()` method to get the value and then examine it via the `typeof` operator. The `toString()` method is present for this object primarily because a string object inherits the method from the root object of JavaScript.

Example

Use The Evaluator (Chapter 13) to test the `valueOf()` method. Enter the following statements into the top text box and examine the values that appear in the Results field:

```
a = new String("hello")
typeof a
b = a.valueOf()
typeof b
```

Because all other JavaScript core objects also have the `valueOf()` method, you can build generic functions that receive a variety of object types as parameters, and the script can branch its code based on the type of value that is stored in the object.

Related Items: `typeof` operator (Chapter 33).

String Utility Functions

Figuring out how to apply the various string object methods to a string manipulation challenge is not always an easy task. The situation is only made worse if you've been tasked to support legacy or mobile browsers with limited JavaScript support. It's also difficult to anticipate every possible way you may need to massage strings in your scripts. But to help you get started, Listing 28-8 contains a fully backward-compatible library of string functions for inserting, deleting, and replacing chunks of text in a string. If your audience uses browsers capable of including external `.js` library files, that would be an excellent way to make these functions available to your scripts.

LISTING 28-8

Utility String Handlers

```
// extract front part of string prior to searchString
function getFront(mainStr,searchStr){
   foundOffset = mainStr.indexOf(searchStr);
   if (foundOffset == -1) {
      return null;
   }
   return mainStr.substring(0,foundOffset);
}
```

```
// extract back end of string after searchString
function getEnd(mainStr,searchStr) {
   foundOffset = mainStr.indexOf(searchStr);
   if (foundOffset == -1) {
      return null;
   }
   return mainStr.substring(foundOffset+searchStr.length,mainStr.length);
}

// insert insertString immediately before searchString
function insertString(mainStr,searchStr,insertStr) {
   var front = getFront(mainStr,searchStr);
   var end = getEnd(mainStr,searchStr);
   if (front != null && end != null) {
      return front + insertStr + searchStr + end;
   }
   return null;
}

// remove deleteString
function deleteString(mainStr,deleteStr) {
   return replaceString(mainStr,deleteStr,"");
}

// replace searchString with replaceString
function replaceString(mainStr,searchStr,replaceStr) {
   var front = getFront(mainStr,searchStr);
   var end = getEnd(mainStr,searchStr);
   if (front != null && end != null) {
      return front + replaceStr + end;
   }
   return null;
}
```

The first two functions extract the front or end components of strings as needed for some of the other functions in this suite. The final three functions are the core of these string-handling functions. If you plan to use these functions in your scripts, be sure to notice the dependence that some functions have on others. Including all five functions as a group ensures that they work as designed.

A modern alternative to Listing 28-8 utilizes a combination of string and array methods to perform a global replace operation in a one-statement function:

```
function replaceString(mainStr, searchStr, replaceStr) {
   return mainStr.split(searchStr).join(replaceStr);
}
```

Going one step further, you can create a custom method to use with all string values or objects in your scripts. Simply let the following statement execute as the page loads:

```
String.prototype.replaceString = function(mainStr, searchStr, replaceStr) {
   return mainStr.split(searchStr).join(replaceStr);
}
```

Then invoke this method of any string value in other scripts on the page, as in:

```
myString = myString.replaceString(" CD ", " MP3 ");
```

Formatting methods

Now we come to the other group of string object methods, which ease the process of creating the numerous string display characteristics when you use JavaScript to assemble HTML code. The following is a list of these methods:

`string.anchor("anchorName")`	`string.link(locationOrURL)`
`string.blink()`	`string.big()`
`string.bold()`	`string.small()`
`string.fixed()`	`string.strike()`
`string.fontcolor(colorValue)`	`string.sub()`
`string.fontsize(integer1to7)`	`string.sup()`
`string.italics()`	

First examine the methods that don't require any parameters. You probably see a pattern: All of these methods are font-style attributes that have settings of on or off. To turn on these attributes in an HTML document, you surround the text in the appropriate tag pairs, such as `<b>...</b>` for boldface text. These methods take the string object, attach those tags, and return the resulting text, which is ready to be put into any HTML that your scripts are building. Therefore, the expression

```
"Good morning!".bold()
```

evaluates to

```
<b>Good morning!</b>
```

Of course, nothing is preventing you from building your HTML by embedding real tags instead of by calling the string methods. The choice is up to you. One advantage to the string methods is that they never forget the ending tag of a tag pair. Listing 28-9 shows an example of incorporating a few simple string methods in a string variable that is eventually written to the page as it loads. Internet Explorer does not support the `<blink>` tag and therefore ignores the `string.blink()` method.

LISTING 28-9

Using Simple String Methods

```
<html>
  <head>
    <title>HTML by JavaScript</title>
  </head>
  <body>
    <script type="text/javascript">
    var page = "";
```

```
        page += "JavaScript can create HTML on the fly.<P>Numerous string object
            methods facilitate creating text that is " +
            "boldfaced".bold() + ", " + "italicized".italics() +
            ", or even the terribly annoying " + "blinking text".blink() + ".";
        document.write(page);
        </script>
    </body>
</html>
```

Of the remaining string methods, two more (string.fontsize() and string.fontcolor()) also affect the font characteristics of strings displayed in the HTML page. The parameters for these items are pretty straightforward — an integer between 1 and 7 corresponding to the seven browser font sizes and a color value (as either a hexadecimal triplet or color constant name) for the designated text. Listing 28-10 adds a line of text to the string of Listing 28-9. This line of text not only adjusts the font size of some parts of the string but also nests multiple attributes inside one another to set the color of one word in a large-font-size string. Because these string methods do not change the content of the string, you can safely nest methods here.

LISTING 28-10

Nested String Methods

```
<html>
    <head>
        <title>HTML by JavaScript</title>
    </head>
    <body>
        <script type="text/javascript">
        var page = "";
        page += "JavaScript can create HTML on the fly.<P>Numerous string object
            methods facilitate creating text that is " + "boldfaced".bold() +
            ", " + "italicized".italics() + ", or even the terribly annoying " +
            "blinking text".blink() + ".<br />";
        page += "We can make " + "some words big".fontsize(5) + " and some words
            both " + ("big and " + "colorful".fontcolor('coral')).fontsize(5) +
            " at the same time.";
        document.write(page);
        </script>
    </body>
</html>
```

The final two string methods let you create an anchor and a link out of a string. The string.anchor() method uses its parameter to create a name for the anchor. Thus, the following expression

```
    "Table of Contents".anchor("toc")
```

evaluates to

```
    <a name="toc">Table of Contents</a>
```

In a similar fashion, the `string.link()` method expects a valid location or URL as its parameter, creating a genuine HTML link out of the string:

```
"Back to Home".link("index.html")
```

This evaluates to the following:

```
<a href="index.html">Back to Home</a>
```

Again, the choice of whether you use string methods to build HTML anchors and links over assembling the actual HTML is up to you. The methods may be a bit easier to work with if the values for the string and the parameters are variables whose content may change based on user input elsewhere in your web site.

URL String Encoding and Decoding

When browsers and servers communicate, some non-alphanumeric characters that we take for granted (such as a space) cannot make the journey in their native form. Only a narrower set of letters, numbers, and punctuation is allowed. To accommodate the rest, the characters must be encoded with a special symbol (%) and their hexadecimal ASCII values. For example, the space character is hex 20 (ASCII decimal 32). When encoded, it looks like %20. You may have seen this symbol in browser history lists or URLs.

JavaScript includes two functions, `encodeURIComponent()` and `decodeURIComponent()`, that offer instant conversion of whole strings. To convert a plain string to one with these escape codes, use the escape function, as in

```
encodeURIComponent("Howdy Pardner"); // result = "Howdy%20Pardner"
```

The `decodeURIComponent()` function converts the escape codes into human-readable form.

CROSS-REF Both of these functions are covered in Chapter 35.

The Math, Number, and Boolean Objects

The introduction to data types and values in Chapter 6's tutorial scratched the surface of JavaScript's numeric and Boolean powers. In this chapter, you look more closely at JavaScript's way of working with numbers and Boolean data.

Math often frightens away budding programmers; but as you've seen so far in this book, you don't really have to be a math genius to program in JavaScript. The powers described in this chapter are here when you need them — if you need them. So if math is not your strong suit, don't freak out over the terminology here.

An important point to remember about the objects described in this chapter is that (like string values and string objects) numbers and Booleans are both values and objects. Fortunately for script writers, the differentiation is rarely, if ever, a factor unless you get into some very sophisticated programming. To those who actually write the JavaScript interpreters inside the browsers we use, the distinctions are vital.

For most scripters, the information about numeric data types and conversions as well as the Math object are important to know.

Numbers in JavaScript

More powerful programming languages have many different kinds of numbers, each related to the amount of memory it occupies in the computer. Managing all these different types may be fun for some, but it gets in the way of quick scripting. A JavaScript number has only two possibilities. It can be an integer or a floating-point value. An *integer* is any whole number within a humongous range that does not have any fractional part. Integers never contain a decimal point in their representation. *Floating-point numbers* in JavaScript spread across the same range, but they are represented with a decimal point and some fractional value. If you are an experienced programmer, refer to the discussion about the number object later in this chapter to see how the JavaScript number type lines up with numeric data types you use in other programming environments.

Integers and floating-point numbers

Deep inside a computer, the microprocessor has an easier time performing math on integer values as compared to any number with a decimal value tacked on it, which requires the microprocessor to go through extra work to add even two such floating-point numbers. We, as scripters, are unfortunately saddled with this historical baggage and must be conscious of the type of number used in certain calculations.

Most internal values generated by JavaScript, such as index values and `length` properties, consist of integers. Floating-point numbers usually come into play as the result of the division of numeric values, special values such as pi, and human-entered values such as dollars and cents. Fortunately, JavaScript is forgiving if you try to perform math operations on mixed numeric data types. Notice how the following examples resolve to the appropriate data type:

```
3 + 4 = 7 // integer result
3 + 4.1 = 7.1 // floating-point result
3.9 + 4.1 = 8 // integer result
```

Of the three examples, perhaps only the last result is unexpected. When two floating-point numbers yield a whole number, the result is rendered as an integer.

When dealing with floating-point numbers, be aware that not all browser versions return the precise same value down to the last digit to the right of the decimal. For example, the following table shows the result of 8/9 as calculated by numerous scriptable browsers and converted for string display:

NN3 & NN4	.8888888888888888
NN6+/Moz+/Safari+	0.8888888888888888
WinIE3	0.888888888888889
WinIE4+	0.8888888888888888

Clearly, from this display, you don't want to use floating-point math in JavaScript browsers to plan space flight trajectories or other highly accurate mission critical calculations. For everyday math, however, you need to be cognizant of floating-point errors that accrue in PC arithmetic.

In Navigator, JavaScript relies on the operating system's floating-point math for its own math. Operating systems that offer accuracy to as many places to the right of the decimal as JavaScript displays are exceedingly rare. As you can detect from the preceding table, modern browsers agree about how many digits to display and how to perform internal rounding for this display. That's good for the math, but not particularly helpful when you need to display numbers in a specific format.

Until you get to IE5.5, Mozilla-based browsers, and other W3C-compatible browsers, JavaScript does not offer built-in facilities for formatting the results of floating-point arithmetic. (For modern browsers, see the `Number` object later in this chapter for formatting methods.) Listing 29-1 demonstrates a generic formatting routine for positive values, plus a specific call that turns a value into a dollar value. Remove the comments and the routine is fairly compact.

> **NOTE** The property assignment event handling technique employed throughout the code in this chapter and much of the book is a deliberate simplification to make the code more readable. It is generally better to use the more modern approach of binding events using the `addEventListener()` (NN6+/Moz/W3C) or `attachEvent()` (IE5+) methods. A modern cross-browser event handling technique is explained in detail in Chapter 25.

LISTING 29-1

A Generic Number-Formatting Routine

```html
<html>
    <head>
        <title>Number Formatting</title>
        <script type="text/javascript">
        // generic positive number decimal formatting function
        function format(expr, decplaces) {
            // raise incoming value by power of 10 times the
            // number of decimal places; round to an integer; convert to string
            var str = "" + Math.round(eval(expr) * Math.pow(10,decplaces));
            // pad small value strings with zeros to the left of rounded number
            while (str.length <= decplaces) {
                str = "0" + str;
            }
            // establish location of decimal point
            var decpoint = str.length - decplaces;
            // assemble final result from: (a) the string up to the position of
            // the decimal point; (b) the decimal point; and (c) the balance
            // of the string. Return finished product.
            return str.substring(0,decpoint) + "." +
                str.substring(decpoint,str.length);
        }
        // turn incoming expression into a dollar value
        function dollarize(expr) {
            return "$" + format(expr,2);
        }
        </script>
    </head>
    <body>
        <h1>How to Make Money</h1>
        <form>
            Enter a positive floating point value or arithmetic expression to be
            converted to a currency format:
            <p><input type="text" name="entry" value="1/3" /> <input type="button"
                id="dollars" value="&gt;Dollars and Cents&gt;"
                onclick="this.form.result.value=dollarize(this.form.entry.value)"
                />
                <input type="text" name="result" /></p>
        </form>
    </body>
</html>
```

This routine may seem like a great deal of work, but it's essential if your application relies on floating-point values and specific formatting for all browsers.

You can also enter floating-point numbers with exponents. An exponent is signified by the letter "e" (upper- or lowercase), followed by a sign (+ or –) and the exponent value. Here are examples of floating-point values expressed as exponents:

```
1e6 // 1,000,000 (the "+" symbol is optional on positive exponents)
1e-4 // 0.0001 (plus some error further to the right of the decimal)
-4e-3 // -0.004
```

For values between 1e-5 and 1e15, JavaScript renders numbers without exponents (although you can force a number to display in exponential notation in modern browsers). All other values outside these boundaries return with exponential notation in all browsers.

Hexadecimal and octal integers

JavaScript enables you to work with values in decimal (base-10), hexadecimal (base-16), and octal (base-8) formats. You have only a few rules to follow when dealing with any of these values.

Decimal values cannot begin with a leading 0. Therefore, if your page asks users to enter decimal values that begin with a 0, your script must strip those zeros from the input string or use the number parsing global functions (described in the next section) before performing any math on the values.

Hexadecimal integer values are expressed with a leading 0x or 0X. (That's a zero, not the letter "o.") The A through F values can appear in upper- or lowercase, as you prefer. Here are some hex values:

```
0X2B
0X1a
0xcc
```

Don't confuse the hex values used in arithmetic with the hexadecimal values used in color property specifications for web documents. Those values are expressed in a special *hexadecimal triplet* format, which begins with a crosshatch symbol followed by the three hex values bunched together (such as #c0c0c0).

Octal values are represented by a leading 0 followed by any digits between 0 and 7. Octal values consist only of integers.

You are free to mix and match base values in arithmetic expressions, but JavaScript renders all results in decimal form. For conversions to other number bases, you have to employ a user-defined function in your script. Listing 29-2, for example, is a function that converts any decimal value from 0 to 255 into a JavaScript hexadecimal value.

LISTING 29-2

Decimal-to-Hexadecimal Converter Function

```
function toHex(dec) {
   hexChars = "0123456789ABCDEF";
   if (dec > 255) {
      return null;
   }
   var i = dec % 16;
   var j = (dec - i) / 16;
   result = "0X";
   result += hexChars.charAt(j);
```

```
result += hexChars.charAt(i);
return result;
}
```

The toHex() conversion function assumes that the value passed to the function is a decimal integer. If you simply need a hexadecimal representation of a number in string format, see the toString() method in Chapter 35.

Converting strings to numbers

What is missing so far from this discussion is a way to convert a number represented as a string to a number with which the JavaScript arithmetic operators can work. Before you get too concerned about this, be aware that most JavaScript operators and math methods gladly accept string representations of numbers and handle them without complaint. You will run into data type incompatibilities most frequently when trying to accomplish addition with the + operator (which is also the string concatenation operator). Also know that if you perform math operations on values retrieved from form text boxes, those object value properties are strings. Therefore, in many cases, you need to convert those values to values of the number type for math operations.

Conversion to numbers requires one of two JavaScript functions:

```
parseInt(string [,radix])
parseFloat(string [,radix])
```

These functions are inspired by the Java language. The term *parsing* has many implied meanings in programming. One meaning is the same as *extracting*. The parseInt() function returns whatever integer value it can extract from the string passed to it; the parseFloat() function returns the floating-point number that can be extracted from the string. Here are some examples and their resulting values:

```
parseInt("42")          // result = 42
parseInt("42.33")       // result = 42
parseFloat("42.33")     // result = 42.33
parseFloat("42")        // result = 42
parseFloat("fred")      // result = NaN
```

Because the parseFloat() function can also work with an integer and return an integer value, you may prefer using this function in scripts that have to deal with either kind of number, depending on the string entered into a text field by a user.

An optional second parameter to both functions enables you to specify the base of the number represented by the string. This comes in handy particularly when you need a decimal number from a string that starts with one or more zeros. Normally, the leading zero indicates an octal value. But if you force the conversion to recognize the string value as a decimal, it is converted the way you expect:

```
parseInt("010")         // result = 8
parseInt("010",10)      // result = 10
parseInt("F2")          // result = NaN
parseInt("F2", 16)      // result = 242
```

Use these functions wherever you need the integer or floating-point value. For example:

```
var result = 3 + parseInt("3");    // result = 6
var ageVal = parseInt(document.forms[0].age.value);
```

The latter technique ensures that the string value of this property is converted to a number (although you should do more data validation — see Chapter 43 on the CD-ROM — before trying any math on a user-entered value).

Both the parseInt() and parseFloat() methods start working on the first character of a string and continue until there are no more numbers or decimal characters. That's why you can use them on strings — such as the one returned by the navigator.appVersion property (for example, 6.0 (Windows; en-US)) — to obtain just the leading, numeric part of the string. If the string does not begin with an acceptable character, the methods return NaN (not a number).

Converting numbers to strings

If you attempt to pass a numeric data type value to many of the string methods discussed in Chapter 28, JavaScript complains. Therefore, you should convert any number to a string before you, for example, find out how many digits make up a number.

Several ways exist to force conversion from any numeric value to a string. The old-fashioned way is to precede the number with an empty string and the concatenation operator. For example, assume that a variable named dollars contains the integer value of 2500. To use the string object's length property (discussed later in this chapter) to find out how many digits the number has, use this construction:

```
("" + dollars).length    // result = 4
```

The parentheses force JavaScript to evaluate the concatenation before attempting to extract the length property.

A more elegant way is to use the toString() method. Construct such statements as you do to invoke any object's method. For example, to convert the dollars variable value to a string, use this statement:

```
dollars.toString()    // result = "2500"
```

This method has one added power in modern browsers: You can specify a number base for the string representation of the number. Called the *radix,* the base number is added as a parameter to the method name. Here is an example of creating a numeric value for conversion to its hexadecimal equivalent as a string:

```
var x = 30;
var y = x.toString(16);    // result = "1e"
```

Use a parameter of 2 for binary results and 8 for octal. The default is base 10. Be careful not to confuse these conversions with true numeric conversions. You cannot use results from the toString() method as numeric operands in other statements.

Finally, in IE5.5+, Mozilla-based browsers, and other W3C browsers, three additional methods of the Number object — toExponential(), toFixed(), and toPrecision() — return string versions of numbers formatted according to the rules and parameters passed to the methods. I describe these in detail later in this chapter.

When a number isn't a number

In a couple of examples in the previous section, you probably noticed that the result of some operations was a value named NaN. That value is not a string but rather a special value that stands for Not a Number. For example, if you try to convert the string "joe" to an integer with parseFloat(), the function cannot possibly complete the operation. It reports back that the source string, when converted, is not a number.

When you design an application that requests user input or retrieves data from a server-side database, you cannot be guaranteed that a value you need to be numeric is, or can be converted to, a number. If that's the case, you need to see if the value is a number before performing some math operation on it. JavaScript provides a special global function, isNaN(), that enables you to test the "numberness" of a value. The function returns true if the value is not a number and false if it is a number. For example, you can examine a form field that should be a number:

```
var ageEntry = parseInt(document.forms[0].age.value);
if (isNaN(ageEntry)) {
    alert("Try entering your age again.");
}
```

Math Object

Whenever you need to perform math that is more demanding than simple arithmetic, look through the list of Math object methods for the solution.

Syntax

Accessing Math object properties and methods:

```
Math.property
Math.method(value [, value])
```

Compatibility: WinIE3+, MacIE3+, NN2+, Moz+, Safari+

About this object

In addition to the typical arithmetic operations (covered in detail in Chapter 33), JavaScript includes more advanced mathematical powers that you can access in a way that may seem odd to you if you have not programmed in true object-oriented environments before. Although most arithmetic takes place on the fly (such as var result = 2 + 2), the rest requires use of the JavaScript internal Math object (with a capital "M"). The Math object brings with it several properties (which behave like some other languages' constants) and many methods (which behave like some other languages' math functions).

The way you use the Math object in statements is the same way you use any JavaScript object: You create a reference beginning with the Math object's name, a period, and the name of the property or method you need:

```
Math.property | method([parameter]. . . [,parameter])
```

Property references return the built-in values (things such as pi). Method references require one or more values to be sent as parameters of the method. Every method returns a result.

Properties

JavaScript Math object properties represent a number of valuable constant values in math. Table 29-1 shows you those methods and their values as displayed to 16 decimal places.

TABLE 29-1

JavaScript Math Properties

Property	Value	Description
Math.E	2.718281828459045091	Euler's constant
Math.LN2	0.6931471805599452862	Natural log of 2
Math.LN10	2.302585092994045901	Natural log of 10
Math.LOG2E	1.442695040888963387	Log base-2 of E
Math.LOG10E	0.4342944819032518167	Log base-10 of E
Math.PI	3.141592653589793116	π
Math.SQRT1_2	0.7071067811865475727	Square root of 0.5
Math.SQRT2	1.414213562373095145	Square root of 2

Because these property expressions return their constant values, you use them in your regular arithmetic expressions. For example, to obtain the circumference of a circle whose diameter is in variable d, employ this statement:

```
circumference = d * Math.PI;
```

Perhaps the most common mistakes scripters make with these properties are failing to capitalize the Math object name and observing the case-sensitivity of property names.

Methods

Methods make up the balance of JavaScript Math object powers. With the exception of the Math.random() method, all Math object methods take one or more values as parameters. Typical trigonometric methods operate on the single values passed as parameters; others determine which of the numbers passed along are the highest or lowest of the group. The Math.random() method takes no parameters but returns a randomized, floating-point value between 0 and 1. Table 29-2 lists all the Math object methods with their syntax and descriptions of the values they return.

TABLE 29-2

Math Object Methods

Method Syntax	Returns
Math.abs(*val*)	Absolute value of *val*
Math.acos(*val*)	Arc cosine (in radians) of *val*
Math.asin(*val*)	Arc sine (in radians) of *val*
Math.atan(*val*)	Arc tangent (in radians) of *val*
Math.atan2(*val1*, *val2*)	Angle of polar coordinates *x* and *y*
Math.ceil(*val*)	Next integer greater than or equal to *val*
Math.cos(*val*)	Cosine of *val*

`Math.exp(val)`	Euler's constant to the power of *val*
`Math.floor(val)`	Next integer less than or equal to *val*
`Math.log(val)`	Natural logarithm (base e) of *val*
`Math.max(val1, val2)`	The greater of *val1* or *val2*
`Math.min(val1, val2)`	The lesser of *val1* or *val2*
`Math.pow(val1, val2)`	*Val1* to the *val2* power
`Math.random()`	Random number between 0 and 1
`Math.round(val)`	N+1 when *val* >= n.5; otherwise N
`Math.sin(val)`	Sine (in radians) of *val*
`Math.sqrt(val)`	Square root of *val*
`Math.tan(val)`	Tangent (in radians) of *val*

HTML is not exactly a graphic artist's dream environment, so using trig functions to obtain a series of values for HTML-generated charting is not a hot JavaScript prospect. Only with the advent of positionable elements have scripters been able to apply their knowledge of using these functions to define fancy trajectories for flying elements. For scripters who are not trained in programming, math is often a major stumbling block. But as you've seen so far, you can accomplish a great deal with JavaScript by using simple arithmetic and a little bit of logic — leaving the heavy-duty math for those who love it.

Creating random numbers

One of the handiest methods in the `Math` object is `Math.random()`, which returns a random floating-point value between 0 and 1. If you design a script to act like a card game, you need random integers between 1 and 52; for dice, the range is 1 to 6 per die. To generate a random integer between zero and any top value (n), use the following formula:

```
Math.floor(Math.random() * n)
```

Here, n is the top number. To generate random numbers between a range that starts somewhere other than zero, use this formula:

```
Math.floor(Math.random() * (n - m + 1)) + m
```

Here, m is the lowest possible integer value of the range and n equals the top number of the range. For the dice game, the formula for each die is

```
newDieValue = Math.floor(Math.random() * 6) + 1;
```

Math object shortcut

In Chapter 32, you see details about a JavaScript construction that enables you to simplify the way you address multiple `Math` object properties and methods in statements. The trick is to use the `with` statement.

In a nutshell, the `with` statement tells JavaScript that the next group of statements (inside the braces) refers to a particular object. In the case of the `Math` object, the basic construction looks like this:

```
with (Math) {
    //statements
}
```

For all intervening statements, you can omit the specific references to the Math object. Compare the long reference way of calculating the area of a circle (with a radius of six units)

```
result = Math.pow(6,2) * Math.PI;
```

to the shortcut reference way:

```
with (Math) {
    result = pow(6,2) * PI;
}
```

Though the latter occupies more lines of code, the object references are shorter and more natural when reading the code. For a longer series of calculations involving Math object properties and methods, the with construction saves keystrokes and reduces the likelihood of a case-sensitive mistake with the object name in a reference. You can also include other full-object references within the with construction; JavaScript attempts to attach the object name only to those references lacking an object name. On the downside, the with construction is not particularly efficient in JavaScript because it must perform a lot of internal tracking in order to work.

Number Object

Properties	Methods
constructor	toExponential()
MAX_VALUE	toFixed()
MIN_VALUE	toLocaleString()
NaN	toString()
NEGATIVE_INFINITY	toPrecision()
POSITIVE_INFINITY	valueOf()
prototype	

Syntax

Creating a number object:

```
var val = new Number(number);
```

Accessing number and Number object properties and methods:

```
number.property | method([parameters])
Number.property | method([parameters])
```

Compatibility: WinIE4+, MacIE4+, NN3+, Moz+, Safari+

About this object

The Number object is rarely used because (for the most part) JavaScript satisfies day-to-day numeric needs with a plain number value. But the Number object contains some information and power of value to serious programmers.

First on the docket are properties that define the ranges for numbers in the language. The largest number is 1.79E+308; the smallest number is 2.22E-308. Any number larger than the maximum is POSITIVE_INFINITY; any number smaller than the minimum is NEGATIVE_INFINITY. Rarely will you accidentally encounter these values.

More to the point of a JavaScript object, however, is the prototype property. Chapter 28 shows how to add a method to a string object's prototype such that every newly created object contains that method. The same goes for the Number.prototype property. If you have a need to add common functionality to every number object, this is where to do it. This prototype facility is unique to full-fledged number objects and does not apply to plain number values. For experienced programmers who care about such matters, JavaScript number objects and values are defined internally as ieee double-precision 64-bit values.

Properties

constructor

(See string.constructor in Chapter 28)

MAX_VALUE
MIN_VALUE
NEGATIVE_INFINITY
POSITIVE_INFINITY

Value: Number.   Read-Only
Compatibility: WinIE4+, MacIE4+, NN3+, Moz+, Safari+

The Number.MAX_VALUE and Number.MIN_VALUE properties belong to the static Number object. They represent constants for the largest and smallest possible positive numbers that JavaScript (and ECMAScript) can work with. Their actual values are $1.7976931348623157 \times 10^{308}$, and 5×10^{-324}, respectively.

A number that falls outside the range of allowable numbers is equal to the constant Number.POSITIVE_INFINITY or Number.NEGATIVE_INFINITY.

Example

Enter each of the four Number object expressions into the top text field of The Evaluator (Chapter 13) to see how the browser reports each value.

```
Number.MAX_VALUE
Number.MIN_VALUE
Number.NEGATIVE_INFINITY
Number.POSITIVE_INFINITY
```

Related Items: NaN property; isNaN() global function.

NaN

Value: NaN.   Read-Only
Compatibility: WinIE4+, MacIE4+, NN3+, Moz+, Safari+

The NaN property is a constant that JavaScript uses to report when a number-related function or method attempts to work on a value other than a number or the result is something other than a number. You encounter the NaN value most commonly as the result of the parseInt() and parseFloat() functions whenever a string undergoing conversion to a number lacks a numeral as the first character. Use the isNaN() global function to see if a value is an NaN value.

Example

See the discussion of the isNaN() function in Chapter 35.

Related Item: isNaN() global function.

prototype

(See String.prototype in Chapter 28)

Methods

`number.toExponential(`*fractionDigits*`)`

`number.toFixed(`*fractionDigits*`)`

`number.toPrecision(`*precisionDigits*`)`

Returns: String.
Compatibility: WinIE5.5+, MacIE-, NN6+, Moz+, Safari+

These three methods let scripts control the formatting of numbers for display as string text. Each method has a unique purpose, but they all return strings. You should perform all math operations as unformatted number objects because the values have the most precision. Only after you are ready to display the results should you use one of these methods to convert the number to a string for display as body text or assignment to a text field.

The toExponential() method forces a number to display in exponential notation, even if the number is in the range in which JavaScript normally uses standard notation. The parameter is an integer specifying how many digits to the right of the decimal should be returned. All digits to the right of the decimal are returned, even if they are zero. For example, if a variable contains the numeric value 345, applying toExponential(3) to that value yields 3.450e+2, which is JavaScript's exponential notation for 3.45×10^2.

Use the toFixed() method when you want to format a number with a specific number of digits to the right of the decimal. This is the method you use, for instance, to display the results of a financial calculation in units and hundredths of units (for example, dollars and cents). The parameter to the method is an integer indicating the number of digits to be displayed to the right of the decimal. If the number being formatted has more numbers to the right of the decimal than the number of digits specified by the parameter, the method rounds the rightmost visible digit — but only with respect to the unrounded value of the next digit. For example, the value 123.455 fixed to two digits to the right of the decimal is rounded up to 123.46. But if the starting value is 123.4549, the method ignores the 9 and sees that the 4 to the right of the 5 should be rounded down; therefore, the result is 123.45. Do not consider the toFixed() method to be an accurate rounder of numbers; however, it does a satisfactory job in most cases.

The final method is `toPrecision()`, which enables you to define how many total digits (including digits to the left and right of the decimal) to display of a number. In other words, you define the precision of a number. The following list demonstrates the results of several parameter values signifying a variety of precisions:

```
var num = 123.45
num.toPrecision(1)    // result = 1e+2
num.toPrecision(2)    // result = 1.2e+2
num.toPrecision(3)    // result = 123
num.toPrecision(4)    // result = 123.5
num.toPrecision(5)    // result = 123.45
num.toPrecision(6)    // result = 123.450
```

Notice that the same kind of rounding can occur with `toPrecision()` as it does for `toFixed()`.

Example

You can use The Evaluator (Chapter 13) to experiment with all three of these methods with a variety of parameter values. Before invoking any method, be sure to assign a numeric value to one of the built-in global variables in The Evaluator (a through z).

```
a = 10/3
a.toFixed(4)
"$" + a.toFixed(2)
```

None of these methods works with number literals (for example, `123.toExponential(2)` does not work).

Related Item: `Math` object.

number.toLocaleString()

Returns: String.
Compatibility: WinIE5.5+, MacIE5+, NN6+, Moz+, Safari+

The `number.toLocaleString()` method returns a string value version of the current number in a format that may vary according to a browser's locale settings. According to the ECMA Edition 3 standard, browsers have some leeway in determining exactly how the `toLocaleString()` method should return a string value that conforms with the language standard of the client system or browser.

Related Items: `number.toFixed()`, `number.toString()` methods.

number.toString([*radix*])

Returns: String.
Compatibility: WinIE4+, MacIE4+, NN4+, Moz+, Safari+

The `number.toString()` method returns a string value version of the current number. The default radix parameter (10) converts the value to base-10 notation if the original number isn't already of that type. Or you can specify other number bases (for example, 2 for binary, 16 for hexadecimal) to convert the original number to the other base — as a string, not a number, for further calculation.

BooleanObject

Example

Use The Evaluator (Chapter 13) to experiment with the `toString()` method. Assign the number 12 to the variable a and see how the number is converted to strings in a variety of number bases:

```
a = 12
a.toString()    // base 10
a.toString(2)
a.toString(16)
```

Related Item: `toLocaleString()` method.

number.`valueOf()`

(See `string.valueOf()` in Chapter 28)

Boolean Object

Properties	Methods
constructor	toString()
prototype	valueOf()

Syntax

Creating a `Boolean` object:

> `var val = new Boolean(BooleanValue);`

Accessing `Boolean` object properties:

> `BooleanObject.property | method`

Compatibility: WinIE4+, MacIE4+, NN3+, Moz+, Safari+

About this object

You work with Boolean values a lot in JavaScript — especially as the result of conditional tests. Just as string values benefit from association with string objects and their properties and methods, so, too, do Boolean values receive aid from the `Boolean` object. For example, when you display a Boolean value in a text box, the `"true"` or `"false"` string is provided by the `Boolean` object's `toString()` method so you don't have to invoke it directly.

The only time you need to even think about a `Boolean` object is if you wish to attach some property or method to `Boolean` objects that you create with the new `Boolean()` constructor. Parameter values for the constructor include the string versions of the values, numbers (0 for `false`; any other integer for `true`), and expressions that evaluate to a Boolean value. Any such new `Boolean` object is imbued with the new properties or methods you add to the `prototype` property of the core `Boolean` object.

For details about the properties and methods of the `Boolean` object, see the corresponding listings for the `String` object in Chapter 28.

Chapter 30

The Date Object

erhaps the most untapped power of JavaScript is its date and time handling. Scripters passed over the Date object with good cause in the early days of JavaScript, because in earlier versions of scriptable browsers, significant bugs and platform-specific anomalies made date and time programming hazardous without significant testing. Even with the improved bug situation, working with dates requires a working knowledge of the world's time zones and their relationships with the standard reference point, known as Greenwich Mean Time (GMT) or Coordinated Universal Time (abbreviated UTC).

Now that date- and time-handling has stabilized in modern browsers, I hope more scripters look into incorporating these kinds of calculations into their pages. In Chapter 54 on the CD-ROM, for example, I show you an application that lets your web site highlight the areas that have been updated since each visitor's last surf ride through your pages — an application that relies heavily on date arithmetic and time zone conversion.

Before getting to the JavaScript part of date discussions, however, the chapter summarizes key facts about time zones and their impact on scripting date and time on a browser. If you're not sure what GMT and UTC mean, the following section is for you.

IN THIS CHAPTER

Working with date and time values in JavaScript

Performing date calculations

Validating date entry form fields

Time Zones and GMT

By international agreement, the world is divided into distinct time zones that allow the inhabitants of each zone to say with confidence that when the Sun appears directly overhead, it is roughly noon, squarely in the middle of the day. The current time in the zone is what we set our clocks to — the local time.

That's fine when your entire existence and scope of life go no further than the width of your own time zone. But with instant communication among all parts of the world, your scope reaches well beyond local time. Periodically you must be

927

aware of the local time in other zones. After all, if you live in New York, you don't want to wake up some-one in Los Angeles before dawn with a phone call from your office.

> **NOTE** For the rest of this section, I speak of the Sun "moving" as if Earth were the center of the solar system. I do so for the convenience of our daily perception of the Sun arcing across what appears to us as a stationary sky. In point of fact, I believe Copernicus's theories, so please delete that e-mail you were about to send me.

From the point of view of the time zone over which the Sun is positioned at any given instant, all time zones to the east have already had their noon, so it is later in the day for them — one hour later per time zone (except for those few time zones offset by fractions of an hour). That's why when U.S. television networks broadcast simultaneously to the eastern and central time zones, the announced schedule for a program is "10 eastern, 9 central."

Many international businesses must coordinate time schedules of far-flung events. Doing so and taking into account the numerous time zone differences (not to mention seasonal national variations, such as daylight saving time) would be a nightmare. To help everyone out, a standard reference point was devised: the time zone running through the celestial observatory at Greenwich (pronounced GREN-itch), England. This time zone is called Greenwich Mean Time, or GMT for short. The "mean" part comes from the fact that on the exact opposite side of the globe (through the Pacific Ocean) is the international date line, another world standard that decrees where the first instance of the next calendar day appears on the planet. Thus, GMT is located at the middle, or mean, of the full circuit of the day. Not that many years ago, GMT was given another abbreviation that is not based on any one language of the planet. The abbreviation is UTC (pronounced as its letters: yu-tee-see), and the English version is Coordinated Universal Time. Whenever you see UTC, it is for all practical purposes the same as GMT.

If your personal computer's system clock is set correctly, the machine ticks away in GMT time. But because you set your local time zone in the appropriate control panel, all file time stamps and clock displays are in your local time. The machine knows what the offset time is between your local time and GMT. For daylight saving time, you may have to check a preference setting so that the offset is adjusted accordingly; in Windows-based operating systems, the system knows when the changeover occurs and prompts you if changing the offset is okay. In any case, if you travel across time zones with a laptop, you should change the computer's time zone setting, not its clock.

JavaScript's inner handling of date and time works a lot like the PC clock (on which your programs rely). Date values that you generate in a script are stored internally in GMT time; however, almost all the displays and extracted values are in the local time of the visitor (not the web site server). And remember that the date values are created on the visitor's machine by virtue of your script's generating that value — you don't send "living" date objects to the client from the server. This concept is perhaps the most difficult to grasp as you work with JavaScript date and time.

Whenever you program time and date in JavaScript for a public web page, you must take the worldview. This view requires knowing that the visitor's computer settings determine the accuracy of the conversion between GMT and local time. You'll also have to do some testing by changing your PC's clock to times in other parts of the world and making believe you are temporarily in those remote locations, which isn't always easy to do. It reminds me of the time I was visiting Sydney, Australia. I was turning in for the night and switched on the television in the hotel. This hotel received a live satellite relay of a long-running U.S. television program, *Today*. The program broadcast from New York was for the morning of the same day I was just finishing in Sydney. Yes, this time zone stuff can make your head hurt.

The Date Object

Like a handful of other objects in JavaScript and the document object models, there is a distinction between the single, static `Date` object that exists in every window (or frame) and a date object that contains a specific date and time. The static `Date` object (uppercase "D") is used in only a few cases: Primarily to create a new instance of a date and to invoke a couple of methods that the `Date` object offers for the sake of some generic conversions.

Most of your date and time work, however, is with instances of the `Date` object. These instances are referred to generically as date objects (lowercase "d"). Each date object is a snapshot of an exact millisecond in time, whether it be for the instant at which you generate the object or for a specific time in the past or future you need for calculations. If you need to have a live clock ticking away, your scripts will repeatedly create new date objects to grab up-to-the-millisecond snapshots of your computer's clock. To show the time on the page, extract the hours, minutes, and seconds from the snapshot date object, and then display the values as you like (for example, a digital readout, a graphical bar chart, and so on). By and large, it is the methods of a date object instance that your scripts invoke to read or modify individual components of a date object (for example, the month or hour).

Despite its name, every date object contains information about date and time. Therefore, even if you're concerned only about the date part of an object's data, time data is standing by as well. As you learn in a bit, the time element can catch you off-guard for some operations.

Creating a date object

The statement that asks JavaScript to make an object for your script uses the special object construction keyword `new`. The basic syntax for generating a new date object is as follows:

```
var dateObjectName = new Date([parameters]);
```

The date object evaluates to an object data type rather than to some string or numeric value.

With the date object's reference safely tucked away in the variable name, you access all date-oriented methods in the dot-syntax fashion with which you're already familiar:

```
var result = dateObjectName.method();
```

With variables, such as `result`, your scripts perform calculations or displays of the date object's data (some methods extract pieces of the date and time data from the object). If you then want to put some new value into the date object (such as adding a year to the date object), you assign the new value to the object by way of the method that lets you set the value:

```
dateObjectName.method(newValue);
```

This example doesn't look like the typical JavaScript assignment statement, which has an equals sign operator. But this statement is the way in which methods that set date object data work.

You cannot get very far into scripting dates without digging into time zone arithmetic. Although JavaScript may render the string equivalent of a date object in your local time zone, the internal storage is strictly GMT.

Even though you haven't yet seen details of a date object's methods, here is how you use two of them to add one year to today's date:

```
var oneDate = new Date();           // creates object with current GMT date
var theYear = oneDate.getYear();    // theYear is now storing the value 2007
theYear = theYear + 1;              // theYear now is 2008
oneDate.setYear(theYear);           // new year value now in the object
```

At the end of this sequence, the `oneDate` object automatically adjusts all the other date components for the next year's date. The day of the week, for example, will be different, and JavaScript takes care of that for you, should you need to extract that data. With next year's data in the `oneDate` object, you may now want to extract that new date as a string value for display in a field on the page or submit it quietly to a CGI program on the server.

The issue of parameters for creating a new date object is a bit complex, mostly because of the flexibility that JavaScript offers the scripter. Recall that the job of the `new Date()` statement is to create a place in memory for all data that a date needs to store. What is missing from that task is the data — what date and time to enter into that memory spot. That's where the parameters come in.

If you leave the parameters empty, JavaScript takes that to mean you want today's date and the current time to be assigned to that new date object. JavaScript isn't any smarter, of course, than the setting of the internal clock of your page visitor's personal computer. If the clock isn't correct, JavaScript won't do any better of a job identifying the date and time.

NOTE   Remember that when you create a new date object, it contains the current time as well. The fact that the current date may include a time of 16:03:19 (in 24-hour time) may throw off things, such as days-between-dates calculations. Be careful.

To create a date object for a specific date or time, you have five ways to send values as a parameter to the `new Date()` constructor function:

```
new Date("Month dd, yyyy hh:mm:ss")
new Date("Month dd, yyyy")
new Date(yy,mm,dd,hh,mm,ss)
new Date(yy,mm,dd)
new Date(milliseconds)
```

The first four variations break down into two styles — a long string versus a comma-delimited list of data — each with optional time settings. If you omit time settings, they are set to 0 (midnight) in the date object for whatever date you entered. You cannot omit date values from the parameters — every date object must have a real date attached to it, whether you need it or not.

In the long string versions, the month is spelled out in full in English. No abbreviations are allowed. The rest of the data is filled with numbers representing the date, year, hours, minutes, and seconds, even if the order is different from your local way of indicating dates. For single-digit values, you can use either a one- or two-digit version (such as 4:05:00). Colons separate hours, minutes, and seconds.

The short versions contain a non-quoted list of integer values in the order indicated. JavaScript cannot know that a 30 means the date if you accidentally place it in the month slot.

You use the last version only when you have the millisecond value of a date and time available. This generally occurs after some math arithmetic (described later in this chapter), leaving you with a date and time in millisecond format. To convert that numeric value to a date object, use the `new Date()` constructor. From the new date object created, you can retrieve more convenient values about the date and time.

Native object properties and methods

Like the String and Array objects, the Date object features a small handful of properties and methods that all native JavaScript objects have in common. On the property side, the Date object has a prototype property, which enables you to apply new properties and methods to every date object created in the current page. You can see examples of how this works in discussions of the prototype property for String and Array objects (Chapters 28 and 31, respectively). At the same time, every instance of a date object in modern browsers has a constructor property that references the constructor function that generated the object.

A date object has numerous methods that convert date object types to strings, most of which are more specific than the generic toString() one. The valueOf() method returns the millisecond integer that is stored for a particular date.

Date methods

The bulk of a date object's methods are for reading parts of the date and time information and for changing the date and time stored in the object. These two categories of methods are easily identifiable because they all begin with the word "get" or "set." Table 30-1 lists all of the methods of both the static Date object and, by inheritance, date object instances. The list is impressive — some would say frightening — but there are patterns you should readily observe. Most methods deal with a single component of a date and time value: year, month, date, and so forth. Each block of "get" and "set" methods also has two sets of methods: one for the local date and time conversion of the date stored in the object; one for the actual UTC date stored in the object. After you see the patterns, the list should be more manageable. Unless otherwise noted, a method has been part of the Date object since the first generation of scriptable browsers, and is therefore also supported in newer browsers.

TABLE 30-1

Date Object Methods

Method	Value Range	Description
dateObj.getFullYear()	1970–...	Specified year (NN4+, Moz1+, IE3+)
dateObj.getYear()	70–...	(See Text)
dateObj.getMonth()	0–11	Month within the year (January = 0)
dateObj.getDate()	1–31	Date within the month
dateObj.getDay()	0–6	Day of week (Sunday = 0)
dateObj.getHours()	0–23	Hour of the day in 24-hour time
dateObj.getMinutes()	0–59	Minute of the specified hour
dateObj.getSeconds()	0–59	Second within the specified minute
dateObj.getTime()	0–...	Milliseconds since 1/1/70 00:00:00 GMT
dateObj.getMilliseconds()	0–999	Milliseconds since the previous full second (NN4+, Moz1+, IE3+)
dateObj.getUTCFullYear()	1970–...	Specified UTC year (NN4+, Moz1+, IE3+)
dateObj.getUTCMonth()	0–11	UTC month within the year (January = 0) (NN4+, Moz1+, IE3+)

continued

TABLE 30-1   *(continued)*

Method	Value Range	Description
dateObj.getUTCDate()	1–31	UTC date within the month (NN4+, Moz1+, IE3+)
dateObj.getUTCDay()	0–6	UTC day of week (Sunday = 0) (NN4+, Moz1+, IE3+)
dateObj.getUTCHours()	0–23	UTC hour of the day in 24-hour time (NN4+, Moz1+, IE3+)
dateObj.getUTCMinutes()	0–59	UTC minute of the specified hour (NN4+, Moz1+, IE3+)
dateObj.getUTCSeconds()	0–59	UTC second within the specified minute (NN4+, Moz1+, IE3+)
dateObj.getUTCMilliseconds()	0–999	UTC milliseconds since the previous full second (NN4+, Moz1+, IE3+)
dateObj.setYear(*val*)	1970–...	Be safe: always specify a four-digit year
dateObj.setFullYear(*val*)	1970–...	Specified year (NN4+, Moz1+, IE3+)
dateObj.setMonth(*val*)	0–11	Month within the year (January = 0)
dateObj.setDate(*val*)	1–31	Date within the month
dateObj.setDay(*val*)	0–6	Day of week (Sunday = 0)
dateObj.setHours(*val*)	0–23	Hour of the day in 24-hour time
dateObj.setMinutes(*val*)	0–59	Minute of the specified hour
dateObj.setSeconds(*val*)	0–59	Second within the specified minute
dateObj.setMilliseconds(*val*)	0–999	Milliseconds since the previous full second (NN4+, Moz1+, IE3+)
dateObj.setTime(*val*)	0–...	Milliseconds since 1/1/70 00:00:00 GMT
dateObj.setUTCFullYear(*val*)	1970–...	Specified UTC year (NN4+, Moz1+, IE3+)
dateObj.setUTCMonth(*val*)	0–11	UTC month within the year (January = 0) (NN4+, Moz1+, IE3+)
dateObj.setUTCDate(*val*)	1–31	UTC date within the month (NN4+, Moz1+, IE3+)
dateObj.setUTCDay(*val*)	0–6	UTC day of week (Sunday = 0) (NN4+, Moz1+, IE3+)
dateObj.setUTCHours(*val*)	0–23	UTC hour of the day in 24-hour time (NN4+, Moz1+, IE3+)
dateObj.setUTCMinutes(*val*)	0–59	UTC minute of the specified hour (NN4+, Moz1+, IE3+)
dateObj.setUTCSeconds(*val*)	0–59	UTC second within the specified minute (NN4+, Moz1+, IE3+)
dateObj.setUTCMilliseconds(*val*)	0–999	UTC milliseconds since the previous full second (NN4+, Moz1+, IE3+)
dateObj.getTimezoneOffset()	0–...	Minutes offset from GMT/UTC
dateObj.toDateString()		Date-only string in a format determined by browser (WinIE5.5+)
dateObj.toGMTString()		Date/time string in universal format
dateObj.toLocaleDateString()		Date-only string in your system's localized format (NN6+, Moz1+, WinIE5.5+)

`dateObj.toLocaleString()`	Date/time string in your system's localized format
`dateObj.toLocaleTimeString()`	Time-only string in your system's localized format (NN6+, Moz1+, WinIE5.5+)
`dateObj.toString()`	Date/time string in a format determined by browser
`dateObj.toTimeString()`	Time-only string in a format determined by browser (WinIE5.5+)
`dateObj.toUTCString()`	Date/time string in universal format (NN4+, Moz1+, IE3+)
`Date.parse("dateString")`	Converts string date to milliseconds integer
`Date.UTC(date values)`	Converts GMT string date to milliseconds integer

Deciding between using the UTC or local versions of the methods depends on several factors. If the browsers you must support go back to the beginning, you will be stuck with the local versions in any case. But even for newer browsers, activities, such as calculating the number of days between dates or creating a countdown timer for a quiz, won't care which set you use, but you must use the same set for all calculations. If you start mixing local and UTC versions of date methods, you'll be destined to get wrong answers. The UTC versions come in most handy when your date calculations must take into account the time zone of the client machine compared to some absolute in another time zone — calculating the time remaining to the chiming of Big Ben signifying the start of the New Year in London.

JavaScript maintains its date information in the form of a count of milliseconds (thousandths of a second) starting from January 1, 1970, in the GMT (UTC) time zone. Dates before that starting point are stored as negative values (but see the section on bugs and gremlins later in this chapter). Regardless of the country you are in or the date and time formats specified for your computer, the millisecond is the JavaScript universal measure of time. Any calculations that involve adding or subtracting times and dates should be performed in the millisecond values to ensure accuracy. Therefore, though you may never display the milliseconds value in a field or dialog box, your scripts will probably work with them from time to time in variables. To derive the millisecond equivalent for any date and time stored in a date object, use the `dateObj.getTime()` method, as in

```
var startDate = new Date();
var started = startDate.getTime();
```

Although the method has the word "time" in its name, the fact that the value is the total number of milliseconds from January 1, 1970, means the value also conveys a date.

Other date object get methods read a specific component of the date or time. You have to exercise some care here, because some values begin counting with 0 when you may not expect it. For example, January is month 0 in JavaScript's scheme; December is month 11. Hours, minutes, and seconds all begin with 0, which, in the end, is logical. Calendar dates, however, use the actual number that would show up on the wall calendar: The first day of the month is date value 1. For the twentieth-century years, the year value is whatever the actual year number is, minus 1900. For 1996, that means the year value is 96. But for years before 1900 and after 1999, JavaScript uses a different formula, showing the full year value. This means you have to check whether a year value is less than 100 and add 1900 to it before displaying that year.

```
var today = new Date();
var thisYear = today.getYear();
if (thisYear < 100) {
   thisYear += 1900;
}
```

This assumes, of course, you won't be working with years before A.D. 100. If you can assume that your audience is using a modern browser, which is quite likely, use only the getFullYear() method. This method returns the complete set of year digits from all ranges.

To adjust any one of the elements of a date value, use the corresponding set method in an assignment statement. If the new value forces the adjustment of other elements, JavaScript takes care of that. For example, consider the following sequence and how some values are changed for us:

```
myBirthday = new Date("July 4, 1776");
result = myBirthday.getDay();  // result = 4, a Thursday
myBirthday.setYear(1777);      // bump up to next year
result = myBirthday.getDay();  // result = 5, a Friday
```

Because the same date in the following year is on a different day, JavaScript tracks that for you.

Accommodating time zones

Understanding the dateObj.getTimezoneOffset() method involves both your operating system's time control panel setting and an internationally recognized (in computerdom, anyway) format for representing dates and times. If you have ignored the control panel stuff about setting your local time zone, the values you get for this property may be off for most dates and times. In the eastern part of North America, for instance, the eastern standard time zone is five hours earlier than Greenwich Mean Time. With the getTimezoneOffset() method producing a value of minutes' difference between GMT and the PC's time zone, the five hours difference of eastern standard time is rendered as a value of 300 minutes. On the Windows platform, the value automatically changes to reflect changes in daylight saving time in the user's area (if applicable). Offsets to the east of GMT (to the date line) are expressed as negative values.

Dates as strings

When you generate a date object, JavaScript automatically applies the toString() method to the object if you attempt to display that date either in a page or alert box. The format of this string varies with browser and operating system platform. For example, in IE6 for Windows XP, the string is in the following format:

```
Tue Dec 05 16:47:20 CDT 2006
```

But in Firefox for Windows XP, the string is

```
Tue Dec 05 2006 16:47:20 GMT-0500 (Central Daylight Time)
```

Other browsers return their own variations on the string. The point is not to rely on a specific format and character location of this string for the components of dates. Use the date object methods to read date object components.

JavaScript does, however, provide two methods that return the date object in more constant string formats. One, dateObj.toGMTString(), converts the date and time to the GMT equivalent on the way to the variable that you use to store the extracted data. Here is what such data looks like:

```
Tue, 05 Dec 2006 16:47:20 GMT
```

If you're not familiar with the workings of GMT and how such conversions can present unexpected dates, exercise great care in testing your application. Eight o'clock on a Friday evening in California in the winter is four o'clock on Saturday morning GMT.

If time zone conversions make your head hurt, you can use the second string method, `dateObj.toLocaleString()`. In Firefox for North American Windows users, the returned value looks like this:

```
Tuesday, December 05, 2006 16:47:20
```

Starting with IE5.5 and NN6/Moz1, you can also have JavaScript convert a date object to just the date or time portions in a nicely formatted version. The best pair of methods for this are `toLocaleDateString()` and `toLocaleTimeString()`, because these methods return values that make the most sense to the user, based on the localization settings of the user's operating system and browser.

Friendly date formats for older browsers

If you don't have the luxury of writing script code only for modern browsers, you can create your own formatting function to do the job for a wide range of browsers. Listing 30-1 demonstrates one way of creating this kind of string from a date object (in a form that will work back to version 4 browsers).

LISTING 30-1

Creating a Friendly Date String

```html
<html>
    <head>
        <title>Date String Maker</title>
        <script type="text/javascript">
        monthNames = ["January", "February", "March", "April", "May", "June",
            "July", "August", "September", "October", "November", "December"];
        dayNames = ["Sunday", "Monday", "Tuesday", "Wednesday", "Thursday",
            "Friday", "Saturday"];

        function customDateString(oneDate) {
            var theDay = dayNames[oneDate.getDay()];
            var theMonth = monthNames[oneDate.getMonth()];
            var theYear = oneDate.getFullYear();
            return theDay + ", " + theMonth + " " + oneDate.getDate() +
                ", " + theYear;
        }
        </script>
    </head>
    <body>
        <h1>
            Welcome!
        </h1>
        <script type="text/javascript">
        document.write(customDateString(new Date()))
        </script>
        <hr />
    </body>
</html>
```

Assuming the user has the PC's clock set correctly (a big assumption), the date appearing just below the opening headline is the current date — making it appear as though the document had been updated today. The downside to this approach (as opposed to the newer `toLocaleDateString()` method) is that international users are forced to view dates in the format you design, which may be different from their local custom.

More conversions

The last two methods shown in Listing 30-1 are methods of the static `Date` object. These utility methods convert dates from string or numeric forms into millisecond values of those dates. The primary beneficiary of these actions is the `dateObj.setTime()` method, which requires a millisecond measure of a date as a parameter. You use this method to throw an entirely different date into an existing `date` object.

`Date.parse()` accepts as a parameter date strings similar to the ones you've seen in this section, including the internationally approved version. `Date.UTC()`, on the other hand, requires the comma-delimited list of values (in proper order: `yy,mm,dd,hh,mm,ss`) in the GMT zone. The `Date.UTC()` method gives you a backward-compatible way to hard-code a GMT time (you can do the same in version 4 browsers via the UTC methods). The following is an example that creates a new date object for 6 p.m. on October 1, 2006, GMT in WinIE6:

```
var newObj = new Date(Date.UTC(2006, 9, 1, 18, 0, 0));
result = newObj.toString();    // result = "Sun Oct 1 13:00:00 CDT 2006"
```

The second statement returns a value in a local time zone, because all non-UTC methods automatically convert the GMT time stored in the object to the client's local time.

Date and time arithmetic

You may need to perform some math with dates for any number of reasons. Perhaps you need to calculate a date at some fixed number of days or weeks in the future or figure out the number of days between two dates. When calculations of these types are required, remember the *lingua franca* of JavaScript date values: milliseconds.

What you may need to do in your date-intensive scripts is establish some variable values representing the number of milliseconds for minutes, hours, days, or weeks, and then use those variables in your calculations. Here is an example that establishes some practical variable values, building on each other:

```
var oneMinute = 60 * 1000;
var oneHour = oneMinute * 60;
var oneDay = oneHour * 24;
var oneWeek = oneDay * 7;
```

With these values established in a script, I can use one to calculate the date one week from today:

```
var targetDate = new Date();
var dateInMs = targetDate.getTime();
dateInMs += oneWeek;
targetDate.setTime(dateInMs);
```

Another example uses components of a date object to assist in deciding what kind of greeting message to place in a document, based on the local time of the user's PC clock. Listing 30-2 adds to the scripting from Listing 30-1, bringing some quasi-intelligence to the proceedings.

LISTING 30-2

A Dynamic Welcome Message

```html
<html>
    <head>
        <title>Date String Maker</title>
        <script type="text/javascript">
        monthNames = ["January", "February", "March", "April", "May", "June", "July",
            "August", "September", "October", "November", "December"];
        dayNames = ["Sunday", "Monday", "Tuesday", "Wednesday", "Thursday",
            "Friday", "Saturday"];

        function customDateString(oneDate) {
            var theDay = dayNames[oneDate.getDay()];
            var theMonth = monthNames[oneDate.getMonth()];
            var theYear = oneDate.getFullYear();
            return theDay + ", " + theMonth + " " + oneDate.getDate() +
                ", " + theYear;
        }
        function dayPart(oneDate) {
            var theHour = oneDate.getHours();
            if (theHour < 6 )
                return "wee hours";
            if (theHour < 12)
                return "morning";
            if (theHour < 18)
                return "afternoon";
            return "evening";
        }
        </script>
    </head>
    <body>
        <h1>Welcome!</h1>
        <script type="text/javascript">
        today = new Date();
        var header = (customDateString(today)).italics();
        header += "<BR>We hope you are enjoying the ";
        header += dayPart(today) + ".";
        document.write(header);
        </script>
        <hr />
    </body>
</html>
```

The script divides the day into four parts and presents a different greeting for each part of the day. The greeting that plays is based, simply enough, on the hour element of a date object representing the time the page is loaded into the browser. Because this greeting is embedded in the page, the greeting does not change no matter how long the user stays logged on to the page.

Counting the days . . .

You may find one or two more date arithmetic applications useful. One displays the number of shopping days left until Christmas (in the user's time zone); the other is a countdown timer to the start of the year 2100.

Listing 30-3 demonstrates how to calculate the number of days between the current day and some fixed date in the future. The assumption in this application is that all calculations take place in the user's time zone. The example shows the display of the number of shopping days before the next Christmas day (December 25). The basic operation entails converting the current date and the next December 25 to milliseconds, calculating the number of days represented by the difference in milliseconds. If you let the millisecond values represent the dates, JavaScript automatically takes care of leap years.

The only somewhat tricky part is setting the year of the next Christmas day correctly. You can't just slap the fixed date with the current year, because if the program is run on December 26, the year of the next Christmas must be incremented by one. That's why the constructor for the Christmas date object doesn't supply a fixed date as its parameters, but rather, sets individual components of the object.

LISTING 30-3

How Many Days Until Christmas

```html
<html>
  <head>
    <title>Christmas Countdown</title>
    <script type="text/javascript">
    function getDaysUntilXmas() {
      var oneMinute = 60 * 1000;
      var oneHour = oneMinute * 60;
      var oneDay = oneHour * 24;
      var today = new Date();
      var nextXmas = new Date();
      nextXmas.setMonth(11);
      nextXmas.setDate(25);
      if (today.getMonth() == 11 && today.getDate() > 25) {
        nextXmas.setFullYear(nextXmas.getFullYear() + 1);
      }
      var diff = nextXmas.getTime() - today.getTime();
      diff = Math.floor(diff/oneDay);
      return diff;
    }
    </script>
  </head>
  <body>
    <h1>
      <script type="text/javascript">
      var header = "You have <i>" + getDaysUntilXmas()  + "<\/i> ";
      header += "shopping days until Christmas.";
      document.write(header);
      </script>
    </h1>
    <hr />
  </body>
</html>
```

The second variation on calculating the amount of time before a certain event takes time zones into account. For this demonstration, the page is supposed to display a countdown timer to the precise moment when the flame for the 2008 Summer Games in Beijing is to be lit. That event takes place in a time zone that may be different from that of the page's viewer, so the countdown timer must calculate the time difference accordingly.

Listing 30-4 shows a simplified version that simply displays the ticking timer in a text field. The output, of course, could be customized in any number of ways, depending on the amount of dynamic HTML you want to employ on a page. The time of the lighting for this demo is set at 11:00 GMT on August 8, 2008 (the date is certainly accurate, but the officials may set a different time closer to the actual event).

Because this application is implemented as a live ticking clock, the code starts by setting some global variables that should be calculated only once so that the function that gets invoked repeatedly has a minimum of calculating to do (to be more efficient). The Date.UTC() method provides the target time and date in standard time. The getTimeUntil() function accepts a millisecond value (as provided by the targetDate variable) and calculates the difference between the target date and the actual internal millisecond value of the client's PC clock.

The core of the getCountDown() function peels off the number of whole days, hours, minutes, and seconds from the total number of milliseconds difference between now and the target date. Notice that each chunk is subtracted from the total so that the next smaller chunk can be calculated from the leftover milliseconds.

One extra touch on this page is a display of the local date and time of the actual event.

LISTING 30-4

Summer Games Countdown

```html
<html>
    <head>
        <title>Summer Games Countdown</title>
        <script type="text/javascript">
        // globals -- calculate only once
        // set target date to 1100GMT on August 8, 2008
        var targetDate = Date.UTC(2008, 7, 8, 11, 0, 0, 0);
        var oneMinute = 60 * 1000;
        var oneHour = oneMinute * 60;
        var oneDay = oneHour * 24;

        function getTimeUntil(targetMS) {
            var today = new Date();
            var diff = targetMS - today.valueOf();
            return Math.floor(diff);
        }
        function getCountDown() {
            var ms = getTimeUntil(targetDate);
            var output = "";
            var days, hrs, mins, secs;
```

continued

LISTING 30-4   *(continued)*

```
        if (ms >= 0) {
            days = Math.floor(ms/oneDay);
            ms -= oneDay * days;
            hrs = Math.floor(ms/oneHour);
            ms -= oneHour * hrs;
            mins = Math.floor(ms/oneMinute);
            ms -= oneMinute * mins;
            secs = Math.floor(ms/1000);
            output += days + " Days, " + hrs + " Hours, " +
                mins + " Minutes, " + secs + " Seconds";
        } else {
            output += "The time has passed.";
        }
        return output;
    }
    function updateCountDown() {
        document.forms[0].timer.value = getCountDown();
        setTimeout("updateCountDown()", 1000);
    }
    </script>
</head>
<body onload="updateCountDown()">
    <h1>Beijing Games Torch Lighting Countdown</h1>
    <p>
        <script type="text/javascript">
        document.write("(" + (new Date(targetDate)).toLocaleString());
        document.write(" in your time zone.)");
        </script>
    </p>
    <form>
        <input type="text" name="timer" size="60" />
    </form>
    <hr />
</body>
</html>
```

Early browser date bugs and gremlins

Each new browser generation improves the stability and reliability of scripted date objects. For example, Netscape Navigator 2 had so many bugs and crash problems that it made scripting complex world-time applications for this browser impossible. NN3 improved matters a bit, but some glaring problems still existed. And lest you think I'm picking on Netscape, rest assured that early versions of Internet Explorer also had plenty of date and time problems. IE3 couldn't handle dates before January 1, 1970 (GMT), and also completely miscalculated the time zone offset, following the erroneous pattern of NN2. Bottom line — you're asking for trouble if you must work extensively with dates and times while supporting legacy browsers.

You should be aware of one more discrepancy between Mac and Windows versions of Navigator through Version 4. In Windows, if you generate a date object for a date in another part of the year, the browser sets the time zone offset for that object according to the time zone setting for that time of year. On the Mac, the current setting of the control panel governs whether the normal or daylight saving time offset is applied to the date, regardless of the actual date within the year. This discrepancy affects Navigator 3 and 4 and can throw off calculations from other parts of the year by one hour.

It may sound as though the road to `Date` object scripting is filled with land mines. Although date and time scripting is far from hassle free, you can put it to good use with careful planning and a lot of testing. Better still, if you make the plausible assumption that the majority of users have a modern browser (WinIE6+, NN6+, Moz1+, FF1+, Cam1+, Safari1+, etc.) then things should go very smoothly.

Validating Date Entries in Forms

Given the bug horror stories in the previous section, you may wonder how you can ever perform data entry validation for dates in forms. The problem is not so much in the calculations as it is in the wide variety of acceptable date formats around the world. No matter how well you instruct users to enter dates in a particular format, many will follow their own habits and conventions. Moreover, how can you know whether an entry of 03/04/2007 is the North American March 4, 2007, or the European April 3, 2007? The answer: You can't.

My recommendation is to divide a date field into three components: month, day, and year. Let the user enter values into each field and validate each field individually for its valid range. Listing 30-5 shows an example of how this is done. The page includes a form that is to be validated before it is submitted. Each component field does its own range checking on the fly as the user enters values. But because this kind of validation can be defeated, the page includes one further check triggered by the form's `onsubmit` event handler. If any field is out of whack, the form submission is cancelled.

> **NOTE** The property assignment event handling technique employed throughout the code in this chapter and much of the book is a deliberate simplification to make the code more readable. It is generally better to use the more modern approach of binding events using the `addEventListener()` (NN6+/Moz/W3C) or `attachEvent()` (IE5+) methods. A modern cross-browser event handling technique is explained in detail in Chapter 25.

LISTING 30-5

Date Validation in a Form

```
<html>
  <head>
    <title>Date Entry Validation</title>
    <script type="text/javascript">
    // **BEGIN GENERIC VALIDATION FUNCTIONS**
    // general purpose function to see if an input value has been entered at all
    function isEmpty(inputStr) {
      if (inputStr == "" || inputStr == null) {
        return true;
      }
      return false;
    }
```

continued

LISTING 30-5 *(continued)*

```javascript
// function to determine if value is in acceptable range for application
function inRange(inputStr, lo, hi) {
    var num = parseInt(inputStr, 10);
    if (num < lo || num > hi) {
        return false;
    }
    return true;
}
// **END GENERIC VALIDATION FUNCTIONS**

function validateMonth(field, bypassUpdate) {
    var input = field.value;
    if (isEmpty(input)) {
        alert("Be sure to enter a month value.");
        select(field);
        return false;
    } else {
        input = parseInt(field.value, 10);
        if (isNaN(input)) {
            alert("Entries must be numbers only.");
            select(field);
            return false;
        } else {
            if (!inRange(input,1,12)) {
                alert("Enter a number between 1 (January) and 12 (December).");
                select(field);
                return false;
            }
        }
    }
    if (!bypassUpdate) {
        calcDate();
    }
    return true;
}

function validateDate(field) {
    var input = field.value;
    if (isEmpty(input)) {
        alert("Be sure to enter a date value.");
        select(field);
        return false;
    } else {
        input = parseInt(field.value, 10);
        if (isNaN(input)) {
            alert("Entries must be numbers only.");
            select(field);
            return false;
        } else {
```

```
            var monthField = document.birthdate.month;
            if (!validateMonth(monthField, true))
                return false;
            var monthVal = parseInt(monthField.value, 10);
            var monthMax = new Array(31,31,29,31,30,31,30,31,31,30,31,30,31);
            var top = monthMax[monthVal];
            if (!inRange(input,1,top)) {
                alert("Enter a number between 1 and " + top + ".");
                select(field);
                return false;
            }
        }
    }
    calcDate();
    return true;
}

function validateYear(field) {
    var input = field.value;
    if (isEmpty(input)) {
        alert("Be sure to enter a year value.");
        select(field);
        return false;
    } else {
        input = parseInt(field.value, 10);
        if (isNaN(input)) {
            alert("Entries must be numbers only.");
            select(field);
            return false;
        } else {
            if (!inRange(input,1900,2007)) {
                alert("Enter a number between 1900 and 2007.");
                select(field);
                return false;
            }
        }
    }
    calcDate();
    return true;
}

function select(field) {
    field.focus();
    field.select();
}

function calcDate() {
    var mm = parseInt(document.birthdate.month.value, 10);
    var dd = parseInt(document.birthdate.date.value, 10);
    var yy = parseInt(document.birthdate.year.value, 10);
    document.birthdate.fullDate.value = mm + "/" + dd + "/" + yy;
}
```

continued

943

LISTING 30-5   *(continued)*

```
        function checkForm(form) {
            if (validateMonth(form.month)) {
                if (validateDate(form.date)) {
                    if (validateYear(form.year)) {
                        return true;
                    }
                }
            }
            return false;
        }
        </script>
    </head>
    <body>
        <form name="birthdate" action="mailto:fun@dannyg.com" method="POST"
            onsubmit="return checkForm(this)">
            Please enter your birthdate...<br />
            Month:<input type="text" name="month" value="1" size="2"
            onchange="validateMonth(this)" /> Date:<input type="text" name="date"
            value="1" size="2" onchange="validateDate(this)" /> Year:<input
            type="text" name="year" value="1900" size="4"
            onchange="validateYear(this)" />
            <p>Thank you for entering:<input type="text" name="fullDate"
                size="10" /></p>
            <p><input type="submit" /> <input type="Reset" /></p>
        </form>
    </body>
</html>
```

The page shows the three entry fields as well as a field that is normally hidden on a form to be submitted to a server-side program. The server program responds only to the hidden field with the complete date, which is in a format for entry into, for example, a MySQL database.

Not every date entry validation must be divided in this way. For example, an intranet application can be more demanding in the way users are to enter data. Therefore, you can have a single field for date entry, but the parsing required for such a validation is quite different from that shown in Listing 30-5. See Chapter 43 on the CD-ROM for an example of such a one-field date validation routine. Data entry validation is also an excellent area of scripting that benefits from asynchronous JavaScript, also known as Ajax.

CROSS-REF   Check out Chapter 27 for more on how Ajax can be used to carry out dynamic data entry validation.

Chapter 31

The Array Object

An array is the sole JavaScript data structure provided for storing and manipulating ordered collections of data. But unlike some other programming languages, JavaScript's arrays are very forgiving as to the kind of data you store in each cell or entry of the array. This allows, for example, an array of arrays, providing the equivalent of multidimensional arrays customized to the kind of data your application needs.

If you have not done a lot of programming in the past, the notion of arrays may seem like an advanced topic. But if you ignore their capabilities, you set yourself up for a harder job when implementing many kinds of tasks. Whenever I approach a script, one of my first thoughts is about the data being controlled by the application and whether handling it as an array will offer some shortcuts for creating the document and handling interactivity with the user.

I hope that by the end of this chapter, you will not only be familiar with the properties and methods of JavaScript arrays, but you will begin to look for ways to make arrays work for you.

Structured Data

In programming, an *array* is defined as an ordered collection of data. You can best visualize an array as a table, not much different from a spreadsheet. In JavaScript, arrays are limited to a table holding one column of data, with as many rows as needed to hold your data. As you have seen in many chapters in Part III, a JavaScript-enabled browser creates a number of internal arrays for the objects in your HTML documents and browser properties. For example, if your document contains five links, the browser maintains a table of those links. You access them by number (with 0 being the first link) in the array syntax: the array name is followed by the index number in square brackets, as in `document.links[0]`, which represents the first link in the document.

For many JavaScript applications, you will want to use an array as an organized warehouse for data that users of your page access, depending on their interaction with form elements. In the application shown in Chapter 50 on the CD-ROM, for example, I demonstrate an extended version of this usage in a page that lets users search a small table of data for a match between the first three digits of their U.S. Social Security numbers and the state in which they registered with the agency. Arrays are the way JavaScript-enhanced pages can re-create the behavior of more sophisticated server-side applications such as CGI scripts and Java servlets. When the collection of data you embed in the script is no larger than a typical .gif image file, the user won't experience significant delays in loading your page; yet he or she has the full power of your small database collection for instant searching without any calls back to the server. Such database-oriented arrays are important applications of JavaScript for what I call *serverless CGIs*.

As you design an application, look for clues as to potential uses of arrays. If you have a number of objects or data points that interact with scripts the same way, you have a good candidate for array structures. For example, you can assign like names to every text field in a column of an order form. In that sequence, like-named objects are treated as elements of an array. To perform repetitive row calculations down an order form, your scripts can use array syntax to perform all the extensions within a handful of JavaScript statements, rather than perhaps dozens of statements hard-coded to each field name. Chapter 51 (on the CD-ROM) shows an example of this application.

You can also create arrays that behave like the Java hash table: a lookup table that gets you to a desired data point instantaneously if you know the name associated with the entry. If you can somehow conceive your data in a table format, an array is in your future.

Creating an Empty Array

Full-fledge array objects in JavaScript go all the way back to NN3 and IE4. It was possible to simulate some array characteristics in even earlier browsers, but since those first-generation browsers have thankfully disappeared from most users' computers, this chapter focuses on the modern array and its hefty powers.

To create a new array object, use the static `Array` object's constructor method. For example:

```
var myArray = new Array();
```

An array object automatically has a `length` property (0 for an empty array).

Should you want to presize the array (for example, preload entries with `null` values), you can specify an initial size as a parameter to the constructor. For example, here is how to create a new array to hold information about a 500-item compact disc collection:

```
var myCDCollection = new Array(500);
```

Unlike with many other programming languages, presizing a JavaScript array does not give you any particular advantage, because you can assign a value to any slot in an array at any time: The `length` property adjusts itself accordingly. For instance, if you assign a value to `myCDCollection[700]`, the array object adjusts its length upward to meet that slot (with the count starting at 0):

```
myCDCollection [700] = "The Smiths/Louder Than Bombs";
collectionSize = myCDCollection.length;     // result = 701
```

Since the count of array elements starts at 0, assigning a value to location 700 results in an array that contains 701 items. A true array object features a number of methods and the capability to add prototype properties, described later in this chapter.

Populating an Array

Entering data into an array is as simple as creating a series of assignment statements, one for each element of the array. Listing 31-1 generates an array containing a list of the nine planets of the solar system.

LISTING 31-1

Generating and Populating a New Array

```
solarSys = new Array(9);
solarSys[0] = "Mercury";
solarSys[1] = "Venus";
solarSys[2] = "Earth";
solarSys[3] = "Mars";
solarSys[4] = "Jupiter";
solarSys[5] = "Saturn";
solarSys[6] = "Uranus";
solarSys[7] = "Neptune";
solarSys[8] = "Pluto";
```

This way of populating a single array is a bit tedious when you're writing the code, but after the array is set, it makes accessing collections of information as easy as any array reference:

```
onePlanet = solarSys[4];      // result = "Jupiter"
```

A more compact way to create an array is available if you know that the data will be in the desired order (such as the preceding solarSys array). Instead of writing a series of assignment statements (as in Listing 31-1), you can create what is called a *dense array* by supplying the data as comma-delimited parameters to the Array() constructor:

```
solarSys = new Array("Mercury","Venus","Earth","Mars","Jupiter","Saturn",
    "Uranus","Neptune","Pluto");
```

The term "dense array" means that data is packed into the array, without gaps, starting at index position 0.

The example in Listing 31-1 shows what you may call a vertical collection of data. Each data point contains the same type of data as the other data points — the name of a planet — and the data points appear in the relative order of the planets from the Sun.

JavaScript Array Creation Enhancements

JavaScript provides one more way to create a dense array and also clears up a bug in the way older browsers handled arrays. This improved approach does not require the Array object constructor. Instead, JavaScript (as of version 1.2) accepts what is called *literal notation* to generate an array. To demonstrate the difference, the following statement is the regular dense array constructor that works all the way back to NN3:

```
solarSys = new Array("Mercury","Venus","Earth","Mars","Jupiter","Saturn",
    "Uranus","Neptune","Pluto");
```

While JavaScript 1.2+ fully accepts the preceding syntax, it also accepts the new literal notation:

```
solarSys = ["Mercury","Venus","Earth","Mars","Jupiter","Saturn",
    "Uranus","Neptune","Pluto"];
```

The square brackets stand in for the call to the `Array` constructor. Unless your audience is stuck using ancient browsers, you should use this streamlined approach to array creation.

The bug fix I mentioned has to do with how to treat the earlier dense array constructor if the scripter enters only the numeric value 1 as the parameter — `new Array(1)`. In NN3 and IE4, JavaScript erroneously creates an array of length 1, but that element is `undefined`. For NN4 and all later browsers, the same statement creates that one-element array and places the value in that element.

Deleting Array Entries

You can easily wipe out any data in an array element by setting the value of the array entry to `null` or an empty string. But until the `delete` operator came along in version 4 browsers, you could not completely remove an element.

Deleting an array element eliminates the index from the list of accessible index values but does not reduce the array's length, as in the following sequence of statements:

```
myArray.length      // result: 5
delete myArray[2]
myArray.length      // result: 5
myArray[2]          // result: undefined
```

The process of deleting an array entry does not necessarily release memory occupied by that data. The JavaScript interpreter's internal garbage collection mechanism (beyond the reach of scripters) is supposed to take care of such activity. See the `delete` operator in Chapter 33 for further details.

If you want tighter control over the removal of array elements, you might want to consider using the `splice()` method, which is supported in modern browsers. The `splice()` method can be used on any array and lets you remove an item (or sequence of items) from the array — causing the array's length to adjust to the new item count. See the `splice()` method later in this chapter.

Parallel Arrays

Using an array to hold data is frequently desirable so that a script can do a lookup to see if a particular value is in the array (perhaps verifying that a value typed into a text box by the user is permissible); however, even more valuable is if, upon finding a match, a script can look up some related information in another array. One way to accomplish this is with two or more parallel arrays: the same indexed slot of each array contains related information.

Consider the following three arrays:

```
var regionalOffices = ["New York", "Chicago", "Houston", "Portland"];
var regionalManagers = ["Shirley Smith", "Todd Gaston",
    "Leslie Jones", "Harold Zoot"];
var regOfficeQuotas = [300000, 250000, 350000, 225000];
```

The assumption for these statements is that Shirley Smith is the regional manager out of the New York office, and her office's quota is 300,000. This represents the data that is included with the document, perhaps retrieved by a server-side program that gets the latest data from a SQL database and embeds the data in the form of array constructors. Listing 31-2 shows how this data appears in a simple page that looks up the manager name and quota values for whichever office is chosen in the select element. The order of the items in the list of select is not accidental: The order is identical to the order of the array for the convenience of the lookup script.

Lookup action in Listing 31-2 is performed by the getData() function. Because the index values of the options inside the select element match those of the parallel arrays index values, the selectedIndex property of the select element makes a convenient way to get directly at the corresponding data in other arrays.

> **NOTE** The property assignment event handling technique employed throughout the code in this chapter and much of the book is a deliberate simplification to make the code more readable. It is generally better to use the more modern approach of binding events using the addEventListener() (NN6+/Moz/W3C) or attachEvent() (IE5+) methods. A modern cross-browser event handling technique is explained in detail in Chapter 25.

LISTING 31-2

A Simple Parallel Array Lookup

```html
<html>
    <head>
        <title>Parallel Array Lookup</title>
        <script type="text/javascript">
        // the data
        var regionalOffices = ["New York", "Chicago", "Houston", "Portland"];
        var regionalManagers = ["Shirley Smith", "Todd Gaston", "Leslie Jones",
            "Harold Zoot"];
        var regOfficeQuotas = [300000, 250000, 350000, 225000];
        // do the lookup into parallel arrays
        function getData(form) {
            var i = form.offices.selectedIndex;
            form.manager.value = regionalManagers[i];
            form.quota.value = regOfficeQuotas[i];
        }
        </script>
    </head>
    <body onload="getData(document.officeData)">
        <h1>Parallel Array Lookup</h1>
        <hr />
        <form name="officeData">
            <p>Select a regional office: <select name="offices"
            onchange="getData(this.form)">
                <option>New York</option>
                <option>Chicago</option>
                <option>Houston</option>
                <option>Portland</option>
```

continued

LISTING 31-2 *(continued)*

```
            </select></p>
            <p>The manager is: <input type="text" name="manager" size="35" /><br />
                The office quota is: <input type="text" name="quota" size="8" /></p>
        </form>
    </body>
</html>
```

On the other hand, if the content to be looked up is typed into a text box by the user, you have to loop through one of the arrays to get the matching index. Listing 31-3 is a variation of Listing 31-2, but instead of the `select` element, a text field asks users to type in the name of the region. Assuming that users will always spell the input correctly (admittedly an outrageous assumption), the version of `getData()` in Listing 31-3 performs actions that more closely resemble what you may think a "lookup" should be doing: looking for a match in one array, and displaying corresponding results from the parallel arrays. The `for` loop iterates through items in the `regionalOffices` array. An `if` condition compares all uppercase versions of both the input and each array entry. If there is a match, the `for` loop breaks, with the value of `i` still pointing to the matching index value. Outside the `for` loop, another `if` condition makes sure that the index value has not reached the length of the array, which means that no match is found. Only when the value of `i` points to one of the array entries does the script retrieve corresponding entries from the other two arrays.

LISTING 31-3

A Looping Array Lookup

```
<html>
    <head>
        <title>Parallel Array Lookup II</title>
        <script type="text/javascript">
        // the data
        var regionalOffices = ["New York", "Chicago", "Houston", "Portland"];
        var regionalManagers = ["Shirley Smith", "Todd Gaston", "Leslie Jones",
            "Harold Zoot"];
        var regOfficeQuotas = [300000, 250000, 350000, 225000];
        // do the lookup into parallel arrays
        function getData(form) {
            // make a copy of the text box contents
            var inputText = form.officeInp.value;
            // loop through all entries of regionalOffices array
            for (var i = 0; i < regionalOffices.length; i++) {
                // compare uppercase versions of entered text against one entry
                // of regionalOffices
                if (inputText.toUpperCase() == regionalOffices[i].toUpperCase()) {
                    // if they're the same, then break out of the for loop
                    break;
                }
            }
            // make sure the i counter hasn't exceeded the max index value
            if (i < regionalOffices.length) {
                // display corresponding entries from parallel arrays
```

```
                  form.manager.value = regionalManagers[i];
                  form.quota.value = regOfficeQuotas[i];
            } else {   // loop went all the way with no matches
                  // empty any previous values
                  form.manager.value = "";
                  form.quota.value = "";
                  // advise user
                  alert("No match found for " + inputText + ".");
            }
      }
      </script>
</head>
<body>
      <h1>Parallel Array Lookup II</h1>
      <hr />
      <form name="officeData">
            <p>Enter a regional office: <input type="text" name="officeInp"
            size="35" /> <input type="button" value="Search"
            onclick="getData(this.form)" /></p>
            <p>The manager is: <input type="text" name="manager"
            size="35" /><br />
            The office quota is: <input type="text" name="quota" size="8" /></p>
      </form>
</body>
</html>
```

Multidimensional Arrays

An alternate to parallel arrays is the simulation of a multidimensional array. While it's true that JavaScript arrays are one-dimensional, you can create a one-dimensional array of other arrays or objects. A logical approach is to make an array of custom objects, because the objects easily allow for naming of object properties, making references to multidimensional array data more readable (custom objects are discussed at length in Chapter 34).

Using the same data from the examples of parallel arrays, the following statements define an object constructor for each "data record." A new object is then assigned to each of four entries in the main array.

```
// custom object constructor
function officeRecord(city, manager, quota) {
    this.city = city;
    this.manager = manager;
    this.quota = quota;
}

// create new main array
var regionalOffices = new Array();
// stuff main array entries with objects
regionalOffices[0] = new officeRecord("New York", "Shirley Smith", 300000);
regionalOffices[1] = new officeRecord("Chicago", "Todd Gaston", 250000);
regionalOffices[2] = new officeRecord("Houston", "Leslie Jones", 350000);
regionalOffices[3] = new officeRecord("Portland", "Harold Zoot", 225000);
```

The object constructor function (officeRecord()) assigns incoming parameter values to properties of the object. Therefore, to access one of the data points in the array, you use both array notations to get to the desired entry in the array and the name of the property for that entry's object:

```
var eastOfficeManager = regionalOffices[0].manager;
```

You can also assign string index values for this kind of array, as in

```
regionalOffices["east"] = new officeRecord("New York", "Shirley Smith",
    300000);
```

and access the data via the same index:

```
var eastOfficeManager = regionalOffices["east"].manager;
```

But if you're more comfortable with the traditional multidimensional array (from your experience in other programming languages), you can also implement the above as an array of arrays with less code:

```
// create new main array
var regionalOffices = new Array();
// stuff main array entries with arrays
regionalOffices[0] = new Array("New York", "Shirley Smith", 300000);
regionalOffices[1] = new Array("Chicago", "Todd Gaston", 250000);
regionalOffices[2] = new Array("Houston", "Leslie Jones", 350000);
regionalOffices[3] = new Array("Portland", "Harold Zoot", 225000);
```

or, for the extreme of unreadable brevity with literal notation:

```
// create new main array
var regionalOffices = [ ["New York", "Shirley Smith", 300000],
                        ["Chicago", "Todd Gaston", 250000],
                        ["Houston", "Leslie Jones", 350000],
                        ["Portland", "Harold Zoot", 225000] ];
```

Accessing a single data point of an array of arrays requires a double array reference. For example, retrieving the manager's name for the Houston office requires the following syntax:

```
var HoustonMgr = regionalOffices[2][1];
```

The first index in brackets is for the outermost array (regionalOffices); the second index in brackets points to the item of the array returned by regionalOffices[2].

Simulating a Hash Table

All arrays shown so far in this chapter have used integers as their index values. A JavaScript array is a special type of object (the object type is covered in Chapter 34). As a result, you can also assign values to customized properties of an array without interfering with the data stored in the array or the length of the array. In other words, you can "piggy-back" data in the array object. You may reference the values of these properties either using "dot" syntax (array.propertyName) or through array-looking syntax consisting of square brackets and the property name as a string inside the brackets (array["propertyName"]). An array used in this fashion is also known as an *associative array*.

Addressing object properties by way of string indexes is sometimes very useful. For example, the multidimensional array described in the previous section consists of four objects. If your page contains a form whose job is to look through the array to find a match for a city chosen from a `select` list, the typical array lookup would loop through the length of the array, compare the chosen value against the `city` property of each object, and then retrieve the other properties when there was a match. For a 4-item list, this isn't a big deal. But for a 100-item list, the process could get time consuming. A faster approach would be to jump directly to the array entry whose `city` property is the chosen value. That's what a simulated hash table can do for you (some programming languages have formal hash table constructions especially designed to act like a lookup table).

Create a simulated hash table after the array is populated by looping through the array and assigning properties to the array object as string values. Use string values that you expect to use for lookup purposes. For example, after the `regionalOffices` array has its component objects assigned, run through the following routine to make the hash table:

```
for (var i = 0; i < regionalOffices.length; i++) {
    regionalOffices[regionalOffices[i].city] = regionalOffices[i];
}
```

You can retrieve the manager property of the Houston office object as follows:

```
var HoustonMgr = regionalOffices["Houston"].manager;
```

With the aid of the hash table component of the array, your scripts have the convenience of both numeric lookup (if the script needs to cycle through all items) and an immediate jump to an item.

Array Object Properties

constructor

(See `string.constructor` in Chapter 28)

length

Value: Integer.   Read/Write
Compatibility: WinIE4+, MacIE4+, NN3+, Moz+, Safari+

A true array object's `length` property reflects the number of entries in the array. An entry can be any kind of JavaScript value, including `null`. If an entry is in the 10th cell and the rest are `null`, the length of that array is 10. Note that because array index values are zero-based, the index of the last cell of an array is one less than the length (9 in this case). This characteristic makes it convenient to use the property as an automatic counter to append a new item to an array:

```
myArray[myArray.length] = valueOfAppendedItem;
```

Thus, a generic function does not have to know which specific index value to apply to an additional item in the array.

prototype

Value: Variable or function.   Read/Write
Compatibility: WinIE4+, MacIE4+, NN3+, Moz+, Safari+

Inside JavaScript, an array object has its dictionary definition of methods and `length` property — items that all array objects have in common. The `prototype` property enables your scripts to ascribe additional properties or methods that apply to all the arrays you create in the currently loaded documents. You can override this prototype, however, for any individual object.

Example

To demonstrate how the `prototype` property works, Listing 31-4 creates a `prototype` property for all array objects generated from the static `Array` object. As the script generates new arrays (instances of the `Array` object, just as a date object is an instance of the `Date` object), the property automatically becomes a part of those arrays. In one array, `c`, you override the value of the prototype `sponsor` property. By changing the value for that one object, you don't alter the value of the prototype for the `Array` object. Therefore, another array created afterward, `d`, still gets the original `sponsor` property value.

LISTING 31-4

Adding a prototype Property

```
<html>
  <head>
    <title>Array prototypes</title>
    <script type="text/javascript">
    // add prototype to all Array objects
    Array.prototype.sponsor = "DG";
    a = new Array(5);
    b = new Array(5);
    c = new Array(5);
    // override prototype property for one 'instance'
    c.sponsor = "JS";
    // this one picks up the original prototype
    d = new Array(5);
    </script>
  </head>
  <body>
    <h2>
      <script type="text/javascript">
      document.write("Array a is brought to you by: " + a.sponsor +
        "<br />");
      document.write("Array b is brought to you by: " + b.sponsor +
        "<br />");
      document.write("Array c is brought to you by: " + c.sponsor +
        "<br />");
      document.write("Array d is brought to you by: " + d.sponsor +
        "<br />");
      </script>
    </h2>
  </body>
</html>
```

You can assign properties and functions to a prototype. To assign a function, define the function as you normally would in JavaScript. Then assign the function to the `prototype` by name:

```
function newFunc(param1) {
    // statements
}
Array.prototype.newMethod = newFunc;  // omit parentheses in this reference
```

When you need to call upon that function (which has essentially become a new temporary method for the `Array` object), invoke it as you would any object method. Therefore, if an array named `CDCollection` has been created and a prototype method `showCoverImage()` has been attached to the array, the call to invoke the method for a tenth listing in the array is

```
CDCollection.showCoverImage(9);
```

where the parameter of the function uses the index value to perhaps retrieve an image whose URL is a property of an object assigned to the 10th item of the array.

Array Object Methods

After you have information stored in an array, JavaScript provides several methods to help you manage that data. These methods, all of which belong to array objects you create, have evolved over time, so pay close attention to browser compatibility if you're in need of supporting legacy (pre-version 4) browsers.

array.concat(*array2*)

Returns: Array object.
Compatibility: WinIE4+, MacIE4+, NN4+, Moz+, Safari+

The `array.concat()` method allows you to join two array objects into a new, third array object. The action of concatenating the arrays does not alter the contents or behavior of the two original arrays. To join the arrays, you refer to the first array object to the left of the period before the method; a reference to the second array is the parameter to the method. For example:

```
var array1 = new Array(1,2,3);
var array2 = new Array("a","b","c");
var array3 = array1.concat(array2);
    // result: array with values 1,2,3,"a","b","c"
```

If an array element is a string or number value (not a string or number object), the values are copied from the original arrays into the new one. All connection with the original arrays ceases for those items. But if an original array element is a reference to an object of any kind, JavaScript copies a reference from the original array's entry into the new array. So if you make a change to either array's entry, the change occurs to the object, and both array entries reflect the change to the object.

Example

Listing 31-5 is a bit complex, but it demonstrates both how arrays can be joined with the `array.concat()` method and how values and objects in the source arrays do or do not propagate based on their data type. The page is shown in Figure 31-1.

array.concat()

FIGURE 31-1

Object references remain "alive" in a concatenated array.

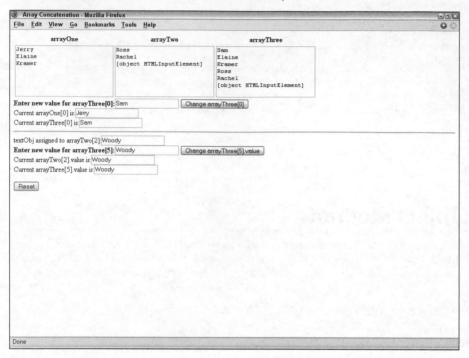

After you load the page, you see readouts of three arrays. The first array consists of all string values; the second array has two string values and a reference to a form object on the page (a text box named "original" in the HTML). In the initialization routine of this page, not only are the two source arrays created, but they are joined with the `array.concat()` method, and the result is shown in the third box. To show the contents of these arrays in columns, I use the `array.join()` method, which brings the elements of an array together as a string delimited in this case by a return character — giving us an instant column of data.

Two series of fields and buttons let you experiment with the way values and object references are linked across concatenated arrays. In the first group, if you enter a new value to be assigned to `arrayThree[0]`, the new value replaces the string value in the combined array. Because regular values do not maintain a link back to the original array, only the entry in the combined array is changed. A call to `showArrays()` proves that only the third array is affected by the change.

More complex is the object relationship for this demonstration. A reference to the first text box of the second grouping has been assigned to the third entry of `arrayTwo`. After concatenation, the same reference is now in the last entry of the combined array. If you enter a new value for a property of the object in the last slot of `arrayThree`, the change goes all the way back to the original object — the first text box in the lower grouping. Thus, the text of the original field changes in response to the change of `arrayThree[5]`. And because all references to that object yield the same result, the reference in `arrayTwo[2]` points to the same text object, yielding the same new answer. The display of the array contents doesn't change, because both arrays still contain a reference to the same object (and the value attribute showing in the `<input>` tag of the column listings refers to the default value of the tag, not to its current algorithmically retrievable value shown in the last two fields of the page).

LISTING 31-5

Array Concatenation

```html
<html>
    <head>
        <title>Array Concatenation</title>
        <script type="text/javascript">
        // global variables
        var arrayOne, arrayTwo, arrayThree, textObj;
        // initialize after load to access text object in form
        function initialize() {
            var form = document.forms[0];
            textObj = form.original;
            arrayOne = new Array("Jerry", "Elaine","Kramer");
            arrayTwo = new Array("Ross", "Rachel",textObj);
            arrayThree = arrayOne.concat(arrayTwo);
            update1(form);
            update2(form);
            showArrays();
        }
        // display current values of all three arrays
        function showArrays() {
            var form = document.forms[0];
            form.array1.value = arrayOne.join("\n");
            form.array2.value = arrayTwo.join("\n");
            form.array3.value = arrayThree.join("\n");
        }
        // change the value of first item in Array Three
        function update1(form) {
            arrayThree[0] = form.source1.value;
            form.result1.value = arrayOne[0];
            form.result2.value = arrayThree[0];
            showArrays();
        }
        // change value of object property pointed to in Array Three
        function update2(form) {
            arrayThree[5].value = form.source2.value;
            form.result3.value = arrayTwo[2].value;
            form.result4.value = arrayThree[5].value;
            showArrays();
        }
        </script>
    </head>
```

continued

LISTING 31-5   *(continued)*

```
<body onload="initialize()">
    <form>
        <table>
            <tr>
                <th>arrayOne</th>
                <th>arrayTwo</th>
                <th>arrayThree</th>
            </tr>
            <tr>
                <td><textarea name="array1" cols="25" rows="6">
                    </textarea></td>
                <td><textarea name="array2" cols="25" rows="6">
                    </textarea></td>
                <td><textarea name="array3" cols="25" rows="6">
                    </textarea></td>
            </tr>
        </table>
        <b>Enter new value for arrayThree[0]:</b><input type="text"
        name="source1" value="Jerry" /> <input type="button"
        value="Change arrayThree[0]" onclick="update1(this.form)" /><br />
        Current arrayOne[0] is:<input type="text" name="result1" /><br />
        Current arrayThree[0] is:<input type="text" name="result2" /><br />
        <hr />
        textObj assigned to arrayTwo[2]:<input type="text" name="original"
        onfocus="this.blur()" /><br />
         <b>Enter new value for arrayThree[5]:</b><input type="text"
        name="source2" value="Phoebe" /> <input type="button"
        value="Change arrayThree[5].value"
        onclick="update2(this.form)" /><br />
        Current arrayTwo[2].value is:<input type="text"
        name="result3" /><br />
        Current arrayThree[5].value is:<input type="text" name="result4" />
        <p><input type="button" value="Reset"
        onclick="location.reload()" /></p>
    </form>
</body>
</html>
```

Related Items: `array.join()` method.

array.`join(`*separatorString*`)`

Returns: String of entries from the array delimited by the *separatorString* value.
Compatibility: WinIE4+, MacIE4+, NN3+, Moz+, Safari+

You cannot directly view data that is stored in an array. Nor can you put an array into a form element for transmittal to a server-side program that expects a string of text. To make the transition from discrete array elements to string, the `array.join()` method handles what would otherwise be a nasty string manipulation exercise.

The sole parameter for this method is a string of one or more characters that you want to act as a delimiter between entries. For example, if you want commas between array items in their text version, the statement is

```
var arrayText = myArray.join(",");
```

Invoking this method does not change the original array in any way. Therefore, you need to assign the results of this method to another variable or a value property of a form element.

Example

The script in Listing 31-6 converts an array of planet names into a text string. The page provides you with a field to enter the delimiter string of your choice and shows the results in a text area.

LISTING 31-6

Using the Array.join() Method

```
<html>
    <head>
        <title>Array.join()</title>
        <script type="text/javascript">
        solarSys = new Array(9);
        solarSys[0] = "Mercury";
        solarSys[1] = "Venus";
        solarSys[2] = "Earth";
        solarSys[3] = "Mars";
        solarSys[4] = "Jupiter";
        solarSys[5] = "Saturn";
        solarSys[6] = "Uranus";
        solarSys[7] = "Neptune";
        solarSys[8] = "Pluto";

        // join array elements into a string
        function convert(form) {
            var delimiter = form.delim.value;
            form.output.value = decodeURIComponent(solarSys.join(delimiter));
        }
        </script>
    </head>
    <body>
        <h2>Converting arrays to strings</h2>
        This document contains an array of planets in our solar system.
        <hr />
        <form>
            Enter a string to act as a delimiter between entries: <input
            type="text" name="delim" value="," size="5" />
            <p><input type="button" value="Display as String"
                onclick="convert(this.form)" /> <input type="reset" /> <textarea
                name="output" rows="4" cols="40" wrap="virtual"></textarea></p>
        </form>
    </body>
</html>
```

---

*array.*pop()

Notice that this method takes the parameter very literally. If you want to include non-alphanumeric characters, such as a newline or tab, do so with URL-encoded characters (%0D for a carriage return; %09 for a tab) instead of inline string literals. Coming up in Listing 31-7, the results of the `array.join()` method are subjected to the `decodeURIComponent()` function in order to display them in the `textarea`.

Related Items: `string.split()` method.

`array.pop()`
`array.push(valueOrObject)`
`array.shift()`
`array.unshift(valueOrObject)`

Returns: One array entry value.
Compatibility: WinIE5.5+, MacIE-, NN4+, Moz+, Safari+

The notion of a *stack* is well known to experienced programmers, especially those who know about the inner workings of assembly language at the CPU level. Even if you've never programmed a stack before, you have encountered the concept in real life many times. The classic analogy is the spring-loaded pile of cafeteria trays. If the pile were created one tray at a time, each tray would be pushed onto the top of the stack of trays. When a customer comes along, the topmost tray (the last one to be pushed onto the stack) gets popped off. The last one to be put on the stack is the first one to be taken off.

JavaScript in modern browsers lets you turn an array into one of these spring-loaded stacks. But instead of placing trays on the pile, you can place any kind of data at either end of the stack, depending on which method you use to do the stacking. Similarly, you can extract an item from either end.

Perhaps the most familiar terminology for this is *push* and *pop*. When you push() a value onto an array, the value is appended as the last entry in the array. When you issue the `array.pop()` method, the last item in the array is removed from the stack and is returned, and the array shrinks in length by one. In the following sequence of statements, watch what happens to the value of the array used as a stack:

```
var source = new Array("Homer","Marge","Bart","Lisa","Maggie");
var stack = new Array();
    // stack = <empty>
stack.push(source[0]);
    // stack = "Homer"
stack.push(source[2]);
    // stack = "Homer","Bart"
var Simpson1 = stack.pop();
    // stack = "Homer" ; Simpson1 = "Bart"
var Simpson2 = stack.pop();
    // stack = <empty> ; Simpson2 = "Homer"
```

While push() and pop() work at the end of an array, another pair of methods works at the front. Their names are not as picturesque as push() and pop(). To insert a value at the front of an array, use the `array.unshift()` method; to grab the first element and remove it from the array, use `array.shift()`. Of course, you are not required to use these methods in matching pairs. If you push() a series of values onto the back end of an array, you can shift() them off from the front end without complaint. It all depends on how you need to process the data.

Related Items: `array.concat()`, `array.slice()` method.

array.reverse()

Returns: Array of entries in the opposite order of the original.
Compatibility: WinIE4+, MacIE4+, NN3+, Moz+, Safari+

Occasionally, you may find it more convenient to work with an array of data in reverse order. Although you can concoct repeat loops to count backward through index values, a server-side program may prefer the data in a sequence opposite to the way it was most convenient for you to script it.

You can have JavaScript switch the contents of an array for you: Whatever element was last in the array becomes the 0 index item in the array. Bear in mind that if you do this, you're restructuring the original array, not copying it, even though the method also returns a copy of the reversed version. A reload of the document restores the order as written in the HTML document.

Example

Listing 31-7 is an enhanced version of Listing 31-6, which includes another button and function that reverse the array and display it as a string in a text area.

LISTING 31-7

Array.reverse() Method

```
<html>
  <head>
    <title>Array.reverse()</title>
    <script type="text/javascript">
    solarSys = new Array(9);
    solarSys[0] = "Mercury";
    solarSys[1] = "Venus";
    solarSys[2] = "Earth";
    solarSys[3] = "Mars";
    solarSys[4] = "Jupiter";
    solarSys[5] = "Saturn";
    solarSys[6] = "Uranus";
    solarSys[7] = "Neptune";
    solarSys[8] = "Pluto";

    // show array as currently in memory
    function showAsIs(form) {
       var delimiter = form.delim.value;
       form.output.value = decodeURIComponent(solarSys.join(delimiter));
    }
    // reverse array order, then display as string
    function reverseIt(form) {
       var delimiter = form.delim.value;
       solarSys.reverse();   // reverses original array
       form.output.value = decodeURIComponent(solarSys.join(delimiter));
    }
```

continued

961

array.slice()

LISTING 31-7   *(continued)*

```
        </script>
    </head>
    <body>
        <h2>Reversing array element order</h2>
        This document contains an array of planets in our solar system.
        <hr />
        <form>
            Enter a string to act as a delimiter between entries: <input
            type="text" name="delim" value="," size="5" />
            <p><input type="button" value="Array as-is"
                onclick="showAsIs(this.form)" /> <input type="button"
                value="Reverse the array" onclick="reverseIt(this.form)" /> <input
                type="reset" /> <input type="button" value="Reload"
                onclick="self.location.reload()" /> <textarea name="output"
                rows="4" cols="60">
                </textarea></p>
        </form>
    </body>
</html>
```

Notice that the `solarSys.reverse()` method stands by itself (meaning, nothing captures the returned value) because the method modifies the `solarSys` array. You then run the now inverted `solarSys` array through the `array.join()` method for your text display.

Related Items: `array.sort()` method.

array.slice(*startIndex* [, *endIndex*])

Returns: Array.
Compatibility: WinIE4+, MacIE4+, NN4+, Moz+, Safari+

Behaving as its like-named string method, `array.slice()` lets you extract a contiguous series of items from an array. The extracted segment becomes an entirely new array object. Values and objects from the original array have the same kind of behavior as arrays created with the `array.concat()` method.

One parameter is required — the starting index point for the extraction. If you don't specify a second parameter, the extraction goes all the way to the end of the array; otherwise the extraction goes to, *but does not include,* the index value supplied as the second parameter. For example, extracting Earth's neighbors from an array of planet names looks like the following:

```
var solarSys = new Array("Mercury","Venus","Earth","Mars",
    "Jupiter","Saturn","Uranus","Neptune","Pluto");
var nearby = solarSys.slice(1,4);
    // result: new array of "Venus", "Earth", "Mars"
```

Related Items: `array.splice()`, `string.slice()` methods.

array.sort([*compareFunction*])

Returns: Array of entries in the order as determined by the *compareFunction* algorithm.
Compatibility: WinIE4+, MacIE4+, NN3+, Moz+, Safari+

JavaScript array sorting is both powerful and a bit complex to script if you haven't had experience with this kind of sorting methodology. The purpose, obviously, is to let your scripts sort entries of an array by almost any kind of criterion that you can associate with an entry. For entries consisting of strings, the criterion may be their alphabetical order or their length; for numeric entries, the criterion may be their numerical order.

Look first at the kind of sorting you can do with the `array.sort()` method by itself (for example, without calling a comparison function). When no parameter is specified, JavaScript takes a snapshot of the contents of the array and converts items to strings. From there, it performs a string sort of the values. ASCII values of characters govern the sort, which means that numbers are sorted by their string values, not their numeric values. This fact has strong implications if your array consists of numeric data: The value 201 sorts before 88, because the sorting mechanism compares the first characters of the strings ("2" versus "8") to determine the sort order. For simple alphabetical sorting of string values in arrays, the plain `array.sort()` method does the trick.

Fortunately, additional intelligence is available that you can add to array sorting. The key tactic is to define a function that helps the `sort()` method compare items in the array. A comparison function is passed two values from the array (what you don't see is that the `array.sort()` method rapidly sends numerous pairs of values from the array to help it sort through all entries). The comparison function lets the `sort()` method know which of the two items comes before the other, based on the value the function returns. Assuming that the function compares two values, a and b, the returned value reveals information to the `sort()` method, as shown in Table 31-1.

TABLE 31-1

Comparison Function Return Values

Return Value Range	Meaning
< 0	Value b should sort later than a
0	The order of a and b should not change
> 0	Value a should sort later than b

Consider the following example:

```
myArray = new Array(12, 5, 200, 80);
function compare(a,b) {
    return a - b;
}
myArray.sort(compare);
```

The array has four numeric values in it. To sort the items in numerical order, you define a comparison function (arbitrarily named `compare()`), which is called from the `sort()` method. Note that unlike invoking other functions, the parameter of the `sort()` method uses a reference to the function, which lacks parentheses.

array.sort()

When the compare() function is called, JavaScript automatically sends two parameters to the function in rapid succession until each element has been compared with the others. Every time compare() is called, JavaScript assigns two of the array's values to the parameter variables (a and b). In the preceding example, the returned value is the difference between a and b. If a is larger than b, then a positive value goes back to the sort() method, telling it to sort a later than b (that is, position a at a higher value index position than b). Therefore, b may end up at myArray[0], whereas a ends up at a higher index-valued location. On the other hand, if a is smaller than b, the returned negative value tells sort() to put a in a lower index value spot than b.

Evaluations within the comparison function can go to great lengths, as long as some data connected with array values can be compared. For example, instead of numerical comparisons, as just shown, you can perform string comparisons. The following function sorts alphabetically by the last character of each array string entry:

```
function compare(a,b) {
    // last character of array strings
    var aComp = a.charAt(a.length - 1);
    var bComp = b.charAt(b.length - 1);
    if (aComp < bComp)
        return -1;
    if (aComp > bComp)
        return 1;
    return 0;
}
```

First, this function extracts the final character from each of the two values passed to it. Then, because strings cannot be added or subtracted like numbers, you compare the ASCII values of the two characters, returning the corresponding values to the sort() method to let it know how to treat the two values being checked at that instant.

When an array's entries happen to be objects, you can even sort by properties of those objects. If you bear in mind that the a and b parameters of the sort function are references to two array entries, then by extension you can refer to properties of those objects. For example, if an array contains objects whose properties define information about employees, one of the properties of those objects can be the employee's age as a string. You can then sort the array based on the numeric equivalent of the age property of the objects by way of the following comparison function:

```
function compare(a,b) {
    return parseInt(a.age) - parseInt(b.age);
}
```

Array sorting, unlike sorting routines you may find in other scripting languages, is not a stable sort. Not being stable means that succeeding sort routines on the same array are not cumulative. Also, remember that sorting changes the sort order of the original array. If you don't want the original array harmed, make a copy of it before sorting or reload the document to restore an array to its original order. Should an array element be null, the method sorts such elements at the end of the sorted array.

JavaScript array sorting is extremely powerful stuff. Array sorting is one reason why it's not uncommon to take the time during the loading of a page containing an IE XML data island, for example, to make a JavaScript copy of the data as an array of objects (see Chapter 57 on the CD-ROM). Converting the XML to JavaScript arrays makes the job of sorting the data much easier and faster than cobbling together your own sorting routines on the XML elements.

Example

You can look to Listing 31-8 for a few examples of sorting an array of string values (see Figure 31-2). Four buttons summon different sorting routines, three of which invoke comparison functions. This listing sorts the planet array alphabetically (forward and backward) by the last character of the planet name and also by the length of the planet name. Each comparison function demonstrates different ways of comparing data sent during a sort.

LISTING 31-8

Array.sort() Possibilities

```
<html>
   <head>
      <title>Array.sort()</title>
      <script type="text/javascript">
      solarSys = new Array(9);
      solarSys[0] = "Mercury";
      solarSys[1] = "Venus";
      solarSys[2] = "Earth";
      solarSys[3] = "Mars";
      solarSys[4] = "Jupiter";
      solarSys[5] = "Saturn";
      solarSys[6] = "Uranus";
      solarSys[7] = "Neptune";
      solarSys[8] = "Pluto";
      // comparison functions
      function compare1(a,b) {
         // reverse alphabetical order
         if (a > b)
            return -1;
         if (b > a)
            return 1;
         return 0;
      }
      function compare2(a,b) {
         // last character of planet names
         var aComp = a.charAt(a.length - 1);
         var bComp = b.charAt(b.length - 1);
         if (aComp < bComp)
            return -1;
         if (aComp > bComp)
            return 1;
         return 0;
```

continued

LISTING 31-8   *(continued)*

```
      }
      function compare3(a,b) {
         // length of planet names
         return a.length - b.length;
      }
      // sort and display array
      function sortIt(form, compFunc) {
         var delimiter = ";";
         if (compFunc == null) {
            solarSys.sort();
         } else {
            solarSys.sort(compFunc);
         }
         // display results in field
         form.output.value = decodeURIComponent(solarSys.join(delimiter));
      }
   </script>
</head>
<body onload="document.forms[0].output.value =
   decodeURIComponent(solarSys.join(';'))">
   <h2>Sorting array elements</h2>
   This document contains an array of planets in our solar system.
   <hr />
   <form>
      Click on a button to sort the array:
      <p><input type="button" value="Alphabetical A-Z"
         onclick="sortIt(this.form)" /> <input type="button"
         value="Alphabetical Z-A" onclick="sortIt(this.form, compare1)" />
         <input type="button" value="Last Character"
         onclick="sortIt(this.form, compare2)" /> <input type="button"
         value="Name Length" onclick="sortIt(this.form, compare3)"/> <input
         type="button" value="Reload Original"
         onclick="self.location.reload()" /> <input type="text"
         name="output" size="62" /></p>
   </form>
</body>
</html>
```

Related Items: `array.reverse()` method.

NOTE   As I show you in Chapter 42 on the CD-ROM, many regular expression object methods generate arrays as their result (for example, an array of matching values in a string). These special
arrays have a custom set of named properties that assist your script in analyzing the findings of the method.
Beyond that, these regular expression result arrays behave like all others.

FIGURE 31-2

Sorting an array of planet names alphabetically by name length.

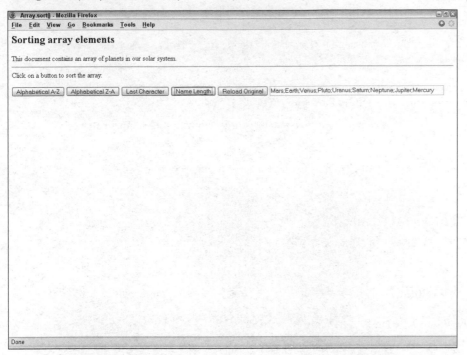

```
array.splice(startIndex , deleteCount[, item1[,
item2[,...itemN]]])
```

Returns: Array.
Compatibility: WinIE5.5+, MacIE-, NN4+, Moz+, Safari+

If you need to remove items from the middle of an array, the `array.splice()` method simplifies a task that would otherwise require assembling a new array from selected items of the original array. The first of two required parameters is a zero-based index integer that points to the first item to be removed from the current array. The second parameter is another integer that indicates how many sequential items are to be removed from the array. Removing array items affects the length of the array, and those items that are removed are returned by the `splice()` method as their own array.

You can also use the `splice()` method to replace array items. Optional parameters beginning with the third let you provide data elements that are to be inserted into the array in place of the items being removed. Each added item can be any JavaScript data type, and the number of new items does not have to be equal to the number of items removed. In fact, by specifying a second parameter of zero, you can use `splice()` to insert one or more items into any position of the array.

*array.*toString()

Example

Use The Evaluator (Chapter 13) to experiment with the splice() method. Begin by creating an array with a sequence of numbers:

```
a = new Array(1,2,3,4,5)
```

Next, remove the center three items, and replace them with one string item:

```
a.splice(1, 3, "two/three/four")
```

The Results box shows a string version of the three-item array returned by the method. To view the current contents of the array, enter a into the top text box.

To put the original numbers back into the array, swap the string item with three numeric items:

```
a.splice(1, 1, 2, 3, 4)
```

The method returns the single string, and the a array now has five items in it again.

Related Items: array.slice() method.

*array.*toLocaleString()

Returns: String.
Compatibility: WinIE5.5+, MacIE-, NN6+, Moz+, Safari+

*array.*toString()

Returns: String.
Compatibility: WinIE4+, MacIE4+, NN3+, Moz+, Safari+

The array.toLocaleString() and the older, more compatible array.toString() are methods to retrieve the contents of an array in string form. Browsers use the toString() method on their own whenever you attempt to display an array in text boxes, in which case the array items are comma-delimited.

The precise string conversion of the toLocaleString() is left up to the specific browser implementation. That browsers differ in some details is not surprising, even in the U.S. English versions of operating systems and browsers. For example, if the array contains integer values, the toLocaleString() method in IE5.5+ returns the numbers comma-and-space-delimited, formatted with two digits to the right of the decimal (as if dollars and cents). Mozilla-based browsers, on the other hand, return just the integers, but these are also comma-delimited.

If you need to convert an array to a string for purposes of passing array data to other venues (for example, as data in a hidden text box submitted to a server or as search string data conveyed to another page), use the array.join() method instead. Array.join() gives you more reliable and flexible control over the item delimiters, and you are assured of the same results regardless of locale.

Related Items: array.join() method.

Chapter 32

Control Structures and Exception Handling

IN THIS CHAPTER

Branching script execution down multiple paths

Looping through ordered collections of data

Applying exception handling techniques

You get up in the morning, go about your day's business, and then turn out the lights at night. That's not much different from what a program does from the time it starts to the time it ends. But along the way, both you and a program take lots of tiny steps, not all of which advance the processing in a straight line. At times, you have to control what's going on by making a decision or repeating tasks until the whole job is finished. Control structures are the facilities that make these tasks possible in JavaScript.

JavaScript control structures follow along the same lines of many programming languages. Basic decision-making and looping constructions satisfy the needs of just about all programming tasks.

Another vital program control mechanism — error (or exception) handling — is formally addressed in Edition 3 of the ECMA-262 language standard. The concept of exception handling was added to the JavaScript version introduced in IE5.5 and NN6, but it is well known to programmers in many other environments. Adopting exception-handling techniques in your code can greatly enhance recovery from processing errors beyond your control, such as those caused by errant user input or network glitches.

If and If. . .Else Decisions

Compatibility: WinIE3+, MacIE3+, NN2+, Moz+, Safari+

JavaScript programs frequently have to make decisions based on the current values of variables or object properties. Such decisions can have only two possible outcomes at a time. The factor that determines the path that the program takes at these decision points is the truth of some statement. For example, when you enter a room of your home at night, the statement under test is something such as "It is too dark to see without a light." If that statement is true, you switch on the light; if that statement is false, you carry on with your primary task.

if

Simple decisions

JavaScript syntax for this kind of simple decision always begins with the keyword `if`, followed by the condition to test, and then the statements that execute if the condition yields a true result. JavaScript uses no "then" keyword (as some other languages do); the keyword is implied by the way parentheses and braces surround the various components of this construction. The formal syntax is

```
if (condition) {
    statementsIfTrue
}
```

This construction means that if the condition is true, program execution takes a detour to execute statements inside the braces. No matter what happens, the program continues executing statements beyond the closing brace (`}`). If household navigation were part of the scripting language, the code would look like this:

```
if (tooDark == true) {
    feel for light switch
    turn on light switch
}
```

If you're not used to C/C++, the double equals sign may have caught your eye. You learn more about this type of operator in the next chapter, but for now, know that this operator compares the equality of items on either side of it. In other words, the `condition` statement of an `if` construction must always yield a Boolean (`true` or `false`) value. Some object properties, you may recall, are Booleans, so you can stick a reference to that property into the `condition` statement by itself. Otherwise, the `condition` statement consists of two values separated by a comparison operator, such as `==` (equals) or `!=` (does not equal).

Next, look at some real JavaScript. The following function receives a form object containing a text object called `entry`:

```
function notTooHigh(form) {
    if (parseInt(form.entry.value) > 100) {
        alert("Sorry, the value you entered is too high. Try again.");
        return false;
    }
    return true;
}
```

The condition (in parentheses) tests the contents of the field against a hard-wired value of 100. If the entered value is larger than that, the function alerts you and returns a `false` value to the calling statement elsewhere in the script. But if the value is less than 100, all intervening code is skipped and the function returns `true`.

About (*condition*) expressions

A lot of condition testing for control structures compares a value against some very specific condition, such as a string's being empty or a value's being `null`. You can use a couple of shortcuts to take care of many circumstances. Table 32-1 details the values that evaluate to a true or false (or equivalent) to satisfy a control structure's *condition* expression.

TABLE 32-1

Condition Value Equivalents

True	False
Nonempty string	Empty string
Nonzero number	0
Nonnull value	Null
Object exists	Object doesn't exist
Property is defined	Undefined property

Instead of having to spell out an equivalency expression for a condition involving these kinds of values, you can simply supply the value to be tested. For example, if a variable named myVal is capable of reaching an if construction with a value of null, an empty string, or a string value for further processing, you can use the following shortcut:

```
if (myVal) {
    // do processing on myVal
}
```

All null or empty string conditions evaluate to false, so that only the cases of myVal's being a processable value get inside the if construction. This mechanism is the same that you have seen elsewhere in this book to employ object detection for browser branching. For example, the code nested inside the following code segment executes only if the document object has an images array property:

```
if (document.images) {
    // do processing on image objects
}
```

Complex decisions

The simple type of if construction described earlier is fine when the decision is to take a small detour before returning to the main path. But not all decisions—in programming or in life—are like that. To present two alternate paths in a JavaScript decision, you can add a component to the construction. The syntax is

```
if (condition) {
    statementsIfTrue
} else {
    statementsIfFalse
}
```

By appending the else keyword, you give the if construction a path to follow in case the condition evaluates to false. The statementsIfTrue and statementsIfFalse do not have to be balanced in any way: One statement can be one line of code, the other 100 lines. But when either one of those branches completes, execution continues after the last closing brace. To demonstrate how this construction can come in handy, the following example is a script fragment that assigns the number of days in February based on whether or not the year is a leap year (using modulo arithmetic, explained in Chapter 33, to determine if the year is evenly divisible by four, and setting aside all other leap year calculation details for the moment):

```
var howMany = 0;
var theYear = 2002;
if (theYear % 4 == 0) {
   howMany = 29;
} else {
   howMany = 28;
}
```

Here is a case where execution has to follow only one of two possible paths to assign the number of days to the howMany variable. Had I not used the else portion, as in

```
var howMany = 0;
var theYear = 2002;
if (theYear % 4 == 0) {
   howMany = 29;
}
howMany = 28;
```

then the variable would always be set to 28, occasionally after momentarily being set to 29. The else construction is essential in this case.

Nesting if. . .else statements

Designing a complex decision process requires painstaking attention to the logic of the decisions your script must process and the statements that must execute for any given set of conditions. The need for repetitive logic disappeared with the advent of switch construction in version 4 browsers (described later in this chapter), but there may still be times when you must fashion complex decision behavior out of a series of nested if. . .else statements. Without a JavaScript-aware text editor to help keep everything properly indented and properly terminated (with closing braces), you have to monitor the authoring process very carefully. Moreover, the error messages that JavaScript provides when a mistake occurs (see Chapter 45 on the CD-ROM) may not point directly to the problem line but only to the region of difficulty.

To demonstrate a deeply nested set of if. . .else constructions, Listing 32-1 presents a simple user interface to a complex problem. A single text object asks the user to enter one of three letters — A, B, or C. The script behind that field processes a different message for each of the following conditions:

- The user enters no value.
- The user enters A.
- The user enters B.
- The user enters C.
- The user enters something entirely different.

NOTE The property assignment event handling technique employed throughout the code in this chapter and much of the book is a deliberate simplification to make the code more readable. It is generally better to use the more modern approach of binding events using the addEventListener() (NN6+/Moz/W3C) or attachEvent() (IE5+) methods. A modern cross-browser event handling technique is explained in detail in Chapter 25.

What's with the Formatting?

Indentation of the if construction and the further indentation of the statements executed on a true condition are not required by JavaScript. What you see here, however, is a convention that most JavaScript scripters follow. As you write the code in your text editor, you can use the Tab key to establish each level of indentation; some developers prefer using a setting in their editor that converts tabs to spaces, which guarantees that indentations are consistent across different editors. The browser ignores these tab characters (and/or spaces) when loading the HTML documents containing your scripts.

LISTING 32-1

Deeply Nested if. . .else Constructions

```
<html>
    <head>
        <title></title>
        <script type="text/javascript">
        function testLetter(form){
            inpVal = form.entry.value;  // assign to shorter variable name
            if (inpVal != "") {  // if entry is not empty then dive in...
                if (inpVal == "A") {  // Is it an "A"?
                    alert("Thanks for the A.");
                } else if (inpVal == "B") {  // No.  Is it a "B"?
                    alert("Thanks for the B.");
                } else if (inpVal == "C") {  // No.  Is it a "C"?
                    alert("Thanks for the C.");
                } else {            // Nope.  None of the above
                    alert("Sorry, wrong letter or case.");
                }
            } else {   // value was empty, so skipped all other stuff above
                alert("You did not enter anything.");
            }
        }
        </script>
    </head>
    <body>
        <form onsubmit="return false">
            Please enter A, B, or C: <input type="text" name="entry"
            onchange="testLetter(this.form)" />
        </form>
    </body>
</html>
```

if. . .else

Each condition executes only the statements that apply to that particular condition, even if it takes several queries to find out what the entry is. You do not need to break out of the nested construction because when a true response is found, the relevant statement executes, and no other statements occur in the execution path to run.

Even if you understand how to construct a hair-raising nested construction, such as the one in Listing 32-1, the trickiest part is making sure that each left brace has a corresponding right brace. My technique for ensuring this pairing is to enter the right brace immediately after I type the left brace. I typically type the left brace, press Enter twice (once to open a free line for the next statement, once for the line that is to receive the right brace); tab, if necessary, to the same indentation as the line containing the left brace; and then type the right brace. Later, if I have to insert something indented, I just push down the right braces that I entered earlier. If I keep up this methodology throughout the process, the right braces appear at the desired indentation after I'm finished, even if the braces end up being dozens of lines below their original spot.

Conditional Expressions

Compatibility: WinIE3+, MacIE3+, NN2+, Moz+, Safari+

While I'm showing you decision-making constructions in JavaScript, now is a good time to introduce a special type of expression that you can use in place of an `if. . .else` control structure for a common type of decision — the instance where you want to assign one of two values to a variable, depending on the outcome of some condition. The formal definition for the conditional expression is as follows:

```
variable = (condition) ? val1 : val2;
```

This expression means that if the Boolean result of the `condition` statement is true, JavaScript assigns `val1` to the variable; otherwise, it assigns `val2` to the variable. Like other instances of condition expressions, this one must also be written inside parentheses. The question mark is key here, as is the colon separating the two possible values.

A conditional expression, though not particularly intuitive or easy to read inside code, is very compact. Compare an `if. . .else` version of an assignment decision that follows

```
var collectorStatus;
if (CDCount > 500) {
   collectorStatus = "fanatic";
} else {
   collectorStatus = "normal";
}
```

with the conditional expression version:

```
var collectorStatus = (CDCount > 500) ? "fanatic" : "normal";
```

The latter saves a lot of code lines (although the internal processing is the same as that of an `if. . .else` construction). Of course, if your decision path contains more statements than just one setting the value of a variable, the `if. . .else` or `switch` construction is preferable. This shortcut, however, is a handy one to remember if you need to perform very binary actions, such as setting a true-or-false flag in a script.

Repeat (for) Loops

Compatibility: WinIE3+, MacIE3+, NN2+, Moz+, Safari+

As you have seen in numerous examples throughout other chapters, the capability to cycle through every entry in an array or through every item of a form element is vital to many JavaScript scripts. Perhaps the most typical operation is inspecting a property of many similar items in search of a specific value, such as to determine which radio button in a group is selected. One JavaScript structure that allows for these repetitious excursions is the for loop, so-named after the keyword that begins the structure. Two other structures, called the while loop and do-while loop, are covered in the following sections.

The JavaScript for loop repeats a series of statements any number of times and includes an optional loop counter that can be used in the execution of the statements. The following is the formal syntax definition:

```
for ( [initial expression]; [condition]; [update expression]) {
    statements
}
```

The three statements inside the parentheses (parameters to the for statement) play a key role in the way a for loop executes.

An initial expression in a for loop is executed one time, the first time the for loop begins to run. The most common application of the initial expression is to assign a name and starting value to a loop counter variable. Thus, seeing a var statement that both declares a variable name and assigns an initial value (generally 0 or 1) to it is not uncommon. An example is

```
var i = 0;
```

You can use any variable name, but conventional usage calls for the letter i, which is short for *index*. If you prefer the word counter or another word that reminds you of what the variable represents, that's fine, too. In any case, the important point to remember about this statement is that it executes once at the outset of the for loop.

The second statement is a *condition*, precisely like the condition statement you saw in if constructions earlier in this chapter. When a loop-counting variable is established in the initial expression, the condition statement usually defines how high the loop counter should go before the looping stops. Therefore, the most common statement here is one that compares the loop counter variable against some fixed value — is the loop counter less than the maximum allowed value? If the condition is false at the start, the body of the loop is not executed. But if the loop does execute, then every time execution comes back around to the top of the loop, JavaScript reevaluates the condition to determine the current result of the expression. If the loop counter increases with each loop, eventually the counter value goes beyond the value in the condition statement, causing the condition statement to yield a Boolean value of false. The instant that happens, execution drops out of the for loop entirely.

The final statement, the *update expression*, is executed at the end of each loop execution — after all statements nested inside the for construction have run. Again, the loop counter variable can be a factor here. If you want the counter value to increase by one the next time through the loop (called incrementing the value), you can use the JavaScript operator that makes that happen: the ++ operator appended to the variable name. That task is the reason for the appearance of all those i++ symbols in the for loops that you've seen already in this book. You're not limited to incrementing by one. You can increment by any multiplier you want or even drive a loop counter backward by decrementing the value (i--).

for

Now, take this knowledge and beef up the formal syntax definition with one that takes into account a typical loop-counting variable, i, and the common ways to use it:

```
//incrementing loop counter
for (var i = minValue; i <= maxValue; i++) {
   statements
}
//decrementing loop counter
for (var i = maxValue; i >= minValue; i--) {
   statements
}
```

In the top format, the variable, i, is initialized at the outset to a value equal to that of minValue. Variable i is immediately compared against maxValue. If i is less than or equal to maxValue, processing continues into the body of the loop. At the end of the loop, the update expression executes. In the top example, the value of i is incremented by 1. Therefore, if i is initialized as 0, then the first time through the loop, the i variable maintains that 0 value during the first execution of statements in the loop. The next time around, the variable has the value of 1.

As you may have noticed in the formal syntax definition, each of the parameters to the for statement is optional. For example, the statements that execute inside the loop may control the value of the loop counter based on data that gets manipulated in the process. Therefore, the update statement would probably interfere with the intended running of the loop. But I suggest that you use all three parameters until such time as you feel absolutely comfortable with their roles in the for loop. If you omit the condition statement, for instance, and you don't program a way for the loop to exit on its own, your script may end up in an infinite loop—which does your users no good.

Putting the loop counter to work

Despite its diminutive appearance, the i loop counter (or whatever name you want to give it) can be a powerful tool for working with data inside a repeat loop. For example, examine a version of the classic JavaScript function that creates an array while initializing entries to a value of 0:

```
// initialize array with n entries
function MakeArray(n) {
   this.length = n;
   for (var i = 1; i <= n; i++) {
      this[i] = 0;
   }
   return this;
}
```

The loop counter, i, is initialized to a value of 1, because you want to create an array of empty entries (with value 0) starting with the one whose index value is 1 (the zeroth entry is assigned to the length property) in the previous line. In the condition statement, the loop continues to execute as long as the value of the counter is less than or equal to the number of entries being created (n). After each loop, the counter increments by 1. In the nested statement that executes within the loop, you use the value of the i variable to substitute for the index value of the assignment statement:

```
this[i] = 0;
```

The first time the loop executes, the value expression evaluates to

```
this[1] = 0;
```

The next time, the expression evaluates to

```
this[2] = 0;
```

and so on, until all entries are created and stuffed with 0.

Recall the HTML page in Listing 31-2, where a user chooses a regional office from a `select` list (triggering a script to look up the manager's name and sales quota for that region). Because the regional office names are stored in an array, the page could be altered so that a script populates the `select` element's options from the array. That way, if there is ever a change to the alignment of regional offices, there need be only one change to the array of offices, and the HTML doesn't have to be modified. As a reminder, here is the definition of the regional offices array, created while the page loads:

```
var regionalOffices = ["New York", "Chicago", "Houston", "Portland"];
```

A script inside the HTML form can be used to dynamically generate the `select` list as follows:

```
<script type="text/javascript">
var elem = ""; // start assembling next part of page and form
elem += "<p>Select a regional office: ";
elem += "<select name='offices' onchange='getData(this.form)'>";
// build options list from array office names
for (var i = 0; i < regionalOffices.length; i++) {
    elem += "<option";    // option tags
    if (i == 0) {         // pre-select first item in list
        elem += " selected='selected'";
    }
    elem += ">" + regionalOffices[i];
}
elem += "</select></p>"; // close select item tag
document.write(elem);    // write element to the page
</script>
```

Notice one important point about the `condition` statement of the `for` loop: JavaScript extracts the `length` property from the array to be used as the loop counter boundary. From a code maintenance and stylistic point of view, this method is preferable to hard-wiring a value there. If the company added a new regional office, you would make the addition to the array "database," whereas everything else in the code would adjust automatically to those changes, including creating a longer pop-up menu in this case.

Notice, too, that the operator for the `condition` statement is less-than (<): The zero-based index values of arrays mean that the maximum index value we can use is one less than the actual count of items in the array. This is vital information, because the index counter variable (`i`) is used as the index to the `regionalOffices` array each time through the loop to read the string for each item's entry. You also use the counter to determine which is the first option, so that you can take a short detour (via the `if` construction) to add the `selected` attribute to the first option's definition.

The utility of the loop counter in `for` loops often influences the way you design data structures, such as two-dimensional arrays (see Chapter 31) for use as databases. Always keep the loop-counter mechanism in the back of your mind when you begin writing JavaScript script that relies on collections of data that you embed in your documents.

Breaking out of a loop

Some loop constructions perform their job as soon as a certain condition is met, at which point they have no further need to continue looping through the rest of the values in the loop counter's range. A common scenario for this is the cycling of a loop through an entire array in search of a single entry that matches some criterion. That criterion test is set up as an `if` construction inside the loop. If that criterion is met, you break out of the loop and let the script continue with the more meaningful processing of succeeding statements in the main flow. To accomplish that exit from the loop, use the `break` statement. The following schematic shows how the `break` statement may appear in a `for` loop:

```
for (var i = 0; i < array.length; i++) {
    if (array[i].property == magicValue) {
        statements that act on entry array[i]
        break;
    }
}
```

The `break` statement tells JavaScript to bail out of the nearest `for` loop (in case you have nested `for` loops). Script execution then picks up immediately after the closing brace of the `for` statement. The variable value of `i` remains whatever it was at the time of the break, so that you can use that variable later in the same script to access, say, that same array entry.

I use a construction similar to this in Chapter 22. There, the discussion of radio buttons demonstrates this construction, where, in Listing 22-6, you see a set of radio buttons whose `value` attributes contain screen sizes, in pixels. A function uses a `for` loop to find out which button was selected and then uses that item's index value — after the `for` loop breaks out of the loop — to alert the user. Listing 32-2 shows the relevant function.

LISTING 32-2

Breaking Out of a for Loop

```
function showMegapixels(form) {
    for (var i = 0; i < form.sizes.length; i++) {
        if (form.sizes[i].checked) {
            break;
        }
    }
    alert("That image size requires " + form.sizes[i].value + " megapixels.");
}
```

In this case, breaking out of the `for` loop was for more than mere efficiency; the value of the loop counter (frozen at the break point) is used to summon a different property outside of the `for` loop. Starting back in version 4 browsers, the `break` statement gained additional powers in cooperation with the new `label` feature of control structures. This subject is covered later in this chapter.

Directing loop traffic with continue

One other possibility in a `for` loop is that you may want to skip execution of the nested statements for just one condition. In other words, as the loop goes merrily on its way round and round, executing statements for each value of the loop counter, one value of that loop counter may exist for which you don't want those statements to execute. To accomplish this task, the nested statements need to include an `if` construction to test for the presence of the value to skip. When that value is reached, the `continue` command tells JavaScript to immediately skip the rest of the body, execute the `update` statement, and loop back around to the top of the loop.

To illustrate this construction, take a look at an artificial example that skips over execution when the counter variable is the superstitious person's unlucky 13:

```
for (var i = 0; i <= 20; i++) {
    if (i == 13) {
        continue;
    }
    statements
}
```

In this example, the `statements` part of the loop executes for all values of i except 13. The `continue` statement forces execution to jump to the `i++` part of the loop structure, incrementing the value of i for the next time through the loop. In the case of nested `for` loops, a `continue` statement affects the `for` loop in whose immediate scope the `if` construction falls. The `continue` statement was enhanced in version 4 browsers with the `label` feature of control structures, which is covered later in this chapter.

The while Loop

Compatibility: WinIE3+, MacIE3+, NN2+, Moz+, Safari+

The `for` loop is not the only kind of repeat loop you can construct in JavaScript. Another statement, called a `while` statement, sets up a loop in a slightly different format. Rather than providing a mechanism for modifying a loop counter, a `while` repeat loop assumes that your script statements will reach a condition that forcibly exits the repeat loop.

The basic syntax for a `while` loop is

```
while (condition) {
    statements
}
```

The `condition` expression is the same kind that you saw in `if` constructions and in the middle parameter of the `for` loop. You introduce this kind of loop if some condition exists in your code (evaluates to `true`) before reaching this loop. The loop then performs some action, which affects that condition repeatedly until that condition becomes `false`. At that point, the loop exits, and script execution continues with statements after the closing brace. If the statements inside the `while` loop do not somehow affect the values being tested in `condition`, your script never exits, and it becomes stuck in an infinite loop.

do-while

Many loops can be rendered with either the `for` or `while` loops. In fact, Listing 32-3 shows a `while` loop version of the `for` loop from Listing 32-2.

LISTING 32-3

A while Loop Version of Listing 32-2

```
function showMegapixels(form) {
   var i = 0;
   while (!form.sizes[i].checked) {
      i++;
   }
   alert("That image size requires " + form.sizes[i].value + " megapixels.");
}
```

One point you may notice is that if the condition of a `while` loop depends on the value of a loop counter, the scripter is responsible for initializing the counter prior to the `while` loop construction and managing its value within the `while` loop.

Should you need their powers, the `break` and `continue` control statements work inside `while` loops as they do in `for` loops. But because the two loop styles treat their loop counters and conditions differently, be extra careful (do lots of testing) when applying `break` and `continue` statements to both kinds of loops.

No hard-and-fast rules exist for which type of loop construction to use in a script. I generally use `while` loops only when the data or object I want to loop through is already a part of my script before the loop. In other words, by virtue of previous statements in the script, the values for any condition or loop counting (if needed) are already initialized. But if I need to cycle through an object's properties or an array's entries to extract some piece of data for use later in the script, I favor the `for` loop. The `for` loop is also generally preferred when the looping involves a simple counter from one value to another.

Another point of style, particularly with the `for` loop, is where a scripter should declare the `i` variable. Some programmers prefer to declare (or initialize if initial values are known) all variables in the opening statements of a script or function. That is why you tend to see a lot of `var` statements in those positions in scripts. If you have only one `for` loop in a function, for example, nothing is wrong with declaring and initializing the `i` loop counter in the initial expression part of the `for` loop (as demonstrated frequently in the previous sections). But if your function utilizes multiple `for` loops that reuse the `i` counter variable (that is, the loops run completely independently of one another), then you can declare the `i` variable once at the start of the function and simply assign a new initial value to `i` in each `for` construction.

The do-while Loop

Compatibility: WinIE4+, MacIE4+, NN4+, Moz+, Safari+

JavaScript brings you one more looping construction, called the `do-while` loop. The formal syntax for this construction is as follows:

```
do {
   statements
} while (condition)
```

An important difference distinguishes the `do-while` loop from the `while` loop. In the `do-while` loop, the statements in the construction always execute at least one time before the condition can be tested; in a `while` loop, the statements may never execute if the condition tested at the outset evaluates to `false`. So, just think of the `do-while` loop as a `while` loop where the first statement gets executed no matter what.

Use a `do-while` loop when you know for certain that the looped statements are free to run at least one time. If the condition may not be met the first time, use the `while` loop. For many instances, the two constructions are interchangeable, although only the `while` loop is compatible with legacy browsers.

Looping through Properties (for-in)

Compatibility: WinIE3+, MacIE3+, NN2+, Moz+, Safari+

JavaScript includes a variation of the `for` loop, called a `for-in` loop, which has special powers of extracting the names and values of any object property currently in the browser's memory. The syntax looks like this:

```
for (var in object) {
    statements
}
```

The `object` parameter is not the string name of an object but a reference to the object itself. JavaScript delivers an object reference if you provide the name of the object as an unquoted string, such as `window` or `document`. Using the `var` variable, you can create a script that extracts and displays the range of properties for any given object.

Listing 32-4 shows a page containing a utility function that you can insert into your HTML documents during the authoring and debugging stages of designing a JavaScript-enhanced page. In the example, the current `window` object is examined and its properties are presented in the page (note that Safari 1.0 doesn't expose `window` object properties).

LISTING 32-4

Property Inspector Function

```
<html>
  <head>
    <title></title>
    <script type="text/javascript">
    function showProps(obj,objName) {
      var result = "";
      for (var i in obj) {
        result += objName + "." + i + " = " + obj[i] + "<br />";
      }
      return result;
    }
    </script>
  </head>
```

continued

LISTING 32-4   *(continued)*

```
<body>
   <b>Here are the properties of the current window:</b>
   <p>
      <script type="text/javascript">
      document.write(showProps(window, "window"));
      </script>
   </p>
</body>
</html>
```

For debugging purposes, you can revise the function slightly to display the results in an alert dialog box. Replace the `<br />` HTML tag with the `\n` carriage return character for a nicely formatted display in the alert dialog box. You can call this function from anywhere in your script, passing both the object reference and a string to it to help you identify the object after the results appear in an alert dialog box. If the `showProps()` function looks familiar to you, it is because it closely resembles the property inspector routines of The Evaluator (see Chapter 13). In Chapter 45 on the CD-ROM, you can see how to embed functionality of The Evaluator into a page under construction so that you can view property values while debugging your scripts.

The with Statement

Compatibility: WinIE3+, MacIE3+, NN2+, Moz+, Safari+

The `with` statement enables you to preface any number of statements by advising JavaScript on precisely which object your scripts will be talking about, so that you don't have to use full, formal addresses to access properties or invoke methods of the same object. The formal syntax definition of the `with` statement is as follows:

```
with (object) {
   statements
}
```

The object reference is a reference to any valid object currently in the browser's memory. An example of this appears in Chapter 29's discussion of the `Math` object. By embracing several `Math`-encrusted statements inside a `with` construction, your scripts can call the properties and methods without having to make the object part of every reference to those properties and methods. Here's an example:

```
with (Math) {
   randInt = round(random() * 100);
}
```

This example uses the `round()` and `random()` methods of the `Math` object to obtain a random integer between 0 and 100. The significance of the code is how the `with` statement allows you to forego using the full notation of `Math.round()` and `Math.random()`.

An advantage of the `with` structure is that it can make heavily object-dependent statements easier to read and understand. Consider this long version of a function that requires multiple calls to the same object (but different properties):

```
function seeColor(form) {
    newColor = (form.colorsList.options[form.colorsList.selectedIndex].text);
    return newColor;
}
```

Using the `with` structure, you can shorten the long statement:

```
function seeColor(form) {
    with (form.colorsList) {
        newColor = (options[selectedIndex].text);
    }
    return newColor;
}
```

When JavaScript encounters an otherwise unknown identifier inside a `with` statement, it tries to build a reference out of the object specified as its parameter and that unknown identifier. You cannot, however, nest `with` statements that build on one another. For instance, in the preceding example, you cannot have a `with` (`colorsList`) nested inside a `with` (`form`) statement and expect JavaScript to create a reference to options out of the two object names.

As clever as the `with` statement may seem, be aware that it introduces some inherent performance penalties in your script (because of the way the JavaScript interpreter must artificially generate references). You probably won't notice degradation with occasional use of this construction, but if it's used inside a loop that must iterate many times, processing speed will almost certainly be affected negatively.

Labeled Statements

Compatibility: WinIE4+, MacIE4+, NN4+, Moz+, Safari+

Crafting multiple nested loops can sometimes be difficult when the final condition your script is looking for is met deep inside the nests. The problem is that the `break` or `continue` statement by itself has scope only to the nearest loop level. Therefore, even if you break out of the inner loop, the outer loop(s) continue to execute. If all you want to do is exit the function after the condition is met, a simple `return` statement performs the same job as some other languages' exit command. But if you also need some further processing within that function after the condition is met, you need the JavaScript facility supported in modern browsers that lets you assign labels to blocks of statements. Your `break` and `continue` statements can then alter their scope to apply to a labeled block other than the one containing the statement.

A *label* is any identifier (that is, name starting with a letter and containing no spaces or odd punctuation other than an underscore) followed by a colon preceding a logical block of executing statements, such as an `if. . .then` or loop construction. The formal syntax looks like the following:

```
labelID:
    statements
```

label

For a `break` or `continue` statement to apply itself to a labeled group, the label is added as a kind of parameter to each statement, as in

```
break labelID;
continue labelID;
```

> **NOTE** If you're arriving at JavaScript from another programming language that has a bit more structure, such as C++ or Java, the thought of labeled code may have you worried about the risks of creating code that is impossible to manage. This worry is likely rooted in the `goto` statement that is found in some languages, such as BASIC, and which is seriously frowned upon in modern structured languages. Labels in JavaScript are much more limited than the infamous `goto` statement in other languages and can only target labels they are nested in. So while I don't necessarily encourage the heavy usage of labels, you can rest easy knowing that they aren't on par with the much maligned `goto` statement.

To demonstrate how valuable this can be in the right situation, Listing 32-5 contains two versions of the same nested loop construction. The goal of each version is to loop through two different index variables until both values equal the target values set outside the loop. When those targets are met, the entire nested loop construction should break off and continue processing afterward. To help you visualize the processing that goes on during the execution of the loops, the scripts output intermediate and final results to a textarea.

In the version without labels, when the targets are met, only the simple `break` statement is issued. This breaks the inner loop at that point, but the outer loop picks up on the next iteration. By the time the entire construction has ended, a lot of wasted processing has gone on. Moreover, the values of the counting variables max themselves out, because the loops execute in their entirety several times after the targets are met.

But in the labeled version, the inner loop breaks out of the labeled outer loop as soon as the targets are met. Far fewer lines of code are executed, and the loop counting variables are equal to the targets, as desired. Experiment with Listing 32-5 by changing the `break` statements to `continue` statements. Then closely analyze the two results in the Results textarea to see how the two versions behave.

LISTING 32-5

Labeled Statements

```html
<html>
  <head>
    <title>Breaking Out of Nested Labeled Loops</title>
    <script type="text/javascript">
    var targetA = 2;
    var targetB = 2;
    var range = 5;
    function run1() {
      var out = document.forms[0].output;
      out.value = "Running WITHOUT labeled break\n";
      for (var i = 0; i <= range; i++) {
        out.value += "Outer loop #" + i + "\n";
        for (var j = 0; j <= range; j++) {
          out.value += "  Inner loop #" + j + "\n";
          if (i == targetA && j == targetB) {
            out.value += "**BREAKING OUT OF INNER LOOP**\n";
```

```
                    break;
            }
        }
    }
    out.value += "After looping, i = " + i + ", j = " + j + "\n";
}
function run2() {
    var out = document.forms[0].output;
    out.value = "Running WITH labeled break\n";
    outerLoop:
    for (var i = 0; i <= range; i++) {
        out.value += "Outer loop #" + i + "\n";
        innerLoop:
        for (var j = 0; j <= range; j++) {
            out.value += "   Inner loop #" + j + "\n";
            if (i == targetA && j == targetB) {
                out.value += "**BREAKING OUT OF OUTER LOOP**\n";
                break outerLoop;
            }
        }
    }
    out.value += "After looping, i = " + i + ", j = " + j + "\n";
}
</script>
</head>
<body>
    <h1>Breaking Out of Nested Labeled Loops</h1>
    <hr />
    <p>Look in the Results field for traces of these button scripts:</p>
    <form>
        <p><input type="button" value="Execute WITHOUT Label"
            onclick="run1()" /></p>
        <p><input type="button" value="Execute WITH Label"
            onclick="run2()" /></p>
        <p>Results:</p>
        <textarea name="output" rows="43" cols="60"></textarea>
    </form>
</body>
</html>
```

The switch Statement

Compatibility: WinIE4+, MacIE4+, NN4+, Moz+, Safari+

In some circumstances, a binary — true or false — decision path is not enough to handle the processing in your script. An `object` property or `variable` value may contain any one of several values, and a separate execution path is required for each one. The most obvious way to establish such a decision path is with a series of `if. . .else` constructions. However, in addition to quickly getting unwieldy with nested code,

switch

the more conditions you must test, the less efficient the processing is, because each condition must be tested. The end result is a sequence of clauses and braces that can get very confusing.

Starting in version 4 browsers, a control structure in use by many languages was introduced to JavaScript. The implementation is similar to that of Java and C/C++, using the `switch` and `case` keywords. The basic premise is that you can create any number of execution paths based on the value of some expression. At the beginning of the structure, you identify what that expression is and then, for each execution path, assign a label matching a particular value.

The formal syntax for the `switch` statement is

```
switch (expression) {
case label1:
    statements
    [break]
case label2:
    statements
    [break]
...
[default:
    statements]
}
```

The `expression` parameter of the `switch` statement can evaluate to any string or number value. Labels are surrounded by quotes when the labels represent string values of the expression. Notice that the `break` statements are optional. A `break` statement forces the switch expression to bypass all other checks of succeeding labels against the expression value. It's important to understand that without a `break` statement at the end of each `case`, every line of code in the `switch` expression will get executed. Another option is the `default` statement, which provides a catchall execution path when the expression value does not match any of the `case` statement labels. If you'd rather not have any execution take place with a non-matching expression value, omit the default part of the construction.

To demonstrate the syntax of a working `switch` statement, Listing 32-6 provides the skeleton of a larger application of this control structure. The page contains two separate arrays of different product categories. Each product has its name and price stored in its respective array. A `select` list displays the product names. After a user chooses a product, the script looks up the product name in the appropriate array and displays the price.

The trick behind this application is the values assigned to each product in the select list. While the displayed text is the product name, the `value` attribute of each `<option>` tag is the array category for the product. That value is the expression used to decide which branch to follow. Notice, too, that I assign a label to the entire switch construction. The purpose of that is to let the deeply nested repeat loops for each case completely bail out of the switch construction (via a labeled `break` statement) whenever a match is made. You can extend this example to any number of product category arrays with additional `case` statements to match.

LISTING 32-6

The switch Construction in Action

```html
<html>
    <head>
        <title>Switch Statement and Labeled Break</title>
        <script type="text/javascript">
        // build two product arrays, simulating two database tables
        function product(name, price) {
            this.name = name;
            this.price = price;
        }
        var ICs = new Array();
        ICs[0] = new product("Septium 900MHz","$149");
        ICs[1] = new product("Septium Pro 1.0GHz","$249");
        ICs[2] = new product("Octium BFD 750MHz","$329");
        var snacks = new Array();
        snacks[0] = new product("Rays Potato Chips","$1.79");
        snacks[1] = new product("Cheezey-ettes","$1.59");
        snacks[2] = new product("Tortilla Flats","$2.29");

        // lookup in the 'table' associated with the product
        function getPrice(selector) {
            var chipName = selector.options[selector.selectedIndex].text;
            var outField = document.forms[0].cost;
            master:
            switch(selector.options[selector.selectedIndex].value) {
            case "ICs":
                for (var i = 0; i < ICs.length; i++) {
                    if (ICs[i].name == chipName) {
                        outField.value = ICs[i].price;
                        break master;
                    }
                }
                break;
            case "snacks":
                for (var i = 0; i < snacks.length; i++) {
                    if (snacks[i].name == chipName) {
                        outField.value = snacks[i].price;
                        break master;
                    }
                }
                break;
            default:
                outField.value = "Not Found";
            }
        }
```

continued

LISTING 32-6 *(continued)*

```
        </script>
    </head>
    <body>
        <b>Branching with the switch Statement</b>
        <hr />
        Select a chip for lookup in the chip price tables:
        <form>
            Chip:<select name="chips" onchange="getPrice(this)">
                <option></option>
                <option value="ICs">Septium 900MHz</option>
                <option value="ICs">Septium Pro 1.0GHz</option>
                <option value="ICs">Octium BFD 750MHz</option>
                <option value="snacks">Rays Potato Chips</option>
                <option value="snacks">Cheezey-ettes</option>
                <option value="snacks">Tortilla Flats</option>
                <option>Poker Chipset</option>
            </select>  Price:<input type="text" name="cost" size="10" />
        </form>
    </body>
</html>
```

Exception Handling

The subject of exception handling is relatively new to JavaScript. Formalized in Edition 3 of ECMA-262, parts of the official mechanism were implemented in IE5, with more complete implementations in IE6 and NN6, and of course in Mozilla, Firefox, Camino, and Safari.

Exceptions and errors

If you've done any scripting, you are certainly aware of JavaScript errors, whether they be from syntax errors in your code, or what are known as *runtime* errors — errors that occur while scripts are processing information. Ideally, a program should be aware of when an error occurs and handle it as gracefully as possible. This self-healing can prevent lost data and help keep users from seeing the ugliness of error messages. Chapter 16 covers the onerror event handler (and window.onerror property), which were early attempts at letting scripts gain a level of control over runtime errors. This event-driven mechanism works on a global level (that is, in the window object) and processes every error that occurs throughout the page. This event handler ends up being used primarily as a last-ditch defense against displaying any error message to the user and is a long way from what programmers consider to be exception handling.

In the English language, the term "exception" can mean something out of the ordinary, or something abnormal. This definition seems quite distant from the word "error," which usually means a mistake. In the realm of programming languages, however, the two words tend to be used interchangeably, and the difference between the two depends primarily on one's point of view.

Consider, for example, a simple script whose job is to multiply numbers that the user enters into two text fields on the page. The script is supposed to display the results in a third text box. If the script contains no data entry validation, JavaScript will attempt to multiply whatever values are entered into the text boxes. If the user enters two numbers, JavaScript is smart enough to recognize that even though the value properties of the two input text fields are strings, the strings contain numbers that can be converted to number types for the proper multiplication. Without complaint, the product of the two numbers gets calculated and displayed into the results.

But what if the user types a letter into one of the text boxes? Again, without any entry validation in the script, JavaScript has a fixed way of responding to such a request: The result of the multiplication operation is the NaN (not a number) constant. If you are an untrained user, you have no idea what NaN means, but your experience with computers tells you that some kind of error has occurred. You may blame the computer or you may blame yourself — the accurate response may in fact be to blame the JavaScript developer!

To shift the point of view to the programmer, however, the script was designed to be run by a user who never makes a typing mistake, intentional or not. That, of course, is not very good programming practice. Users make mistakes. Therefore, anticipating user input that is not what would be expected is the programmer's job — input that is an exception to the rules your program wants to operate by. You must include some additional code that handles the exceptions gracefully so as to not confuse the user with unintelligible output and perhaps even help the user repair the input to get a result. This extra programming code handles the undesirable and erroneous input and makes your scripts considerably more user-friendly and robust.

As it turns out, JavaScript and the W3C Document Object Model liberally mix terms of exception and error within the vocabulary used to handle exceptions. As you see shortly, an exception creates an *error object*, which contains information about the exception. It is safe to say that you can think of exceptions and errors as the same things.

The exception mechanism

Newcomers to JavaScript (or any programming environment, for that matter) may have a difficult time at first creating a mental model of how all this exception stuff runs within the context of the browser. It may be easy enough to understand how pages load and create object models, and how event handlers (or listeners in the W3C DOM terminology) cause script functions to run. But a lot of action also seems to be going on in the background. For example, the event object that is generated automatically with each event action (see Chapter 25) seems to sit "somewhere" while event handler functions run so that they can retrieve details about the event. After the functions finish their processing, the event object disappears, without even leaving behind a Cheshire Cat smile. Mysterious.

Browsers equipped for exception handling have more of this "stuff" running in the background, ready for your scripts when you need it. Because you have certainly viewed the details of at least one scripting error, you have already seen some of the exception-handling mechanism that is built into browsers. If a script error occurs, the browser creates in its memory an error object, whose properties contain details about the error. The precise details (described later in this chapter) vary from one browser brand to the next, but what you see in the error details readout is the default way the browser handles exceptions/errors. As browsers have matured, their makers have gone to great lengths to tone down the intrusion of script errors. For example in NN4+, errors appeared in a separate JavaScript Console window (which must be invoked in NN4 by typing javascript: into the Location field; or opened directly via the Tools menu in NN6+ and Mozilla-based browsers, including Firefox and Camino). In IE4+ for Windows, the status bar comes into play again, as the icon at the bottom-left corner turns into an alert icon: Double-clicking the icon displays more information about the error. MacIE users can turn off scripting error alerts altogether. Safari 1.0 didn't divulge any script errors but a JavaScript console was added as of version 1.3.

try-catch-finally

True exception handling, however, goes further than just displaying error messages. It also provides a uniform way to let scripts guard against unusual occurrences. Ideally, the mechanism makes sure that *all* runtime errors get funneled through the same mechanism to help simplify the scripting of exception handling. The mechanism is also designed to be used intentionally as a way for your own code to generate errors in a uniform way so that other parts of your scripts can handle them quietly and intelligently. In other words, you can use the exception handling mechanism as a kind of "back channel" to communicate from one part of your scripts to another.

The JavaScript exception handling mechanism is built around two groups of program execution statements. The first group consists of the try-catch-finally statement triumvirate; the second group is the single throw statement.

Using try-catch-finally Constructions

The purpose of the try-catch-finally group of related statements is to provide a controlled environment in which script statements that may encounter runtime errors can run, such that if an exception occurs, your scripts can act upon the exception without alarming the rest of the browser's error mechanisms. Each of the three statements precedes a block of code in the following syntax:

```
try {
    statements to run
}
catch (errorInfo) {
    statements to run if exception occurs in try block
}
finally {
    statements to run whether or not an exception occurred [optional]
}
```

Each try block must be mated with a catch and/or finally block at the same nesting level, with no intervening statements. For example, a function can have a one-level try-catch construction inside it as follows:

```
function myFunc() {
    try {
        statements
    }
    catch (e) {
        statements
    }
}
```

But if there were another try block nested one level deeper, a balancing catch or finally block would also have to be present at that deeper level:

```
function myFunc() {
    try {
        statements
        try {
            statements
        }
        catch (e) {
```

```
            statements
        }
    }
    catch (e) {
        statements
    }
}
```

The statements inside the `try` block include statements that you believe are capable of generating a runtime error because of user input errors, the failure of some page component to load, or a similar error. The presence of the `catch` block prevents errors from appearing in the browser's regular script error reporting system (for example, the JavaScript Console of Safari1.3+, NN6+, and Mozilla-based browsers).

An important term to know about exception handling of this type is *throw*. The convention is that when an operation or method call triggers an exception, it is said to "throw an exception." For example, if a script statement attempts to invoke a method of a string object, but that method does not exist for the object (perhaps you mistyped the method name), JavaScript throws an exception. Exceptions have names associated with them — a name that sometimes, but not always, reveals important information about the exception. In the mistyped method example just cited, the name of that exception is a `TypeError` (yet more evidence of how "exception" and "error" become intertwined).

The JavaScript language supported in modern browsers is not the only entity that can throw exceptions. The W3C DOM also defines categories of exceptions for DOM objects. For example, according to the Level 2 specification, the `appendChild()` method (see Chapter 15) can throw (or *raise*, in the W3C terminology) one of three exceptions:

Exception Name	When Thrown
HIERARCHY_REQUEST_ERR	If the current node is of a type that does not allow children of the type of the `newChild` node, or if the node to append is one of this node's ancestors
WRONG_DOCUMENT_ERR	If `newChild` was created from a different document than the one that created the current node
NO_MODIFICATION_ALLOWED_ERR	If the current node is read-only

Because the `appendChild()` method is capable of throwing exceptions, a JavaScript statement that invokes this method should ideally be inside a `try` block. If an exception is thrown, then script execution immediately jumps to the `catch` or `finally` block associated with the `try` block. Execution does not come back to the `try` block.

A `catch` block has special behavior. Its format looks similar to a function in a way, because the `catch` keyword is followed by a pair of parentheses and an arbitrary variable that is assigned a reference to the error object whose properties are filled by the browser when the exception occurs. One of the properties of that error object is the name of the error. Therefore, the code inside the `catch` block can examine the name of the error and perhaps include some branching code to take care of a variety of different errors that are caught.

To see how this construction may look in code, look at a hypothetical generic function whose job is to create a new element and append it to some other node. Both the type of element to be created and a reference to the parent node are passed as parameters. To take care of potential misuses of this function through the passage of improper parameter values, it includes extra error handling to treat all possible exceptions from the two DOM methods: `createElement()` and `appendChild()`. Such a function looks like Listing 32-7.

LISTING 32-7

A Hypothetical try-catch Routine

```
// generic appender
function attachToEnd(theNode, newTag) {
    try {
        var newElem = document.createElement(newTag);
        theNode.appendChild(newElem);
    }
    catch (e) {
        switch (e.name) {
        case "INVALID_CHARACTER_ERR" :
            statements to handle this createElement() error
            break;
        case "HIERARCHY_REQUEST_ERR" :
            statements to handle this appendChild() error
            break;
        case "WRONG_DOCUMENT_ERR" :
            statements to handle this appendChild() error
            break;
        case "NO_MODIFICATION_ALLOWED_ERR" :
            statements to handle this appendChild() error
            break;
        default:
            statements to handle any other error
        }
        return false;
    }
    return true;
}
```

The single catch block in Listing 32-7 executes only if one of the statements in the try block throws an exception. The exceptions may be not only one of the four specific ones named in the catch block but also syntax or other errors that could occur inside the try block. That's why you have a last-ditch case to handle truly unexpected errors. Your job as scripter is to not only anticipate errors but also to provide clean ways for the exceptions to be handled, whether they be through judiciously worded alert dialog boxes or perhaps even some self-repair. For example, in the case of the invalid character error for createElement(), your script may attempt to salvage the data passed to the attachToEnd() function and reinvoke the method passing theNode value as-is and the repaired value originally passed to newTag. If your repairs were successful, the try block would execute without error and carry on with the user's being completely unaware that a nasty problem had been averted. And that's really the goal of exception handling — to save the day when something "unexpected" goes wrong so that the user isn't left confused or frustrated.

A finally block contains code that always executes after a try block, whether or not the try block succeeds without throwing an error. Unlike the catch block, a finally block does not receive an error object as a parameter, so it operates very much in the dark about what transpires inside the try block. If you include both catch and finally blocks after a try block, the execution path depends on whether an exception is thrown. If no exception is thrown, the finally block executes after the last statement of the try block runs. But if the try block throws an exception, program execution runs first to the catch block. After all processing within the catch block finishes, the finally block executes. In development environments that give programmers complete control over resources, such as memory allocation, a finally block may be used to delete some temporary items generated in the try block, whether or not an exception occurs in the try block. Currently, JavaScript's automatic memory management system reduces the need for that kind of maintenance, but you should be aware of the program execution possibilities of the finally block in the try-catch-finally context.

Real-life exceptions

The example shown in Listing 32-7 is a bit idealized. The listing assumes that the browser dutifully reports every W3C DOM exception precisely as defined in the formal specification. Unfortunately, even the latest browsers have yet to fully comply with the DOM when it comes to exception reporting. Most browsers implement additional error naming conventions and layers between actual DOM exceptions and what gets reported with the error object at the time of the exception.

If you think these discrepancies make cross-browser exception handling difficult, you're right. Even simple errors are reported differently among the two major browser brands (IE and Mozilla) and the W3C DOM specification. Until the browsers exhibit a greater unanimity in exception reporting, the smoothest development road will be for those scripters who have the luxury of writing for one of the browser platforms, such as IE for Windows or Safari for Mac.

That said, however, one aspect of exception handling can still be used in all modern browsers without a hitch. You can take advantage of try-catch constructions to throw your own exceptions — a practice that is quite common in advanced programming environments.

Throwing Exceptions

The last exception handling keyword not covered yet — throw — makes it possible to utilize exception-handling facilities for your own management of processes, such as data entry validation. At any point inside a try block, you can manually throw an exception that gets picked up by the associated catch block. The details of the specific exception are up to you.

Syntax for the throw statement is as follows:

```
throw value;
```

The value you throw can be of any type, but good practice suggests that the value be an error object (described more fully later in this chapter). Whatever value you throw is assigned to the parameter of the catch block. Look at the following two examples. In the first, the value is a string message; in the second, the value is an error object.

Listing 32-8 presents one input text box for a number between 1 and 5. Clicking a button looks up a corresponding letter in an array and displays the letter in a second text box. The lookup script has two simple data validation routines to make sure the entry is a number and is in the desired range. Error checking here is done manually by script. If either of the error conditions occurs, throw statements force execution to jump to the catch block. The catch block assigns the incoming string parameter to the variable e. The design here assumes that the message being passed is text for an alert dialog box. Not only does a single catch block take care of both error conditions (and conceivably any others to be added later), but the catch block runs within the same variable scope as the function, so that it can use the reference to the input text box to focus and select the input text if there is an error.

LISTING 32-8

Throwing String Exceptions

```html
<html>
    <head>
        <title>Throwing a String Exception</title>
        <script type="text/javascript">
        var letters = new Array("A","B","C","D","E");
        function getLetter(fld) {
            try {
                var inp = parseInt(fld.value, 10);
                if (isNaN(inp)) {
                    throw "Entry was not a number.";
                }
                if (inp < 1 || inp > 5) {
                    throw "Enter only 1 through 5.";
                }
                fld.form.output.value = letters[inp - 1];
            }
            catch (e) {
                alert(e);
                fld.form.output.value = "";
                fld.focus();
                fld.select();
            }
        }
        </script>
    </head>
    <body>
        <h1>Throwing a String Exception</h1>
        <hr />
        <form>
            Enter a number from 1 to 5: <input type="text" name="input"
            size="5" /> <input type="button" value="Get Letter"
            onclick="getLetter(this.form.input)" /> Matching Letter is:<input
            type="text" name="output" size="5" />
        </form>
    </body>
</html>
```

The flaw with Listing 32-8 is that if some other kind of exception were thrown inside the try block, the value passed to the catch block would be an error object, not a string. The alert dialog box displayed to the user would be meaningless. Therefore, it is better to be uniform in your throw-catch constructions and pass an error object.

Listing 32-9 is an updated version of Listing 32-8, demonstrating how to create an error object that gets sent to the catch block via throw statements.

LISTING 32-9

Throwing an Error Object Exception

```html
<html>
    <head>
        <title>Throwing an Error Object Exception</title>
        <script type="text/javascript">
        var letters = new Array("A","B","C","D","E");
        function getErrorObj(msg) {
            var err = new Error(msg);
            return err;
        }
        function getLetter(fld) {
            try {
                var inp = parseInt(fld.value, 10);
                if (isNaN(inp)) {
                    throw getErrorObj("Entry was not a number.");
                }
                if (inp < 1 || inp > 5) {
                    throw getErrorObj("Enter only 1 through 5.");
                }
                fld.form.output.value = letters[inp - 1];
            }
            catch (e)  {
                alert(e.message);
                fld.form.output.value = "";
                fld.focus();
                fld.select();
            }
        }
        </script>
    </head>
    <body>
        <h1>Throwing an Error Object Exception</h1>
        <hr />
        <form>
            Enter a number from 1 to 5: <input type="text" name="input"
            size="5" /> <input type="button" value="Get Letter"
            onclick="getLetter(this.form.input)" /> Matching Letter is:<input
            type="text" name="output" size="5" />
        </form>
    </body>
</html>
```

The only difference to the catch block is that it now reads the message property of the incoming error object. This means that if some other exception is thrown inside the try block, the browser-generated message will be displayed in the alert dialog box.

throw

In truth, however, the job really isn't complete. In all likelihood, if a browser-generated exception is thrown, the message in the alert dialog box won't mean much to the user. The error message will probably be some kind of syntax or type error — the kind of meaningless error message you often get from your favorite operating system. A better design is to branch the `catch` block so that "intentional" exceptions thrown by your code are handled through the alert dialog box messages you've put there, but other types are treated differently. To accomplish this, you can take over one of the other properties of the error object — `name` — so that your `catch` block treats your custom messages separately.

In Listing 32-10, the `getErrorObj()` function adds a custom value to the `name` property of the newly created error object. The name you assign can be any name, but you want to avoid exception names used by JavaScript or the DOM. Even if you don't know what all of those are, you can probably conjure up a suitably unique name for your error. Down in the `catch` block, a `switch` construction branches to treat the two classes of errors differently. In this simplified example, about the only possible problem other than the ones being trapped for explicitly in the `try` block would be some corruption to the page during downloading. Therefore, for this example, the branch for all other errors simply asks that the user reload the page and try again. The point is, however, that you can have as many classifications of custom and system errors as you want and handle them in a single `catch` block accordingly.

LISTING 32-10

A Custom Object Exception

```
<html>
   <head>
      <title>Throwing a Custom Error Object Exception</title>
      <script type="text/javascript">
      var letters = new Array("A","B","C","D","E");
      function getErrorObj(msg) {
         var err = new Error(msg);
         err.name = "MY_ERROR";
         return err;
      }
      function getLetter(fld) {
         try {
            var inp = parseInt(fld.value, 10);
            if (isNaN(inp)) {
               throw getErrorObj("Entry was not a number.");
            }
            if (inp < 1 || inp > 5) {
               throw getErrorObj("Enter only 1 through 5.");
            }
            fld.form.output.value = letters[inp - 1];
         }
         catch (e) {
            switch (e.name) {
            case "MY_ERROR" :
               alert(e.message);
               fld.form.output.value = "";
               fld.focus();
               fld.select();
```

```
            break;
        default :
            alert("Reload the page and try again.");
        }
    }
}
    </script>
</head>
<body>
    <h1>Throwing a Custom Error Object Exception</h1>
    <hr />
    <form>
        Enter a number from 1 to 5: <input type="text" name="input"
        size="5" /> <input type="button" value="Get Letter"
        onclick="getLetter(this.form.input)" /> Matching Letter is:<input
        type="text" name="output" size="5" />
    </form>
</body>
</html>
```

If you want to see how the alternative branch of Listing 32-10 looks, copy the listing file from the CD-ROM to your hard disk and modify the last line of the try block so that one of the letters is dropped from the name of the array:

```
            fld.form.output.value = letter[inp - 1];
```

This may simulate the faulty loading of the page. If you enter one of the allowable values, the reload alert appears, rather than the actual message of the error object: letter is undefined. Your users will thank you.

All that's left now on this subject are the details on the error object.

Error Object

Properties	Methods
Error.prototype	errorObject.toString()
errorObject.constructor	
errorObject.description	
errorObject.filename	
errorObject.lineNumber	
errorObject.message	
errorObject.name	
errorObject.number	

errorObject.description

Syntax

Creating an error object:

```
var myError = new Error("message");
var myError = Error("message");
```

Accessing static `Error` object property:

```
Error.property
```

Accessing error object properties and methods:

```
errorObject.property | method([parameters])
```

Compatibility: WinIE5+, MacIE-, NN6+, Moz+, Safari+

About this object

An error object instance is created whenever an exception is thrown or when you invoke either of the constructor formats for creating an error object. Properties of the error object instance contain information about the nature of the error so that `catch` blocks can inspect the error and process error handling accordingly.

IE5 implemented an error object in advance of the ECMA-262 formal error object, and the IE5 version ended up having its own set of properties that are not part of the ECMA standard. Those proprietary properties are still part of IE5.5+, which includes the ECMA properties as well. NN6, on the other hand, started with the ECMA properties and adds two proprietary properties of its own. The browser uses these additional properties in its own script error reporting. The unfortunate bottom line for cross-browser developers is that no properties in common among all browsers support the error object. However, two common denominators (`name` and `message`) are between IE5.5+, NN6+, and other Mozilla-based browsers.

As described earlier in this chapter, you are encouraged to create an error object whenever you use the `throw` statement for your own error control. See the discussion surrounding Listing 32-9 about handling missing properties in IE.

Properties

constructor

(See `string.constructor` in Chapter 28)

description

Value: String.   Read/Write
Compatibility: WinIE5+, MacIE-, NN-, Moz-, FF-, Cam-, Safari-

The `description` property contains a descriptive string that provides some level of detail about the error. For errors thrown by the browser, the description is the same text that appears in the script error dialog box in IE. Although this property continues to be supported, the `message` property is preferred.

Related Items: `message` property.

fileName
lineNumber

Value: String.   Read/Write
Compatibility: WinIE-, MacIE-, NN6+, Moz-, FF-, Cam-, Safari-

The NN6 browser uses the `fileName` and `lineNumber` properties of an error object for its own internal script error processing—these values appear as part of the error messages that are listed in the JavaScript Console. The `fileName` is the URL of the document causing the error; the `lineNumber` is the source code line number of the statement that threw the exception. These properties are exposed to JavaScript, as well, so that your error processing may use this information if it is meaningful to your application.

See the discussion of the `window.error` property in Chapter 16 for further ideas on how to use this information for bug reporting from users.

Related Items: `window.error` property.

message

Value: String.   Read/Write
Compatibility: WinIE5.5+, MacIE-, NN6+, Moz+, Safari+

The `message` property contains a descriptive string that provides some level of detail about the error. For errors thrown by the browser, the message is the same text that appears in the script error dialog box in IE and the JavaScript Console in Mozilla. By and large, these messages are more meaningful to scripters than to users. Unfortunately, there are no standards for the wording of a message for a given error. Therefore, it is hazardous at best to use the message content in a `catch` block as a means of branching to handle particular kinds of errors. You may get by with this approach if you are developing for a single browser platform, but you have no assurances that the text of a message for a particular exception may not change in future browser versions.

Custom messages for errors that your code explicitly throws can be in user-friendly language if you intend to display such messages to users. See Listings 32-8 through 32-10 for examples of this usage.

Related Items: `description` property.

name

Value: String.   Read/Write
Compatibility: WinIE5.5+, MacIE-, NN6+, Moz+, Safari+

The `name` property generally contains a word that identifies the type of error that has been thrown. The most general kind of error (and the one that is created via the `new Error()` constructor) has a name `Error`. But JavaScript errors can be of several varieties: `EvalError`, `RangeError`, `ReferenceError`, `SyntaxError`, `TypeError`, and `URIError`. Some of these error types are not necessarily intended for exposure to scripters (they're used primarily in the inner workings of the JavaScript engine), but some browsers do expose them. Unfortunately, there are some discrepancies as to the specific name supplied to this property for script errors.

When JavaScript is being used in a W3C-compatible browser, some DOM exception types are returned via the `name` property. But browsers frequently insert their own error types for this property, and, as is common in this department, little uniformity exists among browser brands.

errorObject.toString()

For custom exceptions that your code explicitly throws, you can assign names as you want. As shown in Listings 32-9 and 32-10, this information can assist a `catch` block in handling multiple categories of errors.

Related Items: `message` property.

number

Value: Number.   Read/Write
Compatibility: WinIE5+, MacIE-, NN-, Moz-, FF-, Cam-, Safari-

IE5+ assigns unique numbers to each error description or message. The value of the `number` property must be massaged somewhat to retrieve a meaningful error description. Following is an example of how you must apply binary arithmetic to an error number to arrive at a meaningful result:

```
var errNum = errorObj.number & 0xFFFF;
```

To find out what an error number means, just look it up on Microsoft's Developer Network (MSDN) site at `http://msdn.microsoft.com/library/en-us/script56/html/js56jsmscRunTimeErrors.asp`.

Related Items: `description` property.

Methods
toString()

Returns: String (see text).
Compatibility: WinIE5+, MacIE-, NN6+, Moz+, Safari+

The `toString()` method for an error object should return a string description of the error. In IE5+, however, the method returns a reference to the very same error object. In Mozilla-based browsers, the method returns the `message` property string, preceded by the string `Error:` (with a space after the colon). Most typically, if you want to retrieve a human-readable expression of an error object, read its `message` (or, in IE5+, `description`) property.

Related Items: `message` property.

Chapter 33

JavaScript Operators

JavaScript is rich in operators: words and symbols in expressions that perform operations on one or two values to arrive at another value. Any value on which an operator performs some action is called an operand. An expression may contain one operand and one operator (called a unary operator), as in a++, or two operands separated by one operator (called a binary operator), as in a + b. Many of the same symbols are used in a variety of operators. The combination and order of those symbols are what distinguish their powers.

NOTE The vast majority of JavaScript operators have been in the language since the very beginning. But, as you may expect from an evolving language, some entries were added to the lexicon as the language matured and gained wider usage. In the rest of this chapter, compatibility charts typically govern an entire category of operator. If there are version anomalies for a particular operator within a category, they are covered in the text. The good news is that modern browsers support the entire set of JavaScript operators.

Operator Categories

To help you grasp the range of JavaScript operators, I group them into seven categories. I assign a wholly untraditional name (connubial) to the second group — but a name that I believe correctly identifies its purpose in the language. Table 33-1 shows the operator types.

TABLE 33-1

JavaScript Operator Categories

Type	What It Does
Comparison	Compares the values of two operands, deriving a result of either true or false (used extensively in condition statements for if...else and for loop constructions)
Connubial	Joins together two operands to produce a single value that is a result of an arithmetical or other operation on the two
Assignment	Stuffs the value of the expression of the right-hand operand into a variable name on the left-hand side, sometimes with minor modification, as determined by the operator symbol
Boolean	Performs Boolean arithmetic on one or two Boolean operands
Bitwise	Performs arithmetic or column-shifting actions on the binary (base-2) representations of two operands
Object	Helps scripts examine the heritage and capabilities of a particular object before they need to invoke the object and its properties or methods
Miscellaneous	A handful of operators that have special behaviors

Any expression that contains an operator evaluates to a value of some kind, meaning that a value is always left behind after an operation. Sometimes the operator changes the value of one of the operands; other times the result is a new value. Even this simple expression

```
5 + 5
```

shows two integer operands joined by the addition operator. This expression evaluates to 10. The operator (+) is what provides the instruction for JavaScript to follow in its never-ending drive to evaluate every expression in a script.

Doing an equality comparison on two operands that, on the surface, look very different is not at all uncommon. JavaScript doesn't care what the operands look like — only how they evaluate. Two very dissimilar-looking values can, in fact, be identical when they are evaluated. Thus, an expression that compares the equality of two values, such as

```
fred == 25
```

does, in fact, evaluate to true if the variable fred has the number 25 stored in it from an earlier statement.

Comparison Operators

Compatibility: WinIE3+, MacIE3+, NN2+, Moz+, Safari+

Anytime you compare two values in JavaScript, the result is a Boolean true or false value. You have a wide selection of comparison operators to choose from, depending on the kind of test you want to apply to the two operands. Table 33-2 lists all comparison operators.

TABLE 33-2

JavaScript Comparison Operators

Syntax	Name	Operand Types	Results
==	Equals	All	Boolean
!=	Does not equal	All	Boolean
===	Strictly equals	All	Boolean (IE4+, NN4+, Moz+, W3C)
!==	Strictly does not equal	All	Boolean (IE4+, NN4+, Moz+, W3C)
>	Is greater than	All	Boolean
>=	Is greater than or equal to	All	Boolean
<	Is less than	All	Boolean
<=	Is less than or equal to	All	Boolean

For numeric values, the results are the same as those you'd expect from your high school algebra class. Some examples follow, including some that may not be obvious.

```
10 == 10        // true
10 == 10.0      // true
9 != 10         // true
9 > 10          // false
9.99 <= 9.98    // false
```

Strings can also be compared on all of these levels:

```
"Fred" == "Fred"    // true
"Fred" == "fred"    // false
"Fred" > "fred"     // false
"Fran" < "Fred"     // true
```

To calculate string comparisons, JavaScript converts each character of a string to its ASCII value. Each letter, beginning with the first of the left-hand operator, is compared to the corresponding letter in the right-hand operator. With ASCII values for uppercase letters being less than those of their lowercase counterparts, an uppercase letter evaluates to being less than its lowercase equivalent. JavaScript takes case-sensitivity very seriously.

Values for comparison can also come from object properties or values passed to functions from event handlers or other functions. A common string comparison used in data-entry validation is the one that sees if the string has anything in it:

```
form.entry.value != ""    // true if something is in the field
```

Equality of Disparate Data Types

For all versions of JavaScript before 1.2 (legacy browsers), when your script tries to compare string values consisting of numerals and real numbers (for example, "123" == 123 or "123" != 123), JavaScript antici-pates that you want to compare apples to apples. Internally it does some data type conversion that does not affect the data type of the original values (for example, if the values are in variables). But the entire situation is more complex, because other data types, such as objects, need to be dealt with. Therefore, prior to JavaScript 1.2, the rules of comparison are as shown in Table 33-3.

TABLE 33-3

Equality Comparisons for JavaScript 1.0 and 1.1

Operand A	Operand B	Internal Comparison Treatment
Object reference	Object reference	Compare object reference evaluations
Any data type	Null	Convert nonnull to its object type and compare against null
Object reference	String	Convert object to string and compare strings
String	Number	Convert string to number and compare numbers

The logic to what goes on in equality comparisons from Table 33-3 requires a lot of forethought on the scripter's part, because you have to be very conscious of the particular way data types may or may not be converted for equality evaluation (even though the values themselves are not converted). In this situation, supplying the proper conversion where necessary in the comparison statement is best. This ensures that what you want to compare — for example, the string versions of two values or the number versions of two values — is compared, rather than leaving the conversion up to JavaScript.

Backward-compatible conversion from a number to string entails concatenating an empty string to a number:

```
var a = "09";
var b = 9;
a == "" + b;  // result: false, because "09" does not equal "9"
```

For converting strings to numbers, you have numerous possibilities. The simplest is subtracting zero from a numeric string:

```
var a = "09";
var b = 9;
a-0 == b;  // result: true because number 9 equals number 9
```

You can also use the parseInt() and parseFloat() functions to convert strings to numbers:

```
var a = "09";
var b = 9;
parseInt(a, 10) == b;  // result: true because number 9 equals number 9
```

Of course, the other solution is to reasonably assume that your user base has a modern web browser that supports JavaScript 1.2+. To clear up the ambiguity of JavaScript's equality internal conversions, in version 1.2 JavaScript added two more operators to force the equality comparison to be extremely literal in its comparison. The strictly equals (===) and strictly does not equal (!==) operators compare both the data type and value. The only time the === operator returns true is if the two operands are of the same data type (for example, both are numbers) and the same value. Therefore, no number is ever automatically equal to a string version of that same number. Data and object types must match before their values are compared.

JavaScript 1.2+ also provides some convenient global functions for converting strings to numbers and vice versa: `String()` and `Number()`. To demonstrate these methods, the following examples use the `typeof` operator to show the data type of expressions using these functions:

```
typeof 9;                // result: number
type of String(9);       // result: string
type of "9";             // result: string
type of Number("9");     // result: number
```

None of these functions alters the data type of the value being converted. But the value of the function is what gets compared in an equality comparison:

```
var a = "09";
var b = 9;
a == String(b);    // result: false, because "09" does not equal "9"
typeof b;          // result: still a number
Number(a) == b;    // result: true, because 9 equals 9
typeof a;          // result: still a string
```

This discussion should impress upon you the importance of considering data types when testing the equality of two values.

Connubial Operators

Compatibility: WinIE3+, MacIE3+, NN2+, Moz+, Safari+

Connubial operators is my terminology for those operators that join two operands to yield a value related to the operands. Table 33-4 lists the connubial operators in JavaScript.

TABLE 33-4

JavaScript Connubial Operators

Syntax	Name	Operand Types	Results
+	Plus	Integer, float, string	Integer, float, string
-	Minus	Integer, float	Integer, float
*	Multiply	Integer, float	Integer, float
/	Divide	Integer, float	Integer, float
%	Modulo	Integer, float	Integer, float
++	Increment	Integer, float	Integer, float
--	Decrement	Integer, float	Integer, float
+*val*	Positive	Integer, float, string	Integer, float
-*val*	Negation	Integer, float, string	Integer, float

Connubial Operators

The four basic arithmetic operators for numbers are straightforward. The plus operator also works on strings to join them together, as in

```
"Scooby " + "Doo" // result = "Scooby Doo"
```

In object-oriented programming terminology, the plus sign is considered *overloaded*, meaning that it performs a different action depending on its context. Remember, too, that string concatenation does not do anything on its own to monitor or insert spaces between words. In the preceding example, the space between the names is part of the first string.

Modulo arithmetic is helpful for those times when you want to know if one number divides evenly into another. You used it in an example in Chapter 32 to figure out if a particular year was a leap year. Although some other leap year considerations exist for the turn of each century, the math in the example simply checked whether the year was evenly divisible by four. The result of the modulo math is the remainder of division of the two values: When the remainder is 0, one divides evenly into the other. Here are some samples of years evenly divisible by four:

```
2002 % 4    // result = 2
2003 % 4    // result = 3
2004 % 4    // result = 0 (Bingo! Leap year!)
```

Thus, I used this modulo operator in a condition statement of an if. . .else structure:

```
var howMany = 0;
today = new Date();
var theYear = today.getYear();
if (theYear % 4 == 0) {
    howMany = 29;
} else {
    howMany = 28;
}
```

The modulo operator is also handy in special cases where you need to carry out some action in a loop at certain intervals, such as every third time through the loop. Here's an example of a loop that increments a counter every third time through while looping to 100:

```
for (var i = 1; i < 100; i++) {
    if (i % 3 == 0)
        threeCounter++;
}
```

Just as the modulo operator gives you the remainder of a division operation, some other languages offer an operator that results in the integer part of a division: integral division, or div. Although JavaScript does not have an explicit operator for this behavior, you can re-create it reliably if you know that your operands are always positive numbers. Use the Math.floor() or Math.ceil() methods with the division operator, as in

```
Math.floor(4/3);    // result = 1
```

In this example, Math.floor() works only with values greater than or equal to 0; Math.ceil() works with values less than 0.

The increment operator (++) is a *unary* operator (only one operand) and displays two different behaviors, depending on the side of the operand on which the symbols lie. Both the increment and decrement (--) operators can be used in conjunction with assignment operators, which I cover next.

As its name implies, the increment operator increases the value of its operand by one. But in an assignment statement, you have to pay close attention to precisely when that increase takes place. An assignment statement stuffs the value of the right operand into a variable on the left. If the ++ operator is located in front of the right operand (prefix), the right operand is incremented before the value is assigned to the variable; if the ++ operator is located after the right operand (postfix), the previous value of the operand is sent to the variable before the value is incremented. Follow this sequence to get a feel for these two behaviors:

```
var a = 10;     // initialize a to 10
var z = 0;      // initialize z to zero
z = a;          // a = 10, so z = 10
z = ++a;        // a becomes 11 before assignment, so a = 11 and z becomes 11
z = a++;        // a is still 11 before assignment, so z = 11; then a becomes 12
z = a++;        // a is still 12 before assignment, so z = 12; then a becomes 13
```

The decrement operator behaves the same way, except that the value of the operand decreases by one. Increment and decrement operators are used most often with loop counters in for and while loops. The simpler ++ or -- symbology is more compact than reassigning a value by adding 1 to it (such as, z = z + 1 or z += 1). Because these are unary operators, you can use the increment and decrement operators without an assignment statement to adjust the value of a counting variable within a loop:

```
function doNothing() {
    var i = 1;
    while (i < 20) {
        ++i;
    }
    alert(i); // breaks out at i = 20
}
```

The last pair of connubial operators are also unary operators (operating on one operand). Both the positive and negation operators can be used as shortcuts to the Number() global function, converting a string operand consisting of number characters to a number data type. The string operand is not changed, but the operation returns a value of the number type, as shown in the following sequence:

```
var a = "123";
var b = +a;     // b is now 123
typeof a;       // result: string
typeof b;       // result: number
```

The negation operator (-val) has additional power. By placing a minus sign in front of any numeric value (no space between the symbol and the value), you instruct JavaScript to evaluate a positive value as its corresponding negative value, and vice versa. The operator does not change the operand's value, but the expression returns the modified value. The following example provides a sequence of statements to demonstrate:

```
var x = 2;
var y = 8;
var z = -x;     // z equals -2, but x still equals 2
z = -(x + y);   // z equals -10, but x still equals 2 and y equals 8
z = -x + y;     // z equals 6, but x still equals 2 and y equals 8
```

To negate a Boolean value, see the Not (!) operator in the discussion of Boolean operators.

Assignment Operators

Compatibility: WinIE3+, MacIE3+, NN2+, Moz+, Safari+

Assignment statements are among the most common statements you write in your JavaScript scripts. These statements appear everywhere you copy a value or the results of an expression into a variable for further manipulation of that value.

You assign values to variables for many reasons, even though you could probably use the original values or expressions several times throughout a script. Here is a sampling of reasons why you should assign values to variables:

- Variable names are usually shorter
- Variable names can be more descriptive
- You may need to preserve the original value for later in the script
- The original value is a property that cannot be changed
- Invoking the same method several times in a script is not efficient

Newcomers to scripting often overlook the last reason. For instance, if a script is writing HTML to a new document, it's more efficient to assemble the string of large chunks of the page into one variable before invoking the document.write() method to send that text to the document. This approach is more efficient than literally sending out one line of HTML at a time with multiple document.writeln() method statements. Table 33-5 shows the range of assignment operators in JavaScript.

TABLE 33-5

JavaScript Assignment Operators

Syntax	Name	Example	Means
=	Equals	x = y	x = y
+=	Add by value	x += y	x = x + y
-=	Subtract by value	x -= y	x = x - y
*=	Multiply by value	x *= y	x = x * y
/=	Divide by value	x /= y	x = x / y
%=	Modulo by value	x %= y	x = x % y
<<=	Left shift by value	x <<= y	x = x << y
>=	Right shift by value	x >= y	x = x > y
>>=	Zero fill by value	x >>= y	x = x >> y
>>>=	Right shift by value	x >>>= y	x = x >>> y
&=	Bitwise and by value	x &= y	x = x & y
|=	Bitwise or by value	x |= y	x = x | y
^=	Bitwise XOR by value	x ^= y	x = x ^ y

As clearly demonstrated in the top group (see "Bitwise Operators" later in the chapter for information on the bottom group), assignment operators beyond the simple equals sign can save some characters in your typing, especially when you have a series of values that you're trying to bring together in subsequent statements. You've seen plenty of examples in previous chapters, where you used the add-by-value operator (+=) to work wonders with strings as you assemble a long string variable that you eventually send to a `document.write()` method. Look at this variation of a segment of Listing 31-3, where you could use JavaScript to create the HTML content of a `select` element on the fly:

```
var elem = "";  // start assembling next part of page and form
elem += "<p>Select a regional office: ";
elem += "<select name='offices' onchange='getData(this.form)'>";
// build options list from array office names
for (var i = 0; i < regionalOffices.length; i++) {
   elem += "<option";          // option tags
   if (i == 0) {               // pre-select first item in list
      elem += " selected='selected'";
   }
   elem += ">" + regionalOffices[i];
}
elem += "</select></p>";     // close select item tag
document.write(elem);        // write element to the page
```

The script segment starts with a plain equals assignment operator to initialize the `elem` variable as an empty string. In many of the succeeding lines, you use the add-by-value operator to tack additional string values onto whatever is in the `elem` variable at the time. Without the add-by-value operator, you are forced to use the plain equals assignment operator for each line of code to concatenate new string data to the existing string data. In that case, the first few lines of code look as shown:

```
var elem = "";  // start assembling next part of page and form
elem = elem + "<p>Select a regional office: ";
elem = elem + "<select name='offices' onchange='getData(this.form)'>";
```

Within the `for` loop, the repetition of `elem +` makes the code very difficult to read, trace, and maintain. These enhanced assignment operators are excellent shortcuts that you should use at every turn.

Boolean Operators

Compatibility: WinIE4+, MacIE4+, NN3+, Moz+, Safari+

Because a great deal of programming involves logic, it is no accident that the arithmetic of the logic world plays an important role. You've already seen dozens of instances where programs make all kinds of decisions based on whether a statement or expression is the Boolean value `true` or `false`. What you haven't seen much of yet is how to combine multiple Boolean values and expressions — a quality that scripts with slightly above average complexity may need to have in them.

In the various condition expressions required throughout JavaScript (such as in an `if` construction), the condition that the program must test for may be more complicated than, say, whether a variable value is greater than a certain fixed value or whether a field is not empty. Look at the case of validating a text field entry for whether the entry contains all the numbers that your script may want. Without some magical JavaScript function to tell you whether or not a string consists of all numbers, you have to break apart the entry character by character and examine whether each character falls within the range of 0 through 9. But that examination actually comprises two tests: You can test for any character whose ASCII value is less than 0 or greater than 9. Alternatively, you can test whether the character is greater than or equal to 0 and is less than or equal to 9. What you need is the bottom-line evaluation of both tests.

Boolean math

That's where the wonder of Boolean math comes into play. With just two values — `true` and `false` — you can assemble a string of expressions that yield Boolean results and then let Boolean arithmetic figure out whether the bottom line is `true` or `false`.

But you don't add or subtract Boolean values the same way you add or subtract numbers. Instead, you use one of three JavaScript Boolean operators at your disposal. Table 33-6 shows the three operator symbols. In case you're unfamiliar with the characters in the table, the symbols for the Or operator are created by typing Shift-backslash.

TABLE 33-6

JavaScript Boolean Operators

Syntax	Name	Operands	Results
&&	And	Boolean	Boolean
||	Or	Boolean	Boolean
!	Not	One Boolean	Boolean

Using Boolean operators with Boolean operands gets tricky if you're not used to it, so I have you start with the simplest Boolean operator: Not. This operator requires only one operand. The Not operator precedes any Boolean value to switch it back to the opposite value (from `true` to `false`, or from `false` to `true`). For instance:

```
!true          // result = false
!(10 > 5)      // result = false
!(10 < 5)      // result = true
!(document.title == "Flintstones")    // result = true
```

As shown here, enclosing the operand of a Not expression inside parentheses is always a good idea. This forces JavaScript to evaluate the expression inside the parentheses before flipping it around with the Not operator. Otherwise, you may accidentally perform the operation on only part of the intended expression, resulting in unexpected consequences.

The And (&&) operator joins two Boolean values to reach a `true` or `false` value based on the results of both values. This brings up something called a *truth table*, which helps you visualize all the possible outcomes for each value of an operand. Table 33-7 is a truth table for the And operator.

TABLE 33-7

Truth Table for the And Operator

Left Operand	And Operator	Right Operand	Result
True	&&	True	True
True	&&	False	False
False	&&	True	False
False	&&	False	False

Only one condition yields a `true` result: Both operands must evaluate to `true`. Which side of the operator a `true` or `false` value lives doesn't matter. Here are examples of each possibility:

```
5 > 1 && 50 > 10    // result = true
5 > 1 && 50 < 10    // result = false
5 < 1 && 50 > 10    // result = false
5 < 1 && 50 < 10    // result = false
```

NOTE You may be wondering why parentheses aren't being used in this code to separate the comparison and Boolean expressions. The reason has to do with operator precedence, which you learn a great deal more about later in the chapter. The short answer is that comparison operators are evaluated before Boolean operators. Even so, it's never a bad idea to use parentheses to group sub-expressions and make absolutely sure you're getting the desired result.

In contrast, the Or (||) operator is more lenient about what it evaluates to `true`. The reason is that if one or the other (or both) operands is `true`, the operation returns `true`. The Or operator's truth table is shown in Table 33-8.

TABLE 33-8

Truth Table for the Or Operator

Left Operand	Or Operator	Right Operand	Result
True	||	True	True
True	||	False	True
False	||	True	True
False	||	False	False

Boolean Operators

Therefore, if a `true` value exists on either side of the operator, a `true` value is the result. Take the previous examples and swap the And operators with Or operators so that you can see the Or operator's impact on the results:

```
5 > 1 || 50 > 10    // result = true
5 > 1 || 50 < 10    // result = true
5 < 1 || 50 > 10    // result = true
5 < 1 || 50 < 10    // result = false
```

Only when both operands are `false` does the Or operator return `false`.

Boolean operators at work

Applying Boolean operators to JavaScript the first time just takes a little time and some sketches on a pad of paper to help you figure out the logic of the expressions. Earlier I talked about using a Boolean operator to see whether a character fell within a range of ASCII values for data-entry validation. Listing 33-1 is a function discussed in more depth in Chapter 43 on the CD-ROM. This function accepts any string and sees whether each character of the string has an ASCII value less than 0 or greater than 9 — meaning that the input string is not a number.

LISTING 33-1

Is the Input String a Number?

```
function isNumber(inputStr) {
   for (var i = 0; i < inputStr.length; i++) {
      var oneChar = inputStr.substring(i, i + 1);
      if (oneChar < "0" || oneChar > "9") {
         alert("Please make sure entries are numerals only.");
         return false;
      }
   }
   return true;
}
```

Combining a number of JavaScript powers to read individual characters (substrings) from a `string` object within a `for` loop, the statement that you're interested in is the condition of the `if` construction:

```
(oneChar < "0" || oneChar > "9")
```

In one condition statement, you use the Or operator to test for both possibilities. If you check the Or truth table (Table 33-8), you see that this expression returns `true` if either one or both tests returns `true`. If that happens, the rest of the function alerts the user about the problem and returns a `false` value to the calling statement. Only if both tests within this condition evaluate to `false` for all characters of the string does the function return a `true` value.

From the simple Or operator, I go to the extreme, where the function checks — in one `condition` statement — whether a number falls within several numeric ranges. The script in Listing 33-2 comes from the array lookup application in Chapter 50 (on the CD-ROM), in which a user enters the first three digits of a U.S. Social Security number.

LISTING 33-2

Is a Number within Discontiguous Ranges?

```
// function to determine if value is in acceptable range for this application
function inRange(inputStr) {
    num = parseInt(inputStr)
    if (num < 1 || (num > 586 && num < 596) || (num > 599 && num < 700) ||
        num > 728) {
        alert("Sorry, the number you entered is not part of our database.  Try
            another three-digit number.");
        return false;
    }
    return true;
}
```

By the time this function is called, the user's data entry has been validated enough for JavaScript to know that the entry is a number. Now the function must check whether the number falls outside of the various ranges for which the application contains matching data. The conditions that the function tests here are whether the number is

- Less than 1
- Greater than 586 and less than 596 (using the And operator)
- Greater than 599 and less than 700 (using the And operator)
- Greater than 728

Each of these tests is joined by an Or operator. Therefore, if any one of these conditions proves `true`, the whole `if` condition is `true`, and the user is alerted accordingly.

The alternative to combining so many Boolean expressions in one `condition` statement would be to nest a series of `if` constructions. But such a construction requires not only a great deal more code but also much repetition of the alert dialog box message for each condition that could possibly fail. The combined Boolean condition is, by far, the best way to go.

Bitwise Operators

Compatibility: WinIE3+, MacIE3+, NN2+, Moz+, Safari+

For scripters, bitwise operations are an advanced subject. Unless you're dealing with external processes on server-side applications or the connection to Java applets, it's rare that you will use bitwise operators. Experienced programmers who concern themselves with more specific data types (such as long integers) are quite comfortable in this arena, so I simply provide an explanation of JavaScript capabilities. Table 33-9 lists JavaScript bitwise operators.

TABLE 33-9

JavaScript's Bitwise Operators

Operator	Name	Left Operand	Right Operand
&	Bitwise And	Integer value	Integer value
|	Bitwise Or	Integer value	Integer value
^	Bitwise XOR	Integer value	Integer value
~	Bitwise Not	(None)	Integer value
<<	Left shift	Integer value	Shift amount
>>	Right shift	Integer value	Shift amount
>>>	Zero fill right shift	Integer value	Shift amount

The numeric value operands can appear in any of the JavaScript language's three numeric literal bases (decimal, octal, or hexadecimal). As soon as the operator has an operand, the value is converted to binary representation (32 bits long). For the first three bitwise operations, the individual bits of one operand are compared with their counterparts in the other operand. The resulting value for each bit depends on the operator:

- **Bitwise And:** 1 if both digits are 1
- **Bitwise Or:** 1 if either digit is 1
- **Bitwise Exclusive Or:** 1 if only one digit is a 1

Bitwise Not, a unary operator, inverts the value of every bit in the single operand. The bitwise shift operators operate on a single operand. The second operand specifies the number of positions to shift the value's binary digits in the direction of the arrows of the operator symbols.

Example

For example, the left shift (<<) operator has the following effect:

```
4 << 2 // result = 16
```

The reason for this shifting is that the binary representation for decimal 4 is 00000100 (to eight digits, anyway). The left shift operator instructs JavaScript to shift all digits two places to the left, giving the binary result 00010000, which converts to 16 in decimal format. If you're interested in experimenting with these operators, use The Evaluator (Chapter 13) to evaluate sample expressions for yourself. More advanced books on C and C++ programming are also of help.

Object Operators

The next group of operators concern themselves with objects (including native JavaScript, DOM, and custom objects) and data types. Most of these have been implemented after the earliest JavaScript browsers, so each one has its own compatibility rating.

delete

Compatibility: WinIE4+, MacIE4+, NN4+, Moz+, Safari+

Array objects do not contain a method to remove an element from the collection, nor do custom objects offer a method to remove a property. You can always empty the data in an array item or property by setting its value to an empty string or `null`, but the array element or property remains in the object. With the `delete` operator, you can completely remove the element or property.

There is special behavior about deleting an array item that you should bear in mind. If your array uses numeric indices, a deletion of a given index removes that index value from the total array but without collapsing the array (which would alter index values of items higher than the deleted item).

Example

For example, consider the following simple dense array:

```
var oceans = new Array("Atlantic", "Pacific", "Indian","Arctic");
```

This kind of array automatically assigns numeric indices to its entries for addressing later in constructions, such as `for` loops:

```
for (var i = 0; i < oceans.length; i++) {
    if (oceans[i] == form.destination.value) {
        // statements
    }
}
```

If you then issue the statement

```
delete oceans[2];
```

the array undergoes significant changes. First, the third element is removed from the array. Note that the length of the array does not change. Even so, the index value (2) is removed from the array, such that schematically the array looks like the following:

```
oceans[0] = "Atlantic";
oceans[1] = "Pacific";
oceans[3] = "Arctic";
```

If you try to reference `oceans[2]` in this collection, the result is `undefined`.

The `delete` operator works best on arrays that have named indices since there is less confusion due to deleted numeric indices. Your scripts will have more control over the remaining entries and their values, because they don't rely on what could be a missing entry of a numeric index sequence.

One aspect of this deletion action that JavaScript doesn't provide is absolute control over memory utilization. All garbage collection is managed by the JavaScript interpreter engine, which tries to recognize when items occupying memory are no longer needed, at which time the unused browser's application memory may be recovered. But you cannot force the browser to perform its garbage collection task. So, deleting an entry from an array doesn't guarantee an immediate release of its associated memory.

instanceof

in

Compatibility: WinIE5.5+, MacIE-, NN6+, Moz+, Safari+

The `in` operator lets a script statement inspect an object to see if it has a named property or method. The operand to the left of the operator is a string reference to the property or method (just the method name, without parentheses); the operand to the right of the operator is the object being inspected. If the object knows the property or method, the expression returns `true`. Thus, you can use the `in` operator in expressions used for conditional expressions.

Example

You can experiment with this operator in The Evaluator (Chapter 13). For example, to prove that the `write()` method is implemented for the `document` object, the expression you type into the top text box of The Evaluator is:

```
"write" in document
```

But compare the implementation of the W3C DOM `document.defaultView` property in IE5.5+ and modern W3C browsers:

```
"defaultView" in document
```

In NN6+, Mozilla (including Firefox and Camino), and Safari, the result is `true`, while in IE5.5 and IE6, the result is `false`.

Having this operator around for conditional expressions lets you go much beyond simple object detection for branching code. For example, if you intend to use `document.defaultView` in your script, you can make sure that the property is supported before referencing it (assuming your users all have browsers that know the `in` operator).

instanceof

Compatibility: WinIE5+, MacIE-, NN6+, Moz+, Safari+

The `instanceof` operator lets a script test whether an object is an instance of a particular JavaScript native object or DOM object. The operand to the left side of the operator is the value under test; the value to the right of the operand is a reference to the root class from which the value is suspected of being constructed.

For native JavaScript classes, the kinds of object references to the right of the operator include such static objects as `Date`, `String`, `Number`, `Boolean`, `Object`, `Array`, and `RegExp`. You sometimes need to be mindful of how native JavaScript classes can sometimes be children of other native classes, which means that a value may be an instance of two different static objects.

Example

For example, consider the following sequence (which you can follow along in The Evaluator):

```
a = new Array(1,2,3);
a instanceof Array;
```

The second statement yields a result of `true`, because the `Array` constructor was used to generate the object. But the JavaScript `Array` is, itself, an instance of the root `Object` object. Therefore both of the following statements evaluate to `true`:

```
a instanceof Object;
Array instanceof Object;
```

new

Compatibility: WinIE3+, MacIE3+, NN2+, Moz+, Safari+

Most JavaScript core objects have constructor functions built into the language. To access those functions, you use the new operator along with the name of the constructor. The function returns a reference to the object instance, which your scripts can then use to get and set properties or invoke object methods. For example, creating a new date object requires invoking the Date object's constructor, as follows:

```
var today = new Date();
```

Some object constructor functions require parameters to help define the object. Others, as in the case of the Date object, can accept a number of different parameter formats, depending on the format of date information you have to set the initial object. The new operator can be used with the following core language objects as of each specified JavaScript version:

JavaScript 1.0	JavaScript 1.1	JavaScript 1.2	JavaScript 1.5
Date	Array	RegExp	Error
Object	Boolean		
(Custom object)	Function		
	Image		
	Number		
	String		

this

Compatibility: WinIE3+, MacIE3+, NN2+, Moz+, Safari+

JavaScript includes an operator that allows script statements to refer to the very object in which they are located. The self-referential operator is this.

The most common application of the this operator is in event handlers that pass references of themselves to functions for further processing, as in

```
<input type="text" name="entry" onchange="process(this)" />
```

A function receiving the value assigns it to a variable that can be used to reference the sender, its properties, and its methods.

Example

Because the this operator references an object, that object's properties can be exposed with the aid of the operator. For example, to send the value property of a text input object to a function, the this operator stands in for the current object reference and appends the proper syntax to reference the value property:

```
<input type="text" name="entry" onchange="process(this.value)" />
```

, (series)

The `this` operator also works inside other objects, such as custom objects. When you define a constructor function for a custom object, using the `this` operator to define properties of the object and assign values to those properties is common practice. Consider the following example of an object creation sequence:

```
function bottledWater(brand, ozSize, flavor) {
    this.brand = brand;
    this.ozSize = ozSize;
    this.flavor = flavor;
}
var myWater = new bottledWater("Crystal Springs", 16, "original");
```

When the new object is created via the constructor function, the `this` operators define each property of the object and then assign the corresponding incoming value to that property. Using the same names for the properties and parameter variables is perfectly fine and makes the constructor easy to maintain.

By extension, if you assign a function as an object's property (to behave as a method for the object), the `this` operator inside that function refers to the object invoking the function, offering an avenue to the object's properties. For example, if I add the following function definition and statement to the `myWater` object created just above, the function can directly access the `brand` property of the object:

```
function adSlogan() {
    return "Drink " + this.brand + ", it's wet and wild!";
}
myWater.getSlogan = adSlogan;
```

When a statement invokes the `myWater.getSlogan()` method, the object invokes the `adSlogan()` function, but all within the context of the `myWater` object. Thus, the `this` operator applies to the surrounding object, making the brand property available via the `this` operator (`this.brand`).

Miscellaneous Operators

The final group of operators doesn't fit into any of the previous categories, but they are no less important.

,

Compatibility: WinIE3+, MacIE3+, NN2+, Moz+, Safari+

The comma operator indicates a series of expressions that are to be evaluated in left-to-right sequence. Most typically, this operator is used to permit multiple variable initializations. For example, you can combine the declaration of several variables in a single `var` statement, as follows:

```
var name, address, serialNumber;
```

Another situation where you could use this operator is within the expressions of a `for` loop construction. In the following example, two different counting variables are initialized and incremented at different rates. When the loop begins, both variables are initialized at zero (they don't have to be, but this example starts that way); for each subsequent trip through the loop, one variable is incremented by one, while the other is incremented by 10:

```
for (var i=0, j=0; i < someLength; i++, j+10) {
    ...
}
```

Don't confuse the comma operator with the semicolon delimiter between statements.

? :

Compatibility: WinIE3+, MacIE3+, NN2+, Moz+, Safari+

The conditional operator is a shortcut way of expressing an `if. . .else` conditional construction covered in Chapter 32. This operator is typically used in concert with an assignment operator to assign one of two values to a variable based on the result of a condition expression. The formal syntax for the conditional operator is:

```
condition ? expressionIfTrue : expressionIfFalse
```

If used with an assignment operator, the syntax is:

```
var = condition ? expressionIfTrue : expressionIfFalse;
```

No matter how you use the operator, the important point to remember is that an expression that contains this operator evaluates to one of the two expressions following the question mark symbol. In truth, either expression could invoke any JavaScript, including calling other functions or even nesting further conditional operators within one of the expressions to achieve the equivalent of nested `if. . .else` constructions. To assure proper resolution of nested conditionals, surround inner expressions with parentheses to make sure that they evaluate before the outer expression evaluates. As an example, the following statement assigns one of three strings to a variable depending on the date within a month:

```
var monthPart = (dateNum <= 10) ? "early" : ((dateNum <= 20) ?
    "middle" : "late");
```

When the statement is evaluated, the inner conditional expression at the right of the first colon is evaluated, returning either `middle` or `late`; then the outer conditional expression is evaluated, returning either `early` or the result of the inner conditional expression.

typeof

Compatibility: WinIE3+, MacIE3+, NN3+, Moz+, Safari+

Unlike most other operators, which are predominantly concerned with arithmetic and logic, the unary `typeof` operator defines the kind of value to which a variable or expression evaluates. Typically, this operator is used to identify whether a variable value is one of the following types: `number`, `string`, `boolean`, `object`, `function`, or `undefined`.

Example

Having this investigative capability in JavaScript is helpful because variables cannot only contain any one of those data types but can change their data type on the fly. Your scripts may need to handle a value differently based on the value's type. The most common use of the `typeof` property is as part of a condition. For example:

```
if (typeof myVal == "number") {
    myVal = parseInt(myVal);
}
```

The evaluated value of the `typeof` operation is, itself, a string.

void

Compatibility: WinIE3+, MacIE3+, NN3+, Moz+, Safari+

In all scriptable browsers you can use the `javascript:` pseudo-protocol to supply the parameter for `href` and `src` attributes in HTML tags, such as links. In the process, you have to be careful that the function or statement being invoked by the URL does not return or evaluate to any values. If a value comes back from such an expression, then that value or sometimes the directory of the client's hard disk often replaces the page content. To avoid this possibility, use the `void` operator in front of the function or expression being invoked by the `javascript:` URL.

Example

The best way to use this construction is to place the operator before the expression or function and separate them by a space, as in

```
javascript: void doSomething();
```

On occasion, you may have to wrap the expression inside parentheses after the `void` operator. Using parentheses is necessary only when the expression contains operators of a lower precedence than the `void` operator (see the following section, "Operator Precedence"). But don't automatically wrap all expressions in parentheses, because some browsers can experience problems with these. Even so, it is common practice to assign the following URL to the `href` attribute of an `a` link whose `onclick` event handler does all of the work:

```
href="javascript: void (0)"
```

The `void` operator makes sure the function or expression returns no value that the HTML attribute can use. Such a link's `onclick` event handler should also inhibit the natural behavior of a clicked link (for example, by evaluating to `return false`).

Operator Precedence

When you start working with complex expressions that hold a number of operators (for example, Listing 33-2), knowing the order in which JavaScript evaluates those expressions is vital. JavaScript assigns different priorities or weights to types of operators in an effort to achieve uniformity in the way it evaluates complex expressions.

In the following expression

```
10 + 4 * 5 // result = 30
```

JavaScript uses its precedence scheme to perform the multiplication before the addition — regardless of where the operators appear in the statement. In other words, JavaScript first multiplies 4 by 5 and then adds that result to 10 to get a result of 30. That may not be the way you want this expression to evaluate. Perhaps your intention was to add the 10 and 4 first and then to multiply that sum by 5. To make that happen, you have to override JavaScript's natural operator precedence. To do that, you must use parentheses to enclose an operator with lower precedence. The following statement shows how you adjust the previous expression to make it behave differently:

```
(10 + 4) * 5 // result = 70
```

That one set of parentheses has a great impact on the outcome. Parentheses have the highest precedence in JavaScript, and if you nest parentheses in an expression, the innermost set evaluates first.

For help in constructing complex expressions, refer to Table 33-10 for JavaScript's operator precedence. My general practice: When in doubt about complex precedence issues, I build the expression with lots of parentheses according to the way I want the internal expressions to evaluate.

TABLE 33-10

JavaScript Operator Precedence

Precedence Level	Operator	Notes
1	( )	From innermost to outermost
	[ ]	Array index value
	function( )	Any remote function call
2	!	Boolean Not
	~	Bitwise Not
	-	Negation
	++	Increment
	--	Decrement
	new	
	typeof	
	void	
	delete	Delete array or object entry
3	*	Multiplication
	/	Division
	%	Modulo
4	+	Addition
	-	Subtraction
5	<<	Bitwise shifts
	>	
	>>	
6	<	Comparison operators
	<=	
	>	
	>=	
7	==	Equality
	!=	
8	&	Bitwise And
9	^	Bitwise XOR
10	|	Bitwise Or

continued

LISTING 33-10   *(continued)*

Precedence Level	Operator	Notes
11	&&	Boolean And
12	||	Boolean Or
13	?	Conditional expression
14	=	Assignment operators
	+=	
	-=	
	*=	
	/=	
	%=	
	<<=	
	>=	
	>>=	
	&=	
	^=	
	|=	
15	,	Comma (parameter delimiter)

This precedence scheme is devised to help you avoid being faced with two operators from the same precedence level that often appear in the same expression. When it happens (such as with addition and subtraction), JavaScript begins evaluating the expression from left to right.

One related fact involves a string of Boolean expressions strung together for a `condition` statement (see Listing 33-2). JavaScript follows what is called *short-circuit evaluation*. As the nested expressions are evaluated left to right, the fate of the entire condition can sometimes be determined before all expressions are evaluated. Anytime JavaScript encounters an And operator, if the left operand evaluates to `false`, the entire expression evaluates to `false` without JavaScript's even bothering to evaluate the right operand. For an Or operator, if the left operand is `true`, JavaScript short-circuits that expression to `true`. This feature can trip you up if you don't perform enough testing on your scripts: If a syntax error or other error exists in a right operand, and you fail to test the expression in a way that forces that right operand to evaluate, you may not know that a bug exists in your code. Users of your page, of course, will find the bug quickly. Do your testing to head bugs off at the pass.

NOTE   Notice, too, that all math and string concatenation is performed prior to any comparison operators. This enables all expressions that act as operands for comparisons to evaluate fully before they are compared.

The key to working with complex expressions is to isolate individual expressions and to try them out by themselves, if you can. See additional debugging tips in Chapter 45 on the CD-ROM.

Chapter 34

Functions and Custom Objects

IN THIS CHAPTER

Creating function blocks

Passing parameters to functions

Creating your own objects

B y now, you've seen dozens of JavaScript functions in action and probably have a pretty good feel for the way they work. This chapter provides the function object specification and delves into the fun prospect of creating objects in your JavaScript code. If you've missed out on the object-oriented programming (OOP) revolution, then now is your chance to join. JavaScript is surprisingly full-featured when it comes to supporting OOP and allowing you to develop scripts that rely heavily on custom objects.

Function Object

Properties	Methods	Event Handlers
arguments	apply()	
arity	call()	
caller	toString()	
constructor	valueOf()	
length		
prototype		

Syntax

Creating a function object:

```
function functionName([arg1,...[,argN]]) {
    statement(s)
}
```

functionObject

```
var funcName = new Function(["argName1",...[,"argNameN"],
   "statement1;...[;statementN]"])
object.eventHandlerName = function([arg1,...[,argN]]) {statement(s)}
```

Accessing function object properties and methods:

```
functionObject.property | method([parameters])
```

Compatibility: WinIE3+, MacIE3+, NN2+, Moz+, Safari+

About this object

JavaScript accommodates what other languages might call procedures, subroutines, and functions all in one type of structure: the *custom function*. A function may return a value (if programmed to do so with the return keyword), but it does not have to return any value. With the exception of JavaScript code that executes as the document loads, all deferred processing takes place in functions.

Although you can create functions that are hundreds of lines long, I recommend you break up longer processes into shorter functions. Among the reasons for doing so: smaller chunks are easier to write and debug; building blocks make it easier to visualize the entire script; you can make functions generalizable and reusable for other scripts; and other parts of the script or other open frames can use the functions.

Learning how to write good, reusable functions takes time and experience. But the earlier you understand the importance of this concept, the more you will be on the lookout for good examples in other people's scripts on the web.

Creating functions

The standard way of defining a function in your script means following a simple pattern and then filling in the details. The formal syntax definition for a function is:

```
function functionName( [arg1] ... [, argN]) {
   statement(s)
}
```

The task of assigning a function name helps you determine the precise scope of activity of the function. If you find that you can't reduce the planned task for the function to a simple one- to three-word name (which is then condensed into one contiguous sequence of characters for the functionName), perhaps you're asking the function to do too much. A better idea may be to break the job into two or more functions. As you start to design a function, be on the lookout for functions that you can call from the one you're writing. If you find yourself copying and pasting lines of code from one part of a function to another because you're performing the same operation in different spots within the function, it may be time to break that segment out into its own function.

Here's a quick example of a simple function that accepts a single argument, a name, and then returns a string greeting that includes the name:

```
function sayHello(name) {
   return ("Hello, " + name + ".");
}
```

You can also create what is called an *anonymous function* using the new Function() constructor. In reality, you assign a name to this anonymous function as follows:

```
var funcName = new Function(["argName1",...[,"argNameN"],
   "statement1;...[;statementN]"]);
```

This other way of building a function is particularly helpful when your scripts need to create a function after a document loads. All the components of a function are present in this definition. Each function parameter name is supplied as a string value, separated from each other by commas. The final parameter string consists of the statements that execute whenever the function is called. Separate each JavaScript statement with a semicolon, and enclose the entire sequence of statements inside quotes, as in the following:

```
var willItFit = new Function("width","height",
    "var sx = screen.availWidth; var sy = screen.availHeight;
    return (sx >= width && sy >= height)");
```

The `willItFit()` function takes two parameters; the body of the function defines two local variables (`sx` and `sy`) and then returns a Boolean value of `true` if the incoming parameters are smaller than the local variables. In traditional form, this function is defined as follows:

```
function willItFit(width, height) {
    var sx = screen.availWidth;
    var sy = screen.availHeight;
    return (sx >= width && sy >= height);
}
```

When this function exists in the browser's memory, you can invoke it like any other function:

```
if (willItFit(400,500)) {
    statements to load image
}
```

One last function creation format is available in IE4+, NN4+, Moz, and other W3C DOM browsers. This advanced technique, called a *lambda expression,* provides a shortcut for creating a reference to an anonymous function (truly anonymous because the function has no name that you can reference later). The common application of this technique is to assign function references to event handlers when an event object also must be passed. The following is an example of how to assign an anonymous function to an `onchange` event handler for a form control:

```
document.forms[0].age.onchange = function(event) {isNumber(document.forms[0].age)}
```

Because an anonymous function evaluates to a reference to a function object, you can use either form of anonymous function in situations where a function reference is called for, including parameters of methods or other functions.

Nesting functions

Modern browsers also provide for nesting functions inside one another. In the absence of nested functions, each function definition is defined at the global level whereby every function is exposed and available to all other script code. With nested functions, you can encapsulate the exposure of a function inside another and make that nested function private to the enclosing function. Of course I don't recommend reusing function names with this technique, although you can create nested functions with the same name inside multiple global-level functions, as the following skeletal structure shows:

```
function outerA() {
    statements
    function innerA() {
        statements
    }
    statements
```

functionObject

```
    }
function outerB() {
    statements
    function innerA() {
        statements
    }
    function innerB() {
        statements
    }
    statements
}
```

A good time to apply a nested function is when a sequence of statements need to be invoked in multiple places within a large function but those statements have meaning only within the context of the larger function. In other words, rather than break out the repeated sequence as a separate global function, you keep it all within the scope of the larger function.

> **NOTE** The premise behind nesting a function is to isolate the function and make it private from the overall script. This results in cleaner script code because nothing is exposed globally without a good reason. As an admittedly strange analogy, the water heater in your house could feasibly be placed outside (global) but it's generally safer and more organized to place it inside (local). Unlike your mailbox, which must interact with the outside (global) world, your water heater plays an internal (local) role, and therefore lives inside your house.

You can access a nested function only from statements in its containing function (and in any order). Moreover, all variables defined in the outer function (including parameter variables) are accessible to the inner function; but variables defined in an inner function are not accessible to the outer function. See the section, "Variable scope: Globals and locals" later in this chapter for details on how variables are visible to various components of a script.

Function parameters

The function definition requires a set of parentheses after the `functionName`. If the function does not rely on any information arriving with it when invoked, the parentheses can be empty. But when some kind of data is arriving with a call to the function, you need to assign names to each parameter. Virtually any kind of value can be a parameter: strings, numbers, Boolean operators, and even complete object references such as a form or form element. Choose names for these variables that help you remember the content of those values; also, avoid reusing existing object names as variable names because it's easy to get confused when objects and variables with the same name appear in the same statements. You must avoid using JavaScript keywords (including the reserved words listed in Appendix B) and any global variable name defined elsewhere in your script. (See more about global variables in the following sections.)

JavaScript is forgiving about matching the number of parameters in the function definition with the number of parameters passed along from the calling statement. If you define a function with three parameters and the calling statement specifies only two, the third parameter variable value in that function is assigned a `null` value. For example:

```
function saveWinners(first, second, third) {
    statements
}
oneFunction("George","Gracie");
```

In the preceding example, the values of first and second inside the function are "George" and "Gracie", respectively; the value of third is null.

At the opposite end of the spectrum, JavaScript also doesn't balk if you send more parameters from the calling statement than the number of parameter variables specified in the function definition. In fact, the language includes a mechanism—the arguments property—that you can add to your function to gather any extraneous parameters that should read your function.

Properties

arguments

Value: Array of arguments.   Read-Only
Compatibility: WinIE4+, MacIE4+, NN3+, Moz+, Safari+

When a function receives parameter values from the statement that invoked the function, those parameter values are silently assigned to the arguments property of the function object. This property is an array of the values, with each parameter value assigned to a zero-based index entry in the array—whether or not parameters are defined for it. You can find out how many parameters are sent by extracting functionName .arguments.length. For example, if four parameters are passed, functionName.arguments.length returns 4. Then, you can use array notation (functionName.arguments[i]) to extract the values of any parameter(s) you want.

Theoretically, you never have to define parameter variables for your functions because you can extract the desired arguments array entry instead. Well-chosen parameter variable names, however, are much more readable, so I recommend them over the arguments property in most cases. But you may run into situations in which a single function definition needs to handle multiple calls to the function when each call may have a different number of parameters. The function knows how to handle any arguments over and above the ones given names as parameter variables.

> **NOTE** It is necessary in some cases to create a function that deliberately accepts a varied number of arguments, in which case the arguments property is the only way to access and process the arguments. For example, if you wanted to create a function that averages test scores, there's a good chance the number of scores may vary, in which case you would write the function so that it loops through the arguments array, adding up the scores as it carries out the calculation.

Example

See Listings 34-1 and 34-2 for a demonstration of both the arguments and caller properties.

arity

Value: Integer.   Read-Only
Compatibility: WinIE-, MacIE-, NN4+, Moz-, Safari-

See the discussion of the length property later in this chapter.

caller

Value: Function object reference.   Read-Only
Compatibility: WinIE4+, MacIE4+, NN3+, Moz+, Safari-

When one function invokes another, a chain is established between the two primarily so that a returned value knows where to go. Therefore, a function invoked by another maintains a reference to the function that called it. Such information is automatically stored in a function object as the `caller` property. This relationship reminds me a bit of a subwindow's `opener` property, which points to the window or frame responsible for the subwindow's creation. The value is valid only while the called function is running at the request of another function; when a function isn't running, its `caller` property is `null`.

The value of the `caller` property is a reference to a function object, so you can inspect its `arguments` and `caller` properties (in case it was called by yet another function). Thus, a function can look back at a calling function to see what values it was passed.

The `functionName.caller` property reveals the contents of an entire function definition if the current function was called from another function (including an event handler). If the call for a function comes from a regular JavaScript statement not originating from inside a function, the `functionName.caller` property is `null`.

Example

To help you grasp all that these two properties yield, study Listing 34-1.

LISTING 34-1

A Function's arguments and caller Properties

```
<html>
  <head>
    <title></title>
    <script type="text/javascript">
    function hansel(x,y) {
        var args = hansel.arguments;
        document.write("<p>hansel.caller is " + hansel.caller + "<br />");
        document.write("hansel.arguments.length is " +
            hansel.arguments.length + "<br />");
        for (var i = 0; i < args.length; i++) {
            document.write("argument " + i + " is " + args[i] + "<br />");
        }
        document.write("<\/p>");
    }

    function gretel(x,y,z) {
        today = new Date();
        thisYear = today.getFullYear();
        hansel(x,y,z,thisYear);
    }
    </script>
```

```
    </head>
    <body>
      <script type="text/javascript">
      hansel(1, "two", 3);
      gretel(4, "five", 6, "seven");
      </script>
    </body>
</html>
```

When you load this page, the following results appear in the browser window (although the `caller` property values show `undefined` for Safari):

```
hansel.caller is null
hansel.arguments.length is 3
argument 0 is 1
argument 1 is two
argument 2 is 3

hansel.caller is function gretel(x, y, z) { today = new Date(); thisYear =
today.getFullYear(); hansel(x, y, z, thisYear); }
hansel.arguments.length is 4
argument 0 is 4
argument 1 is five
argument 2 is 6
argument 3 is 2007 (or whatever the current year is)
```

As the document loads, the `hansel()` function is called directly in the body script. It passes three arguments, even though the `hansel()` function defines only two. The `hansel.arguments` property picks up all three arguments just the same. The main body script then invokes the `gretel()` function, which, in turn, calls `hansel()` again. But when `gretel()` makes the call, it passes four parameters. The `gretel()` function picks up only three of the four arguments sent by the calling statement. It also inserts another value from its own calculations as an extra parameter to be sent to `hansel()`. The `hansel.caller` property reveals the entire content of the `gretel()` function, whereas `hansel.arguments` picks up all four parameters, including the year value introduced by the `gretel()` function.

constructor

(See `string.constructor` in Chapter 28)

length

Value: Integer.   Read-Only
Compatibility: WinIE4+, MacIE4+, NN4+, Moz+, Safari+

As the `arguments` property of a function proves, JavaScript is very forgiving about matching the number of parameters passed to a function with the number of parameter variables defined for the function. But a script can examine the `length` property of a function object to see precisely how many parameter variables are defined for a function. A reference to the property starts with the function name representing the object. For example, consider the following function definition shell:

functionObject.apply()

```
function identify(name, rank, serialNum) {
   ...
}
```

A script statement anywhere outside of the function can read the number of parameters with the reference:

```
identify.length
```

The value of the property in the preceding example is 3. The `length` property supercedes the NN-only `arity` property.

prototype

(See `Array.prototype` in Chapter 31)

Methods

apply([*thisObj*[, *argumentsArray*]])
call([*thisObj*[, *arg1*[, *arg2*[,...*argN*]]]])

Returns: Nothing.
Compatibility: WinIE5.5+, MacIE-, NN6+, Moz+, Safari+

The `apply()` and `call()` methods of a function object invoke the function. This may seem redundant to the normal way in which script statements invoke functions by simply naming the function, following it with parentheses, passing parameters, and so on. The difference with these methods is that you can invoke the function through the `apply()` and `call()` methods using only a reference to the function. For example, if your script defines a function through the `new Function()` constructor (or other anonymous short-cut supported by the browser), you receive a reference to the function as a result of the constructor. To invoke the function later using only that reference (presumably preserved in a global variable), use either the `apply()` or `call()` method. Both of these methods achieve the same result, but choosing one method over the other depends on the form in which the function's parameters are conveyed (more about that in a moment).

The first parameter of both methods is a reference to the object that the function treats as the current object. For garden-variety functions defined in your script, use the keyword `this`, which means that the function's context becomes the current object (just like a regular function). In fact, if there are no parameters to be sent to the function, you can omit parameters to both methods altogether.

The object reference comes into play when the function being invoked is one that is normally defined as a method to a custom object. (I cover some of these concepts later in this chapter, so you may need to return here after you are familiar with custom objects.)

Example

Consider the following code that generates a custom object and assigns a method to the object to display an alert about properties of the object:

```
// function to be invoked as a method from a 'car' object
function showCar() {
   alert(this.make + " : " + this.color);
}
// 'car' object constructor function
```

```
function car(make, color) {
    this.make = make;
    this.color = color;
    this.show = showCar;
}
// create instance of a 'car' object
var myCar = new car("Ford", "blue");
```

The normal way of getting the myCar object to display an alert about its properties is:

```
myCar.show();
```

At that point, the showCar() function runs, picking up the current car object as the context for the this references in the function. In other words, when the showCar() function runs as a method of the object, the function treats the object as the *current object*.

With the call() or apply() methods, however, you don't have to bind the showCar() function to the myCar object. You can omit the statement in the car() constructor that assigns the showCar function to a method name for the object. Instead, a script can invoke the showCar() method and instruct it to treat myCar as the current object:

```
showCar.call(myCar);
```

The showCar() function operates just as before, and the object reference in the call() method's first parameter slot is treated as the current object for the showCar() function.

As for succeeding parameters, the apply() method's second parameter is an array of values to be passed as parameters to the current function. The order of the values must match the order of parameter variables defined for the function. The call() method, on the other hand, enables you to pass individual parameters in a comma-delimited list. Your choice depends on how the parameters are carried along in your script. If they're already in array form, use the apply() method; otherwise, use the call() method. The (ECMA) recommended way to invoke a function through this mechanism when no parameters need to be passed is via the call() method.

NOTE Remember, ECMA is the standards organization that oversees the official JavaScript language standard, which is formally known as ECMAScript. ECMAScript is the language specification, whereas JavaScript is an actual implementation.

toString()
valueOf()

Returns: String.
Compatibility: WinIE4+, MacIE4+, NN4+, Moz+, Safari+

Scripts rarely, if ever, summon the toString() and valueOf() methods of a function object. They work internally to allow debugging scripts to display a string version of the function definition. For example, when you enter the name of a function defined in The Evaluator (see Chapter 13) into the top text box, JavaScript automatically converts the function to a string so that its value can be displayed in the Results box. Using these methods or parsing the text they return has little, if any, practical application.

Function Application Notes

Understanding the ins and outs of JavaScript functions is the key to successful scripting, especially for complex applications. Additional topics covered in this chapter include the ways to invoke functions, variable scope in and around functions, recursion, and the design of reusable functions.

Invoking functions

A function doesn't perform any work until a script calls it by name or reference. Scripts invoke functions (that is, get functions to do something) through four routes: document object event handlers; JavaScript statements; href attributes pointing to a javascript: URL; and the more modern call() and apply() methods of function objects. The one approach not discussed at length yet in this book is the javascript: URL (some say pseudo-URL).

Several HTML tags have href attributes that normally point to Internet URLs for navigating to another page or loading a MIME file that requires a helper application or plug-in. These HTML tags are usually tags for clickable objects, such as links and client-side image map areas.

A JavaScript-enabled browser has a special, built-in URL pseudo-protocol — javascript: — that lets the href attribute point to a JavaScript function or method rather than to a URL on the Net. For example, it is common practice to use the javascript: URL to change the contents of two frames from a single link. Because the href attribute is designed to point to only a single URL, you'd be out of luck without a convenient way to put multiframe navigation into your hands. You implement multiframe navigation by writing a function that sets the location.href properties of the two frames; then invoke that function from the href attribute. The following example shows what the script may look like:

```
function loadPages() {
    parent.frames[1].location.href = "page2.html";
    parent.frames[2].location.href = "instrux2.html";
}
...
<a href="javascript:loadPages()">Next</a>
```

These kinds of function invocations can include parameters, and the functions can do anything you want. One potential side effect to watch out for occurs when the function returns a value (perhaps the function is also invoked from other script locations where a returned value is expected). Because the href attribute sets the target window to whatever the attribute evaluates to, the returned value is assigned to the target window — probably not what you want.

To prevent the assignment of a returned value to the href attribute, prefix the function call with the void operator:

```
<a href="javascript:void loadPages()">
```

If you don't want the href attribute to do anything (that is, let the onclick event handler do all the work), assign a blank function after the operator:

```
<a href="javascript:void (0)">
```

Experienced programmers of many other languages recognize this operator as a way of indicating that no values are returned from a function or procedure. The operator has that precise functionality here, but in a nontraditional location.

Variable scope: Globals and locals

A variable can have two scopes in JavaScript. As you might expect, any variable initialized within the main flow of a script (not inside a function) is a *global variable* in that any statement in the same document's script can access it by name. You can, however, also initialize variables inside a function (in a var statement) so the variable name applies only to statements inside that function. By limiting the scope of the variable to a single function, you can reuse the same variable name in multiple functions thereby enabling the variables to carry very different information in each function. Listing 34-2 demonstrates the various possibilities.

LISTING 34-2

Variable Scope Workbench Page

```
<html>
  <head>
    <title>Variable Scope Trials</title>
    <script type="text/javascript">
    var headGlobal = "Gumby";
    function doNothing() {
        var headLocal = "Pokey";
        return headLocal;
    }
    </script>
  </head>
  <body>
    <script type="text/javascript">
    // two global variables
    var aBoy = "Charlie Brown";
    var hisDog = "Snoopy";
    function testValues() {
        var hisDog = "Gromit";  // initializes local version of "hisDog"
        var page = "";
        page += "headGlobal is: " + headGlobal + "<br />";
        // page += "headLocal is: " + headLocal + "<br />" // won't run:
        // ...headLocal not defined
        page += "headLocal value returned from head function is: " +
            doNothing() + "<br />";
        page += " aBoy is: " + aBoy + "<br />"; // picks up global
        page += "local version of hisDog is: " + hisDog + "<br />"; // "sees"
        // ...only local version
        document.write(page);
    }
    testValues();
    document.write("global version of hisDog is intact: " + hisDog);
    </script>
  </body>
</html>
```

In this page, you define a number of variables — some global, others local — that are spread out in the document's Head and Body sections. When you load this page, it runs the testValues() function, which accounts for the current values of all the variable names. The script then follows up with at least one value extraction that was masked in the function. The results of the page look like this:

```
headGlobal is: Gumby
headLocal value returned from head function is: Pokey
aBoy is: Charlie Brown
local version of hisDog is: Gromit
global version of hisDog is intact: Snoopy
```

Examine the variable initialization throughout this script. In the Head, you define the first variable (headGlobal) as a global style outside of any function definition. The var keyword for the global variable is optional but often helpful for enabling you to see at a glance where you initialize your variables. You then create a short function, which defines a variable (headLocal) that only statements in the function can use.

In the Body, you define two more global variables: aBoy and hisDog. Inside the Body's function (for purposes of demonstration), you reuse the hisDog variable name. By initializing hisDog with the var statement inside the function, you tell JavaScript to create a separate variable whose scope is only within the function. This initialization does not disturb the global variable of the same name. It can, however, make things confusing for you as the script author.

Statements in this script attempt to collect the values of variables scattered around the script. Even from within this script, JavaScript has no problem extracting global variables directly — including the one defined in the Head. But JavaScript cannot get the local variable defined in the other function — that headLocal variable is private to its own function. Trying to run a script that references that variable value will result in an error message saying that the variable name is not defined. In the eyes of everyone else outside of the doNothing() function, that's true. If you really need that value, you can have the function return the value to a calling statement as you do in the testValues() function.

Near the end of the function, the script reads the aBoy global value without a hitch. But because you initialized a separate version of hisDog inside that function, only the localized version is available to the function. If you reassign a global variable name inside a function, you cannot access the global version from inside that function.

As proof that the global variable — whose name was reused inside the testValues() function — remains untouched, the script writes that value to the end of the page for all to see. Charlie Brown and his dog are reunited.

A benefit of this variable-scoping scheme is that you can reuse throwaway variable names in any function you like. For example, you can use the i loop counting variable in every function that employs loops. (In fact, you can reuse it in multiple for loops of the same function because the for loop reinitializes the value at the start of the loop.) If you pass parameters to a function, you can assign to those parameter variables the same names to aid in consistency. For example, a common practice is to pass an entire form object reference as a parameter to a function (using a this.form parameter in the event handler). For every function that catches one of these objects, you can use the variable name form in the parameter:

```
function doSomething(form) {
    statements
}
...
<input type="button" value="Do Something" onclick="doSomething(this.form)" />
```

If five buttons on your page pass their form objects as parameters to five different functions, each function can assign `form` (or whatever you want to use) to that parameter value.

I recommend reusing variable names only for these throwaway variables. In this case, the variables are all local to functions, so the possibility of a mix-up with global variables does not exist. But the thought of reusing a global variable name as, say, a special case inside a function sends shivers up my spine. Such a tactic is doomed to cause confusion and error.

CAUTION Reusing a global variable name locally is one of the most subtle and therefore difficult bugs to find in JavaScript code. The local variable ends up temporarily hiding the global variable without making any effort to let you know. Just do yourself a favor and make sure you don't reuse a global variable name as a local variable in a function.

Some programmers devise naming conventions to avoid reusing global variables as local variables. A popular scheme puts a lowercase g in front of any global variable name. In the example from Listing 34-2, you can name the global variables:

```
gHeadGlobal
gABoy
gHisDog
```

Then, if you define local variables, don't use the leading g. A similar scheme involves using an underscore character (_) instead of a g in front of global variable names. Any scheme you employ to prevent the reuse of variable names in different scopes is fine as long as it does the job.

In a multiframe or multiwindow environment, your scripts can also access global variables from any other document currently loaded into the browser. For details about this level of access, see Chapter 16.

Variable scoping rules apply equally to nested functions in IE4+, NN4+, Moz, and W3C browsers. Any variables defined in an outer function (including parameter variables) are exposed to all functions nested inside. But if you define a new local variable inside a nested function, that variable is not available to the outer function. Instead, you can return a value from the nested function to the statement in the outer function that invokes the nested function.

Parameter variables

When a function receives data in the form of parameters, remember that the values may be copies of the data (in the case of run-of-the-mill data values) or references to real objects (such as a form object). In the latter case, you can change the object's modifiable properties in the function when the function receives the object as a parameter, as shown in the following example:

```
function validateCountry(form) {
    if (form.country.value == "") {
        form.country.value = "USA";
    }
}
```

Therefore, whenever you pass an object reference as a function parameter, be aware that the changes you make to that object in its passed form affect the real object.

As a matter of style, if my function needs to extract properties or results of methods from passed data (such as object properties or string substrings), I like to do that at the start of the function. I initialize as many variables as needed for each piece of data used later in the function. This task enables me to assign meaningful names to the data chunks, rather than rely on potentially long references within the working part of the function (such as using a variable like `inputStr` instead of `form.entry.value`). Here's a quick example:

```
function updateContactInfo(form) {
    var firstName = form.firstname.value;
    var lastName = form.lastname.value;
    var address1 = form.addr1.value;
    var address2 = form.addr2.value;
    var phone = form.phone.value;
    var email = form.email.value;

    // Process contact info using local variables
}
```

Notice in this example how the form field information is first stored in local variables, which are then used to carry out the hypothetical updating of contact information. Throughout the remainder of the function you can use the local variables instead of the longer and less wieldy form fields.

Recursion in functions

In what may come as a strange surprise, it is possible for functions to call themselves — a process known as *recursion*. The classic example of programmed recursion is the calculation of the factorial (the factorial for a value of 4 is 4 * 3 * 2 * 1), shown in Listing 34-3.

In the third line of this function, the statement calls itself, passing along a parameter of the next lower value of n. As this function executes, diving ever deeper into itself, JavaScript watches intermediate values and performs the final evaluations of the nested expressions. If designed properly, a recursive function eventually stops calling itself, and the program flow eventually returns back to the original function call.

Recursive functions are dangerous in a sense that they can easily fall into an infinite state. For this reason, it is very important that you test them carefully. In particular, make sure that the recursion is finite: that a limit exists for the number of times it can recurse. In the case of Listing 34-3, that limit is the initial value of n. Failure to watch out for this limit may cause the recursion to overpower the limits of the browser's memory and even lead to a crash.

LISTING 34-3

A JavaScript Function Utilizing Recursion

```
function factorial(n) {
  if (n > 0) {
    return n * (factorial(n-1));
  } else {
    return 1;
  }
}
```

Turning functions into libraries

As you start writing functions for your scripts, be on the lookout for ways to make functions generalizable (written so that you can reuse the function in other instances, regardless of the object structure of the page). The likeliest candidates for this kind of treatment are functions that perform specific kinds of validation checks (see examples in Chapter 43 on the CD-ROM), data conversions, or iterative math problems.

To make a function generalizable, don't let it make any references to specific objects by name. Object names generally change from document to document. Instead, write the function so that it accepts a named object as a parameter. For example, if you write a function that accepts a `text` object as its parameter, the function can extract the object's data or invoke its methods without knowing anything about its enclosing form or name. Look again, for example, at the `factorial()` function in Listing 34-4 — but now as part of an entire document.

> **NOTE** The property assignment event handling technique employed throughout the code in this chapter and much of the book is a deliberate simplification to make the code more readable. It is generally better to use the more modern approach of binding events using the `addEventListener()` (NN6+/Moz/W3C) or `attachEvent()` (IE5+) methods. A modern cross-browser event handling technique is explained in detail in Chapter 25.

LISTING 34-4

Calling a Generalizable Function

```html
<html>
    <head>
        <title>Variable Scope Trials</title>
        <script type="text/javascript">
        function factorial(n) {
            if (n > 0) {
                return n * (factorial(n - 1));
            } else {
                return 1;
            }
        }
        </script>
    </head>
    <body>
        <form>
            Enter an input value: <input type="text" name="input" value="0" />
            <p><input type="button" value="Calc Factorial"
                onclick="this.form.output.value =
                factorial(this.form.input.value)" /></p>
            <p>Results: <input type="text" name="output" /></p>
        </form>
    </body>
</html>
```

This function is designed to be generalizable, accepting only the input value (n) as a parameter. In the form, the onClick event handler of the button sends only the input value from one of the form's fields to the factorial() function. The returned value is assigned to the output field of the form. The factorial() function is totally ignorant about forms, fields, or buttons in this document. If I need this function in another script, I can copy and paste it into that script knowing that it has been pretested. Any generalizable function is part of my personal library of scripts — from which I can borrow — and saves me time in future scripting tasks.

You cannot always generalize a function. Somewhere along the line in your scripts, you must have references to JavaScript or custom objects. But if you find that you're frequently writing functions that perform the same kind of actions, see how you can generalize the code and put the results in your library of ready-made functions. You should also consider placing these reusable library functions in an external .js library file. See Chapter 13 for details on this convenient way to share utility functions among many documents.

Making sense of closures

A topic that has confused many an aspiring scripter is closures, which may enter the picture when you declare a function within another function. At the core of JavaScript, *closures* refer to the fact that you can keep a local variable defined in a function alive even after the function has executed — which normally signals the end of life for a local variable. That's right, it's possible for a function to return and its local variables to go on living like some kind of strange zombie data. How is this possible? Take a look at an example:

```
function countMe() {
  var count = 1;
  var showCount = function() { alert(count); }
  count++;
  return showCount;
}
```

The unusual thing to note about this code is how the inner function assigned to the showCount variable is returned by the function. When you call the countMe() function, you receive a reference to the inner function that displays the count variable value. That wouldn't be a problem except for the fact that the inner function acts on a variable (count) that is local to the countMe() function.

To see the closure come to life, take a look at this code that calls the countMe() function:

```
var countamatic = countMe();
countamatic();
```

The first line calls the countMe() function, which results in the local count variable being created and a reference to the inner function being passed out and stored in the countamatic variable. The local variable count is also incremented within the countMe() function. Without knowing about closures, you would clearly be in some serious gray area at this point because the countamatic() function defined in the first line is now set to display the value of a variable that is clearly out of scope. But JavaScript works a miracle by keeping the count variable alive in a closure and still allowing the countamatic() function to access it. Thus, the second statement displays an alert with the number 2 in it.

If closures still seem a bit mysterious, just remember that a potential closure is created any time you specify a function within another function. You really only take advantage of a closure when you pass an inner function reference outside the scope of the function in which it is defined.

Okay, so closures reveal a sneaky way to manipulate scope in JavaScript but what good are they? Closures are finding a great deal of usage in Ajax applications because Ajax programming often uses closures to work around inherent limitations in how you normally use the `this` keyword.

CROSS-REF For more on Ajax, check out Chapter 27.

Although I could just pawn everything closure-related off on Ajax, I can demonstrate a simple but practical application of how closures can help you carry out the seemingly impossible. Consider the scenario where you want to set a timer that calls a function after an interval of time has elapsed. You may be thinking no problem — just create a function and pass its reference to the `setTimeout()` function. End of story. What I didn't mention is that you need to pass a couple of parameters to the function. See the problem?

Unless you design with anonymous functions, there is no mechanism for using parameters when you pass a function reference to another function, as in specifying a timer event handler when calling the `setTimeout()` function. Now take a look at this code that uses closures to circumvent the problem:

```
function wakeupCaller(name, roomnum) {
    return (function() {
        alert("Call " + name + " in room #" + roomnum + ".");
    });
}
```

By placing a zero-param function within a parameterized function, you now have the ingredients for a timer handler that can accept parameters. The next step is to create an actual function reference that uses the closure:

```
var wakeWilson = wakeupCaller("Mr. Wilson", 515);
```

At this point, you've passed parameters to a function and received a zero-param function reference in return, which can then be passed along to the `setTimeout()` function:

```
setTimeout(wakeWilson, 600000);
```

Thanks to closures, Mr. Wilson will now get his wake up call!

CAUTION Before you dive into closures and begin exploiting them in all of your code, let me caution you that they can result in some tricky bugs when used incorrectly. Extensive use of closures involving references to DOM objects can also cause memory leaks (gradual increase of memory used by the browser) if the objects are not disposed of (that is, set to `null`) when they are no longer needed. Definitely spend the time to explore closures in more detail before you get too wild with them.

Creating Your Own Objects with Object-Oriented JavaScript

In all the previous chapters of this book, you've seen how conveniently the browser document object models organize all the information about the browser window and its document. More specifically, you learned how to use standard objects as a means of accessing different aspects of the browser window and document. What may not be obvious from the scripting you've done so far is that JavaScript enables you to create your own objects in memory — objects with properties and methods that you define. These objects are not user-interface elements on the page but rather the kinds of objects that may contain data and script functions (behaving as methods) whose results the user can see displayed in the browser window.

You actually had a preview of this power in Chapter 31's discussion about arrays. An array, you recall, is an ordered collection of data. An object typically contains different kinds of data. It doesn't have to be an ordered collection of data — although your scripts can use objects in constructions that strongly resemble arrays. Moreover, you can attach any number of custom functions as methods for that object. You are in total control of the object's structure, data, and behavior.

The practice of employing custom objects in your JavaScript code is known as *object-oriented programming*, or *OOP* for short. OOP has been around a long time and has been used to great success in other programming languages such as C++ and Java. However, the scripted nature of JavaScript has caused OOP to catch on a bit more slowly in the JavaScript world. Even so, support for custom objects is a standard part of modern JavaScript-enabled browsers and is something you should consider taking advantage of whenever prudent.

NOTE To split hairs technically, I have to clarify that JavaScript isn't truly an object-oriented language in a strict sense. Instead, JavaScript is considered an object-based language. The difference between object-oriented and object-based is significant and has to do with how objects can be extended. Even so, conceptually JavaScript's support of objects is enough akin to true OOP languages such that it's not unreasonable to discuss JavaScript in OOP terms. You learn about some of the specific object features that allow JavaScript to approach OOP languages later in the chapter.

There is no magic to knowing when to use a custom object instead of an array in your application. The more you work with and understand the way custom objects work, the more likely you will think about your data-carrying scripts in these terms — especially if an object can benefit from having one or more methods associated with it. This avenue is certainly not one for beginners, but I recommend that you give custom objects more than a casual perusal after you have gained some JavaScripting experience.

The nuts and bolts of objects

An *object* in JavaScript is really just a collection of properties. *Properties* can take on the form of data types, functions (methods), or even other objects. A function assigned to a property is known as a *method*. Methods are no different than other functions except that they are intended to be used in the context of an object, and therefore are assumed to have access to data properties of that object. This connection between data and functions is one of the core concepts prevalent in OOP.

Objects are created using a special function known as a *constructor*, which determines the name of the object — the constructor is named the same as the object. Here's an example of a constructor function:

```
function alien() {
}
```

Although this function doesn't contain any code, it does nonetheless lay the groundwork for creating an `alien` object. You can think of a constructor as a blueprint that is then used to create actual objects. Here's an example of how you create an object using a constructor:

```
var myAlien = new alien();
```

The `new` keyword is used to create JavaScript objects, and it is used in conjunction with a constructor to do so.

Creating properties for custom objects

Earlier I mentioned that properties are key to objects, so you might be wondering how you go about creating a property for a custom object. Custom object properties are created in the constructor with some help from the this keyword, as this code reveals:

```
function alien() {
    this.name = "Clyde";
    this.aggressive = true;
}
```

The this keyword is used to reference the current object, which in this case is the object that is being created by the constructor. So, you use the this keyword to create new properties for the object. The only problem with this example is that it results in all aliens that are created with the alien() constructor having the same name and aggression. The fix is to pass in the property values to the constructor so that each alien can be customized upon creation:

```
function alien(name, aggressive) {
    this.name = name;
    this.aggressive = aggressive;
}
```

Now you can create different aliens that each have their own unique property values:

```
var alien1 = new alien("Ernest", false);
var alien2 = new alien("Wilhelm", true);
```

To get to the properties of the object (for reading or writing after the object has been created), use the same type of dot syntax you use with DOM objects. To change the name property of one of the objects, the statement would be:

```
alien1.name = "Julius";
```

Creating methods for custom objects

Properties are really only half of the JavaScript OOP equation. The other half is methods, which are functions that you tie to objects so that they can access object data. Following is an example of a method that you might use with the alien class:

```
function attack() {
    if (this.aggressive) {
        // Do some attacking and return true to indicate that the attack commenced
        return true;
    }
    else {
        // Don't attack and return false to indicate that the attack didn't happen
        return true;
    }
}
```

Notice that the attack() method references the this.aggressive property to decide if the attack should take place. The only thing missing at this point is the connection between the attack() method and the alien object. Without this connection the this keyword would have no meaning because there would be no associated object. Here's how the connection is made:

```
function alien(name, aggressive) {
    this.name = name;
    this.aggressive = aggressive;
    this.attack = attack;
}
```

This code clearly illustrates how methods are really just properties. A new property named `attack` is created and assigned a reference to the `attack()` function. It's very important to note that the `attack()` function is specified by reference (without the parentheses). Here, then, is the creation of an `alien` object and the invocation of its `attack()` method:

```
var alien1 = new alien("Ernest", false);
alien1.attack();
```

You're now armed with enough of the basics of JavaScript objects to move on to a more complete example, which the next section provides.

An OOP example — planetary objects

Building on your familiarity with the planetary data array created in Chapter 31, this chapter shows you how convenient it is to use the data when it is constructed in the form of an OOP design that utilizes custom objects. The application goal for the extended example in this section is to present a pop-up list of the nine planets of the solar system and display data about the selected planet. From a user-interface perspective (and for more exposure to multiframe environments), the resulting data displays in a separate frame of a two-frame window. This means your object method builds HTML on the fly and plugs it into the display frame. If you implement this application strictly for IE4+, NN6+, Moz, and W3C browsers, you can apply the same data to reconstruct the displayed table data for each user selection. The example as shown, however, is fully backward compatible for all scriptable browsers.

In this chapter, instead of building arrays to hold the data, you build objects—one object for each planet. The design of your planetary object has five properties and one method. The properties of each planet are: name, diameter, distance from the sun, year length, and day length. To assign more intelligence to these objects, you give each of them the capability to display their data in the lower frame of the window. You can conveniently define one function that knows how to behave with any of these planet objects, rather than having to define nine separate functions. When used within the context of an object, a function is actually referred to as a method.

Listing 34-5 shows the source code for the document that creates the frameset for your planetary explorations; Listing 34-6 shows the entire HTML page for the object-oriented planet document, which appears in the top frame.

LISTING 34-5

Framesetting Document for a Two-Frame Window

```
<html>
  <head>
    <title>Solar System Viewer</title>
    <script type="text/javascript">
    function blank() {
        return "<html><body><\/body><\/html>";
    }
```

```
      </script>
   </head>
   <frameset rows="50%,50%" onload="frames['Frame1'].doDisplay(
      frames['Frame1'].document.forms[0].planetsList)">
      <frame name="Frame1" src="lst34-06.htm" />
      <frame name="Frame2" src="javascript:parent.blank()" />
   </frameset>
</html>
```

One item to point out in Listing 34-5 is that because the lower frame isn't filled until the upper frame's document loads, you need to assign some kind of URL for the src attribute of the second frame. Rather than add the extra transaction and file burden of a blank HTML document, here you use the javascript: URL to invoke a function. In this instance, I want the value returned from the function (a blank HTML page) to be reflected into the target frame (no void operator here). This method provides the most efficient way of creating a blank frame in a frameset.

LISTING 34-6

Object-Oriented Planetary Data Presentation

```
<html>
   <head>
      <title>Our Solar System</title>
      <script type="text/javascript">
      // method definition
      function showPlanet() {
         var result = "<html><body><center><table border='2'>";
         result += "<caption align='top'>Planetary data for: <b>" + this.name +
            "</b></caption>";
         result += "<tr><td align='right'>Diameter:</td><td>" + this.diameter +
            "</td></tr>";
         result += "<tr><td align='right'>Distance from Sun:</td><td>" +
            this.distance + "</td></tr>";
         result += "<tr><td align='right'>One Orbit Around Sun:</td><td>" +
            this.year + "</td></tr>";
         result += "<tr><td align='right'>One Revolution (Earth
            Time):</td><td>" + this.day + "</td></tr>";
         result += "</table></center></body></html>";
         // display results in a second frame of the window
         parent.frames["Frame2"].document.write(result);
         parent.frames["Frame2"].document.close();
      }

      // definition of planet object type;
      // 'new' will create a new instance and stuff parameter data into object
      function planet(name, diameter, distance, year, day) {
         this.name = name;
         this.diameter = diameter;
         this.distance = distance;
```

```
        this.year = year;
        this.day = day;
        this.showPlanet = showPlanet; // make showPlanet() function a method
        // ...of planet
    }

    // create new planet objects, and store in a series of variables
    var Mercury = new planet("Mercury","3100 miles", "36 million miles",
        "88 days", "59 days");
    var Venus = new planet("Venus", "7700 miles", "67 million miles",
        "225 days", "244 days");
    var Earth = new planet("Earth", "7920 miles", "93 million miles",
        "365.25 days","24 hours");
    var Mars = new planet("Mars", "4200 miles", "141 million miles",
        "687 days", "24 hours, 24 minutes");
    var Jupiter = new planet("Jupiter","88,640 miles","483 million miles",
        "11.9 years", "9 hours, 50 minutes");
    var Saturn = new planet("Saturn", "74,500 miles","886 million miles",
        "29.5 years", "10 hours, 39 minutes");
    var Uranus = new planet("Uranus", "32,000 miles",
        "1.782 billion miles","84 years", "23 hours");
    var Neptune = new planet("Neptune","31,000 miles",
        "2.793 billion miles","165 years", "15 hours, 48 minutes");
    var Pluto = new planet("Pluto", "1500 miles", "3.67 billion miles",
        "248 years", "6 days, 7 hours");

    // called from push button to invoke planet object method
    function doDisplay(popup) {
        i = popup.selectedIndex;
        eval(popup.options[i].text + ".showPlanet()");
    }
    </script>
</head>
<body>
    <h1>The Daily Planet</h1>
    <hr />
    <form>
        <p>Select a planet to view its planetary data: <select
        name='planetsList' onchange='doDisplay(this)'>
            <option>Mercury</option>
            <option>Venus</option>
            <option selected="selected">Earth</option>
            <option>Mars</option>
            <option>Jupiter</option>
            <option>Saturn</option>
            <option>Uranus</option>
            <option>Neptune</option>
            <option>Pluto</option>
        </select></p>
    </form>
</body>
</html>
```

The first task in the Head is to define the function that becomes a method in each of the objects. You must do this task before scripting any other code that adopts the function as its method. Failure to define the function ahead of time results in an error — the function name is not defined. If you compare the data extraction methodology with the function in the array version, notice that the parameter for the index value is gone and the reference to each property begins with this. Later, I return to the custom method after giving you a look at the rest of the Head code.

Next comes the object constructor function, which performs several important tasks. For one, everything in this function establishes the structure of your custom object: the properties available for data storage and retrieval and any methods that the object can invoke. The name of the function is the name you use later to create new instances of the object. Therefore, choosing a name that truly reflects the nature of the object is important. And, because you probably want to stuff some data into the function's properties to get one or more instances of the object loaded and ready for the page's user, the function definition includes parameters for each of the properties defined in this object definition.

Inside the function, you use the this keyword to assign data that comes in as parameters to labeled properties. For this example, I use the same names for both the incoming parameter variables and the properties. That's primarily for convenience (and is very common practice), but you can assign any variable and property names you want and connect them any way you like. In the planet() constructor function, five property slots are reserved for every instance of the object whether or not any data actually is placed in every property (any unassigned slot has a value of null).

The last entry in the planet() constructor function is a reference to the showPlanet() function defined earlier. Note that the assignment statement doesn't refer to the function with its parentheses — just to the function name. When JavaScript sees this assignment statement, it looks back through existing definitions (those functions defined ahead of the current location in the script) for a match. If it finds a function (as it does here), JavaScript knows to assign the function to the identifier on the left side of the assignment statement. In doing this task with a function, JavaScript automatically sets up the identifier as a method name for this object. As you do in every JavaScript method you encounter, you must invoke a method by using a reference to the object, a period, and the method name followed by a set of parentheses. You see that syntax in a minute.

The next long block of statements creates the individual objects according to the definition established in the planet() constructor. Similar to an array, an assignment statement and the keyword new create an object. I assign names that are not only the real names of planets (the Mercury object name is the Mercury planet object) but that also can come in handy later when the doDisplay() function extracts names from the pop-up list in search of a particular object's data.

The act of creating a new object sets aside space in memory (associated with the current document) for this object and its properties. An object created in memory is known as an *instance*. In this script, you create nine object instances, each with a different set of properties. Note that no parameter is sent (or expected at the function) that corresponds to the showPlanet() method. Omitting that parameter here is fine because the specification of that method in the object definition means that the script automatically attaches the method to every version (instance) of the planet object that it creates. This is important, because it links the function (method) to the object, thereby providing it access to the object's properties.

The last function definition, doDisplay(), is invoked whenever the user makes a choice from the list of planets in the upper frame. This function is also invoked through the frameset's onload event handler so that an initial table is displayed from the default selected item (see Figure 34-1). Invoking the function from the upper frame's onload event handler can cause problems (such as the failure of the other frame) if the frameset is not completely loaded.

FIGURE 34-1

An external and internal face-lift for an earlier application.

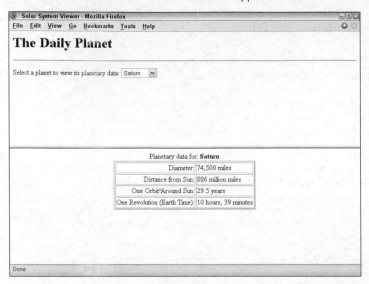

The `onchange` event handler in the `select` list passes that `select` element's reference to the `doDisplay()` function. In that function, the `select` object is assigned to a variable called `popup` to help you visualize that the object is the pop-up list. The first statement extracts the index value of the selected item. Using that index value, the script extracts the text. But things get a little tricky because you need to use that text string as a variable name — the name of the planet — and append it to the call to the `showPlanet()` method. To make the disparate data types come together, use the `eval()` function. Inside the parentheses, extract the string for the planet name and concatenate a string that completes the reference to the object's `showPlanet()` method. The `eval()` function evaluates that string, which turns it into a valid method call. Therefore, if the user selects Jupiter from the pop-up list, the method call becomes `Jupiter.showPlanet()`.

Now it's time to look back to the `showPlanet()` function/method definition at the top of the script. When that method runs in response to a user selection of the planet Jupiter, the method's only scope is of the `Jupiter` object. Therefore, all references to `this.propertyName` in `showPlanet()` refer to `Jupiter` only. The only possibility for `this.name` in the `Jupiter` object is the value assigned to the `name` property for `Jupiter`. The same goes for the rest of the properties extracted in the function/method.

Further encapsulation

One of the benefits of using objects in scripting is that all the "wiring" inside the object — properties and methods — are defined within the local variable scope of the object. It's a concept call *encapsulation*. Thus, when you use the `this` keyword to create object properties and assign values to them inside a constructor function, the property names and any code associated with them are private to the object and never conflict with global variable or object names.

In large scripting projects, especially when multiple programmers are involved, it's fairly easy for global names to clash, sometimes inadvertently. For example, in Internet Explorer, all DOM object IDs become part of the global variable space because that browser allows scripts to reference an element object simply by its ID (unlike the W3C DOM, which uses the `document.getElementById()` method). As a project grows in size and complexity, it is increasingly helpful to avoid piling up more and more objects — including function definitions — in the global variable naming space.

In Listing 34-6, for example, the `showPlanet()` function is defined in the global space. The function is used, however, only as a method of `planet` object instances. Therefore, the `showPlanet()` function is taking up a global object name (`showPlanet`) that might be used elsewhere (perhaps as an ID for a button element). To get the function definition out of the global space, define it within the `planet()` constructor function, either as a nested function, or as an anonymous function assigned directly to the `this.showPlanet` property in the constructor.

Creating an array of objects

In Listing 34-6, each of the planet objects is assigned to a global variable whose name is that of the planet. If the idea of custom objects is new to you, this idea probably doesn't sound so bad because it's easy to visualize each variable representing an object. But, as shown in the `doDisplay()` function, accessing an object by name requires use of the `eval()` function to convert a string representation to a valid object reference. Although it's not too important in this simple example, the `eval()` function is not particularly efficient in JavaScript. If you find yourself using an `eval()` function, look for ways to improve efficiency such that you can reference an object by string. The way to accomplish that streamlining for this application is to place the objects in an array whose index values are the planet names — an associative array.

To assign the custom objects in Listing 34-6 to an array, first create an empty array and then assign the result of each object constructor call to an entry in the array. The modified code section looks like the following (formatted to fit this printed page):

```
// create array
var planets = new Array();
// populate array with new planet objects
planets["Mercury"] =
    new planet("Mercury","3100 miles", "36 million miles",
    "88 days", "59 days");
planets["Venus"] =
    new planet("Venus", "7700 miles", "67 million miles",
    "225 days", "244 days");
planets["Earth"] =
    new planet("Earth", "7920 miles", "93 million miles",
    "365.25 days","24 hours");
planets["Mars"] =
    new planet("Mars", "4200 miles", "141 million miles",
    "687 days", "24 hours, 24 minutes");
planets["Jupiter"] =
    new planet("Jupiter","88,640 miles","483 million miles",
    "11.9 years", "9 hours, 50 minutes");
planets["Saturn"] =
    new planet("Saturn", "74,500 miles","886 million miles",
    "29.5 years", "10 hours, 39 minutes");
```

```
planets["Uranus"] =
   new planet("Uranus", "32,000 miles","1.782 billion miles",
   "84 years", "23 hours");
planets["Neptune"] =
   new planet("Neptune","31,000 miles","2.793 billion miles",
   "165 years", "15 hours, 48 minutes");
planets["Pluto"] =
   new planet("Pluto", "1500 miles", "3.67 billion miles",
   "248 years", "6 days, 7 hours");
```

The supreme advantage to this approach comes in a modified doDisplay() function, which can use the string value from the select element directly without any conversion to an object reference:

```
// called from push button to invoke planet object method
function doDisplay(popup) {
   i = popup.selectedIndex;
   planets[popup.options[i].text].showPlanet();
}
```

The presence of so many similar objects cries out for their storage as an array. Because the names play a key role in their choice for this application, the named index values work best; in other situations, you may prefer to use numeric indexes to facilitate looping through the array.

Taking advantage of embedded objects

One powerful technique for using custom objects is that of embedding an object within another object. When you place one object inside another object, the object being placed is known as an embedded object or object property. Let's extend the planet example to help you understand the implications of using a custom object property.

Say that you want to beef up the planet page with a photo of each planet. Each photo has a URL for the photo file; each photo also contains other information, such as the copyright notice and a reference number, which displays on the page for the user. One way to handle this additional information is to create a separate object definition for a photo database. Such a definition may look like this:

```
function photo(name, URL, copyright, refNum) {
   this.name = name;
   this.URL = URL;
   this.copyright = copyright;
   this.refNum = refNum;
}
```

You then need to create individual photo objects for each picture. One such definition may look like this:

```
mercuryPhoto = new photo("Planet Mercury", "/images/merc44.gif",
   "(c)1990 NASA", 28372);
```

Attaching a photo object to a planet object requires modifying the planet constructor function to accommodate one more property, an object property. The new planet constructor looks like this:

```
function planet(name, diameter, distance, year, day, photo) {
   this.name = name;
   this.diameter = diameter;
   this.distance = distance;
   this.year = year;
```

```
   this.day = day;
   this.showPlanet = showPlanet;
   this.photo = photo; // add photo property
}
```

When the `photo` objects are created, you can then create each `planet` object by passing one more parameter — a `photo` object you want associated with that object:

```
// create new planet objects, and store in a series of variables
Mercury = new planet("Mercury", "3100 miles", "36 million miles",
   "88 days", "59 days", mercuryPhoto);
```

To access a property of a `photo` object, your scripts then have to assemble a reference that works its way through the connection with the `planet` object:

```
copyrightData = Mercury.photo.copyright;
```

The potential of embedded objects of this type is enormous. For example, you can embed all the copy elements and image URLs for an online catalog in a single document. As the user selects items to view (or cycles through them in sequence), a new JavaScript-written page displays the information in an instant. This requires only the image to be downloaded — unless the image was precached, as described in the image object discussion in Chapter 18. In this case, everything works instantaneously — no waiting for page after page of catalog.

If, by now, you think you see a resemblance between this object-within-an-object construction and a relational database, give yourself a gold star. Nothing prevents multiple objects from having the same subobject as their properties — like multiple business contacts having the same company object property.

The modern way to create objects

The examples in Listings 34-5 and 34-6 show a way of creating objects that works with all scriptable browsers. However, there is a much cleaner option available to you. If you can safely assume that your audience consists of users with more modern browsers, then you'll likely want to take advantage of the new `Object()` constructor, which can be used to create any custom object.

From NN3+ and IE4+ onward (including Moz and W3C browsers), you can use the new `Object()` constructor to generate a blank object. From that point on, you can define property and method names by simple assignment, as in the following snippet:

```
var Earth = new Object();
Earth.diameter = "7920 miles";
Earth.distance = "93 million miles";
Earth.year = "365.25";
Earth.day = "24 hours";
Earth.showPlanet = showPlanet;  // function reference
```

When you create a lot of like-structured objects, the custom object constructor shown in Listing 34-6 is more efficient. But for single objects, the new `Object()` constructor is more efficient.

For modern browsers, you can also benefit from a shortcut literal syntax for creating a new object. You can set pairs of property names and their values inside a set of curly braces, and you can assign the whole construction to a variable that becomes the object name. The following script shows how to organize this kind of object constructor:

```
var Earth = {diameter:"7920 miles", distance:"93 million miles", year:"365.25",
        day:"24 hours", showPlanet:showPlanet};
```

Colons link name-value pairs, and commas separate multiple name-value pairs. The value portion of a name-value pair can even be an array (using the [. . .] constructor shortcut) or a nested object (using another pair of curly braces). In fact, you can nest arrays and objects to your heart's content to create exceedingly complex objects. All in all, this is a very compact way to embed data in a page for script manipulation. If your CGI, XML, and database skills are up to the task, consider using a server program to convert XML data into this compact JavaScript version with each XML record being its own JavaScript object. For multiple records, assign the curly-braced object definitions to an array entry. Then your scripts on the client can iterate through the data and generate the HTML to display the data in a variety of forms and sorted according to different criteria (thanks to the JavaScript array-sorting powers).

Defining object property getters and setters

JavaScript 1.5 unofficially added an interesting OOP feature that enables you to create special methods for getting and setting custom object properties. This feature consists of two methods called *getter* and *setter*. I say "unofficially" because getters and setters are not officially part of the current ECMAScript standard and are therefore left to each browser vendor to implement. As of this writing, Mozilla-based browsers are the only browsers that support getters and setters.

The purpose of a getter is to assign a new property to an object and to define how the value returned by the property should be evaluated. A setter does the same, but it also defines how a new value assigned to the property should apply the value to the object. Both definitions are written in the form of anonymous functions, such that reading or writing an object's property value can include sophisticated processing for either operation.

NOTE I introduced the idea of creating a getter and setter for an object briefly in Chapter 14, where the NN6 syntax style extended properties of some W3C DOM objects to include some of the Microsoft-specific (and very convenient) DOM syntax. Most notably, you can define a getter for any container to return an array of nested elements just like the IE-only document.all collection.

Getters and setters are dynamically assigned to the prototype property of an object, thus enabling you to customize native and DOM objects. Following is the syntax used to fashion getters and setters as methods of an object's prototype:

```
object.prototype.__defineGetter__("propName", function)
object.prototype.__defineSetter__("propName", function)
```

Note that the underscores before and after the method names are actually pairs of underscore characters (that is, _, _, defineGetter, _, _). This double underscore was chosen as a syntax that the ECMA standard will not use, so it will not conflict with the eventual syntax for this facility that does make its way into the standard.

The first parameter of the method is the name of the property for which the getter or setter is defined. This can be an existing property name that you want to override. The second parameter can be a function reference; but more likely it will be an anonymous function defined in place. By using an anonymous function, you can take advantage of the context of the object for which the property is defined. For each property, define both a getter and setter—even if the property is meant to be read-only or write-only.

To see how this mechanism works, let's use the getter and setter shown in Chapter 14 to add an innerText property to HTML elements in NN6+/Moz. This property is read/write, so functions are defined for both the getter and setter. The getter definition is as follows:

```
HTMLElement.prototype.__defineGetter__("innerText", function () {
    var rng = document.createRange();
    rng.selectNode(this);
    return rng.toString();
})
```

The modified object is the basic `HTMLElement` object — the object that NN6+ uses to create instances of every HTML element for the page. After the preceding statement executes, every HTML element on the page inherits the new `innerText` property. Each time the `innerText` property is read for an element, the anonymous function in this getter executes. Thus, after a text range object is created, the range is set to the node that is the current element. This is an excellent example of how the context of the current object allows the use of the `this` keyword to refer to the very same object. Finally, the string version of the selected range is returned. It is essential that a getter function include a `return` statement and that the returned value is of the desired data type. Also take notice of the closing of the function's curly brace and the getter method's parenthesis.

By executing this function each time the property is read, the getter always returns the current state of the object. If content of the element has changed since the page loaded, you are still assured of getting the current text inside the element. This is far superior to simply running the statements inside this function when the page loads to capture a static view of the element's text.

The corresponding setter definition is as follows:

```
HTMLElement.prototype.__defineSetter__("innerText", function (txt) {
    var rng = document.createRange();
    rng.selectNodeContents(this);
    rng.deleteContents();
    var newText = document.createTextNode(txt);
    this.appendChild(newText);
    return txt;
})
```

To assign a value to an object's property, the setter function requires that a parameter variable receive the assigned value. That parameter variable plays a role somewhere within the function definition. For this particular setter, the current object (`this`) also manipulates the text range object. The contents of the current element are deleted, and a text node comprising the text passed as a parameter is inserted into the element. To completely simulate the IE behavior of setting the `innerText` property, the text is returned. Although setters don't always return values, this one does so that the expression that assigns a value to the `innerText` property evaluates to the new text.

If you want to create a read-only property, you still define a setter for the property but you also assign an empty function, as in:

```
Node.prototype.__defineSetter__("all", function() {})
```

This prevents assignment statements to a read-only property from generating errors. A write-only property should also have a getter that returns `null` or an empty string, as in:

```
HTMLElement.prototype.__defineGetter__("outerHTML", function() {return ""})
```

Because the getter and setter syntax shown here is unique to NN6+/Moz, you must obviously wrap such statements inside object detection or browser version detection statements. And, to reiterate, this syntax will change in future browser versions when ECMA adopts the formal syntax (look for it in JavaScript 2.0).

Object-Oriented Concepts

As mentioned previously, JavaScript is object-based rather than object-oriented. This means that instead of adhering to the class, subclass, and inheritance schemes of object-oriented languages such as Java, JavaScript uses what is called *prototype inheritance*. This scheme works not only for native and DOM objects but also for custom objects.

Adding a prototype

A custom object is frequently defined by a constructor function, which typically parcels out initial values to properties of the object, as in the following example:

```
function car(plate, model, color) {
    this.plate = plate;
    this.model = model;
    this.color = color;
}
var car1 = new car("AB 123", "Ford", "blue");
```

Modern browsers offer a handy shortcut, as well, to stuff default values into properties if none are provided (the supplied value is null, 0, or an empty string). The OR operator (||) can let the property assignment statement apply the passed value, if present, or a default value you hard-wire into the constructor. Therefore, you can modify the preceding function to offer default values for the properties:

```
function car(plate, model, color) {
    this.plate = plate || "missing";
    this.model = model || "unknown";
    this.color = color || "unknown";
}
var car1 = new car("AB 123", "Ford", "");
```

After the preceding statements run, the `car1` object has the following properties:

```
car1.plate    // value = "AB 123"
car1.model    // value = "Ford"
car1.color    // value = "unknown"
```

If you then add a new property to the constructor's `prototype` property, as in

```
car.prototype.companyOwned = true;
```

any `car` object you already created or are about to create automatically inherits the new `companyOwned` property and its value. You can still override the value of the `companyOwned` property for any individual `car` object. But if you don't override the property for instances of the `car` object, the `car` objects whose `companyOwned` property is not overridden automatically inherit any change to the `prototype.companyOwned` value. This has to do with the way JavaScript looks for `prototype` property values.

Prototype inheritance

Each time your script attempts to read or write a property of an object, JavaScript follows a specific sequence in search of a match for the property name. The sequence is as follows:

1. If the property has a value assigned to the current (local) object, this is the value to use.
2. If there is no local value, check the value of the property's prototype of the object's constructor.
3. Continue up the prototype chain until either a match of the property is found (with a value assigned to it) or the search reaches the native Object object.

Therefore, if you change the value of a constructor's prototype property and you do not override the property value in an instance of that constructor, JavaScript returns the current value of the constructor's prototype property.

Nested objects and prototype inheritance

When you begin nesting objects, especially when one object invokes the constructor of another, there is an added wrinkle to the prototype inheritance chain. Let's continue with the car object defined earlier. In this scenario, consider the car object to be akin to a root object that has properties shared among two other types of objects. One of the object types is a company fleet vehicle, which needs the properties of the root car object (plate, model, color) but also adds some properties of its own. The other object that shares the car object is an object representing a car parked in the company garage — an object that has additional properties regarding the parking of the vehicle. This explains why the car object is defined on its own.

Now look at the constructor function for the parking record, along with the constructor for the basic car object:

```
function car(plate, model, color) {
    this.plate = plate || "missing";
    this.model = model || "unknown";
    this.color = color || "unknown";
}
function carInLot(plate, model, color, timeIn, spaceNum) {
    this.timeIn = timeIn;
    this.spaceNum = spaceNum;
    this.carInfo = car;
    this.carInfo(plate, model, color);
}
```

The carInLot constructor not only assigns values to its unique properties (timeIn and spaceNum) but it also includes a reference to the car constructor arbitrarily assigned to a property called carInfo. This property assignment is merely a conduit that allows property values intended for the car constructor to be passed within the carInLot constructor function. To create a carInLot object, use a statement like the following:

```
var car1 = new carInLot("AA 123", "Ford", "blue", "10:02AM", "31");
```

1053

After this statement, the `car1` object has the following properties and values:

```
car1.timeIn      // value = "10:02AM"
car1.spaceNum    // value = "31"
car1.carInfo     // value = reference to car object constructor function
car1.plate       // value = "AA 123"
car1.model       // value = "Ford"
car1.color       // value = "blue"
```

Let's say that five `carInLot` objects are created in the script (`car1` through `car5`). The prototype wrinkle comes into play if, for example, you assign a new property to the `car` constructor prototype:

```
car.prototype.companyOwned = true;
```

Even though the `carInLot` objects use the `car` constructor, the instances of `carInLot` objects do not have a prototype chain back to the `car` object. As the preceding code stands, even though you've added a `companyOwned` property to the `car` constructor, no `carInLot` object inherits that property (even if you were to create a new `carInLot` object after defining the new `prototype` property for `car`). To get the `carInLot` instances to inherit the `prototype.companyOwned` property, you must explicitly connect the prototype of the `carInLot` constructor to the `car` constructor prior to creating instances of `carInLot` objects:

```
carInLot.prototype = new car();
```

The complete sequence, then, is as follows:

```
function car(plate, model, color) {
    this.plate = plate || "missing";
    this.model = model || "unknown";
    this.color = color || "unknown";
}
function carsInLot(plate, model, color, timeIn, spaceNum) {
    this.timeIn = timeIn;
    this.spaceNum = spaceNum;
    this.carInfo = car;
    this.carInfo(plate, model, color);
}
carsInLot.prototype = new car();
var car1 = new carsInLot("123ABC", "Ford","blue","10:02AM", "32");
car.prototype.companyOwned = true;
```

After this stretch of code runs, the `car1` object has the following properties and values:

```
car1.timeIn        // value = "10:02AM"
car1.spaceNum      // value = "31"
car1.carInfo       // value = reference to car object constructor function
car1.plate         // value = "AA 123"
car1.model         // value = "Ford"
car1.color         // value = "blue"
car1.companyOwned  // value = true
```

NN4+/Moz provides one extra, proprietary bit of syntax in this prototype world. The `__proto__` property (that's with double underscores before and after the word *proto*) returns a reference to the object that is next up the prototype chain. For example, if you inspect the properties of `car1.__proto__` after the preceding code runs, you see that the properties of the object next up the prototype chain are as follows:

```
car1.__proto__.plate          // value = "AA 123"
car1.__proto__.model          // value = "Ford"
car1.__proto__.color          // value = "blue"
car1.__proto__.companyOwned   // value = true
```

This property can be helpful in debugging custom objects and prototype inheritance chain challenges, but the property is not part of the ECMA standard. Therefore, I discourage you from using the property in your production scripts since it isn't available in non-Mozilla-based browsers.

Object Object

Properties	Methods
constructor	hasOwnProperty()
prototype	isPrototypeOf()
	propertyIsEnumerable()
	toSource()
	toString()
	unwatch()
	valueOf()
	watch()

Syntax

Creating an `Object` object:

```
function constructorName([arg1,...[,argN]]) {
    statement(s)
}
var objName = new constructorName(["argName1",...[,"argNameN"]]);
var objName = new Object();
var objName = {propName1:propVal1[, propName2:propVal2[,...N]]}
```

Accessing an `Object` object properties and methods:

```
objectReference.property | method([parameters])
```

Compatibility: WinIE4+, MacIE4+, NN3+, Moz+, Safari+

About this object

Although it might sound like doubletalk, the `Object` object is a vital native object in the JavaScript environment. It is the root object on which all other native objects — such as `Date`, `Array`, `String`, and the like — are based. This object also provides the foundation for creating custom objects, as described earlier in this chapter.

objectObject

By and large, your scripts do not access the properties of the native `Object` object. The same is true for many of its methods, such as `toString()` and `valueOf()`, which internally allow debugging alert dialog boxes (and The Evaluator) to display something when referring to an object or its constructor. Similarly, the `toSource()` method returns a string representation of the source code for an object, which is not something you would typically need to use in a script.

A little more practical are the `watch()` and `unwatch()` methods of the `Object` object, which provide a mechanism for taking action when a property value changes. You can call the `watch()` method and assign a function that is called when a certain property changes. This enables you to handle an internal property change as an event. When you're finished watching a property, the `unwatch()` method is used to stop the watch.

Listing 34-7 contains an example of how the `watch()` and `unwatch()` methods can be used to track the value of a property.

LISTING 34-7

Watching an Object Property

```html
<html>
   <head>
      <title>Object Watching</title>
      <script type="text/javascript">
      function setIt(msg) {
         document.forms[0].entry.value = msg;
      }
      function watchIt(on) {
         var obj = document.forms[0].entry;
         if (on) {
            obj.watch("value",report);
         } else {
            obj.unwatch("value");
         }
      }
      function report(id, oldval, newval) {
         alert("The field's " + id + " property on its way from \n'" +
            oldval + "'\n to \n'" + newval + "'.");
         return newval;
      }
      </script>
   </head>
   <body>
      <b>Watching Over You</b>
      <hr />
      <form>
         Enter text here: <input type="text" name="entry" size="50"
         value="Default Value" />
         <p><input type="button" value="Set to Phrase I"
            onclick="setIt('Four score and seven years ago...')"
            /><br />
            <input type="button" value="Set to Phrase 2"
```

```
           onclick="setIt('When in the course of human events...')"
           /><br />
           <input type="reset" onclick="setIt('Default value')" /></p>
        <p><input type="button" value="Watch It" onclick="watchIt(true)" />
           <input type="button" value="Don't Watch It" onclick="watchIt(false)"
           /></p>
      </form>
   </body>
</html>
```

You can use a trio of methods (hasOwnProperty(), isPrototypeOf(), and propertyIsEnumerable()) to perform some inspection of the prototype environment of an object instance. They are of interest primarily to advanced scripters who are building extensive, simulated object-oriented applications.

Methods

hasOwnProperty("*propName*")

Returns: Boolean.
Compatibility: WinIE5.5+, MacIE-, NN6+, Moz+, Safari-

The hasOwnProperty() method returns true if the current object instance has the property defined in its constructor or in a related constructor function. But if this property is defined externally, as through assignment to the object's prototype property, the method returns false.

Using the example of the car and carInLot objects from earlier in this chapter, the following expressions evaluate to true:

```
      car1.hasOwnProperty("spaceNum");
      car1.hasOwnProperty("model");
```

Even though the model property is defined in a constructor that is invoked by another constructor, the property belongs to the car1 object. The following statement, however, evaluates to false:

```
      car1.hasOwnProperty("companyOwned");
```

This property is defined by way of the prototype of one of the constructor functions and is not a built-in property for the object instance.

isPrototypeOf(*objRef*)

Returns: Boolean.
Compatibility: WinIE5.5+, MacIE-, NN6+, Moz+, Safari-

The isPrototypeOf() method is intended to reveal whether or not the current object has a prototype relation with an object passed as a parameter. In practice, the IE and NN/Moz versions of this method operate differently and return different results.

objectObject.valueOf()

propertyIsEnumerable("*propName*")

Returns: Boolean.
Compatibility: WinIE5.5+, MacIE-, NN6+, Moz+, Safari-

In the terminology of the ECMA-262 language specification, a value is enumerable if constructions such as the for-in property inspection loop (see Chapter 32) can inspect it. Enumerable properties include values such as arrays, strings, and virtually every kind of object. According to the ECMA specification, this method is not supposed to work its way up the prototype chain.

toSource()

Returns: String.
Compatibility: WinIE5.5+, MacIE-, NN6+, Moz+, Safari-

The toSource() method obtains a string representation of the source code for an object. Unlike the toString() method, which returns a string equivalent of the value of an object, the toSource() method returns the underlying code for the object as a string. Seeing as how this is a very specialized, low-level feature, the method is typically only used internally by JavaScript and potentially in some debugging scenarios.

toString()

Returns: String.
Compatibility: WinIE5.5+, MacIE-, NN6+, Moz+, Safari-

The toString() method is used to obtain a string representation of the value of an object. It is fairly common to take advantage of this method in situations where an object needs to be examined as raw text. When creating custom objects, you have the ability to create your own toString() method that reveals whatever information about the object you desire to be seen.

unwatch("*propName*")

Returns: Boolean.
Compatibility: WinIE-, MacIE-, NN6+, Moz+, Safari-

As the counterpart to the watch() method, the unwatch() method terminates a watchpoint that has been set for a particular property.

valueOf()

Returns: Object.
Compatibility: WinIE5.5+, MacIE-, NN6+, Moz+, Safari-

The valueOf() method is used to resolve an object to a primitive data type. This may not always be possible, in which case the method simply returns the object itself. Otherwise, the method returns a primitive value that represents the object.

watch("*propName*")

Returns: Boolean.
Compatibility: WinIE-, MacIE-, NN6+, Moz+, Safari-

The watch() method is the key to a handy little JavaScript debugging feature known as watchpoints. A watchpoint enables you to specify a function that is called whenever the value of a property is set. This enables you to carefully track the state of properties and take action when an important property value changes.

You set a watchpoint by calling the watch() method and passing the name of the property that you want to watch, like this:

```
obj.watch("count",
    function(prop, oldval, newval) {
        document.writeln(prop + " changed from " + oldval + " to " + newval);
        return newval;
    });
```

In this example, a function is created to output a property change notification and then return the new property value. Every watchpoint handler must follow this same convention of using three arguments that specify the property, old value, and new value, respectively.

Chapter 35

Global Functions and Statements

I n addition to all the objects and other language constructs described in the preceding chapters of this reference part of the book, several language items need to be treated on a global scale. These items apply to no particular objects (or any object), and you can use them anywhere in a script. If you read earlier chapters, you were introduced to many of these functions and statements. This chapter serves as a convenient place to highlight these all-important items that are otherwise easily forgotten. At the end of the chapter, note the brief introduction to several objects that are built into the Windows-only versions of Internet Explorer.

This chapter begins with coverage of the following global functions and statements that are part of the core JavaScript language:

Functions	Statements
decodeURI()	// and /*...*/ (comment)
decodeURIComponent()	const
encodeURI()	var
encodeURIComponent()	
escape()	
eval()	
isFinite()	
isNaN()	
Number()	
parseFloat()	
parseInt()	
toString()	
unescape()	
unwatch()	
watch()	

Global functions are not tied to the document object model. Instead, they typically enable you to convert data from one type to another type. The list of global statements is short, but a couple of them appear extensively in your scripting.

Functions

decodeURI("*encodedURI*")
decodeURIComponent("*encodedURIComponent*")
encodeURI("*URIString*")
encodeURIComponent("*URIComponentString*")

Returns: String.
Compatibility: WinIE5.5+, MacIE-, NN6+, Moz+, Safari-

The ECMA-262 Edition 3 standard, as implemented in IE5.5+, NN6+, and Mozilla-based browsers, provides utility functions that perform a more rigorous conversion of strings to valid URI strings and vice versa than was achieved earlier via the escape() and unescape() functions (described later in this chapter). In fact, the modern encodeURI(), encodeURIComponent(), decodeURI(), and decodeURIComponent() functions serve as replacements to the now deprecated escape() and unescape() functions.

The purpose of the encoding functions is to convert any string to a version that you can use as a Uniform Resource Identifier, such as a web page address or an invocation of a server CGI script. Whereas Latin alphanumeric characters pass through the encoding process untouched, you must use the encoding functions to convert some symbols and other Unicode characters to a form (hexadecimal representations of the character numbers) that the Internet can pass from place to place. The space character, for example, must be encoded to its hex version: %20.

Perhaps the biggest difference between the encodeURI() and escape() functions (and their decodeURI() and unescape() counterparts) is that the more modern versions do not encode a wide range of symbols that are perfectly acceptable as URI characters according to the syntax recommended in RFC2396 (http://www.ietf.org/rfc/rfc2396.txt). Thus, the following characters are not encoded via the encodeURI() function:

    ; / ? : @ & = + $, - _ . ! ~ * ' ( ) #

Use the encodeURI() and decodeURI() functions only on complete URIs. Applicable URIs can be relative or absolute, but these two functions are wired especially so symbols that are part of the protocol (://), search string (? and =, for instance), and directory-level delimiters (/) are not encoded. The decodeURI() function should work with URIs that arrive from servers as page locations, but be aware that some server CGIs encode spaces into plus symbols (+) that are not decoded back to spaces by the JavaScript function. If the URIs your script needs to decode contain plus symbols in place of spaces, you need to run your decoded URI through a string replacement method to finish the job (regular expressions come in handy here). If you are decoding URI strings that your scripts encoded, use the decode functions only on URIs that were encoded via the corresponding encode function. Do not attempt to decode a URI that was created via the old escape() function because the conversion processes work according to different rules.

The difference between a URI and a URI component is that a *component* is a single piece of a URI, generally not containing delimiter characters. For example, if you use the encodeURIComponent() function on a complete URI, almost all of the symbols (other than things such as periods) are encoded into hexadecimal versions—including directory delimiters. Therefore, you should use the component-level conversion functions only on quite granular pieces of a URI. For example, if you assemble a search string that has a name-value pair, you can use the encodeURIComponent() function separately on the name and on the value. But if you use that function on the pair that is already in the form name=value, the function encodes the equal symbol to a hexadecimal equivalent.

Since the escape() and unescape() functions were sometimes used on strings that weren't necessarily URL (URI) strings, you will generally use the encodeURIComponent() and decodeURIComponent() functions when modernizing code that utilizes escape() and unescape().

Example

Use The Evaluator (Chapter 13) to experiment with the differences between encoding a full URI and a component, and encoding and escaping a URI string. For example, compare the results of the following three statements:

```
escape("http://www.giantco.com/index.html?code=42")
encodeURI("http://www.giantco.com/index.html?code=42")
encodeURIComponent("http://www.giantco.com/index.html?code=42")
```

Because the sample URI string is valid as is, the encodeURI() version makes no changes. Experiment further by making the search string value into a string with a space, and see how each function treats that character.

escape("*URIString*" [,1])
unescape("*escapedURIString*")

Returns: String.
Compatibility: WinIE3+, MacIE3+, NN2+, Moz+, Safari+

If you watch the content of the Location field in your browser, you may occasionally see URLs that include a lot of % symbols plus some numbers. The format you see is *URL encoding* (more accurately called *URI encoding* — Uniform Resource Identifier rather than Uniform Resource Locator). This format allows even multiple word strings and nonalphanumeric characters to be sent as one contiguous string of a very low, common denominator character set. This encoding turns a character, such as a space, into its hexadecimal equivalent value preceded by a percent symbol. For example, the space character (ASCII value 32) is hexadecimal 20, so the encoded version of a space is %20.

All characters, including tabs and carriage returns, can be encoded in this way and sent as a simple string that can be decoded on the receiving end for reconstruction. You can also use this encoding to preprocess multiple lines of text that must be stored as a character string in databases. To convert a plain-language string to its encoded version, use the escape() method. This function returns a string consisting of the encoded version. For example:

```
var theCode = escape("Hello there");
    // result: "Hello%20there"
```

Most, but not all, non-alphanumeric characters are converted to escaped versions with the escape() function. One exception is the plus sign, which URLs use to separate components of search strings. If you must encode the plus symbol, too, then add the optional second parameter to the function to make the plus symbol convert to its hexadecimal equivalent (2B):

```
var a = escape("Adding 2+2");
    // result: "Adding%202+2
var a = escape("Adding 2+2",1);
    // result: "Adding%202%2B2
```

The unescape() function was used to convert an escaped string back into plain language. I say "was" because the function is now deprecated thanks to decodeURI() and decodeURIComponent() and shouldn't be used.

The escape() function operates in a way that is approximately midway between the newer functions encodeURI() and encodeComponentURI(). However, the function is now deprecated in lieu of the newer functions and shouldn't be used.

eval("*string*")

Returns: Object reference.
Compatibility: WinIE3+, MacIE3+, NN2+, Moz+, Safari+

Expression evaluation, as you probably are well aware by now, is an important concept to grasp in scripting with JavaScript (and programming in general). An expression evaluates to some value. But occasionally you need to force an additional evaluation on an expression to receive the desired results. The eval() function acts on a string value to force an evaluation of that string expression. Perhaps the most common application of the eval() function is to convert a string version of an object reference to a genuine object reference.

Example

The eval() function can evaluate any JavaScript statement or expression stored as a string. This includes string equivalents of arithmetic expressions, object value assignments, and object method invocation. I do not recommend that you rely on the eval() function, however, because this function is inherently inefficient (from the standpoint of performance). Fortunately, you may not need the eval() function to get from a string version of an object's name to a valid object reference. For example, if your script loops through a series of objects whose names include serial numbers, you can use the object names as array indices rather than use eval() to assemble the object references. The inefficient way to set the value of a series of fields named data0, data1, and so on, is as follows:

```
function fillFields() {
    var theObj;
    for (var i = 0; i < 10; i++) {
        theObj = eval("document.forms[0].data" + i);
        theObj.value = i;
    }
}
```

A more efficient way is to perform the concatenation within the index brackets for the object reference:

```
function fillFields() {
    for (var i = 0; i < 10; i++) {
        document.forms[0].elements["data" + i].value = i;
    }
}
```

> **TIP** Whenever you are about to use an eval() function, look for ways to use string index values of arrays of objects instead. The W3C DOM makes it even easier with the help of the document.getElementById() method, which takes a string as a parameter and returns a reference to the named object.

isFinite(*number*)

Returns: Boolean.
Compatibility: WinIE4+, MacIE4+, NN4+, Moz+, Safari+

It is rare that you will ever need the isFinite() function, but its purpose is to advise whether a number is beyond the absolute minimum or maximum values that JavaScript can handle. If a number is outside of that range, the function returns false. The parameter to the function must be a number data type.

isNaN(*expression*)

Returns: Boolean.
Compatibility: WinIE3+, MacIE3+, NN2+, Moz+, Safari+

For those instances in which a calculation relies on data coming from a text field or other string-oriented source, you frequently need to check whether the value is a number. If the value is not a number, the calculation may result in a script error.

Example

Use the `isNaN()` function to test whether a value is a number prior to passing the value onto a calculation. The most common use of this function is to test the result of a `parseInt()` or `parseFloat()` function. If the strings submitted for conversion to those functions cannot be converted to a number, the resulting value is `NaN` (a special symbol indicating "not a number"). The `isNaN()` function returns `true` if the value is not a number.

A convenient way to use this function is to intercept improper data before it can do damage, as follows:

```
function calc(form) {
    var inputValue = parseInt(form.entry.value);
    if (isNaN(inputValue)) {
        alert("You must enter a number to continue.");
    } else {
        statements for calculation
    }
}
```

Probably the biggest mistake scripters make with this function is failing to observe the case of all the letters in the function name. The trailing uppercase "N" is easy to miss.

Number("*string*")
parseFloat("*string*")
parseInt("*string*" [,*radix*])

Returns: Number.
Compatibility: WinIE3+, MacIE3+, NN2+, Moz+, Safari+

All three of these functions convert a string value into a numeric value. The `parseInt()` and `parseFloat()` functions are compatible across all versions of all browsers, including very old browsers; the `Number()` function was introduced in version 4 browsers.

Use the `Number()` function when your script is not concerned with the precision of the value and prefers to let the source string govern whether the returned value is a floating-point number or an integer. The function takes a single parameter — a string to convert to a number value.

The `parseFloat()` function also lets the string source value determine whether the returned value is a floating-point number or an integer. If the source string includes any non-zero value to the right of the decimal, the result is a floating-point number. But if the string value were, say, `"3.00"`, the returned value would be an integer value.

An extra, optional parameter for `parseInt()` enables you to define the number base for use in the conversion. If you don't specify a radix parameter, JavaScript tries to look out for you; but in doing so, JavaScript may cause some difficulty for you. The primary problem arises when the string parameter for `parseInt()` starts with a zero, which a text box entry or database field might do. In JavaScript, numbers starting with zero are treated as octal (base-8) numbers. Therefore, `parseInt("010")` yields the decimal value 8.

When you apply the `parseInt()` function, always specify the radix of 10 if you are working in base-10 numbers. You can, however, specify any radix value from 2 through 36. For example, to convert a binary number string to its decimal equivalent, assign a radix of 2 as follows:

```
var n = parseInt("011",2);
    // result: 3
```

Similarly, you can convert a hexadecimal string to its decimal equivalent by specifying a radix of 16:

```
var n = parseInt("4F",16);
    // result: 79
```

Example

Both `parseInt()` and `parseFloat()` exhibit a very useful behavior: If the string passed as a parameter starts with at least one number followed by, say, letters, the functions do their jobs on the numeric part of the string and ignore the rest. This is why you can use `parseFloat()` on the `navigator.appVersion` string to extract just the reported version number without having to parse the rest of the string. For example, Firefox 1.0 for Windows reports a `navigator.appVersion` value as

```
5.0 (Windows; en-US)
```

But you can get just the numeric part of the string via `parseFloat()`:

```
var ver = parseFloat(navigator.appVersion);
```

> **NOTE** The number stored in the `navigator.appVersion` property refers to the version number of the underlying browser engine, which helps explain why the reported version in this case is 5.0 even though the Firefox browser application is considered version 1.0.

Because the result is a number, you can perform numeric comparisons to see, for instance, whether the version is greater than or equal to 4.

toString([radix])

Returns: String.
Compatibility: WinIE4+, MacIE4+, NN4+, Moz+, Safari+

Every JavaScript core language object and every DOM `document` object has a `toString()` method associated with it. This method is designed to render the contents of the object as a string of text that is as meaningful as possible. Table 35-1 shows the result of applying the `toString()` method on each of the convertible core `language` object types.

TABLE 35-1

toString() Method Results for Object Types

Object Type	Result
String	The same string
Number	String equivalent (but numeric literals cannot be converted)
Boolean	`"true"` or `"false"`
Array	Comma-delimited list of array contents (with no spaces after commas)
Function	Decompiled string version of the function definition

toString()

Many DOM objects can be converted to a string. For example, a location object returns its URL. But when an object has nothing suitable to return for its content as a string, it usually returns a string in the following format:

```
[object objectType]
```

Example

The toString() method is available on all versions of all browsers. By setting the optional radix parameter between 2 and 16, you can convert numbers to string equivalents in different number bases. Listing 35-1 calculates and draws a conversion table for decimal, hexadecimal, and binary numbers between 0 and 20. In this case, the source of each value is the value of the index counter variable each time the for loop's statements execute.

LISTING 35-1

Using toString() with Radix Values

```html
<html>
  <head>
    <title>Number Conversion Table</title>
  </head>
  <body>
    <b>Using toString() to convert to other number bases:</b>
    <hr />
    <table border="1">
      <tr>
        <th>Decimal</th>
        <th>Hexadecimal</th>
        <th>Binary</th>
        <script type="text/javascript">
        var content = "";
        for (var i = 0; i <= 20; i++) {
            content += "<tr>";
            content += "<td>" + i.toString(10) + "<\/td>";
            content += "<td>" + i.toString(16) + "<\/td>";
            content += "<td>" + i.toString(2) + "<\/td><\/tr>";
        }
        document.write(content);
        </script>
      </tr>
    </table>
  </body>
</html>
```

The toString() method of user-defined objects does not convert the object into a meaningful string, but you can create your own method to do just that. For example, if you want to make your custom object's toString() method behave like an array's method, define the action of the method and assign that function to a property of the object (as shown in Listing 35-2).

LISTING 35-2

Creating a Custom toString() Method

```html
<html>
    <head>
        <title>Custom toString()</title>
        <script type="text/javascript">
        function customToString() {
            var dataArray = new Array();
            var count = 0;
            for (var i in this) {
                dataArray[count++] = this[i];
                if (count > 2) {
                    break;
                }
            }
            return dataArray.join(",");
        }
        var book = {title:"The Aeneid", author:"Virgil", pageCount:543};
        book.toString = customToString;
        </script>
    </head>
    <body>
        <b>A user-defined toString() result:</b>
        <hr />
        <script type="text/javascript">
        document.write(book.toString());
        </script>
    </body>
</html>
```

When you run Listing 35-2, you can see how the custom object's toString() handler extracts the values of all elements of the object. You can customize how the data should be labeled and/or formatted.

Keep in mind that you can provide a custom toString() method to any object that you create, not just arrays. This is a handy way to provide a glimpse at the contents of an object for debugging purposes. For example, you could craft a toString() method that carefully formats all of the properties of an object into an easily readable string of text. Then use an alert box or browser debugging console to view the contents of the object if a problem arises.

unwatch(*property*)
watch(*property*, *handler*)

Returns: Nothing.
Compatibility: WinIE-, MacIE-, NN4+, Moz-, Safari-

To supply the right kind of information to external debuggers, JavaScript in NN4+ implements two global functions that belong to every object — including user-defined objects. The watch() function keeps an eye on a desired object and property. If that property is set by assignment, the function invokes another user-defined function that receives information about the property name, its old value, and its new value. The unwatch() function turns off the watch functionality for a particular property.

// (comment)

Statements

//
/*...*/

Compatibility: WinIE3+, MacIE3+, NN2+, Moz+, Safari+

Comments are statements that the JavaScript interpreter (or server-side compiler) ignores. However, these statements enable authors to leave notes about how things work in their scripts. Although lavish comments are useful to authors during a script's creation and maintenance, the full content of a client-side comment is downloaded with the document. Every byte of non-operational content of the page takes a bit more time to download. Still, I recommend lots of comments — particularly as you create a script.

JavaScript offers two styles of comments. One style consists of two forward slashes (no spaces between them), and is useful for creating a comment on a single line. JavaScript ignores any characters to the right of those slashes on the same line, even if they appear in the middle of a line. You can stack as many lines of these single-line comments as is necessary to convey your thoughts. I typically place a space between the second slash and the beginning of my comment. The following are examples of valid, one-line comment formats:

```
// this is a comment line usually about what's to come
var a = "Fred";  // a comment about this line
// You may want to capitalize the first word of a comment
// sentence if it runs across multiple lines.
//
// And you can leave a completely blank line, like the one above.
```

For longer comments, it is usually more convenient to enclose the section in the other style of comment, which is fully capable of spanning multiple lines. The following comment opens with a forward slash and asterisk (/*) and ends with an asterisk and forward slash (*/). JavaScript ignores all statements in between — including multiple lines. If you want to comment out briefly a large segment of your script for debugging purposes, it is easiest to enclose the segment with these comment symbols. To make these comment blocks easier to find, I generally place these symbols on their own lines as follows:

```
/*
some
  commented-out
    statements
*/
```

If you are developing rather complex documents, you might find using comments a convenient way to help you organize segments of your scripts and make each segment easier to find. For example, you can define a comment block above each function and describe what the function is about, as in the following example.

```
/*-------------------------------------------------
    calculate()
    Performs a mortgage calculation based on
    parameters blah, blah, blah.  Called by blah
    blah blah.
-------------------------------------------------*/
function calculate(form) {
    statements
}
```

const

Compatibility: WinIE-, MacIE-, NN6+, Moz+, Safari-

The const keyword initializes a constant. Unlike a variable, whose data is subject to change while a page loads, a constant's value cannot be modified once it is assigned. It is common practice in many programming languages to define constant identifiers with all uppercase letters, usually with underscore characters to delimit multiple words. This style makes it easier to quickly find constants in your code, as well as reminds you that their values are fixed.

Example

Listing 35-3 shows how you can use a constant in NN6+ and other Mozilla-based browsers. The page conveys temperature data for several cities. (Presumably, this data is updated on the server and fashioned into an array of data when the user requests the page.) For temperatures below freezing, the temperature is shown in a distinctive text style. Because the freezing temperature is a constant reference point, it is assigned as a constant.

> **NOTE** The property assignment event handling technique employed throughout the code in this chapter and much of the book is a deliberate simplification to make the code more readable. It is generally better to use the more modern approach of binding events using the addEventListener() (NN6+/Moz/W3C) or attachEvent() (IE5+) methods. A modern cross-browser event handling technique is explained in detail in Chapter 25.

LISTING 35-3

Using the const Keyword

```
<html>
  <head>
    <title>const(ant)</title>
    <style type="text/css">
    .cold {font-weight:bold; color:blue}
    td {text-align:center}
    </style>
    <script type="text/javascript">
    const FREEZING_F = 32;
    var cities = ["London", "Moscow", "New York", "Tokyo", "Sydney"];
    var tempsF = [33, 12, 20, 40, 75];
    function showData() {
      var tableData = "";
      for (var i = 0; i < cities.length; i++) {
        tableData += "<tr><td>" + cities[i] + "<\/td><td ";
        tableData += (tempsF[i] < FREEZING_F) ? "class='cold'" : "";
        tableData += ">" + tempsF[i] + "<\/td><\/tr>";
      }
      document.getElementById("display").innerHTML = tableData;
    }
    </script>
  </head>
```

continued

LISTING 35-3 *(continued)*

```
    <body onload="showData()">
      <h1>The const keyword</h1>
      <hr />
      <table id="temps">
        <tr>
            <th>City</th>
            <th>Temperature</th>
        </tr>
        <tbody id="display"></tbody>
      </table>
  </body>
</html>
```

The const keyword likely will be adopted in the next version of the ECMA-262 standard and will become an official part of the JavaScript vernacular in future browsers. In the meantime, it enjoys full support in Mozilla-based browsers.

var

Compatibility: WinIE3+, MacIE3+, NN2+, Moz+, Safari+

Before using any variable, you should declare it (and optionally initialize it with a value) via the var statement. If you omit the var keyword, the variable is automatically assigned as a global variable within the current document. To keep a variable local to a function, you must declare or initialize the variable with the var keyword inside the function's braces.

If you assign no value to a variable, it evaluates to null. Because a JavaScript variable is not limited to one variable type during its lifetime, you don't need to initialize a variable to an empty string or zero unless that initial value helps your scripting. For example, if you initialize a variable as an empty string, you can then use the add-by-value operator (+=) to append string values to that variable in a future statement in the document.

To save statement lines, you can declare and/or initialize multiple variables with a single var statement. Separate each varName=value pair with a comma, as in

```
var name, age, height;  // declare as null
var color = "green", temperature = 85.6; // initialize
```

Variable names (also known as identifiers) must be one contiguous string of characters, and the first character must be a letter. Many punctuation symbols are also banned, but the underscore character is valid and often is used to separate multiple words in a long variable name. All variable names (like most identifiers in JavaScript) are case-sensitive, so you must name a particular variable identically throughout the variable's scope.

WinIE Objects

Compatibility: WinIE4+, MacIE4+, NN-, Moz-, Safari-

For better or worse, Microsoft prides itself on the integration between web browser functionality and the Windows operating system. The linkage between browser and OS is most apparent in IE's facilities for accessing ActiveX objects. Microsoft has fashioned several such objects for access to scripters — again, provided the deployment is intended only for Windows versions of Internet Explorer. Some objects also exist as a way to expose some Visual Basic Script (VBScript) functionality to JavaScript. Because these objects are more within the realm of Windows and ActiveX programming, the details and quirks of working with them from WinIE is best left to other venues. But in case you are not familiar with these facilities, the following discussions introduce the basic set of WinIE objects. You can find more details at the Microsoft Developer Network (MSDN) web site at `http://msdn.microsoft.com/`.

The objects mentioned here are the `ActiveXObject`, `Dictionary`, `Enumerator`, and `VBArray` objects. Microsoft documents these objects as if they are part of the native JScript language. However, you can be sure that they will remain proprietary certainly to Internet Explorer, if not exclusively for Windows-only versions.

NOTE JScript is Microsoft's proprietary take on JavaScript that is supported by Internet Explorer. JScript is essentially the same as JavaScript with a few Windows-specific extras thrown in, such as support for ActiveX objects.

ActiveXObject

`ActiveXObject` is a generic object that allows your script to open and access what Microsoft sometimes calls *automation objects*. An automation object is an executable program that might run on the client or be served from a server. This can include local applications, such as applications from the Microsoft Office suite, executable DLLs (dynamic-link libraries), and so on.

Use the constructor for the `ActiveXObject` to obtain a reference to the object according to the following syntax:

```
var objRef = new ActiveXObject(appName.className[, remoteServerName]);
```

This JScript syntax is the equivalent of the VBScript `CreateObject()` method. You need to know a bit about Windows programming to determine the application name and the classes or types available for that application. For example, to obtain a reference to an Excel worksheet, use this constructor:

```
var mySheet = new ActiveXObject("Excel.Sheet");
```

Once you have a reference to the desired object, you must also know the names of the properties and methods of the object you'll be addressing. You can access much of this information via Microsoft's developer tools, such as Visual Studio .NET or the tools that come with Visual Basic .NET. These tools enable you to query an object to discover its properties and methods. Unfortunately, an `ActiveXObject`'s properties are not enumerable through a typical JavaScript `for-in` property inspector.

Accessing an `ActiveXObject`, especially one on the client, involves some serious security considerations. The typical security setup for an IE client prevents scripts from accessing client applications, at least not without asking the user if it's okay to do so. While it's foolhardy to state categorically that you cannot perform surreptitious inspection or damage to a client without the user's knowledge (hackers find holes from time to time), it is highly unlikely. In a corporate environment, where some level of access to all clients is desirable, the client may be set up to accept instructions to work with ActiveX objects when they come from trusted sources. The bottom line is that unless you are well versed in Windows programming, don't expect the `ActiveXObject` to become some kind of magic portal that enables you to invade the privacy or security of unsuspecting users.

Dictionary

Although the `Dictionary` object is very helpful to VBScript authors, JavaScript already provides the equivalent functionality natively. A `Dictionary` object behaves very much like a JavaScript array that has string index values (similar to a Java hash table), although numeric index values are also acceptable in the `Dictionary`. Indexes are called *keys* in this environment. VBScript arrays do not have this facility natively, so the `Dictionary` object supplements the language for the sake of convenience. Unlike a JavaScript array, however, you must use the various properties and methods of the `Dictionary` object to add, access, or remove items from it.

You create a `Dictionary` object via `ActiveXObject` as follows:

```
var dict = new ActiveXObject("Scripting.Dictionary");
```

You must create a separate `Dictionary` object for each array. Table 35-2 lists the properties and methods of the `Dictionary` object. After you create a blank `Dictionary` object, populate it via the `Add()` method for each entry. For example, the following statements create a `Dictionary` object to store U.S. state capitals:

```
var stateCaps = new ActiveXObject("Scripting.Dictionary");
stateCaps.Add("Illinois", "Springfield");
```

You can then access an individual item via the `Key` property (which, thanks to its VBScript heritage, looks more like a JavaScript method). One convenience of the `Dictionary` object is the `Keys()` method, which returns an array of all the keys in the dictionary — something that a string-indexed JavaScript array could use.

TABLE 35-2

Dictionary Object Properties and Methods

Property	Description
Count	Integer number of entries in the dictionary (read-only)
Item("key")	Reads or writes a value for an entry whose name is key
Key("key")	Assigns a new key name to an entry

Method	Description
Add("key", value)	Adds a value associated with a unique key name
Exists("key")	Returns Boolean true if key exists in dictionary
Items()	Returns VBArray of values in dictionary
Keys()	Returns VBArray of keys in dictionary
Remove("key")	Removes key and its value
RemoveAll()	Removes all entries

Enumerator

An `Enumerator` object provides JavaScript with access to collections that otherwise do not allow direct access to their items via index number or name. This object isn't necessary when working with DOM collections, such as `document.all`, because you can use the `item()` method to obtain a reference to any member of the collection. But if you are scripting ActiveX objects, some of these objects' methods or properties may return collections that cannot be accessed through this mechanism or the JavaScript `for-in` property inspection technique. Instead, you must wrap the collection inside an `Enumerator` object.

To wrap a collection in an `Enumerator`, invoke the constructor for the object, passing the collection as the parameter:

```
var myEnum = new Enumerator(someCollection);
```

This enumerator instance must be accessed via one of its four methods to position a "pointer" to a particular item and then extract a copy of that item. In other words, you don't access a member directly (that is, by diving into the collection with an item number to retrieve). Instead, you move the pointer to the desired position and then read the item value. As you can see from the list of methods in Table 35-3, this object is truly intended for looping through the collection. Pointer control is limited to positioning it at the start of the collection and incrementing its position along the collection by one:

```
myEnum.moveFirst();
for (; !myEnum.atEnd(); myEnum.moveNext()) {
    val = myEnum.item();
    // more statements that work on value
}
```

TABLE 35-3

Enumerator Object Methods

Method	Description
atEnd()	Returns true if pointer is at end of collection
item()	Returns value at current pointer position
moveFirst()	Moves pointer to first position in collection
moveNext()	Moves pointer to next position in collection

VBArray

The `VBArray` object provides JavaScript access to Visual Basic *safe arrays*. Such an array is read-only and is commonly returned by ActiveX objects. Such arrays can be composed in VBScript sections of client-side scripts. Visual Basic arrays by their very nature can have multiple dimensions. For example, the following code creates a three-by-two VB array:

```
<script type="text/vbscript">
Dim myArray(2, 1)
myArray(0, 0) = "A"
myArray(0, 1) = "a"
myArray(1, 0) = "B"
myArray(1, 1) = "b"
```

```
myArray(2, 1) = "C"
myArray(2, 2) = "c"
</script>
```

Once you have a valid VB array, you can convert it to an object that the JScript interpreter can't choke on:

```
<script type="text/javascript">
var theVBArray = new VBArray(myArray);
</script>
```

Global variables from one script language block can be accessed by another block, even in a different language. But at this point, the array is not in the form of a JavaScript array yet. You can either convert it to such via the VBArray.toArray() method or access information about the VBArray object through its other methods (described briefly in Table 35-4). Once you convert a VBArray to a JavaScript array, you can then iterate through the values just like any JavaScript array.

TABLE 35-4

VBArray Object Methods

Method	Description
dimensions()	Returns number of dimensions of the original array
getItem(dim1[, dim2[,...dimN]])	Returns value at array location defined by dimension addresses
ibound(dim)	Returns lowest index value for a given dimension
toArray()	Returns JavaScript array version of VBArray
ubound(dim)	Returns highest index value for a given dimension

When you use the toArray() method and the source array has multiple dimensions, values from dimensions after the first "row" are simply appended to the JavaScript array with no nesting structure.

Part V

Appendixes

Appendix A

JavaScript and Browser Objects Quick Reference

JavaScript and Browser Objects Quick Reference

String — 28

constructor	anchor("anchorName")
length	big()
prototype	blink()
	bold()
	charAt(index)
	charCodeAt([i])
	concat(string2)
	fixed()
	fontcolor(#rrggbb)
	fontsize(1to7)
	fromCharCode(n1...)*
	indexOf("str" [,i])
	italics()
	lastIndexOf("str" [,i])
	link(url)
	localeCompare()
	match(regexp)
	replace(regexp,str)
	search(regexp)
	slice(i,j)
	small()
	split(char)
	strike()
	sub()
	substr(start,length)
	substring(intA, intB)
	sup()
	toLocaleLowerCase()
	toLocaleUpperCase()
	toLowerCase()
	toString()
	toUpperCase()
	valueOf()

*Method of the static String object.

Regular Expressions — 42

global	compile(regexp)
ignoreCase	exec("string")*
input	test("string")
lastIndex	str.match(regexp)
multiline	str.replace(regexp,"string")
lastMatch	str.search(regexp)
lastParen	str.split(regexp[,limit])
leftContext	
prototype	
rightContext	
source	
$1...$9	

*Returns array with properties: index, input, [0],...[n].

Array — 31

constructor	concat(array2)
length	every(func[, thisObj])M1.8
prototype	filter(func[, thisObj])M1.8
	forEach(func[, thisObj])M1.8
	indexOf(func[, thisObj])M1.8
	join("char")
	lastIndexOf(func[, thisObj])M1.8
	map(func[, thisObj])M1.8
	pop()
	push()
	reverse()
	shift()
	slice(i,[j])
	some(func[, thisObj])M1.8
	sort(compareFunc)
	splice(i,j[,items])
	toLocaleString()
	toString()
	unshift()

Function — 34

arguments	apply(this, argsArray)
caller	call(this[,arg1[,...argN]])
constructor	toString()
length	valueOf()
prototype	

Date — 30

constructor	getFullYear()
prototype	getYear()
	getMonth()
	getDate()
	getDay()
	getHours()
	getMinutes()
	getSeconds()
	getTime()
	getMilliseconds()
	getUTCFullYear()
	getUTCMonth()
	getUTCDate()
	getUTCDay()
	getUTCHours()
	getUTCMinutes()
	getUTCSeconds()
	getUTCMilliseconds()
	parse("dateString")*
	setYear(val)
	setFullYear(val)
	setMonth(val)
	setDate(val)
	setDay(val)
	setHours(val)
	setMinutes(val)
	setSeconds(val)
	setMilliseconds(val)
	setTime(val)
	setUTCFullYear(val)
	setUTCMonth(val)
	setUTCDate(val)
	setUTCDay(val)
	setUTCHours(val)
	setUTCMinutes(val)
	setUTCSeconds(val)
	setUTCMilliseconds(val)
	getTimezoneOffset()
	toDateString()
	toGMTString()
	toLocaleDateString()
	toLocaleString()
	toLocaleTimeString()
	toString()
	toTimeString()
	toUTCString()
	UTC(dateValues)*

*Method of the static Date object.

Math* — 29

E	abs(val)
LN2	acos(val)
LN10	asin(val)
LOG2E	atan(val)
LOG10E	atan2(val1, val2)
PI	ceil(val)
SQRT1_2	cos(val)
SQRT2	exp(val)
	floor(val)
	log(val)
	max(val1, val2)
	min(val1, val2)
	pow(val1, power)
	random()
	round(val)
	sin(val)
	sqrt(val)
	tan(val)

*All properties and methods are of the static Math object.

Error — 32

prototype	toString()
constructor	
descriptionE	
fileNameE	
lineNumber	
message	
name	
numberE	

Control Statements — 32

```
if (condition) {
   statementsIfTrue
}

if (condition) {
   statementsIfTrue
} else {
   statementsIfFalse
}

result = condition ? expr1 : expr2

for ([init expr]; [condition]; [update expr]) {
   statements
}

for (var in object) {
   statements
}

for each ([var] varName in objectRef) {
   statements
}M1.8.1

with (objRef) {
   statements
}

do {
   statements
} while (condition)

yield valueM1.8.1

while (condition) {
   statements
}

return [value]

switch (expression) {
   case labelN :
      statements
      [break]
   ...
   [default :
      statements]
}

label :
continue [label]
break [label]

try {
   statements to test
}
catch (errorInfo) {
   statements if exception occurs in try block
}
[finally {
   statements to run, exception or not
}]

throw value
```

Number — 29

constructor	toExponential(n)
MAX_VALUE	toFixed(n)
MIN_VALUE	toLocaleString()
NaN	toString([radix])
NEGATIVE_INFINITY	toPrecision(n)
POSITIVE_INFINITY	valueOf()
prototype	

Boolean — 29

constructor	toString()
prototype	valueOf()

JavaScript and Browser Objects Quick Reference

Globals 35

Functions
atob()[M]
btoa()[M]
decodeURI("encodedURI")
decodeURIComponent("encComp")
encodeURI("URIString")
encodeURIComponent("compString")
escape("string" [,1])
eval("string")
isFinite(number)
isNaN(expression)
isXMLName("string")[M1.8.1]
Number("string")
parseFloat("string")
parseInt("string" [,radix])
toString([radix])
unescape("string")
unwatch(prop)
watch(prop, handler)

Statements
//   /*...*/
const
var

Appendix A
JavaScript Bible, 6th Edition
by Danny Goodman

How to Use This Quick Reference

This guide contains quick reference info for the core JavaScript language and browser object models starting with IE 5.5, Mozilla, and Safari.

Numbers in the upper right corners of object squares are chapter numbers in which the object is covered in detail.

Each term is supported by all baseline browsers unless noted with a superscript symbol indicating browser brand and version:

  E—Internet Explorer   M—Mozilla   S—Safari

For example, M1.4 means the term is supported only by Mozilla 1.4 or later; E means the term is supported only by Internet Explorer.

Operators 33

Comparison
==	Equals
===	Strictly equals
!=	Does not equal
!==	Strictly does not equal
>	Is greater than
>=	Is greater than or equal to
<	Is less than
<=	Is less than or equal to

Arithmetic
+	Plus (and string concat.)
-	Minus
*	Multiply
/	Divide
%	Modulo
++	Increment
--	Decrement
-val	Negation

Assignment
=	Equals
+=	Add by value
-=	Subtract by value
*=	Multiply by value
/=	Divide by value
%=	Modulo by value
<<=	Left shift by value
>>=	Right shift by value
>>>=	Zero fill by value
&=	Bitwise AND by value
|=	Bitwise OR by value
^=	Bitwise XOR by value

Boolean
&&	AND
||	OR
!	NOT

Bitwise
&	Bitwise AND
		Bitwise OR
^	Bitwise XOR
~	Bitwise NOT
<<	Left shift
>>	Right shift
>>>	Zero fill right shift

Miscellaneous
,	Series delimiter
delete	Property destroyer
in	Item in object
instanceof	Instance of
new	Object creator
this	Object self-reference
typeof	Value type
void	Return no value

frameset 16

border
borderColor[E]
cols
frameBorder[E]
frameSpacing[E]
rows

(None)   onload

iframe 16

align
allowTransparency[E]
contentDocument[MS]
contentWindow[EM]
frameBorder[E]
frameSpacing[E]
height
hspace[E]
longDesc
marginHeight
marginWidth
name
noResize
scrolling
src
vspace[E]
width

frame 16

allowTransparency[E]
borderColor[E]
contentDocument[MS]
contentWindow[EM]
frameBorder
height[E]
longDesc
marginHeight
marginWidth
name
noResize
scrolling
src
width[E]

popup[E] 16

document
isOpen

hide()
show()

location 17

hash	assign("url")
host	reload([unconditional])
hostname	replace("url")
href	
pathname	
port	
protocol	
search	

history 17

current[M(signed)]	back()
length	forward()
next[M(signed)]	go(int | "url")
previous[M(signed)]	

window 16

appCore[M]	addEventListener("evt", func,capt)[MS]	onabort[M]
clientInformation[ES1.2]	alert("msg")	onafterprint[E]
clipboardData[E]	attachEvent("evt", func)[E]	onbeforeprint[E]
closed	back()	onbeforeunload[E]
Components[][M]	blur()	onblur
content[M]	clearInterval(ID)	onclick
controllers[][M]	clearTimeout(ID)	onclose
crypto[M]	close()	onerror
defaultStatus	confirm("msg")	onfocus
dialogArguments[E]	createPopup()[E]	onhelp[E]
dialogHeight[E]	detachEvent("evt", func)[E]	onkeydown
dialogLeft[E]	dispatchEvent()[MS]	onkeypress
dialogTop[E]	dump("msg")[M1.4]	onkeyup
dialogWidth[E]	execScript("exprList"[, lang])[E]	onload
directories[M]	find([str"[, case[, up]])[E]	onmousedown
document	fireEvent("evt"[, evtObj])[E]	onmousemove
event[ES]	focus()	onmouseout
external[E]	forward()[M]	onmouseover
frameElement[EMS1.2]	geckoActiveXObject(ID)[M1.4]	onmouseup
frames[]	getComputedStyle(node, "")[M]	onmove
fullScreen[M1.4]	getSelection()[MS]	onreset
history	home()[M]	onresize[EM]
innerHeight[MS]	moveBy(Δx, Δy)	onscroll[EMS1.3]
innerWidth[MS]	moveTo(x, y)	onunload
length	navigate("url")[E]	
location	open("url","name"[, specs])	
locationbar[M]	openDialog("url", "name"[, specs])[M]	
menubar[M]	print()	
name	prompt("msg", "reply")	
navigator	removeEventListener("evt", func,capt)[MS]	
netscape[M]	resizeBy(Δx, Δy)	
offscreenBuffering[ES1.2]	resizeTo(width, height)	
opener	scroll()	
outerHeight[MS]	scrollBy(Δx, Δy)	
outerWidth[MS]	scrollByLines(n)[M]	
pageXOffset[MS]	scrollByPages(n)[M]	
pageYOffset[MS]	scrollTo(x, y)	
parent	setInterval(func, msecs[, args])	
personalbar[M]	setTimeout(func, msecs[, args])	
pkcs11[M]	showHelp("url")[E]	
prompter[M]	showModalDialog("url"[, args][, features])[ES2.01]	
returnValue[E]	showModelessDialog("url"[, args][, features])[E]	
screen	sizeToContent()[M]	
screenLeft[ES1.2]	stop()[M]	
screenTop[ES1.2]		
screenX[MS1.2]		
screenY[MS1.2]		
scrollbars[M]		
scrollMaxX[M1.4]		
scrollMaxY[M1.4]		
scrollX[MS]		
scrollY[MS]		
self		
sidebar[M]		
status		
statusbar[M]		
toolbar[M]		
top		
window		

JavaScript and Browser Objects Quick Reference

document		18
activeElement^E	clear()	onselectionchange^E
alinkColor	close()	onstop^E
anchors[]	createAttribute("name")^{E6MS}	
applets[]	createCDATASection("data")^M	
baseURI^M	createComment("text")^{E6MS}	
bgColor	createDocumentFragment()^{E6MS}	
body	createElement("tagname")	
charset^E	createElementNS("uri", "tagname")	
characterSet^M	createEvent("evtType")^{MS}	
compatMode^{EM}	createEventObject([evtObj])^E	
contentType^M	createNSResolver(nodeResolver)^M	
cookie	createRange()^M	
defaultCharset^E	createStyleSheet(["url"[, index]])^E	
defaultView^M	createTextNode("text")	
designMode^{EM}	createTreeWalker(root, what, filterfunc, exp)$^{M1.4}$	
doctype^M	elementFromPoint(x, y)	
documentElement	evaluate("expr", node, resolver, type, result)^M	
documentURI$^{M1.7}$	execCommand("cmd"[, UI][, param])$^{EM1.3S1.3}$	
domain	getElementById("ID")	
embeds[]	getElementsByName("name")	
expando[]	importNode(node, deep)^M	
fgColor	open(["mimetype"][, "replace"])	
fileCreatedDate^E	queryCommandEnabled("commandName")$^{EM1.3}$	
fileModifiedDate^E	queryCommandIndterm("commandName")	
fileSize^E	queryCommandState("commandName")	
forms[]	queryCommandSupported("commandName")	
frames[]	queryCommandText("commandName")	
height^{MS}	queryCommandValue("commandName")	
images[]	recalc([all])^E	
implementation^{E6MS}	write("string")	
inputEncoding$^{M1.8}$	writeln("string")	
lastModified		
linkColor		
links[]		
location		
media^E		
mimeType^E		
nameProp^{E6}		
namespaces[]		
parentWindow^E		
plugins[]		
protocol^E		
referrer		
scripts[]^E		
security^E		
selection^E		
strictErrorChecking$^{M1.8}$		
styleSheets[]		
title		
URL		
URLUnencoded^E		
vlinkColor		
width^{MS}		
xmlEncoding$^{M1.8}$		
xmlStandalone$^{M1.8}$		
xmlVersion$^{M1.8}$		

link		37
charset	(None)	onload^E
disabled		
href		
hreflang^{E6MS}		
media		
rel		
rev		
sheet^M		
styleSheet^E		
target		
type		

html	37
version^{E6MS}	

head	37
profile	

title	37
text	

base	37
href	
target	

script	37
defer	
event	
htmlFor	
src	
text	
type	

meta	37
charset^E	
content	
httpEquiv	
name	
url^E	

All HTML Element Objects		15
accessKey	addBehavior("url")^E	onactivate^E
all[]^E	addEventListener("evt", func, capt)^{MS}	onafterupdate^E
attributes[]	appendChild(node)	onbeforecopy$^{ES1.3}$
baseURI^M	applyElement(elem[, type])^E	onbeforecut$^{ES1.3}$
behaviorUrns[]^E	attachEvent("evt", func)^E	onbeforedeactivate^E
canHaveChildren^E	blur()	onbeforeeditfocus^E
canHaveHTML^E	clearAttributes()^E	onbeforepaste$^{ES1.3}$
childNodes[]	click()	onbeforeupdate^E
children$^{ES1.2}$	cloneNode(deep)	onblur
cite^{E6MS}	compareDocumentPosition(node)$^{M1.4}$	oncellchange^E
className	componentFromPoint(x, y)^E	onclick
clientHeight	contains(elem)^E	oncontextmenu^{EM}
clientLeft^E	createControlRange()^E	oncontrolselect^E
clientTop^E	detachEvent("evt", func)^E	oncopy$^{ES1.3}$
clientWidth	dispatchEvent(evtObj)^{MS}	oncut$^{ES1.3}$
contentEditable$^{ES1.2}$	doScroll("action")^E	ondataavailable^E
currentStyle^E	dragDrop()^E	ondatasetchanged^E
dateTime^{E6M}	fireEvent("evtType"[, evtObj])^E	ondatasetcomplete^E
dataFld^E	focus()	ondblclick
dataFormatAs^E	getAdjacentText("where")^E	ondeactivate^E
dataSrc^E	getAttribute("name"[, case])	ondrag$^{ES1.3}$
dir	getAttributeNode("name")^{E6MS}	ondragend$^{ES1.3}$
disabled$^{ES1.2}$	getAttributeNodeNS("uri", "name")^M	ondragenter$^{ES1.3}$
document$^{ES1.2}$	getAttributeNS("uri", "name")^M	ondragleave$^{ES1.3}$
filters[]^E	getBoundingClientRect()^E	ondragover$^{ES1.3}$
firstChild	getClientRects()^E	ondragstart$^{ES1.3}$
height	getElementsByTagName("tagname")	ondrop$^{ES1.3}$
hideFocus^E	getElementsByTagNameNS("uri", "name")^M	onerrorupdate^E
id	getExpression("attrName")^E	onfilterchange^E
innerHTML	getFeature("feature", "version")$^{M1.7.2}$	onfocus
innerText^{ES}	getUserData("key")$^{M1.7.2}$	onfocusin^E
isContentEditable$^{ES1.2}$	hasAttribute("attrName")^{MS}	onfocusout^E
isDisabled^E	hasAttributeNS("uri", "name")^M	onhelp^E
isMultiLine^E	hasAttributes()^{MS}	onkeydown
isTextEdit^E	hasChildNodes()	onkeypress
lang	insertAdjacentElement("where", obj)^E	onkeyup
language^E	insertAdjacentHTML("where", "HTML")^E	onlayoutcomplete^E
lastChild	insertAdjacentText("where", "text")^E	onlosecapture^E
length	insertBefore(newNode, refNode)	onmousedown
localName^{MS}	isDefaultNamespace("uri")$^{M1.7.2}$	onmouseenter^E
namespaceURI^{MS}	isEqualNode(node)$^{M1.7.2}$	onmouseleave^E
nextSibling	isSameNode(node)$^{M1.7.2}$	onmousemove
nodeName	isSupported("feature", "version")^{MS}	onmouseout
nodeType	item(index)	onmouseover
nodeValue	lookupNamespaceURI("prefix")$^{M1.7.2}$	onmouseup
offsetHeight	lookupPrefix("uri")$^{M1.7.2}$	onmousewheel^E
offsetLeft	mergeAttributes(srcObj)^E	onmove^E
offsetParent	normalize()	onmoveend^E
offsetTop	releaseCapture()^E	onmovestart^E
offsetWidth	removeAttribute("attrName"[, case])	onpaste$^{ES1.3}$
outerHTML$^{ES1.3}$	removeAttributeNode(attrNode)^{E6MS}	onpropertychange^E
outerText$^{ES1.3}$	removeAttributeNS("uri", "name")^M	onreadystatechange$^{EMS1.2}$
ownerDocument	removeBehavior(ID)^E	onresize
parentElement$^{ES1.2}$	removeChild(node)	onresizeend^E
parentNode	removeEventListener("evt", func, capt)^{MS}	onresizestart^E
parentTextEdit^E	removeExpression("propName")^E	onrowenter^E
prefix^{MS}	removeNode(childrenFlag)^E	onrowexit^E
previousSibling	replaceAdjacentText("where", "text")^E	onrowsdelete^E
readyState^E	replaceChild(newNode, oldNode)	onrowsinserted^E
recordNumber^E	replaceNode(newNode)^E	onscroll^E
runtimeStyle^E	scrollIntoView(topFlag)$^{EMS2.02}$	onselectstart$^{ES1.3}$
scopeName^E	setActive()^E	
scrollHeight	setAttribute("name", "value"[, case])	
scrollLeft	setAttributeNode(attrNode)^{E6MS}	
scrollTop	setAttributeNodeNS("uri", "name")^M	
scrollWidth	setAttributeNS("uri", "name", "value")^M	
sourceIndex^E	setCapture(containerFlag)^E	
style	setExpression("propName", "expr")^E	
tabIndex	setUserData("key", data, handler)$^{M1.7.2}$	
tagName	swapNode(nodeRef)^E	
tagUrn^E	tags("tagName")^E	
textContent$^{M1.7}$	toString()^E	
title	urns("behaviorURN")^E	
uniqueID^E		
unselectable^E		
width		

JavaScript and Browser Objects Quick Reference

body — 18

alink
background
bgColor
bgProperties[E]
bottomMargin[E]
leftMargin[E]
link
noWrap[E]
rightMargin[E]
scroll[E]
scrollLeft[EM]
scrollTop[EM]
text
topMargin[E]
vLink

createControlRange()[E]
createTextRange()[E]
doScroll("scrollAction")[E]

onafterprint[E]
onbeforeprint[E]
onscroll[E]

h1...h6 — 36

align

br — 36

clear

blockquote, q — 36

cite[E6MS]

font — 36

color
face
size

marquee — 36

behavior[E]
bgColor[E]
direction[EM]
height[EM]
hspace[EM]
loop[E]
scrollAmount[EM]
scrollDelay[EM]
trueSpeed[E]
vspace[E]
width[E]

start()[EM]
stop()[EM]

onbounce[E]
onfinish[E]
onstart[E]

ol — 38

start
type

ul — 38

type

li — 38

type
value

hr — 36

align
color[E]
noShade
size
width

dl, dt, dd — 38

compact

canvas[M1.8S1.3] — 20

fillStyle
globalAlpha
globalCompositeOperation
lineCap
lineJoin
lineWidth
miterLimit
shadowBlur
shadowColor
shadowOffsetX
shadowOffsetY
strokeStyle
target

arc(x, y, radius, start, end, clockwise)
arcTo(x1, y1, x2, y2, radius)
bezierCurveTo(cp1x, cp1y, cp2x, cp2y, x, y)
beginPath()
clearRect(x, y, width, height)
clip()
closePath()
createLinearGradient(x1, y1, x2, y2)
createPattern(img, repetition)
createRadialGradient(x1, y1, radius1, x2, y2, radius2)
drawImage(img, x, y)
drawImage(img, x, y, width, height)
fill()
fillRect(x, y, width, height)
getContext(contextID)
lineTo(x, y)
moveTo(x, y)
quadraticCurveTo(cpx, cpy, x, y)
rect(x, y, width, height)
restore()
rotate(angle)
save()
scale(x, y)
stroke()
strokeRect(x, y, width, height)
translate(x, y)

img — 20

align
alt
border
complete[EM]
dynsrc[E]
fileCreatedDate[E]
fileModifiedDate[E]
fileSize[E]
fileUpdatedDate[E]
height
href
hspace
isMap
longDesc[E6MS]
loop[E]
lowsrc[EM]
mimeType[E6]
name
nameProp[M]
naturalHeight[M]
naturalWidth[M]
protocol[E]
src
start[E]
useMap
vspace
width
x[MS]
y[MS]

(None)

onabort
onerror
onload

Range[MS] — 36

collapsed
commonAncestorContainer
endContainer
endOffset
startContainer
startOffset

cloneContents()
cloneRange()
collapse([start])
compareBoundaryPoints(type, src)
compareNode(node)
comparePoint(node, offset)
createContextualFragment("text")
deleteContents()
detach()
extractContents()
insertNode(node)
intersectsNode(node)
isPointInRange(node, offoffsetset)
selectNode(node)
selectNodeContents(node)
setEnd(node, offset)
setEndAfter(node)
setEndBefore(node)
setStart(node, offset)
setStartAfter(node)
setStartBefore(node)
surroundContents(node)
toString()

TextRange[E] — 36

boundingHeight
boundingLeft
boundingTop
boundingWidth
htmlText
offsetLeft
offsetTop
text

collapse([start])
compareEndPoints("type", range)
duplicate()
execCommand("cmd"[,UI[,val]])
expand("unit")
findText("str"[,scope,flags])
getBookmark()
getBoundingClientRect()
getClientRects()
inRange(range)
isEqual(range)
move("unit"[,count])
moveEnd("unit"[,count])
moveStart("unit"[,count])
moveToBookmark("bookmark")
moveToElementText(elem)
moveToPoint(x,y)
parentElement()
pasteHTML("HTMLText")
queryCommandEnabled("cmd")
queryCommandIndeterm("cmd")
queryCommandState("cmd")
queryCommandSupported("cmd")
queryCommandText("cmd")
queryCommandValue("cmd")
scrollIntoView()
select()
setEndPoint("type", range)

a — 19

charset[E6MS]
coords[E6MS]
hash
host
hostname
href
hreflang[E6MS]
Methods[E]
mimeType[E]
name
nameProp[E]
pathname
port
protocol
rel
rev
search
shape[E6MS]
target
type[E6MS]
urn[E]

selection — 36

anchorNode[M]
anchorOffset[M]
focusNode[M]
focusOffset[M]
isCollapsed[M]
rangeCount[M]
type[E]
typeDetail[E]

addRange(range)[M]
clear()[E]
collapse(node, offset)[M]
collapseToEnd()[M]
collapseToStart()[M]
containsNode(node, entireFlag)[M]
createRange()[E]
deleteFromDocument()[M]
empty()[E]
extend(node, offset)[M]
getRangeAt(rangeIndex)[M]
removeAllRanges()[M]
removeRange(range)[M]
selectAllChildren(elementRef)[M]
toString()[M]

map — 20

areas[]   (None)   onscroll[E]
name

area — 20

alt
coords
hash
host
hostname
href
noHref
pathname
port
protocol
search
shape
target

TextRectangle[E] — 36

bottom
left
right
top

JavaScript and Browser Objects Quick Reference

form   21

acceptCharset	reset()	onreset
action	submit()	onsubmit
autocomplete[E]		
elements[]		
encoding[EM]		
enctype[E6MS]		
length		
method		
name		
target		

input   22/23/24

checked[(checkbox, radio)]	select()[(text, password)]	onchange[(text)]
complete[(image)]		
defaultChecked[(checkbox, radio)]		
defaultValue[(text, password)]		
form		
maxLength[(text)]		
name		
readOnly[(text)]		
size[(text)]		
src[(image)]		
type		
value		

textarea   23

cols	createTextRange()	onchange
form	select()	
name		
readOnly		
rows		
type		
value		
wrap		

select   24

form	add($newOption$[, $index$])[E]	onchange
length	add($newOption$, $optionRef$)[MS]	
multiple	remove($index$)	
name		
options[]		
options[i].defaultSelected		
options[i].index		
options[i].selected		
options[i].text		
options[i].value		
selectedIndex		
size		
type		
value		

option   24

defaultSelected
form
label
selected
text
value

fieldset, legend   21

align
form

label   21

form
htmlFor

optgroup[E6MS]   24

form
label

caption   38

align
vAlign

screen   39

availHeight
availLeft[MS]
availTop[MS]
availWidth
bufferDepth[E]
colorDepth
fontSmoothingEnabled[E]
height
pixelDepth
updateInterval[E]
width

table   38

align	createCaption()	onscroll
background[E]	createTFoot()	
bgColor	createTHead()	
border	deleteCaption()	
borderColor[E]	deleteRow(i)	
borderColorDark[E]	deleteTFoot()	
borderColorLight[E]	deleteTHead()	
caption	firstPage()[E]	
cellPadding	insertRow(i)	
cells[E]	lastPage()[E]	
cellSpacing	moveRow($srcIndex$, $destIndex$)[E]	
cols[E]	nextPage()[E]	
datePageSize[E]	previousPage()[E]	
frame	refresh()[E]	
height		
rows		
rules		
summary[E6MS]		
tbodies		
tFoot		
tHead		
width		

tbody, tfoot, thead   38

align	deleteRow(i)
bgColor	insertRow(i)
ch[E6MS]	moveRow($srcIndex$, $destIndex$)[E]
chOff[E6MS]	
rows	
vAlign	

tr   38

align	deleteCell(i)
bgColor	insertCell(i)
borderColor	
borderColorDark	
borderColorLight	
cells	
ch[E6MS]	
chOff[E6MS]	
height[E]	
rowIndex	
sectionRowIndex	
vAlign	

col, colgroup   38

align
ch[E6MS]
chOff[E6MS]
span
vAlign
width

td, th   38

abbr[E6MS]
align
axis[E6MS]
background[E]
bgColor
borderColor[E]
borderColorDark[E]
borderColorLight[E]
cellIndex
ch[E]
chOff[E]
colSpan
headers
height
noWrap
rowSpan
vAlign
width

navigator   39

appCodeName	javaEnabled()
appMinorVersion[E]	preference($name$[, val])[M(signed)]
appName	
appVersion	
browserLanguage[E]	
cookieEnabled	
cpuClass[E]	
language[MS]	
mimeTypes[MS]	
onLine[E]	
oscpu[MS]	
platform	
plugins[MS]	
product[MS]	
productSub[MS]	
securityPolicy[M]	
systemLanguage[E]	
userAgent	
userLanguage	
userProfile[E]	
vendor[MS]	
vendorSub[MS]	

JavaScript and Browser Objects Quick Reference

event	25

altKey	initEvent()[MS]
altLeft[E]	initKeyEvent()[MS]
behaviorCookie[E6]	initMouseEvent()[MS]
behaviorPart[E]	initMutationEvent()[MS]
bookmarks[E6]	initUIEvent()[MS]
boundElements[E6]	preventDefault()[MS]
bubbles[MS]	stopPropagation()[MS]
button	
cancelable[MS]	
cancelBubble	
charCode[MS]	
clientX	
clientY	
contentOverflow[E]	
ctrlKey	
ctrlLeft[E]	
currentTarget[MS]	
dataFld[E6]	
dataTransfer[ES2]	
detail[MS2]	
eventPhase[MS]	
fromElement[E]	
isChar[MS]	
isTrusted[M1.7.5]	
keyCode	
layerX[MS]	
layerY[MS]	
metaKey[MS]	
nextPage[E]	
offsetX[E]	
offsetY[E]	
originalTarget[M]	
pageX[MS]	
pageY[MS]	
propertyName[E]	
qualifier[E6]	
reason[E6]	
recordset[E6]	
relatedTarget[MS]	
repeat[E]	
returnValue[ES1.2]	
saveType[E]	
screenX	
screenY	
shiftKey	
shiftLeft[E]	
srcElement[ES1.2]	
srcFilter[E]	
srcUrn[E]	
target[MS]	
timeStamp[MS]	
toElement[E]	
type	
view[MS]	
wheelData[E]	
x[E]	
y[E]	

XMLHttpRequest[EMS1.2]		27
readyState	abort()	onreadystatechange
responseText	getAllResponseHeaders()	
responseXML	getResponseHeader("*headerName*")	
status	open("*method*","*url*"[, *asyncFlag*])	
statusText	send(*data*)	
	setRequestHeader("*name*","*value*")	

applet	39
align	(Applet methods)
alt[E6MS]	
altHTML[E]	
archive[E6MS]	
code	
codeBase	
height	
hspace	
name	
object[E]	
vspace	
width	
(Applet variables)	

embed	39
align[M]	
height[EM]	
hidden[E]	
name	
pluginspage[M]	
src[M]	
units[M]	
width[EM]	
(Object variables)	

mimeType[MS]	39
description	
enabledPlugin	
type	
suffixes	

plugin[MS]	39
name	refresh()
filename	
description	
length	

object	39
align[ES]	(Object methods)
alt[E6]	
altHTML[E]	
archive[E6MS]	
baseHref[E]	
baseURI[M]	
border[E6MS]	
classid[E]	
code	
codeBase	
codeType	
contentDocument[M]	
data	
declare[E6MS]	
form	
height	
hspace	
name	
object[E]	
standby[E6MS]	
type	
useMap[E6MS]	
vspace	
width	
(Object variables)	

JavaScript and Browser Objects Quick Reference

style	26

Text & Fonts
color
font
fontFamily
fontSize
fontSizeAdjust[M]
fontStretch[M]
fontStyle
fontVariant[EMS1.3]
fontWeight
letterSpacing
lineBreak[E]
lineHeight
quotes[M]
rubyAlign[E]
rubyOverhang[E]
rubyPosition[E]
textAlign
textAlignLast[E]
textAutospace[E]
textDecoration
textDecorationBlink[E]
textDecorationLineThrough[E]
textDecorationNone[E]
textDecorationOverline[E]
textDecorationUnderline[E]
textIndent
textJustify[E]
textJustifyTrim[E]
textKashidaSpace[E]
textOverflow[E6S1.3]
textShadow[MS1.2]
textTransform
textUnderlinePosition[E]
unicodeBidi
whiteSpace
wordBreak[E]
wordSpacing[E6MS]
wordWrap[ES1.3]
writingMode[E]

Positioning
bottom
height
left
pixelBottom[ES]
pixelHeight[ES]
pixelLeft[ES]
pixelRight[ES]
pixelTop[ES]
pixelWidth[ES]
posBottom[E]
posHeight[E]
posLeft[E]
posRight[E]
posTop[E]
posWidth[E]
position
right
top
width
zIndex

Borders & Edges
border
borderBottom
borderLeft
borderRight
borderTop
borderBottomColor
borderLeftColor
borderRightColor
borderTopColor
borderBottomStyle
borderLeftStyle
borderRightStyle
borderTopStyle
borderBottomWidth
borderLeftWidth
borderRightWidth
borderTopWidth
borderColor
borderStyle
borderWidth
margin
marginBottom
marginLeft
marginRight
marginTop
outline[M1.8.1S1.2]
outlineColor[M1.8.1S1.2]
outlineStyle[M1.8.1S1.2]
outlineOffset[M1.8.1S1.2]
outlineWidth[M1.8.1S1.2]
padding
paddingBottom
paddingLeft
paddingRight
paddingTop

Tables
borderCollapse[EMS1.3]
borderSpacing
captionSide[MS]
emptyCells[MS1.3]
tableLayout

Lists
listStyle
listStyleImage
listStylePosition
listStyleType

Background
background
backgroundAttachment[EMS1.2]
backgroundColor
backgroundImage
gackgroundPosition
backgroundPositionX[ES1.3]
backgroundPositionY[ES1.3]
backgroundRepeat

Inline Display & Layout
clear
clip
clipBottom[E]
clipLeft[E]
clipRight[E]
clipTop[E]
content[MS1.3]
counterIncrement[M1.8]
counterReset[M1.8]
cssFloat[MS]
cursor[EMS1.3]
direction
display
filter[E]
layoutGrid[E]
layoutGridChar[E]
layoutGridLine[E]
layoutGridMode[E]
layoutGridType[E]
markerOffset[M]
marks[M]
maxHeight[E7MS]
maxWidth
minHeight
minWidth
MozOpacity[M]
opacity[M1.7.2S1.2]
overflow
overflowX[EM1.8S1.2]
overflowY[EM1.8S1.2]
styleFloat[M]
verticalAlign[EMS1.2]
visibility
width
zoom[E]

Printing
orphans[M]
widows[M]
page[M]
pageBreakAfter[EMS1.3]
pageBreakBefore[EMS1.3]
pageBreakInside[M]
size[M]

Miscellaneous
accelerator[E]
behavior[E]
cssText[EMS1.3]
imeMode[E]

Scrollbars
scrollbar3dLightColor[E]
scrollbarArrowColor[E]
scrollbarBaseColor[E]
scrollbarDarkShadowColor[E]
scrollbarFaceColor[E]
scrollbarHighlightColor[E]
scrollbarShadowColor[E]
scrollbarTrackColor[E]

styleSheet	26

cssRules[MS]
cssText[E]
disabled
href
id[E]
imports[E]
media
ownerNode[MS]
ownerRule[MS]
owningElement[E]
pages[E]
parentStyleSheet
readOnly[E]
rules
title
type

addImport("url"[, index])[E]
addRule("selector", "spec"[, index])[E]
deleteRule(index)[MS]
insertRule("rule", index)[MS]
removeRule(index)[E]

style (element)	26

media
type

cssRule, rule	26

cssText[MS]
parentStyleSheet[MS]
readOnly[E]
selectorText
style
type[MS]

Appendix B

JavaScript Reserved Words

Every programming language has a built-in vocabulary of keywords that you cannot use for the names of variables and the like. Because a JavaScript function is an object that uses the function name as an identifier for the object, you cannot employ reserved words for function names either. It's worth nothing that many of the keywords in the list are not technically a part of the JavaScript language just yet, but they are reserved for potential future use. Remember that JavaScript keywords are case-sensitive. Although you may get away with using these words in other cases, it may lead to unnecessary confusion for someone reading your scripts.

abstract	boolean	break	byte
case	catch	char	class
const	continue	debugger	default
delete	do	double	else
enum	export	extends	false
final	finally	float	for
function	goto	if	implements
import	in	instanceof	int
interface	long	native	new
null	package	private	protected
public	return	short	static
super	switch	synchronized	this
throw	throws	transient	true
try	typeof	var	void
volatile	while	with	

Appendix C

Answers to Tutorial Exercises

This appendix provides answers to the tutorial exercises that appear in Part II of this book (Chapters 4 through 12).

Chapter 4 Answers

1. The catalog page (a) and temperature calculator (d) are good client-side JavaScript applications. Even though the catalog relies on server storage of the image files, you can create a more engaging and responsive user interface of buttons and swappable images. The temperature calculator is a natural, because all processing is done instantaneously on the client, rather than having to access the server for each conversion.

   The Web site visit counter (b) that accumulates the number of different visitors to a Web site is a server-side application, because the count must be updated and maintained on the server. At best, a client-side counter could keep track of the number of visits the user has made to a site and report to the user how many times he or she has been to the site. The storage requires scripting the cookie (see Chapter 16). A chat room application (c) done properly requires server facilities to open up communication channels among all users connected simultaneously. Client-side scripting by itself cannot create a live chat environment.

2. **a.** Valid, because it is one contiguous word. InterCap spelling is fine.

   b. Valid, because an underscore character is acceptable between words.

   c. Not valid, because an identifier cannot begin with a numeral.

   d. Not valid, because no spaces are allowed.

   e. Not valid, because apostrophes and most other punctuation are not allowed.

3. The diagram is as follows. The paragraph element reference is:

   ```
   document.getElementById("formPar")
   ```

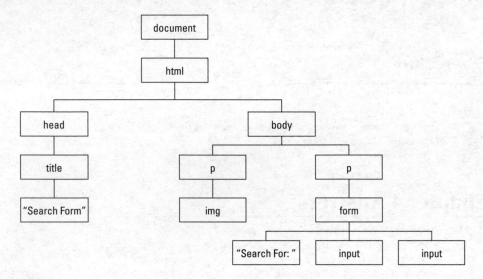

4. In common:

   - Both are types of nodes, derived from the basic DOM node

   - Both may be children of parent nodes that act as containers

   Different:

   - An element node is created by a tag, while a text node has no tag associated with it

   - A text node cannot be a parent to any other node, but an element node can be either a parent (branch node) or end node (leaf node)

5. ```
   <input type="button" name="Hi" value="Howdy" onclick="alert('Hello to you,
   too!')">
   ```

Chapter 5 Answers

1. ```
   <script type="text/javascript">
   <!--
   document.write("Hello, world.");
   // -->
   </script>
   ```

2.
```
<html>
<body>
<script type="text/javascript">
<!--
document.write("Hello, world.");
// -->
</script>
</body>
</html>
```

3.
```
<html>
<body>
<script type="text/javascript">
<!--
// write a welcome message to the world
document.write("Hello, world.");
// -->
</script>
</body>
</html>
```

4. My answer is written so that both event handlers call separate functions. You can also have each event handler invoke the alert() method inline. If you prefer to follow the XHTML format, include a space and forward slash character before the right angle bracket of the input element's tag.

```
<html>
<head>
<title>An onload script</title>
<script type="text/javascript">
<!--
function done() {
    alert("The page has finished loading.");
}
function alertUser() {
    alert("Ouch!");
}
// -->
</script>
</head>
<body onload="done()">
Here is some body text.
<form>
    <input type="button" name="oneButton" value="Press Me!"
onclick="alertUser()">
</form>
</body>
</html>
```

5. **a.** The page displays two text fields.

   b. The user enters text into the first field and either clicks or tabs out of the field to trigger the onchange event handler.

   c. The function displays an all-uppercase version of one field into the other.

Chapter 6 Answers

1. **a.** Valid.

    b. Not valid. The variable needs to be a single word, such as howMany or how_many.

    c. Valid. The trailing semicolon is missing, but because it is optional for a one-line statement, browsers accept the statement as written.

    d. Not valid. The variable name cannot begin with a numeral. If the variable needs a number to help distinguish it from other similar variables, then put the numeral at the end: address1.

2. **a.** 4

    b. 40

    c. "4020"

    d. "Robert"

3. The functions are parseInt() and parseFloat(). Strings to be converted are passed as parameters to the functions: parseInt(document.getElementById("entry").value).

4. Both text field values are strings that must be converted to numbers before they can be arithmetically added together. You can use the parseFloat() functions either on the variable assignment expressions (for example, var value1 = parseFloat(document.getElementById("inputA").value)) or in the addition expression (document.getElementById("output").value = parseFloat(value1) + parseFloat(value2)).

5. Concatenate means to join together two strings to become one string.

Chapter 7 Answers

1. The following answer shows the HTML markup portion in XHTML, where elements not acting as containers (notably the input elements) include a space and forward slash to simulate XHTML's required close tag.

```
<html>
<head>
<script type="text/javascript">
var USStates = new Array(51);
USStates[0] = "Alabama";
USStates[1] = "Alaska";
USStates[2] = "Arizona";
USStates[3] = "Arkansas";
USStates[4] = "California";
USStates[5] = "Colorado";
USStates[6] = "Connecticut";
USStates[7] = "Delaware";
USStates[8] = "District of Columbia";
USStates[9] = "Florida";
USStates[10] = "Georgia";
USStates[11] = "Hawaii";
USStates[12] = "Idaho";
USStates[13] = "Illinois";
USStates[14] = "Indiana";
USStates[15] = "Iowa";
```

```
USStates[16] = "Kansas";
USStates[17] = "Kentucky";
USStates[18] = "Louisiana";
USStates[19] = "Maine";
USStates[20] = "Maryland";
USStates[21] = "Massachusetts";
USStates[22] = "Michigan";
USStates[23] = "Minnesota";
USStates[24] = "Mississippi";
USStates[25] = "Missouri";
USStates[26] = "Montana";
USStates[27] = "Nebraska";
USStates[28] = "Nevada";
USStates[29] = "New Hampshire";
USStates[30] = "New Jersey";
USStates[31] = "New Mexico";
USStates[32] = "New York";
USStates[33] = "North Carolina";
USStates[34] = "North Dakota";
USStates[35] = "Ohio";
USStates[36] = "Oklahoma";
USStates[37] = "Oregon";
USStates[38] = "Pennsylvania";
USStates[39] = "Rhode Island";
USStates[40] = "South Carolina";
USStates[41] = "South Dakota";
USStates[42] = "Tennessee";
USStates[43] = "Texas";
USStates[44] = "Utah";
USStates[45] = "Vermont";
USStates[46] = "Virginia";
USStates[47] = "Washington";
USStates[48] = "West Virginia";
USStates[49] = "Wisconsin";
USStates[50] = "Wyoming";

var stateEntered = new Array(51);
stateEntered[0] = 1819;
stateEntered[1] = 1959;
stateEntered[2] = 1912;
stateEntered[3] = 1836;
stateEntered[4] = 1850;
stateEntered[5] = 1876;
stateEntered[6] = 1788;
stateEntered[7] = 1787;
stateEntered[8] = 0000;
stateEntered[9] = 1845;
stateEntered[10] = 1788;
stateEntered[11] = 1959;
stateEntered[12] = 1890;
stateEntered[13] = 1818;
stateEntered[14] = 1816;
stateEntered[15] = 1846;
```

```
stateEntered[16] = 1861;
stateEntered[17] = 1792;
stateEntered[18] = 1812;
stateEntered[19] = 1820;
stateEntered[20] = 1788;
stateEntered[21] = 1788;
stateEntered[22] = 1837;
stateEntered[23] = 1858;
stateEntered[24] = 1817;
stateEntered[25] = 1821;
stateEntered[26] = 1889;
stateEntered[27] = 1867;
stateEntered[28] = 1864;
stateEntered[29] = 1788;
stateEntered[30] = 1787;
stateEntered[31] = 1912;
stateEntered[32] = 1788;
stateEntered[33] = 1789;
stateEntered[34] = 1889;
stateEntered[35] = 1803;
stateEntered[36] = 1907;
stateEntered[37] = 1859;
stateEntered[38] = 1787;
stateEntered[39] = 1790;
stateEntered[40] = 1788;
stateEntered[41] = 1889;
stateEntered[42] = 1796;
stateEntered[43] = 1845;
stateEntered[44] = 1896;
stateEntered[45] = 1791;
stateEntered[46] = 1788;
stateEntered[47] = 1889;
stateEntered[48] = 1863;
stateEntered[49] = 1848;
stateEntered[50] = 1890;

function getStateDate() {
   var selectedState = document.getElementById("entry").value;
   for ( var i = 0; i < USStates.length; i++) {
      if (USStates[i] == selectedState) {
         break;
      }
   }
   alert("That state entered the Union in " + stateEntered[i] + ".");
}
</script>
</head>
<body>
<form name="entryForm">
Enter the name of a state:
<input type="text" name="entry" />
```

```
<input type="button" value="Look Up Entry Date" onclick="getStateDate()"
/>
</form>
</body>
</html>
```

2. Several problems plague this function definition. Parentheses are missing from the first `if` construction's condition statement. Curly braces are missing from the second nested `if...else` construction. A mismatch of curly braces also exists for the entire function. The following is the correct form (changes and additions in boldface):

```
function format(ohmage) {
   var result;
   if (ohmage >= 10e6) {
      ohmage = ohmage / 10e6;
      result = ohmage + " Mohms";
   } else {
      if (ohmage >= 10e3) {
         ohmage = ohmage / 10e3;
         result = ohmage + " Kohms";
      } else {
         result = ohmage + " ohms";
      }
   }
   alert(result);
}
```

3. Here is one possibility:

```
for (var i = 1; i < tomatoes.length; i++) {
   if (tomatoes[i].looks == "mighty tasty") {
      break;
   }
}
var myTomato = tomatoes[i]
```

4. The new version defines a different local variable name for the dog.

```
<html>
<head>
<script type="text/javascript">
var aBoy = "Charlie Brown";    // global
var hisDog = "Snoopy";         // global
function demo() {
   var WallacesDog = "Gromit"; // local version of hisDog
   var output = WallacesDog + " does not belong to " + aBoy + ".<br>";
   document.write(output);
}
</script>
<body>
<script type="text/javascript">
demo();         // runs as document loads
document.write(hisDog + " belongs to " + aBoy + ".");
</script>
</body>
</html>
```

5. The application uses three parallel arrays and is structured very much like the solution to question 1. Learn to reuse code whenever you can.

```html
<html>
<head>
<script type="text/javascript">
var planets = new Array(4);
planets[0] = "Mercury";
planets[1] = "Venus";
planets[2] = "Earth";
planets[3] = "Mars";

var distance = new Array(4);
distance[0] = "36 million miles";
distance[1] = "67 million miles";
distance[2] = "93 million miles";
distance[3] = "141 million miles";

var diameter = new Array(4);
diameter[0] = "3100 miles";
diameter[1] = "7700 miles";
diameter[2] = "7920 miles";
diameter[3] = "4200 miles";

function getPlanetData() {
    var selectedPlanet = document.getElementById("entry").value;
    for ( var i = 0; i < planets.length; i++) {
        if (planets[i] == selectedPlanet) {
            break;
        }
    }
    var msg = planets[i] + " is " + distance[i];
    msg += " from the Sun and ";
    msg += diameter[i] + " in diameter.";
    document.getElementById("output").value = msg;
}
</script>
</head>
<body>
<form name="entryForm">
Enter the name of a planet:
<input type="text" name="entry" id="entry" />
<input type="button" value="Look Up a Planet" onclick="getPlanetData()"
/>
<br />
<input type="text" size="70" name="output" id="output" />
</form>
</body>
</html>
```

Chapter 8 Answers

1. **a.** Close, but no cigar. Array references are always plural:
   ```
   window.document.forms[0]
   ```

   b. Not valid: `self` refers to a window and `entryForm` must refer to a form. Where's the document? It should be `self.document.entryForm.entryField.value`.

   c. Valid. This reference points to the `name` property of the third form in the document.

   d. Not valid. The uppercase "D" in the method name is incorrect.

   e. Valid, assuming that `newWindow` is a variable holding a reference to a subwindow.

2. `window.alert("Welcome to my Web page.");`

3. `document.write("<h1>Welcome to my Web page.</h1>");`

4. A script in the Body portion invokes a function that returns the text entered in a `prompt()` dialog box.
   ```
   <html>
   <head>
   <script type="text/javascript">
   function askName() {
       var name = prompt("What is your name, please?","");
       return name;
   }
   </script>
   </head>
   <body>
   <script type="text/javascript">
   document.write("Welcome to my web page, " + askName() + ".");
   </script>
   </body>
   </html>
   ```

5. The URL can be derived from the `href` property of the `location` object.
   ```
   <html>
   <head>
   <script type="text/javascript">
   function showLocation() {
       alert("This page is at: " + location.href);
   }
   </script>
   </head>
   <body onload="showLocation()">
   Blah, blah, blah.
   </body>
   </html>
   ```

Chapter 9 Answers

1. For Listing 9-1, pass the text input element object because that's the only object involved in the entire transaction.

```
<html>
<head>
<title>Text Object value Property</title>
<script type="text/javascript">
function upperMe(field) {
   field.value = field.value.toUpperCase();
}
</script>
</head>
<body>
<form onsubmit="return false">
<input type="text" name="convertor" value="sample"
onchange="upperMe(this)">
</form>
</body>
</html>
```

For Listing 9-2, the button invokes a function that communicates with a different element in the form. Pass the form object.

```
<html>
<head>
<title>Checkbox Inspector</title>
<script type="text/javascript">
function inspectBox(form) {
   if (form.checkThis.checked) {
      alert("The box is checked.");
   } else {
      alert("The box is not checked at the moment.");
   }
}
</script>
</head>
<body>
<form>
<input type="checkbox" name="checkThis">Check here<br>
<input type="button" value="Inspect Box" onclick="inspectBox(this.form)">
</form>
</body>
</html>
```

For Listing 9-3, again the button invokes a function that looks at other elements in the form. Pass the form object.

```html
<html>
<head>
<title>Extracting Highlighted Radio Button</title>
<script type="text/javascript">
function fullName(form) {
    for (var i = 0; i < form.stooges.length; i++) {
        if (form.stooges[i].checked) {
            break;
        }
    }
    alert("You chose " + form.stooges[i].value + ".");
}
</script>
</head>

<body>
<form>
<p>Select your favorite Stooge:
<input type="radio" name="stooges" value="Moe Howard" checked>Moe
<input type="radio" name="stooges" value="Larry Fine"> Larry
<input type="radio" name="stooges" value="Curly Howard"> Curly<br>
<input type="button" name="Viewer" value="View Full Name..."
onclick="fullName(this.form)"></p>
</form>
</body>
</html>
```

For Listing 9-4, all action is triggered by and confined to the `select` object. Pass only that object to the function.

```html
<html>
<head>
<title>Select Navigation</title>
<script type="text/javascript">
function goThere(list) {
    location = list.options[list.selectedIndex].value;
}
</script>
</head>

<body>
<form>
Choose a place to go:
<select name="urlList" onchange="goThere(this)">
    <option selected value="index.html">Home Page
    <option value="store.html">Shop Our Store
    <option value="policies">Shipping Policies
    <option value="http://www.google.com">Search the Web
</select>
</form>
</body>
</html>
```

2. Here are the most likely ways to reference the text box object:

```
document.getElementById("email")
document.forms[0].elements[0]
document.forms["subscription"].elements[0]
document.subscription.elements[0]
document.forms[0].elements["email"]
document.forms["subscription"].elements["email"]
document.subscription.elements["email"]
document.forms[0].email
document.forms["subscription"].email
document.subscription.email
```

The reference `document.all.email` (or any reference starting with `document.all`) works only in Internet Explorer and other browsers that emulate IE, but not in Mozilla or Safari, as requested. Other valid references may include the W3C DOM `getElementsByTagName()` method. Since the question indicates that there is only one form on the page, the text box is the first `input` element in the page, indicating that `document.body.getElementsByTagName("input")[0]` would be valid for this page.

3. The `this` keyword refers to the text input object, so that `this.value` refers to the `value` property of that object.

```
function showText(txt) {
    alert(txt);
}
```

4.
```
document.accessories.acc1.value = "Leather Carrying Case";

document.forms[1].acc1.value = "Leather Carrying Case";
```

5. The `select` object invokes a function that does the job.

```
<html>
<head>
<title>Color Changer</title>
<script type="text/javascript">
function setColor(list) {
    var newColor = list.options[list.selectedIndex].value;
    document.bgColor = newColor;
}
</script>
</head>

<body>
<form>
Select a background color:
<select onchange="setColor(this)">
<option value="red">Stop
<option value="yellow">Caution
<option value="green">Go
</select>
</form>
</body>
</html>
```

Chapter 10 Answers

1. Use `string.indexOf()` to see if the field contains the "@" symbol.

```
<html>
<head>
<title>E-mail @ Validator</title>
<script type="text/javascript">
function checkAddress(form) {
    if (form.email.value.indexOf("@") == -1) {
        alert("Check the e-mail address for accuracy.");
        return false;
    }
    return true;
}
</script>
</head>

<body>
<form onsubmit="return checkAddress(this)">
Enter your e-mail address:
<input type="text" name="email" size="30"><br>
<input type="submit">
</form>
</body>
</html>
```

2. Remember that the substring goes up to, but does not include, the index of the second parameter. Spaces count as characters.

```
myString.substring(0,3)    // result = "Int"
myString.substring(11,17)  // result = "plorer"
myString.substring(5,12)   // result = "net Exp"
```

3. The missing `for` loop is in boldface. You could also use the increment operator on the `count` variable (++count) to add 1 to it for each letter "e."

```
function countE(form) {
    var count = 0;
    var inputString = form.mainstring.value.toLowerCase();
    for (var i = 0; i < inputString.length; i++) {
        if (inputString.charAt(i) == "e") {
            count += 1;
        }
    }
    var msg = "The string has " + count;
    msg += " instances of the letter e.";
    alert(msg);
}
```

4. The formula for the random throw of one die is in the chapter.

```
<html>
<head>
<title>Roll the Dice</title>
<script type="text/javascript">
function roll(form) {
    form.die1.value = Math.floor(Math.random() * 6) + 1
    form.die2.value = Math.floor(Math.random() * 6) + 1
}
</script>
</head>

<body>
<form>
<input type="text" name="die1" size="2">
<input type="text" name="die2" size="2"><br>
<input type="button" value="Roll the Dice" onclick="roll(this.form)">
</form>
</body>
</html>
```

5. If you used the `Math.round()` method in your calculations, that is fine for your current exposure to the `Math` object. Another method, `Math.ceil()`, may be more valuable because it rounds up any fractional value.

```
<html>
<head>
<title>Waiting for Santa</title>
<script type="text/javascript">
function daysToXMAS() {
    var oneDay = 1000 * 60 * 60 * 24;
    var today = new Date();
    var XMAS = new Date("December 25, 2001");
    var diff = XMAS.getTime() - today.getTime();
    return Math.ceil(diff/oneDay);
}
</script>
</head>

<body>
<script type="text/javascript">
document.write(daysToXMAS() + " days until Christmas.");
</script>
</body>
</html>
```

Chapter 11 Answers

1. `onload="parent.currCourse = 'history101'"`

2.

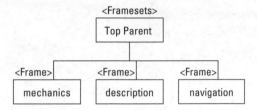

3. All three frames are siblings, so references include the parent.

   ```
   parent.mechanics.location.href = "french201M.html";
   parent.description.location.href = "french201D.html";
   ```

4. A script in one of the documents is attempting to reference the `selector` object in one of the frames but the document has not fully loaded, causing the object to not yet be in the browser's object model. Rearrange the script so that it fires in response to the `onload` event handler of the framesetting document.

5. From the subwindow, the `opener` property refers back to the frame containing the `window.open()` method. To extend the reference to the frame's parent, the reference includes both pieces: `opener.parent.location`.

Chapter 12 Answers

1. As the document loads, the `<img>` tag creates a document image object. A memory image object is created with the `new Image()` constructor. Both objects have the same properties, and assigning a URL to the `src` property of a memory object loads the image into the browser's image cache.

2. ```
   var janeImg = new Image(100,120);
   janeImg.src = "jane.jpg";
   ```

3. `document.images["people"].src = janeImg.src;`

4. Surround `<img>` tags with link (`<a>`) tags, and use the link's `onclick`, `onmouseover`, and `onmouseout` event handlers. Set the image's `border` attribute to zero if you don't want the link highlight to appear around the image.

5. The following works in all W3C DOM-compatible browsers. The order of the first two statements may be swapped without affecting the script.

   ```
   var newElem = document.createElement("a");
   var newText = document.createTextNode("Next Page");
   newElem.href = "page4.html";
   newElem.appendChild(newText);
   document.getElementById("forwardLink").appendChild(newElem);
   ```
   ```

Appendix D

JavaScript and DOM Internet Resources

As an online technology, JavaScript has plenty of support online for scripters. Items recommended here were taken as a snapshot of Internet offerings in late 2006. But beware! Sites tend to change. URLs can change too. Be prepared to hunt around for these items if the information provided here is updated or moved around by the time you read this.

Support and Updates for This Book

The most up-to-date list of errata and other notes of interest pertaining to this edition of *JavaScript Bible* can be found at the official Support Center, located at:

```
http://www.dannyg.com/support/index.html
```

If you are experiencing difficulty with the example listings in this book, first check with the Support Center to see if your question has been answered. As mentioned earlier, you are encouraged to enter the tutorial listings yourself to get used to typing JavaScript (and HTML) code. If, after copying the examples from Part II, you can't make something work (and a fix hasn't already been posted to the Support Center), send the file you've typed to me via e-mail, along with a description of what's not working for you. Also tell me the browser version and operating system that you're using. My e-mail address is `dannyg@dannyg.com`. Regretfully, I am unable to answer general questions about JavaScript or how to apply examples from the book to your own projects.

Newsgroups

The best places to get quick answers to your pressing questions are online newsgroups. Here are the top JavaScript-related newsgroups:

On most news servers:

```
comp.lang.javascript
```

On news://msnews.microsoft.com:

```
microsoft.public.scripting.jscript
microsoft.public.windows.inetexplorer.ie55.programming.dhtml
microsoft.public.windows.inetexplorer.ie55.programming.dhtml.scripting
microsoft.public.inetsdk.programming.scripting.jscript
```

On news://news.mozilla.org:

```
mozilla.dev.tech.javascript
mozilla.dev.tech.js-engine
mozilla.dev.apps.js-debugger
mozilla.dev.ajax
netscape.public.mozilla.jseng
netscape.public.mozilla.jsdebugger
```

Before you post a question to a newsgroup, however, read about FAQs in the following section and also use the extremely valuable newsgroup archive search facility of Google Groups. Visit the Google Groups search page at:

```
http://groups.google.com/
```

Enter the keyword or phrase into the top text box, but then also try to narrow your search by limiting the newsgroup(s) to search. For example, if you have a question about weird behavior you are experiencing with the borderCollapse style property in IE, enter borderCollapse into the search field, and then try narrowing the search to a specific newsgroup (forum) such as comp.lang.javascript.

If you post a question to a newsgroup, you will most likely get a quick and intelligent response if you also provide either some sample code that's giving you a problem, or a link to a temporary file on your server that others can check out. Visualizing a problem you've spent days on is very hard for others. Be as specific as possible, including the browser(s) on which the code must run and the nature of the problem.

FAQs

One situation that arises with a popular and accessible technology, such as JavaScript and DHTML authoring, is that the same questions get asked over and over, as newcomers arrive on the scene daily. Rather than invoke the ire of newsgroup users, look through existing FAQ files to see if your concern has already been raised and answered. Here are some of the best JavaScript FAQ sites:

```
javascript.faqts.com
developer.irt.org/script/script.htm
javascripter.net/faq/index.htm
```

For less-frequently asked questions — but previously asked and answered in a public form — use the Google Groups search, described earlier in this appendix.

Online Documentation

Locations of Web sites that dispense official documentation for one browser or another are extremely fluid. Therefore, the following information contains links only to top-level areas of appropriate Web sites, along with tips on what to look for after you are at the site.

Microsoft has condensed its developer documentation into a massive site called MSDN (Microsoft Developer Network). The place to begin is:

```
http://msdn.microsoft.com/library/
```

This page is the portal to many technologies, but the one most applicable to JavaScript and client-side scripting is one labeled "Library." Within the MSDN Library, you can then click "Web Development" to access information related to JavaScript and other Web development technologies. Inside the Wed Development area of the library you'll find a section named "Scripting." Here you'll find plenty of documentation and technical articles for Microsoft scripting technologies, including JScript (Microsoft's flavor of JavaScript).

For Mozilla-based browser technologies, start at:

```
http://www.mozilla.org/docs
```

Finally, you can read the industry standards for HTML, CSS, and ECMAScript technologies online. Be aware that these documents are primarily intended for developers of tools that we use — browsers, WYSIWYG editors, and so forth — to direct them on how their products should respond to tags, stylesheets, scripts, and so on. Reading these documents has frequently been cited as a cure for insomnia.

```
http://www.ecma-international.org/publications/standards/Ecma-262.htm
http://www.w3.org/TR/html4/
http://www.w3.org/MarkUp/
http://www.w3.org/TR/REC-CSS2/
http://www.w3.org/DOM/
```

Please note that just because a particular item is described in an industry standard doesn't mean that it is implemented in any or all browsers. In the real world, we must develop for the way the technologies are actually implemented in browsers.

World Wide Web

The number of Web sites devoted to JavaScript tips and tricks is mind-boggling. Many sites come and go in the middle of the night, leaving no trace of their former existence. If you are looking for more example code for applications not covered in this book, perhaps the best place to begin your journey is through the traditional search engines. Narrowing your search through careful keyword choice is vital. In addition to the Mozilla and (heavily Windows-oriented) Microsoft developer Web sites (plus numerous online articles of mine listed at `http://www.dannyg.com/pubs/index.html`), a few other venerable sites are:

```
http://www.javascript.com/
http://www.w3schools.com/js/
http://www.webreference.com/js/
http://en.wikipedia.org/wiki/Javascript
```

These sites are by no means the only worthwhile JavaScript and DHTML destinations on the Web. Sometimes having too many sources is as terrifying as having not enough. The links and newsgroups described in this appendix should take you a long way.

Appendix E

What's on the CD-ROM

The accompanying Windows–Macintosh CD-ROM contains additional chapters including many more JavaScript examples, an electronic version of the Quick Reference shown in Appendix A for printing, a complete, searchable version of the entire book, and the Adobe Reader.

System Requirements

To derive the most benefit from the example listings, you should have a Mozilla-based browser (for example, Firefox 1+, Netscape Navigator 7+, or Camino 1+) or Internet Explorer 6+ installed on your computer. Although many scripts run in these and other browsers, several scripts demonstrate features that are available on only a limited range of browsers. To write scripts, you can use a simple text editor, word processor, or dedicated HTML editor.

To use the Adobe Reader (version 7.0), you need the following:

- For Windows XP Pro/Home, or Windows XP Table PC Edition, you should be using a Pentium computer with 128 MB of RAM and 90 MB of hard disk space.
- Macintosh users require a PowerPC G3, G4, or G5 processor, OS X v10.2.8 or later, at least 128 MB of RAM, and 110 MB of disk space.

Disc Contents

When you view the contents of the CD-ROM, you will see files tailored for your operating system. The contents include the following items.

JavaScript listings for text editors

Starting with Part III of the book, almost all example listings are on the CD-ROM in the form of complete HTML files, which you can load into a browser to see the JavaScript item in operation. A directory called Listings contains the example files, with nested folders named for each chapter. The name of each HTML file is keyed to the listing number in the book. For example, the file for Listing 15-1 is named lst15-01.htm. Note that no listing files are provided for the tutorial chapters of Part II, because you are encouraged to enter HTML and scripting code manually.

For your convenience, the _index.html file in the Listings folder provides a front-end table of contents to the HTML files for the book's program listings. Open that file from your browser whenever you want to access the program listing files. If you intend to access that index page frequently, you can bookmark it in your browser(s). Using the index file to access the listing files can be very important in some cases, because several individual files must be opened within their associated framesets to work properly. Accessing the files through the _index.html file ensures that you open the frameset. The _index.html file also shows browser compatibility ratings for all the listings. This saves you time from opening listings that are not intended to run on your browser. To examine and modify the HTML source files, open them from your favorite text editor program (for Windows editors, be sure to specify the .htm file extension in the Open File dialog box).

You can open all example files directly from the CD-ROM, but if you copy them to your hard drive, access is faster and you will be able to experiment with modifying the files more readily. Copy the folder named Listings from the CD-ROM to any location on your hard drive.

Printable version of the JavaScript and Browser Object Quick Reference from Appendix A

If you like the quick reference in Appendix A, you can print it out with the help of the Adobe Reader, included with the CD-ROM.

Adobe Reader

The Adobe Reader is a helpful program that enables you to view the Quick Reference from Appendix A and the searchable version of this book, both of which are in PDF format on the CD-ROM. To install and run Adobe Reader, follow these steps:

For Windows

1. Navigate to the Adobe_Reader folder on the CD-ROM.
2. In the Adobe_Reader folder, double-click the lone executable file and follow the instructions presented on-screen for installing Adobe Acrobat Reader.

For Macintosh

1. Open the Adobe_Reader folder on the CD-ROM.

2. In the Adobe_Reader folder, double-click the Adobe Reader disk image icon; this will mount the disk image on your computer. Then open the mounted image and copy the Adobe Reader folder to the Applications directory of your computer.

PDF version of book with topical references

In many places throughout the reference chapters of Parts III and IV, you see notations directing you to the CD-ROM for a particular topic being discussed. All of these topics are located in the chapters as they appear in complete Adobe Acrobat form on the CD-ROM. A single PDF file is located on the CD-ROM, and it serves as an electronic version of the entire book, complete with full topics that are listed as CD-ROM references in the printed book. For the fastest access to these topics, copy the entire PDF file for the book to your hard disk.

Like any PDF document, the PDF version of the book is searchable. Current versions of Adobe Reader should automatically load the index file (with the .pdx extension) to supply indexed search capabilities (which is much faster than Acrobat's Find command).

To begin an actual search, click the Search icon (binoculars in front of a sheet of paper). Enter the text for which you're searching. To access the index and search facilities in future sessions, the CD-ROM must be in your CD-ROM drive; unless, of course, you've copied both the .pdx and .pdf files to your hard drive.

Troubleshooting

If you have difficulty installing or using the CD-ROM programs, try the following solutions:

■ **Turn off any anti-virus software that you may have running.** Installers sometimes mimic virus activity and can make your computer incorrectly believe that a virus is infecting it. (Be sure to turn the anti-virus software back on later.)

■ **Close all running programs.** The more programs you're running, the less memory is available to other programs. Installers also typically update files and programs; if you keep other programs running, installation may not work properly.

■ **Reference the ReadMe file.** Refer to the ReadMe file located at the root of the CD-ROM for the latest product information at the time of publication.

Customer Care

If you have trouble with the CD-ROM, please call the Customer Support phone number at (800) 762-2974. Outside the United States, call 1(317) 572-3994. You can also contact Wiley Product Technical Support at http://support.wiley.com. John Wiley & Sons will provide technical support only for installation and other general quality control items. For technical support on the applications themselves, consult the program's vendor or author.

To place additional orders or to request information about other Wiley products, please call (877) 762-2974.

Index

Note: Page numbers preceded by BC refer to Bonus Chapters 36–58 on the CD-ROM.

Numbers

0 (zero), avoiding with Date objects, 115

1-12 nodeType property values, descriptions of, 235

32-bit Windows operating systems, using Internet Explorer with, 173

Symbols

- (hyphens), prohibition in JavaScript, 173

! (Not) Boolean operator, operand and result for, 1010

!= (does not equal) comparison operator, meaning of, 65, 1003

!== (strictly does not equal) comparison operator, operand and result for, 1003

(hash mark) URL convention, property for, 498–500

placeholder, using with rollovers, 137

$ positional metacharacter, using in regular expressions, BC243

$1...$9 property, using with RegExp object, BC259–BC260

% (modulo) connubial operator, operand and result for, 1005

%= (modulo by value) assignment operator, example of, 1008

& (bitwise And) operator, operands for, 1014

&& (And) Boolean operator
 operand and result for, 1010
 truth table for, 1011

&= (bitwise and by value) assignment operator, example of, 1008

() (parentheses), using with regular expressions, BC244

* (multiply) connubial operator, operand and result for, 1005

* counting metacharacter, using in regular expressions, BC243

*= (multiply by value) assignment operator, example of, 1008

, (comma) operator
 description of, 1018
 evaluating left-to-right expressions with, 1018–1019

. (dot) matching metacharacter, using in regular expressions, BC242

// (comment) global statement, explanation of, 1070

/ (divide) connubial operator, operand and result for, 1005

// (forward slashes), purpose of, 48–49, 147

/*...*/ (comment) global statement, explanation of, 1070

/= (divide by value) assignment operator, example of, 1008

? : operator, explanation of, 1019

? counting metacharacter, using in regular expressions, BC243

@ (at) symbol, ensuring inclusion in e-mail addresses, 29–30

– (minus) connubial operator, operand and result for, 1005

– (minus) sign, checking for, BC266

– – (decrement) connubial operator, operand and result for, 1005

–= (subtract by value) assignment operator, example of, 1008

[...] matching metacharacter, using in regular expressions, BC242

[] (square brackets)
 using in Internet Explorer, 202
 using with repeat loops, 70

[^...] matching metacharacter, using in regular expressions, BC242

\ (backslash) pairs, examples of, 885

^ (bitwise XOR) operator, operands for, 1014

^ positional metacharacter, using in regular expressions, BC243

^= (bitwise XOR by value) assignment operator, example of, 1008

_ (underscore), using with variable names, 59–60

{} (curly braces), using, 74

{n,} counting metacharacters, using in regular expressions, BC243

| (bitwise Or) operator, operands for, 1014

|| (Or) Boolean operator
 operand and result for, 1010
 truth table for, 1011

|= (bitwise or by value) assignment operator, example of, 1008

S

T

W

X

Y

Z

Wiley Publishing, Inc.
End-User License Agreement

READ THIS. You should carefully read these terms and conditions before opening the software packet(s) included with this book "Book". This is a license agreement "Agreement" between you and Wiley Publishing, Inc. "WPI". By opening the accompanying software packet(s), you acknowledge that you have read and accept the following terms and conditions. If you do not agree and do not want to be bound by such terms and conditions, promptly return the Book and the unopened software packet(s) to the place you obtained them for a full refund.

1. **License Grant.** WPI grants to you (either an individual or entity) a nonexclusive license to use one copy of the enclosed software program(s) (collectively, the "Software") solely for your own personal or business purposes on a single computer (whether a standard computer or a work-station component of a multi-user network). The Software is in use on a computer when it is loaded into temporary memory (RAM) or installed into permanent memory (hard disk, CD-ROM, or other storage device). WPI reserves all rights not expressly granted herein.

2. **Ownership.** WPI is the owner of all right, title, and interest, including copyright, in and to the compilation of the Software recorded on the physical packet included with this Book "Software Media". Copyright to the individual programs recorded on the Software Media is owned by the author or other authorized copyright owner of each program. Ownership of the Software and all proprietary rights relating thereto remain with WPI and its licensers.

3. **Restrictions on Use and Transfer.**

   (a) You may only (i) make one copy of the Software for backup or archival purposes, or (ii) transfer the Software to a single hard disk, provided that you keep the original for backup or archival purposes. You may not (i) rent or lease the Software, (ii) copy or reproduce the Software through a LAN or other network system or through any computer subscriber system or bulletin-board system, or (iii) modify, adapt, or create derivative works based on the Software.

   (b) You may not reverse engineer, decompile, or disassemble the Software. You may transfer the Software and user documentation on a permanent basis, provided that the transferee agrees to accept the terms and conditions of this Agreement and you retain no copies. If the Software is an update or has been updated, any transfer must include the most recent update and all prior versions.

4. **Restrictions on Use of Individual Programs.** You must follow the individual requirements and restrictions detailed for each individual program in the "What's on the CD-ROM" appendix of this Book or on the Software Media. These limitations are also contained in the individual license agreements recorded on the Software Media. These limitations may include a requirement that after using the program for a specified period of time, the user must pay a registration fee or discontinue use. By opening the Software packet(s), you agree to abide by the licenses and restrictions for these individual programs that are detailed in the "What's on the CD-ROM" appendix and/or on the Software Media. None of the material on this Software Media or listed in this Book may ever be redistributed, in original or modified form, for commercial purposes.

5. **Limited Warranty.**

   (a) WPI warrants that the Software and Software Media are free from defects in materials and workmanship under normal use for a period of sixty (60) days from the date of purchase of this Book. If WPI receives notification within the warranty period of defects in materials or workmanship, WPI will replace the defective Software Media.

The books you read to succeed.

Get the most out of the latest software and leading-edge technologies with a Wiley Bible—your one-stop reference.

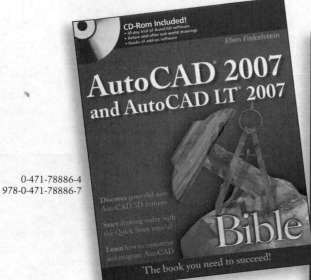

CD-Rom Included!
- 30 day trial of AutoCAD software
- Before-and-after real-world drawings
- Stacks of add-on software

Ellen Finkelstein

AutoCAD 2007 and AutoCAD LT 2007

Discover powerful new AutoCAD 3D features

Start drawing today with the Quick Start tutorial

Learn how to customize and program AutoCAD

Bible

The book you need to succeed!

0-471-78886-4
978-0-471-78886-7

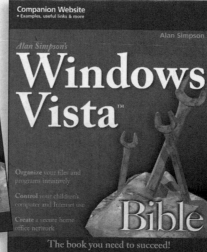

Companion Website
- Examples, useful links & more

Alan Simpson

Alan Simpson's

Windows Vista™

Organize your files and programs intuitively

Control your children's computer and Internet use

Create a secure home office network

Bible

The book you need to succeed!

0-470-04030-0
978-0-470-04030-0

"Paul is a data architect, database developer, and trainer. All three of his areas of expertise are embodied in the book with great examples. If you want to learn SQL Server 2005, this book is for you."
— Wayne Snyder, Managing Consultant, Mariner

Paul Nielsen

SQL Server™ 2005

Discover expanded features for DBAs and programmers

Write stored procedures and increase productivity

Integrate XML and Web servers

Bible

The book you need to succeed!

0-7645-4256-7
978-0-7645-4256-5

DVD Included!
- Examples and content from the book
- Models and textures you can customize
- Searchable PDF of book

Full-color Insert
- 16-page full-color insert with cutting-edge examples

Kelly L. Murdock

3ds Max® 9

Model and animate from day one with Quick Start

Create red-hot gaming animations

Discover 3ds Max 9's new features

Bible

The book you need to succeed!

0-470-10089-3
978-0-470-10089-9